Finest Hour

OTHER BOOKS BY MARTIN GILBERT

The Appeasers (*with Richard Gott*)
The European Powers, 1900–1945
The Roots of Appeasement
Recent History Atlas, 1860–1960
British History Atlas
American History Atlas
Jewish History Atlas
First World War Atlas
Russian Imperial History Atlas
Soviet History Atlas
The Arab–Israeli Conflict: Its History in Maps
Sir Horace Rumbold: Portrait of a Diplomat
Churchill: A Photographic Portrait
The Jews of Russia: Their History in Maps and Photographs
Jerusalem Illustrated History Atlas
Exile and Return: The Struggle for Jewish Statehood
Children's Illustrated Bible Atlas
Auschwitz and the Allies
The Macmillan Atlas of the Holocaust
Churchill's Political Philosophy

Editions of documents

Britain and Germany Between the Wars
Plough My Own Furrow, the Life of Lord Allen of Hurtwood
Servant of India: Diaries of the Viceroy's Private Secretary, 1905–1910

FINEST HOUR

WINSTON S. CHURCHILL
1939–1941

by

Martin Gilbert

HEINEMANN : LONDON

William Heinemann Ltd
10 Upper Grosvenor Street, London W1X 9PA

LONDON   MELBOURNE   TORONTO

JOHANNESBURG   AUCKLAND

434 29187 0
First published 1983
© 1983 C & T Publications Ltd

Reprinted 1983

Printed and bound in Great Britain by
Richard Clay (The Chaucer Press) Ltd
Bungay, Suffolk

Contents

PART THREE: BRITAIN ALONE

PART FOUR: WORLD WAR

Maps

Illustrations

Front Jacket

1 Churchill during an inspection of units of the Czechoslovak Army, 19 April 1941 (*Czechoslovak Army News Service*).

Section 1

2 Churchill leaving Admiralty House on the morning of 5 September 1939, on his way to the War Cabinet (*The Associated Press Limited*).

3 Churchill's first wartime broadcast, 1 October 1939 (*Fox Photos Limited*).

4 Churchill visits the Advanced Air Striking Force headquarters near Rheims, 7 January 1940 (*Imperial War Museum*).

5 Halifax, Daladier, Chamberlain, Churchill and Kingsley Wood in Paris, 5 February 1940 (*H. Roger-Viollet, photo Harlinque-Viollet*).

6 Churchill at the garden gate of 10 Downing Street on 4 April 1940 (*Radio Times Hulton Picture Library*).

7 Churchill in Paris, 31 May 1940, three weeks after becoming Prime Minister (*Keystone Press Agency Limited*).

8 Churchill at Dover, 28 August 1940, during a visit to the south-east coast defences (*Imperial War Museum*).

9 Admiralty Arch; defending Whitehall against an attack by German parachutists landing in Trafalgar Square (*Imperial War Museum*).

10 Horse Guards Parade, from the Admiralty (*Imperial War Museum*).

11 Churchill inspecting air raid damage in London on 8 September 1940 (*Central Press Photos Limited*).

12 Churchill in the East End, 8 September 1940 (*Imperial War Museum*).

13 Churchill in London during the Blitz, 10 September 1940 (*Fox Photos Limited*).

14 Churchill inspects a bomb crater, 10 September 1940. (*Fox Photos Limited*).

Back Jacket

Dedicated to
Yuly Kosharovsky
and
Aba Taratuta
in friendship, and in hope

Preface

M Y aim in this volume has been to tell Churchill's personal story from September 1939 to December 1941. Since the war, many diaries, memoirs and historical accounts have been published about these years, including the first three volumes of Churchill's own war memoirs. Each of these books has given its own insight. I have tried to weave together all the available sources, unpublished as well as published, to present a new perspective on Churchill's contribution, setting his thoughts and policies, his hopes and fears, in the context of the daily, and at times hourly, pressures of war.

As with each of the earlier volumes of this biography, I am grateful to Her Majesty the Queen, who graciously gave me permission to seek guidance on various points from the Royal Archives, and to quote from a letter which she wrote to Churchill in the Spring of 1941. For help in answering my various queries relating to the Royal Archives, I should like to thank Sir Robin Mackworth Young, Librarian, Windsor Castle, for his courtesy over many years, and Jane Langton, Registrar.

I am once again grateful to the Warden and Fellows of Merton College, Oxford, for their patience and consideration towards a colleague whose work has forced him for more than fourteen years to be more noticeable by his absence than by his participation, and for their generosity in giving me substantial photocopying facilities.

I am grateful to Churchill's daughter, Lady Soames, who recalled several personal episodes of her father's wartime Premiership.

I was also able to use a number of recollections set down one evening in February 1963 by Churchill's son Randolph, when he was in the process of mapping out what would have been, but for his untimely death five years later, his own chapters of the Second World War period of this biography.

In telling Churchill's story, my initial and basic source was Churchill's private papers in the custody of the Chartwell Trust. These papers include important personal and political material not available elsewhere. They also contain copies of a considerable number of documents from the official archives of Churchill's Premiership, selected by Churchill's research assistants when they were helping him to prepare his memoirs of the Second World War. For access to this material, now housed at Churchill College, Cambridge, I am grateful to the Trustees of the Chartwell Trust, Sir John Colville and Sir William Deakin.

I am indebted to Bodley's Librarian and the Bodleian Library, Oxford, for providing increasingly valuable floor space for these papers during the course of my researches.

Despite the wealth and extent of the Chartwell Trust papers, it would not have been possible to tell the full story of how Churchill worked as Prime Minister without access to the official archives of the Prime Minister's Office at the Public Record Office, Kew. These 'Premier papers' contain Churchill's working files for each day of his premiership.

The papers of the Cabinet Office, also at Kew, were likewise indispensable, Churchill's Defence Office papers being an important part of them, as are the records of the War Cabinet and its Committees. These Public Records, which include the archives of the Admiralty, the Foreign Office, the War Office, the Air Ministry, and other Government departments, also contain the Halifax, Eden and Ismay papers cited here. For the convenience of access to this material, I should like to thank the Keeper of the Public Record Office, G. H. Martin, and his staff, particularly those of the Search Rooms and the Stacks.

The help and guidance which I have received from members of Churchill's wartime Private Office and Defence Office have been substantial:

Sir John Martin, Churchill's Principal Private Secretary for the latter part of the period covered in this volume, and a member of his Private Office from May 1940, put at my disposal his wartime diary and letters, and other notes, and patiently answered my many queries, as well as reading the book both in typescript and page proof.

Sir John Peck, a member of Churchill's Private Office during his last month at the Admiralty and throughout his Premiership, gave me the original typescript of his memoirs, read my own typescript and proofs, and made many valuable suggestions.

Three members of Churchill's Private Office at the Admiralty, Bernard Sendall, John Higham and Sir Clifford Jarrett, likewise gave me the benefit of their personal recollections; John Higham also scrutinized the typescript of the Admiralty section.

Lieutenant-General Sir Ian Jacob, Military Assistant Secretary to the War Cabinet and a member of Churchill's Defence Office, not only gave me access to his diary of the first meeting between Churchill and Roosevelt in August 1941, but also read the book both in typescript and page proof and advised me on many aspects relating to Churchill's work as Minister of Defence.

One of the most important contributions to any understanding of Churchill during this period emerges from the diary of Sir John Colville, the junior member of Churchill's Private Office during the first year and a half of his Premiership. From this diary it has been possible not only to describe Churchill's actions, thoughts and moods more fully than has been hitherto possible, but also to set them in the context of the pressures and problems of the war. The twenty-six-year-old Colville was the Boswell of Churchill's Premiership, illuminating, through his record of Churchill's conversation, many previously unknown and important details of Churchill's war years.

I am extremely grateful to Kathleen Hill, Churchill's principal personal secretary throughout the Second World War, for the help, recollections and materials which she made available to me.

From the spring of 1941, Mrs Hill was assisted by Elizabeth Layton, who put at my disposal the many letters which she sent to her parents and her own diary, setting down from a secretary's perspective, the Prime Minister's daily pattern of work, and the atmosphere surrounding it.

From August 1941, when Churchill first met President Roosevelt off Newfoundland, he was accompanied on his journeys by a male secretary and shorthand writer, Peter Kinna, to whom I am grateful for his willingness to share with me the memory of this exacting, but also exhilarating work.

From his first weeks at the Admiralty until his last day as Prime Minister, Churchill used a specially prepared Map Room in which to follow the military, naval and air dispositions from day to day. The work of organizing the Map Room in its various locations was the responsibility of Sir Richard Pim, who gave me access to the typescript of his recollections, and answered my queries.

Several of those who came in contact with Churchill during his nine months as First Lord of the Admiralty have given me their recollections, including Admiral Sir Guy Grantham, Captain Lewis, Captain Swinley and Hubert Fox.

For the period of the fall of Chamberlain's Government I am grateful to Sir Charles Taylor for his recollections of the Parliamentary crisis of May 1940. For the early months of Churchill's Premiership I am grateful for the recollections of Lord Boothby, Lieutenant-General Sir Harold Redman, Professor R. V. Jones, and Barbara Cartland.

Churchill's nephew John S. Churchill kindly gave me an account of his journey from the beachhead of Dunkirk to his uncle's bedside, and John Wheldon added a Staff Officer's perspective to this same episode. Lord Paget of Northampton QC and Alastair Forbes gave me their recollections of the Dakar expedition, and David Wedgwood Benn sent me an account of his refusal to be evacuated to Canada.

Among those who have spoken to me about episodes described in this volume during the first year and a half of Churchill's wartime Premiership were Lord Geoffrey-Lloyd, Lord Balfour of Inchrye, General Sir James Marshall-Cornwall and Helen Robbins Milbank (formerly Helen Kirkpatrick).

Two of the Battle of Britain pilots who met Churchill at this time, Wing Commander Kayll and Group Captain Gillam, also gave me their recollections. I am grateful to Whitelaw Reid for his note of a luncheon conversation with Churchill at 10 Downing Street, and to Squadron Leader Ladbrooke for his recollections of Churchill's visit to Iceland in August 1941. Marshal of the Royal Air Force Sir Arthur Harris discussed with me British bombing policy, and his own mission to the United States in 1941.

In November 1940 Churchill visited his old school, Harrow; I am grateful to two of the boys at the school, Sir Michael Thomas and Sir Anthony Royle, for setting down their recollections of the occasion for me.

Sir George Harvie-Watt kindly gave me access to his Parliamentary Private Secretary's reports to the Prime Minister.

From the outset of his Premiership, Churchill was considerably helped in all questions of United States' supply by a leading Canadian industrialist, Arthur Purvis, who was killed in an air crash in August 1941. I am extremely grateful to Arthur Purvis' widow, Mrs A. B. Purvis, and his secretary Miss E. Lucille Brady, and to his son Blaikie Purvis, who helped me to reconstruct several important aspects of Purvis' mission to the United States.

Since 1968, when I succeeded Randolph Churchill as author of this biography, many of Churchill's contemporaries who have since died helped me with background information and general guidance for the early years of Churchill's wartime Premiership. I should like to mention

in particular Lord Avon, Lord Beaverbrook, Lord Butler of Saffron
Walden, Lord Chandos, Sir Geoffrey Shakespeare and General Sir
Edward Spears.

It has only recently been possible to tell the story of the 'most secret
source' of British Intelligence in the Second World War. In the context
of the Churchill biography this source is of considerable importance,
and I have tried to indicate the principal occasions on which it influenced Churchill and his advisers in their decisions. Some of this
material emerged during my own work at the Public Record Office.
But my understanding of its influence could not have been completed,
nor put to the fullest use without the help of the first two volumes of
the official history of British Intelligence in the Second World War, by
F. H. Hinsley and others, nor the personal guidance of one of those
'others', Edward Thomas. At the sacrifice of much time, Edward
Thomas made it possible for me to establish the links between Churchill's policy throughout the period, and the 'most secret source', his
cherished 'Boniface'.

I am grateful to Commander Christopher Seal, RN, for giving me
access to the letters and other papers of his father, Sir Eric Seal, Churchill's Principal Private Secretary both at the Admiralty and for the
first year of his Premiership.

I am also grateful to Lord Henley for letting me see the letters which
his father, the 7th Baron Henley, wrote home from Chequers at the
end of 1940, to Simon Ward Thompson for allowing me to see Commander Thompson's set of Churchill's monthly engagement cards; and
to Professor Warren F. Kimball, who let me see in advance of publication his edition of the Churchill–Roosevelt correspondence.

As well as the Churchill papers and other archives in the Public
Record Office, and the Churchill papers of the Chartwell Trust, I
have consulted and used material from the following archives: the
Royal Archives; BBC Written Archives; National Archives, Washington;
Archives of the United Grand Lodge of England, Baldwin papers, Bal-
four of Inchrye papers, Barrington-Ward papers, Baruch papers,
Beaverbrook papers, Butler of Saffron Walden papers, Camrose papers,
Cazalet papers, Chamberlain papers, Chequers Trust (Chequers
visitors book), Cherwell papers, Colville papers, Cunningham papers,
Ditchley Trust (Ditchley visitors book), Downing Street papers,
Eadon papers, Flemming papers, Fox papers, Grigg papers, Hankey
papers, Harvie-Watt papers, Jacob papers, Captain Lewis papers,
Lloyd papers, Lothian papers, Loveday papers, Marshall-Cornwall
papers, Martin papers, Maydwell papers, Maze papers, Menzies

papers, Morgenthau papers, Nel papers, Nicolson papers, Pearman papers, Pim papers, Quickswood papers, Roosevelt papers, Roskill papers, Seal papers, Shakespeare papers, Simon papers, Baroness Spencer-Churchill papers, Storrs papers, Templewood papers, Thompson papers, Tompkinson papers, Wedgwood papers, David Wedgwood Benn papers, and the Duchess of Windsor papers.

For access to these papers I am grateful to the Cambridge University Library (Baldwin and Templewood papers), the Beaverbrook Library and A. J. P. Taylor (Beaverbrook papers), the late Donald McLachlan (Barrington-Ward papers), Lord Hartwell (Camrose papers), Birmingham University Library (Chamberlain papers), Nuffield College Oxford (Cherwell papers), British Library (Cunningham papers), Churchill College Cambridge (Grigg, Spears and Hankey papers), Scottish National Library (Lothian papers), National Library of Australia (Menzies papers), Pembroke College Cambridge (Storrs papers), Balliol College Oxford and Nigel Nicolson (Nicolson papers) and Dame Mary Soames (Baroness Spencer-Churchill papers).

I am grateful to the copyright holders of the documents reproduced here for permission to publish them, and wish to apologize to any whose permission may have been overlooked. For the text of the Bernard Shaw letter to Churchill, copyright Shaw text 1983, I am grateful to the Trustees of the British Museum, the Governors and Guardians of the National Gallery of Ireland and the Royal Academy of Dramatic Art.

During the course of my researches on this volume many people have answered my specific queries. I should like to thank, for their knowledge and expertise: Benedict S. Benedikz, Sub-Librarian, Special Collections, the Library, University of Birmingham; Michael Bloch; P. B. D. Bunyan; Thelma Cazalet-Keir; Sybil, Lady Cholmondeley; Air Marshal Sir Edward Chilton; John Costello; Francis Cuss; Nicholas Piers Eadon; Baroness Elliot of Harwood; Lady Flemming; Richard Gott; J. P. de C. Hamilton; Lord Harvey of Prestbury; Lady Harvie-Watt; Valerie Helson; Mrs P. Henderson; Alison A. S. Hunter; Jacqueline Kavanagh, Written Archives Officer, British Broadcasting Corporation Written Archives Centre; Sir John Langford Holt; Dan Laurence; D. H. Leadbetter; the Hon. Davina Lloyd; the late Valerie Maydwell; Charles Mold; George Munster; Captain Milewski; the late Donald McLachlan; Alan Palmer; General C. G. Phillips; Alison Pilkington; John Profumo; John Raad; Pam Ray, Acting Manuscript Librarian, National Library of Australia; Dr Norman Rose; Captain Stephen Roskill; Martin Russell; Ivor Samuels; Leonard Sinclair; Giles

Smith; John Sparrow; Penina Stone; Lady Vansittart; Jon Wenzel, Research and Information Office, Imperial War Museum; and Roma Woodnutt, the Society of Authors.

I am grateful to the copyright owners and custodians of the photographs which I have selected, and for permission to reproduce them: the Czechoslovak Army News Service, Associated Press Limited, Fox Photos Limited, the Imperial War Museum, H. Roger-Viollet, Radio Times Hulton Picture Library, Keystone Press Agency Limited, Central Press Photos Limited, Camera Press Limited, the Topical Press Agency Limited, the Broadwater Collection (Winston Churchill MP), George Rance, and Lieutenant-Colonel M. J. Evetts.

I am grateful to Per Beck-Andersen for being at my side throughout the indexing of this volume; and to Terry Bicknell, the cartographer, for transforming my rough map drafts into artwork of the highest quality.

I have listed in the footnotes all those published works from which quotation has been made, and should like to thank the authors, editors, copyright holders and publishers for permission; as also for all quotations from Parliamentary debates, newspapers, magazines and gramophone records cited in this volume.

One of the pleasures of preparing successive volumes of the Churchill Biography for publication has been my personal contact with the printers, Richard Clay and Company Limited, Bungay, whose continuing interest in the text has led to printing of the highest order.

When full time work on preparing this volume began, shortly after the completion of Volume V in 1976, I was helped in the photocopying and sorting of material by William Sturge and Taffy Sassoon.

Special thanks are due to Dr Christopher Dowling, Keeper of the Department of Education and Publications at the Imperial War Museum, for help on all military, air and naval matters; and to those members of the staff at the Imperial War Museum whose help he enlisted. I should like in this context to thank Mike Willis of the Photographic Department, not only for his photographic guidance, but for his expert help on matters relating to the weaponry of the Second World War.

At the typescript and proof stage I was considerably helped by the rigorous scrutiny of Lloyd Thomas, John Cruesemann and Larry Arnn. I was also helped in the completion of the work by Erica Hunningher, who made important suggestions of form and presentation.

For some years my typescripts have been scrutinized by Sir David Hunt, himself Churchill's Private Secretary from 1951 to 1954, and an expert on many aspects of the history of the Second World War. I am very grateful to him for having been so willing to put his experience at the disposal of the biography and spend so many hours advising on its content.

In seeking to tell the full story of Churchill's personal contribution to the war I have covered several topics which Churchill himself did not cover, or was unable to write about, in his war memoirs. From the outset of my work I have been helped in this regard by Churchill's personal research assistant on the war memoirs, Sir William Deakin, who discussed with me the principal topics on which he felt further illumination was possible, and guided my steps along new paths. Throughout the long and at times difficult years of research his personal friendship has been a constant and valued source of encouragement.

Throughout the writing of this volume I have been helped by the secretarial work of Sue Rampton, who not only undertook the typing of more than half a million words, in itself a formidable task, but who also managed the enormous extra volume of typing involved in the correspondence generated by the research. Her help in the typing and organization of this material has been of considerable importance to the speedy conclusion of the work.

I was also helped in the typing of the book by Judy Holdsworth, whose contribution was substantial, and in the final stages by Rosemary Nixon, Pam Brogan and Anne Collings.

I should particularly like to thank my children, Natalie, David and Joshua, for being so patient with an often distracted father.

For the past twelve years my principal guide in all matters connected with the biography has been my wife Susie. Her historical guidance and personal enthusiasm have been the main force ensuring that the work was as comprehensive as the subject demanded, and as thorough as our researches together could make it. It is to her, therefore, as much as to myself, that the thanks of the contented reader should be addressed.

Merton College,   Martin Gilbert
Oxford
15 March 1983

Part One
At the Admiralty

1

The First Week of War:
'I cannot doubt our victory'

AT eleven o'clock on the morning of 3 September 1939, as German troops advanced through Poland for the third successive day, Britain declared war on Germany. Throughout the day, the fighting in Poland continued, intense but inconclusive. At five o'clock that afternoon, when the British War Cabinet held its first meeting of the war, there was some discussion as to who should be appointed Chief of the Imperial General Staff. The War Office favoured General Sir Edmund Ironside, whose name was pressed by the Secretary of State for War, Leslie Hore-Belisha.[1] 'There was some opposition to Ironside's appointment,' Hore-Belisha wrote in his diary that night, 'but Winston came down on my side and strongly supported it; and that settled it.'[2]

As well as his support for Ironside, Churchill suggested to the War Cabinet that the War Office prepare a survey of current British gun production. Such a survey already existed, Hore-Belisha replied, and he would circulate it at once. While this discussion was in progress the latest air reconnaissance reports were brought in. These were then read out by the Secretary to the Committee of Imperial Defence, Major-General Ismay. Four or five German battleships, he reported, were putting out to sea, together with four cruisers and five destroyers.[3]

It was not known where these German warships were headed: Churchill thought it might be the Baltic. From the point of view of the

[1] War Cabinet No. 1 of 1939, 3 September 1939, 5 p.m.: Cabinet papers, 65/1.
[2] Hore-Belisha diary, 3 September 1939: quoted in R. J. Minney, *The Private Papers of Hore-Belisha*, London 1960, pages 229–30. Before the outbreak of war, Churchill had been much impressed by Ironside's energy and ability.
[3] 'Central War Room, Summary of Information Received, No. 1 B', timed at 6.30 p.m., 3 September 1939: Cabinet papers, 100/1.

Royal Air Force, commented the Secretary of State for Air, Sir Kingsley Wood, there could not be a 'fairer target'.[1]

The War Cabinet thereupon authorized an air attack on the German Fleet. The attack itself, however, by 27 Blenheims and 9 Wellingtons, proved of importance not for what it achieved but for what it revealed. As one of the Secretaries present at that first War Cabinet later recalled, this air initiative 'showed how ineffective and ill-designed our aircraft and bombs were against strong defences and well-armoured ships'.[2]

As soon as the War Cabinet of September 3 was over, Churchill walked at once across Horse Guards Parade to the Admiralty. 'I met him at the private entrance,' Captain Guy Grantham, the Naval Assistant to the First Sea Lord, later recalled, 'and escorted him to the room he knew so well.' As they entered the Admiralty building, Grantham wrote:

The first thing he said was 'Where is the octagonal table?' I got hold of the Office Keeper and said Winston wanted the table back – it was soon produced.

He also told me that on the back of the sofa there should be a chart box. It was there with charts in it, which I showed him. He said 'I thought so. These are the same charts I used in this room in 1915!'[3]

Kathleen Hill, Churchill's secretary since the summer of 1937, has also recalled that moment of Churchill's return to the Admiralty. 'He rushed up the steps and flung open the panelling. There were the charts. The ships were still there.'[4]

Churchill now began work again in the same room, and at the same desk, where he had worked as First Lord from October 1911 until the crisis at the Dardanelles of May 1915. Then, Prince Louis of Battenberg and Admiral of the Fleet Lord Fisher had been his senior advisers. Now it was Admiral of the Fleet Sir Dudley Pound, a former Assistant to Fisher, who was First Sea Lord; and it was with Pound that Churchill now discussed the disposition of the German Fleet, and Britain's own naval preparations. In 1939, when Italy had invaded and occupied Albania, Pound had been in command of the Mediterranean Fleet, and Churchill had been a severe critic of that Fleet's disposition. 'Now,' Churchill recalled, 'we met as colleagues upon whose intimate relations and fundamental agreement the smooth-working of the vast Admiralty machine would depend,' and he added: 'We eyed each other doubt-

[1] Manuscript notes taken at the War Cabinet meeting of 3 September 1939 by Lieutenant-Colonel Jacob: Jacob papers.

[2] Lieutenant-General Sir Ian Jacob, notes for the author, 1 July 1982.

[3] Admiral Sir Guy Grantham, letter to the author, 10 March 1982.

[4] Kathleen Hill, conversation with the author, 15 October 1982.

fully. But from the earliest days our friendship and mutual confidence ripened.'[1]

That evening, Pound introduced Churchill to the senior Admiralty officials with whom he would have to work from day to day, and hour to hour. Among those present was the Third Sea Lord and Controller, Rear-Admiral Bruce Fraser, who later recalled:

As he once again took the First Lord's chair in the famous Board Room, Churchill was filled with emotion. To a few words of welcome from the First Sea Lord he replied by saying what a privilege and honour it was to be again in that chair, that there were many difficulties ahead but together we would overcome them.

He surveyed critically each one of us in turn and then, adding that he would see us all personally later on, he adjourned the meeting. 'Gentlemen,' he said, 'to your tasks and duties.'[2]

On the morning of September 4, as German aeroplanes bombarded Warsaw, killing hundreds of civilians, and as German troops continued to advance across Polish soil, the British War Cabinet held its second meeting, with the Prime Minister, Neville Chamberlain, in the Chair. During the discussion Churchill, after noting that the 'main German effort' was concentrated on the Polish front, suggested that 'every means possible should be employed to relieve the pressure'. His suggestion was an attack against the Siegfried Line, carried out jointly by the French Army and the Royal Air Force. The War Cabinet agreed that such a combined plan of action 'was a vital necessity'.

Later in the same meeting, Churchill gave his War Cabinet colleagues an account of the sinking of the steamship *Athenia* by a German submarine, two hundred miles north-west of Ireland, on the previous afternoon. 'It was understood,' he said, 'that the passengers and crew were in the ship's boats. Two destroyers were hastening to the rescue and should be near the scene.' Churchill added: 'The occurrence should have a helpful effect as regards public opinion in the United States.'[3] Later it was learnt that 112 passengers had been drowned, including twenty-eight Americans. The German Government at once announced

[1] Draft paragraphs of Churchill's war memoirs: Churchill papers, 4/95.

[2] Admiral of the Fleet Lord Fraser of North Cape, 'Churchill and the Navy', in Sir James Marchant (editor), *Winston Spencer Churchill: Servant of Crown and Commonwealth*, London 1954, pages 78–9.

[3] War Cabinet No. 2 of 1939, 4 September 1939, 11.30 a.m.: Cabinet papers, 65/1.

that it was Churchill who had personally ordered a bomb to be placed on board. 'This falsehood,' he later wrote, 'received some credence in unfriendly quarters.'[1]

At half past nine that evening, September 4, Churchill held a conference with Dudley Pound and several other senior Admiralty officials. According to the notes of the meeting, which he marked 'Most Secret', Churchill spoke of how, 'with Japan placid, and Italy neutral though indeterminate', the first phase of the naval war, and the 'prime attack', would be in the Atlantic approaches to Britain. A convoy system was being set up, to protect merchant shipping from submarine attack. For this purpose, Churchill noted, the First Sea Lord was examining whether as many as twelve destroyers and escort vessels could be 'scraped' from the Mediterranean and Eastern Theatres, until the completion, in about a month's time, of special trawlers then being fitted with anti-submarine devices. Churchill wanted a statement prepared for him, to show the date of deliveries of these trawlers, expected in October, and he added: 'It would seem well at any rate in the earliest deliveries, not to wait for the arming of them with guns, but to rely upon depth-charges. Gun-arming can be recommenced when the pressure eases.'

Churchill then proposed to the conference the immediate establishment of a scheme under which every captain or master of a merchant ship coming from the Atlantic would be visited 'by a competent naval authority', who would examine the records of his course, 'including zig-zags'. Then, Churchill proposed, all 'infractions or divergences from Admiralty instructions should be pointed out, and all serious departures should be punished, examples being made of dismissal'. The Admiralty had assumed responsibility for the safety of merchant shipping, Churchill commented, 'and merchant-skippers must be made to obey'.

Discussing the diversion of merchant shipping from the Mediterranean to the Cape route, Churchill advised that this diversion, ordered automatically on September 3, should be maintained until Italy's intentions become less obscure. But 'no expectation', he told his advisers, 'can be based by us that the Italian uncertainty will be cleared up in the next six weeks', though he felt that the Admiralty should 'press' the Government 'to bring it to a head in a favourable sense as soon as possible'.

Churchill ended the conference by explaining that he wished his

---

[1] Winston S. Churchill, *The Second World War*, volume 1, London 1948, page 331.

officials to treat his ideas as a basis for discussion, rather than the last word: 'The First Lord,' he ended, 'submits these notes to his naval colleagues for consideration, *for criticism and correction*, and hopes to receive proposals for action in the sense desired.'[1]

From his first day at the Admiralty, Churchill instituted a method of work which was to be his hallmark throughout the war, and to be much misunderstood and even resented by some. This was the minute, a dictated note sent to one or more of his advisers, or even to Cabinet colleagues, containing a question, or a series of questions, some long and argumentative, others short and brisk.

These minutes, numbering several a day and several thousand a year, constituted the bulk of Churchill's written output during the Second World War. They were intended, in the main, not as mere statements of fact, or exhortations, but as a means of entering into a dialogue with the recipient: they were instead of, or a supplement to, conversation; initiating or carrying on debate and enquiry into the myriad topics of the Navy, and of the nation at war.

More so than other Ministers and officials, Churchill used these minutes to acquire information, to initiate discussion, and to propose schemes and stratagems. Some contain words of rebuke, some words of encouragement; some are stern, some witty; some are weighty, some light. But from each of his minutes, Churchill expected to learn what was happening over the full range of his responsibilities, and to probe every area of potential war policy and action.

Three of Churchill's minutes of September 3 showed his concern to equip himself with the facts needed to form a coherent picture of the naval situation. The first was addressed to the Director of Naval Intelligence, Rear-Admiral Godfrey, to whom he wrote: 'Let me have a statement of the German U-boat force, actual and prospective, for the next few months. Please distinguish between ocean-going and small-size U-boats. Give the estimated radius of action in days and miles in each case.' To the Fourth Sea Lord he minuted: 'Please let me have a return showing the number of rifles in the possession of the Navy both afloat and ashore. Also return of the mines of different natures.' And to the Deputy Chief of the Naval Staff, Rear-Admiral Tom Phillips, he minuted: 'Kindly let me know the escorts which will be provided for the big convoy to the Mediterranean (a) from England to Gibraltar,

---

[1] 'Most Secret', 'Notes on Conference, 9.30 p.m. on 4th September, 1939': Admiralty papers, 205/2. The words in italics were underlined by Churchill himself. All subsequent italicized words in the quotations in this volume were underlined in the original, unless otherwise stated.

and (b) through the Mediterranean. I understand these escorts are only against U-boat attack.'[1]

One of Churchill's minutes on September 4 showed his concern for the well-being of those who worked under him. 'You must be very uncomfortable,' he minuted to Pound, 'in that over-crowded, over-heated small room, and the conditions there cannot be favourable to the important work that has to be conducted. I suggest that you should consider going back to the old war room at Admiralty House, where the last war was fought from, and only use the underground room after an air-raid warning has been received.' Churchill ended this minute, as so many were to end, 'Pray let me know your views.'[2] Within the Admiralty these minutes quickly became known as 'First Lord's prayers'.

One such early 'prayer' concerned the setting up of a special Map Room at Admiralty House. The need for such a Room arose at once, as Churchill sought to grapple with the seriousness of the U-boat threat to Britain's food and raw material life-lines. Seeking to follow from day to day the progress of hundreds of merchant ships and their destroyer escorts, as well as to keep track of unescorted ships, he asked on September 5 for 'a room and additional staff' to be established, to set up and display a chart 'of large size' on which, each morning, could be shown 'all vessels within two, or better still, three days distance from our shores'.

The guidance or control of each of these vessels, Churchill minuted, 'must be foreseen and prescribed so that there is not one whose case has not been individually dealt with, as far as our resources allow. Pray let me have proposals to implement this, which should come into being within twenty-four hours, and work up later.'[3]

The required Map Room, Captain Grantham later recalled, 'I got organised in the Library of Admiralty House, where large-scale charts of the oceans of the world were mounted in wooden frames.'[4]

Looking back after the war on these early days, with their many War Cabinets, and Admiralty Conferences, Churchill wrote:

I do not recall any period when the weather was so hot – I had a black alpaca jacket made to wear over only a linen shirt. It was indeed just the weather that Hitler wanted for his invasion of Poland. The great rivers on which the Poles had counted in their defensive plan were nearly everywhere fordable,

[1] Minutes dated 3 September 1939: Churchill papers, 19/3.
[2] Minute dated 4 September 1939: Churchill papers, 19/3.
[3] Note dated 5 September 1939: Admiralty papers, 205/2.
[4] Admiral Sir Guy Grantham, letter to the author, 10 March 1982.

and the ground was hard and firm for the movement of tanks and vehicles of all kinds.

Each morning the CIGS, General Ironside, standing before the map, gave long reports and appreciations which very soon left no doubt in our minds that the resistance of Poland would speedily be crushed. Each day I reported to the Cabinet the Admiralty tale, which usually consisted of a list of British merchant ships sunk by the U-boats. . . .[1]

When the War Cabinet met on the morning of September 5, Churchill warned of the danger of an incident arising in the Mediterranean, where there was 'the risk that an Italian submarine would be mistaken for a German submarine'. It was agreed that the Foreign Secretary, Lord Halifax, would inform the Italian Government of this danger, and 'invite them' to take action to avoid it.

During the meeting, General Ironside informed the War Cabinet that several German motorized divisions had broken through the Polish defences at Częstochowa, a breakthrough 'that might result in Germany capturing Poland's main industrial area'. It might also mean, Ironside declared, 'that the Polish army would have to withdraw to the line of the Vistula'.

A discussion then took place as to whether the Germans would continue deliberately to attack merchant shipping and unarmed steamers; whether the sinking of the *Athenia* was a unique and unfortunate episode, or the start of an ocean-wide terror tactic.

The Chief of the Air Staff, Sir Cyril Newall, stated that 'personally' he was 'by no means convinced that the attack on the *Athenia* was part of a deliberate policy laid down by the German Government'. Churchill disagreed, pointing out, as the notes of the discussion recorded, 'that the attack on the *Athenia* was not an isolated incident. There was definite evidence that four ships had been attacked. The most recent of which he had information was the sinking of a British tramp ship in the Bay of Biscay. This vessel had been sunk by gunfire.'[2]

The discussion then turned to the question of a possible Franco-British attack on the Siegfried line. Sir Cyril Newall doubted whether air power could, by itself, do more than delay the arrival of German land reinforcements, once the attack had been launched. Churchill agreed, telling the War Cabinet, as the minutes recorded, 'that he did not believe that the essential elements of war would be altered by the

---

[1] Draft paragraphs of Churchill's war memoirs: Churchill papers, 4/95.

[2] Following the sinking of the *Athenia* on September 3, German submarines sank the *Bosnia* and the *Royal Sceptre* on September 5, the *Bosnia* in the Bay of Biscay.

air arm'. The Spanish Civil War had been cited as an example of the supremacy of air power; but, he said, 'it should be remembered that the Republican Armies had for many weeks maintained themselves on the south bank of the Ebro, notwithstanding the fact that the bridges across the river were subject to continuous and powerful air attack'.

At the end of its meeting the War Cabinet agreed that, if French troops were ordered to advance against Germany, the Royal Air Force would be 'available to assist'.[1] Despite this decision, no such French advance took place, although German troops continued to advance across Poland, supported by repeated air attacks on both military targets and civilian centres.

Returning to the Admiralty after the War Cabinet of September 5, Churchill sent a minute to his senior officials asking all heads of departments to draw up a report 'upon the question arising from the so-called neutrality of the so-called Eire'. He was worried that 'Irish malcontents', as he described them, might be willing to give help and shelter to U-boats in the inlets of the west of Ireland. 'If they throw bombs in Ireland,' he asked, 'why should they not supply petrol to U-boats?'

In May 1938 Chamberlain's Government had returned to Eire the control of several southern Irish ports, over which Britain had retained sovereign rights under the Irish Treaty of 1922. Churchill had opposed this action, arguing that if Eire remained neutral during the war, and refused to allow Britain to use the ports, 'we should find the greatest difficulty in conducting our supply'.[2] Eire had indeed declared itself neutral on the outbreak of war, and in his minute Churchill asked his advisers to prepare a study of 'the advantage to be gained' by a British return to the control of the former Treaty Ports. But, he added, the Board of Admiralty must realize 'that we may not be able to obtain satisfaction, as the question of Eirish neutrality raises political issues which have not yet been faced, and which the First Lord is not certain he can solve'.[3]

Also on September 5, Churchill sent a minute to Dudley Pound 'and others concerned' about the possibility, which he had already explored with partial success in 1914, of making a number of 'dummy reproductions' of naval vessels 'in order that enemy reconnaissance might mistake the false for the true'. In 1914, air reconnaissance had been in its infancy. 'Now,' he wrote, 'the argument is vastly increased. Air reconnaissance can sweep over every harbour, and obtain a photograph of

[1] War Cabinet No. 3 of 1939, 5 September 1939, 11.30 a.m.: Cabinet papers, 61/1.
[2] *Hansard*, 5 May 1938.
[3] Minute dated 5 September 1939: Churchill papers, 19/3.

the deck plan, though not of the silhouette, of every vessel. In a few hours they can know what we have at Scapa, or the Thames, or Portsmouth.' It was therefore important to try to introduce 'this element of mystery which, if rightly used, might draw long exhausting and futile attacks upon worthless targets, while the real ships are doing their work elsewhere'.[1]

The dummy ships were duly built; proof, as one of Churchill's Private Secretaries, John Higham, later reflected, 'that Winston's practical ideas were often sound'.[2] Churchill's energies were quickly appreciated; on September 5, the newspaper proprietor, Lord Camrose, noted the view of the Conservative MP, Leo Amery, 'that the present War Cabinet was, with the exception of Winston himself, entirely devoid of the offensive fighting spirit, and did not think they could last more than a few months'.[3]

At the War Cabinet of September 6, which met that morning, Churchill reported that five merchant ships, four British and one French, had been sunk by German submarines on the previous day. 'Rigorous steps were being taken,' he added, 'to ensure that merchant ship captains obeyed the instructions given them.' As for the activities of British warships, Churchill told his colleagues, two German merchant ships had been sunk by HMS *Ajax* on the previous day. 'The sinking had been in accordance with the rules of warfare,' Churchill reported, 'but it was not clear why HMS *Ajax* had been unable to find the prize crews and to take the ship into port.'

In future, Churchill promised, the Admiralty would take steps to ensure that wherever possible 'enemy merchant ships were captured and not sunk'.[4]

Returning to the Admiralty, Churchill again addressed a series of minutes to his senior officials. To the Director of Naval Intelligence he minuted: 'It is of the highest importance that the Admiralty bulletin should maintain its reputation for truthfulness, and the tone should not be forced.'[5] Asking that Lord Stanhope, the man whom he had replaced as First Lord three days before, should be kept informed on those naval matters in which he had been interested, Churchill wrote: 'He should not be cut off from the course of events at the Admiralty with which he had been so intimately concerned.'[6]

---

[1] Minute dated 5 September 1939: Churchill papers, 19/3.
[2] John Higham, notes for the author, 16 September 1982.
[3] Note of 5 September 1939: Camrose papers.
[4] War Cabinet No. 5 of 1939, 6 September 1939, 11.30 a.m.: Cabinet papers, 65/1.
[5] Minute dated 6 September 1939: Churchill papers, 19/3.
[6] Minute dated 6 September 1939: Churchill papers, 19/3.

Before the war Churchill had been a public critic of the various naval treaties, including the London Treaty of 1930, which had restricted the scale of British warship construction in the interests of naval disarmament. His criticisms of these Treaties had led him to a detailed study of British and German cruiser design. In one of his minutes of September 6, he returned to this theme, noting for Pound, Phillips and Fraser: 'Now that we are free from all treaty restrictions, if any cruisers are built they should be of a new type, and capable of dominating the five German 8-inch cruisers now under construction.'[1] In a further minute to Pound, he asked the Naval Staff to prepare an appreciation on the possibility of the Royal Navy forcing a passage into the Baltic.[2] This had been a project much discussed, but never tried, during Churchill's early wartime months at the Admiralty in 1914; it was also a plan which Churchill had discussed with one of his closest friends, Professor Frederick Lindemann, before the outbreak of war.

The War Cabinet met for the second time on September 6 at six o'clock in the evening, when it had before it a memorandum prepared by the Chiefs of Staff Committee, and signed by Newall, Pound and Ironside, which set out the measures needed to improve the air defences of the fleet in Scapa Flow against attack from German aircraft based in North West Germany. Their report warned that although 'the early provision of fighter squadrons' was an urgent priority, 'We cannot, however, recommend that the air defence of Great Britain, which is still short of 15 squadrons, should be further depleted by taking two for Scapa.' The two fighter squadrons needed at Scapa, the Chiefs of Staff noted, 'cannot be provided until next summer'.[3]

At half past nine that evening, September 6, Churchill held a merchant shipping conference with his senior Admiralty officials. Outward bound convoys, it was agreed, were to start on the following day, leaving both the Thames and Liverpool, with each convoy to be escorted 'by three escorting vessels'.[4] Thus after only three days of war, and with no dispute, was enacted a policy which had not been put into effect in the First World War until after three years of severe shipping losses and bitter debate.

On the third day of the war Churchill also received a personal appeal from the Duke of Windsor, who wrote to Churchill from his villa in the

[1] Minute dated 6 September 1939: Admiralty papers, 205/2.

[2] Minute dated 6 September 1939: Churchill papers, 19/3.

[3] War Cabinet No. 6 of 1939, 6 September 1939, 6 p.m., Chiefs of Staff Committee Memorandum No. 8 of 1939, 'Air Defence of Scapa': Cabinet papers 61/1, folios 82–6.

[4] Conference Notes, 6 September 1939: Admiralty papers, 205/2.

South of France that it would 'greatly facilitate' his and the Duchess of Windsor's return to England 'if you could send a destroyer or other naval vessel to any French Channel port Monday or Tuesday that you designate'. The Duke added: 'This would enable us to bring our whole party of five and our small amount of luggage in one journey.'[1]

The Duke of Windsor had not set foot on English soil since his abdication nearly three years before. Churchill now made the necessary plans, asking his son Randolph to be among those who would greet the Duke at Cherbourg, and escort him to Portsmouth, and detailing the destroyer *Kelly*, commanded by Lord Louis Mountbatten, 'to be at Cherbourg by 1500 on Tues 12th'.[2] Churchill advised his son: 'You should wear uniform, and look your best,'[3] and in a letter which he gave Randolph to be handed to the Duke of Windsor at Cherbourg he wrote: 'Welcome home! Your Royal Highness knows how much I have looked forward to this day: I know you will forgive me for not coming to meet you, but I cannot leave my post.' Churchill ended his letter: 'We are plunged in a long and grievous struggle. But all will come right if we all work together to the end.'[4]

This phrase, 'all will come right', was to become a frequent exhortation in Churchill's letters and speeches; he remembered it from the Boer War, when it had been a much quoted saying of the Orange Free State President, Martinus Steyn. For Churchill, it served as a means of raising morale at times when there seemed little cause for optimism. Convinced that morale was a subject of paramount importance in wartime, Churchill neglected no means, however small they might seem, of seeking to rally individual and collective spirits. Thus on September 7, while reflecting on the proposal for dummy ships which he had outlined to Dudley Pound two days before, he suggested looking into the possibility of using the dummy hulls to the benefit of the sailors, asking Pound to consider 'whether a recreation room or cinema' could not be fitted in the dummy hulls 'without, of course delaying the completion'. Churchill added: 'I like to think that in a long dark winter at Scapa they might add to the amenities as well as the protection of the Fleet.'[5]

---

[1] Letter dated 6 September 1939, from La Cröe, Cap d'Antibes, Alpes Maritimes: Churchill papers, 19/2.

[2] Minute of 10 September 1939: Churchill papers, 19/2.

[3] 'Private and Personal', 10 September 1939: Churchill papers, 19/2.

[4] Letter of 10 September 1939, sent from Chartwell: Churchill papers, 19/2.

[5] Minute of 7 September 1939: Churchill papers, 19/3.

On a further question of morale, Churchill wrote direct to Neville Chamberlain on September 7. This concerned the problems created by the blackout. Churchill accepted that the civil population had to be drilled 'in completely putting out their private lights'. But he proposed to mitigate the adverse effect on morale by what he called 'great installations of lights' controlled from two or three city centres. As he wrote to Chamberlain:

While enforcing the household blackouts, why not let the controllable lighting burn until an air-warning is received? Then when the hooters sound, the whole of these widespread systems of lighting would go out at once together. This would reinforce the air-raid warning, and when the all-clear was sounded, they would all go up together, telling everyone. Immense inconvenience would be removed, and the depressing effect of needless darkness; and as there are at least ten minutes to spare, there would be plenty of time to make the blackout complete.[1]

While seeking to anticipate the problems of war, Churchill was at times prompted, or provoked, to reflect upon past errors and omissions. One such reflection came when he re-read a letter from Vice-Admiral Sir Reginald Henderson, in the pre-war years a leading gunnery expert, about shortcomings in the design of some of the more recent British ships. Bitterly, Churchill wrote to Dudley Pound of how:

All the constructive genius and commanding reputation of the Royal Navy has been besmirched and crippled by Treaty restrictions for twenty years. A warship should be the embodiment of a tactical conception. All our cruisers are the results of trying to conform to Treaty limitations and 'gentlemen's agreements'. The masterly letter of Admiral Henderson throws a clear light on our policy and present position.

Churchill added, disarmingly: 'Pray do not allow the reading of this to be a burden to you in your heavy work, but let me have it back when it has passed round.'[2]

At the evening War Cabinet of September 6, Churchill was given his first official responsibility outside Admiralty matters, when he was appointed a member of a special War Cabinet Committee, the Land Forces Committee, under the chairmanship of the Lord Privy Seal, Sir Samuel Hoare. This Committee was instructed to report to the Cabinet

[1] Letter of 7 September 1939: Churchill papers, 19/3.
[2] Minute of 7 September 1939: Churchill papers, 19/3.

'as quickly as possible' on what should be the size of Britain's land forces, and on the 'date of completion of equipment for the various contingents'.

The first meeting of the Land Forces Committee was held on September 7. 'I was a member of this small body,' Churchill later recalled, 'which met at the Home Office, and in one single sweltering afternoon agreed, after hearing the generals, that we should forthwith begin the creation of a fifty-five division Army, together with all the munition factories, plants, and supply services of every kind necessary to sustain it in action.'[1]

At its first meeting, Churchill told the Committee that Britain should aim to provide for 20 divisions within six months, 40 divisions within a year, and a grand total by 1941 of some 50 to 60 divisions. 'The promise of any effort smaller than this,' he argued, 'might fail to hold the French during the difficult time approaching.'[2]

On the following day, at a second meeting of the Land Forces Committee, Churchill undertook to accept a 'temporary reduction' in the Royal Navy's ammunition scales for the next few months, 'so as to assist the Ministry of Supply over a difficult period, by transferring naval cordite to the Army'.[3] That same day Churchill set out in a secret memorandum his thoughts on the necessary scale of the proposed continental army. 'I cannot think that less than 20 divisions by March 1, 1940 would be fair to the French army,' he wrote, even if, to achieve this size, it might be necessary 'to accept lesser standards of equipment than those to which we shall work up at a later date'. Churchill added: 'We must take our place in the Line if we are to hold the Alliance together and win the War.'[4]

It was ten years since the Cabinet room had resounded with Churchill's contribution, and some of those who heard him speak were not used to his vigorous counsel. 'He is writing his new memoirs,' one observer commented to Hoare after a discussion on Press correspondents, while the President of the Board of Trade, Oliver Stanley, asked scathingly: 'Why did he not bring his "World War"?'[5]

This scathing comment hid a deep truth; Churchill's six volume history of the First World War, *The World Crisis*, was more than a narrative history of the war, and Churchill's part in it. Published between 1923 and 1931, it encapsulated Churchill's thoughts on war-

---

[1] Winston S. Churchill, *The Second World War*, volume 1, London 1948, page 355.
[2] Land Forces Committee No. 1 of 1939, 7 September 1939: Cabinet papers, 92/111.
[3] Land Forces Committee No. 2 of 1939, 8 September 1939: Cabinet papers, 92/111.
[4] Land Forces Memorandum No. 4 of 1939, 8 September 1939: Cabinet papers, 92/111.
[5] Sir Samuel Hoare, diary entry for 7 September 1939: Templewood papers.

direction. In writing it during the nineteen-twenties, he relived the crises and setbacks of the war, and once more thought through the policies which he believed ought to have been carried out, and the methods of control which he felt would have averted the many setbacks and disasters, from the Dardanelles to Passchendaele, which had so bedevilled the British policymakers.

In *The World Crisis* Churchill had argued in favour of a decision-making body where decisions, once reached, would be carried out efficiently, and without fear of abrupt reversal. He had urged the need for clear-cut decisions on war policy, which those responsible for giving effect to them could understand; decisions that could then be acted upon with confidence, the commander in the field knowing that, if things began to go badly, the enterprise would not be prematurely changed or abandoned, but given the necessary extra support to see it through. This required an autonomous decision-making body, presided over by a decisive Prime Minister.

Such were the echoes and warnings of *The World Crisis*. There was no way that Churchill, who had lived through the events first as a participant and then as a historian, could shake them out of his mind. Yet in the first days of war, he sensed that the confusions and lack of direction that had characterized, and in his view cursed, the first two years of the First World War would recur with equal danger. 'Was I,' he had written in the Dardanelles section of his second volume, 'in the light of all that followed, "wrong to worry and excite myself"? Await the sequel. It is right to feel the things that matter: and to feel them while time remains.'[1]

At sea, German submarines, having sunk two British merchant ships on September 6, sank a further three on September 7, a total of more than 20,000 tons in forty-eight hours.[2] At the War Cabinet on September 8 Churchill told his colleagues that there had been no loss of life, 'as the ships had been sunk by gunfire after the crews had been removed'. As for the measures being taken to protect Britain's trading lifelines, not only was the convoy system being introduced, but the Admiralty were proposing 'to restrict the sailings of valuable fast ships until they had been armed'. He also suggested that two squadrons of long-range flying-boats, then in the Mediterranean, should be moved to the south-western approaches, and to the coast of Spain, 'where they could assist in the protection of trade'.

[1] Winston S. Churchill, *The World Crisis*, volume 2, London 1923, page 237.
[2] The merchant ships sunk on September 6 were the *Rio Claro* and the *Manaar*, on September 7 the *Pukkastan*, *Olivegrove* and *Gartavon*.

The Chief of the Air Staff accepted this suggestion. Meanwhile, from Poland, the news seemed hopeful; indeed, Ironside reported to the War Cabinet that the Polish Army 'was fighting well and had not been broken'.[1]

But members of the War Cabinet had also received that morning a report that although the Polish Army was 'not demoralized', its withdrawals were being 'much impeded by the overwhelming German superiority in the air and in armoured vehicles'.[2] The Poles, wrote a former Prime Minister of Holland, Dr Colijn, to Churchill that day, 'do not seem to be as good as was expected'. In Holland itself, Colijn reported, '300,000 men, still somewhat weak in artillery, are standing by'.[3]

On this fifth day of the war, the War Cabinet received a pointer to the future in the report of the Land Forces Committee. For planning of all kinds, the report recommended, 'we should assume that the war will last for at least three years, and that the maximum publicity should be given to this assumption'. Britain should aim to equip 55 divisions by the end of the second year of the war, twenty of which should be ready 'within the first twelve months'.

One disturbing note in the report of the Land Forces Committee was the information that the French army was likely 'to require assistance' in equipping itself 'after the first four months of the war'. Even more disturbing, perhaps, was the suggestion that the French might be able to 'assist us with certain of our deficiencies'.[4] These deficiencies were considerable, shrouded in such secrecy that even the members of the War Cabinet only learned of them on September 9, when it discussed the report of the Land Forces Committee. Reading of these deficiencies after the war, Clementine Churchill commented: 'It shews the interminable distance we had to travel before we could fight.'[5]

Meanwhile, on September 8, Churchill discovered that no ship in the Royal Navy had been fitted with radar.[6] Not technical reasons, but lack of finance and priority had been the cause of this. Churchill at once sent a minute to Admiral Fraser, in which he urged that the fitting of radar in all naval ships, 'especially those engaged in the U-

[1] War Cabinet No. 8 of 1939, 8 September 1939, 11.30 a.m.: Cabinet papers, 65/1.
[2] 'Central War Room, Summary of Information Received, No. 3', timed at 7 a.m., 7 September 1939: Cabinet papers, 100/1.
[3] Letter dated 7 September 1939: Churchill papers, 19/2.
[4] War Cabinet Paper No. 14 of 1939, 8 September 1939: Cabinet papers, 66/1.
[5] Churchill papers, 4/131.
[6] Then known as Radio Direction-Finding (RDF).

boat fighting, is of high urgency'. And he added: 'Our submarines should certainly be fitted with this distinguishing apparatus.'[1]

Another anxiety revealed by Churchill's minutes for September 9 concerned what he saw as the slow pace of naval construction, both in the previous year, and as planned for the year to come. 'It is most disconcerting,' he wrote to Admiral Fraser, 'that we get only six destroyers in the present year, then no more for nine months, and only three more in the whole of 1940.' This meant only nine destroyers in prospect in sixteen months. Such a programme, Churchill commented, 'cannot possibly be accepted'.

Churchill then set out for Fraser his own suggestions, as to both types and numbers. Having regard to the 'U-boat menace, which must be expected to renew itself on a much larger scale towards the end of 1940', Churchill wrote, the type of destroyer to be constructed 'must aim at numbers and celerity of construction rather than size or power'. It ought to be possible, Churchill added, to design destroyers which could be completed in under a year, 'in which case', he told Henderson, '50 at least should be begun forthwith'.

Drawing upon his own long experience of naval construction, Churchill ended his minute: 'I am well aware of the need of a proportion of flotilla leaders and large destroyers capable of ocean service, but the arrival in our Fleets of 50 destroyers of the medium emergency type I am contemplating would liberate all larger vessels for ocean work and for combat.'[2]

To Admiral Fraser on September 9, Churchill expressed his concern on a matter of Foreign Policy. He was determined, if possible, to maintain such relations with Italy as might preserve Italian neutrality, and to this end informed Fraser that when the War Cabinet had considered the possibility of developing trade with Italy, the Air Ministry had suggested that the Italians might buy some British aircraft. During the discussion Sir Samuel Hoare had wondered whether 'we might buy some motor boats', and it was this thought which Churchill wished to follow up. 'The matter has some political value,' he told Fraser, 'in building a bridge of mutual interests, and also showing to the world that Italy is not above selling arms to us.'[3]

The War Cabinet had now to discuss the proposal of the Land Forces Committee that Britain should arm and equip 55 divisions for despatch abroad within the next two years. The Secretary of State for War,

[1] Minute dated 8 September 1939: Churchill papers, 19/3.
[2] Minute dated 9 September 1939: Churchill papers, 19/3.
[3] Minute dated 9 September 1939: Churchill papers, 19/3.

Leslie Hore-Belisha, told his colleagues that he was 'satisfied with the proposals of the Committee', and that eleven of the 55 divisions would be able to go overseas within six months, although, he warned, 'their equipment would be deficient in certain respects'. Churchill took the view, however, that the figure for the next twelve months proposed by the Committee should not be 20, but 40 divisions, and that 20 divisions in the first year was 'inadequate'. In any case, he said, they should go overseas 'at considerably earlier dates' than proposed. The Committee's target of 55 divisions within two years, Churchill believed, 'should be the minimum objective', and was an objective 'within our powers'.

During the Land Forces Committee discussions on September 8, the Minister of Supply, Leslie Burgin, had spoken of a shortage of cordite as 'one of his difficulties'. Churchill now told the War Cabinet, as he had told the Committee, that he thought the Admiralty could supply the army with fifty tons of naval cordite a week 'by delaying the completion of reserves of ammunition for heavy guns'.

The Chief of the Imperial General Staff, Sir Edmund Ironside, had also given evidence to the Land Forces Committee during its afternoon session on September 8. Referring to this evidence, Churchill told his War Cabinet colleagues that much of Ironside's information had been 'highly secret', but that he felt nevertheless that one feature, 'the deficiency in heavy guns—should be brought to the notice of the Cabinet'. Once more, Churchill offered 'to see if the Admiralty could help', and he mentioned the possibility of handing over 'some obsolescent naval ordnance', as well as diverting some naval heavy gun production 'to army purposes', provided these suggestions were approved by the Admiralty Board.

At the end of the discussion, Churchill 'emphasized', as the minutes recorded, 'the importance of the Ministry of Supply making rapid progress with planning on the basis of 55 divisions'. But although this sense of priority was embodied in the War Cabinet's conclusions, Churchill's argument in favour of an accelerated pace of troop preparation was not. Although Hoare, the Committee's Chairman, had supported Churchill's view, the Secretary of State for Air, Sir Kingsley Wood, had asked that nothing should be done that might affect adversely the pace of aircraft production.

Once more, the deficiencies in pre-war policy, of which Churchill had been so severe a critic, now inhibited war policy; indeed it was Neville Chamberlain himself who, referring to news of the sudden retreat of Polish forces in western and southern Poland, told the War

Cabinet of September 9 that the Germans had 'a superiority in air armaments', and that the recent fighting in Poland 'showed how such a superiority could be employed to the detriment of land operations'. To meet this superiority, Chamberlain argued, 'we should have to increase materially our productive capacity for aircraft', and it was this argument which persuaded the War Cabinet to defer any final decision on any increase in Army expenditure until the Land Forces Committee could report on the needs of all three Services.[1]

Churchill's work as a member of the Land Forces Committee had led him to ponder the problems of the French Army, as well as those of the British. The need for a close working partnership with France had been a theme of many of Churchill's pre-war speeches and articles. Now he was in a position to ensure that, as far at least as the Admiralty was concerned, such a partnership could be worked for at the highest level. Less than a month before the outbreak of war, while still out of office, he had been invited by the French Government to visit the Maginot Line, and to examine a section of the Franco-German frontier which ran along the Rhine. There, in sight of the German frontier guns, he had discussed with his host, General Georges, the possibility of Monitors—ships without superstructures, but with guns mounted on their protected decks—being used on the Rhine to help hold back any German assault.

On September 9 Churchill wrote to Georges, who had just been appointed Commander of the Forces and Operations in the North East, to explain that he had 'talked to the Admiralty' before he had taken Office about the use of Monitors on the sector of the Rhine frontier which he and Georges had inspected in August. 'I find,' Churchill wrote, 'they have already sent over a couple of engineers to get particulars from your people. I did not know till yesterday that this had happened or I would have written to you beforehand. If it is a nuisance do not hesitate to say so.' Churchill added: 'I think I will make some Monitors for action on rivers—if not the Rhine, then, perhaps, the Danube!'

Churchill ended his letter to Georges: 'I wondered when we last met how long it would be before we should be working in the same affair together, and I beg you to consider me always at your service, either personally or officially, if there is anything you think I can do.'[2] That same day Churchill wrote to the French Ambassador in London,

---

[1] War Cabinet No. 9 of 1939, 9 September 1939, 11.30 a.m.: Cabinet papers, 65/1.
[2] 'Private & Personal', 9 September 1939: Churchill papers, 19/2.

Charles Corbin: 'We have a hard struggle before us, but if there is full comradeship I cannot doubt our victory.'[1]

That night, in utmost secrecy, the first troops of the British Expeditionary Force sailed in convoy to France. The crossing was unchallenged, repeating what was for Churchill one of his proudest achievements of August 1914. News of the success of this first cross-Channel convoy was circulated to the War Cabinet two days later.[2] Twice in twenty-five years Churchill had borne the responsibility of the safe transit of British troops across the Channel.

[1] Letter of 9 September 1939: Churchill papers, 19/2.
[2] 'Central War Room Record No. 7', information up to 11 a.m., 11 September 1939: Cabinet papers, 100/1.

2

'One who treads alone'

THROUGHOUT the early weeks of the war Churchill was quick to point out any signs of what he considered to be unnecessary weakness in British policy, whether military, naval, air or diplomatic. As a member of the War Cabinet, he received copies of all the main Foreign Office telegrams, and it was as a result of reading one of these that on September 10, in a personal letter to the Foreign Secretary, Lord Halifax, he protested about a conversation between the British Ambassador in Rome, Sir Percy Loraine, and the Italian Foreign Minister, Count Ciano. 'From his latest telegram,' Churchill wrote, 'Loraine does not seem to understand our resolve. Surely he could be rallied to a more robust mood.'

Loraine had hinted to Ciano that, if Poland were to sign a peace with Germany, Britain might not need to continue the struggle, initiated as it had been by the German attack on Poland. 'It would make no difference to our action,' Churchill told Halifax, 'if Poland were forced into a defeated peace'; indeed, Loraine ought to make it clear 'that we intend to see the war through to a victorious end, whatever happens to Poland'. Once Ciano realized Britain's 'inflexible purpose', Churchill commented, 'he will be less likely to toy with the idea of an Italian mediation, coupled with veiled menaces of intervention against us'.

A second telegram which had disturbed Churchill was one which implied that Egypt should not enter the war at Britain's side, in order to make use of Egyptian neutral ports for supplies from the United States. 'I thought our policy was to bring Egypt into the war as a belligerent at the earliest moment,' he wrote, 'and we certainly have no need to keep her neutral for the purpose of war purchases from the United States who'—he added—'will very soon give us all we want direct.'

Churchill ended his letter to Halifax on what he intended to be a reassuring note. 'I hope,' he wrote, 'you will not mind my drawing your attention from time to time to points which strike me in the Foreign Office telegrams, as it is so much better than that I should raise them in Cabinet.'[1]

Churchill had not been present at a meeting of the War Cabinet on September 10 which discussed the 'observance of the rules of war'. But he did write later that day to Neville Chamberlain, setting out his own feeling 'that we should not take the initiative in bombing, except in the immediate zone in which the French armies are operating, where we must of course help'. Churchill added:

It is to our interest that the war should be conducted in accordance with the more humane conceptions of war, and that we should follow and not precede the Germans in the process, no doubt inevitable, of deepening severity and violence. Every day that passes gives more shelter to the population of London and the big cities, and in a fortnight or so there will be far more comparatively safe refuges than now.

Churchill went on to tell Chamberlain of one area of continuing concern. He was, he said, reluctant to accept Sir Kingsley Wood's opposition to the creation of a fifty-five division Army within two years, on the grounds, insisted upon by Kingsley Wood, that such a commitment would be detrimental to Air Force and Admiralty expansion. At the War Cabinet on September 9 Chamberlain had been influenced by Kingsley Wood's argument. Now Churchill, in seeking to persuade him to change his mind, wrote: 'pardon me if I put my experience and knowledge, which were bought, not taught, at your disposal'.

Churchill pointed out that the preliminary work involved in building the factories needed for the supply side of such a long-term Army programme 'will not for many months require skilled labour; there are months of digging foundations, laying concrete, bricks and mortar, drainage etc., for which the ordinary building-trade labourers suffice', enabling the skilled men to continue to produce the existing priorities for the Navy and Air Force. If the Ministry of Supply did not 'make a big lay-out at the beginning', there would inevitably be 'vexatious delays when existing factories have to be enlarged'. Churchill added: 'A factory once set up need not be used until it is necessary, but if it is not in existence you may be helpless if you need a further effort.'

[1] 'Secret', 'Personal and Private', 10 September 1939: Churchill papers, 4/143. Churchill's responsibilities as a member of the War Cabinet included, as he saw it, a watching brief over all matters of war policy, including foreign affairs. But his exercise of what he regarded as his responsibility was, Sir Ian Jacob reflected on reading this letter to Halifax, an 'illustration of how Churchill impinged on other Minister's concerns' (Sir Ian Jacob, notes for the author, 1 July 1982).

Churchill based his arguments on his own two years' experience as Minister of Munitions in the First World War, when he had supervised munitions production for several war fronts, and had coordinated the munitions supplies of the Allies. Recalling his work at another of his previous Ministerial posts, Churchill was able to make a further suggestion. 'In 1919,' he told Chamberlain, 'after the war, when I was Secretary of State for War, I ordered a mass of cannon to be stored, oiled, and carefully kept; and I also remember making in 1918 two 12-inch howitzers at the request of GHQ to support their advance into Germany in 1919. They were never used, but they were the last word at the time. They are not easy things to lose . . .' It was, Churchill added, 'vitally urgent, first, to see what there is in the cupboard.'[1]

On September 11 both the President of the Board of Trade, Oliver Stanley, and the President of the Chamber of Shipping, at a meeting of the Shipping Defence Advisory Committee, pressed Churchill to support the creation of a Ministry of Shipping. Churchill wrote at once, within a few hours, direct to Chamberlain, supporting the request in detail, and adding that it also seemed to him important 'that the step of creating a Ministry of Shipping should be taken by the Government before pressure is applied in Parliament and from shipping circles, and before we are told that there is valid complaint against the existing system'.[2]

That evening, September 11, Churchill dined at the Other Club—the Club he had founded with his friend F. E. Smith twenty-eight years before. The dinner was a special one, to say goodbye to the Commander-in-Chief of the British Expeditionary Force, Lord Gort, who was about to cross to France. Among those present were the former Prime Minister of Canada, R. B. Bennett, Churchill's friend Brendan Bracken, and the newspaper proprietor, Lord Camrose. In a note of the conversation, Camrose wrote of how 'Winston prophesied that while we would get the submarine menace in hand fairly quickly, there would be a very large recrudescence of submarine warfare in about a year's time. He said this was what happened in the last war. Bennett, Gort and I disagreed with him.'[3]

---

[1] 'Private and Personal', despatched at 1 a.m. on 11 September 1939: Churchill papers, 19/2.

[2] Letter of 11 September 1939: Churchill papers, 19/2. On 13 October 1939 a Ministry of Shipping was created. Its first Minister was Sir John Gilmour, who was succeeded in April 1940 by Robert Hudson, and in May 1940 by Ronald Cross.

[3] Notes of interviews, 11 September 1939: Camrose papers. Churchill was right, as the Battle of the Atlantic was eventually to show. Only a most secret intelligence source enabled that battle to be won (see pages 609–13).

That night Churchill prepared his now routine note for the Admiralty Board meeting of the following morning. His notes were brief and brisk, intended to probe all areas where errors or waste could be avoided, and to suggest new areas of construction and research. Of the projected expansion of *Fiji* class cruisers he wrote: 'Please No! This policy of scattering over the seas weak cruisers which can neither fight nor flee the German 8-inch 10,000 ton cruisers—of which they will quite soon have five—should be abandoned. The idea of two *Fijis* fighting an 8-inch gun cruiser will never come off. All experience shows that a cluster of weak ships will not fight one strong one.' Churchill gave as an example of this his own failure, in August 1914, to prevent the escape of the German battle cruiser *Goeben* from the Adriatic to the Dardanelles.

In his note of September 11, Churchill had asked for an Admiralty committee to be set up to see if a special 'anti-submarine and anti-air vessel' could be built, based on 'the greatest simplicity of armament and equipment', capable of being mass-produced, and able to take over anti-submarine duties from destroyers and fast escort vessels which would be needed elsewhere. These new ships, he wrote, 'will be deemed "Cheap and Nasties" (cheap to us, nasty to the U-Boat).' They would, he added, 'being built for a particular but urgent job', be of little value to the Navy once that job had been done, but, he urged, 'let us get the job done'.[1]

Writing to Pound on September 12, Churchill proposed the setting up of a special 'Unit of Search', based on a single cruiser and an aircraft-carrier, to seek out and destroy German cruisers which were sinking British merchant ships. 'The mere multiplication of small, weak cruisers,' he wrote, 'is no means of ridding the seas of powerful raiders. Indeed, they are only an easy prey. The raider, cornered at length, will overwhelm one weak vessel and escape from the cordon.' Churchill wanted a formation which would have the speed and power to search 'an enormous area' and to destroy 'any single raider' once detected. 'Each Unit of Search,' he wrote, 'must be able to find, to catch, and to kill.'[2]

Also on September 12, Churchill sent his most senior naval advisers a five-page outline of the project he had mentioned to Dudley Pound

---

[1] 'Secret', 11 September 1939: Churchill papers, 19/3. Three British merchant ships had been sunk on September 9 (the *Winkleigh*, the *Regent Tiger*, and the *Kennebec*), and two on September 10 (the *Goodwood* and the *Magdapur*). A further three were sunk on the day of Churchill's note (the *Blairlogie*, the *Firby* and the *Inverliffey*), a total of more than 50,000 tons in four days.

[2] Minute of 12 September 1939: Admiralty papers, 205/2.

six days before, a British naval attack into the Baltic, aimed at 'command' of Germany's only sea link with Norway, Sweden and Finland.

The scheme was to be given the code name 'Catherine'. Since first broaching it to Pound, Churchill had already discussed with Sir Stanley Goodall, the Director of Naval Construction, some of the special designs needed to enable a substantial naval force to navigate the narrow waters linking the North Sea with the Baltic. 'It would also be necessary,' Churchill noted, 'to strengthen the armour deck so as to give exceptional protection against air attack.' Plans would need to be put in hand almost at once, with the orders for all necessary work being given 'by October 1', and the operation itself planned for March 1940, when 'the ice in the theatre concerned melts'. It would, Churchill added, 'be a great pity to waste the summer, therefore the highest priority would be required'.

In preparation for 'Catherine', Churchill suggested, two 15-inch gun battleships would be prepared ('but of course 3 would be better') to be pitted against 'their only possible antagonists', the *Scharnhorst* and *Gneisenau*. These two warships were 'the sole resources of Germany' in the battleship class; the superior guns of the British battleships would 'out-range them and would shatter them'. The British battleships would be protected in their voyage into the Baltic by a dozen specially prepared 'mine-bumpers' designed with 'a heavy fore end to take the shock of any exploding mine'. The whole 'expeditionary fleet' was to take with it a three months' supply of fuel oil, in tankers prepared for this task.

Churchill then set out for his senior advisers the objectives of 'Catherine', an operation which he described to them as 'the supreme naval offensive open to the Royal Navy'. Above all, he wrote, the 'isolation' of Germany from Norway and Sweden 'would intercept the supplies of iron ore, food and all other trade'. The very arrival of the force in the Baltic 'would probably determine' the entry of Denmark, Norway and Sweden into the war on the side of Britain and France, 'in which case a convenient base could be found capable of being supplied overland'. The three months' oil supply would give the Scandinavian States time to decide, but 'if the worst comes to the worst, it is not seen why the Fleet should not return as it came'.

But if 'Catherine' succeeded, Churchill believed, the mere presence of so dominant a British naval power 'would hold all enemy forces on the spot. They would not dare to send them on the trade routes, except as a measure of despair.' In addition, the influence on Russia of a British Fleet in the Baltic 'would be far-reaching', although, as Churchill wrote, 'we cannot count on this'.

Churchill's 'Catherine' was headed 'Most Secret', and given its limited circulation on September 12. 'I commend these ideas to your study,' he wrote, 'hoping that the intention will be to solve the difficulties.'[1]

Two personal matters concerned with the war also engaged Churchill's attention during September 12. Having heard that Sir Samuel Hoare had recommended Brendan Bracken to be Under-Secretary at the Ministry of Information, Churchill wrote to Chamberlain to press his friend's appointment. 'I need not say how very agreeable this would be to me,' Churchill wrote, 'he being one of my best friends. But I am sure he would serve you with equal loyalty.' People who were reluctant to criticize the fighting departments, Churchill noted, 'will work off their feelings on the Ministry of Information'. The post of Under-Secretary would be 'much under fire'. At the start of the First World War, Churchill recalled, he himself had appointed F. E. Smith to this post, 'and he had a very rough ride in which all his parliamentary skill was needed. I believe Bracken has the ability and personal qualities to fill this place. He is an exceptional man, and is very good in the personal relations. . . .'[2]

To Lord Beaverbrook, who had also pressed Bracken's claim, Churchill wrote that same day, 'I have written as strongly as I can to Neville about Brendan. I hope it will do more good than harm.'[3] But a week later Chamberlain appointed Sir Edward Grigg to the position, whereupon Churchill decided to use Bracken's services and talents as his own Parliamentary Private Secretary at the Admiralty.

Another personal matter arose when one of Churchill's closest friends, 'Bendor', the 2nd Duke of Westminster, alleged, at a private meeting on September 12, that Britain need not be at war with Germany at all. The war, declared the Duke, was part of a Jewish and Masonic plot to destroy Christian civilization.[4] A report of the Duke's remarks had been sent to Chamberlain, and was mentioned by several

[1] Churchill made eight copies of this proposal, 'Of which all except one,' he wrote, 'will be destroyed after the necessary examination has been made': Admiralty papers, 199/1928.

[2] 'Private and Personal', 12 September 1939: Churchill papers, 2/364.

[3] 'Private and Personal', 12 September 1939: Beaverbrook papers.

[4] Unknown perhaps to the Duke of Westminster, Churchill himself had been a Freemason. On 24 May 1901 Brother Winston Leonard Spencer Churchill had been initiated in the United Studholme Lodge No. 1591, London, on the same evening as George Cave, later Home Secretary in Lloyd George's wartime coalition, and Viscount Mersey. Churchill was Raised on 25 March 1902, and resigned from the Craft 'in good faith and order with all dues paid up' in July 1912 (Archives of the United Grand Lodge of England). In his memoirs, Lord Mersey wrote: 'That month I was initiated as a Freemason at Studholme Lodge. While waiting for the ceremony I walked round and round Golden Square with Winston Churchill, another candidate' (Viscount Mersey, A Picture of Life, 1872–1940, London 1941, page 188).

War Cabinet Ministers at their meeting of September 13. 'It gave me great distress to read it,' Churchill wrote to the Duke later that day, 'being one of your oldest friends,' and he added: 'I am sure that pursuance of this line would lead you into measureless odium and vexation. When a country is fighting a war of this kind, very hard experiences lie before those who preach defeatism and set themselves against the will of the nation.'

Churchill ended his letter: 'I beg you not to spurn the counsels of a life-long friend.'[1]

Churchill continued to exhort his War Cabinet colleagues to a robust prosecution of the war, and on September 12, after General Ironside had reported that the Belgians were unwilling to enter into military discussions with France and Britain, or even to allow reconnaissance by French and British officers, Churchill intervened to describe the Belgian Government's attitude as 'indefensible'. The Belgians, he said, 'owed everything to us, and their retention of their Colonial Empire would entirely depend on our victory'. It was essential, he added, 'that, whatever outward attitude they might adopt, they should consent to close relations between the three countries'.[2]

At a further War Cabinet on the morning of September 14, Churchill argued in favour of making 'the fullest possible use of the offensive power of our air force'. Attacks should be made, he suggested, on 'strictly military objectives—such as synthetic petrol plants in Germany which were vital to her prosecution of the war, and which, at the same time, were isolated from the civil population'. Such attacks should be made, Churchill suggested, 'even if this was to draw German fire on ourselves'. But in reply, the Secretary of State for Air, Sir Kingsley Wood, stressing the very air weakness of which Churchill had warned in vain for so many years, told the War Cabinet that, above all, 'we must keep our small and inferior Air Force "in being" against the time when its existence might be vital to us'. Britain's air position, Kingsley Wood added, would be 'immeasurably better' by March 1940.[3]

No one could doubt the dangers which this weakness in the air foreshadowed. That morning all members of the War Cabinet received a report from the British Ambassador to Poland, giving details of the

[1] 'Secret and Personal', 13 September 1939: Churchill papers, 19/2.
[2] War Cabinet No. 13 of 1939, 12 September 1939, 11.30 a.m.: Cabinet papers, 65/1.
[3] War Cabinet No. 15 of 1939, 14 September 1939, 11.30 a.m.: Cabinet papers, 65/1.

extent to which Poland was being 'deliberately and systematically devastated by air attack'.[1]

In his daily survey of military developments, General Ironside told the War Cabinet on September 15 that the French were convinced the Germans 'would stage a big attack on the Western Front' in a month's time. Ironside himself felt that such an attack might be possible at the end of October.[2] But in a letter to Chamberlain later that day, Churchill felt that it was 'most unlikely' that the Germans would strike westward 'at this late season'. More likely, he wrote, was a continual advance eastwards and south, 'through Poland, Hungary and Rumania', or, he added, 'it may be that he has some understanding with Russia by which she will take part of Poland and recover Bessarabia'.

Churchill doubted whether Hitler would move west until, as he wrote to Chamberlain, 'he has collected the easy spoils which await him in the East', thus enabling him to give the German people 'the spectacle of repeated successes'. None the less, Churchill argued, 'I am strongly of opinion that we should make every preparation to defend ourselves in the West.' It was essential, he wrote, that the French frontier 'behind Belgium should be fortified night and day by every conceivable resource'. In particular, 'the obstacles to tank attack, planting railway rails upright, digging deep ditches, erecting concrete dolls, land-mines in some parts and inundations all ready to let out in others, etc., should be combined in a deep system of defence'. The attack of three or four German armoured divisions which had been so effective in Poland, 'can only be stopped', Churchill asserted 'by physical obstacles defended by resolute troops and a powerful artillery'. Without such physical obstacles, Churchill warned, 'the attack of armoured vehicles cannot be resisted'.

In his letter of September 15 Churchill gave Chamberlain an item of good news: 'the mass of war-time artillery which I stored in 1919', he wrote, had now been discovered. There were in the store so many howitzers, including 32 twelve-inch, 145 nine-inch and nearly 200 six-inch, with large quantities of ammunition, to constitute 'the heavy artillery, not of our small Expeditionary Force, but of a great army'. Churchill advised Chamberlain that no time should be lost 'in bringing some of these guns into the field, so that whatever else our troops lack they will not suffer from want of heavy artillery'.

Churchill's letter ended: 'I hope you will consider carefully what I

[1] 'Central War Room Record No. 10', information up to 7 a.m., 14 September 1939: Cabinet papers, 100/1. The Ambassador was Sir Howard Kennard.
[2] War Cabinet No. 16 of 1939, 15 September 1939, 11.45 a.m., Confidential Annex: Cabinet papers, 65/3.

write to you. I do so only in my desire to aid you in your responsibilities and discharge my own.'[1] In answer, Chamberlain told Churchill that all his letters were 'carefully read and considered by me'. If he had not replied to them, it was because 'I am seeing you every day, and moreover because, as far as I have been able to observe, your views and mine have very closely coincided.' Chamberlain added, however, that contrary to Churchill's view, he believed that the extent of Britain's effort on land should be determined by Britain's resources '*after* we have provided for Air Force extension'.[2] Thus once again the priorities of war policy were imposed not by the needs of the strategic situation, but by the dictates of pre-war neglect.

On the night of September 15, Churchill left London by train for Wick, and thence to Scapa Flow, to discuss the naval situation with the Commander-in-Chief, Sir Charles Forbes. He travelled north with Sir Archibald Sinclair, Brendan Bracken and the Admiralty Flag Lieutenant, Lieutenant-Commander 'Tommy' Thompson. With Churchill, in his locked box of papers, were the secret minutes of a meeting of the Chiefs of Staff Committee, held on September 15, at which the defence of Scapa had been discussed. It was clear from these minutes that the full scheme of defences would only be ready 'by the spring of 1940'. As for Scapa's Air defences, the minutes recorded, 'it was agreed that a start should be made with the work straight away. The searchlights and guns should be provided step by step, as and when equipments became available. . . .'[3]

On the way to Wick on the morning of September 16, Churchill reached the naval base at Invergordon. From there he sent a messenger back to London with a letter for the Foreign Secretary, Lord Halifax. Once more, it was the reading of Foreign Office telegrams that had, during the train journey north, excited his concern. In his letter to Halifax he stressed the need to bring Bulgaria into the Balkan defence system, if only to allow Turkish troops to be able to march overland, across Bulgaria, to the defence of Rumania. A German attack on Rumania might, he feared, follow the defeat of Poland.[4] The Greeks as

---

[1] 'Secret and Personal', 15 September 1939: Churchill papers, 19/2.

[2] Letter of 16 September 1939, marked in red ink, 'read 18.9. WSC': Churchill papers, 19/2.

[3] Chiefs of Staff Committee No. 17 of 1939, 15 September 1939: Cabinet papers, 79/1.

[4] It did not; but in the spring of 1941, after considerable German pressure, Rumania joined the Axis powers, and in June 1942 Rumanian forces fought alongside the German Army in the invasion of the Soviet Union.

well as the Rumanians, Churchill wrote, 'if they are to enjoy our protection, should also pay a price which indeed is no more than justice',
and he suggested that Greece meet Bulgarian claims for an outlet on
the Aegean Sea. Assuming Turkey would be willing to help Rumania,
he added, 'it would seem' that Britain's representatives in Yugoslavia,
Rumania, Bulgaria, Greece and Turkey 'should all sing one tune,
namely, gain Bulgaria by threats and concessions'.

Churchill ended his letter by thanking Lord Halifax for his permission 'to write to you freely my views', and he added: 'pray believe that
I shall equally welcome any suggestions about the Admiralty which at
any time occur to you'.[1]

From Invergordon, Churchill went on by train to Wick, and thence
to Scapa Flow, where Sir Charles Forbes described the plans being
put into effect for the protection of merchant shipping convoys. As
Churchill reported to the War Cabinet on his return to London, these
convoys would receive Royal Navy protection against submarine attack
in the approaches to Britain, 'though for some time the anti-submarine
escorts will be weaker than desired'. Henceforth, however, Churchill
wrote, all the Navy's defence measures 'will progressively increase in
power'.

Churchill also reported to the War Cabinet on the morale of the
merchant seamen. In spite of the early heavy sinkings, he wrote, 'there
will be no reluctance to proceed to sea and an increasing readiness to
obey Admiralty instructions'.[2]

From Scapa Flow, Churchill sailed in the *Nelson* to Loch Ewe, where
the rest of the Fleet was sheltering. Leaving Scapa for the open sea, he
was surprised to see no escort of destroyers 'for this great ship', and, as
he later recalled, told Admiral Forbes: 'I thought you never went to
sea without at least two, even for a single battleship.' Of course, Forbes
replied, that was 'what we should like'. But, Forbes added, 'we haven't
got the destroyers to carry out any such rule'.

As he sailed around the northern coast of Scotland from Scapa to
Loch Ewe, Churchill remembered how, in August 1914, he had visited
the Fleet at Loch Ewe at the outbreak of the First World War. Then,
he recalled, he had found the ships 'a prey to the same uncertainties as
now afflicted us'. The Admirals and Captains who now paced the decks
had been young Lieutenants 'or even Midshipmen in those far off days'.

---

[1] 'Sent from Invergordon by hand', 16 September 1939; Churchill papers, 4/143.
[2] 'Secret', 'Report of the First Lord of the Admiralty to the War Cabinet, No. 1', War Cabinet
Paper No. 36 of 1939, 17 September 1939: Cabinet papers, 66/1. One merchant ship had been
sunk on September 13, two on September 14 and three on September 17.

Then, Churchill had already been First Lord of the Admiralty for nearly three years, and had been able to make the appointments he believed to be the best in preparation for war. Now, he wrote, 'all these were new figures and new faces . . . an entirely different generation filled the uniforms and the posts'. Only the ships were old; many being those which Churchill himself had ordered to be built between 1911 and 1915. 'It was a strange experience,' he reflected, 'like suddenly resuming a previous incarnation. It seemed that I was all that had survived in the same position I had held so long ago. But no; the dangers had survived too. . . .'

Churchill stayed overnight on board the *Nelson*, leaving Loch Ewe on the morning of September 17, and driving across the Highlands to Inverness. 'We had a picnic lunch on the way,' he recalled, 'by a stream sparkling in hot sunshine. I felt oddly oppressed with my memories.' No one, he reflected, 'had ever been over the same terrible course twice with such an interval between. No one had felt its dangers and responsibilities from the summit,' or understood, from personal experience, 'how First Lords of the Admiralty are treated when great ships are sunk or things go wrong'.

Churchill was stirred to sombre reflections: 'If we were in fact going over the same cycle a second time, should I have once again to endure the pangs of dismissal? Fisher, Wilson, Battenberg, Jellicoe, Beatty, Pakenham, Sturdee, all gone!' and he recalled the lines:

> I feel like one
> Who treads alone
> Some banquet-hall deserted,
> Whose lights are fled,
> Whose garlands dead,
> And all but he departed.[1]

As Churchill's reflections intensified, he asked himself:

And what of the supreme, measureless ordeal in which we were again irrevocably plunged? Poland in its agony; France but a pale reflection of her former warlike ardour: the Russian Colossus no longer an ally, not even neutral, possibly to become a foe. Italy no friend. Japan no ally. Would America ever come in again? The British Empire remained intact and gloriously united, but ill-prepared, unready. We still had command of the sea. We were woefully outmatched in numbers in this new mortal weapon of the air.

'Somehow,' Churchill added, 'the light faded out of the landscape.'[2]

[1] From *National Airs, Oft in the Stilly Night* by Thomas Moore (1779–1852).
[2] Winston S. Churchill, *The Second World War*, volume 1, London 1948, pages 339–40.

The disaster foreshadowed by Churchill's musings while he was driving across Scotland on September 17 was quickly upon him. Even as he arrived in London in the early hours of the morning, after the long journey from Inverness, Pound was waiting for him at the station with the news of the sinking of the aircraft carrier *Courageous*. The carrier had been on temporary convoy escort duty. More than 500 of her crew of 1,260 had been drowned, together with her Captain.

At that morning's War Cabinet, Churchill noted that the sinking had 'drawn attention once more to the shortage of destroyers from which we were suffering'. He then made two suggestions. The first was that Britain should do everything in its power 'to purchase destroyers from the United States'. The second was that the Government of Eire should make available the former Treaty Port of Berehaven, as a base for 'long-range flying boats and destroyers'. The situation as far as Eire was concerned, Churchill added, was 'profoundly unsatisfactory'. But it was generally agreed, the minutes recorded, that it was 'very undesirable' for there to be any 'open difference' at the moment between Britain and Eire.[1]

As far as purchases from the United States were concerned, Churchill recognized the limitations. 'There is, of course, no objection to exploring American possibilities,' he noted that day on an earlier Admiralty suggestion for such purchases, 'but the dollar stringency will be very great, and nothing should be bought abroad which we can make at home.'[2]

The news that dominated the War Cabinet's discussion on September 18 was the Soviet military occupation of eastern Poland: this move, agreed upon secretly in the Nazi–Soviet Pact negotiations a week before the outbreak of war, effectively destroyed all chance of Polish resistance to the continuing German advance in the west.

With Poland virtually defeated, and on the verge of partition between Germany and the Soviet Union, Churchill feared a German air attack on Britain's aircraft factories 'before the weather seriously deteriorates', as he wrote to Kingsley Wood that same day, September 18. Such an air offensive, Churchill felt, was 'far more likely than a land offensive in the West', and he suggested that the Air Ministry take some of the balloons and anti-aircraft guns from London, 'for the

---

[1] War Cabinet No. 19 of 1939, 18 September 1939, 11 a.m.: Cabinet papers, 65/1.

[2] 'First Lord's Comments on Captain Tennant's notes of Staff Conference of September 12', 18 September 1939: Admiralty papers, 205/2.

defence of the principal aircraft factories at Coventry, Derby, Bristol, etc.'. Were such a policy to be proposed, he added, he would support it.[1]

Later on September 18, at a meeting of senior Admiralty officials in Churchill's room at the Admiralty, he expressed his belief that 'Germany's best interests would be to push on to the Black Sea', unless Russia were to impose a veto. The threat of such a move by Germany might, however, help to form a 'Balkan Front', and he was 'still hopeful' that Britain could persuade Turkey to join such a front. If Germany 'got into Rumania', Churchill declared, 'it would be essential for Britain to have command of the Black Sea'.

Britain must also be prepared, Churchill told his advisers, for an eventual German move in the west. What he envisaged was 'an attack via Belgium'. The advance of four or five German armoured divisions through Belgium would be 'a great danger', and he reiterated his conviction that 'special trenches, barricades and palisades' should be dug 'forthwith' on the Franco-Belgian frontier.

The Naval Staff also shared Churchill's concern about the Irish ports, stating 'how invaluable' it would be for Britain to get the use of Berehaven with regard to the operation of destroyers in the Western Approaches.

During the meeting, Churchill told his admirals that, in his view, as a general principle, 'the search for Naval offensives should be pursued'. Admiral Drax[2] had spoken of the need to prevent the Germans bringing Swedish iron ore, vital for their war effort, across the Gulf of Bothnia to Germany. It was suggested, the notes of the meeting do not say by whom, that 'every possible effort' should be made to stop the movement of iron ore from Sweden by diplomatic means, but that if all other methods failed, including a British offer to buy the ore, 'we should be prepared to violate Norwegian neutrality'.

The possibility of trying to halt Swedish iron ore from its routes across the Baltic Sea or along the Norwegian coast raised once again the question of a British naval presence in the Baltic, and at a further meeting in Churchill's room on September 18, the Director of Plans, Captain C. S. Daniel, described the result of his investigations into 'Catherine'. The minutes of the meeting recorded that these investigations 'were generally approved and it was decided that planning should continue'.[3]

---

[1] 'Secret', 18 September 1939: Churchill papers, 19/2.
[2] Commander-in-Chief, the Nore.
[3] 'Minutes of Meetings in First Lord's Room, 18th September, 1939': Admiralty papers, 205/2.

Churchill was determined to follow up the iron ore question without delay, and at the War Cabinet on the morning of September 19 he described the ore as 'vital for the German munitions industry'. Whereas, he explained, this ore in summer could cross the Gulf of Bothnia, in winter it had to go from Sweden to the Norwegian port of Narvik, and from Narvik 'along the whole length of the Norwegian coast', from north to south.

The German ships, Churchill explained, protected themselves from attack from the Royal Navy by remaining within the three-mile limit of Norwegian territorial waters. And yet, he pointed out, British policy 'must be to stop this trade going to Germany'.

Churchill went on to warn the War Cabinet that if the iron ore could not be stopped 'by pressure on the Norwegian Government, he would be compelled to propose the remedy which had been adopted in the last war, namely, the laying of mines inside Norwegian territorial waters, which had drawn the ore-carrying vessels outside the three-mile limit'. This measure, however, he pointed out to his colleagues, had not been adopted in the First World War until after the entry of the United States in the spring of 1917.[1]

In a letter to Pound on his return to the Admiralty, Churchill noted that he had advised the War Cabinet to 'repeat this process' of mining Norwegian territorial waters, as had been done in 1918 'with the approval and co-operation of the United States', and to do so 'very shortly'. The Cabinet, he added, including Lord Halifax, 'appeared strongly favourable to this action'. Churchill therefore instructed the Admiralty staff concerned to study the operation. 'Pray let me be continually informed of the progress of this plan', he wrote, 'which is of the highest importance in crippling the enemy's war industry.' A further Cabinet decision would of course be necessary, 'when all is in readiness'.[2]

Churchill immediately set out for the War Cabinet his reasons for seeking action against Germany by laying mines inside Norwegian territorial waters. The Swedish port of Oxelösund, he pointed out, could export only one fifth of the weight of iron ore which Germany required from Sweden. The main winter trade was therefore through Narvik. 'It must be understood,' Churchill wrote, 'that an adequate supply of Swedish iron ore is vital to Germany and the interception or prevention of these Narvik supplies during the winter months, i.e. from October to the end of April, will greatly reduce her power of resistance.'

[1] War Cabinet No. 20 of 1939, 19 September 1939, 11 a.m.: Cabinet papers, 65/1.
[2] 'Most Secret', 19 September 1939: Churchill papers, 19/3.

The need for action might not arise at all, Churchill pointed out, for during the first three weeks of war 'no iron ore ships left Narvik owing to the reluctance of crews to sail'. Should this 'happy state of affairs continue', he added, 'no special action would be demanded from the Admiralty in regard to this problem'. At the same time, negotiations were proceeding with the Swedish Government which might 'effectively reduce' the supplies of Scandinavian ore to Germany by diplomatic means. 'Should however the supplies from Narvik start moving once more,' Churchill warned, 'the situation will need to be reconsidered with a view to more drastic action.'[1]

What Churchill now sought was the War Cabinet's approval to 'remit the question to the various Departments concerned in order that detailed plans may be made for prompt action'.[2]

The War Cabinet did not share Churchill's sense of urgency about the problem of the Narvik ore convoy; it would be at least six months before the Norwegian waters would be free from the hazards of winter ice. But Churchill had trained himself to look ahead; this had been his method of thought for more than forty years, and he could not abandon it now. He therefore continued, within the Admiralty, to keep up his questioning. One such minute, written a month after he had first raised the iron ore issue, consisted of six specific requests for 'detailed information' about the convoy or iron ore ships which would sail from Narvik to Germany. His questions were: 'When does it start? How many ships are in it? What is the escort? How long does the voyage take? What is the nationality of the various ships included? What is their cargo?'[3]

Not the distant project to mine Norwegian waters, however, but the immediate state of Britain's air defences, was the dominant concern at the War Cabinet of September 19. In a discussion so secret that it was recorded only in the 'Most Secret' confidential annex to the War Cabinet's conclusions, Ministers heard expert opinion about Britain's ability to take the offensive. The Chief of the Air Staff, Sir Cyril Newall, warned that Britain's air defences were 'far from complete', while Sir Samuel Hoare told his colleagues that 'a considerable time would elapse under our present programme before we even achieved parity with the Germans'.

---

[1] For a map of the Scandinavian region, see page 177.

[2] 'Norway and Sweden', 23 September 1939 (Memorandum for the War Cabinet): Admiralty papers, 205/2.

[3] Minute of 25 October 1939, addressed to Admiral Phillips, and to Captain Mansergh, Director of the Trade Division: Churchill papers, 19/3.

Churchill's own forecast of the development of the war was not, however, a pessimistic one. Although the German and Allied populations were 'approximately equal', he told his colleagues, the Germans started with 'the disadvantage' that they were short 'of certain vital materials, and some at least of their population was gravely disaffected'. It therefore seemed to him probable, he added, 'that after a few months, weaknesses would begin to show in the German military machine, however formidable it might appear now'.[1]

Churchill also spoke optimistically later that same day, at a meeting of the War Cabinet to discuss the second report of the Land Forces Committee, when he once more argued in support of a 55 division army, believing that there would be 'no clash' between the demands of the Army, the Air Ministry and the Admiralty, even with the need to equip such an army, as the Committee now recommended, within a period of two years, and at the same time to maintain a steady output of 2,550 aircraft a month.

First, Churchill argued, Britain's naval demands would 'probably be less than in the last war'. Secondly, the 55 divisions now aimed at for 1941 should be compared with the 100 divisions in existence in 1918. Thirdly, 'the population of our country was substantially higher than during the last war, and we had the possibility of employing about 2 million more work people than we had then', despite the high percentage of people in the older age groups.[2]

Churchill's wider perspective, based as it was upon his long ministerial experience, especially during the First World War, served even in personal conversation to rally his colleagues. 'Yesterday,' wrote Lord Hankey to his wife on September 19, 'was a bad day, what with the *Courageous* and the Russian defection. But one has these shocks in war. For example Winston has reminded me how, about 25 years ago almost to the day we lost the *Aboukir*, *Cressy* and *Hogue*, sunk by German submarines. And this is not the first time Russia has "defected". So we must not worry too much.'[3]

Russia was much on Churchill's mind that week, when Pound gave him a series of notes on 'Catherine'. 'There can be little doubt,' Pound wrote, 'that if we could maintain control of the Baltic for a considerable period it would greatly enhance our prestige.' Its success would depend, however, in his view, on Russia not having joined Germany, and on

---

[1] War Cabinet No. 20 of 1939, 19 September 1939, 11 a.m., Confidential Annex: Cabinet papers, 65/3.

[2] Land Forces Committee No. 3 of 1939, 19 September 1939, 4 p.m.: Cabinet papers, 92/111.

[3] Letter of 19 September 1939: Hankey papers.

'the *active* co-operation of Sweden for the supply of oil and the use of a base and her repair facilities', within a 'measureable time' of the British ships arriving in the Baltic. In addition, Pound wrote, the force which Britain sent into the Baltic '*must* be such that we can with our Allies at that time win the war without it, in spite of any probable combination against us'.[1]

Reading Pound's notes on September 20, Churchill wrote at the bottom of them: 'I entirely agree.' And he added: 'At present the decision is only for exploration; & no question of *action* arises. But the search for a naval offensive must be incessant.'[2]

Churchill now sought a senior Admiral who, supported by a small staff, could examine 'Catherine' in detail, gathering all the necessary information, and drafting the technical plans. In October 1914 he had given similar planning duties to the seventy-two-year-old Sir Arthur Wilson, whom he had brought out of retirement. Now he proposed that Admiral of the Fleet the Earl of Cork and Orrery should be put in charge of the new task. Pound agreed, and the sixty-five-year-old Admiral took up his duties at once, with a room at the Admiralty.

At the War Cabinet on September 21 Churchill raised again the danger of an autumn invasion. 'The next fortnight,' he said, 'while there was a good moon, and before the weather broke up, might be a time of particular danger.' He feared that a recent German complaint to Switzerland about the 'inhumane' British naval blockade 'sounded like a German manoeuvre to justify an air attack on this country'.[3]

Later in the discussion, Lord Halifax told the War Cabinet that the Rumanian Government had begun to intern many leading Poles, who had crossed into Rumania in an attempt to escape the German advance. Such conduct, Churchill said, was 'odious', and would 'create a deplorable impression' in both Britain and the United States. The Rumanian Government, he said, 'should be asked to explain their present actions with the position which they occupied towards us in view of our having guaranteed their country against invasion by Germany'.

[1] 'Most Secret', 'To be passed round only in a box', 'Notes on "C" ', 19 September 1939: Admiralty papers, 205/4.
[2] Note of 20 September 1939: Admiralty papers, 205/4.
[3] War Cabinet No. 22 of 1939, 21 September 1939, 11 a.m.: Cabinet papers, 65/1.

Churchill then emphasized that he wished to see 'all the Balkan countries and Turkey' brought into the war, ideally with Italy's acquiescence. 'We needed as many Allies in the Balkans as we could secure,' he argued, 'and it was not at all to our interest that the Balkans should be kept in a state of quiet, whilst France and ourselves were left to bear the full brunt of the German assault on the Western Front.'

Halifax challenged Churchill's view, fearing the danger of presenting Germany with what he described as a series 'of additional cheap victories'. But Churchill countered with the argument that 'if Yugoslavia and Turkey joined us in hostilities with Germany', no such easy victories would be possible on Germany's part.

It was now the turn of the Air Force and Army Chiefs of Staff, whose presence during all military discussions of the War Cabinet had become a matter of routine, to challenge Churchill's concept of an active Balkan bloc which might redress the military balance in favour of Britain and France. According to the Chief of the Air Staff, Sir Cyril Newall, it was the view of the Chiefs of Staff Committee that 'it was not to our advantage at present that the war should be extended to the Balkans', particularly in view of Italy's position as a potential ally of Germany.

Ironside also argued against trying to create an active Balkan alliance, reminding the War Cabinet of 'our experience in the last war', when Rumania, encouraged by France to enter the war 'prematurely', had been quickly overcome by Germany. 'If we were to draw the Balkan countries into the present war on our side,' Ironside warned, 'it was essential that we should make certain that they came in at the right moment.'

Churchill was angered by these remarks; they showed, he said, 'that we appeared unwilling to encourage an extension of the war in the East while, at the same time, we did not look forward to the forthcoming war in the West'.[1] As soon as the War Cabinet was over, he therefore dictated a letter to Chamberlain, asking him to consider having 'an occasional meeting of the War Cabinet Ministers to talk among themselves without either secretaries or military experts'. The War Cabinet consisted of 'the responsible Ministers for the conduct of the war'; in Churchill's view, it would be 'in the public interest' if they were to meet from time to time 'as a body'. Churchill's letter continued: 'Much is being thrown upon the Chiefs of the Staffs which falls outside

[1] War Cabinet No. 22 of 1939, 21 September 1939, 11 a.m., Confidential Annex: Cabinet papers, 65/3.

the professional sphere. We have had the advantage of many valuable
and illuminating reports from them. But I venture to represent to you
that we ought sometimes to discuss the general position alone.'

'I do not feel,' Churchill added, 'that we are getting to the root of
the matter on many points.'[1]

It was the Minister for the Co-ordination of Defence, Lord Chatfield,
who proposed, as a solution to this problem, the establishment of a
permanent War Cabinet committee on which the three Service Ministers and Lord Chatfield would sit, and which, assisted by the Service
chiefs or their deputies, would scrutinize strategic proposals for
presentation to the War Cabinet. This small committee would be able
to co-ordinate the strategic ideas of the Chiefs of Staff with political
and diplomatic considerations, as well as strategic thought, in the minds
of the Service Ministers.

Chatfield's proposal, Churchill wrote privately to Chamberlain, was
'good and useful' and he added: 'I should welcome it myself—I believe
it would enable a number of questions which are too technical for
Cabinet discussion to be thrashed out at length and in detail.' The new
Committee, he believed, should come into operation 'as soon as possible';[2] and within three weeks, the Military Co-ordination Committee,
as it was called, was holding regular meetings, with Chatfield in the
Chair, and Churchill an active member.

As envisaged by Chatfield, the Military Co-ordination Committee
was potentially the most effective body for the evolution of war policy.
But without the Prime Minister as its Chairman, no real authority
existed to override the disputes which might arise between the four
Ministers. Each, if unwilling to concede in an argument, could fall
back upon his Departmental authority. But without the ultimate
authority of the Prime Minister to decide, the Commitee could, and
did at times, dissolve into a clash of wills and personalities, a procedure
which, as one of its military secretaries, Lieutenant-Colonel Jacob, later
recalled, 'caused endless rows'.

When Churchill and the other Service Ministers quarrelled, Jacob
added, but 'he wasn't the boss', the result echoed the situation at the
time of the Dardanelles. Jacob commented, in retrospect: 'Winston's
mind was so immensely active, he could only be Prime Minister.'[3]

Churchill was able at times to escape, if only momentarily, from the

[1] Letter of 21 September 1939: Churchill papers, 19/2.
[2] Letter of 22 October 1939: Premier papers, 1/404, folio 81.
[3] Sir Ian Jacob, notes for the author, 1 July 1982.

turmoil of high policy. After the stormy War Cabinet meeting of September 21 he had gone to Portsmouth, with Brendan Bracken, Admiral Phillips and his Principal Private Secretary, Eric Seal, to visit HMS *Vernon*, the shore station on whose minesweeping responsibilities so much depended.[1] There he was shown a model of the Actaeon net, designed in 1918 to protect merchant ships against 18-inch torpedoes. At *Vernon*, Commander Currey was eager to see the use of the net revived. Churchill's interest was effective. The nets were redesigned to stop 21-inch torpedoes, and, within three months, fitted and tested.[2]

Churchill returned to London, and on the following day, at the next meeting of the War Cabinet, urged the scrutiny of the conduct of the war in all its aspects, including the question of the rapidly rising expenditure, with which Ministers were much concerned: 'we were already spending as much as in 1918', he told his colleagues, 'although the war effort was nothing like as great', and he went on to ask why 'we apparently had so little to show for this expenditure'.[3]

Churchill's own instinct was to seek economies wherever possible. 'I am trying,' he wrote to Sir John Simon, the Chancellor of the Exchequer, on September 24, 'to prune the Admiralty of large schemes of naval improvements which cannot operate until after 1941 . . .' and he added: 'Beware lest these fortifications people and other departments do not consume our strength upon long-scale developments which cannot mature until after the climax which settles our fate.' Churchill's letter ended:

I see the departments full of loose fat, following on undue starvation. It would be much better from your point of view to come along with your alguazils *as critics* upon wasteful exhibitions, rather than delaying action. Don't hamper departments acting in a time of crisis; give them the responsibility; but call them swiftly to account for any failure in thrift.

I hope you will not mind me writing to you upon this subject, because I feel just as strongly about the husbanding of the money-powers as I do about the war effort, of which it is indeed an integral part. In all these matters you can count on my support, and also, as the head of a spending department, upon my submission to searching superintendence.[4]

[1] *Vernon* contained the Admiralty's Torpedo Experimental Department, as well as the Mining, Mine Design, Electrical Experimental and Instructional Mining Departments.

[2] Commander E. D. Webb, *HMS Vernon, A Short History from 1930 to 1955*, HMS *Vernon*, 1956, page 31. The Actaeon net was eventually mass produced in the United States, where it was fitted to some 800 'Liberty' ships, fifteen of which were saved from torpedoes by the nets.

[3] War Cabinet No. 23 of 1939, 22 September 1939, 6 p.m., Minute 6, Confidential Annex: Cabinet papers, 66/1.

[4] 'Private', 24 September 1939: Churchill papers, 19/2.

Churchill's method of work involved taking up in writing whatever struck him as needing comment or redress: for forty years he had been in the habit of dictating at once to a shorthand writer the ideas that came to him as he read the newspapers, travelled, studied documents or was told something that disturbed him. On his return from Portsmouth it was quite natural to him, therefore, to send a series of minutes to his naval advisers, arising out of what he had seen. He had been struck, he wrote, by the concentration of wireless research and development, as well as radar, at the Signal School at Portsmouth, and was worried 'that we are running a grave risk in leaving all this valuable plant and work in such a vulnerable spot'. Security, he felt, lay in the 'dispersal' of whatever research did not need to be carried out in the vicinity of ships.[1]

The urgency of such dispersal arose in Churchill's mind from the continuing fear of a possible German attack. 'I consider,' he minuted that same day, 'there is imminent danger of attack upon our dockyards, especially Chatham.'[2]

The range of Churchill's concerns was considerable: learning that forty or fifty officers and men of the merchant ship *Royal Sceptre* had been left to die in their open boats in the Atlantic after the ship had been torpedoed by a German submarine, he minuted: 'Let this outrage be given the fullest publicity. The names of the murdered men should be published and everything done to excite world reprehension against this odious act of bestial piracy on the high seas.' Whenever U-Boat captains had shown 'some poor civility to the men they have cast adrift', Churchill noted, the newspapers were quick to record it. 'Here is the other side of the medal.'[3]

That same day, September 24, Churchill was angered to read an assertion by one of the Eire Government ministers, J. W. Dulanty, that the existing friction between Britain and Eire would be lessened, if Britain could see its way to support an eventual union between northern and southern Ireland. Churchill recalled that Dulanty, who was personally 'thoroughly friendly to England', had served under him in 1917 at the Ministry of Munitions, but that he had 'no control or authority in Southern Ireland (so-called Eire)', acting only as 'a general smoother, representing everything Irish in the most favourable light'. Churchill's minute continued:

[1] Minute of 22 September 1939: Admiralty papers, 205/2.
[2] Minute of 22 September 1939: Churchill papers, 19/3.
[3] Minute to Director of Naval Intelligence, and to Press Section, Admiralty, 24 September 1939: Churchill papers, 19/3.

Three-quarters of the people of Southern Ireland are with us, but the implacable, malignant minority can make so much trouble that De Valera dare not do anything to offend them.

All this talk about Partition and the bitterness that would be healed by a union of Northern and Southern Ireland will amount to nothing. They will not unite at the present time, and we cannot in any circumstances sell the loyalists of Northern Ireland.

There was 'a good deal of evidence', Churchill added, 'or at any rate suspicion', that German submarines were being 'succoured' from the west of Ireland ports. Yet under the 1938 agreement, Britain was debarred from using Berehaven, or any of the other Treaty Ports. 'If the U-Boat campaign became more dangerous,' Churchill noted, 'we should coerce Southern Ireland both about coast watching and the use of Berehaven etc.' If, however, the U-Boat campaign were to slacken off, the Cabinet would not be inclined 'to face the serious issues' which 'forcible' measures against Eire would entail. The Admiralty, Churchill believed, 'should never cease to formulate through every channel its complaints' against Eire, while he himself would 'from time to time bring our grievances before the Cabinet'. On no account, Churchill told his advisers, 'must we appear to acquiesce in, still less be contented with, the odious treatment we are receiving'.[1]

On September 24 Churchill wrote to Major Davies, the Deputy Editor of the *News of the World*, which before the war had published many of Churchill's principal articles, and now wanted more: 'During the last three weeks I have not had a minute to think of anything but my task. They are the longest three weeks I have ever lived.'[2]

---

[1] 'Most Secret', 'For general guidance', 24 September 1939: Churchill papers, 19/3.
[2] Letter of 24 September 1939: Churchill papers, 8/629.

3

'We have now found our leader'

WITH the opening of the fourth week of war, Soviet troops began to take up their positions across the centre of Poland, dividing Poland's territory with Germany. As Churchill saw it, this act held certain advantages for the Western Allies. It created, he wrote to his War Cabinet colleagues on September 25, an eastern front to which the Germans would be forced to despatch a large army, if only 'to watch it', and which it would be impossible for the Germans to 'denude'. As many as twenty-five German divisions, he believed, would now be forced to remain on guard in the east.

Churchill saw further advantages to Britain in the Soviet occupation of eastern Poland. This move, he wrote, might help to create his hoped for Balkan front, as 'Russian interest in the Slavonic peoples of the Balkans is traditional', whereas the arrival of German troops on the Black Sea would be 'a deadly threat to Russia', as well as to Turkey; so much so that Russia and Turkey might, in his view, 'make common cause to prevent this', an event in 'direct fulfilment of our wishes'.

The ideal of any Balkan bloc, Churchill argued, was 'that all these countries should fall at once upon the sole and common foe, Nazi Germany'. To this end, it was in Britain's interest to see 'a renewal of relations with Russia'. Balkan neutrality would in itself be 'a great deal', but 'hostile action' by the Balkan States against Germany was what was needed 'to prevent the whole strain being thrown on the Western front'.

In his War Cabinet memorandum, Churchill saw Hitler being confronted with three choices, if he was 'barred' in the East. The first, an attack on France, through Belgium, 'collecting Holland on the way', would, he felt, be imminent only when 'at least' thirty German divisions had been concentrated on Germany's western border. The second, 'an intensive attack by air' on British factories and naval ports, 'seems a very likely thing for that man to do', but, Churchill added, 'he may not be allowed to do it by his generals, who now are presumably more powerful, for fear of making a mortal blood-feud with Great Britain, and perhaps drawing in the United States by the air massacres which would be inevitable'. The third possibility was for Hitler to launch a 'peace offensive'. Of this Churchill wrote, 'it would seem our duty and policy to agree to nothing that will help him out of his troubles, and to leave him to stew in his own juice during the winter while speeding forward our armaments and weaving-up our alliances'.

In conclusion, Churchill wrote, the 'immediate pinch' was the danger of the second possibility, the air attack, which 'always remains'.[1]

On September 26 Churchill spoke in the House of Commons of the Royal Navy's successes in setting up the convoy system, in arming merchant ships, in attacking the U-Boats, and in reducing the tonnage of British shipping losses from 65,000 in the first week of the war, to 46,000 in the second week, 21,000 in the third week, and only 9,000 in the week that was just ending. And yet, he warned, 'one must not dwell upon these reassuring figures too much, for war is full of un-pleasant surprises'. He had mentioned them because, as he said, 'I am entitled to say that so far as they go, these figures need not cause any undue despondency or alarm.'

Churchill went on to describe the British attack on German submar-ines as 'only just beginning'. The Royal Navy's 'hunting force' was gaining strength each day. And with the submarine danger 'falling into its proper confines', Britain and the Empire and all their 'friends' in every quarter of the world would be able to develop their resources and manpower 'in ever growing intensity upon the task we have in hand, in which task we have only to persevere to conquer'.[2]

The impact of Churchill's speech was considerable: 'one of your very best of recent years', wrote Anthony Eden, '& that is saying "summat" ',[3] while Harold Nicolson contrasted Chamberlain's speech with Churchill's, writing in his diary, first of Chamberlain's remarks:

During the whole speech Winston Churchill had sat hunched beside him. Then he gets up. He is greeted by a loud cheer from all the benches. . . .

I notice that Hansard does not reproduce his opening phrases. He began by saying how strange an experience it was for him after a quarter of a century to find himself once more in the same room in front of the same maps, fighting

---

[1] War Cabinet Paper No. 52 of 1939, 'Notes on the General Situation', 25 September 1939: Churchill papers, 20/15.

[2] *Hansard*, 26 September 1939.

[3] Letter of 28 September 1939: Churchill papers, 2/394.

the same enemy and dealing with the same problems. His face then creases into an enormous grin and he adds, glancing down at the Prime Minister, 'I have no conception how this curious change in my fortunes occurred'.

The whole House roared with laughter and the Prime Minister had not the decency even to raise a sickly smile. He just looked sulky.

The effect of Winston's speech was infinitely greater than could be derived from any reading of the text. His delivery was amazing, and he sounded every note from deep preoccupation to flippancy, from resolution to sheer boyishness. One could feel the spirit of the House rising with every word. It was obvious afterwards that the PM's inadequacy and lack of inspiration had been demonstrated even to his warmest supporters.

In those 20 minutes Churchill brought himself nearer the Post of Prime Minister than he has even been before. In the lobbies afterwards even Chamberlainites were saying 'we have now found our leader'. Old Parliamentary hands confessed that never in their experience had they seen a single speech so change the temper of the House.[1]

Nicolson's conclusion was borne out by other MPs who listened to Churchill's speech. In a letter to his sister Barbara, Ronald Cartland described how Churchill 'smashed and confounded his critics, who had been whispering that the years had been taking their toll'. Cartland added: 'He revealed to a delighted House all the weapons of leadership that his armoury contains. I know that the *nation* will never let him go now that, at long last, he is back in the Cabinet.'[2]

Churchill's speech stirred varied reflections. On September 28 one of Neville Chamberlain's private secretaries, John Colville, noted in his diary: 'It would probably be a good thing if Chamberlain resigned soon and left the conduct of the war to some younger, forceful successor. Unfortunately I can see no Lloyd George on the horizon at present: Winston is a national figure, but is rather too old; and the younger politicians do not seem to include any outstanding personality.'[3]

Another onlooker, Thomas Jones, a former Deputy Secretary to the Cabinet, wrote to a friend on September 30: 'Winston is the only Cabinet Minister who can put things across in an arresting way to our people. The PM is costive and dull and talks of endurance and victory in the most defeatist tones.'[4] That same day P. J. Grigg, Churchill's former private secretary at the Treasury, wrote to his father: 'I am told

---

[1] Nicolson diary, 26 September 1939, quoted in: Nigel Nicolson (editor), *Harold Nicolson, Diaries and Letters 1939–1945*, London 1967, page 37.

[2] Letter of 26 September 1939, quoted in: Barbara Cartland, *Ronald Cartland*, London 1945, page 142.

[3] Colville diary, 28 September 1939: Colville papers.

[4] Letter of 30 September 1939, quoted in: Thomas Jones, *A Diary with Letters 1931–1950*, London 1954, page 440.

that Winston's stock is going up & that people are expecting him to be PM before long.'[1]

Not all observers approved of this development. Indeed, the idea of Churchill as Prime Minister prompted the publisher Sir Ernest Benn to write to the Chancellor of the Exchequer, Sir John Simon: 'I pray that such a catastrophe will be averted.' Churchill, he warned, would succeed as Lloyd George had done twenty-five years before, only 'in rousing the lower instincts of the nation'. Benn feared the transfer of power from the 'restraint and breeding' of men like Chamberlain and Simon, to those 'who like flagwagging or epigramming'.[2]

The return of Churchill to the centre of policymaking was a source of conflicting emotions, often within the mind of a single individual. Thus Sir Samuel Hoare, erstwhile opponent, now colleague, and fellow Parliamentarian for more than thirty years, wrote to Lord Beaverbrook on October 1:

Winston has been much as you expected he would be, very rhetorical, very emotional and, most of all, very reminiscent. He strikes me as an old man who easily gets tired. Certainly in the country he has a very big position. He made a great success of his Naval statement in the House last week and he is taking a great deal of trouble with a broadcast for tonight. I should say that at the moment he is the one popular figure in the Cabinet.[3]

On the fringes of the War Cabinet itself, among members of the Cabinet Secretariat, there was considerable comment about Churchill's future. As one member of the Secretariat, Gilbert Flemming, later recalled: 'From the beginning we speculated on his chances of becoming PM and on his behaviour at this time. We were not happy at the prospect. His drive and pugnacity were obvious, but we could not foresee how far, once he was in command, these would outweigh the disadvantage of his impulsive imagination.'

Flemming recalled a discussion in the War Cabinet on the possible introduction of rationing. As the complex arguments proceeded, as to whether imports would continue to arrive 'in full flow', as they were then doing, Ministers hesitated to reject rationing outright. But Churchill, as Flemming recalled, 'brushed the question aside', telling his colleagues bluntly: 'The country wants positive action, not negative restrictions.'[4]

[1] Letter of 30 September 1939: Grigg papers.
[2] Letter of 2 October 1939: Simon papers (I am grateful to Dr Norman Rose of the Hebrew University of Jerusalem for this reference).
[3] Letter of 1 October 1939: Beaverbrook papers.
[4] Sir Gilbert Flemming, recollections, typescript, Part 1, 'To the Cabinet Office, Sept. 1939': Flemming papers.

Churchill's search for positive action depended upon his being able to have at his fingertips the facts and above all the figures needed to form a clear view of the actual state of naval preparedness. Within two weeks of reaching the Admiralty, he had asked for details of the existing statistical facilities. The report, which he read on September 30, 'constitutes', he wrote, 'the case for a central body which should grip together all Admiralty statistics, and present them to me in a form increasingly simplified and graphic'. Churchill went on to explain in his minute of September 30:

I want to know at the end of each week everything we have got, all the people we are employing, the progress of all vessels, works of construction, the progress of all munitions affecting us, the state of our merchant tonnage, together with losses, and numbers, of every Branch of the RN and RM.[1]

The whole should be presented in a small book such as was kept for me by Sir Walter Layton when he was my statistical officer at the Ministry of Munitions in 1917 and 1918. Every week I had this book, which showed the past and weekly progress, and also drew attention to what was lagging. In an hour or two I was able to cover the whole ground, as I knew exactly what to look for and where.

Churchill ended his minute: 'How do you propose this want of mine should be met?'[2]

Three weeks earlier, Churchill's close friend and confidant, Professor Frederick Lindemann had been appointed 'Personal Adviser to the First Lord in Scientific Matters'. Within another week Lindemann was offered and accepted the post of head of a new Statistical Department in Churchill's Private Office. What was now needed, Churchill minuted on October 12, was 'a weekly picture of the progress of all new construction, showing delays from contract dates'. It would not be for Lindemann to enquire into the reasons for these delays; Churchill would make his 'own enquiries'. At the same time he wanted a return of all British merchant ships together with weekly losses, details of all new construction, and a forecast of future deliveries. Further charts were also to be prepared for him to show the weekly state of all ammunition, torpedo and oil consumption, together with new deliveries.[3]

Such were to be Lindemann's duties. When, after a week, the Statis-

---

[1] The Royal Navy and the Royal Marines.
[2] Minute of September 30: Admiralty papers, 1/10459.
[3] Minute of 12 October 1939: Admiralty papers, 1/10459.

tical Branch still remained a mere paper scheme, Churchill minuted again: 'The formation of the "S" Branch is of the highest urgency. I cannot cover the ground for which I am responsible without it.'[1] A team of eight university statisticians was quickly assembled: many of whom were to have distinguished post-war careers.[2]

Twenty-three permanent charts were soon devised, the first of which enabled Churchill to see a daily presentation of British merchant vessels sunk by enemy action, showing in each case the type of action. There was also work to be done outside the Admiralty sphere; what Churchill himself described as 'special enquiries' analysing the Cabinet papers which reached him from other departments, and which had a 'statistical character'.[3]

Reflecting on Churchill's use of Lindemann within the Admiralty, one of the young statisticians of 'S' Branch, Roy Harrod, later recalled: 'Churchill felt that he wanted an independent mind to digest and criticize these papers. It was not enough, amid the heavy pressure of his duties at the Admiralty, to have a cursory knowledge of matters outside his province; he wanted to have a deeply critical knowledge, and what better person to aid him towards getting that than the Prof?'[4]

On October 1 Churchill made his first wartime radio broadcast. It was exactly a month since the German invasion of Poland, a country which had, he said, 'again been overrun by two of the great Powers which held her in bondage for a hundred and fifty years, but were unable to quench the spirit of the Polish nation'. The heroic defence of Warsaw showed 'that the soul of Poland is indestructible, and that she will rise again like a rock, which may for a spell be submerged by a tidal wave, but which remains a rock'.

Churchill went on to speak of the Russian occupation of eastern Poland, based upon 'a cold policy of self-interest'. Reflecting the reasoning of his War Cabinet memorandum of September 25, Churchill told his listeners: 'We could have wished that the Russian armies should be standing on their present line as the friends and allies of Poland instead of as invaders. But that the Russian armies should stand on the

---

[1] Minute of 20 October 1939: Admiralty papers, 1/10459.

[2] The team included D. G. Champerdowne (Professor of Economics and Statistics at Cambridge University from 1970 to 1978), G. L. S. Shackle (Professor of Economic Sciences in the University of Liverpool, 1951 to 1969), G. D. A. MacDougall (Chief Economic Adviser to the Treasury, 1969 to 1973) and Roy Harrod (Economic Adviser to the International Monetary Fund, 1952 to 1953).

[3] Minute of 9 October 1939: Churchill papers, 19/3.

[4] Roy Harrod, *The Prof, A Personal Memoir of Lord Cherwell*, London 1959, page 179.

line was clearly necessary for the safety of Russia against the Nazi menace. At any rate,' he added, 'the line is there, and an Eastern Front has been created which Nazi Germany does not dare assail.' Churchill continued:

I cannot forecast to you the action of Russia. It is a riddle wrapped in a mystery inside an enigma; but perhaps there is a key. That key is Russian national interest. It cannot be in accordance with the interest or the safety of Russia that Germany should plant itself upon the shores of the Black Sea, or that it should overrun the Balkan States and subjugate the Slavonic peoples of southeastern Europe. That would be contrary to the historic life-interests of Russia.

There was, Churchill argued, a 'community of interests' between Britain, France and Russia, which could be seen quite plainly through 'the fog of confusion and uncertainty'. It was in the interest of each of these powers 'to prevent the Nazis carrying the flames of war into the Balkans and Turkey'.

Churchill then spoke of the war at sea. To protect British merchant ships, some two thousand of which were 'in constant movement every day upon the seas', the Royal Navy had immediately taken the offensive, attacking German submarines where it could find them, and was 'hunting them night and day—I will not say without mercy, because God forbid we should ever part company with that—but at any rate with zeal and not altogether without relish'.

Describing Parliament as 'the shield and expression of democracy', Churchill argued that 'all grievances or muddles or scandals, if such there be', could be debated openly. As to the 'great ordeals' that might be coming, especially from the air, he declared: 'We shall do our best to give a good account of ourselves; and we must always remember that the command of the seas will enable us to bring the immense resources of Canada into play as a decisive ultimate air factor. . . .'

Preparations were being made, Churchill said, for a war of at least three years. But victory could come sooner than that; how soon would depend upon how long Hitler 'and his group of wicked men, whose hands are stained with blood and soiled with corruption, can keep their grip upon the docile, unhappy German people'. Britain would go on with the fight to the end, 'convinced that we are the defenders of civilisation and freedom'.

Churchill then cast his mind back, as he had done so often during the past four weeks, to the events of the First World War, and to his own memories:

Here I am in the same post as I was twenty-five years ago. Rough times lie ahead; but how different is the scene from that of October, 1914! Then the French Front, with its British Army fighting in the line, seemed to be about to break under the terrible impact of German Imperialism. Then Russia had been laid low at Tannenberg; then the whole might of the Austro-Hungarian Empire was in battle against us; then the brave, warlike Turks were about to join our enemies. Then we had to be ready night and day to fight a decisive sea battle with a formidable German fleet almost, in many respects, the equal of our own.

We faced those adverse conditions then; we have nothing worse to face tonight.[1]

Churchill's broadcast was widely praised. 'I take the same view as Winston,' Chamberlain wrote to his sister, 'to whose excellent broadcast we have just been listening. I believe Russia will always act as she thinks her own interests demand, and I cannot believe she would think her interests served by a German victory followed by a German domination of Europe.'[2]

That night Sir Samuel Hoare, who had spoken to Churchill during the day, noted how he was 'very exhilarated', and he added: 'The Press talked of him as Prime Minister,'[3] while Chamberlain's junior Private Secretary, John Colville, wrote in his diary:

Heard Winston Churchill's inspiring speech on the wireless. He certainly gives one confidence and will, I suspect, be Prime Minister before the war is over. Nevertheless, judging from his record of untrustworthiness and instability, he may in that case lead us into the most dangerous paths. But he is the only man in the country who commands anything like universal respect, and perhaps with age he has become less inclined to undertake rash adventures.[4]

Among the personal friends who wrote to Churchill after his broadcast was Lady Desborough, two of whose three sons had been killed in the First World War. 'Your broadcast last night was a touchstone,' she wrote, 'lifting up our hearts—& your beautiful Navy speech last week. Bless you. You made one feel that all that matters most is unconquerable, serenely sheltered somewhere—to hold us all together.'[5]

* * *

[1] Speech of 1 October 1939: Churchill papers, 9/138.
[2] Letter of 1 October 1939: Chamberlain papers.
[3] Hoare diary, 1 October 1939: Templewood papers.
[4] Colville diary, 1 October 1939: Colville papers.
[5] Letter of 2 October 1939: Churchill papers, 2/364.

During the first month of the war, Churchill had frequently reflected on the position of the United States, both as a neutral power and as a source of material and moral support for Britain's war effort. Several years before the outbreak of war, when President Roosevelt's son James had visited Churchill at Chartwell, Churchill had already written a number of newspaper articles praising Roosevelt's effort to revive the United States' economy. At their meeting, Churchill drew for Roosevelt's son a design for linking the pound and the dollar. He had also sent Roosevelt the successive volumes of his biography of Marlborough.

On September 11 Roosevelt wrote direct to Churchill, from the White House:

My dear Churchill,

It is because you and I occupied similar positions in the World War that I want you to know how glad I am that you are back again in the Admiralty. Your problems are, I realise, complicated by new factors, but the essential is not very different. What I want you and the Prime Minister to know is that I shall at all times welcome it if you will keep me in touch personally with anything you want me to know about. You can always send sealed letters through your pouch or my pouch.

I am glad you did the Marlboro volumes before this thing started—and I much enjoyed reading them.

With my sincere regards,
Faithfully yours,
Franklin D. Roosevelt [1]

Churchill did not receive this letter until the first week of October. As soon as it reached him, he circulated a copy to his War Cabinet colleagues, to whom he proposed, on October 5, that his 'exchange of correspondence' with Roosevelt should take place 'in sealed envelopes conveyed by diplomatic bag'. Churchill went on to explain to the War Cabinet that the President was not only Commander-in-Chief of the United States Navy, but took 'an immense pride in his tenure of this post', being personally responsible for 'many of the moves of his ships'. Indeed, on the previous day Roosevelt had given an order 'forbidding any publicity' for such moves, an order, Churchill told his colleagues, 'which in normal circumstances was only given when a country was on the point of declaring war'.

Churchill then proposed that in his reply to Roosevelt's letter, he would use as his theme the Pan-American Conference being held that same week in Panama City, at which it had been proposed that a

[1] Letter dated 11 September 1939: Admiralty papers: 199/1928.

'safety belt' area should be declared around the Americas, extending 300 miles out to sea, within which all 'belligerent activities' would be outlawed, and all passenger and merchant ships of whatever nationality, moving from one American port to another, 'would be immune from attack'.

Churchill explained to the War Cabinet that this proposal would 'relieve the Royal Navy of a great load of responsibility'. It would set more British ships free to take part in the Atlantic convoys. It would mean that the German Navy could not attack a British ship 'approaching, say, Jamaica or Trinidad without risking hostilities with the United States'.[1]

Before drafting his reply to Roosevelt, Churchill discussed the Panama Conference both with his own Naval Staff, and with the United States Ambassador, Joseph Kennedy. Churchill and the Naval Staff then prepared an answer to the President. Churchill proposed beginning on a personal note. 'Your letter,' he wrote, 'takes me back to 1914 and it is certainly a most unusual experience to occupy the same post fighting the same enemy 25 years later.' But this opening sentence was lost when the full reply, concerned entirely with the Panama proposals, was redrafted by Admiral Phillips.[2]

'We like the idea of a wide limit of say 300 miles within which no submarines of any belligerent country should act,' the final draft declared. But it went on to warn of the difficulties that would be created if a German raider were to operate from, or take refuge in, the American zone. In such an event, Churchill's telegram read, 'we should have to be protected or allowed to protect ourselves'. There would also be 'great difficulty' in Britain accepting a zone 'which was only policed by some weak neutral. But of course if the American Navy takes care of it, that is all right.'

Churchill's first wartime telegram to Roosevelt ended: 'We wish to help you in every way in keeping the war out of American waters.'[3]

The War Cabinet of October 5 approved Churchill's reply to Roosevelt. Henceforth, both as First Lord and then as Prime Minister, Churchill and Roosevelt were to exchange several thousand telegrams on every aspect of war policy. That same night, Churchill dined at his

[1] War Cabinet No. 38 of 1939, 5 October 1939, 11.30 a.m., Minute 5, Confidential Annex: Cabinet papers, 65/3.

[2] Admiralty papers, 199/1928.

[3] 'The following from Naval person', sent 5 October 1939, 'Most Secret': Cabinet papers, 65/3, folios 95-6.

flat in Morpeth Mansions with the Third Sea Lord, Rear-Admiral Fraser and the Director of Naval Construction, Sir Stanley Goodall, to discuss the shipbuilding programme. Fifteen years later Fraser recalled how, towards the end of dinner, the telephone rang, and the butler came in. Churchill, 'who rather disliked telephones', asked the butler:

'Who is it?'
'I don't know, sir,' said the butler.
'Well, say I can't attend to it now.'
'I think you ought to come, sir,' said the butler, and Churchill got up rather testily. Then we heard his replies, 'Yes, sir . . . No, sir.'
The telephone conversation was on some question concerning the *Athenia* incident. The First Lord said: 'Admiral, I think you must now excuse me. This is very important and I must go and see the Prime Minister at once.'[1]

Roosevelt had telephoned because of a warning given over the German wireless by Admiral Raeder, that the United States ship *Iroquois*, which had left Cork on September 3 bound for the United States, would be sunk 'in similar circumstances' to the sinking of the *Athenia*, the implication being that it would be the work of the Royal Navy, and indeed of Churchill himself.

Churchill understood the danger of these accusations; not only the sinking of the *Athenia* in 1939, but of the *Lusitania* in 1915, had been laid at his door by German propaganda. Churchill therefore jotted down at once the gist of his own remarks to Roosevelt during their telephone conversation:

Iroquois is probably a thousand miles West of Ireland. Presume you could not meet her before 50th meridian. There remains about a thousand miles in which outrage might be committed. U-boat danger inconceivable in these broad waters. Only method can be time-bomb planted at Queenstown. We think this not impossible.

Am convinced full exposure of all facts known to United States Government, including sources of information, especially if official, only way of frustrating plot. Action seems urgent. Presume you have warned *Iroquois* to search ship.[2]

Churchill discussed this German 'warning' with Neville Chamberlain that same night, and on the following morning he told the War Cabinet that the Germans might well have secreted a bomb on board the *Iroquois*, 'timed to explode when she was in mid-Atlantic'. Should this

---

[1] Quoted in Sir James Marchant (editor), *Winston Spencer Churchill: Servant of Crown and Commonwealth*, London 1954, pages 80–1.
[2] 'Telegrams and Letters Exchanged between the Naval Person and President Roosevelt, 11th September, 1939–7th May 1940', 'Most Secret': Churchill papers, 4/123.

happen, Churchill commented, 'the Germans no doubt hoped to claim credit for the friendly gesture of having warned the Americans and so enabled them to save the crew'.[1] But in the event, the *Iroquois* reached port safely.[2]

Having conquered Poland and partitioned it with Russia, Hitler now proposed to negotiate peace with Britain and France. On October 5 Lord Halifax told the War Cabinet that a Swedish businessman, Birger Dahlerus, had come to see him, having already seen Hitler and Goering, with a proposal that Goering himself would meet 'in some neutral country' an intermediary 'nominated by the British Government'. It had been suggested that General Ironside should be that intermediary.

Lord Halifax told the War Cabinet that in his view 'we should not absolutely shut the door', while leaving all initiative to the Germans. Sir Samuel Hoare asked whether, 'in the circumstances, it might not be well to damp down a little over *anti*-Goering propaganda?', a proposal which Halifax approved 'since', he said, 'our real object was to destroy Hitler'. Churchill, who spoke immediately after Halifax and Hoare, told the War Cabinet, as the official minutes recorded:

. . . that these German feelers might not be sincere and their real object might be to spread division and doubt amongst us. If they were insincere, it was likely that they would shortly be followed by a suggestion of some time limit, and when that time limit was passed we should certainly expect the most bitter fighting.

If, on the other hand, these feelers were sincere, they came, not from any sense of magnanimity, but from weakness, the present German leaders finding themselves unable to drag the German people into a war to destroy the Western Democracies.

In that event we should need to be most provident stewards of the national interest, and to take every step to ensure that we were not deceived.

Speaking at the end of the discussion, Kingsley Wood said that in his opinion Goering 'would be glad to secure the removal of Herr Hitler, as he wished himself to live in peace and luxury', at which

---

[1] War Cabinet No. 39 of 1939, 6 October 1939, 11 a.m.: Cabinet papers, 65/1.
[2] Two British merchant ships were not so lucky: on October 5 *Stonegate* was sunk by the *Deutschland* and *Newton Beach* by *Admiral Graf Spee*. Within the next five days the *Graf Spee* had claimed two further British merchant ships as its victims, *Ashlea* on October 7 and *Huntsman* on October 10.

Churchill agreed 'that Marshal Goering might well cherish the idea of playing the role of General Monk'.[1]

General George Monk, Cromwell's commander in Scotland, had been instrumental in the restoration of the British monarchy in 1660. Churchill's reference to him had not been accidental, for, amid the daily pressures of war, he still somehow grasped every spare half hour to try to complete his four volume literary work, *A History of the English-Speaking Peoples*. His research assistant, F. W. Deakin, while training with the 63rd Oxfordshire Yeomanry Anti-Tank Regiment, was correcting the proofs of one of the final chapters, on the Victorian Age, while a young Oxford don, Alan Bullock, was preparing the section on Canada. On October 6 Churchill asked Deakin to divide what had been done into chapters, and sent him by special messenger several sections to be corrected. 'I do hope you will be able to get on with this during the week,' he wrote, 'as the matter is so important and the stress here is very great.'[2]

To speed the task, Deakin enlisted the help of Churchill's first research assistant, Maurice Ashley, who agreed to write 10,000 words on Cromwell. He also obtained a further 10,000 words from Alan Bullock on the origins of the Empire in Australia and New Zealand.

By December only Waterloo and Trafalgar remained to be done. His research assistants having sent him their drafts, Churchill found time to add at least a few passages in his own style.

It was the imminent German 'peace' offer that now became the focus of British attention, and on October 6, in a speech to the Reichstag, Hitler did indeed propose a negotiated peace with Britain and France. His condition was that Germany retained 'effective hegemony' in central and eastern Europe.

Two days after Hitler's speech, Churchill sent his Cabinet colleagues a note in which he argued that, with Czechoslovakia and Poland both 'subjected to a foreign yoke', no negotiations should begin until 're-paration' had been offered 'to the states and peoples who have been so wrongfully conquered', and until their 'effective life and sovereignty is unmistakably to be restored'.[3]

Sending this note to Chamberlain on October 9, Churchill wrote that the condition he laid down 'does not close the door upon any genuine offer', but he added: 'I think opinion is hardening against the

---

[1] War Cabinet No. 38 of 1939, 5 October 1939, 11.30 a.m., Minute 5, Confidential Annex: Cabinet papers, 65/3.

[2] Letter of 6 October 1939: Churchill papers, 8/626.

[3] 'A Note on the German Peace Suggestions', 8 October 1939: Churchill papers, 19/2.

Hitler terms, and the Press seems unanimous.'[1] Churchill reiterated this view at the War Cabinet that same day, when he said that British, Dominion and neutral opinion was 'clear' that it was 'no use holding discussions with Herr Hitler until he showed by his actions that his policy had changed'. Churchill's personal view was: 'we should not attempt to manoeuvre in order to gain time'.[2]

While not wishing to enter into discussions with Hitler, Churchill was eager to continue to try to talk to the Italians, in the hope 'of drawing Italy to our side', and to this end he proposed, to both Pound and Phillips, that Britain should try to build up 'a policy of cooperation' with Italy in the Balkans, in the Mediterranean, and by means of mutual reductions of the Italian garrison in Libya and the French garrison in Tunis. 'The Cabinet showed itself much disposed to favour this policy yesterday,' Churchill noted. Any such agreement, he added, would also have to include an agreement with Italy 'to ensure that Germany does not receive appreciable supplies from Italian sources'. The aim of the agreement would be a Convention, signed by Britain, France and Italy, 'making the Mediterranean free for all traffic, forbidding submarine war in those waters and guaranteeing each other against interruption'. Only submarines of the Convention signatories would be allowed in the Mediterranean, thus ensuring 'the effective extirpation of the U-Boats'.[3]

Churchill's note was sent on to the Foreign Office, which agreed to send the Admiralty any draft telegram to Rome on the subject of such a Convention, and a few days later a telegram to Sir Percy Loraine in Rome contained a section written by Churchill, in similar terms to his note, and ending with a direct appeal from Churchill to Loraine: 'Pray let them see the full advantages of the friendly arrangement we have in mind.'[4] But neither Hitler's speech of October 6, nor the attempts to neutralize Italy, deflected Churchill from his main task, for he continued to be alert to any German plans for an attack in the west, and to be ready to try to counter those plans to the fullest extent possible. Many contingencies were discussed, and plans laid; on October 7 he told the War Cabinet that a Captain had been chosen to go 'to each of the main ports in the Low Countries', to study at first hand 'the resources of Holland and Belgium', and that details were being worked out, in the event of a German attack, to move the Dutch and Belgian

---

[1] 'Private', 9 October 1939: Churchill papers, 19/2.
[2] War Cabinet No. 42 of 1939, 9 October 1939, 11.30 a.m.: Cabinet papers, 65/1.
[3] Note of 7 October 1939: Admiralty papers, 116/4177.
[4] Telegram No. 115 to Rome (draft), 11 October 1939: Admiralty papers, 116/4177.

gold bullion either to Britain or to the United States.[1] But on October 10 Lord Halifax reported to the War Cabinet that as far as any military staff conversations between Britain and Belgium were concerned, the Belgian Government was not ready for them, 'since they would constitute a derogation from Belgium's neutrality'.[2]

The hesitations of Belgium were one cause for concern in the second week of October. A second cause for concern that week emerged when Pound sent Churchill details of substantial lags in the naval construction due for 1940, under the Naval Estimates of 1936. 'These are the ships we want to fight the war with,' Churchill commented, 'and it is lamentable that they should all be breaking down on contract dates. It's far more important to have some ships to fight with, and to have ships that Parliament has paid for, delivered to date, than to squander effort upon remote construction which has no relation to our dangers!'

Churchill was particularly worried, as he wrote to Pound, that the *King George V* and the *Prince of Wales* should be ready by their contract dates, July 1940 and October 1940 respectively. To reach this target would now require a 'supreme effort'. Above all, Churchill wrote, the 'Peace-time habit of contractors in booking orders, and executing them when they please', could not be allowed to continue in time of war. 'Advise me,' he added, 'of the penalties that may be enforced.'

Churchill had his own solution to this vexatious lag. It too derived from his First World War experiences, both at the Admiralty, and at the Ministry of Munitions. 'I will see the contractors personally at the Admiralty in your presence,' he wrote to Pound. 'Pray arrange these meetings from 5 p.m. onwards. It is no use the contractors saying it cannot be done. I have seen it done when full pressure is applied, and every resource and contrivance utilized.'

As for the naval construction programme of 1937, with its ships laid down for 1941, that programme, Churchill wrote, 'may jog along as fast as it can, but the ships we need to win the war must be in commission in 1940'. His minute ended: 'Pray thrust yourselves into this and give me your aid to smooth away the obstacles.'[3]

Churchill's exhortations to Pound were accepted as the legitimate concern of an energetic First Lord; his was, in the end, the ultimate responsibility in the event of naval unpreparedness, or the neglect of

[1] War Cabinet No. 40 of 1939, 7 October 1939, 11.30 a.m., Minute 6, Confidential Annex: Cabinet papers, 65/3.
[2] War Cabinet No. 43 of 1939, 10 October 1939, 11.30 a.m., Minute 10, Confidential Annex: Cabinet papers, 65/3.
[3] Minute of 8 October 1939: Admiralty papers, 205/2.

future war construction. But as Churchill saw it, his responsibilities extended far beyond the confines, if such they were, of the Royal Navy, and of Britain's sea-borne lifelines. This sense of responsibility pervaded his thoughts on Foreign Affairs, and also on domestic policy in connection with the war. He was, after all, a member of the War Cabinet, and it was in pursuance of what he saw as his War Cabinet responsibilities that he wrote on October 8 to the Lord Privy Seal, Sir Samuel Hoare:

In spite of having a full day's work usually here, I cannot help feeling anxious about the Home Front. You know my views about the needless and, in most parts of the country, senseless, severities of these black-outs, entertainment restrictions and the rest. But what about petrol? Have the Navy failed to bring in the supplies? Are there not more supplies on the water approaching and probably arriving than would have been ordered had peace remained unbroken?

I am told that very large numbers of people and a large part of the business of the country is hampered by the stinting. Surely the proper way to deal with this is to have a ration at the standard rate, and allow free purchasing, subject to a heavy tax, beyond it. People will pay for locomotion, the Revenue will benefit by the tax, more cars will come out with registration fees, and the business of the country can go forward.

Churchill now turned to the new food rations, which he had earlier opposed, and was still uneasy about:

Then look at these rations, all devised by the Ministry of Food to win the war. By all means have rations, but I am told that the meat ration for instance is very little better than that of Germany. Is there any need of this when the seas are open?

If we have a heavy set-back from Air attack or surface attack, it might be necessary to inflict these severities. Up to the present there is no reason to suppose that the Navy has failed in bringing in the supplies, or that it will fail.

Churchill turned next to the question of manpower, and put forward a novel scheme:

... what about all these people of middle-age, many of whom served in the last war, who are full of vigour and experience and who are being told by tens of thousands that they are not wanted, and that there is nothing for them, except to register at the local Labour Exchange. Surely this is very foolish.

Why do we not form a Home Guard of half-a-million men over forty (if they like to volunteer) and put all our elderly stars at the head and in the structure of these new formations. Let these five hundred thousand men come along and push the young and active out of all the home billets. If uniforms are lacking, a brassard would suffice, and I am assured there are plenty of rifles at any rate. I thought from what you said to me the other day that you liked this idea. If so, let us make it work.

'I hear continual complaints from every quarter,' Churchill ended, 'of the lack of organization on the Home Front. Can't we get at it?'[1]

On October 11 an attempt to shake public confidence in Chamberlain had been made by the *Daily Mirror*, in an article stating that it was only Churchill's 'brilliant memorandum' that had persuaded the Cabinet to stiffen Chamberlain's proposed reply to Hitler. As soon as he read the article, Churchill sent a copy to Chamberlain, describing it as 'evidently designed by them to make mischief between us'. Churchill added: 'I spoke to no one about my draft article outside the secret circle. I gave copies of it to five Cabinet colleagues including yrself & Edward.'[2] Chamberlain replied at once; 'I should pay no attention to it,'[3] and the episode was over.

Chamberlain rejected Hitler's proposals in a statement in the House of Commons on October 12; part of his statement was indeed based on Churchill's draft. 'The reception of the Prime Minister's speech by the House,' Churchill minuted to Pound that same day, 'so clearly endorsed a firm attitude that one must expect a violent reaction from Herr Hitler. Perhaps quite soon. Everyone seems to think that it will be on a naval force, convoys, shipping in the docks etc.' All this was now Churchill's responsibility. 'It seems to me,' he told Pound, 'that special vigilance should be enjoined at Chatham, Devonport and Portsmouth, and that the Fleet at Scapa should be loose and easy in its movements. Not tethered particularly.'

Churchill also suggested that the Admiralty 'go over' its arrangements with the Air Force for the defence of these various threatened points, making the Air Force feel 'how much we are relying on them to strike back hard at the assailant'. Churchill ended: 'Pray let me know anything else you think we can do, and how best to have everything toned up to concert pitch. These next few days are full of danger.'[4]

[1] 'Private & Personal', 8 October 1939: Churchill papers, 19/2.
[2] 'Private', 11 October 1939: Churchill papers, 19/2. Edward = Lord Halifax.
[3] Undated note, on a Cabinet Room slip: Churchill papers, 19/2.
[4] Minute of 12 October 1939: Admiralty papers, 205/2.

4

'Fire and Stimulus'

THE 'danger' of which Churchill had warned on October 12 was indeed near; at one o'clock in the morning of October 14 a German submarine, having penetrated the anti-submarine defences at Scapa Flow, torpedoed and sank the battleship *Royal Oak*, then at anchor. The Admiral and more than eight hundred officers and men were drowned. 'The loss of this ship,' Churchill told the War Cabinet that morning, 'though an extremely regrettable disaster, did not materially affect the general naval position.'[1] It had, however, affected him personally, for, as John Higham later recalled, 'when I brought the news to Churchill, tears sprang to his eyes and he muttered, "Poor fellows, poor fellows, trapped in those black depths" . . .'[2]

Churchill's daughter Mary, then aged seventeen, also remembered the impact of the sinking of the *Royal Oak*. 'You couldn't conceive it was possible,' she recalled. 'It wasn't on the high seas. Just down to the bottom.' Her father, she added, 'felt the loss of life very much. He realized what it all meant, the loss of the great ships, the loss of the men—and what it meant in terms of the war.'[3]

The Air Ministry, Churchill told his War Cabinet colleagues on October 14, had been asked whether they would reinforce the air defences of Scapa. Additional anti-submarine defences would be ready by November 7. Meanwhile, the Fleet had been moved from Scapa to Rosyth.

At the end of Churchill's survey, Chamberlain asked 'whether there was any possibility of retaliating', and suggested 'a submarine attack on German warships in harbour'. But Dudley Pound pointed out that

---

[1] War Cabinet No. 47 of 1939, 14 October 1939, 11.30 a.m.: Cabinet papers, 65/1.
[2] John Higham, notes for the author, 16 September 1982.
[3] Lady Soames, conversation with the author, 19 October 1982.

this was considered 'impracticable', owing to the narrow, shallow-water approaches to the German naval bases.

The War Cabinet then discussed the part to be played by the Royal Air Force in the event of a German invasion of Belgium. Churchill was emphatic that the 'violation' of Belgium would, as he expressed it, 'afford a moral justification for our bombing the Ruhr, even if this involved civilian casualties', and he added: 'The idea of causing civilian casualties among the German population of the Ruhr was to him less shocking than the civilian casualties which the Belgians would incur if we bombed the German Army while it was moving through Belgium.'

By the end of the discussion there was 'general agreement', as the official minutes recorded, 'that an attack on the Ruhr would have a very big moral, as well as military, effect'.[1]

Following the sinking of the *Royal Oak*, Churchill prepared an account of the naval situation for President Roosevelt. 'I think we ought to send something more to our American friend,' he explained in a note to Pound on October 16, 'in order to keep him interested in our affairs. If you agree, I will show this to the PM before sending it to the American Ambassador for transmission.' Churchill's note continued: 'If you think of anything else which could be added with advantage, please pencil it in. We must not let the liaison lapse.'[2]

Both Pound and Chamberlain approved of Churchill's telegram, his second to Roosevelt since he had become First Lord. 'We have been hitting the U-Boats hard with our new apparatus,' Churchill explained, 'and on Friday 13th four, including two of the largest and latest, were destroyed.' Speculating on the future course of the war, Churchill told Roosevelt: 'Our accounts of Hitler's oil position make us feel he is up against time limits. This means that either he will make a vehement attack on us for which we are prepared, or that he is being held back by counsellors who see the red light. Either way we propose to see what happens, being fairly confident that all will be well.' Churchill also offered to give the United States Navy access to Britain's 'Asdic' anti-submarine location device 'whenever you feel they would be of use to the United States Navy'.[3]

As each day passed, Churchill studied the secret information available to members of the War Cabinet; information which showed the

[1] War Cabinet No. 47 of 1939, 14 October 1939, 11.30 a.m., Minute 4, Confidential Annex: Cabinet papers, 65/3.

[2] Minute of 16 October 1939, marked 'Secret to you': Admiralty papers, 199/1928.

[3] 'Naval Person to President Roosevelt', 16 October 1939: Churchill papers, 20/15. But Roosevelt declined this offer, being unwilling in return to provide Britain with the secrets of the Norden bombsight, which the Air Ministry was keen to acquire.

extent of Britain's weakness. On the same day that he prepared this telegram for Roosevelt with its assertion that 'all will be well', he studied an Air Ministry paper on aircraft production. Then, recalling his own warnings from 1934 to 1937, and how they had been dismissed at the time by Baldwin, Chamberlain and their Ministers, Churchill wrote to his War Cabinet colleagues:

We were told in 1937 that there would be 1,750 first-line aircraft modernly equipped by April 1, 1938 (see Sir Thomas Inskip's speeches). However the House of Commons was content with the statement that this position had in fact been realised by April 1, 1939.

We were throughout assured that reserves far above the German scale were the feature of the British system. We now have apparently only about 1,500 first-line aircraft with good reserves ready for action. On mobilization the 125 squadrons of April 1, 1939 shrank to 96.

The Air Ministry paper also showed that only half the aircraft output from factories would be available for action by April 1940. 'It may be impossible to remedy this,' Churchill wrote, 'but at any rate we ought to examine it without delay.'[1]

In the third week of October, Churchill again pressed his colleagues not to neglect the possibility of creating a 'friendly' Italy. Once a common Anglo-Italian policy began to be evolved, he wrote on October 18, 'one thing leads to another, and confidence ripens into comradeship'. A good relationship with Italy would enable Britain, France and Italy 'to bring home an equal number of divisions from the Middle East', a move which would be 'all to the good'. No one, he wrote, would want to keep a large British army in Egypt 'simply to build up what is called a reserve in the Middle East, irrespective of the general military situation'. Italy's friendship, and what he described as Britain's desire 'to draw Italy into our system', would strengthen Britain's military and naval position at home and in western Europe.[2]

Given an agreement with Italy to 'keep the U-boat warfare out of the Mediterranean'—Churchill's phrase in his War Cabinet memorandum of October 18—he did see another area in which British naval activity might be needed. Turkey had just signed an alliance with Britain. Russia might try to put pressure on Turkey for control of the Bosphorus. A British Fleet in the Black Sea could prevent the Russians from actually attacking Turkey.

---

[1] War Cabinet Paper No. 43 of 1939, 16 October 1939, 'Air Supply': Churchill papers, 4/143.
[2] War Cabinet Paper No. 92 of 1939, 18 October 1939, 'Possible Détente with Italy in the Mediterranean': Cabinet papers, 66/2.

This was Churchill's line of thought in a minute which he sent to Dudley Pound and Tom Phillips on October 19. 'What is the strength of the Russian Black Sea marine,' he asked them, 'and what would be sufficient to master them?' The Naval Staff should study the question 'in all its military bearings', and should work out the means 'of finding and maintaining' such a force. 'Clearly,' Churchill concluded, 'if Russia declares war upon us, we must hold the Black Sea.'[1]

Holding the Black Sea was hypothetical; maintaining the safety of the oceanic convoys, armed merchant ships, or isolated vessels, was the urgent need. On October 18 Churchill asked for a 'special chart' to be marked up, showing all unarmed merchant ships 'of any size' that were approaching Britain unescorted. This chart, he said, should be 'kept up to date daily'.[2] Five days later he wrote privately to Pound:

Do you think the arrangement for routing and escorting the convoys is sufficiently well-organised? There is no question of interference with the C in C Western Approaches, but ought there not to be a group of officers in the Admiralty whose sole function is to worry about the safety, from hour to hour, of particular convoys?—and make suggestions to higher authority.

'Ought we not,' Churchill added, 'to have a daily report of every convoy as regularly worked out as the block-signal system on the railway?'[3]

Despite the Admiralty's vigilance, there were insufficient warships either to escort all convoys, or to ensure the full safety of an escorted convoy once it was attacked. In the week following Churchill's letter to Pound, six more British merchant ships were sunk by U-boats.[4] On November 9 Churchill summoned his senior advisers, together with Lindemann, and Major Desmond Morton of the Ministry of Economic Warfare, his principal pre-war source of information about German military preparedness. He also asked Frederick Leathers, whom he described to Pound as 'a great shipping expert, known personally to me'.[5]

The aim of this meeting was to discuss the 'immense slowing down of trade' in the first ten weeks of war, a fact which left Churchill 'deeply

[1] 'Most Secret' minute, 18 October 1939: Admiralty papers, 205/2.
[2] Minute of 18 October 1939: Admiralty papers, 205/2.
[3] 'Private', 23 October 1939: Admiralty papers, 205/2.
[4] *Ledbury*, *Menin Ridge* and *Tafna* on October 24, *Brontë* on October 27, *Malabar* on October 29 and *Cairnmona* on October 30.
[5] The Chairman of more than fifty companies connected with shipping, in May 1940 Leathers joined the Ministry of Shipping as adviser on all matters relating to cost. In 1941 Churchill appointed him Minister of War Transport, a position he held for the rest of the war.

disturbed'. As Churchill remarked: 'We shall have failed in our task if we merely substitute delays for sinkings,' and he added: 'I frankly admit I had not appreciated this aspect, but in this War we must learn from day to day. We must secretly loosen up the convoy system (while boasting about it publicly), especially on the outer routes.'

The solution, as Churchill saw it, lay in accepting 'a higher degree of risk', and he told the meeting: 'This is possible now that so many of our ships are armed,' as even on the Atlantic routes, they could cross 'in smaller parties'.[1]

One item of hope that week had come from France, and offered to lessen the risk that the secret loosening up of the convoy system would create, at least on the Halifax convoys. For on November 6 the British Naval Attaché in France, Captain Holland, saw the French naval Commander-in-Chief, Admiral Darlan, and reported that Darlan was 'extremely ready to cooperate' with Britain by sending six large French submarines to the Halifax convoy route. These six submarines, Holland noted, would be sent off to convoy duty 'as soon as they can, though it will probably entail taking two from Martinique'.[2]

When, and how, would the German offensive in the west begin? These were the questions which were continually on Churchill's mind during the late autumn of 1939. At an evening War Cabinet on October 19, held in Chamberlain's room in the House of Commons, he 'strongly urged', as the minutes recorded, that the Canadian, Australian and New Zealand troops then being prepared for service overseas 'should take their places in the line in France by the opening of the Spring campaign'.[3] At a further War Cabinet held at 10 Downing Street on the morning of October 20, Churchill told his colleagues that he thought that Britain herself 'should make every effort to get as large a force as possible into the line by the Spring, when decisive operations might be expected to start'. It would be better, he argued, 'to send troops over with a lower scale of equipment, than to leave the French Army with insufficient forces to withstand the whole weight of the German Army'.[4]

To his two most senior Naval Staff colleagues, Pound and Phillips, Churchill minuted on October 21 that, much as he deprecated 'invasion scares', and had combated them 'so constantly' in the early months

[1] Minute of 9 November 1939: Admiralty papers, 205/2.
[2] Signal of 6 November 1939: Admiralty papers, 205/4.
[3] War Cabinet No. 53 of 1939, 19 October 1939, 5.45 p.m.: Cabinet papers, 65/1.
[4] War Cabinet No. 54 of 1939, 20 October 1939, 11.30 a.m.: Cabinet papers, 65/1.

of the First World War, he still felt that it 'might be well for the Chiefs of Staff to consider what would happen' if twenty thousand men were 'run across and landed say, at Harwich, or at Webburn Hook,[1] where there is deep water close inshore'. The long, dark nights of the oncoming winter 'would help such designs'. Had the War Office made plans, he asked, 'to provide against this contingency?' He did not think such a landing likely, but was it 'physically possible?'[2] Two days later Churchill wrote again to Pound: 'I have, of course, no knowledge of the military arrangements, but it seems to me there ought to be a certain number of mobile columns or organised forces that can be thrown rapidly against any descent.' Equally, he added, it might be 'that the Air service will be able to assume full responsibility'.[3]

On October 21 Churchill urged upon Pound the need for 'a squadron of heavy ships that can stand up to the battery from the Air', and of extra decoy ships 'to mix and baffle' air reconnaissance. 'It looks to me,' Churchill wrote, 'as if the war would lag through the winter with token fighting in all spheres & theatres, but that it will begin with mortal intensity in the Spring'. To encourage Pound, he added: 'Remember no-one can gainsay what we together decide,' writing at the top of this minute, '*Alone*', and at its end, 'Trafalgar day!'[4]

In the context of the coming conflict, Churchill continued to be alarmed by the ambiguity of Eire's position, and took exception, at the War Cabinet of October 22, to a remark by Lord Halifax that 'Eire is to be regarded as a neutral state.' That same day Churchill wrote personally to Halifax, doubting that 'the neutrality wh Mr De Valera has proclaimed' was in any way the same as the neutrality of Holland or Switzerland. 'What is the international juridical status of Southern Ireland?' Churchill asked. 'It is not a Dominion. They themselves repudiate the idea. It is certainly under the Crown. Nothing has been defined. Legally I believe they are "At war but skulking".'[5]

The Dominions Secretary, Anthony Eden, while sympathetic to Churchill's distress, understood the strength of feeling in Eire against even the leasing of naval bases. 'I fear that it has become every day

---

[1] Pronounced 'Webburn', spelt 'Weybourne'. According to a Norfolk rhyme: 'He that would Old England win, Must at Weybourne Hook begin.'

[2] 'Most Secret and Private', 21 October 1939: Churchill papers, 19/3.

[3] Minute of 23 October 1939: Churchill papers, 19/3.

[4] Minute of 21 October 1939 (which began, 'I address this first of all to you alone, because together we can do what is needful'): Admiralty papers, 205/2.

[5] Letter of 22 October 1940: Foreign Office papers, 800/310.

clearer,' he wrote to Lord Halifax, 'that it is scarcely possible for "Dev" to square neutrality with the grant of the facilities for which the Admiralty ask, and at least 80% of the Irish people favour neutrality.' Altogether Eden added, 'a pretty problem'.[1]

At the War Cabinet on October 24 Churchill argued that Britain 'should challenge the constitutional position of Eire's neutrality'. Unlike the other Dominions, he said, which were separated from Britain by thousands of miles, 'Eire was an integral part of the British Isles'. As the German submarine menace grew, Britain would have to 'insist' on the use of the southern Irish harbours. At present, Churchill told his colleagues, Eire 'was having the best of both worlds'. She should now be told that she was at 'the parting of the ways, and it should be brought home to her what she stood to lose in being declared a foreign power'.

Replying to Churchill, Chamberlain feared that seizure of the southern Irish ports 'would have most unfortunate repercussions in the United States and in India, where it would be hailed as a high-handed and unwarranted action'. But it should be possible, Chamberlain added, to make the Dominions realize 'the dangers to them of Eire's attitude'.[2]

It was the question of air support for the army that was uppermost in Churchill's mind at the fourth and final meeting of the Land Forces Committee, held on October 23. The pioneer aviator, and Conservative MP, Colonel Moore-Brabazon, whom Churchill had known for more than forty years, had proposed to the Committee the provision of cheap aircraft by mass production, both to provide close support for the Continental Army, and 'to achieve surprise on the battlefield'. Arguing that this proposal should be examined further, Churchill stressed 'that everything possible should be done to give the Army the intimate air support which was necessary in modern conditions'.[3]

Three days later, foreign affairs again intruded on Churchill's work, when he was invited by Chamberlain to a special War Cabinet Committee to discuss British aid to Turkey in the event of a German or Russian attack. Under a Treaty of Mutual Assistance signed seven days before, between Britain, France and Turkey, both France and Britain were pledged to lend Turkey 'all aid and assistance in their power' against the aggression of any European power. Turkey's pledge

[1] Letter of 20 October 1939: Foreign Office papers, 800/310.
[2] War Cabinet No. 58 of 1939, 24 October 1939, 11.30 a.m.: Cabinet papers, 65/1.
[3] Land Forces Committee No. 4 of 1939, 23 October 1939, 5 p.m.: Cabinet papers, 92/111.

was somewhat less demanding: no more than 'at least a benevolent neutrality'.[1]

As far as a possible Russian attack on Turkey was concerned, Churchill told the Committee, while it was important to prevent the Russians from seizing the mouth of the Bosphorus, this 'could easily be done by our Fleet'. Once Turkey was the victim of aggression, Churchill pointed out, Britain would be entitled, under the pre-war Montreux Convention, 'to send naval forces through the Dardanelles', to implement Britain's obligations not only to Turkey, but also to Greece and Rumania.[2]

Churchill proposed telling the Turks, through their Ambassador in London, General Orbay, 'that we contemplated being able to give them immediate naval support in the event of their being threatened by Russia, and that such support would be considerably more effective if the Turkish naval bases were adequately defended for use by our fleet'. His suggestion was approved, on condition that, as the Committee's report noted, 'in no circumstances should our forces be placed under the command of a Turkish Commander-in-Chief'.[3]

Danger seemed suddenly to come much closer to home when, in the early hours of October 27, a telegram reached the Foreign Office from Belgrade, with details, said to have come from the German General Staff, of an alleged German plan to invade Britain. A total of 5,200 aircraft divided into four sections; one would parachute 12,000 men on the East Coast, one would neutralize British aerodromes, aircraft factories and railways by bombing, one would neutralize the Navy, and one would protect the transport of troops by sea, and cover their disembarkation. At the same time, a mass of small merchant ships would transport a further 23,000 men, including armoured detachments. On the following night, a further 45,000 men would be landed. A diversionary attack would be made on the Maginot Line, using a 'new type of flame thrower' and armour-piercing aerial torpedoes 'launched from aircraft'.[4]

A special Committee of the War Cabinet, headed by the Minister for Co-ordination of Defence, Lord Chatfield, met at 9.30 on the evening

[1] 'Treaty of Mutual Assistance Between Britain, France and Turkey, 19 October 1939', printed in J. A. S. Grenville, *The Major International Treaties 1914–1973: A history and guide with texts*, London 1974, pages 197–8.

[2] 'Convention regarding the régime of the Straits', known as the Montreux Convention, signed on 20 July 1936.

[3] 'Assistance to Turkey against German and/or Russian Aggression': Cabinet papers, 83/1.

[4] Sir R. Campbell to Foreign Office, No. 305, sent 8.45 p.m., 26 October 1939, received 1.40 a.m., 27 October 1939: Cabinet papers, 83/1. These invasion details were false.

of October 27. The War Cabinet was represented by Hore-Belisha, Kingsley Wood, the Minister without Portfolio, Lord Hankey, and Churchill. It was Churchill who warned that in the event of such an assault by Germany, as far as naval forces were concerned: 'The East coast was bare.' Many of the 'great ships' needed to combat such an invasion were 'away hunting' German commerce raiders. The majority of the Royal Navy's destroyers 'were engaged on hunting U-boats and on convoy work'.

Churchill did not rule out the possibility of such an attack, telling his colleagues, as the Committee's minutes recorded, that:

The Germans were faced with the necessity of undertaking some great operation, either against ourselves or against the French. They might shrink from sacrificing vast numbers in an attack on the Maginot Line, whereas they might well gamble on a hazardous venture against Great Britain, which, if it succeeded, would cause us great loss and confusion, and, if it failed, would only entail the loss of 80,000 men. He thought, therefore, that we should treat the possibility seriously, and take due precautions.

'If an invasion materialized,' Churchill pointed out, 'it might even be necessary to bring back Divisions from France,' and he suggested that 'plans for doing so' should be prepared.

It was the Secretary of State for War, Leslie Hore-Belisha, who cautioned that the source of the information was 'highly unreliable'. It might, he said, be a ' "red herring", designed to draw us off the track of a real operation, planned elsewhere, possibly against Holland'.[1]

At the War Cabinet on October 28, it was Chatfield who reported on the Committee's discussion. The Air Ministry had confirmed that Germany did indeed possess the necessary 5,200 aircraft 'if all types were taken into account', and also the 'trained parachute infantry'. It would therefore be 'unwise to ignore the possibility' of such an invasion plan.

Churchill then told the War Cabinet of the naval measures recommended 'to meet the possibility of this invasion'. On these measures would depend Britain's ability to hamper, if not to prevent, a German landing. One submarine, he explained, would be sent to reconnoitre the Heligoland Bight. Ten submarines would form a screen along the western edge of the German minefield, 'across the possible route of an expedition'. Four cruisers would be placed at Rosyth, ready to move against the German troop transports. At the cost of 'a great strain' to

[1] 'Invasion of Great Britain', War Cabinet Committee of 27 October 1939, 9.30 p.m.: Cabinet papers, 83/1.

the existing convoy, escort and anti-submarine forces, the destroyer force on the Humber and at Harwich would be brought up to a strength of 35; this measure was in fact already in progress. But the heavy ships of the Home Fleet would remain in the north, to protect them from the 'heavy damage' to which they would be exposed by the aerial attack envisaged in the German invasion plan, if such it was.

Churchill then warned his colleagues 'that we were fighting this war with last war's ships, which were not designed against heavy air attack'. But Lord Chatfield pointed out that, whatever the risk, it was wrong to leave the East Coast 'devoid of Capital Ships'.[1]

Churchill pondered Chatfield's criticism; then, at midnight on October 28, sent Pound a letter supporting what Chatfield had said. 'It seems to me serious,' Churchill wrote, 'for all heavy ships to yield up the North Sea for two and a half days by going to the Clyde.' They would, he felt, be safer in the Forth, protected by sixty-four guns as against twenty-four in the Clyde. 'Why then should we choose the Clyde,' he asked, 'at the cost of uncovering the Island?'

Churchill had another reason for opposing the move to the Clyde, telling Pound:

There are plenty of Irish traitors in the Glasgow area; telephone communication with Ireland is, I believe, unrestricted; there is a German ambassador in Dublin. I should expect that within a few hours of the arrival of these ships it would be known in Berlin that the British heavy ships were definitely out of the North Sea, and could not return for more than sixty hours.[2]

Within twenty-four hours Churchill had decided to follow Chatfield's advice. 'Every effort should be made,' he wrote to Pound and Chatfield on the morning of Sunday October 29, 'to make Rosyth the strongest defended war-harbour in the world', while at least one heavy ship should be posted on the East Coast 'as an effective deterrent against any attempt to dominate the North Sea by enemy surface craft'. Churchill's letter ended: 'Thus we may await attack with confidence.'[3]

At noon that same day, Sunday October 29, the War Cabinet renewed its discussion on the possibility of a German invasion. Churchill suggested that the London parks might be a good place for an enemy parachute landing, and asked for an urgent review of the British

[1] War Cabinet No. 63 of 1939, 28 October 1939, 11.30 a.m., Confidential Annex: Cabinet papers, 65/3.
[2] 'Secret', 28 October 1939, 'midnight': Admiralty papers, 205/2.
[3] Minute of 29 October 1939: Admiralty papers, 205/2.

troops available in London itself.[1] For his own part, Churchill took immediate action, instructing Phillips to arrange for 'a stand of arms' to be placed in the basement of the Admiralty, and for all officers and 'able-bodied personnel' employed in the Admiralty building to have a rifle, a bayonet and ammunition. Fifty such armed men, he wrote 'would be enough'. And he added: 'Let this be done in forty-eight hours.'[2]

On October 31 Churchill went up to Scapa Flow for a second time to discuss the northern defences with the Commander-in-Chief, Admiral Forbes. On November 1, on his return to London, Churchill gave instructions to Phillips, for 'the camouflaging of the oil tanks and the creation of dummy oil tanks' at Scapa. At the same time, the defences of Rosyth would continue, he wrote, 'to be worked up in every way until it is a place where the strong ships of the Fleet can rest in security'. After setting out various detailed proposals for improving the defences of Rosyth, Churchill added that he would be 'glad' if Phillips would 'vet this minute and make sure it is correct and solid in every detail'; only then was it to go to Pound for his assent, and made 'operative' in all Departments.[3]

Preparations had now been made, for both the immediate defences of Rosyth, and the longer term defences of Scapa Flow. But at the same time, Churchill was distressed by the continuing talk about a possible peace with Germany. At the War Cabinet on November 1 he listened uneasily while Halifax told his colleagues that a message had been given to a Swedish intermediary, to the effect that Britain could not come to terms with any Government in Germany 'unless Hitler ceased to hold a position where he could influence the course of events'.[4] Such a message, Churchill warned Halifax privately on November 1, would mean, by implication, 'that we were prepared to accept a Government in Germany which reserved a ceremonial and honourable position for Hitler'. Such an arrangement, Churchill believed, would 'not be accepted for a moment' by the British nation. It would, in addition, be contrary 'to the whole basis of our public declarations and Cabinet co-operation'. Churchill's letter continued:

... I do not see any advantage in our dealing with German suggestions in

[1] War Cabinet No. 64 of 1939, 29 October 1939, 12 noon, Minute 4, Confidential Annex: Cabinet papers, 65/3.

[2] Minute of 29 October 1939: Churchill papers, 19/3.

[3] 'Most Secret', 1 November 1939: Admiralty papers, 1/10317.

[4] War Cabinet No. 67 of 1939, 1 November 1939, 11.30 a.m., Minute 15, Confidential Annex: Cabinet papers, 65/4.

detail. We have said that the restoration of confidence is the prerequisite of peace negotiations. It is for the Germans to establish conditions which when viewed as a whole would engender that feeling in our breasts.

There is great danger in these secret communications. If, for instance, you said anything like what you suggested, the Germans could use it to undermine French confidence in us with possibly fatal effects.

'On the other hand,' Churchill told Halifax, 'if you stand firm in accordance with our public declarations, the Germans may themselves disintegrate.'[1]

Churchill left England for France on the afternoon of Thursday November 2, driving from London to Dover, and crossing to Boulogne by destroyer. From Boulogne he took the train to Paris.[2] It was his first wartime visit across the Channel, his hundredth visit or more to France since he had first gone there, as a boy, with his father, more than fifty years before. His love of France was profound; he had many personal friendships with individual Frenchmen, and for the whole of his political life had been an advocate of close Franco-British friendship. During the First World War he had been in intimate contact, first in 1914–15, and again in 1917–18, with those at the highest levels of French war policy.

Reaching Paris late in the evening of November 2, Churchill slept at the Ritz. On the following morning he was driven to French Naval headquarters, at Marceau, to the east of Paris, where for two hours he discussed the naval situation with Admiral Darlan. As the official British notes of the meeting recorded, Churchill opened the meeting 'by making a speech in French'. This speech 'was closely followed by the French, who were visibly affected by the offers of cooperation and assistance'.[3]

In his speech, Churchill offered 'to supply and fit every French anti-submarine craft with asdics'. Any French vessels sent to England for fitting 'will be immediately taken in hand', he promised. Britain would also arrange for 'imparting of the method' to the French, and training.

---

[1] 'Private', 1 November 1939 ('shown to Lord Chatfield by 1st Lord's authority', 3 November 1939): Churchill papers, 19/2.

[2] It was Admiral Darlan's special train: Admiralty papers, 1/10250. Churchill was accompanied by his son-in-law Duncan Sandys, and by Admiral Phillips. Also on the journey were Eric Seal, Commander Thompson, Detective Inspector Thompson and Kathleen Hill.

[3] 'Notes of Meetings held at Marceau on 3rd November 1939': Admiralty papers, 116/5458.

Churchill was confident that by continuing the joint Franco-British strategy of blockade 'no temptation will be offered to Italy to enter the war against us, and that the German power of resistance will certainly be brought to an end'.[1] There followed a series of detailed discussions, mostly on convoy co-operation, in which Phillips was the senior British naval officer present. These discussions continued in the afternoon.

Returning to Paris, Churchill called on the Prime Minister, Edouard Daladier, whom he found, as he told the War Cabinet on his return, 'labouring under a sense of imminent crisis'. Churchill told Daladier that Britain wished 'to go better than our word' in the number of divisions to be sent to France, and he stressed 'that the whole strength of the country was being thrown into the struggle'. With this, Churchill noted, he felt he had left Daladier 'in a more optimistic frame of mind'.[2]

That night Churchill gave a small dinner to his French opposite number, Campinchi, the French Minister of Marine, in a private room at the Ritz. Looking back after the war, Churchill recalled his 'high opinion' of Campinchi, and he added: 'His patriotism, his ardour, his acute intelligence, and above all his resolve to conquer or die, hit home.'

As for Darlan, Churchill later wrote, he was fighting 'on quite a different front from ours'. For seven years he had been the head and the 'reviver' of the French Navy, 'while shifting Ministerial phantoms had filled the office of Minister of Marine. It was his obsession to keep the politicians in their places as chatterboxes in the Chamber.'

Phillips, like Churchill, had been impressed chiefly by Campinchi, this 'tough Corsican', Churchill called him, 'who never flinched or failed'. When Campinchi died, Churchill added, 'broken and under the scowl of Vichy towards the beginning of 1941, his last words were of hope in me. I shall always deem them an honour.'[3]

That night Churchill again slept at the Ritz, and on the morning of November 4, using his room at the Ritz as an office, he dictated a number of departmental minutes. In one, he commented on his own journey to France: 'I was not entirely satisfied with the state of the mine-field at Dover. Although it has been laid with remarkable and praiseworthy activity, a large gap exists in the Western field through which U-boats can easily pass.' Indeed, there was no doubt that the mine-field was being 'traversed' by U-boats, 'and that the majority got

[1] 'Statement by the First Lord to the French Admiralty', War Cabinet paper No. 116 of 1939: Cabinet papers, 66/3.

[2] As reported by Churchill to the War Cabinet on 6 November 1939: Cabinet papers, 65/2.

[3] Winston S. Churchill, *The Second World War*, volume 1, London 1948, pages 392-3.

through'. Churchill then proposed a remedy which he recalled from the First World War, to have the barrage 'lighted and buoyed'.

Churchill also noted, having been much impressed by the French Admiralty's 'very complete installation' at Marceau, that it was British policy not to leave the capital, as the French had done, but 'to stay in London until it becomes really impossible'. Nevertheless he hoped that the British Admiralty's 'alternative installation' would be brought up 'to a high level of efficiency', and he went on to ask:

Pray let me know how it stands, and whether we could in fact shift at a moment's notice without any break in control. Have the telephones, &c., been laid effectively? Are there underground wires as well as others? Do they connect with exchanges other than London, or are they dependent upon the main London exchange? If so, it is a great danger.[1]

At noon on November 4 Churchill lunched with General Gamelin, and in the afternoon he visited General Georges at his headquarters. They discussed the possibility, as Churchill told the War Cabinet on his return, of releasing 'an appreciable number of destroyers' from escort duty by using the Channel ports for as many troop movements as possible, while at the same time sending British units 'still under training' to districts such as Provence, 'where French Army training areas would be placed at our disposal'. Not only was the climate favourable and the terrain 'well adapted' for training, but the presence of British troops 'would have a most heartening effect on Italian opinion'.[2]

Returning to Paris on the evening of November 4, Churchill gave a dinner at the Ritz for Campinchi and Darlan. Also invited were three of his French friends of the pre-war years: Léon Blum, Paul Reynaud and Georges Mandel, together with a senior Foreign Ministry official, Alexis Léger. Then, at midnight, Churchill took a special train to Amiens, sleeping in the train, and leaving it after breakfast for Arras, to visit Lord Gort's headquarters. After lunching with Gort, Churchill returned to London via Boulogne and Dover.[3]

'I hope,' Churchill wrote to Darlan on his return, 'that the development of the French Fleet, which is due so greatly to yourself, may be continued in association with the British Fleet until the war is brought to a successful conclusion.'[4]

[1] Minute to Pound, Phillips and the Assistant Chief of the Naval Staff 'to initiate action', 4 November 1939: Churchill papers, 19/3.
[2] As reported by Churchill to the War Cabinet on 6 November 1939: Cabinet papers, 65/2.
[3] 'First Lord's Visit to France, 2nd–6th November, 1939': Admiralty papers, 1/10250.
[4] Letter of 10 November 1939: Admiralty papers, 1/10250.

On the morning of November 6 Churchill gave the War Cabinet an account of his visit to France. The discussion then turned to a report by the Chiefs of Staff Committee on the military implications of a German invasion of Holland. Their conclusion was that the aim of such an invasion would be to use Holland, as Chamberlain put it, 'solely as a base for attack against this country', and Kingsley Wood confirmed that a German occupation of the Dutch islands at the mouth of the Scheldt 'would constitute a very serious menace in placing the German medium bombers and fighters within range of London'. Churchill agreed; a German advance into Holland, avoiding the Dutch 'fortress' north of Antwerp, and concentrating on the area between Rotterdam and Antwerp, would, he said 'make it easier for them to carry out a mortal attack on this country'.

Churchill saw no way to prevent a German occupation of southern Holland. He therefore advocated, as the official minutes recorded, 'that we ought to be prepared if necessary, to retaliate immediately by attacking the Ruhr'. At the same time, once German troops entered Holland, the Belgians were likely to invite both France and Britain 'to enter Belgium'. From his conversation with General Georges, it was clear, Churchill said, that 'every preparation for such a move had been made'. In addition, he reported, General Georges had spoken highly of the eighteen Belgian divisions, 'which he considered were better material than some of the less well-equipped German divisions'.[1]

At the War Cabinet on the following day, November 7, Churchill told his colleagues about the sinking of the *Royal Oak*. There should, he said, be no enquiry; and he went on to explain that 'the Senior Naval Officer in Scotland had reported the previous April that the defences of Scapa were inadequate. In May, the Admiralty had replied to the effect that they were satisfied with the arrangements that had been made.'[2] When Hore-Belisha expressed his concern about hostile feeling in the House of Commons, Churchill 'expressed himself confident' that he would be able to 'satisfy' the House of Commons, and at a further War Cabinet on the morning of November 8 Churchill argued that over the whole naval story it was 'right to give the House the complete picture, not slurring over our setbacks, but leading up to a happy conclusion'.[3]

[1] War Cabinet No. 72 of 1939, 6 November 1939, 11.30 a.m., Minute 5, Confidential Annex: Cabinet papers, 65/4.

[2] In May 1939 the First Lord was Churchill's predecessor, Lord Stanhope.

[3] War Cabinet No. 74 of 1939, 7 November 1939, 11.30 a.m., Minute 3, Confidential Annex: Cabinet papers, 65/4.

That afternoon Churchill gave the House of Commons an account of the sinking of the *Royal Oak*. The 'long and famed immunity', he said, which Scapa Flow had gained in the First World War had led 'to a too easy valuation of the dangers which were present. An undue degree of risk was accepted, both at the Admiralty and in the Fleet.' The Admiralty, he added 'upon whom the broad responsibility rests, are resolved to learn this bitter lesson, namely, that in this new war, with its many novel complications, nothing must be taken for granted; and that every joint in our harness must be tested and strengthened so far as our resources and ingenuity allow'.

Churchill went on to speak of the successes both of the convoy system and of the offensive against German submarines. 'Three times as many hunting craft are now at work,' he said, 'as at the outbreak of the war.' And yet, Churchill continued, striking that measured balance between realism and hope which was to become the hallmark of all his wartime speeches:

I must warn the House again that continual losses must be expected. No immunity can be guaranteed at any time. There will not be in this war any period when the seas will be completely safe; but neither will there be, I believe and I trust, any period when the full necessary traffic of the Allies cannot be carried on.

We shall suffer and we shall suffer continually, but by perseverance, and by taking measures on the largest scale, I feel no doubt that in the end we shall break their hearts.[1]

Once more, Churchill's speech was effective; its 'candour' and 'impressive confidence' being praised that afternoon in the House of Commons by the leader of the Liberal Party, Sir Archibald Sinclair. But those around Chamberlain were still suspicious of Churchill's judgment. On November 9 John Colville noted in his diary that although Chamberlain was now suffering 'rather badly' from gout there was 'really nobody to take his place: Halifax hasn't the forcefulness and Winston is too unstable'.[2]

Churchill's public warning of November 8 that 'nothing must be taken for granted' was rapidly translated into a spate of enquiries into new and old areas of concern. 'It appears to me,' he minuted to Phillips on November 9, 'that St Helena and Ascension must be made effectively secure against seizure by landing parties from, say, a Deutschland. We should look very foolish if we found them in possession of

---

[1] *Hansard*, 8 November 1939.
[2] Colville diary, 9 November 1939: Colville papers.

the two 6-inch guns with a supply ship in the harbour. I don't feel
the garrisons there are strong enough.'[1] That same day, studying figures
which showed that the convoy system had resulted in a slowing down
of both imports and exports, Churchill proposed an 'intricate study' to
be made of the convoy problem, and to do this he once more enlisted
the help both of Professor Lindemann, and of Desmond Morton, to
whom he had often turned before the war for help on matters of trade
and defence.[2]

Still concerned about the possibility of some sudden German move
against Britain, at the War Cabinet that evening Churchill argued that,
given the 'considerable number' of enemy agents 'still at large', it would
seem prudent 'to establish military pickets and patrols in Whitehall
and Downing Street'.[3] But the principal concern of that evening's
War Cabinet was to decide what action Britain's bomber force should
take if Germany invaded Holland. Kingsley Wood spoke of the
'gap' between British and German air strength and suggested that,
'owing to our relative inferiority in numbers at the present time', it
would better 'suit our book' for Germany to attack Britain, and lose
many of their bombers, 'rather than for us to launch a heavy attack on
Germany'. Meanwhile, by avoiding British bomber actions, 'we might
gradually reduce the gap between the strengths of the two air forces'.

Churchill opposed this reasoning. Once the Germans were allowed
to occupy Holland and Belgium, he said, they would be in 'a far better
position' to attack Britain's industrial centres, while at the same time
building up 'a heavy scale of defence' for the Ruhr. As Germany's
object in attacking the Low Countries was to 'make it easier' for them
to attack Britain 'we ought', he argued, 'to throw in everything we
have to prevent this'.

As an immediate measure in the event of a German invasion of
Holland, or of Belgium, Churchill advocated a British bombing offensive against the Ruhr. Even if half of the British force involved were
destroyed in such an effort, he said, this would be 'trivial' compared
with the advantage to Germany of establishing herself in Holland and
Belgium. If the losses were 'even heavier than anticipated', he said, the
project could be abandoned after the first day.

---

[1] Minute of 9 November 1939: Churchill papers, 19/3.
[2] Minute of 9 November 1939: Churchill papers, 19/3.
[3] War Cabinet No. 77 of 1939, 9 November 1939, 9.30 p.m.: Cabinet papers, 65/2. No such
agents were in fact 'at large'.

Churchill was supported by Hore-Belisha and Sir John Simon; so much so that the War Cabinet, in Neville Chamberlain's absence, agreed formally that Chamberlain should be told that they 'felt strongly the weight of argument in favour of retaliating against a German invasion of Belgium, as of Holland and Belgium, by an immediate heavy air attack on military objectives in the Ruhr'.[1]

Five days later, when the War Cabinet again discussed bombing the Ruhr, Churchill spoke of how 'finely balanced' the arguments were. On the one hand, he warned, 'we might sustain severe losses in bombers which we could not afford' as well as laying Britain open to 'heavy retaliation'. On the other hand, he felt that what he described as 'our blow on Germany's industrial' life might prove 'mortal'. Summing up his feelings, Churchill thought that, on balance, 'the great concentration of industry presented to us in the Ruhr would justify the hope that our attack would be more formidable than theirs, especially as we could confidently hope to exact a fearful toll from the enemy's bombing squadrons'.

At the end of this second discussion both Churchill and Hankey told their colleagues that they felt that 'it would be impossible to take any final decision' until the actual German attack took place. In this they were supported by Chamberlain, who added that if the bombing of the Ruhr might prove necessary, 'he would not shrink from it'.[2]

Amid these daily, and indeed hourly pressures of planning and preparation, Churchill reflected on the wider issues of the war. On November 9 the Vice-Chancellor of Bristol University, of which Churchill was Chancellor, had written in some perturbation about the need for some 'assurance', especially for the 'great mass of decent thinking young men' that the war was going to be 'ultimately worth while'.

The Vice-Chancellor, Thomas Loveday, was especially concerned to answer the question which a young man had posed to him, having applied for a commission in the Tank Corps. The question was: 'Is any progress coming out of this war?' The young man had gone on to write: 'I want to know what I am doing and to see an attainable and concrete objective.'[3] To this, Churchill replied: 'I cannot tell you

---

[1] War Cabinet No. 77 of 1939, 9 November 1939, 9.30 p.m., Minute 1, Confidential Annex: Cabinet papers, 65/4.

[2] War Cabinet No. 82 of 1939, 14 November 1939, 11.30 a.m., Minute 6, Confidential Annex: Cabinet papers, 65/4.

[3] Letter of 9 November 1939, 'Personal': Loveday papers.

whether any "progress" is coming out of this War, but I am quite sure there will be a considerable set-back if England is beaten, and the British Commonwealth of Nations destroyed.'[1]

On the following evening Churchill again addressed himself to the question of the reason for the war, when he made his second wartime broadcast. The power of Britain and France, he said, 'to restore and revive' the life of the Poles, Czechs and Slovaks, had been 'growing every day'. In peacetime Britain had put up with a lot of things 'which ought not to have happened'. Such was often the case in parliamentary countries 'which aim at freedom for the individual and abundance for the mass'. But now Britain was at war, and was going to make war, 'until the other side have had enough of it.'

Nothing had ever impressed him so much, Churchill said, 'as the calm steady, business-like resolution with which the masses of our wage-earning folk and ordinary people in our great cities faced what they imagined would be a fearful storm about to fall on them and their families at the very first moment'. They had prepared themselves for the worst and had 'braced themselves for the ordeal. They did not see what else there was to do.'

Now, after ten weeks of war, Britain was 'far better prepared' than at the beginning of September 'to endure the worst malice of Hitler and his Huns'. The U-boats had paid 'a heavy toll'. The army was improving in training every day. Fifteen German aeroplanes had been shot down without the loss of one British plane. 'Now the mists and storms of winter wrap our Island,' making German bombing raids 'far more difficult.'

If 'violent and dire events' should occur, Churchill said, Britain would 'confront them with resolution'. There would be 'very rough weather' ahead. At the same time, he added, 'I have this feeling: that the Germany which assaults us today is a far less strongly built and solidly founded organism than that which the Allies and the United States forced to beg for an armistice twenty-one years ago.'

Churchill then spoke of the German leaders:

As they look out tonight from their blatant, panoplied, clattering Nazi Germany, they cannot find one single friendly eye in the whole circumference of the globe. Not one! Russia returns them a flinty stare; Italy averts her gaze; Japan is puzzled and thinks herself betrayed. Turkey and the whole of Islam have ranged themselves instinctively but decisively on the side of progress. The hundreds of millions of people in India and in China, whatever their

---

[1] Letter of 11 November 1939: Loveday papers.

other feelings, would regard with undisguised dread a Nazi triumph, well knowing what their fate would soon be. The great English-speaking Republic across the Atlantic Ocean makes no secret of its sympathies or of its self-questionings, and translates these sentiments into actions of a character which anyone may judge for himself.

Churchill ended his speech with words of defiance and hope:

The whole world is against Hitler and Hitlerism. Men of every race and clime feel that this monstrous apparition stands between them and the forward move which is their due, and for which the age is ripe. Even in Germany itself there are millions who stand aloof from the seething mass of criminality and corruption constituted by the Nazi Party machine. Let them take courage amid perplexities and perils, for it may well be that the final extinction of a baleful domination will pave the way to a broader solidarity of all the men in all the lands than we could ever have planned if we had not marched together through the fire.[1]

'This last broadcast of yours is beyond praise,' the Labour MP Josiah Wedgwood, one of the heroes of the Gallipoli landings, wrote to Churchill on November 13: 'the concluding paragraphs should be historic, and moved one as nothing has since 1918. Do get them issued in pamphlet form for propaganda & for inspiration.'[2] But not everyone was impressed by Churchill's oratory: 'very boastful', John Colville noted in his diary, 'over-confident and indiscreet (especially about Italy and the USA)'; and yet, he added, 'certainly most amusing'.[3] On the following day Colville wrote again: 'Winston's speech has made a very bad effect at No. 10, but the FO and the City take a favourable view.' The Italian and Dutch representatives, he added, had 'protested at the FO', while R. A. Butler, the Under-Secretary of State at the Foreign Office, and a supporter of Baldwin and Chamberlain for the past decade, told Colville he thought Churchill's speech 'beyond words vulgar'.[4]

Not so Thomas Loveday, who wrote to Churchill on November 13, of the questions raised by the young officer-to-be, that the German threat to Holland and Belgium 'must have resolved doubts' and adding: 'I am sure that your speech last night gave the fire and stimulus which were so badly needed.'[5]

[1] Broadcast of 12 November 1939: Churchill papers, 9/138.
[2] Letter of 13 November 1939: Churchill papers, 2/368.
[3] Colville diary, 13 November 1939: Colville papers.
[4] Colville diary, 14 November 1939: Colville papers.
[5] Letter of 13 November 1939, 'Personal': Loveday papers.

5

Hitler's Secret Weapon

ON 10 September 1939 a merchant ship, the *Magdapur*, had been sunk by a mine off the Suffolk coast in circumstances which, it was later noted, 'could not be satisfactorily explained'. Following two further such sinkings, the *City of Paris* on September 18 and the *Phryne* on September 24, a Committee was set up at the Admiralty, under instructions to inquire into the mysterious mine, and to develop counter-measures.

This Committee held its first meeting on October 8. It soon became clear that the mines were triggered by the magnetic field of any ship which passed beside or above them. But even as the Committee examined the evidence, a further eighteen ships were blown up by these mysterious magnetic mines.[1]

On November 14 Churchill reported this bad news to his War Cabinet colleagues. Recently, he said, a U-boat had laid a minefield 'opposite the entrance to the Thames estuary, and a British warship, HMS *Adventure*, had been badly damaged, and twelve sailors killed. The damage, Churchill revealed, had been caused by a magnetic mine. Such mines, he warned, were 'likely to prove a great vexation'.[2]

Five days later, Churchill reported to the War Cabinet that the number of ships sunk by these magnetic mines had increased 'with alarming rapidity'. The Admiralty's technical experts, he said, 'were doing their utmost to discover a remedy; and the counter would no doubt be found in time', but in the meantime Britain was confronted 'with a grave menace which might well be Hitler's "Secret weapon" '.[3]

The success of the German magnetic mine led Churchill to propose,

[1] 'Suggested Memorandum on the Development of Magnetic Mine Counter-measures', September 1941, unclassified, 15 November 1976: Captain Lewis papers.

[2] War Cabinet No. 82 of 1939, 14 November 1939, 11.30 a.m.: Cabinet papers, 65/2.

[3] War Cabinet No. 88 of 1939, 19 November 1939, 11.30 a.m.: Cabinet papers, 65/2.

on November 19, 'a measure of retaliation', and in a minute to Admiral Fraser and Captain Boyd, he reverted to an idea that he had discussed with General Gamelin during his visit to France: 'to feed large numbers of floating mines into the Rhine'. This could 'easily be done' above Strasbourg, he pointed out, where the left-bank was French territory. The Rhine below Strasbourg was 'the main artery of German trade and life'. At least twelve new bridges of boats had been thrown across the Rhine since the outbreak of war, 'upon which the German armies concentrated in the Saarbrücken–Luxemburg area depend'.

The British mine, Churchill added, should be designed so as 'to spread the terror further down the Rhine to its confluence with the Moselle, or beyond'. Before reaching Dutch territory, it should either sink automatically 'or preferably explode'. Very large numbers of mines would be used, and the process 'kept up night after night for months on end', to deny the Germans the use of their principal waterway.[1]

Explaining his proposals that same day to Pound and Phillips, Churchill noted that nine British ships had been sunk in the mouth of the Thames in the previous three days, an act which was, he added, 'an outrage upon the accepted International Law'. One of the ships was a Dutch passenger liner, and many lives had been lost. Churchill therefore wanted the Law Officers to report at once on the legal position. 'Not an hour should be lost,' he wrote. It was essential, publicly, to condemn 'this odious practice' as soon as possible.

Churchill told Pound and Phillips of his idea for mines in the Rhine. 'Professor Lindemann has pressed these ideas upon me,' he noted, 'and is ready with plans.'[2]

The toll of the magnetic mine continued to be a severe one. On November 19 alone five merchant ships were sunk, two British, one French, one Swedish and one Italian: losses which Churchill reported to the War Cabinet on the morning of November 20. No effort would be spared, he said, 'to direct the fullest scientific investigation on to the problem'.[3]

At ten o'clock that night Churchill's senior advisers gathered in his room at the Admiralty to discuss with him 'steps to meet the enemy's magnetic mine'. Those present included Admirals Pound, Phillips and Fraser. Lindemann had also been invited at Churchill's request. It was agreed that the East Coast convoys would have to be given up temporarily between the Humber and the Thames, 'ships to proceed

---

[1] 'Most Secret', 19 November 1939: Admiralty papers, 116/4239.
[2] Minute of 19 November 1939: Admiralty papers, 205/2.
[3] War Cabinet No. 89 of 1939, 20 November 1939, 11.30 a.m.: Cabinet papers, 65/2. The British merchant ships sunk were the *Blackhill* (2,492 tons) and the *Torchbearer* (1,267 tons).

independently'. There would be a new combined sea and air offensive against U-boats in the North Sea, for which escort vessels, released from convoying, would be 'used for hunting'. Special aircraft would be equipped. Destroyers, and special wooden trawlers, would tow a special 'skid' to detonate mines. A new type of sweep would be prepared, an electric current 'being passed along it from generators with towing vessels'. And a magnetic device would be provided to project a magnetic field in front of the ship in which it was installed: the first of these to be ready by the second week of 1940.[1]

Churchill reported these decisions to the War Cabinet on the morning of November 21. In addition, he explained, all East Coast navigational lights would be extinguished 'so that U-boats would have no leading marks by which to lay mines at night'. All merchant shipping would therefore have to anchor during the hours of darkness. Churchill also told the War Cabinet of another magnetic mine casualty, the minesweeper *Mastiff*, blown up while sweeping for mines in the Thames estuary on the previous day.[2]

There were four further magnetic mine casualties to report to the War Cabinet on the morning of November 22:[3] there was 'no doubt now', Churchill told his War Cabinet colleagues, that these magnetic mines were being dropped from aeroplanes.

Churchill asked his colleagues whether, 'in view of the uneasiness resulting from the large number of sinkings', he should make a short statement in the House of Commons that afternoon, on the balance-sheet of shipping losses. Chamberlain thought it would be 'preferable' to defer any such statement until the following day, 'when Parliament would be prorogued'.[4]

Halifax was opposed altogether to Churchill's statement. 'If I remember right,' he wrote to Churchill later that day, 'the conclusion of your argument was to be that we had really done wonderfully well and that the damage inflicted by the Germans was negligible.' This was, of course, 'most satisfactory', Halifax added, but it would not look well

[1] Most Secret', 20 November 1939: Admiralty papers, 205/4.

[2] War Cabinet No. 90 of 1939, 21 November 1939, 11.30 a.m.: Cabinet papers, 65/2. Captain Lewis notes: 'The *Mastiff* was trying to get a magnetic mine specimen. She was a trawler. They trawled round the wrecks with their nets hoping to find the twin of a pair. They found one, and the *Mastiff* blew up while they were hoisting it on board'. (Captain Lewis, conversation with the author, 18 March 1982.)

[3] HMS *Belfast*, damaged but successfully docked; HMS *Gipsy*, struck by a mine on leaving Harwich, severely damaged, and then beached; the steamship *Geraldus*, mined and sunk off the mouth of the Thames; and the Japanese steamship *Terukuni Maru*, mined and sunk off the entrance to the Thames.

[4] War Cabinet No. 91 of 1939, 22 November 1939, 11.30 a.m.: Cabinet papers, 65/2.

when contrasted with the justification being used to stop all German exports to neutral States. The neutrals had been told that the German submarine attack was 'grave enough' to justify the British in stopping even neutral ships from reaching Germany.[1]

Churchill decided not to make his proposed statement, 'largely', as he wrote to Halifax later on November 22, 'because of the reasons which you mentioned in your letter'. Churchill added: 'My information is that the public are not really rattled, and from every other point of view it is much better that the grievance should dominate our thoughts and speech at this juncture. We must let the grievance have a good run in order to cover the economic reprisal.' Once that point had been 'put over', Churchill felt, it would be possible 'to strike the reassuring note'.[2]

Searching for every possible means of combating the magnetic mine, Churchill proposed to Pound and Phillips on November 22 'a special Section' to collect all the evidence about the mines from survivors, to experiment with counter-measures, to produce the various materials needed, and to put them into action.[3] Within twenty-four hours this Section had been set up, headed first by Admiral Lyster, then by Admiral Wake-Walker, with instructions 'to co-ordinate and direct all measures for dealing with the German magnetic mine'.[4]

Meanwhile, the reprisal action was being further advanced. On November 23 Churchill interviewed a Major in the Royal Engineers, Major Jefferis, who had already constructed a pilot model of a small floating mine weighing only five pounds, which could be used in rivers or canals against barges. A considerable number could be carried by aeroplane.[5]

In preparation for the War Cabinet on November 24, Lindemann provided Churchill with a note on the importance of the Rhine to Germany 'as a traffic artery'. More than 40% of Germany's exports passed down the Rhine, he wrote, 'as against 25% by sea and 30% by rail'. Lindemann's conclusion was: 'If this traffic could be stopped or even seriously impeded, it would probably have as great an economic effect as any other measure which could be taken'.[6]

[1] Letter of 22 November 1939: Foreign Office papers, 800/325.
[2] 'Private', 22 November 1939: Foreign Office papers, 800/325.
[3] Minute of 22 November 1939: Churchill papers, 19/3.
[4] 'Suggested Memorandum on the Development of Magnetic Mine Counter-measures', September 1941, unclassified, 15 November 1976: Captain Lewis papers.
[5] 'Royal Marine Operation': Cabinet papers, 120/418.
[6] 'Secret', 24 November 1939: Admiralty papers, 116/4239.

At the War Cabinet of November 24 Churchill sought approval for the Rhine project. If the operation were to go ahead, he explained, it would be made clear 'that we were doing so as a reprisal for the sinkings caused by the illegal use of mines by the Germans'. He went on to explain that the mines would be dropped from the air, 'and for a single aircraft to carry 400 to 500 of them at a time'. A large-scale operation 'might do tremendous damage'. Admiral Fraser, was already in consultation with the Air Ministry, and it was estimated that some 10,000 mines would be ready by the end of January 1940.

The War Cabinet authorized work on the scheme 'to proceed forthwith', on the understanding that a final decision would be 'reserved' until the project was ready to be put into execution. Lord Hankey added that Churchill 'should include the Danube, as well as the Rhine, in the investigations which he would be ordering'.[1]

Five days after the War Cabinet's approval for the plans to proceed, the idea of mining the River Rhine received a setback: a note prepared at Churchill's own request by Desmond Morton's experts at the Intelligence Department of the Ministry of Economic Warfare. The note stressed the fall in German imports and exports traffic on the Rhine since 1938, a fall that was likely to continue still further 'with the application of the Allies' Reprisal Order against German exports'. For the traffic that existed, there was no shortage of barges. If Rhine traffic were interrupted or blocked, most of the essential supplies could be transferred by canal or rail. To mine the river 'is unlikely by itself to have a decisive effect, or even an effect so serious as would be produced on Ruhr output by the stoppage of traffic on one of the high level sections of the Dortmund–Ems Canal, through which now passes, inter alia, the greater part of the iron ore destined for the Ruhr'.[2]

Here at least was a possible alternative area of action: so secret was it considered that Morton only sent Churchill six copies, four of which were subsequently destroyed to ensure the maximum secrecy.

On the night of November 22 the magnetic mine problem took a sudden turn towards a solution. 'A number of magnetic mines had now been located,' Churchill told the War Cabinet two days later, 'one of which had fallen on the mud near Shoeburyness, where it was uncovered at low tide.' Two naval officers were examining it. Two protu-

---

[1] War Cabinet 93 of 1939, 24 November 1939, 11.30 a.m., Minute 3, Confidential Annex: Cabinet papers, 65/4.

[2] 'Most Secret', 'Germany, Traffic on the Rhine', I/503/1 of 29 November 1939: Admiralty papers, 116/4239.

berances—'which it was assumed were detonators'—had been detached, and taken away, with the mine itself, for detailed examination.[1]

At eleven o'clock on the night of November 23 Lieutenant-Commander Lewis, one of the four men who had recovered the mine, reported to Churchill at the Admiralty. 'I gathered together eighty or a hundred officers and officials in our largest room,' Churchill later recalled, 'and a thrilled audience listened to the tale, deeply conscious of all that was at stake.'[2]

The meeting was held in the cinema room at the Admiralty. 'I was terrified,' Lieutenant-Commander Lewis later recalled. 'I'd never seen so many Admirals and Captains in my life.'[3] As Lewis told his tale, Churchill cross-examined him as to times and details. 'Did you lay your hands on it?' 'There was no parachute attached to the mine?' 'Had the tide receded?' 'Did you use force?' 'Where is the explosive?' 'Where is the charge?' And as Lewis set out his account, Churchill commented: 'To sum up, you have dissected this monster, divided it into pieces and now you can examine it at leisure!'

When questioned as to what the mechanism of the mine might be, Lewis answered Churchill: 'I personally think it is accoustic.'[4] With the mine and its mechanism in their possession, Churchill asked Lewis, 'you will be able to find out all the life history of this animal?' To which Lewis replied: 'We hope so.'

It was now midnight, and the meeting was at an end. 'We have got our prize,' Churchill told the assembled sailors, 'as good a ship as ever sailed the seas, and we owe a great deal to the public spirit of Lieut. Commander Lewis and his colleague Lieut. Commander Ouvry who have been up against it today.'[5]

No obstacle now stood in the way of combating the magnetic mine, and the technical plans discussed a few days earlier at the Admiralty were now geared to the exact specifications of the mine itself. 'Suitable apparatus for sweeping up the mines would be completed as soon as

[1] War Cabinet 93 of 1939, 24 November 1939, 11.30 a.m.: Cabinet papers, 65/2.

[2] Winston S. Churchill, *The Second World War*, volume 1, London 1948, page 397. The four who recovered the mine were Lieutenant-Commanders Ouvry and Lewis, Chief Petty Officer Baldwin and Able Seaman Vearncombe.

[3] Captain Lewis, conversation with the author, 18 March 1982.

[4] It was not; within 24 hours *Vernon* had found that it was magnetic.

[5] Commander G. Thistleton-Smith, 'The Personal Side of Some Vernon Mine Recovery and Investigation Operations, September 1939–December 1940', typescript dated 10 May 1942: Captain Lewis papers. One result of the recovery of the mine was the award of the first naval decorations of the war, two DSOs, one DSC and two DSMs, bestowed personally by King George VI at HMS *Vernon* on 19 December 1939.

possible,' Churchill was able to tell the War Cabinet on November 25;[1] and at a series of meetings during the last week of November Churchill and his advisers initiated experiments and discussed progress. Later on November 25, three most senior Air Force officers, Sir Cyril Newall, Air Marshal Dowding and Air Vice-Marshal Peck, meeting with Churchill and his advisers at the Admiralty, promised to give whatever help was possible, including radar, as soon as a radar set was available. But at the same time Dowding warned that there were bound to be 'teething troubles and delays'.[2]

At a meeting of Admiralty officials on November 27, there was a discussion of all the methods being developed; 'work on all the proposals', it was reported 'was being carried out simultaneously'.[3] But the public knew nothing of this. The daily sinkings of merchant ships, both British and neutral, provided a gloomy diet of news, broadcast daily over the BBC, giving a depressing prominence to Hitler's successes. Nor was the political atmosphere entirely conducive to national unity. Earlier that same week Lady Astor had written to Lord Lothian of how, at a 1922 Club Dinner in London, Neville Chamberlain had 'sneered at the Labour Party for not coming in, and then said we were better without them'. Lady Astor added: 'The whole thing was so absolutely lacking in statesmanship, uplift or vision of any kind, it really got one down for the moment. . . . I am sure he meant it to be a fighting speech, but its effect on me was to make me wish that Winston were PM (This was only momentary, and I knew it was wrong, but that was my reaction).'[4]

On 30 November 1939 Churchill celebrated his sixty-fifth birthday. 'You need no blood-transfusions,' Lady Violet Bonham Carter wrote to him, 'unlike some of your colleagues!'[5] During the day Churchill continued to scrutinize several areas of Admiralty activity. 'I am much disturbed,' he minuted to Admiral Fraser, 'to find that only 25 of the medium destroyers (escort vessels) will be delivered during the whole of 1940. I understood these vessels were specially simplified and

---

[1] War Cabinet No. 94 of 1939, 25 November 1939, 11.30 a.m.: Cabinet papers, 65/2.

[2] 'Most Secret', 'Meeting in First Lord's room on 25th November, 1939', 26 November 1939: Admiralty papers, 1/10315.

[3] 'Most Secret', 'Draft Report on a Meeting held on November 27th, 1939 to review the action being taken to counter the German magnetic mine': Admiralty papers, 1/10315.

[4] Letter of 22 November 1939: Lothian papers.

[5] Letter of 30 November 1939: Churchill papers, 2/363.

designed to be capable of production in 9 months.' Why then, Churchill asked, 'do we only have 25 sixteen months after the war has begun?' and he added: 'Even more depressing is the very late arrival of the whalers, which we were assured could be made under 6 months.'[1]

Churchill was also concerned during November 30 to learn that only two Royal Navy escort vessels were to guard the Australian troop transports on their way to Britain. A third escort vessel was, he felt, essential. 'The transportation of the Australian Divisions is an historic episode in Imperial history,' he minuted to Pound and Phillips. 'An accident would be a disaster.'[2] On his mind was the sinking six days earlier of HMS *Rawalpindi* with heavy loss of life.[3]

At the War Cabinet on November 30 Churchill again spoke of his Balkan concerns, and hopes. It was his belief, he said, that the Balkans 'were gradually veering towards the Allies', and that if Greece, Rumania and Yugoslavia were to join the war against Germany, 'it might even be possible that Italy would eventually declare war in favour of the Allies'.[4]

Searching for areas of possible action, Churchill again discussed the mining of the Rhine with senior Admiralty and Air Force officers on December 4, when the Director of Plans at the Air Ministry, Air Commodore Slessor, agreed to prepare 'within three days' a comprehensive scheme of operation. At this same meeting, Admiral Wake-Walker described trials carried out with models in the Thames: 'The test had been severe, but the results were considered hopeful.' Three days later a draft outline plan was ready, code named 'Royal Marine'.[5] On receiving it, Churchill noted: 'Keep in an "O" (offensive) box w other similar affairs in wh I am interested.'[6]

On December 6 Churchill gave the House of Commons an account

---

[1] Minute of 30 November 1939: Churchill papers, 19/3.

[2] Minute of 30 November 1939: Churchill papers, 19/3.

[3] The *Rawalpindi*, an armed merchant cruiser, ex-P and O liner, had been sunk by the German battlecruiser *Scharnhorst* after a fourteen-minute engagement, having refused the battlecruiser's signal to heave to and abandon ship. Some 270 officers and men were lost, including the Captain, Edward Coverley Kennedy RN. There were only 38 survivors, 27 of whom were picked up by the Germans. A tribute to Captain Kennedy was published in 1942 by his son, Ludovic Kennedy, entitled *Sub-Lieutenant: A Personal Record of the War at Sea*. During the engagement, the *Rawalpindi* had managed one hit on the *Gneisenau*, the sister ship of the *Scharnhorst*.

[4] War Cabinet No. 99 of 1939, 30 November 1939, 11.30 a.m.: Cabinet papers, 65/2.

[5] 'Most Secret', 'The RM: Draft Report of a meeting, held in the First Lord's room on December 4th, 1939': Admiralty papers, 116/4239. The operation was given the code name 'Royal Marine' because the initials 'RM' were those of 'Rhine Mines'.

[6] Note by Churchill on a letter from Air Commodore Slessor to Captain H. L. Barrow, 'Most Secret', 7 December 1939: Admiralty papers, 116/4239.

of the war at sea. The struggle was proceeding, he said, 'upon a margin which, though adequate, is not extravagant'. He wished to repeat his earlier warning, 'that a steady flow of losses must be expected, that occasional disasters will occur, and that any failure upon our part to act up to the level of circumstances would immediately be attended by grave dangers'. It was, however, his 'sure belief' that, as he expressed it, 'we are getting the better of this menace to our life. We are buffeted by the waves, but the ocean tides flow steady and strong in our favour.'[1]

That evening Harold Nicolson noted in his diary: 'Winston makes a statement on our naval position. When estimating our existing tonnage he adds in the ships operating on the Canadian lakes. But he is vigorous and eloquent.'[2]

At his meeting with General Gamelin on November 4 Churchill had mentioned the project to put mines into the Rhine, and had discussed with Gamelin some of the political, as well as the technical problems involved. However, as he wrote to Gamelin on November 26, the War Cabinet had 'approved in principle of the preparation, and the technical difficulties are being rapidly solved, so that I hope soon to go on to large-scale production'. Churchill added: 'In view of the unbridled attacks which the Germans are making by their magnetic mines upon our shipping in the Thames, an act of reprisal on the largest scale will be fully justified.'[3]

Churchill was determined to see the scheme for the mining of the Rhine put into action. He was therefore angered to read a legal note prepared for the Air Staff, opposing any such reprisal action both for legal reasons, and for fear of counter-reprisals. Crossing out the heading on his copy—'Note on the Use of Mines laid by Aircraft in Inland Waterways'—Churchill replaced it with the words: 'Some funkstick in the Air Ministry running for shelter under Malkin's petticoat.' Sir William Malkin was the Legal Adviser at the Foreign Office.

Churchill then scribbled a series of irate comments on the Air Staff

[1] *Hansard*, 6 December 1939.

[2] Nicolson diary, 6 December 1939: Nicolson papers.

[3] Letter of 26 November 1939, 'Secret': Admiralty papers, 1/10250. Churchill sent a copy of this letter to General Georges, adding in his covering note: 'I am hoping to have a good talk with you, should you be able to spare me some of your valuable time.' Churchill planned a three-day visit to France, beginning on 15 December 1939. It was eventually postponed until the first week of January 1940.

note. Where the note stated: 'The conclusion thus appears to be . . .'
Churchill had inserted after the word conclusion: 'based on false
premises, & carefully designed to hamper British action, while leaving
the enemy free'. Where the Air Staff had commented: 'Far the best
way of dislocating traffic in the canals would be by destroying the
three aqueducts,' Churchill wrote: 'Why don't you try it?' Where the
Air Staff had described retaliation as 'unprofitable', Churchill exclaimed: 'Don't irritate them dear!'[1]

Undeterred, even provoked by these Air Staff hesitations, Churchill
emphasized, at the War Cabinet on December 10 'the need for offensive
action'. His appeal was generally supported by his colleagues, who
concluded that, in view of Germany's 'complete disregard of international undertakings', Britain's retaliatory measures should be determined by the expediency of the measures open to Britain, rather than
by reference to the extent of the retaliation which would be justified
'on a strictly legal view of the problem'.[2]

Encouraged by this conclusion, and relieved that the Air Staff opinion had not been supported by the Secretary of State for Air, Sir
Kingsley Wood, or by his two senior advisers, Sir Cyril Newall and Air-
Marshal Peirse, Churchill wrote to Kingsley Wood on December 11:
'It would be better to have the operation argued out solely as to
whether it could be carried out with success, and what the military
retaliation would be. If this study of the technical aspects in their integrity and in isolation reveals a good case, it would then be for the
Cabinet to consider the wider aspects of law and policy involved.' First,
Churchill argued, 'let us see if we can make the ship float, and then let
the War Cabinet decide whether she is to be sent to sea, and in what
circumstances, and when.'[3]

The planning of 'Royal Marine' continued. Vickers were given
orders to produce two thousand special mines, and further river trials
took place. At a meeting in Churchill's room on December 12, Air
Vice-Marshal Tedder envisaged 'no difficulty' in having ten thousand
mines ready by 1 February 1940. Further experiments were to be
conducted, and the help of the French authorities enlisted, to provide
the operation with its forward bases. 'The aim,' Churchill told those
present, 'should be to have all material and plans ready for a big
offensive by the middle of February, 1940, so that whenever the Cabi-

---

[1] Legal Note attached to the Air Staff's study of Operation 'Royal Marine', 'Secret', 7 December
1939: Admiralty papers, 116/4239.
[2] War Cabinet 110 of 1939, 10 December 1939, 5 p.m.: Cabinet papers, 65/2.
[3] 'Private and Personal', 11 December 1939: Admiralty papers, 116/4239.

net should give authority the plans could be immediately put into operation.'[1]

Churchill had ended his letter to Kingsley Wood of December 11 with a concise statement of his philosophy of the offensive, and of his belief in making as detailed and far-seeing plans as possible, not only well in advance of action, but even in advance of final, formal approval. 'The offensive,' he wrote, 'is three or four times as hard as passively enduring from day to day. It therefore requires all possible help in early stages. Nothing is easier than to smother it in the cradle. Yet here perhaps lies safety.'[2]

By the beginning of December, strenuous efforts were being made by day and by night to find an answer to the daily toll which continued to be inflicted by the magnetic mine. At a meeting in Churchill's room on December 1 the idea of 'placing the ship in a coil' was discussed. 'The problem was difficult,' the minutes recorded, but investigations would proceed.[3] The idea was that, by girdling the ship in a magnetic cable, the ships own magnetization would be so drastically reduced that it would not activate the mine.

Meanwhile, the magnetic mine sinkings continued: at the War Cabinet on December 2 Churchill reported the latest toll.[4] He also reported 'success' in the Admiralty anti-mine experiments,[5] and at the War Cabinet on the evening of Sunday December 3 he was able to tell his colleagues that despite bad weather having hampered the practical tests, 'a number of devices would shortly be at work'.[6]

On December 4 Churchill had again to report a magnetic mine casualty: the battleship *Nelson* damaged and at least thirty of her crew injured.[7] It was later agreed, at a meeting of the War Cabinet on December 8, to keep this news secret 'as long as possible'; even, Churchill advised, 'from the Dominion Prime Ministers'.[8]

[1] 'Secret', 'Review of Measures taken for the Production of RM': Admiralty papers, 116/4239.
[2] 'Private and Personal', 11 December 1939: Admiralty papers, 116/4239.
[3] 'Secret', 1 December 1939: Admiralty papers, 205/4.
[4] The *Sheafcrest*, sunk in the Thames Estuary, had, Churchill said, 'been 600 yards off the course given to her'. In addition, a Norwegian tanker, ordered into British waters by the Contraband Control Service, had been struck by a mine off the Humber.
[5] War Cabinet No. 101 of 1939, 2 December 1939, 11.30 a.m.: Cabinet papers, 65/2.
[6] War Cabinet No. 102 of 1939, 3 December 1939, 5.30 p.m.: Cabinet papers, 65/2.
[7] War Cabinet No. 103 of 1939, 4 December 1939, 11.30 a.m.: Cabinet papers, 65/2.
[8] War Cabinet No. 108 of 1939, 8 December 1939, 11.30 a.m.: Cabinet papers, 65/2.

At a meeting in the Admiralty on December 4, an important step was taken towards finding a solution when it was proposed 'that certain ships be de-magnetized', to be used as mine-sweepers, while at the same time pressing on with experiments to develop 'a method of self-protection for ships themselves'. This method involved altering the magnetism of the ship herself, so 'that she will not activate the firing mechanism of the mine when she passes over it'.[1] This would also have the great advantage that each ship would provide its own protection.

As the experiments continued, so did the sinkings. Making his daily survey of naval affairs to the War Cabinet on December 5, Churchill reported a British collier sunk by a mine, and the steamship *Eskdene* mined but still afloat. But on the question of bringing in outside experts, which Lindemann opposed, despite protests from Pound and Phillips, Churchill adhered to his previous decision to keep them out. The 'theoretic aspects' of the problem were known, he told the War Cabinet. It was the 'practical application' on which a solution now depended, and this was being worked on by a sub-committee of experts, whose work it would be 'undesirable in any way to interrupt'. If, however, 'after, say, a fortnight', no satisfactory results had been achieved, 'it might be necessary to broaden the scope of the investigations'. But following a suggestion by Halifax, Churchill did agree that outside scientists could be told of the progress of Admiralty investigations, 'in order that they might be aware of the position', if, as Halifax phrased it, 'it was decided to call on their services', at a later stage.[2]

One ill effect of the magnetic mine casualties was explained to the War Cabinet on December 6 by the Director-General of the Ministry of Shipping, Sir Cyril Hurcomb. 'Since the magnetic mine campaign had started,' he said, 'the Greeks had ceased to offer their ships to us. The crews were now unwilling to come to this country.' The Danes likewise were no longer keen to allow the British to charter Danish ships. Yet these neutral charters were essential if Britain's sea-borne trade was to be maintained.

When the War Cabinet of December 6 went on to discuss the possibility of sugar rationing, Churchill opposed any such measure. Not only was he 'not satisfied' that the state of British merchant shipping

[1] Note by Admiral Phillips dated 5 December 1939: Admiralty papers, 205/2.

[2] War Cabinet No. 104 of 1939, 5 December 1939, 11.30 a.m.: Cabinet papers, 65/2. Lindemann seemed mainly concerned to keep his long-time rival, Professor Sir Henry Tizard, away from these experiments.

justified rationing, but he thought that the adoption of rationing 'would be used as an argument to prove the success of the German campaign against our trade'.[1]

At a further magnetic mine meeting in Churchill's room on December 8, progress was reported in all areas, including the proposed detonation of the mine by three specially equipped aircraft, the first one of which 'should be ready by Christmas day', the remaining two at intervals of a week or ten days. But the most promising news was in the experiment for individual ship de-magnetization—or 'de-gaussing'—in which a trawler had had its magnetic field 'reduced to one third of its original amount'. It was therefore intended, as the report recorded, 'to de-magnetize as many trawlers as necessary, and to go on to de-magnetize larger ships'.[2]

A race was now in progress between the continuing German success in dropping magnetic mines, and the British researches to combat them. The race did not seem to be going well for Britain. On December 12 Churchill told the War Cabinet that it was becoming 'increasingly necessary to deal with the menace of the magnetic mine', and he went on to explain that the Commander-in-Chief at the Nore, Admiral Sir Reginald Drax, 'had reported that the position was not improving'. There were at the moment only two channels open; and if these were closed, as they might be at any moment, a very serious situation would arise. Meanwhile, the German aircraft were coming over, not only by night but also by day, when they had the great advantage, denied to them in the dark, of being able to see the channels marked out by the buoys, 'which were a necessity for the guidance of shipping'.

Churchill asked whether one way of dealing with the day-time German aircraft might be 'to attack the German bases with bombs?'[3] But at the War Cabinet on December 13, before any discussions could take place on a bombing initiative, Churchill reported two more merchant ships mined in the North Sea.[4] A similar tale of German successes

---

[1] War Cabinet No. 106 of 1939, 6 December 1939, 4.30 p.m.: Cabinet papers, 65/2.

[2] Draft Report, 'Most Secret', 8 December 1939: Admiralty papers, 205/4. 'It seems ironical,' commented an official publication later in the war, 'that the unit of magnetic flux, which is one of the means of countering the magnetic mine, should derive its name from a German scientist, Carl Frederick Gaus (1777–1855)': Ministry of Information, *His Majesty's Minesweepers*, London 1943, page 28.

[3] War Cabinet No. 112 of 1939, 12 December 1939, 11.30 a.m., Minute 2, Confidential Annex: Cabinet papers, 65/4.

[4] The *King Egbert* off the Happisburgh lightship and the *Marwick Head* off Yarmouth. War Cabinet No. 113 of 1939, 13 December 1939, 11.30 a.m.: Cabinet papers, 65/2.

was reported on December 14, when Churchill spoke of three ships sunk by magnetic mines.[1] As a result, the Tyne had been temporarily closed to shipping.[2]

In the South Atlantic there was a similar tale of shipping losses, as the depredations of the German raider, the pocket battleship *Graf Spee*, continued. On December 2 she sunk the *Doric Star*, on December 3 the *Tairoa*, and on December 7 the *Streonshalh*. Suddenly, however, her raiding days were ended, as, on December 13, three British cruisers, *Achilles*, *Ajax* and *Exeter*, tracked down and engaged the pocket battleship. 'It had been most exciting,' Churchill later recalled, 'to follow the drama of this brilliant action from the Admiralty War Room.'[3] The *Graf Spee*, having been hit more than fifty times, sought sanctuary in Uruguayan territorial waters.[4]

That evening, at a further magnetic mine meeting in Churchill's room, success was reported on the de-magnetization experiment. The magnetic field of the trawler experimented on 'was down to a quarter of its original value', making it safe from mines in any water more than five or six fathoms deep. It was now intended 'to attempt to de-magnetise' both a destroyer, a battleship and the cruiser *Manchester*.[5]

At the War Cabinet on December 15 there was further news of German successes: two British oil tankers, one Swedish tanker and three trawlers sunk by mines. Shipping losses, Churchill warned, 'were assuming serious proportions'. Nevertheless, he told his colleagues, he was 'satisfied with the progress which was being made with the experiments to deal with magnetic mines'; indeed, he hoped to have 'the first of the new devices' ready for use by 1 January 1940.[6]

At the War Cabinet on December 16, Lord Halifax spoke of 'the depressing accounts' of Britain's recent shipping losses, 'which had been unduly advertised in neutral countries'. Churchill agreed, telling his colleagues that in particular 'he deplored the unrelieved pessimism of the BBC broadcasts, which unfailingly opened with a long account of ships sunk'. These broadcasts, he said, were having 'a demoralising effect' on the fleet itself, and it would be sufficient, he said, to broadcast shipping losses once a week.[7]

---

[1] A British trawler—'Only one survivor', the Belgian steamship *Rosa* sunk off the Tyne, and the Danish steamship *Magnus* sunk off Peterhead.

[2] War Cabinet No. 114 of 1939, 14 December 1939, 10 a.m.: Cabinet papers, 65/2.

[3] Winston S. Churchill, *The Second World War*, volume 1, London 1948, page 410.

[4] British losses were 64 killed in *Exeter*, 7 in *Ajax* and 4 in *Achilles*.

[5] 'Most Secret', 13 December 1939: Admiralty papers, 205/4.

[6] War Cabinet No. 116 of 1939, 15 December 1939, 11.30 a.m.: Cabinet papers, 65/2.

[7] War Cabinet No. 117 of 1939, 16 December 1939, 10.30 a.m.: Cabinet papers, 65/2.

A chance to change the daily impression of recurring disaster came on the evening of December 17, when the badly damaged *Graf Spee* blew herself up inside Uruguayan waters some six miles south west of Montevideo harbour.[1] On the following evening Churchill broadcast to the nation. The raider's end, he said, meant that 'for a spell at least' the shipping of many nations would enjoy the freedom of the seas. At the same time, in the North Sea, several German warships had been sunk or severely damaged by British submarines. In reply to these heavy blows, Churchill added, the 'Nazi Navy and Air Force' were redoubling their efforts 'to sink the fishing-smacks and drown the fishermen in the North Sea'. Throughout December 17 and 18 they had bombed merchant ships moving up and down the east coast of Britain, 'including an Italian ship'. Churchill went on: 'I am glad to tell you, however, that the heat of their fury has far exceeded the accuracy of their aim. Out of twenty-four ships attacked by bombs yesterday and today, only six small boats engaged in fishing and one small coasting vessel have been sunk, and the bulk of the others, including the Italian, have not even been hit.'

Churchill went on to praise the work of Pound and Phillips, and the support given to the naval leadership 'by the whole body of officers and men of the Navy'. It was, he said, 'upon these faithful, trusty servants in the great ships and cruisers that the burden falls directly day after day'. His broadcast ended: 'Many vexatious tasks lie before the Royal Navy and before its comrades in the Merchant Navy, and, as I always warn you, rough and violent times lie ahead, but everything that has happened since the beginning of this war should give the nation confidence that in the end the difficulties will be surmounted, the problems solved, and duty done.'[2]

Among the letters which Churchill received after his broadcast was one from the Conservative MP Sir Ralph Glyn, who wrote: 'your language, & the spirit behind it, matched the great exploits of the Fleet during this wonderful week'.[3] Another Conservative MP, Vyvyan

---

[1] Captain Lewis writes: 'I was in Admiral Wake-Walker's office the morning after the *Graf Spee* was sunk. An FO telegram in a yellow envelope (envelope addressed to 1st Lord) was handed into W-W's office; on the envelope was scribbled "Admiral W-W . . . . . Do something WSC." Inside was the telegram from British Ambassador in Montevideo to FO: "Have purchased wreck of *Graf Spee*, presume Admiralty interested". Lt. Kilroy & two of the Navy's best Artificer Divers left in plain clothes under false passports for Montevideo via Lisbon that afternoon!! Some six weeks later when they had finished diving & collecting what info they could, (they were ostensibly seeing if they could refloat her) it was reported locally, that salvage was possible but the particular firm concerned to whom the divers had been attached was not large enough for the job, so the wreck was put up for sale again . . .' (Captain Lewis, letter to the author, 27 March 1982).

[2] Broadcast of 18 December 1939: Churchill papers, 9/139.

[3] Letter of 18 December 1939: Churchill papers, 2/365.

Adams, wrote that same evening: 'Your broadcast tonight was as fine as ever. Though there might be difficulties, I wish you could talk to us every night! I know you would be equal to the task and the theme.' He was writing to thank Churchill 'for filling our hearts with legitimate pride'. Adams ended his letter: 'You are right, if I may say it, to emphasise the hardness of the struggle ahead.'[1]

To the War Cabinet of December 18, Churchill had been able to report that a channel one mile wide had been swept through the mine-field opposite the Tyne, and that a magnetic mine had been successfully exploded.[2] On the following day, at a meeting in the Admiralty Board Room, further progress was reported on all aspects of anti-mine experiment. De-magnetization of the *Manchester* had proved 'easier than had been expected', so much so that it was now hoped 'to de-magnetize her almost completely', and there seemed to be 'a good chance of making ships immune by this means', except in very shallow waters.[3]

So successful were the de-magnetization experiments that on December 24 Churchill telegraphed to President Roosevelt: 'Magnetic mines were deadly weapons on account of possibility of varying sensitiveness of discharge, but we think we have got hold of its tail, though we do not want them to know this'.[4] That same day, in an attempt to keep the success of the counter-measures secret, Churchill minuted to Phillips: 'Wherever ships are lost by mines in future it will be well to state that they are sunk by *magnetic* mines whenever this possibility exists.'[5]

On Christmas day 1939, after a month of intense worry and unceasing experimentation, Churchill was able to write to Chamberlain of the 'marked success' which was being achieved against the magnetic mine, telling Chamberlain that the sweep and the coils had both proved effective. Two mines had already been blown up by the magnetic sweep, and two by lighters carrying heavy coils. In addition, Churchill wrote, 'it looks as if the de-magnetization of warships and merchant ships can be accomplished by a simple, speedy, and inexpensive process'. The aeroplanes, and the special magnetic ship, the *Borde*, would both be at work 'within the next ten days', and the Admiralty were

[1] Letter of 18 December 1939: Churchill papers, 2/365.

[2] War Cabinet No. 118 of 1939, 18 December 1939, 10.30 a.m.: Cabinet papers, 65/2.

[3] Report dated 20 December 1939, 'Most Secret': Admiralty papers, 205/4.

[4] Sent to United States Embassy, 24 December 1939, transmitted to Washington, 25 December 1939: Admiralty papers, 199/1928.

[5] Minute No. 97 (First Lord's Personal Minutes, numbered series), 24 December 1939: Churchill papers, 19/3.

'pretty sure', as Churchill phrased it, 'that the danger from magnetic mines will soon be out of the way'.[1]

Hitler's first 'secret weapon' had been mastered. Three months of worry and uncertainty gave way to the hard but manageable task of combating the known and the understood. Of the Merchant Navy, which had suffered so severely from the magnetic mine, and was still to have to face five years of hazard, Churchill later wrote: 'their spirits rose with the deadly complications of the mining attack, & our effective measures for countering it. Their unnoticed toils and tireless courage were our salvation. The sea traffic on which we depended for our existence proceeded without interruption'.[2]

---

[1] Letter of 25 December 1939: Churchill papers, 4/99.

[2] Draft paragraphs of Churchill's war memoirs: Churchill papers, 4/99. On one magnetic mine captured intact were painted the words: 'Geb ich ein gut Geleite, Churchill hat dann grosse Pleite': ('Guide me on my way aright. Then Churchill will be in sad plight').

6

The Widening War

B Y the end of September 1939 Poland had been partitioned between Germany and the Soviet Union. In November the Russians and Germans had consolidated their power in the occupied areas:
the Germans by methods of barbaric cruelty, against Polish civilians,
and against the two million Polish Jews who, coming now under Nazi
rule, were beaten and tormented, and several thousand Jews and
Christians murdered.[1]

Throughout October, Russia had begun to apply pressure on Finland, demanding special privileges in certain of Finland's ports. The
Finns had rejected the Soviet demands, to the delight of many in Britain and France, who were stirred by the sight of so small a nation
standing up to its vast neighbour.

Churchill, for more than twenty years an opponent of the Soviet
system, was nevertheless in favour of the Soviet demands for naval
bases in Finland. These bases, he had told Pound and Phillips on
October 27 'are only needed against Germany'. Britain should point
out to Finland that her 'preservation' as a country would not be
affected by Russian bases in the Gulf of Finland or the Gulf of Bothnia.
Russian naval power in the Baltic, Churchill told his two senior advisers, 'could never be formidable', and he added: 'It is Germany alone
that is the danger and the enemy there.'

It was 'quite natural', Churchill wrote in his memorandum of October 27, for Russia to need bases 'which prevent German aggression in
the Baltic Provinces or against Petrograd', and he felt that, if his reas-

---

[1] In the first six weeks of the German occupation of Poland, more than 15,000 Polish civilians
were murdered, of whom at least 5,000 were Jews, a ratio of 3 to 1. The ratio of non-Jews to Jews
in Poland was 10 to 1. In a number of instances, Jews were locked inside their local synagogue,
and the synagogue then set on fire. These facts were made public by the Polish Government in
Exile in London, and some of them were referred to by Churchill in a speech at Manchester on
27 January 1940 (see page 143 of this volume).

oning was 'right', Britain ought to let the Russian Government know 'what our outlook is', while at the same time 'trying to persuade the Finns to make concessions, and Russia to be content with strategic points'.[1]

The Finns refused to make the concessions which Russia demanded, being unconvinced that Russia would be content with bases alone. In Britain there continued to be strong sympathy for Finland's plight, and her decision to resist Soviet pressure was much praised. But Churchill still argued, as at the War Cabinet of November 16, that 'it was to our interests' that the Soviet Union should 'increase their strength in the Baltic', thereby limiting, as he saw it, 'the risk of German domination in that area'. For this reason, he said, it would be a 'mistake' for Britain to stiffen the Finnish mood of defiance.[2] In any case, he noted on November 30, while he favoured 'expressing disapproval', it should be remembered that the Russians were 'impervious to words'.[3]

The Russian pressure on Finland was taking place near the very region, the Baltic, which Churchill had long envisaged as a possible area of British interest, and action. Since the first week of the war, Churchill had argued that the Baltic and Scandinavia were areas in which Britain would eventually become embroiled. The reason for this was, primarily, the danger to Britain of Germany's ability to bring essential iron ore, without interruption, along the Norwegian coast. The Germans had two possible routes, one along the Norwegian coast, sheltering behind Norwegian neutrality, the other direct across the Baltic Sea from the iron mines in Sweden, to Germany. Another danger, as Churchill saw it, was Germany's ability, while in complete and unchallenged control of the Baltic, to shelter her warships until such time as they chose to attack British shipping in the North Sea or the Atlantic.

In an attempt to find some feasible method of British action inside the Baltic, 'Catherine', the plan to send a British naval force into the Baltic had been discussed within the Admiralty on an almost daily basis since mid-September, and a special planning group, headed by the Earl of Cork and Orrery, had reported regularly to Churchill on the progress of its deliberations. On November 9 plan 'Catherine' had been put before the Minister for Co-ordination of Defence, Lord Chatfield, who gave his 'warm approval of the general principle',[4] and on

---

[1] Note of 27 October 1939: Churchill papers, 19/3. Churchill wrote at the top of this note: 'Pray consider this note which I wrote with the idea of circulating it to the Cabinet.'

[2] War Cabinet No. 85 of 1939, 16 November 1939, 11.30 a.m.: Cabinet papers, 65/2.

[3] War Cabinet No. 99 of 1939, 30 November 1939, 11.30 a.m.: Cabinet papers, 65/2.

[4] Minute from Lord Cork to Churchill, 9 November 1939, 'Personal': Admiralty papers, 199/1928.

November 23 it had been allocated a date after which it could be ready to be put into effect, 31 March 1940.

Given the size of the force that would have to be assembled, and the technical difficulties still to be overcome by special designs, no earlier date had been possible.

On November 30 the Red Army invaded Finland. There were many people in Britain who wanted the British Government to go at once to Finland's aid, even by declaring war on Russia. Plan 'Catherine', of which the public knew nothing, provided at least a means whereby a British naval force could reach the Baltic. But Churchill saw the plan as one to be used solely against Germany.

Plan 'Catherine' was under attack, however, even within the secret circle of Churchill's advisers. On December 3 it had been challenged by Pound in a twelve-point memorandum. Although Churchill had asked for a programme to be drawn up with 31 March 1940 as its starting date, Pound wrote that no programme had in fact been drawn up 'as it is quite impossible to do so under existing conditions when every available ship of whatever class is required with the Fleet'.

Pound suggested that no attempt should be made 'to achieve the impossible' by working to any specific date, that 'no further preparations' be made as regards stores, that 'all work' on special heating arrangements be stopped, and that even Lord Cork's committee might be 'disbanded for the time being as a considerable number of very able officers now employed on the Committee are urgently required for other duties'.

Churchill returned Pound's memorandum two days later, with the comment: 'An absolute defensive is for weaker forces. If we go on indefinitely like this we shall simply be worried & worn down, while making huge demands upon the national resources.' Churchill added: 'I cd never be responsible for a naval strategy wh excluded the offensive principle, & relegated us to keeping open the lines of communication. Presently, you will see the U boats in the outer seas. What then?'[1]

During the first week of December the Soviet offensive against Finland intensified. But still the Finns resisted with tenacity, and in Britain the question continued to be debated as to whether Russia was now an enemy against whom action should be taken. On December 5, Lord Cork, deep in his plans for 'Catherine', wrote to Churchill that the Russian attack on Finland 'affords us a wonderful chance—and per-

---

[1] Memorandum by Pound, 'Most Secret', 3 December 1939, and Churchill's comment: Admiralty papers, 199/1929.

haps the last—of mobilising the anti-Bolshevik forces of the world on
our side'. In contrast to Pound's hesitations, Cork wanted 'Catherine'
to be accelerated and put into operation at once. 'It would, no doubt,
call for tremendous effort and courage,' he wrote, 'but what great result
can be gained without?'

Churchill rejected Cork's advice. 'I still hope war with Russia may
be avoided,' he noted, '& it is my policy to try to avoid it.'[1] And in
answer to Pound's criticisms Churchill wrote: 'Obviously these issues
do not arise at the present time, & we can discuss them at our leisure.'[2]

For Churchill, the urgent question during the first week of December
was not the possible confrontation with Russia, which he hoped to
avoid, but the growing German use of Norwegian territorial waters. It
was the transport of the iron ore needed to maintain Germany's war
effort and preparations that alarmed him. This sense of urgency was
heightened by a single-page intelligence report from the Director of
Naval Intelligence, Rear-Admiral Godfrey, setting out the statistics of
iron ore movement from Norway to Germany. The report showed that
seven German iron ore ships had reached Narvik during the week,
that one ship had left Kirkenes with ore, passing Tromso on December
3, and that during the previous eight weeks seven German ships
had loaded ore at the head of Trondheim fiord, where 5,000 tons
of ore were stocked at the quayside. At Trondheim the iron ore
mines were only half a mile from the quayside. In addition, Godfrey
reported, another iron ore mine, at Farnes in South Norway, had
been re-opened 'with German capital' after having been closed since
1918. There, 2,800 tons of iron ore were already awaiting shipment to
Germany.[3]

Churchill realized the extent to which this ore would sustain Germany's ability to open an attack in the west. 'We must now make our
case for action,' he minuted to Pound and Phillips on December 7.
'Please speak to me about it.'[4]

The most effective action open to Britain was to lay mines in Norwegian territorial waters. This, although a breach of Norwegian neutrality, would force the German ore ships out into the open sea, where
British warships could attack them. Alternatively, the British warships
could themselves enter the neutral waterway.

[1] Note of 5 December 1939: Admiralty papers, 199/1928.
[2] Memorandum of 11 December 1939, 'Secret': Admiralty papers, 199/1928.
[3] Report of 5 December 1939: Admiralty papers, 205/2.
[4] Minute of 7 December 1939: Admiralty papers, 205/2.

The German government had no scruples in entering neutral waters, in one instance even to help the Soviet attack on Finland. For, as Churchill reported to the War Cabinet on December 10, a Swedish oil tanker, steaming in Swedish territorial waters, had been stopped by a German warship with orders, explained by the warship itself, 'to stop supplies of oil from reaching Finland'.[1]

Anxious to take rapid steps against the German ore ships, Churchill asked Joseph Kennedy to find out, 'privately' what President Roosevelt's reaction would be 'to the suggestion that we should mine Norwegian territorial waters in order to interrupt the passage of iron ore to Germany from Narvik'. On December 11 Churchill was able to report to the War Cabinet that he had received a message from Washington 'which indicated that the President's reactions were more favourable than he had hoped'.

Later in the War Cabinet's discussion on December 11 Churchill gave his opinion that it would be to Britain's advantage if 'the trend of events in Scandinavia' forced Norway and Sweden into war with Russia. 'We would then be able to gain a foothold in Scandinavia,' he explained, 'with the object of helping them, but without having to go to the extent of ourselves declaring war on Russia.' Once Britain were allied to Norway and Sweden, ostensibly against Russia, Britain would be able to use Norwegian and Swedish ports, including the Baltic ports, against Germany: a prospect, he said, 'which might be most fruitful'.[2] But he did not elaborate, or refer openly to plan 'Catherine'.

The idea of some future naval action in the Baltic was, however, very much on Churchill's mind. Reflecting further on Pound's critical memorandum of December 3, on the changing situation following the Russian attack on Finland, and on a proposal for offensive action put forward by the Commander-in-Chief at the Nore, Admiral Drax, on December 7, Churchill wrote again to Pound and Phillips on December 11 that if action did become urgent in the Baltic, perhaps with Britain allied to Sweden, Norway, Finland and Italy, all at war with Russia, 'it would be grievous if the need and opportunity came and found us without the necessary preparation'. It was more likely, however, that the situation would remain obscure. Yet Britain, 'having been thrown so completely on the defensive, and the initiative having passed to the enemy', had suffered heavy shipping losses and been forced 'to disperse its naval strength'. Even worse, Churchill wrote: 'We have no safe

[1] War Cabinet No. 110 of 1939, Sunday 10 December 1939, 5 p.m.: Cabinet papers, 65/2.
[2] War Cabinet No. 111 of 1939, 11 December 1939, 11.30 a.m.: Cabinet papers, 65/2.

harbour where the Fleet can shelter in security. We have, for the time being, evacuated the North Sea. Our harbours are insulted and mined with impunity, requiring terrific efforts merely to keep the traffic moving.'

Churchill accepted that with these problems, it would be difficult to find the opportunity to fit vessels for 'Catherine'. But he felt that even this difficulty 'should be reviewed at leisure, and certainly before the end of the year'. Meanwhile, Lord Cork's Committee must remain in being; indeed, Churchill wrote, its functions should be extended to include the examination of all projects being studied by the Admiralty Plans Division. 'I am by no means satisfied,' Churchill declared, 'that the offensive side receives the full effort which it requires.' Churchill added: 'I therefore propose to you that Lord Cork, assisted by his group of officers, should go through all the offensive ideas of our Plans Division, and that Admiral Drax should be invited to submit his schemes orally to Lord Cork, and be cross-examined about them with a view to arriving at the best possible plans for regaining the initiative.'[1]

On December 14 Churchill informed the War Cabinet that in the past three days the Germans had sunk three merchant ships inside the three mile limit of Norwegian territorial waters.[2] These sinkings, Churchill felt, gave Britain 'the strongest possible case for retaliatory action'.[3] and at the War Cabinet on the following morning he elaborated this advice. This action 'on the part of the enemy', he said, 'made it necessary that we should, in our own interest, claim and make use of a similar latitude, without delay'.

Churchill told his War Cabinet colleagues that the need for 'prompt action' was now increased, as the Norwegian government was said to be proposing to provide a convoy escort for all shipping within the Norwegian three mile limit. Such a convoy system would enable all traffic to and from Germany 'to pass without hindrance'. He therefore proposed the immediate despatch of four or five British destroyers into 'the more lonely parts' of Norwegian territorial waters 'for the purpose of arresting all ships carrying ore to Germany'.

These ships would not be sunk, but taken as prizes. There would undoubtedly be 'a violent protest' from the Norwegians against the entry into their waters of British warships, but Churchill felt 'that such

---

[1] Minute No. 55 (First Lord's Personal Minutes, numbered series), 'Most Secret', 11 December 1939: Churchill papers, 19/3.

[2] One of these ships was Greek. Another was the British steamship *Deptford*, which had been carrying iron ore to Britain.

[3] War Cabinet No. 114 of 1939, 14 December 1939, 10 a.m.: Cabinet papers, 65/2.

protests could be satisfactorily disposed of by reference to diplomatic channels'.

Churchill's proposal was supported by the Lord Privy Seal, Sir Samuel Hoare. But the Chancellor of the Exchequer, Sir John Simon, 'foresaw strong objections from the neutrals' if Britain were to seize any neutral, as opposed to only German ships, and Churchill was asked to prepare a memorandum setting out his proposals.[1] Before he could do so, a review of the situation by the Naval Staff led Churchill to report to the War Cabinet of December 16 that 'it would be wiser', in the view of the Naval Staff, to adopt the plan to lay a mine-field in Norwegian territorial waters, 'rather than to send in our own destroyers'. In this way, as Phillips explained to the War Cabinet, a clash between the British and Norwegian navies could be avoided, and, with the ore-carrying ships forced by the mines out of Norwegian waters, 'we would be able to exercise our rights by intercepting contraband in the usual manner on the high seas'.

At the end of the discussion Churchill stated that the 'great principle' to be observed was that, 'if we decided to go for the ore, we must do it wholeheartedly. We should use any and every means to stop the traffic not only from Narvik, but from Luleå and other ports, so as to create a real shortage.' By doing so, he said, 'we should shorten the war and save many thousands of lives'.[2]

On December 16 Churchill circulated the War Cabinet with his memorandum on the Norwegian iron ore traffic. The stoppage of this traffic, he argued, would rank 'as a major offensive operation of war'. No other method was open to Britain 'for many months to come' which would give so good a chance 'of abridging the waste and destruction of the conflict, or of perhaps preventing the vast slaughters which will attend the grapple of the main armies'.

Not only would Germany be denied 'a mere million tons' between December and May, but, by the cutting off of all but a negligible amount of her whole winter ore supply she would undergo 'a severe deprivation, tending to crisis before the summer'. If it were possible to cut Germany off from all Swedish iron ore supplies until the end of 1940 'a blow will have been struck at her war-making capacity equal to a first-class victory in the field or from the air, and without any serious sacrifice of life'. It might, indeed, be 'immediately decisive'.

If, by German 'brute force', the war were to spread to Norway and

Sweden, there was no reason why, with Britain's command of the seas, British and French troops should not 'meet the German invaders' on Scandinavian soil. 'At any rate,' Churchill added, 'we can certainly take and hold whatever islands or suitable points on the Norwegian coast we choose.' The northern blockade of Germany would then become complete.

A British occupation of Narvik or Bergen, Churchill argued, would keep these ports open for British trade, while 'closing them completely' to Germany. Britain would also secure 'a large and long-continued' supply of iron ore from Sweden through Narvik, 'while at the same time diverting all supplies of ore from Germany'. This, Churchill declared, 'must be our aim'.

On the legal aspect, and that of world opinion, Churchill suggested in his memorandum that as Britain had entered the war in accordance with the principles of the Covenant of the League of Nations, no infringement of International Law, 'so long as it is unaccompanied by inhumanity of any kind', could deprive Britain of the 'good wishes' of the neutrals. In particular, 'No evil effect will be produced upon the greatest of all neutrals, the United States.' Churchill added: 'We have reason to believe that they will handle the matter in the way most calculated to help us. And they are very resourceful.'

Churchill went on to argue that the 'final tribunal' as far as the morality of the scheme was concerned 'is our own conscience', and he ended his call for action by telling his War Cabinet colleagues:

We are fighting to re-establish the reign of law and to protect the liberties of small countries. Our defeat would mean an age of barbaric violence, and would be fatal not only to ourselves, but to the independent life of every small country in Europe. Acting in the name of the Covenant, and as virtual mandatories of the League and all it stands for, we have a right, and, indeed, are bound in duty, to abrogate for a space some of the Conventions of the very laws we seek to consolidate and reaffirm.

Churchill's memorandum continued:

Small nations must not tie our hands when we are fighting for their rights and freedom. The letter of the law must not in supreme emergency obstruct those who are charged with its protection and enforcement. It would not be right or rational that the Aggressor Power should gain one set of advantages by tearing up all laws, and another set by sheltering behind the innate respect for law of their opponents. Humanity, rather than legality, must be our guide.[1]

[1] 'Norway—Iron-Ore Traffic', War Cabinet paper No. 162 of 1939, 16 December 1939: Cabinet papers, 66/4.

At the War Cabinet of December 18, Halifax spoke of the possibility of Russia, angered by Swedish help to Finland, making demands on Sweden. These demands would force Germany to invade Sweden 'in order to safeguard her supplies of iron ore from the threat of a Soviet invasion'. Churchill argued that the neutrality of Norway and Sweden 'was a source of embarrassment to us, and of considerable advantage and profit to Germany'. But if Germany attempted to secure the 'over-lordship' of Scandinavia, this would give Britain the opportunity 'to take what we wanted, and this, with our sea power, we could do'. If Narvik and its ore supplies were to fall, 'it would be to us and not the enemy', an operation which, he suggested, 'should be studied in advance'. The mountainous nature of the Norwegian countryside, 'which excluded the use of tanks and similar mechanised equipment of which we were short' might even be 'an advantage to us'. At a later stage of such a conflict Britain might be able to establish air bases in the south of the peninsula, 'and so intervene in the Baltic'.[1]

Churchill did not confine his search for areas of possible offensive action to the Norwegian coast alone, although that was the area in which he felt action would be most immediately advantageous. During a War Cabinet discussion on December 19, after Kingsley Wood had reported a British air attack on German seaplane bases at Borkum and Sylt, Churchill urged further attacks on these bases 'with the object of destroying them'. But the Chief of the Air Staff, Sir Cyril Newall, explained that any such attack on a scale envisaged by Churchill came 'within the War Cabinet prohibition against any bombing which might cause loss of civilian life'.

Churchill replied that in his belief 'German morale was becoming shaken, and that a few blows of this kind might be sufficient to destroy it'. If justification were needed for bombing the bases at Borkum and Sylt, the 'unwarrantable murder' of British fishermen provided it. 'We could thus associate a specific operation with a specific crime.' But Kingsley Wood felt 'that it might be unwise to disturb the present situation, since by doing so we might lose more than we gain'.[2]

The question of stopping Swedish iron ore supplies to Germany arose again at a meeting of the War Cabinet's Military Co-ordination Committee on December 20. It was, Churchill said, 'the most urgent matter' under discussion, and he wished to proceed at once, 'stage by stage',

[1] War Cabinet No. 118 of 1939, 18 December 1939, 10.30 a.m.: Cabinet papers, 65/2.
[2] War Cabinet No. 119 of 1939, 19 December 1939, 11.30 a.m.: Cabinet papers, 65/2.

first stopping the traffic from Narvik, and then dealing with the other routes. Above all, Churchill said, 'we should not nibble at the problem, but go whole-heartedly for stopping Germany's supplies'.

Support for Churchill came when the Secretary of the War Cabinet, Sir Edward Bridges, read out extracts from a report on the importance of Swedish iron ore to Germany, 'to the effect that the Swedish iron-ore would be a deciding factor in the war and that victory would go to the side which obtained control over these important mines'. If this were true, Churchill said, the stoppage of the ore 'was vital to us', and he repeated that success 'might shorten the war and save an enormous number of lives'.

Churchill was supported in this argument by the Secretary of State for War, Leslie Hore-Belisha. But a far more ambitious scheme was about to be put forward, involving a military expedition entering neutral Sweden and occupying the iron ore fields themselves. This scheme was favoured by the French Government, and put forward at the War Cabinet by a senior Foreign Office official, Sir Orme Sargent, who read out a joint Anglo-French draft, promising 'to co-operate with Norway and Sweden'. This promise, Sargent explained, 'might be developed with the despatch of an expeditionary force, which in that case would be able to occupy Narvik and the Swedish iron ore fields as part of the process of assisting Finland and defending Sweden'. All this would arise, Sargent explained, as a result of a resolution just adopted by the League of Nations, 'calling upon Member States to assist Finland'.

Churchill was so impressed by this proposal that he urged that plans for the despatch of a military force to Scandinavia 'should be put in hand at once', together with orders to hold the Swedish iron ore mines. Such a move, he said, 'would not make war with Russia inevitable', and he told the Military Co-ordination Committee:

Russia might hold back from further aggression if she found us already in occupation; and even if she did come in, it did not necessarily mean that we should be engaged in general hostilities with Russia. It was the Russian practice to engage in local hostilities without a general declaration of war, as for example in Manchuria.[1]

There was undoubtedly a risk that we might ultimately be drawn into a general war with Russia, but this was a risk which we should have to run. He thought that we should make a friendly offer of assistance to the Scandinavian countries, as was proposed by the French, but that we should make it quite

[1] Where Soviet forces had recently clashed with Japanese forces, and several battles been fought, without any declaration of war.

clear that whether they accepted it or not we should come in and take possession of the minefields.[1]

A decision on whether or not to take action to try to deprive Germany of its iron ore was to be reached at the War Cabinet of December
22. On the previous day, in preparation for this meeting, Churchill
discussed with Pound the arguments he would put forward, and in a
note to Pound on the morning of the War Cabinet, he set out the
points he intended to make. 'Urge Sweden and Norway to help Finland,' the note began, 'and offer them an Anglo-French guarantee
that if they are consequently or subsequently invaded, either by Russia
or Germany, we will come to their aid with adequate forces.'
Churchill's second point was: 'Tell Norway at the same time that we
intend to stop the ore traffic, and indeed all enemy commerce on the
west coast of Norway forthwith. This action to be put into effect at the
same time that the Note is delivered, but in any case no later than one
week from today.'
Churchill's third point concerned the end of April 1940, by which
time Germany's need of iron ore 'will have become desperate', but the
Gulf of Bothnia would be ice-free, enabling the ore to be transported
across the Baltic Sea. 'It may by then be possible,' he argued, 'to take
further measures, either military or naval or both, to prevent Germany
or Russia getting possession of or working the Swedish iron fields, with
consequences that may be decisive for the war effort.'[2]
To cut off German supplies of Swedish ore, Churchill re-iterated at
the War Cabinet on December 22, 'was worth all the rest of the blockade, and provided a great chance of shortening the war and possibly
saving immeasurable bloodshed on the Western Front'. He then put
forward in detail each of the arguments of his memorandum of December 16, his remarks at the Military Co-ordination Committee on
December 20, and his discussion with Pound on December 21. These
arguments were, however, to no avail. Speaking immediately after
Churchill, Halifax told the War Cabinet that he felt 'very doubtful'
whether either Norway or Sweden 'would welcome any guarantee of
assistance from us against Germany, whatever might be their attitude
to an offer of assistance against Russia'.
Even Chamberlain, who favoured the halting of Germany's iron ore
supplies, and believed that it might 'be one of the turning points of the

---

[1] Military Co-ordination Committee No. 10 of 1939, 20 December 1939, 5.30 p.m.: Cabinet
papers, 83/1. Churchill was referring to the iron ore fields at Gällivare (also called 'orefields').
[2] 'Most Secret', 'Note used & followed by me at Cabinet', 22 December 1939: Admiralty
papers, 116/4471.

war' offering a chance 'of dealing a mortal blow to Germany', warned that any such action must depend on Swedish support. He was afraid, he said, that 'unless we had the goodwill of Sweden', it would be 'impracticable' to proceed with the first part of Churchill's plan, a force landed at Narvik.

The problem, Chamberlain stressed, seemed to him that of 'getting Sweden into the war on our side', and of doing nothing against Norway first which might have an adverse effect on Sweden.

The danger of alienating Sweden was also raised by the Minister of Supply, Leslie Burgin, who 'emphasized the importance of Sweden's friendship from the supply point of view', as Britain depended on Sweden both for ferro-chrome and calcium-carbide. 'If the Swedish supplies were cut off,' he warned, 'the position would be rather serious.' Kingsley Wood also cautioned delay, at least 'until the Chiefs of Staff had made their report'.

As the discussion continued, Churchill was supported in his call for immediate action both by the Minister without Portfolio, Lord Hankey, who feared losing 'an opportunity of inflicting a serious embarrassment on Germany', and by the Minister of Economic Warfare, Ronald Cross, who said that some German ironworks in Northern Bohemia had already shut down 'owing to lack of ore'. Lord Chatfield, the Minister for Co-ordination of Defence, also favoured 'the opening up of the Baltic front', arguing that this would prevent the Germans from invading the Balkans, where it would be much harder for Britain to maintain troops than in Scandinavia.

As the meeting of December 22 drew to its close, Churchill told his colleagues that, whatever the outcome of the discussions about the means of winning over Sweden and Norway to the Allies, he 'felt very strongly that we should seize the iron ore fields at all costs'.

Churchill's plea was finally turned down, however. Although the War Cabinet agreed to instruct the Chiefs of Staff to examine 'the military implications of a policy which aimed at stopping the export of Swedish iron ore to Germany', it laid down specifically that 'no action should be taken by the Admiralty towards stopping the exports of iron ore from Narvik to Germany'.[1]

Churchill had wanted this military and naval action against the German ore-bearing ships to begin on December 29. Instead, the War Cabinet initiated a series of prolonged examinations and discussions. These, while approving the general principle of stopping Germany's

[1] War Cabinet No. 122 of 1939, 22 December 1939, 11 a.m., Minute 1, Confidential Annex: Cabinet papers, 65/4.

iron ore supplies, and believing this to be of the highest importance, were nevertheless in disagreement as to what scheme ought to go ahead, and thereby delayed any action at all for more than three months. Churchill continued, however, to put foward the arguments for speedy action against the ore ships in Norwegian territorial waters, and the seizure of the Swedish ore fields, fearing any British delay would result in Germany becoming so powerful that no action could then succeed.

Writing to Neville Chamberlain on Christmas Day from the Admiralty, Churchill stressed that, 'Everyone here, and all the colleagues I have seen, are dead set upon the ironfields, and think it may be the shortest and surest road to the end.' All the Naval Intelligence reports, Churchill added, pointed to the Germans becoming 'increasingly interested' in Scandinavia. The matter, Churchill wrote, 'seems urgent and might well be ripe for a Cabinet discussion on Thursday if you saw fit'.[1]

That same day, while working in his study at Admiralty House, Churchill wrote an eight-point survey of 'the War in 1940' for Dudley Pound. 'This is the best I can do for a Christmas Card in these hard times,' he wrote in a covering note.[2] In his survey, Churchill set out his argument for a military and naval offensive against the ore fields. The amphibious operations to seize 'Narvik and the great ironfield', he told Pound, present themselves 'in a light of decisive action. I have been very glad to see the astonishing harmony of thought which prevails in Government circles on this theme'.

Churchill told Pound that the Baltic scheme, plan 'Catherine', ought also to be kept at the highest pitch of readiness, as it 'may well be' that Britain would, as a result of Scandinavian developments, 'be keeping a force in the Baltic after the summer of 1940 is over'. Churchill added: 'this will be equally true of the White Sea; for if a great operation is launched for the ironfields, one cannot say when it will end, or how large it will become'. Far from 'slackening-off' the preparations for 'Catherine', Churchill argued, these plans 'seem to have acquired a far greater measure of strategic relevance and urgency'. Warming to the theme of the wider Scandinavian operation, Churchill told Pound:

The supreme strategy is to carry the war into a theatre where we can bring superior forces to bear, and where a decision can be obtained which rules all other theatres. We have to select from a host of dangers the one which can best be dealt with, and which, if dealt with, causes all the others to fall away.

[1] Letter of 25 December 1939: Churchill papers, 4/99.
[2] Note of 25 December 1939: Churchill papers, 19/3.

Such a strategy may well be open to us now. And the enemy must know it.

With Britain able to secure 'the friendship, if not the alliance' of Sweden and Norway, Churchill envisaged, in this wider operation, a British naval base at Stockholm, supplied by oil and stores brought across the North Sea, and then by rail across Scandinavia. This, he believed, could be started in March or April 1940. A 'strong flotilla' of British submarines, thus based in the Baltic on a friendly shore, could 'hamper, if not deter' a German military attack on the Swedish iron-fields, by then already in British hands. But it would be wrong, he felt, to try to maintain a British Fleet in the Baltic 'unless we can see our way to maintaining it under air attack'.

It would be 'still more wrong', Churchill told Pound, to make the relatively limited operation of seizing the ironfields dependent upon sending a surface fleet to the Baltic. 'Catherine' was thus to be an addition to the iron ore operation, not the precondition for it. It was to offer, as Churchill saw it, wider possibilities going far beyond the benefits of seizing the ore fields.

Churchill therefore urged Pound to continue the plans and preparations for 'Catherine', so that if it became a possibility, it could be put into operation without crippling delays. 'Let us advance with confidence,' Churchill ended, 'and see how the Naval side develops as events unfold.'[1]

The goodwill of the United States had for some time seemed to Churchill essential if the Scandinavian operation were to go ahead. On December 27 he noted for the British Ambassador in Washington, Lord Lothian, that he had already asked Joseph Kennedy to find out 'in strictest privacy' the views of President Roosevelt. In his note to Lothian, Churchill set out the sequence of four distinct operations which he now envisaged: a British occupation of the port of Narvik, an expedition to seize and occupy the Swedish ironfields at Gällivare, the seizure of the port of Luleå and the railway leading to it from Gällivare, and 'the sending of a fleet into the Baltic'.[2]

The reply which Kennedy had brought was 'that President did not wish to be consulted'. Negative though this might seem, Churchill told Lothian that he had 'good reason to interpret this reply as meaning that no great trouble will arise in United States'.[3]

The War Cabinet's decision of December 22 had prevented Chur-

---

[1] 'A Note on the War in 1940', 25 December 1939: Churchill papers, 19/3.
[2] Note of 27 December 1939: Admiralty papers, 199/1928.
[3] 'Most Secret': Admiralty papers, 116/4471.

chill from taking any immediate naval action against the German iron ore ships in Norwegian waters. But, as he told the War Cabinet on December 27, 'the Admiralty were ready to send a force of destroyers to intercept the traffic as soon as the War Cabinet authorised it'. He also thought that as soon as the Germans realized 'that we were laying our hands on the iron ore from Narvik', they would take action against southern Scandinavia. Such action, Churchill declared, would give Britain 'full justification for the larger operation'.

The War Cabinet of December 27 concluded that 'preparation should now be made' which would enable Britain to follow up its imminent diplomatic approach to Norway and Sweden, proposing an end to 'coastwise traffic from Norwegian ports to Germany', by 'action at very short notice'. But at the same time the minutes recorded 'that no final decision should be taken to order Naval vessels to enter Norwegian territorial waters'.[1] Thus the action which Churchill had orginally proposed for December 29 was yet further postponed, in the interests of a wider plan which had to await diplomatic negotiations.

Churchill remained determined to press for early action in the limited naval sphere, and in a note prepared for the War Cabinet on December 29 he drew attention to a report from Narvik 'that the Swedish ore company is working 24 hours a day instead of 16, and that eighteen trains a day instead of 10 will run from the mines to Narvik'.

Nearly a month had passed, Churchill noted, since the Germans had sunk British and neutral ships in Norwegian territorial waters. Two weeks had passed since his own proposal for action by December 29. 'Thus the German ore is flowing down and the British grievance is getting cold.'

Churchill still hoped that the smaller plan—which now envisaged both the mining of Norwegian waters, and the destruction of the Swedish iron ore transit facilities at the Baltic port of Oxelösund—could go ahead with the least possible delay. He therefore proposed, in his note for the War Cabinet of December 29, a timetable of action. The first stage would be an immediate promise to Norway and Sweden of help from Britain and France; then, on December 30, the completion of a technical report by the Chiefs of Staff 'on the larger plan' of a British expeditionary force to Scandinavia; then, on January 1, 'notification to Norway of our intention to retaliate for the German sinkings in Norwegian territorial waters'; then, on January 3, 'flotillas start for Norwegian coast'; then, on January 4, 'we begin arresting German

[1] War Cabinet No. 123 of 1939, 27 December 1939, 11.30 a.m., Minute 1, Confidential Annex: Cabinet papers, 65/4.

ships and turning others into our contraband control inside Norwegian territorial waters'; then, on January 30 'at latest', measures to destroy the iron ore transit facilities at Oxelösund.

This plan, Churchill wrote, need not 'impede' the development of the larger plan. Nor, if the larger plan 'were adopted or abandoned', would the smaller plan be upset. It would indeed, he wrote, 'be the best means of setting in train those German reactions, Swedish & Norwegian reactions, which must guide us *inter alia* in our future decisions'.[1]

On December 31, before Churchill could circulate this note, the wider Scandinavian plan received qualified support in a twenty-two page report by the Chiefs of Staff, Newall, Pound and Ironside. 'The opportunity is a great one,' they wrote, 'and we see no prospect of an equal chance being afforded us elsewhere.' Offensive operations initiated in March 'might well prove decisive'. The strategy of operating in Scandinavia was 'sound', as long as both the front in France and Britain's sea-borne trade, could be kept secure. This, they thought, could be done. A Scandinavian operation would involve risk. Nevertheless, 'in view of the possibility of obtaining decisive results we think this risk can be accepted'.

There was always a danger, the Chiefs of Staff noted, that the Germans 'might attempt to forestall us'. To meet this, a German invasion of Scandinavia would have to be hampered and delayed 'by submarine forces operating in the Baltic', and a hastily improvised force landed at Narvik, to picket the Narvik railway, seize the Boden aerodrome and destroy the port facilities at Luleå. Such a force would later be reinforced 'by an adequately equipped and properly prepared expedition'.[2]

Although the Chiefs of Staff supported the wider scheme under certain conditions, they did not agree with Churchill's proposal to start the whole scheme at once by the stoppage of German iron ore ships in Norwegian territorial waters. 'We must emphasise,' the Chiefs of Staff wrote in a separate memorandum, 'that the consequences of stopping the Narvik trade now must be to prejudice the subsequent execution of the major operation. For this reason, we do not recommend this course of action.'[3]

Reading both these Chiefs of Staff's reports, Churchill was cast down. 'The self-contained minor operation of stopping the ore from Narvik and at Oxelösund,' he wrote caustically, 'must not be tried because it would jeopardise the larger plan. The larger plan must not

[1] Note of 29 December 1939: Admiralty papers, 116/4471.
[2] War Cabinet Paper No. 179 of 1939, 31 December 1939: Cabinet papers, 66/4.
[3] War Cabinet Paper No. 180 of 1939, 31 December 1939: Cabinet papers, 66/4.

be attempted unless Sweden and Norway co-operate. Not merely must they not resist militarily, or adopt a purely passive attitude, but they must actively co-operate.' Churchill added:

But is there any prospect of Sweden and Norway actively co-operating with us of their own free will to bring about a series of operations which, as is well set out in the paper, will—
(a) Ruin the trade of their ironfield and the shipping which carries it.
(b) Involve them in war with Germany.
(c) Expose the whole southern part of both countries to German invasion and occupation.
Left to themselves they will certainly refuse, and, if pressed diplomatically, they will protest loudly to the world. Thus the minor operation is knocked out for the sake of the bigger, and the bigger is only declared practicable upon conditions which will not occur.

Churchill's reply to the Chiefs of Staff continued:

The only way in which the desired train of events can, perhaps, be set in motion is by the practical step of stopping the Narvik ore. This causes little injury to Norway and Sweden and is the minimum violation of their neutrality. It is not comparable to an act of invasion of their soil. Nevertheless, as this paper shows, it may bring about a violent German reaction.

If this reaction takes the form of the invasion of southern Norway and southern Sweden, then alone will the offence be given to those countries, which will make them take up arms in self-defence, and this will be the moment when they will look to us for aid and be willing to open to us the passage to the northern orefields. Thus the minor operation, far from jeopardising the major, is, in fact, the only way by which the major is likely to become possible.

In short, the object of the minor operation is to provoke a German reaction which will secure us the Norwegian and Swedish co-operation deemed essential.

Churchill was keen to embark quickly on positive action which offered definite results. But he realized that the impact of the Chiefs of Staff's report of December 31, which although in its central arguments supported his own proposals, would lead to an even greater degree of hesitation and postponement than the War Cabinet's decision of nine days before. 'With many of the larger arguments of the Chiefs of Staff I am in full accord,' he wrote in his own memorandum of December 31. 'But I fear that the effect will lead to a purely negative conclusion, and that nothing will be done.'[1]

[1] Memorandum entitled 'Swedish Iron-ore', 31 December 1939, circulated to the War Cabinet as War Cabinet Paper No. 3 of 1940: Cabinet papers, 66/5.

The last week of 1939 saw Churchill disappointed, not only in the postponement of his plans to deprive Germany of iron ore, but also in his hopes of a closer and constructive relationship with the United States. After the battle of the River Plate, and the scuttling of the *Graf Spee*, the United States had supported protests from several South American Governments complaining that the British warships involved had entered the special three hundred mile non-combatant zone. This zone had recently been established by the Panama Conference of American States, including the United States. There had also been complaints, which the United States had supported, of British warships seizing German supply ships within this newly-created non-combatant zone so far beyond the International three-mile limit.

Anxious to avoid friction with the United States, on December 24 Churchill had drafted a telegram for President Roosevelt, apologizing for 'recent incidents' in which this had taken place. 'We cannot always refrain,' Churchill explained, 'from stopping enemy ships outside International three-mile limit when these may well be supply ships for U-Boats or surface raiders.' Nevertheless, Churchill told the President, instructions had now been given 'only to arrest or fire upon them out of sight of United States shore'.

Churchill went on to defend the British warships which had closed with the *Graf Spee* off Montevideo. As a result of the scuttling of the *Graf Spee*, Churchill wrote, the whole of the South Atlantic 'is now clear and may perhaps continue clear of warlike operations'. This fact, Churchill commented, 'must be a blessing to South American Republics whose trade was hampered by activities of raiders and whose ports were used for his supply ships and information centres'.

As Britain had 'rescued all this vast area from disturbance', Churchill hoped that there would be no more criticism of the British action, even if it had involved the appearance of British warships inside the Panama Zone, but not, he hastened to assure the President, inside the three mile territorial limits of the South American States. As Churchill explained to Roosevelt, the 'Laws of War' had given the *Graf Spee* the right to 'capture, or sink' all ships trading with Britain in the South Atlantic. 'No protest was made about this,' he pointed out, 'although it injured Argentine commercial interests,' and he went on to ask:

Why then should complaints be made of our action in ridding seas of this raider in strict accordance with same International Laws from which we had been suffering. Trust matter can be allowed to die down and see no reason why any trouble should occur unless another raider is sent which is unlikely after fate of first. South American States should see in Plate action their deliverance perhaps indefinitely from all annoyance. Much of world duty is being thrown on Admiralty. Hope burden will not be made too heavy for us to bear.

Even a single German raider 'loose in the North Atlantic,' Churchill pointed out, required the use of half of Britain's battle fleet 'to give sure protection' to the merchant ships. If Britain 'should break under load,' he warned, 'South American Republics would soon have many worse enemies than the sound of one day's distant seaward cannonade. And you also, Sir'—Churchill added—'in quite a short time would have more direct cares.'

Churchill went on to ask Roosevelt that 'full consideration' should be given to Britain 'at this crucial period', and that the United States should put the 'best construction' upon British action 'indispensable to end war shortly in right way'.

On a personal note, Churchill told Roosevelt that he was sending him by air mail various reports of the battle of the River Plate. The damage to the *Exeter* from the *Graf Spee*'s 11-inch guns was 'most severe', he noted, 'and ship must be largely rebuilt. Marvel is she stood up to it so well.'

Churchill ended his telegram to Roosevelt with the reflection: 'Generally speaking, think war will soon begin now.'[1]

While working at the Admiralty on Christmas Day, Churchill sent Chamberlain a copy of his telegram to Roosevelt. 'Everything is very quiet here,' he wrote to Chamberlain during the day. But he was worried about the 'stiff attitude' being taken in Washington about the Panama Congress Zone. Of course, Churchill wrote, Roosevelt 'is our best friend, but I expect he wants to be re-elected and I fear that isolationism is the winning ticket'.[2]

Churchill's telegram to Roosevelt, and his acknowledgment of the strength of American isolationist feeling, coincided with a development which was to prove of considerable importance to Britain's war effort, and to America's contribution to that effort: the establishment in the United States of an Anglo-French Purchasing Board. The Chairman of this Board was a British-born industrialist, Arthur Purvis, whose task was to persuade the United States administration both to sell

---

[1] Draft dated 24 December 1939; sent to United States Embassy, 24 December 1939; 'transmitted to President' 25 December 1939: Admiralty papers, 199/1928.
[2] Letter of 25 December 1939: Churchill papers, 4/99.

Britain essential munitions of war and raw materials, and to deny those raw materials to the Germans.[1]

Purvis had one strong ally close to Roosevelt, the Secretary to the Treasury, Henry Morgenthau junior, whose senior officials shared Morgenthau's willingness to help the British cause. All the Treasury experts were agreed, Purvis reported to London on December 24, 'that effective action' on restricting supplies of molybdenum, nickel and tungsten to Germany 'would be sufficiently serious to slow up enemy war effort'.[2] That same week, Morgenthau decided to put immediate pressure on raw material manufacturers throughout the United States not to ship essential raw materials to two neutral States, the Soviet Union and Japan, through both of whom Germany could legally receive American supplies. This pressure was effective, constituting what Purvis later called a 'moral embargo'.[3]

Churchill's career had been through an extraordinary revolution during the twelve months of 1939. In January he had been isolated and abused. Neville Chamberlain had publicly belittled his judgment. Parliament had rejected his appeals for a more war-oriented economy. He was approaching his tenth year in the political wilderness. Aged sixty-four, his political career was believed by many to be over. He was an elder statesman without a future. His own advice on defence and rearmament having been consistently rejected, he saw his country militarily weak, and its diplomacy crippled by that weakness. His calls for an alliance of threatened States having been ignored, he saw Europe divided, an easy prey for Nazi aggression. He could see no way in which his own abilities would now be used to help the nation, or in which the nation itself would be able to play a part in resisting the steady onward march of Nazi tyranny.

Within a year he had become a senior member of the Government, active in the War Cabinet, listened to with growing respect both in Parliament and over the wireless, able it seemed to raise the hopes and

[1] In 1914 Purvis, then aged 24, and an explosives expert, had been sent from Britain to the United States to buy up all available supplies of acetone, the scarcity of which in Britain was seriously impeding the manufacture of explosives. He was thus the first British purchaser of war supplies in the United States of the First World War. In 1924 he settled in Canada, as President of Canadian Explosives, Limited. His wife was American born.

[2] 'Purco' No. 1, Washington Telegram No. 960, 24 December 1939: Cabinet papers, 85/14, folio 11.

[3] 'Purco' No. 74: Cabinet papers, 85/14, folios 113–15.

courage of tens of thousands of people, looked up to as one of the few politicians able to lead the nation to victory.

Churchill knew the limitations to his power. He also recognized the strength of the obstacles to actions he wished to see carried out. He was not a member of the Supreme War Council, at which the British and French leaders worked out a common strategy. He also knew the extent to which the old suspicions of his reliability remained strong, especially in political circles. The Prime Minister had other confidants. Those who sought the emergence of a younger leadership looked elsewhere. Nevertheless, the revolution in Churchill's life was complete, awaiting only the steady unfolding of events to reach its climax.

7

January 1940:
'the tremendous array of
negative arguments'

THE year 1940 opened with a political crisis, the dismissal of Leslie Hore-Belisha from the War Office. According to Sir Samuel Hoare's diary notes, Churchill 'had told LG and Kingsley Wood that the Government would be stronger without HB'. Hoare also noted, of 2 January 1940, 'Neville Chamberlain's disclosures on Tuesday to me about Belisha. Winston agreed.'[1]

Friction between Hore-Belisha and the War Office had grown during December to such an extent that, in Chamberlain's view, it was impeding the development of Britain's war effort, especially in France. Hore-Belisha had expressed lack of confidence in the Commander-in-Chief of the British Expeditionary Force, Lord Gort. After Chamberlain had visited Gort's headquarters on December 15, and listened to Gort's account of the deficiencies of equipment in the BEF, he realised that no confidence existed between the senior British officers in France, and their Minister.

Churchill himself had for more than a month been planning a four day visit to Paris, the Maginot Line, and Gort's headquarters. On the morning of January 4, only an hour or so before Churchill left for France, Chamberlain told him that Hore-Belisha was to be replaced.

Churchill left London by train at 1.15 on January 4. An hour and a half later, shortly before Churchill's train reached Folkestone, Chamberlain summoned Hore-Belisha to the Cabinet Room, and informed him that he was to leave the War Office.

Chamberlain offered Hore-Belisha either the Presidency of the Board

[1] Sir Samuel Hoare, diary notes for 2 January 1940: Templewood papers.

of Trade, or the Ministry of Information, both posts being outside the War Cabinet. Late that night Hore-Belisha telephoned Churchill, who had reached the British Embassy in Paris at eleven o'clock, and told him of his removal from the War Office. Churchill advised Hore-Belisha to accept the Board of Trade, but Hore-Belisha rejected this advice. He therefore withdrew to the back benches.[1]

Churchill was now at Dover, where HMS *Codrington*, one of the Dover Patrol Destroyers, awaited him. The ship's Captain, Casper Swinley, later recalled:

... he was wearing an overcoat with an astrakhan collar and his 1st Lord's (Trinity House) cap, the peak and badge of which were slightly out of place. I heard later that someone had sat on it in the car on the way to Dover! I presented my officers to him and as he was some three quarters of an hour late, I suggested he should come on the bridge. But he said, 'No, I'd rather go to your cabin.'

I had left my cabin furnished as usual with my pictures in place. Mr Churchill at once noticed a photograph of my step-mother-in-law, Mrs Carnegie, who had been Mrs Joseph Chamberlain, and asked me what the connection was. He was very complimentary about her. I offered him a cigar (I had brought a special box for the occasion), but he politely refused and said 'No, thank you, I'd rather have one of my own.' (I didn't make the mistake that one destroyer captain made in offering him a cigarette!)

Sitting in my only arm chair he then noticed a framed quotation on my desk and asked me what it was. I told him it was a quotation from Alston's seamanship manual of 1865 which I always kept on my desk. He said 'I've never heard of it, do you mind reading it out to me?', which I accordingly did.[2]

After I had finished reading the quotation, there was a pause, and it seemed to me that Mr Churchill was impressed for he then said 'That's a fine piece of English. Now I should like to go on the bridge and see you take the ship out of harbour.' On the bridge Mr Churchill took a keen interest until half way to Boulogne when he said 'I know it is not usual for ladies to be on the bridge of a destroyer in wartime, but, I would be glad if you would give my secretary[3] a cup of tea. I am going down to your cabin to do some work.'

[1] Churchill never wavered in his view that Hore-Belisha should have accepted the Board of Trade: indeed he later averred that had Hore-Belisha done so, and thus still been a Cabinet Minister in May 1940, there would have been every chance of his having received office in Churchill's own administration. Hore-Belisha did not return to Government office until Churchill's caretaker Government of May to July 1945, as Minister of National Insurance, a Ministry not in the Cabinet.

[2] The quotation read: 'Remember, then, that your life's vocation, deliberately chosen, is war—war as I have said as the means of peace but still war: and in singleness of purpose, for England's fame, prepare for the time when the welfare and honour of the Service may come to be in your keeping: that by your skill and valour when that time arrives, and fortune comes your way, you may revive the spirit, and perpetuate the glory of the days that tingle in our hearts and fill our memories.'

[3] Kathleen Hill.

The *Codrington* was unaccompanied and proceeded at 25 knots and it was pitch dark when we reached Boulogne. There was much coming of French Admirals and Generals, and when we had secured I left the bridge and made my way to my cabin.

I shall always remember the spectacle—my cabin full of people and smoke—and my small table set in the middle with Mr Churchill seated at one end with the French Admiral on his right and others gathered round the table, seated and standing up. On the table were ink pots, mustard pots, india rubbers and so on. I saw Mr Churchill pick up one of these and turning to the French Admiral said 'This is the mistake the *Graf Spee* made!'

'We were witnessing a demonstration,' Swinley noted, 'of the Battle of the River Plate.'[1]

Churchill was accompanied during his visit to France by his son Randolph, Professor Lindemann, Lieutenant-Commander 'Tommy' Thompson, Detective Thompson, two police inspectors, and Kathleen Hill.[2] His aim was to discuss, both with the French and British Air Force experts, the 'Royal Marine' plan to sow mines in the river Rhine. For this reason he was also accompanied by the Director of Torpedoes and Mining, Captain FitzGerald.

On January 5 Churchill and FitzGerald discussed 'Royal Marine' at Vincennes with General Gamelin and Admiral Darlan. 'Various demonstrations were made of the scheme,' FitzGerald noted in his official report, whereupon Churchill placed FitzGerald directly under Darlan's orders, for the purposes of advancing the project as quickly as possible.[3]

On January 6 Churchill visited the Maginot Line. That night he dined with General Georges at the headquarters of the French Army Staff at La Ferté. French military opinion was in favour of the mining project. Indeed, as Churchill minuted to Pound, Lindemann and others six days later, 'French Military even point out that they control the head waters of the Saar and the Moselle, in addition to the Rhine, and that many possibilities are open there', provided that 'a really large supply of the needful is in hand'. Churchill's minute continued:

Not only must the first go-off be on the largest scale at all points, but the daily and weekly supply thereafter must be such as to keep the tension at the highest pitch indefinitely.

[1] Captain Casper S. B. Swinley, letter to the author, 5 December 1981.
[2] Churchill had written to Lord Gort on 28 December 1939 that he would like to bring with him 'my son Randolph who is now a 4th Hussar, and Professor Lindemann who is in all my secrets': Admiralty papers, 1/10250.
[3] 'Most Secret', 5 January 1940: Admiralty papers, 116/4239.

It is, of course, understood that while all action is to be prepared the final decision rests with the Governments.

In all circumstances I am prepared to postpone the date from the February moon to the March moon. Meanwhile every exertion is to be made to perfect the plan and accumulate the greatest store.

'Above all,' Churchill ended, 'any obstacle or cause of undue delay is to be reported, so that the operations can be brought to full readiness as soon as possible. We may be forced to act before the March moon.'[1]

After spending the night of January 6 in a hotel near La Ferté, Churchill travelled the following day to the headquarters of the Advanced Air Striking Force in France, near Rheims, where he was met by Air Vice Marshall Barratt. His programme was a full one: visiting squadron headquarters, talking to the officers of the Operations Room and Intelligence Section, and inspecting various gun positions and aerodromes. After staying overnight with the Advanced Air Striking Force, Churchill travelled to Arras where, on January 8, he lunched with Gort, and visited units of the British forces in France.[2]

Before leaving for England on the morning of January 9, Churchill issued a statement to the Press. 'I have visited a British Brigade,' he said, 'which is in direct contact with the enemy and found them in splendid spirits.' Everything was 'very quiet' except for the sound 'of distant cannon fire over and again'. Visiting a number of Royal Air Force squadrons, he had been 'struck with the state of instant readiness which prevailed', dull though it was for all concerned 'waiting about on the starting point week after week'.

Churchill's statement continued: 'Anyone at home who feels a bit gloomy or fretful would benefit very much by spending a few days with the British and French Armies. They would find it at once a tonic and a sedative.' Unhappily, Churchill added, 'the Admiralty cannot guarantee to provide transport for them all'.[3]

Churchill returned to the Admiralty on the evening of January 9.[4]

---

[1] 'Secret', 'Royal Marine', 12 January 1940: Admiralty papers, 116/4239.

[2] 'Programme, Sunday, 7th January, 1940': Admiralty papers, 1/10250.

[3] Press Statement, 9 January 1940: Admiralty papers, 1/10250.

[4] On his return to London, Churchill asked 'Tommy' Thompson to draw up a list of those to whom French translations of *My Early Life* should be sent. 'The officer who entertained us at dinner at Metz,' he suggested, 'and Lieutenant Chauvey at the Maginot fortress occur to me. Perhaps you may think of one or two others . . .' As for the officer who had looked after them at the Air Force headquarters, he 'might have a copy of the abridged edition of *The World Crisis*' (Churchill papers, 19/6).

On January 11, Churchill wrote to Hore-Belisha:

My dear Leslie,

I much regret that our brief association as colleagues has ended. In the last war I went through the same experience as you have suffered, and I know how bitter and painful it is to anyone with his heart in the job. I was not consulted in the changes that were proposed. I was only informed after they had been decided. At the same time, I should fail in candour if I did not let you know that I thought it would have been better if you had gone to the Board of Trade or the Ministry of Information, and I am very sorry that you did not see your way to accept the first of these important offices.

Churchill's letter continued:

The outstanding achievement of your tenure of the War Office was the passage of conscription in time of peace. You may rest with confidence upon this, and I hope that it will not be long before we are colleagues again, and that this temporary set-back will prove no serious obstacle to your opportunities of serving the country.[1]

Hore-Belisha replied that same day:

My dear Winston,

My first instinct after hearing from Neville was to get in touch with you. I rang you up, but you had gone. As you know I subsequently spoke to you in Paris. The fact that you had, unjustly, undergone the same experience was not the only reason why I had a natural recourse to you.

I never had any doubt as to the course I should take.

I know you will do much to win the war & that is the only thing that matters.

Thank you for writing.[2]

Five days later, after the debate on the sacking of Hore-Belisha, Churchill received a fascinating postscript to the episode. 'I think you ought to know,' wrote Robert Boothby from the House of Commons, 'that the House is—not unnaturally—restless and dis-satisfied; and that this afternoon has weakened the position of the PM.' Boothby had dined a week earlier with the new Secretary of State for War, Oliver Stanley. 'He told me then' Boothby wrote, 'that when he was offered the post of S. of S. for War it was made clear to him that the choice before the PM lay between the dismissal of HB, and a request from Gort *and the 2 Corps Commanders* to be relieved of their appointments. . . .'

---

[1] 'Private', 11 January 1940: Churchill papers, 19/2.
[2] Letter of 11 January 1940: Churchill papers, 19/2.

The whole episode, Boothby concluded, 'strikes the layman as a very rum business—and one that, to say the least, has been shockingly handled'.[1]

One result of Churchill's visit to the British Expeditionary Force was his proposal, at a meeting of the Military Co-ordination Committee on January 12, to replace the 3-inch anti-aircraft guns then with the forces in France by 3.7-inch guns. The 3-inch, he said, should be brought back to Britain 'for use in the quieter areas'. Churchill also pointed out to his Committee colleagues, Lord Chatfield, Kingsley Wood, and Oliver Stanley, that although the French forces 'were equipped almost entirely with artillery from the last war', they had modernized this artillery 'so as to get extra range, and even to out-range the new German types'.[2] But the impression made on Churchill by the French preparations had not been entirely favourable. As he later recalled:

Throughout the winter there were many tasks that needed doing: training demanded continuous attention: defences were far from satisfactory or complete—even the Maginot Line lacked many supplementary field works; physical fitness demands exercise.

Yet visitors to the French Front were often struck by the prevailing atmosphere of calm aloofness, by the seemingly poor quality of the work in hand, by the lack of visible activity of any kind. The emptiness of the roads behind the line was in great contrast to the continual coming and going which extended for miles behind the British sector.

'There can be no doubt,' Churchill concluded, 'that the quality of the French Army was allowed to deteriorate during the winter', and that it would have fought better in the autumn of 1939 than in the spring of 1940.[3]

A further weakness of the Maginot Line was that its fortifications ended at the Belgian border, leaving a gap of more than 150 miles between the north end of the French defences, and the North Sea. One means of helping to make this gap a less inviting target for a German assault was to persuade the Belgian Government to invite British troops into Belgium.

A sudden opportunity to do this arose in the second week of January, when a German aeroplane crash-landed on Belgian soil. In it were two German Staff Officers carrying what appeared to be genuine, and were certainly detailed, plans for a German invasion of Belgium.[4]

---

[1] 'Personal & Secret', 16 January 1940: Churchill papers, 19/2.

[2] Military Co-ordination Committee No. 12 of 1939–40, 12 January 1940, 5 p.m.: Cabinet papers, 83/3.

[3] Winston S. Churchill, *The Second World War*, volume 1, London 1948, pages 441–2.

[4] The plans were indeed genuine.

The British and Belgian Governments both believed that a German invasion of Belgium might be imminent. Admiral Sir Roger Keyes, a Conservative MP, and a personal friend of Churchill, was sent to Brussels to see Leopold, King of the Belgians. Keyes saw the King, then drove across the Belgian border into France to telephone Churchill with Leopold's proposals. If Britain would agree to the 'complete restoration' of Belgium and her colonies, and financial help for this restoration in the event of Belgium being conquered by Germany, then the King, for his part, thought that he could 'persuade his Ministers' to invite French and British troops into Belgium 'at once'.

Churchill immediately took this message to Chamberlain. Both men believed that 'at once' must mean that Allied troops would be invited to enter Belgium before any German attack, provided the King's conditions were met. The War Cabinet discussed the suggestion on the morning of January 14, a Sunday.[1] At this meeting, Churchill told his colleagues that Chamberlain, who was not present, 'had strongly disliked the suggestion that the Belgians should, at this late hour, attach conditions to receiving help from us'. The only guarantees possible, Chamberlain believed, were those 'implicit in a military alliance', and Churchill had passed this message back to Keyes, who had already returned to Belgium to see Leopold once more.

Oliver Stanley told the War Cabinet that in his view the Belgian conditions were already 'more or less implicit in our alliance', and that if the Belgians really were prepared to allow the Allied armies to enter Belgium before any invasion took place, 'this would be to our very great military advantage'. General Ironside agreed: even 'a few hours' start' over the Germans would, he believed, enable the British to form a defensible line along the Wavre-Namur axis.[2]

In a telegram from Brussels on January 15, to the Foreign Office, Keyes reported that King Leopold was 'not prepared to issue the invitation' in advance of a German attack. Yet this was the sole assumption on which the invitation had been so welcomed by the War Cabinet. The King felt that his country could not be induced to enter the war 'while there was any hope of keeping out'. He also told Keyes that it was both a Belgian and a British interest 'that the onus for the breaking of Belgian neutrality' should be left to Germany. The King also expressed his fear that once British and French forces entered Belgium, his country

---

[1] Only four members of the War Cabinet were present, Lord Chatfield (in the Chair), Oliver Stanley, Churchill and Sir Kingsley Wood.

[2] Report of Keyes' visit, and subsequent discussion, War Cabinet No. 12 of 1940, 14 January 1940, 11.30 a.m., Minute 1, Confidential Annex: Cabinet papers, 65/11.

would be made 'once again the battlefield of Europe—a matter of terrible concern to the unfortunate Belgian people, who though 90% pro-Ally, were desperately keen to be kept out of the war'.[1]

As this Belgian opportunity faded away, the Scandinavian option seemed to gain once more in importance. Churchill still believed that stopping all German iron ore movements along the Norwegian coast should be the most immediate British war objective, and at the War Cabinet on January 2 the arguments for and against the Norwegian coast operation were again rehearsed in detail.

At the start of the discussion Chamberlain asked whether it was accurate to say that 'the duration of the war would be profoundly affected' by depriving Germany of Swedish ore. The Director-General of the Ministry of Economic Warfare, Sir Frederick Leith-Ross, replied that it might take up to a year to cut off the supply altogether, but that once it were done it would be 'decisive'. Chamberlain then spoke of his concern that once British warships moved into Norwegian waters, the Germans would retaliate by 'seizing' bases in southern Norway, 'from which they could develop a most serious air threat'. Britain would not be able to prevent such a move.

Churchill argued that a German invasion of Norway 'would be vexatious but would in no way be decisive'. It would open the way for Britain's own 'next action', the occupation of the northern Swedish ore fields. The Norwegians, he said, 'would undoubtedly resist a German invasion which would be a violation incomparably greater than the violation of territorial waters of which we should be guilty'.

Chamberlain summed up the discussion by stating that while he was 'very anxious to undertake the limited project of stopping the Narvik traffic', and saw 'no serious difficulty' in doing so either from the point of view of international law 'or from the reactions of Sweden', he was nevertheless 'seriously concerned' by the emphasis which the Chiefs of Staff had laid in their report on the possibility of German counter-action in southern Norway. He was afraid also that once Germany occupied southern Norway, Sweden 'might be induced to come over into the German camp'.

Churchill intervened to say that if Sweden 'gave way to German threats', it would then be open to Britain 'to go in and seize the Northern Swedish orefields at once'. But the Chief of the Imperial General Staff, Sir Edmund Ironside, warned that an expedition to Scandinavia in face of opposition by the inhabitants 'would be a very hazardous

[1] Foreign Office memorandum of 6 July 1948 (prepared for Churchill when he was writing his war memoirs): Churchill papers, 4/143.

affair', Britain had no ski-troops immediately available, and the Swedes 'might adopt the same tactics against us as the Finns had so successfully pursued against the Russians'.

Another objection to the type of wider action which Churchill envisaged came from the Dominions Secretary, Anthony Eden. He pointed out that the Canadians, who had hoped to organize a force of between five thousand and seven thousand troops for operations in Northern Scandinavia in March, had no troops 'at present trained' to work on skis. But now it was Ironside's turn to support the scheme, at least as far as the Canadians were concerned. A 'very large number' of their troops, he said, 'were used to working on snow shoes. Such troops could operate in deep snow just as well as ski troops.' In addition, Ironside said, somewhat reversing his earlier remarks, there were 'a very considerable number of British personnel already trained in the use of skis who could also be made available' in the spring.[1]

A further War Cabinet meeting on January 3 rehearsed the same arguments at length, with Halifax saying that he did not think a German seizure of bases in southern Norway 'a vital factor', nor did he attach what he called 'undue importance' to the probable Swedish reaction. Nor did Norway's response alarm him. She would 'no doubt show considerable annoyance', he said, 'but she would probably get over this'. Halifax's concern was that the stopping of the Narvik traffic might affect 'our chances of carrying through the bigger project of stopping all the ore supplies to Germany'.[2]

There were four further discussions on the Narvik scheme at the War Cabinet in the second week of January. On January 9 Chatfield suggested that Britain should open negotiations with the Swedes about possible cooperation. But Halifax warned against 'giving ground to those in Sweden who already claimed we were trying to bring Sweden into the War',[3] and on January 10 Churchill likewise argued against any such negotiations with Sweden. The neutral countries, he said, should not be permitted 'to tie our hands when we were, in fact, fighting to maintain their liberties'. In order to obtain both Swedish and Norwegian cooperation, Churchill added, Britain should confront both

[1] War Cabinet No. 1 of 1940, 2 January 1940, 11 a.m., Minute 1, Confidential Annex: Cabinet papers, 65/11.

[2] War Cabinet No. 2 of 1940, 3 January 1940, 11.30 a.m., Minute 1, Confidential Annex: Cabinet papers, 65/11.

[3] War Cabinet No. 7 of 1940, 9 January 1940, 12 noon, Minute 8, Confidential Annex: Cabinet papers, 65/11.

countries 'with a choice of two evils', and he went on to explain: 'We should have to make them more frightened of us than they were of Germany.'

At the War Cabinet on January 10, Sir Samuel Hoare stressed 'the urgency of taking action to stop the Narvik trade', arguing that every week that passed without any British action 'allowed a further quantity of ore to sail to Germany'. Churchill agreed with Hoare, and went on to warn his colleagues: 'Every week the prize was melting. Time would be consumed in the proposed negotiations, and if we failed, we should be back again just where we started.'

The War Cabinet of January 10 decided, however, 'to defer a decision on the Narvik project' until the arrival in Britain of a Swedish diplomat, who was expected later that same day. At the same time, the Chiefs of Staff were invited to advise the War Cabinet 'as to what instructions and authority the Service Departments required to enable detailed plans and preparations to be made' for the two wider schemes of a despatch of a British force via Narvik to the northern Swedish orefields, and for the despatch of a force 'to co-operate in the defence of Southern Sweden'.[1]

On January 11 the War Cabinet discussed the possible reaction of Norway to any British action. When Halifax expressed fears that the Norwegian Government would cut off all ore supplies to Britain, Churchill stated that he 'did not believe' this would be so. The Norwegians had 'done nothing,' he pointed out, 'when Germany had sunk three ships in their territorial waters'.

Chamberlain agreed with Churchill, adding that he was 'not greatly concerned with the effect on Norway of any action we might take'. But he went on to tell the War Cabinet that he did, however, 'attach great importance' to Britain 'not alienating Sweden', especially as Swedish support would be 'essential if later we were to proceed with the larger project'.

Churchill now reiterated his almost daily plea: 'Whatever course was decided upon,' he said, 'it was essential that we should now act decisively.'[2]

At the War Cabinet of January 12 Lord Halifax reported that the Swedish diplomat had warned of Sweden's fears of German retaliation, should Sweden cooperate in any way with Britain. Even a British action

[1] War Cabinet No. 8 of 1940, 10 January 1940, 11.30 a.m., Minute 1, Confidential Annex: Cabinet papers, 65/11.
[2] War Cabinet No. 9 of 1940, 11 January 1940, 11.30 a.m., Minute 5, Confidential Annex: Cabinet papers, 65/11.

in Norwegian territorial waters 'would be seriously damaging to the Allied cause', the diplomat had declared. Nor did he see how Britain could help supply Sweden with arms to replace those which Sweden was giving to Finland. 'At the present time,' he explained, Germany was replacing these arms.

Halifax told the War Cabinet that his conversation with the Swedish diplomat 'had definitely weighted the balance of his judgement against the Narvik project'. Churchill was furious. The discussion of this subject, he said, 'had now been proceeding for six weeks and every argument had been brought forward in favour of doing nothing . . .' It was not right, he reiterated, 'that we should bear the whole burden of fighting the Germans on behalf of the small neutral countries while they did nothing to help us'.

Churchill argued that the British 'should brace ourselves to accept the hazards of action'; otherwise Germany would go on getting her ore indefinitely, without interruption. He was not, he said, 'impatient for action merely for action's sake', but ever since the beginning of the war 'we had let the initiative rest with Germany'. Britain had waited for Germany to develop 'each form of attack against us', and had contented herself 'with devising means of meeting these attacks as they arose'.

It was Churchill's conviction that, by opening up 'a new theatre of operations' in Scandinavia, Britain would have 'a fine chance of forcing Germany into situations which she had not foreseen, and of seizing the initiative for ourselves'. But once again there was a challenge, this time from a newcomer to the discussions, and a distant observer. For Chamberlain now read the War Cabinet a telegram he had just received from the Prime Minister of Australia, Robert Menzies, who asked that no decision should be taken about action in Norwegian territorial waters 'until the Dominions had had an opportunity to express their views'.

Menzies added that he wished to be 'fully informed of the arguments in favour of and against the proposed action'. He also wanted to be given a summary of the Chiefs of Staff's report. And he concluded, as Chamberlain reported, 'by expressing the opinion that the suggested action would have a bad effect in neutral countries and would present arguments to Germany which she would not otherwise have'.

The War Cabinet of January 12 then discussed Chamberlain's suggestion that a senior British Minister should go to Sweden 'to open negotiations' on a high level. Sir Samuel Hoare was suggested: 'His conversations with the Swedish Government,' Chamberlain thought, 'might well open the way to securing their active co-operation.' Once that was secured, Chamberlain added, and Britain had 'a friendly country on the shores of the Baltic', wide possibilities 'of offensive action against the enemy would be opened up'.

Chamberlain felt that such a mission 'seemed to offer a very good prospect of success', both for the wider scheme, and in securing support for the Narvik plan. In any case, he said, in view of the telegram from Menzies, 'it would be out of the question to take any immediate action against the Narvik traffic'.

Churchill's anger mounted as each reason for delay was produced. 'It would surely be better,' he told the War Cabinet, 'to take naval action first and then to send our Mission, nominally on the pretext of dealing with the protests which would certainly follow.' By sending a mission in advance of action, he stressed, the Swedes would only be 'emboldened to continue their protests'. The Scandinavian countries were 'dominated by fear'. As soon as they saw that Britain had dropped the Narvik project as a result of their protests, they would resist even the suggested mission 'with redoubled vigour'.

As the meeting drew to an end, an acrimonious tone entered the discussion. Churchill still could not accept that because of Swedish protests the scheme must be postponed: 'a flotilla,' he said, 'could be sent in the teeth of a protest, but not a Mission'. But in view of the various opinions expressed, and what he described caustically as 'the evident necessity to carry the Dominions with us in any direction', he did not propose 'to pursue the matter further'.

Churchill wished, however, as the minutes recorded, 'to emphasise one point'; and he did so in a way that reminded his colleagues of the bitter Parliamentary battles of the previous five years. Until that moment, Churchill said, he had felt 'that time was on our side'. But he was not sure that this could continue to be so. 'We had hoped,' he noted, 'that our Air Force would gradually overhaul that of Germany.' But, he asked, 'was it certain that after six months of war we should, in fact, have improved our position in this respect?'

The response was frosty. 'French air strength must be taken into account with our own,' Chamberlain said. And Kingsley Wood replied curtly that 'so many factors were involved' that he would like 'time to consider his reply'.

Churchill had touched upon what was, for him, the central theme, linking his pre-war warnings of potential air inferiority with the war-time reality. Germany, he said, in her 'central position', could deliver threats in several directions. 'We might well have a much graver situation ahead of us and we must redouble our efforts to guard against it.'

Chamberlain did not reject Churchill's warning. Indeed, he said, 'he agreed' with its tone; and he now suggested that the Chiefs of Staff 'should examine the possibility of capturing the ore fields' in the face of both Norwegian and Swedish opposition. But it was Halifax's turn to introduce a critical note. On military grounds, he said, 'he personally was unable to contemplate war with Norway to capture Narvik'.

The discussion ended with Sir Samuel Hoare suggesting that 'as the first step' of his Mission, Britain might suggest 'buying the mines'. But even this suggestion found a critic, Kingsley Wood, who felt that 'the Swedes would be too much afraid of Germany's reactions to agree to sell. . . .'

The War Cabinet had now to reach a conclusion on the Narvik scheme. It decided, as the minutes recorded, 'that no action should be taken for the time being to stop the traffic between Germany and Narvik by sending a Flotilla into Norwegian territorial waters'. In reaching this decision, the minutes added, the War Cabinet were 'impressed by the risk' that such an action 'might imperil the success of the larger project, i.e., the complete stoppage of supplies to Germany from the Northern orefields'. At the same time, the Chiefs of Staff were invited to consider one aspect of the larger project, 'the possibility of capturing the Gällivare orefields in the face of Norwegian and Swedish opposition', and then to say, if they thought the idea was practicable, 'what forces would it involve?'[1]

Churchill's sense of frustration was acute: had his original advice been taken, the interception of German ore-bearing ships would have begun ten days earlier. His anger during the War Cabinet of January 12 had been obvious. It had also caused a certain unease, and on the following day Halifax wrote to him from the Foreign Office:

My dear Winston

I have felt very unhappy at finding myself taking a different line to you on the Narvik project: not only because I realise all the force of the argument you deployed, and appreciate how disastrous it may be to refrain from positive action in such a struggle as this, but also because I have too great a respect for you and for all that you bring to this business of saving civilisation, to feel other than uncomfortable when my mind does not go with yours. And you have been always so willing to help me on my side of the job, that I hate being less helpful to you.

Yet one can but do one's best to form a judgment, and reach a decision, to the best of one's capacity, as the problem presents itself. But I wanted to tell

[1] War Cabinet No. 10 of 1940, 12 January 1940, 11.30 a.m., Minute 1, Confidential Annex: Cabinet papers, 65/11.

you how strong had been, and is, my feeling on personal grounds about finding myself in any matter differing from you—especially when I reflect—as I constantly do—upon the hourly anxiety that your particular responsibilities impose.

Yrs ever
Edward[1]

Churchill was visiting Portsmouth when this letter was written, having returned to HMS *Vernon* to inspect a German magnetic mine that had been retrieved intact, and to discuss the continuing progress in protecting merchant ships. In his reply to Halifax two days later, he expressed his deepest fears about the conduct of the war:

My dear Edward,

I am most grateful to you for the kindness of your letter.

My disquiet at the decision taken was due mainly to the awful difficulties which our machinery of war-conduct presents to positive action. I see such immense walls of prevention, all built and building, that I wonder whether any plan will have a chance of climbing over them.

Just look at the arguments which have had to be surmounted in the seven weeks we have discussed this Narvik operation.

First, the objections of the other Economic Departments, Supply, B. of T.,[2] etc. Secondly, the Joint Planning Committee. Thirdly, the Chiefs of Staff Committee. Fourthly, the insidious argument, 'don't spoil the big plan for the sake of the small', when there is really very little chance of the big plan being resolutely attempted. Fifthly, the juridicial and moral objections, all gradually worn down. Sixthly, the attitude of neutrals, and above all, the United States. But see how well the United States have responded to your démarche. Seventhly, the Cabinet itself, with its many angles of criticism. Eighthly, when all this had been smoothed out, the French have to be consulted. Finally, the Dominions and their consciences have to be squared, they not having gone through the process by which opinion has advanced at home.

All this makes me feel that under the present arrangements we shall be reduced to waiting upon the terrible attacks of the enemy, against which it is impossible to prepare in every quarter simultaneously without fatal dissipation of strength.

Churchill's letter continued:

I have two or three projects moving forward, but all I fear will succumb before the tremendous array of negative arguments and forces. Pardon me, therefore, if I showed distress. One thing is absolutely certain, namely, that victory will never be found by taking the line of least resistance.

---

[1] Letter of 13 January 1940: Churchill papers, 19/2.
[2] Board of Trade.

Churchill went on to tell Halifax of the possible imminent invasion of Belgium and Holland. 'It may indeed be argued,' he wrote, 'though I do not think much of it, that if we had violated Norwegian territorial waters, the Germans would have claimed they were only doing the same thing in invading Holland and Belgium.' But, he added, 'it is a better sequence that our peccadilloes should follow their crimes, instead of the other way round'. Even if a German attack on Belgium and Holland ended in a stalemate, the Germans 'may feel far more free', and then for Britain 'a diversion may become even more needful'.[1]

The Belgian alarm proved to be a false one, and within forty-eight hours the War Cabinet had returned to the discussion of Narvik, and of the wider Scandinavian project. Churchill no longer saw any hope of a swift or uncircumscribed decision. But, with a never diminishing sense of urgency, he continued to put forward his argument for immediate action at each successive meeting. The Scandinavian Governments, he declared at the War Cabinet of January 17, should be told 'that we would not for an indefinite period tolerate their supplying the enemy with the means of continuing the war'. The Swedish supply of ore, he added, 'would become the means of sending hundreds of thousands of British and French soldiers to their death'. But when Chamberlain supported Churchill's argument, as he did on this occasion, it was, nevertheless, always with reservations. Any such message to Norway or Sweden, he said, while important in itself, must be 'minus the threat of Naval action on our part'.

Churchill had once again to accept the more cautious ruling. But at the end of the meeting his distress was evident. 'He only regretted,' the minutes recorded, 'that it was not possible for us to use the threat of taking the ore fields by force. . . .'[2]

There were other causes of distress for Churchill at these War Cabinet meetings, more especially when, on January 15, Kingsley Wood announced that the total British first line air strength as of 1 January 1940 was 1,745 aircraft, as against 4,330 German first line aircraft. Even adding the 1,625 French aircraft to the British total, the Germans still had a superiority of nearly a thousand aircraft. But in an attempt to lessen the burden of the facts, Kingsley Wood gave as 'his impression' that Germany, in concentrating on numbers, 'had sacrificed something

---

[1] 'Private', 15 January 1940: Foreign Office papers, 800/328, folios 405–7.

[2] War Cabinet No. 16 of 1940, 17 January 1940, 11.30 a.m., Minute 9, Confidential Annex: Cabinet papers, 65/11.

in quality', while Britain had aimed at producing 'a somewhat higher quality'.[1]

Four days later, on January 18, Churchill was again brought up against the legacies of the pre-war policies when the Chancellor of the Exchequer, Sir John Simon, drew the War Cabinet's attention to 'the estimated deficiencies' in the production of munitions by 'the main industrial groups concerned in the summers of 1940 and 1941'. These deficiencies, Simon warned, would have to be overcome 'if the war programme was to be completed by the date contemplated'.

During the ensuing discussion Churchill drew attention to the success of the 'area organisation' developed by the Ministry of Munitions 'in the last war' to handle the problems of large scale munitions production, and he asked bluntly: 'Had this organisation been reproduced to-day?' In reply the Minister of Supply, Leslie Burgin, said that the area organization was 'already far advanced', and that the Committee which would deal with the Birmingham area 'would be inaugurated the next day'.

Burgin went on to say that the Area Committees would not have the authority actually to place orders, as they had done when Churchill was Minister of Munitions, but would be 'only advisory'. In that case, Churchill replied, the Committees 'would have little influence over firms in their areas'.[2]

Churchill's intervention derived from his own two-year experience as Minister of Munitions in the First World War, and from his persistent demands before the war, from 1936 onwards, for the setting up of a Ministry of Supply to anticipate, and to try to avert, just such a crisis.[3] Now, in January 1940, all Britain's plans to take the initiative were overshadowed by deficiencies in every branch of war production. Yet the developments of the war outside Britain could not simply be ignored.

On January 20 the widening war seemed likely to impede British plans still further; for on that day the War Cabinet was informed of an appeal for immediate help from Finland. This appeal followed fierce battles between the attacking Soviet force and the Finnish Army, and was for 'a small unit of Hurricane fighters' to be sent to Finland manned with British pilots, and with a nucleus of British maintenance

---

[1] War Cabinet No. 14 of 1940, 15 January 1940, 3 p.m., Minute 1, Confidential Annex: Cabinet papers, 65/11.

[2] War Cabinet No. 17 of 1940, 18 January 1940, 11.30 a.m.: Cabinet papers, 65/5.

[3] Churchill had first urged setting up a Ministry of Supply on 23 April 1936. The Ministry had not been set up until 14 July 1939, a month and a half before the outbreak of war.

personnel.[1] The Deputy Chief of the Air Staff explained that the British pilots and personnel would be 'volunteers from the Air Force, but proceeding as civilians'. The Royal Air Force, he added, could actually spare 'a few pilots of high quality'.

Chamberlain supported the despatch of the Hurricanes, but not of their pilots. But Churchill 'emphasised', as the minutes recorded, 'the great moral value of successful operations against the Russian Air Force by a British flight of volunteers'.[2]

Churchill's concern with the moral value of British pilots being in action reflected his general worry that the 'phoney war' was creating a sense of unease and demoralization. This worry was clear when he broadcast that same evening, opening with the words: 'Everyone wonders what is happening about the war.'

The U-boats, Churchill said, were being conquered. 'Our faithful Asdic detector smells them out in the depths of the sea, and, with the potent aid of the Royal Air Force, I do not doubt that we shall break their strength and break their purpose.' The *Graf Spee*, he added, 'still sticks up in the harbour of Montevideo as a grisly monument and as a measure of the fate in store for any Nazi warship which dabbles in piracy in the broad waters'. Much neutral shipping was being sunk, as a result of Hitler's 'hate and spite', but the convoy system was gaining in efficiency, 'steadily keeping the seas open'. All Europe was arming. The Dutch, 'whose services to European freedom will be remembered long after the smear of Hitler has been wiped from the human path—stand along their dykes, as they did against the tyrants of bygone days'. No one knew who would be 'the next victim' against whom the 'criminal adventurers of Berlin will cast their rending stroke'.

Churchill then spoke of Finland, telling his radio listeners:

Only Finland—superb, nay, sublime—in the jaws of peril—Finland shows what free men can do. The service rendered by Finland to mankind is magnificent. They have exposed, for all the world to see, the military incapacity of the Red Army and of the Red Air Force. Many illusions about Soviet Russia have been dispelled in these few fierce weeks of fighting in the Arctic Circle. Everyone can see how Communism rots the soul of a nation; how it makes it abject and hungry in peace, and proves it base and abominable in war.

We cannot tell what the fate of Finland may be, but no more mournful spectacle could be presented to what is left to civilized mankind than that this

---

[1] The size of the unit suggested was a single Flight of six Hurricanes with two Immediate Reserve, 'and four more reserve aircraft to follow later'.

[2] War Cabinet No. 19 of 1940, 20 January 1940, 12 noon: Cabinet papers, 65/5.

splendid Northern race should be at last worn down and reduced to servitude worse than death by the dull brutish force of overwhelming numbers. If the light of freedom which still burns so brightly in the frozen North should be finally quenched, it might well herald a return to the Dark Ages, when every vestige of human progress during two thousand years would be engulfed.

Churchill then urged the neutral States 'with one simultaneous impulse to do their duty' in accordance with the League of Nations Covenant, and to stand together 'against aggression and wrong'. At present, he said, 'their plight is lamentable; and it will become much worse'. At present their policy was to 'bow humbly and in fear to German threats of violence', knowing that Britain and France would always observe 'all the laws and conventions', while breaches of these laws 'are only to be expected from the German side'.

Churchill then spoke critically of the neutral States. 'Each one hopes that if he feeds the crocodile enough, the crocodile will eat him last', and he added:

All of them hope that the storm will pass before their turn comes to be devoured. But I fear—I fear greatly—the storm will not pass. It will rage and it will roar, ever more loudly, ever more widely. It will spread to the South; it will spread to the North.

There is no chance of a speedy end except through united action; and if at any time Britain and France, wearying of the struggle, were to make a shameful peace, nothing would remain for the smaller States of Europe, with their shipping and their possessions, but to be divided between the opposite, though similar, barbarisms of Nazidom and Bolshevism.

Churchill went on to express his faith in victory, despite the 'numerical odds' at present against Britain and France. The 'decisive factors', he believed, would not be numbers, but 'Quality, willpower, geographical advantages, natural and financial resources, the command of the sea, and, above all, a cause which rouses the spontaneous surgings of the human spirit in millions of hearts'.

If it had not been otherwise, Churchill said, 'how would the race of men have risen above the apes; how otherwise would they have conquered and extirpated the dragons and monsters; how would they have ever evolved the moral theme. . . .'

From the first hours of the war, the question of maintaining moral standards, and thus also the morale of the Allies was of supreme importance to Churchill. Morality and morale: these were to be the twin themes both of his public speeches, and of his secret advice. The British and French, he told his listeners on January 20, must look 'behind the brazen fronts of Nazidom', to see the signs of psychological and physical disintegration, the shortage of raw materials, the 'hesitancy & divided counsels' and the doubts which 'assail and undermine those who count on force and force alone'.

Churchill ended his broadcast with words of hope of those who were suffering under Nazi rule:

> In the bitter and increasingly exacting conflict which lies before us we are resolved to keep nothing back, and not to be outstripped by any in service to the common cause. Let the great cities of Warsaw, of Prague, of Vienna banish despair even in the midst of their agony. Their liberation is sure. The day will come when the joybells will ring again throughout Europe, and when victorious nations, masters not only of their foes but of themselves, will plan and build in justice, in tradition, and in freedom a house of many mansions where there will be room for all.[1]

Among the neutral States, reaction to Churchill's speech was hostile. 'Winston's broadcast to the neutrals,' Hoare noted in his diary, 'Bad effect.'[2] In Norway, the *Morgenbladet* wrote that it had no knowledge that either Scandinavia or the other neutral states had 'yielded humbly to German threats'. In Holland, *Het Handelsblad* stated that Churchill had gone too far in telling the neutrals 'that it is their duty to join the Allies according to League principles', nor could they be expected to 'lend their countries for "battlefields" '. In Switzerland, the *Journal de Genève* warned that the neutral states 'have no desire to be dragged into war'. In Denmark, *Politiken* felt that 'the best friend of the neutral states is he who acknowledges their strong determination to secure and maintain their neutrality'.

Within the Foreign Office, these criticisms were circulated together with a letter from the man who had collected them, Professor E. H. Carr, in charge of the Foreign Publicity Department at the Ministry of Information. 'If it were, in fact,' Carr wrote, 'the object of H.M.G. to bring in as many of the neutrals as possible into the War on our side at the earliest possible moment, it would be safe to say that the method adopted by Mr Churchill would be the one least calculated to promote that result. Here we cannot help feeling that our efforts to increase sympathy for our cause in the neutral countries have received a severe set back.'[3]

On receiving Professor Carr's ten-page digest of the neutral press,

---

[1] Broadcast of 20 January 1940: Churchill papers, 9/143.

[2] Hoare diary, 26 January 1940: Templewood papers.

[3] 'Foreign Reaction to Mr. Churchill's Speech': Churchill papers, 23/3. In 1947, in preparation for the writing of his war memoirs, Churchill asked his literary assistant, Denis Kelly, to find these quotations from among his wartime papers. Kelly's covering letter is dated 25 August 1947.

Halifax sent both the digest, and Carr's letter, to Churchill, writing in a covering note, on January 26:

I must send you the enclosed note which has been put up to me by my Department: for you ought to see it.

I am afraid I think the effect of your broadcast in the countries which you no doubt had principally in mind has been very different from what you anticipated—though if I had seen your speech myself, I should have expected some such reactions.

Would you think it unreasonable of me to ask that in future, if you are going to speak with particular reference to Foreign policy, you might let me see in advance what you had it in mind to say?

Halifax's rebuke continued:

It puts me in an impossible position if a member of the Gov. like yourself takes a line in public which differs from that taken by the PM or myself: and I think, as I have to be in daily touch with these tiresome neutrals, I ought to be able to predict how their minds will work.

We are all concerned to get the same results—and I would always be ready to discuss any time with you, but it won't help if we speak with two voices. And I have no doubt that you would feel the same if the roles were reversed, and I was making general speeches about Naval policy etc.

There is a great difference between what one can say to these people in public and in private.[1]

To this strong criticism Churchill replied that same day:

This is undoubtedly a disagreeable bouquet. I certainly thought I was expressing yr view & Neville's. To make certain I asked Sir O. Sargent to look through what I had written; but I did not take his advice on one point—viz, the reference to the L. of N.[2] In this I was wrong. For the rest I never intended to make any pronouncement on Foreign affairs, least of all ones differing from yours. I thought (& still think) that the statement of these truths wd be beneficial in neutral opinion, after the natural resentment had passed away. After all it is the facts that dominate.

I wd gladly have shown you what I was going to say beforehand if I had thought there was any need to trouble you; & you will always find me ready to do this. No Foreign Secretary cd ask less.

Do not however be quite sure that my line will prove so inconvenient as now appears. What the neutrals say is vy different from what they feel: or from what is going to happen.

This however touches upon prophecy.

In a postscript, Churchill asked Halifax not to mention to Orme Sar-

[1] 'Personal & Confidential', 26 January 1940: Churchill papers, 23/3.
[2] League of Nations.

gent 'that I consulted him'. He had asked, he said, for either Sargent or Sir Alexander Cadogan to help him with the speech, and Sargent had actually come to Admiralty House. 'But,' Churchill added, 'I alone am responsible.'[1]

Halifax had made no mention to Churchill of the favourable French reaction to Churchill's remarks. Yet in a telegram from Paris, a senior diplomat, Oliver Harvey, had reported that Churchill's broadcast had been received in France 'with a chorus of praise for its realism and resolution'. Churchill's warnings to the neutrals, Harvey added, were considered to be both 'timely and carefully phrased'. As to the attacks on Churchill in the neutral Press, these, Harvey reported, were said by the French newspapers to be 'clearly inspired by German propaganda', and were based either on misrepresentation or 'on the same errors which have contributed to leading neutral countries in Europe into their present dangerous position'.[2]

Despite Professor Carr's digest of hostile neutral responses, Churchill did have some intimation that his broadcast had been well received in Allied France when he was sent a copy of the *Petit Journal*, which called it 'a wise and necessary warning'.[3] Several of his friends also sent him words of encouragement. 'I am persuaded,' wrote his friend and literary adviser Emery Reves, from Paris, 'that this broadcast is the beginning of very important developments since it is a signal to start a movement in all the neutral countries to change their utterly immoral and unreasonable attitude.'[4]

There was also praise from listeners in Britain. 'I cannot resist telling you how absolutely splendid & inspiring your speech was,' wrote Lady Ribblesdale. 'Every word true, powerful, compelling—hitting the nail hard on the head & the message to neutrals especially—what one had longed to hear for a long time. It smothers every other speech since the war.'[5] 'What a wonderful speech you made last Saturday,' wrote Nathan Laski, 'and how many millions of people you heartened!'[6]

---

[1] 'Private', 26 January 1940: Foreign Office papers, 800/322, folios 61–2.

[2] Paris Telegram No. 61, 23 January 1940: Foreign Office papers, 371/24297, C.1195.

[3] Churchill papers, 23/3.

[4] Churchill papers, 2/410.

[5] Letter of 21 January 1940: Churchill papers, 2/398. Lady Ribbelsdale was the American-born Ava Willings, former wife of Colonel Jacob Astor. Her second husband, the 4th Baron Ribbelsdale, had died in 1925.

[6] Letter of 22 January 1940: Churchill papers, 2/394. Laski had been a constituent of Churchill at North-West Manchester, from 1906 to 1908, and a leading member of the Jewish community there. He was the father of the socialist writer, Harold Laski.

8

'Let us to the task'

ONE of the most important questions throughout the early months of 1940 was that of the size and equipment of Britain's future army. After less than five months of war there was daily evidence of the inhibiting effect of poor pre-war planning and insufficient pre-war production. At a meeting of the War Cabinet's Military Co-ordination Committee on January 23, Churchill was perturbed to hear the Secretary to the Ministry of Supply, Sir Arthur Robinson, state that 'the full army programme could not be realised in the time limit of two years now laid down without serious interference with the air programme'. The burden of Robinson's statement was that the target date of 1942 for full army readiness, with 55 divisions equipped for a European war, should be delayed.[1] At the same time, Kingsley Wood warned on behalf of the Air Ministry that 'he could not acquiesce in the erection and equipping of factories on a 55-division basis if this entailed interference with the Air Ministry programme'.

Churchill now sought to act as a mediator between the conflicting claims of an under-equipped army and an air force with so serious a numerical inferiority to Germany. An Army weapons factory, he explained, would take a year to erect, and 'it was not until this point' that it would need machine tools. 'Hence a clash with the Air Ministry programme,' he pointed out, 'should not arise for many months.' But if the plants were to be able to come into operation when needed, he said, 'it was essential that they should be laid down now'. At some future date the War Cabinet might decide to put only 32 divisions in the field.

Churchill then spoke a word of warning. If 'circumstances', he said, 'forced them to engage a larger force, and in his view it was certain

[1] Robinson had been Permanent Secretary at the Air Ministry during Churchill's two years (1919 and 1920) as Secretary of State for War and Air.

that they would, the necessary resources would not be available, unless action were taken now'. He realized that 'every sort of difficulty' would have to be met. But this, he insisted, 'was no excuse for not pressing on with the task'.

Drawing on his earlier experience, Churchill went on to point out that the 'great shell plants' laid down by Lloyd George in the summer of 1915 had not come into full production until the autumn of 1917. The 'enormous increase' achieved then 'was solely due to the fact that the foundations had been laid early'. For this reason 'he was pressing for long-term construction to begin immediately'.[1]

On the afternoon of January 27, four days after this exhortation to the Military Co-ordination Committee, Churchill spoke in public at Manchester. His theme was: 'we have to make a huge expansion of our labour force, and especially of those capable of performing skilled or semi-skilled operations'. To achieve this expansion, 'we must especially count for aid and guidance upon our Labour colleagues and trade union leaders'. On this subject, he pointed out, 'I can speak with some knowledge,' having presided over the Ministry of Munitions 'in its culminating phases' in the First World War. Agriculture also, he stressed, must be organised 'upon at least the 1918 scale'.

Churchill urged his listeners not to be disheartened when they read 'of daily losses', or heard them 'reiterated by the BBC'. The convoy system was working so well that out of nearly 7,500 ships convoyed, 'only fifteen have been lost'. In addition, the convoy system was becoming 'more refined and rapid as the weeks go by'.

Churchill went on to speak of the importance of public and parliamentary criticism. 'Criticism in the body politic,' he said, 'is like pain in the human body. It is not pleasant, but where would the body be without it?' It was the 'Nazi and Bolshevik dictatorships' that feared criticism, and in fearing it 'run their greatest risk'. Wherever criticism was silenced 'by the concentration camp, the rubber truncheon, or the firing party', the men at the top would be fed only with the facts 'which are palatable to them'. Scandals and shortcomings, instead of being exposed, 'continue to fester behind the pompous frontage of the State'. These men at the top 'may be very fierce and powerful, but their ears are deaf, their fingers are numb; they cannot feel their feet as they move forward in the fog and darkness of the immeasurable and the unknown'.

Churchill then spoke of the nature of Nazi tyranny in Czechoslovakia

[1] Military Co-ordination Committee No. 8 of 1939–40, 23 January 1940, 5.30 p.m.: Cabinet papers, 83/3.

and Poland. All Czech universities had been closed down. 'Students are shot by scores and tormented in concentration camps by thousands.' The Czech lands had been plundered. A hundred thousand Czech workmen had been 'led off into slavery to be toiled to death in Germany'. Yet even all this, Churchill declared, 'pales in comparison with the atrocities which, as I speak here this afternoon, are being perpetrated upon the Poles', and he went on to explain the 'two distinct phases' of Nazi occupation:

In the first the Germans tried to cow the population by shooting individuals picked at random from the towns. At one place where they had decided to shoot thirty-five people they collected thirty-four, and then, finding themselves one short, went into a chemist's shop and seized the first person they saw to make up the tally.

But later on they became more discriminating—they made careful search for the natural leaders of Polish life: the nobles, the landowners, the priests, as well as prominent workmen and peasants. It is estimated that upwards of fifteen thousand intellectual leaders have been shot. These horrible mass executions are a frequent occurrence. At one place three hundred were lined up against the wall; at another a group of drunken German officers are said to have shot seventy hostages in prison; at another a hundred and thirty-six Polish students, some of whom were only twelve or thirteen years old, were butchered.

Torture has been used. Press gangs seize men and women in the streets and drive them off in droves to forced labour in Germany. Famine stalks not only amid the ruins of Warsaw, but far and wide throughout the ancient country which a few months ago was the home of a people of over thirty-five millions, with a history extending back far beyond anything that Germany can boast.

From these 'shameful records', Churchill warned, 'we may judge what our own fate would be if we fell into their clutches'. Yet from these same records, he believed, 'we may draw the force and inspiration to carry us forward upon our journey and not to pause or rest till liberation is achieved and justice done'.

Churchill ended his speech with a clarion call to action:

Come then: let us to the task, to the battle, to the toil—each to our part, each to our station. Fill the armies, rule the air, pour out the munitions, strangle the U-boats, sweep the mines, plough the land, build the ships, guard the streets, succour the wounded, uplift the downcast, and honour the brave.

Let us go forward together in all parts of the Empire, in all parts of the Island. There is not a week, nor a day, nor an hour to lose.[1]

Churchill's speech was broadcast not only throughout Britain, but

[1] Speech of 27 January 1940: Churchill papers, 9/143.

also to Canada. That same night the Canadian Prime Minister, Mackenzie King, telegraphed from Ottawa: 'A magnificent interpretation of the present conflict, and its significance should deeply stir the conscience of mankind.'[1]

'. . . not a week, nor a day, nor an hour to lose'; more than anything else, these words reflected Churchill's frustration at the delay in coming to any firm decision about Norway and Sweden. But as January drew to a close, the wider action in Scandinavia which the War Cabinet had now been discussing for more than two months seemed slowly to draw nearer. On January 28 the Chiefs of Staff reported to the War Cabinet that they did not consider 'that undue weight should be given to the inherent difficulties of the enterprise. The stakes are high, but the prize of success is great.' If the opportunity to occupy the Gällivare ore fields 'should be presented, or could be created', Britain should, in their opinion, 'seize it with both hands'. Their report went on to warn: 'Unless our preparations are timely and complete, we will be unable to do so.'

The Chiefs of Staff then explained the nature of the expedition which they wished to see carried out: a force landed at Narvik, they wrote, could move up the Narvik–Gällivare–Luleå railway, occupy the Gällivare ore fields, secure, 'and if necessary destroy', the port of Luleå, in the event of a German counter-landing.

As a 'preliminary' to the despatch of this force, the report stated, bases would have to be obtained at Trondheim and Namsos. It would also be necessary 'to deny to the Germans' Bergen and Stavanger. Up to forty destroyers would be required 'continuously for close escort duty'. Two brigades would be needed to seize Gällivare and Luleå, and five allied divisions at Trondheim and Namsos. But to achieve all this, the report warned, the cooperation of Norway and Sweden in this plan was 'essential'; otherwise 'the price which we might have to pay . . . might be the opening of unrestricted air warfare'.[2]

At the War Cabinet on January 29 the Secretary of State for War, Oliver Stanley, announced that as General Gamelin now wanted 'direct Allied intervention in Finland', discussion of the Chiefs of Staff report would have to be 'deferred' until after this new French idea had been further discussed in Paris. Churchill pointed out, however, that the Chiefs of Staff had just circulated the War Cabinet with a further report which 'deprecated the particular proposals put forward by

[1] Telegram, 27 January 1940: Churchill papers, 2/395.
[2] Chiefs of Staff Paper No. 218 of 1939–40, 28 January 1940: Cabinet papers, 80/7.

General Gamelin'. For his part, Chamberlain supported the new French proposal, suggesting 'that Allied assistance to Finland might be the only way of getting a foothold in Scandinavia'.[1]

Thus the area of potential action was widened still further, and the decision on the Chiefs of Staff's already ambitious Scandinavian plan was further deferred. Yet the urgency seemed unabated, and on January 30 Churchill sent Chamberlain confirmation, from the Ministry of Economic Warfare, of what appeared to be Norwegian preparations to prevent British ships from trying to strike at German ore carriers in Norwegian territorial waters. 'This seems to fit in with what you said the other day about a minefield,' Churchill wrote. And he added: 'Minefield or Flotilla—it is all one. But surely we shd move. The traffic is growing every week.'[2]

Chamberlain, however, still deprecated immediate action, replying to Churchill that same day, that it would be 'better' to wait for confirmation from the Swedish Minister to London, Bjorn Prytz, as to whether the Norwegians really were planning some anti-British action. 'I believe,' Chamberlain noted, 'he is back today or to-morrow.'[3]

While the British leaders delayed action, the Germans continued to take the initiative, launching, on January 30, a series of air attacks on British cargo ships plying along the East Coast. At the War Cabinet on January 31, Churchill reported, for the previous day, air attacks of 'great severity' carried out with bomb and machine gun. 'A brutal feature of these attacks,' he said, 'was that they were directed almost entirely against small unarmed vessels. . . .' A number of casualties had been caused by machine-gun fire from the aeroplanes, while at the same time 'comparatively few survivors had been saved'. Seven ships in all had been attacked. 'The essence of the problem,' Rear-Admiral Phillips explained, 'was a shortage of anti-aircraft guns.'[4]

As far as naval deficiencies generally were concerned, on February 2 Phillips informed Churchill that one weakness was a lack of battleship strength. This, he explained, had arisen because of the London Naval Treaty of 1930, which bound Britain not to build until 1937, when, as a result, 'we started considerably behind' the other naval powers. As a result, Phillips wrote, 'our relative capital ship strength has been

[1] War Cabinet No. 26 of 1940, 29 January 1940, 11.30 a.m.: Cabinet papers, 65/5.
[2] Letter of 30 January 1940: Admiralty papers, 116/4471.
[3] Letter of 30 January 1940: Admiralty papers, 116/4471.
[4] War Cabinet No. 28 of 1940, 31 January 1940, 11.30 a.m.: Cabinet papers, 65/5. Five of the seven merchant ships attacked on January 30 were sunk, *Giralda*, *Vaclite*, *Bancrest*, *Voreda* and *Highwave*.

steadily deteriorating since 1936 and we are now in a weaker position relative to other Powers than the Board of Admiralty were willing to accept at the conclusion of the Great War when the Washington Treaty was negotiated'.[1]

Churchill made no comment: he had at the time of the London Naval Treaty been an outspoken critic, having told the House of Commons on 15 May 1930 that the Treaty represented 'a formal acceptance by Great Britain of definitely inferior seapower'. At the end of his speech Churchill had declared, bitterly: 'We are the passive matrix on which others imprint their claims.'[2]

There was to be nothing 'passive' about Churchill's outlook, nor any narrow focus to his gaze. At the end of January he took up again his correspondence with President Roosevelt. 'I gave orders last night,' he telegraphed to the President on January 29, 'that no American ship should in any circumstances be diverted into the combat zone round the British Islands declared by you. I trust this will be satisfactory.'[3] On the following day, when complications arose, Churchill telegraphed again: 'It has been pointed out to me that my signal to Fleet can only be maintained if measures are taken in advance of their departure that US ships carry no objectionable cargo.' Moreover, he explained, 'in exceptional cases it may be necessary to divert United States ships if we have definite ground for suspicion against them'.[4]

Roosevelt replied by letter on 1 February 1940, thanking Churchill first for the 'tremendously interesting account' of the *Graf Spee* action. As for the 'search and detention of American ships', the conversations on this were, he believed, 'working out satisfactorily'. Roosevelt added, however: 'I would not be frank unless I told you that there has been much public criticism here. The general feeling is that the net benefit to your people and to France is hardly worth the definite annoyance caused to us. That is always found to be so, in a nation which is 3,000 miles away from the fact of war.'

Roosevelt ended his letter: 'I wish much that I could talk things over with you in person—but I am grateful to you for keeping me in touch, as you do.'[5]

*   *   *

---

[1] Minute of 2 February 1940: Admiralty papers, 205/6.

[2] *Hansard*, 15 May 1930.

[3] Foreign Office telegram No. 128 of 29 January 1940: Churchill papers, 20/15.

[4] Foreign Office telegram No. 131 of 30 January 1940: Admiralty papers, 199/1928.

[5] Letter of 1 February 1940 (from The White House, Washington): Admiralty papers, 199/1928.

In the first week of February 1940, Chamberlain asked Churchill to accompany him to Paris, to a meeting of the Supreme War Council. This joint Anglo-French Council, headed by the two Prime Ministers, had already met four times since the outbreak of war. Churchill accepted this, his first invitation to join the Council, and at his own suggestion the British Ministers sailed from Dover in a destroyer, reaching Paris on the evening of February 5.

The discussion at the Supreme War Council centred upon 'Aid to Finland', with Chamberlain and Daladier the principal speakers. The fourteen-page official minutes do not record Churchill as having spoken at all. By the end of the meeting it had been agreed that Britain and France would together make 'immediate preparations' for three or four divisions—amounting in all to thirty or forty thousand trained troops—to be sent to Finland, while at the same time persuading Norway and Sweden to allow Britain and France to send supplies and re-inforcements to the Finns. It was also agreed that the Allies should take control of the Swedish ore fields at Gällivare.

At the Supreme War Council of February 5 Daladier described Norway's outlook as 'selfish and isolationist', and counselled his colleagues that the Norwegians 'still kept an illusion of safety and were disinclined to abandon it'. The mood of the meeting was not, however, one that could easily be influenced by such problems. 'Finland must not be allowed to disappear off the map,' Chamberlain had insisted. 'If she did,' he added, 'a feeling of great depression, and perhaps of resentment, would be roused among the peoples of France and Great Britain.' Although Finland was not fighting against 'the enemy with whom the Allies were engaged', nevertheless, Chamberlain asserted, 'her collapse would be regarded throughout the world as an Allied defeat', and would lead to 'a serious loss of morale' not only among the Allies, but 'in every neutral quarter, and particularly in the United States'. To land a force at Narvik, help Finland, and at the same time take the Gällivare ore fields was a plan, Chamberlain said, which he 'much preferred' as it offered the prospect 'of killing two birds with one stone'.

One result of the Supreme War Council discussions on February 5 was that two British divisions, which were to have started for France on the following day, were held back in England, to be prepared for operations in Scandinavia. It was also agreed that Finland would be asked to appeal for help from Britain and France, whereupon the Allies would 'demand passage across Norway and Sweden for their contingents'. If Norway and Sweden were to object, and to object sufficiently strongly so as to make it 'impossible for the Allies to get control of the Swedish ore fields', then another project altogether, an Allied landing on Finnish soil at Petsamo, could be considered.[1] This would mean that the wider Scandinavian scheme would have to be abandoned, or at least postponed, while the landing in Finland was undertaken.

The British Ministers at the Supreme War Council—Churchill, Chamberlain, Halifax, Oliver Stanley and Kingsley Wood—returned to London on February 6. HMS *Boadicea* awaited them at Boulogne. As they crossed the Channel, Churchill later recalled, 'an amusing incident' occurred:

We sighted a floating mine. So I said to the captain, 'Let's blow it up by gunfire.' It burst with a good bang, and a large piece of wreckage sailed over towards us and seemed for an instant as if it were going to settle on the bridge, where all the politicians and some of the other swells were clustered. However, it landed on the forecastle, which was happily bare, and no one was hurt. Thus everything passed off pleasantly.

From time to time, Churchill added, he was invited back to Paris with Chamberlain: 'But I could not provide an equal entertainment each time.'[2]

Another eye-witness to this event was First Lieutenant Hubert Fox, the Gunnery Officer of the *Boadicea*, who wrote to his father on the following day:

We lay at the quay at Boulogne waiting to take them back. Presently the neat figure of Neville Chamberlain approached, surrounded by his retinue like a popular master at a preparatory school conducting the Sunday walk. One or two of the boys preferred to trudge along by themselves. Among these was Winston Churchill.

They came on board, most of them going up to the bridge where they watched all that happened with great animation. The Prime Minister got cold so we had some soup brought up to him. Warm in the wardroom, Churchill growled, 'Tell the Prime Minister to come and have some gin.'

Churchill sat in the wardroom at the long polished table drinking port and sucking a cigar. He was flicking over the pages of 'Blighty', a popular magazine with pictures of ladies without clothes. Later we lost him altogether for a time and eventually found him on the stokers' mess deck, sitting on a mess table swapping yarns.

---

[1] Supreme War Council, 5th Meeting of 1939–40, 5 February 1940, 10 a.m.: Cabinet papers, 99/3, folios 24–5.
[2] Winston S. Churchill, *The Second World War*, volume 1, London 1948, page 443.

There was one satisfactory incident. A mine was sighted and we blew it sky high first shot, bits of it very nearly descending on the Big Noises. Everyone was very gratified at the good marksmanship.[1]

Returning to the Admiralty, Churchill's frustration at the conduct of the war was heightened when he read a paper by Lord Stamp, the Government's Adviser on Economic Co-ordination, on the financial dangers of the Government's war programme. If the advice of this memorandum was accepted, Churchill wrote 'we must now definitely curtail our war objective in men and material, and the impression will be spread in all quarters, including French quarters, that we are definitely recoiling from the task we set ourselves'. Such an impression, he warned, 'would have a most depressing effect, and would lead at once to relaxation at home, and reproach from abroad'.

Churchill felt that the war effort should at least equal 'our own effort last time'. To allow any lesser standards 'would be unworthy of our cause, and unequal to our dangers'. After analysing in detail Lord Stamp's criticisms, especially in regard to what Stamp regarded as excessive expenditure on the Army, Churchill asked his colleagues to consider 'the very grave danger to our alliance with France if we do not do our fair share of the actual fighting on land, i.e. at least half of what they will be doing'. His note ended:

It is upon the forces actually brought to bear upon the enemy that our eyes must be fixed. For all its vast expenditure, we have only added twenty or thirty squadrons to the Air Force in the last two years. Out of a million and three-quarter men, maintained at the most expensive rate and rationed on the highest scale, we are only producing 10 divisions by the sixth month and 20 divisions at the twelfth month. We aim at only 55 divisions by the twenty-fourth month. Now it is argued that even this is too much for us.

'So far from accepting any diminution of objective,' Churchill wrote, 'we ought to hurl ourselves into the task with a new surge of impulse, and face all the sacrifices, hardships and exertions which this entails.'[2]

Within the Admiralty, Churchill fought to maintain as forceful a momentum as possible. 'Time is passing rapidly,' he wrote on February 8, having studied a note of experiments to construct concrete barges. 'I had hoped to receive definite proposals for action in an experimental sense by February 24'; but now, Churchill added, 'it appears that only

[1] Letter of 7 February 1940: Fox papers.
[2] 'Lord Stamp's Paper, Note by the First Lord of the Admiralty', printed for the War Cabinet, 7 February 1940: Churchill papers, 19/8.

the opinions of the concrete firms will be ready by that date, if then. Can nothing be done to accelerate matters?'[1]

The mood of delay and retrenchment was pervasive: so much so that at a meeting of the Military Co-ordination Committee on February 9 Churchill found himself in a minority when he reiterated his earlier insistence that he was 'not prepared in any circumstances to abandon the target of 55 divisions to be equipped at least by the spring of 1942'. The War Office had wanted, in view of the expense, to concentrate on the 36 divisions already in being, and to make them the focus for supply priorities. Indeed, it appeared that the existing plans for munitions and supply production were such that even these 36 divisions could not be fully equipped for service overseas by September 1941. There was 'a great danger', Churchill told Chatfield, Stanley and Kingsley Wood, 'in mentioning a figure of 36 divisions. It would lead to a tendency to relax all round and not to put forth our maximum effort.' Churchill added, angrily: 'It would be a most dishonourable thing if the size of our Army were reduced to a mere 36 divisions when the French, with a much smaller population and only half the manufacturing capacity, had 110 in the field.' The political consequences of such a reduction, 'in our effort on land', Churchill warned, 'might be disastrous. . . . We should be failing in our duty as a nation if we aimed at anything less.'[2]

Churchill had yet another cause for complaint at the Military Coordination Committee of February 9. He had been 'gravely disturbed', he said, to see that the production of both heavy and light anti-aircraft guns 'was apparently falling far behind the forecast given by the Ministry of Supply'. Out of 120 heavy guns forecast for January 'only 81 had materialized,' and out of 102 light anti-aircraft barrels 'only 26'. It emerged, according to the Minister of Supply, Leslie Burgin, that the forecasts had in fact been changed, but that the new forecast had not been supplied to the Deputy Chiefs of Staff. This, Churchill commented, was 'unfortunate'; particularly, he noted sarcastically, as the Deputy Chiefs of Staff 'were responsible for the allocation of the guns'.[3]

---

[1] Minute No. 182, 8 February 1940: Churchill papers, 19/6.

[2] Churchill also warned, in a memorandum for this meeting of the Military Co-ordination Committee, that in all calculations of the scale of munitions supply to guns in the field, 'air bombing of communications may be expected to diminish the forward movement of ammunition' (Military Co-ordination Committee Memorandum No. 47 of 1940: Cabinet papers, 83/4).

[3] Military Co-ordination Committee No. 9 of 1939–40, 8 February 1940, 5.30 p.m.: Cabinet papers, 83/3.

Churchill's mood of frustration at this time led him to institute a system of special labels, printed in capitals 'ACTION THIS DAY', which he stuck with glue at the top of his own minutes whenever he wanted to speed up matters which were either urgent in themselves, or had fallen in his view unduly behind. One of the first of these was sent to the Parliamentary Secretary to the Admiralty, Geoffrey Shakespeare. It read:

The attached telegram from Portsmouth Dockyard is a confession of complete failure to deal with labour supply by dilution. It admits that 'the number of fitters is slightly less than before the war'. No wonder then it is impossible to meet the war-time repairs, conversions, and other work.

I am astonished that this condition has not been reported, so that measures could have been taken with the Ministry of Labour to obtain the necessary supplies of labour; or, if it is said that they do not exist, to begin training them. The repair and maintenance of the Fleet must have a very high priority assigned to it.

Churchill continued his exhortation with a series of instructions to Shakespeare to take up the question, to confer with the relevant authorities, and to 'report directly to me weekly'. His minute ended: 'It is shocking that after six months helpless telegrams of this kind should be all that we have to show.'[1]

Amid these frustrations, a naval drama in the third week of February did much to revive the national mood, dulled somewhat since the Battle of the River Plate, and depressed by the continuing Russian successes against Finland. For on the morning of February 16 Churchill learned that the German warship, the *Altmark*, with nearly three hundred captured British merchant seamen locked in its hold, had been sighted by British aircraft, inside Norwegian territorial waters. These prisoners were all men who had been taken aboard after the merchant ships in which they were sailing had been sunk by the *Graf Spee*.

Churchill, determined to rescue the seamen, ordered the British cruisers and destroyers in the area to enter Norwegian waters and 'sweep northwards during the day'. They should not hesitate, he wrote, to arrest the *Altmark* inside these waters 'should she be found'. The ship was, he pointed out, violating Norwegian neutrality 'in carrying British prisoners-of-war to Germany'.[2]

Later that same day HMS *Cossack*, commanded by Captain Philip Vian, sighted the *Altmark* and followed her to the mouth of Jösing Fiord, where she took shelter. Two British destroyers then approached

[1] Minute No. 185, 10 February 1940: Shakespeare papers.
[2] Minute No. 206, 16 February 1940: Churchill papers, 19/6.

the fiord, intending to send boarding parties aboard, but were met by two Norwegian gunboats. The senior Norwegian Captain, of the gunboat *Kjell*, came on board the *Cossack*. 'I demanded the right to visit and search,' Captain Vian later recalled, 'asking him to come with me. In his reply he stated that the German ship had been examined three times since her entry into Norwegian waters, and that no prisoners had been found. His instructions were to resist entry by force: as I might see, his ships had their torpedo-tubes trained on *Cossack*. Deadlock.'[1]

Vian then signalled for instructions. As soon as his signal reached the Admiralty, it was shown to Churchill. Hitherto, operational orders had come, not from the First Lord himself, but from the Admiralty War Staff. Now Churchill intervened directly, drafting a signal to Vian on the afternoon of Friday, February 16:

> You should board *Altmark*, liberate the prisoners and take possession of the ship pending further instructions. If Norwegian torpedo-boat interferes you should warn her to stand off. If she fires upon you, you should not reply unless attack is serious, in which case you should defend yourself using no more force than is necessary, and ceasing fire when she desists.

Realizing the seriousness of the entry of British warships into Norwegian waters, Churchill decided to read this signal to Halifax. As a result of their talk, Churchill added an extra sentence to the opening of the message, which now began: 'Unless Norwegian torpedo boat undertakes to convoy *Altmark* to Bergen with a joint Anglo-Norwegian guard on board, & a joint escort, you should board . . .'[2]

This signal was sent from the Admiralty at 5.25 p.m. Thereafter, Churchill and Pound sat up through the evening and night in the Admiralty War Room, 'in some anxiety', as Churchill later recalled, for both men were 'fully aware of the technical gravity of the measures taken'.[3]

Acting on Churchill's telegram, Captain Vian entered the fiord and asked the captain of the Norwegian gunboat *Kjell* to agree to a joint escort into Bergen. The captain refused, denying that there were any British prisoners at all on board the *Altmark*. Vian then announced that he was going to board the *Altmark*, and invited the Norwegian officer to join him, an offer which the Norwegian declined.

The *Altmark* now tried to ram the *Cossack*, but ran herself aground. The *Cossack* then came alongside, sending a boarding party across.

---

[1] Admiral of the Fleet Sir Philip Vian, *Action This Day, A War Memoir*, London 1960, page 26.
[2] Note of 16 February 1940, 5.25 p.m.: Churchill papers, 19/5.
[3] Winston S. Churchill, *The Second World War*, volume 1, London 1948, page 445.

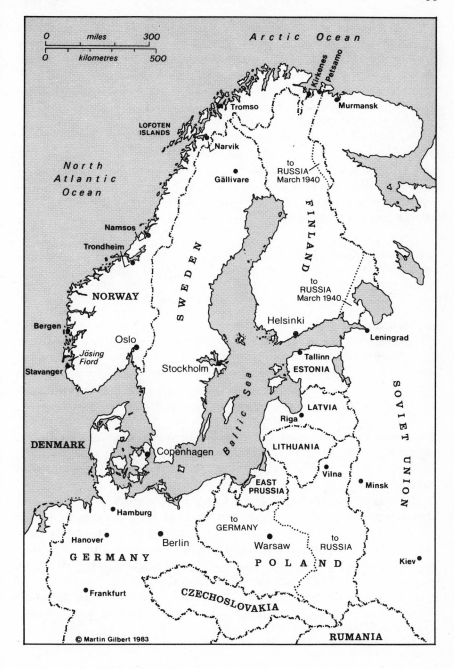

© Martin Gilbert 1983

There was a fight, four Germans were killed, the rest surrendered or fled ashore. The ship was found to be armed: although earlier boarded by the Norwegians, she had not in fact been searched. Locked below were 299 British prisoners. By midnight they had all been transferred to the *Cossack*, which sailed out of the fiord and headed back across the North Sea.

As soon as the news of the *Cossack*'s triumph was released, there was unrestrained excitement throughout Britain. 'Winston deserves much credit,' Lord Lloyd, a former High Commissioner in Egypt, wrote to his son on February 18: 'had it been any other Ministers courage would have failed them.'[1]

A special message of congratulation reached Churchill from King George VI. Churchill replied at once:

Sir,

It is a vy gt encouragement & gratification to me to receive Your Majesty's most gracious & kindly message of approval through my Naval Secretary about the rescue of our poor merchant seamen from the clutches of the enemy. The knowledge wh we all have at the Admiralty that Your Majesty watches every step we take with keen & experienced eye is a stimulus in the heavy & anxious work we have in hand. By none is Your Majesty's compliment more treasured than by the vy old servant of Your Royal House and of your father & yr grandfather who now subscribes himself

Your Majesty's faithful & devoted subject

Winston S. Churchill[2]

The rescued seamen were landed from the *Cossack* at Leith. Among those who saw them land was Randolph Churchill's wife Pamela, who wrote to her father-in-law on February 19: 'You must have had a very thrilling & anxious night on Friday. It's comforting to know we can be ferocious.'[3]

Unpublicised, but equally 'thrilling' for Churchill, on the day of the rescue of the *Altmark* prisoners, two convoys had reached British ports safely. Both had crossed the Atlantic from the Canadian port of Halifax: one a large convoy of 44 ships, including eleven oil tankers, escorted by the *Royal Sovereign*, the other a fast ocean convoy of eight ships, including three tankers, escorted by the armed merchant cruiser *Alaunia*.[4]

[1] Letter of 18 February 1940: Lloyd papers.
[2] Letter of 18 February 1940: Royal Archives.
[3] Letter of 19 February 1940: Churchill papers, 1/355.
[4] 'Central War Room Record No. 167', timed at 7 a.m., 17 February 1940: Cabinet papers, 100/2.

9

Churchill's Admiralty

T HE two successful trans-Atlantic convoys, and the rescue of the prisoners of the *Altmark*, marked a high point of Churchill's work as First Lord. Nearly five and a half months had passed since his return to the Cabinet, and to the Admiralty. Ten years in the political wilderness had done nothing to blunt his departmental abilities. But those same years had given him a deep knowledge and wide perspective of the issues at stake. A week after the outbreak of war, the *News of the World* had commented: 'Mr Churchill was born for Government, and on rising to address the House for the first time in his new Office he placed his elbows on the despatch box with such easy familiarity that one could not imagine that he had been a back bencher for a decade.'[1]

Churchill's First World War ministerial, as well as front line, experiences ensured a continuity of outlook and method, and a range of experience, shared by no other member of Chamberlain's War Cabinet. This special status was recognized by many observers. 'There is a general feeling of relief that you are at the Admiralty,' a former First Lord, Leo Amery, had written to him on 19 October 1939, 'and an equally general feeling that you ought not to stay there too long, but presently make yourself free to attend to the problems of the war as a whole.'[2]

The officials at the Admiralty, and the sailors themselves, had been quick to recognize Churchill's qualities, and to respond to his persistent promptings. One of those who was at the Admiralty when Churchill became First Lord was the Deputy Director of the Trade Division, G. R. G. Allen. Some twenty-five years later Allen recalled:

One thing that remains firmly in my mind about Winston's arrival in the

---

[1] *News of the World*, 10 September 1939.
[2] 'Private and Personal', 19 October 1939: Churchill papers, 23/1.

Admiralty was the immediate impact which his personality made on the staff at all levels, both service and civilian.

From the very first day even I in my subordinate situation became aware of this presence and I amongst others began to receive little notes signed 'WSC' from the private office demanding weekly reports of progress direct to him.

Allen added:

If the required report was a good one (and it would not necessarily be one's fault if it were not) one might get a reply in red ink—'v.g. press on'. It was like the stone thrown into the pond, the ripples got out in all directions, galvanising people at all levels to 'press on'—and they did.[1]

This impression was widely shared. 'He practically killed people by overwork,' Clifford Jarrett, a Principal in the Department of the Secretary of the Admiralty, later recalled, 'and at the same time inspired people to extreme devotion. He was a manifestly human person every moment of the day.' Churchill's 'supreme talent', Jarrett stressed, was 'his ability to speak to people'; his next talent was 'in goading people into giving up their cherished reasons for not doing anything at all'.[2]

Those closest to Churchill from day to day were the members of his Private Office. One of them, Bernard Sendall, later recalled Churchill's particular concern for the three Private Secretaries—his senior Eric Seal, himself, and his deputy John Higham. 'One got caught up into the family,' Sendall recalled, 'You were treated as part of the family on the basis of complete trust, whether it was personal or official. One realised that if one did drop a clanger which incurred his wrath, it wouldn't last long and he wouldn't bear a grudge against you, as long as you were doing your duty as best you could.'[3]

John Higham likewise remembered, more than forty years later, the atmosphere of those autumn months at the Admiralty. 'Everybody realised what a wider responsibility he had,' and Higham added:

He was a great man for seeing the people who had done the job. This did a tremendous amount of good.

Certainly everyone was very conscious that he was regarded by his colleagues as trying to take the war over. They were pretty sensitive about that. There was a feeling that the war was being run from the Admiralty War Room.

---

[1] G. R. G. Allen, recollections, in a letter to Arthur Marder, 1966: Arthur J. Marder, *From the Dardanelles to Oran*, London 1974, pages 106–7. After the war Allen became Churchill's research assistant on the naval aspects of Churchill's Second World War memoirs.

[2] Sir Clifford Jarrett, recollections, in conversation with the author, 31 October 1979.

[3] Bernard Sendall, recollections, in conversation with the author, 14 November 1979.

He was also a tremendous nuisance. But there wasn't any resentment. 'The Old Man's off again.'

His baits were very real. They did lead him off on false tracks. But I don't think anyone ever felt he was an impossible man to deal with.

The Admirals felt he had to be handled very carefully, but they weren't frightened of him. He was a tremendous tonic, everybody saw that.[1]

The inspiration of Churchill's character and concern was felt by all his staff. 'When Winston was at the Admiralty,' his secretary Kathleen Hill later recalled, 'the place was buzzing with atmosphere, with electricity. When he was away, on tour, it was dead, dead, dead.'[2]

Not only those who worked with Churchill within the Admiralty building, but those who saw him at work outside it, were impressed. Lieutenant-Colonel Jacob, one of the Secretaries of the Military Co-ordination Committee, later recalled how, 'while at the Admiralty, Churchill studied all the telegrams, not only the naval telegrams. He came well prepared to all the meetings. The other Ministers may not have read the telegrams—their senior officials had read them of course, and briefed them on that basis—but Churchill had read them himself.'

It was Churchill's 'immense power of work' which Jacob remembered most vividly.[3] For the sailors, it was the buoyant spirit which his presence imparted. 'The Dockyard men love him,' the Commander-in-Chief, Portsmouth, wrote after Churchill's visit there on 13 January 1940, 'and turned out in thousands to cheer. Wherever he was, frowns gave way to smiles.'[4]

As First Lord, Churchill was continuously involved in questions of conduct. In March 1940 he learned that during the liberation of the prisoners of the *Altmark*, a watch, a chronometer and the Iron Cross belonging to the ship's captain had been taken as souvenirs. 'Anything of this kind,' he minuted to Pound and Phillips on March 25, 'must be stopped with the utmost strictness. No souvenir of any value can be preserved without being reported and permission obtained.' Churchill added: 'Personal property of enemies may be confiscated by the State, but never by individuals.'[5]

[1] John Higham recollections, in conversation with the author, 1 March 1982.
[2] Kathleen Hill, conversation with the author, 15 October 1982.
[3] Lieutenant-General Sir Ian Jacob, conversation with the author, 18 November 1979.
[4] Admiral Sir William James, *The Portsmouth Letters*, London 1946, page 30.
[5] Minute No. 267, 25 March 1940: Churchill papers, 19/6.

Five months earlier, on 14 October 1939, Churchill had argued, in a minute to Phillips about Indian sailors serving in the Royal Navy: 'There must be no discrimination on grounds of race or colour.' He added, however, that 'much inconvenience' would be caused in practice 'if this theoretical equality had many examples'. His minute ended: 'I cannot see any objections to Indians serving on HM Ships where they are qualified or needed, or if their virtues so deserve rising to be Admirals of the Fleet. But not too many of them, please.'[1]

On the following day, commenting to Pound about the use of ruses to destroy German submarines, Churchill warned that no ruse should be carried out which abandoned mercy. Of a recent case, that of the *Baralong*, which had sunk a U-boat by the stratagem of pretending to abandon ship, and then, when the U-boat surfaced, attacking. This 'stratagem' itself, Churchill wrote, was acceptable. 'What was odious was allowing the survivors of the U-boat, who had been received aboard the *Baralong*, to be murdered one by one during the next twelve hours, the last two found hiding in the screw alley.' Churchill's minute continued:

Mercy should always be shown to men in the water, and once a man is received on board he is a prisoner of war and can be dealt with by the tribunals according to law and custom. However, there is this corrective, that no risks need be run in picking up men from the water in cases where the rescuing ship may still be exposed to the danger of renewed U-boat attack. A brave officer will always be humane.[2]

Churchill's concern for the law and custom of war was paralleled by his keenness to break out of the bounds of current orthodoxy. In 1915 he had done this by sponsoring from the Admiralty the first experiments in tank design, for which he put forward Admiralty funds, and assembled and encouraged naval and technical experts. At the end of October 1939 he had sought to encourage a similar innovative leap among his new Admiralty experts, asking the Director of Naval Construction, Sir Stanley Goodall, to initiate experiments for a mechanical trench digger. The aim of this machine was to give the British and French forces on the western front a means of advance 'up to and through the hostile lines without undue or prohibitive casualties'.

To ensure secrecy, the scheme was given the code name 'White Rabbit No. 6'. On November 29 the code name was changed to 'Cultivator No. 6'. That same week a model was ready, and was dem-

[1] Minute (unnumbered series) of 14 October 1939: Churchill papers, 19/3.

[2] 'Employment of Ruses to destroy Enemy Submarines', 15 October 1939: Churchill papers, 19/3.

onstrated in Chamberlain's presence on a floor of sand in the Admiralty basement. Ironside gave the scheme his 'active support', and Churchill took the model to Paris where he showed it to both Gamelin and Georges, both of whom expressed what Churchill later recalled as 'approving interest'.

On December 6 Churchill was told that if orders for 'Cultivator No. 6' were given 'absolute priority', as many as 200 of these trench diggers could be operational by March 1941; and on 7 February 1940 both Cabinet and Treasury approval was given both for these, as well as for forty even larger machines which could dig a trench wide enough for tanks to pass through. In March 1940 the manufacture of these diggers was transferred to the Ministry of Supply. Two months later, the German conquest of France made the production of such a machine no longer relevant.[1] 'Such was the tale of "Cultivator No. 6",' Churchill later wrote, and he added: 'I am responsible but impenitent.'[2]

The effort involved in Churchill's work as First Lord of the Admiralty, and as a member of the War Council, could not have been sustained without a strict daily routine, and the support of a devoted personal staff. The routine involved a long working day, but a disciplined one, essential for a man of sixty-five, who had suffered in his late fifties both a severe car accident and the recurring ill-effects of typhoid fever. Beginning work while still in bed at six or seven o'clock, Churchill would take a short rest after lunch, when he would undress and go to bed, after which he would begin work again in the early afternoon, and work on, with a break for dinner, until two or three in the morning.

Two props of this rigorous daily routine were individuals: Lieutenant-Commander 'Tommy' Thompson, who had the task of organizing the daily budget of travel, and Captain Richard Pim, who was in charge of Churchill's Upper War Room, established in the library of Admiralty House, on the floor below Churchill's bedroom. Pim's job was to ensure that the daily developments of the war were plotted on the maps and charts with which the room had been equipped in the second week of September, as a result of one of Churchill's earliest wartime minutes.

---

[1] On 19 June 1940 Churchill minuted to the Minister of Supply: 'I have already asked that the Cultivator No. 6 should be cut down to a quarter, i.e., 60. I now think one-eighth will be sufficient, i.e., 30—25 privates and 5 officers' (Churchill papers, 20/13).

[2] 'Cultivator No. 6', Appendix O: Winston S. Churchill, *The Second World War*, volume 1, London 1948, pages, 566–8.

Both Thompson and Pim joined Churchill during his first week at the Admiralty, and remained with him until the end of the war. A second Thompson who was at his side throughout his time both as First Lord and as Prime Minister was his detective, W. H. Thompson, who had first guarded Churchill in 1921, had remained with him until 1929, accompanied him to the United States in 1931, and had been recalled to his duties ten days before the outbreak of war in 1939.

One of the responsibilities of Commander Thompson was to arrange each Tuesday a dinner party of some fourteen people at Admiralty House to which Churchill invited Cabinet Ministers, members of the Board of Admiralty, the Army Council and the Air Councils, senior civil servants, politicians and others whom he wished to bring together, the ice being broken by a Swedish milk punch. On the day after one of these dinners, the Minister of Transport, Euan Wallace, who had been invited for the first time, wrote on 3 January 1940:

Dear Winston,
Thank you ever so much for last night. It was a great honour to be asked to one of your 'Tuesdays' and I enjoyed your company at dinner and that of old friends afterwards more than I can tell you.
It was after 11 by the time Morton and I left after the CNS[1] had given us a most interesting time in the 'Bridge' and basement war rooms.
More power to your elbow![2]

The War Room tours were a noted feature of Churchill's Tuesday dinners. Often Churchill himself would accompany the guests to what was, in effect, the only operational headquarters situated inside any Government department; for it was from the Admiralty building itself that all operational orders were sent to the scattered Fleet, in which a twenty-four hour watch was kept on the hour-by-hour developments of the war, and to which the coded signals came.

In the Upper War Room, Captain Pim had transformed an elegant three-hundred-year-old library into a focal point of information, the maps and charts being covered with curtains so that their secrets would not be seen by members of the Admiralty Staff not authorized to use them, or by cleaners. Churchill, who slept in the room above, could consult Pim's maps at any hour, whenever a plan had to be made, or an urgent signal was received. In his draft memoirs, Pim later recalled Churchill's first inspection of his efforts. 'Very good, very good,' Churchill told him. 'But the maps will all have to be

---

[1] Chief of the Naval Staff: Sir Dudley Pound.
[2] Letter of 3 January 1940: Churchill papers, 2/399.

replaced. When you know me better you will know that I only paint in pastel shades, and those strong colours under the lamps would give me and you a headache.'

Pim was momentarily depressed that his efforts had not met with Churchill's approval. But the colours were quickly muted, and the maps approved. Henceforth the War Room was manned day and night, there always being two naval officers and one military officer, on duty. One wall was covered with a map of the world, the other by regional maps. Ship symbols, mounted on pins, showed the day-by-day position of every British and Allied warship, convoy and merchantman on the high seas, and every known position of a German vessel. As Pim later recalled:

The positions were plotted from signals which came in day and night in a continuous stream and reached me after being decoded elsewhere. Records of attacks on our shipping by U-boat, aircraft or raider were kept showing the tonnage sunk and also details of attacks by our ships on enemy surface vessels and U-boats and graphs of imports, month by month, into the UK.

Mr Churchill lived in the top flat of Admiralty House and he was working almost continuously by day and night.

If any signal of importance arrived, a very few moments would elapse before he arrived in the War Room and was in complete possession of all the facts. I had always heard that he was an indefatigable worker and there is no other word to describe his activities. His day started with a visit in his multi-coloured dressing gown to the War Room, generally soon after seven—although often it was a far earlier hour—or, alternatively I (or in my absence the duty officer) went up to his room to report on the events of the night.

This duty of visiting Mr Churchill as soon as he woke up each morning was continued throughout the war both in England and overseas. With the exception of about two hours' rest each afternoon he continued hard at it with a short respite for meals until one or two o'clock next morning when he used to pay us a final visit on his way to bed.

Pim recalled many of the visitors to the Upper War Room, Churchill's friends and colleagues for whom a tour of this secret sanctuary would be a high point of their evening at Admiralty House. There was Sumner Welles, on his European mission, who called the room 'the second most interesting thing he had seen in Europe', without revealing what the first had been. As he had just come from Germany, Pim recalled, 'we felt it must have had something to do with Hitler'. The High Commissioner to Eire, Sir John Maffey, visited the room on the eve of his departure for Dublin, spending some time, as Pim recalled, 'seeing for himself the terrible handicap which the loss of the use of certain harbours in Eire was to the British Navy, and indeed to all who met disaster in the North Atlantic'. Neville Chamberlain, Sir John Simon and Leslie Hore-Belisha were three regular visitors; so too were Sir Archibald Sinclair and Lord Beaverbrook, neither of them members of the Government, but both of them in Churchill's confidence. Another visitor was the Solicitor-General, Sir Terence O'Connor, who 'seemed to feel', so Pim recalled, 'that we had got to be "good haters" without squeamishness if we were to pull through'.

Pim later recalled, of the events in the Upper War Room:

If a Raider was reported in any specific area we were able in a few moments to say what British ships were in its vicinity and what was their speed so that a wireless signal could be sent ordering them, if necessary, to alter course to avoid the danger.

This picture also enabled the First Lord to see at a glance if ships were being delayed in any specific part of the world and to take remedial action. As an example of this I remember Mr Churchill ringing up Sir John Gilmour, then Minister of Shipping, at 2 a.m. to find out whether there was not perhaps some unnecessary delay in loading ships in the River Plate.

From what I heard later, some high officials were badly shaken at being called upon to discuss official business in the early hours.[1]

The dramas and secrets of the Upper War Room had a quieter but equally influential counterpart in the First Lord's Statistical Branch directed by Professor Lindemann. It too had a room at the Admiralty, a small staff, and a part to play in Churchill's concept of how the war should be conducted. It too remained as a part of his personal system until the war was won.

Lindemann's advice, with its statistical backing, reached Churchill almost daily in the form of terse, normally single page notes. On the basis of one such set of notes, Churchill argued successfully in the War Cabinet of 28 October 1939 against the introduction of food rationing, despite the support given to rationing by both the Minister of Food and the Minister of Labour. On that occasion, dealing with the wider, non-statistical aspect, Churchill told his colleagues that there were signs in the Press of all political shades 'that public opinion was becoming increasingly critical of governmental control and interference with liberty of the individual'.[2]

But Churchill did not regard statistics as things to be manipulated in order to advance a particular policy. Indeed, although he had strenu-

---

[1] Sir Richard Pim, draft memoirs: Pim papers.
[2] War Cabinet No. 63 of 1939, 28 October 1939, 11.30 a.m.: Cabinet papers, 65/1.

ously opposed rationing when he believed, on Lindemann's figures, that it would be premature, he was still willing to be convinced to the contrary. 'Please examine this at once,' he minuted to Lindemann on 4 December 1939, about new figures that he had been shown concerning falling imports of food, paper, sugar and meat, 'comparing it with previous calculations. Do not think of making a case for a particular point of view, or sustaining what we said last time. Let us just have the cold-blooded facts.'[1]

Churchill used Lindemann to scrutinize the statistics and needs of a dozen Government departments. One area of his concern was overseas food supply. 'This shipping,' he wrote to Robert Hudson on the day after Hudson's appointment as Minister of Shipping, 'is a nerve centre which has rusted in a dull way.' And he added: 'Please keep in touch with Lindemann who has a mass of vital figures and ideas.'[2]

On 15 February 1940 Lindemann advocated the pursuit of research into a torpedo which would seek out its target. The weapon, he informed Churchill, 'would be an adaptation of the ordinary torpedo, fitted with the acoustical device in the head and arranged to sit quiescent in the bottom until stimulated by the noise of a passing vessel'. This device, he explained, would 'release the mechanism and the torpedo moving at a speed of about 40 knots would chase the ship'.[3]

Four days later Lindemann suggested using neutral shipping, 'e.g. American, which would otherwise lie idle', to carry British goods out-side the Atlantic war zone. His minute, as usual a personal one to Churchill alone, continued, with a careful balance of the pros and cons: 'If we could get American ships to carry goods from Australia, New Zealand and Chile, even only as far as Panama, it would set free British shipping capacity enough to bring an extra 4 to 6 million ton annually to this country. We should, of course, have to pay freights in dollars. But this might be off-set by the possibility of buying in soft currencies rather than hard. If the shipping position is really acute, this may well offer a chance of easement.'[4]

Not all Churchill's Private Office approved of Lindemann's in-fluence. Bernard Sendall later recalled: 'Prof used to feed Winston with all sorts of nonsense, very often culled from Whitaker or some simple

---

[1] 'Food, Paper, Sugar and Meat', 4 December 1939: Churchill papers, 19/3.
[2] Letter of 4 April 1940, 'Personal': Churchill papers, 2/395. Hudson had succeeded Sir John Gilmour as Minister of Shipping on 3 April 1940.
[3] Minute of 15 February 1940: Churchill papers, 19/7.
[4] Minute of 19 February 1940: Churchill papers, 19/7.

book of reference.' But of Lindemann's intimacy with the First Lord there could be no doubt. 'He came in most evenings,' Sendall recalled, 'and would sit himself down on the settee in front of the fire, and be with Winston until Winston went to bed—at about 2 or 3.' Before bed, there was usually a tour of the operational rooms in the basement. 'These tours,' Sendall recalled, were 'terribly good for the naval staff. Then he would look in to the map room—Pim's sacred domain.'[1]

Another of those who worked with Churchill throughout his eight months as First Lord was the Parliamentary Secretary to the Admiralty, Geoffrey Shakespeare. He also has recalled the pattern of evenings at Admiralty House:

> Usually after dinner he held a Naval conference from 9 to 11 p.m. But after 11 p.m. he devoted himself to speech making. Having been closely associated with Lloyd George in the preparation of his speeches, I was interested to observe Churchill's technique. He used no notes or headlines giving the sequence of his points. He dictated directly and firmly to an expert typist who used a silent machine. One night he remarked: 'Are you all ready? I'm feeling very fertile tonight.'
>
> As each page was finished he scanned it rapidly, altering a word here and there, thus softening or accentuating the meaning. As he dictated he padded up and down in soft bedroom slippers, arms behind his back, head thrust forward, a cigar protruding from his mouth. The argument flowed in smooth and logical sequence. Now and again he paused to ask me a question or I made a suggestion and he replenished his glass from a whisky decanter on the table. On he went. Crisp scintillating phrases that next day re-echoed round the free world, came hissing out through clouds of cigar smoke.
>
> Later, perhaps next morning, the typist would prepare condensed notes from the dictated draft, but starting each paragraph precisely as dictated and adding a key word or two. Churchill had such a phenomenal memory that from these pointers he would recite the speech next day almost verbatim and with an air of spontaneity that concealed the fact that it had been so carefully prepared.
>
> If he finished dictating by 2 a.m. he usually wanted to visit the War Room to study the position of warships on the oceans of the world. It was very difficult to get him to bed. Once early in the morning I remember him asking his secretary—'Where is the OIL?' 'What OIL?' said the puzzled secretary. 'I want,' replied Churchill, 'Admiral the OIL [Earl] of Cork and Orrery.' It was nearly 3 a.m. We were dropping with fatigue.[2]

Geoffrey Shakespeare was rapidly captivated by his new master, contrasting him with his first political chief, Lloyd George, for whom

---

[1] Bernard Sendall, recollections, in conversation with the author, 14 November 1979.
[2] Sir Geoffrey Shakespeare's recollections, 'Winston at War': Shakespeare papers.

he had worked at 10 Downing Street in 1921 and 1922. 'Of the two men,' he later wrote, 'Churchill has been, in my opinion, more loyal to his colleagues than Lloyd George was.' While Lloyd George often neglected his friends, Churchill 'never forgets a service rendered to him, and delights in rewarding his friends for their loyalty, sometimes even to his own disadvantage'. As to Churchill's relations with the Service Chiefs, Shakespeare wrote, 'He was accepted as one of them; he spoke the same language.'

Of Churchill's departmental method as First Lord, Shakespeare wrote: 'If he summoned anyone to discuss a problem he would throw out a number of alternative solutions. In cases where decisions were outstanding he gave them instantly. He expected immediate action to be taken on every occasion and often his directions were couched in a form impossible of fulfilment, but he was always satisfied as long as some action was taken and he accepted advice provided it was clear that his advisers were competent to advise.'

Shakespeare added:

Though he had an inflexible purpose, he had no rigidity of mind. He was, in fact, an empiricist. If one experiment proved unsuccessful, another was suggested. The only unpardonable sin was to sit back and accept the seemingly inevitable. . . .

He knew from experience that war was a thing of hazards and dangers, disappointments and disasters, and was not unduly despondent when they occurred. He loved, too, the excitements and the tense situations which war always brings in its train. 'What a dull naval war this will be,' he said to me once with a spark of prophetic intuition. 'We have only Germany to fight. Now if we fought Germany, Italy and Japan together, that would be much more interesting.'

Shakespeare also recalled a particular Churchill minute, which was to become legendary in Admiralty circles and beyond; the instruction: 'utmost fish'. As Shakespeare wrote:

One morning I was surprised to find on my desk a pink tab with a memo to this effect: 'I am concerned about the shortage of fish. Parliamentary Secretary will immediately take up the matter with the ACNS[1] and the head of the Mine Sweeping Division to see if any trawlers can be released for fishing.

'We must have a policy of "utmost fish". Parliamentary Secretary will report to me by midnight with his proposals. WSC.'

This was indeed a poser. I had no knowledge of, or responsibility for, the fishing industry. That question came within the purview of the Ministry of Agriculture and Fisheries. I got busy, however, and arranged with the

[1] The Assistant Chief of the Naval Staff, Rear-Admiral H. M. Burrough.

Ministry of Agriculture to call a conference of trawler owners from Hull, Grimsby and elsewhere, and ACNS—Rear-Adml. Burrough, whose name later in the war was brilliantly associated with the Malta convoys—came to the rescue by releasing a few trawlers.

After many hours of intensive study of the problem, I dictated a comprehensive memorandum on the essential facts of the industry, the number of trawlers and drifters still used for fishing and the numbers taken over by the Admiralty, daily catches, difficulties of protecting fishing fleets from aircraft and mines, and I concluded by suggesting the formation of a new Fishing Promotion Council, composed of representatives of the Admiralty, Ministry of Agriculture, trawler and drifter owners, and of the trades unions concerned.

I completed the memorandum just after midnight and took it into the presence. Churchill read it, asked numerous questions and concurred in the formation of the new council and instructed me to constitute it forthwith. He also asked me to approach Ernest Bevin to secure his interest. Churchill himself promised to preside at the first meeting to be held in a week's time.

So a policy of 'utmost fish' was fostered by the Admiralty in war-time.[1]

Within the Admiralty, Churchill's devotion to his responsibilities as First Lord were not to meet with universal approval. And yet his energies impressed themselves favourably even on the critics. As one naval officer, Captain Ralph Edwards, wrote in his diary at a time when he was acting Director of Operations (Home): 'Winston Churchill is taking a great personal interest and tends to interfere with the sailor's business. He is an extraordinary man and has an astonishing grasp on the situation, but I wish he would keep to his own sphere. . . .'[2]

Churchill's 'sphere' was whatever he could see, sense or remember; it was everything he heard and everything that was on his mind. From his room at the Admiralty, as he looked across Horse Guards Parade to 10 Downing Street, every facet of war policy seemed to him a part of his legitimate concern, matters large and matters small. The very Admiralty building was within range of his enquiry or exhortation. In December 1939 work had begun on strengthening the Admiralty basement. 'The work below,' he minuted on February 16, 'seems to be progressing very slowly indeed. Pray let me have a report.'

Yet although First Lord's 'prayers' were a daily feature of Churchill's conduct of Admiralty business, he never sought to burden unduly those to whom they were addressed. As he explained in April 1940 to Admiral Phillips: 'I am going in future to mark a number of my queries "Naval

---

[1] Sir Geoffrey Shakespeare, *Let Candles Be Brought In*, London 1949, pages 67, 69 and 230–2.

[2] Edwards diary, 7 April 1940: Stephen Roskill, *Churchill and the Admirals*, London 1977, page 102.

Staff" where they simply relate to facts or messages I do not understand.' This would relieve Phillips personally 'of the necessity of looking at them'.[1]

Despite the pressure of problems and events, there were still moments which Churchill could devote to family matters. The marriage of his son Randolph to the nineteen-year-old Pamela Digby, daughter of the 11th Baron Digby, had been one such occasion. 'I expect he will be in action in the early spring,' Churchill wrote to the Duke of Westminster five days before the wedding, 'and therefore I am very glad that he should be married before he goes. She is a charming girl, and they both seem very pleased about it.'[2]

The moments of leisure were few, but they did exist. On 9 December 1939 Churchill's desk diary noted: 'Cinema with Mrs Churchill',[3] and on 24 February 1940: 'Mr and Mrs Churchill dine with Mr and Mrs Eden. (Ice Hockey Match at Wembley afterwards.)'[4] On one occasion Neville Chamberlain and his wife came to Admiralty House for a quiet, private evening. It was 13 October 1939. 'We were a party of four,' Churchill later recalled, and he added: 'Although we had been colleagues under Mr Baldwin for five years, my wife and I had never met the Chamberlains in such circumstances before. By happy chance I turned the conversation on to his life in the Bahamas, and I was delighted to find my guest expand in personal reminiscence to a degree I had not noticed before. He told us the whole story, of which I knew only the barest outline, of his six years' struggle to grow sisal on a barren West Indian islet. . . .'

Churchill listened fascinated while Chamberlain spoke at length of his earlier, and unsuccessful struggles, culminating in the loss of £50,000 of his family's fortune. It was, Churchill recalled, a tale 'of gallant endeavour'. As he listened to it he thought to himself: 'What a pity Hitler did not know when he met this sober English politician with his umbrella at Berchtesgaden, Godesberg, and Munich that he was actually talking to a hard-bitten pioneer from the outer marches of the British Empire!'

Looking back on this evening, Churchill recalled: 'This was really the only intimate social conversation that I can remember with Neville Chamberlain amid all the business we did together over nearly twenty years.' His account continued:

---

[1] Minute of 15 April 1940: Churchill papers, 19/2.
[2] Letter of 29 September 1939: Churchill papers, 19/2.
[3] Churchill's engagement cards: Lieutenant-Commander Thompson papers.
[4] Churchill's engagement cards: Lieutenant-Commander Thompson papers.

During dinner the war went on and things happened. With the soup an officer came up from the War Room below to report that a U-boat had been sunk. With the sweet he came again and reported that a second U-boat had been sunk; and just before the ladies left the dining-room he came a third time reporting that a third U-boat had been sunk. Nothing like this had ever happened before in a single day, and it was more than a year before such a record was repeated.

As the ladies left us, Mrs Chamberlain, with a naïve and charming glance, said to me, 'Did you arrange all this on purpose?' I assured her that if she would come again we would produce a similar result.[1]

As he followed so closely the developments of the war at sea, and watched on the maps of the Upper War Room the German U-boat losses, and their successes, Churchill also invited to Admiralty House some of the officers whose exploits had struck his imagination. 'Mentally,' Commander Thompson later recalled, 'he drew fresh inspiration from the gravity of his task and his close contact with men of action.'[2] One such officer was Lieutenant-Commander Bickford, Captain of the submarine *Salmon*, whose successful exploits early in the war, in torpedoing and seriously damaging two German cruisers, had provided a major boost to public morale during a week when the Press was full of the triumphs of the German magnetic mine.

On 19 December 1939 Churchill suggested that the King might like to see Bickford, 'and conclude the audience by pinning on the DSO'. Churchill added: 'Naval Secretary might find out what they think about this at the Palace.' In suggesting similar awards to the Captain and crew members of HMS *Ursula*, Churchill wrote: 'Every effort must be made to announce the awards to the men at the same time as the officers. The whole should be put through in 48 hours at the latest.'[3]

Churchill's admiration for Bickford was stirred by the signal which Bickford had sent the Admiralty after his fight, a signal which began: 'Have attacked enemy Battle Fleet. . . .' Nor had this been an idle boast: as Bickford surveyed the scene through his periscope, he had seen five German warships, including two cruisers, in his field of vision.[4]

---

[1] Winston S. Churchill, *The Second World War*, volume 1, London 1948, pages 388–9.

[2] Commander Thompson, recollection: Gerald Pawle, *The War and Colonel Warden, Based on the recollections of Commander C. R. Thompson*, London 1963, page 40.

[3] First Lord's Personal Minute No. 83, 19 December 1939: Admiralty papers, 205/2.

[4] 'War Patrol Narrative of HMS *Salmon*', 'Most Secret', 17 December 1939: Admiralty papers, 205/2. The torpedoed cruisers were the *Leipzig* and the *Nürnberg*. The *Nürnberg* was out of action until May 1940, the *Leipzig* until December 1940, when she was restricted to training duties.

On 25 February 1940 Churchill invited Bickford to tell him at first hand, over lunch at Admiralty House, of his exploits. He also encouraged others to listen to Bickford's stirring tale, and sought to find him an advisory position at the Admiralty where he could both rest for a while from the strains and dangers of his hazardous work, and could at the same time give others the benefit of his advice and zeal. With this in mind Churchill minuted to Pound and Phillips after his lunch with Bickford:

There would be advantages in having Commander Bickford in the Plans Division of the Admiralty for, say, six months in order to bring them in close and direct contact with the very latest conditions prevailing in Heligoland Bight. This Officer seems to me to be very able, and he has many things to say about anti-U-boat warfare which I trust will be gathered at the earliest opportunity.[1]

Bickford himself asked not to be taken away from active duty, and his request was granted. In May he was married; and returned to sea, where he and his submarine saw active service in Norwegian waters.

Churchill's return to the Admiralty, and to the Cabinet, in September 1939, had been a cause of puzzlement and even of concern to many of those who felt that his great days were past, that his Ministerial career had surely ended ten years before, or that his judgment was flawed. Writing to Lord Beaverbrook on 1 October 1939, Sir Samuel Hoare, one of Churchill's War Cabinet colleagues, had described him as 'very much as you expected he would be, very rhetorical, very emotional and, most of all, very reminiscent'. In addition, Hoare wrote: 'He strikes me as an old man who easily gets tired.' Yet there was another side even to Hoare's portrait. 'Certainly,' he wrote, 'in the country he has a very big position. ... I should say that at the moment he is the one popular figure in the Cabinet.'[2]

This combination of the negative and positive was seen by all observers. But the balance tilted most often in Churchill's favour. 'I have the greatest admiration for WC,' Dudley Pound wrote to Sir Charles Forbes on 20 January 1940, 'and his good qualities are such and his desire to hit the enemy so overwhelming, that I feel one must hesitate in turning down any of his proposals.'[3]

On 23 February 1940 Churchill welcomed back, at a special cere-

---

[1] Minute of 25 February 1940: Churchill papers, 19/6.
[2] Letter of 1 October 1939: Beaverbrook papers.
[3] Letter of 20 January 1940: Cunningham papers.

mony at the Guildhall, the crews of HMS *Exeter* and *Ajax*, heroes of
the battle of the River Plate. It was, he said, a 'brilliant sea fight', and
he added 'that in a dark, cold winter it warmed the cockles of the
British heart'.[1] One observer, Sir Samuel Hoare, commented critically
in his diary: 'Winston overbidding the market in his speeches.'[2] But
Churchill's former Private Secretary, Sir Edward Marsh, wrote to him
on the following day:

> What times you've been having! I got a letter from Siegfried Sassoon this
> morning, in which he says: 'What an apotheosis Winston is enjoying! I suppose
> he is the most popular—as well as being the ablest—political figure in Eng-
> land. He must be glorying in the deeds of the Navy, who are indeed superb.
> And W himself has certainly put up a grand performance.'
> I hope you may be pleased with this tribute from a former opponent![3]

Three days after his Guildhall speech, Churchill received a letter
from Neville Lytton, the painter with whom he had travelled on the
western front during the First World War, immediately after the
German breakthrough of March 1918. 'I want to tell you,' Lytton
wrote from Paris, 'that fate has chosen you to be the Clemenceau of
this war. France as well as England puts herself under your auspices &
your leadership.' Lytton added: 'Drive us to victory with all the force
of your will to conquer.'[4] It was only after three years of war, however,
that Clemenceau had taken over the French Premiership and central
war direction.

On February 27 Churchill introduced the Navy Estimates debate
to Parliament. 'It seems to me,' he said, 'since I last presented Navy
Estimates in war-time—25 years ago, almost to a day—there has grown
up a very much wider comprehension of the conditions under which
the Navy and the Admiralty do their duty; of their difficulties, and of
the certainty that mistakes will be made both at Whitehall and on salt
water, and that, however hard we try, a painful drain of losses will be
sustained.' The Labour and Liberal opposition, he added, were to be
thanked 'for this spirit of tolerance, of understanding, and even indulgence with which we have been and are being treated'. No precise
facts or figures of the proposed strength and cost of the Navy could be
laid before the House: 'there is no need to tell the enemy more than is
good for him about what we are doing'.

Speaking for more than an hour and a half, Churchill spoke of the

---

[1] Speech of 23 February 1940: Churchill papers, 9/143.
[2] Hoare diary, 25 February 1940: Templewood papers.
[3] Letter of 26 February 1940: Churchill papers, 8/658.
[4] Letter of 26 February 1940: Churchill papers, 2/396.

dangers and difficulties of war at sea, of the U-boat depredations, of the 'inevitable losses' of merchant ships, and of German attacks on fishing fleets, lightships and unarmed merchantmen, denouncing:

... the outrages they have committed upon the fishing fleets and upon small unarmed merchant vessels and upon the lightships which warn the mariners of all countries off the rocks and shoals. So execrable has been the behaviour of some of the German aviators in attacking harmless, unarmed vessels, in machine-gunning their crews when in the boats, and in describing on the radio what fun it was to see a little ship 'crackling in flames like a Christmas tree', that we have had to set about arming all our fishing boats and small craft with the means of defending themselves, because it was found that nothing gives better results in respect to one of these raiders than to fire upon it at once.

Churchill went on to speak of 'one of the most extraordinary things that I have ever known', the way in which German illegalities, atrocities and brutalities 'are coming to be accepted as if they were part of the ordinary day-to-day conditions of war'. 'Why, Sir,' he continued:

... the neutral Press makes more fuss when I make a speech telling them what is their duty than they have done when hundreds of their ships have been sunk and many thousands of their sailors have been drowned or murdered, for that is the right word, on the open sea. Apparently, according to the present doctrine of neutral States, strongly endorsed by the German Government, Germany is to gain one set of advantages by breaking all the rules and committing foul outrages upon the seas, and then go on and gain another set of advantages through insisting whenever it suits her, upon the strictest interpretation of the International Code she has torn to pieces. It is not at all odd that His Majesty's Government are getting rather tired of it. I am getting rather tired of it myself.

At the end of six months of war, Churchill told the House of Commons, 63,000 tons of warships, and 200,000 tons of merchant shipping had been lost. Both figures were less than half the equivalent figures in the First World War. At the same time, Britain had captured more cargoes destined for Germany than she herself had lost. His task, and that of the Admiralty was to make 'prudent preparations against the unknown', and to raise the British war effort 'to the highest pitch'. Churchill's speech ended:

I will not make any prophecies about the future which is doubly veiled by the obscurities and uncertainties of war. But personally I shall not be content, nor do I think the House should be content, if we do not reach and maintain a control of the seas equal to the highest standards of the last war and en-able the Navy once again to play a decisive part in the general victory of the Allies.[1]

Hardly was Churchill's speech over than he set off northwards by night train on another visit to the Fleet, accompanied by Eric Seal, and a typist, Mary Shearburn. 'We have had a terribly busy time since Sunday over the speech,' Seal wrote home that night, 'today has been a nightmare. We only just had time, after the speech, to gather up our papers & things & dash for the train. But all's well that ends well, & now I'm in my pyjamas, in a very comfy cabin, writing to you!' His letter, Seal added, would be sent back by hand of Miss Shearburn: 'She's getting out at Crewe (I wish I were) & going back in a sleeper with the papers we have done since the train started.'[2]

Among the letters of congratulation which Churchill received after his Navy Estimates speech was one from his secretary of ten years, Violet Pearman, who now, a sick woman, lived at Spitals Cross near Chartwell. 'Your speech in Parliament yesterday,' she wrote, 'was very heartening, and must have had several shocks in it for Hitler and his gang.' Her letter continued:

I think that the country relies on you more than any other Member of the Cabinet to express national feeling in a way that Germany only understands, standing up to a bully and proving him the coward that he is. Thank God, our Navy has you with your heart of gold to lead our 'hearts of oak and jolly tars'.

If I wrote to you every time to praise and bless you it would be very often, but I refrain except on special occasions from doing so because your mail is already burdened by such letters. But you know that here in Edenbridge one humble person follows your joys and griefs with a very full heart. I am very proud to hear your name spoken frequently in this small market town by all sorts and conditions of men, and to hear the pride and confidence which your presence in so vital a post brings to all.[3]

---

[1] *Hansard*, 27 February 1940, 3.59 p.m. to 4.37 p.m. columns 1923-35.

[2] Letter of 27 February 1940 ('nearly midnight'): Seal papers. Churchill was also accompanied by his wife and son. At Barrow-in-Furness Clementine Churchill launched a new aircraft carrier, the *Indomitable*. After the ceremony, Eric Seal wrote home: 'Winston made a most eloquent & rousing speech, which delighted everyone, especially as by that time a good many bottles & decanters had been opened! Mrs C was given a very expensive jewelled clip, in an expensive ivory box, with a gold inscription. The party broke up with more cheers; & much elated, we all climbed into a special train, feeling that we had done a good day's work for winning the war! We got back to town about 10 pm, after a journey whose worst feature was that Vickers' minions kept on waking us up to give us more drinks, or more cigars!!' (Seal papers).

[3] Letter of 28 February 1940: Pearman papers. Mrs Pearman died in 1941, aged 45.

Churchill's speech had been well received in France, where, according to the British Ambassador, Sir Ronald Campbell, it had caused 'great satisfaction'. Once again, it was Churchill's criticisms of the neutral States that had been singled out for comment, and 'unanimously approved by all sections of the Press'.[1]

On 5 March 1940 Churchill's friend Maxine Elliot died in the South of France. Her villa to the east of Cannes, the Château de L'Horizon, had been a place of rest and refuge for Churchill during the wilderness years; it was there that he had brooded on his own inability to deflect the appeasement policy, or to persuade Chamberlain's Government to adopt the measures of rearmament and alliance which, if adopted in time, Churchill was convinced could have deterred Hitler from war.

Maxine Elliot's devoted companion of her latter years, Doctor Brès, had been with her on the day of her death. 'I have in the ears,' he wrote to Churchill that evening, 'her last words said this morning about you. "Winston knows how to take his responsibilities—nothing can frighten him—he should be Prime Minister."'[2]

'I heard with deep sorrow that dear Maxine has passed away,' Churchill replied. 'I shall always feel grateful to you for the tender care and skill with which you watched over her.' 'In this grim world,' Churchill added, 'the lights are being put out one by one, and sunlight days at the Château de L'Horizon are gone for ever.'[3]

[1] Paris Telegram No. 164, 29 February 1940: Foreign Office papers, 371/24297, C.3194.
[2] Letter of 5 March 1940: Churchill papers, 2/394.
[3] Letter of 15 March 1940: Churchill papers, 2/394.

10

Scandinavia: The Failure
to Decide

T HE Supreme War Council of February 5 had decided to take
control of the Swedish ore fields, as well as to prepare a military
expedition to help Finland. The operation was to begin with the occupation of three Norwegian ports, Stavanger, Bergen and Trondheim.
The troops undertaking this operation were to be known as Force
'Stratford'. Reporting this decision to the War Cabinet on February 7,
Chamberlain noted that March 20 was 'the critical date' by which the
first echelons of 'Stratford' would have to be ready to arrive in Scandinavia 'if we were to be sure of forestalling the Germans'.

The War Cabinet of February 7 authorized the Service Departments to make their preparations 'with a view to being ready for
military intervention in Scandinavia' by March 20.[1] At a further
War Cabinet on February 9, Hankey pointed out that the question
of subsequent reinforcements 'had not been fully examined', while
Churchill stressed 'the urgency of pressing on with our preparations
as fast as possible'.

Churchill also asked whether the War Cabinet could be provided
'with a timetable'. It would be of 'special interest', he said, to see 'how
soon the leading elements of our forces would be ready to move'.[2]

In Finland, Soviet forces continued to suffer heavy losses, and at
some points to be driven back. On February 10 Ironside told the War
Cabinet that in the extreme north the Russians 'were reported to be
very short of food'. The War Cabinet also learned that two Labour

[1] War Cabinet No. 35 of 1940, 7 February 1940, 11.30 a.m., Minute 1, Confidential Annex:
Cabinet papers, 65/11.
[2] War Cabinet No. 37 of 1940, 9 February 1940, 11.30 a.m., Minute 5, Confidential Annex:
Cabinet papers, 65/11.

leaders, Sir Walter Citrine and Philip Noel Baker, 'had formed a very low opinion of Russian morale'.[1]

After five months of war with Germany, it was in Scandinavia alone that Britain and France were committed to initiate military action. Yet barriers to action continued to appear, as on February 12, when Halifax drew the War Cabinet's attention to a telegram from Victor Mallet in Sweden, in which the diplomat saw 'no present prospect' of Sweden 'and still less Norway' permitting an influx of armed forces through Narvik. The most which Mallet envisaged being allowed by Sweden was that 'several thousand' volunteers for Finland might be permitted 'to filter through by that route in bodies of about 150 a time'.

Halifax himself feared, and reported the agreement in this of the French Ambassador, 'that when we had prepared our expedition, we might be met by a refusal from Norway and Sweden to allow it to pass'. Oliver Stanley pointed out that the Finns 'required 30 or 40 thousand men to save the situation in the Spring', yet only 350 volunteers had been found so far 'who could work in the snow'.

Churchill again attacked what he saw as attitudes of negation. It would, he said, be worth investigating 'the possibility of working fairly small bodies of men through as soon as possible'. The 'great thing' from the point of view of strategy, he stressed, 'was to get our foot into the doorway into Scandinavia'; to this end, advanced parties on the Gällivare railway 'would be very valuable'.

Churchill also asked the War Cabinet of February 12 to send a British officer, Brigadier Ling, to Finland, 'to give moral support' to General Mannerheim, and to provide Britain 'with full and accurate information'. Halifax approved this proposal, which was then authorized by the War Cabinet.[2]

On February 17 the Chiefs of Staff produced a timetable of events whereby the landing in Norway could take place on March 20. This was the 'earliest date' possible, but would need the War Cabinet's decision to go ahead on March 11 at the latest, if it were to be carried out in time.

The last possible date for landing in Norway in order to reach Gällivare and Luleå before the ice melted would be April 3, and would require a War Cabinet decision on March 25.

[1] War Cabinet No. 38 of 1940, 10 February 1940, 10.30 a.m., Minute 4, Confidential Annex: Cabinet papers, 65/11.
[2] War Cabinet No. 39 of 1940, 12 February 1940, 11.30 a.m., Minute 6, Confidential Annex: Cabinet papers, 65/11.

For the operation of this plan, giving Britain and France their reason for landing, the Finns would first 'have to be persuaded to issue an appeal for help'. But the Finns might be reluctant to do this, the Chiefs of Staff noted, as by accepting Allied help they would be 'risking war with Germany'. Once the Finnish appeal for help had been issued, the neutral Norwegian and Swedish Governments would still 'have to be persuaded' to grant passage to the Allied troops, and if they refused to do so, 'an ultimatum might have to be delivered'.

The Chiefs of Staff calculated that to enable the War Cabinet to take its final decision for action by March 25, the Finns would have to 'issue their appeal' on March 5: scarcely two weeks away.[1]

On February 18 the War Cabinet had the Chiefs of Staff report before them. At the start of the discussion, Kingsley Wood asked about the German ability to bomb any British force which landed in Scandinavia. He had been told, he said, that Trondheim was within range of 1,400 German aircraft, 'which might drop up to 100 tons of bombs a day on the port'. In reply, the Chief of the Air Staff, Sir Cyril Newall, agreed that 'considerable risks' were involved, but he went on to inform the War Cabinet that the Chiefs of Staff 'felt that the risk was worth accepting for the sake of the great advantage which we should obtain if we secured possession of the Swedish ore fields'.

Newall suggested that if the Germans could be forestalled at Stavanger 'with a small force', this would lessen the danger of a German air attack on Trondheim. If this small force was heavily attacked, 'it could destroy the aerodrome and be withdrawn by sea'.

At this same War Cabinet, Churchill again argued in favour of his first and least ambitious proposal, to stop the traffic of Swedish iron ore to Germany 'by naval action in Norwegian territorial waters'.[2] This was the plan he had originally proposed, and which he had always hoped would be carried out before the larger Scandinavian operation.[3]

At this same meeting, Ironside added the warning that if Norway refused to cooperate with the landing force, it would be impossible to operate the Narvik to Gällivare railway 'for several months', and in the event of neither Sweden nor Norway cooperating with the Allies, 'it would clearly be impossible to achieve our object of occupying the

[1] Chiefs of Staff Committee, 32nd Meeting of 1940, 17 February 1940, 11 a.m., Confidential Annex: Cabinet papers, 79/85.

[2] War Cabinet No. 45 of 1940, 18 February 1940, 6.30 p.m., Minute 1, Confidential Annex: Cabinet papers, 65/11.

[3] Chiefs of Staff Committee No. 34 of 1940, 19 February 1940, 10.30 a.m., Confidential Annex: Cabinet papers, 79/85.

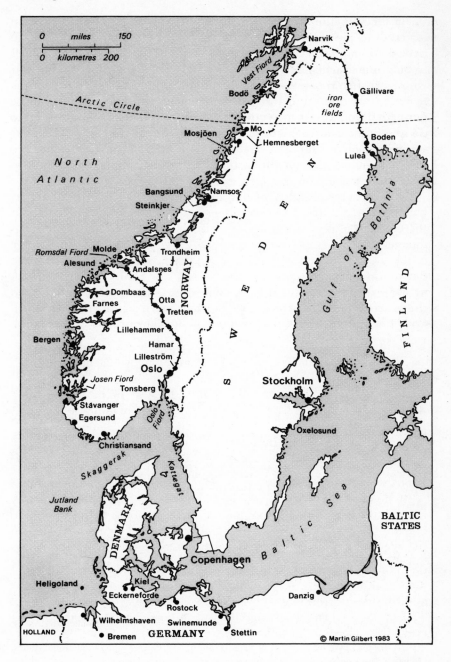

orefields at Gällivare before the melting of the ice allowed the Germans to forestall us by using the sea route via the Gulf of Bothnia'.[1]

At the War Cabinet an hour later, Churchill again pressed for his original, limited scheme. He was anxious, he said, to be given 'authority to make all the preparations'. If so, the ships could be ready to sail in five days. 'No opportunity so good as the present one might recur.' Britain could point out to Norway that she was 'not prepared' to run the risk of a second *Altmark*. Norwegian territorial waters were being used both to obtain supplies, and for the passage of warships. Norway had been unable to stop this action. By laying a minefield, Britain would 'force traffic into the open sea, and thus relieve the Norwegians of their heavy responsibility'. Churchill continued:

. . . by laying a minefield, we should not prejudice the larger operation which was being planned. On the contrary, we might succeed in provoking Germany into an imprudent action which would open the door for us. It was essential to link our action with the *Altmark* incident, and not to allow time to elapse in hesitation and argument.

If preparations were begun now, the War Cabinet would have, at the least, five days before a decision needed to be made, and no great inconvenience would be caused if the operation were put off from day to day thereafter.

It would be necessary, Churchill added, 'to give notice of our intention to lay a minefield'. But, he told his colleagues, 'he would not favour a diplomatic argument with the Norwegians on the subject'.

Halifax agreed with Churchill's request to start preparations; but only on condition that it was 'fully understood that, in doing so, he was not giving any measure of consent to the proposal'. The general feeling, as expressed by the official minutes, was that laying a minefield 'might be unfavourable for our chances of getting in to help Finland and seizing the orefields . . .' but that if Germany reacted to the laying of a minefield this might provide Britain with the 'opening' needed to embark on the wider scheme.

It was therefore decided that the 'small forces' designed to occupy Stavanger, Bergen and Trondheim as part of the larger scheme should be ready to move 'when the minefield was laid'. But whether or not either plan would in fact be put into operation was to be decided later.

One fear, that these forces 'might suffer severely from air attack', was dismissed by Ironside, who said that 'they would be quite capable of looking after themselves after they were landed, and could not be dislodged by German air action'.

---

[1] Chiefs of Staff Committee No. 34, Minutes of Meeting: Cabinet papers, 79/3.

The War Cabinet of February 19 gave Churchill the authority 'to make all the preparations' to lay a minefield in Norwegian territorial waters so that, if the mining were subsequently approved, 'there would be no delay in carrying out the operation'.[1] Following this decision, Churchill instructed Pound and Phillips that all preparations should be made 'as soon as possible'. The operation being 'minor and innocent', he added, 'it may be called "Wilfred".'[2]

That same day the Joint Planning Staffs reported to the Chiefs of Staff Committee that troops would be ready to leave for Stavanger, Bergen and Trondheim in six days time, on February 26. But Ironside expressed his concern that sending 'these small forces' to Norwegian ports 'some considerable time before the main operation was due to begin, might not be a wise thing to do'. It would give the Germans 'a long start' in which to prepare counter measures.[3]

Churchill shared Ironside's apprehensions, and at the War Cabinet on February 22 he insisted that it would be 'a grave error' to authorize a military landing in Norway 'in the face of opposition', merely 'as a mark of displeasure' at Norway's attitude over the *Altmark*. 'Even the firing of a few shots between British and Norwegian forces,' he said, 'would be a most unfortunate affair.' The course of action which he favoured, however, the laying of a minefield in Norwegian waters, 'could almost certainly be accomplished without any kind of collision with Norwegian forces'. Indeed, Churchill added, as there were several different places where a minefield could be laid, if Norwegian warships happened to be present at one of them 'it would be an easy matter for our mine-laying vessels to remove their operations elsewhere', and thus avoid even a naval confrontation.[4]

At the War Cabinet on February 23 Halifax spoke of the legal and foreign aspects of the mining of Norwegian territorial waters. As a result of Germany's effort 'to stop all sea-borne trade of any sort which might in any way be of advantage to us', Britain could not feel herself bound to keep 'all the rules of war'. Nor could Hitler be allowed to have what Halifax called 'the double advantage of disregarding those

[1] War Cabinet No. 46 of 1940, 19 February 1940, 11.30 a.m., Minute 9, Confidential Annex: Cabinet papers, 65/11.

[2] 'Secret', Minute No. 216, 20 February 1940: Churchill papers, 19/6. Wilfred was the smallest of three characters, Pip, Squeak and Wilfred, in a strip cartoon then being published daily in the *Daily Mirror*.

[3] Chiefs of Staff Committee No. 36 of 1940, 20 February 1940, 10.30 a.m., Confidential Annex: Cabinet papers, 79/85.

[4] War Cabinet No. 49 of 1940, 22 February 1940, 10.30 a.m., Minute 6, Confidential Annex: Cabinet papers, 65/11.

rules which suited him, while sheltering behind the strict observance of the rules by us'.

Halifax warned however that in the United States, Lord Lothian had reported that the proposed action against Norway might be regarded 'as bullying a small neutral'. It would be 'resented', Lothian reported, and it would strengthen 'the growing sentiment for maintaining American neutral rights against us'. Halifax himself concluded that if Britain took 'further belligerent action in Norwegian waters', it was probable that neutral opinion 'would swing against us'.

Churchill, speaking next, pointed out that no one could make an accurate statement of 'all the pros and cons' in advance. It might more be a question 'of following an instinct'. He 'pleaded earnestly', the minutes recorded, 'for action to be taken immediately'. Such action, he said 'would be more than a naval foray: it might well prove the main fulcrum on which the whole course of the war would turn'.

Summing up, Chamberlain said that 'his instincts were in favour of taking action'. But he then spoke of his concern that 'we might lose the support of the world' by a move against a neutral. In any case, he said, 'it would be necessary to make quite certain that the Dominions were with us'. It would also be necessary to consult the Leaders of the Opposition in Britain. Churchill agreed with all this, but 'besought' the War Cabinet not to withhold their agreement to the plan. He was convinced, he said, 'that in the present situation of the war as a whole, if we did not make a move, we should regret it'.[1]

Churchill's words betrayed his unease at the continuing hesitations and lack of urgency. It was a feeling which increased six days later when, at the War Cabinet of February 29, Chamberlain reported that whereas the Leader of the Liberal Party, Sir Archibald Sinclair, had expressed himself 'in favour' of taking action in Norwegian territorial waters, the two most senior Labour politicians, Clement Attlee and Arthur Greenwood, had taken the view that Britain 'would not be justified in taking action which would injure a third party'. To lay a minefield in Norwegian waters would, they said, 'expose that country to attacks by Germany'. In addition, Attlee had doubted whether Britain would gain by the proposed action 'any advantage sufficient to outweigh the moral disadvantages that we should incur'.

Chamberlain also reported on the reaction of the Dominion Governments, who were, he said, 'not, on the whole, in favour of the project'. He himself, while still in favour of 'taking the initiative whenever a

[1] War Cabinet No. 50 of 1940, 23 February 1940, 3.30 p.m.: Cabinet papers, 65/5.

good opportunity occurred', was 'not at all convinced' that the measures proposed would be 'opportune at the present moment'. German brutality, Chamberlain pointed out, 'would no doubt continue', giving Britain 'other opportunities' for putting the plan into operation. But for the present he believed it would be 'advisable' to postpone it. One consideration which weighed with Chamberlain was, he said, that the United States 'would regard the laying of a minefield in neutral territorial waters as an attack on neutral rights which might later prejudice their own interests'. Churchill argued that the mining operation was 'justified', and that it could 'do more to hasten the defeat of Germany than any other single measure within our power at the present time'. It would, he added, have been even more effective 'if it had been carried out three months ago', as he had proposed originally. Personally, he greatly regretted Chamberlain's decision. But the 'principal burden of the conduct of the war' fell on Chamberlain's shoulders, and there could be no question of embarking on the operation against the Prime Minister's 'better judgement'.

Everyone in the War Cabinet, Churchill said, was 'equally anxious to strike a blow at Germany'. But he went on to say, in recognition of Chamberlain's position, that it was better not to act 'when one was in grave doubt as to the consequences of one's act'. Churchill's own fear was that Britain's northern policy 'was now petering out', and he went on to tell his colleagues:

We were now enjoying an interlude of quiescence, but that interlude would not necessarily be prolonged by virtue of the decision which was being taken that morning.

His belief was that it was dangerous to give Germany an opportunity of quietly preparing and perfecting plans for large-scale operations. The carrying through of our Northern policy would not necessarily have compelled Germany to abandon any big offensive which she might be contemplating. On the other hand, it was always possible that our action might have put Germany's preparations out of joint to such an extent as to upset her plans.

Chamberlain thanked Churchill for his 'very generous reference' to his position as Prime Minister; knowing Churchill's own strong views, he said, 'he appreciated his attitude all the more'.[1]

In spite of all the hesitations and debate, Force 'Stratford', the troops selected to occupy Bergen, Trondheim and Stavanger, had, as instructed by the War Cabinet on February 7, been fully mobilized 'and ready to move' since midnight on February 25. All store ships

[1] War Cabinet No. 55 of 1940, 29 February 1940, 11.30 a.m.: Cabinet papers, 65/5.

were ready to be loaded on March 1. A portable runway had been ordered for use at Bodö, and a mobile hydrogen plant had been bought from the French for possible use for the Trondheim balloon barrage. Anti-torpedo baffles were being provided for Narvik, and anti-submarine trawlers for Trondheim and Namsos. To confuse the Germans, 'cover' plans were being developed for a supposed landing in the Middle East.[1]

A blow to all these plans came on March 1 when the Finnish Minister in London told Halifax that help for Finland, the object of the Supreme War Council's plan on February 5, and of 'Stratford', would come 'too late'. At the same time, the Finnish Government had 'professed themselves somewhat disappointed', Halifax told the War Cabinet, as to the extent of the Anglo-French assistance proposed. The Finns now wanted a force of 50,000 fighting men, as well as a hundred bombers. In addition to this, Pound told the War Cabinet, an extra 20,000 men would be needed to hold the lines of communication. Even 'mild' opposition from Swedish forces, warned Newall, would make it 'impossible for our forces to reach Finland in time', or to reach the Gällivare ore fields 'before a German force could get there'.

For Churchill, the over-riding fear was the possibility that by the end of April, 'when the ice broke, Germany might send forces up the Gulf of Bothnia. Finland could then be taken in the rear and over-whelmed, and Germany, in collusion with Russia, could entirely cut us out of Northern Scandinavia'. This, Churchill said, 'would be a heavy reverse for us'.

It was Halifax who now proposed four different possible courses. The first was an ultimatum to Norway and Sweden to say that if British troops were not given permission to cross their countries, 'we should force our way through'. The second was a 'strong request' for passage across Scandinavia backed up 'by arriving off Narvik with the expedition'. The third course was to send through strong forces of unarmed volunteers to be followed 'at a short interval' by arms and munitions. The fourth and final course was that, if Allied troops were not allowed to pass through Scandinavia, the Allies should send Finland the war material that these troops 'would have used'.

Churchill, who spoke immediately after Halifax, said that he favoured the second course, the strong request for passage across Scan-

[1] 'Aide Memoire', 'Most Secret', 'Progress Report – Week Ending Wednesday, 28th February, 1940': Cabinet papers, 65/11, folios 320–2.

dinavia, backed up by the actual arrival off Narvik of the Allied expedition. This course, Churchill said, had 'been suggested by General Smuts'. Churchill went on to tell the War Cabinet: 'we should arrive off Narvik with our force and demand passage. In that event he did not think the Norwegians would fire on our troops. It was possible, of course, that when our expedition arrived off Narvik, the Norwegians would adopt so strong and menacing an attitude that we should have to return without landing.'

Churchill would not, however, regard this 'as too humiliating a rebuff'. It would make it clear, he said, 'that we were determined on caution, that we had done all we could, had behaved honourably, and had only withdrawn because to force a passage would involve the risk of serious hostilities with the Norwegians'.

'At the same time,' Churchill told his colleagues, 'he would not entirely exclude, at this stage, the use of some force in order to make our way through.'

It was Newall who then warned that if an 'opposed landing' were contemplated, it would be necessary to 're-organize' the expedition. Even if there were 'relatively mild opposition' from the Swedes, 'it would be impossible for our forces to reach Finland in time to render effective help', or even to reach the Gällivare ore fields 'before a German force could get there'.

The War Cabinet made no decision on which military plan it preferred. It did however decide to inform the Swedish and Norwegian Governments that preparations were being made for the despatch of an Allied force to Finland 'through Norway and Sweden', and seeking their 'active co-operation essential for the success of the scheme'.

If this cooperation involved Norway and Sweden in 'hostilities with Germany' then the Allied Governments, the War Cabinet decided, 'were willing to afford extensive military assistance to Norway and Sweden, and were actively preparing to do so'.[1]

Such was the decision, and the message to Norway and Sweden. But in reply three days later the Swedish Government warned Britain that Sweden was 'emphatically opposed to the whole proposition'. In the face of this opposition from Sweden, and given Finland's demands for greater help, the Chiefs of Staff concluded on March 4 that any Scandinavian operation to help Finland had now become 'impracticable'.[2]

---

[1] War Cabinet No. 56 of 1940, 1 March 1940, 11.30 a.m., Minute 1, Confidential Annex: Cabinet papers, 65/12.
[2] Chiefs of Staff Committee No. 44 of 1940, 4 March 1940, Minute 4, Confidential Annex: Cabinet papers, 79/85.

Churchill was relieved. The Finnish war, he told the War Cabinet on March 5, could not be regarded as a profitable diversion, since German forces were not engaged', and he 'deprecated' sending further aircraft to Finland, since the British would thereby 'weaken ourselves against Germany'.[1]

On March 6 Churchill left London for a visit to the Fleet, sailing on March 7 from the Clyde to Scapa Flow. While he was with the Fleet, the War Cabinet continued to discuss the problem of aid to Finland, now that Sweden had refused to cooperate. 'The Norwegians,' Churchill had instructed Pound in a note for use in Cabinet, 'and later the Swedes, ought to be put to the proof. We should not be turned from our purpose in going to the aid of Finland by mere protests extorted by German intimidation.' Having got Narvik, Churchill added, 'we have got our foot in the door'.[2]

At the War Cabinet on March 8, in Churchill's absence, Chamberlain suggested offering to send the Finns fifty British bombers, in return for a definite Finnish appeal for help. Such an appeal was needed, Chamberlain explained, to justify the despatch of an expeditionary force to Scandinavia, despite Swedish opposition. Chatfield suggested sending 'test' forces to the Norwegian ports, 'and, if they were successful in getting ashore, the remainder of the expedition could follow after them'.

Pound then told the War Cabinet that Churchill 'was very anxious that the idea of securing the Gällivare ore fields should not be given up, unless and until we encountered actual resistance from the Scandinavians'. Failure to give effective help to Finland would certainly lose Britain 'prestige', Churchill believed, 'but this loss would be much less if our expedition had actually arrived off Narvik and then turned back owing to Scandinavian resistance'.

Churchill added, in Pound's words on his behalf: 'It would be a mistake to cancel the expedition altogether merely because the Swedes *said* they would not co-operate. The arrival of the expedition might change the atmosphere altogether, and we might find that the Scandinavian peoples were, after all, prepared to co-operate, despite what their Governments had said.'

[1] War Cabinet No. 60 of 1940, 5 March 1940, 11.30 a.m.: Cabinet papers, 65/6.
[2] Note dated 6 March 1940: Admiralty papers, 116/4471.

On the morning of March 11 Chamberlain told the War Cabinet that a Finnish delegation in Moscow was faced 'with very stiff terms by the Soviets'. A public announcement, he said, was 'urgently required to give Finland some moral support'. Newall reported that the first eight British aircraft were ready to leave, and Chamberlain thought they should be sent to Finland 'at the earliest possible moment'. As for the Scandinavian expedition, Chamberlain said, 'it would be fatal' to abandon it. It would be said that Britain 'had never meant business at all and that our offer of assistance had been a sham'.

Churchill, who had travelled back from Scotland overnight, reiterated his view that the Norwegians would not oppose a Narvik landing by any 'vigorous' show of arms. 'Once ashore,' he said, 'we should have secured a valuable prize not only of about a million and a half tons of iron ore but also in our occupation of the harbour which would be of the greatest use for naval purposes.' Even if the railway to Gällivare had been sabotaged, 'ultimately we might persuade the Scandinavians to give us railway facilities for a further advance'.[1]

At a special meeting that same afternoon, the Chiefs of Staff concluded that it was 'most desirable to obtain a foothold at Trondheim as well as at Narvik'. In addition, a landing at Stavanger 'was most important', in order to deny the Germans the use of the airport. A simultaneous landing at Bergen would also be of advantage, they said, 'in tending to confuse the enemy', as well as depriving him of a base for his minesweepers.

The Chiefs of Staff were supported in their conclusion by Admiral Evans, who, on being asked for his opinion on the basis of 'his knowledge of the Norwegian people', stated that the British troops 'would not meet with active opposition at any of the Norwegian ports'.[2]

Thus the Chiefs of Staff, despite their decision of a week earlier that the Bergen, Stavanger and Trondheim decisions were 'impracticable' to help Finland, now supported action designed to obtain a 'foothold' on the Norwegian coast, and approved both the 'Stratford' plan to seize Trondheim, Stavanger and Bergen, and the 'Wilfred' attack at Narvik.

It was not only at Narvik that Churchill wished to see action initiated. On March 6 he had brought before the War Cabinet the plan to float mines down the river Rhine. He was 'now ready to begin

[1] War Cabinet No. 65 of 1940, 11 March 1940, 11.30 a.m., Minute 6, Confidential Annex: Cabinet papers, 65/12.
[2] Chiefs of Staff Committee No. 51 of 1940, 11 March 1940, 3 p.m., Confidential Annex: Cabinet papers, 79/85. Evans, the author of *South with Scott*, and Scott's successor on the British Antarctic Expedition in 1913, was a Commander of the Order of St Olaf of Norway.

operations with the river mine', he said, and proposed beginning the operation in six days time.

The War Cabinet gave its 'general approval' to the scheme and its timetable, the Minutes noting that it was to go ahead 'as a method of retaliation for German methods of sea warfare'.[1] The French Government gave it approval two days later. Meanwhile, Churchill had already sent the Fifth Sea Lord, Admiral Royle, instructions to travel to France to supervise 'the execution and launching of this enterprise'. To General Gamelin, Churchill wrote that same day to emphasize 'that this operation, as we conceive it, is not a temporary or occasional blow, but is designed to be a permanent feature of the war, to be applied and extended by every means and with many variations and novelties unfolding . . .' The mines would be supplied by the Admiralty 'so as to provide an unceasing flow'.[2]

Such were Churchill's hopes; but on March 8, while he had been on his way to Scapa Flow, Churchill had received a personal wireless message from Admiral Royle, reporting that Gamelin, while 'agreeing in principle' to the proposed operation, was doubtful whether the French were prepared 'for possible reprisals' and whether it should not be delayed until it could be combined 'with some other unspecified operation'. Gamelin was to hold a meeting of the Chiefs of Staff of the French Armies that Sunday, March 10, which Royle would attend, and the matter would be considered by the French Cabinet on Monday, March 11, 'Royle considerably disappointed', Pound reported, 'at Gamelin's attitude but hopes with Darlan's support to gain adherence to our programme'.[3]

Churchill had returned to London from Scotland on the morning of March 11. That same afternoon, while the Chiefs of Staff were discussing plans to land at Trondheim, Bergen and Stavanger, Churchill flew to Paris, hoping by a direct intervention with Gamelin to revive the plan on which so much time and effort had been spent, and in which so many hopes reposed: Royal Marine.

As soon as he reached Paris, Churchill drove to see Gamelin, who told him that he 'had strongly supported the execution of this operation', but that the Council had asked 'for more time'. Churchill then dined with Daladier, and asked the reason for this delay. Daladier said that he himself had been 'fully prepared to support the immediate launching of the operation', as had 'all who were present' at the Coun-

---

[1] War Cabinet No. 61 of 1940, 6 March 1940, 11.30 a.m.: Cabinet papers, 65/12.

[2] Letter of 6 March 1940: Admiralty papers, 116/4239.

[3] Naval Message 43912, 121 H, sent 2.20 a.m., received 6.10 a.m.: Admiralty papers, 116/4239.

cil meeting, with the sole exception of the French Air Minister, Guy la Chambre, 'who had made a special case for a postponement of three weeks', as he feared German reprisals on some 300 French aircraft assembled at Villacoublay. When Churchill pointed out that 'it should not take three weeks to remove these aircraft', Daladier promised to 'look into the matter' as Churchill reported on the following day to the War Cabinet.[1]

Writing after the war, in his memoirs, Churchill recalled:

In all their wars and troubles in my lifetime I have been bound up with the French, and I believed that they would do as much for me as for any other foreigner alive. But in this phase of the Twilight War I could not move them. When I pressed very hard they used a method of refusal which I never met before or since. M. Daladier told me with an air of exceptional formality that 'The President of the Republic himself had intervened, and that no aggressive action must be taken which might only draw reprisals upon France'.

This idea of not irritating the enemy did not commend itself to me. Hitler had done his best to strangle our commerce by the indiscriminate mining of our harbours. We had beaten him by defensive means alone. Good, decent, civilised people, it appeared, must never themselves strike till after they have been struck dead.

Churchill's reflection continued:

In these days the fearful German volcano and all its subterranean fires drew near to their explosion-point. There were still months of pretended war. On the one side endless discussions about trivial points, no decisions taken, or if taken rescinded, and the rule 'Don't be unkind to the enemy; you will only make him angry.' On the other, doom preparing—a vast machine grinding forward ready to break upon us![2]

Churchill flew back to London on the morning of March 12. Later that same morning the Scandinavian expedition was taken another stage forward when the Chiefs of Staff informed the War Cabinet that Admiral Evans had been selected as the Naval Commander, and Major-General Mackesy as the Military Commander. Churchill was worried about the Chiefs of Staff decision of the previous afternoon to attack Bergen and Stavanger, and 'deprecated' both these expeditions. To attack Bergen and Stavanger, as well as Narvik and Trondheim, he argued, 'would savour too much of a general attack'. After all, he added, Stavanger and Bergen 'were not on the way to Finland'.

---

[1] War Cabinet No. 66 of 1940, 12 March 1940, 11.30 a.m., Minute 3, Confidential Annex: Cabinet papers, 65/12.

[2] Winston S. Churchill, *The Second World War*, volume 1, London 1948, page 454.

Chamberlain commented that there was 'considerable force' in Churchill's argument, whereupon the War Cabinet decided that the forces for Bergen and Stavanger should be held in readiness 'but not despatched'. This decision was made despite Newall's protest that if the Germans were allowed to hold Stavanger, their air forces could operate from it 'against our shipping and the fleet at Scapa'.

The War Cabinet of March 12 gave its authority to an operation which 'should be confined to the landing at Narvik in the first instance'. Once news was received 'of a successful landing' at Narvik, a second force, its departure timed in advance, would land at Trondheim. The forces for Stavanger and Bergen 'should not leave this country until further orders, but should be available to sail at short notice'. It was also agreed that no communication should be made to the Norwegian Government 'as to our intention to land a force at Narvik', until the ships had actually arrived.[1]

On March 13, the day after this British decision to attack Narvik was made, the Finnish Government gave up the unequal struggle against the Soviets, signing a Russo-Finnish Treaty, whereby large tracts of Finnish territory were ceded to the Soviet Union. That night Chamberlain gave a 'stand still' order on Britain's Scandinavian expedition, and on the following morning the War Cabinet discussed what was now to be done.

Churchill wanted to go on with the plan to seize Narvik: 'Our real objective', he said, 'was, of course, to secure possession of the Gällivare ore fields, which would certainly shorten the war and save great bloodshed later on.' Up till now, he added, Britain had 'had assistance to Finland as "cover" for such a move on our part, but we had now lost this justification for intervention in Scandinavia'.

Churchill feared that Russia, victorious over Finland, would now be able to threaten British national interests directly by 'making her way through Scandinavia to the Atlantic'. A decision to seize Narvik by force was, he said, 'a very unpleasant one to take, but it had to be balanced against the much worse propect of very costly fighting on the Western Front later on'.

Chamberlain opposed Churchill's suggestion. 'If we took such action,' he said, 'we should completely alienate the sympathies of Norway and Sweden at the very moment when they were feeling a sense of relief from the danger of being involved in hostilities.' Now, he believed, might be a good time to send a mission to Norway and

[1] War Cabinet No. 66 of 1940, 12 March 1940, 11.30 a.m., Minute 2, Confidential Annex: Cabinet papers, 65/12. Evans was replaced as naval commander after two days.

Sweden, headed by a member of the War Cabinet, in the hope of 'improving our relations' with those two countries. Later on, 'they might even ask for our support'.

Halifax likewise opposed Churchill's suggestion. Its 'only effect', he told the War Cabinet, 'would be to drive the Norwegians and the Swedes into the arms of the Germans'.

Churchill's desire to continue with the Narvik landing received little support. Simon, Stanley, and Hoare were against it, while Kingsley Wood felt that Norway and Sweden 'might very probably be more impressed with the might of Germany and Russia than with the wish to cultivate good relations with us'. Only Hankey shared Churchill's view that there was a danger of Russian aggression in Scandinavia, and felt that the Norwegians and Swedes 'would do well to concert measures with us for meeting it'.

Towards the end of the meeting, Churchill, desperate to secure a favourable decision, reiterated yet again his arguments in favour of the Narvik landing. 'It was the only hope of securing the iron ore,' he said, 'and of thus shortening the length of the war, and perhaps of obviating the slaughter which would otherwise ensue on the Western Front, which would justify that course.'

Guided by Chamberlain, however, the War Cabinet decided that within a few hours, as soon as it was clear that the Finnish policy of peace with Russia could not be reversed, 'steps should be taken to disperse the forces prepared for the Scandinavian expedition'.[1] Amazed and angered by this decision, Churchill wrote later that same day to Lord Halifax:

My dear Edward,

I feel I ought to let you know that I am vy deeply concerned about the way the war is going. It is not less deadly because it is silent. The days are full of absorbing work: but they cost six millions each. Never was less result seen for money. There is no possibility of any positive project to gain the initiative, and acquire direction of events, getting through the critical and obstructive apparatus which covers up on every side. There never was any chance of giving effective help to Finland; but this hope—or rather illusion—might have been the means of enabling us to get to Gällivare. All has now fallen to the ground; because so cumbrous are our processes that we were too late.

Now the ice will melt; & the Germans are the masters of the North.

Can we suppose they have not been thinking about what to do? Surely they have a plan. We have none. There is no sort of action in view except to wait

---

[1] War Cabinet No. 68 of 1940, 14 March 1940, 11.30 a.m., Minute 4, Confidential Annex: Cabinet papers, 65/12.

on events. These I fear are taking an increasingly adverse turn. In spite of all their brutality the Germans are making more headway with the neutrals than we with all our scruples. The Air Force is not catching up. The Army causes me much anxiety. The money-drain is grievous. There is no effective intimacy with the French. Public opinion is far from trustful of the Government. We have never done anything but follow the line of least resistance. That leads only to perdition. Considering the discomfort & sacrifice imposed upon the nation, public men charged with the conduct of the war sh'd live in a continual stress of soul. Faithful discharge of duty is no excuse for Ministers: we have to contrive & compel victory.

Excuse me writing like this—wh I so seldom do—but I am bound to tell you that we have sustained a major disaster in the North; & that this has put the Germans more at their ease than they have ever been. Whether they have some positive plan of their own wh will open upon us, I cannot tell. It w'd seem to me astonishing if they have not.[1]

In his reply on the following day, Halifax told Churchill: 'You have never been willing to recognize what has always seemed to me the hard and inexorable fact that it was not possible for France and ourselves to exercise an influence upon the Eastern Baltic and Baltic countries generally comparable to that of Germany and Russia—*if they were acting together.*'[2]

The tone of Churchill's letter to Halifax derived not only from the failures to reach any clear Scandinavian decision. Churchill was also upset to discover that the instinct for peacemaking was still evident, stimulated by the visit, first to Berlin and then to London, of Roosevelt's emissary, Sumner Welles. On March 13 Halifax had discussed the outlook for a negotiated peace with his Under-Secretary of State, R. A. Butler, who noted in his diary: 'I said I would not exclude a truce if Mussolini, the Pope and Roosevelt would come in, to which Halifax replied: "You are very bold, what a challenging statement, but I agree with you." '[3]

Butler was far from being alone in his hopes for a 'truce'. In a letter to Chamberlain, several leading members of the National Peace Council also took the opportunity of Sumner Welles' visit to urge the Government 'to give sympathetic consideration to any proposals for a basis of negotiation which neutral States choose to sponsor'; the signatories included G. D. H. Cole, John Gielgud, George Bernard Shaw and Sybil Thorndike.[4]

[1] 'Private & Personal', 14 March 1940: Foreign Office papers, 800/328, folios 424–6.
[2] 'Private', 15 March 1940: Foreign Office papers, 800/328, folios 428–9.
[3] Butler diary, 13 March 1940: Butler of Saffron Walden papers.
[4] Premier papers, 4/25/2, folios 106–7.

At the War Cabinet on March 13 Chamberlain had explained that Sumner Welles, having visited both Berlin and London, intended to tell Roosevelt that any peace proposals, to be successful, must be such as to give 'the necessary sense of security to the Allies', while at the same time not requiring 'the elimination of Herr Hitler'. This sense of security, Welles believed, would be obtained 'by general disarmament'. But Chamberlain had told Welles that no such scheme could work. There had, instead, to be 'a complete change of heart in Germany'.

Churchill had also seen Welles, on the previous afternoon, and he too gave the War Cabinet of March 13 an account of their conversation. 'Now that we had entered the war', Churchill had told Welles, 'we must, and should fight it to a finish. If we and the French were to become separated, it would never be possible again to achieve security in Europe.' Churchill had 'taken the line', he told the War Cabinet, 'that our only course now was to fight to a finish, even though this meant putting all to the stake'.[1]

Just how much risk was involved in 'putting all to the stake' had been made clear five days earlier by the Chiefs of Staff, who, in a memorandum for the Military Co-ordination Committee on the shortage of anti-aircraft guns, pointed out that in September 1939 the Ministry of Supply had budgeted for a production of 1,250 light anti-aircraft guns by 1 September 1940. This forecast, they pointed out, 'was later scaled down to 770', but even so, production 'does not seem to be keeping up even to this drastically reduced forecast'.

The Chiefs of Staff also revealed that the British Expeditionary Force in France had only 152 instead of the 352 anti-aircraft guns authorised for its present strength, and that in France the British Advanced Air Striking Force, which should have had 48 light anti-aircraft guns for its protection, had 'none at all'. Out of a further 1,860 anti-aircraft guns authorized for the Air Defence of Great Britain, no more than 108 were deployed, 'all of which' the Chiefs of Staff noted, 'have perforce to be concentrated' around the naval bases and radar stations, leaving air industries 'and other vital points unprotected against the very form of attack which is likely to fall upon them'. It was a 'hard fact', the Chiefs of Staff concluded, that out of the total requirement on 1 March 1940 of well over 3,000 light anti-aircraft guns, only 388 had been issued'.[2]

On March 15, at a meeting of the Military Co-ordination Committee, Churchill also learnt of serious delays in the delivery of heavy

[1] War Cabinet No. 67 of 1940, 13 March 1940, 11.30 a.m.: Cabinet papers, 65/6.
[2] Report signed by Newall, Pound and Ironside, Military Co-ordination Committee Memorandum No. 61 of 1940, 8 March 1940: Cabinet papers, 83/5.

guns. 'It was proving very difficult,' he was told by the Minister of Supply, Leslie Burgin, 'to get skilled labour to work night shifts at Coventry.' In addition, there was a six week 'time lag' between the despatch of a gun from the factory, and its arrival with the Army. There was also a delay in the supply of machine tools. As for the output of aircraft for the previous twelve months, Kingsley Wood reported a German production of 12,000, compared with 9,000 for Britain and 4,900 for France.[1]

Churchill was also disturbed by the postponement of mining the Rhine. After the 'fiasco in Scandinavia', he wrote to Gamelin on March 16, 'and of the sinister lull now prevailing, the effect of our appearing bankrupt in all forms of positive or offensive action may be bad upon the neutrals, and give encouragement to the movements for a patched up peace, which gather round the mission of Mr Sumner Welles'.

The Germans would not be concerned, Churchill added, to find 'a pretext' to attack 'the factories of France and Great Britain'. They would do it 'when it pays them'.[2]

The British now awaited the next German initiative. It came on March 16, when fifteen German aircraft attacked the ships at Scapa Flow. HMS *Norfolk* was hit by a bomb, and three officers were killed. One civilian had been killed by a bomb dropped on land, and five cottages had been damaged. 'There was considerable feeling in the country,' Churchill told the War Cabinet on March 18, 'that while the Germans used bombs we only dropped leaflets.' But as a result of this raid on Scapa Flow, he said, there seemed 'ample justification' for a British attack 'on a military objective such as the island of Sylt, which might cause civilian casualties'.[3] The raid on Sylt was carried out on March 19, when the air base of Hornum and the naval harbour of List were 'heavily bombed for more than six hours', and 'severe damage' reported as a result of the raid.[4]

Anxious to take some initiative in Scandinavia, Churchill now put forward a quite new plan, which would not involve any military landing in Scandinavia, but which might hamper Germany's ore imports by another means. During the War Cabinet of March 18 he reported on this new plan, which was, he said, being examined by the Naval Staff. Its aim was to stop the supply of iron ore to Germany through

---

[1] Military Co-ordination Committee No. 14 of 1940, 15 March 1940, 5 p.m.: Cabinet papers, 83/3.

[2] 'Secret', 16 March 1940: Admiralty papers, 116/4240.

[3] War Cabinet No. 71 of 1940, 18 March 1940, 11.30 a.m.: Cabinet papers, 65/12.

[4] *Daily Telegraph*, 6 April 1940.

Luleå, on the Gulf of Bothnia, once that port became ice free and the Germans could use the security of the Baltic Sea for the transfer of the ore.

This new proposal was to send an aircraft carrier 'up the Norwegian coast', and then for aircraft from the carrier to fly across Norway and Sweden, to launch torpedoes against ships in Luleå harbour, 'and to block it'. This plan, Churchill told the War Cabinet, would be submitted to the Chiefs of Staff as soon as it was ready.

The War Cabinet of March 18 was also told of indications that the Germans might be planning an attack on Holland, and Chamberlain raised the question of whether, if Belgium remained neutral, she would agree to the passage of Allied troops across Belgium, into Holland. 'At present,' Oliver Stanley told his colleagues, no such move was possible, 'since no plan had been prepared for such an operation'. If Holland were attacked, Churchill commented, it was in Britain's interest 'that Belgium should declare war on Germany and should call on us for help'. It was important that the Belgians should know that Britain would 'demand a passage for our troops across Belgian soil', he said, for in that event 'clearly Belgium would not be able to maintain her neutrality at the expense of the Netherlands'.[1]

That same afternoon, at a meeting of the Military Co-ordination Committee, Churchill spoke of the weaknesses of Britain's army in France. The proportion of fighting troops to the total number of men transported to France 'was very low indeed'. Britain had only eight divisions in France, compared with sixteen in February 1915: 'it was therefore all the more necessary that they should be of the very highest quality'. It was essential, also, to press on 'with their military training and education'.

When Stanley explained that within the army there was a shortage of labour, but that he hoped to 'make good the deficiency' by August 1940, Churchill argued that the demand for labour 'should be drastically cut down by reducing the general standard of accommodation and maintenance'. Indeed, Churchill said, 'additional fighting formations' might well be formed out of the 'very large numbers of personnel' employed in the bases and lines of communication. 'He felt very strongly,' Churchill told the Committee, 'that we were working on the wrong lines altogether at present.'[2]

---

[1] War Cabinet No. 71 of 1940, 18 March 1940, 11.30 a.m., Minute 6, Confidential Annex: Cabinet papers, 65/12.

[2] Military Co-ordination Committee No. 15 of 1940, 18 March 1940, 5 p.m.: Cabinet papers, 83/3.

The instinct for the negative was so strong that on March 19 Halifax was able to tell the War Cabinet that whereas the French 'were anxious that action should be taken against the Narvik iron ore traffic', the French arguments for carrying it out at this juncture 'were not convincing', with the result that 'the idea had not been pursued'. It was the 'Royal Marine' operation to float mines down the Rhine that Halifax felt was 'the most promising idea, and likely to have valuable effects'; but here it was the French who were hesitating.[1]

Reflecting on the failure of the Scandinavian plans, Churchill wrote to Lord Cork on March 20: 'If we had had the power in the early days of the war to enter those waters, we might immediately have secured the allegiance of the Scandinavian States, who are now thinking of nothing but a selfish and injurious neutrality.' But plans for such a move, he added, 'would have entailed careful preparation in time of peace, which it did not fall to me to make'. One day, he believed, even the Baltic operation, Plan 'Catherine', 'may play its part, and I am doing everything in my power to nourish it'.[2]

During the third week of March 1940, Paul Reynaud succeeded Edouard Daladier as Prime Minister of France. Churchill had known and admired Reynaud for many years. Together with Georges Mandel, who now became Minister of Colonies, Reynaud had been drawn close to Churchill during Churchill's visits to France during the 'wilderness years', and particularly at the time of Munich. They had met, briefly, during Churchill's recent visit to Paris. 'I rejoice that you are at the helm,' Churchill wrote on March 22, 'and that Mandel is with you, and I look forward to the very closest and most active cooperation between our two Governments'. Churchill's letter continued:

I share, as you know, all the anxieties you expressed to me the other night about the general course of the war, and the need for strenuous and drastic measures; but I little thought when we spoke that events would so soon take a decisive turn for you. We have thought so much alike during the last three or four years that I am most hopeful that the closest understanding will prevail, and that I may contribute to it.

I now send you the letter which I wrote to Gamelin upon the business which brought me to Paris last week, and I beg you to give the project your immediate sympathetic consideration. Both the Prime Minister and Lord Halifax have become very keen upon this operation, and we were all three about to press it strongly upon your predecessor. It seems a great pity to lose this valuable time. I have now upwards of 6,000 mines ready and moving

[1] War Cabinet No. 72 of 1940, 19 March 1940, 11.30 a.m.: Cabinet papers, 65/6.
[2] 'Secret', 20 March 1940: Admiralty papers, 199/1928.

forward in an endless flow,—alas only on land—and of course there is always danger of secrecy being lost when delays occur.

I look forward to an early meeting of the Supreme Council, where I trust concerted action may be arranged between French and English *colleagues*—for that is what we are.

Pray give my kind regards to Mandel, and believe me, with the warmest wishes for your success in which our common safety is deeply involved.[1]

Having urged Reynaud to revive the mining of the Rhine, Churchill prepared an eight point note for Pound on March 23, seeking to revive earlier proposals for action. Britain's 'prime and imperative task', he wrote, was to blockade Germany and to keep the seas open 'for ourselves and our allies', but, he added, 'we must also continually ask ourselves whether as the war unfolds we cannot, without prejudice to our first duty, strike further blows at the enemy'.

To this end, Churchill set out what he described as the two 'supreme strategic operations': the entry and domination of both the Baltic and the Black Seas. 'As a possible extension of the latter,' he wrote, 'the command of the Caspian may come upon the scene.'

If Pound were to support him in regarding the Baltic and Black Seas as 'the two main objectives of Naval strategy', Churchill hoped that their 'view of our task' could be impressed upon all those branches of the Naval Staff concerned with plans, intelligence and operations. Above all, 'Catherine' should be kept up to date, not only for possible use in 1941, but even in 1942. 'The aim of a proportion of vessels equipped for Arctic conditions,' he wrote, 'must be steadily pursued.' If Russia's attitude remained 'aloof and indeterminate', Britain's ability to seize the command of the Baltic, even temporarily, 'would certainly be a mortal blow to Germany'. All should therefore be prepared, so that advantage could be taken of any favourable political situation that might develop: 'Only in this way can we acquire the power to guide the war as we desire.'[2]

The power to direct an active, sustained war policy, was the issue of central importance to the future of Britain's war effort. As the much-discussed, much-postponed, much-changed and now suspended Scandinavian plans awaited new meetings and new decisions, the question of Churchill's personal power had also become a subject of speculation in Whitehall. On March 26 one of Chamberlain's Private Secretaries, John Colville, noted in his diary that there had been some discussion

---

[1] 'Private and Personal', 22 March 1940: Churchill papers, 19/2.

[2] 'Secret and Personal', 23 March 1940, marked by Churchill 'lie in a locked box': Churchill papers, 19/6.

of removing Chatfield, Hankey and Stanley from the Cabinet, and appointing Churchill in Chatfield's place as Minister for Co-ordination of Defence. At the same time, Churchill would remain First Lord.

Such a change would give Churchill at least some of the authority without which, in his view, a coherent war policy could not emerge. But would it be enough? In France, although mining the Rhine was not favoured, Churchill's other, and indeed principal hope, the expedition to Narvik, had now become a French scheme also. The French desire to prosecute the war more vigorously, Colville noted, was supported by Churchill, 'whose policy,' he wrote, 'is one of action for action's sake'.[1]

It was not action for action's sake, however, but the desire for a logical, coherent plan of action, speedily adopted and rigorously pushed ahead, which had made Churchill press for the stopping of iron ore supplies by means of naval action off Narvik, and a possible landing to reach and destroy the railway from Narvik to Gällivare, and the Gällivare ore field installations.

The failure throughout March to reach any decision on this, or on the Supreme War Council's wider plan to send troops across southern Scandinavia in support of Finland, was to prove a costly one; it was also to provide Churchill personally with clear evidence of how unwieldy a machine of war policy was Chamberlain's War Cabinet.

[1] Colville diary, 26 March 1940: Colville papers.

11

Narvik: 'all is moving'

A T three o'clock in the afternoon of 26 March 1940 a telegram
reached London from the British Air Attaché in Stockholm to
the Director of Intelligence at the Air Ministry. The telegram reported,
through a high Swedish source, the news that the Swedish Staff believed
that the Germans were 'concentrating aircraft and shipping for operation which Swedish intelligence consider *might* consist of seizure of
Norwegian aerodromes and ports'.[1]

The Swedish source seemed reliable: a man known in England to
the Directors of both Air and Military Intelligence. The news was
indeed true: Hitler had in fact decided earlier in March to invade
Norway. Had Churchill's original proposal of the previous September
been followed, had even the War Cabinet's decision on March 12 to go
ahead not been reversed two days later, the German invasion would
have been set to begin after British forces had taken control of
northern Norway. As it was, Britain was left once more to respond
to a German initiative; one that would cut off Britain herself from
the Swedish iron ore, and give Germany a dominant position in the
North Sea.

That same day, March 26, Pound gave Churchill a copy of a letter
he had just sent to the Deputy Secretary to the War Cabinet, General
Ismay. The letter informed the War Cabinet that the Chiefs of Staff
were now considering the question 'of stopping the iron ore trade from
Gällivare by certain naval operations'. These operations would
involve 'infringing both Norwegian and Swedish territorial waters'.
Pound had gone on to suggest that 'if we go as far as this we should
simultaneously infringe the neutrality of Eire', by forcibly making use
of Berehaven as a submarine base. Churchill noted in the margin of

[1] Mallet (Stockholm) to Foreign Office, No. 140 DIPP, Limited Distribution, 26 March 1940:
Admiralty papers, 116/4471.

this latter suggestion: 'I deprecate loading Narvik with this just now.'[1]

At the War Cabinet on March 27, before the Air Attaché's telegram had reached London, Churchill had again urged that the Supreme War Council, due to meet in London on the following day, should agree 'to the stoppage of traffic in Norwegian waters'. Already, by operating at the weekend 'on the fringe of the 3-mile limit', the Royal Navy had secured 'an appreciable check to the ore supplies, and the crews of the German ships had shown an extremely nervous state of mind'. He was, however, 'strongly opposed to the French suggestion of occupying Norwegian soil'.[2]

During the late afternoon of March 27, Churchill received at the Admiralty the 'Daily Secret Situation Report' of the Joint Intelligence Sub-Committee, all copies of which were to be 'destroyed as soon as they have been read'.[3] It was from this that he learnt of the report from Sweden that the Germans might be planning an operation against Norway.

The Supreme War Council met at 10 Downing Street at ten in the morning of March 28.[4] Chamberlain opened the discussion by stressing that, 'in order to maintain the courage and determination of their peoples, and also in order to impress neutrals, the Allies should take active measures'. His first proposal was that the plan to float mines down the Rhine 'should be put into operation immediately'. His second proposal was to 'take all possible steps' to prevent Germany from obtaining Swedish iron ore. It would be 'a comparatively simple naval operation', Chamberlain said, 'to block the route, at any particular moment, with a minefield. This would force the oreships into the open sea, where they would be seized by a British naval squadron.'

As well as ore, Germany needed oil to continue the war. Chamberlain told the Supreme War Council of the possibility of striking at the sources of German oil supply in Russia. A successful attack on the Baku oilfields, he said, 'would have the double advantage of paralysing Russia's economic structure and effectively preventing her from carrying out military operations outside her own territory, but also of denying Germany supplies of oil of which she was very much in need'. The

[1] Letter of 26 March 1940: Admiralty papers, 116/4471. To ensure Churchill saw this paper quickly, it had been marked 'Top of Box'.

[2] War Cabinet No. 76 of 1940, 27 March 1940, 11 a.m.: Cabinet papers, 65/6.

[3] Joint Intelligence Sub-Committee, Daily Secret Situation Report, 27 March 1940, 3 p.m.: Admiralty papers, 116/4471.

[4] The Council members present were (for Britain) Chamberlain, Halifax, Churchill, Stanley and Kingsley Wood; (for France) Reynaud (President of the Council), Campinchi (Minister of Marine) and Laurent-Eynac (Minister of Air). The senior British officials present were Newall, Pound, Ironside and Sir Alexander Cadogan.

attack on Baku, he said, could be made either through Iraq and Syria, or through Iran.

Chamberlain had at last argued in favour of the policy—the mining of Norwegian waters—which Churchill had been advocating for so many months. 'I listened to this powerful argument with increasing pleasure,' Churchill later wrote. 'I had not realised how fully Mr Chamberlain and I were agreed.'[1] At the end of the meeting, Reynaud had also been convinced.

It was therefore agreed that minefields were to be laid in Norwegian territorial waters on April 5. Mines were also to be launched into the Rhine on April 4, and dropped into the canals of Germany by air on April 15. In addition, if Germany invaded Belgium, the Allies would move in 'without waiting for a formal invitation to do so', while if Germany invaded Holland, and Belgium did not go to her assistance, the Allies would 'regard themselves as entitled' to enter Belgium for the purpose of helping Holland.

The mood of the meeting had been one of defiance and optimism. As a sign of their unity of purpose, the two Governments agreed that 'they will neither negotiate nor conclude an armistice or treaty of peace except by mutual agreement'; and this decision was made public in their press communiqué.[2]

Immediately after the Supreme War Council meeting, Phillips sent Churchill a note to say that the information about German plans against Norway in the Daily Secret Situation Report was borne out by a second report which had just reached the Admiralty. Phillips saw the news as 'a last opportunity' for Britain 'to try to get to the Swedish orefields via Narvik before the ice breaks up'. If such an opportunity did occur, he wrote, 'I feel that it would be absolutely vital to seize it immediately and to improvise the expedition with what we could make available in the time taken to load the ships and to send them off at once.'

Phillips wanted no considerations of 'proper organisation and pre-paration' to stand in the way of a Narvik operation. The expedition, 'starting at this late hour', would, he wrote, 'be a gambler's bid for a really vital stake which, if successful, might lead to the end of the war within a measureable period.'[3]

Churchill took Phillips' note with him to the War Cabinet on March 29, when Chamberlain confirmed that minelaying in the Rhine would begin on the evening of April 4, and the laying of mines in Norwegian

---

[1] Winston S. Churchill, *The Second World War*, volume 1, London 1948, page 456.
[2] Supreme War Council No. 6 of 1939–40, 28 March 1940, 10 a.m.: Cabinet papers, 99/3.
[3] Note of 28 March 1940: Admiralty papers, 116/4471.

territorial waters on the following day, April 5. It had also been agreed, Chamberlain reported, that plans were to be prepared by the British and French Staffs 'for interrupting traffic from Luleå as soon as the Gulf of Bothnia became ice-free'.

After outlining the actual minelaying plans, whereby each of the three proposed minefields would extend for six miles from the Norwegian shore and be laid 'in a period of half an hour', Churchill drew his colleagues' attention to the possibility that the minelaying operation 'might lead the Germans to take forcible action against Norwegian territory, and so give us an opportunity for landing forces on Norwegian soil with the consent of the Norwegian Government'. He made no reference to the secret information about existing German plans to seize Norwegian aerodromes and ports, the news of which had reached London three days before. But, drawing on Phillips' note, he did stress that 'we should continue in a state of readiness to despatch a light force to Narvik', and possibly also the force that had been planned for Stavanger.

No forces were available for any larger scale operation, however, the War Cabinet of March 14 having cancelled all earlier plans for the four-port landing. Indeed, at the meeting of March 29 Stanley said that it was 'now out of the question' to send the two divisions previously prepared 'for the main Scandinavian expedition'. All that was 'still available' was the brigade which had been intended for Narvik, and the force for Stavanger.[1]

There was now general agreement that the Supreme War Council's decision to mine Norwegian territorial waters would lead to a military landing. Three quarters of an hour earlier, at the Chiefs of Staff Committee, the Director of Plans at the War Office, Brigadier Playfair, had described it as 'clearly necessary' to take the opportunity 'to be prepared to seize the Norwegian ports, and even to take advantage of any opportunity which might occur to get to Gällivare'. There could, however, he added, be 'no question of landing in Norwegian ports' unless the Germans made some move 'which turned Norway into a theatre of operations'.

The Chiefs of Staff Committee were also agreed that it would be 'only prudent' to hold Bergen and Trondheim 'in sufficient force to secure them as bridgeheads for possible extended operations in Scandinavia'. The troops assembled for these landings had, however, been dispersed after the War Council of March 14. Now, the Chiefs of Staff

[1] War Cabinet No. 77 of 1940, 29 March 1940, 11.30 a.m., Minute 2, Confidential Annex: Cabinet papers, 65/12.

noted, 'there was at least a possibility that it might be necessary to reconstitute a force of this character'.[1]

At the War Cabinet that morning, this conclusion had been upheld. A military expedition had become a matter, not of principle, but of timing. It was at this moment of decision that Churchill made a further broadcast, his fifth in five months. 'It seems rather hard,' he said, 'when spring is caressing the land, and when, after the rigours of winter, our fields and woodlands are reviving, that all our thoughts must be turned and bent upon sterner war.' The past six months of preparation had been an 'invaluable help' to the Allies, with Britain and France 'now joined together in an indissoluble union, so that their full purposes may be accomplished'.

Up to the present, Churchill warned, time had been on Britain's side: 'but time is a changeable ally. He may be with you in one period and against you in another, and then if you come through that other, he may return again more faithful than before'. There was, Churchill felt, 'an intensification of the struggle' to be expected, 'and we are certainly by no means inclined to shrink from it'.

Churchill was often asked, he said, 'will the war be long or short?', and he answered:

It might have been a very short war—perhaps indeed there might have been no war—if all the neutral States who share our convictions upon fundamental matters, and who openly or secretly sympathize with us, had stood together at one signal and in one line.

We did not count on this, we did not expect it, and therefore we are not disappointed or dismayed. We trust in God and in our own arm uplifted in a cause which we devoutly feel carries with it the larger hopes and harmonies of mankind.

But the fact that many of the smaller States of Europe are terrorized by Nazi violence and brutality into supplying Germany with the materials of modern war—this fact may condemn the whole world to a prolonged ordeal with grievous unmeasured consequences in many lands. Therefore I cannot assure you that the war will be short, and still less that it will be easy.

Every day, Churchill continued, the ships of neutral States were being sunk by mine and torpedo, and their crews murdered 'or left to perish', unless rescued by British ships. 'Swedes, Norwegians, Danes, and even Italians, and many more I could mention, have been the victims of Hitler's murderous rage'. Yet these neutral States, he said, were being forced to supply Hitler's régime 'with the means of future aggression'.

[1] Chiefs of Staff Committee No. 60 of 1940, 29 March 1940, 10.45 a.m., Confidential Annex: Cabinet papers, 79/85.

The 'outrages upon the sea, which are so clearly visible', paled, Churchill declared, before Germany's 'villainous deeds' against the Czechs, the Austrians and above all the Poles, whose people had become 'an incoherent multitude of tortured and starving men, women and children, ground beneath the heel of two rival forms of withering and blasting tyranny'. He had, he said, recently inspected the crew of a Polish destroyer: 'I have rarely seen a finer body of men. I was stirred by their discipline and bearing. Yet how tragic was their plight! Their ship was afloat, but their country had foundered.'

Although the fate of Poland stared people in the face, Churchill commented, there were still 'thoughtless dilettanti or purblind world-lings who sometimes ask us: "What is it that Britain and France are fighting for?" To this I answer: "If we left off fighting you would soon find out." '

More than a million German soldiers, Churchill told his listeners, were 'drawn up ready to attack, at few hours' notice', all along the frontiers of Luxembourg, Belgium and Holland. At any moment these three neutral countries 'may be subjected to an avalanche of steel and fire'. Could anyone wonder that Britain and France were determined 'to bring such a hideous state of alarm and menace to an end, and to bring it to an end as soon as may be, and to bring it to an end once and for all?'[1]

As Churchill spoke, the Admiralty were busy with their plans to mine Norwegian territorial waters, and to float mines down the Rhine. On March 31 Churchill informed Admiral Royle that he would take the clock mechanism of the Rhine mine to show to the War Cabinet on the following day, telling Royle: 'it is a very nice piece of work'.[2] But that same morning a wireless message from the British Ambassador in Paris, Sir Ronald Campbell, warned that the French War Commit-tee had 'decided yesterday evening' against the 'Royal Marine' operation.[3] This was indeed so; later that day Corbin, the French Ambassador to London, reported to Chamberlain that the French Government had decided to postpone the operation for three months. 'The ground was fear of reprisals,' Chamberlain noted, 'and the objec-tion came from Monsieur Daladier.'

Angered by this decision, Chamberlain told Corbin: 'No mines—no Narvik,' to which Corbin replied that 'if both were abandoned we should be doing exactly nothing'.[4]

[1] Broadcast of 30 March 1940: Churchill papers, 9/144.
[2] Minute No. 270, 31 March 1940: Churchill papers, 19/6.
[3] Campbell to Foreign Office, No. 83 DIPP, 'Most Immediate', received on 31 March 1940, 10.53 a.m.: Admiralty papers, 116/4240.
[4] 'Most Secret', 'Note by the Prime Minister', 31 March 1940: Admiralty papers, 116/4240.

Thus, to Churchill's astonishment, only four days before both operations were to begin, Narvik was precipitately postponed and the mining of the Rhine put at risk. As Cadogan wrote to Halifax later that day, 'Royal Marine' and 'Wilfred' had been designed to proceed together so that any ' "moral" loss' incurred by the Norwegian operation could be faced by showing at the same time 'that we were hitting hard at *Germany*'. It was in this setting, Cadogan added, that the British had been prepared 'to carry out the "Wilfred" operation'; but if 'Royal Marine' now disappeared, 'we are back where we were before the Supreme War Council meeting'.[1]

Before this new crisis could be resolved, Neville Chamberlain announced certain Cabinet changes, with Hoare becoming Secretary of State for Air, and Chatfield resigning as Minister for the Co-ordination of Defence. Anthony Eden, who remained at the Dominions Office, noted in his diary: 'Winston saddened and disgusted. He has not been consulted, only informed. He much wanted me to go to the Air Ministry....' Churchill told Eden that when Pound learned that Hoare was to go to the Air Ministry, the Admiral 'had been unable to conceal his consternation'.

Eden's view was that Chamberlain had his particular friends, and 'would stick to them as long as he could, and longer than the country wished'. He had only accepted Churchill and Eden 'because he could not avoid it'. Eden noted: 'Winston maintained that there would be more chances, many more, on this rough voyage and sought to hearten himself in this strain, and no doubt me too. But he was worried and depressed....'[2]

To Chamberlain himself, Churchill wrote on April 1: 'It is a very good thing that Sam has come up to the scratch in good form. He has a stiff job and difficult start before him. I will help him in every way possible.' Churchill ended his letter: 'I value highly the confidence which you are showing in me; and will try my best to deserve it.'[3]

Two days earlier, Chamberlain had written to his sister:

Winston, in spite of his violence and impulsiveness, is very responsive to a sympathetic handling. To me personally he is absolutely loyal and I am continually hearing from others of the admiration he expresses for the PM. This week I had an hour's talk alone with him—the best talk with the PM he had

[1] 'Argument Against Postponement of RM Operation', 31 March 1940: Foreign Office papers, 800/312, folio 30.

[2] Eden diary, 1 April 1940, quoted in The Earl of Avon, *The Eden Memoirs, The Reckoning*, London 1965, page 90.

[3] 'Private', 1 April 1940: Churchill papers, 19/2.

ever had, he told a friend—about Cabinet changes and he warmly concurred in what I proposed to do even though I refused both his pet suggestions for taking Archie Sinclair & Max Beaverbrook into the Government. Even he had not suggested Ll G![1]

One important result of the Cabinet changes was an increase in Churchill's own responsibilities. Since the end of October 1939 Chatfield had presided over the War Cabinet's Military Co-ordination Committee. With Chatfield's resignation, Chamberlain asked Churchill, as the senior Service Minister, to preside. This new arrangement, *The Times* commented on April 4, 'will strengthen the organisation of the War Cabinet'.[2] But, as Churchill later recalled, although he was now 'first among equals' with the three other Service Ministers, 'I had however no power to take or enforce decisions. I had to carry with me both the Service Ministers and their professional chiefs. Thus many important and able men had a right and a duty to express their views. . . .'[3]

In France, the news was interpreted as Churchill's promotion 'to the head of a Ministry of National Defence', as the French Minister of Marine, Campinchi, telegraphed on April 4. 'The concentration in your hands of the general control of the armed forces of Britain,' Campinchi added, 'is one more guarantee for our joint victory.'[4] Graciously, Churchill replied: 'I am deeply grateful for your generous message of congratulation on my assumption of new responsibilities,' and he added: 'I derive encouragement from the knowledge that my relations with fellow Ministers in France are those of complete sympathy and understanding.'[5]

Six years later, General Ismay set out, in a private note for Churchill, the result of the new arrangements. 'Mr Churchill,' he wrote, 'took the Chair at meetings of the Military Co-ordination Committee held daily, and sometimes twice a day, from Monday 8th April to Monday 15th April.' The principal topic of all these meetings, Ismay wrote, 'was the campaign in Norway', and he added laconically: 'The above arrangements were not satisfactory.'[6]

Even at the time, it is clear that Churchill shared Ismay's doubts. As

[1] Letter of 30 March 1940: Chamberlain papers.

[2] *The Times*, 4 April 1940.

[3] Winston S. Churchill, *The Second World War*, volume 1, London 1948, page 463. The Minister of Supply, Leslie Burgin, was added to the Committee as its fourth member, to replace the Minister for the Co-ordination of Defence.

[4] Telegram No.088, 4 April 1940, passed by Censor No. 107: Churchill papers, 2/393.

[5] Telegram of 8 April 1940: Churchill papers, 2/393.

[6] 'Higher Defence Organisation, April–May, 1940', note by Ismay enclosed with his letter to Churchill of 30 May 1946: Churchill papers, 4/143.

Sir Edward Bridges was to note only four weeks after the new powers had been conferred on Churchill, he and Ismay had 'several conversations' with Churchill about how the Committee would function, and about Churchill's own 'duties'. On Sunday April 7 there had been 'one such discusion', at which Churchill told Bridges that Chamberlain ought 'on occasion' to take the Chair, especially 'when some very important matter came up for discussion'.

The Military Co-ordination Committee were told of Churchill's doubts, and of his suggestion that Chamberlain might also take the Chair, at their meeting on April 8, the first meeting at which Churchill himself was in the Chair. But no decision was made, and Churchill found himself with a heavier burden of work and of responsibility than at any time since May 1915, for, as Bridges noted, 'while the War Cabinet must retain final responsibility, the Military Co-ordination Committee was a body for pre-digestion of Defence topics'.[1]

At least two of Churchill's friends were sceptical of the meaning of his new responsibilities. Brendan Bracken, who had been at Churchill's side since the outbreak of war, wrote to the Labour MP Josiah Wedgwood on April 9:

I do not altogether share your satisfaction about the new Committee over which Winston presides. This office, if one can use such a word, adds to his responsibilities, but gives him no real powers. The new arrangement may work out all right, but I am rather distrustful.

There is another consideration which has not been properly weighed by Winston or any of his friends. The Admiralty abounds in heavy administrative responsibilities. Winston works from about 7.30 a.m. until 2 a.m. The Chairmanship of this new Committee will certainly take four or five hours of his working day. I think he needs more help, both at the Admiralty and on the new Committee.[2]

Five days earlier, Churchill's friend 'Crinks' Johnstone, a former Liberal MP, had written direct to Churchill: 'I can't help wondering whether it isn't deliberately calculated, as was your original appointment at the Admiralty, so as to load you with work as to make things impossible.' Nevertheless, Johnstone felt, the new position might enable Churchill 'to galvanise Hoare into doing something about aircraft production, poor creature though he is'.[3] From South Africa, one of

---

[1] Note by Sir Edward Bridges, dated 25 April 1940: Premier papers, 1/404, folios 22–5.

[2] Letter of 9 April 1940: Wedgwood papers.

[3] Letter of 4 April 1940: Churchill papers, 2/395. Brendan Bracken wrote direct to Hoare: 'You are taking on a great but very tough job. You and our Neptune ought to find many ways of harrying Hitler. May your combination prosper' (letter of 4 April 1940, Templewood papers).

Churchill's oldest friends, Abe Bailey, wrote: 'You have indeed great responsibility now, you are practically at the top of the tree,' but he added: 'what a terrible job you have Winston. Your helpmates do not strike me as being very good.'[1]

From the Theatre Royal, Bath, where she was pursuing her chosen career as an actress, Churchill's daughter Sarah wrote, on hearing of her father's new task:

Darling Papa

This letter is just to tell you that wherever I go, people rush up to me and shake me by the hand, congratulate me, and smile on me—because of you, and I felt I must pass on some of their wishes and good will to you.

There was such a lovely picture of you on the Newsreel the other day, and the buzz and excitement that swept through the theatre, suddenly made me feel so inordinately proud that I was your daughter, and it suddenly occurred to me that I had never really told you, through shyness and inarticulateness— *how much* I love you, and how much I will try to make this career that I have chosen—with some pain to the people I love, and not a little to myself— worthy of your name—one day—

Your loving Sarah[2]

The news of Churchill's new responsibilities was made public on the evening of April 3. That same night Berlin radio declared that Churchill had been 'elevated from warmonger to grand warmonger'. 'Mr Churchill Becomes Super War Chief', the *Daily Mail* headline read on the following day, while one of the paper's columnists pointed out that Churchill had become 'in effect, Britain's Supreme Defence Minister'. The *Daily Mail*'s leading article saw however, as those inside Whitehall had seen, the essential weakness of Churchill's new position, and the problems of war direction which still remained:

The appointment will be welcomed. But it illustrates again the Government's ineradicable habit of compromise. Mr Chamberlain has not brought himself to appoint Mr Churchill as Defence Minister. As Chairman of the Defence Committee, the First Lord will occupy a commanding position in the councils of the experts, but it leaves him still with the weight of the Admiralty upon his shoulders.

The *Dail Mail* leader continued: 'The demand for a real War Cabinet will grow, and it is bound to be granted if the war drags on.

[1] Letter of 6 April 1940: Churchill papers, 2/392.
[2] Letter of 4 April 1940: Churchill papers, 1/355.

Victory will not come easily if our war effort comes to be directed by a Council of Tired Men.'[1]

On April 2, as the moment of decision drew near for 'Wilfred', Chamberlain expressed his confidence in the course of the war at a speech to the Council of the National Union of the Conservative and Unionist Party. Hitler, he declared, had 'missed the bus'.[2] Chamberlain's audience was not to know that the British plan to mine Norwegian territorial waters was imminent, if still not finally approved, and that, as far as Chamberlain and his colleagues knew, it would when launched catch the Germans unawares, cutting them off from an essential war supply.

In his letter to Chamberlain of April 1, Churchill had suggested that even if the French Government 'do not give way' over mining the Rhine, the sooner the mining of Norwegian territorial waters took place 'the better'. The Admiralty, Churchill pointed out, were still working towards the starting date of April 5, 'but can hold it a few days if desirable, or if weather forces us'.

A decision was needed, Churchill suggested, by April 3 'at latest'. Nor should the mining of the Rhine be abandoned, although it could be postponed from April 4 to the week beginning April 12. 'I might perhaps go over Friday & Sat and try to educate them,' Churchill added. 'I think I might do some good with Daladier.'[3] But when Corbin, the French Ambassador, went to discuss 'Royal Marine' at the Foreign Office on the morning of April 2 he was, as one official, Roger Makins, wrote, 'rather sphinxlike and depressed, and was evidently trying to convey that there was little chance of his Government changing their opinion. . . .'[4]

At the War Cabinet on the morning of April 3 there was ominous news from Norway, when Stanley reported that 'a somewhat garbled account had been received at the War Office' that the Germans had been collecting 'a strong force of troops' at the Baltic port of Rostock, 'with the avowed intention of taking action in Scandinavia, if necessary'. Halifax noted that the most recent telegram from Stockholm 'tended to confirm' the War Office account, as, according to the Swedish Legation in Berlin, substantial numbers of German troops were already on board ship in Stettin and Swinemünde harbours.

[1] *Daily Mail*, 4 April 1940.
[2] *The Times*, 3 April 1940.
[3] 'Private', 1 April 1940: Churchill papers, 19/2.
[4] R. M. Makins to Sir R. Campbell, No. 734, 'Most Secret', 2 April 1940: Admiralty papers, 116/4240.

Speaking after Halifax, Churchill repeated what he had said earlier to Chamberlain, that whatever decision the French might take over mines in the Rhine, 'we should proceed with the laying of mines in Norwegian Territorial Waters'. Neville Chamberlain agreed. 'Matters had now gone too far,' he said, 'for us not to take action,' even if the Rhine operation had to be abandoned because of French opposition.[1] The French would be given one more chance to co-ordinate the two plans. But the War Cabinet agreed that if the Rhine plan was postponed again, the Norwegian mining would go ahead, and with only a three-day delay, on April 8.

On April 4, in one last effort to persuade the French to agree to go ahead with 'Royal Marine', Chamberlain sent a long personal appeal to Daladier, explaining that in view of possible neutral, and above all United States objections to the mining of Norwegian waters, the mining of the Rhine was 'highly desirable as a counterpart'. It would be a direct attack on Germany itself, and it should have 'a considerable effect on German morale, by carrying the war for the first time into their midst and seriously hampering their principal waterway', while at the same time it 'deflects attention in the United States' away from the Norwegian operation, and 'makes it quite clear that we are only acting thus as part of a general and concerted effort to win the war as soon as we could'.

If 'Royal Marine' and 'Wilfred' took place simultaneously, Chamberlain argued, 'attention would be concentrated on the attack on Germany'. If 'Wilfred' alone went ahead, it would be said 'no doubt very unjustly, that there was little or nothing to choose between the morality of the Allies and that of their enemies'.[2]

Chamberlain asked the British Ambassador in Paris, Sir Ronald Campbell, not to deliver his message to Daladier until he had shown it to Reynaud. Rather to Campbell's surprise, Reynaud refused to let Daladier have the message, on the grounds that it would worsen his own relations with Daladier. But Reynaud did have a suggestion of his own, which he put to the Ambassador, and which Campbell at once telephoned to the Foreign Office, 'to the effect that the First Lord of the Admiralty, in his new capacity as Chairman of the War Committee, might pay a visit to Paris and, after seeing M. Reynaud, might call on M. Daladier and do his best to bring the latter round'.[3]

[1] War Cabinet No. 80 of 1940, 3 April 1940, 10.30 a.m., Minute 5, Confidential Annex: Cabinet papers, 65/12.

[2] Foreign Office to Sir R. Campbell, No. 58, 4 April 1940, 3.30 a.m., by telephone, 'Most Immediate': Admiralty papers, 116/4240.

[3] Note from Ralph Skrine Stevenson to Halifax, 4 April 1940: Admiralty papers, 116/4240.

As soon as Halifax saw this message, he showed it to Churchill, who said that he was 'prepared to go to Paris' that same afternoon if necessary.[1] 'I am not quite sure that I like your going over to persuade D,' wrote Chamberlain. 'But perhaps you could find some other reason for the journey and work in RM incidentally.'[2]

Just before leaving for Paris, Churchill sent a message to Sir Horace Wilson, through Eric Seal. 'The First Lord intends,' wrote Seal, 'to preach the gospel, as set forth in the Prime Minister's telegram of last night, as strongly as he can. He cannot however guarantee success; he feels there may be a solid core of opposition in France. He hopes, at least, to establish easy relations with Daladier, and to get on a good footing with him.'[3]

Horace Wilson showed this message to Chamberlain on the evening of April 4. Churchill, meanwhile, had set off early that same evening by air, accompanied by Admiral Royle, Commander Thompson, a secretary, a typist, and his friend General Spears, whose knowledge of internal French politics was formidable, and whose friendship with the leading political and military figures was as deep as Churchill's own. After the war Spears recalled:

We were shaken in our old de Havilland as if we were a salad in a colander manipulated by a particularly energetic cook. Churchill showed me a letter he was taking to Daladier from the Prime Minister in much the same terms as that sent to Reynaud. It was clear and strong on the subject of 'Royal Marine'. There was to be no mining of Norwegian waters unless the French agreed to our floating-mines operation. . . .

I did my best, as we capered and caracoled our windy way over the Channel, to explain how I thought this tricky question should be dealt with. The man in whose hands the decision lay was Daladier. Although Prime Minister, Reynaud was at the moment only a passenger in his own Government. Further, the two men detested each other, and Daladier was determined to exert his utmost power to humiliate Reynaud in every possible way. . . .

The mere fact that Reynaud had agreed to sponsor 'Royal Marine' was enough, apart from Daladier's general objection to anything savouring of bellicosity near the French border, to make Daladier veto it. This was, I thought, the main reason why 'Royal Marine' had been turned down.[4]

On reaching Paris, Churchill dined with Reynaud at the British Embassy. Daladier, who had also been invited, pleaded a previous

[1] Note on Skrine Stevenson minute of 4 April 1940: Admiralty papers, 116/4240.
[2] Letter of 4 April 1940: Admiralty papers, 116/4240.
[3] Letter of 4 April 1940: Premier papers, 1/419.
[4] Major-General Sir Edward Spears, *Assignment to Catastrophe*, volume 1, London 1954, page 97.

engagement, but said that he would see Churchill on the following morning. During the dinner, Reynaud told Churchill that he had spent three hours at the French War Committee trying to overcome Daladier's objections. But he 'could not overrule his Minister of Defence on a point of strategy'.[1]

On the morning of April 5 Churchill saw Daladier, who argued that the French air force needed three more months until it would be ready to meet any possible German reprisal attack as a result of the mining of the Rhine. 'For this,' Churchill later recalled, 'he was prepared to give a firm date in writing. He made a strong case about the defencelessness of French factories. Finally he assured me that the political crisis in France was over, and that he would work in harmony with M. Reynaud. On this we parted.'[2]

Churchill telephoned at once to 10 Downing Street, where the War Cabinet was in session. Halifax was called to the telephone, and learnt from Churchill of Daladier's decision. 'The First Lord,' Halifax reported, 'felt strongly that it would be a very great mistake to force the French to fall in with our wishes.'[3] One of Chamberlain's Private Secretaries noted in his diary: 'Winston went over to Paris to try to convert Daladier to the RM operation and then telephoned in the middle of the Cabinet meeting to say that *he* had been converted by Daladier! The PM commented that it was like the story of the pious parrot, bought to teach good language to the parrot which swore, that ended by learning to swear itself.'[4]

The War Cabinet, having discussed Daladier's insistence on delay, and Churchill's support for the French hesitations, decided to go ahead nevertheless with the mining of Norwegian waters, despite the inability now to link the operation with mining the Rhine. It was also decided that April 8, in four days' time, would remain the starting point. Pound then described the actual process of the proposed minelaying off Narvik, while Phillips gave details of the ships that were being 'held in readiness' should the Germans react by invading Norway, and British troops be needed to counter any German invasion by landings at Narvik, Stavanger, Bergen and Trondheim.[5]

Churchill lunched that day in Paris with General Georges, who had

---

[1] Sir R. Campbell to Lord Halifax, 4 April 1940, sent by telephone, 5 April 1940, 5.45 a.m., 'Most Immediate' No. 88: Admiralty papers: 116/4240.

[2] Winston S. Churchill, *The Second World War*, volume 1, London 1948, page 460.

[3] War Cabinet No. 82 of 1940, 5 April 1940, 11.30 a.m.: Cabinet papers, 65/6.

[4] Colville diary, 5 April 1940: Colville papers.

[5] War Cabinet No. 82 of 1940, 5 April 1940, 11.30 a.m., Minute 6, Confidential Annex: Cabinet papers, 65/12.

hurried back specially from eastern France to see him. Spears, who was present, later recorded how:

We were three friends enjoying each other's company and remarkable food and wine. Georges was tranquil, gay and confident. We discussed the war, but I have no precise memories of what was said, beyond that old ground was gone over. There was speculation as to what the Germans' next move would be; the possibility of their invading Scandinavia (a theatre, it will be remembered, outside Georges' responsibilities) was considered, the difficulties they would encounter were stressed, and Churchill drew vivid pictures of the disorganisation 'Royal Marine' would inflict on such a plan. He spoke of the folly of delaying this operation with such emphasis that I felt sure he had failed with Daladier. I remember his saying we showed a lamentable tendency to miss the bus (*'Nous allons perdre l'omnibus,'* he said). . . .

Georges told us that the Government had decided to send home several of the older classes. This was the equivalent of suppressing some divisions, and he did not disguise the fact that the morale of certain units, particularly of the older men, was not too good, *'pas fameux'*.

Churchill and I drove to the Embassy after lunch. He was so pleased with his talk with Georges that his discomfiture with Daladier was almost forgotten. 'Georges is quite different when you are there,' he said. 'What a splendid type he is!'[1]

Eager to try to reconcile the conflict between Daladier and Reynaud, Churchill had already suggested that he should remain in Paris that night, and dine with both men together. Churchill's suggestion, the Ambassador reported by telephone to Halifax, had been made 'with a view to facilitating a reconciliation between Daladier and Monsieur Reynaud'.[2] The dinner, however, did not take place as Churchill had hoped. Once more, Daladier decided to stay away: indeed, at their meeting that morning he had intimated that he would not come, and Spears later recorded how Churchill was 'shocked at this, said it made him very sad, and added: "What will centuries to come say if we lose this war through lack of understanding?" '[3]

On the morning of April 6 Churchill set off by air from Paris, lunching with Lord Gort at the headquarters of the British Expeditionary Force, and discussing the military situation both with Gort and with the commander of the 1st Army Corps, General Sir John Dill. In a

[1] Major-General Sir Edward Spears, *Assignment to Catastrophe*, volume 1, London 1954, page 99.

[2] Sir R. Campbell to Lord Halifax, sent by telephone, 5 April 1940, 5.45 a.m., 'Most Immediate' No. 88: Admiralty papers, 116/2420.

[3] Major-General Sir Edward Spears, *Assignment to Catastrophe*, volume 1, London 1954, page 100.

letter to Stanley, Gort described Churchill's arrival at his headquarters as 'as gust of the freshest air, brimming over with ideas, information and encouragement, and looking years younger than he had done a few months before'.[1]

From Gort's headquarters Churchill flew north again, reaching London at eleven in the evening. No sooner had he reached his room at the Admiralty than he wrote at once to Chamberlain:

My dear PM,

Here is the answer from Daladier to yr note wh I imparted to him in an informal manner. It is vy long-winded; but they are serious in their alarm about their aviation; & it wd be dangerous to press them against their judgment.

I stopped my Flamingo (air plane) at Gort's HQ for luncheon to-day & was much impressed by all I heard. There are a lot of things which want attending to. I was vy glad to have a long talk with Dill. He put before me some points wh I had not heard of before: but wh wd become vy important if an offensive shd be launched against us in the West.

Perhaps you wld spare me $\frac{1}{2}$ an hour Monday as I wd like to tell you abt my journey etc.

'I am so glad you stuck to Wilfred,' Churchill wrote in a postscript, and he added: 'All is moving.'[2]

The mining of Norwegian waters had indeed begun. On April 5, while Churchill was in Paris, the special naval force had at last left Scapa, and throughout April 6 had continued to steam across the North Sea. But the decision had come too late. The Germans were also on the move; on the night of April 6 Bomber Command reconnaissance aircraft reported 'intense shipping activity and brilliantly lit wharves' at Eckernförde, near Kiel, and at twenty-five minutes to midnight a large German ship, 'possibly a battlecruiser', was sighted twenty miles north of Heligoland.[3] The clash of forces was about to begin.

---

[1] Quoted in J. R. Colville, *Man of Valour: Field-Marshal Lord Gort VC*, London 1972, page 179.
[2] Letter of 6 April 1940, 11 p.m.: Chamberlain papers.
[3] 'Summary of Events': Admiralty papers, 116/4471.

12

Narvik: 'We have been completely outwitted'

THROUGHOUT Sunday 7 April 1940 units of the British Home Fleet steamed eastward across the North Sea, towards the Norwegian coast. Simultaneously, German warships moved northwards along the Danish coast. Shortly after midday, the Admiralty Intelligence Department signalled to the Commander-in-Chief of the Home Fleet, Admiral Forbes:

Recent reports suggest that a German expedition is being prepared. Hitler is reported from Copenhagen to have ordered the unostentatious movement of one division in ten ships by night to land at Narvik with simultaneous occupation of Jutland. Sweden to be left alone. Moderates said to be opposing the plan. Date given for arrival Narvik was 8th April.

'All these reports,' the signal added, 'are of doubtful value and may well be only a further move in the war of nerves.'[1]

This message, with its reassuring comment, was sent to Admiral Forbes with the approval of Phillips.[2] Even as it was being coded for despatch, aircraft of Bomber Command located and attacked 'a force of enemy ships' off Jutland Bank, but according to the pilots' own report, the bombing was 'ineffective'.

That evening Admiral Forbes ordered his ships at Scapa and Rosyth 'to raise steam'. At the same time, an outward bound Norwegian convoy was ordered to reverse its course and all submarines in the North Sea were ordered to intercepting positions. To avoid a possible clash with the German ships steaming northward, however, the British naval force that was to have laid the southern minefield off the Nor-

---

[1] Signal 796, timed at 12.59 p.m., 7 April 1940: Seal papers.
[2] After being sent, it was circulated to Churchill, Pound and other senior officers.

wegian coast was ordered to turn back.[1] The northern minefield force continued, however, on its course.

Churchill had still not given up hope of persuading the French to mine the Rhine, and during April 7, in a letter to Halifax, he urged that the plans for the mining of the Rhine should still go forward. 'It appears urgent,' he wrote, 'to consider the possibility of a German offensive against Holland and Belgium in the April moon which is favourable from the 15th onward.' Such an offensive would at once lead to French approval for the mining scheme, which would serve as an important counter-measure. It was therefore essential, Churchill wrote, to keep the mines ready for action.[2]

In a note for the Military Co-ordination Committee, Churchill set out the French reasons for hesitation, as he had gathered them while in Paris. 'The French declare,' he wrote, 'that their aviation is passing through a crisis. Not only is the dispersion of the factories and materials unachieved, but they expect to be far stronger in a few months and to have a faster fighter than the Germans.' The French, Churchill added 'name July 1' as the new date on which they would be ready to launch 'Royal Marine'.[3] Reynaud, as Churchill told Chamberlain, had offered 'to give this assurance in writing, and Monsieur Daladier independently promised to try even to improve upon it'.[4]

The preparations to mine the Rhine were proceeding at a steady pace. Four thousand mines were ready to be sent to France immediately, with sufficient extra supplies available in England so that once the operation began, as Churchill explained to Pound that same day, 'it may be continued indefinitely'.[5]

When the War Cabinet met on the morning of April 8, Churchill was able to report that off the Norwegian coast, minefields had been laid in the Vest Fiord during the early hours of the morning. 'Wilfred' had begun. But at the same time he had to inform his colleagues that a German naval force 'was undoubtedly making towards Narvik'. The force might well be intercepted, before it reached Narvik, by the British ships which had been laying the minefield. This confrontation, he said, 'might take place very shortly', and he added: 'it was impossible to foretell the risks of war, but such an action should not be on terms unfavourable to us'.

---

[1] 'Summary of Events': Admiralty papers, 116/4471.

[2] 'Secret', 7 April 1940: Foreign Office papers, 800/312, folios 41-3.

[3] Military Co-ordination Committee Memorandum No. 70 of 1940, 7 April 1940: Cabinet papers, 83/5.

[4] Letter of 7 April 1940: Premier papers, 1/419.

[5] 'RM Operation', 7 April 1940: Admiralty papers, 116/4240.

The Admiralty 'judged it desirable', Churchill told the War Cabinet, to do everything they could 'to ensure that the German ships would not be able to return home'. To this end, every possible ship had been ordered out to sea, and the First Cruiser Squadron, which had been taking on troops at Rosyth 'for the possible operation of occupying Norwegian ports', had disembarked both the troops and explosives, and would shortly be sailing eastwards without them.

Even as Churchill was telling his colleagues that the warships were to leave for Norway without troops on board, a signal was sent from the Admiralty to the Commanding Officer of the Force intended for Narvik: '*Aurora* is to proceed with all despatch without troops on board, repeat, without troops on board. . . .'[1]

The naval emergency had eclipsed and negated all plans for an unopposed landing.

The War Cabinet then discussed Hitler's motive in ordering the capture of Narvik. Perhaps, it was argued, this was a 'preparatory measure' to the occupation of Luleå when the ice melted. 'In any case,' the War Cabinet concluded, the whole German operation 'seemed to be a most hazardous venture'.[2]

It was the state of French political disarray which most perturbed the War Cabinet on April 8, when Halifax read out a letter from Sir Ronald Campbell, attributing Daladier's opposition to mining the Rhine to his 'vindictiveness' and pointing out that Daladier was 'determined to embarrass M. Reynaud in every possible way'. Indeed, he had gone so far as to describe the proposed operation, once Reynaud had agreed to it, as 'dangerous to France'. It must be remembered, Campbell added, 'that M. Daladier was a peasant, and that he had all the bad, as well as all the good qualities of the class from which he had sprung'.[3]

Distressed by the conflict between Reynaud and Daladier, and the postponement of 'Royal Marine', Churchill was further troubled on the afternoon of April 8 to learn, during the meeting of the Military Co-ordination Committee at which he was in the Chair for the first time, that the War Office's estimates of tank delivery during 1940 had been far too optimistic, and that it was now 'too late to take effective steps to increase production for the campaigning season of 1940'. In

---

[1] Signal timed at 11.37 a.m., 8 April 1940: Seal papers. The signal was authorized by the acting Director of Operations (Home), Captain Ralph Edwards.

[2] War Cabinet No. 84 of 1940, 8 April 1940, 11.30 a.m.: Cabinet papers, 65/6.

[3] War Cabinet No. 84 of 1940, 8 April 1940, 11.30 a.m., Minute 5, Confidential Annex: Cabinet papers, 65/12.

view of these 'gloomy prospects', Churchill said, 'which it would appear we should have to accept, every effort must be made to get into the best possible position for the campaigning season of 1941'.

In addition to learning of tank deficiencies, the Military Co-ordination Committee of April 8 discussed grenades, the 'Royal Marine' Operation—which Churchill said the French High Command were anxious to keep ready for use 'in case of a major German land attack on the Western Front'—and British air operations in the event of a German offensive in the west. There was so much to be discussed, Churchill said, that the Committee should now meet twice a week, and sometimes three times. He also suggested that Hankey should take over from him the chairmanship of the Priority Sub-Committee, and that Neville Chamberlain himself should be asked to preside over the main Committee 'say once a month'.[1]

Churchill's area of responsibility had widened considerably in the previous week. So too had the problems with which he was confronted. Yet he was still hopeful that his principal concern, the mining of Norwegian territorial waters, would succeed. That night he dined with Hoare and Stanley. Hoare, the host, wrote in his diary: 'Winston very optimistic, delighted with mine laying, and sure he had scored off the Germans. He went off completely confident and happy at 10.30.'[2]

But on returning to the Admiralty, Churchill was confronted with alarming news. From the Intelligence reports even then being decoded, it seemed certain that a substantial force of German warships had put to sea, and were steaming northwards towards Norway.[3] At that very moment, a new member was about to join his Secretariat. His name was John Peck, and he had been working since the outbreak of war as Chatfield's Private Secretary in the Office of the Minister for the Co-ordination of Defence. Now his Minister was gone, and Churchill had taken over Chatfield's responsibilities at the Military Co-ordination Committee. It was to help with these responsibilities that Peck was summoned to the Admiralty, to be co-opted into Churchill's Private Secretariat. 'When I arrived,' he later wrote, 'the Admiralty was tense. All that Eric Seal had time for was, "The entire German Navy seems

---

[1] Military Co-ordination Committee No. 16 of 1940, 8 April 1940, 5 p.m.: Cabinet papers, 83/3.

[2] Hoare diary, 8 April 1940: Templewood papers.

[3] At 6.50 p.m. on 8 April 1940 HMS *Sunfish* signalled to the Admiralty: 'At 18.15 sighted 1 Blücher class, 2 Cruisers, 1 Destroyer course and speed 320° 15 in position MBA Q57 17′.' This signal was received at the Admiralty at 8.36 p.m., and sent as soon as it had been decoded to Churchill, Pound, Phillips and other senior naval officers (Seal papers).

to be heading for Norway. Winston's in the Map Room. He'll probably be there for hours. You'd better wait." So I waited. By midnight it was apparent that a new phase of the war had begun, that Winston Churchill was totally absorbed in it, and that he would not be taking time off to see a new junior member of his Staff. So I went home. . . .'[1]

That night, the fact that German naval action had coincided with Britain's long delayed naval initiative did not weaken Churchill's earlier dinner-time confidence. Indeed, as John Colville noted in his diary, 'the First Lord is jubilant and maintains that our failure to destroy the German fleet up to the present is only due to the bad visibility and rough weather, while if the Germans fly for home ports, they will leave their garrisons exposed to our expeditionary forces'.[2]

Within hours these hopes proved illusory, as the news from Norway worsened with alarming rapidity during the night. In the early hours of April 9 German warships were reported off Trondheim, Bergen and Stavanger, and an hour later four German warships were also reported entering Oslo Fiord. By five in the morning it was clear that German land forces had occupied Denmark and were invading Norway. That same morning the Admiralty were sent the text of an intercepted telegram, sent from the Norwegian Minister of Foreign Affairs to the Norwegian Legation in Spain, which read: 'German Minister handed over note demanding surrender of whole of Norway to German administration. In event of refusal all resistance will be crushed. The demand was refused. Hostilities already broken out. Bergen occupied.'[3] Two hours later MI6 informed the War Office that the Norwegian Government was evacuating Oslo, its capital.[4]

The Chiefs of Staff were summoned for 7.30 that same morning, and the War Cabinet for 8.30. 'I vividly remember being awakened very early in the morning,' Eric Seal wrote to Churchill fourteen years later, 'and seeing you off to the Cabinet from Admiralty House in a dressing gown.'[5]

At that early morning War Cabinet, Churchill reported that British destroyers were covering the mouth of Vest Fiord 'to stop enemy transport entering Narvik'. Ironside suggested 'that our first immediate action should be to go ahead with our plan for seizing Narvik'; one battalion, he said, was ready to sail that day, and could be at Narvik

[1] John Peck, *Dublin from Downing Street*, London 1978, pages 65–6.
[2] Colville diary, 8 April 1940: Colville papers.
[3] 'Time, 4.30 a.m.': Admiralty papers, 116/4471.
[4] M.I.3B, reference M.I.3/6519, 'Diary of Events in Scandinavia': Premier papers, 1/419.
[5] 'Draft Minute to the Prime Minister', 2 June 1954: Seal papers.

in three days' time. It was also important, Ironside argued, to prevent the Germans from establishing themselves at Trondheim and Bergen: their forces there were probably not more than two thousand men, 'and these had possibly accomplished little more than the taking of the docks'.

Churchill agreed with Ironside. Immediate steps would be taken, he said, 'to have transports ready to proceed' both to Trondheim and Bergen. 'No large forces would be required in the initial stages. Minefields could be laid to prevent further access by German forces.' Meanwhile, 'he strongly advocated that we should proceed with the operation against Narvik'.

The War Cabinet accepted these arguments, and instructed Churchill to authorize the Home Fleet 'to take all steps to clear Bergen and Trondheim of enemy forces'. At the same time, the Chiefs of Staff were asked to 'set on foot preparations for military expeditions to recapture Trondheim and Bergen, and to occupy Narvik'. But these expeditions were not to move until 'the Naval situation had been cleared up'.

Before the War Cabinet had met, its members received a summary of the most recent Intelligence reports, up to 7 a.m. that morning. At 2.35 a.m. 'five large German warships' had entered Oslo Fiord and were now at anchor at Tönsberg. An hour and a half later, at 4.07 a.m., two German warships had entered Trondheim harbour.[1]

At the War Cabinet on the morning of April 9, Churchill suggested that the 'present events' in Scandinavia might well be the prelude to the opening of a German offensive against western Europe. It was therefore important, he said, to press the Belgian Government 'to come into the open before it was too late, and to allow the Allied troops into their country'. When the meeting ended, Halifax was asked to consider, in consultation with the French, 'whether the present was a suitable time' for trying to persuade the Belgian Government 'to declare their attitude'.[2]

When the War Cabinet met again at noon on April 9 it had become clear that 'a small German force had landed at Narvik'. This news was a blow to the hopes for a swift British success. 'We were all terribly despondent,' Eric Seal wrote to his wife on the following day, 'because

---

[1] 'Cabinet War Room Record No. 209', up to 7 a.m., 9 April 1940: Cabinet papers, 100/3. As for British naval activity off the Norwegian coast, all that the Intelligence reports could tell was that two destroyers, *Kashmir* and *Kelvin*, had been in collision, and with 'considerable damage' done to both, were limping back to Scapa Flow.

[2] War Cabinet No. 84 of 1940, 9 April 1940, 8.30 a.m.: Cabinet papers, 65/6.

of the news that the Germans had got to Narvik, which is the prize they were really after, because of the iron ore up there.'[1] But Churchill was still optimistic, telling his colleagues: 'As regards the general situation in Scandinavia, he felt that we were in a far better position than we had been up to date. Our hands were now free, and we could apply our over-whelming sea power on the Norwegian coast.' As Churchill saw it, and went on to explain to his colleagues:

The German forces which had been landed were commitments for them, but potential prizes for us. We could not have prevented these landings without maintaining large patrols continuously off the Norwegian coast, which would have been wasteful of our naval strength; but we would liquidate them in a week or two.

It was heartening to find that the Norwegians were resisting and we should proclaim to the world our intention to go to their assistance. The Norwegians would hem in the German forces on land, and we could do the same on the sea, either by laying mines or other naval action.[2]

Churchill informed the War Cabinet that orders had been given to the naval forces to force their way into Narvik and Bergen, but that Trondheim would be left until the situation had been clarified. 'This,' wrote Eric Seal fourteen years later, 'is undoubtedly the Cabinet you remember so vividly, on the return from which you were waylaid by the First Sea Lord who told you that it had been decided to cancel the Bergen attack.'

Recalling the decision, Seal wrote to Churchill fourteen years later:

It seems possible that the First Sea Lord was concerned about the size of the force which Admiral Forbes had detached for the purpose of entering Bergen, which consisted of seven destroyers supported by four cruisers which were to remain outside. There was a doubt as to whether there were one or two German cruisers inside, and there was a strong possibility that the defences were in German hands.

'Another factor,' Seal added, 'was the intention to attack Bergen by air, which seemed to offer a better prospect of success.'

'I have a clear personal recollection,' Seal commented, 'that you spoke to me after lunch saying that the decision to abandon the attack had been pressed on you, and that you hoped the decision taken had been the correct one.'[3]

The naval attack on the two German cruisers reported to be at

[1] Letter of 10 April 1940: Seal papers.
[2] War Cabinet No. 85 of 1940, 9 April 1940, noon: Cabinet papers, 65/6.
[3] 'Draft Minute to the Prime Minister', 2 June 1954: Seal papers.

Bergen was cancelled. It was thought that the Germans had already gained possession of the fixed defences, and that British ships would have 'little chance' of sinking the cruisers, if, as had been reported by aircraft, they were already 'tucked in under the cliffs'.[1] The order to cancel the operation was sent to Forbes from the Admiralty a few minutes before two o'clock. It consisted of three words: 'Cancel Bergen Operation.'[2]

Further air reconaissance during April 9 revealed German warships at Trondheim, Bergen, Christiansand and Stavanger. Throughout the day, German aircraft bombed British ships, and British aircraft attacked German ships, with damage and casualties on both sides. Frustrated at the way in which the British initiative had been forestalled, Lord Cork wrote to Churchill that same day: 'If only "Catherine" had gone ahead. What an ideal force we should have had together to go right in & break up the German invading fleet. It would have been ready according to your last date on March 31st—9 days ago!'[3]

All morning, John Peck, the potential new member of Churchill's Private Secretariat, had waited to be admitted to an introductory session with his would-be master. 'In the afternoon,' Peck later recalled, 'Seal said that the First Lord was working in bed and the best thing would be to take him some papers and act as if I had been working for him for months.' Peck's account continued:

It was the first time I had seen Winston Churchill at close range. He was sitting up in bed with a large cigar in his mouth, studying some maps. He took no notice of me, but at intervals he reached forward to stroke a fine black cat sleeping at the foot of the bed. 'Poor Pussy,' he said, 'poor Pussy.' I stood in silence for what seemed an age, while he comforted the cat. He then said 'Poor Pussy. He's just had a painful operation. His name is Nelson. So you've come to work for me.' 'Yes please, Sir.' 'Good, what have you got there?' I told him. He looked through the papers. A gentle, almost paternal smile. 'Thank you very much.' I was in.[4]

On the afternoon of April 9 the Supreme War Council met in London, Reynaud, Daladier and Darlan having flown over from Paris. It was agreed that 'strong forces' should be sent to Norway, these forces to include a French Alpine Division, the leading elements of which

---

[1] 'Summary of Events': Admiralty papers, 116/4471.
[2] Signal timed at 1.57 p.m., 9 April 1940: Seal papers.
[3] Letter of 9 April 1940: Admiralty papers, 199/1928.
[4] John Peck, *Dublin from Downing Street*, London 1978, pages 65–6. Peck was to remain a member of Churchill's Private Office for the rest of the war.

would be ready to sail within two or three days. The British contribution would be two battalions ready to sail that night from Scapa, a further five battalions ready to sail within three days, and a further four battalions ready to sail within two weeks.

Churchill wanted the destination of these forces to be Narvik. 'The actual operation of clearing any Germans out of Narvik,' he told the Council, 'should not present great difficulty. What had to be decided was what was to happen subsequently, when the Allied forces reached the Swedish border.'

Churchill was challenged at this meeting by Oliver Stanley, the Secretary of State for War, who, while he accepted 'the importance of occupying Narvik', warned that the Supreme War Council 'must not be blind to the value of re-occupying Trondheim and Bergen'. It would be a 'mistake to throw away an opportunity' of capturing Trondheim and Bergen. Without the occupation of Bergen, he felt, 'it was difficult to see how Norwegian resistance could continue'.

The Council thereupon agreed that the forces available should be sent to 'ports on the Norwegian seaboard'. No place names were mentioned. But the aim in each case, the Council concluded, would be to recapture each port from the Germans, and hold both port and railhead 'securely'. No forces should be despatched, however, 'until the Naval situation had been cleared up'.

The Council also agreed that if Germany were to attack in the west, the mining of the Rhine would be begun 'as quickly as possible'.

Churchill was not entirely satisfied with this last decision. Even if no German attack took place in the west there was still some need, he said, 'for striking at Germany', and he went on to explain that in his view, in order to influence neutral opinion, and especially Italian opinion, 'it was important that the Allies should show that they were not afraid to strike at Germany herself'.[1]

In an attempt to discover just how near such a strike might be, Churchill telegraphed that afternoon to Admiral Forbes:

We should be able to help you better in your great task if whenever you find it possible to break wireless silence you could add a few sentences explaining main decisions you are taking. We have a great deal of information here, and events are moving very rapidly, and it is sometimes difficult to understand what you are doing and why. When we know the reasons we can contribute more effectively.

[1] Supreme War Council No. 7 of 1939–40, 9 April 1940, 4.20 p.m.: Cabinet papers 99/3, folios 45–51.

Churchill went on to tell Forbes: 'I consider Germans have made strategic error in incurring commitments on Norwegian coast which we can probably wipe out in a short time,' and he added: 'It seems to me very likely that the great land battle in the West will soon begin.'[1]

At nine-thirty that evening Churchill again presided over a meeting of the Military Co-ordination Committee. Narvik, he reported, was being held by six German destroyers and one submarine, and a force of approximately three to four thousand men. A destroyer flotilla of nine ships had therefore been ordered to move into Narvik at dawn on the following morning, April 10. At dusk on April 10, torpedo carrying aircraft would attack the two German cruisers at Bergen. Both these measures were 'imperative', if Britain was to prevent the Norwegians 'from collapsing and making peace'.

The Military Co-ordination Committee then discussed the 'immediate steps which might be taken' to counter the German military occupation of so many Norwegian ports. Churchill, as the Minutes recorded, 'proposed that no action should be taken at Trondheim', while Ironside stressed that with the British and French forces at the Allies' disposal it would be 'impossible' to attempt to 'dislodge the Germans from more than one point on the Norwegian coast. We must, therefore, concentrate our attack on Narvik.' Not until Narvik had been captured, Ironside added, 'should we attempt to expel the Germans from elsewhere'. Meanwhile, he warned, even this single operation 'would be doomed to failure if it were rushed'.

Ironside's judgment was accepted by all present, having regard, as the official conclusions of the meeting noted, 'to the strategic importance of Narvik in relation to the Gällivare ore fields'. The Chiefs of Staff were therefore instructed to 'put in hand' the preparation of a plan 'for the capture of Narvik'. At the same time, the conclusions noted, 'this plan should take into consideration the possibility of establishing a foothold by Allied forces at Namsos and Andalsnes (Romsdal fiord)'.

Summing up the discussion, Churchill pointed out what he described as 'the paramount necessity' of carrying out the operation with the 'utmost expedition'. Every day's delay, he warned, 'would mean that the operation would assume the character of a siege and that we should require a larger force for it'.[2]

---

[1] 'Private Office', signal sent out at 7.14 p.m., 9 April 1940: Seal papers.

[2] Military Co-ordination Committee No. 17 of 1940, 9 April 1940, 9.30 p.m.: Cabinet papers, 83/3.

The discussions of April 9 had been overshadowed by the German landing at Narvik. 'I was very worried too about Winston,' Eric Seal wrote home on the following day. Churchill, he explained, 'was knocked out last night. I had to manoeuvre him to bed; he had a good night, & this morning is in wonderful fighting trim. He is to make a statement about it all in the House tomorrow. I have to be a sort of nurse at times!! He's very like a spoilt child in many ways. I got to bed about 2 . . .' Seal added:

Poor little Admiral Phillips had a rotten time. He was worrying about whether we had done right, & couldn't sleep at all. However, we're getting the situation in hand; & the general feeling is that with a little bit of luck we *may* be in a better position as a result of this German outrage. I won't discuss details with you in an open letter, naturally; but I really am optimistic, & so is Phillips, & also Winston, at heart.[1]

One wider hope that seemed to hinge upon the events in Norway was that of keeping Italy neutral. On March 30 the British Ambassador in Rome, Sir Percy Loraine, had reported that Mussolini was 'fully aware of the risks involved by over-hasty decision on his part', and this report had been circulated to members of the War Cabinet. But by the time this report had been commented on inside the Foreign Office, a difficult perspective had opened up. 'I fear,' noted Orme Sargent on April 9, 'that today's "diversion" culminating in the capture by Germany of Bergen and Trondheim under the nose of the British Fleet is not likely to impress Mussolini in the way we should wish.'

'Yes,' commented the Under Secretary of State at the Foreign Office, R. A. Butler, 'but the Fleet may yet do us credit.'[2] Many people shared this hope.

In the early hours of April 10 news of the full extent of the German success in Scandinavia reached the members of the War Cabinet. German troops had landed at Trondheim, Bergen, Egersund, Stavanger and Narvik. Oslo had capitulated after 'some resistance', and the Norwegian Government had left the capital for Hamar, eighty miles to the North. German bombers had struck at many targets. The town of Lilleström was in flames.

South of Norway, German forces occupied the whole of Denmark 'under protest, but without untoward incident'.[3]

---

[1] Letter of 10 April 1940: Seal papers.
[2] Rome Telegram No. 287 DIPP, 30 March 1940 (received 31 March 1940): Foreign Office papers, 371/24939.
[3] 'Cabinet War Room Record No. 220', up to 7 a.m., 10 April 1940: Cabinet papers, 100/3.

April 9 had been Germany's day of triumph. On the following morning, off Narvik, five British destroyers went into action against the German naval forces. The British warships, commanded by Captain Warburton-Lee, had an initial success, but then the Germans succeeded in beating off the attack. One of the British destroyers, HMS *Hardy*, was sunk, one beached, and two damaged; Warburton-Lee was among those killed.

That evening, the evening of April 10, the commander-designate of the British Field Force, Major-General Mackesy, who was then in London, was instructed 'to eject the Germans from the Narvik area and establish control of Narvik itself', while Ironside wrote to Mackesy personally: 'You may have a chance of taking advantage of naval action, and should do so if you can. Boldness is required.'[1]

Churchill decided to entrust the command of the naval forces to Lord Cork. 'My impression on leaving London,' Cork wrote in his official despatch, 'was quite clear, that it was desired by His Majesty's Government to turn the enemy out of Narvik at the earliest possible moment, and that I was to act with all promptitude in order to obtain this result.'[2]

Now that the Germans had gained the initiative, Churchill was under no illusion as to the seriousness of the task with which Mackesy and Cork had been entrusted, writing to Pound on April 10: 'We must seal up Bergen with a watched minefield, and concentrate on Narvik, for which long and severe fighting will be required.' Churchill added: 'Narvik must be fought for. Although we have been completely outwitted, there is no reason to suppose that prolonged and serious fighting in this area will not impose a greater drain on the enemy than on ourselves.' But at least one fuelling base would have to be found and seized on the Norwegian coast: 'now that the enemy have bases there we cannot carry on without it'. The Naval Staff were at work 'selecting various alternatives'. Unless such a base were acquired soon, 'we cannot compete with the Germans in their new position'.[3]

At the Military Co-ordination Committee at five o'clock that afternoon, Ironside explained that General Mackesy had been informed that his 'primary duty' was to prevent the Germans who had already landed at Narvik from obtaining 'any reinforcements by sea'. To this end, a patrol had already been established across the mouth of Vest Fiord.

---

[1] Message 'written out in manuscript' by Ironside, 11.30 p.m., 10 April 1940, and taken to Mackesy by Brigadier Lund: copy, War Office papers, 106/1875.

[2] Final draft report, Section 1, Paragraph 1: War Office papers, 32/9624.

[3] Minute to Pound '& all concerned', 10 April 1940: Admiralty papers, 116/4471.

The 'first step' of the operation, Ironside told the Committee, would be 'to establish an advanced base somewhere in the vicinity of Narvik', where the military expedition could be 'sorted out' in preparation for the landing operation against Narvik itself. Two battalions were 'immediately available' to establish this base: the question was, where should it be. This would be decided, he said, 'by the Naval Staff and the General Staff in consultation'.

The Military Co-ordination Committee of April 10 also agreed that the 'first object' in seizing Narvik and destroying or capturing the German force there 'was to establish a naval base for ourselves'. The 'second object' would be to use Narvik as a base 'from which to reach out to the Gällivare ore fields'.[1] The whole operation was to have the code name 'Rupert'.

During April 10 it became clear that the Chiefs of Staff also wanted action other than at Narvik. At their morning meeting on April 10 Ironside had proposed, to forestall a German advance into Holland, an air attack on Germany. There were German ammunition dumps and troop concentrations close to the Rhine, he said, 'which provided good targets for air attack'. Newall wanted to hold back any such attack until after the Germans had marched into Holland, but Ismay warned that once the British bombing force was 'fully occupied with attacks on the German Army' it would be unable to carry out bombing operations in Germany as well. The British public, Ismay believed, were expecting 'forceful action against the Germans' as a result of their attack on Norway and Denmark. An immmediate air attack would therefore 'kill two birds with one stone'.[2]

This was also Pound's view. 'I feel most strongly,' he minuted to Churchill, 'that we should commence bombing. If we do not bomb the Germans we should bomb Germany—the latter is much more use,' and he added: 'I am sure we must do something drastic.'[3]

Hoare, the new Air Minister, was less certain about the need for an immediate bombardment of Germany, preferring, like Newall, to wait until after any German attack on Holland. That night Anthony Eden noted in his diary, after he had looked in to the Admiralty War Room after dinner to study the charts of the latest naval situation: 'Winston found me there and carried me off to his room. He is indignant with Sam, whom he suspects of being eager to score off him, and whom he

---

[1] Military Co-ordination Committee No. 18 of 1940, 10 April 1940, 5 p.m.: Cabinet papers 83/3.

[2] Chiefs of Staff Committee No. 72 of 1940, 10 April 1940, 10 a.m.: Cabinet papers, 79/3.

[3] Minute of 10 April 1940: Admiralty papers: 116/4471.

regards as unsuited to inspire the Air Force at a time like this. "A snake" and some stronger epithets. . . .'[1]

On the morning of April 11 Churchill learned of the previous day's combat: an unsuccessful German air raid on Scapa Flow, in which four German aircraft had been shot down by British fighters; and a successful attack by a single British fighter on Stavanger airport, when a German bomber had been destroyed on the ground, and several other aircraft damaged. At Bergen, a German cruiser had been sunk by a Fleet Air Arm attack, while British destroyers were systematically combing the west coast of Norway for German ships. In the north Atlantic, a British force had occupied the Danish-ruled Faroe Islands, to deny them to the Germans.[2] 'The British Navy,' the *Daily Mail* declared that morning in its comment on the main Norwegian engagement, 'has embarked on a glorious enterprise.' Hitler, the newspaper added, 'is shaken by the hammer blows of our sailors and airmen.'[3]

That morning Churchill was present at Downing Street when a French Mission, headed by Ambassador Coulondre and General Mittelhauser, gave an account of its intention to proceed to Sweden, and to urge the Swedish Government to 'invite' both Britain and France 'to go to their assistance' as soon as the Germans attacked, as it was assumed they would, the southern Swedish coast. Chamberlain expressed his agreement with the need both 'to stiffen' Sweden's attitude, 'and to help her preserve her independence'. He also mentioned the value to the Allies if the Swedish Government 'could be induced to send forces overland to assist the Allies at Narvik'. In that event, Narvik might be recaptured 'very much sooner', and an Allied expeditionary force sent through Narvik to Sweden 'at an earlier date'. He doubted, however, whether the Germans would attack Sweden, as her 'real objective', the iron ore mines, would be likely to be destroyed the moment such an attack took place.

At Chamberlain's request, Churchill then gave the French Mission an account of the situation at Narvik. The first troops, he said, were to leave Britain on the following day, April 12, 'in order to establish a base to which further reinforcements might be sent'. He hoped that it

---

[1] Eden diary, 10 April 1940: The Earl of Avon, *The Eden Memoirs, The Reckoning*, London 1965, pages 95–6.

[2] This was operation 'Valentine', carried out by a force of Royal Marines, followed by armoured units.

[3] *Daily Mail*, 11 April 1940.

would be possible to recapture Narvik 'within one or two weeks'. Until then, no serious operations could be undertaken against Bergen or Trondheim. 'In the meantime, we were attacking German warships and supply ships by sea and air.' What the Swedes could do to help, he said, was to interrupt the land communications by which the Germans could reinforce Bergen and Trondheim. Britain could not at present promise the Swedes a military expedition, but the Allies could tell the Swedes 'that if they fought on our side they would share with us in the final victory'.[1]

The French Mission then withdrew, and the War Cabinet assembled. Churchill had returned briefly to the Admiralty, and when he got back to 10 Downing Street a discussion was already in progress, critical of the French desire to bring Sweden into the war. But Churchill was emphatic, as he told his colleagues, that 'we should do all we could to persuade the Swedes to declare war on Germany', while at the same time not making 'any specific promises', such as the 'immediate bombing of Berlin' if the Germans bombed Stockholm.[2]

Chamberlain and Halifax had already deprecated the involvement of Sweden in the way which Churchill proposed. Early that afternoon, Churchill wrote to them both, at length, arguing that it was not Swedish neutrality, but a Swedish declaration of war on Germany, which Britain wanted. 'It seems to me,' he wrote, 'we must not throw cold water on the French idea of trying to induce the Swedes to enter the war.' It would, he warned, be 'disastrous' if the Swedes remained neutral, 'and bought Germany off with ore from Gällivare, down the Gulf of Bothnia'. Churchill added: 'I must apologize for not having sufficiently gripped this issue in my mind this morning, but I only came in after the discussion had begun, and did not address myself properly to it.'[3]

In reply, Halifax stated that he and Chamberlain were both agreed that any representations to Sweden 'that can be readily translated in their minds into an attempt by us to drag them into the war will be likely to have an effect opposite to that which we want', and Churchill deferred to this view.[4]

That afternoon, Churchill went to the House of Commons to give an account of the events of the past four days. 'A thousand people packed

---

[1] 'Scandinavia, Notes of Informal Meeting', 11 April 1940, 9.45 a.m.: Admiralty papers, 205/4.
[2] War Cabinet No. 88 of 1940, 11 April 1940, 11.30 a.m.: Cabinet papers, 65/6.
[3] Notes by Churchill, 11 April 1940: Premier papers, 1/419.
[4] Letter of 11 April 1940: Premier papers, 1/419.

the pavements outside the House of Commons,' reported the *Daily Mail*, waiting to see Churchill's face. '"Where's Winnie?" they asked, after other Ministers had arrived. "Wonder if he'll be smiling. You can always tell what's in the air by Winnie's face".'[1] But when Churchill reached the chamber, as he later recalled, 'I had to face a disturbed and indignant House of Commons.'[2] The nature of this mood, and Churchill's own reaction to it, is clear from Harold Nicolson's account, written later that same day:

Winston comes in. He is not looking well and sits there hunched as usual with his papers in his hand. When he rises to speak it is obvious that he is very tired. He starts off by giving an imitation of himself making a speech, and he indulges in vague oratory coupled with tired gibes. I have seldom seen him to less advantage.

The majority of the House were expecting tales of victory and triumph, and when he tells them that the news of our re-occupation of Bergen, Trondheim and Oslo is untrue, a cold wave of disappointment passes through the House. He hesitates, gets his notes in the wrong order, puts on the wrong pair of spectacles, fumbles for the right pair, keeps on saying 'Sweden' when he means 'Denmark', and one way and another makes a lamentable performance. He gives no real explanation of how the Germans managed to slip through to Narvik. We have sunk some eight German transports and two cruisers have been damaged. He claims that this has 'crippled' the German Navy. He says that the Faroe Islands have been seized and that Iceland will be protected. His references to the Norwegian Army and Navy are vague in the extreme.

One has the impression that he is playing for time and expects that at any moment some dramatic news will be brought to him. It is a feeble, tired speech and it leaves the House in a mood of grave anxiety.[3]

In his speech, Churchill set out at length the history of the past four days following the German invasion of Denmark and Norway. In having to defend what he knew to be a failed policy, he was not indeed at his most inspired. But he did refer to a theme that had long been his particular concern. 'It is not the slightest use blaming the Allies,' he said, 'for not being able to give substantial help and protection to neutral countries if they are held at arm's length by the neutral countries until those countries are actually attacked on a scientifically prepared plan by Germany.' It was his hope, he added, that the fact that Norway's 'strict observance of neutrality' had been a contributory cause to her present sufferings and the 'limits of aid which we can give her'

[1] *Daily Mail*, 12 April 1940.

[2] Winston S. Churchill, *The Second World War*, volume 1, London 1948, page 474.

[3] Nicolson diary, 11 April 1940: Nigel Nicolson (editor), *Harold Nicolson, Diaries and Letters 1939–1945*, London 1967, page 70.

would be meditated on 'by other countries who may to-morrow, or a week hence, or a month hence find themselves the victims of an equally elaborately worked out staff plan for their destruction and enslavement'.

Churchill then described in detail the battles that had taken place, including the sinking of four German cruisers, and the defeat of Warburton-Lee's destroyer force. 'I do not think we ought to have a kind of mealy-mouthed attitude towards these matters,' he said. 'We have embarked on this war and we must take our blows,' and a few moments later he declared: 'We are not children to be kept in the dark, and we can take what is coming to us as well as any other country.'

Churchill then spoke of the 'recklessness' with which 'Hitler and his advisers had cast the interests of the German Navy upon the wild waters', and he went on:

. . . this very recklessness makes me feel that these audacious, costly operations may be only the prelude to far larger events which impend on land.

We have probably arrived now at the first main crunch of the war. But we certainly find no reason in the fact of what has just happened, and still less in our own hearts, to deter us from entering upon any further trials that may lie before us.

While we will not prophesy or boast about battles still to be fought, we feel ourselves ready to encounter the utmost malice of the enemy and to devote all our life strength to achieve the victory in what is a world cause.[1]

Churchill's friends saw how hard it had been for Churchill to make his speech, to a troubled and at times hostile House of Commons. 'You had so many obvious difficulties to contend with,' the Solicitor-General, Sir Terence O'Connor, wrote: 'the need to deflate wild press appreciations of the position; lack of a chance to prepare etc.' And yet, O'Connor wrote, 'the speech didn't suffer, it gained from the circumstances. There weren't so many gothic periods, but it was all the better for that & in its toughness & baldness caught the mood of the country and gave inspiration.'[2]

'He was witty,' noted Chamberlain's Private Secretary, John Colville, 'but less polished than usual. He caused amusement by saying that Denmark had had most to fear of all the neutrals, because she had been the most recent to negotiate a non-aggression pact with Germany.' Churchill, Colville added, had 'wisely damped down the absurd over-optimism of this morning's newspapers, but made a good case for the Navy's achievements during the last three days'.[3]

[1] *Hansard*, 11 April 1940.
[2] Letter of 11 April 1940: Churchill papers, 2/397.
[3] Colville diary, 11 April 1940: Colville papers.

There is a glimpse of the background to Churchill's speech in a letter which Eric Seal wrote to his wife on the following morning. Yesterday, he said, 'was a beast', and he added:

I was on from 9.30 am until 12.45 am—with only an hour & a half for dinner, & no lunch time. The speech was only written—finished a quarter of an hour before it was due for delivery. We had to improvise arrangements for getting it to France, & to Stanhope for the Lords. I had to correct it sheet by sheet as the First Lord dictated it.

When finally we left for the House I could only pray that it had been put together in the proper order!! It was.[1]

From the House of Commons, Churchill again returned to the Admiralty, before going at half-past six to Ismay's room in Richmond Terrace, for a meeting of the Military Co-ordination Committee. At this meeting Churchill stressed, as the minutes recorded, 'the need for constant harassing attacks from the air on Stavanger aerodrome, so as to prevent the peaceful consolidation of the position gained by the Germans'. But the Committee, while agreeing that it was important 'not to leave the Germans in peace', warned that action by the Royal Air Force 'must be governed by the necessity for avoiding undue dissipation of our air striking force which would be required to meet the main German attack, which might soon materialize'.[2]

Thus, once again, Britain's air weakness was an inhibiting factor in determining a war plan. Churchill could do no more than bow to the realities which he himself had for so long pointed out. Yet at the same time, Britain was making a considerable air commitment to France. This was Operation 'Alphonse', a plan for British heavy bomber intervention on German lines of communication, in the event of a German attack in the West.[3] This much was agreed by the Military Co-ordination Committee on April 9. Three days later, in his Chairman's summary, Churchill noted the Committee's decision that it would be for the French High Command 'to indicate the targets which they require to be attacked'.[4]

At the evening Military Co-ordination Committee on April 11 Newall had brought up a question on which the Chiefs of Staff had formed a firm opinion: that if 'Rupert'—the attack on Narvik by ships

[1] Letter of 12 April 1940: Seal papers.
[2] Military Co-ordination Committee No. 19 of 1940, 11 April 1940, 6.30 p.m.: Cabinet papers, 83/3.
[3] 'Operation Alphonse', Military Co-ordination Committee Memorandum No. 71 of 1940, 9 April 1940: Cabinet papers, 83/5.
[4] 'Operation Alphonse', Military Co-ordination Committee Memorandum No. 72 of 1940, 12 April 1940: Cabinet papers, 83/5.

and troops—were to succeed, 'it might be desirable to follow it up' by further attacks 'against either Trondheim or Bergen'.

Ironside commented on the difficulties involved at Trondheim because of the 'mountainous cliffs running straight down into the water', which meant that 'there was no possible landing place'. But he went on to tell the Committee that this plan was nevertheless being studied by the Staffs 'since it would be the most valuable objective, giving access to the interior of the country'.

Churchill was not entirely opposed to this Trondheim plan, which now received the operational code name 'Maurice'. The 'study of this operation', he told the Committee 'should proceed'; but he added the caveat that 'no action should be taken' until it was seen what would be involved in operation 'Rupert' at Narvik, where it was intended first to dislodge the German troops, and then to provide the Allied force with a base from which the Gällivare railway and ore field could be immobilized.

The Military Co-ordination Committee then agreed that while the 'Maurice' operation against Trondheim should be 'studied in detail' by the Service Staffs, 'no actual preparations should begin' until it was known 'what would be involved' in the assault on Narvik.[1]

There remained for Churchill one more meeting on the evening of April 11, in the War Room at the Admiralty. One of those present, Captain Ralph Edwards, who wrote the meeting up a short time later, noted in his diary: 'There was a very long meeting with WSC in the evening. He was half-cocked as usual.' Those present, Edwards added, 'came to the conclusion about 2315 that they ought to attack Trondheim'.

It was decided therefore to go and see Ironside. 'The meeting was going well,' Edwards added, 'when Winston lost his temper and spoilt the whole show.' On the following day Edwards wrote in his diary: 'Everyone is very indignant about the conduct of affairs and Winston appears to be the chief target. He will try and be a naval strategist if not an actual tactician.'[2]

There is a second contemporary account of this final evening meeting in the letter which Eric Seal wrote to his wife:

In the evening I attended a staff conference, at which Winston & I were the only people not covered all over with gold braid. The bullion round the table would have (almost) paid my salary for a year.

[1] Military Co-ordination Committee No. 19 of 1940, 11 April 1940, 6.30 p.m.: Cabinet papers, 83/3.
[2] Note of a meeting of 11 April 1940 and Edwards diary for 12 April 1940: Stephen Roskill, *Churchill and the Admirals*, London 1977, page 102.

Everybody was tired out; & only little Tom[1] & Winston really showed a grip. However, a great deal of good came out of it. Winston is marvellous at picking up all the threads & giving them coherent shape & form.

Of the Norwegian situation, Seal commented to his wife: 'As things are, they are not at all bad. Hitler has thrown away a large part of his Fleet—for what? A big & vulnerable commitment, which may kill him in the end. The moral effect upon neutrals of such a big success will tend to diminish when its empty character & its cost come more & more into view.'[2]

For the neutral Swedes, it was not the tardiness of Britain's attack that caused concern, but its destination. Early on April 12 both Ismay and the Minister of Economic Warfare, Ronald Cross, met two Swedish businessmen, who strongly urged that not Narvik but Trondheim should be Britain's first, and indeed sole objective. According to the Swedes, 'British troops at so remote a spot as Narvik would not have a great effect,' whereas 'If only Trondheim were in British hands, Narvik would be bound to fall at a later date.' Above all, said the Swedes, the arrival of British troops at Trondheim 'would have an important effect in stiffening the morale of the Norwegian people'.[3]

But Narvik was now the first aim and focus of all British efforts as, at noon on April 12, both Cork and Mackesy sailed for Scandinavia. 'It was hoped,' Churchill told the War Cabinet that morning, 'to get ashore and make touch with the Norwegian troops in the neighbourhood of Narvik. A base for naval operations would also be established. . . .' Ironside pointed out that men had been included in the expedition whose task once ashore would be the destruction of the Gällivare ore fields, but that these men were 'debarred from crossing the border into Sweden' without the sanction of the War Cabinet.

Norway was no longer the innocent neutral, but the outraged victim; and Norwegian troops were fighting the Germans at every landing point. The 'most important need' at the present time, Churchill told the War Cabinet, was to encourage the Norwegians in their fight, 'to urge them to hem the Germans in, to break up communications, and to tell them that we were coming quickly to their assistance'.

Halifax, however, was critical of the Narvik plan, which would, he said, 'have very much less political effect' than an attempt 'to clear the Germans out of the Southern part of Norway'. The Germans were

---

[1] Admiral Phillips.

[2] Letter of 12 April 1940: Seal papers.

[3] Note by Ismay, 'Operation Maurice', circulated as Co-ordination Committee Memorandum No. 73 of 1940, 12 April 1940: Cabinet papers, 83/5.

'thrusting forward' from Trondheim southwards, and from Oslo northwards. But Churchill strongly opposed changing the plans at this late stage, and attempting to counter this substantial German force; he told his colleagues that an opposed landing at Trondheim would be 'a very difficult operation, and if mounted without proper preparation might only lead to a bloody repulse'. Plans for the Narvik expedition, Churchill pointed out, 'were well advanced, and the landing could be made within a few days'.

Churchill spoke with confidence of the Narvik plans. 'We could be reasonably sure of success at that point,' he told the War Cabinet, 'and a success would show that we should be able ultimately to clear the Germans out of all the ports in which they had obtained a foothold.'[1]

At the Military Co-ordination Committee meeting that afternoon, it was agreed that there should be 'no interference' with the Narvik plan.[2] Anticipating the success of that plan, Churchill set out for the Joint Planning Staff his ideas for the next phase. 'If Namsos could be occupied within the next week,' he wrote, 'it would give encouragement to Norway and Sweden.' This was an idea which Chamberlain himself had proposed at the War Cabinet that morning, and which the War Cabinet had endorsed. Churchill's note continued:

It is suggested that we should be active on the whole coast from Namsos to Molde; cleansing the leads with cruisers and flotillas; using coastal motor boats to rouse the population and puzzle the enemy; so that we can make landings at Namsos or Molde with forces incapable of serious action inland, and which can be taken off if heavily attacked. Publicity would be given to these enterprises, and the idea spread about that a large Anglo-French army was preparing to attack Trondheim, and generally establish itself in the teeth of the enemy on this part of the Norwegian coast.

It is neither necessary nor possible at this stage to look beyond these minor operations. It might be that if a heavy German concentration had been induced at Trondheim, Bergen could be attacked instead. The use of flexible amphibious power may give remarkable rewards.

The Joint Planning Staff should work incessantly during the next twenty-four hours upon the implementing of these ideas, having regard to the small forces available from the army and the Royal Marines, to the Naval power to dominate these waters with small craft, to the use of mines to baffle serious

[1] War Cabinet No. 89 of 1940, 12 April 1940, 11.30 a.m., Minute 3, Confidential Annex: Cabinet papers, 65/12.
[2] Military Co-ordination Committee No. 20 of 1940, 12 April 1940, 5.30 p.m. (with Churchill in the Chair, and Oliver Stanley, Sir Samuel Hoare and Leslie Burgin present, with the three Service Chiefs, Sir Cyril Newall, Sir Dudley Pound and Sir Edmund Ironside also present): Cabinet papers, 83/3.

enemy attack, to the choice of the places for landing, to the manner of effecting surprise, to the security of the forces when landed, and to their withdrawal if they are seriously attacked.

It by no means follows that only two parties should be landed or that parties landed should remain where they first set foot. All this is a matter of tactics and manoeuvre.[1]

That evening, Churchill sent a minute to Pound and Phillips, summarizing his expectations. 'Once Narvik is cleared up,' he wrote, 'and we are established there, very good forces will be available for other enterprises.' His thoughts were also on the widening war. 'Nothing,' he wrote, 'will steady Italy so much as a speedy success at Narvik.'[2]

The Foreign Office was also concerned about the effect of the Narvik battle upon Italy's decision to remain neutral, and on the evening of April 12 a telegram was sent to Sir Noel Charles, the British Counsellor in Rome, urging him to point out to the Italian Government that Hitler had committed a 'grave strategic error' in invading Norway. 'German forces landed at various points in Norway,' he was told, 'are now isolated by British naval units except round Oslo and even there their communications are seriously interrupted.' The telegram continued:

Result of naval and air action since April 7th is loss to Germans of four cruisers a very large percentage of German cruiser strength, at least that number of destroyers, and at least three submarines, while one of the two German battle-cruisers, though supported by a large cruiser, was considerably damaged in action with one British battle-cruiser.

German fleet only escaped greater losses through weather conditions preventing further opportunities for action. Nearly a dozen transport and supply ships have been sunk or captured, chiefly in the Kattegat, and many more sinkings are probable, though not yet reported.

Allied losses were superficial damage to one battle cruiser, three destroyers sunk and another run ashore, damaged.

As for the counter-attack at Narvik, five British destroyers had engaged 'six of the largest type German destroyers and shore batteries and sunk at least seven store and ammunition ships besides some of the destroyers'. Allied forces were 'now on their way to Norway', and the Norwegians themselves were resisting the German invasion, 'which has

---

[1] 'Note by the Chairman of the Military Co-ordination Committee', 12 April 1940: Admiralty papers, 199/1929. The original note as received by Neville Chamberlain is in Premier papers, 1/419.

[2] Minute of 12 April 1940: Churchill papers, 19/6.

not progressed from coast except in south, in spite of indiscriminate bombing'. The telegram ended:

Economically, German action has greatly helped Allied blockade. Denmark will be a liability rather than an asset in a few months' time.

Germans have always maintained that extension of war to Scandinavia would be to advantage of Allies, and it is only in desperation that they could have determined to bring about such a situation.

Events of next few weeks should prove this, and Italian Government would be well advised to await them.

An identical telegram was sent to the British Ambassador in Tokyo.[1]

Encouragement for Churchill's efforts reached him on April 12 from King George VI. 'I know what a great strain has been placed upon you,' the King wrote by hand from Buckingham Palace, 'by your increased responsibilities as Chairman of the Co-ordination Committee. I shall however ask you to come and see me as soon as there is a lull. In the meantime,' the King added, 'I would like to congratulate you on the splendid way in which, under your direction, the Navy is countering the German move against Scandinavia. I also beg of you to take care of yourself & get as much rest as you possibly can in these critical days.'[2]

---

[1] Telegrams No. 223 and 289 (to Rome and Tokyo respectively), 12 April 1940: Foreign Office papers, 371/24939, R 4548/58/2.
[2] Letter of 12 April 1940: Churchill papers, 19/2.

13

Divided Counsels

D URING April 13 the news from Narvik boded extremely well for the Allied cause. '*Warspite*,[1] *Cossack*, *Foxhound* in Narvik Bay,' an Admiralty telegram reported to the world. 'Little opposition. All German destroyers sunk (seven). Three of them after retiring up Rombaks Fiord. One submarine sunk by *Warspite*'s aircraft. Parties of men possibly soldiers retreating over hill. One field howitzer silenced by *Cossack*.'

Even the damage to British ships seemed relatively slight. '*Eskimo* bow blown off by torpedo,' the telegram stated. '*Cossack* damaged and ashore in Narvik Bay. *Punjabi* one boiler out of action.'[2]

That afternoon Churchill was in the Chair at the Military Co-ordination Committee where it was decided that, the German naval forces in Narvik Bay having apparently been destroyed, and German troops having retired from Narvik town, the British landing might therefore be made in the town itself.

This encouraging prospect led the Committee to discuss how best to use the forces which had been assembled for a possible landing near Trondheim. There, according to the minutes of the meeting, the Naval Staff expected 'no difficulty in silencing the shore batteries'; 300 of these men were 'in any event' about to be landed at Namsos within twenty-four hours, while a small naval force was to land at Ålesund, landings which 'would tend to attract the Germans away from Trondheim itself and lead to their dispersal'.

The Committee agreed that the Service Staffs should at once study 'all the implications' of a direct landing at Trondheim by part at least of this southern force.[3] Meanwhile, the Commander-designate of this

---

[1] *Warspite* was Vice-Admiral Whitworth's flagship.

[2] Admiralty telegram, 13 April 1940: Foreign Office papers, 371/24939.

[3] Military Co-ordination Committee No. 21 of 1940, 13 April 1940, 5 p.m.: Cabinet papers, 83/3. For maps of the Narvik and Trondheim areas, see pages 265 and 266.

force, General Carton de Wiart, was to be flown out to Namsos on the following day.

Since the German invasion of Norway on April 9, Churchill himself had regarded the Narvik operation as the paramount one, to which all else should be subordinate. But the Trondheim operation now began to be pressed for by the French, two strong advocates of it being the French Mission in Sweden, and Admiral Darlan.

At the War Cabinet on April 13, while the Narvik expedition was actually on its way across the North Sea, Halifax again sought to give Trondheim the priority, telling his colleagues that he thought 'that the most important point was to secure Trondheim, and the railways leading from that port across the peninsula'. Halifax's view was challenged by Ironside, who at once pointed out that not only would a major operation against Trondheim 'require additional troops', but that these troops could only be obtained by withdrawing them from France. Chamberlain, however, drawing attention to a telegram from the French Mission in Sweden, said that he was 'impressed with the urgency of obtaining a foothold at Trondheim, particularly from the political point of view'. If we 'merely concentrated' on Narvik, Chamberlain added, 'there was a danger lest the Norwegians and Swedes would feel that our only interest was the iron ore'. In that event, he added, 'they might become disheartened and give up the struggle'.

Halifax then spoke again; not only was 'early action' against Trondheim 'imperative from the political point of view', but if necessary, as he put it, 'the operation at Narvik could wait'.

Churchill was strongly opposed to this change of priority. No alteration should be made, he urged, 'in the present plans for the capture of Narvik, which were, in fact, already in the process of being carried out'. But Chamberlain reiterated the views of the French Mission in Sweden, that Trondheim should 'stand first' in the order of Allied objectives, and he suggested that the French troops—the Chasseurs Alpins—then on their way to Narvik, should be diverted in due course to Trondheim. Churchill again spoke against the new objective, telling his colleagues he was:

... very apprehensive of any proposals which might tend to weaken our intention to seize Narvik. Nothing must be allowed to deflect us from making the capture of this place as certain as possible. Our plans against Narvik had been very carefully laid, and there seemed every chance that they would be successful if they were allowed to proceed without being tampered with. Trondheim was, on the other hand, a much more speculative affair, and he deprecated any suggestion which might lead to the diversion of the Chasseurs

Alpins until we had definitely established ourselves at Narvik. Otherwise we might find ourselves committed to a number of ineffectual operations along the Norwegian coast, none of which would succeed.

Once the British force at Narvik had succeeded in its objective, Churchill pointed out, General Mackesy 'would be free to address his mind to the possibility of carrying out further operations to the south'. He was no longer to try to advance to Gällivare, 'since, if Sweden was friendly, we should have no need to be apprehensive about the orefields, and, if hostile, the difficulty of pushing on would be too great'.

Chamberlain and Halifax were supported by the Chancellor of the Exchequer, Sir John Simon, who felt that the Norwegians and Swedes 'were disposed to wilt because they thought that we were only interested in Narvik'. Churchill was a minority voice, supported only by Stanley, who wanted the French to be told that the capture of Narvik was 'an essential prerequisite' to operations in the Trondheim area.

The War Cabinet now decided, against Churchill's judgment, to undertake a further commitment.[1] As Churchill himself informed Reynaud and Daladier that same day: 'We are proposing in the next few days to land 4,000 infantry, additional to those going to Narvik, at a suitable point on the coast to secure a lodgment from which larger forces may be directed upon Trondheim.' If the Chasseurs Alpins were not required 'to clinch matters at Narvik', Churchill added, the British Government wanted now 'permission to divert them when the time comes to the Trondheim operation'.[2]

At a second meeting of the Military Co-ordination Committee that day, the Trondheim landing, code name 'Maurice', was discussed in detail. Five battalions were to be prepared for it, and the 127th Infantry Brigade, which was about to go to France, was ordered to be held back in England for at least a week. In the meantime, 'the first road movements of the brigade to the ports of embarkation should be begun immediately', with a view to its 'possible arrival' in Norway on April 26 or the following day.[3]

---

[1] War Cabinet No. 91 of 1940, 13 April 1940, 11.30 a.m., Minute 3, Confidential Annex: Cabinet papers, 65/12.

[2] 'Most Secret', 13 April 1940: Cabinet papers, 21/1388. In his original message Churchill had written that full details of the Trondheim operations 'are now being worked out *and will be sent to you before the decision becomes necessary*' (author's italics). Lord Halifax had insisted, however, as Ismay informed Neville Chamberlain's office, on the deletion of the passage in italics before the message was sent. Ismay added: 'In view of the secrecy of this telegram, I am arranging for it to be sent by aeroplane in charge of an officer.'

[3] Military Co-ordination Committee No. 22 of 1940, 13 April 1940, 10.30 p.m.: Cabinet papers, 83/3.

Deeply concerned about the military implications of this second, and now major landing, Churchill wrote that evening to Stanley about the number and quality of the British troops involved:

My dear Oliver,

We are being irresistibly drawn into all kinds of improvised operations with raw, half-trained troops, and it is quite possible that the Germans are using carefully-selected units, or units accompanied by a large proportion of care-fully-selected men, with whom in a few days we may be in contact. I wonder therefore whether it is not possible to stiffen the 'Maurice' force by one or two regular regiments of mechanised cavalry. Take the mobile division in York-shire, for example. Here you have high-grade regular units. It is true they are despicably armed so far as fighting in Flanders is concerned, but at any rate they are highly-trained. Their addition to the Territorials it is proposed to use would give a sprinkling of competent officers and men to hold strong points or reconnoitre. Even their wretched tanks are quite good as far as movement and machine-gunning is concerned. As the cruiser tanks with which they are to be equipped in the future are still many months away, there would be time to get them over, with or without their vehicles, in time to help this improvised adventure and they could be withdrawn when the position is established.

'Pray let me know,' Churchill ended, 'what your advisers think of this.'[1]

The primacy of the Norwegian plans in Britain's war strategy was unchallenged, and in the second week of April was underlined by a report, prepared at the request of Simon and Kingsley Wood, by the economist Lord Stamp, who came to the conclusion that if Germany occupied Norway, she 'would be relieved of all anxiety on the score of supplies of iron ore so long as she retained control of the Baltic'. Stamp also pointed out that Germany would secure 'for her own use' the skilled engineering and shipbuilding labour 'available in Scandinavia, and the plants in which they are employed'.[2]

April 13, the day on which Lord Stamp's report was circulated to the members of the War Cabinet, was the day on which all seven German destroyers in Narvik Bay had been sunk, and a successful British landing seemed imminent. 'On the assumption that Narvik falls into our hands in the near future,' Churchill minuted on the following morning, 'we must consider the uses to which we intend to put it.' Above all, it should be made 'a convenient oiling base', where the British flotillas acting on the Norwegian coast 'can refuel at the highest

[1] 'Urgent', 'Secret', 'By Box', 13 April 1940, 7.30 p.m.: Churchill papers, 19/2.
[2] War Cabinet Paper No. 103 of 1940, 13 April 1940, 'Secret', circulated by the Chancellor of the Exchequer (Sir John Simon) on behalf of himself and the Lord Privy Seal (Sir Kingsley Wood): Cabinet papers, 67/6.

economy'. Secondly, the 'masses of ore' at Narvik should be shipped to Britain 'in a very active manner'. For both these ends, a 'moderate garrison' was needed 'about a thousand Territorial troops', Churchill suggested, protected by anti-aircraft guns. Britain's object, he concluded, 'must be to make Narvik self-supporting and self-defended at the earliest moment after we have it in our power. . . .'[1]

At the War Cabinet on April 14 Chamberlain offered 'the congratulations of the War Cabinet' to Churchill and Pound for the 'brilliant operation' carried out at Narvik on the previous day. This success seemed a prelude, not only to a military landing, but to wider advantages to Britain. Halifax hoped that the interruption being caused to German sea traffic would force the Germans to demand the right of passage through Sweden. 'It was most important,' he said, 'that everything possible should be done to intensify our operations so as to force the Germans to take action against Sweden.' Looking further afield, it was Churchill who commented that 'the heavy German losses' in the previous week would create 'a profound impression' on Mussolini.

The Italian perspective remained an important one, with the preservation of Italian neutrality a main object of British and French policy.[2] That same day, the Foreign Office studied a report from Rome to the effect that the Fascist leaders were impressed by German accounts of the operations in Scandinavia. According to one source, however, Mussolini had decided to enter the war on the German side 'but is still waiting until he is sure of German success in Scandinavia'.[3]

Reading this report, Orme Sargent commented: 'Mussolini's decision may well depend on the result of the race between ourselves and the Germans to get to Trondheim. If we don't win the race Mussolini will conclude that Hitler has succeeded in his conquest of Norway.' Sargent added, somewhat cynically, or perhaps realistically: 'I fear that yesterday's successful operations at Narvik will not impress him in the least.' 'Still,' added Cadogan, 'we must play it up.'[4]

A further telegram was now sent to Rome and Tokyo, stressing Britain's successes. 'Result of action at Narvik,' it read, 'is complete de-

[1] Minute No. 287, 14 April 1940: Churchill papers, 19/6.

[2] See Sir William Deakin, 'Les Relations Franco-Anglaises et le Problème de la Neutralité Italienne (Septembre 1939–Juin 1940)', a paper delivered in Paris in December 1975 and published in Français et Britanniques dans la Drôle de Guerre, Paris 1979.

[3] The source was André François-Poncet, French Ambassador in Rome (and formerly French Ambassador in Berlin).

[4] Foreign Office papers, 371/24939. A widely held Foreign Office fear was that 'in the event of matters moving badly for the Allies in the North and possibly in the West', Mussolini would invade Yugoslavia (Telegram No. 94 and 233 DIPP to Paris and Ankara, 14 April 1940, 11.55 p.m.: Foreign Office papers, 371/24939).

struction of remainder of German naval forces there, seven destroyers and one submarine, making surrender of land forces inevitable. Allies thus obtain invaluable base which will control whole of North Norway and greatly facilitate land operations in South Norway now about to begin.' The telegram continued, with a passage added by Sargent: 'Thus the action at Narvik is not an end in itself but merely its first step towards the early expulsion of Germans from all the strategic points which they hold on the North Sea & the reinforcement of the Norwegian Army now operating in the interior of the country.'[1]

That such confident assertions were effective, and that the news that they reported was impressive to some, was clear from a telegram from the British Minister at the Vatican, sent to London two days later. 'I am told,' wrote the Minister, 'that Signor Mussolini is in a very bad mood today presumably owing to news of British successes in Scandinavia.' Although Mussolini was 'obsessed by desire to go to war and is liable to order attack on Greece from Albania at any moment', on the other hand, 'news of latest German naval losses and of British landing in Norway (reported in this evening's Press) may exercise a moderating and deterrent effect. . . .' And yet, the Minister added, 'in his abnormal condition of excitability' Mussolini was 'capable of any folly'.[2] This telegram was subsequently circulated to the members of the War Cabinet.

The naval success at Narvik began to convince Churchill, in spite of his previous caution, that Halifax's persistent pressure for an attack on Trondheim might not be so ill-advised as he had at first believed. During the War Cabinet of April 14, Churchill explained that the Narvik military force would arrive in the area 'during the course of that day', and that there was an unconfirmed report that the German forces 'were in retreat and were being rounded up by the Norwegians'. This 'altered' situation, he said, permitted 'a more hopeful view to be taken' with regard to operations in the Trondheim area. He had spoken on the telephone to Reynaud, who was 'prepared to give us a free hand' in the employment of the Chasseurs Alpins division.[3]

Churchill then told the War Cabinet that the Naval Staff had suggested that 'it might be possible' to land at Trondheim itself. Three hundred seamen and marines would be landed 'in any event' at Namsos later that day: operation 'Henry'. At dawn on April 16, six hundred

[1] Telegrams to Rome and Tokyo, 14 April 1940: Foreign Office papers, 371/24939.
[2] Telegram No. 40 DIPP, from the Vatican, 16 April 1940: Foreign Office papers, 371/24939.
[3] The Chasseurs Alpins division reached the Clyde on 15 April 1940. Its despatch to Norway was given the code name 'Gerard'.

marines and seamen would land at Ålesund: operation 'Primrose'. These landings, Churchill reported, would 'tend to attract the Germans away from Trondheim itself', and lead to their dispersal.

Churchill also noted that some 23,000 men would be available for the Trondheim operation, while the Germans 'had only some 3,500 men' at Trondheim. He felt therefore that a landing there 'did not appear to involve unjustifiable risks', particularly, 'as seemed possible', the Norwegians still held the railway to the port.[1]

Further hope of a speedy victory at Narvik reached the War Cabinet during the afternoon of April 14, when Admiral Whitworth telegraphed, as the Military Co-ordination Committee recorded, 'that he was convinced that Narvik could be taken by direct assault without fear of meeting serious opposition on landing'. The main landing force, Whitworth judged, 'need only be small', if supported by ships and destroyers with 'the best available' anti-aircraft armament.

The Military Co-ordination Committee noted that Whitworth's telegram had been sent to the ships carrying both the naval and military commanders into the area, but that the question of whether or not to act on the Admiral's advice 'must be left to Lord Cork and General Mackesy to decide after they had consulted together'.[2] The Committee did decide, however, at a further meeting that afternoon, that one of the Brigades for Narvik, the 146th, comprising 2,500 troops, should be, and indeed was already being diverted southwards towards Namsos.

The Chiefs of Staff had been emphatic that 'owing to the necessity of getting to the Trondheim area as quickly as possible', it was, as they expressed it, 'better to divert one of the Narvik brigades there immediately'. During the discussion at the Military Co-ordination Committee it was pointed out that the 146th Brigade were Territorial troops 'whose training was not yet advanced', a fact which, the minutes recorded, 'tended to increase the risk of the operation'. The Committee were agreed, however, 'that in the circumstances these risks must be accepted and the position fully explained to the War Cabinet'.

Both Norwegian landings were now about to be carried out; the landing at Narvik, code name 'Rupert', at daylight on the following morning, April 15, and 'Maurice' at Trondheim also on April 15. At the same time, 'Maurice' was to be supported by 'Henry' at Namsos on the night of April 15, and by 'Primrose' at Ålesund, timed for the early hours of April 17. The Military Co-ordination Committee also

---

[1] War Cabinet No. 92 of 1940, 14 April 1940, 11.30 a.m.: Cabinet papers, 65/5.
[2] Telegram sent at 1.54 p.m., 14 April 1940: Military Co-ordination Committee No. 23 of 1940, 14 April 1940, 4.30 p.m.: Cabinet papers, 83/3.

confirmed that air attacks would be made on Stavanger aerodrome 'to synchronise with the landings at Namsos'.[1]

The Norwegian plan, although much revised and amended, seemed to be on the eve of fulfilment. On the morning of April 15, in reply to the King's letter of April 12, Churchill wrote of how, since he had received that letter, 'we have had a good success' at sea, and that he hoped to have 'something more & better to say about Narvik before long'. Churchill's letter continued:

These have indeed been most crowded days & I have had to do my utmost to keep pace with the ceaseless flow of telegrams. We are aiming at Trondheim which wd be an even greater prize than Narvik. It will be an operation of much difficulty & risk; but we must not fail to profit by success & speed.[2]

As the telegrams reached the Admiralty during April 15, it was clear that all was not well. Off Narvik, after consulting with General Mackesy in Vaags Fiord, Lord Cork telegraphed that Mackesy 'did not consider an immediate attack practicable'.[3] They had therefore decided not to attempt to land at Narvik itself. Three hundred men of the Scots Guards had, however, landed at Salangen, on the mainland thirty miles to the north of Narvik, a unit of Irish Guardsmen had landed at Bogen, while Mackesy had established his base at Harstad, on Hinnöy island.

At Namsos, a report from the Naval landing party of three hundred men stressed 'that it would be unwise, in the absence of air defences', to put any large number of troop transports into Namsos, 'where there were no unloading facilities'.[4] In addition, as Churchill reported to the War Cabinet on the morning of April 15, Namsos itself 'was under four feet of snow and offered no concealment from the air'. It was also short of fresh water.

As for operation 'Primrose', this had not even sailed, as the six hundred sailors and marines due to land at Ålesund had been 'held up' all day by a gale at Invergordon, and when they did set sail across the North Sea on the following morning, it was not known whether or not Ålesund was 'in German hands'; they were therefore to be diverted to Andalsnes.

In his report to the War Cabinet on April 15, Churchill had warned

---

[1] Military Co-ordination Committee No. 24 of 1940, 14 April 1940, 5.45 p.m.: Cabinet papers, 83/3.

[2] Letter of 15 April 1940: Royal Archives.

[3] Signal sent at 8 p.m., 15 April 1940: Admiralty papers, 199/1929. See maps on pages 265 and 266.

[4] 'Most Secret', 'Summary of impending operations', 16 April 1940: Admiralty papers, 199/1929.

that the Narvik operation was not going as well as had been hoped. HMS *Kimberley*, which had been operating off Narvik on the previous day, had reported 'that the defence was stiffening and that she had suffered casualties from enemy machine-gun fire from the shore'. There were general indications, Churchill added, that Narvik 'was going to prove a military proposition, and that we could not count on taking it without resistance'.

In his survey on April 15, Churchill also stressed the 'very hazardous nature' of the Trondheim operation, not only on account of the terrain, 'and of the exposure of the landing forces to air attack', but also because 'the majority of the troops to be employed were not highly trained'.[1]

Churchill's warnings were not intended to cast doubt on 'Rupert' or on 'Maurice'. But early that afternoon, at a meeting of the Chiefs of Staff, it was felt that 'Maurice', the direct attack on Trondheim, 'would be costly in execution' and would be 'unlikely' to result in the capture of Trondheim. The Chiefs of Staff therefore proposed postponing the direct Trondheim attack for at least a week.

Wishing, however, 'to keep up activity' in the Trondheim area, the Chiefs of Staff suggested, in a draft memorandum for discussion at the next meeting of the Military Co-ordination Committee, that 'Henry' and 'Primrose' should be continued, with these twin attacks, on Namsos and Andalsnes, having as their aim the 'isolating' of the German forces in Trondheim, prior to a direct attack.

Trondheim was not therefore to be abandoned, but only, and briefly, postponed. Nevertheless, it was Chamberlain who expressed his 'great disappointment' at even this short delay.[2] 'Capture of Trondheim considered essential,' Ironside telegraphed to de Wiart shortly before midnight on April 15.[3]

The news from 'Henry' had been bad throughout the day, however, and during the evening the Admiralty learnt that although de Wiart had arrived off Namsos, he had been 'unable for the moment to disembark', owing to enemy gunfire.[4]

Early on the morning of April 16 Churchill saw Ismay, to tell him that he 'disagreed entirely' with the Chiefs of Staff 'as to the plan for the attack on Trondheim': that is, to postpone the frontal assault in

---

[1] War Cabinet No. 93 of 1940, 15 April 1940, 11 a.m., Minute 4, Confidential Annex: Cabinet papers, 65/12.

[2] Military Co-ordination Committee No. 25 of 1940, 15 April 1940, 5.30 p.m.: Cabinet papers, 83/3.

[3] Military Co-ordination Committee No. 26 of 1940, 16 April 1940, noon, Confidential Annex: Cabinet papers, 83/3, folio 246.

[4] Admiralty papers, 199/1929. De Wiart had arrived by flying boat.

order first to isolate Trondheim by the pincer attacks at Namsos and Andalsnes.

It emerged during Churchill's discussion with Ismay that Pound had not yet shown Churchill the draft memorandum of the previous afternoon setting out the views of the Chiefs of Staff 'as to how the attack should be carried out'. As Ismay talked to Churchill, it became clear to him that the difference was 'at the most no more than one of emphasis'.

Ismay then wrote to Chamberlain that his fear was not for the Trondheim plan itself, but on the clash of personalities. Having regard 'to the strained feelings which understandably existed' on the Military Co-ordination Committee, there was, he warned, 'every chance of a first-class row' if Churchill were to chair the meeting that day, April 16, during the discussion of the proposed delay in the direct attack on Trondheim.

Ismay also told Sir Edward Bridges of his fears. Bridges went at once to see Churchill, and Churchill then went to see Chamberlain. At their meeting, Churchill asked Chamberlain to chair the meeting. Bridges had also taken steps to avert a crisis, and, at that morning's Chiefs of Staff meeting, having cleared the room of Assistant Secretaries, 'implored the Chiefs of Staff to exercise the most rigid control over themselves and at all costs to keep their tempers'. Otherwise, Bridges warned, there would be 'a first-class political row'.[1]

On April 16 the news from the Narvik area was of deep snow, a night-time temperature of zero degrees fahrenheit, and the danger of casualties from frostbite. In preparation for that day's Military Co-ordination Committee, at which Chamberlain was to preside for the first time, Churchill prepared a summary of the situation, approved by the Naval Staff, which tried, as he wrote to Chamberlain that morning, 'to clamp together the various & changing plans wh are now afoot'. Churchill added that in the event of 'difficulties arising' during the Committee meeting, 'I shall have to involve yr assistance'.[2]

In his note, Churchill pointed out that the Namsos and Andalsnes landings were to be regarded 'as diversions to confuse the enemy', and also as the 'speediest means' to bring British troops to 'join and encourage' the Norwegian forces 'which stand between us and the enemy'. For the postponed Trondheim landing, it was hoped that the Guards Brigade then at Salangen, north of Narvik, the one brigade of regular troops in the region, would be available after April 20, and that the

[1] Memorandum by Sir Edward Bridges, dated 25 April 1940: Premier papers, 1/404.
[2] 'Private', 16 April 1940: Admiralty papers, 199/1929.

Trondheim landing itself could now take place on April 22 or April 23, with 'not less than 7,000 or 8,000 men composed of the best fighting troops available'.

To help the Trondheim attack, Stavanger aerodrome would be bombarded by the guns of HMS *Suffolk*, with the hope of putting it 'out of action' entirely.[1]

'We are managing to keep going quite reasonably at the moment,' Eric Seal wrote to his wife that day, '& we are all quietly optimistic, albeit perhaps a trifle impatient at the time it takes to get going. However, it's only a week since the Norwegian trouble started, & we haven't done so badly.' His own fear 'all along', Seal added, had been 'that we should allow the enemy too long to consolidate'.[2]

That same day one of Neville Chamberlain's Private Secretaries, John Colville, noted in his diary: 'Our forces at Narvik, under Lord Cork, are rather loth to make an attack because of the snow, but Winston feels that a long delay would be disastrous both for military and psychological reasons.' There were signs, Colville added, that the Norwegians 'will lose heart unless quickly assured of substantial support'.[3]

News of the disagreements over the postponement of the direct Trondheim attack had spread beyond those actually involved in the postponement, for or against. When the War Cabinet met on the morning of April 16, there was a feeling among certain Ministers that decisions of war policy were being made at the Military Co-ordination Committee, without the War Cabinet having the chance to question them in any detail, or to examine the background to them.

There was considerable discontent among Ministers who had not been consulted about the postponement of Trondheim, or about the wisdom of the newly scheduled attack of April 22. In a note for Chamberlain, Sir Horace Wilson reported a conversation between Simon, the Chancellor of the Exchequer, Kingsley Wood, now Lord Privy Seal, and Hankey, the Minister without Portfolio. These three Ministers, Wilson wrote, had agreed that it was 'most unsatisfactory' that the Cabinet should be invited 'to acquiesce in naval and military operations which are obviously of a hazardous character', having before them, as Simon told Wilson, 'only oral statements made at the Cabinet and not having the customary written appreciations of the Chiefs of Staff'.

---

[1] 'Most Secret', Note by the Chairman of the Military Co-ordination Committee, 16 April 1940: Admiralty papers, 199/1929.

[2] Letter of 16 April 1940: Seal papers.

[3] Colville diary, 16 April 1940: Colville papers.

Horace Wilson suggested to Simon that he should see Chamberlain 'at once' to tell him his views. At the ensuing meeting Chamberlain told Simon, to set his mind at rest, that he 'had it in mind' to take the Chairmanship of the Military Co-ordination Committee, 'at any rate for the time being'.[1]

The Military Co-ordination Committee thus met, at noon, at 10 Downing Street, with Chamberlain in the chair. At the outset, the Prime Minister 'emphasised', as the minutes recorded, 'the need for carrying out the main operation on Trondheim with the least possible delay'. It was essential, he added, to 'make contact' with the Norwegian forces holding Steinkjer, north of Trondheim, 'at the earliest possible moment'.

Churchill, however, was worried about the small scale and lack of quality of the troops being made available for the main Trondheim assault. Twenty-five years earlier, the Dardanelles expedition had in his view come to grief because Kitchener, as Secretary of State for War, had delayed sending first class troops to the Peninsula. Now Churchill saw the same danger at Trondheim: that the troops needed to make the landings a success, and to push through to Steinkjer as Chamberlain wanted, would be kept back at Narvik and Namsos, and that Trondheim and its hinterland would be lost through lack of a sufficiently concentrated military force.

As Churchill told the Military Co-ordination Committee on April 16:

Time was necessary to plan what was a hazardous and, if successful, would be a brilliant operation. He thought, however, it was essential to have a large force of well trained troops. For this reason, he was disposed to question the use of the first demi-brigade of Chasseurs Alpins at Namsos. He was afraid that we might find ourselves with appreciable forces held up, both at Narvik and Namsos, and with insufficiency of seasoned troops for the central thrust. This was rather confirmed by the latest news as to the position at Narvik.

The Narvik 'position' was that the British headquarters were at Harstad, the Scots Guards across Vaags Fiord at Salangen, but Narvik itself still under German control.

During the discussion that followed Churchill's warning, it was agreed that 'only troops of the first quality' should be used in the Trondheim operation, and that to make this possible a regular brigade should be withdrawn from France. The Committee were 'reluctant', as the minutes recorded, 'to weaken Lord Gort's forces at a time when

[1] Memorandum by Sir Horace Wilson, dated 25 April 1940: Premier papers, 1/404, folio 20.

a German attack appeared imminent, but it was considered essential that one regular brigade should be added to the forces available for the attack on Trondheim'. The planning of the attack should proceed, Chamberlain himself declared, 'on the assumption that this regular brigade would be available'.[1]

As soon as this meeting was over, Neville Chamberlain told Sir Horace Wilson 'that the First Lord had expressed to him his gratification at the way in which the business before the Committee had been transacted; Mr Churchill added that he hoped that the Prime Minister would be able to continue to take the Chair, at any rate while the present affair was in progress'.[2]

For Churchill, the appearance of Chamberlain as Chairman had, as he expressed it to Ismay and Bridges, 'got him out of a hole'.[3] But early the following morning, April 17, Hankey again discussed the Scandinavian plans while walking with Chamberlain in St James's Park, and in a note of their discussion submitted immediately afterwards, Hankey put in writing his verbal caution, noting that the Dardanelles Royal Commission had criticized the Ministers of 1915 for not eliciting the views of their naval and military advisers. It was essential now, Hankey stressed, to know the 'collective opinion' of the Chiefs of Staff. Hankey added: 'an attack on coast fortifications and a landing in a foreign country are probably the most difficult kind of operation that can be undertaken. Attacks on coast forts have scarcely ever succeeded unless either there was treachery within (as apparently at Oslo) or markedly superior force available (as at Alexandria).'[4]

Chamberlain heeded Hankey's warning, and at once sent for Sir Cyril Newall to ask him whether, at the forthcoming meeting of the Military Co-ordination Committee, scheduled for ten o'clock that same morning, the Chiefs of Staff would be ready to express their true views. Newall replied in the affirmative, whereupon Chamberlain reminded him that 'he must regard himself as responsible for expressing disagreement, if he or the Chiefs of Staffs did disagree', about what was 'about to be settled' in the Military Co-ordination Committee and, an hour later, at the War Cabinet.

Newall then asked Chamberlain if he could tell his colleagues what Chamberlain had said, and Chamberlain agreed that he should do so.

---

[1] Military Co-ordination Committee No. 26, of 1940, 16 April 1940, noon: Cabinet papers, 83/3.

[2] Note by Sir Horace Wilson, 25 April 1940: Premier papers, 1/404, folio 19.

[3] Note by Sir Edward Bridges, 25 April 1940: Premier papers, 1/404, folio 32.

[4] Note by Sir Maurice Hankey, 17 April 1940: Premier papers, 1/404, folios 29–31.

There would now be no doubt as to whether or not the Chiefs of Staff supported the plans which the politicians believed should be carried out, and at the War Cabinet itself, as Sir Horace Wilson noted that same day, questions were put to Newall 'which elicited the fact that the Chiefs of Staff were in agreement with the military plans which had been decided upon at the meeting of the Military Co-ordination Committee'.[1] The direct attack on Trondheim was thus to go ahead, assisted by a regular brigade of British troops, as Churchill had urged and Chamberlain endorsed.

Reflecting that day upon Chamberlain's Chairmanship of the Military Co-ordination Committee, Ronald Harris, Sir Edward Bridges' Secretary, told John Colville 'that Winston has been presiding over innumerable Committees, talking a lot and getting nothing done, but that now the PM has begun to preside over the Military Co-ordination Committee, things are beginning to move, more practical plans are being made and there are signs that the difficulties and opportunities of the situation are being handled in a realistic manner'.[2]

This realism centred upon the imminent British naval attack on Trondheim, an attack which was based upon the prior landing of British troops at Narvik, and the subsequent transfer of the Guards Brigade from Narvik to the Trondheim area by April 20. But on the morning of April 17 the whole plan was put in jeopardy when General Mackesy, reporting from his island headquarters at Harstad, decided that he would not make a direct assault on Narvik until the snows had melted. This, he explained, might not be until the end of the month. In the meantime he would hold on to Harstad and Salangen, and possibly a further unoccupied position on the approaches to Narvik. Mackesy also asked to be sent further troops, including the Chasseurs Alpins who had been diverted to the Trondheim operation, and for HMS *Warspite* to remain as his principal naval support.

Mackesy's decision to delay caused consternation to Churchill, who described it, in a note for the Military Co-ordination Committee, as 'at once unexpected and disagreeable'. Churchill went on to point out that one of 'the best regular brigades in the Army', the Guards Brigade, 'will be wasting away, losing men by sickness, and playing no part'.[3]

Churchill's view was endorsed by the Chiefs of Staff, at whose

[1] Note by Sir Horace Wilson, 17 April 1940: Premier papers, 1/404, folios 26–7.

[2] Colville diary, 17 April 1940: Colville papers.

[3] 'Military Co-ordination Committee, Note by the Chairman', 17 April 1940, 1.45 a.m.: Admiralty papers, 199/1929. Circulated to the Chiefs of Staff and Military Co-ordination Committees as Military Co-ordination Committee Memorandum No. 77 of 1940, 17 April 1940: Cabinet papers, 83/5.

meeting, at nine o'clock that morning, there was what the minutes described as 'general agreement on the need for urging General Mackesy to press on, if possible, with the capture of Narvik'.[1] The Chiefs of Staff had before them Churchill's note, in which he proposed to send a telegram to Cork and Mackesy urging a reconsideration of the General's decision. The Chiefs of Staff agreed that the telegram should be sent. It began: 'Your proposals involved damaging deadlock at Narvik and the neutralisation of one of our best brigades,' and went on to inform Mackesy that he could not be sent the Chasseurs Alpins, nor could he have the support of HMS *Warspite* for more than two or three days. 'The capture of the port and town would be an important success,' the telegram continued. 'Send us your appreciation and act at once if you consider right. Matter most urgent.'[2]

Churchill's telegram was again considered, together with the Chiefs of Staff endorsement, by the Military Co-ordination Committee which met at ten o'clock that morning, with Chamberlain in the chair. The other committee members, Chamberlain, Stanley and Hoare, 'endorsed' Churchill's opinion that 'it was of the highest importance to liquidate the position at Narvik as early as possible', and they too agreed with the text of the telegram to be sent to Cork and Mackesy.[3]

The War Cabinet met at 11.30 that morning to discuss the Norwegian situation. The point had been made at the Military Co-ordination Committee, Churchill told them, 'that the casualties in General Mackesy's force caused by exposure in the next few weeks might well be as severe as those which would be suffered in an immediate assault'. For this reason, the Committee had agreed to send the telegram to Cork and Mackesy which, 'while in no way over-ruling their judgement, put before them arguments in favour of an early assault'.

Apart from the new possibility of delay at Narvik, all else, Churchill reported, was proceeding well. Troops were being landed at Namsos, and General de Wiart had spoken 'of being able to begin his thrust towards Trondheim' from Namsos on April 21. Some six hundred marines would arrive at Andalsnes that night, followed by a further thousand troops on April 18, to take part in the second Trondheim diversion. For the Trondheim landing itself 2,500 French troops and a thousand Canadians were available for a landing on April 22, with a

[1] Chiefs of Staff Committee No. 83 of 1940, 17 April 1940, 10 a.m., Minute 2, Confidential Annex: Cabinet papers, 79/85.

[2] 'Most Secret', 'Most Immediate', 17 April 1940, 1.50 p.m., approved by 1st Sea Lord (Sir Dudley Pound): Admiralty papers, 199/1929.

[3] Military Co-ordination Committee No. 27 of 1940, 17 April 1940, 10 a.m.: Cabinet papers, 83/3.

further thousand British Territorials who could 'exploit any success achieved' by the first landing.

Although these landings would involve 'considerable' risk, Newall told the War Cabinet, they were 'not out of proportion to the value of success if achieved'. The military value of such a success, Newall added, 'should not perhaps be rated too highly, but it was clear that the political and moral advantages which would result from the capture of Trondheim would be very great', a view with which Chamberlain at once expressed his agreement.[1]

Churchill was still confident that success could be achieved in the Norwegian operation, and in a letter that afternoon to Admiral Forbes, he expressed that confidence clearly. 'All that has happened,' he wrote, 'makes me sure that Hitler had made a grave strategic blunder in giving us the right, as we have always had the power, to take what we like on the Norwegian coast.' There were already 25,000 men available 'to support the Navy' on the western seaboard of Norway, Churchill wrote, but he was trying to get at least 50,000 by the end of May, 'irrespective of whether or not the great battle opens in Flanders'. Churchill's letter continued:

I look forward to an increasingly vigorous campaign being fought along the Norwegian coast during the summer, and I trust we shall be able to beat them out of all their lodgments and establish ourselves in their place right down to Bergen.

Naturally we were taken aback by General Mackesy's proposal to sit down in front of Narvik, and convert the operation into a kind of siege. We have sent him and Lord Cork a telegram which I trust will lead to resolute action, although of course the risk must be run and the price must be paid. We are still awaiting the response to this.[2]

Shortly before midnight, in an attempt to ensure that Mackesy's decision might be reversed, Churchill sent a personal telegram to Cork. 'Should you consider that situation is being mishandled,' he wrote, 'it is your duty to report either to me personally or to the Admiralty upon it, and what you would do yourself.' In this event, Churchill added, 'you should of course inform the General of the action you have taken, so that he will have an opportunity of expressing his views to the War Office.'[3]

---

[1] War Cabinet No. 95 of 1940, 17 April 1940, 11.30 a.m., Minute 3, Confidential Annex: Cabinet papers, 65/12.

[2] 'Secret & Personal', 17 April 1940: Churchill papers, 19/2.

[3] 'Action This Day', 'Most Immediate', 'Personal and Private', 17 April 1940, despatched to Narvik as Signal No. 2332, timed at 11.32 p.m.: Churchill papers, 19/2.

This attempt by Churchill to reactivate the earliest possible action at Narvik was unsuccessful. 'I have urged assault,' Cork replied on the afternoon of April 18, 'but feel obliged to accept soldiers' view, which seems unanimous, at least until snow disappears.' The soldiers, Cork added, 'refuse to entertain idea of assault'.[1]

Sometimes there was a moment of direct contact between the events at Narvik and the men in London who had set these events in motion. On April 19 Churchill himself welcomed back to Britain the survivors of the destroyer *Hardy*, which had been beached during the destroyer action in Vest Fiord on April 10. Many of her crew had managed to get ashore, and then been rescued by other Royal Naval ships. Captain Warburton-Lee had been killed on the bridge by German naval gunfire. His last instruction had been: 'continue to engage the enemy'. Posthumously he was awarded the Victoria Cross.

In welcoming the survivors back to Britain, Churchill praised their 'readiness to take opportunities by the hand', and described them as 'the vanguard of the Army which we and our French allies will use this summer to purge and cleanse the soil of the Vikings, the soil of Norway, from the filthy pollution of Nazi tyranny'. We know, Churchill added, 'that after a short rest you will be anxious to resume your duties in this conflict. In the name of the Board of the Admiralty I wish you good fortune and success.'

It was, Churchill told the survivors of the *Hardy*, a 'hard and obstinate war'.[2] But other than at Narvik, the operations appeared to be proceeding according to plan. At Namsos, Churchill had reported to the Military Co-ordination Committee on the morning of April 18, Brigadier Phillips' brigade[3] was ashore 'complete without loss', while the Chasseurs Alpins were expected there 'at dusk'. Advancing from Namsos, these forces should, Churchill added, 'be exercising considerable pressure on the Germans north of Trondheim' by April 21. Also ashore by the morning of April 18 were the seven hundred men sent to Andalsnes, who landed 'without incident'[4] and more would be landed within the next twenty-four hours. Meanwhile, a petrol and ammunition dump, established by the Germans near Bjerkvik, north of Narvik, had been destroyed by a landing party from HMS *Faulkner*, with the loss of one rating killed.

---

[1] Signal timed at 1.17 p.m., 18 April 1940: Admiralty papers, 199/1929.
[2] Speech of 19 April 1940: *The Times*, 20 April 1940.
[3] The 146th Brigade.
[4] Lieutenant-Colonel H. W. Simpson, RM, 'Situation Report No. 1', 19 April 1940: Admiralty papers, 202/422.

The Norwegians, meanwhile, had appealed for Allied reinforcements further to the south, at Lillehammer, and it was Chamberlain himself who told the Military Co-ordination Committee of these 'urgent appeals' for troops. The Norwegians, he added, 'were saying that if these did not arrive soon, they would not be able to hold out'. In reply, Ironside spoke with a certain optimism. Although it would not be possible, he said, to send troops 'in the next few days', he did feel that if 'the operations around Trondheim developed successfully', Britain's object would then be to establish a front 'as far south as possible', so that 'we might divert troops from Dombaas towards Lillehammer'.[1]

Ironside had already telegraphed to Mackesy on April 18, to inform him that no Chasseurs Alpins could be sent to him 'owing to other operations in Scandinavia', and he added: 'Your action should be based upon having no more troops than you have at present.'[2] This telegram effectively confirmed Mackesy in his resolve not to advance on Narvik until the snows had melted, and on the morning of April 19 he set out his reasons for delay in a wireless message to the War Office. 'I must point out,' the message read, 'that I have not even one field gun and I have not even one anti-aircraft gun. I have practically no mortar ammunition. My force is probably inferior to the enemy.' He needed more troops, nor could he undertake for 'some weeks' any tactical movements with the troops he did have, 'owing to snow conditions'. As for any offensive operation, this, he said, 'without artillery must be ruled out'.[3]

This message reached the Admiralty shortly before midday, and effectively ended any chance that Churchill still had of persuading Mackesy to attack Narvik without delay, the original landing having been planned for April 15, four days before. Two hours after Mackesy's message had been decoded and circulated, the Chiefs of Staff met to discuss the Trondheim operations, planned for April 22. It was Pound who now proposed that instead of a direct assault on Trondheim, helped by the pincer attacks at Namsos and Andalsnes, only the pincer movements should be attempted.

The Chiefs of Staff accepted Pound's proposal, being influenced in their decision by the 'dangers' of German air attacks on the landing forces, and by the risk to so many British warships within the confined

---

[1] Military Co-ordination Committee No. 28 of 1940, 18 April 1940, 10 a.m.: Cabinet papers, 83/3.

[2] 'Most Immediate', 18 April 1940: Cabinet papers, 83/3, folio 260.

[3] 'Most Immediate', from HMS *Aurora*, by Wireless Telegraph, sent 9.43 a.m., received 11.29 a.m., 19 April 1940: Admiralty papers, 199/1929.

waters of the fiord. This was the view not only of Ironside, Newall and Pound, but also of their deputies, Dill, Peirse and Phillips.[1]

'When I became aware of this right-about-turn,' Churchill later recalled, 'I was indignant, and questioned searchingly the officers concerned.' But the harder he questioned them, the clearer it became that 'all professional opinion was now adverse to the operation which only a few days before it had spontaneously espoused'.[2]

The full extent of the Chiefs of Staff's change of plan was explained by Churchill himself to the War Cabinet in a memorandum which he circulated late that afternoon. The Chiefs of Staff and their Deputies, Churchill wrote, had advised 'a complete alteration of the emphasis between the two pincer attacks and the centre attack'. Under the new plan, the 'main weight was to be thrown into the Northern and Southern pincers', and the central attack on Trondheim 'should be reduced to a demonstration'.

Churchill then listed the four reasons which had led the Chiefs of Staff and their Deputies to this change. First, the 'considerable advance' of de Wiart from Namsos. Second, the 'very easy landings' at Andalsnes and the other ports in the southern fiord. Third, 'the indiscretions of the Press pointing to a storm of Trondheim' and fourth, the 'very heavy naval forces' required for the postponed but enlarged Trondheim assault—its code name now changed from 'Maurice' to 'Hammer'—with the 'undoubted major risks' connected with keeping 'so many valuable ships so many hours under close air attack'.

In order to give the pincer attacks immediate priority, Churchill pointed out, de Wiart's force would have to be strengthened with artillery, 'without which his force is not well-composed'. Troops already under orders for the Trondheim assault would now be 'shoved in as quickly as possible, mostly in warships, at the various ports of the Romsdal Fiord', with orders to 'press on to Dombaas'. Some of these troops would fight their way south towards the main Norwegian front, but 'the bulk' would move north towards Trondheim. Churchill added:

Although this change of emphasis is to be deprecated on account of its being a change, it must be recognised that we move from a more hazardous to a less hazardous operation, and greatly reduce the strain upon the Navy involved in 'Hammer'.

---

[1] Chiefs of Staff Committee No. 87 of 1940, 19 April 1940, 2 p.m., Confidential Annex: Cabinet papers, 79/85. Dill, hitherto commanding the First Corps in France, had just been appointed Vice-Chief of the Imperial General Staff.

[2] Winston S. Churchill, *The Second World War*, volume 1, London 1948, page 495.

It would seem that our results would be equally achieved by the safer plan, and it does not follow that they will be delayed.[1]

In describing the change of policy to the War Cabinet on the following day, Churchill recalled that the Chiefs of Staff decision 'to shift the emphasis from the Trondheim landing to the enveloping movement from the north and south' had been made in the morning, and that in the afternoon he had found the Chiefs of Staff 'unanimous in their opinion that the direct assault on Trondheim should be called off'. As a result of this unanimity, and 'in order that time and labour might not be wasted in loading the ships for this operation, if it was to be called off, he had obtained an immediate decision to the effect from the Prime Minister'.[2]

There was one advantage which Churchill believed could now be derived from this decision to abandon the main Trondheim assault. HMS *Warspite*, which Mackesy had asked for off Narvik, but which had been tied to the Trondheim assault, was now free, together with her escorting destroyers, to take part in the Narvik operation. 'This seemed,' to the members of the Military Co-ordination Committee at their meeting at ten o'clock that night, 'to open up the possibility of earlier and more direct operations for the capture of Narvik itself.' Churchill himself suggested that the Canadian troops, who were also no longer needed for the Trondheim assault, should likewise be transferred to Narvik where they 'might well turn the scale and enable the Commander to undertake the necessary offensive steps'.

The Committee reiterated its view of the importance of 'clearing up' the situation at Narvik 'as soon as possible', in order to release the first line troops there for service further south.[3] Given the imminent despatch of HMS *Warspite* to Narvik, and the release of the troops formerly needed for the direct assault on Trondheim, Churchill now sought to provide Mackesy with any further reinforcements he needed. The General had already decided to proceed with a bombardment aimed at 'isolating Narvik', to be followed by reconnaissances 'to test the possibility of making landings in force'.[4] In a personal telegram earlier that evening to Lord Cork, Churchill tried to encourage action

---

[1] 'Operations in Norway', Military Co-ordination Committee Paper No. 80 of 1940, 19 April 1940: Cabinet papers, 83/5.

[2] War Cabinet No. 98 of 1940, 20 April 1940, 10.30 a.m., Minute 3, Confidential Annex: Cabinet papers, 65/12.

[3] Military Co-ordination Committee No. 30 of 1940, 19 April 1940, 10 p.m.: Cabinet papers, 83/3.

[4] War Cabinet No. 97 of 1940, 19 April 1940, 11.30 a.m., Minute 3, Confidential Annex: Cabinet papers, 65/12.

at Narvik as soon as possible. 'I thought,' he wrote, 'that the tongue of land, especially its tip occupied by Narvik port and town, could certainly be dominated by the fire of warships, and that the houses could be occupied with the forces you possess. Once this is achieved we have the trophy at which all Europe is looking, we have a bridge-head for further landings, and our men sleep under such shelter as may be left, while the enemy sleep in the snow.' Churchill's message to Cork continued:

As I see it, once you have got the Narvik tip, and are ensconced in the houses and wrecked pill-boxes, all his detachments in the country are ruined, and can be reduced at leisure. Now if you can get this tongue-tip, all is well, and the snow is only the enemy's trouble. I am trying to find other troops to aid you in clearing up the outlying detachments.

Pray regard this telegram as my own personal opinion to enable you, after consultation with the General, to let me know what you severally and jointly advise, and if you do not agree, what are the main obstacles. The movements which you are now carrying out with the General seem admirable preparatories for what we have in mind. Send also a timetable of operations, and if you require more infantry we will try to find them. There seems no need to delay opening harassing fire. We are sending you an ammunition ship as fast as possible. Of course the less the town is knocked about the better for our own accommodation, but we must get in to Narvik or its ruins as soon as possible.[1]

Churchill's hopes were considerable. As he wrote in a memorandum to the Military Co-ordination Committee on April 20, it should now be possible, with the guns of *Warspite* and the extra troops from the abandoned Trondheim attack, to ensure not only that Narvik was captured, and the Germans who were there taken prisoner, but also that troops could 'get up the railway to the Swedish frontier' and secure 'an effective but well defended seaplane base on some lake'. Then, Churchill explained, even 'if we cannot obtain control of the ore-fields', it would be possible to prevent them 'being worked under German control'.

Churchill's memorandum ended: 'We have therefore at the moment only a month to spare.'[2]

Churchill's hopes were not fulfilled. As each day passed, new decisions were made in London, and new doubts received from Narvik

---

[1] 'Personal and Private', signal despatched at 7.26 p.m., 20 April 1940: Admiralty papers, 199/1929.

[2] 'Operation "Rupert"', Military Co-ordination Committee Paper No. 82 of 1940, 20 April 1940: Cabinet papers, 83/5.

itself. On April 20, at Churchill's suggestion, Lord Cork was appointed the commander of all the forces in the Narvik area. 'Starting harassing fire today,' he had signalled to Churchill that morning, and he added: 'HMS *Warspite* much appreciated. Intend her to engage pill-boxes at point blank range. Hope to make first try 23rd April and obtain footing ashore.'

As for Mackesy, Cork added, he 'would be glad of more infantry and particularly desires some artillery'.[1] But in the signal appointing Cork to the 'absolute command' of the Narvik operation later that day, Churchill stated emphatically: 'No further troops can be made available for at least a fortnight.' In passing on this news he had asked both Cork and Mackesy to report as soon as possible whether they would 'act now or delay for reinforcements', while stressing that it was 'highly desirable for both political and military reasons that there should not be any delay in the capture of Narvik'.[2]

At five minutes after midnight, Churchill signalled to Cork: 'It seems to me that you can feel your way and yet strike hard. Please keep us informed as much as possible. Ask for what you want. Remember Luleå is open in about a month. Count on unflinching support of your friends at the Admiralty.'[3]

---

[1] 'Personal', signal despatched 9.53 a.m., 20 April 1940: Admiralty papers, 199/1929.

[2] Signal despatched at 8.27 p.m., 20 April 1940, 'Immediate', 'Personal for Admiral of the Fleet Lord Cork and General Mackesy': Admiralty papers, 199/1929.

[3] Signal despatched at 12.55 a.m., 21 April 1940, 'Secret', 'Personal and Private': Admiralty papers, 199/1929.

14

The Face of Failure

THE primacy of the Narvik operation remained uppermost in Churchill's mind; at the War Cabinet of April 20 he told his colleagues that although there might now be as many as five thousand German troops in the area, 'Narvik was of vital importance to us.' Churchill added:

> Unless we had the area in our control and our forces established on the Swedish frontier, and were in a position immediately to interfere with the ore-fields if necessary, the Germans would be very likely to demand from Sweden the right to reinforce their troops as soon as their shipping could get up to Luleå. We had therefore only a month in which to liquidate the position at Narvik, and it was of the utmost importance not to have our attention diverted by operations elsewhere from our principal objective, which had always from the very start been the control of the Gällivare ore-fields.

During the War Cabinet of April 20, Stanley criticized the new pincer plan at Namsos and Andalsnes. It was, he said, 'little less hazardous' than that of the direct assault on Trondheim. In addition, he warned, until Trondheim airfield was secured, 'little could be done to offset the heavy scale of air attack to which our bases might be subjected'. The southern force would have first of all to secure themselves against attack from German forces to the south, and it might well be a month before it could make 'any serious move' against Trondheim.[1]

On April 21 there was bad news from both Namsos and Narvik. At Namsos, further disembarkation of men and materials had become impossible, de Wiart reported, 'unless enemy air activity is restricted'. Because of German air attacks, de Wiart had been unable to receive the *Ville d'Alger*, carrying the Chasseurs Alpins, 'anywhere near Namsos', and owing to what he called 'the difficulties which he was

[1] War Cabinet No. 98 of 1940, 20 April 1940, 10.30 a.m.: Cabinet papers, 65/6.

experiencing in feeding and supplying his troops', it might even be necessary 'to contemplate the possibility' of evacuating Namsos itself.

At Andalsnes, although the force under Brigadier Morgan had landed successfully, the Norwegians had pressed for it to move south to Lillehammer. This Morgan had done, 'after mopping up the parachutists at Dombaas'.[1]

At the War Cabinet of April 21, Chamberlain asked whether it might not be possible 'to stage an operation to capture Stavanger', but it was generally agreed that this would not only be an 'extremely difficult operation' but that the maintenance problems would be 'much worse than at Namsos', while Stanley wanted the French to be told 'what a hazardous operation we were undertaking'. Churchill agreed, telling his colleagues: 'The position in Norway certainly gave rise to some anxiety, but was not by any means desperate. We had taken a risk with our eyes open, knowing that it was a very hazardous operation to throw lightly equipped forces ashore without proper maintenance facilities. This, however, had been the only way possible of bolstering up the Norwegians, and as a result of what we had done the Norwegians were still holding out.'[2]

At Narvik, as Cork wrote to Churchill that same day—although his letter did not reach Churchill until May 6: 'The inertia is difficult to overcome, and of course the obstacles to the movement of troops are considerable, particularly the snow, which on northern slopes of hills is still many feet deep.' Cork's letter, written from Harstad, continued:

I myself have tested that, & as it has been snowing on & off for two days the position has not improved. The initial error was that the original force started on the assumption they would meet with no resistance, a mistake we often make . . . .

As it is, the soldiers have not yet got their reserves of small arms ammunition, or mortars, but tons of stuff and personnel they do not want. . . .

What is really our one pressing need is fighters; we are so overmatched in the air. There is a daily inspection of this place, & they come when there are transports or steamers to bomb.

Sooner or later they must get a hit. I flew over Narvik yesterday, but it was very difficult to see much. The rocky cliff is covered with snow, except for rock outcrops, round which the drifts must be deep.

It is snow down to the water's edge which makes it impossible to see the nature of the foreshore.

---

[1] 'Operations in Scandinavia', War Office Note: Cabinet papers, 83/3, folios 286–8.
[2] War Cabinet No. 99 of 1940, 21 April 1940, 4.30 p.m.: Cabinet papers, 65/6.

It was 'exasperating', Cork added, 'not being able to get on, & I quite understand your wondering why we do not, but I assure you that it is not from want of desire to do so'.[1]

Cork's account of the difficulties was no less formidable than that of General Mackesy, whose telegram to the War Office, sent on the afternoon of April 20, had reached London in the early hours of April 21. 'My original opinion,' he wrote, 'that the conditions essential for a successful opposed landing do not at present exist is fully confirmed,' and he added: 'Owing to nature of ground, flat trajectory of naval gun, and impossibility of locating the concealed machine guns, I am convinced that naval bombardment cannot be militarily effective, and that a landing from open boats in above conditions must be ruled out absolutely. Any attempt of the sort would involve not neutralisation but destruction of 24th Guards Brigade.'[2]

Churchill had been encouraged in his hopes for Narvik by Cork's firm belief in the demoralizing effect which the British Naval bombardment would have on the German forces.[3] But in his telegram on April 20, Mackesy had specifically challenged even this hopeful assessment. 'Those of us,' he warned, 'who have seen and experienced far heavier and better directed bombardment than this one must know only too well that British and German troops are not so easily demoralized and that machine gun detachments always come up when bombardment ceases.'[4]

Mackesy's telegram ended with the statement that he would be 'unable to continue with the plan' unless he had an assurance that 'no last minute action' was taken 'to try and force my hand against my judgement'.[5]

At eight on the evening of April 21, a signal from Cork reinforced Mackesy's hesitations. 'It is not my intention,' the Admiral informed Churchill, 'to attempt an opposed landing, climate conditions are against it. As I write this message it is snowing heavily.'[6] Four and a half hours later, a telegram from Mackesy raised new doubts and obstacles to an immediate, or even a substantial attack. Mackesy's telegram read:

[1] Letter of 21 April 1940 (received on 6 May 1940): Churchill papers, 19/2.

[2] Signal from HMS *Aurora*, despatched 2.51 p.m., 20 April 1940, received 5.14 a.m., 21 April 1940: Admiralty papers, 199/1929.

[3] At the Dardanelles in 1915 it had been expected that the British Naval bombardment would, likewise, demoralize and dislodge the Turks.

[4] Mackesy had served on the Western Front from 1915 to 1918.

[5] Signal from HMS *Aurora*, despatched 2.51 p.m., 20 April 1940, received 5.14 a.m., 21 April 1940: Admiralty papers: 199/1929.

[6] Signal sent 10.15 a.m., received 8.36 p.m., 21 April 1940: Admiralty papers, 199/1929.

Before proposed action against Narvik commences I have the honour to inform you that I feel it my duty to represent to you that I am convinced that there is not one Officer or man under my command who will not feel shame for himself and his country if thousands of Norwegian men, women and children in Narvik are subject to bombardment proposed.[1]

That night, before Mackesy's telegram reached him, Churchill set out for Chamberlain his view of what could still be done. The French Division should be brought to Norway 'as speedily as possible', to be landed 'in spite of enemy opposition' in the Andalsnes–Molde area, and then sent via Dombaas to the Norwegian southern front. Two British brigades were already going south 'with all speed' from Andalsnes 'to enable the Norwegians to hold out meanwhile'. This would 'for the moment' preclude the Trondheim pincer action, but Dombaas should still be held, and the Namsos port and terminal restored and protected. In addition, Mosjöen should be held as 'an alternative line of supply, or of retreat', for the forces at Namsos.

Above all, Churchill argued, the 'great importance' of the Narvik enterprise, 'our original quest, must not be lost sight of'. More troops should be sent there 'immediately', including French troops, 'capable of exploiting any success that may be achieved there, and of rounding up the enemy who have spread out in the surrounding countryside or sit astride the Narvik-Gällivare railway'.

Churchill was anxious that Chamberlain should make it clear to the French that all disembarkations, 'except at Narvik', would be a matter of 'extreme difficulty in the teeth of U-boat and Air attack'. His letter ended:

It will be a severe and perhaps protracted struggle to land and supply the increasing forces which are available, and to build up the southern front. We must expect losses and misfortunes in this complicated task, and no one can guarantee that forces so large as those it is desired to use on the southern front can arrive at their stations in time. We can but try our best to execute a sound conception.[2]

On receiving Mackesy's telegram, in which the General so strongly opposed the bombardment of Narvik, Churchill was angered almost beyond endurance, so much so that he at once telegraphed to Cork: 'If this Officer appears to be spreading a bad spirit through the higher ranks of the land force, do not hesitate to relieve him or place him under arrest.'

[1] Signal sent 10.29 p.m., received 11.59 p.m., 21 April 1940, 'Immediate': Admiralty papers, 199/1929.
[2] Note of 21 April 1940, marked by Churchill, 'midnight': Admiralty papers, 116/4471.

Churchill then set out ways of preceding the bombardment with warnings 'by every means', including if possible leaflets, 'that all civilians must leave the town', and that the German commander would be 'held responsible if he obstructs their departure'. Such a warning, he said, might itself demoralize the Germans, 'and in any case will be to our credit if we have to bombard'. It might even be possible, he said, for Cork to arrange for the evacuation of Norwegians with ships, or to promise not to bombard the railway line for six hours 'in order to allow the civilians to depart'. Churchill ended his message: 'Just off to Paris to get you more soldiers.'[1]

The Supreme War Council met in Paris, at the Quai d'Orsay, at three o'clock in the afternoon of April 22.[2] Churchill asked that as many as possible of the Chasseurs Alpins should be diverted to Narvik, 'so as to give our forces there a balanced composition, and make it possible to round up the Germans when they retreated to the hills'. His request was accepted, for the mood of the meeting was strongly in favour of the whole Norwegian campaign, both in order 'to deprive Germany of iron ore supplies from Sweden' and having regard, as the minutes recorded, 'to the effect which an Allied success in Scandinavia would have on world opinion'. To this end, the Supreme War Council decided, the Norwegian campaign 'should be prosecuted with the utmost vigour', with the capture of Trondheim and the capture of Narvik as the 'immediate military objectives'. After the capture of Narvik, there was to be an immediate concentration 'of an adequate Allied force' on the Swedish frontier, astride the iron ore railway route from Gällivare.[3]

Churchill remained in Paris overnight, for a second meeting of the Supreme War Council on the morning of April 23.[4] The theme of the discussion was the possibility of a German attack on Holland and Belgium, in which event the Allied armies would advance into Belgium without further communication with the Belgians, while at the same time the British Government, without further consultation with France, was authorised 'immediately to attack marshalling yards and oil refineries in the Ruhr'. Churchill warned, however, that any attempt to

---

[1] 'Immediate', sent 2.29 p.m., 22 April 1940: Admiralty papers, 199/1929.

[2] The British Members of the Council were Chamberlain and Churchill; the French Members were Reynaud, Daladier and Campinchi. Among the other senior British and French officials present were Pound and Ironside, Gamelin, Darlan, and the head of the French War Cabinet Secretariat, Paul Baudouin.

[3] Supreme War Council No. 8 of 1939–40, First Session, 22 April 1940, 3 p.m.: Churchill papers, 23/2.

[4] Chamberlain and Churchill were joined by Halifax and Hoare; Reynaud, Daladier and Campinchi by the Air Minister, Laurent-Eynac.

keep Italy neutral by a show of naval force in the eastern Mediterranean would be hampered because of the 'tremendous strain' which
the Norwegian campaign was putting 'on our Naval resources'.[1]

Returning to London, Churchill was present at a meeting of the
Military Co-ordination Committee—it was then ten o'clock in the
evening—and learned further bad news from Norway. At Namsos,
Phillips' brigade had been 'roughly handled' by mortars, light artillery,
machine-guns, aircraft and destroyers, and was being withdrawn to a
bridgehead at Bangsund.[2]

During April 23, as a result of fierce and unopposed German air
bombardment, British troops of the Trondheim 'pincer' were forced to
abandon the strategically pivotal town of Steinkjer, and fall back towards Bangsund from the south. With the abandonment of Steinkjer,
the attempt by 'Henry' to advance on Trondheim from the north
had failed. That same day, south of Trondheim, the Germans captured
Tretten, forcing the British troops there back towards Otta, and
threatening the whole southern flank of the Trondheim pincer. The
Italians, meanwhile, watching the spectacle of Britain's military discomfiture, were making threatening noises to invade Yugoslavia, and
to dominate the eastern Mediterranean.

Inside Whitehall, there was growing concern about Churchill's part
in the decisions and developments of the Norwegian campaign. On
April 23 Colville noted in his diary a comment by Edward Bridges,
that 'Winston was being maddening, making the most unreasonable
proposals'. Colville added: 'The PM is depressed, more by Winston's
rampages than by the inherent strategic difficulties.'[3]

The strategic difficulties were considerable, however, and augmented
by tactical setbacks. On the morning of April 24 Churchill himself
reported to the War Cabinet that, in a 'regrettable incident', a battle
flight of three Hudsons, flying over Romsdal Fiord 'in order to provide
air protection and support for our own forces', had been fired on, and
one machine shot down. Three further Hudsons had also been shot
down, 'by enemy fighters', while searching for three missing French
anti-torpedo boats in the Skagerrak.[4]

Confronted by the Norwegian setbacks—what Clementine Churchill

---

[1] Supreme War Council No. 8 of 1939–40, Second Session, 23 April 1940, 9.30 a.m.: Churchill
papers, 23/2.
[2] Military Co-ordination Committee No. 32 of 1940, 23 April 1940, 10 p.m.: Cabinet papers,
83/3.
[3] Colville diary, 23 April 1940: Colville papers.
[4] War Cabinet No. 102 of 1940, 24 April 1940, 11 a.m.: Cabinet papers, 65/6.

was later to call 'sickening disappointments'[1]—and their wider implications, Churchill sought to stimulate his advisers and colleagues into some further decision. To Pound he noted:

It seems to me a. that we must take Trondheim or face expulsion from Southern Norway & b. that we must succeed at Narvik quite soon or face a German force both on the orefield & to help their people in Narvik. The main reason why we abandoned the 'Hammer' was because the good progress made by the 'pincers' N & S, offered the possibility of a safer way & a less important stake for taking Trondheim. Now the Northern pincer is repulsed, & the Southern has been turned to the South. The question of a revival in some form or other of Hammer is therefore raised. Without Trondheim it is difficult to believe that the Norwegian Southern front can be held, or reinforced by the French in time.[2]

Lord Cork's Harstad signals continued to tell of ill-fortune. 'Weather bad,' he reported on the afternoon of April 24. 'Heavy snow, which is our worst enemy, prevents all movements.'[3] For his part, Churchill had already informed Cork, in a signal late the previous night, that 'Affairs have gone badly' on the southern Norwegian front near Lillehammer, and that 'it is by no means certain we can take Trondheim before the main German advance from Oslo reaches it'.[4]

Fearful of the outcome of the Norwegian campaign, and distressed at the way in which every decision made seemed to be almost as swiftly altered or abandoned, Churchill set out his feelings in a letter which he drafted for Chamberlain. 'Being anxious to sustain you to the best of my ability,' he wrote, 'I must warn you that you are approaching a head-on smash in Norway.'[5]

Churchill then deleted this sentence, and began again:

My dear Neville,

I am vy grateful to you for having at my request taken over the day to day management of the Military Co-ordination Cte.

I think I ought however to let you know that I shall not be willing to receive the responsibility back from you without the necessary powers. At present no one has the power. There are six Chiefs of the Staff, three Ministers,

---

[1] Churchill papers, 4/131.

[2] Handwritten note: Seal papers. In a further note to Chamberlain, Churchill wrote: If the combination of 'secondary difficulties' became 'unduly exhausting, strike with Air Force at vital key points in Germany'.

[3] 'Secret', sent at 2.07 p.m. and received at 4.36 p.m., 24 April 1940: Admiralty papers, 199/1929.

[4] 'Most Secret', 'Immediate', sent at 12.44 a.m., 24 April 1940: Admiralty papers, 199/1929.

[5] Draft of letter of 24 April 1940: Churchill papers, 19/2.

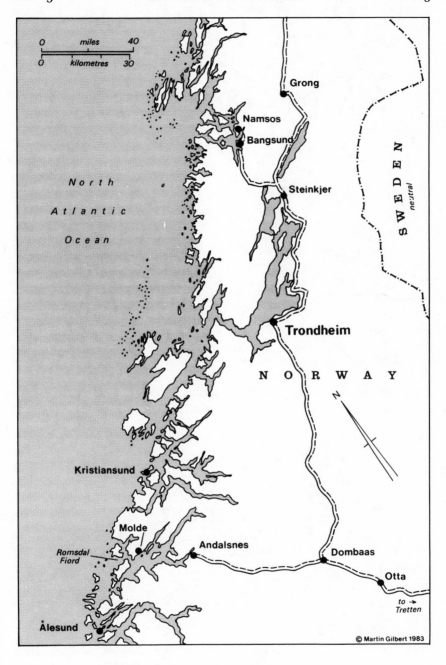

© Martin Gilbert 1983

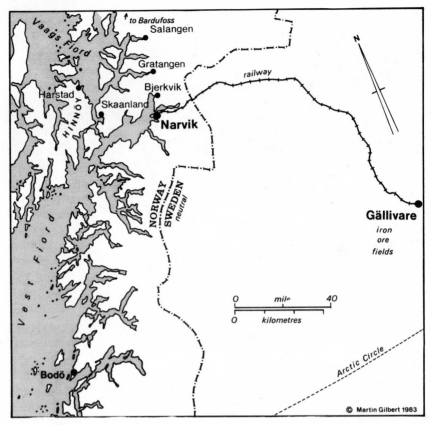

to Bardufoss
Salangen
Gratangen
Bjerkvik
Skaanland
Narvik
Harstad
HINNÖY
Vaags Fiord
railway
N
NORWAY
SWEDEN *neutral*
Vest Fiord
Gällivare
*iron
ore
fields*

O	*mile*	40

O	*kilometres*	

Arctic Circle

Bodö

© Martin Gilbert 1983

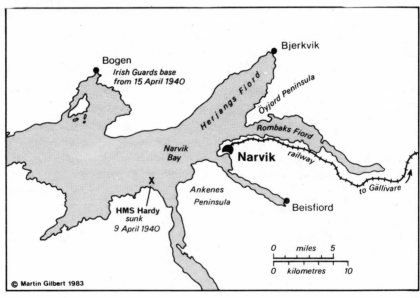

Bogen
*Irish Guards base
from 15 April 1940*

Bjerkvik
Herjangs Fiord
Öyjord Peninsula
Rombaks Fiord
Narvik Bay
Narvik
railway
X
HMS Hardy
*sunk
9 April 1940*
Ankenes
Peninsula
Beisfiord
to Gällivare

O	*miles*	5

O	*kilometres*	10

© Martin Gilbert 1983

two C-in-Cs & General Ismay who all have a voice in Norwegian operations, apart from Narvik. But no one is now responsible for the creation & direction of military policy except yourself. If you feel able to bear this burden, you may count upon my unswerving loyalty as First Lord of the Admiralty. If you do not feel you can bear it, with all yr other duties, you will have to delegate yr powers to a deputy who can concert & direct the general movement of our war action, & who will enjoy yr support & that of the War Cabinet, unless vy good reason is shown to the contrary. Believe me

Yours ever
Winston S. Churchill[1]

While Churchill was sending this letter, Chamberlain himself had written along similar lines:

My dear Winston,

I have been thinking over the Scandinavian situation and the rather un-satisfactory position in which it stands. I dont feel that I get your whole mind in Committee and should very much like to discuss it all with you in private.

I cant manage it before 7 as I have to see the King. Could you spare the time to come across to Downing Street after dinner say at 9.30?

Yours ever
Neville Chamberlain[2]

At seven o'clock that evening the Military Co-ordination Committee met at 10 Downing Street. A signal from Lord Cork was read out describing the situation at Narvik 'where operations were considerably impeded by bad weather', and a telegram from the British troops twenty-five miles south of Dombaas, who were being 'attacked from the air and by armoured fighting vehicles'.

Churchill spoke forcefully of the sequence of events since the original German landing, so carefully prepared beforehand. 'Our first reaction,' he said, 'had been to concentrate on securing Narvik from which we might ultimately hope to gain possession of the Gällivare ore fields, which constituted our primary objective in Scandinavia.' But, as he went on to recall:

We had then received an urgent appeal from many quarters to go to the assistance of the Norwegians in the South. The original conception of such assistance had been comparatively small landings on the coast with small numbers of troops, mainly as a demonstration of our loyalty to the Norwegian people.

[1] Final draft, 24 April 1940, marked 'Not sent, 1L saw PM at 9.30 p.m.': Churchill papers, 19/2.
[2] 'Secret', 24 April 1940: Churchill papers, 19/2.

We had taken a great risk in throwing light forces ashore without adequate administrative arrangements, without proper transport, and without even anti-aircraft defences. At first we had encountered no opposition and our forces had advanced. Consequently, our hopes had risen and we had been agreeably surprised to find, when our troops reached Dombaas, that the Norwegians had formed a fighting front to the North of Oslo. Brigadier Morgan had pushed forward and joined the Norwegians on this front.

This meant a considerable extension of our liabilities. But now, if the worst came to the worst, and we were pushed right back in the South, we were intrinsically no worse off than we thought we should be when the enemy made his first landings two weeks previously.

Churchill concluded by suggesting a limitation of Britain's Norwegian objectives, telling the Committee:

We might now have to adjust our plans and concentrate all our efforts on Narvik once more. Leaving aside the question of support to the Norwegian people, our only requirement in Southern Norway was a lodgment on the coast to which the mine barrage could be 'hooked'. To secure this, we might have to carry out a carefully prepared and rehearsed combined operation in a part of the coast remote from communications inland.

Chamberlain 'agreed' with Churchill's summary. 'If we had to evacuate,' he said, 'there would be no reason for us to be ashamed or to regret the effort we had made. We must, however, face the fact that we should have incurred a psychological reverse and a blow to our prestige.'[1]

In a note on the following day, Churchill wrote of what he felt was at least one continuing advantage in the Norwegian campaign: 'diversion of German army strength wh has already relieved the Western Front by 9 divisions – & will continue'. He had added this in the margin of a paper by Hankey, who had given three further advantages: the 'substantial reduction' in the German surface fleet; 'some damage' to the German Air Force; and the beneficial effect on Italy and some of the Balkan States 'of our stubborn resistance'.[2]

These advantages seemed of little weight to those at the Military Co-ordination Committee of April 26, when there was a discussion on the idea of evacuating all British forces from southern Norway. The Chiefs of Staff felt that 'preparations for such a withdrawal should be put in hand at once'. Nor would it be possible, they advised, to continue

[1] Military Co-ordination Committee No. 33 of 1940, 24 April 1940, 7 p.m.: Cabinet papers, 83/3.

[2] Paper by Lord Hankey, 'Scandinavia – 25th April 1940', 'Most Secret': Admiralty papers, 116/4471.

with any of the plans to capture Trondheim, whose air defences would involve, with those of Narvik, the taking up of almost the whole of Britain's anti-aircraft gun resources.

Chamberlain was worried that a 'precipitate withdrawal' would have 'a very bad effect on the neutrals, particularly on Italy'. But he did feel that if done well, a withdrawal could be claimed as a 'strategical triumph', and it could also be stressed 'that it was all part of our plan for concentrating our efforts at Narvik'.

Churchill endorsed Chamberlain's view. Narvik had always been 'our principal objective' in Norway. The aim of the Trondheim expedition had been no more than to 'bolster up the Norwegians if they seemed to be putting up any sort of resistance'. The capture of Trondheim would, he felt, be 'a very heavy drain on our naval resources', making it impossible to fulfil the needs of Narvik. He therefore advised a withdrawal from Trondheim, 'after giving the Germans as hard a knock as we could with the Regular troops which had been put in on that front'.[1]

Churchill reiterated his advice to withdraw from Trondheim at the Supreme War Council meeting in London later that day. Even if the town were captured by direct assault, he said, 'we would not be able in the face of air attack to maintain the forces which would be necessary to keep it in our hands'. Nor, he said, could the British Government possibly undertake to establish 'a strong defensive front' to hold back the advance of the Germans from the south: any such idea, he stressed, 'must be ruled out'.

At Chamberlain's request, Churchill gave the Supreme War Council, whose French delegation was led by General Gamelin, an account of the increasing difficulties of the campaign:

The German air power had developed to a far greater extent than had been anticipated. We had at our disposal only a few small ports on the Norwegian coast. These were being continuously bombed. We had had to keep ships with anti-aircraft guns continuously in these ports to protect the landing-places. Some of these ships had been hit and damaged.[2] The task of passing a

---

[1] Military Co-ordination Committee No. 34 of 1940, 26 April 1940, 10 a.m.: Cabinet papers, 83/3.

[2] Contemplating these naval losses, and the continual U-boat sinkings of British merchant ships in the Atlantic, Churchill asked his War Cabinet colleagues, on the day of this Supreme War Council, that in future the published details of ships sunk by enemy action 'shall be confined to a weekly statement, seven days in arrear', giving the numbers of ships sunk and their tonnage 'but not the name, the tonnage of each ship, the date or the cause of loss'. Such details, Churchill wrote, would be 'of value to the enemy', as was happening 'at present' when shipping losses by enemy action were released for publication immediately. 'I have reviewed our policy in this respect,' Churchill wrote. 'Prompt announcement of our shipping losses only convey to the enemy valuable intelligence of the efficiency of any particular operation against shipping' (War Cabinet Paper No. 113 of 1940, 26 April 1940: Cabinet papers, 67/6).

force into Norway was clearly a matter of great difficulty. This task could only be carried out at a high cost and over a long period of time, and it was bound to involve serious losses.[1]

As the Norwegian crisis intensified, Churchill was being pressed by the hero of the Zeebrugge raid of 1918, Admiral of the Fleet Sir Roger Keyes, to appoint him to the command of a special force to seize Trondheim by direct assault. Churchill had known and admired Keyes for more than forty years. It was Keyes' willingness to risk all at the Dardanelles by a renewed naval attack on the Narrows that had marked him out in Churchill's mind as a man of action and decision.[2]

Now Lady Keyes was likewise pressing her husband's claim for control of a naval force to seize Trondheim, urging in her husband's favour 'his great qualities and power of leadership and genius for war'.[3] But Churchill could not take up his friend's cause, writing to him direct on April 25:

Dear Roger,

It astonishes me that you should think that all this has not been examined by people who know exactly what resources are available, and what the dangers would be. I will however ask the First Sea Lord whether he can receive you.

You will, I hope appreciate the fact that I have to be guided by my responsible Naval advisers, and that it is not open to me to make the kind of appointments you and Eva have in mind on grounds of friendship.[4]

Keyes did not accept Churchill's argument, and insisted upon seeing him again on the morning of Sunday April 28.[5] After their talk, Keyes wrote to Churchill of the Admiralty's 'deplorably pusillanimous and short-sighted' conduct of the war at sea; a description, he said which was shared 'with bitter resentment' by many naval officers with whom

---

[1] Supreme War Council No. 9 of 1939–40, 26 April 1940, 9.30 p.m.: Cabinet papers, 99/3.

[2] Only six months before the outbreak of war Churchill had written, in a foreword to Keyes' book *Adventures Ashore and Afloat*: 'We sail with the author about the world from China to Brazil and back again. We mount with him the rungs of the ladder of promotion, some of which are slippery indeed. When most of his contemporaries are still at their books he plays his part in skirmish and foray afloat and ashore in command of men who have real jobs to do. When barely twenty-seven he commands the torpedo-boats which cut out the Chinese destroyers near the Taku forts. Those great teachers of youth, Responsibility and Work which is a Joy, stood ever at his side.' (Foreword dated 9 March 1939, written from Chartwell: Admiral of the Fleet Sir Roger Keyes, *Adventures Ashore and Afloat*, London *1939*).

[3] 'Private and Personal, For your eye only please', 23 April 1940: Churchill papers, 2/395.

[4] Letter of 25 April 1940: Churchill papers, 2/395.

[5] Churchill Engagement Cards, 28 April 1940: Thompson papers.

he had recently been in contact. The 'delay in taking action, when Germany first seized several Norwegian ports, before they had time to organise defences, is angrily commented on'. Keyes added: 'Steinkjer will stink in our nostrils until this disgrace is wiped out.'

The immediate need, Keyes insisted, was a 'smashing naval blow' at Trondheim, which 'could, and should have been in our hands'. Chamberlain himself, Keyes declared, had sent him a message to say 'that if I could get your support, the Cabinet would support you'.[1]

Had Chamberlain given Keyes such a message? Churchill at once sent the Admiral's letter to 10 Downing Street, where Chamberlain's Principal Private Secretary wrote in the margin: 'This is not true,' and Chamberlain himself added: 'I never sent any such message as is alleged here.'

Enquiries were made at once and it emerged that Keyes had indeed been to 10 Downing Street in order to see Chamberlain. But one of Chamberlain's Private Secretaries, Arthur Rucker, and Lord Dunglass, had intercepted the Admiral, and told him, as Rucker noted a few days later, 'that the position wd no doubt be different if the First Lord were persuaded to accept Keyes' views'.

As Lord Dunglass recalled it, five days after the event, 'I pointed out that Churchill was, after all, not merely First Lord but Chairman of the Military Co-ordination Committee, and that if he were to bring forward a scheme backed by his full authority, then obviously there would be a very good chance that his word would go with the War Cabinet.' But Keyes was, as Dunglass wrote, 'so excited' when he came to Downing Street 'as to be almost incoherent, and apparently heading for a brainstorm, so he may generally have misunderstood'.[2]

Keyes was undeterred by these reactions. 'If you will back me,' he wrote to Churchill on May 1, 'you will soon have the power as well as the responsibility.'[3]

At 10 Downing Street, more than Keyes' appearance was being discussed. On April 25 Colville noted in his diary: 'The trouble about Winston which has been brewing for the last few days, arises from his demand to be appointed Chairman of the Chiefs of Staff Committee.' Were Chamberlain to refuse this demand, Colville added, 'W threatens to go down to the House and say he can take no responsibility for what is happening.'

[1] Letter of 29 April 1940: Premier papers, 1/418.
[2] Correspondence and comments of the Prime Minister's Private Office: Premier papers, 1/418. Lord Dunglass (later Lord Home) was Chamberlain's Parliamentary Private Secretary.
[3] Letter of 1 May 1940: Churchill papers, 19/2.

Churchill, for his part, 'professes absolute loyalty to the PM', Colville wrote, 'and indeed they get on admirably'; it was the Chiefs of Staff and the Joint Planners, Churchill claimed, who were 'making a hopeless muddle'.[1] The proposed solution, Colville commented on the following day, 'if W accepts it', was that he should have a Secretariat of his own, headed by General Ismay, who would become a member of the Chiefs of Staff Committee 'and there represent Winston's views'.

As a result of this plan, Colville wrote, Churchill would become 'a kind of deputy PM in matters connected with Defence'. Chamberlain, he added, 'is wisely humouring Winston, whose position in the country is unassailable'.[2]

Churchill sought these wider powers in order, as he saw it, to enable essential decisions of war policy to be carried out with clarity and authority. Even while such substantial changes were being mooted, the reports from Norway continued to provide evidence of the precariousness of the situation. Andalsnes had been 'heavily bombed' on the previous day, the War Cabinet were told on the morning of April 27, and HMS *Flamingo*, 'the only ship at the port, had expended all her ammunition'. For three hours, until the ship had been relieved by HMS *Black Swan*, there had been no anti-aircraft ship at the port, and 'severe damage' had been done to the port area. A jetty and store houses had been burnt out, 'with considerable loss of small arms, ammunition and explosives'.

A message had just been received from General Paget 'stating that under existing air conditions the continued maintenance of his force through Andalsnes was not feasible; artillery was urgently required'. Churchill now veered, however, away from his earlier support for evacuation. He 'demurred', he said, to an immediate withdrawal, 'and wished further consideration to be given to leaving the troops now in Norway to put up the best fight they could, in conjunction with the Norwegians'.[3]

That afternoon the Supreme War Council met again in London, with Reynaud, Daladier, Campinchi and Laurent-Eynac as the French representatives.[4] Reynaud envisaged that 'as a result of our failure in Central Norway', the Norwegian Government might capitulate and come to terms with Germany. An Allied failure in Central Norway, he

---

[1] Colville diary, 25 April 1940: Colville papers.

[2] Colville diary, 26 April 1940: Colville papers.

[3] War Cabinet No. 105 of 1940, 27 April 1940, 10.30 a.m.: Cabinet papers, 65/6.

[4] The British Members of the Council were Chamberlain, Halifax, Churchill, Stanley and Hoare. The British officials present were Pound, Ironside, Newall and Cadogan. The French officials included Gamelin, Darlan, and the Chief of the Air Staff, General Vuillemin.

added, 'would come as a great shock to public opinion'. The Council agreed, however, that Trondheim 'must be abandoned'; because of Germany's 'air superiority', its capture and subsequent retention would represent 'an undue strain on Allied resources'. In addition, a withdrawal from Andalsnes 'might at any time become an urgent necessity', although it should be delayed as long as possible, 'having regard to the loss of prestige'. There remained Narvik, whose capture 'as quickly as possible', the Council concluded, 'remained a most important military objective'.[1]

That evening the Military Co-ordination Committee discussed the withdrawals, the first of which, General Paget's 15th Brigade at Andalsnes, would begin in three days time. On the same night, April 30, the bulk of the French would be withdrawn from Namsos; and by May 3 the Namsos evacuation would be completed.

Unwilling now to accept without a fight the stigma of withdrawal, Churchill asked whether the troops to be evacuated from Andalsnes could not remain, and be 'dispersed into small parties', in order 'to continue the struggle on guerilla lines'. But Ironside said that this would be 'out of the question' with the present troops, and Chamberlain argued that if the Committee did not approve the evacuation they would be taking on 'a grave responsibility'.

The withdrawals from Namsos and Andalsnes were agreed. So too was Ironside's proposal to set up, as a quite separate operation, special companies which, after the withdrawal, would be landed from destroyers 'with the object of carrying out guerilla operations'. Such a proposal, Churchill said, 'should be carried out with the utmost vigour'.[2]

Two days after the withdrawals were agreed, General Paget telegraphed to the War Office that he had explained the evacuation plans to the Norwegian commander, General Ruge, who had warned that unless the Norwegians could hope for some 'further Allied intervention', he would advise the Norwegian Government to begin 'peace negotiations'.[3] This telegram was at once sent on to Chamberlain, who showed it to Churchill. General Ruge 'ought to know', Churchill minuted, 'what we have decided', to which Chamberlain noted, 'I agree'. Three and a half hours later, at one minute before midnight, a telegram was sent back to General Paget, signed by Ironside, to inform the Norwegians that the evacuation of Namsos and Andalsnes constituted a 'strategic withdrawal', but that the Allies were already operating in

---

[1] Supreme War Council No. 10 of 1939–40, 27 April 1940, 2.30 p.m.: Cabinet papers, 99/3.
[2] Military Co-ordination Committee No. 35 of 1940, 27 April 1940, 6 p.m.: Cabinet papers, 83/3.
[3] Telegram sent at 7.40 p.m., received at 8.25 p.m., 29 April 1940: Premier papers, 1/419.

northern Norway, and that their forces there 'are being rapidly rein-forced', with a view, Ironside added at Chamberlain and Churchill's request, to holding the area north of Namsos 'as a preliminary to counter-attack southwards'.[1]

On the night of April 27, for a few hours, Churchill was able to break off momentarily from the pressures of the Norwegian campaign. Under his contract with Cassell & Company, the publishers, he had still to complete the final sections of his history of the English-speaking Peoples. At 11 o'clock that night his research assistant, F. W. Deakin, presented himself at Admiralty House, it being Churchill's habit, as Deakin later recalled, 'to spend an hour or so in the afternoon or in the early morning hours completing his chapters on the Norman Conquest and mediaeval England'. Deakin's account continued:

Naval signals awaited attention, admirals tapped impatiently on the door of the First Lord's room, while on one occasion talk inside ranged round the spreading shadows of the Norman invasion and the figure of Edward the Confessor who, as Churchill wrote, 'comes down to us faint, misty, frail'. I can still see the map on the wall, with the dispositions of the British Fleet off Norway, and hear the voice of the First Lord as he grasped with his usual insight the strategic position in 1066. But this was no lack of attention to current business. It was the measure of the man with the supreme historical eye. The distant episodes were as close and real as the mighty events on hand.[2]

With the capture of Narvik now the focal point of Britain's Norwegian effort, Churchill cast about for means to ensure its retention once captured. In a minute to the Naval Staff on April 28 he urged the preparation of a proper plan for the anti-aircraft defence of the area. The scale to be worked to, he said, 'should be half-Scapa in guns and searchlights'. In addition, the aerodrome should be extended, and other aerodrome sites searched for in the neighbourhood. The camouflage of oil tanks was another priority, as were anti-submarine defences. It was his intention, he wrote, that Narvik would become the base 'for a considerable army', as well as 'a resting place for a squadron and a flotilla'.[3]

In a signal to Cork on April 28, Churchill explained that it was now 'beyond our strength' to capture Trondheim, or to use it as a base. The Germans, he explained, 'disregarding many thousands of losses in crossing the Skagerrak have developed an overwhelming northerly

---

[1] Telegram sent at 23.59 p.m., 29 April 1940: Premier papers, 1/419.
[2] F. W. Deakin, 'Churchill The Historian', in *Schweizer Monatshefte*, issue 4, Zurich, 1970.
[3] Minute No. 315, 28 April 1940: Churchill papers, 19/6.

thrust from Oslo, and well-equipped, audacious gangs have advanced with great rapidity far ahead of the main army along roads and railways which the Norwegians failed to break up'. It was therefore upon Narvik and the Gällivare orefields 'that all efforts must now be centred. . . . Here it is we must fight and persevere on the largest scale possible'. Further French troops were already on their way as reinforcements. Churchill's signal continued:

We must expect Hitler to make vehement effort to rescue his Narvik garrison either by the favour or coercion of Sweden. Enemy reinforcements may appear long before the end of May. Troops already sent or coming to you amount to nearly thirteen thousand men. But plans are being made to develop Narvik and its environs into a fortified base capable of maintaining the utmost forces the region can carry, up to thirty thousand men or more for operations on or possibly beyond the Swedish frontier during the summer.

It seems most vital to get the Air defence by guns and aircraft mounted at earliest moment. When Germans have thoroughly organized Trondheim aerodrome they will no doubt intensify their air attack thence and from intermediate bases. Plan out your scheme for establishing strongly-defended base and ask for all you want to which high priority will be given. We are making parallel studies here.

'Please keep us informed daily,' Churchill added. 'It is so difficult to help you if we cannot follow events.'[1]

Shortly before midnight on April 28, Cork informed Churchill that the French General who had just arrived 'appears to be a live-wire', but that his troops had arrived 'without guns'. Cork's hope, however, was to capture Narvik 'before middle of May', and he added: 'Am urging necessity for speed.'[2]

Churchill now sought to draw some positive advantages from the continuation of the Narvik expedition. It should be 'the object of our operations throughout the summer', he told the Military Co-ordination Committee on April 29, 'to force the Germans to keep as large an army as possible in Norway and to subject them to constant attacks at different points'. These attacks, he believed, if 'carefully planned in advance and executed when conditions were favourable', should be able not only to achieve 'a certain measure of local success', but also to 'retain large German forces at many points on the coast'.

It was at this meeting of the Military Co-ordination Committee on

---

[1] 'Personal', sent at 1.48 a.m., 28 April 1940: Admiralty papers, 199/1929.

[2] Signal sent at 11.27 p.m. 28 April 1940, arrived 5.12 a.m., 29 April 1940: Admiralty papers, 199/1929. The French General was Antoine Béthouart, who had graduated from the same class at Saint-Cyr as General de Gaulle.

April 29 that the first mention was made of the possibility of a German invasion of Britain, when, according to the minutes of the meeting, 'it was pointed out that our aerodromes were very lightly defended and that there was a shortage of trained and equipped troops'. In contrast, however, there were 'excellent roads' in every part of Britain, and 'much artillery, all of which was mechanized'. It might be desirable, however, to bring back some troops from France, and to 'hold up' the departure to France of the 4th Corps, which was expected to complete its equipment and training 'early in June'.[1] Discussing troop shortages at the War Cabinet on the following day, Churchill recalled that early in September 1939 he had raised the question of recalling to Britain the regular British battalions then serving in India, and replacing them by Territorial battalions. This idea, he said, 'should again be examined'.

The War Cabinet of April 30 was told that the news from Narvik was hopeful: two battalions of the 24th Guards Brigade and two battalions of Chasseurs Alpins were gradually 'closing in' on the town. South of Dombaas, the 15th Infantry Brigade was covering the withdrawal of the Norwegian troops, despite 'severe bombing by low-flying aircraft'. At Otta, the same brigade had destroyed three German tanks. At Molde, the *Glasgow* had embarked the King of Norway, the British and French Ministers to Norway, their wives, and twenty-three tons of gold. The evacuation of Andalsnes would begin that same night.[2]

The setbacks and failures of the Norwegian campaign had begun to focus political criticism on the Government's conduct of the war; so much so that on April 29 a Watching Committee of Peers and Members of Parliament sent a deputation of their senior members to the Foreign Office, to protest to Halifax about 'the want of initiative shown by the Government' in almost every sphere of war policy. The leader of the deputation, Lord Salisbury, spoke about the harmful effect on neutral opinion 'of Germany's spectacular successes and our failure to retort, except at sea'. If the Germans succeeded in occupying southern Norway, Salisbury warned, 'the effect on neutrals would be very serious', and it was therefore 'essential' for the Government to take the initiative somewhere. The 'only possible sphere', Salisbury argued, 'seemed to be the air. A formidable air offensive against German military objectives would have a profound and, he thought, favourable effect on neutrals, including the United States.'

---

[1] Military Co-ordination Committee No. 36 of 1940, 29 April 1940, 6 p.m.: Cabinet papers, 83/3.

[2] War Cabinet No. 108 of 1940, 30 April 1940, 11.30 a.m.: Cabinet papers, 65/6.

Salisbury's appeal was echoed by a former Secretary of State for Air, Lord Swinton, who urged the Government to embark on 'offensive air action against selected targets' in Germany. If it were thought, he said, that the Government 'were holding back' because of fear of German retaliation, 'the people would be furious'.[1]

The deputation left the Foreign Office as dissatisfied as they had arrived, and on the same day they reported on their discussion to their members. The discussion continued on April 30, at Lord Salisbury's house off Piccadilly. 'I go to Arlington Street for the Watching Committee,' Harold Nicolson wrote in his diary on April 30, 'and find a glum crowd. The general impression is that we may lose the war.' At the meeting, members were told of an 'appalling' shortage of tanks. 'We part in gloom,' Nicolson added. 'Black Week in the Boer War can hardly have been more depressing. They think that this will mean the fall of Chamberlain, and Lloyd George as Prime Minister. The Whips are putting it about that it is all the fault of Winston who has made another forlorn failure. That is hell.'[2]

The Government were conscious of what Anthony Eden recalled as 'the mounting tide of opinion against them'. Indeed, at the full Cabinet on May 1, Eden wrote, 'much of the time was spent by colleagues rehearsing their defence of our withdrawal from southern Norway'.[3]

In an attempt to give the public a sense of the Government's determination to wage effective war, on May 1 Chamberlain informed the War Cabinet of a reorganization of the upper direction of the war. Churchill was to become responsible, on behalf of the Military Coordination Committee, 'for giving guidance and directions' to the Chiefs of Staff Committee. For this purpose, it would be open to Churchill 'to summon that Committee for personal consultation at any time when he considers it necessary'. For their part, the Chiefs of Staff would prepare plans 'to achieve any objectives indicated to them by the First Lord' on behalf of the Military Co-ordination Committee.[4]

---

[1] 'Record of a discussion with Lord Salisbury and Members of a Watching Committee, held at the Foreign Office, April 29th', marked 'Seen by PM & Lord Hankey': Foreign Office papers, 800/326, folios 102–7. Other speakers in similar vein were Lord Trenchard, Leo Amery, Lord Hailsham, Lord Lloyd, Brigadier-General Spears, Lord Horne, Lord Londonderry, Lord Cecil of Chelwood, and Richard Law.

[2] Nicolson diary, 30 April 1940: Nigel Nicolson (editor), *Harold Nicolson, Diaries and Letters*, London 1967, page. 74.

[3] The Earl of Avon, *The Eden Memoirs, The Reckoning*, London 1965, page 96.

[4] War Cabinet Papers No. 120 of 1940, drafted 30 April 1940, circulated 1 May 1940 entitled 'Defence Organisation': Cabinet papers, 120/3. The copy in the Churchill papers is marked by Churchill: 'Make 3 copies & keep under lock, Ap 30 1940' (Churchill papers, 4/143).

Churchill had obtained the minimum powers which he felt were essential if war decisions were to be made with the firmness and authority needed to carry them through. In the War Cabinet paper setting out his new position it was noted that in 'urgent cases' it might be necessary 'to omit submission' of the plans prepared by the Chiefs of Staff to a formal meeting of the Military Co-ordination Committee. In such cases, Churchill would 'no doubt find means of consulting the Service Ministers informally and in case of dissent the decision will be referred to the Prime Minister'.[1]

To make the new organization effective, a Central Staff was created, under the control of a specially designated 'Senior Staff Officer', Major-General Ismay. 'I had known Ismay for many years,' Churchill later wrote, 'but now for the first time we became hand-in-glove, and much more.' To strengthen Churchill's position in giving 'guidance and direction' to the Chiefs of Staff Committee, Ismay was now made a full member of that Committee. Churchill himself was to derive his authority over the Chiefs of Staff 'on behalf' of the Military Co-ordination Committee, and, as the War Cabinet paper explained, would, in Chamberlain's absence from the Military Co-ordination Committee, 'act as his deputy'.

These were substantial additions of authority and control. And yet, as Churchill wrote eight years later, looking back on them, 'I was thus to have immense responsibilities, without effective power in my own hands to discharge them'. At the time, however, 'I had a feeling that I might be able to make the new organisation work'.[2]

To Neville Chamberlain, Churchill wrote on April 30: 'I am much obliged to you for the arrangements you have made. I accept them & I have every hope they will afford a working basis for action. I shall try my best to make all go smoothly.' As for Ismay, Churchill added, he would be 'most acceptable to me in the capacity you propose'.[3]

In retrospect, Ismay was less impressed with Churchill's new powers, writing in a private note six years later:

... on the 1st May the new Defence Organisation was brought into being. The new departure was that Mr Churchill was given responsibility for giving guidance and directions to the Chiefs of Staff Committee. General Ismay was appointed to the post of Senior Staff Officer in charge of the central staff placed at his disposal and was made a member of the Chiefs of Staff Committee. This arrangement lasted only ten days, since on the 10th May, Mr Churchill

[1] War Cabinet Paper No. 120 of 1940, 1 May 1940: Cabinet papers, 67/6.
[2] Winston S. Churchill, *The Second World War*, volume 1, London 1948, page 507.
[3] Letter of 30 April 1940: Premier papers, 1/401, folios 10–11.

became Prime Minister and Minister of Defence. It never worked satisfactor-ily, since Mr Churchill had not the power to *give orders* to Service Ministers or to the Chiefs of Staff.[1]

Behind Churchill's back, there was considerable criticism. On May 1 Chamberlain spoke to a recent recruit to his Cabinet, John Reith, the Minister of Information, referring, if Reith's record of two days later is to be believed, 'to Churchill's reputation, so inflated, and based on broadcasts (I said this latter). . . .' According to Reith, Chamberlain also said that 'if there was to be a debunking it would have to be done by someone else'. There was 'no doubt', Reith added, 'how he feels about Churchill'.[2]

That evening, the first evening of his new powers, Churchill gazed out from 10 Downing Street across Horse Guards Parade and St James's Park, where a sudden dark squall had descended. Then, turning to John Colville, he remarked: 'If I were the first of May, I should be ashamed of myself.'

Colville, a devoted supporter of Chamberlain, commented in his diary: 'Personally, I think he ought to be ashamed of himself. . . .'[3]

At the War Cabinet on May 1 the Chiefs of Staff reported that small landings were to be made south of Narvik, at Bodö, Mosjöen and Mo, with instructions 'to dispute the advance of German forces by guerilla tactics'. But the relief at this positive news was seriously dimin-ished when the War Cabinet heard a report from Major Jefferis, who had been sent to Andalsnes to blow up the railway leading to central Norway, and had witnessed the effect on the British troops of German air superiority: 'the moral effect', Jefferis reported, 'of seeing the aircraft coming, of being unable to take cover, of being able to observe the bomb dropping, and of the terrific explosion, had been overwhelming'.

It was 'quite impossible', Jefferis concluded, for land forces to with-stand 'complete air superiority of the kind the Germans had enjoyed in Norway'. Even at Narvik, Jefferis warned, the operations could not succeed without air bases for both fighters and bombers. Unknown to Jefferis, the Chiefs of Staff Committee had pointed out a few hours earlier that the provision of 'adequate anti-aircraft defences' at Narvik 'would make very heavy demands indeed upon our resources in these weapons'.[4]

[1] 'Higher Defence Organisation, April–May, 1940', note by Ismay enclosed with his letter to Churchill of 30 May 1946: Churchill papers, 4/143. Ismay had underlined the words in italics.
[2] Reith diary, 3 May 1940: Charles Stuart (editor), *The Reith Diaries*, London 1975, page 249. Reith had entered the Cabinet on 5 January 1940; it was his first Cabinet appointment.
[3] Colville diary, 1 May 1940: Colville papers.
[4] Chiefs of Staff Committee No. 105 of 1940, 1 May 1940, 10 a.m., Confidential Annex: Cabinet papers, 79/85.

At the War Cabinet on May 1 Churchill reported on a new and sinister development, 'the exceptionally large number of mine-laying air-raids' on the previous evening, which seemed to indicate an imminent German invasion of Belgium or Holland. It was essential, he argued, to have 'at least one highly trained Division' in Britain 'available to meet a German landing'. To ensure this, it was agreed to recall the rest of the 5th Division from France on the following day.[1]

The suggestion of an imminent German invasion of Holland derived from specific reports that the Germans planned to seize the Dutch island of Texel. During the discussion, Churchill pointed out 'that in any previous war we should have been able to seize Texel; but, in view of the development of the air arm, it was not desirable to expose war ships to continual air attack in this manner. This objection did not apply, however, to the use of submarines. The most effective answer to a German attack on Texel would be an immediate air attack by ourselves on the Ruhr.'

Churchill was supported both by Halifax, who said that it would be right for Britain 'to assume that such action by the Germans would constitute an invasion of the Netherlands, and would thus free our hands to attack the Ruhr', and by Chamberlain who also 'agreed, and added that this was fully understood by the French Government'.[2]

At Westminster, political speculation now centred on a possible change of Government. On May 1 Harold Nicolson had noted in his diary, after a talk with Lord De la Warr, the recently appointed First Commissioner of Works: 'Buck seems to think that if Norway is lost, the PM will have to resign. I say that what will happen is that Reynaud will resign and the PM will stay put. The Tapers and Tadpoles are putting it around that the whole Norwegian episode is due to Winston.' Nicolson added: 'there is a theory going round that Lloyd George may head a Coalition Cabinet. What worries people is that everybody asks, 'But whom could you put in Chamberlain's place?'[3]

On May 2, Churchill's new powers came into effect, and in a note that day to Ismay he asked for arrangements to be made 'to combine

[1] War Cabinet No. 109 of 1940, 1 May 1940, 11.30 a.m.: Cabinet papers, 65/7.

[2] War Cabinet No. 109 of 1940, 1 May 1940, 11.30 a.m., Minute 9, Confidential Annex: Cabinet papers, 65/13, folio 12.

[3] Nicolson diary, 1 May 1940: Nigel Nicolson (editor), *Harold Nicolson, Diaries and Letters 1939–1945*, London 1967, pages 74–5. Taper and Tadpole were characters in Disraeli's *Coningsby*. Both were typical Party wire-pullers.

the work of all concerned in the preparation of the Narvik base, in so far as this still remains to be done'. Churchill also suggested setting up a small controlling group, representing the three Services. As for the scale of the Narvik defences, he wrote, 'We must be careful not to indulge in disproportionate and extravagant views.' The Navy must choose an anchorage which derived protection from the guns and balloons already assigned to the defence of the main army base, and it was on this that the main anti-aircraft strength should be concentrated. No more than 'deterrent protection' could be provided to the outlying places, nor should the anti-aircraft protection of the three aerodromes 'be on a greater scale than those in France or England which are in proximity to the main German bombing force'.

During May 2 news had reached London of German air attacks on British hospital ships. In his note to Ismay, Churchill suggested that the 'best protection' for hospital ships would be 'to moor the German prisoners (when and if we get them) from Narvik in one or two transports intermingled with the hospital ships, and publish the fact'.[1]

The War Cabinet on May 2 reviewed the situation throughout the Norwegian theatres of operation. At Namsos, fog was delaying the evacuation, which it was now hoped to complete by May 4. Once the fog lifted the 'main danger', Stanley reported, 'was concentrated air attack'. Fighter protection was virtually impossible, as Namsos was out of range for RAF fighters operating from bases in Britain. Air protection would only be provided if three or four fighters were sent to Namsos 'under orders to remain there until their fuel was exhausted'. The aircraft-carriers *Ark Royal* and *Glorious* were 'short of aircraft', and would have to return to Scapa to take on more. Nor could the carriers operate 'close enough to the shore' to support the troops.

At Mosjöen, fog had prevented the landing of the small guerilla party. At Andalsnes and Molde the last of the British troops had been evacuated. At Narvik, the town still remained in German hands, but 'it was hoped' that British troops already ashore on the Ankenes peninsula would soon be able to 'block the railway between Narvik and the frontier'.[2]

It was on Narvik that the hopes of an Allied victory now centred. On May 2, at Churchill's suggestion, an inter-Service Committee was set up to implement 'as rapidly and efficiently as possible' the plans laid down by the Chiefs of Staff. Known as the Narvik Committee, at

[1] Military Co-ordination Committee, 'Note by the Chairman', 2 May 1940: Admiralty papers, 199/1929.
[2] War Cabinet No. 110 of 1940, 2 May 1940, 11.30 a.m.: Cabinet papers, 65/7.

its second meeting on May 3 it optimistically discussed the eventual export of iron ore from Narvik to Britain, while at the same time noting that no British aircraft would be able to land at the three Narvik aerodromes until May 15 as neither the airstrips themselves nor their anti-aircraft defences were yet ready.[1] That same day Churchill informed Cork that according to weather reports, May 8 was the 'normal date' of the thaw, but that there might be 'at least a fornight's delay this year'; a delay which would postpone the assault on Narvik itself until May 22 at the earliest. 'Everything,' Churchill added, 'is being done here to send men and materials to you with the highest priority.' But, he warned:

We must expect that intense efforts will be made by the enemy either from the Air or through Sweden or both to attack you before Narvik falls. Violation of Swedish neutrality by Germany would not necessarily be unhelpful to us, but every day that Narvik remains untaken, even at severe cost, imperils the whole enterprise. I must regard the next six or seven days as possibly decisive.[2]

On the morning of May 3 the War Cabinet was told that at Mosjöen the British force of 128 men, delayed earlier by fog, had now been landed 'without opposition and apparently unobserved'. At Namsos, 6,400 troops had been embarked 'without any hitch' and the evacuation was complete: 'a very successful military operation' it was called in the minutes of the War Cabinet. At Narvik, a German attack on the British troops in the Ankenes peninsula had been repulsed 'with considerable loss to the enemy', and with few British casualties.[3]

That night Churchill telegraphed to Cork: 'Urgency of Narvik is extreme. Trust you will use all available strength and press hard for decision. I shall be glad to share your responsibilities.' With reference to an idea which had been put to him by Lindemann, Churchill added: 'Presume you have considered use of smoke screens from one or other of the Fiords according to wind.'[4]

At the War Cabinet on the morning of May 4, Churchill gave his colleagues an optimistic account of the situation outside Narvik. There had been some fighting, he said, and 'our troops were gradually closing in'. It was 'very desirable', he added, that matters should be brought

---

[1] Narvik Committee No. 2 of 1940, 3 May 1940, 5 p.m.: Admiralty papers, 116/4305. The Civil Lord of Admiralty was in the Chair. The nineteen members present were all senior officials from the Admiralty, Air Ministry and War Office.

[2] 'Personal', sent at 12.31 a.m., 3 May 1940: Admiralty papers, 119/1929.

[3] War Cabinet No. 111 of 1940, 3 May 1940, 11.30 a.m.: Cabinet papers, 65–7.

[4] 'Personal', 'Most Immediate', signal sent at 12.38 a.m., 4 May 1940: Admiralty papers, 199/1929.

to a 'definite conclusion' there as soon as possible; indeed, Cork intended to seek a decision 'in the coming week', despite the intensive German air attack that was now likely. Cork's intention, Churchill said, was a 'wise' one, which he hoped would be supported 'whatever the outcome'.[1]

The War Cabinet approved of Cork's resolve, while the Chiefs of Staff Committee continued to consider every possible means of providing him with the air and sea support which he needed; at their meeting on the morning of May 4 they had already advised that even without Cork's specific requests, there should be no delay 'in preparing whatever could be foreseen and despatching it'.[2]

While the War Cabinet and the Chiefs of Staff Committee looked forward to the imminent capture of Narvik, General Mackesy's senior military advisers were preparing to challenge the whole operation. 'In view of their unanimity,' Cork telegraphed to Churchill shortly before midnight on May 5, 'I feel bound to refer the matter to the judgement of HM Government which I do with great reluctance.'

Cork then set out the soldiers' arguments against a Narvik landing. There were 'insufficient assault landing craft' to put ashore an adequate force to cover the landing of troops 'in unprotected craft', and only half of the fourteen landing craft required were available. To supplement the motor landing craft, 'of which there are only five', local trawlers would have to be used, but they would need a steeply sloping beach, and with the 'limited information and bad charts' available, it was uncertain 'whether they will ground within reach of rocks'. Only one small beach was available for each of the two assaulting battalions; yet each was bordered 'by high rocks and steep slopes over which men could barely clamber let alone assault'. As it was daylight that far north 'throughout the 24 hours', surprise of any sort was 'impossible'. No smoke shells were carried by the ships, leaving only smoke floats and funnel smoke, both of which were dependent 'on remote chance of a suitable wind'. Nor could the troops dig in against air attack 'on account of rocks and frost'; yet there was no other adequate defence.

Cork added that 'all the military officers experienced in war' fully agreed with these points, while General Mackesy, who had 'no previous knowledge that these representations were going to be made', and who had been doing his 'utmost' to carry out Cork's orders, felt that since

---

[1] War Cabinet No. 112 of 1940, 4 May 1940, 10.30 a.m.: Cabinet papers, 65/7.
[2] Chiefs of Staff Committee No. 110 of 1940, 4 May 1940, 9.30 a.m.: Cabinet papers, 79/4.

his earlier protest the situation in the air had grown worse, and regarded 'an opposed landing in face of unopposed enemy aircraft as being absolutely unjustified'.[1]

For Churchill, this protest was a blow to the plans which had seemed to be so near to fulfilment. He at once brought it to the attention of the Chiefs of Staff Committee, which met at 10.15 on the morning of May 6, and then to the War Cabinet, which met at 11.30. Both the Chiefs of Staff and the War Cabinet were also told that Lieutenant-Colonel Trappes-Lomax, who was in charge of the actual troops who would carry out the landing operation, 'was of the opinion that a direct assault on Narvik in present circumstances was not justified'.[2]

The War Cabinet agreed that it was 'most important' not to send Cork any message which might 'bring pressure to bear' on him, or might cause him 'to take action against his better judgement'. Churchill then read out a reply that had been prepared by the Chiefs of Staff, and which was approved. The telegram was sent from the Admiralty early that same afternoon, and read:

Whilst grounds for taking Narvik speedily are weighty especially in view of effect on neutrals and probability of increasing air attacks, the military views expressed in your telegram cannot be lightly set aside.

Cabinet desire to know your personal appreciation without seeking to bias your judgement in any way.

General Auchinleck who will ultimately command the troops should join you on 12th May.[3]

The Chiefs of Staff, at their morning meeting, had stressed that 'both on political and military grounds the capture of Narvik had become more urgent', and this view was reiterated at the War Cabinet by Churchill, who, as the minutes recorded, 'emphasised how very serious would be the repercussions of a defeat at Narvik'. It would show, he said, 'that our will to win and our fighting capacity were less than those of the enemy'. If Britain accepted defeat, he warned, 'without a bitter struggle', it would have 'a devastating effect on world opinion'.[4]

---

[1] 'Immediate', signal sent at 11.55 p.m., 5 May 1940, received at 4.21 a.m., 6 May 1940: Admiralty papers, 199/1929.

[2] Chiefs of Staff Committee No. 112 of 1940, 6 May 1940, 10.15 a.m.: Cabinet papers, 79/4.

[3] 'Immediate', signal sent at 2.18 p.m., 6 May 1940: Admiralty papers, 199/1929.

[4] War Cabinet No. 113 of 1940, 6 May 1940, 11.30 a.m., Minute 3, Confidential Annex: Cabinet papers, 65/13.

15

'I Think I Shall be Prime Minister Tomorrow'

THE failures in Norway, and the precarious situation of the troops still ashore, created during the first week of May a demand for a full Parliamentary debate. Anger had been caused by Chamberlain's confident assertion at the beginning of April, that Hitler had 'missed the bus', a remark which Clementine Churchill later described as 'a monument of ignorance and obstinacy'.[1] One of those who were exploiting that anger was Sir Roger Keyes, who was denouncing what he regarded as too timid a naval policy, and the folly of not having made a direct attack on Trondheim. 'Roger Keyes accosts me in the Lobby,' Harold Nicolson noted in his diary on April 30. 'He is in despair. He says that if only we had struck quickly with the Navy all would have been well.' Nicolson added:

He says that the Admiralty Board refused to take naval risks since they were frightened by the possible attitude of Italy. He says that we have been outmanoeuvred and beaten because we were too afraid. He says that Winston's drive and initiative have been undermined by the legend of his recklessness. Today he cannot dare to do the things he could have dared in 1915.[2]

The Conservative MP Henry Channon was also in the Lobby during April 30, where he found, as he noted in his diary, 'more talk of a cabal against poor Neville'. Channon added: ' "They" are saying that it is 1915 over again, that Winston should be Prime Minister as he has more vigour and the country behind him.'[3]

---

[1] Churchill papers, 4/131 (Clementine Churchill's comments in the margin of the proofs of Churchill's war memoirs).

[2] Nicolson diary, 30 April 1940: Nigel Nicolson (editor), *Harold Nicolson, Diaries and Letters 1939–1945*, London 1967, page 74.

[3] Channon diary, 30 April 1940: Robert Rhodes James (editor), *Chips, The Diaries of Sir Henry Channon*, London 1967, page 243.

Lord Salisbury's Watching Committee had continued, after its meeting with Lord Halifax on April 29, to serve as a focus of Conservative Parliamentary discontent, and a growing number of Tory MPs now felt that there had to be a change. Some turned towards Churchill. 'Winston is being lauded by both the Socialist and Liberal oppositions,' Channon noted in his diary on May 1, 'and being tempted to lead a revolt against the PM'. But Chamberlain, Channon added, was playing 'a deep game', and to 'gain time he has given Winston more rope, and made him what amounts to Director of Operations'. That evening, Channon noted, Churchill was 'joking and drinking' in the Smoking Room, 'surrounded by A. V. Alexander and Archie Sinclair, the new Shadow Cabinet'.[1]

On May 2 a Liberal Peer, Lord Davies, one of the pre-war stalwarts of the League of Nations Union, wrote to Churchill: 'You, I believe, are the only person in the Cabinet who is not responsible for this War. You are not tarred with the Munich brush. Your advice to re-arm went unheeded. You did not let down the small nations or throw our friends to the wolves.' It was for this reason, Davies added, that Churchill could 'restore our prestige and confidence at home and inspire us for further sacrifices abroad'. Davies' letter continued:

Now, in addition to your heavy responsibilities at the Admiralty, you have taken on the Chairmanship of the Committee for the Co-ordination of our War effort. May I respectfully submit that this is a full time job. All the thanks you get from the Central Office is a 'go-about' saying you are a tired man. Bah! Some of your colleagues will doubtless try and shift the responsibility on to your shoulders, without conferring upon you the necessary powers and authority. If anything goes wrong, you will be blamed. It seems to me that such an arrangement is unfair both to you and to the country.[2]

Speculation mounted both in the Service Ministries, and in the Parliamentary Lobbies. 'I hear that there is a first-class row commencing in the House,' Ironside noted in his diary on May 3, 'and that there is a strong movement to get rid of the PM'. Ironside added: 'Naturally the only man who can succeed is Winston and he is too unstable, though he has the genius to bring the war to an end.'[3]

Clementine Churchill was aware of the precariousness of her hus-

---

[1] Channon diary, 1 May 1940: Robert Rhodes James (editor), *Chips, The Diaries of Sir Henry Channon*, London 1967, pages 243–4.

[2] Letter of 2 May 1940: Churchill papers, 2/393.

[3] Ironside diary, 3 May 1940: Colonel Roderick Macleod and Denis Kelly (editors), *The Ironside Diaries 1937–1940*, London 1962, page 293.

band's position. 'Had it not been for your years of exile & repeated warnings re. the German peril,' she later wrote, 'Norway might well have ruined you.'[1]

In Whitehall, there was speculation as to Churchill's part in the movement to replace Chamberlain. During May 3, Colville discussed the growing crisis with Lord Portal of Laverstoke, the Regional Commissioner for Wales. Portal's information, Colville noted in his diary, 'went to shew that Winston himself was being loyal to the PM, but his satellites (e.g. Duff Cooper, Amery etc) were doing all in their power to create mischief and ill-feeling'.[2]

The move against Chamberlain was growing rapidly. 'I find there is grave suspicion of the Prime Minister,' Harold Nicolson wrote in his diary on May 4. 'His speech about the Norwegian expedition has created disquiet. The House knows very well that it was a major defeat. But the PM said that "the balance of advantage rested with us" and that "Germany has not attained her objective".' People knew, Nicolson reflected, 'that this is simply not true' and he noted: 'People are so distressed by the whole thing that they are talking of Lloyd George as a possible PM. Eden is out of it.' Churchill, Nicolson added, 'is undermined by the Conservative caucus'.[3]

At the War Cabinet on May 4 there was a discussion about the adverse publicity which might be expected when the troops who had been evacuated from Norway reached Britain. The evacuation was to be debated in Parliament in three days' time, and much criticism of the conduct of the Norwegian campaign was expected both in the Press and Parliament. Churchill told his colleagues that the Press should be reminded:

... that we must learn courageously to endure reverses and not to react to them in such a way as to give the enemy encouragement at a critical stage of the struggle. It was difficult, in any case, to have to debate the conduct of the campaign in the House of Commons, but it would be almost impossible for the Government adequately to state their case without giving the enemy information as to the reasons for our actions, &c.

It would be intolerable that the House of Commons or the Press should make the task of the Government more difficult by insisting on revelations of a kind which would assist the enemy and by making defamatory statements which were eagerly utilised by the enemy.

---

[1] Churchill papers, 4/131 (Clementine Churchill's comments in the margin of the proofs of Churchill's war memoirs).

[2] Colville diary, 3 May 1940: Colville papers.

[3] Nicolson diary, 4 May 1940: Nigel Nicolson (editor) *Harold Nicolson, Diaries and Letters, 1939–1945*, London 1967, page 75.

If the position were properly explained to the Press, he was sure that the Press would respond well, and would realise that they had their part to play in helping us to achieve victory.[1]

Churchill had no illusions about the weakness of Britain's position. During May 4 he had been perturbed by a report from Gort to the effect that whereas the military efficiency of the five Regular divisions with the British Expeditionary Force in France had improved in the past six months, the standard of training of the Territorial divisions which had arrived was 'low'. Indeed, in Gort's opinion, 'against a first class enemy' these Territorial troops were fit only for 'static' warfare.[2] Writing that same day to Stanley, Churchill described Gort's report as 'serious'.[3]

The strain of events was beginning to tell on Churchill. After the Military Co-ordination Committee on May 4, Ironside noted in his diary: 'we found him very tired and sleepy and hardly did anything at all. He took quietly what we said without demur.'[4] On the following day Ironside noted again: 'Winston seems to me to be a little weighed down by the cares of being solely responsible for Narvik. He wants it taken and yet doesn't dare to give any direct order to Cork.'[5]

With evidence of British air weakness being presented daily by the Chiefs of Staff, Churchill also felt it necessary, at the War Cabinet on May 6, to warn his colleagues that it would be 'very dangerous and undesirable' for Britain to take the initiative in air warfare 'at a time when we possessed only a quarter of the striking power of the German Air Force'. Even a 'limited initiative' on Britain's part might, he feared, 'result in a wholesale indiscriminate bombing of this country'. If this were to happen, 'we should not be able to appeal to the United States, who would be able to retort that it was we who had taken the first step'.

British policy, Churchill believed, should be to press on with the production of 'small incendiary capsules for the destruction of German harvests and forests', not in order to use them, but in order to use the

---

[1] War Cabinet No. 112 of 1940, 4 May 1940, 10.30 a.m.: Cabinet papers, 65/7.

[2] 'Most Secret', Gort to Oliver Stanley, letter dated 11 April 1940: Admiralty papers, 199/1929.

[3] Letter of 4 May 1940: Admiralty papers, 199/1929.

[4] Ironside diary, 4 May 1940: Colonel Roderick Macleod and Denis Kelly (editors), *The Ironside Diaries 1937–1940*, London 1962, page 294.

[5] Ironside diary, 5 May 1940: Colonel Roderick Macleod and Denis Kelly (editors), *The Ironside Diaries 1937–1940*, London 1962, page 295.

fact of their existence 'to induce our enemies to confine air bombing to the zone of operations'.[1]

That evening, while presiding over the Military Co-ordination Committee, Churchill learnt with dismay of further weaknesses and problems in both Army and Air Force needs. Munitions production had fallen so far that according to the Ministry of Supply, 'the figures for the last two months were below the corresponding figures for 1915'. The training of women had been 'slower than expected'. Machinery which had been left out of use 'was not yet working efficiently'. Present requirements of rifle ammunition 'were in excess of production', a serious situation relieved only 'somewhat' by purchases from Canada, India, South Africa and Greece. But there were still 'deficiencies', and a French appeal for ten million rounds for the Lewis Guns they had obtained from Britain for the defence of aerodromes could not be provided without further deficiencies building up. Tank production had also failed to reach the expected level, so that 'the supply fell far short of requirements'. Existing production 'was already handicapped by a shortage of jigs and tools', a shortage of which Churchill had warned repeatedly before the war.

The worst deficiency revealed at the Military Co-ordination Committee meeting of May 6 concerned aviation spirit. While in France, Churchill told the Committee, 'his attention had been drawn to the wastage caused by deterioration in aviation spirit that was stored in tins'. This wastage, he had been told, had assumed 'alarming proportions'. Speaking for the Air Ministry, Air Marshal Sir Christopher Courtney informed the Committee that 'at the estimated scale for active operations', the reserves of petrol 'would only last some 10–11 weeks'.[2]

On the morning of May 7 Churchill, ever mindful of the importance of the attitude of the United States, wrote personally to Roosevelt from the Admiralty: 'My dear Mr President, In view of the interest you displayed in the Battle of the River Plate, I thought you would like to see an advance copy of the official account of the Battle which we shall shortly be publishing.'[3] That same morning, from his base at Harstad, Lord Cork sent his reply to the War Cabinet's request that he should give his own assessment of the Narvik prospects. 'My view is,' he wrote, 'that while every difficulty has been stressed, little weight has been given to favourable factors.' Given that it was important to take Narvik,

[1] War Cabinet No. 113 of 1940, 6 May 1940, 11.30 a.m., Minute 3, Confidential Annex: Cabinet papers, 65/13.

[2] Military Co-ordination Committee No. 37 of 1940, 6 May 1940, 5 p.m.: Cabinet papers, 83/3.

[3] Letter of 7 May 1940: Admiralty papers, 199/1928.

Cork added, 'my opinion is that a decided effort should be made to do so'. The Admiral did not minimize the difficulties. But he was determined to try to overcome them. 'I do not consider success certain,' he wrote, 'but believe there is a good chance, whereas it is quite certain by not trying no success can be gained.'[1]

Cork's determination came too late to avert the political crisis. That same day, May 7, the Parliamentary Debate was to open, awaited with trepidation by the Government and uncertainty by its critics. 'I am much afraid,' Lord Lloyd wrote to his son that morning, 'that the weakness of the Opposition and subservience of the Commons majority will leave Chamberlain at the head of affairs until some further blunder brings fresh humiliation and disaster to our armies.' Lloyd added: 'It is the terrible complacency of Neville, Simon and Sam Hoare that alarms me so much. We all behave as if we had three years or more in which to win the war, whereas it is certain that it is in the next 4 or at latest 5 months that Hitler will stake his all in an attempt to administer a knock-out blow. . . .'[2]

In his diary, Harold Nicolson recorded the opening stages of the debate, intended as a Motion for Adjournment:

> The House is crowded, and when Chamberlain comes in, he is greeted with shouts of 'Missed the bus!' He makes a very feeble speech and is only applauded by the Yes-men. He makes some reference to the complacency of the country, at which the whole House cheers vociferously and ironically, inducing him to make a little, rather feminine, gesture of irritation. Attlee makes a feeble speech and Archie Sinclair a good one. . . .[3]

In his speech, Sinclair praised 'the efficiency of our Naval Staff', and said that the Norwegian failure arose because 'there had been no foresight in the political direction of the war and in the instructions given to the Staffs to prepare for these very difficult operations in due time'. As a result of this lack of foresight, he said, the Staffs were 'hastily improvising instead of working to long and carefully-matured plans'.

Sinclair urged the setting up of a smaller War Cabinet, 'free from departmental responsibility', which would do the necessary 'thinking, planning and imparting through all the departments, drive and thrust to our war effort'. Throughout the country, he said, in all the constitu-

---

[1] 'Immediate', signal sent at 6.31 a.m. and received at 7.41 p.m., 7 May 1940: Admiralty papers, 199/1929.

[2] Letter of 7 May 1940: Lloyd papers.

[3] Nicolson diary, 7 May 1940: Nigel Nicolson (editor), *Harold Nicolson, Diaries and Letters 1939–1945*. London 1967, page 76.

encies, people were becoming 'more and more disturbed with the direction of the war'. They had been 'profoundly shocked' by the Norwegian episode, and 'misled by optimistic speeches'. Sinclair then spoke of the speech that Churchill, his friend of more than thirty years, would be making on the second day of the debate:

I have no doubt that the right hon. Gentleman the First Lord to-morrow night, with a debating power which I myself shall never attain, will be able to explain; but is it not the fact that the Prime Minister and the First Lord have led the people to believe the impossible about this adventure which was never thought out and which was never taken to the end?

Is it not the case that, through lack of direction by the Government—and I am not in favour of censorship, but I would like these matters straightened out—the Press led the public to believe that day by day we were winning magnificent victories, when those people who looked at the map and thought about the situation knew that those things could not be?

The right hon. Gentleman to-day told us that south of Trondheim and north of Trondheim we had succeeded, by a masterly policy, in evacuation with no losses. Wars are not won on masterly evacuations.

'In the first major effort of this war,' Sinclair commented, 'whatever the reasons may be, justifiable or not, we have had to creep back to our lairs, which is against the spirit of the men who are over the waters.'[1]

Shortly after Sinclair had spoken these damaging words, Sir Roger Keyes entered the House, dressed in the full uniform of an Admiral of the Fleet, with six rows of medals, to make what Nicolson described in his diary as 'an absolutely devastating attack upon the naval conduct of the Narvik episode and the Naval General Staff. The House listens in breathless silence when he tells us how the Naval General Staff had assured him that a naval action at Trondheim was easy but unnecessary owing to the success of the military. There is a great gasp of astonishment.' Nicolson added: 'It is by far the most dramatic speech I have ever heard, and when Keyes sits down there is thunderous applause.'[2]

There was yet more drama to come, when Leo Amery recalled the days of the Civil War three hundred years before, when the Parliamentary troops were being beaten, and Oliver Cromwell told John Hampden: 'Your troops are most of them old, decayed serving men and tapsters, and such kind of fellows.' Then, looking down on the Conservative front bench, and towards Chamberlain, Amery continued:

[1] *Hansard*, 7 May 1940.

[2] Nicolson diary, 7 May 1940: Nigel Nicolson (editor), *Harold Nicolson, Diaries and Letters 1939–1945*, London 1967, page 77.

I have quoted certain words of Oliver Cromwell. I will quote certain other words. I do it with great reluctance, because I am speaking of those who are old friends and associates of mine, but they are words which, I think, are applicable to the present situation. This is what Cromwell said to the Long Parliament when he thought it was no longer fit to conduct the affairs of the nation: 'You have sat too long for any good you have been doing. Depart, I say, and let us have done with you. In the name of God, go!'[1]

'These were terrible words,' Churchill later wrote, 'coming from a friend and colleague of many years, a fellow Birmingham Member, and a Privy Councillor of distinction and experience.'[2]

After this first day's debate, Nicolson noted that night in his diary, there was a general impression 'that we are unprepared to meet the appalling attack which we know is about to be delivered against us. The atmosphere is something more than anxiety; it is one of actual fear, but it is a very resolute fear. . . .'[3] There were political fears also, especially among Chamberlain's supporters. 'The atmosphere was intense,' Henry Channon noted in his diary that night, 'and everywhere one heard whispers: "What will Winston do?"'[4]

The debate was to resume on May 8. Throughout the morning Churchill worked at the Admiralty. While he worked, the Chiefs of Staff Committee informed Lord Cork that according to 'our information', the German defence of Narvik was 'weakening', and that in those circumstances the capture of Narvik 'should be pressed with vigour', even before General Auchinleck's arrival, now delayed until May 12.[5]

But the willingness of Cork to attack, the determination of the Chiefs of Staff to support him, and the approval of the War Cabinet for a rapid offensive, were all unknown to the House of Commons when it reassembled that afternoon, its mood as hostile to the Government as it had been on the previous day. 'The present agitation,' Nicolson noted in his diary, 'is not solely due to Norway, but to very widespread

---

[1] *Hansard*, 7 May 1940.

[2] Winston S. Churchill, *The Second World War*, volume 1, London 1948, page 521.

[3] Nicolson diary, 7 May 1940: Nigel Nicolson (editor), *Harold Nicolson, Diaries and Letters 1939–1945*, London 1967, page 77.

[4] Channon diary, 7 May 1940: Robert Rhodes James (editor), *Chips, The Diaries of Sir Henry Channon*, London 1967, page 245.

[5] Chiefs of Staff Committee No. 116 of 1940, 8 May 1940, 10 a.m., Annex II: Cabinet papers, 79/4, folio 86. This signal was sent, as 'Most Immediate', at 12.34 p.m.: Admiralty papers, 199/1929.

anxiety about supply and labour conditions'[1]—the very conditions in fact which Churchill had heard described in the secrecy of the Military Co-ordination Committee two days before.

The second day's debate was opened by Herbert Morrison, who declared that the Labour Opposition now wished to call for a Vote of Censure on the Government. Chamberlain replied that he had 'friends' in the House, an assertion that shocked many of those present, and provoked Lloyd George into a devastating attack. 'It is not a question of who are the Prime Minister's friends,' he said. 'It is a far bigger issue,' and Lloyd George went on to say, of Chamberlain:

> He has appealed for sacrifice. The nation is prepared for every sacrifice so long as it has leadership, so long as the Government show clearly what they are aiming at, and so long as the nation is confident that those who are leading it are doing their best.
>
> I say solemnly that the Prime Minister should give an example of sacrifice, because there is nothing which can contribute more to victory in this war than that he should sacrifice the seals of office.[2]

Churchill's position in the debate was an uneasy one. Some of the criticism during both days had been against the Narvik expedition, and against him as First Lord. But most of the criticism had been aimed at Chamberlain, at alleged perpetuation of peace time moods in war time, and at the alleged continuation in wartime of the pre-war appeasement policy of which Churchill himself had been such a prominent critic.

Some Conservative MPs were nervous of criticizing the Narvik operation too severely, for fear that Churchill would be a victim of the debate, rather than in some way its beneficiary. As Harold Macmillan later recalled:

> Our chief anxiety concerned Churchill. We knew he had determined to stand loyally by his colleagues and would close the debate as the spokesman for the Government. We were determined to bring down the Government, and as every hour passed, we seemed more likely to achieve our purpose. But how could Churchill be disentangled from the ruins? If the chief issue of the first day had been the overthrow of the Government, the chief anxiety of the second was the rescue of Churchill.[3]

Among those who tried to 'rescue' Churchill had been Lloyd George himself. 'I do not think,' he had said towards the end of his speech,

[1] Nicolson diary, 8 May 1940: Nigel Nicolson (editor), *Harold Nicolson, Diaries and Letters 1939–1945*, London 1967, page 78.

[2] *Hansard*, 8 May 1940.

[3] Harold Macmillan, *The Blast of War 1939–1945*, London 1967, page 72.

'that the First Lord was entirely responsible for all the things which happened in Norway.' But Churchill had at once risen in his seat to tell the House: 'I take complete responsibility for everything that has been done at the Admiralty, and I take my full share of the burden.' This had prompted a sharp riposte from Lloyd George, that Churchill 'must not allow himself to be converted into an air-raid shelter to keep the splinters from hitting his colleagues'.[1]

Chamberlain had asked Churchill to wind up the debate for the Government. What had begun as a motion for the Adjournment of the House was now a Vote of Censure. During the evening, as the debate continued, Churchill went to the smoking room, where he saw Harold Macmillan. 'He beckoned to me,' Macmillan later recalled, 'and I moved to speak to him. I wished him luck, but added that I hoped his speech would not be too convincing. "Why not?" he asked. "Because," I replied, "we must have a new Prime Minister, and it must be you." He answered gruffly that he had signed on for the voyage and would stick to the ship. But I don't think he was angry with me.'[2]

Shortly after ten o'clock Churchill rose to speak. 'One saw at once,' Channon noted in his diary, 'that he was in bellicose mood, alive and enjoying himself, relishing the ironical position in which he found himself: i.e. that of defending his enemies, and a cause in which he did not believe.' It was, Channon added, 'a slashing, vigorous speech, a magnificent piece of oratory. I was in the gallery behind him, with Rab, who was, several times, convulsed with laughter.'[3]

Churchill made no reference in his speech either to his own attempts for seven months to persuade the War Cabinet to initiate prompt action at Narvik, or to his original doubts about the Trondheim attack. But he did tell the House of Commons: 'My eye has always been fixed on Narvik.' This, he added, 'is a port which may lead to some decisive achievement in the war'. But once the Germans had invaded Norway, there was 'no dispute that we were bound to go to the aid of the Norwegians and that Trondheim was the place'. That was undoubtedly, he said, 'a hazardous operation', and once the Germans began to advance north of Oslo, and the Norwegians were unable to hold the mountain passes, and did not destroy the roads and railways, then it became necessary to withdraw the troops 'or leave them to be destroyed by overwhelming force'.

[1] *Hansard*, 8 May 1940.

[2] Harold Macmillan, *The Blast of War 1939–1945*, London 1967, page 74.

[3] Channon diary, 8 May 1940: Robert Rhodes James (editor), *Chips, The Diaries of Sir Henry Channon*, London 1967, page 246. 'Rab' was R. A. Butler, Under-Secretary of State for Foreign Affairs.

The decision to withdraw, Churchill insisted, 'was undoubtedly sound'. To have tried to remain in the Trondheim region against a German army of more than 120,000 able to move up unmolested from Oslo would have committed the far smaller British forces 'to a forlorn operation on an ever-increasing scale'. Churchill then warned the House of the dangers involved in continuing the Trondheim plan:

We must be careful not to exhaust our Air Force, in view of the much graver dangers which might come upon us at any time, and also not to throw such a strain on our flotillas and anti-aircraft cruisers as might hamper the general mobility of the Fleet.

There are other waters of which we have to think besides the Norwegian waters, and I can think of nothing more likely to bring new adversaries down upon us in other waters than the spectacle of our being too largely absorbed under the most unfavourable conditions in a protracted struggle around Trondheim.

Of course, if Sweden had come to the rescue of Norway, if her troops had entered, as they could easily have done, and if her air bases had been at the disposal of the Royal Air Force, very different positions might have been established.

There has, unhappily, never been any chance of that. The Swedish Government, like many other people, have been confined to adverse criticism of His Majesty's Government.

At Narvik, Churchill went on, the conditions were 'much more equal' so far as the ability to send reinforcements was concerned, and there the struggle continued.

Labour members in particular were concerned to find out whether Churchill and the War Cabinet had overruled the advice of the Chiefs of Staff. Herbert Morrison asked whether the naval authorities who wanted to enter Trondheim had been 'overruled' by Whitehall. Churchill was angered by the implications of such questioning, which formed a part of what he called 'the cataract of unworthy suggestions and of actual falsehoods which have been poured out to the public during the last few days', and he told the House:

A picture has been drawn of craven politicians hampering their admirals and generals in their bold designs. Others have suggested that I have personally overruled them, or that they themselves are inept and cowardly. Others again have suggested—for if truth is many-sided, mendacity is many-tongued—that I, personally, proposed to the Prime Minister and the War Cabinet more violent action and that they shrank from it and restrained it.

There is not a word of truth in all that. [An HON. MEMBER: 'Who said it?'] After all, you said you wanted the truth.

As for Keyes' criticisms, 'I sympathise intensely,' Churchill said, 'with his desire to lead a valiant attack, and to repeat in Scandinavian waters the immortal glories of the Zeebrugge Mole, but I am sorry that this natural impulse should have led him to cast aspersions upon his old shipmates and his old staff officers, Sir Dudley Pound and Vice-Admiral Phillips. . . .' When Keyes had come to see him with his own plan for 'forcing an entrance in Trondheim, I could only tell him that there was already a plan very similar to his, though his was to some extent to be preferred; but that we had abandoned the plan'.

Churchill said no more about Keyes and his plan. But in his notes for the speech he had intended to include the following remarks, which he omitted at the last moment. 'However,' he had written in his notes, 'remembering what I felt all those years in not being allowed to take any part in the work of preparations, so far as I am concerned I forgive him freely.'[1]

While talking about the Trondheim operation, Churchill was interrupted by Arthur Greenwood, one of Labour's principal critics of the evacuation, who demanded to know whether it was the War Cabinet which had 'delayed taking a decision about Trondheim?' Churchill replied: 'Do dismiss these illusions,' and went on to try to convince the House that there was another, more positive, more hopeful aspect to the whole Norwegian campaign, for all its tale of delay and difficulty and evacuation. The German invasion of Norway, he said, had been for Hitler 'a cardinal political and strategic error', and he continued:

In the brown hours, when baffling news comes, and disappointing news, I always turn for refreshment to the reports of the German wireless. I love to read the lies they tell of all the British ships they have sunk so many times over, and to survey the fools' paradise in which they find it necessary to keep their deluded serfs and robots.

The Germans have claimed to have sunk or damaged 11 battleships: actually, two have been slightly damaged—neither of them withdrawn for a day from the service. They have claimed three aircraft carriers heavily damaged; the facts are that one was slightly injured by a near miss, and that it is still going on in the service. They have declared that they have sunk or damaged 28 cruisers; actually, one anti-aircraft cruiser has sustained damage. As to destroyers, and so forth—I could go on, but I will not.

The only point on which they have not exaggerated is the sinking of trawlers. We have, unhappily, lost 11 trawlers in the Government service at one time or another; and that explains all these 'battleships' in the German accounts.

Lloyd George had argued in his own speech that it was wrong to

[1] Speech notes, 8 May 1940: Churchill papers, 9/139.

mention such calculations of profit and loss. 'I do not agree,' Churchill continued. 'Calculations of profit and loss are our life. We win by these calculations of the ships we sink.'[1]

In Churchill's notes for his speech, written on the back of an envelope, Churchill had written the following sentences, which he did not deliver:

> L G said he wished I was
>   back in my corner seat.
> Well perhaps I shall be.
> I shall not complain. I have done my best.
>   At any rate I do not
>   see how any Govt is
>   to be carried on
>   under these conditions
>   or how head is to be made
>   against the tremendous
>   power of the enemy.

In red ink Churchill had added: 'Do not forget the enemy.'[2]

Churchill had intended to bring his speech to an end by referring to the Labour Party's Vote of Censure. But as he spoke, his remarks brought him in direct collision with the Labour Opposition, and led to uproar. At one point Churchill commented angrily, of the Labour MP Emanuel Shinwell: 'He skulks in the corner,'[3] whereupon there was a burst of indignation on the Labour benches. Another Labour MP— 'rather the worse for drink',[4] as Channon noted in his diary, and who had never heard the word 'skulking' before, thought Churchill had said 'skunking'. He thereupon accused Churchill of unparliamentary language.

Amid the ensuing clamour, Churchill was unable to continue. 'Honourable Members,' he called out, 'dare not listen to the argument. All day long we have had abuse, and now honourable Members opposite will not even listen.'

The point Churchill wished to make was one in favour of the withdrawal from the Trondheim area. Had Britain continued with the Trondheim plan, he argued, the eight or nine divisions withdrawn from the western front in order to carry it out would have been 'locked

---

[1] *Hansard*, 8 May 1940.

[2] Speech notes, 8 May 1940: Churchill papers, 9/139.

[3] *Hansard*, 8 May 1940, column 1360.

[4] Channon diary, 8 May 1940: Robert Rhodes James (editor), *Chips, The Diaries of Sir Henry Channon*, London 1967, page 246.

up in that country all the summer, defending a coast 800 miles long and indented in a most extraordinary manner'.

Churchill then turned to those who had criticized Chamberlain's appeal to his friends. 'He *thought* he had some friends,' Churchill said, 'and I *hope* he has some friends. He certainly had a good many when things were going well.' It would, he added, be 'most ungenerous and unworthy of the British character', and of the Conservative Party, to turn against the Government 'in a moment of difficulty' without all the processes of 'grave debate', but on the 'precipitate' decision of the Opposition 'after such little notice', to call for a Vote of Censure. Churchill's speech ended:

Let me say that I am not advocating controversy. We have stood it for the last two days, and if I have broken out, it is not because I mean to seek a quarrel with hon. Gentlemen.

On the contrary, I say, let pre-war feuds die; let personal quarrels be forgotten, and let us keep our hatreds for the common enemy. Let party interest be ignored, let all our energies be harnessed, let the whole ability and forces of the nation be hurled into the struggle, and let all the strong horses be pulling on the collar.

At no time in the last war were we in greater peril than we are now, and I urge the House strongly to deal with these matters not in a precipitate vote, ill debated and on a widely discursive field, but in grave time and due time in accordance with the dignity of Parliament.[1]

'How much of the fire was real,' Channon wrote in his diary, 'how much ersatz, we shall never know, but he amused and dazzled everyone with his virtuosity.'[2]

The most recent addition to Churchill's Private Secretariat, John Peck, was in the official box during the closing phase of the debate. 'I listened fascinated to Churchill's winding up speech,' he later wrote:

He was constantly heckled by the Labour opposition, and he tore into them vehemently and often angrily. I had never heard him in action in the House of Commons and I was strangely uneasy. My instant reaction was that it was a fine speech and that he was a superb actor, but that somehow it did not ring entirely true. I still believe this to be corrrect, but in the circumstances of the hour it would have been humanly impossible to make a completely sincere and heartfelt reply to the attacks on the Chamberlain Government.

Churchill knew that he was defending positions which were, in many respects, indefensible. He knew that if the bitterest critics had their way, Cham-

---

[1] *Hansard*, 8 May 1940.

[2] Channon diary, 8 May 1940: Robert Rhodes James (editor), *Chips, The Diaries of Sir Henry Channon*, London 1967, page 246.

berlain would resign. He knew that, in that case, he would probably become Prime Minister himself. But throughout the entire political crisis he never spoke or acted except in absolute loyalty to his Prime Minister.[1]

As soon as the debate ended, MPs milled about, discussing who, and how many, would vote against the Government. Roy Wise, the Conservative MP for Oldham—the constituency for which Churchill had first been elected to Parliament in 1900—told Channon that he, for one, would vote against Chamberlain, as it was 'the only way to shock us out of our complacency'. Channon commented that Wise was 'playing with dynamite'. Another Conservative MP, Charles Taylor, who had been one of the younger Conservatives to support Churchill over India ten years before, told Channon emphatically: 'We are trying to get your Government out tonight.'[2]

Four decades later, Charles Taylor recalled how, that evening, 'friends were split', and 'terrible pressure' was put upon those who had made it plain that they intended to vote against the Government. It was the Chief Whip, David Margesson, who pointed out to Taylor: 'Do you realize Winston Churchill is going to support Neville Chamberlain tonight.' But Taylor did not allow this argument to deter him, telling Margesson: 'Of course he will. He must. He is First Lord.'[3]

Despite a three-line Whip, 33 Conservatives and 8 of their supporters voted with the Opposition.[4] A further 60 abstained. The voting was 281 for the Government and 200 against, a Government majority of 81. A united Conservative Party vote would have given Chamberlain a majority of 213.

The majority of 81 was indeed a hollow one. As soon as the figures were announced, the Labour MP Josiah Wedgwood led the Government's opponents in the singing of *Rule Britannia*. But even this unprecedented demonstration was drowned in cries of 'Go! Go! Go! Go!' directed at Chamberlain as he left the Chamber.[5]

That same evening Chamberlain went to see the King. He had not come to offer his resignation, he said, and he had not yet given up

---

[1] John Peck, 'Bull and Benediction', unpublished typescript, pages 96–7.

[2] Channon diary, 8 May 1940: Robert Rhodes James (editor), *Chips, The Diaries of Sir Henry Channon*, London 1967, page 246.

[3] Sir Charles Taylor, conversation with the author, 19 March 1982.

[4] The Conservative back-benchers who defied the three-line Whip and voted against their Leader included Leo Amery, Alfred Duff Cooper, Lord Wolmer, Leslie Hore-Belisha, Lady Astor (Nancy Astor), Paul Emrys-Evans, Sir Roger Keyes, Richard Law, Quintin Hogg, Robert Boothby, Sir Derrick Gunston, Brigadier-General Spears, Charles Taylor, Ronald Tree, John Profumo, Sir Ralph Glyn and Harold Macmillan (*The Times*, 9 May 1940).

[5] Harold Nicolson diary, 8 May 1940: Nigel Nicolson (editor), *Harold Nicolson, Diaries and Letters, 1939–1945*, London 1967, page 79.

hope of forming a National Coalition Government. It was hoped that the Labour opposition would agree to join the Government, and their leaders accept Ministerial Office. But on the following morning, May 9, it seemed that Chamberlain was prepared to give up the Premiership altogether, if the Labour Party refused to serve under him. This was the same line of thought that had occurred to Churchill, who asked Anthony Eden to come to see him at the Admiralty that morning, and, while shaving, told Eden that Chamberlain 'would not be able to bring in Labour and that a National Government must be formed'.

Later that day, Churchill lunched with Eden. Also present was Kingsley Wood. 'They told me,' Eden noted in his diary, 'that Neville had decided to go. The future was discussed. Kingsley thought that W should succeed, and urged that he should make plain his willingness.'

Kingsley Wood had been Chamberlain's protégé, colleague and friend for nearly twenty years; Eden was therefore shocked when he heard him warning Churchill that Chamberlain would want Halifax to succeed him as Prime Minister, and would ask Churchill to agree; but that Churchill should refuse. 'Don't agree,' Kingsley Wood insisted, 'and don't say anything.' Eden noted in his diary: 'I was shocked that Wood should talk in this way, for he had been so much Chamberlain's man, but it was good counsel and I seconded it.'[1]

That afternoon Chamberlain asked Churchill and Halifax to discuss the situation with him at 10 Downing Street. According to the account of the conversation which Halifax gave to Cadogan—and which Cadogan recorded in his diary—Chamberlain began the discussion by saying that the 'main thing' was national unity, that Labour must come into the Government, and that if Labour would not agree to serve under him, then he was 'quite ready to resign'.

Chamberlain then asked the Labour leaders, Clement Attlee and Arthur Greenwood, to join them, and when they arrived, asked if they would enter the Government under his Premiership, or, if they refused that, under another Conservative Prime Minister. Both said that the decision would depend on the views of the Labour Party, then at its annual conference at Bournemouth, but that they thought the answer would be 'almost certainly "No" ' to serving under Chamberlain, and 'probably "Yes" ' to serving under someone else.[2]

'The conversation was most polite,' Churchill later recalled, 'but it

---

[1] Eden diary, 9 May 1940, and Eden's subsequent reflections: The Earl of Avon, *The Eden Memoirs, The Reckoning*, London 1965, pages 96–7.

[2] Cadogan diary, 9 May 1940: David Dilks (editor), *The Diaries of Sir Alexander Cadogan OM, 1938–1945*, London 1971, page 280.

2. Churchill leaving Admiralty House on the morning of 5 September 1939, on his way to the War Cabinet (see page 9). With him is his Principal Private Secretary, Eric Seal

3. Churchill's first wartime broadcast, 1 October 1939 (see page 49)

4. Churchill visits the Advanced Air Striking Force headquarters near Rheims, 7 January 1940 (see page 123). With him is Air Vice Marshal Barratt. Professor Lindemann, in bowler hat, is behind Churchill and Barratt

5. Lord Halifax, Edouard Daladier, Neville Chamberlain, Churchill and Sir Kingsley Wood at the Ministry of War, Paris, during a meeting of the Supreme War Council, 5 February 1940 (see page 147). Sir Alexander Cadogan is between Daladier and Chamberlain

6. Churchill arriving at the garden gate of 10 Downing Street on 4 April 1940, the morning after it was announced that he was to preside over the newly created Defence Committee (see pages 204–7)

7. Churchill in Paris, 31 May 1940, three weeks after becoming Prime Minister. With him, at a meeting of the Supreme War Council, are General Sir John Dill (Chief of the Imperial General Staff), Clement Attlee (Lord Privy Seal) and the French Prime Minister, Paul Reynaud. Behind Reynaud are General Ismay and General Spears (see pages 437–46)

8. Churchill at Dover, 28 August 1940, during a visit to the south-east coast defences (see pages 760–1)

9. Admiralty Arch: defending Whitehall against an attack by German parachutists landing in Trafalgar Square. Through the Arch are St James's Park and the Mall, and, through the centre arch, the Admiralty (see page 372)

10. Horse Guards Parade, from the Admiralty. Across the parade can be seen the trees in the garden of 10 Downing Street, and the Foreign Office (above the barrage balloon). St James's Park is to the right (see page 372)

11. Churchill inspecting air raid damage in London on 8 September 1940 (see page 775)

12. Churchill in the East End, 8 September 1940 (see page 775)

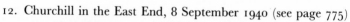

13. 'Huge crowds followed Mr Winston Churchill today when he inspected the damage and bomb craters caused by last night's raid. Mr Churchill asked the crowd as a whole if they were disheartened, and cries of "No" were heard from one and all.' Press Agency caption after Churchill inspected bomb damage on 10 September 1940 (see page 776). On Churchill's right, in army uniform, is his son-in-law, Captain Duncan Sandys

14. Churchill inspects a bomb crater on 10 September 1940

15. Churchill views bomb damage from the river Thames, 25 September 1940 (page 811)

16. Churchill and his wife during their journey down the Thames on 25 September 1940

was clear that the Labour leaders would not commit themselves without consulting their people, and they hinted, not obscurely, that they thought the response'—to serving under Chamberlain—'would be unfavourable.'

The Labour leaders then left, to begin their consultations. Churchill, Chamberlain and Halifax remained behind. Two accounts survive of the ensuing conversation. According to Churchill's account, Chamberlain told them 'that he was satisfied that it was beyond his power to form a National Government'. The response he had received from the Labour leaders left him 'in no doubt' of that. The question therefore was, 'whom he should advise the King to send for after his own resignation had been accepted?' Churchill's account continued:

I have had many important interviews in my public life, and this was certainly the most important. Usually I talk a great deal, but on this occasion I was silent. Mr Chamberlain evidently had in his mind the stormy scene in the House of Commons ... when I had seemed to be in such heated controversy with the Labour Party. Although this had been in his support and defence, he nevertheless felt that it might be an obstacle to my obtaining their adherence at this juncture. I do not recall the actual words he used, but this was the implication. His biographer, Mr Feiling, states definitely that he preferred Lord Halifax.

As I remained silent a very long pause ensued. It certainly seemed longer than the two minutes which one observes in the commemorations of Armistice Day. Then at length Halifax spoke. He said that he felt that his position as a Peer, out of the House of Commons, would make it very difficult for him to discharge the duties of Prime Minister in a war like this. He would be held responsible for everything, but would not have the power to guide the assembly upon whose confidence the life of every Government depended. He spoke for some minutes in this sense, and by the time he had finished it was clear that the duty would fall upon me—had in fact fallen upon me.

Then for the first time I spoke. I said I would have no communication with either of the Opposition parties until I had the King's Commission to form a Government. On this the momentous conversation came to an end, and we reverted to our ordinary easy and familiar manners of men who had worked for years together and whose lives in and out of office had been spent in all the friendliness of British politics.[1]

Churchill's account was written more than six years after the event. Halifax's account, which he gave to Cadogan on his return to the Foreign Office, was written down later that same day. According to Halifax:

[1] Winston S. Churchill, *The Second World War*, volume 1, London 1948, pages 523–4. Churchill has mistakenly placed this interview on 10 May 1940.

PM said I was the man mentioned as the most acceptable. I said it would be hopeless position. If I was not in charge of the war (operations) and if I didn't lead in the House, I should be a cypher. I thought Winston was a better choice. Winston did *not* demur. Was very kind and polite but showed that he thought this right solution.

The Chief Whip, David Margesson, believed, as Halifax also told Cadogan, that the feeling in the House of Commons had been 'veering towards' Churchill. Halifax did not disagree, commenting only that if Chamberlain were to remain in the Government, 'as he is ready to do', his advice and judgement 'would steady Winston'.[1]

The crucial interview was over. 'It was a bright, sunny afternoon,' Churchill recalled, 'and Lord Halifax and I sat for a while on a seat in the garden of Number 10 and talked about nothing in particular. I then returned to the Admiralty, and was occupied during the evening and a large part of the night in heavy business.'[2]

Throughout May 9 the Conservative rebels of the previous night's vote were discussing what should be done to exploit the impact of their protest. That evening Robert Boothby wrote to Churchill from the House of Commons:

Dear Winston,
    I have been in the House all day.
    This is the situation, as I see it.
    (1) The Labour party won't touch Chamberlain, at any price.
    (2) Nor will Archie.[3]
    (3) Nor will our group.
Therefore it is inconceivable that Chamberlain can carry through a reconstruction of the Government.
    A majority of the House is, nevertheless, determined on a *radical* reconstruction, which will involve ('inter alia') the elimination of Simon and Hoare.
    (4) Opinion is hardening against Halifax as Prime Minister. I am doing my best to foster this, because I cannot feel he is, in any circumstances, the right man.

Boothby's letter continued, of the prospect of Halifax as Prime Minister:

    At the moment of writing, our group would oppose his appointment, unless it commanded universal assent. It is quite a powerful group. It is now led by Amery; and includes Duff Cooper, Eddie Winterton, Belisha, Hammers-

---

[1] Cadogan diary, 9 May 1940: David Dilks (editor), *The Diaries of Sir Alexander Cadogan OM, 1938–1945*, London 1971, page 280.
[2] Winston S. Churchill, *The Second World War*, volume 1, London 1948, page 523.
[3] Sir Archibald Sinclair, Leader of the Liberal Party.

ley, Dick Law, Harold Macmillan, Henderson Stewart, Emrys Evans, Mrs Tate, R. Tree, Russell, Harold Nicolson, Gunston, Clem Davies, & King-Hall.

At a meeting held this afternoon, at which all the above were present, it was unanimously agreed:—

(a) that there must be a genuine National Government, comprised of all parties;

(b) that the Prime Minister, whoever he may be, should choose his colleagues on grounds of merit alone, without undue reference to the various Whips' offices. For this reason it was felt that it would be an advantage rather than a handicap that the War Premier should not himself be a party leader;

(c) that we would give full support to any Prime Minister who could form such a Government, *and none to one who couldn't.*

In fact, I find a gathering concensus of opinion in all quarters that you are the necessary and inevitable Prime Minister—as I wrote to you some weeks ago.

God knows it is a terrible prospect for you. But I don't see how you can avoid it.

Boothby added in his postscript that he had talked to a leading Liberal MP, Clement Davies, who reported 'that Attlee & Greenwood are unable to distinguish between the PM & Halifax, and are *not* prepared to serve under the latter'.[1]

Another letter that was sent to Churchill during May 9 was from Violet Bonham Carter, Asquith's daughter, whose devotion to Churchill had never flagged, even at times of deep political disagreement: 'Dearest Winston,' she wrote, 'I know what a heavy strain the last month must have been & what a heavy burden you have been bearing. I have made no sign, for I know that you cannot have had a spare moment for anything outside your work. I have sat through the debate, & I think you know where my hopes have lain.' Her letter continued: 'I wish that your present ship may sink—& I look forward to the launching of a greater one, of which you will hold the supreme command. There is a great tide flowing which *you* can direct.'[2]

As the political crisis intensified during May 9, Churchill worked at the Admiralty, seeking to ensure the success of the attack on Narvik. The telegrams from Lord Cork confirmed the difficulties with which the attack would be faced. Progress at Skaanland aerodrome was slow, Cork had reported in his first signal to arrive in the early hours of May

---

[1] Letter of 9 May 1940, marked by Churchill, 'Secret, for dinner, in a box': Churchill papers, 2/392.

[2] Letter of 9 May 1940: Churchill papers, 2/392.

9, 'and at least nine days will it is thought be required to allow of planes using it'. The arrival of the aircraft carrier *Ark Royal* had been effective for twenty-four hours, 'but bombing has begun again, all anchorages being attacked p.m. today 8th May as well as ships off Narvik'. An operation involving the landing of British troops at Bjerkvik was to take place on the night of May 10 'having as its object capture of Öyjord Peninsula and establishment of artillery there and cleaning up of enemy opposing French and Norwegians south of Gratangen'. At the same time, the 24th Brigade would occupy the Ankenes Peninsula and Beisfiord.

Lord Cork concluded his telegram: 'I am now committed to this operation but shall prepare for more direct attack in case there is no apparent result. . . .'[1]

A further wireless message reached Churchill from Cork early on the evening of May 9. In it he pointed out that the first eight long-range anti-aircraft guns to reach him had not arrived until May 6, that four of them had been in action that day, but that the four being sent to Bardufoss, twenty-five miles away, 'cannot be ready for two or three days on account of bad roads'.[2]

During May 9 the French Government had been pressing for greater British activity along the Norwegian coast to the south of Narvik, including the rapid occupation of the Mosjöen, Hemnesberget, Mo and Bodö regions. A note from Ismay to Churchill commented tersely: 'Neither the French Government nor the French High Command appear to have any conception of the difficulties of maintaining overseas forces which are dependent upon a long line of communication vulnerable to both submarine and air attack.'[3]

The question of German air superiority had been a principal cause of the failure to take Trondheim, or to achieve the pincer plan. Churchill had intended to refer to this in his speech on May 8. At the last moment he had deleted the passage, which read, in its note form:

> In Naval circles the power of the Air
> was underrated,
> and fact that up to present
> we are fighting largely with ships
> built with little regard to Air menace,

---

[1] Signal sent at 9.54 p.m., 8 May 1940, received at 3.18 a.m., 9 May 1940: Admiralty papers, 199/1929.

[2] Signal sent at 2.16 p.m., and received at 8.25 p.m., 9 May 1940: Admiralty papers, 199/1929.

[3] 'Secret', 9 May 1940: Admiralty papers, 116/4471.

or built before it developed
fully,
has affected for the time being
our Naval strategy.[1]

At half-past eight that evening Churchill dined at Admiralty House with Sir Archibald Sinclair, Eden, Bracken and Lindemann.[2] According to Eden's diary, Churchill stated that 'he thought it plain' that Chamberlain would advise the King to send for him, since Halifax 'did not wish to succeed'.

There was even some talk at dinner that evening of the composition of the new Cabinet, with Churchill, whom Eden described as 'quiet and calm', wanting Chamberlain to remain in the Government as leader of the House of Commons. Eden himself, Churchill suggested, should become Secretary of State for War, with Churchill as 'Minister of Defence as well as PM'.[3]

Across Horse Guards Parade, the mood at 10 Downing Street was confused. 'I left about 8 o'clock,' Channon noted in his diary, and he added: 'Neville still reigns, but only just.'[4] That night Randolph Churchill telephoned his father from Kettering, where his Territorial unit was stationed, and asked for the latest news, to which Churchill replied: 'I think I shall be Prime Minister tomorrow.'[5]

---

[1] Speech notes, 8 May 1940: Churchill papers, 9/139.
[2] Kathleen Hill's engagement diary: Churchill papers, 2/413.
[3] Eden diary, 9 May 1940: The Earl of Avon, *The Eden Memoirs, The Reckoning*, London 1965, page 97.
[4] Channon diary, 9 May 1940: Robert Rhodes James (editor), *Chips, The Diaries of Sir Henry Channon*, London 1967, page 248.
[5] Randolph Churchill recollections, dictated at Stour, East Bergholt on 13 February 1963.

16

The Tenth of May 1940

I N the early hours of Friday 10 May 1940 the Germans invaded Holland and Belgium. The western *Blitzkrieg* had begun. Shortly after half-past five in the morning Churchill was woken up and told the news. 'Boxes with telegrams poured in,' he later recalled, 'from the Admiralty, the War Office and the Foreign Office.'[1]

At six o'clock that morning Churchill telephoned the French Ambassador, Charles Corbin, and asked him to find out if the Allied armies would move into Belgium on the information, then available, that the attack 'was on Holland alone'. Twenty minutes later Corbin telephoned back to say that Belgium had been invaded as well as Holland, and that the Belgian Government had 'asked for help' from the Allies. The French and British could therefore move their forces forward to meet the German advance.[2]

At seven o'clock that morning Randolph Churchill was breakfasting in camp when he heard on the wireless the news of the invasion of Belgium and Holland. He at once telephoned his father at the Admiralty. 'What's happening?' asked Randolph. 'Well,' replied Churchill, 'the German hordes are pouring into the Low Countries, but the British and French armies are advancing to meet them, and in a day or two there will be a head-on collision.'

Randolph then asked his father: 'What about what you told me last night about you becoming Prime Minister today?' to which Churchill replied: 'Oh, I don't know about that. Nothing matters now except beating the enemy.'[3]

At six o'clock that morning the Secretaries of State for War and for Air, Stanley and Hoare, went to Admiralty House to discuss the im-

[1] Winston S. Churchill, *The Second World War*, volume 1, London 1948, page 523.
[2] Reported by Churchill to the War Cabinet at 8 o'clock that morning: Cabinet papers, 65/7.
[3] Randolph Churchill recollections, dictated at Stour, East Bergholt, on 13 February 1963.

mediate military, air and naval measures needed. In his memoirs, Hoare recalled the scene: 'Churchill whose spirit, so far from being shaken by failure or disaster, gathered strength in a crisis, was ready as always with his confident advice.'

Churchill, Stanley and Hoare breakfasted together. 'We had had little or no sleep,' Hoare's account continued, 'and the news could not have been worse. Yet there he was, smoking his large cigar and eating fried eggs and bacon, as if he had just returned from an early morning ride.' [1]

A few moments after seven o'clock, the Military Co-ordination Committee met in the Upper War Room at the Admiralty, with Churchill in the Chair. Hoare and Stanley were the other two Ministers present, together with seven of their senior advisers.[2] At the meeting it was reported that the Governments of both Belgium and Holland 'had appealed to the Allies for help'. The German Air Force was bombing aerodromes in Belgium and northern France, and German parachute troops had been dropped into Belgium. At the same time, British and French troops 'had begun their march into Belgium', British shipping having sailed from all Dutch and Belgian ports.

That morning, two British fighter squadrons had been ordered from Britain to France 'in accordance with the pre-arranged plan'. The Committee learnt, however, that two further squadrons intended for France were 'in process of being sent to Narvik'.

Two decisions were taken by the Committee at once: to send two additional fighter squadrons from Britain to France to replace those that were 'on their way to Narvik'; and to authorize the immediate execution of 'Royal Marine', the long-planned, much-delayed operation of mining the River Rhine.[3]

The War Cabinet met at eight o'clock at 10 Downing Street, with Churchill, Stanley and Hoare walking there from the Admiralty, across Horse Guards Parade. The most recent news was that German parachute troops had been dropped between Leyden and The Hague, and in the Rotterdam area; that German troops had crossed the Luxembourg frontier; and that the French town of Nancy had been bombed.

---

[1] Viscount Templewood, *Nine Troubled Years*, London 1954, pages 431–2.

[2] Also present at this meeting were Air Vice Marshal Sir Cyril Newall (Chief of the Air Staff), General Sir Edmund Ironside (Chief of the Imperial General Staff), Admiral of the Fleet Sir Dudley Pound (Chief of the Naval Staff), two of the three Vice Chiefs (Vice-Admiral Tom Phillips, Air Marshal Richard Peirse), Air Commodore Slessor, Major-General Ismay and two members of the War Cabinet Secretariat, Colonel Hollis and Lieutenant-Colonel Jacob.

[3] Military Co-ordination Committee No. 38 of 1940, 10 May 1940, 7 a.m.: Cabinet papers, 83/3.

At sea, HMS *Kelly* had been hit by a torpedo off the Belgian coast, 'but was being towed home'. German aircraft had dropped magnetic mines in the Scheldt, but the Admiralty was sending sweeping gear to clear the waterway for Dutch and Belgian shipping.

Churchill reported that the whole plan for the advance of the Allied forces into the Low Countries 'had been set in motion'. The troops, he said, 'were not at the highest state of readiness, but would certainly be on the move quickly'. At the same time, a special operation, code name 'XD', was authorized, to demolish port installations in Holland and Belgium in the event of a German thrust to the mouths of the Rhine or the Scheldt.[1]

It was nine o'clock in the morning; all Britain now knew that the Germans had invaded Holland and Belgium. At Bournemouth, the Labour Party were discussing whether or not to serve under Chamberlain, with the mass of opinion hostile, as Attlee and Greenwood had told Chamberlain on the previous day. But when Hoare went to 10 Downing Street he found, as he recalled in his memoirs, that 'Chamberlain's first inclination was to withhold his resignation until the French battle was finished'.[2]

For a brief while that morning, the imminence of the removal of Chamberlain seemed momentarily to recede. In his diary, Nicolson recorded a meeting with the young Conservative MP, Paul Emrys Evans, who had been told by Brendan Bracken 'that in view of the military crisis, the political crisis had been postponed, and that Hoare was insisting on remaining at the Air Ministry'. Angered by the thought of Chamberlain remaining Prime Minister, Emrys Evans telephoned Lord Salisbury, who told him, as Nicolson noted, 'that we must maintain our point of view, namely that Winston should be made Prime Minister during the course of the day'.[3]

At about ten o'clock, while Churchill was at the Admiralty, Kingsley Wood asked to see him. 'He told me,' Churchill later recalled, 'that Mr Chamberlain was inclined to feel that the great battle which had broken upon us made it necessary for him to remain at his post'.[4] This had also been Chamberlain's view when he had spoken earlier to Hoare. But whereas Hoare had accepted Chamberlain's new resolve, Kingsley Wood had told him bluntly 'that, on the contrary, the new

[1] War Cabinet No. 117 of 1940, 10 May 1940, 8 a.m.: Cabinet papers, 65/7.
[2] Viscount Templewood, *Nine Troubled Years*, London 1954, page 432.
[3] Nicolson diary, 10 May 1940: Nigel Nicolson (editor), *Harold Nicolson, Diaries and Letters 1939–1945*, London 1967, page 82.
[4] Winston S. Churchill, *The Second World War*, volume 1, London 1948, page 523.

crisis made it all the more necessary to have a National Government, which alone could confront it'. Kingsley Wood added that Chamberlain had 'accepted' this view.[1] In later years, Sir Horace Wilson was to speak bitterly of this act of 'betrayal' by Chamberlain's protégé, friend and colleague.[2]

Churchill remained at the Admiralty, where he was visited by the Ministers of the Dutch Government, who had just flown from Amsterdam, 'haggard and worn', as Churchill recalled, 'with horror in their eyes'. The Germans, they said, had already reached the causeway which enclosed the Zuider Zee. British help was urgently needed. 'Luckily,' Churchill wrote, 'we had a flotilla not far away, and this was immediately ordered to sweep the causeway with fire and take the heaviest toll possible of the swarming invaders.'[3]

A second War Cabinet was summoned for half-past eleven that same morning. Before it met, there was much political talk among Ministers. Eden has recalled how he was talking to Hankey shortly before the War Cabinet was to assemble, when Simon came up to them and said 'that he understood that despite the attacks in Flanders, Churchill was pressing for early changes in the Government'. Simon, as Eden recalled, was 'indignant' at this, but Hankey commented,—'quietly and firmly'—'Personally, I think that if there are to be changes, the sooner they are made the better.'[4]

When the War Cabinet met again at half-past eleven, it was learned that sixteen people, most if not all of them civilians, had been killed in the German air attack on Nancy. Several other French towns, including Lille, Lyon, Colmar, Pontoise and Luxeuil, had also been bombed, as well as aerodromes at Calais and Dunkirk, and an aircraft factory at Clermont-Ferrand. Bombs had also fallen on The Hague and Brussels. German parachute troops had landed 'at numerous places throughout Holland'.

During the meeting, Churchill suggested to his colleagues that Sir Roger Keyes should be sent on a mission to Brussels, with instructions 'to offer his counsel and support to the King of the Belgians, with whom he was on terms of close personal friendship'. The War Cabinet approved this proposal, and Keyes was at last found some outlet for his pent-up energies.[5]

[1] Winston S. Churchill, *The Second World War*, volume 1, London 1948, page 523.
[2] Sir Horace Wilson, conversation with the author and Richard Gott, Bournemouth, October 1962.
[3] Winston S. Churchill, *The Second World War*, volume 1, London 1948, page 524.
[4] The Earl of Avon, *The Eden Memoirs: The Reckoning*, London 1965, pages 97–8.
[5] War Cabinet No. 118 of 1940, 10 May 1940, 11.30 a.m.: Cabinet papers, 65/7.

During the meeting, Churchill offered to show the War Cabinet an anti-aircraft homing fuse. 'It wouldn't take a minute,' he said.[1] Watching the demonstration, the Minister of Information, Sir John Reith, who was among several other Ministers at the meeting, noted in his diary: 'Ironside very snotty about a homing rocket which Churchill's tame scientist, Lindemann, was demonstrating on a side table. "Do you think this is the time for showing off toys?" he asked me.'[2]

Churchill also informed the War Cabinet of steps that were being taken for 'the removal of the gold still left in Holland'.

The Military Co-ordination Committee held its second meeting of May 10 at one o'clock, with Churchill in the Chair, and Hoare the only other Minister present.[3] It was agreed that the British Government should respond favourably to a Belgian appeal for an announcement 'that the bombing of open towns in Belgium would be regarded as if open towns in France and England were being bombed'. At Churchill's suggestion, it was also agreed to draw the French Government's attention to one of the conclusions of the Supreme War Council, in which it had been agreed that in the event of invasion of Holland and/or Belgium, Britain should attack German oil refineries and marshalling yards. The British note to France should go on to say, the minutes recorded, 'that if the accumulated evidence went to show that the Germans had "taken off the gloves", the British Government were inclined to commence attacks tonight, on oil refineries and marshalling yards in Germany'.[4]

After this meeting, Churchill lunched at Admiralty House with Beaverbrook. A week earlier, after a note of encouragement from Beaverbrook, Churchill had replied in his own hand: 'My dear Max, I am vy grateful to you for yr letter. It is a real help & spur.'[5]

A third War Cabinet had been summoned for four-thirty that afternoon. Once again Churchill crossed the Horse Guards Parade to where his colleagues and their advisers were assembled. The meeting began with a report from the Joint Intelligence Sub-Committee that five incendiary bombs had been dropped in Kent; while in Europe the Ger-

---

[1] Ironside diary, 10 May 1940: Roderick Macleod and Denis Kelly (editors), *The Ironside Diaries 1937–1940*, London 1962, pages 301–2.

[2] Reith diary, 10 May 1940: Charles Stuart (editor), *The Reith Diaries*, London 1975, page 250.

[3] The Service advisers present were Pound, Dill and Newall. Ismay was also present.

[4] Military Co-ordination Committee No. 39 of 1940, 10 May 1940, 1 p.m.: Cabinet papers, 83/3.

[5] Letter of 2 May 1940, 10.25 p.m.: Beaverbrook papers.

mans had bombed 'a large number of places', not only in Holland and Belgium, 'but also in France and Switzerland'. The Chief of the Air Staff, Sir Cyril Newall, reported that Rotterdam aerodrome had been seized by the Germans, 'who were landing troop-carrying aircraft on it'; that six Blenheim fighters had been sent to intercept the troop-carriers; but that only one Blenheim had returned. 'It was feared that the other 5 Blenheims might have been shot down by the Messer-schmitts, though they would probably have done considerable damage to the troop-carrying aircraft.' Ironside commented that it was 'doubtful whether an invasion of Belgium in strength was actually taking place'. It might begin that night. The leading British troops were already on the line of the Dyle.

The discussion turned to the possibility of sending British heavy bombers to bomb the oil refineries and marshalling yards of the Ruhr. Newall was in favour, telling the War Cabinet: 'The psychological effect of an immediate blow at the enemy's most vulnerable spot would be very great throughout the world.' But Ironside reported Gort's view that such an attack 'would have no effect on the land battle', and that if the bombers first attacked the Ruhr and had then to be switched to attacking the German army, 'we might end by achieving nothing de-cisive against either objective'. Churchill was himself in favour of delay, suggesting to the War Cabinet:

... that it would be wise to wait for 24 hours before attacking the targets in the Ruhr. There was no doubt that we should shortly have to attack the oil refineries, and we had full justification for doing so. Nevertheless, the effect of a 24-hour delay could not make any appreciable difference to the difficulty or danger of the attack, but it might enable a clearer view to be obtained of the situation on land.

Hoare favoured an immediate bombing raid, and he was supported in this by Pound. About forty heavy bombers, Newall told the War Cabinet in answer to a question by Churchill, would take part in the attack on the first night, followed each night by a similar number 'until results were achieved'.

Churchill was still reluctant to agree to an immediate raid, and pointed out to his colleagues 'that if we delayed our attack and the Germans bombed our bomber aerodromes that night, they would not have a much better target than they would have if these 40 bombers had been despatched'. He therefore felt, as the minutes recorded, 'that this was a risk which would be present each night, and must be accepted'.

Chamberlain agreed with Churchill, and it was decided that no air attack should take place east of the Rhine that night.

A message, brought in from the War Office, was then read out by Ironside. More German parachutists, it reported, had landed at various points behind the Belgian defences, and at eleven that morning German infantry and tanks had crossed the Belgian border east of Liège.

There was a brief discussion about the need to warn troops in Britain about what action they should take 'against parachutists attempting to land in this country', and it was also agreed to move a Pioneer Corps unit, 'which comprised German refugees in British uniform', from its camp near Dover 'to a more suitable area'.

It was then, as the fifth item on the War Cabinet's agenda, that Chamberlain spoke of the political situation. He had now received, he said, the Labour Party's answer to his questions; they had indeed been passed to him while the War Cabinet was in session. No members of the Labour Party were prepared to serve 'under the present Prime Minister', but they were willing to 'take their share of responsibility as a full partner in a new Government, under a new Prime Minister, which would command the confidence of the nation'. Chamberlain then continued, as the War Cabinet minutes recorded:

. . . in the light of this answer, he had reached the conclusion that the right course was that he should at once tender his resignation to The King. He proposed to do so that evening. He thought it would be convenient that the new Prime Minister should be authorised to assume that all members of the War Cabinet placed their resignations at the disposal of the new Prime Minister, when sent for by The King, and that there was no necessity for this to be confirmed in writing. In the meantime, of course, Ministers remained in office and would continue to discharge their functions until a new Administration had been formed.

The minutes ended with eight words: 'The War Cabinet agreed to the course suggested.'[1] Chamberlain said nothing about whom he would favour as his successor, or about his discussion the previous afternoon with Halifax and Churchill; only, as Eden recorded in his diary, that 'he proposed to see the King that evening'.[2]

Churchill returned to the Admiralty. Within half an hour, Chamberlain was on his way to Buckingham Palace to tender his resignation.

[1] War Cabinet No. 119 of 1940, 10 May 1940, 4.30 p.m.: Cabinet papers, 65/7.
[2] Eden diary, 10 May 1940: The Earl of Avon, *The Eden Memoirs: The Reckoning*, London 1965, page 98.

In his diary the King recorded how, having accepted, he told Chamberlain:

... how grossly unfairly I thought he had been treated, & that I was terribly sorry that all this controversy had happened. We then had an informal talk over his successor. I, of course, suggested Halifax, but he told me that H was not enthusiastic, as being in the Lords he could only act as a shadow or a ghost in the Commons, where all the real work took place. I was disappointed over this statement, as I thought H was the obvious man, & that his peerage could be placed in abeyance for the time being. Then I knew that there was only one person whom I could send for to form a Government who had the confidence of the country, & that was Winston. I asked Chamberlain his advice, & he told me Winston was the man to send for.[1]

Chamberlain returned to 10 Downing Street, and Churchill was summoned to Buckingham Palace. 'I was taken immediately to the King,' he later recalled. 'His Majesty received me most graciously and bade me sit down.' Churchill's account continued:

He looked at me searchingly and quizzically for some moments, and then said, 'I suppose you don't know why I have sent for you?' Adopting his mood, I replied, 'Sir, I simply couldn't imagine why.' He laughed and said, 'I want to ask you to form a Government.' I said I would certainly do so.

The King had made no stipulation about the Government being National in character, and I felt that my commission was in no formal way dependent upon this point. But in view of what had happened, and the conditions which had led to Mr Chamberlain's resignation, a Government of National character was obviously inherent in the situation.

If I found it impossible to come to terms with the Opposition parties, I should not have been constitutionally debarred from trying to form the strongest Government possible of all who would stand by the country in the hour of peril, provided that such a Government could command a majority in the House of Commons.

I told the King that I would immediately send for the leaders of the Labour and Liberal Parties, that I proposed to form a War Cabinet of five or six Ministers, and that I hoped to let him have at least five names before midnight.[2]

During their discussion, Churchill gave the King the names of some of those whom he hoped to have in his Government. While the two men were talking, Randolph Churchill, at camp, had found a message in the Adjutant's office asking him to telephone Admiralty House. 'I

[1] King George VI, diary, 10 May 1940: John W. Wheeler-Bennett, *King George VI, His Life and Reign*, London 1958, pages 443–4.
[2] Winston S. Churchill, *The Second World War*, volume 1, London 1948, page 525.

did so forthwith,' Randolph later recalled. 'The Private Secretary in the private office said: "Only just to say that your father has gone to the Palace and when he comes back he will be Prime Minister." ' [1]

Churchill drove back from Buckingham Palace to the Admiralty, accompanied only by his detective, W. H. Thompson. The journey was made, as Thompson later recalled, 'in complete silence'. Then, as Churchill was getting out of the car, he turned to his detective and said: 'You know why I have been to Buckingham Palace, Thompson?' 'Yes, sir,' replied Thompson, and proceeded to congratulate him. 'I only wish,' he added, 'that the position had come your way in better times, for you have an enormous task.' Tears came into Churchill's eyes. 'God alone knows how great it is,' he said. 'I hope that it is not too late. I am very much afraid that it is. We can only do our best.'

Thompson's account continued: 'That was all I heard. As he turned away he muttered something to himself. Then he set his jaw and with a look of determination, mastering all emotion, he began to climb the stairs of the Admiralty.' [2]

As soon as Churchill had returned to his room at the Admiralty, he began the work of forming a Government. He was sixty-five years old. For more than forty years he had believed that the destiny of Britain would be well guarded in his hands. In the First World War, after he had almost been killed by a German shell on the western front, he had written to his wife: '20 yards more to the left & no more tangles to unravel, no more hatreds & injustices to encounter: joy of all my foes, . . . a good ending to a chequered life, a final gift—unvalued—to an ungrateful country—*an impoverishment of the war-making power of Britain which no one would ever know or measure or mourn.*' [3] Now all his qualities, all his energies, all his experience, and his faith in himself, were to be put to the test.

On his return to the Admiralty, Churchill wrote at once to the man whom he had just succeeded:

My dear Neville,

My first act on coming back from the Palace is to write and tell you how grateful I am to you for promising to stand by me and to aid the country at this extremely grievous and formidable moment. I am under no illusions about what lies ahead, and of the long dangerous defile through which we must march for many months. With your help and counsel and with the support of the great party of which you are the leader, I trust that I shall succeed. The

[1] Randolph Churchill recollections, dictated at Stour, East Bergholt, on 13 February 1963.

[2] W. H. Thompson, *Sixty Minutes with Winston Churchill*, London 1953, pages 44–5.

[3] Letter of 28 March 1916: Spencer-Churchill papers. The italics are mine (author).

example which you have set of self-forgetting dignity and public spirit will govern the action of many and be an inspiration to all.

In these eight months we have worked together I am proud to have won your friendship and your confidence in an increasing measure. To a very large extent I am in your hands—and I feel no fear of that. For the rest I have faith in our cause which I feel sure will not be suffered to fail among men.

I will write to you again to-night after I have seen the Labour Leaders.

'I am so glad,' Churchill ended, 'you will broadcast to our anxious people.'[1]

Having written this letter, Churchill telephoned Chamberlain to ask if he would be willing to remain in the Government as leader of the House of Commons and as Lord President of the Council. Chamberlain accepted. Churchill also asked Halifax to remain as Foreign Secretary. He then, in his second letter as Prime Minister, wrote to Halifax:

My dear Edward,

Now that I have taken up this task, I write to thank you for the chivalry and kindness with which you have treated me. The task I have assumed is one of sombre and dire consequence. No one knows better than I what weaknesses lie undisclosed, and we both have a full realization of the dangers which crowd in upon us, and their problems, from every side. However, with your help and Neville's, I do not shrink from the ordeal.

It gives me so much pleasure to feel that we shall be fighting this business through together to the end. I feel sure your conduct of Foreign Affairs is an essential element in our war strength. I am so grateful to you for being willing to continue your work in this great office of which you are at once the slave and the master: and that you will of course lead the H of L.

I am assuming that I may count on this, and that no formal invitation is required from

Your sincere friend
Winston S. Churchill[2]

As soon as he had returned to the Admiralty from the Palace, Churchill had sent a message to Clement Attlee, asking to see him. Attlee came, together with Arthur Greenwood, and when Churchill asked if the Labour Party would join his Government, Attlee gave his assent. Mentioning Ernest Bevin, A. V. Alexander, Herbert Morrison and Hugh Dalton as 'men whose services in high office were immediately required', Churchill asked Attlee to let him have a list of Labour men to consider for particular offices. 'We had a pleasant talk for a little

[1] Letter of 10 May 1940: Churchill papers, 19/2.
[2] Letter of 10 May 1940: Churchill papers, 20/2.

while,' Churchill later recalled, 'and they went off to report by telephone to their friends and followers at Bournemouth. . . .'[1]

During his talk with the King at Buckingham Palace, while discussing the possible composition of his Government, Churchill had mentioned his wish to bring in Beaverbrook, as Minister of Aircraft Production. But the King shared neither Churchill's fascination with
Beaverbrook, nor his admiration for him; indeed, during the evening
he felt strongly enough about Beaverbrook's possible inclusion in
the Government to send Churchill a letter in his own hand, his first
letter to the new war leader:

My dear Prime Minister,

I have been thinking over the names you suggested to me this evening in
forming your Government, which I think are very good, but I would like to
warn you of the repercussions, which I am sure will occur, especially in
Canada, at the inclusion of the name of Lord Beaverbrook for aircraft production in the Air Ministry. You are no doubt aware that the Canadians do not
appreciate him, & I feel that as the Air Training Scheme for pilots & aircraft is
in Canada, I must tell you this fact. I wonder if you would not reconsider your
intention of selecting Lord Beaverbrook for this post. I am sending this round
to you at once, as I fear that this appointment might be misconstrued.

I hope you will understand why I am doing this, as I want to be a help to
you in the very important & onerous office which you have just accepted at
my hands.

                    Believe me

                                        Yours very sincerely
                                        George RI.[2]

At nine o'clock that evening Chamberlain broadcast to the nation.
Recent events had made it clear, he said, that a Coalition Government
was needed, and he had since understood that the only opposition to
such a Coalition was himself. He had therefore tendered his resignation,
and Churchill was the new Prime Minister.[3]

Even while Chamberlain was making this announcement, Churchill
was writing to the former Prime Minister to inform him of both the
political and military events of the day. Clement Attlee and Arthur
Greenwood, Churchill wrote, had made it clear earlier that evening
that 'they would both expect places', and he went on to point out that
there were three other Labour men he himself would want: A. V.
Alexander, Herbert Morrison and Ernest Bevin. 'I hope to have the

---

[1] Winston S. Churchill, *The Second World War*, volume 1, London 1948, page 526.
[2] Letter of 10 May 1940: Churchill papers, 20/11.
[3] Broadcast of 10 May 1940, 9 p.m.: BBC Written Archives.

War Cabinet and the Fighting Services complete tonight for the King,' Churchill added. 'The haste is necessitated by the battle.'

During May 10 British and French forces had already taken up positions on the Antwerp–Namur line, and 'there seems to be very good hope', Churchill explained to Chamberlain, 'that this line will be strongly occupied by the Allied Armies before it can be assailed. This should be achieved in about 48 hours . . .' Meanwhile, the Germans had not yet forced the Albert Canal, the Belgians were reported to be fighting well', and, Churchill noted, the Dutch also 'are making stubborn resistance'.[1]

That evening Churchill sent the King the list of five senior Ministers. Eden was to go to the War Office, Sinclair to the Air Ministry, and A. V. Alexander to the Admiralty. Thus, with a Conservative, a Liberal and a Socialist as heads of the three Service Ministries, the all-Party nature of Churchill's Coalition was established. Lord Halifax would remain Foreign Secretary, and Chamberlain would become Lord President of the Council. There was to be no vindictiveness against the man who, less than a year before, had derided in public Churchill's judgment and fitness for high office.

Nor was Churchill to succumb to the cry of those who urged the immediate ousting of Chamberlain, Halifax, Simon and others, the 'Men of Munich'. A year earlier he had been the severest of their critics. Now he rejected all pressures for a cutting off of heads. 'No one,' he later reflected, 'had more right than I to pass a sponge across the past. I therefore resisted these disruptive tendencies.'[2]

It was nearly three o'clock in the early hours of May 11 before Churchill went to bed. At that moment, he later recalled:

I was conscious of a profound sense of relief. At last I had the authority to give directions over the whole scene. I felt as if I were walking with destiny, and that all my past life had been but a preparation for this hour and for this trial.

Ten years in the political wilderness had freed me from ordinary party antagonisms. My warnings over the last six years had been so numerous, so detailed, and were now so terribly vindicated, that no one could gainsay me. I could not be reproached either for making the war or with want of preparation for it.

I thought I knew a good deal about it all, and I was sure I should not fail. Therefore, although impatient for the morning, I slept soundly and had no need for cheering dreams. Facts are better than dreams.[3]

[1] Letter of 10 May 1940: Churchill papers, 20/11.
[2] Winston S. Churchill, *The Second World War*, volume 2, London 1949, page 10.
[3] Winston S. Churchill, *The Second World War*, volume 1, London 1948, page 527.

Fourteen years later, before both Houses of Parliament assembled to honour him on his eightieth birthday, Churchill reflected on this change in his fortunes. 'It was,' he said, 'the nation and the race dwelling all round the globe that had the lion's heart. I had the luck to be called upon to give the roar.'[1]

---

[1] Speech in Westminster Hall, 30 November 1954: Churchill papers, 5/56.

Part Two

'Darkest Hour'

BRITAIN

Yarmouth

North Sea

Zuider Zee

Leyden

The Hague

Doorn

Hook of Holland

Rotterdam

Maas

Rhine

HOLLAND

Ostend

Antwerp

Albert Canal

GERMANY

Dunkirk

Scheldt

Dyle

Calais

B
E
L
G
I
U
M

Dendre

Brussels

Tongres

Maastricht

Lille

Wavre

Meuse

Liège

Lens

Namur

Arras

Denain

Cambrai

Abbeville

Bapaume

Le Cateau

LUXEMBOURG

Amiens

Somme

St Quentin

Chauny

Sedan

Luxembourg

F R A N C E

Reims

Verdun

Metz

Pontoise

Villacoublay

La Ferté

Paris

Vincennes

Marceau

M
A
G
I
N
O
T

L
I
N
E

Moselle

Meuse

Nancy

| 0 | *miles* | 50 |
| 0 | *kilometres* | 80 |

© Martin Gilbert 1983

17

Prime Minister: 'blood, toil, tears and sweat'

C HURCHILL'S appointment as Prime Minister had been announced over the wireless by Chamberlain on the evening of May 10. 'Your old, old friends must be among the very first to rejoice with you,' wrote Lady Desborough, whom he had known for more than forty years, 'and how truly we do—what a pinnacle it is, the summit of so many dreams, attained by how few.'[1] 'How one wishes that your wise counsel had been listened to all these years,' Lady Cranborne wrote on the following morning, and she added: 'if only we had begun rearming then',[2] while Asquith's daughter Violet wrote to her friend of thirty-five years:

My wish is now realized. I can now face all that is to come with faith and confidence.

I know, as you do, that the wind has been sown, and that, for a time at least, we must *all* reap the whirlwind. But you will ride it—instead of being driven before it.

Thank Heaven that you are there, and at the helm of our destiny—and may the nation's spirit be kindled by your own.[3]

From France, a French friend, the painter Paul Maze, wrote of how 'every Frenchman shares my joy, and your name is on every lip, especially today when all the confidence is needed to meet the new threat',[4] while from Hoare came private words of admiration for Churchill's 'vision and grip' in facing the enormous problems of war. 'I

[1] Letter of 11 May 1940: Churchill papers, 2/393.
[2] Letter of 11 May 1940: Churchill papers, 1/393.
[3] Letter of 11 May 1940: Churchill papers, 2/392.
[4] Letter of 11 May 1940, from the Moulin de Moutreuil, St Georges Motel, Eure: Churchill

am sure,' Hoare added, 'that your energy and brilliance will now have
the freest possible scope, and I send this line to wish strength to your
elbow and success to your efforts.'[1]

As well as becoming Prime Minister, Churchill became Minister of
Defence, a post unknown in the inter-war years, or during the First
World War. It was in his combined capacity as Prime Minister and
Minister of Defence that he was able to supervise the war effort both
as the ultimate authority, and as specific overlord of defence policy.
Yet his control of defence was not through a great department of
State with its myriad officials, its national and local offices, its agents
and its emissaries. Instead, it was a single office headed by Ismay,
and with a small staff. 'I clearly remember,' Ismay wrote to Churchill six years later, 'that one of the first things that you said to me
after you had assumed the office of Minister of Defence was "we
must be very careful not to define our powers too precisely". In point
of fact, they were, as you know, never defined, but the system worked
admirably.'[2]

Reflecting on his new powers, Churchill later wrote, in an unpublished note originally intended for his war memoirs:

By all these processes and by the confidence, indulgence, and loyalty by which
I was upborne, I was soon able to give an integral direction to almost every aspect of the war. This was really necessary because times were so very bad. It was
accepted because everyone realised how near death and ruin we stood. Not only
individual death, which is the universal experience, stood near, but, incomparably more commanding, the life of Britain, her message and her glory.[3]

The emotion of words and phrases was very real to Churchill; his
reflection that Britain herself, 'her message and her glory', was in mortal
danger was no mere literary flourish. Churchill felt these concepts as
realities. But if emotion provided an impetus for action, that action
itself was governed by severe practical needs. It was to meet these
needs that his assumption of the title Minister of Defence in addition
to that of Prime Minister was to be an essential arm of war policy.

Five weeks after he had become Prime Minister, Churchill set out in
a short minute how the Defence Office had begun to work. Ismay, he

---

papers, 2/396. It was to the Moulin, with Paul Maze, that Churchill had gone to paint in the
third week of August 1939. As they painted, he told Maze: 'This is the last picture we shall paint
in peace for a very long time' (Maze diary, 20 August 1939: Maze papers).
[1] Letter of 11 May 1940, sent from the Air Ministry: Churchill papers, 2/406.
[2] Letter dated 30 May 1946: Churchill papers, 4/143.
[3] Churchill papers, 4/194.

wrote, was to continue as hitherto to represent him at the Chiefs of Staff meetings, 'and generally to act as my Staff Officer through whom I am accustomed to pass the bulk of my communications to the three fighting departments'. His own son-in-law, Duncan Sandys, would act as his 'special liaison' with Home Defence and Air Raid Precautions. Oliver Lyttelton would be his liaison with 'the whole field of munitions production', with a seat on the Supply Council.[1]

In one particular, this plan did not go unopposed: the employment of Lyttelton was objected to by the Minister of Supply, Herbert Morrison, one of Churchill's most senior Labour Party appointments, who felt that it would be 'derogatory' to him for Lyttelton to be a member of the Supply Council. But as Churchill minuted to Ismay four days later: 'I must have an effective liaison with his Department just as I have with the Services through you.'[2]

Four days later, Ismay set out for Churchill, in a personal minute, the aims of the Secretariat which had been set up to assist Churchill as Minister of Defence. First, wrote Ismay, it was to keep Churchill 'in close touch with all important activities of Departments and other bodies concerned with defence', and at the same time to bring to his notice 'matters requiring your special attention'. Secondly it was to 'convey Churchill's instructions to those responsible for taking action, and to follow matters up to ensure that there is no stagnation'. Thirdly, whenever more than one Department was involved in a decision, the Secretariat would arrange the necessary links and actions between them.[3]

The central feature of Churchill's position as Minister of Defence was to be his direct link with the Chiefs of Staff Committee. It was this Committee which examined all possible courses of action, rejected or supported them, and ensured that once approved by Churchill or the War Cabinet they were put into operation. On the Chiefs of Staff Committee, Ismay served as Churchill's 'Chief Staff Officer', and as his personal representative. In this capacity Ismay was a full member of the Committee, although he did not sign its reports.

The four members of the Chiefs of Staff Committee met daily, usually

---

[1] Minute of 24 June 1940: Cabinet papers, 120/3.

[2] Minute of 28 June 1940: Cabinet papers, 120/3.

[3] Minute of 1 July 1940: Cabinet papers, 120/3. Ismay also listed the names and functions of the Secretariat officials as Captain Nicholl RN (Naval matters, Oil, Air Defence), Colonel Dykes RE, Colonel Jacob RE and Major Price RE (Army, Home Defence, Defence Supply Committee, Colonial Defence Matters, Dominions Defence Matters including Ireland), Group Captain Elliot (Air Matters, Research and Experiment, Bacteriological Warfare) and Captain Clarke RN (Military Relations with the Allies). Ismay's deputy in the Defence Office was Colonel Hollis.

in the morning. Churchill rarely attended their routine meetings; but he presided over the Committee when he felt it necessary, or when he summoned them specially. The three Deputy Chiefs of Staff also formed a separate Committee, which relieved the Chiefs of Staff on many military, air and naval matters of lesser importance, which nevertheless called for a decision.

From day to day, Ismay was to keep Churchill informed of the proceedings of the Chiefs of Staff Committee, and to submit reports and plans to him for approval. Sometimes Churchill would give his approval without further meetings. Sometimes he summoned the Chiefs of Staff to discuss the action which they proposed, or some problem on which Ministerial or political guidance was required. On these occasions Churchill might call a full meeting of the Defence Committee, or of the War Cabinet; but increasingly as the war continued the War Cabinet was content to leave the conduct of the war to the Prime Minister and the Chiefs of Staff, and did not wish to be brought into strategic discussions. The formal Defence Committee eventually came less and less into the picture, and was later superseded by what Churchill called 'Staff Conferences': meetings of a few Ministers with particular interests, together with himself and the Chiefs of Staff.

The decisions reached by this continuous process were communicated to those who were required to implement them. All such communication was done by those members of the War Cabinet Office who constituted the Office of the Minister of Defence. This Office was headed by Ismay, with Colonel Hollis as his deputy dealing primarily with the strategic side, and Lieutenant-Colonel Jacob dealing primarily with manpower, supply and procurement. These three were in effect interchangeable; one or two of them always accompanied the Prime Minister on his frequent journeys abroad.

'The days of mere "co-ordination" were out for good and all,' Hollis has recorded. 'We were now going to get direction, leadership, action— with a snap in it!'

Churchill's control of the Defence Office, and his direct involvement as Minister of Defence with the Chiefs of Staff Committee, altered the process of decision-making within days of Churchill becoming Prime Minister. Hitherto, as Hollis noted, the Defence Secretariat, and before it the Committee of Imperial Defence, had seemed to Churchill to represent 'the maximum of study and the minimum of action'. It was 'all very well', Hollis added, 'to say that everything had been thought of. The crux of the matter was—had anything been done?' [1]

[1] General Sir Leslie Hollis, *One Marine's Tale*, London 1956, pages 66–71.

There was another aspect of Churchill's new position as Minister of Defence, and of his direct access to the Chiefs of Staff. 'It was the Dardanelles complex,' John Peck has recalled.[1] At the Dardanelles, as Churchill himself later reflected, 'a supreme enterprise was cast away, through my trying to carry out a major and cardinal operation of war from a subordinate position. Men are ill-advised to try such ventures.' This lesson, he added, 'had sunk into my nature'.[2] So also had the recent lesson of Narvik and Trondheim.

As Minister of Defence, Churchill 'was determined', wrote Ian Jacob, whose work on the Defence Secretariat brought him in frequent contact with Churchill's enquiries and energies, 'to be No. 1 and to use all the political powers of a No. 1 directly'.[3]

It was through the close working relationship between Churchill as Minister of Defence and his Chiefs of Staff that the principal decisions of war policy were evolved. As we shall see again and again, Churchill deferred to their collective advice, even when he disagreed with it, at times under formal protest. But he did not overrule them. Sometimes, indeed, it was they who turned to him. As John Peck later recalled:

... I have the clearest possible recollection of General Ismay talking to me about a meeting of the Chiefs of Staff Committee at which they got completely stuck and admitted that they just did not know what was the right course to pursue; so on a purely military matter they had to come to Churchill, civilian, for his advice. He introduced some further facts into the equation that had escaped their notice and the solution became obvious.

'The point of the story,' Peck added, 'is that one of the reasons for the success of the working relationship between Churchill and the Chiefs of Staff was their deep respect, even on the frequent occasions when they disagreed with him, for his *military* talents if not genius.'[4]

The interaction of Churchill and the Chiefs of Staff, more than any other combination, provided Britain with its war direction. The relationship between Churchill and the Chiefs of Staff, with Ismay as both a formal and a personal link, was of mutual, and of national benefit. After having observed this process in action from day to day, Ian Jacob wrote of Churchill:

[1] Sir John Peck, conversation with the author, 15 October 1982.
[2] Winston S. Churchill, *The Second World War*, volume 2, London 1949, page 15.
[3] Lieutenant-General Sir Ian Jacob, letter to the author, 19 October 1982.
[4] Sir John Peck, note for the author, 20 October 1982. The word in italics was underlined by Sir John Peck.

His pugnacious spirit demanded constant action. The enemy must be assailed continuously: the Germans must be made to 'bleed and burn'.

Hence it was vital that Churchill should be firmly harnessed to a strong and capable military staff. This he found to his hands in the British Chiefs of Staff. He provided the flow of ideas, the stimulus and drive, and the political guidance. They turned all this into a consistent military policy and saw to it that plans were matched by resources.

'The Prime Minister and his military staff,' Jacob added, 'made a formidable combination.'[1]

May 11 marked the inception of Churchill's powers. Shortly before midday, he, Chamberlain and Halifax met at the Admiralty together with Pound, Ironside, Newall, and the Vice-Chief of the Imperial General Staff, Sir John Dill. At this meeting Churchill raised two questions: whether 'the Police should be armed' in connection with the internment of enemy aliens, and whether it was possible to persuade Sweden 'to come into the war on our side'.[2]

A further suggestion put forward on May 11, at a second War Cabinet held that evening, was that the British Government should ask the United States for aircraft from its own supplies: aircraft which would later be replaced 'from orders which we had already placed in the United States'. This suggestion was passed on at once to Arthur Purvis, head of the Anglo-French Purchasing Commission in Washington.

There was also bad news from Norway: the Allied forces, Churchill was told, were 'seriously hampered by snow', while at Harstad the Allied base was being bombed daily by German aircraft operating from the Trondheim area. In addition, it was reported that German troops were being transferred to Murmansk along the Soviet railway, for a pincer move into northern Norway.[3]

Studying these facts, Churchill urged the reinforcement of Mosjöen by Allied troops from Harstad. Mosjöen, he minuted for the Chiefs of Staff, must not be 'given up'.[4] But the Chiefs of Staff replied that no forces were now available to hold Mosjöen 'in strength', as well

[1] Lieutenant-General Sir Ian Jacob, 'His Finest Hour', in *The Atlantic*, volume 215, number 3, March 1965, page 84 (essay written in 1958).

[2] War Cabinet No. 119A of 1940, 11 May 1940, 11.30 a.m.: Cabinet papers, 65/7.

[3] War Cabinet No. 119B of 1940, 11 May 1940, 10.30 p.m.: Cabinet papers, 65/7.

[4] Minute of 11 May 1940: Premier papers, 4/32/2, folios 53–54.

as Bodö, in view of the 'life and death struggle on the western front'.

Churchill now entered into the hour by hour conduct of the war: pushing forward his own ideas, and scrutinizing the work of others. Reflecting on this moment of his new authority, he later wrote: 'Power, for the sake of lording it over fellow-creatures or adding to personal pomp, is rightly judged base. But power in a national crisis, when a man believes he knows what orders should be given, is a blessing.'[1]

The urgency of the hour could not, however, entirely obliterate old dislikes and suspicions. During May 11 Lord Davidson wrote to Stanley Baldwin: 'the Tories don't trust Winston', and he added: 'After the first clash of war is over it may well be that a sounder Government may emerge.'[2]

That same evening Colville, who had remained as the junior Private Secretary at Downing Street after the fall of Chamberlain, noted in his diary: 'There seems to be some inclination in Whitehall to believe that Winston will be a complete failure and that Neville will return.'[3]

On Sunday May 12 many more letters were written to congratulate Churchill on becoming Prime Minister. 'The news that you have accepted to form a Government at this supreme hour of trial for our nation', wrote the Duke of Windsor from France, 'is dramatic indeed',[4] while Pamela Lytton, Churchill's girl friend of Victorian times, wrote: 'All your life I have known you would become PM, ever since Hansom Cab days! Yet, now that you *are*, the news sets one's heart beating like a sudden surprise. Your task is stupendous . . .'[5] That same day Churchill's son Randolph wrote from his army camp:

At last you have the power and authority out of which the caucus have cheated you and England for nine long years! I cannot tell you how proud and happy I am. I only hope that it is not too late.

---

[1] Winston S. Churchill, *The Second World War*, volume 2, London 1949, page 14. In 1915, having been removed from the Admiralty during the Dardanelles campaign, and going to the western front as a battalion commander, Churchill had written to his wife: 'God for a month of power—and a good shorthand writer' (Letter of 3 January 1916: Baroness Spencer-Churchill papers).

[2] Letter of 11 May 1940: Baldwin papers.

[3] Colville diary, 11 May 1940: Colville papers. Colville later recalled 'I think that the horror of Winston's arrival was such that people were clutching at straws' (Conversation with the author, 14 May 1981).

[4] Letter of 12 May 1940, from No. 1 British Military Mission, France: Churchill papers, 2/399.

[5] Letter of 12 May 1940: Churchill papers, 2/396. Churchill replied by telegram 'Thank you so much dear Pamela'.

'It is certainly a tremendous moment at which to take over,' Randolph added. 'I send you all my deepest wishes for good fortune in the anxious days ahead.'[1]

As the names of Churchill's Government Ministers were announced, Beaverbrook, whom he had appointed Minister of Aircraft Production despite the King's concern, wrote to Churchill: 'The list goes well, because you carry everything before you now, with the British public. I remember a trainload of bluejackets in Victoria Station cheering you wildly after you were dismissed from the Admiralty in 1915. Your popularity has reached the same high again.'[2]

There were also Ministers to be dismissed, a task essential to the forming of any Government, but one full of danger in the creation of animosity and disaffection. There were those who understood Churchill's dilemma. In expressing his confidence that 'you will bring us through safely', Lord Hankey wrote that Churchill should not feel 'any misgivings' about dropping him. 'I should never feel any bitterness or resentment,' he added, 'because I know from long experience the difficulties of a Prime Minister.'[3]

Hankey had been Minister without Portfolio since the outbreak of war. On May 14 Churchill appointed him Chancellor of the Duchy of Lancaster, on Halifax's suggestion.

As the changes were decided upon, Churchill tried to find time, amid the developments of the war, to write personally to those who were to leave their departments. To Sir John Reith, who had been Minister of Information for the past four months, Churchill wrote on May 12:

By the time you receive this letter, you will have been informed of the change which is taking place in the office you have so capably fulfilled at the Ministry of Information.

I take this opportunity of expressing my high sense of appreciation of the services you have rendered.

I am sure you will forgive me for not giving you previous intimation of the change I have thought it necessary to make. It is a matter of extreme national importance that the new Administration should be installed with the least possible delay; and I have been overlaid not only with the difficult task of forming a new Government, but with the course of a battle of considerable importance.[4]

---

[1] Letter of 12 May 1940: Churchill papers, 1/355.
[2] Letter of 12 May 1940: Churchill papers, 20/40.
[3] Letter of 11 May 1940: Cabinet papers, 63/91, folio 91.
[4] Letter of 12 May 1940: Churchill papers: 2/398. Two days later, Reith was appointed Minister of Transport, a post which he held until October 1940.

The new Minister of Information was to be Churchill's friend, Alfred Duff Cooper, who had resigned from Chamberlain's Cabinet in October 1938, in protest against the Munich Agreement.

It had become clear during May 12 that the course of the battle was going badly. At the War Cabinet[1] that evening, Newall spoke of 76 British aircraft lost in two days of fighting, and warned of 'undue losses of medium bombers in relation to the results attained'. Although there was still a 'very good prospect' of French and British forces establishing themselves on the Antwerp–Namur line in Belgium, the situation in Holland was 'more difficult'. Churchill himself spoke of the 'rapid German progress' in Norway, as a result of which the British force at Mosjöen had withdrawn to Bodö. The situation revealed by this, he added, 'was far from satisfactory'.[2]

During this War Cabinet, Newall pointed out that it was possible that the German invasion of Belgium and Holland was intended to gain air bases from which Germany 'could launch an intensive air attack on Great Britain', and he went on to warn that since the outbreak of war eight months before 'the enemy had so far seized the initiative every time, and we had been forced to follow his lead'. Newall then proposed that Britain should take the initiative, and bomb the Ruhr. If this were done, he said, and the Germans were to retaliate immediately by bombing Britain, 'we should at one and the same time be striking at the enemy's vital spot, and drawing off his bombers from the land battle to attacking targets in England, where our air defences were ready to meet him'.

The War Cabinet then discussed whether 'on moral grounds' there was justification 'for carrying the air war into the enemy's country', and came to what the official record described as 'general agreement' that there was such a moral justification. Churchill, 'summing up' the discussion, told his colleagues:

> ... that we were no longer bound by our previously held scruples as to initiating 'unrestricted' air warfare. The enemy had already given us ample justification for retaliation on his country. Opinion in the United States of America would not now be adverse if we carried out the operations proposed. The Germans would attack us in this country when, and where, it suited them.

From the arguments put forward by the Chiefs of Staff it seemed that our

[1] Those Ministers present were: Churchill (in the Chair), Neville Chamberlain (Lord President of the Council), A. V. Alexander (First Lord), Anthony Eden (Secretary of State for War), Lord Halifax (Secretary of State for Foreign Affairs) and Sir Archibald Sinclair (Secretary of State for Air).

[2] War Cabinet No. 119C of 1940, 12 May 1940, 10.30 p.m.: Cabinet papers, 65/7.

position would be worse the longer we waited. It was, moreover, significant that the Germans had so far held off, and the reason for this could be interpreted as being because it was not in their interests to be attacked in their own country.

Churchill added, however, that as neither Attlee nor Greenwood were present, 'it would hardly be right' for the War Cabinet to take 'an immediate decision', which must therefore wait until the following evening's meeting.[1]

On the morning of May 13 the Chiefs of Staff Committee met at Admiralty House, with Churchill in the Chair for the first time as Minister of Defence. Appeals for air support had just been received from the Dutch, the Belgians and the French. During the discussion it was agreed that no further air support could be given 'without unduly weakening the defence of this country, upon which so much depended', although 'a certain number' of aircraft and pilots might perhaps be added to the ten British fighter squadrons already in France.

The Committee learnt that the Allied armies had at last successfully reached the line Namur–Antwerp in their full strength, and that every day 'which could be gained' would enable them to dig in more strongly. 'It was not yet certain,' the official minutes recorded, where the main German attack would come: whether through Maastricht-Tongres, or through Luxembourg.

Churchill was not entirely satisfied at the Chiefs of Staff's opposition to the French, Dutch and Belgian appeals for air support, telling them 'that although we should not reduce our home defence resources below a minimum safety figure, there was a great deal to be said for making further efforts to give additional support to the Allied armies who were establishing themselves on the Dyle'. Churchill then invited Newall to consider, in consultation with the Secretary of State for Air, 'whether any further measures could be taken'.[2]

As Churchill spoke, a special operation approved by the first War Cabinet of his Premiership was being carried out at Antwerp. With the code-name of operation 'XD', for Explosive Demolition, 'Party D' for Antwerp, it involved the successful evacuation of a hundred British subjects by HMS *Brilliant*, and the setting of explosive charges to destroy the oil tanks, cranes and locks of Antwerp port.[3]

[1] War Cabinet No. 119C of 1940, 12 May 1940, 10.30 p.m., Confidential Annex ('Most Secret'): Cabinet papers, 65/13.

[2] Chiefs of Staff Committee No. 128 of 1940, 13 May 1940, 11.30 a.m.: Cabinet papers, 79/4.

[3] The demolitions were carried out on 16 May 1940 by Lieutenant Cadzow, RNVR and 2nd Lieutenant Wells, RE; as a result of their efforts, 150,000 tons of fuel were drained off into the river Scheldt: Premier papers, 3/324/4.

In London, the formation of the Government continued throughout May 13. During the day, Ernest Bevin, after consultation with other Trade Union leaders, accepted the post of Minister of Labour and National Service. But he agreed to do so only on four conditions. The first was that his Ministry would not be regarded merely as an institution to supply personnel but would also 'make its contribution to the actual organisation of production so as to secure the right utilisation of labour'. The second was that in accepting the office it must not be assumed 'that I can accept the status quo in the matter of the social services for which it is responsible'. The third was that the 'present difficulties' in the Trade Union Act should 'be dealt with'. And the fourth was 'a complete revision of our attitude to the question of International labour policy'.[1]

Churchill accepted Bevin's conditions, to the anger of many Conservatives. But he could not always secure the acceptance of those who felt that they were being slighted, particularly if they were being offered a more lowly position than they held already. In bringing in so many Labour men, however, it was inevitable that some Conservatives should have to take a step down. One of these was Oliver Stanley, whom Neville Chamberlain had appointed Secretary of State for War in January 1940. Churchill, having moved Eden to the War Office, offered to make Stanley Secretary of State for the Dominions in Eden's place. But Stanley was aggrieved, writing to Churchill on May 13:

The contemptuous, if frank way in which the appointment was offered, revealed the position only too clearly.

You may be quite right when you say I lack drive and initiative, but, if I do, I ought not to be a Minister, and, if you think I do, then you ought not to ask me to be one. In any case such a lack of confidence on your part would make my position intolerable.

'I had felt from the beginning,' Stanley added, 'that the obvious antipathy of mind and outlook, which had led to increasing tension between the two of us during the last few months, would make proper relationship between a Minister and his Chief almost impossible. You have made it abundantly clear on many occasions that you mistrusted my capacity, while I must confess there were a number of times on which I questioned your judgement.'

Churchill persevered, seeing Stanley personally, but in vain: 'any doubts I had were removed at our interview', Stanley wrote, in finally

---

[1] Letter of 13 May 1940, from Transport House: Churchill papers, 20/11.

declining the office.[1] Another who declined office was Lloyd George, to whom Churchill offered the Ministry of Agriculture. 'He refused it,' Colville noted in his diary, 'because he thinks the country is in a hopeless condition, and is generally despondent.'[2]

Most of Churchill's appointment interviews were more successful and during May 13 most of the senior posts were filled. Chamberlain was to be Lord President of the Council, Halifax was to remain as Foreign Secretary. Eden was to go to the War Office, and Sinclair to the Air Ministry. From the Labour Party, Attlee was to be Lord Privy Seal, A. V. Alexander First Lord of the Admiralty, and Herbert Morrison Minister of Supply. That afternoon Churchill summoned his Ministers to Admiralty House, and told them: 'I have nothing to offer but blood, toil, tears and sweat.'

Churchill repeated this phrase a few hours later, when he spoke to the House of Commons for the first time as Prime Minister. But then, and on the next few occasions when he spoke in Parliament, the Conservative members treated him, as he later recalled, 'with some reserve', their cheering being in fact held back until Chamberlain entered, while the 'warmest welcome' came from the much less numerous Labour members.[3]

'Winston got a poor reception compared with Neville,' Davidson wrote to Stanley Baldwin on the following day, 'and in the House of Lords Neville's name was received with a full-throated cheer, whereas Winston's name was received in silence.' Churchill's Ministerial appointments, Davidson added, 'are being heavily criticized in private'.[4] Lord Chatfield, who had been Minister for Co-ordination of Defence until the previous month, wrote to Hoare: 'Winston seems indeed to have challenged fate by the selection of some of his colleagues. I am really glad that I am out of the picture.'[5]

'To form an Administration of this scale and complexity,' Churchill told the House of Commons, 'is a serious undertaking in itself, but it must be remembered that we are in the preliminary stage of one of the greatest battles in history . . .' and he went on:

[1] Letter of 13 May 1940: Churchill papers, 20/11.

[2] Colville diary, 13 May 1940: Colville papers. Reflecting after the war on this offer to Lloyd George, Clementine Churchill commented: 'I was in an agony for fear he should accept' (note on a proof sheet of Churchill's memoirs: Churchill papers, 4/175).

[3] Winston S. Churchill, *The Second World War*, volume 2, London 1949, page 211. Following the General Election of 1935, 432 Conservative, 154 Labour and 21 Liberal candidates had been elected. Between 1935 and 1940 there had been thirteen Labour gains from Conservatives at by-elections.

[4] Letter of 14 May 1940: Baldwin papers.

[5] Letter of 13 May 1940: Templewood papers.

In this crisis I hope I may be pardoned if I do not address the House at any length today. I hope that any of my friends and colleagues, or former colleagues, who are affected by the political reconstruction, will make allowance, all allowance, for any lack of ceremony with which it has been necessary to act. I would say to the House, as I said to those who have joined this Government: 'I have nothing to offer but blood, toil, tears and sweat.'

We have before us an ordeal of the most grievous kind. We have before us many, many long months of struggle and of suffering. You ask, what is our policy? I will say: It is to wage war, by sea, land and air, with all our might and with all the strength that God can give us; to wage war against a monstrous tyranny, never surpassed in the dark, lamentable catalogue of human crime. That is our policy.

You ask, what is our aim? I can answer in one word: It is victory, victory at all costs, victory in spite of all terror, victory, however long and hard the road may be; for without victory, there is no survival. Let that be realised; no survival for the British Empire, no survival for all that the British Empire has stood for, no survival for the urge and impulse of the ages, that mankind will move forward towards its goal.

But I take up my task with buoyancy and hope. I feel sure that our cause will not be suffered to fail among men. At this time I feel entitled to claim the aid of all, and I say, 'Come then, let us go forward together with our united strength.'[1]

Many Members of Parliament were eager to know Churchill's inner mood at this time of crisis. Brendan Bracken, who had been at Churchill's side throughout the Cabinet-making process, told Harold Macmillan that Churchill felt 'profound anxiety',[2] while Ismay later recalled how, two or three days after Churchill had become Prime Minister:

I walked with him from Downing Street to the Admiralty. A number of people waiting outside the private entrance greeted him with cries of 'Good luck, Winnie. God bless you.' He was visibly moved, and as soon as we were inside the building, he dissolved into tears. 'Poor people,' he said, 'poor people. They trust me, and I can give them nothing but disaster for quite a long time.'[3]

All the news reaching London on May 13 bore out this dire forecast. Late that afternoon, at a meeting of the War Cabinet, Ironside spoke

---

[1] *Hansard*, 13 May 1940, columns 1501-2.

[2] Nicolson diary, 13 May 1940: Nigel Nicolson (editor), *Harold Nicolson, Diaries and Letters 1939-1945*, London 1967, pages 85-6. On 15 May 1940 Harold Macmillan was appointed Parliamentary Secretary to Herbert Morrison at the Ministry of Supply; it was his first Government appointment.

[3] *The Memoirs of General the Lord Ismay*, London 1960, page 116.

of 'strong German forces advancing in a number of directions' along
the whole western front, although there were as yet 'no signs of infantry
columns' in support. In addition, he said, the Belgian army 'did not
appear to be putting up a strong resistance, and Liège was probably
isolated', while at the same time 'the situation in Fortress Holland was
very precarious': the Germans were landing 'more and more troops' in
the Rotterdam area.

The new Secretary of State for War, Anthony Eden, then asked for
'discretion' to withdraw the British battalion from the Hook of Holland.
For his part, Churchill hoped it would not be withdrawn 'if it were
successfully providing a nucleus to rally Dutch resistance'. But he
agreed to leave the decision to Eden, as Eden had asked.

It was still not known, Ironside reported, whether the main German
effort was to be against Maastricht, or against the Maginot Line.
Churchill commented, as the minutes of the meeting recorded,
that:

> . . . the picture which had been placed before the War Cabinet of the present
> situation showed that there were two alternatives. The Germans might either
> be launching their great land attack with the object of trying to defeat the
> Franco-British armies, or they might content themselves with making contact
> along the line which the Allied armies had taken up in Belgium, and with
> consolidating their position in Holland preparatory to their great attack on
> this country.

Ironside believed, however, that the extent of the German air and
mechanized commitment indicated 'that the land battle was beginning', and that once their mechanized forces had completed their preparations, 'the advance of their main columns might be expected to
begin'.[1]

The War Cabinet then discussed again its earlier tentative decision
to bomb Germany. Chamberlain was opposed to any such action: 'If
we now bombed the Ruhr,' he said, 'the Germans would be forced to
retaliate and might go for our aircraft factories and aerodromes, the
defences of which were not as strong as they might be.' Recent events,
Chamberlain added, 'had shown the effect of a lack of anti-aircraft
defences'. By attracting German bombers to Britain, he argued, it would
make it 'impossible to release further fighters for France'.

Sinclair also opposed the bombing of Germany. He too argued on
the basis of British air weakness. The Air Staff, he warned, had estimated that sixty fighter squadrons were needed 'for the adequate de-

---

[1] War Cabinet No. 120 of 1940, 13 May 1940, 6.30 p.m.: Cabinet papers, 65/7.

fence of this country', whereas 'we only had 39 squadrons'. Even sixty squadrons would not be sufficient, added Newall, 'if the Germans were able to operate from air bases in Holland'.

Halifax also stressed the theme of Britain's weakness. It was, he said, 'to the interest of the nation in the weaker position, especially if it had great potential development, to refrain from exposing that potential to damage'.

Churchill bowed to the logic of this argument: whatever course the battle in France took, he told the War Cabinet, 'we could not afford to use up our fighters day by day, until the defences of this country were seriously impaired'. He went on to warn that if Britain's fighter strength were to be weakened 'we would lay ourselves open to the far greater accuracy' of German daylight attack.

Not only would it be impossible 'to send large numbers of fighters to France', Churchill added, but similarly 'we should not allow our heavy bomber force to be frittered away, and thus deprive ourselves of its principal deterrent effect, and of the ability to deliver its heavy blow'.

The main problem remained, however, that of German intentions. Churchill felt, and told the War Cabinet on May 13, that he was 'by no means sure that the great battle was developing'. No great masses of German troops had yet come forward, and the position 'was quite compatible with German anxiety not to engage the full strength of their army, but only to use specialised troops'. Ironside disagreed, believing that the advance of the German Army would soon follow in the wake of the mechanized forces. Churchill therefore accepted that any decision about an air attack on the Ruhr should be put off for three or four days 'in order to make sure whether the great battle had started or not'.[1]

At the end of the evening War Cabinet of May 13 Churchill asked his colleagues if they would agree to him sending a personal message to President Roosevelt, 'informing him of the seriousness of the situation'. This was at once approved, and a discussion ensued as to 'what action President Roosevelt could take' to help the Allies. The conclusion was that the President should 'let us have aircraft at once from their own supplies', including aircraft which according to the American Ambassador had been ordered by the Swedish Government but had not yet been shipped across the Atlantic.

The immediate hope of American aircraft to offset the British de-

[1] War Cabinet No. 120 of 1940, 13 May 1940, 6.30 p.m., Confidential Annex: Cabinet papers, 65/13.

ficiencies was to prove a vain one. Equally fraught with disappointment was the War Cabinet's decision not to send more fighters to France. It was a decision made in the full knowledge of Britain's air weakness; a weakness stressed by both Chamberlain and Halifax. Churchill deferred to their advice, and to that of Sir Archibald Sinclair, the Liberal leader, his own choice as Secretary of State for Air.

That night Churchill returned to Admiralty House from 10 Downing Street, having decided to sleep for another month or more in his old room, until Chamberlain was ready to leave No. 10. 'At the side of his desk,' Colville noted in his diary at the end of a long evening, 'stands a table laden with bottles of whisky, etc.[1] On the desk itself are all manner of things: tooth picks, gold medals which he uses as paperweights, special cuffs to save his coat sleeves becoming dirty, and innumerable pills and powders.'[2]

There was further news on May 13 from Norway, where French forces, commanded by General Béthouart, had landed at Bjerkvik, a tiny fishing village, eight miles from Narvik as the crow flies but more than thirty by road. With these forces, but 'in the capacity of a spectator only', was General Auchinleck, who had embarked for Norway a week before, and who, on finding that Mackesy and Cork were at loggerheads, had superseded Mackesy 'there and then'.[3]

The new commander of all the forces in the Narvik area was General Béthouart, whose appointment was made only fifteen days before the intended landing at Narvik itself. This Narvik landing was to be the only remaining military activity planned in Norway, for on the following day, in London, the Chiefs of Staff had decided that any further action in the Namsos, Mosjöen and Bodö region to the south should be restricted to 'small independent forces, specially

[1] Colville diary, 13 May 1940: Colville papers. Colville later reflected in conversation with the author: 'Winston's whisky was very much a whisky and *soda*. It was really a mouthwash. He used to get frightfully cross if it was too strong' (conversation with the author, 14 May 1981). Sir David Hunt, one of Churchill's Private Secretaries during his second Premiership, has written of Churchill's drinking: 'To my mind, and from my own observation, he was remarkably moderate. He certainly drank the weakest whisky-and-sodas that I have ever known. This was brought home to me early on, in fact on 30 November 1951, his seventy-seventh birthday. After his birthday party he came down to the Cabinet Room to work just the same and with his usual thoughtfulness invited me to have a drink with him. ... The whiskies had been poured by a messenger, not by one of his own servants; mine tasted normal enough to me, but he was deeply indignant with the messenger for mixing it far too strong. In truth in his normal drink the whisky only faintly tinged the soda' (Sir David Hunt, *On the Spot, An Ambassador Remembers*, London 1975, page 63).

[2] Colville diary, 13 May 1940: Colville papers.

[3] 'Operations in Northern Norway from May 13, 1940 to June 8, 1940', 19 June 1940 (General Auchinleck's Report): Premier papers, 3/328/5.

equipped', and with the aim of making Mosjöen and Bodö a 'no-man's land'.[1]

Yet the Norwegian coast was to remain for another three weeks the focus of Allied hopes, and of progressive disappointment. On May 14 Churchill signalled to Cork: 'I hope you will get Narvik cleaned up as soon as possible, and then work southwards with increasing force.'[2] On the following night Cork sent Churchill good news of the Bjerkvik landing: the French Foreign Legion had captured the village, taking '70 prisoners and many machine guns, stores etc'. Despite German dive-bombing successes, Cork added, 'I feel we must hold on and fight at Mo: if that goes, the whole Narvik situation becomes precarious.'[3]

Yet the news from Mo worsened in the coming week, and on May 19 Brigadier Gubbins, commanding at Mo, reported to Harstad via a blockade runner: 'further withdrawals inevitable'.[4] That same day, Cork reminded the Chiefs of Staff: 'Narvik is not yet actually in our hands. No precise date can be given for its occupation.' Even with the capture of Narvik, Cork added, no progress could be made in retaining Bodö, or in establishing control of the northern Norwegian coast, without the supply and maintenance of a 'sufficient Air Force' and 'ample' anti-aircraft artillery.[5] Two days later, Harstad was attacked with incendiary bombs, oil tanks set on fire, two Allied ships burnt out, and several houses destroyed. German air mastery was almost complete, its most serious single blow having been the sinking of the Polish liner *Chobry* on the evening of May 14, with more than 700 British troops on board, on their way from Harstad to Bodö.[6]

On May 21, on learning that his requests for air reinforcements, and particularly bombers, could not be met, Cork sent a personal signal to Churchill: 'I deplore decision not to send any bombers here, which means we cannot delay enemy advance North by road, and, apparent to all, have no means of striking back.'[7]

No further air reinforcements had been available from Norway for

[1] Chiefs of Staff Minute dated 14 May 1940: Premier papers, 4/32/2.
[2] Signal sent at 5.29 p.m., 14 May 1940: Premier papers, 3/328/4, folio 57.
[3] Signal sent at 11.58 p.m., 15 May 1940, received at 5.28 a.m., 16 May 1940: Premier papers, 3/328/4, folio 54.
[4] Signal received in London at 12.05 p.m., 19 May 1940: Premier papers, 3/328/4, folio 46.
[5] Signal sent at 10.17 p.m., 18 May 1940, received in London at 4.31 p.m., 19 May 1940: Premier papers, 3/328/4, folio 42.
[6] The troops were a battalion of the Irish Guards. 694 were saved. The twenty men killed included every senior officer of the battalion, one of them being the Commanding Officer.
[7] Signal sent at 3.06 p.m., received at 5.31 p.m., 21 May 1940: Premier papers, 3/328/4, folio 41.

several days, nor would they become available in the days ahead. Every spare aircraft was in daily demand for France. During the night of May 13, Anthony Eden sent Churchill a telegram from Gort, in which Gort stressed the need for additional fighter squadrons. 'We have to support in the air not only the BEF,' Gort explained, 'but also our Allies who have suffered heavy air attacks.' Reinforcing squadrons could, Gort added, 'be called home at short notice if required', and additional squadrons could be maintained temporarily, for a limited period, by ground staffs already in France. 'I earnestly hope,' he ended, 'War Cabinet will decide to give additional air assistance which in my judgement is essential for Allied success in the coming battle.'[1]

When the War Cabinet met on May 14, Gort's appeal was reinforced by a telephone message from Reynaud; a message which Churchill himself read out to his Ministers. In it Reynaud reported that the Germans had broken through the French defences at Sedan, and asked for the immediate despatch of ten more British fighter squadrons. 'I am confident,' Reynaud said, 'that in this crisis English help will not fail us.'

The German aim, Reynaud warned, was to bring the maximum military and air pressure between the Meuse and the Moselle, 'to try to open up the road to Paris'. And he went on to remind Churchill that at one of the last meetings of the Supreme War Council, Chamberlain, then Prime Minister, had said that when Germany engaged her forces in a great offensive, in order perhaps to try to secure the supreme decision, 'Great Britain would direct to the threatened point the whole of her available reserves'. That time had now come; nor did Reynaud doubt, as Corbin, the French Ambassador, wrote to Churchill in sending him Reynaud's message, 'that you will reply to his appeal by providing for our Armies the fighters which are indispensable to buttress their resistance'.[2]

Churchill read out Reynaud's message at the Chiefs of Staff Committee at six o'clock that evening, when Newall reiterated that it would be 'difficult to put additional fighter squadrons into France', and Churchill told his advisers that he himself 'was not yet convinced that we could afford to divert more resources from this country', but that 'this vital matter' must be discussed at once by the War Cabinet.[3]

[1] Telegram sent from Lord Gort at 12.15 a.m., received in London at 1.45 p.m., 13 May 1940: Premier papers, 3/188/1.

[2] Letter dated 14 May 1940: Premier papers, 3/188/1, folio 40.

[3] Chiefs of Staff Committee No. 132 of 1940, 14 May 1940, 6 p.m.: Cabinet papers, 79/4. Those present were Churchill (in the Chair), Newall, Pound, Ironside and Ismay, together with Lieutenant-Colonel Jacob of the War Cabinet Secretariat.

The War Cabinet met at seven o'clock that same evening, when Churchill gave it as his view 'that we should hesitate before we denuded still further the heart of the Empire'. Newall supported Churchill; that very night, he pointed out, thirty-six British bombers would be leaving Britain to bomb targets in northern France previously selected by the French High Command, and the fact that these targets had not been changed 'was perhaps an indication that they did not regard the situation in the south as being quite as desperate as was suggested by M. Reynaud'. In addition, Newall warned, in contrast to Gort's view, he was personally convinced that these ten extra squadrons 'would never return to this country once they were established on the other side of the Channel, as the majority of them would be lost'.[1]

Churchill's reply to Reynaud gave little hope that immediate extra air support could be sent from Britain to France. 'No time is being lost,' the message read, 'in studying what we can do to meet the situation.'[2] This was not the answer for which Reynaud had begged. But it was the limit of what the Chiefs of Staff, the War Cabinet and Churchill believed themselves able to do.

That night, as Churchill also worked to complete the junior Ministerial appointments with the Chief Whip, David Margesson, several friends arrived: Eden, Sinclair, Ismay and Beaverbrook. The American Ambassador, Joseph Kennedy, also called, and greatly alarmed Colville by talking 'the most disquieting nonsense' that Italy was about to enter the war on Germany's side.

Churchill's visitors, Colville noted in his diary, made 'a motley crew', and he added: 'they walked about, talking to each other, while Winston popped in and out, first through one door and then the next, appointing Under-Secretaries with David, talking about the German threat to Sedan with Eden, and listening to the alarmist, and, I think untrustworthy opinions of Mr Kennedy'.[3]

Shortly after seven o'clock on the morning of May 15, Churchill was woken by a telephone call from Reynaud. As Eric Seal noted, the French Prime Minister was in 'a very excited mood', telling Churchill that the counter attack on the Germans who had broken through at Sedan had failed, that 'the road to Paris was open', and that 'the battle was lost'. Reynaud then talked 'of giving up the struggle', to which Churchill replied that 'he must not be misled by panic-stricken

[1] War Cabinet No. 122 of 1940, 14 May 1940, 7 p.m.: Cabinet papers, 65/7.
[2] 'Message for M. Reynaud from Mr Churchill', 14 May 1940: Premier papers, 3/188/1, folio 35.
[3] Colville diary, 14 May 1940: Colville papers.

messages of this kind', that only a 'small proportion of the French Army was engaged', and that the Germans who had broken through would be in a 'vulnerable position'.[1]

Reynaud then pointed to what he called 'the small number of British troops in France', and 'begged for assistance'. But Churchill replied that Britain could not send troops to France 'quicker than the schedule to which we were working, and in any case nothing could arrive in time to influence the present battle'. Churchill also 'found it necessary', as he told the Chiefs of Staff later that morning, to point out to Reynaud 'that whatever the French might do, we should continue the fight—if necessary alone'.

Stressing that the German penetration was on a narrow front' and could not possibly be 'rapidly exploited in strength' Churchill told Reynaud that it was essential that he speak to General Georges. This he did, again by telephone, at 10.30 that morning and, as he reported to the Chiefs of Staff, had found General Georges 'calm'. Georges told Churchill that there had indeed been a serious breach of more than 15 kilometres on the front at Sedan, but it was now plugged. Georges had also been very warm in his praise of the assistance given by the Royal Air Force, and had asked for nothing.

Churchill then told Georges that 'we would continue to give full assistance, but could not unguard ourselves beyond a certain point'. This, Churchill noted, General Georges 'had quite understood'.

In reporting these two conversations to the Chiefs of Staff, Churchill added that he might have to go to Paris that same day 'to sustain the French Government'. The Deputy Chief of the Air Staff, Air Marshal Peirse, then recalled Reynaud's request of the previous day for ten British fighter squadrons, three of which had in fact been sent to the Sedan front. But these had now been recalled to 'their proper task' with the British forces in France, owing to the shortage of fighters.

The head of Fighter Command, Air Chief Marshal Sir Hugh Dowding, then told the Chiefs of Staff that 'if things went badly' in France, 'we would then have to face an attack directed against this country, possibly from France in addition to Holland and Germany'. Provided no more fighters were 'removed' from the Air Defence of Great Britain, 'he was confident that the Navy and the Royal Air Force would be able to keep the Germans out of this country'. But if more fighters were taken from him 'they would not achieve decisive results in France, and he would be left too weak to carry on over here.

[1] 'Record of telephone conversation between the Prime Minister and Monsieur Reynaud', 'Most Secret', 15 May 1940: Premier papers, 3/188/1, folios 27–8.

He was absolutely opposed to parting with a single additional Hurricane.'

Numerically, Churchill noted, the Germans 'could afford heavy losses'.[1]

Not only the battle in France, but also the future of Italian neutrality, were urgent questions on the morning of May 15. When the War Cabinet met at 11 a.m., Halifax reported on the Italian situation and suggested that 'it might be of value' if Churchill sent a personal message to Mussolini. Churchill replied that he had already thought of doing so, and proposed to assure Mussolini 'of his hope that this country and Italy should not be divided by bloodshed; we were finding the war hard, but we were confident of ultimate victory; it would be a disaster of the first magnitude if any irrevocable step were taken, but, if this should happen, we should have no choice but to pursue the matter to the end, and this we should do'. Churchill's message to Mussolini, as finally sent on the following day, read:

Now that I have taken up my office as Prime Minister and Minister of Defence I look back to our meetings in Rome and feel a desire to speak words of goodwill to you as chief of the Italian nation across what seems to be a swiftly-widening gulf. Is it too late to stop a river of blood from flowing between the British and Italian peoples? We can no doubt inflict grievous injuries upon one another and maul each other cruelly, and darken the Mediterranean with our strife. If you so decree it must be so; but I declare that I have never been the enemy of Italian greatness, nor ever at heart the foe of the Italian law-giver. It is idle to predict the course of the great battles now raging in Europe, but I am sure that whatever may happen on the Continent, England will go on to the end, even quite alone, as we have done before, and I believe with some assurance that we shall be aided in increasing measure by the United States, and, indeed, by all the Americas.

I beg you to believe that it is in no spirit of weakness or of fear that I make this solemn appeal which will remain on record. Down the ages above all other calls comes the cry that the joint heirs of Latin and Christian civilisation must not be ranged against one another in mortal strife. Hearken to it I beseech you in all honour and respect before the dread signal is given. It will never be given by us.[2]

On receiving this message, Count Ciano, who was both Foreign Minister and Mussolini's son-in-law, noted in his diary: 'It is a message

[1] Chiefs of Staff Committee No. 133 of 1940, 15 May 1940, 10.30 a.m.: Cabinet papers, 79/4.
[2] Telegram sent on 16 May 1940: Premier papers, 4/19/5, folios 699–700. In sending the final draft of this telegram to Ismay, one of Churchill's Private Secretaries, Anthony Bevir, wrote: 'I gathered if you thought it was all right, he proposed to send it off.'

of goodwill, couched in vague terms, but none the less dignified and noble.' Even Mussolini, Ciano added, 'appreciated the tone of it'.

But Mussolini's reply two days later was, so Ciano described it, 'brief and needlessly harsh in tone'.[1] It harked back to 1935, when Britain had taken the initiative at the League of Nations to organize sanctions against Italy because of the Abyssinian war: Italy's effort, as Mussolini expressed it, at 'securing for herself a small piece in the African sun without causing the slightest injury to your interests or territories, or those of others'. Mussolini ended his reply: 'If it was to honour your signature that your Government declared war on Germany, you will understand that the same sense of honour and of respect for engagements assumed in the Italian-German Treaty guides Italian policy today and tomorrow in the face of any event whatsoever.'[2]

A third question raised as a matter of urgency at the War Cabinet on May 15 was that of possible enemy agents in Britain. Halifax referred to a report alleging that the German advance into Holland had been helped considerably by cooperation between German parachutists and fifth column 'elements', such as a German maid who had led a party of parachutists to a particular house. In the existing circumstances, Churchill advised, he thought it 'important if the machine was not to be overtaxed, that the most urgent action should be taken first'. The groups which he had 'particularly' in mind were:

(i)   Italians and British subjects of Italian origin.
(ii) Czech refugees in this country who were not enemy aliens.
(iii) Refugees from the Netherlands and Belgium, some of whom might be German agents.
(iv) The British Fascists.
(v)   The Communists in this country.

It was much better, Churchill added, 'that these persons should be behind barbed-wire, and internment would probably be much safer for all German-speaking persons themselves since, when air attacks developed, public temper in this country would be such that such persons would be in great danger if at liberty'.[3]

There was also some discussion at the War Cabinet of a British

[1] Ciano diary, entries for 16 and 18 May 1940: Malcolm Muggeridge (editor), *Ciano's Diary 1939–1943*, London 1947, pages 251–2.

[2] Premier papers, 4/19/5 (both Churchill's letter and Mussolini's reply were published in full in *The Times* on 24 December 1940, on the day after Churchill's broadcast to the Italian people, see pages 948–9).

[3] War Cabinet No. 123 of 1940, 15 May 1940, 11 a.m.: Cabinet papers, 65/7.

bomber attack on the Ruhr, which Dowding described as 'the soundest action which we could take in the present situation', even if Germany took air reprisals. Churchill agreed with Dowding. To attract German bombers over Britain would, he added, 'have the advantage of relieving the pressure over France'.[1]

For most of that afternoon Churchill worked at 10 Downing Street completing the formation of his Government, and offering various Under-Secretaryships. When he asked R. A. Butler to remain at the Foreign Office, Butler reminded him that they had 'often sparred in the past, and disagreed on many things'. Yes, Churchill had replied, 'but you invited me to your private residence'.[2] Others were told that they were no longer to be in the Government. 'To tell one of them the news,' Colville later recalled, 'I had to have the train stopped at Crewe.'[3]

It was not only former Ministers to whom messages had to be sent; during May 15 Churchill sent a telegraphic message to all officers and men of the Royal Navy, to say how proud he had been 'to come again to the Admiralty in the hour of peril'. The sorrow he felt on leaving, he added, 'is tempered by feeling I shall not be far away'.[4]

For Churchill, the part which the United States would play in the war had always been a central feature of his concern, and of his faith in eventual victory. He had long accepted that the American Ambassador in London, Joseph Kennedy, would take a pessimistic view of Britain's prospects. But from Washington also there was news of a distressing nature when, on May 14, Arthur Purvis, the head of the Anglo-French Purchasing Commission in the United States, reported that British and French experts who had been studying the aircraft types then in service in the United States were reported to be 'unanimous' that 'nothing is suitable for European combat conditions'. No planes were armoured. None had self-sealing fuel tanks. All were 'obsolete'.

In the long-term, despite these initial disappointments, the scale of United States help promised to be considerable. Of the 524 Curtiss

[1] War Cabinet No. 123 of 1940, 15 May 1940, 11 a.m., Confidential Annex: Cabinet papers, 65/13. The first British bombing raid on the Ruhr took place that night.
[2] Channon diary, 15 May 1940: Robert Rhodes James (editor), *Chips: The Diaries of Sir Henry Channon*, London 1967, page 253.
[3] Sir John Colville, conversation with the author, 5 July 1980.
[4] Telegram, 15 May 1940: Admiralty papers, 1/10570.

P. 40 aircraft already on order to the United States forces, Britain, Purvis telegraphed, had obtained the release of 324, delivery of which would begin 'within two or three months'. At the same time, of the hundred Grumann fighters being built in and for the United States, Britain had secured delivery of 81. 'This represents real sacrifices by United States Services,' Purvis commented, 'as many squadrons on account of this will not be able to get their complement of modern planes.' Purvis added: '. . . it is certain that the goodwill of President and Morgenthau is higher than ever and yesterday Morgenthau told us that they were only anxious to prove this to us more fully than ever before. . . .'

Morgenthau had gone so far, Purvis reported, as to give an 'emphatic assurance' that the new United States Army Air Force orders, which would result from the increased United States armaments programme, would not be allowed to interfere with Britain's existing orders.[1]

A week earlier Churchill had asked Roosevelt if a British aircraft carrier could be permitted to enter a United States port, in order to enable aircraft being bought by Britain in the United States to be shipped uncrated, and 'ready to fly'. On May 15, however, Roosevelt telephoned Purvis to say that Churchill's request could not be granted under the Neutrality Act.

This was a blow to Churchill's hopes for the most rapid and effective transport possible of these essential aircraft. But it was Roosevelt himself who suggested, as Purvis telegraphed to London on May 15, that the British aircraft carrier 'be sent to Botwood, Newfoundland, which incidentally would be the shorter trip. We could then arrange to have the aircraft flown to the Canadian border, pushed across that border and flown on to Botwood'. Such was Roosevelt's suggestion to circumvent his own Neutrality Act. 'We already know,' Purvis added, 'that this method is feasible and legal.'[2]

In a second telegram on May 15, Purvis reported that Roosevelt had told him of another request from Churchill, 'as to the possibilities of arranging further aircraft priorities'. It was Roosevelt himself who had suggested to Purvis the possibility 'of utilising reserve civil transport planes and private-owner planes', for Allied transport and light bombing purposes.

That same evening Purvis had arranged, with the help of Morgenthau, that the delivery of 35 such aircraft would be switched from American

---

[1] 'Purco' No. 118, 14 May 1940: Cabinet papers, 85/14, folios 236–7.
[2] 'Purco' No. 125, 'Most Secret and Urgent', 15 May 1940: Cabinet papers, 85/14, folio 250.

to Allied purchasers over the next three months.[1] But three days later he warned that stocks of military aircraft in the United States 'which our technical people feel would have value' were limited to 150 pursuit planes and 144 bombers, and that the United States Army had advised Roosevelt 'that the former represent the only planes available for training purposes and that their release would delay the pilot training programme for 4 to 6 months'. Nor, Purvis added, was United States public opinion 'yet considered ripe' to allow the release of naval equipment which Britain had requested, although opinion was 'moving rapidly in that direction'.[2]

Churchill had decided to intervene directly in Britain's search for material help from the United States, and in a telegram to Roosevelt on May 15, the first since he had become Prime Minister, he told the President:

Although I have changed my offfice, I am sure you would not wish me to discontinue our intimate, private correspondence. As you are no doubt aware, the scene has darkened swiftly. The enemy have a marked preponderance in the air, and their new technique is making a deep impression upon the French.

I think myself the battle on land has only just begun, and I should like to see the masses engage. Up to the present, Hitler is working with specialized units in tanks and air.

The small countries are simply smashed up, one by one, like matchwood. We must expect, though it is not yet certain, that Mussolini will hurry in to share the loot of civilisation. We expect to be attacked here ourselves, both from the air and by parachute and air-borne troops in the near future, and are getting ready for them.

If necessary, we shall continue the war alone, and we are not afraid of that. But I trust you realise, Mr. President, that the voice and force of the United States may count for nothing if they are withheld too long. You may have a completely subjugated Nazified Europe established with astonishing swiftness, and the weight may be more than we can bear.

All I ask now is that you should proclaim non-belligerency, which would mean that you would help us with everything, short of actually engaging armed forces.

For the second part of this message to Roosevelt, Churchill had obtained, through Sir Edward Bridges, details of all that was most urgently required by the Admiralty, the Air Ministry, the Ministry of Supply and the War Office. Basing himself upon these facts, and adding two extra points of his own, Churchill declared:

---

[1] 'Purco' No. 127, 'Secret and Immediate', 15 May 1940: Cabinet papers, 85/14, folio 254.
[2] 'Purco' No. 131, 18 May 1940: Cabinet papers, 85/14, folio 262.

Immediate needs are:

First of all, the loan of 40 or 50 of your older destroyers to bridge gap between what we have now and the large new construction we put in hand at the beginning of the war. This time next year we shall have plenty. But if in the interval Italy comes in against us with another 100 submarines, we may be strained to breaking-point.

Secondly, we want several hundred of the latest types of aircraft, of which you are now getting delivery. These can be repaid by those now being constructed in the United States for us.

Thirdly, anti-aircraft equipment and ammunition, of which again there will be plenty next year, if we are alive to see it.

Fourthly, the fact that our ore supply is being compromised from Sweden, from North Africa, and perhaps from Northern Spain makes it necessary to purchase steel in the United States. This also applies to other materials. We shall go on paying dollars for as long as we can, but I should like to feel reasonably sure that when we can pay no more, you will give us the stuff all the same.

Fifthly, we have many reports of possible German parachute or air-borne descents in Ireland. The visit of a United States Squadron to Irish ports, which might well be prolonged, would be invaluable.

Sixthly, I am looking to you to keep that Japanese dog quiet in the Pacific, using Singapore in any way convenient.

'The details of the materials which we have in hand,' Churchill ended, 'will be communicated to you separately. With all good wishes and respect.'[1]

The pace of events in Europe was swifter even than these telegraphic exchanges. During the course of the Chiefs of Staff meeting on the morning of May 16, a message was brought in to the effect that the Germans had broken through the Maginot Line. Newall then read out a message from Gamelin asking for ten fighter squadrons 'at once', and stating that 'if they did not come, the battle would be lost'. In the light of the 'new and critical situation', Newall advised the despatch of additional fighter squadrons to France, and was supported in this request by the three other members of the Committee, Pound, Ironside and Ismay.

Churchill, who joined the meeting at this stage, 'agreed that in the circumstances with which we were now faced it was right to send further fighters to France',[2] and this proposal was put to the War Cabinet an hour later. To send fighter aircraft out of Britain 'at a time when we were most likely to be attacked ourselves in response to the attacks on military targets in the Ruhr the previous night', Churchill

[1] Telegram of 15 May 1940: Premier papers, 3/468, folios 204–21.
[2] Chiefs of Staff Committee No. 134 of 1940, 15 May 1940, 10.15 a.m.: Cabinet papers, 73/4.

said, 'was taking a very grave risk, but it seemed essential to do something to bolster up the French'. The 'first necessity', as he saw it, 'was to support the French morale and give them a chance to recover themselves and deal with German armoured forces by the use of their own Army'.

Churchill urged acceptance of Newall's proposal to send four squadrons, and advised sending two further squadrons, at present allocated to the defence of Scapa Flow. But Sinclair, after reporting Dowding's 'strong representations' on the previous day 'against sending any fighters out of the country', agreed that four was a maximum, and would in itself be 'a very serious risk', taken 'contrary to the advice' of Dowding, 'who was responsible for the defence of this country'.

The War Cabinet decided to send four squadrons at once, and to hold two more in readiness for despatch, 'if it was so decided'.[1] Sir John Dill then reported that the French had just given orders for a withdrawal of the line that night. Churchill, as the War Cabinet minutes recorded, 'took an extremely grave view of this news', and considered 'that a withdrawal from our line on account of the penetration of the French line by a force of some 120 German armoured vehicles was quite unjustifiable and would expose the British Army to far more serious risks than if they remained in their present position and fought'. He therefore felt that the order to withdraw 'was one which could not possibly be accepted without further consultation', and he accordingly proposed that 'he should himself go to France that very afternoon to discuss the matter with the French'.

The War Cabinet then invited Churchill 'to proceed that afternoon to France', both to find out the actual military situation, and to put forward on behalf of Britain 'strong objections to such a withdrawal'.[2]

Before leaving for France, Churchill wrote to Chamberlain, who, as leader of the Conservative Party since 1937, had suggested that Churchill should now, as Prime Minister, take over the position. 'I am of course a Conservative,' Churchill wrote. 'But as Prime Minister of a National Government, formed on the widest basis, and comprising the three Parties, I feel that it would be better for me not to undertake the Leadership of any one political Party. I therefore express the hope that your own Leadership of our Party will remain undisturbed by the change of Government or Premiership, and I feel sure that by this

[1] War Cabinet No. 124 of 1940, 16 May 1940, 11.30 a.m., Confidential Annex: Cabinet papers, 65/13.
[2] War Cabinet No. 124 of 1940, 16 May 1940, 11.30 a.m.: Cabinet papers, 65/7.

arrangement the cause of national unity will best be served.' Churchill added: 'The relations of perfect confidence which have grown up between us makes this division of duties and responsibilities, very agreeable to me.'[1]

[1] Letter of 16 May 1940: Churchill papers, 2/402.

18

Mission to Paris

A T three o'clock on the afternoon of 16 May 1940 Churchill flew
to Paris, together with Dill and Ismay. At Le Bourget airport they were told that all movement of troops to the front was being
disrupted by a strike of Belgian railway workers. Churchill's immediate
reaction was, as Ismay later recalled: 'shoot the strikers'.[1] In a further
recollection, Ismay wrote to Churchill:

> From the moment that we got out of the Flamingo at Le Bourget, it was
> obvious that the situation was far more critical than we had suspected. The
> officers who met us said that the Germans were expected in Paris in a few
> days at most. With the memory of 1914–18 in our minds, none of us could
> believe it.[2]

From the airport, the three Englishmen were driven to the British
Embassy, and then on to the Quai d'Orsay. By 5.30 they were in
Reynaud's study. 'Everybody was standing,' Churchill later recalled.
'At no time did we sit down around a table. Utter dejection was written
on every face.'[3]

This was also Ismay's recollection. As he later wrote:

I have never forgotten the complete dejection on the faces of Reynaud, Daladier and Gamelin as we entered the room at the Quai d'Orsay. I remember
saying to myself 'The French High Command are beaten already'. M. Reynaud cheered up under your influence, but Daladier and Gamelin remained
the picture of misery and despair throughout.[4]

---

[1] Ismay to Churchill, 8 September 1948: Churchill papers, 4/44.
[2] 'Notes on Meetings of the Supreme War Council between 16th May and 16th June 1940',
enclosed with letter dated 20 May 1946: Churchill papers, 4/44.
[3] Winston S. Churchill, *The Second World War*, volume 2, London 1949, page 42.
[4] 'Notes on Meetings of the Supreme War Council between 16th May and 16th June 1940',
enclosed with letter dated 20 May 1946: Churchill papers, 4/44.

For the first ten minutes of the meeting, no one was present to record the proceedings. As Churchill himself later recalled, Gamelin explained in some detail how and where the Germans had broken through the French defences. 'The General talked perhaps five minutes without anyone saying a word,' Churchill wrote, and he went on:

When he stopped there was a considerable silence. I then asked: 'Where is the strategic reserve?' and breaking into French, which I used indifferently (in every sense): 'Ou est la masse de manoeuvre?' General Gamelin turned to me and, with a shake of the head and a shrug, said: 'Aucune.'

There was another long pause. Outside in the garden of the Quai d'Orsay clouds of smoke arose from large bonfires, and I saw from the window venerable officials pushing wheelbarrows of archives on to them. Already therefore the evacuation of Paris was being prepared.[1]

A British officer, Colonel Redman, now entered, and later that evening set down the gist of the rest of the discussion from his notes. Redman himself later recalled how throughout the meeting, Churchill was 'aggressively trying to find out the exact state of affairs, which Reynaud, Gamelin and the others hardly knew themselves'.[2]

According to Redman's notes of the meeting, Gamelin now made it clear that the French might have to withdraw from the Namur–Wavre line in Belgium. Churchill at once pointed out that 'we have always been told that the object of getting the line Namur–Antwerp was that by doing so we would shorten our front and economise 20 Divisions. Now we had got there, why should we retire? Let us fight on that line.' But Reynaud interjected to say that 'we had lost Namur', and Gamelin said that it had been impossible to bring troops from the north 'because of the strike in Belgium'. To which Churchill declared, as he had already done at the airport: 'shoot the strikers'.

Gamelin then explained that troops were being taken from the right flank 'to fill the gap', and that he had begun to collect divisions 'forward of Paris'. In that case, said Churchill, 'we should attack'. But Gamelin replied that the armoured divisions were 'very exhausted', and the infantry had 'suffered very heavily' owing to attack from the air and by armoured fighting vehicles. It was necessary, Gamelin said, to bomb the advancing German columns, and the bridges of the Meuse behind them. Above all, he said, 'there must be fighters to protect the infantry'.

To this Churchill replied 'that the British had only 39 squadrons of

---

[1] Winston S. Churchill, *The Second World War*, volume 2, London 1949, page 42.
[2] Lieutenant-General Sir Harold Redman, letter to the author, 14 July 1980.

fighters for the protection of England. These were the life of the country and guarded our vitals from attack. We must conserve them.' As regards bombing, he pointed out, the British had sent four squadrons which had attacked near Sedan: 'We had taken great risks in order to destroy the bridges over the Meuse and had lost 36 aircraft in doing so. You can replace bridges,' Churchill said, 'but not fighters.' The fighter losses were 'much to be regretted', he added, 'and it seemed wrong to destroy the whole British effort unless targets were very well worthwhile'.

Churchill then told Gamelin that the four extra Fighter squadrons whose despatch had been agreed to by the War Cabinet would arrive in France 'in the course of the day', while at the same time arrangements were being made 'to fill up existing squadrons to their original strength'.

The discussion continued, and was acrimonious. The French now pressed for six further British fighter squadrons, in addition to the four already in France, and the four on their way. When Churchill said that he did not think six more squadrons 'would make the difference', Daladier replied that 'the French believed the contrary'. If the French infantry could feel that fighters were above, protecting them, 'they would be given confidence, and would not be taking cover when the tanks came along'.

Reynaud then told the members of the Council that they had to choose between 'two big risks': either they must leave the English factories without fighter protection, 'like the French factories', or they must be prepared 'to see the German armies continue their advance towards Paris'. The minutes of the meeting recorded Churchill's reply, 'that as long as the British could hold command of the air over England and could control the seas of the world, they were confident of the ultimate results, and it would always be possible to carry on'.

A few minutes later, when Gamelin asked 'where shall we be able to find another French Army?' Churchill asked in reply 'where the rest of the French Army was'.

At the end of the meeting Churchill commented that 'certain pre-war prophets had been proved wrong, as the offensive was coming into its own again'. It had not seemed 'in the least possible', he added, 'that great Armies in fortified positions could be pierced and thrust aside'.[1]

Six years later, General Ismay sent Churchill his recollections of this stormy meeting:

[1] Supreme War Council, 11th Meeting of 1939–40, 16 May 1940, 5.30 p.m.: Cabinet papers, 99/3, folios 76–8.

The following is typical of General Gamelin's state of mind throughout the meeting. You asked him when and where he proposed to counter attack the flanks of the bulge. His reply was: 'Inferiority of numbers, inferiority of equipment, inferiority of method'—and then a hopeless shrug of the shoulders.

The burden of General Gamelin's, and indeed of all the French High Command's subsequent remarks was insistence on their inferiority in the air and earnest entreaties for more squadrons of the Royal Air Force—bomber as well as fighter, but chiefly the latter. This prayer for fighter support was destined to be repeated at every subsequent Conference until France fell.

In the course of his appeal, General Gamelin remarked that fighters were needed not only to give confidence to the French Army, but also to stop the tanks. At this you said: 'No: it is the business of the artillery to stop the tanks; It is the business of the fighters to cleanse the skies (nettoyer le ciel) over the battle.' [1]

Returning to the British Embassy, Churchill discussed with Dill the French request for six further fighter squadrons, and for British bomber activity along the Meuse; and at nine that evening he telegraphed to the War Cabinet to explain 'situation grave in the last degree', with the Germans having driven a fifty kilometre bulge into the French front line. Unless this battle of the bulge were won, Churchill warned, 'French resistance may be broken up as rapidly as that of Poland.' Even if British long range heavy bombers were to be employed, as the French wished, 'upon the German masses crossing the Meuse', the results, Churchill commented, 'cannot be guaranteed'. His telegram to the War Cabinet continued:

I personally feel that we should send squadrons of fighters demanded (i.e., six more) tomorrow, and, concentrating all available French and British aviation, dominate the air above the Bulge for the next two or three days, not for any local purpose, but to give the last chance to the French Army to rally its bravery and strength.

It would not be good historically if their requests were denied and their ruin resulted. Also night bombardment by a strong force of heavy bombers can no doubt be arranged.

It looks as if the enemy was by now fully extended both in the air and tanks. We must not underrate the increasing difficulties of his advance if strongly counter-attacked. I imagine that if all fails here we could still shift what is left of our own air striking force to assist the BEF should it be forced to withdraw.

I again emphasise the mortal gravity of the hour, and express my opinion as above. Kindly inform me what you will do. Dill agrees.

---

[1] 'Notes on Meetings of the Supreme War Council between 16th May and 16th June 1940', enclosed with letter dated 20 May 1946: Churchill papers, 4/44.

'I must have answer by midnight,' Churchill warned, 'in order to encourage the French.'[1]

The War Cabinet met at eleven that night. 'Winston's telegram was decyphered in driblets,' Colville noted in his diary. 'I rushed it into the Cabinet in instalments.' Some of Churchill's Private Office were sceptical. Reading Churchill's phrase 'the mortal gravity of the hour', one of them commented: 'he's still thinking of his books', while another referred to Churchill's 'blasted rhetoric'.[2]

It was, Colville himself added, 'a terrifying telegram'. So much so that within half an hour the War Cabinet had agreed to the French request. After Newall's warning that there now remained in the United Kingdom 'only six *complete* Hurricane squadrons', it was agreed that three of these squadrons should 'work in France from dawn until noon'. They would have then to return to aerodromes in Kent, to be relieved by the other three squadrons 'for the afternoon'. The effect, Newall noted, 'would be the same as if the whole of the six squadrons were sent to work from French aerodromes'. In addition, they would be in less danger of attack on the ground.[3]

To preserve secrecy, the War Cabinet's decision was communicated by telephone to Ismay by means of the Hindustani word for 'yes'. Then, as Ismay later recalled in a letter to Churchill:

You immediately took me off in a car to M. Reynaud's flat. We found it more or less in darkness, the only sign of life in the sitting room being a lady's fur coat. M. Reynaud emerged from his bedroom in his dressing gown and you told him the glad news. You then persuaded him to send for M. Daladier, who was duly woken up and brought to the flat to hear the decision of the British Cabinet.[4]

'Daladier never spoke a word,' Churchill himself recalled. 'He rose slowly from his chair and wrung my hand.' It was nearly two in the morning. Returning to the British Embassy, Churchill 'slept well, though the cannon fire in petty aeroplane raids made one roll over from time to time'.[5]

Early on May 17 Churchill flew back to London, reaching Hendon airport shortly before nine o'clock. 'He looked quite cheerful,' noted Colville, who met him at Hendon, 'having slept and breakfasted well'

[1] Paris telegram No. 206D1PP, by telephone, 16 May 1940: Churchill papers, 4/149.
[2] Colville diary, 16 May 1940: Colville papers.
[3] War Cabinet No. 125 of 1940, 16 May 1940, 11 p.m.: Cabinet papers, 65/7.
[4] 'Notes on Meetings of the Supreme War Council between 16th May and 16th June 1940', enclosed with letter dated 20 May 1946: Churchill papers, 4/44.
[5] Winston S. Churchill, *The Second World War*, volume 2, London 1949, page 46.

at the Embassy in Paris. But the impact of the German onslaught gave
no cause for cheer. 'Winston is depressed,' Colville added. 'He says the
French are crumpling up as completely as did the Poles, and that our
forces in Belgium will inevitably have to withdraw in order to maintain
contact with the French.'

Churchill feared, as Colville noted in his diary, a further risk that
the British Expeditionary Force 'will be cut off if the French do not
rally in time', and this gloomy prognosis seemed confirmed by Ismay's
remarks to Colville that the French were not merely retreating 'but
were routed'. Ismay added: 'Their nerves were shattered by this
armoured warfare and by the German air mastery.' The Deputy
Director of Operations at the War Office, Brigadier Lund, was however
'more optimistic' about the situation, provided that the British and
French could concentrate their air power 'over the battle front'.[1]

From Hendon airport, Churchill drove to 10 Downing Street for a
meeting of the War Cabinet. There was no doubt, he told his colleagues, 'that the 9th French Army had sustained a heavy defeat'.
Their smaller anti-tank guns have been unable to stop the German
tanks, while the flame-throwing guns on their tanks had been particularly effective 'even against block houses'. Some of the French
troops, he had been told, 'had retreated without sufficient cause'.

Of those whom he had met, Churchill reported, Daladier and
Gamelin had been 'depressed', but Reynaud 'in rather better heart'.
Churchill had also seen Brigadier Swayne, the British representative
with General Georges. During their talk, Swayne told Churchill that
Georges, commanding the French North-East theatre of Operations,
'was dealing calmly with the situation'.

Churchill told the War Cabinet that he had made it clear to the
French that unless they made 'a supreme effort', the British Government would not feel justified 'in accepting the grave risk to the safety
of this country which would be entailed by the despatch of more fighters
to France'. If the French would 'fight their hardest', then the British
Government would do 'everything possible' to help them. As to the
War Cabinet's decision the previous night to send air squadrons to
France, this, Churchill said, had been 'the gravest decision that a British Cabinet had ever had to take'. It had heartened the French 'to a
very considerable degree'.

The outcome of the battle was still uncertain: there was a reasonable
hope, Churchill told his colleagues that with a four or five days' respite

[1] Colville diary, 17 May 1940: Colville papers.

from German air attack, the French Army 'would be able to rally and re-establish the position'. Some 'comfort' might be taken, added Dill, that the 'flower of the French Army' was not in the part of the line 'where the blow had fallen'. Everything possible, said Chamberlain, 'must be done to give the French a chance to rally'. Indeed, as Newall reported, six of the eight fighter squadrons which the War Cabinet had decided to send to France had reached there at dusk on the previous day, while the other two would arrive that very morning. At the same time, British heavy bombers had struck at German road, rail and air communications, including the marshalling yards at Düsseldorf, the railway sidings at Hamburg, and the aerodrome at Duisburg. But there was bad news of the British Advanced Air Striking Force, which was reported to be 'virtually out of action', and its position 'precarious'.[1]

Hardly had the War Cabinet ended when the American Ambassador, Joseph Kennedy, reached 10 Downing Street. Cadogan, who was present when Kennedy spoke to Churchill, recorded in his diary his conviction that the President 'will do all he can, but he can't go ahead of his public'. And even then, Cadogan added, 'what can they do to affect *this* battle'.[2]

The message which Kennedy had brought was a personal telegram from Roosevelt to Churchill. In it Roosevelt stated 'that the loan or gift of forty or fifty older destroyers', which Churchill had requested, would require the authorisation of Congress, 'and I am not certain that it would be wise for that suggestion to be made to the Congress at this moment'. Furthermore, Roosevelt added, it seemed doubtful to him 'from the standpoint of our own defence requirements', including American obligations in the Pacific, 'whether we could dispose even temporarily of these destroyers'. He was, however, doing all in his power to make it possible for the Allied Governments, 'to obtain the latest types of aircraft in the United States', and to discuss the question of possible purchases of anti-aircraft equipment, ammunition and steel. As for Japan, the American fleet 'is now concentrated at Hawaii', where it would remain 'at least for the time being'.[3]

Disappointed about the destroyers, Churchill replied to Roosevelt on May 18: 'I do not need to tell you about the gravity of what has happened. We are determined to persevere to the very end whatever the result of the great battle raging in France may be. We must expect

---

[1] War Cabinet No. 126 of 1940, 17 May 1940, 10 a.m.: Cabinet papers: 65/7.

[2] Cadogan diary, 17 May 1940: David Dilks (editor), *The Diaries of Sir Alexander Cadogan, OM, 1938–1945*, London 1971, page 285.

[3] Telegram, 17 May 1940: Premier papers, 3/468, folios 201–2.

in any case to be attacked here on the Dutch model before very long, and we hope to give a good account of ourselves.' But, Churchill added, 'if American assistance is to play any part it must be available soon'.[1]

During May 17 the British 3rd Division, commanded by General Montgomery, was ordered to retire through Brussels to the line of the river Dendre: the first move, as General Brooke later wrote, of his plan of retirement for II Corps, 'straight to the rear, through successive defensive positions'.[2]

Even as the news of the first details of these British withdrawals reached London, Churchill hurried to complete the formation of his Government. Twelve junior Ministerial posts were allotted on May 17, and immediately following Kennedy's visit to Downing Street, Churchill telephoned to as many of these new appointees as he could. Among them was Harold Nicolson, a National Labour MP, who recorded his conversation with Churchill:

'Harold, I think it would be wise if you joined the Government and helped Duff at the Ministry of Information.'
'There is nothing I should like better.'
'Well, fall in tomorrow. The list will be out tonight. That all right?'
'Very much all right.'
'OK.'[3]

Churchill rang off, to make the next call. Among those who accepted positions that morning were David Margesson, Parliamentary Secretary to the Treasury; Sir Edward Grigg, Under-Secretary of State at the War Office; and Ellen Wilkinson, the Labour MP and social reformer, Parliamentary Secretary, Ministry of Pensions.

Only one person declined an offer of an Under-Secretaryship: Emanuel Shinwell, whom Churchill had offered the post at the Ministry of Food.[4] It was accepted that same day by Robert Boothby, who wrote to Churchill:

---

[1] Telegram, 18 May 1940: Premier papers, 3/468, folio 200.

[2] 'Operations of II Corps during retreat from Louvain to Dunkirk', notes prepared for Churchill by Field Marshal Viscount Alanbrooke, OM, GCB, DSO, and sent to Churchill on 31 October 1946: Churchill papers, 4/196.

[3] Nicolson diary, 17 May 1940: Nigel Nicolson (editor), *Harold Nicolson, Diaries and Letters 1939–1945*, London 1967, page 86.

[4] 'Under-Secretaries & Parliamentary Secretaries': Churchill papers, 20/11. Against Shinwell's name, Churchill added the single word: 'refused'. Leslie Burgin, who had been Minister of Supply since 1939, was offered the Chairmanship of the Cultivator Committee. He declined, on the grounds that 'this would not be a wise use of manpower', and that he had handed over the whole Supply organisation, including that of 'Cultivator No. 6', 'in good order and condition'. That he was not to remain a Minister, Burgin added, 'came, as you can readily imagine, as both a disappointment and a shock' (letter of 16 May 1940: Churchill papers, 20/11).

I'm afraid I must have appeared ungracious yesterday; but it was one of the rare occasions in my life when I felt shy—and I found great difficulty in saying anything.

I very much appreciate the offer you have been able to make to me, and am particularly glad that I go to a Department so closely concerned with our war effort.

I will do my best to justify your choice. Meanwhile my thoughts, together with those of every man and woman in this country, are constantly with you. All good wishes—and 'au revoir'.[1]

During May 17 Churchill also set up a wide group of economic committees to deal with trade, transport, shipping, food and agriculture, over all of which Chamberlain, as Lord President, would exercise what Churchill called 'a large measure of executive control'.[2] At the same time Churchill established a direct liaison between himself and the French Government on all matters connected with British supply of armaments. This liaison he entrusted to Desmond Morton.[3]

Other concerns during May 17 included the danger that neutral States, encouraged by the German military successes, might be tempted to throw in their lot with Germany. That day Churchill appointed Sir Samuel Hoare Ambassador to Spain, charging Hoare, a former Foreign Secretary, with the task of preserving Spanish neutrality. There was also the problem of Japan. Immediately after he had completed his Junior Ministerial appointments that day, Churchill had gone to the Japanese Embassy for lunch with the Ambassador, Shigemutsu, toward whose Government the utmost amiability appeared necessary, despite its military dominance of China.

Throughout the afternoon of May 17 a series of telegrams from France reported a continuing German advance. That evening, at Churchill's urgent request, Chamberlain examined 'the consequences of the withdrawal of the French Government from Paris and the fall of that city'. He was also asked by Churchill to study the problems which would arise if it were necessary to withdraw the British Expeditionary Force from France altogether, possibly 'by the Belgian and Channel ports'.[4]

That night Churchill dined at Admiralty House with Beaverbrook and Bracken. The United States' hesitations were much on his mind, and on the morning of May 18 an echo of his concern, but also of his

[1] 'Personal', 18 May 1940: Churchill papers, 20/11.
[2] Minute to Sir Edward Bridges, 17 May 1940: Churchill papers, 20/13.
[3] Morton minute to Churchill, initialled by Churchill, 17 May 1940: Premier papers 7/1.
[4] Premier papers: 3/188/2.

ultimate conviction of joint Anglo-American action, was witnessed by his son Randolph, who later recorded how, on leave from his unit, he arrived at Admiralty House:

I went up to my father's bedroom. He was standing in front of his basin and was shaving with his old fashioned Valet razor. He had a tough beard, and as usual he was hacking away.

'Sit down, dear boy, and read the papers while I finish shaving.' I did as told. After two or three minutes of hacking away, he half turned and said: 'I think I see my way through.' He resumed his shaving. I was astounded, and said: 'Do you mean that we can avoid defeat? (which seemed credible) or beat the bastards' (which seemed incredible).

He flung his Valet razor in to the basin, swung around, and said:—'Of course I mean we can beat them.'

Me: 'Well, I'm all for it, but I don't see how you can do it.'

By this time he had dried and sponged his face and turning round to me, said with great intensity:—'I shall drag the United States in.'[1]

At that morning's War Cabinet the news from France seemed less desperate. The French were bringing up troops, Churchill reported, and French artillery had had 'some success' in destroying German tanks. As for the Royal Air Force, its pilots 'had covered themselves with glory'.

Eden then reported that the Russians were 'uneasy at the German advance', and it might therefore be possible to 'make some arrangements with them'. To this end, with Churchill's approval, the War Cabinet agreed to send Sir Stafford Cripps to Moscow on what Churchill called an 'exploratory mission'.[2]

The War Cabinet was to meet again that evening. During the day the news from France worsened. At five o'clock Colville spoke on the telephone to Brigadier Swayne, Gort's representative at General Georges' headquarters. Swayne, anxious to report to Churchill on the situation of the French forces, gave his message in a simple but graphic code. The 'Patient' he said, referring to the French forces, 'is rather lower and depressed. The lower part of the wound continues to heal, but as I expected, the upper part has started to suppurate again . . .' Swayne added: 'The effect of the injection will not be known for some time, but I have asked the Doctors to let me know as soon as possible the general effect which, as you will realise, must be the combined result of many local injections.' There had, Swayne reported, been a

---

[1] Randolph Churchill recollections, dictated at Stour, East Bergholt, on 13 February 1963.
[2] War Cabinet No. 127 of 1940, 18 May 1940, 11.30 a.m.: Cabinet papers, 65/7.

'number of incidents'; by which, Colville noted, he probably meant 'air raids on headquarters etc'.[1]

'The German thrust towards the sea continues,' Eden wrote in his diary, 'and the French 1st and 9th Armies seem badly broken up'.[2]

The question now arose as to whether the Armoured Division about to be sent to France should in fact be sent in its entirety. Through Ismay, Churchill asked the Chiefs of Staff whether 'it would not be well' to send only half the Division. 'One must always be prepared,' he wrote, 'for the fact that the French may be offered very advantageous terms of peace, and the whole weight be thrown on us.'

Worried that there might not be 'enough trustworthy troops in England' in view of the large number of German troops that might be landed from air carriers 'preceded by parachutists', Churchill also wanted the Chiefs of Staff to consider the bringing of eight battalions of regular British infantry from Palestine, and eight further battalions from India, by the fastest possible convoy.[3]

These suggestions were taken to Ismay that afternoon by Desmond Morton, who also reported to Churchill that in the other matter raised by Churchill, the internment of 'very considerable numbers' of Communists and Fascists, 'including the leaders', the Ministry of Home Security, 'do not wish to be precipitate'.[4]

It was to discuss both this issue of internment, and the measures to be taken in the event of the defeat of France, that the War Cabinet met again an hour later, at 5.30 p.m. The Home Secretary, Sir John Anderson, spoke of his regret at having to receive a second influx of 100,000 Belgian refugees, and hoped 'that this number might be cut down'. Any Germans found among them would be interned on arrival. As regards the British Fascists, Anderson explained the difficulty of taking any effective action 'in the absence of evidence which indicated that the organization as such was engaged in disloyal activities'. But the general view of the War Cabinet, which Churchill himself summed up, 'was that it would be desirable to stiffen up the measures already taken'.[5]

On the question of the possible defeat of France, Neville Chamberlain told the War Cabinet that until America 'could be induced to

---

[1] 'Message from Brigadier Swayne—17.00 hours', 18 May 1940: Premier papers, 3/188/3, folio 26.

[2] Eden diary, 18 May 1940: The Earl of Avon, *The Eden Memoirs: The Reckoning*, London 1965, page 106.

[3] Minute of 18 May 1940: Churchill papers, 20/13.

[4] Note of 18 May 1940, 4.30. p.m.: Premier papers, 7/1.

[5] War Cabinet No. 128 of 1940, 18 May 1940, 5.30 p.m.: Cabinet papers, 65/7.

come to our help' it would be 'imperative' for Britain to abandon its 'present rather easy-going methods' and to resolve on a form of Government 'which would approach the totalitarian'. As a preliminary step for public acceptance of such measures, it was desirable, Chamberlain added, for Churchill to broadcast to the nation on the following day, and to indicate 'that we were in a tight fix and that no personal considerations must be allowed to stand in the way of measures necessary for victory'. The situation might deteriorate, and if so, 'further sacrifices would be called for'.

The War Cabinet agreed that Churchill should broadcast to the nation on the lines indicated by Chamberlain. Of the nature of the emergency legislation, Churchill told his colleagues that the proposed emergency powers 'would be transitory and would be related to the declaration of a supreme emergency'. When this emergency arose, he said, the Government 'would claim the right to take service and property as it might think right'. But when the emergency had passed, 'the reinstatement of former rights would be considered in accordance with the constitutional usage of this country'.[1]

No decision was taken, as the news from France was still obscure. At 10.30 that night Churchill, Eden and the Chiefs of Staff, meeting at Admiralty House, decided to send the Vice Chief of the Imperial General Staff, Sir John Dill, to France 'tomorrow at dawn' to see Reynaud and General Georges, to try to learn Georges' plan 'and give him our views'.[2]

Churchill then wrote a letter to Georges, for Dill to take with him. Colville, who was present, noted in his diary that Churchill 'is full of fight in times of crisis and adversity'.

During the evening Mussolini's rejection of Churchill's appeal for Italian neutrality reached London. The First Lord of the Admiralty, A. V. Alexander, to whom Churchill showed Mussolini's reply, wanted to seize the initiative and occupy Crete, even before Mussolini declared war on Britain. Churchill answered, as Colville noted in his diary, 'that our hands were too full elsewhere to enable us to embark on adventures'. 'Such,' reflected Colville, 'is the change that high office can work on a man's inherent love of rash and spectacular action.'[3] Such also was the ability of a statesman to vary his advice and temper to suit the circumstances in which he operated.

[1] War Cabinet No. 128 of 1940, 18 May 1940, 5.30 p.m., Confidential Annex: Cabinet papers, 65/13.

[2] Eden diary, 18 May 1940: The Earl of Avon, *The Eden Memoirs*, *The Reckoning*, London 1965, page 106.

[3] Colville diary, 18 May 1940: Colville papers.

19

The Battle for France

WHEN the War Cabinet met on the morning of Sunday May 19, Ironside reported on the continuing German advances, the evacuation of Arras by the British, and the danger of the British and Belgian forces 'being cut off from the main French armies'. Once this happened, he warned, supplies could only reach the British troops through Boulogne, Calais and Dunkirk, 'all of which had been attacked from the air on the previous night'.

It was Churchill who pointed out that although the British Army was under the orders of General Georges, it was right that Gort and Ironside, 'should concert as to the plans which should be taken in various eventualities to safeguard the position of the British Expeditionary Force'.[1]

Two plans existed: to move south and link up with the French forces falling back on Paris, or to move north to the Channel ports, give up the battle, and try to return to Britain. Much would depend on the opinion of Sir John Dill, whom the War Cabinet had sent to France to consult with Gort and the French, and to report back as a matter of urgency.

While awaiting Dill's report, Churchill returned first to Admiralty House, where his wife told him of a 'pacifist' sermon which she had just heard preached at St Martin's in the Fields. Clementine Churchill had walked out. 'You ought,' Churchill remarked, 'to have cried "Shame, desecrating the house of God with lies."'[2]

At noon, in search of a few hours' sunshine, and the quiet in which to prepare his evening's broadcast, Churchill was driven to Chartwell. There, as Colville has written, he sought distraction 'by feeding his surviving black swan (the remainder had been eaten by foxes) and his

[1] War Cabinet No. 129 of 1940, 19 May 1940, 10 a.m.: Cabinet papers, 65/7.
[2] Colville diary, 19 May 1940: Colville papers.

greatly cherished goldfish'. But the tranquil scene was soon interrupted. 'Almost before the last ant's egg had been offered,' Colville wrote, 'the telephone rang . . .'[1]

The cause of concern was a telephone message which had reached Eden at the War Office. It was from Gort, asking for an immediate decision: the French 1st Army on his right had faded away, Gort reported, and he proposed to base himself on Dunkirk, holding a semi-circular line, to 'fight it out with his back to the sea'. But a second telephone message from Gort explained that this was only contemplated 'as a last resort' if the French fall back further, abandoning Cambrai.[2]

As Churchill hurried back to London, Eden discussed Gort's dilemma with Ironside. Both were agreed that Gort must try to re-establish contact with the French, and informed Gort of their decisions. If only the French would stage a 'good counter-attack from Chauny', Eden noted in his diary, 'Gort's very dangerous position would be eased'.[3]

At 4.30 that afternoon, with Churchill back in London, the War Cabinet discussed Gort's intention to withdraw towards Dunkirk if the gap between him and the French forces on his right were to widen. Ironside told the War Cabinet that he had already replied to Gort that 'this proposal could not be accepted at all'. Supplies might be sent 'at a pinch' to a British bridgehead resting on the Channel ports, but this could only be 'for a limited time', as no such force could be evacuated 'complete'.

Ironside believed that if Gort were to move his force southward to the Somme, 'to regain touch with the French there', it might then be possible to 'secure our position'.

Churchill supported Ironside. If the British Expeditionary Force fell back on the Channel ports, he said, it would be 'closely invested in a bomb-trap, and its total loss would be only a matter of time'. By moving south to Amiens, the possibility would remain of a further retirement 'back through Rouen, moving always towards our bases and reserves'.

The Belgian Army had appealed for the British to remain in their northerly position. But the War Cabinet must 'face the fact', Churchill warned, 'that the Belgian Army might be lost altogether, but we should do them no service by sacrificing our own Army'. At worst, Britain

---

[1] J. R. Colville, *Man of Valour: The Life of Field-Marshal The Viscount Gort VC, GCB, DSO, MVO, MC*, London 1972, page 204.

[2] Eden diary, 19 May 1940: The Earl of Avon, *The Eden Memoirs*, *The Reckoning*, London 1965, page 106.

[3] Eden diary, 19 May 1940: The Earl of Avon, *The Eden Memoirs*, *The Reckoning*, London 1965, page 106.

could make 'every endeavour' to evacuate as many Belgian troops as possible.

The War Cabinet agreed that Gort's forces should move in a south-westerly direction on the Arras–Amiens axis 'to join up with the French Army'.[1] During the meeting, according to Colville, Churchill told his colleagues that he had 'decided to fly to see Gort' himself, and he at once prepared to leave, accompanied by Ismay and Colville, who was, as he himself later recorded, 'standing expectantly on the doorstep, clutching a small suitcase, when he learned that the Prime Minister had with difficulty been dissuaded from going, and Ironside chosen as bearer of the War Cabinet's instructions'.[2]

Churchill's wish to set out for France himself greatly impressed itself upon the young Colville. 'His spirit is indomitable,' he noted in his diary that evening, 'and even if France and England should be lost I feel he will carry on the crusade himself with a band of privateers.'[3]

At 8.15 that evening the Defence Committee met to consider a letter which had just been brought from France, giving Dill's assessment of the situation. Dill's letter made it clear, Churchill told the Committee, that the French 'were entirely opposed to any suggestion that the British Expeditionary Force should take independent action by withdrawing to Boulogne'. Gort should therefore be instructed 'to move his forces as quickly as possible' southwards towards Amiens, 'brushing through such enemy forces as he might encounter and leaving rearguards as necessary to fulfil his withdrawal'.

Ironside supported Churchill, as did Eden. Since the French took the same view of what was necessary as did the War Cabinet, Churchill commented, 'there should be no difficulty in convincing them of the advantage of a plan which sought to bring back a fine and intact army of nine Divisions over a distance of 70 miles along its own communications for the purpose of ranging alongside the French Army'.[4]

With Gort having been ordered southwards to link up with the French, Churchill made the broadcast which, on the previous day, Chamberlain had felt to be so essential to national morale. It was broadcast live. 'I speak to you,' Churchill said, 'for the first time as Prime Minister, in a solemn hour for the life of our country, of our Empire, of our Allies, and, above all, of the cause of Freedom.' There was still a possibility of a 'sudden transformation' of the battle in

---

[1] War Cabinet No. 130 of 1940, 19 May 1940, Confidential Annex: Cabinet papers: 65/13.
[2] J. R. Colville, *Man of Valour*, London 1972, page 205.
[3] Colville diary, 19 May 1940: Colville papers.
[4] Defence Committee No. 4 of 1940, 19 May 1940, 8.15 p.m.: Cabinet papers, 69/1.

France. Although it would be foolish to 'disguise the gravity of the hour', it would be 'still more foolish to lose heart', or to suppose 'that well-trained, well-equipped armies numbering three or four millions of men can be overcome in the space of a few weeks, or even months, by a scoop or raid of mechanized vehicles, however formidable'.

We may look, Churchill added, 'with confidence' to the stabilization of the front in France. But once that happened, German aggression would then be turned 'in a few days' upon Britain.

This then was the moment of which the War Cabinet had wanted Churchill to speak, and he now sought to rally the nation in the event of such a German assault, telling his millions of listeners:

I am sure I speak for all when I say we are ready to face it; to endure it; and to retaliate against it—to any extent that the unwritten laws of war permit. There will be many men and many women in this Island who when the ordeal comes upon them, as come it will, will feel comfort, and even a pride, that they are sharing the perils of our lads at the Front—soldiers, sailors and airmen, God bless them—and are drawing away from them a part at least of the onslaught they have to bear. Is not this the appointed time for all to make the utmost exertions in their power?

Churchill exhorted his listeners to heed 'the imperious need' for munitions of all kinds. Once the battle for France 'abates its force', there would come 'the battle for our Island—for all that Britain is, and Britain means', and he went on to warn: 'That will be the struggle. In that supreme emergency we shall not hesitate to take every step, even the most drastic, to call forth from our people the last ounce and the last inch of effort of which they are capable. The interests of property, the hours of labour, are nothing compared with the struggle for life and honour, for right and freedom, to which we have vowed ourselves.'

Churchill then spoke of Reynaud's pledge 'that whatever happens', France would fight on to the end, and of the composition of his own new administration. 'We have differed and quarrelled in the past,' Churchill said, 'but now one bond unites us all—to wage war until victory is won, and never to surrender ourselves to servitude and shame, whatever the cost and the agony must be.' His broadcast ended:

This is one of the most awe-striking periods in the long history of France and Britain. It is also beyond doubt the most sublime. Side by side, unaided except by their kith and kin in the great Dominions and by the wide Empires which rest beneath their shield—side by side, the British and French peoples have advanced to rescue not only Europe but mankind from the foulest and most soul-destroying tyranny which has ever darkened and stained the pages of history. Behind them—behind us—behind the Armies and Fleets of Britain and France—gather a group of shattered States and bludgeoned races: the Czechs, the Poles, the Norwegians, the Danes, the Dutch, the Belgians—upon all of whom the long night of barbarism will descend, unbroken even by a star of hope, unless we conquer, as conquer we must; as conquer we shall.

Today is Trinity Sunday. Centuries ago words were written to be a call and a spur to the faithful servants of Truth and Justice: 'Arm yourselves, and be ye men of valour, and be in readiness for the conflict; for it is better for us to perish in battle than to look upon the outrage of our nation and our altar. As the Will of God is in Heaven, even so let it be.'[1]

Churchill's first broadcast as Prime Minister caught the imagination of millions. It was his first attempt as Prime Minister to point the way through setbacks and disasters to the ultimate, essential victory. That evening Eden wrote to Churchill: 'My dear Winston, You have never done anything as good or as great. Thank you, and thank God for you.'[2] Among the letters of congratulation was one from Churchill's former chief, later his adversary, Lord Baldwin, who wrote from his home in Worcestershire:

My dear PM,

I listened to your well known voice last night and I should have liked to have shaken your hand for a brief moment and to tell you that from the bottom of my heart I wish you all that is good—health and strength of mind and body—for the intolerable burden that now lies on you.

Yours always sincerely,
SB[3]

'It was worth a lot,' Halifax wrote from the Foreign Office, 'and we owe you much for that, as for a great deal else, in these dark days.'[4] It was a speech, the *Evening Standard* reported, that had been described as one 'of imperishable resolve'.[5]

Churchill's day was not over. Immediately after his broadcast, he was in conference with the Air Officer Commanding-in-Chief of Bomber Command, Air Chief Marshal Sir Edgar Ludlow-Hewitt, who had been in his Private Office at the Air Ministry twenty years before. From that conference there emerged a decision, strongly urged by Churchill, that, as he minuted to Ismay at midnight, no more squad-

[1] Broadcast of 19 May 1940 speech notes: Churchill papers, 9/144; speech printed in full in *The Listener*, 23 May 1940. The quotation is a shortened version of 1 Maccabees, chapter 3, verses 58–60.
[2] Letter of 19 May 1940: Churchill papers, 2/394.
[3] Letter of 20 May 1940: Churchill papers, 20/1.
[4] Letter of 20 May 1940: Churchill papers, 20/11.
[5] *Evening Standard*, 20 May 1940.

rons of fighters would leave Britain 'whatever the need in France'. Churchill's minute continued:

If it becomes necessary to evacuate the BEF a very strong covering operation will be necessary from English bases against the German bombers who will most certainly do their best to prevent re-embarkation. This should be studied today. From the point of view of the future resistance it makes no difference whether we strike down German bombers here or in France. Indeed the latter is to be preferred so long as the home bases are not voided. AOC in C should be told the above and make his plans accordingly.

But I also request that within a month from today at least ten squadrons of fighters for home defence shall be formed from the Schools from spare machines. Also that plans should be made to use the Battles etc. to bombard German factories if it is possible to reach them.

In the event of a withdrawal of the BEF or a collapse in France we ought to get a good many of our aircraft, now fighting there, back. It must be borne in mind that since the battle began the Germans have lost far more heavily in aircraft than we, and that the actual proportion of strength has moved in our favour.

I see no reason why with these resources we should not fight it out with them on better terms than were possible at the beginning of the war. Once individual and unit superiority is established very great advantages will follow.

Churchill now sought to locate the area of greatest danger, and to focus activity upon that. The 'utmost available' anti-aircraft strength, he ordered, 'should be concentrated on the aircraft factories. These are more important than anything else at the moment'.[1]

Reading this minute, it was Lindemann who challenged the decision not to allow any more fighter squadrons to be sent to France. His angry note was addressed to Desmond Morton, to be shown by Morton to Churchill. It read, in its final draft:

In the watches of the night I had great misgivings about the midnight decision not to comply with our allies request for certain assistance. If Germany fails now she will lose the war. It is worth taking great risks to make sure she does.

If our friends are blinded and exposed to unresisted bombing they may crack. Surely we should not chance this in order to have a few more units here to defend the civilians in case we are attacked. Even 1/10th of our force would make a real difference if we cannot send 1/4.

If you think there is anything in these views a word from you would be much more effective than pages from a mere layman.[2]

[1] Minute of 19 May 1940: copy, Cherwell papers, G.4.
[2] Letter, undated, on notepaper of the Carlton Hotel, London: Cherwell papers, G.4.

Lindemann's anguish was shared by all who contemplated the decision not to send more fighters to France. But Churchill alone had the responsibility for the decision. There is no doubt that it weighed heavily on him, and was a cause of considerable distress, highlighting as it did Britain's weakness and isolation.

That night Churchill summoned the Chiefs of Staff, Eden and Beaverbrook, and prepared a telegram to be sent as a matter of urgency to President Roosevelt. 'Considering the soothing words he always uses to Americans,' Colville noted, 'and particularly to the President, I was somewhat taken aback when he said to me: "Here's a telegram for those bloody Yankees. Send it off tonight." '[1]

The telegram to Roosevelt was sent to the American Embassy towards midnight. Then, in the early hours of May 20, Churchill decided to look at it again. A messenger was sent to the American Embassy to bring it back. But with the new dawn Churchill decided to send it after all, minuting to Ismay: 'I fetched this back during the night for a final view; but decided not to alter anything. Now despatch.'[2]

The reason for Churchill's telegram to Roosevelt, and the reason for his momentary hesitation about it, was that the British Ambassador in Washington, Lord Lothian, had confirmed that Roosevelt could not yet provide even the minimum of destroyers for which Churchill had asked as a matter of urgency. It was also clear to Lothian that there was little faith in Washington in Britain's ability to withstand a German attack. In his telegram, Churchill addressed himself to both these questions, seeking to stress the urgency and the dangers, even the possiblity of surrender. His telegram read, in full:

Lothian has reported his conversation with you. I understand your difficulties, but I am very sorry about the destroyers. If they were here in six weeks they would play an invaluable part. The battle in France is full of danger to both sides. Though we have taken heavy toll of enemy in the air and are clawing down two or three to one of their planes, they have still a formidable numerical superiority. Our most vital need is, therefore, the delivery at the earliest possible date of the largest possible number of Curtiss P. 40 fighters now in course of delivery to your Army.

---

[1] Colville diary, 19 May 1940: Colville papers.

[2] Premier papers, 3/468, folio 193. In sending this telegram to the United States Embassy for transmission to Washington, Colville wrote to the Counsellor of Embassy, Herschel B. Johnson: 'A Former Naval Person would be very grateful if you could arrange for the enclosed Private and Personal telegram to be sent to the President at your earliest convenience' (Premier papers, 3/468, folio 192). As First Lord, Churchill had sent his telegrams to Roosevelt as from 'Naval Person'. Henceforth, until the end of the war, almost all his messages to the President were to come from 'Former Naval Person'.

With regard to the closing part of your talk with Lothian, our intention is, whatever happens, to fight on to the end in this Island, and, provided we can get the help for which we ask, we hope to run them very close in the air battles in view of individual superiority. Members of the present Administration would likely go down during this process should it result adversely, but in no conceivable circumstances will we consent to surrender. If members of the present Administration were finished and others came in to parley amid the ruins, you must not be blind to the fact that the sole remaining bargaining counter with Germany would be the Fleet, and, if this country was left by the United States to its fate, no one would have the right to blame those then responsible if they made the best terms they could for the surviving inhabitants.

Excuse me, Mr President, putting this nightmare bluntly. Evidently I could not answer for my successors, who in utter despair and helplessness might well have to accommodate themselves to the German will.

'However,' Churchill added, 'there is happily no need at present to dwell upon such ideas. Once more thanking you for your goodwill.'[1]

When the Chiefs of Staff Committee met at 10.15 on the morning of May 20, the Assistant Chief of the Imperial General Staff, Major-General Percival, estimated that it would take between seven and ten days to get the whole British Expeditionary Force 'clear' and behind the line of the Somme. Churchill then reported that he had spoken on the telephone to both Dill and Swayne, who had reported that, 'in principle', the French were 'pushing up from the south', particularly in the Cambrai–Le Cateau area. Ironside was shortly to see Gort; until then at least the orders to Gort to fall back and link up with the French forces 'must stand'.

Another area of concern was Narvik, where the new First Lord of the Admiralty, A. V. Alexander, felt that Cork was not doing enough to capture the port. The Chiefs of Staff approved a telegram which Churchill proposed to send, 'in continuation' of an exhortation which had already been sent from the Admiralty. 'I am increasingly disappointed,' the telegram began, 'by the stagnation which appears to rule in the military operations around Narvik, and at the delay in occupying the town itself.' Churchill's telegram continued:

According to all reports, there are very few Germans in Narvik, and only forces of about 1,500 in the surrounding country. Yet these seem to hold up three or four times their number, who refrain from coming to grips with them and keeping them under constant fire at close quarters. It is necessary to

[1] Telegram sent on 20 May 1940: Premier papers, 3/468, folios 194–5.

reach a decision in this theatre in view of larger events. Expedition is eating up large quantities of shipping and other essential supplies. More destroyers will be needed in the South very soon. It is, indeed, lamentable that slowness in repairing Bardu Aerodrome has forced *Glorious* to return to Scapa to refuel. Delay is costing more men and ships than vigorous action.

'I should be very much obliged,' Churchill ended, 'if you would enable me to understand what is holding you back.'[1]

A. V. Alexander welcomed Churchill's intervention. 'I was more than grateful,' he wrote later that day, 'for your personal signal to the Earl of Cork in support of the Admiralty's telegrams.'[2] He was, however, worried about the future of the Narvik operation. To continue it, he wrote in a five page memorandum for Churchill, would hold up a large number of troops, guns and planes which would otherwise be valuable in home defence in a time not only of danger, but 'possibly of immediate threat to our Island security'. But to withdraw from Narvik also had drawbacks. 'What would be the situation,' Alexander asked Churchill, 'if within the next three or four days, or even the next two or three weeks, we reach the situation in France comparable to the Battle of the Marne in 1914, and the tide was turned, if in the meantime we had fled from our commitments in Norway,' and had then to settle down to a long economic struggle, 'not with the support but with the enmity of peoples we had promised to assist?'[3]

Churchill did not know the answer. The news from France was so bad as to suggest that little time remained for a calm decision. According to Churchill's Principal Private Secretary, Eric Seal, 'the whole thing is dropping to pieces through sheer ineptitude'.[4] At the War Cabinet that morning both Churchill and Halifax asked that the Chiefs of Staff 'should consider carefully whether we were likely to get a dividend out of our occupation of Narvik, even after we had succeeded in capturing it'. It was clear, they added, that the troops, ships and equipment occupied in the Narvik operation 'were urgently needed elsewhere'.

Churchill also told the War Cabinet that he had spoken on the telephone that morning to Ironside, who reported that Gort was moving three divisions down to the Lens area, but anticipated it would take forty-eight hours to complete the move as the roads 'were very badly congested with refugees'.

[1] 'Most Secret', sent at 6.48 p.m., 20 May 1940: Admiralty papers, 199/1929.
[2] 'Secret', 20 May 1940: Admiralty papers, 116/4471.
[3] Memorandum of 20 May 1940: Admiralty papers, 116/4471.
[4] As reported by Seal to Colville, Colville diary, 20 May 1940: Colville papers.

How far it would be possible to link up with the French at all seemed suddenly in doubt, for Major-General Percival told the War Cabinet that the Germans had already captured Bapaume, more than twenty miles south of Lens. It was clear that this German success further threatened Gort's move towards Amiens, as well as resulting in the loss of an important ammunition depot.

The main German thrust, Percival reported, was in the direction of Arras, which lay on Gort's route south. The staff of the British Armoured Division being sent to help the French forces had landed at Le Havre, but the convoy with the first units of the Division had been diverted to Cherbourg. They were not expected to be ready for action for at least four days.

It was becoming increasingly difficult to assess Gort's chances of linking up with the French, or the French chances of halting the German thrust. As a 'precautionary measure', Churchill told the War Cabinet, 'the Admiralty should assemble a large number of small vessels in readiness to proceed to ports and inlets on the French coast'.[1]

Churchill then told the War Cabinet he had already suggested to the Chiefs of Staff that they should prepare a study of the covering operations which would be necessary from bases in England, in the event 'of it being necessary to withdraw the British Expeditionary Force from France'. In addition, he agreed with Newall that, as Churchill expressed it, 'we had reached the limit of the air assistance which we could send to France, and that we could not consider despatching further resources permanently to France, thus denuding our defences at home'.[2]

The War Cabinet meeting of May 20 ended with a report from Eden, that he had spoken to Ironside on the telephone, and that 'a start was being made with the withdrawal to the south of three Divisions'. Two of these Divisions had been ordered to attack Arras, 'and were at that moment on the move'.

Gort's main difficulty, Ironside reported from France, would be 'to extricate himself' from his present position on the Scheldt. According to Eden, Ironside had seen 'no reason why the situation should not be put right, but that it would take time'.[3]

Time, however, was running out: on May 14 General Brooke had

[1] War Cabinet No. 131 of 1940, 20 May 1940, 11.30 a.m.: Cabinet papers, 65/7.

[2] War Cabinet No. 131 of 1940, 20 May 1940, 11.30 a.m., Confidential Annex, Minute 10: Cabinet papers: 65/13.

[3] War Cabinet No. 131 of 140, 20 May 1940, Confidential Annex, Minute 13: Cabinet papers, 65/13.

ordered a further retreat in the north, from the river Dendre to the river Scheldt, and only with heavy fighting had managed to drive back German units which had crossed the Scheldt in several places. At 3.20 p.m. on the afternoon of May 20 a telegram from Dill reached Churchill, in which Dill reported that he had urged upon Weygand and Georges the need for 'some energetic action' by the French forces. Without such action, Dill warned, the communications of the British Expeditionary Force would be cut, 'and we would then be forced to consider our own security'.

Georges had then told Dill that the commanding general in the north, General Billotte had as his 'first preoccupation' a number of 'holes' in his front line. But after remonstrances from Dill, Weygand telephoned Billotte and told him that it was 'essential to thrust south in the direction of Cambrai'; the 'decisive moment' of the battle had arrived, and 'whatever the cost this drive must be made'. Infantry must attack tanks, and 'every gun' should be put forward.

Dill then spoke on the telephone to Ironside, who was with Billotte, and who reported these 'energetic orders' just issued by Weygand. But Ironside also told Dill that in his view both Weygand and Georges had 'lost confidence in Billotte's ability to carry out any orders energetically'.

As Dill told Churchill, one way out seemed to be the possibility 'of investing Ironside with Billotte's power', and putting Ironside himself under Georges' command. But for the Chief of the Imperial General Staff to leave his central position of authority in London and take a subordinate command in France would require the sanction of the British Cabinet. Meanwhile both Weygand and Georges were insisting that they had 'complete confidence' in Billotte, whose 'apparent failure' in initiating the southward drive on the previous day was due, they said, to 'Uncertainty yesterday of British intentions'.[1]

At a meeting of the Defence Committee at 6.30 that evening scarcely an hour after the arrival of Dill's telegram, General Percival reported 'further news' to the effect that rail communications at Amiens and Abbeville had been cut during the day by German air attack, so that the Expeditionary Force would have to rely on its forward supplies, adequate only for between twenty-four and forty-eight hours.

The Defence Committee went on to discuss the preparation of plans to evacuate Narvik, and the report 'on the amount of equipment to be abandoned' if Narvik were evacuated.

[1] No. 2 (Swayne) Military Mission, Telegram No. 245, despatched 3.07 p.m., received 5.20 p.m., 20 May 1940: Premier papers, 3/188/3, folios 22–3.

The final discussion that evening was about the possible invasion of Britain itself. The main area of concern was the lack of small arms ammunition, and trained riflemen. There were soldiers in infantry depots who had never taken even a musketry course. All such men, Churchill told the Committee, 'should be exercised in the firing of a few rounds of ball ammunition, even if they could not do a full course'.

It was the view of the Defence Committee that the danger of invasion was greater from Holland than from the Channel ports. 'Action' would be taken against such an 'expedition', the minutes recorded, 'with motor torpedo boats and destroyers'. It was thought 'improbable' that the Germans would land troops at night, but parachutists might well be used. There were, however, 'mobile columns' available in Britain to reinforce airport guards. Two airports, at Wick and Lossiemouth, were mentioned as particularly vulnerable, but local volunteers might be recruited to guard them.[1]

Even Whitehall was not considered immune from the possibility of a German parachute assault. Indeed, for four days plans had been drawn up specifically to protect the Government Offices in Whitehall from a German attempt to capture them. The main defence was to consist of eight bren gun posts, set up at road blocks throughout Whitehall, including the entrance to Downing Street. Two bren guns situated above the roadway on Admiralty Arch were to cover any German attack from the direction either of Trafalgar Square or of Buckingham Palace.[2]

'Good,' Churchill minuted on May 20, after he had studied this plan.[3]

On the night of May 20 the first German armoured columns passed Amiens on the road to Abbeville, cutting off the British Expeditionary Force both from the main French armies, and from its bases and supplies. Ironside, returning that night to Britain, had a narrow escape when his hotel at Calais received a direct hit from a German bomb, and he himself had been blown out of bed.

At the Chiefs of Staff Committee on the morning of May 21, Churchill heard Ironside report that when he had impressed on Billotte, whose eight divisions were still 'more or less intact', the need to move south from Denain to Cambrai to try to break the German thrust to the sea, Billotte 'had taken heart at his words and had undertaken to attack today'. At the same time, Ironside reported two British divisions

[1] Defence Committee, No. 5 of 1940, 20 May 1940, 6.30 p.m.: Cabinet papers, 69/1.
[2] 'London Area Operation Order No. 2', 16 May 1940: Premier papers, 3/263/1.
[3] Minute of 20 May 1940: Premier papers, 3/263/1.

had already moved south to the Arras area, and a third was on its way.[1]

Ironside's report seemed to Churchill cause for hope. 'I saw Winston,' Ironside noted in his diary, 'who persists in thinking the position no worse,'[2] and when the War Cabinet met an hour later, Churchill expressed the opinion 'that the situation was more favourable than certain of the more obvious symptoms could indicate'. One German armoured column, he said, had entered Abbeville. Another had been seen passing Frévent, 'probably making for Boulogne'. But two battalions of Guards were, as Churchill had been told at the Chiefs of Staff Committee, being sent to Boulogne in destroyers, in order to hold the town against the German column. Above all, Churchill commented, the British forces 'still enjoyed an overwhelming superiority of numbers in this theatre of operations. We must now be ready to fight hard under open warfare conditions.'

Churchill's hopeful assessment seemed borne out by Ironside himself, when he told the War Cabinet of his visit to France. Although Billotte 'had failed to carry out his duties of co-ordination for the last eight days, and appeared to have no plans', Ironside said, he had also spoken while in France to the new French Commander-in-Chief, General Weygand, who had 'spoken sharply' to Billotte. There was 'nothing wrong with the French troops themselves', Ironside declared, while the British troops 'were in very good heart, and ready for the fight'.

The British troops, Ironside reported, had seen practically no fighting so far, and their total casualties in the field 'were only of the order of 500'. After nine low flying German aircraft had been brought down by British troops with their bren guns, the low-flying attack had ceased. The urgent need was to clear the refugees from all the main strategic towns, block the entrances to those towns, and then 'hold them with our troops', even if some of those towns were 'strictly speaking' in the French sector.

Newall then spoke of various 'successful attacks' made on the previous afternoon by 23 British aircraft on German transport and troops. Only one British plane had been shot down. During the night, a further ninety-one British bombers had attacked German troop concentrations between Cambrai and St Quentin.

A sense of the coming danger did emerge, however, at the end of the War Cabinet of May 21, when the question arose of the despatch of·

---

[1] Chiefs of Staff Committee No. 142 of 1940, 21 May 1940, 10.15 a.m.: Cabinet papers, 79/4.
[2] Ironside diary, 21 May 1940: Roderick Macleod and Denis Kelly (editors), *The Ironside Diaries 1937–1940*, London 1962, page 326.

Anson and Battle aircraft to Canada, to be used for training pilots, observers and air gunners. During the discussion, Churchill pointed out the Battle aircraft were being used on the front 'today', and would become even more useful during the coming two months if the Germans were to 'obtain a foothold' on the French coast. His remarks continued:

The types of aircraft now in question were not those of the first efficiency, but if we ran short of the better types it would be unwise to deprive ourselves of the second-best in the life-and-death struggle which we might have to face in the next few weeks.

Although the number of machines involved was inconsiderable, he thought that it would be dangerous to send away from the country even a small number of aircraft, if they could be used for operational purposes in the near future.

The supply of pilots, though of immense value, was remote in comparison with the needs of the moment, when the enemy appeared to be staking everything on reaching a quick decision.[1]

Churchill's principal concern during May 21 was the situation of the French forces. According to Cadogan's note of the War Cabinet discussion, Ironside had reported that the French troops in the north were 'trained and with good material, but the command paralysed'. If Weygand could 'get a grip' however, Cadogan added, 'we may yet do something'.[2]

The exact intentions of the leading French soldiers were unclear. At eleven o'clock on the morning of May 21 Dill saw General Georges, and reported 'that this is not time for plugging holes but for making them'. Georges himself, Dill told Churchill, was in 'better form' than on May 20. This, Dill added, was because Weygand was now in the north, and would relieve Georges of the need to exercise his authority there.

Dill also gave Churchill the apparent good news that the Belgian Army was extending its front to the south, and thus relieving the British divisions in that area. Billotte, he reported, was 'said to be regrouping' for a 'strong offensive' southward, but was 'not yet ready to strike'.

Georges could give Dill neither the timing nor any other details of Billotte's proposed southward offensive. But he did confirm that 'some Germans' were in Abbeville, and that there was a German bridgehead south of Amiens. The French were attempting to regain this bridgehead by counter attack, Georges assured Dill. But French troop concentra-

---

[1] War Cabinet No. 132 of 1940, 21 May 1940, 11.30 a.m.: Cabinet papers, 65/7.

[2] Cadogan diary, 21 May 1940: David Dilks (editor), *The Diaries of Sir Alexander Cadogan, 1938–1945*, London 1971, page 287.

tions between Paris and the river Somme were being delayed by German bombing of their communications.

Reporting these details to Churchill, Dill cautioned that although it was the French intention to use the divisions between Paris and the Somme for a northward offensive, any such action 'early' was, in Dill's view, 'improbable'.[1]

Having sent this telegram, Dill set off from France to return to Britain. As he was returning, Churchill, in the hope of encouraging the new French offensive, telegraphed to Reynaud: 'Many congratulations upon appointing Weygand, in whom we have entire confidence here.' Churchill had been troubled, however, by Reynaud's assertion to him, in a telegram on the previous day, that wherever German tanks tried to pierce holes in the French lines, those holes would be stopped, and the invading force hemmed in. 'It is not possible,' Churchill declared, 'to stop columns of tanks from piercing thin lines and penetrating deeply. All ideas of stopping holes and hemming in these intruders are vicious. Principle should be, on the contrary, to punch holes.'

Churchill's telegram continued:

Undue importance should not be attached to the arrival of a few tanks at any particular point. What can they do if they enter a town? Towns should be held with riflemen, and tank personnel should be fired upon should they attempt to leave vehicles. If they cannot get food or drink or petrol, they can only make a mess and depart. Where possible, buildings should be blown down upon them. Every town with valuable cross-roads should be held in this fashion.

Secondly, the tank columns in the open must be hunted down and attacked with a few cannon. Their tracks must be wearing out, and their energy must abate. This is the one way to deal with the armoured intruders. As for the main body, which does not seem to be coming on very quickly, the only method is to drive in upon the flanks.

The confusion of this battle can only be cleared by being aggravated, so that it becomes a *mêlée*. They strike at our communications; we should strike at theirs. I feel more confident than I did at the beginning of the battle; but all the armies must fight at the same time and I hope the British will have a chance soon.

'Above is only my personal view,' Churchill ended, 'and I trust it will give no offence if I state it to you.'[2]

One decision which Churchill was being pressed to take immediately

[1] No. 2 (Swayne) Military Mission, Telegram No. 246, despatched 1.35 p.m., received 1.50 p.m., 21 May 1940: Premier papers, 3/188/3, folio 18.
[2] Telegram of 21 May 1940: Premier papers, 3/188/1.

concerned the exchange of technical naval information with the United States. This course had been suggested on the previous day, as a matter of urgency, and in order 'to show our goodwill towards the United States', by the First Lord of the Admiralty, A. V. Alexander.[1] 'I do of course appreciate very forcibly,' Churchill wrote on Alexander's letter, 'the importance of retaining the goodwill of the United States authorities and of extracting from them all the material assistance they can give.' But he added that he would prefer to wait a few days before taking any such decision. 'I made an offer previously,' he explained, 'to give them the secret of the Asdics in exchange for their bomb sight, but it was not accepted.'[2]

The United States was already serving, however, as the essential arsenal for British war supplies. Twice on May 21 Britain's dependence upon the manufacture of arms and aircraft in the United States was made clear: first, as far as future supplies were concerned, when Churchill asked Desmond Morton to find out 'what rifles of all kinds we have got in store' in Britain, and learned that there were at that moment, according to Eden, only 150,000 rifles 'of all types' being examined and reconditioned.[3] If any substantial supply of rifles was to be obtained, and obtained quickly, it was clear that the United States must be the main supplier.

The second decision on May 21 which concerned United States supplies was on the question of whether to give publicity to the current production of Rolls Royce aeroplane engines in the United States. 'What do Air Ministry say?' Churchill minuted three days later, and after discussing the question with Beaverbrook, agreed that secrecy should be maintained.[4]

At seven o'clock that evening, for the second time in four days, Churchill went to Buckingham Palace to report on the war situation to the King.[5] Returning to Admiralty House, he telephoned Ironside to discuss the continuing German thrust towards Boulogne. 'They expect to be able to hold Boulogne,' Colville noted, 'but it is a shock that the Germans should have penetrated so far, and the BEF's communications are in danger.'[6]

It was proving difficult to know exactly what the military situation

[1] 'Most Secret and Urgent', 'Letter sent in a box', 20 May 1940: Premier papers, 3/475/1, folios 66–8.

[2] Note dated 21 May 1940: Premier papers, 3/475/1, folio 68.

[3] Minute of 21 May 1940 (Morton to Churchill): Premier papers, 7/2.

[4] Minutes of 21 May 1940 (Morton) and 24 May 1940 (Churchill): Premier papers, 7/2.

[5] Churchill desk diary, 21 May 1940: Thompson papers.

[6] Colville diary, 21 May 1940: Colville papers.

was; yet without adequate information, the necessary hour by hour scrutiny of the changing face of the battle was impossible. Telephone communication with France had almost totally broken down. 'In all the history of war,' Churchill told Colville, as they tried in vain to put through a telephone call to Reynaud, 'I have never known such mismanagement.' Colville added: 'I have not seen Winston so depressed.'[1]

What then was to be done? According to Colville's diary, Churchill decided, 'against the advice of the Chiefs of Staff', to go to Paris early on the following morning to see Weygand and Reynaud, 'and to impress on them that it is no use concentrating on the destruction of German mechanical columns which had penetrated far into France, but that we must withstand the main German advance, and ourselves attack'.

Would a British attack be possible? Newall, as Colville noted, thought that the British Expeditionary Force was already 'in grave danger', although fighting well 'unlike their French allies'.[2]

There was further bad news that night, when it was learned in London that Billotte, having assured first Ironside and then Weygand that he would deploy his eight divisions with greater energy, had been killed in a car crash while driving back to his headquarters. When Colville broke the news to Churchill, the Prime Minister was much moved. 'Poor man, poor man,' he repeated, 'I am indeed sorry.'[3]

At dawn, Churchill prepared for his second visit to France since he had become Prime Minister only twelve days before; twelve of the most fateful days in British history. The outcome of the battle was still uncertain. The German armies, for all their speed and strength, were not yet either within striking distance of Paris, or within strangling distance of the Channel ports. But the situation was changing from hour to hour.

---

[1] Colville diary, 21 May 1940: Colville papers.
[2] Colville diary, 21 May 1940: Colville papers.
[3] Colville diary, 21 May 1940: Colville papers.

20

The Weygand Plan

<hr>

EFORE leaving for France, Churchill wrote to Chamberlain, about the arrest of British Fascist and enemy aliens: 'I will agree to whatever the Cabinet thinks best.'[1] Two hours later, as Churchill was airborne, the War Cabinet met to approve special emergency power regulations over individuals and property. Chamberlain, who took the Chair, told his colleagues that Churchill had left a message 'that if any doubt existed, the persons in question should be detained without delay'. This view, the War Cabinet minutes recorded, 'met with general approval'.[2]

Accompanied by Dill, Peirse and Ismay, Churchill reached Paris shortly before midday. They were met by Reynaud, who was now both Prime Minister and Minister of War, and driven, together with the British Ambassador, Sir Ronald Campbell, to Weygand's headquarters at Vincennes. 'Weygand's appearance was a pleasant surprise,' Ismay later recalled. 'He gave the impression of being a fighter—resolute, decisive and amazingly active, in spite of his wizened face and advanced years.'

Weygand was seventy-three years old, almost the age of Admiral Fisher when Churchill had recalled him to be First Sea Lord in 1914. 'One dared to hope,' Ismay added, 'that the Allied armies would now have the leadership that had hitherto seemed lacking.'[3]

The meeting at Vincennes opened with a survey of the military situation by a French officer, Colonel Simon, who also reported that Billotte had now been replaced by General Blanchard as Commander-in-Chief of the British, French and Belgian forces in the North. The

<hr>

[1] Minute of 22 May 1940: Churchill papers: 20/13. Some 1,500 enemy aliens and Fascists were thought likely to be interned, compared with 29,000 enemy aliens in 1914.

[2] War Cabinet No. 133 of 1940, 22 May 1940, 10.30 a.m.: Cabinet papers, 65/7.

[3] *The Memoirs of General the Lord Ismay*, London 1960, page 130.

two Guards battalions which had been landed at Boulogne, Churchill noted, were 'the last units of the active Army still in England'. In addition, steps had been taken to protect Calais and Dunkirk. The commander at Dunkirk, commented Weygand, was 'a particularly vigorous Admiral', who had, in addition to his personal qualities, 'sufficient forces at his disposal to protect the town'.[1]

Weygand's proposal for the northern armies, was, however, not to fall back on the Channel ports, nor even 'simply to retreat' southwards to join up with the main French army. What was required, he said, was that all the available French and British forces should 'take offensive action', covered to the east, and even to the north, by the Belgian army. This offensive would be helped at the same time by a northward 'push' of the French army then south of the Somme in the Beauvais region against the German armoured forces in the Amiens, Abbeville, Arras triangle. In this way, Weygand hoped that the Allied armies could halt the onward thrust of the German advance, and take the initiative against it.

According to the minute of this meeting, 'Mr Churchill and Sir John Dill gave numerous signs of approval' throughout Weygand's survey of the action needed, and showed by their questions and comments that 'their own conception of the battle was in exact correlation' with his, particularly 'in the matter of the task to be assigned to the Belgian army'.

During Weygand's presentation of his plan, Churchill 'repeatedly stated', as the minutes recorded, 'that the restoring of communications between the armies in the north and the main forces in the south, through Arras, was essential. The British forces under Gort, he said, had no more than four days' food left. All the supplies and war stores of the Expeditionary Force were concentrated along the coast from Calais southwards towards St Nazaire; 'and that General Gort's paramount concern was to preserve this line of communication, which was absolutely vital for him'.

Two days previously, Churchill explained, Gort had begun to move certain forces behind the line towards his right flank 'with the object of proceeding gradually towards Arras and Bapaume'. The outcome of this battle was 'vital to the further conduct of the war, for the maintenance of the British forces through the Channel ports was becoming exceedingly hazardous'. It was for this reason that Allied control of the Cambrai–St Quentin area 'assumed decisive importance'.

Weygand now asked, 'in firm and exact, although courteous, terms',

[1] This was Admiral Abrial.

for British fighter and bomber forces to be engaged 'up to the hilt' in the present theatre of war. After what was politely called in the minutes 'an exchange of views' between Weygand and Peirse, it was agreed that Weygand's wishes should be met.

The Vincennes meeting was drawing to its close. If 'suitable methods' were applied, Churchill concluded, 'and if a calm determination was maintained', it should be possible to resist attacks by armoured German units even when they were supported by bomber activity. What mattered 'was now to hold on everywhere at every single point where an Allied force was in possession'.

It was also, Weygand added, 'necessary to act'. Every time an attack was launched by the Allies, 'some part of the enemy force found itself faced with difficulties'.

As the Vincennes meeting came to an end, the Weygand plan was agreed in writing. Both the British Expeditionary Force and the French First Army would attack south-west towards Bapaume and Cambrai 'at the earliest moment—certainly tomorrow', with a view to freeing Amiens, and in order to 'join hands' with the new French Army group which was advancing upon Amiens from the south.[1]

Churchill prepared to return to London, having telegraphed the Weygand plan to Gort, whose headquarters were then at Premesques. These conclusions, Churchill telegraphed, 'which were reached between Reynaud, Weygand and ourselves', were also in exact accord with the 'general directions' which Gort had already received from the War Office. 'You have our best wishes,' Churchill added, 'in the vital battle now opening towards Bapaume and Cambrai.'[2]

Six hours later, at 10 Downing Street, Churchill gave the War Cabinet an account of the Vincennes meeting. 'He was almost in buoyant spirits,' Ironside noted in his diary, 'having been impressed by Weygand.' Churchill told the Cabinet that Weygand 'looked like a man of fifty'.[3] But 'when it came down to things', Ironside noted, 'it was still all *projets*'.[4]

'Provided the French fought well,' Churchill commented, 'there seemed a good prospect of success.' Dill, however, drew the conclusion that 'from the fact that the French forces had not fought much any-

---

[1] Supreme War Council, 12th meeting of 1939–40, 22 May 1940 (translated from the French text): Cabinet papers, 99/3, folios 80–2.

[2] Telegram of 22 May 1940: Churchill papers, 20/14.

[3] Weygand was seventy-three.

[4] Ironside diary, 22 May 1940: Roderick Macleod and Denis Kelly (editors), *The Ironside Diaries 1937–1940*, London 1962, page 328.

where, it seemed likely that the morale of the units', as well as the morale of their commanders, 'was not too good'.[1]

An even more serious obstacle to the Weygand plan was then read out by Eden. It was a note of his telephone conversation with Gort's Aide-de-Camp, Lord Munster, at five o'clock that same afternoon. According to Munster's message, the situation 'was very grave'. All the lines of communication of the British Expeditionary Force were cut. Even telephone conversation was impossible, either with London or Paris. Munster himself was telephoning from 'some point' on the Belgian coast some two hours drive from Gort's headquarters. There was a 'severe shortage of the essential commodities for war both in respect of food and munitions'. Above all, Munster reported, 'there was no co-ordination between ourselves and the French on our right. "The Co-ordinator has had an accident and co-ordinates no longer".' After three hours' conversation with the French, Gort himself had 'received the impression that there was "very little doing".'

As yet, Munster added, the French forces 'were not prepared to fight, nor did they show any sign of doing so'. As for the British supplies of food and ammunition, 'they could not be sufficient', he told Eden, 'for any large number of days'.[2]

The Weygand plan thus seemed in doubt, even before its opening moves had been put into effect. As Cadogan noted in his diary: 'Counter offensive should start tomorrow. But will the French fight?'[3] Both Dill and Ismay were pessimistic, despite Weygand's own apparent zeal. According to Ismay, Weygand himself had been 'magnificent'. When asked point blank if he could get the French Army to fight, he had replied, 'I will try.' But Ismay added that reports of the French fighting spirit 'were bad', and he was afraid, Colville noted in his diary, that the Germans would offer the French 'generous terms'. What Britain had to do, Ismay concluded, was 'to prepare for the worst'.[4]

One further question which the War Cabinet discussed on the evening of May 22 was the future of the Anglo-French forces in Norway. 'M. Reynaud took the view,' Churchill reported, 'that if we lost the battle in France, a success at Narvik would be of little avail. On the

---

[1] War Cabinet No. 134 of 1940, 22 May 1940, 7.30 p.m., Confidential Annex: Cabinet papers, 65/13.

[2] War Cabinet No. 134 of 1940, 22 May 1940, 7.30 p.m., Confidential Annex, Appendix II, 'note by the Secretary of State for War recording a conversation with Lord Munster (ADC to Lord Gort)': Cabinet papers, 65/13, folio 114.

[3] Cadogan diary, 22 May 1940: David Dilks (editor), *The Diaries of Sir Alexander Cadogan, 1938–1945*, London 1971, page 288.

[4] Colville diary, 22 May 1940: Colville papers.

other hand, if this battle were even indeterminate, a small success at Narvik would be an enheartening contribution.' Such a view, Churchill commented, was 'good common sense'.[1]

In reply to Churchill's earlier rebuke, Lord Cork had already telegraphed to stress the need to establish aerodromes before attempting to attack Narvik itself. Cork added: 'I do not require spurring, for I am doing my best in order to attain object and do not doubt achieving it.'[2] Churchill now replied, in a personal message drafted by the Admiralty: 'The capture of Narvik town will have a special significance and I note your intention to achieve this as soon as you have established the aerodromes.'[3]

On the morning of May 23 the three Chiefs of Staff proposed to the War Cabinet 'that we should capture Narvik and then withdraw from Norway'. Churchill was puzzled by this proposal, telling the War Cabinet that he 'deprecated asking troops to incur heavy losses in assaulting a town which it was proposed to evacuate immediately afterwards'.

On behalf of the Chiefs of Staff, Newall then referred to the 'political advantage of being able to say that we had captured Narvik'. But Churchill replied that he thought that these advantages 'had been considerably minimized' by the situation in France.

It was a Labour member of the War Cabinet, A. V. Alexander, who reiterated the 'grave political considerations' involved in a decision 'to abandon Norway'. But both Attlee and Halifax supported Churchill. The possession of Narvik, Halifax said, would be a 'valueless lever' if it was known that Britain intended to withdraw.

Churchill agreed to postpone an immediate decision. But he did ask for plans to be worked out 'at once' for the evacuation of Norway, should the War Cabinet eventually decide to evacuate, and in a minute that same day to Ismay he wrote: 'Narvik must be wound up at once. Lord Cork should be ordered to prepare scheme for evacuation.' This scheme, he added, should be ready in three days, together with a scheme from the Planning Committee in London. These three days, Churchill added, 'will give time for the present operations at Narvik to reach a conclusion if they have any chance of doing so'.[4]

As the War Cabinet discussion continued on the morning of May

[1] War Cabinet No. 134 of 1940, 22 May 1940, 7.30 p.m.: Cabinet papers, 65/7.
[2] Telegram No. 303, by wireless telegraph, received London 5.31 p.m., 21 May 1940: Admiralty papers, 199/1929.
[3] Telegram No. 83, 21 May 1940: Admiralty papers, 199/1929.
[4] Minute of 23 May 1940: Premier papers, 3/348.

23, Churchill informed his colleagues that he had 'no doubt that this country would shortly be subjected to heavy attack'. The guns, destroyers, aircraft carriers, shipping and troops 'at present devoted to the Norwegian project', he added, 'were urgently needed for our own defences'.[1]

Basing himself on the most recent information from France, Churchill warned the War Cabinet that 'very much larger German forces' than had at first been supposed had succeeded in getting through the gap between the Allied armies. The situation around the Channel ports had become so critical that he had instructed Ironside to remain at the War Office 'in order that he might in person supervise the conduct of these operations'. The whole success of the Weygand plan, he added, 'depended on the French forces taking the offensive. At present they showed no signs of doing so.'[2]

Gort was in agreement with Churchill that if the Weygand plan were to succeed, 'the weight of attack in closing the gap must come from the south'. These were his words to Blanchard at 7.30 on the morning of May 23. Gort added that his own beleaguered garrison could do no more 'than make a sortie'.[3]

In London, Churchill had also seen, in the continuing German advance towards Boulogne, a threat to Gort's line of communication, and a barrier to any southward movement by Gort, as envisaged by the Weygand plan. The German advance towards Boulogne, Churchill minuted for Ironside, was a 'peril'. The coastal area 'must be cleared up if the major operation of withdrawal is to have any chance'. Churchill added: 'The intruders behind the line must be struck at and brought to bay. The refugees should be driven into the fields and parked there, as proposed by General Weygand, so that the roads can be kept clear.'[4]

From the perspective of London, it seemed that it was Weygand who most needed exhortation. That morning Churchill telegraphed to Reynaud, pointing out that the communications of the northern armies had been cut 'by strong enemy armoured forces'. The 'salvation' of these armies, he warned, could only be obtained by the 'immediate execution' of the Weygand plan, and he added: 'I demand the issue to French commanders in north and south and Belgian GHQ of

[1] War Cabinet No. 135 of 1940, 23 May 1940, Confidential Annex, Minute 9: Cabinet papers, 65/13.
[2] War Cabinet No. 135 of 1940, 23 May 1940, 11.30 a.m.: Cabinet papers, 65/7.
[3] J. R. Colville, Man of Valour, London 1972, page 211.
[4] Minute of 23 May 1940: Churchill papers, 20/13.

the most stringent orders to carry this out and turn defeat into victory. Time is vital as supplies are short.'[1]

The initial phases of the Weygand plan depended not only upon Gort's ability to carry out the British drive southward, but also upon Weygand's ability to deliver the northward punch. As Cadogan noted in his diary, '*if* Weygand can stage a good counter attack in next 24 hours, we *may* avert complete disaster. But that is all the time we have.'[2]

At 3.45 that afternoon Churchill went to the House of Commons, where he announced that German armoured forces had 'penetrated into the rear of the Allied defences and are now attempting to derange their communications'. At the same time, he said, Weygand, 'who is in supreme command, is conducting the operation involving all the Allied armies, with a view to restoring and reconstituting their combined front'.[3]

It was while he was, briefly, in his room at the House of Commons that Churchill was introduced to John Martin, a young man from the Colonial Office who had been recommended as a possible Private Secretary. Martin had met Churchill three years earlier at the time of the Palestine Royal Commission, on which he had served as Secretary. 'I was taken into his room at the House of Commons,' Martin later recalled. 'There was no conversation, but I remember his geniality and air of brisk confidence. He told me to stand over in the window and looked me up and down searchingly, then without further ado said, "I understand that you are to be one of my Private Secretaries." '

With a 'friendly smile', Martin added, 'I was dismissed.'[4]

Returning to Downing Street, Churchill studied the latest information from France: the Germans were already in Boulogne, Gort's attack southwards to Arras had made no progress, the British Expeditionary

---

[1] Telegram of 23 May 1940: Churchill papers, 20/14.

[2] Cadogan diary, 23 May 1940: David Dilks (editor), *The Diaries of Sir Alexander Cadogan 1938–1945*, London 1971, page 289.

[3] *Hansard*, 23 May 1940.

[4] Sir John Martin, letter to the author, 22 December 1981. Martin added: 'Churchill believed he could sum up a man in such a swift scrutiny. Later I was to see him reject a candidate after an equally abrupt examination. In the ordinary way candidates for such vacancies at No. 10 were nominated by the Treasury, but Churchill would not have accepted Sir Horace Wilson's nominations and I suspect that I owed my selection to Brendan Bracken, who often showed his admiration for the Palestine Royal Commission and indicated that he was familiar with the Commissioners' tribute to me as their Private Secretary.' Martin was then 36 years old. The age of Churchill's other Private Secretaries at that time was Seal 42, Peck 27, Colville 25 and Anthony Bevir, then responsible for Civil List Pensions, later the Patronage Secretary, 44.

Force had been forced through lack of supplies to go on half rations, and Weygand's northward offensive had not yet begun. Yet twenty-four hours earlier, at Vincennes, Weygand had assured Churchill that he was assembling eighteen to twenty fresh divisions along the Somme, for the northward thrust.

Fearing that the Weygand plan might not even be in prospect, Churchill telephoned to Reynaud at 4.50 that afternoon to say, as Reynaud recalled, 'that Gort had received no information from Blanchard', and that because of the position of the German armoured divisions moving towards Boulogne and Calais 'he was wondering whether it would not be better if the British army fought in retreat towards the coast'.

Reynaud assured Churchill: 'Weygand is satisfied. We ought not to change anything. We must follow the path which we have traced out. *We must go on.*' [1]

As proof that the Weygand plan was actually in operation, Weygand himself was brought to the telephone at six that evening, and assured Churchill that a re-formed French Army had already begun its northward assault, and that it had already recaptured Amiens, Albert and Péronne. This information was false. But, as Colville later recalled, 'there was no reason to doubt Weygand's report, and gloom gave way to elation. The Germans must have shot their bolt; perhaps the Miracle of the Marne, that historical parallel of which everybody had been daydreaming, was going to be repeated.' [2]

The reason for Weygand's deception has been a matter of considerable concern to those who were involved in the crisis of May 23, or who witnessed it at the time. Colville, who was at Downing Street throughout that day, and who was later to write a biography of Gort, later reflected: 'Weygand was determined, if the BEF could not go southward, that *we* should go under if *they* did.' [3]

Having spoken to Churchill, Weygand then spoke to Ironside. Not only had Amiens, Albert and Péronne been taken, but, Weygand said, 'the manoeuvre was continuing under good conditions'. To continue this manoeuvre was 'the only solution'. The rest 'was disaster'. Ironside noted: 'He was quite unmoved when I told him of the weight of the forces moving up on the line Béthune–St Omer. He said that the German Armoured Divisions were reduced by casualties.' Ironside's re-

[1] Paul Reynaud, *In The Thick of the Fight*, London 1955, page 369. The italics are Reynaud's own.
[2] J. R. Colville, *Man of Valour*, London 1972, page 213.
[3] Sir John Colville, conversation with the author, 21 January 1981.

port of the conversation concluded tersely: 'Weygand was confident.'[1]

When the War Cabinet met at seven o'clock that evening, only an hour after Ironside's talk with Weygand, there was no reason to doubt that the French Army's northward thrust was still in progress, as Weygand had asserted. The bad news came from the Channel ports. One of the forts at Boulogne had been captured by the Germans, who were shelling the town. 'There was no doubt,' Churchill warned, 'that our troops were undergoing a great ordeal.'

Churchill also told the War Cabinet that a Tank Regiment, which had been sent across the Channel to help Gort, had disembarked at Calais and ordered to clear the route to St Omer, 'but had encountered enemy forces three miles out of Calais'.

Summing up the situation, and bearing in mind Weygand's telephonic assurances both to himself and to Ironside, Churchill thought that, 'while there was as yet little ground for confidence', the British Government 'had no choice in the matter but to do our best to conform to General Weygand's plan'. Any other course, he added, 'would wreck the chance of General Weygand's plan succeeding'.

Confronted by Weygand's demand that Gort's southward advance should continue, and by the supreme commander's assurance that his own northward thrust was in progress, both Ironside and Dill were of the view, as the War Cabinet minutes recorded, 'that it was better that the operation should continue'. If Gort's troops were to retire on the Channel ports, they added, 'it was unlikely that more than a small part of the force could be got away'.[2]

Thus, for the War Cabinet and its senior military advisers, the Weygand plan was still in existence, and still favoured, on the evening of May 23. But the threat to the plan by the German advance towards Boulogne and Calais was clear, and, as Colville noted in his diary, at dinner that night Ismay, always a good guide to the true situation, 'was dismal and depressing'.[3]

Churchill understood what was at stake should the Weygand plan prove to be an illusion, and in a telegram to the four Dominion Prime Ministers, Menzies, Smuts, Fraser and Mackenzie King, he sought on May 23 to warn of the possibility of an 'early heavy attack' on Britain. For such an attack, Churchill said, 'we are preparing, and we hope that our naval defence will be effective against large bodies, and that

---

[1] War Cabinet No. 136 of 1940, 23 May 1940, Confidential Annex (report by Churchill of Ironside's conversation with Weygand): Cabinet papers, 65/13, folio 124.

[2] War Cabinet No. 136 of 1940, 23 May 1940, Confidential Annex, Cabinet papers: 65/13.

[3] Colville diary, 23 May 1940: Colville papers.

our land defence will deal with any sea-borne survivors after some rough work'.

The final result, Churchill warned, would depend on the ability of the Royal Air Force 'to make head against superior numbers, and help destroy airborne descents'. His telegram continued:

Our Air Force will be far more effective in this country, for many technical reasons which I cannot give, than operating overseas, and we believe we are capable of limiting daylight raids on ports and factories to manageable proportions on account of the number of casualties we shall inflict on German aviation being out of all proportion to our own Air losses. Night raids far less dangerous to precise targets.

'Anyhow,' Churchill added, 'everyone' in Britain was 'resolved to fight it out.'

The Canadian troops already in Britain would, Churchill told the Dominion Premiers, be used in the battle against invasion. He was also very glad to see a 'fast convoy of Australians approaching'. As for aid from the United States, every form of 'intimate personal appeal', he wrote, and the 'most cogent arguments', had already been sent to Roosevelt. 'He is doing his best,' Churchill added, 'but must carry Congress and public opinion still much diverted by impending Presidential Election.' In these circumstances, Churchill could not at that moment recommend 'a public appeal' to Roosevelt such as Menzies had suggested, 'for it would give an impression of weakness' beyond that which the situation in France, 'grave though it be', yet justified.

Before sending this telegram, Churchill deleted the reference to the 'grave' situation in France. Instead, he told the Dominion Prime Ministers that Britain had been acting in France under Gamelin's orders, 'and conforming to the French plans'. His telegram ended: 'I saw Weygand yesterday, who is attempting to execute important operations in entire accord with us. Weygand made an excellent impression upon us, and has full control.'[1]

At ten o'clock that night, at the King's request, Churchill went to Buckingham Palace. 'He told me,' the King noted in his diary, 'that if the French plan made out by Weygand did not come off, he would have to order the BEF back to England.' This operation, the King added, 'would mean the loss of all guns, tanks, ammunition, & all stores in France'.[2]

[1] Telegram sent to the Dominions Office for despatch on 23 May 1940: Premier papers, 4/43B/1, folios 483–4.

[2] King George VI's diary, 23 May 1940, quoted in John W. Wheeler-Bennett, *King George VI, His Life and Reign*, London 1958, page 456.

Returning from Buckingham Palace to Admiralty House, Churchill prepared yet another appeal to Reynaud. This further telegram reached the French Prime Minister at five o'clock on the morning of May 24. It contained two stern warnings intended 'for General Weygand': first, there was no co-ordination between the French, Belgian and British armies on the northern front, while second, a telephone message from Keyes, now Churchill's personal representative at Belgian headquarters, had made it clear that the Belgian forces 'had received no directive' from the French as to what they should be doing. 'How does this agree,' Churchill asked, 'with your statement that Blanchard and Gort are *main dans la main*?'[1]

Churchill went on to warn Reynaud that he could feel 'no effective concert of operations' in the northern area, where the Germans were concentrating the attack. 'Trust you will be able to rectify this,' Churchill wrote, adding that in Gort's opinion any advance by him 'must be in nature of sortie and that relief must come from south, as he has not (*repeat* not) ammunition for serious attack.'

Such was the reality; and yet, Churchill assured Reynaud, the British Government had instructed Gort 'to persevere in carrying out your plan'. The problem was to ascertain the particulars of that plan. 'We have not here even seen your own directive,' Churchill wrote, 'and have no knowledge of the details of your northern operations.'[2]

Angrily, Reynaud replied at midday with several accusations. Weygand, he said, 'has noted with surprise' that contrary to his plan 'Arras was evacuated yesterday by British troops', while at the same time the evacuation of heavy units of the British Army from Le Havre was having 'a serious effect on the morale of the rear areas'. Reynaud added that Weygand was 'surprised, as I myself am, that he was not previously advised of this'.

The burden of Reynaud's telegram was stated bluntly in the six words: 'General Weygand's orders should be obeyed.'[3]

In an attempt to find out the exact situation among the French strategists, Churchill asked Reynaud if Major-General Spears, who in 1918 had acted as liaison officer between the British and French High

[1] The official British military historian writes: 'It never occurred to Lord Gort to question the intentions or good faith of the French commanders, but by now [May 24] he had been led seriously to distrust their capacity to control a swiftly changing situation or make effective ripostes to the enemy's thrusts' (Major L. F. Ellis, *The War in France and Flanders 1939–1940*, London 1953, page 144).

[2] Telegram of 23 May 1940, received in Paris at 5 a.m., 24 May 1940: Churchill papers, 20/40.

[3] Quoted in Paul Reynaud, *In The Thick of the Fight, 1930–1945*, London 1955, pages 370–1.

Commands, could go to France and report on the situation at first hand. To this Reynaud agreed.[1]

Meanwhile, at the morning War Cabinet on May 24, Churchill reported the evacuation of British troops from Boulogne on the previous night: '1,000 men had been got away, but 200 had been left behind.' The troops in Calais were being shelled, but had been unable to clear the roads out of the town, or to get a food convoy through to St Omer. Further north, the Belgians had tried to persuade two French divisions to occupy Gravelines, but, as Keyes had told Churchill on the telephone that morning, 'on hearing that German tanks were in the vicinity, the French had turned back'.

As on previous days, the War Cabinet also discussed the question of the danger to Britain itself of enemy aliens, many of whom were German Jews and other anti-Nazi refugees. 'The proper method by which Germans opposed to the Nazi regime could contribute to the common cause,' Churchill told the War Cabinet, 'was by work in the factories or fields of this country, or, best of all, under discipline in the Pioneer Corps.' The German fifth-column techniques in the Low Countries had shown, Churchill added, 'the weakness to which we were exposed', and he was 'strongly in favour' of removing all internees out of the United Kingdom.

At Neville Chamberlain's suggestion, the Isle of Man was chosen as the principal detention centre for all German and Austrian women between the ages of 16 and 60. All other aliens had to surrender their cars or bicycles and also remain at their place of residence from 10 p.m. to 8 a.m., while every householder was obliged to report to the police 'particulars of any alien who spends a night in his house'.[2]

As the situation in France worsened, so the imminence of direct danger to Britain seemed to increase. But the exact situation in France had become obscure. On learning that the British forces inside Calais were trapped, but having no information about Gort's difficulties, Churchill minuted to Ismay: 'I cannot understand the situation around Calais. The Germans are blocking all exits, and one regiment of tanks is boxed up in the town because it cannot face the field guns planted

---

[1] On the morning of May 24 Churchill wrote to Reynaud: 'It is not easy for either of us to leave our posts frequently in order to visit each other, and I have therefore appointed an old friend of yours, Major-General Spears, by whose hand I shall send this letter, to be the personal liaison officer between us on matters relating to defence' (Churchill papers: 20/2). On May 25 Churchill telegraphed to Reynaud: 'General Spears will be with you tomorrow morning, and it will probably be quickest to send him back when the position is clear' (Churchill papers: 20/14).

[2] War Cabinet No. 137 of 1940, 24 May 1940, 11.30 a.m.: Cabinet papers, 65/7.

on the outskirts. Yet I expect the forces achieving this are very modest. Why then, are they not attacked?'

Churchill went on to ask why Gort did not attack the Germans surrounding Calais from the rear, while the British troops inside Calais made a simultaneous sortie. 'Surely Gort can spare a brigade or two,' he asked, 'to clear his communications and to secure the supplies vital to his armies?' Here was a General 'with nine divisions about to be starved out, and yet he cannot send a force to clear his communications'. Where else could a reserve be better employed? If German motorized artillery, far from its base, could block British tanks, 'why cannot we, with the artillery of a great army, block them?' Churchill added, bitterly: 'Of course if one side fights and the other does not, the war is apt to become somewhat unequal.'[1]

Churchill's questions reflected the anguish, and lack of information, of the hour. In fact, during May 24, Gort did send one of his divisions, the 48th, to relieve the troops then hemmed in at Cassel, more than twenty-five miles from Calais. At the same time the 5th Division was fighting to prevent the Germans north of Arras from taking the Vimy ridge.

In London, certain members of the Government, among them Beaverbrook, had decided that somebody ought to 'keep an eye' on Churchill's health. The Prime Minister was sixty-five years old. Nine years earlier he had been severely battered in New York, when knocked over by a motor car. In 1932 he had suffered an attack of paratyphoid, and in the years that followed had been a victim of painful dyspepsia.

The doctor chosen to keep a watch on Churchill was a General Practitioner, Sir Charles Wilson, later Lord Moran, who duly presented himself at Admiralty House. In his diary for that day, the new doctor recorded:

Though it was noon, I found him in bed reading a document. He went on reading while I stood by the bedside. After what seemed quite a long time, he put down his papers and said impatiently:

'I don't know why they are making such a fuss. There's nothing wrong with me.'

He picked up the papers and resumed his reading. At last he pushed his bed-rest away and, throwing back the bed-clothes, said abruptly:

'I suffer from dyspepsia, and this is the treatment.'

With that he proceeded to demonstrate to me some breathing exercises. His

[1] Minute of 24 May 1940: Churchill papers: 4/150. This last sentence was omitted in the text of this telegram as published in Churchill's war memoirs, where he added the comment, about the rest of the telegram: 'This did less than justice to our troops. But I print it as I wrote it at the time.'

big white belly was moving up and down when there was a knock on the door, and the PM grabbed at the sheet as Mrs Hill came into the room. Soon after I took my leave . . .[1]

Such was the doctor's view of that dramatic and difficult day, during which so many decisions, and so many preparations, had to be made. Of these, of course, the doctor could know nothing. But as Churchill's minutes show, two particular worries predominated. 'Now that the war is coming so close,' Churchill minuted to Beaverbrook, 'the object must be to prepare the largest number of aircraft.' It was essential now, as Beaverbrook himself had suggested, to prepare training and civil aircraft 'to carry bombs to enemy aerodromes on the Dutch, Belgian and French coasts'.[2]

During May 24 it was also decided, upon the advice of the Chiefs of Staff, to evacuate Narvik as soon as Cork's forces had captured it. The Allied assault on the town was planned for May 28, and was to go ahead as planned. But on the evening of May 24, Cork was told of the Government's decision 'to evacuate Northern Norway at the earliest moment'. The reason for this, he was told, was that the troops, ships, guns and certain equipment were 'urgently required for the United Kingdom'.[3]

Plans were now made to evacuate Bodö by May 31 and Narvik itself, once it had been captured, by June 8. Before these evacuations had been completed, Churchill minuted to Ismay, plans should be made to ensure that 'the largest possible number of mines should be laid in the approaches to Luleå', to deny the Germans the easy passage of ships with iron ore. 'Let a plan be prepared,' Churchill wrote, for laying these mines 'by flights from aircraft carriers'.[4]

There were other minutes dictated on May 24, as every day, scanning and probing each facet of war policy and organization. Colville in whose presence this particular morning's dictation was done, noted in his diary how Churchill was dressed 'in the most brilliant of fancy dressing gowns, puffing a long cigar'.[5] One of his minutes was to the Cabinet Secretary, Sir Edward Bridges. 'I am sure,' it began, 'there are far too many Committees of one kind or another which Ministers

---

[1] Charles Wilson diary, 24 May 1940: Lord Moran, *Winston Churchill: The Struggle for Survival 1940–1965*, London 1965, page 5.

[2] Minute of 24 May 1940: Churchill papers, 20/13.

[3] 'Most Secret', Telegram No. 99, 8.05 p.m., 24 May 1940: Premier papers, 3/328/4, folio 36. On May 27 the evacuation of Narvik was given the code name 'Alphabet'.

[4] Minute of 24 May 1940: Churchill papers, 20/17. The mining of the approaches to Luleå was given the code name 'Paul'.

[5] Colville diary, 24 May 1940: Colville papers.

have to attend, and which do not yield a sufficient result. These should be reduced by suppression or amalgamation . . .'[1] To Lindemann, Churchill wrote that same day: 'Let me have on one sheet of paper a statement about the Tanks,' and he went on to ask five questions: 'How many have we got with the Army? How many of each kind are being made each month? How many are there with manufacturers? What are the forecasts? What are the plans for heavier Tanks?'[2]

At five o'clock on the evening of May 24 Churchill presided over a meeting of the Defence Committee.[3] During the discussion, on the evacuation of Narvik, it was noted that if an invasion of the United Kingdom began while the evacuation from Narvik was still in process, all naval forces would have to be ordered back to the British coast. To get the destroyers back, however, and to refuel them, would take 'about four days'. Meanwhile, with Churchill's strong support, fifty aircraft would be used to carry out Operation 'Paul', the mining of the sea lanes from Luleå. 'No political consideration,' Churchill remarked, 'should stand in the way of this operation.' It was essential to deprive the Germans of 'at least part' of the iron ore they could hope to get out through Luleå during the summer months.

In discussing the defence of Britain in the event of invasion, Ironside warned the Defence Committee that 'much of the British Expeditionary Force might be lost' in the battle in northern France. Churchill thereupon told the Committee that in view of 'the danger of an invasion of the United Kingdom we could not possibly send any more troops to France, and M. Reynaud was being informed accordingly'.

Invasion was now the dominant concern of those at the centre of war policy. It was important, Churchill stressed, with the example of the German successes in France much in his mind, to find 'some means of dealing with the enemy's tanks', possibly by some form of mine. As for a German invasion across the Channel, 'short of the sea passage being made in fog', Churchill told his colleagues, the Royal Navy and the Royal Air Force 'should be able to deal with a sea-borne expedition'.[4]

That same evening, from Paris, came a further telegram of re-

---

[1] Minute of 24 May 1940: Churchill papers, 20/13.

[2] Minute of 24 May 1940: Churchill papers, 20/13.

[3] Consisting of Churchill, A. V. Alexander (First Lord of the Admiralty) Anthony Eden (Secretary of State for War), Sir Archibald Sinclair (Secretary of State for Air), Air Chief Marshal Sir Cyril Newall (Chief of the Air Staff), Admiral of the Fleet Sir Dudley Pound (First Sea Lord and Chief of Naval Staff), General Sir Edmund Ironside (Chief of the Imperial General Staff) and Major-General H. L. Ismay (War Cabinet Officer).

[4] Defence Committee No. 7 of 1940, 24 May 1940, 5 p.m.: Cabinet papers, 69/1.

crimination from Reynaud to Churchill. Far from carrying out the Weygand plan, so Reynaud alleged, the British Army had 'decided on and carried out a withdrawal of forty kilometres towards the ports, at a time when our troops, moving up from the south, are gaining ground towards the north . . .'

The British withdrawal, Reynaud added, 'has naturally compelled General Weygand to modify his arrangements', to the extent that he must, as a result, give up 'any idea' of closing the gap between the armies.[1]

Reynaud's telegram of complaint was considered at the War Cabinet during its morning meeting on May 25. Little was known of the precise military situation. 'Just as gloomy as usual,' Cadogan noted in his diary. 'Gort seems—inexplicably, rather—to have withdrawn 40 Kms! But everything is complete confusion: no communications and no one knows what's going on, except that everything's as black as black.'[2]

Commenting on Reynaud's allegation, Churchill told the War Cabinet: 'No doubt the action had been forced on Lord Gort by the position in which he had found himself.' Of course, Churchill added, Gort should have informed London of the action which he had taken, and there was no doubt that the French 'had grounds for complaint'. But this was 'no time for recriminations'. All that was necessary was to tell the French that Gort's reported withdrawal 'had now been confirmed'.

In defence of Gort, Chamberlain hoped that 'no hasty judgement' would be passed on the Commander-in-Chief's failure to keep the Government informed. There might, after all, be 'some explanation for his apparent omission to let us know what he was doing'. For his part, Ironside noted that it was almost certain that Gort's communications 'had been almost completely severed'. The War Office's only direct link was with Dunkirk. Ironside himself had sent a message to Gort 'asking him to say whether he was (i) advancing on the ports, (ii) advancing on Amiens, or (iii) fighting it out on his present position'.[3]

As yet, no reply to these questions had been received from Gort. But in his own reply to Reynaud, Churchill sought to justify Gort's action, pointing out that the British Commander-in-Chief had been forced by the pressure on his western flank, and by the need to keep Dunkirk open for essential supplies, 'to place parts of two divisions' between himself and the increasing pressure of the German armoured

---

[1] Quoted in Paul Reynaud, *In the Thick of the Fight, 1930–45*, London 1955, page 371.

[2] Cadogan diary, 25 May 1940: David Dilks (editor), *The Diaries of Sir Alexander Cadogan, 1938–1945*, London 1971, pages 289–90.

[3] War Cabinet No. 138 of 1940, 25 May 1940, 11.30 a.m.: Cabinet papers, 65/7.

forces. These forces, Churchill wrote, 'in apparently irresistible strength have successively captured Abbeville and Boulogne, are menacing Calais and Dunkirk, and have taken St Omer'. How, he went on to ask, could Gort move southwards according to the Weygand plan, and disengage his northern front, 'unless he throws out this shield on his right hand?'

Churchill added, however, that nothing in Gort's movements could be 'any excuse for the abandonment of the strong pressure of your northward move across the Somme', a move, Churchill wrote, which 'we trust will develop'.

That very morning, Churchill confided to Reynaud, Dill had called the southward move 'the sole hope of any effective extrication of our Army'. But Reynaud must understand that Britain now found its troops 'ripped from the coast by the mass of the enemy's armoured vehicles'. The southward move would continue, but in conjunction with 'such flank guard protection to the westward as is necessary'.[1]

Still unaware of Gort's specific reasoning, or plans, Churchill minuted to Ironside on May 25: 'I must know at earliest why Gort gave up Arras, and what actually he is doing with the rest of his Army.' Churchill went on to ask: 'Is he still persevering in Weygand's plan, or has he become largely stationary? If the latter, what do you consider the probable course of events in the next few days, and what course do you recommend?'

Clearly, Churchill commented, Gort 'must not allow himself to be encircled and surrender without fighting a battle'. The question was, 'should he not do this by fighting his way to the coast and destroying the armoured troops which stand between him and the sea with over-whelming force of artillery . . .' This decision, Churchill added, must be taken 'tomorrow at latest'.[2]

As soon as 'we know what has happened', Churchill telegraphed to Reynaud, 'I will report fully.' It was clear, however, 'that the Northern Army is practically surrounded and that all its communications are cut except through Dunkirk and Ostend'.[3]

It was through Dunkirk that Dill now returned to London. But before he left France he was able to report back further details of the German successes. 'Have just seen Gort,' he telegraphed to Churchill and Eden on May 25. 'There is no blinking seriousness of situation in Northern Area.' The British line on the western flank, he reported, now

[1] Telegram of 25 May 1940: Churchill papers, 20/14.
[2] Minute of 25 May 1940: Churchill papers, 4/150.
[3] Telegram of 25 May 1940: Churchill papers, 20/14.

ran from Dunkirk to St Omer to Aire to Bethune to Carvin, while on the eastern flank the Germans were said to have penetrated the eastern sector of the line held by the Belgians to the north-east of Courtrai.[1]

Dill's telegram reached London on the afternoon of May 25. In a second telegram which reached London ten minutes after the first, Dill reported that he had just seen the King of the Belgians, together with the King's Chief Military Adviser, General van Overstraeten. Both men had expressed 'great anxiety' regarding the situation on the Menin-Courtrai Front, where the German attack was being made by four infantry divisions supported by tanks. Both men, Dill warned, fearing that the Belgian line might break, had asked for help. But he had explained to them that 'no British General reserves' were available, as 'nothing must be done to weaken impending attack'.

As for the few British and Belgian troops he had seen, Dill added, they 'look fit and business-like'.[2]

Outside the Dunkirk perimeter, communications were still possible with the British troops in Calais. But the city was surrounded by considerable German forces, including armoured units diverted to Calais from Gort's southern flank. In London, the War Cabinet and the Chiefs of Staff had decided that the British troops at Calais should not be evacuated, but should continue to act as a barrier to the German advance towards Dunkirk. Reading a War Office order which mistakenly implied the imminent evacuation of Calais, Churchill minuted to Eden and Ironside: 'This is not the way to encourage men to fight to the end,' and he went on to ask: 'Are you sure there is no streak of defeatist opinion in the General Staff?'[3]

Churchill then drafted a message for the brigadier defending Calais, Brigadier Nicholson, in which he explained that the defence of the city 'is of the highest importance to our country and our Army now', tying down as it did a large part of the German armoured forces which might otherwise be attacking Gort's line of communication, and preserving a 'sally port' from which portions of the British Army 'may make their way home'. Churchill's message ended: 'The eyes of the Empire are upon the defence of Calais, and His Majesty's Government are confident you and your gallant Regiment will perform an exploit worthy of the British name.'[4]

[1] Telegram despatched at 8.10 a.m., received at 2.15 p.m., 25 May 1940: Premier papers, 3/188/3, folio 15.

[2] Telegram received at 2.25 p.m., 25 May 1940: Premier papers, 3/188/3, folio 17.

[3] Minute of 25 May 1940: Churchill papers, 4/150.

[4] Message of 25 May 1940: Churchill papers, 4/150. This message was sent to Nicholson shortly after midday.

As message after message arrived from France and Belgium, a confused picture emerged which Churchill sought to clarify in his own mind by frequent visits to his Map Room at the Admiralty. But even this source of carefully collated information was strongly challenged on May 25, by Desmond Morton. 'I strongly recommend you,' wrote Morton, 'to pay at least one visit a day to the Map Room in the Cabinet War Room. The most up to date information about the fighting in France is shown on this map, compared to which the one in the Upper War Room in the Admiralty is in my opinion definitely misleading.'[1]

The most vigilant man, and that Churchill certainly was, still lay at the mercy of inaccurate 'facts' and out-of-date information.

That night Churchill dined with Beaverbrook, Lindemann and Bracken, three friends with whom he could share his innermost fears and hopes. Unknown as yet in London, Gort had been continuing his preparations for a southward thrust, according to the Weygand plan, and intended to begin it on the following day. In preparation for this, Gort had set aside two British Divisions to join with three of Blanchard's French Divisions. But throughout May 25 Gort had also been weighing up the cruel facts, as known to him, but not yet known in London: the continuing lack of communication or direction from his French Allies; the flight of Blanchard's Moroccan troops from the battlefield at Carvin, only eleven miles south of Gort's own headquarters; the gap created by French troops retreating northwards to the Scheldt rather than southwards to link up with his own lines; the destruction of the tank force of the 50th (Motor) Division, whereby of Major-General Martel's sixteen Mark II tanks on May 21, only two were left by May 25, with his sixty more lightly armed Mark I tanks reduced by May 25 to fifteen;[2] and the news, reported to him that afternoon by a senior British officer, that 'the Belgians had no fighting spirit left'.[3]

It was this Belgian news that proved decisive, for it was at the point where the Belgian and British forces linked, between Ypres and Menin, that the German armoured thrust was at its most severe. Here, at

---

[1] Minute of 25 May 1940: Premier papers, 7/2.

[2] The Mark II was armed with a 2-pounder gun; the Mark I with nothing more than a machine-gun.

[3] J. R. Colville, *Man of Valour*, London 1972, page 217. The officer, who had just reached Gort's headquarters from the Belgian lines, was the Colonel of the 12th Lancers, Lieutenant-Colonel Herbert Lumsden. For his action on Montgomery's Staff during the subsequent retreat to Dunkirk he was awarded the DSO. In the First World War he had received the Military Cross. Commanded X Corps at Alamein.

the very point where the Belgians were withdrawing, the Germans had ordered a full scale attack. Their orders had, by chance, fallen into British hands. Reading them, it became clear that afternoon that two German Corps were about to attack a single British Corps.

As the Intelligence Branch at General Headquarters, near Armentières, studied the captured orders, the exact German plan of attack became clear. One Corps was to strike at Ypres, another at Wytschaete. 'We had at that time,' General Brooke later wrote, 'nothing on the Ypres-Comines Canal except one brigade I had obtained from GHQ the previous day. I knew for certain that the Belgians would offer no resistance, consequently a German thrust through Ypres, unless stopped, must inevitably cut off the BEF from the sea.'[1]

Once these facts had been presented to him, Gort had no alternative but to abandon his part of the Weygand plan. At 6.30 that evening he made his decision, cancelling the British southward offensive planned for the following day, and ordering the two divisions earmarked for that attack, the 5th and 50th, to move northwards into the gap between the British and Belgian forces. Thus alone could the British Expeditionary Force avoid encirclement, and the road to Dunkirk be kept open.

Three hours later, at the very moment when Churchill and his friends were dining at Admiralty House unaware of these developments, the news of Gort's decision reached General Blanchard. The Weygand plan was dead. 'Thus at Britain's gravest hour,' writes Gort's biographer, 'it fell to Gort, deprived of all instructions from higher authority, outnumbered and outgunned but not outwitted, to take a prompt and solitary decision which thwarted von Bock and saved the whole British Expeditionary Force from death or captivity.'[2]

At ten o'clock that evening of May 25, at the very moment when Blanchard was learning of Gort's decision to go north, not south, the Defence Committee met in London at Admiralty House.[3] There was no news from Gort, and no knowledge of his decision three hours earlier

[1] 'Operations of II Corps during the Retreat from Louvain to Dunkirk', enclosed with a letter to Churchill from Field Marshal Viscount Alanbrooke, OM, GCB, DSO, 31 October 1946: Churchill papers, 4/196.

[2] J. R. Colville, *Man of Valour*, London 1972, page 217. The official historian earlier wrote of Gort's decision to move the 5th and 50th Divisions to the Ypres-Menin gap: 'By doing so he saved the British Expeditionary Force' (Major L. F. Ellis, *The War In France and Flanders 1939–1940*, London 1953, page 149).

[3] Those present were: Churchill (in the Chair), A. V. Alexander, Anthony Eden, Sir Archibald Sinclair, Admiral of the Fleet Sir Dudley Pound, General Sir Edmund Ironside, Vice-Admiral T. S. V. Phillips, General Sir John Dill and Lieutenant-General Sir Henry Karslake.

not to attack southward on the following day. But Sir Henry Karslake, who had just returned from General Georges' headquarters, told the meeting that even Weygand's side of the plan did not seem to be operative, for he had received 'a very gloomy picture of the chances of any effective attack being launched from south of the Somme in the next few days'. This was a sure indication that the southern thrust of the Weygand plan was still not in prospect.

Karslake also reported that at the very moment when Weygand had informed the British that French troops had recaptured Amiens, Albert and Péronne, they had in fact done no more 'than send a small force forward to the southern outskirts of Amiens'.

Churchill, although ignorant of Gort's decision to abandon the Weygand plan, now spoke critically of the plan itself. 'It was clear,' he told his colleagues, basing himself on a letter he had just received from Spears, 'that there was no chance of General Weygand striking north in sufficient strength to disengage the Blanchard group in the north.'

Even Weygand, it now appeared, was no longer a supporter of his much-pressed plan, believing, as Spears had reported 'that attacks to the south by the group of armies in the north, including the British Army, could serve no other purpose than to gain breathing space before falling back to a line covering the harbours'.

The Defence Committee then asked Dill, who, like Karslake, had just returned from France, to report on the situation in the north. Dill, likewise knowing nothing of Gort's decision to abandon the attack southward, did know, however, of the diversion of one of the two British divisions, the 5th, to the region of Ypres, and stressed that when Gort had found that the Germans were round his right flank, 'he had had no option but to withdraw his forces in this area'.

Dill still believed that another division could be found, possibly from the fortified line to the east of Lille, to replace the 5th, and reactivate the Weygand plan. But he went on to warn the Defence Committee that if a British drive to the south was tried and failed, Gort would not then have sufficient strength to try the other course open to him, 'namely to cut his way north to the coast'.

Churchill had now to give his opinion on the basis of what Karslake and Dill had reported. He did so without hesitation, putting the points, as the minutes describe it, 'in favour of an advance north to the ports and the beaches'.

Thus, within four hours of each other, first Gort in France and then Churchill in London had come to the same conclusion, but with each unaware of the other's decision. In London, the Defence Committee concluded that, having regard 'to the practical certainty that no effective French offensive is likely to be launched from south of the Somme for some considerable time', an immediate march to the coast 'was the right course'.

Churchill then set out the action that must be taken at once in order to implement this decision: Gort to march 'north to the coast, in battle order, under strong rearguards, striking at all forces between himself and the sea'; the Navy to prepare 'all possible means for re-embarkation, not only at the ports but on the beaches'; the Air Force to 'dominate the air' above the area involved; a warning telegram to be sent to Gort to draw up a scheme to begin the march to the sea on the night of May 26; and six divisions of troops now in Britain to be 'brought to full strength' and provided with equipment.

There seemed no future success in prospect, not only for the British Expeditionary Force, but for the French armies north and south. From Karslake, the Defence Committee learned that Brigadier Swayne, at French General Headquarters, had reported 'that the French were very down-hearted and did not mean to stay in the war'. Churchill accepted this assessment. He would not be 'at all surprised', he told the Defence Committee that night, if the Germans made a peace offer to the French, given France's weak position, and the likelihood of an Italian attack. But if France went out of the war, he said, she must make it a condition of any agreement with Germany 'that our Army was allowed to leave France intact, and to take away its munitions, and that the soil of France was not used for an attack on England'.

All this supposed that France could secure an armistice with freely negotiated terms, and without a German occupation. If this were possible, Churchill said, France must also make it a condition that she should 'retain her Fleet'. If the Germans made France an offer on these terms, so the minutes of the Defence Committee recorded, 'he (the Prime Minister) would accept it'. In such circumstances, Churchill added, 'he thought that we could hold out in this country once we had got our Army back from France'.[1]

The decision to evacuate the British Expeditionary Force from France forced Churchill and his advisers to turn to new problems: the examination of the myriad questions of evacuation. Among Churchill's staff as he worked on these questions on the night of May 25 was his new Private Secretary, John Martin. 'There are three of us,' Martin wrote home, 'working in the room next to the Cabinet Room—Seal,

[1] Defence Committee No. 9 of 1940, 25 May 1940, 10 p.m.: Cabinet papers, 69/1.

Bevir and myself, while there are two younger secretaries[1] in another room and also Miss Watson,[2] so we are quite a crowd; but with the stream of phone calls and alarms and excursions everyone is needed, particularly while the PM alternates between Admiralty House (where he still lives) and No. 10.'[3]

Churchill's Private Office worked round the clock to assemble the incoming papers and telegrams, to prepare the minutes for despatch, to answer letters and queries, and to ensure that his instructions were circulated and followed up. It was an arduous task: John Martin's first day 'began at ¼ to 10 in the morning', he wrote home, 'and ended at the Admiralty, where I was lucky to find a taxi, at 3.15 a.m. on the following morning'.[4]

That night Churchill had to consider a proposal by Sir Robert Vansittart inviting French cooperation 'in the Home Defence of this Island by the despatch to England of a division of French troops'.[5] That same night he was asked by Desmond Morton about experiments into Butane gas as a filling for bombs. 'Pursue incessantly on my full authority,' he minuted, with an added note that Lindemann should be shown the file.[6] And on a proposal to remove all wireless sets in private cars, Churchill minuted on the following day: 'Let action be taken at once: report what is being done tomorrow.'[7]

Churchill also learnt on May 25 of the decision of the Canadian Government to send its No. 112 Army Co-operation Squadron for service overseas. This squadron consisted of twelve Lysander aircraft, 'the only Lysander aircraft available', as the Canadian Prime Minister explained. Canada would also send No. 1 Fighter Squadron, 'together with all the available Hurricane fighters, fourteen in number', to the United Kingdom. At the same time, the Canadians pledged that the whole of the output of Hurricane fighters from the Fort William factory 'should be directed to the Royal Air Force. . . .'[8]

At the Dominions Office it was felt that a personal message of thanks should be sent to the Canadians. This message was drafted by Norman Archer, the Private Secretary to the Secretary of State for the Dom-

[1] John Peck and John Colville.
[2] Edith Watson, who had served at 10 Downing Street under every Prime Minister since Lloyd George.
[3] John Martin, letter of 25 May 1940: Martin papers.
[4] John Martin, letter of 25 May 1940 (referring to the previous day): Martin papers.
[5] Minute of 25 May 1940: Premier papers, 7/2.
[6] Minute of 26 May 1940: Premier papers, 7/2.
[7] Minute of 26 May 1940: Premier papers, 7/2.
[8] Vincent Massey (Canadian High Commissioner) to Dominions Office, telegram sent on 24 May 1940: Premier papers, 4/44/4, folio 158.

inions, and was approved by Churchill without alteration. The proofs of Canada's readiness 'to stand with us at all costs against our determined and ruthless enemy', the message read, 'are a source of the greatest encouragement'.[1]

Late that night Ironside, Dill and Ismay were among those with whom Churchill discussed the implications of the impending disaster in France. For some weeks there had been what Churchill described as 'a very strong feeling' in the War Cabinet and high military circles for Dill to succeed Ironside as Chief of the Imperial General Staff. At the same time, a Commander-in-Chief was needed to take on the massive responsibilities which a German invasion of Britain would entail.

As the discussion proceeded, Ironside volunteered the proposal that he should 'cease to be CIGS' and offered to command the British Home Forces instead. 'Considering the unpromising task that such a command was at the time thought to involve', Churchill later wrote, 'this was a spirited and selfless offer'. Indeed, Churchill added, the 'high dignities and honours' which were later conferred on Ironside 'arose from my appreciation of his bearing at this moment in our affairs'.[2]

The news of Dill's elevation made an immediate impact. 'Fortunately Ironside is gone,' noted Colville on the following day, 'and Dill who inspires great confidence is to take his place.'[3]

---

[1] Churchill to Massey, telegram dated 25 May 1940: Premier papers, 4/44/4, folio 157.

[2] Winston S. Churchill, *The Second World War*, volume 2, page 65. The principal honours and dignities subsequently granted to Ironside were: Field-Marshal (1940) and Baron (1941).

[3] Colville diary, 27 May 1940: Colville papers.

21

Dunkirk

A S dawn broke on May 26, the news from France dominated Churchill's thoughts, and those of his advisers and staff. The road to Dunkirk was open. The race to the sea was about to begin. There was a 'good chance', Churchill told the War Cabinet at nine o'clock that morning, 'of getting off a considerable proportion of the British Expeditionary Force'. Yet the future of the war was bleak; Halifax went so far as to tell his colleagues that 'it was not so much now a question of imposing a complete defeat upon Germany, but of safeguarding the independence of our own Empire . . .'. In this context, Halifax added, the Italian Ambassador in London, Signor Bastianini, had asked for an interview in order to put forward 'fresh proposals' for a peace conference.

Peace and security, Churchill commented, might indeed be achieved 'under a German domination of Europe'. That was an outcome, however, that, as he told the War Cabinet, 'we could never accept'. He was opposed, he said, to any negotiations 'which might lead to a derogation of our rights and power'.[1]

Churchill lunched that day with Reynaud, who had just flown to London from France, bringing with him, as Eden later recalled, 'disturbing accounts of Marshal Pétain's already burgeoning defeatism'. According to Eden, Reynaud went so far as to warn that if Germany were to occupy a large part of France, 'Pétain would be likely to come out in favour of an armistice'.[2]

During their lunchtime discussion, Reynaud told Churchill that the French had placed fifty divisions between the Maginot Line and the sea. But against these divisions, he added, the Germans could put three times that number. From this it was clear, Reynaud said, 'that the war

[1] War Cabinet No. 139 of 1940, 26 May 1940, 9 a.m., Confidential Annex: Cabinet papers, 65/13.
[2] The Earl of Avon, *The Eden Memoirs, The Reckoning*, London 1965, page 111.

could not be won on land'. But Churchill argued that as soon as the situation in North-eastern France had been 'cleared up', the Germans would make no further attacks on the French line south of the Somme, but would 'immediately start attacking' Britain itself.

Reynaud disagreed. The 'dream of all Germans', he told Churchill, 'was to conquer Paris'. After reaching the Channel ports, the Germans would turn southward and march on Paris. Whatever happened, Churchill replied, 'we were not prepared to give in. We would rather go down fighting than be enslaved to Germany.'

Churchill went on to urge on Reynaud that 'if only' the Allies could 'stick things out for another three months', the position would be 'entirely different'. But Reynaud reiterated that, although Weygand himself was prepared to fight on, he 'could hold out no hope that France had sufficient power of resistance'.

At two o'clock that afternoon, Churchill gave the War Cabinet an account of his discussion with Reynaud. He added that it was necessary, in his view, to 'persuade' Reynaud that Weygand 'should be instructed to issue' an order for the British Expeditionary Force to march to the coast. Only by such an order, Churchill felt, could Britain make sure 'that the French had no complaint against us on the score that, by cutting our way to the coast, we were letting them down militarily'. It was important, he added, that such an order should be issued 'as soon as possible'.[1]

The War Cabinet agreed, and in a second talk with Reynaud, Churchill explained the War Cabinet's concurrence in the previous day's decision to authorize Gort to abandon the Weygand plan. For his part, Reynaud agreed to send a telegram to Weygand, asking that General Blanchard be given formal authority at once 'to order a withdrawal towards the ports'.[2] That same afternoon, Eden telegraphed to Gort: 'You are now authorized to operate towards coast forthwith, in conjunction with French and Belgian armies.'[3]

The message to Weygand having been despatched, Reynaud returned to France. At the Admiralty, an informal meeting of Ministers listened to Churchill's assessment of the situation.[4] 'In the first place,' he told them, 'we still had powers of resistance and attack, which they had not. In the second place, they would be likely to be offered decent

[1] War Cabinet No. 140 of 1940, 26 May 1940, 2 p.m., Confidential Annex: Cabinet papers, 65/13.
[2] Report of a conversation, 26 May 1940: Cabinet papers, 65/13, folio 154.
[3] Telegram of 26 May 1940: quoted in Major L. F. Ellis, *The War in France and Flanders, 1939–1940*, London 1953, page 174.
[4] Those present included Halifax, Chamberlain, Greenwood and Attlee.

terms by Germany, which we should not.' There was 'no limit', he
believed, to the terms which Germany would impose on Britain 'if she
had her way'.

Churchill still hoped that France might be able to secure the sort of
peace terms with Germany which would stop short of occupation.
'From our point of view,' he explained, 'he would rather France was
out of the war before she was broken up, and retained the position of a
strong neutral whose factories could not be used against us.'

Later in the discussion, Churchill doubted whether Germany was
likely to try to subject France to the Gestapo. But Halifax replied 'that
he was not so sure'.

As the discussion continued, Halifax raised again the question of
peace negotiations under Italian supervision. But Churchill argued that
the suggested approach to Mussolini 'implied that if we were prepared
to give Germany back her colonies and make certain concessions in the
Mediterranean, it was possible to get out of our present difficulties'.[1]
Churchill's view was 'that no such option was open to us'. The terms
offered would, he pointed out, 'certainly prevent us from completing
our rearmament'.

The discussion had been proceeding for about half an hour when Sir
Alexander Cadogan arrived from the Foreign Office. Churchill, he
noted in his diary, was 'too rambling and romantic and sentimental
and temperamental'.[2]

As the meeting drew to a close, Churchill remarked 'that Herr Hitler
thought he had the whip hand'. The only thing to do was to show him
'that he could not conquer this country'. If, as Reynaud's remarks had
suggested, France could not continue with the war, 'we must part
company'. But at the same time, as the minutes recorded, 'he did not
raise objection to some approach being made to Signor Mussolini'. If
Mussolini were to offer terms for a general settlement 'which did not
postulate the destruction of our independence', Halifax added, 'we
should be foolish if we did not accept them'.

In the final phase of the Ministers' discussion, Churchill was called
out of the room to speak on the telephone to Sir Roger Keyes, who
reported the encouraging news that the Belgians 'were determined to
act as the left flank to assist our re-embarkation'. He also reported that

---

[1] During the discussion, Arthur Greenwood (Minister without Portfolio) suggested that Mussolini would want Malta, Gibraltar and Suez as part of the peace conference. Chamberlain
believed that he would want Kenya, Somaliland or Uganda.

[2] Cadogan diary, 26 May 1940: David Dilks (editor), *The Diaries of Sir Alexander Cadogan, OM,
1938–1945*, London 1971, page 290.

he had been at Gort's headquarters when the orders to march to the coast had arrived. These orders, he said, 'had been received with acclamation at GHQ, where it was held that the march to the south held out no prospect of success'.[1]

At six o'clock, after more than four hours, this meeting of Ministers came to an end. An hour later a signal was sent from the Admiralty to the Flag Officer commanding Dover, Vice-Admiral Bertram Ramsay. The signal consisted of five words: 'Operation Dynamo is to commence.'[2] 'Dynamo' was the code name for the evacuation by sea of as many soldiers as could be taken off the quaysides, jetties and beaches of Dunkirk.

That night Churchill dined at Admiralty House with Eden, Ironside and Ismay. The decision that had now to be made was the future of the garrison besieged inside Calais. For three days, destroyers had been held in readiness to attempt a rescue. But, as Gort proceeded to turn his force towards Dunkirk, it seemed essential to put all Britain's military, air and naval strength into the single, perhaps impossible, task of holding Dunkirk, and to maintain for as long as possible the flanks of the land corridor leading to Dunkirk. This was, as Ismay later wrote, a 'grim decision', for it involved abandoning the garrison at Calais to its fate. Eden's own regiment, with which he had fought in the First World War, was among the forces inside the Calais perimeter.

With a sense almost of despair, Churchill approved the telegram to Brigadier Nicholson. This telegram, which was finally sent from the War Office shortly before midnight, informed the Brigadier that every hour his troops continued to exist was of the 'greatest help' to the British Expeditionary Force. The telegram ended: 'Government has therefore decided that you must continue to fight. Have greatest admiration for your splendid stand.'[3]

'The decision affected us all very deeply,' Ismay later recalled, 'especially perhaps Churchill. He was unusually silent during dinner that evening, and he ate and drank with evident distaste.'[4]

---

[1] There is a substantial report of the discussion at the meeting of Ministers at 2 p.m. on 26 May 1940 in the Conclusions of War Cabinet No. 140 of 1940, Confidential Annex: Cabinet papers, 65/13, folios 146–153.

[2] Signal sent at 7 p.m., 26 May 1940: quoted in Major L. F. Ellis, *The War in France and Flanders, 1939–1940*, London 1953, page 182.

[3] Telegram of 26 May 1940: quoted in Major L. F. Ellis, *The War in France and Flanders 1939–1940*, London 1953, page 167. In Churchill's war memoirs published three years before the official history, an added sentence appears in this telegram and reads: 'Evacuation will not (*repeat* not) take place, and craft required for above purpose are to return to Dover.' (Winston S. Churchill, *The Second World War*, volume 2, London 1949, page 73.)

[4] *The Memoirs of General the Lord Ismay*, London 1960, page 131.

As they rose from the table, Churchill later recalled, he told Eden, Ironside and Ismay that he felt 'physically sick'.[1] Ismay later commented: 'He has quoted these words in his memoirs, but he does not mention how sad he looked as he uttered them.'[2]

At times of stress, Churchill often recalled some particular quotation which expressed his feelings. On May 26 he asked John Martin to look out for him a passage in George Borrow's prayer for England at Gibraltar. Martin gave Churchill the quotation on the following day, and, as he later recalled: 'it matched his mood'.[3] The quotation read: 'Fear not the result, for either shall thy end be a majestic and an enviable one, or God shall perpetuate thy reign upon the waters.'[4]

As the British Expeditionary Force moved back towards Dunkirk, the focus of attention and of danger was on the northern flank, where two British divisions were moving on parallel lines behind the front, northward from Arras to Dunkirk. The divisions moved through some of the battlefields of the First World War, scenes of four years of courage and slaughter: through Armentières, over the Wytschaete Ridge, and west of Ypres.

At one moment General Brooke, while travelling to inspect various II Corps positions along this line of retreat, narrowly escaped capture; the battle, he later wrote, 'was raging and fluctuating unpleasantly'. At the same time, the roads essential to a speedy British withdrawal were 'badly congested with civilians and portions of the French Army'. Yet the moves had to be made wherever possible at night; otherwise, Brooke wrote, the British troops 'would be fully exposed to German air attacks at low altitude, as we had no fighters and little AA artillery'.[5]

With such dangers, no sector of the front could be allowed to collapse. Between Lille and Ypres the front was held by British forces; but north-east of Ypres it was upon the Belgian Army that the eastern flank of the Dunkirk perimeter depended.

On the evening of May 26 Belgian forces still held Roulers, and a substantial protective bulge stretching to the east of Bruges. But, that same night, fears of a Belgian surrender suddenly gripped the British leaders, as, in London, the Counsellor of the Belgian Embassy went to

---

[1] Winston S. Churchill, *The Second World War*, volume 2, London 1949, page 73.

[2] *The Memoirs of General the Lord Ismay*, London 1960, page 131.

[3] Sir John Martin, letter to the author, 24 October 1982.

[4] From *The Bible in Spain*, by George Borrow (1803–1881).

[5] 'Operations of II Corps during the Retreat from Louvain to Dunkirk', enclosed with a letter to Churchill from Field Marshal Viscount Alanbrooke, OM, GCB, DSO, 31 October 1946: Churchill papers, 4/196.

the Foreign Office to say that the King of the Belgians appeared to consider 'that the war was lost' and that he 'was contemplating a separate peace with Germany'.[1]

As soon as he learned of the possibility of a Belgian surrender, Churchill asked Sir Roger Keyes to press upon the King of the Belgians the importance of remaining at war, and in particular of ensuring Belgian support for the Dunkirk evacuation. 'Certainly we cannot serve Belgium's cause,' Churchill's message read, 'by being hemmed in and starved out.' The only hope was victory, and Britain would 'never quit the war whatever happens till Hitler is beat or we cease to be a State'.

Churchill went on to advise the King to leave Belgium by aeroplane for Britain 'before too late'. Should the Dunkirk operation succeed in establishing an 'effective bridgehead' for evacuation, he added, 'we would try, if desired, to carry some Belgian divisions to France by sea'. Above all, Churchill stressed, it was 'vitally important' for Belgium to continue in the war.[2]

From the moment of the decision to evacuate the British Expeditionary Force, Churchill had been forced to contemplate a situation in which France would be 'unable to continue the war' and would become neutral. With the German forces still holding 'their present position', the Belgian Army would likewise be forced to capitulate, but only, as Churchill minuted to Ismay, 'after assisting the British Expeditionary Force to reach the coast'. At that point, Britain would be alone; and on the morning of May 27 Churchill asked the Chiefs of Staff Committee, and the Vice-Chiefs of Staff, to examine, and to report 'what are the prospects of our continuing the war alone against Germany and probably Italy'.

As Churchill saw it, once France and Belgium were out of the war, Germany would offer peace terms to Britain 'which would place her entirely at the mercy of Germany through disarmament, cession of naval bases in the Orkneys etc'. If these terms were offered, Britain would have to decide whether it was possible to carry on fighting. 'Can the Navy and Air Force hold out reasonable hopes,' Churchill wanted to know, 'of preventing serious invasion, and could the forces gathered in this Island cope with raids from the air involving detachments not greater than 10,000 men.' One factor to be considered in this, Churchill believed, was that a prolongation of British resistance 'might be very

[1] Report of Lord Halifax to the War Cabinet on the morning of 27 May 1940: Cabinet papers, 65/7, folio 172A.
[2] Telegram of 26 May 1940: Churchill papers, 20/14.

dangerous' for a Germany that was already 'holding down the greater part of Europe'.[1]

The Chiefs of Staff and the Vice-Chiefs studied Churchill's question during the morning of May 27. Their answer was set out in eleven terse and conclusive paragraphs. For as long as the British Air Force was 'in being', they wrote, the Navy and Air Force together 'should be able to prevent Germany carrying out a serious sea-borne invasion of this country'. If Germany obtained air superiority, the Navy could hold up an invasion 'for a time', but not, however, 'for an indefinite period'.

Once such an invasion began, Churchill was told, the coast and beach defences 'could not prevent German tanks and infantry getting a firm footing on our shores'. Thereafter, Britain's land defences would be 'insufficient' to deal with a serious invasion. The 'crux of the matter' was air superiority. Once Germany attained that, 'she might attempt to subjugate this country by air attack alone'. But air superiority would require the destruction both of the Royal Air Force and the aircraft industries, 'some vital portions of which are concentrated at Coventry and Birmingham'. Success in this would depend 'not only on the material damage by bombs' but on the 'moral effect' of the bombing on the aircraft factory workers 'and their determination to carry on in the face of wholesale havoc and destruction'.

If the Germans were to press home night attacks on the aircraft industry, they were 'likely to achieve such material and moral damage' in the industrial area as to 'bring all work to a standstill'. Their superiority in the air was 'four to one', and their own aircraft factories 'well dispersed and relatively inaccessible'. Some counter bombing could be carried out, however, and, by a similar 'moral and material effect', bring at least a proportion of the German aircraft factories to a 'standstill'.

The Chiefs of Staff and the Vice-Chiefs concluded that '*prima facie* Germany has most of the cards'. But they went on to advise Churchill: 'the real test is whether the morale of our fighting personnel and civil population will counter-balance the numerical and material advantages which Germany enjoys. We believe it will.'[2]

The War Cabinet discussed this report at its morning meeting on May 27, when Churchill expressed his doubts as to whether the German air superiority really was as high as 4 to 1. The more likely ratio, he said, was that suggested by the respective aircraft production figures during the past three years, of 25,000 German aircraft to 15,000 British, or a ratio of 5 to 3. 'Our whole policy,' he warned, 'might depend on

[1] Minute of 27 May 1940: Churchill papers, 20/13.
[2] Chiefs of Staff Paper No. 168 of 1940, 27 May 1940: Cabinet papers, 80/11.

our assessment of the German air strength.' It was therefore essential that all estimates 'should be subjected to the most detailed scrutiny'.

The Vice-Chief of the Air Staff, Air Marshal Richard Peirse, now produced new figures which had been prepared by his experts 'to arrive at a true basis of comparison'. Studying these, Churchill pointed out to the War Cabinet that it now appeared 'that the odds against us were only 2½ to 1'. If the British airmen were shooting down German planes at a ratio of 3 to 1, 'the balance was on our side'. But this, as Newall pointed out, was only by day. At night the balance 'would be very much less favourable to us'.

After a long discussion the War Cabinet accepted the Chiefs of Staff report: British morale would be the decisive factor. Many emergency measures were now proposed to supplement and enhance morale, including further pressure on the United States for 'active financial and economic assistance', and the immediate release of American destroyers, motor torpedo boats and aircraft. Steps were to be taken at once to prevent Fifth Column activities. The Eire Government must be asked for the use of the port of Berehaven by the Royal Navy. Defence measures must be strengthened in all aircraft and munitions factories. Experiments must be pressed forward for the production of smoke screens to cover industrial areas.[1]

Churchill had already written to Ismay on May 26 about the danger of German parachute attacks on aircraft factories and aerodromes. 'Not nearly enough is being done,' he stated. 'Get in touch w Lord Beaverbrook & then speak to me.'[2] Action was swift; two days later Ismay was able to report back to Churchill that Admiral Evans, then London Regional Commissioner for Civil Defence, was to be put in charge of this essential task.[3]

Among those putting forward suggestions for home defence was Desmond Morton, who proposed on May 27 'a curfew for aliens'. But Churchill was chary of rash action, minuting to Morton: 'Discrimination is needed.'[4] Morton also proposed making all possible German landing grounds in Norfolk 'unserviceable'.[5]

---

[1] War Cabinet No. 141 of 1940, 27 May 1940, 11 a.m., Minute 9, Confidential Annex: Cabinet papers, 65/13, folios 165–73.

[2] Minute of 26 May 1940: Premier papers, 3/93/1, folio 22.

[3] Minute of 28 May 1940: Premier papers, 3/93/1, folio 21. In 1913 Evans had commanded the British Antarctic expedition after the death of Captain Scott. In 1917, while commanding HMS *Broke*, his ship, together with HMS *Swift*, had defeated six German destroyers. He retired from the Navy in 1939, after four years as Commander-in-Chief, the Nore.

[4] Minute of 27 May 1940: Premier papers, 7/2.

[5] Minute of 27 May 1940: Premier papers, 7/2.

Morton reported later that same day, informing Churchill that he had spoken on the telephone to the Director of Air Intelligence, Air-Commodore Boyle, who told him that the Local Authorities in Norfolk had already begun 'ploughing up certain parts of the land and scattering suitable obstacles over other parts'. Boyle was satisfied, Morton added, 'that the steps taken are adequate'.[1]

One encouraging telegram which reached Churchill on the morning of May 27 was from the Australian Prime Minister, Robert Menzies, who wanted to know 'what use' the British Government wanted to make of Australian troops 'both trained and in training'. It should be assumed, Menzies added, that the Australian Government 'will pledge the whole of their resources to victory'.[2] Reading this message, Churchill noted on the bottom: 'Reply: It will be a splendid episode in the history of the Empire if Australian, New Zealand & Canadian troops defend the Motherland against invasion.'

Numerous urgent problems now pressed upon Churchill, his Ministers, and his military advisers. All those at the centre accepted the responsibilities of their respective offices. But all looked also to Churchill for guidance and inspiration. The news from hour to hour added to the pressure, continually opening up new matters for immediate decision.

At that very morning's War Cabinet on May 27, a message from Lord Lothian, the British Ambassador in Washington, proposed leasing British landing grounds at Trinidad, Newfoundland and Bermuda to the Government of the United States, in order to 'add to our security'. But Churchill was opposed to any such offer, except as part of a deal whereby Britain would receive something tangible in return. The United States had 'given us practically no help in the war', he told the War Cabinet, 'and now they saw how great was the danger, their attitude was that they wanted to keep everything that would help us for their own defence'.[3]

During this same War Cabinet, Neville Chamberlain reported a conversation the previous evening with the Australian High Commissioner, Stanley Bruce, who, in contrast to Menzies, had taken 'a most gloomy view' of Britain's prospects if France were defeated, and had urged the mediation of Roosevelt and Mussolini. Chamberlain suggested that he should see Bruce again, and tell him that, even if France went out of the war, 'there was no prospect of our giving in'. It would be as well,

[1] Minute of 27 May 1940: Premier papers, 3/222/5, folio 20.
[2] Telegram No. 171, received at 3.16 a.m. on 27 May 1940: Premier papers, 4/43B/1, folio 334.
[3] War Cabinet No. 141 of 1940, 27 May 1940, 11.30 a.m.: Cabinet papers, 65/7.

Churchill added, to issue 'a general injunction to Ministers to use confident language'. He was convinced, he told the War Cabinet, 'that the bulk of the people of this country would refuse to accept the possibility of defeat'.[1]

Earlier in this same morning's Cabinet, the new Chief of the Imperial General Staff, Sir John Dill, reported that the British troops in Calais were 'still holding out with great gallantry'.[2] Calais was also in Churchill's mind when, in a telegram to Gort, he suggested that the German tanks attacking Calais were probably both tired and busy in their task, so that a British tank column 'directed on Calais' by Gort 'might have a good chance'. Perhaps, Churchill added, the German tanks 'will be less formidable when attacked themselves'.

The purpose of Churchill's message was to send his good wishes at 'this solemn moment', and to tell Gort that the British Government was asking the Belgians 'to sacrifice themselves for us'. Churchill added: 'Presume troops know they are cutting their way home to Blighty. Never was there such a spur for fighting. We shall give you all that the Navy and Air Force can do.'[3]

When the War Cabinet met again at 4.30 that afternoon the discussion was dominated by Halifax's support for an Anglo-French approach to Italy, with a view to persuading Mussolini to act as a mediator, at least for a 'general discussion'. Among those opposed to any such approach was Sir Archibald Sinclair, who warned that 'any weakness on our part' would encourage the Germans and Italians, and would 'tend to undermine morale both in this country and in the Dominions'. Clement Attlee believed that any such approach 'would be very damaging to us', as it would inevitably lead 'to our asking Signor Mussolini to intercede to obtain peace-terms for us'. Neville Chamberlain also opposed Halifax's suggestion; to go any further with such approaches, he said, would be 'heading for disaster'.

Churchill spoke with similar force against any such mediation plan. He was, he said, 'increasingly oppressed with the futility of the suggested approach to Signor Mussolini'. Such an approach would 'ruin the integrity of our fighting position in this country'. Anyway, he added, 'let us not be dragged down with France'. If the French were not prepared to go on with the struggle, 'let them give up', although

[1] War Cabinet No. 141 of 1940, 27 May 1940, 11.30 a.m., Confidential Annex: Cabinet papers, 65/13, folio 163.
[2] War Cabinet No. 141 of 1940, 27 May 1940, 11.30 a.m., Confidential Annex: Cabinet papers, 65/13, folio 161.
[3] Telegram of 27 May 1940: Churchill papers, 20/14.

he personally doubted whether they would do so. If Britain were beaten, France would became 'a vassal State'. But if Britain won, 'we might save them'. The best help that Britain could give Reynaud, Churchill argued, was to let him feel that, whatever happened to France, 'we were going to fight it out to the end'.

Churchill then spoke with considerable emotion. 'At the moment,' he said, 'our prestige in Europe was very low. The only way we could get it back was by showing the world that Germany had not beaten us. If, after two or three months, we could show that we were still unbeaten, our prestige would return. Even if we were beaten, we should be no worse off than we should be if we were now to abandon the struggle. Let us therefore avoid being dragged down the slippery slope with France.'

Chamberlain now seemed to change his mind, and to speak somewhat in favour of Halifax's suggestion. Although, he said, the proposed approach to Mussolini 'would not serve any useful purpose', he thought that 'we ought to go a little further with it, in order to keep the French in a good temper'. Halifax went further. If it were possible to 'obtain a settlement' which did not come up against 'fundamental conditions which were essential to us', he, 'for his part, doubted if he would be able to accept the view now put forward by the Prime Minister'. Provided Britain's 'independence' were not at stake, Halifax said, he would 'think it right', rather than to take the risk of two to three months of air attack, 'to accept an offer which would save the country from avoidable disaster'.

Churchill now sought to draw a distinction between a British offer to negotiate, which would betoken weakness, and circumstances in which some sort of negotiations might prove inevitable. 'If Herr Hitler was prepared,' he said, 'to make peace on the terms of the restoration of the German colonies and the overlordship of Central Europe, that was one thing. But it was quite unlikely that he would make any such offer.'

Would Churchill be prepared, Halifax asked, to discuss terms offered to France and England by Hitler—'anxious to end the war through knowledge of his own internal weakness'—to which Churchill replied that 'he would not join France in asking for terms: but if he were told what the terms offered were, he would be prepared to consider them'.

If, however, as Chamberlain suggested might happen, Hitler's tactics were to make a 'definite offer' to France, and then, when the French said they had allies, reply: 'I am here, let them send a delegate to Paris,' the War Cabinet thought, as its minutes recorded, 'that the answer to such an offer could only be "No".'

At the end of the War Cabinet there was some discussion on the attitude of President Roosevelt, who seemed, the minutes noted, 'to be taking the view that it would be very nice of him to pick up the bits of the British Empire if this country was overrun'. It was important, declared Sinclair, 'to get it realised in the United States that we meant to fight on'.[1]

Although the War Cabinet ended on this note of unanimity, the earlier discussion of peace terms, the French proposals, and Mussolini's mediation had led to heated words between Churchill and Halifax. 'I thought Winston talked the most frightful rot . . .' Halifax wrote in his diary that night. So too, he added, had Arthur Greenwood, with the result that 'I said exactly what I thought of them, adding that if that was really their view, and if it came to the point, our ways must separate'.

This threat of resignation had certainly caught Churchill unawares, for, as Halifax noted in his diary, 'when I repeated the same thing in the garden' he was 'surprised and mellowed', and 'full of apologies and affection'. But, Halifax added, 'it does drive one to despair when he works himself up into a passion of emotion when he ought to make his brain think and reason'.[2]

Rumours of what had occurred at this emotion-charged meeting spread quickly among the Downing Street circle. The War Cabinet, noted Colville, 'are feverishly considering our ability to carry on the war in such circumstances and there are signs that Halifax is being defeatist. He says our aim can no longer be to crush Germany, but rather to preserve our own integrity and independence.'[3]

To Sir Alexander Cadogan, Halifax declared as soon as the War Cabinet of May 27 was over: 'I can't work with Winston any longer,' to which Cadogan replied, in dissuading Halifax from resignation: 'Nonsense: his rhodomontades probably bore you as much as they do me, but don't do anything silly under the stress of that.' Later Halifax told Cadogan that Churchill had 'of course' been 'very affectionate'.[4]

* * *

[1] War Cabinet No. 142 of 1940, 27 May 1940, 4.30 p.m., Confidential Annex: Cabinet papers, 65/13.

[2] Halifax diary, 27 May 1940: quoted in The 2nd Earl of Birkenhead, *Halifax: The Life of Lord Halifax*, London 1965, page 458. 'At that time,' Colville later reflected, 'Winston could be terrifyingly explosive—and remarkably paternal. He stood up to the strain incredibly well.' (Conversation with the author, 20 May 1981.)

[3] Colville diary, 27 May 1940: Colville papers.

[4] Cadogan diary, 27 May 1940: David Dilks (editor), *The Diaries of Sir Alexander Cadogan 1938–1945*, page 291.

Throughout May 27 it was clear that the Belgian Government was in imminent danger of collapse. On the battlefield, General Brooke noted tersely: 'Belgians seem to have vanished off the map,'[1] while in London the Belgian Embassy assumed that the latest decision of the King of the Belgians to remain in Belgium, despite the British offer to give him asylum, meant that he regarded the war as lost, 'and contemplates separate peace'.

Churchill reported this assumption in a telephone message to Sir Roger Keyes, adding that the Belgian Government had 'reassembled itself on foreign soil', in order to dissociate itself from the King's decision. Even if the Belgian army had to lay down its arms, Churchill added, 'there are 200,000 Belgians of military age in France, and greater resources than Belgium had in 1914 with which to fight'. By his decision not to leave Belgium and form the nucleus of a fighting force, and continued resistance, the King 'is dividing the nation and delivering it into Hitler's protection'.

Churchill wanted Keyes to 'convey these considerations' to the King himself, and to impress on him 'the disastrous consequences to the Allies and to Belgium of his present choice'.[2] But this exhortation came too late, and when the Defence Committee met at seven o'clock that evening, Churchill told the meeting of 'disturbing news' which had been received from Keyes. The King of the Belgians had ordered his Commander-in-Chief to ask for an armistice, to take effect from midnight that night.

The dominant consideration was the effect of the Belgian armistice on the British troops, whose situation, Churchill commented, would become 'even more desperate', with their only choice 'to fight their way back to the coast, taking as heavy a toll of the enemy as they could on the way'. As for the King of the Belgians, Churchill added, while he 'could not be reproached' for the action which he was now taking, this action 'completed the full circle of misfortune into which our Allies had landed us while we had loyally carried out our obligations and undertakings to them'.[3]

At ten o'clock that night, Churchill gave the news of the Belgian surrender to a specially summoned War Cabinet at 10 Downing Street.

---

[1] Brooke diary, 27 May 1940, 'Lt-Gen Brooke's Diary, 10th May 1940–30th May 1940': War Office papers, 106/1708.

[2] 'Message from Prime Minister to Admiral Keyes', 27 May 1940: Churchill papers, 20/14.

[3] Defence Committee No. 10 of 1940, 27 May 1940, 7 p.m.: Cabinet papers, 69/1. Those present during this discussion were Churchill (in the Chair), Halifax, Air Chief Marshal Sir Cyril Newall, Admiral of the Fleet Sir Dudley Pound, General Sir John Dill and Major-General Ismay.

The King's action, Churchill said, 'was certainly not heroic', but if he now made a separate peace with Germany, and carried on as a puppet monarch, this 'might well be the best that he could do for his country'. In France, Churchill commented, the news of the Belgian action 'might sting the French to anger, in which case they would be very much more formidable opponents to the Germans than in their present stunned and bewildered state'. As for the British, the announcement of the Belgian armistice would, he believed, 'go a long way to prepare the public for bad news'.[1]

The War Cabinet over, Churchill walked from Downing Street to Admiralty House, accompanied by Colville. 'He said he did not think the French would give in,' Colville wrote in his diary, 'and at any rate they ought not to so do.' Colville added: 'At midnight, after reading a few papers and saying "Pour me out a whisky and soda, very weak, there's a good boy," he went to bed.'[2]

During the early hours of May 28, while Churchill slept, the long-awaited Allied landing took place at Narvik. After fierce fighting, in which a hundred and fifty British, French, Norwegian and Polish soldiers were killed, Narvik was under Allied control. Few of the officers who celebrated the successful landing knew that they had, without delay, to prepare for evacuation. Yet this was now General Béthouart's immediate task.

At five o'clock that morning, in France, Lord Gort's forces began their own preparations for a further day of withdrawal towards the beaches east of Dunkirk. In London, when the War Cabinet met at 11 a.m., Sir Roger Keyes reported on yet another blow to Allied hopes; the Belgian surrender had come into effect at dawn.

While Keyes gave his report, a note was handed to Churchill by John Martin. It was the text of a telephone message which had been sent to Downing Street from the Operations and Intelligence Centre at the Admiralty, having been sent to the Admiralty from the Chief Censor. This message was an intercepted telephone conversation between the head of the French Military Mission at Belgian headquarters, General Champon, who was then at La Panne, and his superiors in Paris. During this conversation, Champon had given Paris the terms of the Belgian Armistice. These were, as intercepted: 'Belgian troop movements forbidden. Troops to line up on the side of roads and await orders, showing white flags. . . . German troops to be allowed to proceed

---

[1] War Cabinet No. 143 of 1940, 27 May 1940, 10 p.m.: Cabinet papers, 65/7.
[2] Colville diary, 27 May 1940: Colville papers.

to coast. Free passage to Ostend demanded. No destruction permitted. All resistance will be overcome.'[1]

The King of the Belgians, Churchill commented, 'would now presumably become the puppet of Hitler, and might possibly obtain better treatment for his people than if he had left the country and continued to resist from foreign soil'. But Churchill was unwilling to condemn Leopold's decision outright. 'No doubt history would criticize the King,' he said, 'for having involved us and the French in Belgium's ruin. But it was not for us to pass judgment on him.'

Later in the meeting a British officer, Lieutenant-Colonel Davy, gave the War Cabinet an account of the bravery of the Belgian troops, and of the King's order that his artillery remain at their guns until overrun. Davy also reported that a Belgian battalion which had been sent to try to fill the gap between the Belgians and the British east of Ypres 'had been wiped out by a wave of 60 enemy bombers'.

The discussion then turned to the continuing evacuation from Dunkirk. The latest news was that 11,400 men had been rescued during the night, and that a further 2,500 were at that very moment crossing the Channel. But some 200,000 were still encircled, and with them an additional 160,000 Frenchmen. Fighter Command had, as the Chief of the Air Staff, Sir Cyril Newall, reported, been ordered to maintain 'continuous patrols in strength' over Dunkirk and the adjacent beaches. But, Newall added, the Air Officer Commanding-in-Chief of Fighter Command, Sir Hugh Dowding, was deeply concerned at the effect of this order on the air defence of Great Britain. 'Our fighter defences,' Dowding wished it to be known, 'were almost at cracking point. If this exceptional effort had to be repeated over Dunkirk on the following day, the situation would be serious.'

After reporting Dowding's fears, the Chief of the Air Staff said he 'could not accept' them. Churchill was likewise sceptical of Dowding's assessment, feeling that the Germans were 'no doubt' as fully extended as the British.[2]

Before going to the House of Commons to make a statement on the Belgian surrender, and on the situation at Dunkirk, Churchill spoke privately to Keyes, who said that Gort did not 'rate very highly' the chance of saving the British Expeditionary Force.[3] To the House of Commons, basing himself on Colonel Davy's eye-witness report, Churchill praised the Belgian Army, which 'has fought very bravely and has

---

[1] Message of 28 May 1940: Premier papers, 3/69A, folio 152.
[2] War Cabinet No. 144 of 1940, 28 May 1940, 11 a.m.: Cabinet papers, 65/7.
[3] Colville diary, 28 May 1940: Colville papers.

both suffered and inflicted heavy losses'. It was not the time to attempt to 'pass judgment' on King Leopold's action. 'Whatever our feeling may be,' he said, 'upon the facts so far as they are known to us, we must remember that the sense of brotherhood between the many peoples who have fallen into the power of the aggressor and those who still confront him will play its part in better days than those through which we are passing.'[1]

The situation of the British troops withdrawing to Dunkirk, Churchill warned, was 'extremely grave'. The surrender of the Belgian Army 'adds appreciably to their grievous peril'. But the troops were in good heart, and were fighting 'with the utmost discipline and tenacity'. Meanwhile, the House of Commons should prepare itself for 'hard and heavy tidings'. His statement ended:

I have only to add that nothing which may happen in this battle can in any way relieve us of our duty to defend the world cause to which we have vowed ourselves; nor should it destroy our confidence in our power to make our way, as on former occasions in our history, through disaster and through grief to the ultimate defeat of our enemies.

The House responded to Churchill's mood of defiance. Whatever Churchill might have to report in the next days or weeks, declared the Labour MP for Keighley, Hastings Lees-Smith, 'we have not yet touched the fringe of the resolution of this country', while the Liberal Chief Whip, Sir Percy Harris, said of Churchill's 'dignified' statement that it reflected 'not only the feeling of the whole House but the feeling of the whole nation'.[2]

Having made his statement, Churchill went to his room in the House

---

[1] But four years later Churchill wrote to Eden, about the Belgians: 'Considering that there are millions of French and British graves in Belgium, and that she was saved from all the horrors of German incorporation by our exertions, I thought her attitude in the years preceding the war singularly ungrateful and detached. Had she acted vigorously with France, French action might have been stimulated. Anyhow at the outbreak of War, her armies could have been placed in a far better strategical position than was subsequently possible, and the hideous gap at Sedan might have presented a very different aspect to the enemy. Without going so far as to say that Belgian action might have changed the sombre course of events, I have no doubt whatever that, up till the time they were fallen upon and invaded, our account with them was expressed by "Thank you for nothing". Indeed I think they were the most contemptible of all the neutrals at that time.' Churchill added: 'This however did not prevent me from speaking in more considerate tones about the surrender of the Belgian Army by the King of the Belgians without the slightest regard to what happened to all the forces that had come as fast as they could, in view of Belgian policy, to the rescue of that country. In fact I have very little sympathy with them beyond what I feel for all countries invaded and trampled down by the Huns.' (Prime Minister's Personal Minute, M.639/4, 27 May 1944: Premier papers, 3/69A.)

[2] *Hansard*, 28 May 1940.

of Commons, for a meeting with the four other members of the War
Cabinet, to discuss the repeated Italian request to act as an intermediary.[1] According to Halifax, the current proposal, which had been
discussed with Reynaud, was that, provided Britain's independence
could be secured, 'there were certain concessions' that Britain would
be prepared to make to Italy, as regards Italian efforts to begin a
general negotiation to end the war. But Churchill feared that the
French Government 'were trying to get us on to the slippery slope';
only after the Germans had attempted to invade Britain, he said,
and their attempt had failed, would the situation be 'entirely different'.

Halifax disagreed; he was reluctant to give up the idea of possible
negotiations: 'we must not ignore the fact', he said, 'that we might get
better terms before France went out of the war and our aircraft factories
were bombed, than we might get in three months time'.

After Neville Chamberlain had warned that the French proposals
seemed 'another attempt to run out', Churchill spoke emphatically
against any negotiations, telling his War Cabinet colleagues:

It was impossible to imagine that Herr Hitler would be so foolish as to let us
continue our re-armament. In effect, his terms would put us completely at his
mercy. We should get no worse terms if we went on fighting, even if we were
beaten, than were open to us now. If, however, we continued the war and
Germany attacked us, no doubt we should suffer some damage, but they also
would suffer severe losses. Their oil supplies might be reduced. A time might
come when we felt that we had to put an end to the struggle, but the terms
would not then be more mortal than those offered to us now.

Churchill's emphatic conclusion did not end the discussion. Opinion
was divided on the merits of such negotiations. Halifax reiterated that
he did not see what Churchill felt was 'so wrong' in the possibility of
Italian mediation, and even Chamberlain did not see 'what we should
lose if we said openly that, while we would fight to the end to preserve
our independence, we were ready to consider decent terms if such were
offered to us'.

Churchill replied that the chances of being offered any such 'decent
terms' seemed to him a thousand to one against 'at the present time',

[1] The War Cabinet Ministers present were Churchill (in the Chair), Neville Chamberlain
(Lord President of the Council), Lord Halifax (Secretary of State for Foreign Affairs), Clement
Attlee (Lord Privy Seal) and Arthur Greenwood (Minister without Portfolio). Also present were
Sir Archibald Sinclair (Secretary of State for Air), Sir Alexander Cadogan (Permanent Under-
Secretary of State for Foreign Affairs, for part of the meeting only) and Sir Edward Bridges
(Secretary).

and he warned his colleagues: 'nations which went down fighting rose again, but those which surrendered tamely were finished'.

It was Attlee who then supported Churchill, warning of the 'grave danger' to the morale of the British public if the Government were to embark on negotiations. Once any such negotiations began, he said, 'we should find it impossible to rally the morale of the people'. The other Labour member of the War Council, Arthur Greenwood, then warned that the industrial centres of Britain 'would regard anything like weakening on the part of the Government as a disaster'.[1]

The meeting adjourned shortly after six o'clock. As soon as the War Cabinet Ministers had left, the room was filled with all those Ministers who were not members of the War Cabinet, some twenty-five in all. There now occurred one of the most extraordinary scenes of the war. Churchill, tired after more than two hours of combating the talk of mediation and negotiation, explained the situation at Dunkirk. He then explained that Hitler would probably 'take Paris and offer terms', followed by the Italians who would 'threaten and offer terms'. There was no doubt whatever, Churchill commented, 'that we must decline anything like this and fight on'.[2]

Among those present as Churchill urged 'fight on' was Hugh Dalton, who had just become Minister of Economic Warfare, and who noted in his diary, of Churchill's remarks:

He was quite magnificent. The man, and the only man we have, for this hour. He gave a full, frank, and completely calm account of events in France. Now it was necessary to fight our way through to the Channel ports and get away all we could. How many would get away we could not tell. We should certainly be able to get 50,000 away. If we could get 100,000 away, that would be a wonderful performance. Only Dunkirk was left to us. Calais had been defended by a British force which had refused to surrender, and it was said that there were no survivors.

He was determined to prepare public opinion for bad tidings. We must now expect the sudden turning of the war against this island, and we must not be taken by surprise by any events. Attempts to invade us would no doubt be made, but they would be beset with immense difficulty. We should mine all round our coast; our Navy was extremely strong; our air defences were much more easily organised from this island than across the Channel; our supplies of food and oil were ample; we had good troops in this island, and others were on the way by sea, both British Army units coming from remote garrisons and

[1] War Cabinet No. 145 of 1940, 29 May 1940, 4 p.m., Confidential Annex: Cabinet papers, 65/13, folios 184–9.
[2] Reith diary, 28 May 1940: Charles Stuart (editor), *The Reith Diaries*, London 1975, page 254. Reith had been appointed Minister of Transport two weeks earlier.

excellent Dominion troops, and, as to aircraft, we were now more than making good our current losses, and the Germans were not.

And then he said: 'I have thought carefully in these last days whether it was part of my duty to consider entering into negotiations with That Man.' But it was idle to think that, if we tried to make peace now, we should get better terms than if we fought it out. The Germans would demand our fleet—that would be called 'disarmament'—our naval bases, and much else. We should become a slave state, though a British Government which would be Hitler's puppet would be set up—'under Mosley or some such person'. And where should we be at the end of all that? On the other hand, we had immense reserves and advantages.

'And I am convinced,' he concluded, 'that every man of you would rise up and tear me down from my place if I were for one moment to contemplate parley or surrender. If this long island story of ours is to end at last, let it end only when each one of us lies choking in his own blood upon the ground.'

There were loud cries of approval all round the table, in which, I think, Amery, George Lloyd and I were loudest.

Not much more was said. No one expressed even the faintest flicker of dissent. Morrison asked about the evacuation of the Government, and hoped that it would not be hurried. The PM said he was all against evacuation, unless things became utterly impossible in London. 'But,' he said, 'mere bombing will not make us go.'

As we separated several of us went up and spoke to him. He had risen from the long table and was standing in front of the fireplace. I patted him on the back and said: 'Well done, Prime Minister! You ought to get that cartoon of Low, showing us all rolling up our sleeves and falling in behind you, and frame it and stick it up there.' He answered with a broad grin, 'Yes, that was a good one, wasn't it?'[1]

Churchill was fortified in his opposition to a negotiated peace by this spontaneous surge of support for continuing war. 'He did not re-member,' he told the re-assembled War Cabinet at seven o'clock, 'having ever before heard a gathering of persons occupying high places in political life express themselves so emphatically.'[2] In his memoirs Churchill recalled the emotion of that occasion. 'There then occurred,' he wrote, 'a demonstration which, considering the character of the gathering—twenty-five experienced politicians and Parliament men, who represented all the different points of view, whether right or wrong, before the war—surprised me. Quite a number seemed to jump up

[1] Dalton diary, 28 May 1940: Hugh Dalton, *The Fateful Years, Memoirs 1939–1945*, London 1957, pages 335–6. Amery had been appointed Secretary of State for India and Burma on May 13, Lord Lloyd Secretary of State for the Colonies on May 12, and Herbert Morrison Minister of Supply on May 12.

[2] War Cabinet No. 145 of 1940, 28 May 1940, 7 p.m., Confidential Annex: Cabinet papers, 65/13, folio 189.

from the table and come running to my chair, shouting and patting me on the back.' There was no doubt, Churchill added, 'that had I at this juncture faltered at all in the leading of the nation I should have been hurled out of office. I was sure that every Minister was ready to be killed quite soon, and have all his family and possessions destroyed, rather than give in. In this they represented the House of Commons and almost all the people. There was a white glow, overpowering, sublime, which ran through our Island from end to end.'[1]

Churchill had been Prime Minister for less than three weeks. No hour had been free from bad news, worry, and the need for immediate decisions. There had been no time for contact with any but a handful of senior Ministers, the Service chiefs, their deputies, and senior civil servants. The twenty-five other Ministers and their demonstration represented contact with the public at large. Churchill had not even seen most of them since their appointment as Ministers; even these appointments had mostly been made on the telephone. The effect of their demonstration was considerable on Churchill's own resolve.

The War Cabinet of May 28 resumed its earlier discussion of the Franco-Italian mediation plan. Neville Chamberlain now shared fully Churchill's sense of determination, telling his four War Cabinet colleagues that Reynaud should be persuaded 'that it was worth his while to go on fighting'. As for involving the United States, even in a firm declaration, as Lord Halifax suggested, Churchill disagreed. Such an appeal would, he said, be 'premature'. If Britain were to make 'a bold stand against Germany', that action would itself command 'admiration and respect' in the United States. But 'a grovelling appeal', made at such a moment, would have 'the worst possible effect'.[2]

There were to be no negotiations, no appeal to the United States, no flinching of British resolve. By midnight on May 28, a further 25,000 British troops had been brought back safely from Dunkirk. 'When we heard the score that night,' General Ismay later recalled, 'the Prime Minister asked me how I would feel if I were told that a total of 50,000 could be saved. I replied without hesitation that I would be absolutely delighted, and Churchill did not upbraid me for pessimism.'[3]

There was further bad news from France on the night of May 28. In Paris, as Desmond Morton reported direct to Churchill, 'confidence in Monsieur Reynaud was waning'. The people of France were 'solid' in

[1] Winston S. Churchill, *The Second World War*, volume 2, London 1949, page 88.
[2] War Cabinet No. 145 of 1940, 28 May 1940, 7 p.m., Confidential Annex: Cabinet papers, 65/13, folio 190.
[3] *The Memoirs of General the Lord Ismay*, London 1960, page 132.

their desire to continue the war, but political intrigue in Paris was 'rife'.[1] According to the British Ambassador in Paris, Sir Ronald Campbell, Reynaud was 'firm', but Daladier 'cannot be counted on'. The 'best' of the French Ministers, Campbell reported, was Georges Mandel, who was 'both efficient and determined'.[2] Campbell added that he was 'satisfied with the spirit of the French Government as a whole'.[3]

That night Churchill rejected Reynaud's proposed acceptance of Italian mediation. In a firm message, telephoned to the British Ambassador in Paris twenty minutes before midnight, Churchill argued that if Britain and France could show that 'after the loss of our two armies and the support of our Belgian ally we still have stout hearts and confidence in ourselves, we shall at once strengthen our hands in negotiations and draw the admiration and perhaps the material help of the USA'. Churchill added that as long as Britain and France stood together, Britain's 'undefeated' Navy and Air Force 'afford us the means of exercising in our common interest a continuous pressure upon Germany's internal life'. Churchill's message ended:

We have reason to believe that the Germans too are working to a time-table and that their losses and the hardships imposed on them together with the fear of our air raids is undermining their courage. It would indeed be a tragedy if by too hasty an acceptance of defeat we threw away a chance that was almost within our grasp of securing an honourable issue from the struggle.

In my view if we both stand out we may yet save ourselves from the fate of Denmark or Poland. Our success must depend first on our unity, then on our courage and endurance.[4]

The effect of this message on Reynaud was 'magical', General Spears recalled: 'It evidently re-inforced his own inner conviction that this was the right course to pursue, and he straightway vetoed any further communication being sent to Rome.'[5]

At the War Cabinet on the morning of May 29 Churchill reported that 40,000 British troops had now been brought back from France, and that the evacuation was continuing 'at the rate of about 2,000 an hour'.[6] In answer to a request from Gort, over the telephone to Sir John Dill the previous night, Churchill said that British troops 'should

[1] Report of 28 May 1940: Premier papers, 3/188/4, folio 14. Morton's source of information was Jean Monnet, who wanted Weygand to replace Reynaud as Prime Minister 'without delay'.

[2] Colville diary, 28 May 1940: Colville papers.

[3] Telegram of 28 May 1940, shown to War Cabinet No. 146 of 1940, 29 May 1940, 11.30 a.m.: Cabinet papers, 65/7, folio 192.

[4] Message of 28 May 1940, 11.40 p.m., to Sir R. Campbell (Paris), No. 255 DIPP, Most Immediate, by telephone: Churchill papers, 4/152.

[5] Major-General Sir Edward Spears, *Assignment to Catastrophe*, London 1954, volume 1, page 255.

[6] War Cabinet No. 146 of 1940, 29 May 1940, 11.30 a.m.: Cabinet papers, 65/7.

on no account delay their withdrawal to conform with the French, otherwise there would be a danger of getting no troops off'.

The War Cabinet then turned to the question of what instructions should be sent to Gort, in the event of his communications with London being cut. Cadogan, who was present, recorded in his diary: 'WSC rather theatrically bulldogish.'[1] In Halifax's view it would 'not be dishonourable to relinquish the struggle in order to save a handful of men from massacre'. But Churchill felt that a Commander, in circumstances 'as desperate and distressing' as those in which Gort now found himself, 'should not be offered the difficult choice between resistance and capitulation'; that is to say, that Gort's existing orders to fight on should be maintained.

In answer to worries expressed first by Chamberlain, then by Dill and finally by Eden, Churchill stated that Gort's instructions had not been intended to convey the impression 'that troops which were cut off from hope of relief and were without food or without water or without ammunition should attempt to continue the struggle', and it was agreed to make this clear in new instructions.[2]

These instructions were sent by Churchill to Gort that evening. 'If you are cut off from all communication with us,' they read, 'and all evacuation from Dunkirk and beaches had in your judgment been finally prevented, after every attempt to reopen it had failed, you would become the sole judge of when it was impossible to inflict further damage upon the enemy.' His Majesty's Government were 'sure', the message ended, 'that the repute of the British Army is safe in your hands'.[3]

That night Churchill dined with his wife and General Ironside. 'He was in great form,' Ironside noted in his diary, and he added:

He showed me Louis Spears' letter that had come in from Paris. There is a good deal of defeatist attitude amongst the French. Weygand is a good hard conscientious worker. Georges is purely 'negative' and does not function very much.

Very little chance of the whole BEF coming off. They have now sunk three ships in Dunkirk harbour[4] and so there is very little more chance of getting any units off. . . .[5]

[1] Cadogan dairy, 29 May 1940: David Dilks (editor), *The Diaries of Sir Alexander Cadogan, OM, 1938–1945*, London 1971, page 292.

[2] War Cabinet No. 146 of 1940, 29 May 1940, 11.30 a.m., Confidential Annex: Cabinet papers: 65/13.

[3] Telegram No. 72519, despatched 9.40 p.m., 29 May 1940: Premier papers, 3/175, folio 19.

[4] Among the ships that had gone down on 28 May 1940 was the paddle steamer *Brighton Belle* (sunk in collision with a wreck). On 29 May 1940 the paddle steamer *Waverley* was sunk by a German bomb, and the paddle steamer *Gracie Fields* damaged by bombs. In all, four ships were sunk off Dunkirk on May 28 and ten on May 29 (War Cabinet, Chiefs of Staff Committee, *Weekly Résumé* (*No. 40*) *of the Naval Military and Air Situation*, Appendix II, pages 13–14: Churchill papers, 23/5).

[5] Ironside diary, 29 May 1940: Roderick Macleod and Denis Kelly (editors), *The Ironside Diaries, 1937–1940*, London 1962, pages 344–5.

Particularly concerned about a future French grievance if those French troops who might still be evacuated were to be left to their fate, Churchill minuted, during May 29, for Eden, Ismay and Dill, that it was 'essential' that the French should share 'in such evacuations from Dunkirk as may be possible'. Nor should they be dependent only upon their own shipping resources. Everything must be done 'so that no reproaches, or as few as possible, arise'.[1] That same evening Churchill telegraphed to Reynaud, for communication to General Weygand and General Georges: 'We wish French troops to share in evacuation to fullest possible extent, and Admiralty have been instructed to aid French Marine as required. We do not know how many will be forced to capitulate, but we must share this loss together as best we can, and, above all, bear it without reproaches arising from inevitable confusion, stresses and strains.'

Churchill then outlined to the French leaders a scheme to 'build up a new BEF' from St Nazaire, on the Atlantic coast. Equipment sufficient for five divisions was being moved south of Amiens. Reinforcements were on their way from India and Palestine: regular British troops who would be able, together with Australians and Canadians 'arriving soon', to 'get into order and meet impending shock'. A new scheme would soon be sent 'for reinforcement of our troops in France'.

These plans, sent in good faith, were a desperate attempt to boost Reynaud's morale, and through him, to sustain the will to fight of Weygand and Georges, even as the Dunkirk evacuation was accelerating. 'I send this in all comradeship,' Churchill ended. 'Do not hesitate to speak frankly to me.'[2]

This message was sent from the War Office shortly before midnight, reaching the British Military Attaché in Paris before dawn. There, in the British Embassy, it was deciphered, and handed to Spears, who had been summoned from his bed, for immediate transmission to Reynaud. But as an act of conciliation the message was a failure. Whereas Churchill's previous message to Reynaud had immediately revivified the French Prime Minister, this one only angered him. As Spears later recalled: 'This message evidently gave Reynaud neither satisfaction nor solace. In fact, he showed a degree of ill-temper very unusual in him. He said sourly, almost sarcastically, that he was very glad Churchill had emphasized that the French would be evacuated in equal

[1] Minute of 29 May 1940, flagged 'Action this day': Premier papers, 3/175, folio 25.
[2] Telegram No. 72522, despatched 11.45 p.m., 29 May 1940: Premier papers, 3/175, folios 20–21.

numbers with the British. If this were not so, French opinion would be déchaînée'—unleashed—'against Britain.'[1]

Spears knew that Churchill was serious in his offer of joint evacuation, and in his plans to regroup and to fight on in France. But he could not convey this resolve to Reynaud. Spears could only do as Churchill had asked him earlier that same evening in a message personal to himself. 'Meanwhile,' Churchill had told his emissary, 'reiterate our inflexible resolve to continue, whatever they do.'[2]

During May 29 Churchill was angered by a demand by the Egyptian Prime Minister that all British troops should move out of Cairo, and that the city should then be declared an unfortified town, in order to seek its immunity from air attack. 'We should surely take a strong line with the Egyptian Government,' Churchill minuted to Halifax, 'who must not be allowed to hamper our military measures when we are their sole defence against Italian annexation. We ought on no account to tolerate any Egyptian efforts to contract out of the war.'

Churchill added an apology for seeking to guide policy by a short dictated note. 'I do hope you do not mind me sending you "chits" like this,' he added. 'There is so much going on.' And seeing, before his message was actually sent across to the Foreign Office, that Halifax had already replied to Cairo in a similar sense, Churchill added a short postscript, 'I am so glad you are acting already.'[3]

It was on May 29 that Churchill also learned, finally, of Lloyd George's attitude towards joining the Government. On the previous day he had offered Lloyd George a place in the War Cabinet, but on condition that Neville Chamberlain agreed. In answering Churchill's offer, Lloyd George said that because of this condition, it did not constitute a firm offer. 'Until it is definite,' he added, 'I cannot consider it.' Lloyd George ended his letter:

I am no office seeker. I am genuinely anxious to help to extricate my country from the most terrible disaster into which it has ever been plunged by the ineptitude of her rulers. Several of the architects of this catastrophe are still leading members of your Government, and two of them are in the Cabinet that directs the war.

Like millions of my fellow-countrymen I say to you that, if in any way you

---

[1] Major-General Sir Edward Spears, *Assignment to Catastrophe*, London 1954, page 279.
[2] Telegram despatched at 11.40 p.m., 29 May 1940: Foreign Office papers, 800/312, folio 73.
[3] Note of 29 May 1940: Foreign Office papers, 800/310, folio 194.

think I can help, I am at your call. But if that call is tentative and qualified I shall not know what answer to give.[1]

At 10 Downing Street it was noted that Lloyd George had refused to accept office, 'except on the most unqualified terms', and that Churchill had replied that he 'would not abandon the loyalty he felt for Chamberlain'.[2]

A third problem which presented itself on May 29 concerned military aid from the United States. For several days the Chairman of the Anglo-French Purchasing Board in the United States, Arthur Purvis, had been trying to obtain the release of American war materials for immediate despatch to Britain and France. Five days earlier he had been urged to secure, in particular, such anti-aircraft guns, anti-tank guns, Bofors guns, small arms ammunition and tanks as could be bought from existing United States stocks. But on May 29 Purvis telegraphed to London that he had just been told, by Morgenthau, the Secretary to the Treasury, that 'the President has decided that it would be impossible at this time to obtain from Congress a modification of the Law which at present prevents the sale to belligerents of existing United States Army and Navy stocks of equipment'.

Morgenthau had gone on to warn Purvis that it would be both 'useless and dangerous' for Britain to take any action to 'attempt the impossible'. But there was one glimmer of hope, at least for the long term, if such were to be vouchsafed. The American Chief of Staff, General Marshall, was, Purvis reported, 'sympathetic to the Allied cause', and was even at that moment trying to find a solution to the supply of arms to Britain and France 'within the existing law'.[3]

On reading Purvis' report, the Secretary to the Cabinet, Sir Edward Bridges, had drafted a telegram for Churchill to send to Roosevelt, setting out Britain's most 'urgent needs'. These needs, Bridges reminded Roosevelt, had been sent to Purvis 'as you suggested'. Nevertheless, the draft continued:

I feel justified in asking for the release to us of 200 Curtiss P. 40 fighters now being delivered to your Army. The courage and success of our pilots against numerical superiority are a guarantee that they will be well used. At the present rate of comparative losses, they would account for something like 800 German machines.

[1] Letter of 29 May 1940: Churchill papers, 20/10.
[2] Colville diary, 29 May 1940: Colville papers.
[3] 'Purco' No. 157A, 29 May 1940: Cabinet papers, 115/83.

Bridges' draft went on to say, again as if written by Churchill: 'I also understand your difficulties, legal, political and financial regarding destroyers.'

Churchill agreed to send the message almost as drafted. He deleted, however, Bridges penultimate sentence: 'I leave any request with you and know that, if you see a possibility of meeting it, you will,' and he amended Bridges final sentence, 'The need is very great' to read: 'But the need is extreme.'[1]

Even in the interval between the drafting and sending of this telegram, Purvis had continued to follow up specific British requests. On May 30, following an appeal from Churchill's Supply Co-ordinator, Oliver Lyttelton, for the urgent purchase of 12,700 tons of steel bars, Purvis replied that he had been able to purchase 4,300 tons for shipment to Britain in June, July and August, with a further 8,400 tons to come by the end of August, some of it from orders being carried out for despatch to Chile.[2]

This success was rapidly followed by another, for on the following day, May 31, Purvis was able to telegraph to London that General Marshall would be 'prepared to stretch a point' in declaring substantial quantities of munitions 'as surplus', and therefore 'available to us'.[3] There was also, Purvis reported, a prospect of Britain getting a 'priority' for the purchase of 15,000 tons of new Trinitrotoluol explosive (TNT).[4]

It was not the quest for arms supplies from America however, but recent disagreements within the War Cabinet, that stirred Cadogan to confide to his diary that night. Cadogan feared that Churchill's relations with Chamberlain and Halifax would become 'rather strained'. Churchill's 'fault' in this regard, he noted, was his 'theatricality'.[5] But Colville, who had worked throughout that day in Downing Street, saw another characteristic as predominant. 'Winston's ceaseless industry is impressive,' he wrote in his diary. 'He is always having ideas which he puts down on paper in the form of questions and despatches to Ismay and the Chief of the Imperial General Staff. Sometimes they relate to matters of major importance and sometimes to quite trivial questions.'[6]

[1] Draft dated 29 May 1940: Premier papers, 3/468, folio 184. The telegram was sent on 1 June 1940.

[2] 'Purco' No. 161, 30 May 1940: Cabinet papers, 85/14, folio 328.

[3] These supplies were: 100 million rounds of Lee machine gun and rifle ammunition; 500,000 Lee Enfield rifles; 25,000 automatic rifles; 10,000 Browning machine guns; 500 75-millimetre field guns; 500 3-inch Stokes mortars, 'some thousands' of anti-aircraft and tank machine guns, and 'some thousands' of revolvers.

[4] 'Purco' No. 163, 31 May 1940: Cabinet papers, 85/14, folio 331.

[5] Cadogan diary, 29 May 1940: David Dilks (editor), The Diaries of Sir Alexander Cadogan OM, 1938–1945, London 1971, page 292.

[6] Colville diary, 29 May 1940: Colville papers.

It was difficult to know what could be called trivial. Amid the perils of the Dunkirk evacuation, and the growing fears of an imminent German assault on Britain, clearly almost any other issue, whether the question of the defence of Egypt, or a War Cabinet post for Lloyd George, or arms supplies from the United States, might be considered trivial. Yet the issues and perspectives were changing so quickly that one of Churchill's tasks was to take note of the smaller issues which, if neglected, might with the passage of time and changing circumstances become dominant. As Prime Minister, his was the ultimate responsibility to ensure that such issues did not slip into neglect or oblivion.

As serious as any issue with which Churchill was confronted on May 29 was one on which he felt the need to assert his greatest possible personal influence: the question of morale; the ability of the British people, or of any people, to maintain their resolve in the face of rumour and uncertainty, against a background of retreat, following the surrender of one Ally and the obvious weakness of another.

In an attempt to stiffen the resolve of his own Ministers and senior civil servants, on May 29 Churchill issued a single page exhortation which read:

> In these dark days the Prime Minister would be grateful if all his colleagues in the Government, as well as high officials, would maintain a high morale in their circles; not minimising the gravity of events, but showing confidence in our ability and inflexible resolve to continue the war till we have broken the will of the enemy to bring all Europe under his domination.
>
> No tolerance should be given to the idea that France will make a separate peace; but whatever may happen on the Continent, we cannot doubt our duty and we shall certainly use all our power to defend the Island, the Empire and our Cause.

This message, signed 'WSC', was circulated to all thirty-five War Cabinet and other Ministers, all thirty-nine Junior Ministers, forty-six 'High Officials', and the six Dominion Representatives.[1]

That evening, in France, the situation had worsened considerably. 'French Army now a rabble, and complete loss of discipline,' General Brooke noted in his war diary. 'Troops dejected and surly, refusing to clear road and panicking every time German planes come over.' Brooke had gone to the coast at La Panne 'to see how embarkation was proceeding', but had found 'everything quite inadequate'. He had then gone to see Gort, 'and asked him to apply pressure on Admiralty'.[2]

---

[1] 'Strictly Confidential', minute of 29 May 1940: Premier papers, 4/68/9, folios 954–60.
[2] Brooke diary, 29 May 1940, 'Lt-Gen Brooke's Diary, 10th May 1940–30th May 1940': War Office papers, 106/1708.

Both General Gort, and the commander of the First Division, Major-General Alexander, now decided to take steps to inform Churchill personally about their problems, and in particular about the lack of small craft. Gort sent his ADC, Lord Munster, back to London, while Alexander despatched Churchill's nephew Johnny.

The despatch of Johnny Churchill was widely approved. A junior officer on the Staff of the 1st Division, John Wheldon, who had been Churchill's literary assistant at Chartwell in 1934 and 1935, later recalled how 'for day after day in the perimeter' the Staff officers had expected 'to hear something about arrangements for embarkation. No news came out. GHQ and the Admiralty seemed totally constipated. We felt the decision to send Johnny Churchill (who in 1935 at Chartwell had done the frescoes which are still in the Loggia and was now Corps Camouflage Officer) was probably in consequence of very strong pressures from below. I think that even the troops knew that he had left on a special mission to Winston.' 'It seemed to us,' Wheldon added, 'that GHQ & the Navy could not have made clear in Whitehall what the conditions were, viz the 1 Div. was in a position of strength (comparatively) so that ships were very unlikely to be shot at by enemy artillery and so the whole BEF, or virtually the whole, ought to be embarked . . .'[1]

The two Dunkirk emissaries, Munster and Churchill, reached England on the morning of May 30. Twenty years later Johnny Churchill set down an account of their joint efforts:

Still soaking wet, and in full battle kit, I got on a train at Dover and travelled up to London. I noticed two Staff officers in the same railway coach. They were General Pownall and Captain Lord Munster, ADC to General Lord Gort, who looked very smartly dressed and 'Staff'. I felt terribly unkempt by comparison, especially considering that my mission was to the Prime Minister.

Not knowing Lord Munster very well, I did not talk to him on the journey. On arrival at Victoria Station I went straight to the adjoining Grosvenor Hotel and shaved. Then, without wasting further time, I took a taxi to the Admiralty. I arrived and stepped into the lift for the Prime Minister's apartments at the same moment as Lord Munster who, it turned out, had been sent over by Lord Gort on a similar mission.

Our reception at 8 a.m. by my uncle and aunt, both of whom were in dressing gowns, was a moment never to be forgotten. The contrast between Lord Munster's uniform and mine was rather acute because he, I recollect, was in jackboots and Staff dress appropriate to his function as ADC to the Commander-in-Chief of the BEF, and dry, having been put aboard a special

[1] John Wheldon, notes for the author, 4 March 1982.

boat I suppose. I was in ordinary battledress, absolutely sodden and thoroughly shaken by my ordeals.

'Johnny!' exclaimed my uncle delightedly, 'I see you have come straight from battle!'

Preferring to give way to my fellow-emissary, whom I considered to be far more important, I replied: 'I think Lord Munster has also come . . .' But my uncle was determined to hear my story first. 'Who sent you and what have you got to say about the situation?' he asked. 'I believe we have taken off about eighty thousand men and still have another two hundred and fifty thousand.'

'I have been sent by General Alexander, 1st Division Commander,' I said, 'to say that in his opinion the most urgent need is for small boats to get the troops off the beaches out to the bigger ships.'

My uncle next wanted to know why I was so wet. 'Have you come straight out of the sea?' he asked.

'Yes,' I told him, 'and I will be pleased to go back again in a fast motor-boat to give everyone encouragement.'

At long last Lord Munster was able to get a word in edgeways, 'I have exactly the same message to report,' he said. 'The C in C thinks that the small boats can be our salvation.'[1]

Two naval signals from the Dunkirk beaches, both of which were shown to Churchill that morning, reinforced the messages that had been brought by his own nephew and by Gort's ADC. 'Boats urgently required,' one of the signals read, 'Only two whalers, one cutter, one motor boat; and about 60,000 soldiers to embark. Matter most urgent.'[2] The other signal, from the destroyer *Vimy*, was more outspoken: 'Request continuous fighter action in the air,' it read, 'No Beauforts are left. If these conditions are not complied with a scandal, repetition scandal, reflecting on the present British Cabinet forever, will pass to history.'[3]

Throughout May 30, the Defence Committee, the Chiefs of Staff Committee and the War Cabinet received a series of messages from Dunkirk, and sought, as best they could, to follow if not to guide events, and to consider the wider implications of the collapse of the Allied forces in northern France.

In his account, Johnny Churchill had recalled Lieutenant-General Pownall as one of those returning from Dunkirk on the morning of May 30, and it was at the first of the Defence Committee meetings of

[1] John Spencer Churchill, *Crowded Canvas*, London 1961, pages 162–3.

[2] Lieutenant Fletcher (La Panne) to Admiralty, telephoned at 8.50 a.m., 30 May 1940: Premier papers, 3/175, folio 18.

[3] HMS *Vimy* to Vice-Admiral Dover (Bertram H. Ramsay), telephoned at 8.15 a.m., 30 May 1940: Premier papers, 3/175, folio 16.

that morning that Pownall, Gort's Chief of Staff, read out the signal from the *Vimy* and insisted that there was 'no truth whatever in the insinuations made in it'.

Pownall then described in detail the plans for holding the Dunkirk perimeter to enable the embarkations to continue. Eighteen years later Ian Jacob, who was present at the Defence Committee meeting as Military Assistant Secretary to the War Cabinet, recalled how:

> The Prime Minister questioned General Pownall and listened to the plans. No one in the room imagined that they could be successful if the German armoured divisions supported by the Luftwaffe pressed their attack. The perimeter would be broken as it thinned out, and there would be carnage on the beaches. Churchill never gave a sign of weakness. Nothing but encouragement and resolve showed in his face or his voice.

'We felt,' Jacob added, 'that he would have liked to be fighting on the beaches himself.' [1]

The Munster mission, Alexander's emissary, and Pownall had achieved their purpose; for Dudley Pound was able to report to the Defence Committee that 'every possible small craft' was being collected in British harbours and sent across to Dunkirk. 'Very many were on the way,' he said, 'but there had been a number of unfortunate accidents in the darkness, leading to the loss of considerable numbers on the passage.'

Seeking to answer French criticisms of the withdrawal to Dunkirk, Pownall told the Committee: 'There could be no foundation whatever for a suggestion that we had left the 1st French Army in the lurch. We had guarded their flanks to the last, but they had no spirit to continue the fight.' The British evacuation itself, Pownall added, was being made more difficult because the whole area 'was a congested mass of disorganized Frenchmen, refugees and Belgians'. At one moment it had seemed likely 'that a body of about 1,500 Frenchmen would attempt to storm the boats'. Now, however, one-third of the beach to the east of Dunkirk had been 'allotted' to the French.

Churchill approved this decision. The principle must also be established, he said, that the British and French 'share the available shipping', although he recognized, as the notes of the Defence Committee recorded, 'that the embarkation of French soldiers might reduce the number of British who could be saved, but for the good of the common cause this must be accepted'.

[1] Lieutenant-General Sir Ian Jacob, 'His Finest Hour', in *The Atlantic*, March 1965, page 82. The article was written in the spring of 1958, as part of a pre-obituary issue planned by the editor, Edward Weeks.

The evacuation figures belied the earlier pessimism. Up to the early hours of that morning, the Committee was told, 80,000 men had been evacuated, including troops from Boulogne.[1] But although withdrawal was proceeding 'all the time', as Churchill reported to the War Cabinet shortly after midday, 'the conditions were difficult', and the War Cabinet approved Churchill's draft of a further telegram to Gort, which was sent from the War Office at two o'clock that afternoon, instructing Gort that once his fighting force was reduced to the equivalent of three Divisions, he should hand over command and return to England. 'On political grounds,' the message explained, 'it would be a needless triumph to the enemy to capture you when only a small force remained under your orders.'

This message to Gort, which Churchill had drafted in his own hand, ended with a clear transfer of authority from the War Cabinet to the senior officer at Dunkirk itself. 'The Corps Commander chosen by you,' the message read, 'should be ordered to carry on the defence, in conjunction with the French, and evacuation whether from Dunkirk or the beaches, but when in his judgment no further organized resistance is possible and no further proportionate damage can be inflicted upon the enemy, he is authorised in consultation with the Senior French Commander to capitulate formally to avoid useless slaughter.'[2]

There was one other urgent matter to be discussed before the War Cabinet ended, the increase of activity by members of the Irish Republican Army in southern Ireland. It was Chamberlain who raised the matter, telling his four colleagues, as well as Eden and Cadogan, that the IRA forces now seemed 'almost strong enough to over-run the

[1] Defence Committee No. 11 of 1940, 30 May 1940, 10.15 a.m.: Cabinet papers, 69/1. General Brooke returned to Britain that evening, having handed over command of II Corps to General Montgomery. His last entry in his war diary was: 'Embarkation still proceeding too slowly. Heavy bombing of beaches' (Brooke diary, 30 May 1940, 'Lt Gen Brooke's Diary, 10th May 1940–30th May 1940': War Office papers, 106/1708).

[2] Message of 30 May 1940: Cabinet papers: 65/7, folio 199. In *The Second World War*, volume 2, London 1949, page 96, Churchill commented: 'It is possible that this last message influenced other great events and the fortunes of another valiant Commander. When I was at the White House at the end of December 1941 I learned from the President and Mr Stimson of the approaching fate of General MacArthur and the American garrison at Corregidor. I thought it right to show them the way in which we had dealt with the position of a Commander-in-Chief whose force was reduced to a small fraction of his original command. The President and Mr Stimson both read the telegram with profound attention, and I was struck by the impression it seemed to make upon them. A little later in the day Mr Stimson came back and asked for a copy of it, which I immediately gave him. It may be (for I do not know) that this influenced them in the right decision which they took in ordering General MacArthur to hand over his command to one of his subordinate generals, and thus saved for all his future glorious services the great Commander who would otherwise have perished or passed the war as a Japanese captive. I should like to think this was true.'

weak Eire forces', and he advised that Britain must be 'ready to send forces to southern Ireland'.[1]

Churchill realized the danger to Britain of a civil war in Ireland, arising most probably out of a German landing. But such a landing, he minuted to Ismay, for the Chiefs of Staff Committee on the following day, would also bring 'various advantages to us'. These he listed as:

1 We should bomb and fight the German Air Force under conditions specially favourable to us, and costly to them.

2 We should take Berehaven, & c., for our own use.

3 We should have split the Sinn Feiners effectively and should have the greater part of the population on our side for the first time in history.

Much would of course depend, Churchill added, 'on prompt attack upon the enemy Air Force', either after the German invasion of Eire, or 'on their way there'.[2]

It was the Minister of Labour, Ernest Bevin, who, three weeks later, sought some constitutional change for Ireland, as a feature and outcome of the war, proposing, in a private letter to Churchill, a 'joint Defence Council' for Ireland, immediate consultations between the British and Eire General Staffs, and agreement by Britain and Eire for a new constitution 'on the basis of a united Ireland at the end of hostilities'. The Chairman of the constitution-making body, Bevin added, should be selected by the President of the United States.

Churchill noted on the bottom of Bevin's letter: 'I certainly shd welcome any approach to Irish unity: but I have 40 years experience of its difficulties. I cd never be a party to the coercion of Ulster to join the Southern counties: but I am much in favour of their being persuaded. The key to this is de Valera showing some loyalty to Crown & Empire.'[3]

As soon as the midday War Cabinet of May 30 was over, Churchill lunched with his cousins the Duke and Duchess of Marlborough, his brother John and sister-in-law Lady Gwendeline Churchill, and their daughter Clarissa, together with his naval aide, Commander Thompson.[4] Hardly had lunch ended, than news reached Churchill that half the British Expeditionary Force 'were now away', but that Dunkirk as a port of evacuation was 'scarcely usable any more'.[5]

[1] War Cabinet No. 147 of 1940, 30 May 1940, 12.30 p.m.: Cabinet papers, 65/7, folio 197.

[2] Minute of 31 May 1940, General Ismay for the Chiefs of Staff Committee: Churchill papers, 20/13.

[3] Letter and Minute of 18 June 1940: Premier papers, 4/53/2, folios 118–20.

[4] Churchill engagement diary, 30 May 1940: Churchill papers, 2/413.

[5] Colville diary, 4 p.m., 30 May 1940: Colville papers. At the War Cabinet an hour and a half later it was learned that 105,241 men had already been evacuated (War Office figure). The Admiralty figure was given as 86,000, then, during the meeting, increased to 101,154 (Cabinet papers, 65/7, folio 202).

At the War Cabinet later that afternoon it was the question of a German invasion of Britain that dominated the discussion, after Pound had reported German naval activity on the Norwegian coast, and German motor-boats collected at Bremen and Hamburg. The Navy, Churchill commented, 'would have to endeavour to intercept such raids on the high seas'. But it became clear during the discussion that, particularly in the event of a night crossing, some of the raiding craft 'would probably get through'. To this Churchill replied, as the minutes recorded, 'that we should not hesitate to contaminate our beaches with gas if this course would be to our advantage'. And he added: 'We had the right to do what we liked with our own territory.'[1]

Churchill then read to the War Cabinet a series of French requests, sent through General Spears, who had flown back from Paris to London. The French were appealing for further British divisions to help on the Somme front, where there had been hard and continuous fighting for eight days; for more Royal Air Force assistance; for joint Anglo-French appeals to Roosevelt, and 'for concessions to Italy'. He could not resist the conclusion, Churchill said, that 'when we refused these requests, as we must, the French would use these refusals as an excuse for giving up the struggle'.

In Churchill's view it would, he said, be 'quite unreasonable to denude the essential defences of this country to send such small fully trained and equipped forces as were available to fight on the Somme front', where they could not possibly make any appreciable effect in relation to the large German forces 'which would shortly be available for pressing the attack'. If the French could hold out until the forces evacuated from Dunkirk had been re-equipped, and further Dominion forces had arrived in Britain, then 'we should send them help'.

All this, Churchill suggested, he could himself explain to the French, and he proposed flying to Paris on the following morning, with Attlee and Dill, for this purpose. Effectively, Churchill's mission would be to keep France in the war, for the War Cabinet also learned, through the British Ambassador in Paris, that Daladier was still eager to pursue the idea of negotiations through Italy, despite Reynaud's veto of the idea. The War Cabinet accepted that 'it would be impossible to dissuade the French', but it was agreed, and this gave urgency to Churchill's visit, that the French 'should not commit us by anything which they said to Signor Mussolini'.

The War Cabinet then discussed another evacuation. Earlier that week, almost unnoticed amid the drama of Dunkirk, Allied troops had

[1] War Cabinet No. 148 of 1940, 30 May 1940, 5.30 p.m.: Cabinet papers: 65/7.

occupied Narvik. Now it was decided to withdraw not only from Narvik itself, but from northern Norway altogether. Britain could discharge its 'moral obligations' to the Norwegians, said Halifax, 'by giving notice to them in advance of our intentions, so as to free ourselves from the charge which had been levelled against King Leopold'. It was agreed to begin the withdrawal on June 2, for completion on June 7.[1]

The War Cabinet ended at eight o'clock that evening, after two and a half hours' discussion. That night Churchill dined with Neville Chamberlain and his wife.[2] Then, at eleven o'clock, he took the Chair at a further Defence Committee meeting, at which it was learned, from a message timed 8.15 p.m., that 120,000 men had now been taken off from Dunkirk, and its easterly beaches, 'including 6,000 French', that 860 vessels were involved in the evacuation, and that in spite of intense bombardment and air attack, '4,000 men had been embarked in the previous hour'. Churchill again emphasized 'the urgent necessity of getting off more French troops. If we failed to do so it might do irreparable harm to the relations between ourselves and the Allies'.[3] So urgent did this factor seem, that Churchill repeated it that same day in a telephone conversation direct with Lord Gort.[4]

This then was the fear that night; that the French, assisted by an upsurge of anti-British feeling, would seek a sudden peace. Nor was the idea of peacemaking confined to France. During May 30 Desmond Morton sent Churchill a seven page note by the Australian High Commissioner in London, Stanley Bruce, arguing, in one of its paragraphs, in favour of an international conference 'to formulate a peace settlement'. Churchill struck out this paragraph, and wrote in the margin: 'No'. Crossing out Bruce's final point, that 'the further shedding of blood and the continuance of hideous suffering is unnecessary' and

[1] War Cabinet No. 148 of 1940, 30 May 1940, Confidential Annex, Minute 9: Cabinet papers, 65/13. Churchill's distress at the conduct of the Narvik operation was expressed most forcefully two weeks later, when he minuted to Anthony Eden: 'I hope before any fresh appointment is given to General Auchinleck, the whole story of the slack and feeble manner in which the operations at Narvik were conducted, and the failure to make an earlier assault on Narvik Town, will be considered. Let me know the dates when General Auchinleck was in effective command of the military. I regard the operations at Narvik as a shocking example of costly over-caution and feebleness, all the more lamentable in contrast with German fortitude in defence and vigour in attack. When the whole story is complete, the question of disciplinary action against General Mackesy must also be considered. Rewards to brave and skilful Officers have no meaning unless severe and public punishment is also inflicted on those who fall below the standard of determination without which we cannot win this war' (Minute of 14 June 1940: Churchill papers, 20/13).

[2] Churchill's monthly engagement cards, entry for 30 May 1940: Commander Thompson papers.

[3] Defence Committee No. 12 of 1940, 30 May 1940, 11 p.m.: Cabinet papers, 69/1.

[4] Reported by Churchill to Reynaud on the following day, telegram of 31 May 1940: Churchill papers, 23/2.

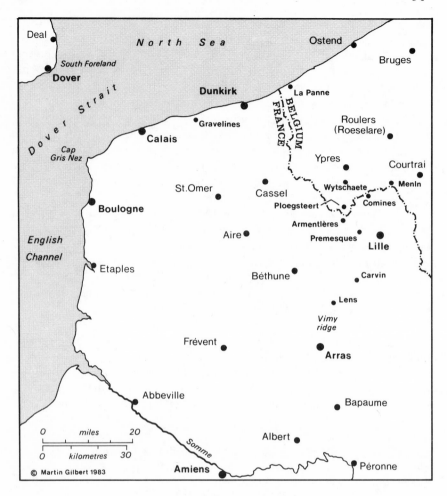

that the belligerents should 'cease the struggle', Churchill wrote: 'Rot,' and went on to note, for Morton: 'The end is rotten.'[1]

That night one of Churchill's private secretaries, John Martin, wrote home: 'The PM's confidence and energy are amazing. "Nobody left his presence without feeling a braver man" was said of Pitt; but it is no less true of him.'[2]

---

[1] Bruce note, undated; Morton note of 30 May 1940; Churchill note, undated: Premier papers, 7/2.

[2] Martin letter, 30 May 1940: Martin papers.

22

'The British People Will Fight On'

A S Churchill prepared to fly to France on the morning of Friday 31 May 1940, the news of the Dunkirk evacuation gave considerable cause for relief: 133,878 British troops, and 11,666 Allied troops, mostly French, had been successfully evacuated up to seven o'clock that morning.[1]

As the evacuation continued throughout the morning of May 31, Churchill flew across the Channel to France. With him were Attlee, Dill and Ismay. As their plane and its fighter escort approached Paris, the presence of German fighters north of the city forced a substantial detour.

Those gathered at the airport at Villacoublay feared the worst, as the arrival time, ten o'clock, came and went. 'After a painful period of waiting,' recalled one of those, Louis Spears, who was at the airport, 'some keen-eyed fellow cried that he saw them, then we all did, and almost at once there was a mighty roar, the plane landed, and out stepped the rather hunched but resilient figure of Winston, a stick on which he did not lean in his hand'. Spears went on to recall how Churchill:

was as fresh as a daisy, obviously in grand form. He might not have had a care in the world. This was perhaps due to the fact that he had had a rest in the plane, but was more likely generated by the sense of the danger inherent in such a journey. Danger, the evocation of battle, invariably acted as a tonic and a stimulant to Winston Churchill.

As a sign of good humour which was very gratifying to me, for I took it to denote satisfaction with my work, he stood and looked at me with an enormous grin, then poked me in the stomach. This was far more eloquent than any phrase even he might have coined.[2]

[1] Report of 31 May 1940: Cabinet papers, 65/7, folio 208.
[2] Major-General Sir Edward Spears, *Assignment to Catastrophe*, volume 1, London 1954, page 293.

After Churchill had 'waved his stick and beamed at the escorting pilots', he was driven to the British Embassy in the Rue Saint-Honoré, for lunch with the Ambassador, Sir Ronald Campbell, and then on to the Rue Saint-Dominique, to Reynaud's own room at the Ministry of War. It was Ismay who later recalled, of the opening moments of this emergency conference, how, 'As we were standing round the table waiting for the discussion to begin, a dejected-looking old man in plain clothes shuffled towards me, stretched out his hand and said: "Pétain". It was hard to believe that this was the great Marshal of France whose name was associated with the epic of Verdun and who had done more than anyone else to restore the morale of the French Army after the mutinies of 1917. He now looked senile, uninspiring, and defeatist.'[1]

The meeting opened at half past two, and was formally the thirteenth meeting of the Supreme War Council.[2] Churchill reported the latest, midday, figure of 165,000 men evacuated from Dunkirk. These figures included 10,000 wounded, 'but so far only 15,000 French soldiers'. Reynaud at once 'drew attention', as the official minutes recorded, to the 'disparity' in numbers, warning that unless French troops were withdrawn in greater number the French public 'might draw unfortunate conclusions'.[3] But it was not only Reynaud who had been upset by the figures of only 15,000 French soldiers among the 165,000 soldiers evacuated so far, for at this very moment, as Spears wrote:

Weygand chimed in, 'But how many French? The French are being left behind?' His voice was high, querulous and aggressive.

The Prime Minister looked at him for a moment. The light had died out of his face, his fingers were playing a tune on the edge of the table; out came his lower lip as if he were going to retort, and I expected one of those sentences that hit like a blow, but his expression changed again. It was evident that he

[1] *The Memoirs of General The Lord Ismay*, London 1960, page 133.

[2] The two British representatives were Churchill and Attlee, the two French representatives, Reynaud (President of the Council) and Pétain (Vice-President of the Council). Also present were, on the British side, Sir Ronald Campbell (the British Ambassador in Paris), General Sir John G. Dill (Chief of the Imperial General Staff), Major-General H. L. Ismay (Deputy Secretary, Military, of the War Cabinet) and Major-General E. L. Spears MP. On the French side were also present General Weygand (Chief of the General Staff), Admiral Darlan (Chief of the Naval Staff) and Captain Roland de Margerie, Reynaud's Chef de Cabinet.

[3] All quotations from the Official Minutes of the 13th Supreme War Council meeting are from Cabinet papers, 99/3, folios 83–90. All quotations specifically referred to as the notes or recollections of Major-General Spears are taken from his summary of his notes, and subsequent recollections, published in *Assignment to Catastrophe*, volume 1, London 1954, pages 294–319. Of his personal role at the Council, Spears wrote: 'I was busy throughout taking voluminous notes' (page 294).

felt every indulgence must be shown to people so highly tried, undergoing so fearful an ordeal. He looked very sad, and as he spoke a wave of deep emotion swept from his heart to his eyes, where tears appeared not for the only time that afternoon. 'We are companions in misfortune,' he said, 'there is nothing to be gained from recrimination over our common miseries.'

The note he had struck was so true, went so deep, that a stillness fell over the room, something different from silence, it was like the hush that falls on men at the opening of a great national pageant. I imagine all thoughts were turned inwards, questioning whether each one was observing that precept. It was important in its results, for the note it struck was maintained throughout the meeting; goodwill, courtesy and mutual generosity prevailed.

Churchill then explained that the evacuation of Narvik could begin on June 2, involving some 16,000 men, mostly Polish and French troops, apart from the British troops. There were also a hundred anti-aircraft guns to be evacuated, all badly needed in Britain. As many troops as possible, Churchill agreed with Reynaud, would be sent, after regrouping in the Clyde, to the Somme–Aisne front, for the defence of Paris. The Norwegian expedition was at an end.

Returning to the second item on the agenda, the Dunkirk evacuation, Churchill defended the predominance of British troops among those rescued on the grounds that 'up to the present' the French troops had received no orders to evacuate. This was indeed so. When General Blanchard had visited Gort's headquarters on May 29 he was, as Gort later recorded, 'obviously very upset at the suggestion that the BEF was to embark. It was clear to me that whereas we had both received similar instructions from our own Government for the establishment of a bridgehead, he had as yet received no instructions to correspond with those I had received to evacuate my troops.' General Blanchard, noted Gort, 'would not contemplate evacuation'.[1]

'One of the chief reasons he had come to Paris,' Churchill told Reynaud, 'was to make sure that the same orders were now given to the French troops as had been given to the British.'

Instructions in this sense, commented Weygand, 'were already being acted upon', and Gort, Blanchard, and the French Commander-in-Chief at Dunkirk, Admiral Abrial, 'were in close touch'. Churchill then gave the French an assurance 'that the British would keep their three divisions on the perimeter in order to enable as many French troops to get away as possible. This would be the British contribution to the heavy Allied losses that must inevitably be suffered under such

---

[1] *Despatches of the Operations of the British Expeditionary Force 3rd September 1939 to 19th June 1940*, page 46, Secret Document No. A.5307: Premier papers, 3/188/5.

conditions. There would, he hoped, be no reproaches as between comrades-in-arms faced with a great disaster.'

The British troops, Churchill insisted, would 'fight their way back to the very edge of the sea', even though a part of the rearguard, whose defensive action alone could ensure this, would be 'crushed'.[1]

Churchill then went on to explain that the British Government had 'found itself compelled to order Lord Gort to evacuate the fighting troops before the wounded, of which there were many thousands within the perimeter. It was only the dire circumstances of the war that had made such an order necessary for the sake of the future: the able-bodied could be taken off in greater number than stretcher cases, and numbers were vital for continuing the struggle.' It was hoped, however, Churchill added, 'that American aid might perhaps be enlisted to look after and succour the wounded left behind'.

The evacuation, as now seemed likely, of 200,000 able-bodied troops, would, Churchill said, be 'almost a miracle'. Four days ago he would not have wagered on more than 50,000 'as a maximum'. But he felt he must point out that the British would lose all their equipment, with the exception of small arms and personal equipment. 'Some 1,000 British field guns, all the heavy guns, and all the mechanical transport would have to be left behind'; yet this was precisely the equipment of which the British 'were so terribly short'. They had now lost, Churchill said, more than double the number of guns that existed in the United Kingdom.

At one point in the discussion, according to Spears' account, Churchill pressed upon Admiral Darlan the need to block Dunkirk harbour 'in good time', to prevent its use by the Germans in the immediate aftermath of the evacuation. At this, Spears wrote:

... there was another dismal sound from Darlan, as of a flapping sail on a dying breeze: 'We have not the means to block the harbour.' The Prime Minister's voice now was like a cracking whip. He evidently did not intend that an answer be given him. 'We have the means and we will block the harbour, and we will do it in good time. The Germans shall not have the opportunity of using Dunkirk harbour.'

[1] Such was the official record. Spears gives the following version of these same remarks: 'Churchill was speaking again: "we have hopes", he said, "hopes which may be destroyed by enemy action, of avoiding anything in the nature of a capitulation". Then, with his jaw well forward, he said: "we will fight to the water's edge. The rear-guard may of course be *assommée*," he used the French word. Wiped out was the meaning. "There will be no capitulation", echoed Weygand, "though there may be extermination", and his hands went up and he looked down with the gesture and expression of a man watching his wallet fall down a well. This remark did not happen to strike the right note, perhaps because, whatever else had happened so far, none sitting at that table had heard of any French Army being massacred rather than surrender.'

As the discussion continued, Reynaud 'begged' Churchill, as the official minutes recorded, to send at once 'the largest possible number' of British troops to help hold the French front line along the Somme. But Churchill pointed out that of the nine divisions which had previously made up the British Expeditionary Force, 'there might perhaps be 4 or 5 divisions left', for which it would be 'very difficult to find fresh equipment'. As for further forces, he said, in the last three weeks one Regiment of Guards had been sent to Belgium, of which one half had been lost; and of two Rifle Brigade battalions, some three thousand men strong, sent to Calais, only 30 men had survived. 'There were now no forces left,' he warned, 'that could be sent at once. Something had to be kept within the United Kingdom to deal with a possible invasion by sea or air.' In this connection, Churchill added, 'the danger had become much more pressing, since Germany could now debouch not only from the mouths of the German rivers but from ports in Holland, Belgium and, within a matter of days, France itself'.

Churchill also pointed out to Reynaud that of the thirty-nine squadrons originally allocated to the Air Defence of Great Britain, ten had been sent to France, 'originally for a few days only; but as matters had turned out there was now very little of these ten squadrons left'. As a result of this decision to send Britain's own air support to the French, Churchill explained, Britain was left with only twenty-nine squadrons to meet a concentrated attack, 'not so much upon the civilian population of the islands—for such an attack would be stoutly resisted and he did not fear it—as upon the factories engaged in the production of new aircraft'. He felt confident, Churchill added, that the Royal Air Force 'would continue to give a good account of itself against the present heavy odds; but if the factories were put out of action, then the situation would indeed become hopeless. It was impossible to run any further risk; he was neither authorised, nor would he be willing, to expose the vital British aircraft industry to greater danger than was already being run.'

Churchill now returned to the question of British troops who might be sent to western France, as part of an effort to build up a 'land force' there, for the defence of Paris. There were already two British divisions, he pointed out, 'in position on the new front', and one of them was armoured. In Britain itself, interjected Dill, there were only three divisions left, and these were 'not fully equipped'.

Churchill now sought to encourage Reynaud to persevere, holding out hope for an 'increasing *tempo*' of further British divisions for France 'in the future'. There were at present, Churchill pointed out, fourteen divisions undergoing training in the United Kingdom. But these were equipped only with rifles, 'and therefore totally unfit for modern warfare'. As he saw it, however, the future was not so bleak, for, as he told Reynaud: 'When guns, anti-tank equipment and other supplies began to come in, the situation would alter very rapidly.' Meanwhile, 'every effort' was being made to draw as fully as possible upon the resources of the British Empire. Eight battalions were at that very moment being brought back to England from Palestine, to be replaced by Indian battalions, and a further eight battalions were on their way from India itself. A further force of some 14,000 Australian troops was also due to reach Britain on June 12, and the second Canadian division would be landing 'in about a month's time'. Both the latter forces, Churchill commented, 'were of the highest quality, but not fully trained or equipped'.

The present emergency, Churchill reflected, could not have arisen at a worse moment: 'there was nothing ready, though a great deal was on its way'. If a minimum of troops was not kept in the United Kingdom 'to resist an invasion', he warned, 'then all would be lost'. For this reason, whatever Britain might be able to do in terms of troops or military supplies, 'he felt bound to utter the warning that the immediate contribution would of necessity be small'.

A telegram was then drafted by the French, to be sent to Admiral Abrial at Dunkirk. Reynaud read out the draft, in French, to the British delegation. French troops were to make their way to the points of embarkation, 'the British forces embarking first'.

At this moment Churchill interrupted, without waiting for a translation. Spears recorded the Prime Minister's intervention: ' "Nong," he roared, *"Partage—bras dessus, bras dessous."* ' The gesture Churchill made, Spears added, 'effectively camouflaging his accent, conveyed, better than the words, that he wished the French and British soldiers to leave Dunkirk arm in arm'.

As the official record noted, Churchill had insisted that the evacuation proceed 'on equal terms between the British and the French, "bras dessus bras dessous".' The telegram to Admiral Abrial was amended. A few moments later Churchill told Reynaud 'that every effort would be made to restore equilibrium by getting the French off first from now on'.

There was little time left for these plans to be put into effect. Gort was handing over his command that night, and leaving Dunkirk for Britain, although, as Dill pointed out, 'he had not wanted to leave'.[1]

---

[1] Gort was succeeded in command of the remaining troops at Dunkirk by Major-General Alexander, commander of the 1st Division, now in temporary command of 1 Corps.

The discussion then turned to Italy. It was no longer a question of negotiations to secure a general peace, but of military action against Italy as soon as Italy came into the war. The official minutes of the Supreme War Council record Churchill's determination, and Anglo-French unanimity, on this score:

Mr Churchill said that the British view was that if Italy came in against the Allies we should strike at her at once in the most effective manner. Many Italians were opposed to war, and all should be made to realise its severity. He proposed that we should strike at the North Western industrial triangle enclosed by the three cities of Milan, Turin and Genoa. Such an attack could be delivered without undue hardship to civilians. The British had four heavy Bomber Squadrons available for the purpose and the French Government had already authorised the sending of an advance party, which had in fact left England for South-Eastern France. The Royal Air Force believed strongly that great results would be gained by making this attack. Would M. Reynaud now agree to it, or did he still fear retaliation on French territory? He (Mr Churchill) did not think that the retaliation would be as serious as the damage the Royal Air Force could inflict.

M. Reynaud agreed that from the political point of view it was important to strike hard, to bring home to the Italian people the mistake they had made in entering the war when it was quite unnecessary for them to do so. As for the damage that might be inflicted on France, recriminations might take place; but he agreed that the Allies must strike at once.

Admiral Darlan said that along the coast between the Italo-French frontier and Naples, one-third of Italy's oil supplies was stored. A naval and aerial bombardment of these stores would cripple Italy seriously. The French Admiralty had a plan ready.

M. Reynaud suggested that representatives of the two Admiralties and Air Forces should meet to plan this operation. . . .

The Supreme War Council meeting of May 31 had reached the end of its agenda. 'To mark the fact,' Spears later recalled, Churchill said, in French, 'which was generally with him a sign of either exhilaration or good humour, "Fini l'Agenda". He beamed as he said it and this caused general relaxation, a feeling enhanced by the predisposition to pleased amusement among the French whenever he spoke their language, for they delighted in his accent, intonation and, above all, the supreme democracy of his repertoire which denied the right of one article rather than another to precede any given noun, and repudiated the protocol which regulates the orderly sequence of words. But he was speaking English again and his tone was expository.'

Seeking to stress the 'general outlook', as the official minutes recorded, Churchill argued that behind the German technical troops who had made possible the recent advance was a conscript army 'very far from the standard of 1914'. He could not believe that the German Army 'was as good as the French'. If the Allies could hold out through the summer, Britain would emerge as 'a most important factor', able to contribute militarily to the battles in France. Both countries must maintain 'an unflinching front against all their enemies'. The United States, he said, had been 'roused' by recent events, and even if they did not enter the war, 'they would soon be prepared to give us powerful aid'. Steel and other essentials should be ordered 'in vast quantities'. Payment should be no obstacle. If the British or French were unable to pay, 'America would nevertheless continue to deliver'.

Inspired by the solemnity of the occasion Churchill now spoke with considerable passion and emphasis, telling Reynaud, Weygand and Darlan, as the official minutes recorded, that:

An invasion of England, if it took place, would have a still profounder effect on the United States, especially in those many towns in the New World which bore the same names as towns in the British Isles. England did not fear invasion, and would resist it most fiercely in every village and hamlet. To put up a stout resistance she must have troops, and it was only after her essential and urgent needs had been met that the balance of her armed forces could be put at the disposal of her French ally.

In the present emergency, it was vital that England and France should remain in the closest accord. By doing so, they could best ensure that their spirits remained high. He was absolutely convinced that they had only to carry on the fight to conquer.

Even if one of them should be struck down, the other must not abandon the struggle. The British Government were prepared to wage war from the New World if, through some disaster, England herself was laid waste. It must be realised that if Germany defeated either Ally, or both, she would give no quarter: they would be reduced to the status of vassals and slaves for ever.

It would be better far that the civilisation of Western Europe, with all its achievements, should come to a tragic but splendid end, than that the two great Democracies should linger on, stripped of all that made life worth living. That, he knew, was the deep conviction of the whole British people, and he would himself be proclaiming it in the British Parliament within a few days.

'The British people will fight on,' Churchill had said—according to Spears' version—'until the New World reconquers the Old. Better far that the last of the English should fall fighting and *finis* to be written to our history than to linger on as vassals and slaves.'

Everyone in the room, Spears later recalled, 'was deeply moved, carried away by the emotion that surged from Winston Churchill in great torrents. It was not necessary to understand his words to seize his meaning. The interpreters were silent, it never occurred to them to translate the sentences as they poured from him, hot and passionately sincere. When they did translate, even the pale echo of the original words was formidable as is a great storm passing from sight and hearing beyond a mountain range.'

Attlee followed Churchill, telling the French leaders, as the official record noted, that he 'entirely agreed' with what Churchill had said. The British people knew that in the event of a German victory, 'everything they had built up would be destroyed'. The Germans, said Attlee, 'killed not only men but ideas'. The British people were resolved 'as never before in their history'.

Reynaud responded in kind, thanking Churchill and Attlee for their 'inspiring' words. If France could hold the Somme, he said, with the help of Britain, and if American industry came in to 'make good the disparity in arms' now that a great part of France's industrial areas were occupied by Germany, 'then they could be certain of victory'. If one country went under, Reynaud concluded, 'the other would not abandon the struggle; he was most grateful for Mr Churchill's renewed assurance on this point. Never before had their two countries been so united and determined as in the present hour of danger.'

No one knew how far Reynaud would adhere to this mood of confidence and courage. On the previous day the British Ambassador in Paris had reported to Lord Halifax: 'Reynaud is in better heart but he is a bundle of nerves and is hardly up to the herculean task of galvanizing his rather flabby team (always excepting MM Mandel, Dautry and perhaps Campinchi) into activity.' But in the postscript to this report, the Ambassador added: 'Since I began this letter, which was interrupted, the Prime Minister has come and gone. He came at a psychological moment and his visit was of supreme value. He handled the French magnificently.' At the end of the Supreme War Council meeting, the Ambassador added, Churchill had made 'the most magnificent peroration on the implacable will of the British people to fight on to the bitter end, and to go down fighting rather than to succumb to bondage'. Reynaud had responded in the same vein. But, the Ambassador warned, 'one felt that it came rather from his head than from his heart'.[1]

Although the Supreme War Council was over, for a short while those present continued to talk informally. Churchill found himself in

[1] Sir Ronald Campbell to Viscount Halifax, 31 May 1940: Foreign Office papers, 800/312.

the bay window with Pétain, Spears and de Margerie, who spoke of fighting it out in Africa if France fell. But Pétain's attitude to the young Frenchman's determination was, as Churchill later recalled, 'detached and sombre, giving me the feeling that he would face a separate peace'. There was no doubt of the danger; the influence of Pétain's personality, Churchill reflected, 'his reputation, his serene acceptance of the march of adverse events, apart from any words he used, was almost overpowering to those under his spell'.

Another of the French officials present then spoke ominously of how 'a continuance of military reverses' might necessitate 'a modification of foreign policy' upon France. It was Spears who answered him, addressing himself particularly to Pétain, and warning that any such change would mean a British blockade of France; not only blockade, but bombardment of all French ports in German hands. 'I was glad to have this said,' Churchill later wrote. 'I sang my usual song: we would fight on whatever happened or whoever fell out.'[1]

That night, following Gort's departure from Dunkirk, General Alexander was supervising the final phase of the evacuation. There remained only 20,000 British and 60,000 French troops to be taken off. At the same time, the long-term outlook did not seem so bleak. 'The Secret Service reports from Germany,' noted Churchill's junior Private Secretary, John Colville, 'show that the difficulties there are increasing and that the Nazis are terrified of failing to win the war that same year.' There was general apathy throughout Germany, 'and casualties have been heavy, the shortages of food and raw materials are making themselves felt, and the production of tanks and aircraft is falling off by about 40 percent'. If this were true, Colville added, 'the war may be over by Christmas'. At the same time, indirect attempts were being made through the Dominion High Commissioners 'to bring the United States into the war', by painting to the members of Roosevelt's administration 'the most sombre portrait of what we expect from Germany, and by harping on the possibility of France giving up the struggle'.[2]

Churchill, Attlee, Dill and Ismay remained overnight in Paris, dining and sleeping at the British Embassy. During dinner, Reynaud, Mandel and Dautry were the French guests, joining Churchill, Attlee, Dill, and Spears at the Ambassador's residence. During the dinner, as Spears later recalled, Churchill's mind 'was running on the creation of bands to attack German tank columns'. He evidently believed, Spears reflected,

[1] Winston S. Churchill, *The Second World War*, volume 2, London 1949, page 100.
[2] Colville diary, 31 May 1940: Colville papers.

in the tactical and even strategical value such operations might have, 'but it was obvious that his real hope was that they would serve to awaken France'. The French, however, were not impressed. Visualizing as they did 'colossal armoured columns advancing with irresistible force on parallel lines, like a Martian invasion, under a swarm of Stukas', for them, as Spears phrased it, Churchill's suggestions appeared 'in the nature of trying to stop a charging elephant with a pea-shooter'.

The French guests left, and Churchill said goodnight to his fellow Britons. 'I knew,' Spears later recalled, 'more from his tone than from the few words Winston said when he walked over to me as I stood alone for a moment before taking leave, that he realized in his heart that the French were beaten, that they knew it, and were resigned to defeat. He had not said so, it was as if he would not permit the thought to dwell consciously in his mind. But he knew.'

Before falling asleep, Spears jotted down in his diary a note about the Supreme War Council meeting. 'One sentence,' he wrote, 'seems to float over the conference in my memory—like a wisp of cigarette smoke circling over the table—Winston's phrase: "The partner that survives will go on", and an impression remains, more vivid than others, the way Reynaud clutched at those words as if to a lifeline.'[1]

After a night disturbed by a 'petty raid', as Churchill later recalled,[2] the British representatives returned by air to London, and shortly before noon on June 1 Churchill reached Downing Street. There, a meeting of the War Cabinet was already in progress. Churchill reported on his visit to Paris, and on Reynaud's appeal for help on the Somme front. Now that 'we had got off such a large proportion' of British troops from Dunkirk, Churchill said, 'we should send some additional troops to France, complete with the necessary air component'. Every effort should also be made 'to re-open our long-range air attacks on German industry'.

As for Dunkirk itself, it was clear from a report from General Alexander that, as Churchill expressed it, 'the embarkation must be finished that night', and that there was 'no hope for any French troops that were still outside the perimeter'. The operation for the evacuation at Dunkirk, he added, had been a 'trial of strength' between the British and German Air Forces. 'We had achieved our purpose and saved our

[1] Major General Sir Edward Spears, *Assignment to Catastrophe*, volume 1, London 1954, pages 318-9.
[2] Winston S. Churchill, *The Second World War*, volume 2, London 1949, page 100.

Army'. There could be 'no doubt', he said, 'that this constituted a signal victory for the Royal Air Force, which gave cause for high hopes for our success in the future'.[1]

While the War Cabinet was still in session, Gort arrived at Downing Street. 'Cabinet rose and greeted him,' Cadogan recorded in his diary, 'and PM said 3 or 4 sentences very well.'[2]

Churchill returned to Admiralty House, and awaited the arrival of the Chiefs of Staff, for their daily meeting. But in the confusion of the rearranged day, they were not there when he wanted them. When they did finally arrive there was 'an unpleasant scene', for, as Colville noted that night in his diary: 'He always pitches in upon the first available person to display his wrath, irrespective of who is to blame— but he bears no grudge.'[3]

At the Chiefs of Staff meeting itself, a telegram was drafted, informing Weygand that the evacuation would end that same night. Churchill tried to resist this conclusion, emphasizing to Eden, Gort and the Chiefs of Staff, 'the importance of holding on as long as possible'. Churchill argued that the Germans might not break through, and that it might therefore be possible to continue the evacuation 'for another night'. The success or failure of British efforts to rescue the remnants of the French Army, he said, 'might have great results on the Alliance'. As long as the front held, the evacuation should be continued, 'even at the cost of naval losses'. The flow of ships should therefore be maintained, 'at any rate at certain periods', during the following day.

After further discussion, it was agreed that 'nobody but the Commander on the spot', General Alexander, could decide 'whether the time had come to go, or whether the position could be held to allow evacuation to continue longer',[4] whereupon Churchill redrafted and then signed the telegram to Weygand, informing the French Commander-in-Chief that a crisis in the evacuation from Dunkirk had been reached; that the Royal Air Force was unable to provide more than five Fighter squadrons 'acting almost continuously' over the beachhead; that six ships, 'several filled with troops', had been sunk by bombing that morning; and that by trying to hold the beachhead until

---

[1] War Cabinet No. 151 of 1940, 11.30 a.m., 1 June 1940: Cabinet papers, 65/7.

[2] Cadogan diary, 1 June 1940: David Dilks (editor), *The Diaries of Sir Alexander Cadogan, OM, 1938–1945*, London 1971, page 293.

[3] Colville diary, 1 June 1940: Colville papers. Sir John Colville comments: 'He never, never bore a grudge. If he had been unpleasant to me he always made it up before the end of the day, by doing something especially nice' (conversation with the author, 20 May 1981).

[4] Chiefs of Staff Committee No. 162 of 1940, 1 June 1940, 3.30 p.m.: Cabinet papers, 79/4. Also present were the Vice Chief of the Imperial General Staff (Lieutenant-General R. H. Haining) and the Deputy Chief of the Air Staff (Air Vice Marshal W. S. Douglas).

the following day, 'we may lose all'. By a final withdrawal that night, Weygand was told, 'much may certainly be saved, though much will be lost'.

Churchill's message to Weygand ended: 'Situation cannot be fully judged only by Admiral Abrial in the fortress, nor by you, nor by us here. We have therefore ordered General Alexander commanding British sector of bridgehead to judge in consultation with Admiral Abrial whether to try to stay over tomorrow or not.'[1]

Churchill dealt with two other urgent matters during June 1. The first was brought to his attention by Desmond Morton, who pointed out that there were no War Cabinet committees to scrutinize or push the production of small inventions. Before the war, as a member of a Committee of Imperial Defence sub-committee on Air Defence Research, Churchill had taken a strong personal interest in such matters. Morton now proposed that he and Lindemann should do it. 'Get to it, both of you,' Churchill replied, '& report to me what we shd push out for full blast production.'[2]

The second matter concerned evacuation in the event of invasion, or even before invasion. This had been raised in several forms. The Foreign Office had put forward a suggestion to prepare to evacuate the Royal Family, and also the Government, to 'some part of the Overseas Empire, where the war would continue to be waged'. When Morton passed on this request to Churchill, the Prime Minister answered: 'I believe we shall make them rue the day they try to invade our island. No such discussion can be permitted.'[3]

At this same moment, the Director of the National Gallery, Kenneth Clark, suggested that the paintings in the National Gallery should be sent from London to Canada. Churchill was likewise against this suggestion, and emphatically so. 'No,' he minuted, 'bury them in caves and cellars. None must go. We are going to beat them.'[4]

---

[1] Telegram No. 72794, despatched 6.45 p.m., 1 June 1940: Premier papers, 3/175, folio 12.

[2] Morton note of 30 May 1940, Churchill Minute of 1 June 1940: Premier papers, 7/2.

[3] Submission of D. J. M. D. Scott, 30 May 1940 and Churchill minute, 1 June 1940: Premier papers, 7/2.

[4] Quoted in John Colville's diary, 1 June 1940: Colville papers. In November 1939, during Chamberlain's premiership, the 'Lincoln' copy of Magna Carta had been sent from England to be deposited in the Library of Congress 'for safe keeping during the war'. On 11 November 1940 the British Embassy in Washington telegraphed to the Foreign Office: 'Magna Carta now in Embassy safe' (Washington Telegram No. 2623, 11 November 1940: Foreign Office papers, 371/24245).

23

'I Expect Worse to Come. . . .'

IN the late afternoon of Saturday 1 June 1940 Churchill left London for Chequers. It was his first weekend visit to the house which was to become his main weekend retreat of the war. But it was to be only a brief escape from the drama of the final stages of the evacuation from Dunkirk. On the Sunday he lunched with his wife, Eric Seal and Desmond Morton, before returning to London for the second part of a meeting of the Chiefs of Staff Committee at 5.15 and for the War Cabinet at 6.30.

At their evening meeting on June 2, the Chiefs of Staff reported that the evacuation from Dunkirk was continuing, but only in the hours of darkness. It had been halted at seven that morning, but would continue from 9 p.m., when it was expected that 22,000 would be 'got off' during the night. The French had asked for the evacuation to continue on Monday night as well, to take off the remaining 25,000.

The Committee then considered an appeal from Reynaud to Churchill, sent just after midday through General Spears, for the despatch back to France, to the Somme front, of three divisions of Dunkirk evacuees, all of whom were, as Reynaud phrased it, 'of tested fighting value'. Reynaud also asked for British fighting aircraft to operate henceforth not from British but from French air fields, and he added: 'We are constructing new grounds for our own aeroplanes.'[1]

This new appeal from Reynaud, as Colville noted, 'annoys Winston who considers the French grasping and whose main energies are now turned to consolidating our home defences, conserving our air strength and building up a new army from the remnants of the old, and from the troops now in India and Palestine'. At the same time, it was clear

[1] Chiefs of Staff Committee No. 163 of 1940, held in the Admiralty, 2 June 1940: Cabinet papers: 79/4.

to Churchill and to all those present that it was 'vital to sustain French morale and give no excuse for their collapse'.[1]

According to Ian Jacob, who was present at this particular meeting, 'never for one minute did Churchill contemplate denuding this Island of the fighter strength it needed. The question was, how much *could* be spared without weakening the British defences.' On this question, Jacob later recalled, Churchill and the Chiefs of Staff 'kept receiving conflicting views' as to the number of aircraft available, and in immediate prospect.[2]

This same question dominated the War Cabinet which met at 6.30 that same evening. There was a general feeling, expressed by Halifax and Chamberlain, against sending further aid to France, and a feeling of the need to 'cut loose and concentrate on the defence of these islands', as Cadogan summed it up in his diary that night. Cadogan added: 'sentimental Winston rather doubtful'.[3]

Churchill's actual arguments were recorded in the official minutes. If Britain failed to respond to Reynaud's appeal, he said, 'there was a considerable danger that a point might be reached at which French resistance might collapse; and, if Paris fell, they might be tempted to conclude a separate peace'. Such a peace would mean the establishment in France 'of a Government friendly to the Nazis', with the result that Britain would then 'have to bomb aerodromes in France, occupied by German air forces, and to exercise economic pressure against France'. Indeed, he warned, Britain might eventually be faced with a French Government 'not merely out of the war, but actually hostile to us'.

Churchill was supported in part by Attlee who, while not wishing to send any fighter aircraft to France, did suggest the offer of 'one or two divisions', both as a 'token of our sincerity', and as a means of doing at least something 'to hearten the French'. As for air support, Sir Archibald Sinclair suggested that French demands for bombing assistance could probably be met by the use of Polish pilots based in Britain, but the risk of sending any further fighter squadron overseas 'would be very difficult to justify'.

---

[1] Colville diary, 2 June 1940: Colville papers.

[2] Lieutenant-General Sir Ian Jacob, conversation with the author, 6 December 1979. Sir Ian Jacob's recollection was correct; on 5 June 1940 Churchill minuted to Ismay: 'How was it when I went to Paris and asked for the ten additional squadrons I was told we had only 39, so that the ten reduced them to 29? Please look up the papers on this point. The Air Ministry change their figures every single day' (Minute of 5 June 1940: Churchill papers, 20/13).

[3] Cadogan diary, 2 June 1940: David Dilks (editor), *The Diaries of Sir Alexander Cadogan, OM, 1938–1945*, London 1971, page 293.

Churchill sought no final decision, but proposed waiting for the appreciation of the situation by the Chiefs of Staff. Personally, he said, he would like to be able to send three divisions to France within the next five to six weeks, starting with the Canadians. He also wanted British bombers to bomb by night, wherever possible, 'targets as indicated by the French Commander-in-Chief', rather than the existing British targets in the Ruhr. But he doubted whether any additional fighter squadrons should be sent across the Channel, 'unless it was found possible to operate them from west of Abbeville'. Churchill's conclusion was that Britain should give 'the greatest possible' support to France, 'without leaving the defence forces of the United Kingdom dangerously reduced in face of the risk of invasion'.[1]

Focusing his mind increasingly on the danger of a German invasion, Churchill also told the War Cabinet of June 2 of the need for the 'most intensive study' of how to defeat the type of swift German tank advance which had proved so effective in France. On the one hand, he said, 'there was the probability of adopting special weapons for this purpose, while on the other hand, it should be possible to devise some system for harrying and pursuing tanks'. It should be possible, Churchill added, 'to cut off tank crews from supplies of food, water and petrol'.[2]

In a note that same day to Ismay, for consideration by the Chiefs of Staff, Churchill expressed some optimism on the prospect for Britain once the units returned from Dunkirk could be re-formed. Even 200,000 men, he wrote, based on the 'mass of trained troops' returned from Dunkirk, 'would not be beyond our compass', and would constitute a serious obstacle to any German invasion attempt, except one that would have to be executed 'on a prohibitively large scale'.

Churchill then set out for the Chiefs of Staff the reasons for his confidence. 'As I have personally felt less afraid,' he wrote, 'of a German attempt at invasion than of the piercing of the French line on the Somme or Aisne and the fall of Paris, I have naturally believed the Germans would choose the latter.' This probability, he added, was 'greatly increased by the fact that they will realise that the armed forces in Great Britain are now far stronger than they have ever been, and that their raiding parties would not have to meet half-trained formations, but the men whose mettle they have already tested, and from whom they have recoiled, not daring seriously to molest their departure'.

[1] War Cabinet No. 152 of 1940, 2 June 1940, 6.30 p.m., Confidential Annex: Cabinet papers, 65/13.
[2] War Cabinet No. 152 of 1940, 2 June 1940, 6.30 p.m., Item 6: Cabinet papers, 65/7.

From this hopeful assessment, Churchill returned to his scheme for helping the French to resist, by reconstructing those units of the British Expeditionary Force which were still in western and central France. Unless this were done, he feared, 'the French will not continue in the war'. Even if Paris were captured by the Germans, he believed, the French 'must be adjured to continue a gigantic guerilla', supported by British forces holding a bridgehead in Britanny, 'where a large army can be developed'.

Despite his experiences with Pétain and Darlan in Paris two days earlier, Churchill still envisaged the possibility of a continuing French military resistance. 'We must have plans worked out,' he told Ismay, 'which will show the French that there is a way through if only they will be steadfast.'[1] British heavy bomber squadrons, he wrote that same day to Sinclair and Newall, should be flown at once to aerodromes in southern France, 'to strike back at Italy' the moment Italy entered the war.[2]

There remained for Churchill on June 2 one further delicate and personal task. Three days earlier, he had learned from the King's Private Secretary, Alexander Hardinge, that the King did not wish to admit Brendan Bracken to the Privy Council, an honour that 'up till now' had been reserved 'as the lists will show, for those who have attained high office in, or rendered long service to, the state'.[3] In his reply, Churchill recalled the ten wilderness years so recently ended during which Bracken had been his staunch parliamentary and personal supporter, and when many of those now still in power had been the foe. His letter read:

My dear Hardinge,

I much regret to receive your letter of May 30. I should have thought that in the terrible circumstances which press upon us, and the burden of disaster and responsibility which has been cast upon me after my warnings have been so long rejected I might be helped as much as possible. I had it in mind to submit Mr Bracken's name to the King for a post in the Government, which would have carried with it a Privy Councillorship. But he preferred to remain a private member, giving me the personal assistance as my Parliamentary Private Secretary which he has done for so many years. In these circumstances and as he is privy necessarily to many secret matters I counted with confidence upon His Majesty's gracious favour in making the submission. One precedent which rises in my mind is that of Mr Balfour's Private Secretary, Mr Sandars,

---

[1] Minute of 2 June 1940: Churchill papers, 20/13.
[2] Minute of 2 June 1940: Churchill papers, 20/13.
[3] Letter of 30 May 1940, 'Personal', from Buckingham Palace: Churchill papers, 20/7.

who was not even a Member of Parliament, but in 1902 was sworn to the Privy Council in the reign of King Edward VII. In Mr Bracken's case the Committee of the Privy Council has seen no objection to the proposal.

Mr Bracken is a Member of Parliament of distinguished standing and exceptional ability. He has sometimes been almost my sole supporter in the years when I have been striving to get this country properly defended, especially from the air. He has suffered as I have done every form of official hostility. Had he joined the ranks of the time-servers and careerists who were assuring the public that our Air Force was larger than that of Germany, I have no doubt he would long ago have attained high Office. The fact that this is known to the public will be one of the reasons why his name will receive wide-spread approval.[1]

Within twenty-four hours the King had agreed to confer a Privy Councillorship on Brendan Bracken. 'The last thing that His Majesty wants to do,' Hardinge replied on the following day, 'is to create difficulties for you when you are bearing such an overwhelming burden of responsibility and anxiety—indeed his sympathy for you is beyond measure.'[2]

Two of the letters which Churchill was sent on Sunday June 2 were of encouragement from members of his own family, his son Randolph, and his son-in-law Duncan Sandys. Randolph, who wrote from Nottinghamshire to thank his father for being willing to pay his clothing and other bills up to £100, ended his letter by saying that he and his wife Pamela were thinking of Churchill constantly 'at this grim moment'. Randolph added: 'We pray that you will find strength to sustain you so that you may continue to lead us heroically to whatever may befall.'[3] Duncan Sandys, writing from Norway, where he was on active service, told his father-in-law: 'The one and only thing which makes us all cheerful and confident of ultimate victory is the knowledge that you are at the wheel. However badly things may seem to be going, everyone is firmly assured that somehow you will pull us through. I *know* you will.' Sandys ended: 'Good luck to you dear Winston. You are, I feel, our one solid & visible war asset. All else may fail. But so long as you are there, somehow you will bring us through to victory.'[4]

Although still living at Admiralty House, Churchill had, after a mere three weeks as Prime Minister, evolved a pattern of war direction conducive to long hours and sudden crises. An account of Churchill's day

[1] Letter of 2 June 1940: Churchill papers, 20/7.
[2] Letter of 3 June 1940: Churchill papers, 20/7.
[3] Letter of 2 June 1940: Churchill papers, 1/355.
[4] Letter of 2 June 1940: Churchill papers, 1/355.

was set down that weekend by one of his Private Secretaries, John Martin, who wrote of the 'elaborate arrangement of shifts' which had been worked out to enable each Private Secretary to have a weekend off once, if not twice, a fortnight. As Martin explained in a letter home:

It is really necessary for any but supermen like the PM himself (though even he goes to sleep most days for about an hour after lunch). He has a boxful of papers left outside his room each night and works through this in bed in the morning, dictating to a shorthand-writer, and generally does not get up and dress till quite late. About 11 he comes over to No 10 for the daily Cabinet meeting, which lasts till about 2. There is much coming and going of Ministers and Chiefs of Staff etc. for this. (Yesterday we had Lord Gort on his return from France.)

Then the PM returns to Admiralty House for lunch and rest, usually working in Downing Street (or having another meeting of Ministers there or in the House of Commons) from about 4.30 until dinner time. He dines at Admiralty House and there sees a succession of Ministers until bed-time not much before midnight and may be a good deal later.

There is going to be little time for amusements or for private reading. Bevir and I take days out helping the younger PS[1] who remains in attendance until the PM actually goes to bed, i.e. we stay at Admiralty House till 11.30 or later. On the alternate day we get away 'early' but that is not before about 8.15.

The chief difficulty is understanding what he says and great skill is required in interpreting inarticulate grunts or single words thrown out without explanation. I think he is consciously odd in these ways. Anyhow he is certainly a 'character' and I shan't soon forget an interview with him in his bedroom walking about clad only in a vest.

It has been an anxious week, waiting hour by hour for the latest news of the BEF. . . .[2]

By first light on the morning of June 3 the Dunkirk evacuation came effectively to an end, with the last of 222,568 British troops being taken off. Less than 70,000 French troops had been evacuated, however, and, when Sir Dudley Pound spoke that morning at the Chiefs of Staff Committee, he warned that every effort should be made to persuade the French to complete the evacuation 'that night'.[3]

Churchill was not present at this meeting, but when the War Cabinet met later that morning he pointed out that the French 'had not made anything like full use of the facilities available for the evacuation of

---

[1] John Peck or John Colville.
[2] Letter of 2 June 1940: Martin papers:
[3] Chiefs of Staff Committee No. 165 of 1940, 3 June 1940, 10 a.m.: Cabinets papers, 79/4.

their troops on the previous night and day'.[1] The War Cabinet then
approved his draft of a telegram to Reynaud and Weygand which
read: 'We are coming back for your men to-night. Pray make sure that
all facilities are used promptly. Last night for three hours many ships
waited idly at much cost and danger.'[2]

The facts then emerging from Dunkirk gave an indication both of
the cost, and of the achievement. During June 3 an Admiralty communiqué told of 222 naval vessels and 665 other British ships engaged
in the evacuation. Six destroyers had been sunk, and twenty-four smaller war vessels lost.[3] Churchill's own map room organizer, Captain
Pim, who had slipped away from his desk job to take part in the
evacuation, and who was now back safely, reported direct to Churchill
on June 2 that according to the War Office, in addition to more than a
quarter of a million troops, 'up to midnight last night we had brought off
71 guns and 595 vehicles'.[4]

It was the question of further military and air support for France,
however, which dominated the War Cabinet discussion on June 3. In
their report, submitted that morning, the Chiefs of Staff had recommended sending out two divisions. Churchill thought 'that we should
promise to send a third division, provided the French could supply the
artillery for it'. Neville Chamberlain, after pointing out that the situation might have changed considerably in the next three or four weeks,
said that he therefore 'saw no harm' in promising to send a third division. Churchill's proposition was then agreed.

There was no agreement, however, about the air forces that could or
could not be sent. The Chiefs of Staff Committee had recommended
limiting the British air forces in France to six bomber squadrons and
three fighter squadrons. At the War Cabinet, this was specifically recommended by the Chief of the Air Staff, Sir Cyril Newall, who pointed
out that the fighters previously sent to France, a total of more than two
hundred and fifty aircraft,[5] had been sent 'against the advice' of the

[1] War Cabinet No. 153 of 1940, 3 June 1940, 11.30 a.m.: Cabinet papers, 65/7.

[2] Telegram of 3 June 1940: Premier papers 3/175, folio 9.

[3] Admiralty communiqué, 3 June 1940: published in *The Times* on 4 June 1940. The destroyers
sunk were *Basilisk, Havant, Keith, Grafton, Grenade* and *Wakeful*.

[4] Message of 2 June 1940: Premier papers 3/175, folio 11.

[5] 'First four squadrons (64 aircraft), then 8 flights (48 aircraft), then 32 aircraft from the first
line at Home, making a total of 144 aircraft to operate "for a few days", in addition to 6
squadrons which had been ordered to operate in relays over France and Belgium at an early stage
of the battle.' All these aircraft sent to France, Sir Cyril Newall pointed out, 'had been operating
at maximum intensity ever since the 10th of May'. From half to three-quarters of a squadron had
been lost 'every day' (Cabinet papers, 65/13, folio 237).

Air Officer Commanding-in-Chief, Fighter Command, Air Chief Marshal Sir Hugh Dowding.

Dowding himself then produced a graph, illustrating the 'wastage' in Hurricanes in the ten days from 8 to 18 May 1940: 250 had been 'permanently lost', an expenditure rate of twenty-five a day, against four received from production. Had this rate of wastage continued throughout May, he said, 'we should have expended all our Hurricanes by the end of May'.

The fighting over Dunkirk, said Dowding, had involved 'a tremendous strain' on Britain's fighter resources. If the Germans were to develop 'a heavy attack on this country at this moment, he could not guarantee air superiority for more than 48 hours'. The number of fighters serviceable as of the previous day was 224 Hurricanes and 280 Spitfires. But even this low figure did not represent the 'true picture', for, as he told the War Cabinet, a number of the pilots already with their squadrons 'had not yet done their first solo on 8-gun fighters', and would need up to six weeks to become sufficiently proficient to take part in 'active operations'.

Dowding ended his ominous survey by pointing out that 'quite apart from the tremendous drain which would be involved in the despatch of any large numbers of Fighters to France', he was faced with a 'very formidable task' in reconstructing the Home Defence squadrons which had 'suffered heavily' as a result of recent operations in France, and that this had to be done at a time 'when he had to be prepared for an air attack on this country which might be launched at any moment'.

After Dowding's survey, no one present was prepared to challenge the Chiefs of Staff's recommendation. All were agreed, as far as British bombers were concerned, that French nominated targets still had to be given priority: Sinclair, Eden and Newall all argued this, 'though this was a procedure', Newall pointed out, 'which he himself had felt could not be justified on military but on psychological grounds'. But as for further fighter support, although the existing three Hurricane squadrons then in France would be brought up to full operational strength 'as soon as possible', all now accepted that no further squadrons could be sent out.

To the French, Churchill told his colleagues, 'it looked as if we had some 500 fighters of incomparable quality which we would be withholding at a moment when they would be making a supreme effort on land. It would therefore have to be pointed out to them that we were at this moment staggering under the enormous strain of recent operations in France and would recover if we were given sufficient respite.'

But until then, all we could do was to bring existing squadrons up to strength. To send any more would be 'uneconomical, because it would be impossible to maintain them'.[1]

Dowding's intervention had proved decisive, and the Chiefs of Staff report was adopted. As soon as the War Cabinet was over, Churchill telegraphed to Spears, who had the task of giving Reynaud and Weygand the War Cabinet's decision, 'You should prepare them for favourable response Army but disappointment about Air.'[2]

Dowding himself was pleased with this decision, telephoning Ironside on the following day to say that he had 'had a good day with the Cabinet', and sounding, Ironside noted, 'much less lugubrious' than he had done earlier. But Ironside also commented, critically, that Dowding was 'very much inclined to regard himself as outside the operations in France, which is quite impossible'.[3]

During the War Cabinet meeting of June 3, in the course of the discussion of fighter strength, Churchill had been 'distressed', as he wrote to Sinclair, by a statement from Sinclair that the Royal Air Force was now running short of fighter pilots, and that it was this shortage of pilots which had now become 'the limiting factor'. As soon as the War Cabinet was over, Churchill wrote to Sinclair:

This is the first time that this particular admission of failure has been made by the Air Ministry. We know that immense masses of aircraft are devoted to the making of pilots, far beyond the proportion adopted by the Germans. We heard some months ago of many thousands of pilots for whom the Air Ministry declared they had no machines, and who consequently had to be 're-mustered': as many as 7,000 were mentioned, all of whom had done many more hours of flying than those done by German pilots now frequently captured. How then, therefore, is this new shortage to be explained?

Churchill's letter continued: 'Lord Beaverbrook has made a surprising improvement in the supply and repair of aeroplanes, and in clearing up the muddle and scandal of the aircraft production branch,' and he ended: 'I greatly hope that you will be able to do as much on the Personnel side, for it will indeed be lamentable if we have machines standing idle for want of pilots to fly them.'[4]

Churchill now turned to the problems of the home front, which were

[1] War Cabinet No. 153 of 1940, 3 June 1940, Confidential Annex, Minute 10: Cabinet papers, 65/13, folios 235–40.

[2] 'Private', 'for General Spears only', 3 June 1940: Premier papers, 3/175.

[3] Ironside diary, 4 June 1940: Roderick Macleod and Denis Kelly (editors), *The Ironside Diaries 1937–1940*, London 1962, page 351.

[4] Letter of 3 June 1940: Churchill papers, 4/201.

increasingly to dominate his time. One of his concerns on June 3 was
the danger of fifth column activity among the interned aliens. 'Has
anything been done about shipping 20,000 internees to Newfoundland
or St Helena?' he minuted that day to Sir Edward Bridges. 'I should
like to get them on the seas as soon as possible . . .'[1] And on the same
day he authorized Desmond Morton to ensure 'that all military communications in England should *at once* be organized in a fool proof
way'.[2] To Lindemann he minuted: 'You are not presenting me as
I should like every few days, or every week, with a short clear statement of the falling off or improvement in munitions production,'
and he added: 'I am not able to form a clear view unless you do
this.'[3]

Churchill also issued instructions on June 3 for keeping in view the
last remaining sphere of action against German ore shipments from
Sweden: the planting of mines in the approaches to the Swedish port of
Luleå. 'This operation called *Paul* is indispensable,' he minuted to
Ismay. 'Make sure we do not find ourselves prevented by any neutrality
argument.'[4]

As the full scale of the disaster in France forced British thought to
focus on the question of meeting a German invasion, Churchill himself,
as Colville noted, was 'tired about always being on the defensive'. He
was indeed, so it appeared, 'contemplating raids on enemy territory'.[5]

In a sternly worded letter to Halifax that same day Churchill gave
his considered opinion that 'I have a large measure of responsibility as
Minister of Defence for advising the Cabinet upon the main grouping
and development of our Forces'. Were France to go 'out of the war',
Churchill told Halifax, it would be because Britain had been unable to
make 'anything like the military effort which we made in the first year
of the last war'. The least that could now be done was, 'the moment
the invasion danger has been parried', to try to build up 'a new and
stronger Expeditionary Force'. The build up of such a force would be
indispensable, and would require all the 'regular British cadres'. Churchill's letter ended: 'I hope I may be given some help in this, and be
allowed to view the War situation as a whole.'[6]

'How wonderful it would be,' Churchill minuted to Ismay on June
4, 'if the Germans could be made to wonder where they were going to

[1] Minute of 3 June 1940: Churchill papers, 20/13.
[2] Minute of 3 June 1940: Premier papers, 3/222/1.
[3] Minute of 3 June 1940: Churchill papers, 20/13.
[4] Minute of 3 June 1940: Churchill papers, 20/17.
[5] Colville diary, 3 June 1940: Colville papers.
[6] Letter of 3 June 1940: Churchill papers, 4/201.

be struck next, instead of forcing us to try to wall in the Island and roof it over.' And Churchill added: 'An effort must be made to shake off the mental and moral prostration to the will and initiative of the enemy from which we suffer.'[1]

Churchill's mood was contagious. Randolph Churchill, visiting his father for a few hours at Admiralty House, wrote to him on the following day: 'I cannot tell you how stimulating & reassuring it was to see you again & to find you so full of courage & determination.'[2]

At the War Cabinet on the morning of June 4 there was further discussion of Reynaud's appeal for more British fighters, and some criticism of France's own air policy. It emerged that the French had ignored a twenty-four hour warning from Britain of an air raid on Paris, and, as Cadogan noted in his diary, 'the pilots were all at lunch. 40 machines on the ground, and 4 got off.'[3] There was further bad news from France that day about the French air force: according to Reynaud, as reported by the British Ambassador, the French were losing aircraft at the rate of thirty-seven a day, but their 'daily intake' only amounted to eighteen, which included eight a day from America.[4]

Churchill now told his War Cabinet colleagues that he wished to reconsider the previous day's decision not to send any more fighters to France. 'His own view,' he said, 'was that we could not refuse to maintain in France the same number of squadrons as we had had there before the last battle started, while keeping a larger number of squadrons than ever in this country.' At one point during the battle in France we had been down to 29 fighter squadrons in the Air Defence of Great Britain, 'whereas now we had about 45'. According to new figures just produced by Lord Beaverbrook, the Minister of Aircraft Production, there were now more aircraft available in Britain than before the German assault on western Europe on May 10. 'We could never keep all that we wanted for our own defence,' Churchill declared, 'while the French were fighting for their lives.'

Beaverbrook now intervened to tell the War Cabinet that fighters were being manufactured at a rate of fifteen a day, with a weekly

---

[1] Minute of 4 June 1940: Churchill papers, 20/13.

[2] Letter of 5 June 1940: Churchill papers, 1/355.

[3] Cadogan diary, 4 June 1940: David Dilks (editor), *The Diaries of Sir Alexander Cadogan, OM, 1938–1945*, London 1971, page 294. The figure given to the War Cabinet by the Secretary of State for Air was 40 machines on the ground, but only *three* had taken off to intercept.

[4] Sir Ronald Campbell, Telegram No. 339 DIPP, 4 June 1940, quoted by Churchill at the War Cabinet of 4 June 1940, figures confirmed by Air Marshal Barratt.

production rate of all types of 400 aircraft.[1] But Sinclair, in a direct challenge to Churchill's hopes, argued at length against sending any further fighter squadrons to France. Despite the numerical gain, he said, 'the overall efficiency' of Fighter Command was very much less. Squadrons were now 'greatly disorganized', and many of the leaders had been lost. Britain would run 'the risk of disasters' by throwing into the battle 'unorganized units'. If additional squadrons were sent to France, more leaders would be required, and the reorganization of the fighter defences of Britain would be 'correspondingly delayed'.

Churchill deferred to Sinclair's arguments, and a telegram was sent to Reynaud, in which the Chiefs of Staff's earlier advice was upheld: the three squadrons already in France would be 'brought up to strength immediately', but in view of the 'very serious losses of the last three weeks', it would take 'some time' to overhaul the squadrons, to replace the losses, and 'to determine what further help we can send and when'. After listing the scale of Britain's recent engagements in France, and the extent of the losses, Churchill told Reynaud: 'I would most urgently ask you to appreciate that the above points materially affect the assistance that we can immediately render.'[2]

The British, like the French, looked to the United States for their essential military, air and raw material supplies. By June 1940 Arthur Purvis had built up, in Washington, more than five months' goodwill and understanding of British and French needs among those who regarded it as essential to the United States that Britain should survive. The planning departments of five Ministries at the centre of Britain's war effort—Supply, Aircraft Production, the Air Ministry, the Admiralty and the War Office—depended in large measure for the fulfilment of their programmes upon the success of these Washington endeavours. Nor would all Purvis' technical expertise have been effective in Britain's case had he not been able, by patient diplomacy and the winning of minds already attuned to Britain's cause, to enlist the help of the United States Chief of Staff, General Marshall, and the Secretary to the Treasury, Henry Morgenthau. Both men were willing to authorize the despatch of essential and costly war materials to nations that might not preserve their independence for another six months, or even six weeks. Of Morgenthau throughout this time, Purvis later wrote: 'He is the

[1] Beaverbrook gave the figures of 453 aircraft of all types produced, and 436 aircraft of all types lost, between 19 May and 1 June 1940. Of *Hurricanes* 151 had been produced and 119 lost. Of *Spitfires*, however, 39 had been produced and 75 lost.

[2] War Cabinet No. 154 of 1940, 4 June 1940, 11.30 a.m., Confidential Annex, minute 1: Cabinet papers, 65/13.

one whose responsibility has been to surmount resistance to our demands from the various US Departments, Army or others.' Purvis added: 'It is he who is regarded by the President and the other Departments as responsible for the representation of British needs and to paint in United States Government circles the picture of the British supply position.'[1]

Copper, explosives, steel, cannon, powder, aircraft engines—these were the needs of the late spring and early summer of 1940, and each was in the Purvis pipeline from before the first days of Churchill's Premiership. At the same time, at Britain's request, the export from the Americas of raw materials judged essential to Germany or Japan was deliberately held up, with United States approval, although United States, Canadian and Mexican stocks of these materials were readily available for such export. The Americans agreed to these programmes and restraints in the name of what Purvis had described to them, rightly, as 'the indefinite nature of Allied military necessity'.[2] Here was a discreet, persistent and essential life-line, news of which, reaching Churchill regularly, give him added cause for confidence in Britain's ability to survive.

For Britain, the most recent and most secret news of future supplies from the United States, while it could do nothing to ameliorate the immediate dangers, was of considerable importance for the future. On the morning of June 4 Churchill had been given details of a telegram from Washington, in which Purvis reported on a law, about to be submitted to Congress, which would enable the United States Administration to deliver war material from United States stocks to France and Britain. In his telegram, Purvis had listed the war material that was even then ready for shipment, including half a million rifles and five hundred 75-millimetre field guns.[3]

In passing on to Churchill the gist of a telephone conversation with Purvis late on the previous night, Jean Monnet, the Chairman of the Anglo-French Co-ordinating Committee in London, noted that General Marshall was already arranging for those armaments which were about to be made available to be collected, and to be 'directed to New York, ready for shipment immediately the amendment is passed'. But the course of the purchasing procedure did not always run smoothly.

[1] 'Pursa' No. 128, 2 October 1940 (Ministry of Aircraft Production No. APX 29): Premier papers, 3/483/2.

[2] 'Purco' No. 80, 11 April 1940: Cabinet papers, 85/14, folios 131–2. A week earlier the Supreme War Council had set aside $614 million for Anglo-American aircraft purchases ('Purco' No. 30, Monnet to Purvis, 4 April 1940: Cabinet papers, 85/13).

[3] Sir Edward Bridges to Eric Seal, 'Secret', 4 June 1940: Premier papers, 3/468, folio 176.

One worry, Purvis reported on June 4, was that Roosevelt had decided 'to his regret' that as far as destroyers were concerned, 'the United States of America could not spare any'.[1]

In the immediate aftermath of Dunkirk, Churchill was caught up, not only in the political, but also in the personal perspective. Among those whom he had known, and who had fought at Dunkirk were Michael Fleming, the son of his friend Valentine Fleming. 'Val' had been killed in action in the First World War; his son was severely wounded in the line near Cassel, holding the town as the other troops fell back. Captured by the Germans, Michael Fleming died in captivity within four months.[2] Ronald Cartland, one of the young Conservative MPs who had followed Churchill's star in the 'wilderness years', was killed on May 30.[3] Colonel Denning, one of several serving officers who had brought Churchill information about military deficiencies in the late nineteen thirties, was killed on June 1.

Churchill had now to prepare to tell the House of Commons, and the nation, of the Dunkirk evacuation. For two hours he received suggestions and material. Desmond Morton asked him to make clear in his speech that there were certain French individuals 'who really desire to continue the struggle come what may'.[4] Dudley Pound sent Churchill the final evacuation figures: 224,318 British evacuees, 111,172 Allied evacuees.[5] That same day, Admiral Phillips sent Churchill, through Pound, the equivalent figures for the Gallipoli evacuation at the end of 1915: 118,316 British and Empire troops evacuated from Cape Helles, Anzac Cove and Suvla Bay.[6]

In his speech in the House of Commons, a speech which lasted for just over half an hour, Churchill first outlined the course of the German advance from the French and Belgian frontiers to the sea. Then he

[1] 'Note by M. Jean Monnet', 'Secret', 'Urgent', 4 June 1940: Premier papers, 3/468, folio 178.

[2] Among his brothers were Peter Fleming, the explorer, and Ian Fleming the inventor of 'James Bond'.

[3] Forty-two years later, Ronald Cartland's sister Barbara recalled: 'Winston rang up three times during Dunkirk. He was going to give Ronald a Ministry' (Barbara Cartland, conversation with the author, 12 August 1982).

[4] Note of 4 June 1940: Premier papers, 7/2. Morton had been speaking to Jean Monnet, Chairman of the Anglo-French Co-ordinating Committee, whose headquarters were in Richmond Terrace, Whitehall.

[5] Note of 3 June 1940: Premier papers, 3/175, folio 58.

[6] Note dated 3 June 1940: Premier papers, 3/175, folio 32.

recalled his earlier statement to the House of Commons. 'When,' he said, 'a week ago today, I asked the House to fix this afternoon as the occasion for a statement, I feared it would be my lot to announce the greatest military disaster in our long history.' He had thought—'and some good judges agreed with me'—that perhaps 20,000 or 30,000 men might be re-embarked. 'The whole root and core and brain of the British Army,' he said, 'on which and around which we were to build, and are to build, the great British Armies in the later years of the war, seemed about to perish upon the field or be led into an ignominious and starving captivity.'

There was still to come 'another blow which might well have proved final', the surrender of the Belgian Army. Churchill spoke bitterly of what had proved to be, he said, Belgium's 'fatal neutrality' between the wars, and of the King's 'personal act' of capitulation. He then described the course of the Dunkirk battle, by land, sea and in the air. This struggle, he said, was 'protracted and fierce'. Now, suddenly, 'the scene has cleared, the crash and thunder has for the moment—but only for the moment—died away. A miracle of deliverance, achieved by valour, by perseverance, by perfect discipline, by faultless service, by resource, by skill, by unconquerable fidelity, is manifest to all.'[1]

More than 335,000 men, French and British, had been carried 'out of the jaws of death and shame, to their native land and to the tasks which lie immediately ahead'. But, Churchill warned: 'We must be very careful not to assign to this deliverance the attributes of a victory. Wars are not won by evacuations.' But there was a victory, he added, 'inside this deliverance', and he went on to explain that this victory:

. . . was gained by the Air Force. Many of our soldiers coming back have not seen the Air Force at work; they saw only the bombers which escaped its protective attack. They underrate its achievements. I have heard much talk of this; that is why I go out of my way to say this. I will tell you about it.

This was a great trial of strength between the British and German Air Forces. Can you conceive a greater objective for the Germans in the air than to make evacuation from these beaches impossible, and to sink all these ships which were displayed, almost to the extent of thousands? Could there have been an objective of greater military importance and significance for the whole purpose of the war than this? They tried hard, and they were beaten back;

[1] When all the eye-witness reports from Dunkirk were studied, the honours and awards granted were substantial, including 119 DSCs and 252 DSMs. Admiral Ramsay was awarded the KCB (Military). Subsequently he was Allied Naval Commander-in-Chief, Expeditionary Force (1944) before being killed in an aeroplane accident in France in January 1945.

they were frustrated in their task. We got the Army away; and they have paid fourfold for any losses which they have inflicted.

Very large formations of German aeroplanes—and we know that they are a very brave race—have turned on several occasions from the attack of one-quarter of their number of the Royal Air Force, and have dispersed in different directions. Twelve aeroplanes have been hunted by two. One aeroplane was driven into the water and cast away, by the mere charge of a British aeroplane, which had no more ammunition. All of our types—the Hurricane, the Spitfire and the new Defiant—and all our pilots have been vindicated as superior to what they have at present to face.

When we consider how much greater would be our advantage in defending the air above this island against an overseas attack, I must say that I find in these facts a sure basis upon which practical and reassuring thoughts may rest.

The 'great French Army', Churchill pointed out, had been very largely 'cast back and disturbed by the onrush of a few thousands of armoured vehicles'. And he went on to ask:

May it also be that the cause of civilisation itself will be defended by the skill and devotion of a few thousand airmen? There never had been, I suppose, in all the world, in all the history of war, such an opportunity for youth. The Knights of the Round Table, the Crusaders, all fall back into a prosaic past: not only distant but prosaic; but these young men, going forth every morn to guard their native land and all that we stand for, holding in their hands these instruments of colossal and shattering power, of whom it may be said that 'When every morning brought a noble chance, And every chance brought out a noble knight,' deserve our gratitude, as do all the brave men who, in so many ways and on so many occasions, are ready, and continue ready, to give life and all for their native land.[1]

Churchill now spoke of the deeds and sufferings of the Army, fighting on 'some of the old grounds that so many of us knew so well',[2] and sustaining 30,000 losses in killed, wounded and missing. The House offered its sympathy, he said, 'to all who have suffered bereavement' or who were 'still anxious' about the fate of the thousands who had merely been reported 'missing'. The President of the Board of Trade, Sir An-

[1] Of the part played by the Royal Air Force at Dunkirk, David Divine, who was himself awarded the DSM at Dunkirk, and whose motor boat the *Little Ann* was sunk on rescue work, has written: 'Between May 25th and June 5th, 394 German planes were destroyed for the loss of 114 aircraft of the RAF—a superiority of substantially more than three to one. This was the first great qualitative victory of the Allied air. It was the pattern for the Battle of Britain and for the great air defeats of Africa and the Mediterranean, of Italy and of France' (A. D. Divine, *Dunkirk*, London 1945, page 240).

[2] Churchill's own battalion headquarters, and front line trenches, between January and May 1916, had been at the village of Ploegsteert ('Plug Street') on the Ypres–Armentières road. Churchill had then been a Lieutenant-Colonel Commanding the 6th battalion, Royal Scots Fusiliers. This area had been overrun by the Germans on 29 May 1940.

drew Duncan, was not in the House. 'His son has been killed, and many in the House have felt the pangs of affliction in the sharpest form.'

Churchill then spoke of the transformation of Britain. Factories were now working night and day, weekdays and Sundays. 'Capital and labour have cast aside their interests, rights and customs and put them into the common stock.' Munitions production had already 'leapt forward':

Nevertheless, our thankfulness at the escape of our Army and so many men, whose loved ones have passed through an agonising week, must not blind us to the fact that what has happened in France and Belgium is a colossal military disaster. The French Army has been weakened, the Belgian Army has been lost, a large part of those fortified lines upon which so much faith had been reposed is gone, many valuable mining districts and factories have passed into the enemy's possession, the whole of the Channel ports are in his hands, with all the tragic consequences that follow from that, and we must expect another blow to be struck almost immediately at us or at France.

We are told that Herr Hitler has a plan for invading the British Isles. This has often been thought of before. When Napoleon lay at Boulogne for a year with his flat-bottomed boats and his Grand Army, he was told by someone, 'There are bitter weeds in England.' There are certainly a great many more of them since the British Expeditionary Force returned.

Turning again to the question of invasion, Churchill told the House of Commons:

The whole question of home defence against invasion is, of course, powerfully affected by the fact that we have for the time being in this island incomparably more powerful military forces than we have ever had at any moment in this war or the last. But this will not continue. We shall not be content with a defensive war. We have our duty to our Ally. We have to reconstitute and build up the British Expeditionary Force once again, under its gallant Commander-in-Chief, Lord Gort. All this is in train; but in the interval we must put our defences in this island into such a high state of organisation that the fewest possible numbers will be required to give effective security and that the largest possible potential of offensive effort may be realised. On this we are now engaged. It will be very convenient, if it be the desire of the House, to enter upon this subject in a secret Session. Not that the Government would necessarily be able to reveal in very great detail military secrets, but we like to have our discussions free, without the restraint imposed by the fact that they will be read the next day by the enemy, and the Government would benefit by views freely expressed in all parts of the House by Members with their knowledge of so many different parts of the country. I understand that some request is to be made upon this subject, which will be readily acceded to by His Majesty's Government.

There had been concern at the widespread internment of aliens; to this
subject Churchill now addressed the House:

> We have found it necessary to take measures of increasing stringency, not
> only against enemy aliens and suspicious characters of other nationalities, but
> also against British subjects who may become a danger or a nuisance should
> the war be transported to the United Kingdom. I know there are a great
> many people affected by the orders which we have made who are the passion-
> ate enemies of Nazi Germany. I am very sorry for them, but we cannot, at the
> present time and under the present stress, draw all the distinctions which we
> should like to do. If parachute landings were attempted and fierce fighting
> attendant upon them followed, these unfortunate people would be far better
> out of the way, for their own sakes as well as for ours.
>
> There is, however, another class, for which I feel not the slightest sympathy.
> Parliament has given us the powers to put down Fifth Column activities with
> a strong hand, and we shall use those powers, subject to the supervision and
> correction of the House, without the slightest hesitation until we are satisfied,
> and more than satisfied, that this malignancy in our midst has been effectively
> stamped out.

Balancing his words between tones of warning and confidence, Churchill continued:

> I would observe that there has never been a period in all these long centuries
> of which we boast when an absolute guarantee against invasion, still less
> against serious raids, could have been given to our people. In the days of
> Napoleon, of which I was speaking just now, the same wind which would
> have carried his transport across the Channel might have driven away the
> blockading fleet. There was always the chance, and it is that chance which
> has excited and befooled the imagination of many Continental tyrants. Many
> are the tales that are told. We are assured that novel methods will be adopted,
> and when we see the originality of malice, the ingenuity of aggression, which
> our enemy displays, we may certainly prepare ourselves for every kind of
> novel stratagem and every kind of brutal and treacherous manoeuvre. I think
> that no idea is so outlandish that it should not be considered and viewed with
> a searching, but at the same time, I hope, with a steady eye. We must never
> forget the solid assurances of sea power and those which belong to air power if
> it can be locally exercised.

Churchill ended his speech with a stirring peroration:

> I have, myself, full confidence that if all do their duty, if nothing is neglec-
> ted, and if the best arrangements are made, as they are being made, we shall
> prove ourselves once again able to defend our island home, to ride out the
> storm of war, and to outlive the menace of tyranny, if necessary for years, if
> necessary alone. At any rate, that is what we are going to try to do. That is
> the resolve of His Majesty's Government—every man of them. That is the will

of Parliament and the nation. The British Empire and the French Republic, linked together in their cause and in their need, will defend to the death their native soil, aiding each other like good comrades to the utmost of their strength.

Even though large tracts of Europe and many old and famous States have fallen or may fall into the grip of the Gestapo and all the odious apparatus of Nazi rule, we shall not flag or fail. We shall go on to the end. We shall fight in France, we shall fight on the seas and oceans, we shall fight with growing confidence and growing strength in the air, we shall defend our island, whatever the cost may be. We shall fight on the beaches, we shall fight on the landing grounds, we shall fight in the fields and in the streets, we shall fight in the hills; we shall never surrender, and even if, which I do not for a moment believe, this island or a large part of it were subjugated and starving, then our Empire beyond the seas, armed and guarded by the British Fleet, would carry on the struggle, until, in God's good time, the new world, with all its power and might, steps forth to the rescue and the liberation of the old.[1]

The House of Commons, and the many Peers who had crowded into the Peers' gallery, responded to Churchill's speech with enthusiasm: 'another good rousing speech', commented Viscount Mersey, a Deputy Speaker of the House of Lords. 'He is head and shoulders above them all.'[2] And Churchill's friend Josiah Wedgwood, a Labour MP who, like Lord Mersey, had served at the Dardanelles, wrote: 'My dear Winston. That was worth 1,000 guns, & the speeches of 1,000 years.'[3]

'A magnificent oration,' John Colville noted, 'which obviously moved the House,'[4] and the Conservative MP, Henry 'Chips' Channon commented in his diary: 'he was eloquent, and oratorical, and used magnificent English; several Labour members cried. He hinted that we might be obliged to fight alone, without France, and that England might well be invaded.'[5]

The French Ambassador in London had been so alarmed by Churchill's phrase that Britain would fight on 'if necessary alone', that he had asked for an interview. What did these words mean, he asked? They meant just what they said, he was told.[6]

---

[1] Speech begun at 3.40 p.m., ended at 4.15 p.m., 4 June 1940: *Hansard*, columns 787–796.
[2] Mersey diary, 4 June 1940: Viscount Mersey, *Journal and Memories*, London 1952, page 434.
[3] Letter of 4 June 1940: Churchill papers, 2/399.
[4] Colville diary, 4 June 1940: Colville papers.
[5] Channon diary, 4 June 1940: Robert Rhodes James (editor), *Chips: The Diaries of Sir Henry Channon*, London 1967, page 256. Channon added: 'Jock Colville tells me that the Admiralty is fantastic now; people who were at each other's throats a few weeks ago are now intimate and on the best of terms. Winston darts in and out, a mountain of energy and good-nature, the Labour leaders, Brendan Bracken and Prof. Lindemann, sometimes Randolph, Beaverbrook, the Defence Ministers, etc.—the new racket all much in evidence, but no Neville and no Horace Wilson.'
[6] Colville diary, 4 June 1940: Colville papers.

Many of those who were not in the Commons to hear it were exhilarated by Churchill's speech. 'Even repeated by the announcer,' Vita Sackville-West wrote to her husband, Harold Nicolson, 'it sent shivers (not of fear) down my spine. I think that one of the reasons why one is stirred by his Elizabethan phrases is that one feels the whole massive backing of power and resolve behind them, like a great fortress: they are never words for words' sake.' Replying a day later, Nicolson told his wife: 'I feel so much in the spirit of Winston's great speech that I could face a world of enemies.'[1]

That evening Churchill was, as Colville noted, 'a little on edge'. As work proceeded in his Private Office, and he himself worked in the next room, he kept ringing the bell to complain about the noise, asking pointedly at one moment about the source of 'this bloody Jaw'. On being told 'It's the First Lord,' he mumbled 'Oh . . .' and returned to his work.[2]

Among the letters which Churchill sent that evening was one to the King, thanking him for approving of Brendan Bracken's Privy Councillorship, and adding: 'Better days will come—though not yet.'[3] And to Stanley Baldwin he wrote, thanking him for a letter of good wishes 'which reached me—I am ashamed to say—nearly a fortnight ago': 'We are going through vy hard times & I expect worse to come: but I feel quite sure better days will come: though whether we shall live to see them is more doubtful.'

Churchill ended his letter to Baldwin: 'I do not feel the burden weigh too heavily, but I cannot say that I have enjoyed being Prime Minister vy much so far.'[4]

[1] Letters of 4 and 5 June 1940: Nigel Nicolson (editor), *Harold Nicolson Diaries and Letters 1939–1945*, London 1967, pages 93 and 94.
[2] Colville diary, 4 June 1940: Colville papers.
[3] Letter of 4 June 1940: Churchill papers, 20/7.
[4] Letter of 4 June 1940: Baldwin papers, volume 174, folio 264.

24

'The Common Cause'

A T four o'clock on the morning of 5 June 1940 the German forces
assembled on the Somme began their offensive towards Paris.
Although opposed principally by French troops, the line on their right
flank, between Abbeville and the sea, was held by the 51st Highland
Division, commanded by Major-General Fortune. These British troops,
'though they fought with dogged tenacity', as the Official History records, were forced back, or overwhelmed as a result of mounting
casualties, dwindling ammunition and 'the superior numbers of the
enemy'.[1]

In Paris, news of the German offensive led to immediate Cabinet
changes. Daladier was dropped altogether, and a serving officer, General Charles de Gaulle, was appointed Under-Secretary for Defence.
From Paris, Reynaud at once appealed, yet again, for the immediate
despatch of more British fighter squadrons. At eleven that morning
Churchill discussed this appeal with Sinclair, Beaverbrook, and the
three senior airmen, Newall, Peirse and Dowding. Ismay, who was
also present, took notes of the discussion. 'How can we help the French
in the battle?' Churchill asked, 'without hurting ourselves mortally,
and in a way that will encourage the French to feel that we are doing
all in our power.' The British 'must do something'.

It was Dowding who spoke in answer to Churchill's question, and
who again opposed the despatch of any more fighters. Following Churchill's persistent questioning as to the numbers of planes and pilots
available, or in prospect, Dowding agreed to produce the detailed
figures early that same afternoon.[2] 'Winston would like to send more
than the experts agree,' Colville noted in his diary. 'The latter say we

---

[1] Major L. F. Ellis, *The War in France and Flanders, 1939–1940*, London 1953, page 271.
[2] 'Notes of a Meeting held at 10 Downing Street at 11 a.m. on Wednesday, 5th June 1940':
Cabinet papers, 127/13.

must have time for reorganization and that we cannot leave this country exposed.'[1]

Nevertheless, in an attempt to preserve French fighting morale, Churchill decided that morning, and reported at once to Reynaud, that Britain would hold two squadrons of fighters, as well as four squadrons of bombers, 'at full strength ready to intervene from this country'. To do this, Churchill pointed out, 'We have had to break up many squadrons and suspend the whole process of re-organization after the stress and confusion of Dunkirk.'[2]

Hardly had this difficult decision to put two of Britain's fighter squadrons at the disposal of the French been taken, than a second appeal arrived from France, urging an even greater commitment, of ten squadrons of fighters to be sent to France 'immediately', followed 'as soon as possible by ten further squadrons'.[3] This request came from General Vuillemin, whose letter also contained a scathing reference to British air support in the earlier battles as 'tardy, inadequate but nevertheless of value'.[4] 'You don't seem to understand at all,' Churchill telegraphed to Reynaud and Weygand in reply, 'that British fighter aviation has been worn to a shred and frightfully mixed up by the need of maintaining standing patrols of forty-eight fighters over Dunkirk without which the evacuation would have been impossible.' The mere sorting out of the aeroplanes from the various squadrons, Churchill added, 'practically paralyses the force for four or five days'.[5]

In response to Reynaud's requests for more British troops, Churchill had agreed to send the 52nd Division to France, and had instructed, as Sir John Dill noted, 'that the first elements should leave on 6th June'. At the same time, Newall agreed to draw up a programme showing how many squadrons it would be necessary to amalgamate 'to send overseas one, two, three or four effective fighter squadrons', and the dates by which these squadrons could operate in France.[6]

The effect of these enquiries would depend as much on the course of the new German offensive as on their own merits. Meanwhile, at the War Cabinet that day, Churchill reported that he had received an

[1] Colville diary, 5 June 1940: Colville papers.
[2] Telegram of 5 June 1940, 'Most Immediate', No. 73066, despatched at 4.15 p.m.: Premier papers, 3/188/1.
[3] This request for 20 squadrons represented, as Reynaud himself recognized, 'one half of the total fighter strength based in the United Kingdom' (Cabinet papers, 65/13, folios 252–3).
[4] Colville diary, 5 June 1940: Colville papers.
[5] Telegram No. 297 DIPP, 5 June 1940, despatched 5.45 p.m.: Cabinet papers, 65/13, folio 255.
[6] Chiefs of Staff Committee No. 169 of 1940, 5 June 1940, 3.45 p.m.: Cabinet papers, 79/4. Churchill was not present at this meeting.

encouraging letter from Spears, to the effect that the number of French divisions on the Somme–Aisne front 'was now considerably larger than the number previously reported to us'.[1]

Turning briefly to events in Norway, the Cabinet learned that 4,500 Allied troops had been 'successfully embarked' from Narvik on the night of June 3, and that, as Lord Cork had reported to Churchill, the evacuation would continue 'under favourable conditions of low cloud and rain'.[2] It was also reported to the War Cabinet that the King of Norway, on the eve of his departure into exile in England, 'believed that the Allies would win in the end'.[3]

Despite the news of the evacuations from Norway, and the ending of what had only six weeks earlier been a major British initiative, Churchill was, as Colville noted, 'still full of offensive zeal', thinking that the Australian troops about to reach Britain 'should be used for small forays on the coasts of occupied countries such as Belgium and Holland'.[4] These ideas were set out, and expanded, on June 5 in a minute to Ismay, suggesting the creation of detachments of 250 Australians each, 'equipped with grenades, trench mortars, tommy guns, armoured vehicles and the like, capable of acting against an attack on this country, but also capable of landing on the friendly coasts now held by the enemy'. It was essential, Churchill added, 'to get out of our minds the idea that the Channel ports and all the country between them are enemy territory'.

Searching for some means of a British initiative, Churchill continued:

Enterprises must be prepared, with specially trained troops of the hunter class, who can develop a reign of terror down these coasts, first of all on the 'butcher and bolt' policy, but later on, or perhaps as soon as we are organized, we should surprise Calais or Boulogne, kill and capture the Hun garrison and hold the place until all the preparations to reduce it by siege or heavy storm have been made, and then away.

The passive resistance war, which we have acquitted ourselves so well in, must come to an end. I look to the Joint Chiefs of the Staff to propose me measures for a vigorous, enterprising and ceaseless offensive against the whole German occupied coastline. Tanks and AFVs[5] must be carried in flat-bottomed

[1] War Cabinet No. 155 of 1940, 12.30 p.m., 5 June 1940: Cabinet papers, 65/7.

[2] Signal sent at 10.04 p.m., 4 June 1940, received at 00.12 a.m., 5 June 1940: Premier papers, 3/328/4, folio 29.

[3] War Cabinet No. 155 of 1940, 5 June 1940, 12.30 p.m., Confidential Annex, Minute 6: Cabinet papers, 65/13.

[4] Colville diary, 5 June 1940: Colville papers.

[5] Armoured Fighting Vehicles.

boats, out of which they can crawl ashore, do a deep raid inland, cutting a vital communication, and then back, leaving a trail of German corpses behind them.

It was possible, Churchill added, that when the 'best' German troops went on to the attack on Paris, only the 'ordinary German troops of the line' would be left. And he told Ismay: 'The lives of these must be made an intense torment.'[1]

On Churchill's mind throughout these days of danger was the question of aid from the United States. This question was brought to the forefront by a telegram from the Prime Minister of Canada, Mackenzie King, on the possible transfer of the British Fleet across the Atlantic, in the event of Britain's defeat. In his reply on June 5, Churchill stressed his 'solid confidence' in Britain's ability to continue the war, to defend the Empire, and to maintain the naval blockade against Germany. The 'principal remaining danger' to Britain was German air attack on the Air factories, he explained, but 'if our Air defence is so strong that enemy can only come on dark nights', German precision bombing would not be easy. Even the French, after defeat, might be able to maintain 'a gigantic guerilla'. Churchill's telegram to Mackenzie King continued:

We must be careful not to let Americans view too complacently prospect of a British collapse, out of which they would get the British Fleet and the guardianship of the British Empire, minus Great Britain. If United States were in the war and England conquered locally, it would be natural that events should follow like you describe.

But if America continued neutral, and we were overpowered, I cannot tell what policy might be adopted by a pro-German administration such as would undoubtedly be set up.

Although President is our best friend, no practical help has been forthcoming from the United States as yet. We have not expected them to send military aid, but they have not even sent any worthy contribution in destroyers or planes, or by a visit of a squadron of their Fleet to Southern Irish ports.[2]

Churchill's vexation at the American attitude emerged again on June 6, after Lindemann had urged taking up once more the possibility of 'exchanging information' with the American Services. Lindemann's immediate concern was the Norden bombsight, not, as he explained, because there was any reason 'to suppose it is superior to our own', but because it would, as he told Churchill, be worth paying a large price,

[1] Minute of 5 June 1940: Churchill papers, 20/13.
[2] Both Chamberlain and Halifax concurred in this message: Premier papers, 4/43B/1, folios 301 and 305-7.

in terms of secrets given to the Americans, 'to get *immediate delivery* of a thousand or more' of these bombsights, 'which would be installed in our machines, since there seems little prospect of stabilizing our own automatic sights this summer'. To be able to 'hit our targets from great heights', Lindemann added, 'might make all the difference'.[1]

As he had been two weeks earlier, in reply to A. V. Alexander's similar suggestion, Churchill was cool. 'I am still disinclined to do this at this moment,' he noted on the bottom of Lindemann's proposal, 'I am waiting for a further development of the American attitude.'[2]

That evening Churchill again asked Neville Chamberlain if he would agree to allow Lloyd George to be found a place in the War Cabinet, and on the afternoon of June 6, Churchill wrote to thank Chamberlain for putting aside the deep dislikes of two decades. 'Lloyd George would,' wrote Churchill, 'be a valuable counsellor, and a help to me and to the Cabinet.' But being treated 'as an outcast', he would become, so Churchill felt, 'the focus for regathering discontents'. Churchill believed that Lloyd George was ready to put aside 'all personal feuds or prejudices', and he added: 'In this terrible hour, with all that impends, the country ought to be satisfied that all its oldest and best-known leaders are playing their part, and I certainly do not think that one should be set against another.'[3]

Chamberlain replied that same day. 'When men are giving their lives for their country,' he wrote, 'any baser sacrifice doesn't count.' But he wished to set two conditions. The first was that Lloyd George would give Churchill his personal assurance to 'drop his personal feud & prejudice against me' and work with Chamberlain 'for the national interest only'. The second was that the criticisms of Chamberlain which were being voiced by the *Daily Herald*, the *News Chronicle* and 'some members of Parliament' should be stopped '*before* any announcement is made of Lloyd George's inclusion'. Chamberlain went on to explain: 'I cannot allow it to be said that his inclusion in the Government is part of a bargain between you & me in return for which you have agreed to protect me.'[4]

The move against Chamberlain had been growing for more than a week. On May 21 the leading article in the Labour *Daily Herald*, headed 'No Room for Deadweight', declared: 'If a man has been incapable of estimating the probabilities of the war up to now, of what

---

[1] Minute dated 5 June 1940: Premier papers, 3/475/1, folio 60.
[2] Note of 6 June 1940: Premier papers, 3/475/1, folio 62.
[3] 'Private', 6 June 1940: Churchill papers, 20/11.
[4] 'Private', 6 June 1940: Churchill papers, 20/11.

use will he be when—as must happen soon—its problems become infinitely more complex, its surprises more frequent, its dangers more dire?' If there was 'deadweight' in the Government 'it could easily be replaced, and should be'. The article continued: 'One object animates this people: the arrest and reversal of the Nazi march across civilization. Nothing and nobody, however honestly he blunders, must be allowed to impede our effort for an instant.'[1]

Each day brought new articles in the *Daily Herald* on the same theme, but the culminating attack came in the Liberal *News Chronicle* on June 6. Under the headline 'Resignations of Ministers are Expected', the newspaper wrote:

... there is a rising tide of indignation at Westminster about the unpreparedness of the BEF to meet Germany's total strength.

I have met many MPs—they used to support Mr Chamberlain's Administration through thick and thin—who confess now that it must have been guilty either of culpable negligence or a complete misunderstanding of Germany's strength and intentions both before and since the war began. Either fault, they say, should be punished.[2]

It was 'striking to note', the *News Chronicle* added, how many Members of Parliament were discussing 'quite openly' the possible resignation of Neville Chamberlain, and also of Kingsley Wood.

Churchill could make no 'bargain' to protect Chamberlain against such attacks, even though they were damaging to the Government politically. Nor did he intend to embark upon a 'Munich' vendetta by dropping either Chamberlain or Kingsley Wood. At the same time, he could not overcome Chamberlain's objection to Lloyd George's inclusion in the Government.

Churchill spent his first working hours on June 6 in bed, as had become his habit. His dictation covered several urgent aspects of future military and air needs. In a minute to the Minister of Supply, Herbert Morrison, he asked for weekly reports, 'if possible not exceeding one sheet of paper', on the progress made with Proximity Fuses and the Unrotating Projectile weapon. To Ismay he asked for someone to 'concentrate attention' on finding some projectile which could be fired from a rifle at a tank, 'like a rifle grenade', or from an anti-tank rifle, like a trench-mortar bomb. From Sinclair and Newall he wanted to know the result

[1] *Daily Herald*, 31 May 1940.
[2] *News Chronicle*, 6 June 1940.

of a discussion on the previous day on the temporary transfer of trained and half-trained pilots from the Fleet Air Arm to the Fighter Force. 'I was considering,' he explained, 'that at least fifty should be found at once as a minimum. Pray let me know what has happened.' And he added: 'Was Air Marshal Dowding consulted and is he satisfied?' [1]

In a minute to Lord Halifax on June 6, Churchill reflected on the possibility of encouraging Yugoslavia to commit itself to the Allies by some reciprocal promise of help in the event of an Italian invasion. 'I have hitherto argued,' he wrote, 'against going to war with Italy because she attacked Yugoslavia, and have wished to see whether it was a serious attack upon Yugoslavian independence or merely taking some naval bases in the Adriatic.' However, he noted, this situation had changed: 'Italy is continually threatening to go to war with England and France, and not by "the back door". We are so near a break with Italy on grounds which have nothing to do with Yugoslavia that it would seem that our main aim might well be now to procure this Balkan mobilisation.' Churchill ended his minute: 'Will you think it over?' [2]

On the previous day Churchill had spoken to the senior Ministers of the Dutch Government in exile. In one of his minutes on June 6 he supported their request for the formation and equipping of a Dutch Brigade, telling both Halifax and Eden: 'If there is no Foreign Office objection, it seems important to get on with this as quickly as possible, and I shall be very glad to receive a weekly report.' To Pound he pressed for further information on 'Paul', the plan to mine the sea approaches to Luleå, the port of embarkation for Swedish iron ore bought by Germany. 'Pray let me have a report of how this is progressing, and when it is intended to begin.' He also asked Pound whether plans had been made to 'render unusable' the Norwegian aerodromes at Bardufoss and Skaanland, by means of delayed action bombs. 'Have we got these bombs?' he asked. 'And can they be sent to Lord Cork in time?' And he added somewhat sourly: 'This ought to have been thought of before.' [3]

Against Pound's suggestion that mining action should be confined to those channels where a 'block' would occur if a ship were mined there, Churchill wrote: 'When will the action be taken? Or will this peter out like the rest?' Against Pound's comment that, according to Lord Cork, the Norwegians would need Bardufoss, Churchill noted: 'But the Ger-

---

[1] It emerged that Dowding was satisfied, and on the following day the First Lord of the Admiralty, A. V. Alexander, wrote to Churchill to say how proud the Navy was, 'at your request, to supply pilots on loan to the Air Force at a crucial moment in our history' (Letter of 7 June 1940: Premier papers, 3/24/1, folio 7).

[2] 'Private', 6 June 1940: Churchill papers, 4/153.

[3] Minutes of 6 June 1940: Churchill papers, 4/153.

mans will take it at once.' And on the top of Pound's minute Churchill wrote: 'We seem quite incapable of *action*.'[1]

As Churchill dictated his minutes on the morning of June 6, Colville noted: 'The PM was in an impatient frame of mind,' especially with Pound, and also with Eden.[2] On the question of eight Indian battalions which were said to be able to reach England forty-two days after the order being given to transport them, Churchill minuted to Eden: 'I am much disappointed with your letter, which shows how everything gets smaller and is slowed down so far as British action is concerned.'[3] The order had been given. But the troops would take more than sixty days. As to the 'virtual deadlock' caused by Wavell's refusal to allow British battalions in Palestine to be transferred to Britain, and replaced locally by Indian troops, Churchill's anger was considerable, and he minuted, again for Eden:

It is quite natural that General Wavell should look at the situation only from his own viewpoint. Here we have to think of building up a good Army in order to make up, as far as possible, for the lamentable failure to support the French by an adequate BEF, during the first year of the war. Do you realise that in the first year of the late war we brought forty-seven divisions into action, and that these were divisions of twelve battalions plus one Pioneer battalion, not nine as now? We are indeed the victims of a feeble and weary departmentalism.

Looking back at what had been done in the First World War, Churchill told Eden that he found very apparent now 'Our weakness, slowness, lack of grip and drive', and he went on to exhort Eden to work with Lord Lloyd at the Colonial Office and Leo Amery at the India Office 'to lift our affairs in the Middle East out of the catalepsy by which they are smitten'.[4]

One final minute on June 6 revealed Churchill's sense of frustration. Noting 'a lot of valuable ships' then in Malta harbour under repair, he asked Pound for a list of these ships and the dates when they would be ready for sea, commenting sarcastically that the Admiral responsible 'does not seem to have been much concerned about the fate of all these ships'.[5]

[1] Minute and Note of 6 June 1940: Churchill papers, 20/17.

[2] Colville diary, 6 June 1940: Colville papers.

[3] Minute of 6 June 1940: Churchill papers, 20/13. In printing the rest of this minute in his war memoirs (volume 2, pages 145–6), Churchill omitted this opening sentence.

[4] Minute of 6 June 1940: Churchill papers, 20/13.

[5] Minute of 6 June 1940: Churchill papers: 20/13. The Admiral was Sir Andrew Cunningham, Commander-in-Chief, Mediterranean from 1939 to 1942, and First Sea Lord and Chief of the Naval Staff from 1943 to 1946.

It was not until shortly after midday on June 6 that the War Cabinet met at 10 Downing Street. But when it met the news from France seemed more hopeful. According to a report from Spears, which Churchill read out, the French Command 'seemed to be gaining more confidence'. If the fighting were to develop into 'old-style infantry battles', Churchill remarked, the Germans 'might not relish the prospect of pressing home their attacks'.[1] But there was also a reminder at that War Cabinet of just how weakened the British forces were when details were given of British material losses as a result of the Dunkirk evacuation: 7,000 tons of ammunition, 90,000 rifles, 1,000 heavy guns, 2,000 tractors, 8,000 Bren guns and 400 anti-tank guns.[2]

For Churchill, knowledge of these losses was combined with an awareness of how long it would take to replace them. Three days earlier he had asked Ismay for a list of the 'principal items of equipment' that had been lost, and on June 6 Ismay had sent it to him. It was a staggering total, including, in addition to the war supplies itemized above, 475 tanks, 38,000 vehicles, 12,000 motor cycles, 8,000 telephones and 1,855 wireless sets.

As for the loss of the 90,000 rifles and more than 8,000 Bren guns, this meant, the War Cabinet were told, that there were now less than 600,000 rifles and 12,000 Bren guns in the United Kingdom. Yet the figures for maximum production in June, which Churchill studied minutely, were for 2,040 Bren guns and 124,000 rifles. Similar problems existed for every other item of essential equipment. The losses would take between three and six months to make up.[3]

By the late afternoon of June 6, Churchill was able to report to Reynaud that the plans to which the War Cabinet had agreed in order to help France were all in train. The 52nd Division was to embark for France on the following morning, to be followed by the Canadians on June 11. British air forces, Churchill informed Reynaud, bomber as well as fighter, were again intervening in the battle, 'taking off from English bases'. The British fighters were filling up with petrol at French air fields, 'and are thus able to undertake sorties of a longer duration'.[4]

That night Churchill worked until one o'clock; 'he is cross with the French', Colville noted, in their continued demands for air support,

[1] War Cabinet No. 156 of 1940, 6 June 1940, 12.30 p.m.: Cabinet papers, 65/7.
[2] War Cabinet No. 156 of 1940, 6 June 1940, 12.30 p.m., Confidential Annex: Cabinet papers, 65/13.
[3] Note of 6 June 1940, and enclosures: Premier papers, 3/183, folios 16–23.
[4] Telegram of 6 June 1940: Churchill papers, 20/14.

and was 'justifiably angry' with General Vuillemin's earlier remarks about Britain's 'inadequate' efforts.[1]

Churchill was particularly angered when he read a remark by Weygand, a remark which was telegraphed to London by General Spears on June 6, that 'Mr Churchill may think General Vuillemin's demands unreasonable. Perhaps if he saw the condition of our army he would think we were unreasonable to go on fighting.' Spears added the 'astonishing' fact that Weygand had not yet even spoken to Air Marshal Barratt, the Air Officer Commanding-in-Chief of the British Air Force in France. He, Spears, had arranged that Weygand should meet Barratt that afternoon, for the first time.[2]

The extent of German superiority in air strength was made clear to Churchill on June 6, when he received from the Anglo-French Executive Committee for Air Production and Supply a detailed note of the respective British, German and French air strengths as of 24 May 1940. The British fighter strength stood on May 24 at 1,668, with 194 having been shot down between May 10 and May 24, and 138 having been built during that same period. The French fighter strength stood at 1,224, with 354 having been shot down and 154 constructed between May 10 and May 24. The total Anglo-French first line strength of all types on May 24 stood at 7,621. The German figure for all types of operational aircraft was estimated at 11,675 in the last week of May.[3]

That evening, Jean Monnet, in his capacity as Reynaud's personal representative in London, went to see Churchill to make a 'special appeal' for additional air support.[4] But after Monnet had gone, Ismay took the view that the French were, as Colville recorded, 'nothing short of outrageous, doing nothing but slinging mud at us'. Ismay added: 'We should be insane to send them all our fighters because if they were lost the country would be beaten in two days, whereas even if France surrenders we should still win the war—provided our air defences are intact.'[5]

For Churchill, the belief that the best form of air defence was attack had long been paramount. Thus on June 7 he urged Lindemann to 'go forward with the stabilising bomb sight', on the grounds that 'we must knock out their aircraft factories at the same rate that they affect ours'.

[1] Colville diary, 6 June 1940: Colville papers.
[2] Spears to Ismay, 6 June 1940, for the Prime Minister's information: Premier papers, 3/188/3, folio 10.
[3] Note of 6 June 1940: Premier papers, 3/188/4, folios 3–6.
[4] Reported by Churchill to the War Cabinet on the following day, 7 June 1940: Cabinet papers, 65/13, folio 259.
[5] Colville diary, 6 June 1940: Colville papers.

Once all those concerned were gathered together, Churchill wrote, 'I will next week receive their reports and urge them on.'[1]

The French demands for more British fighter support continued throughout June 7. Indeed, one of the first messages that Churchill saw that morning was from Spears, who had telegraphed to London during the night that Reynaud urgently wanted information for the Army Committee of the Senate on how many British fighters had been engaged on June 6, 'and will be tomorrow'.[2]

Churchill replied, through Ismay, that he 'strongly deprecated' the precise figures for June 6 being given, and that to disclose the strength of fighters to be employed on June 7 'is still more to be deprecated'. But, Ismay added, on Churchill's instructions, in order that Reynaud 'may be aware of the scale of our effort', he could be told for his personal information that 144 British fighters were engaged in France on June 6, 'and that a still larger number will be operating today'.[3]

Half an hour after this telegram had been sent off, the War Cabinet met to discuss the French position. It was 'clear', Churchill commented, 'that they would try and put the blame on us if they lost this critical battle'. In point of fact, he added, 'we had had 144 fighters operating over France the previous day', mainly from British aerodromes, but using advanced landing grounds in France. 'This was the equivalent of 12 squadrons,' he pointed out, 'and more than they had originally asked for.' An even larger number would be operating that day.[4]

The War Cabinet agreed that Churchill should inform Reynaud in detail of the scale and nature of British fighter support. The first three paragraphs read:

I am now able to tell you that during the last 24 hours we have increased our effort in the air for the assistance of France. During the night our heavy bombers attacked in strength (59 tons of bombs) all the targets indicated by the French High Command. In addition, to-day the medium bombers from Britain have so far undertaken 60 sorties.

2. The fighters working from this country and using forward landing grounds south of the Somme have operated for the purpose of escorts to medium bombers and as independent fighter patrols at a strength of 192 aircraft sorties, exclusive of protection for troop transport movements between Southampton and Cherbourg, &c.

[1] Minute of 7 June 1940: Churchill papers, 20/13.

[2] Telegram despatched from Paris at 11.35 p.m., received in London at 2 a.m., 7 June 1940: Premier papers, 3/188/3, folio 9.

[3] Telegram No. 73242, despatched at 12 noon, 7 June 1940: Premier papers, 3/188/3, folio 8.

[4] War Cabinet No. 157 of 1940, 7 June 1940, 12.30 p.m., Confidential Annex, Minute 2: Cabinet papers, 65/3.

3. To-morrow it is proposed, by amalgamating three fighter squadrons, to send two additional fighter squadrons at full strength to be based in France in the Advance Air Striking Force area under the orders of Commander-in-Chief, BAFF.[1] This will bring his strength up to five full fighter squadrons. In addition, we hope to be able to operate four fighter squadrons daily based in this country from the advanced refuelling landing grounds south of the Somme.

'Our recent experience has shown,' Churchill warned 'that we cannot at present maintain more than this number of squadrons at the high battle wastage experienced in the Flanders battle.'

Churchill took the opportunity of this telegram to defend the conduct of General Fortune, the commander of the 51st Division, whom Reynaud had criticized. The General, Churchill added in a note at the end of the telegram, 'has a wide front to hold & has had vy heavy losses'.

In this same telegram to Reynaud, Churchill agreed to a French request for twenty-four complete barrage balloon outfits, with crews, for the defence of Paris. 'It may be relevant to observe,' Churchill added, 'that attacks on objectives in this country have been undertaken during the last two nights at a strength of approximately 100 aircraft per night . . .'[2]

That evening a meeting took place in Pound's room at the Admiralty, presided over by the Chancellor of the Duchy of Lancaster, Lord Hankey. The purpose of the meeting was to decide 'what should be done with the French Fleet in the event of France going out of the war'. Hankey warned that the Germans were now only seventy miles from Paris, that they might reach the City 'within a week', and that if the Government changed, and Flandin and Laval came in, 'conversations with Germany might start fairly soon'. It was Pound who, in agreeing that Britain must stop the Germans getting control of the French naval forces, told those present: 'the only way to do that properly was to sink the French fleet'.[3]

On the morning of June 8, Hankey and his colleagues presented their conclusion to Churchill.[4] That same morning, Churchill pressed Eden about War Office plans for reconstituting the British Expedi-

---

[1] The British Air Forces in France, commanded by Air Marshal Barratt.

[2] Telegram No. 308 DIPP, 11.15 p.m., 7 June 1940: Premier papers, 3/188/1, folio 12.

[3] Meeting of 7 June 1940 (evening): Admiralty papers, 205/4. Those present were Hankey, Pound, Sir Alexander Cadogan (Permanent Under-Secretary of State, Foreign Office) and William Strang (Assistant Under-Secretary of State, Foreign Office).

[4] Churchill's monthly engagement cards, entry for 8 June 1940: Commander Thompson papers.

tionary Force. 'There is a great opportunity now,' he wrote, 'for picking leaders, not only among those who have had the opportunity of meeting the enemy, but also in those who have prepared themselves to do so.' Men of 'force and intelligence and personality', who would in normal times make their way to leading positions in civilian life, should be given their chance as soon as they had acquired the minimum of training. 'We want live wires,' Churchill wrote, 'and not conventional types.' Of course, 'qualities shown in action' would take precedence, and give 'fine opportunities' of promoting men in their twenties to the command of battalions.[1]

In France, the French forces were being driven back along the road to Rouen and the Seine. Off Norway, as the evacuation of Narvik reached its final day, the aircraft carrier *Glorious* and two destroyers, *Ardent* and *Acasta*, were sunk, and more than 1,500 killed.[2]

The Defence Committee met at 5.15 that afternoon, to take the final decision about the renewed French appeals for further British fighter squadrons to be sent to France. There were now five Hurricane squadrons based in France, under Barratt's command, and a further four squadrons operating during the day from aerodromes near Rouen, and returning to bases in Britain at night. Earlier that day, two of these latter squadrons, eighteen aircraft in all, had encountered a large Messerschmitt formation, and ten of the eighteen British fighters had been lost. Also on June 8, three of the French-based fighters had been shot down.

Churchill now gave his colleagues his assessment, and his conclusion. There were, he said:

... two alternatives open to us at the present time. We could regard the present battle as decisive for France and ourselves, and throw in the whole of our fighter resources in an attempt to save the situation, and bring about victory. If we failed, we should then have to surrender.

Alternatively, we should recognise that whereas the present land battle was of great importance, it would not be decisive one way or the other for Great Britain. If it were lost, and France was forced to submit, we could continue the struggle with good hopes of ultimate victory, provided we ensured that our fighter defences in this country were not impaired; but if we cast away our defence the war would be lost, even if the front in France were stabilised, since Germany would be free to turn her air force against this country, and would have us at her mercy.

[1] Minute of 8 June 1940: Churchill papers, 20/13. When Churchill had taken command of his battalion on the western front in 1916, he had just celebrated his forty-first birthday.

[2] There were 40 survivors from *Glorious*, two from *Ardent*, and only one, Able Seaman Carter, from *Acasta*.

'One thing was certain,' Churchill added. 'If this country were defeated, the war would be lost for France no less than for ourselves, whereas, provided we were strong ourselves, we could win the war, and, in so doing, restore France to her position.' He felt, in conclusion, that it would be 'fatal to yield to the French demands and jeopardise our own safety'.

The issue was no longer one of balancing home and continental forces, but of survival. 'Unanimous agreement,' the minutes recorded, was expressed with Churchill's view.[1] It only remained to inform Reynaud of the conclusion.

It was Churchill who first drafted the reply to Reynaud. All his earlier hopes having been dashed of being able to send a stream of British fighters to France, to stiffen French resolve, and to sustain those in the French Government who wished to fight on, he now intended to warn Reynaud that although yet more fighters might give 'temporary relief' for a few days, they would then be 'burnt up and cast away', whereas, if not cast away, 'they afford the means by which we expect to prolong the war until the United States comes in, or even indefinitely, thus saving in the end not only ourselves but France'.

The present battle, Churchill wished to tell Reynaud, need not be decisive for France, and certainly 'it must not be the end of the resistance in England, for then all hope of final victory would be gone'.

Churchill's draft message continued:

We believe that if we do not by an act of strategic folly leave ourselves utterly defenceless Hitler will break his Air weapon in trying to invade us. The score of squadrons or so which you would like to have melted down in the next few days as a mere makeweight or episode in your splendid struggle will we believe if properly used in this country enable us to break his Air attack, and thus break him.

That is what we are going to try.

Churchill proposed to end the message to Reynaud with the following paragraph:

It would be madness for us to cast aside the entire future, and the surest hope of our common victory, for the sake of what could only be a comparatively minor intervention. I have not an Officer or colleague who would

---

[1] Defence Committee No. 14 of 1940, 8 June 1940, 5.15 p.m.: Cabinet paper, 69/1. Those present were Churchill, Sir Archibald Sinclair, Lord Beaverbrook, General Sir John Dill, Air Marshal Peirse, Sir Edward Bridges (Secretary to the War Cabinet) and Lieutenant-Colonel Jacob (Secretary).

remain with me if I took so improvident a step. But even if it rested with me alone, I would not be guilty of such weakness and despair.[1]

After some discussion, it was agreed to send a far shorter, and less personal message. But its burden was the same. 'We are giving you all the support we can in this great battle,' it read, 'short of ruining the capacity of this country to continue the war.' And the message ended: 'We have had very heavy and disproportionate loss in the air today but we shall continue tomorrow.'

Churchill approved the despatch of this message at 7.55 that evening. It was confirmed by General Dill ten minutes later, and sent to Reynaud at 8.30.[2] As far as the British leaders were concerned, the battle in France was almost lost.

Yet even at this eleventh hour, not all those in Britain had abandoned the struggle in France, and on June 8 Jean Monnet, Chairman of the Anglo-French Co-ordinating Committee, telegraphed from London to Arthur Purvis in the United States: 'Rush with utmost speed 347 field guns, 75mm, with limbercaisson and caisson limber to France, with all the HE shells. This is a most urgent need, with absolute priority. . . .' Monnet added two further instructions: 'Ship to France all the Browning ground machine guns with half of the machine gun ammunition' and 'Ship 15,638 Marlin anti-aircraft machine guns and 14,000 Lewis aircraft machine guns to France. . . .' Speaking on behalf of the Anglo-French Co-ordinating Committee, Monnet added: 'We are very appreciative of your success in obtaining the release of this material and please express our gratitude to Mr Morgenthau for his inspiring efforts.'[3]

Guns and munitions could still go to France, but aircraft could not. Defending his refusal to send any further fighter squadrons to France, Churchill telegraphed to General Smuts, who had urged Churchill to comply with the French appeals:

We are of course doing all we can both from the Air and by sending divisions as fast as they can be equipped to France. It would be wrong to send the bulk of our fighters to this battle and when it was lost, as is probable, be left with no means of carrying on the war. I think we have a harder, longer, and more hopeful duty to perform.

Advantages of resisting German air attack in this Island, where we can concentrate very powerful fighter strength, and hope to knock out four or five

[1] Draft message, 8 June 1940, not sent: Premier papers, 3/188/1, folios 20–21.
[2] 'Most Immediate', 'Secret', 8 June 1940: Premier papers: 3/188/1, folio 16.
[3] 'Purco' No. 119, 'Most Immediate', 8 June 1940: Cabinet papers, 85/13.

hostiles to one of ours, are far superior to fighting in France, where we are inevitably outnumbered and rarely exceed two to one ratio of destruction, and where our aircraft are often destroyed at exposed aerodromes.

This battle does not turn on the score or so of fighter squadrons we could transport with their plant in the next month. Even if by using them up we held the enemy, Hitler could immediately throw his whole air strength against our undefended Island and destroy our means of future production by daylight attack.

The classical principles of war which you mention are in this case modified by the actual quantitative data.

Churchill ended his telegram to Smuts:

I see only one sure way through now, to wit, that Hitler should attack this country, and in so doing break his air weapon. If this happens he will be left to face the winter with Europe writhing under his heel, and probably with the United States against him after the Presidential election is over.[1]

In a private note to the Secretary of State for the Dominions, Lord Caldecote,[2] who was to despatch this telegram to Smuts, Churchill commented: 'It is vital to our safety that United States should be involved in totalitarian war.'[3]

Churchill's recognition of the extent to which Roosevelt's hands might be tied until after the Presidential Election in November 1940 had already led to one British effort to curb any exacerbation of isolationist feeling. Three weeks earlier, on May 20, MI5 had arrested an employee of the United States Embassy, Tyler Kent, who over the previous seven months had stolen more than 1,500 documents from the Embassy, including copies of eight messages from Churchill to Roosevelt. Kent had intended to smuggle these documents back to the United States, in order to give them as ammunition to isolationist groups opposed to Roosevelt's pro-British policies.

Two days after Kent's arrest, the War Cabinet had authorized the arrest of Sir Oswald Mosley and more than two hundred of his followers, as well as of a Conservative MP, Captain Archibald Ramsay, who Kent had hoped would raise in the House of Commons the whole question of Churchill's links with Roosevelt. But although they had arrested Kent, who was an American citizen, the British authorities held him incommunicado for five months; in order, as Joseph Ken-

---

[1] 'Personal & Secret', 9 June 1940: Premier papers, 4/43B/1, folios 442–3. The Presidential Election was to be held on 5 November 1940.

[2] Formerly Sir Thomas Inskip, Minister for Co-ordination of Defence from 1936 to 1939.

[3] Note dated 9 June 1940: Premier papers, 4/43B/1, folio 454.

nedy informed the State Department, to avoid embarrassing Roosevelt during the election campaign.[1]

It was the precise attitude of the United States which led Churchill to telegraph, also on June 9, to Lord Lothian, the British Ambassador in Washington, who had raised the question of what Churchill had meant in his 'Dunkirk' speech about the New World eventually stepping forth 'to the rescue and liberation of the Old'. As Churchill now explained:

My last words in my speech were of course addressed primarily to Germany and Italy, to whom the idea of a war of Continents and a long war are at present obnoxious; also to Dominions, for whom we are trustees. . . .

If Great Britain broke under invasion, a pro-German Government might obtain far easier terms from Germany by surrendering the Fleet, thus making Germany and Japan masters of the New World. This dastard deed would not be done by His Majesty's present advisers, but, if Mosley were Prime Minister or some other Quisling Government were set up it is exactly what they would do, and perhaps the only thing they could do, and the President should bear this very clearly in mind.

You should talk to him in this sense and thus discourage any complacent assumption on United States' part that they will pick up the *débris* of the British Empire by their present policy.

On the contrary, they run the terrible risk that their sea-power will be completely over-matched. Moreover, islands and naval bases to hold the United States in awe should certainly be claimed by the Nazis.

'If we go down,' Churchill added, 'Hitler has a very good chance of conquering the world.'[2]

On the afternoon of June 9 Churchill received a visitor from France, the recently appointed Under-Secretary for National Defence, General Charles de Gaulle, who had flown to Britain at Reynaud's request. It was their first meeting. That same evening Churchill reported to the War Cabinet that de Gaulle had given 'a more favourable impression of French morale and determination'. He had come, Churchill explained, to outline the French regroupment plans and to urge that the further British divisions which were being moved to France 'should be sent as rapidly as possible'.

Churchill had told de Gaulle 'why we could not engage the whole of

---

[1] I am grateful to John Costello for the reference to Kennedy's telegrams. The story of Kent's activities, arrest and trial is in: Robert Harris, 'The American tearoom spy', *The Times*, 4 December 1982. Tyler was tried in secret at the end of October 1940. On 7 November 1940, two days after Roosevelt's re-election, the Press were admitted for the first time to the court, to see Kent sentenced to seven years in prison. In 1945 he was deported to the United States.

[2] Telegram of 9 June 1940: Churchill papers, 20/14. In the version of this telegram as finally sent to Roosevelt, Churchill omitted the phrase 'if Mosley were Prime Minister' (Premier papers, 3/462/2/3, folios 164–5).

our Air Force in the battle in France'. To this de Gaulle had replied that, 'speaking for himself', he 'agreed with our policy'.[1]

According to de Gaulle's recollection of the meeting, Churchill had expressed satisfaction at de Gaulle's statement that the French Government was determined to continue the struggle, if necessary from the French territories overseas, but had told the General 'that he no longer believed in the possibility of a victory in France'.[2]

At the War Cabinet that evening, it became clear that de Gaulle had not been uncritical of the British efforts. He had first told Eden that it was important both to give the French 'a definite programme' of the troops we intended to send to France, and to organize the fullest possible cooperation in the provision of equipment. He had then told Dill that the British tanks in the Armoured Division about to be sent to France 'were not heavily enough armoured'.

During the War Cabinet of June 9, Churchill also raised an issue which he had first raised in the House of Commons on June 4: the accusations by soldiers returned from Dunkirk that the Royal Air Force had let them down. He had recently been told, he said, of an Air Force officer having been 'insulted' by troops at Dover, and he asked Dill 'to carry out a vigorous campaign, which should include propaganda', in all army units to ensure 'that the gallantry and heroism shown by the Royal Air Force in recent operations was known and appreciated'.[3]

From hour to hour, Churchill cast about for some means of counteracting the relentless German thrusts into France. A month earlier, just as he had become Prime Minister, Operation 'Royal Marine' had been activated in order to drop aerial mines into the Rhine, and to disrupt river traffic. 'By midnight tonight,' Churchill had been told on May 13, 'the whole of the Rhine may be infected,'[4] and a week later he learned that 1,184 mines had been dropped into the Rhine, with a further 360 in the Moselle.[5] At least one bridge had been destroyed, leaving '7 miles of lorries waiting to go over'.[6] On June 8 Churchill was told that, following the destruction by mines of two barrages over the Rhine, aerial reconnaisance had shown that traffic between Karlsruhe and Mainz was 'totally suspended'.[7]

---

[1] War Cabinet No. 159 of 1940, 9 June 1940, 7 p.m.: Cabinet papers, 65/7, Minute 3 (second part), folios 402–3.

[2] Charles de Gaulle, l'Appel, Paris 1954, pages 47–8.

[3] War Cabinet No. 159 of 1940, 9 June 1940, 7 p.m.: Cabinet papers, 65/7.

[4] 'Operation RM', 'Report of 13 May 1940': Premier papers, 3/375, folio 47.

[5] 'Operation RM', 'Report of 17 May 1940': Premier papers, 3/375, folios 42–3.

[6] 'Operation RM', 'Night of 22nd May': Premier papers, 3/375, folio 36.

[7] 'Secret', 8 June 1940: Premier papers, 3/375, folio 34.

It was at this moment that Churchill learned of a French request that the British minelaying party under Admiral Fitzgerald, which General Georges had been using to lay mines on roads as anti-tank devices, was no longer needed for road work, and had been told to return to Britain. He at once telegraphed to Reynaud:

> Our aerial reconnaissance shows that all traffic on the Rhine between Karlsruhe and Mainz is stopped. Not one barge was seen in transit by our aviators. Why not keep it stopped? We have not hitherto been able owing to battle needs to lay the air fluvials in the lower reaches, especially from Mainz to Coblenz and Cologne. Traffic on this section is vital to the enemy's industry and military supplies. It requires only a squadron or two of night-bombers and will not affect our night support of your Army. The moon is getting good. Propose therefore to continue streaming into the Rhine from French territory in order to poison river down to Mainz, and open up by air attack on lower reaches.

'Pray let me know what reasons you have to the contrary,' Churchill added; then deleted the sentence. His telegram ended: 'It would be most improvident to throw this attack on pontoon bridges and munition traffic away.'[1]

Even as Churchill prepared to send this telegram, the news from France worsened considerably, nor were any further 'Royal Marine' activities possible.[2] On June 9, German armoured troops had reached the outskirts of Rouen, and on the following day General Fortune and the 51st Division were driven back to the sea, at St Valéry en Caux, where they were quickly surrounded by German forces. Because of fog, evacuation that night was impossible, and although the General refused to surrender, he was under considerable pressure to do so from the French forces at the beachhead. At one point, as the 5th Gordon Highlanders were about to open fire on the advancing German tanks, French troops carrying white flags marched directly across the Highlanders' front, making it impossible for them to open fire. During June 10, to the south, German armoured columns entered Rouen, and in two places crossed the Seine. The road to Paris was opening up to the invader.

---

[1] Draft of 9 June 1940, sent at 2 a.m. on 11 June 1940 as telegram No. 329 DIPP to Sir R. Campbell in Paris: Premier papers, 3/375, folios 25 (draft) and 21 (telegram as sent).

[2] Following the return of the 'Royal Marine' expedition to Britain, Rear-Admiral Fitzgerald was awarded the CB and Commander Wellby the DSO. According to the citation, Wellby had worked within 'a few hundred yards' of the German positions, despite harassing shell-fire, and had succeeded in stopping 'all traffic' of barges between Karlsruhe and Mainz. Two DSCs and seventeen DSMs were also awarded ('Mine-laying on Rhine; 21 awards to Naval Expeditionary Force Personnel': Admiralty papers, 1/10494).

In London, Churchill and the Chiefs of Staff Committee were considering the question of defence against invasion. 'It is impossible,' Churchill wrote to the Committee on June 9, 'to provide protection everywhere against mere threats of possible descent by parachute.' His note continued:

The only sound principle of defence is to have vigilant, widespread local watch and such protection as can be organized on the spot, and to hold well-organized, mobile forces at hand at short notice to attack the assailants. The Commander-in-Chief, Home Forces, should be supported in his sound decision not to dissipate or distribute his striking force. Unless he is sustained you will presently have no army at all, only a vast swarm of sentries. No universal protection can be given, but examples can be made of assailants.

The only exception to this rule, Churchill added, was the 'key aircraft factories', and he commented: 'I presume some of the mobile columns are very close to these areas. They might *live* in the handiest places.'

Surely, Churchill asked, without deviating from 'the general principle of no dispersion', defence parties could be organized from the working staff at the factories, and also 'from the local parashooters'. These defence parties could apply not only to aircraft factories, but to 'unoccupied aerodromes, coal mines etc'. Churchill's minute ended: '*Don't disperse the army*. Keep strong strike forces in hand. Have good communications.'[1]

That same day, June 9, as French troops on the Seine fell back towards Paris, more than 11,000 British and French troops at the Channel port of Le Havre were being taken off by ship and evacuated to Britain. This operation, code named 'Cycle', had been ordered on the previous afternoon, and was completed within three days, despite the evacuation armada being 'heavily bombed' on the evening of June 10.

Plans were also being made to evacuate the British and French troops surrounded at St Valéry.[2]

At the Defence Committee meeting on June 10, the discussion was dominated by plans to meet a German invasion. A complete new issue of rifles was being made to the British Expeditionary Force evacuees, and would be concluded in a few days. Bren guns were also being

---

[1] Minute of 9 June 1940, circulated as Chiefs of Staff Paper No. 370 of 1940: Premier papers, 3/93/1. folios 11–12.

[2] 'Operation Cycle', Report of 18 June 1940: Admiralty papers, 1/10481. Twelve ships were sunk during the Havre and St Valéry evacuations: the passenger vessel *Bruges* and No. 2 Train Ferry (both by air attack), two Dutch schoots (one mined, one shelled by shore batteries) and eight small motor craft. The naval personnel involved in these two evacuations were to receive one DSO (Commander C. A. N. Chatwin, RN), eleven DSCs, and 16 DCMs.

issued although, as Ironside explained, 'we had not got enough in hand to complete all the Divisions'. Special bodies of men 'who would know the country intimately' were being organized for coast watching. Defensive positions in places 'where we could not afford to give up any ground to the enemy' had been designated, and 32,000 men allotted to their defence. Beach defences, barbed-wire barricades and pill-boxes were all being constructed. There was, however, 'a great shortage of artillery and anti-tank guns'.

Turning to the situation in France, the Minister of Information, Duff Cooper, warned of German propaganda to the effect that, as the British 'were not giving them any support', the French should make peace with Germany. There was, Churchill himself pointed out, 'considerable feeling' in certain circles in France 'that we had given inadequate support on land, and had only paid attention to rescuing our own Army from Dunkirk'.

By contrast, Churchill commented, while the British 'had some reason' to feel that matters had not been very well handled by the French, and recent events on the left flank in France had been 'a repetition of what had occurred in Flanders', it was nevertheless 'essential' that nothing should be said in Britain 'which might be construed as criticism of the French'. Furthermore, it was agreed to broadcast within the next three hours a statement of Britain's current support for France.[1]

The message as broadcast referred to the 'maximum possible support' being given by the British, the rapid organization of 'further extensive reinforcements' which would shortly be available, and the activities of the Royal Air Force which 'has been continuously engaged over the battlefield'.[2]

During the rest of June 10, as Churchill followed the worsening news from France, he presided over the War Cabinet at 12.30, lunched with Sinclair, saw Dill and Spears—just returned from France—at 3.15, Halifax and A. V. Alexander at 5, General Alan Brooke at 5.30, the Ministers not in the Cabinet at 6, and the American Ambassador an hour later.[3]

---

[1] Defence Committee No. 15 of 1940, 10 June 1940, 10.30 a.m.: Cabinet papers, 69/1.

[2] Annex to Defence Committee 15 of 1940: Cabinet papers, 69/1.

[3] Churchill's monthly engagement cards, entry for 10 June 1940: Commander Thompson papers; and Kathleen Hill's engagement diary: Churchill papers, 2/413. General Brooke was about to cross back to France, having commanded the II Corps in the retreat to Dunkirk. His new command was the first Corps of the new British Expeditionary Force, promised by Churchill to Reynaud. On June 10 he received his instructions, including an assurance that, when circumstances demanded, he would have 'the full support of the Royal Air Force as a whole' (Instructions of 10 June 1940: Cabinet papers, 65/7, folio 414).

The focus of Churchill's attention now turned momentarily to Italy, where Mussolini was expected to declare war on Britain at any time. At a quarter to five on the afternoon of June 10, the British Ambassador in Rome, Sir Percy Loraine, was summoned to the Italian Foreign Ministry. There he was given, by Mussolini's son-in-law Count Ciano, a 'declaration of war' by Italy.[1]

Loraine's telegram did not reach London until late that evening. But a clear intimation that war with Italy was only a matter of hours had reached Churchill's Private Office while Churchill was still having his 'afternoon slumber'. He was awakened at once. But, as Colville noted, 'the possibility of the *French* being defeated or giving in was of more interest to him than Italy coming in'. Pressed for some private comment, all he would say was: 'People who go to Italy to look at ruins won't have to go so far as Naples and Pompeii again.'[2]

That evening, as soon as official confirmation of Italy's declaration of war arrived, Churchill instructed the Minister of Home Security, Sir John Anderson, 'to arrange for a general internment of male Italians in Britain'.[3]

Italy's entry into the war was of considerable concern; her troops were poised in the Alps to strike at France, and in North and East Africa to threaten British interests at several points, including Egypt. At the same time, Italy's air, sea and submarine forces constituted a cause for anxiety to Britain's lines of communication throughout the eastern and central Mediterranean.

At the very moment when Britain's last Ally seemed on the verge of disaster, Hitler had gained a co-belligerent. However small Italy's powers might be in comparison to Germany's, they constituted nevertheless, at this time of danger, an added threat to Britain, and an added burden to Churchill. But it was fear of a French collapse that tormented Churchill throughout the evening of June 10. 'He was in a bad temper,' Colville wrote in his diary, 'snapped everybody's head off, wrote angry minutes to the First Sea Lord, and refused to pay any attention to messages given him orally.'[4]

That night, as German troops continued their advance towards Paris,

---

[1] Telegram No. 901(R), despatched 5.55 p.m., received 10.40 p.m., 10 June 1940: Foreign Office papers, 371/24948.

[2] Colville diary, 10 June 1940, Colville papers.

[3] Churchill's report to the War Cabinet of 11 June 1940: Cabinet papers, 65/13, folio 419. At this meeting of June 11 Halifax told his colleagues: 'it was to our advantage to get rid of as many Italians as possible. Italy would have to feed them, and they would probably form centres of disaffection in Italy, since many of them had no desire to return to that country'.

[4] Colville diary, 10 June 1940: Colville papers.

and the Italian army prepared to invade south-eastern France, Churchill decided to fly to Paris on the following morning in an attempt to persuade the French to defend their capital. But as he began to make his plans, a telegram arrived with the news that the French Government was leaving Paris. 'What the hell,' was Churchill's immediate comment. 'It seemed,' wrote Colville, 'that there was no perch on which he could alight.'

Following the German crossings of the Seine, further appeals reached London for greater fighter support. There was no way, however, that the previous day's decision, reached with such difficulty, and yet with such conviction and unanimity, could be revoked. As to the French Government's decision to move the seat of Government out of Paris, Churchill thought it was, if anything, a good omen, 'because it shows', as Colville recorded, 'that they intend to go on fighting'. But he was at the same time 'afraid that Flandin and other Quislings may stay behind and make terms with the invader'.[1]

Towards midnight Churchill, who was working in the Admiralty War Room, listened to a broadcast of a speech by Roosevelt at the University of Virginia. 'We will extend to the opponents of force,' said Roosevelt, 'the material resources of this nation. We will not slow down or detour. Signs and signals call for speed: full speed ahead.' And he added: 'I call for effort, courage, sacrifice, devotion, and the love of freedom. All these are possible.'[2]

It was, Churchill later wrote, 'a magnificent speech, instinct with passion, and carrying to us a message of hope'.[3] Churchill at once dictated a message to the President, for approval by the War Cabinet. All who listened, Churchill told Roosevelt, 'were fortified by the grand scope of your declaration'. The statement that the material aid of the United States would be given to the Allies in their struggle was, he wrote, 'a strong encouragement in a dark but not unhopeful hour'. Everything should be done 'to keep France in the fight and to prevent any idea of the fall of Paris, should it occur, becoming the occasion of any kind of parley'.

Churchill then outlined to Roosevelt the British plan: to defend Britain against a German invasion once Hitler, 'baffled of quick results' in France, turned upon Britain; then to equip divisions on the 'much higher scale' needed for Continental service, and to send them to

---

[1] Colville diary, 10 June 1940: Colville papers.

[2] Speech of 10 June 1940: Samuel I. Roseman (editor), *The Public Papers and Addresses of Franklin D. Roosevelt*, volume 9, New York 1941, number 58.

[3] Winston S. Churchill, *The Second World War*, volume 2, London 1949, page 116.

France; and to have 'a strong army' fighting in France 'for the campaign of 1941'.

All this assumed, of course, that by 1941 the French army would still be holding a portion of French soil.

Churchill now turned to Britain's immediate needs, telling Roosevelt that airplanes and flying boats were essential 'in the impending struggle for the life of Great Britain'. But even more pressing, he urged, was the need for destroyers. Churchill's appeal continued:

The Italian outrage makes it necessary for us to cope with a much larger number of submarines, which may come out into the Atlantic and perhaps be based on Spanish ports. To this the only counter is destroyers. Nothing is so important as for us to have the thirty or forty old destroyers you have already had reconditioned. We can fit them very rapidly with our Asdics, and they will bridge the gap of six months before our wartime new construction comes into play. We will return them or their equivalents to you, without fail, at six months' notice if at any time you need them.

The next six months are vital. If while we have to guard the East Coast against invasion a new heavy German–Italian submarine attack is launched against our commerce the strain may be beyond our resources.

Reading this telegram before it was sent off, Churchill added at this point, in his own handwriting: '& the ocean's traffic by which we live may be strangled. Not a day shd be lost.'

'I send you my heartfelt thanks,' Churchill ended, '& those of my colleagues, for all you are doing & seeking to do for what we may now indeed call the Common Cause.'[1]

Churchill's appeal for destroyers crossed with a telegram from Lothian which raised serious questions of how Roosevelt might respond. 'Have just learned from authoritative source,' Lothian wrote, 'that the President is not convinced that our need for destroyers is serious, and is therefore concentrating on the Allies' other needs.'

Lothian believed that it was 'imperative' for Churchill to inform Roosevelt 'as soon as possible' of the numbers, types and tonnages of destroyers lost, of the numbers damaged, of the time taken to repair these, 'and any other information necessary to convince him of our case'. The American Press, Lothian added ominously, had been carrying a statement 'that we have already made good all destroyers lost'.[2]

Not so easily was Churchill to win United States' adherence to the 'Common Cause'. Not so quickly was the new Italian threat to be

---

[1] 'Personal & Private', 11 June 1940: Premier papers, 3/468, folios 170–72.

[2] Telegram No. 967, sent 0.25 a.m., received 10 a.m., 12 June 1940: Premier papers, 3/468, folio 165.

overcome. Not so swiftly was the battle in France to be stabilized or won. But Churchill's own courage was fortified by his conviction that disaster, to Britain at least, might be averted; and in displaying such conviction, he inspired even the French leaders. He certainly did not fear to confront them, nor flinch from urging them to continue the struggle, even amid the hourly reports of retreat and lack of resolve. Indeed, it was the blackness of the reports that seemed to draw from Churchill most strongly the will-power needed to confront the dissolving scene around him.

25

Briare: 'the break-up'

THROUGHOUT the first ten days of June 1940 each hour's news brought drama and uncertainty. Yet despite the added worries caused by Italy's entry into the war, and the relentless German advance on Paris, in general Churchill maintained a calm nerve and steady temper. 'Winston is standing up to the strain very well,' Beaverbrook wrote to Hoare, who was in Madrid as Ambassador, on June 11. 'He is like Atlas with two worlds to carry. With one hand he bears up the British Empire, with the other he sustains the French Republic. And the French Republic takes a bit of supporting too, let me tell you.'[1]

In a note to Halifax that morning, Churchill stated that he did not expect 'an immediate collapse' of France. But he wanted the French situation watched 'from day to day' by someone who had access to both Reynaud and Darlan. 'I do not know at present where our Ambassador has gone to,' Churchill wrote, 'or what means of communication exist. If we have to go to France this afternoon, I will take the memorandum with me.'

The 'memorandum' was Hankey's report on the action to be taken by Britain 'in the event of a French military collapse'. The first action proposed was to ensure that France's gold reserves were shipped to the United States. The second action concerned the future of the French Fleet. As Pound had told Hankey, and as Hankey reported, 'it would be better if the French Fleet were sunk' before German pressure to force it to return to bases in France. Hankey added that it had 'accordingly been arranged' that Pound would, at the appropriate moment, get in touch with Darlan 'with a view of inducing him to sink the French Fleet'.

The third and final action concerned French aircraft. Those being

[1] Letter of 11 June 1940: Beaverbrook papers.

assembled in France or Casablanca 'could, if necessary, be flown across British territory in Africa to the Middle East', or a British ship would be sent to Casablanca 'to take possession of them'. Aircraft on board ship on the high seas could be 'diverted to British ports', or intercepted. The future of the 2,000 to 3,000 aircraft being constructed for France in the United States 'will be a matter for discussion between the American Government and ourselves'. The French Government itself, Hankey added, would be responsible for destroying all internal stocks of oil.[1]

The basis of Hankey's plan was that the French Government would be taking active steps in Britain's interest to ensure that a French collapse did not give the German's undue advantage. Nor, at that moment, was this hope far-fetched. Even as Hankey wrote his memorandum, Canadian troops were on their way to France, to try to give new strength to the French military struggle. In view of the Canadian commitment, Churchill approved a draft telegram to the Prime Minister of Canada, Mackenzie King, which said, as if in Churchill's words: 'Of Canada's own thoughts it is not for me to speak, but I know well the profound emotion with which in due time the people of this country will learn of the Canadians' arrival in France.'[2] A similar telegram of thanks went to the Prime Minister of Australia, for placing at Britain's disposal the battleship *Australia* and two cruisers, further proof, Churchill wrote, of Australia's determination 'to support our efforts by every means in her power in these critical hours'.[3]

Once more, Churchill's minutes reveal the urgency of the hour and the extent of the need. Learning of delay in an improvement in bombsight design decided upon more than three months earlier, he minuted to Beaverbrook: 'I would be very glad if you would look at the files and ascertain who was responsible for stifling action.'[4]

Seeking every means to anticipate invasion, in a second minute to Beaverbrook, about the production of reconnaissance aircraft, Churchill noted that these machines were of 'tremendous value in enabling us to find out if any expedition is preparing in the German harbours or river mouths'.[5] In a minute to Pound on June 11, Churchill asserted the need for naval action against a German artillery battery at Fécamp on the French coast. This battery had shelled and driven off a British

---

[1] 'Most Secret', 'Action by His Majesty's Government in the event of a French military collapse', 11 June 1940: Premier papers, 3/188/2, folios 3–6.

[2] Message drafted by Norman Archer, Assistant Secretary, Dominions Office, and approved by Churchill in its entirety, 11 June 1940: Premier papers, 4/44/4.

[3] Telegram of 11 June 1940: Churchill papers, 20/14.

[4] Minute of 11 June 1940: Churchill papers, 20/13.

[5] Minute of 11 June 1940: Churchill papers, 20/13.

destroyer, causing casualties on board. 'Why has a cruiser not been sent,' Churchill asked, 'or other suitable bombarding vessel, and why is this battery that is in the track of our retreating troops not knocked out or driven away. It is the duty of the Navy to give proper support at the present time.'[1]

At 10.30 that morning, at a meeting of the Defence Committee, Churchill's mind was still very much on his midnight message to Roosevelt, in which he had talked of a British army ready to go to France in 1941. What he now required, he told the Committee, was a programme whereby 500 to 600 heavy tanks 'could be produced, and in the hands of troops, by the end of March 1941'. Every consideration should be sacrificed to speed up production, 'all refinements being eliminated'. No modification in design would be accepted which would delay production 'in the slightest degree'.[2]

Even while the Defence Committee was meeting, a message had arrived for Churchill from Reynaud. Although he and Churchill could no longer meet in Paris, they could meet at the new Army Headquarters at Briare, on the Loire, eighty miles south of Paris, 'The French have sent for me again,' Churchill telegraphed to Roosevelt during the morning, 'which means that crisis has arrived. Am just off. Anything you can say or do to help them now may make the difference.'[3]

At the War Cabinet that morning, doubts had been expressed about the ability of Eire to remain neutral. With Italy now a belligerent against Britain, the spectre of a German-dominated Ireland was alarming. 'We are also worried about Ireland,' Churchill informed Roosevelt. 'An American Squadron at Berehaven would do no end of good I am sure.'[4] But Roosevelt made no reply to this request to commit the United States to put pressure upon de Valera's Ireland.

During the midday War Cabinet on June 11, Churchill told his colleagues what he expected to achieve in his talks with the French at Briare. 'We should have to concert with them,' he said, 'a grand strategic plan for the future conduct of the war and to find out what their intentions were.' If the French were driven from Paris, Churchill said, it seemed possible that they 'would be prepared to fight on in the more difficult country' to the south of the capital. 'He would of course,' as the minutes recorded, 'give them every encouragement to continue the struggle and discourage any signs of a movement towards making a

[1] Minute of 11 June 1940: Churchill papers, 20/13.
[2] Defence Committee No. 16 of 1940, 11 June 1940 10.30 a.m.: Cabinet papers, 70/1.
[3] Telegram of 11 June 1940: Churchill papers, 20/14.
[4] 'Secret and Personal', 11 June 1940: Premier papers, 3/468, folio 117.

separate peace.' He would 'impress on them' that if they could continue fighting, and thus prevent the Germans from achieving the 'quick decisions' which they required, 'we should hold out, even if the whole resources of the enemy were turned on the United Kingdom'.

The War Cabinet then approved Churchill's proposed message to Roosevelt, and also his instruction of the previous day to intern all Italian subjects then in Britain. Halifax was particularly emphatic that the measures against Italians should be comprehensive, and Sir John Anderson spoke of a hard core of '1,500 desperate characters' who were about to be seized. Churchill agreed with Halifax and Anderson, adding the general principle that the Government 'should endeavour to round up all enemy aliens as quickly as possible, so as to place them out of harm's way'. Subsequently, the Government should examine individual cases, 'and release those who were found to be well-disposed to this country'.

The discussion turned to the question of an Egyptian declaration of war on Italy. Churchill had suggested to Halifax that there was 'something to be said' for not forcing the Egyptian Government to declare war, but rather to wait until some 'direct action' by Italy would 'seem' to force war upon Egypt. If the Italians were to bomb Cairo, Churchill ventured, 'then we should be entitled to bomb Rome'.[1]

On a second bombing matter, the War Cabinet of June 11 agreed, with Churchill's approval, to proceed with a Royal Air Force attack on the Black Forest, 'with incendiary bombs'.[2]

Churchill now prepared to leave for France, for the meeting upon which so much depended, and yet from which only the imminent surrender of France, and Britain finding herself alone against Germany, was the likely outcome. He was accompanied by Eden, Dill, Brigadier Lund,[3] General Spears, and an interpreter, Captain Berkeley. It was a day, as Eden later recalled, of 'unbroken sunshine'.[4] Setting off from Hendon airport at 2.30 that afternoon, they flew by Flamingo, escorted by twelve Hurricanes. Also on board was Ismay, who later recalled:

[1] War Cabinet No. 161 of 1940, 11 June 1940, 12.30 p.m.: Cabinet papers, 65/7.

[2] War Cabinet No. 161 of 1940, 11 June 1940, Confidential Annex, Minute 3: Cabinet papers, 63/13. On June 25 the Operation was given the code name 'Razzle'.

[3] Deputy Director of Military Operations and Plans.

[4] Eden's recollections here, and for the rest of the Briare visit, are from the Earl of Avon, *The Eden Memoirs: The Reckoning*, London 1965, pages 115–16.

Early in the morning the Prime Minister had told me that I had better stay behind and 'mind the shop'. Presumably some well-meaning friend had said that I was worn out and needed a rest. Since this was untrue, I did not take the instructions too seriously, but to be on the safe side I got to Hendon well ahead of Churchill and hid behind the aeroplane.

As soon as he embarked, I followed close on his heels, and sat in the seat immediately behind him. I felt like a stowaway, and it was a relief when we took off. After we had been flying for about five minutes, Churchill turned round and barked out, 'You're here, are you?' There was not much that I could say, so I remained silent.

He turned his back on me and continued reading. After a further pause he turned round again and, with an expression of fury, said, 'I knew you'd come.' Another pause, and he was handing me papers to read and comment upon. I was forgiven.

But we were not yet out of the wood. The Prime Minister suddenly realised that we were heading west instead of south. He protested that he wanted to get to Briare as quickly as possible. 'Why don't we fly direct over France?'

I suspect that he had a faint hope of being able to see something of the battle! However, the pilot was able to convince him that both he and the fighter escort had had precise instructions from the Air Ministry, and that it was impossible to change the route.[1]

Spears, who was also on the flight to Briare, later recorded how, during the journey, Churchill 'brooded in his arm-chair, his eyes on the horizon. Occasionally he beckoned to one of us to ask a question, then relapsed into silence.' As for Ismay, Spears recalled, he, like Dill, 'had an enormous number of folders in his dispatch-cases. He never took his eyes off them save when called by Churchill or Dill, when he would look-up, wide-eyed, put his hand to his ear to hear through the vibrations of the machine, and smile as soon as he had grasped what was wanted of him.'[2]

The Flamingo reached Briare in the late afternoon. 'I felt almost ashamed,' Eden recalled, 'of our ordered escort of Hurricanes as we landed on the airfield, with its scattered confusion of odds and ends of aircraft.' The airfield itself, wrote Spears, 'seemed particularly flat and deserted'. Churchill however, 'in black, leaning on his stick, strolled about beaming as if he had left all his preoccupations in the plane and had reached the one spot in the world he most wished to visit at that particular moment'. He conveyed the impression, Spears commented

---

[1] Ismay's recollections here, and for the rest of the Briare visit are from *The Memoirs of General The Lord Ismay*, London 1960, pages 137–40.

[2] Spears' recollections here, and for the rest of the Briare visit, are from Major-General Sir Edward Spears, *Assignment to Catastrophe*, volume 2, London 1954, pages 137–71.

wryly, that the long journey had been well worth while, 'since at last it was vouchsafed to him to walk about the aerodrome of Briare'.

A French Colonel arrived by car, and the British left. From the Colonel's expression, Spears wrote, he might have been welcoming poor relations 'at a funeral reception'. The drive, some six miles to the east of Briare, took the British to Weygand's headquarters residence at the Château du Muguet. Walking in to the Château, wrote Spears, 'was like walking into a house thinking one was expected, to find one had been invited for the following week. Our presence was not really desired.'

After being given tea, the British visitors were ushered into a large dining-room where the conference was to be held. It was seven o'clock in the evening. The Frenchmen present, as Spears later recalled, 'sat with set white faces, their eyes on the table', looking like prisoners 'hauled up from some deep dungeon to hear an inevitable verdict'. Only one of the Frenchmen, Charles de Gaulle 'had a look of confidence and self-possession'. According to Eden, Reynaud, who presided, 'was firm and courteous despite the strain', while Ismay recalled, of Reynaud, that in spite of the 'apparent hopelessness of the situation, and of the defeatism around him, he was, as ever, friendly, militant and a bundle of energy'. But Weygand seemed to Ismay 'to have abandoned all hope', while Pétain 'looked more woe-begone than ever'.

After an awkward pause, and before the actual conference started, Reynaud raised a point of some delicacy, and, as Spears wrote, 'he evidently found considerable difficulty in doing so'. The episode was not recorded in the minutes. It concerned the combined Anglo-French sea and air operation which was to take place that very night against Italian military objectives in Genoa, Turin and Milan. British bombers were to fly to Salon, near Marseilles, refuel, and fly on immediately to their Italian targets. As Spears later recalled, Reynaud asked, with great embarrassment, that the operation should be called off. 'Lyons was completely unprotected,' he said 'so were the great petrol depots near Marseilles. The Italians were sure to retaliate, with disastrous results.'

Churchill was dismayed. But then, after consulting Ismay, he looked up, as Spears recalled, 'beaming'. For, as Ismay wrote, having done a 'quick calculation', it was clear that the bombers had already started from England, and it was no longer possible to countermand them. 'On Churchill's instructions,' Ismay added, 'I explained this elementary but decisive fact. There was nothing more to be said.'

Roland de Margerie translated, in 'cold, precise words', as Spears recalled, 'that fell like silver coins on a counter. Reynaud's eyebrows arched higher, but he made no comment. Weygand looked at Pug[1] with faint distaste but said nothing either, nor did Pétain, in comparison with whom Lazarus would have looked skittish and high in colour.'

After a further, awkward pause, Reynaud turned to Churchill, and asked him to address the conference. The fourteenth meeting of the Supreme War Council had begun. He wished to make it clear at the outset, Churchill declared, 'that Britain would continue the struggle in all circumstances'.[2] It was his expectation, 'even his hope', that as soon as the Germans 'stabilised' a position in France, they would turn against the United Kingdom, and give the Royal Air Force 'an opportunity of breaking Germany's might in the air'. He felt confident that the air force 'would succeed'.

As for British military help in France, if the French forces could hold out, militarily, even for a few weeks, Churchill said, the British military contribution 'would grow apace'; the immediate problem was one of 'tiding over the lean weeks', until the potential strength of the Allies 'became actual'.

Churchill's words, as Spears later recalled, 'came slowly, carefully selected but hammered together sharply into a vivid mosaic'. Spears also noted, as the official record did not, the military details which Churchill gave of Britain's current and prospective help: a Canadian division and 72 guns were landing that very night, bringing the number of divisions already in France up to four. Another division would arrive in about nine days time. Yet a further division would be available if the French could provide the guns. Then there were the troops being withdrawn from Narvik. If the French Army could hold out in France for nine months, until the Spring of 1941, the British would have from twenty to twenty-five divisions 'to place at the disposal of the French command, to employ anywhere'.

As Spears took his notes, he was aware of Reynaud's 'suppressed irritation', and that of the other Frenchmen present, 'at the inadequacy of this trickle to halt a conflagration whose flames were fast spreading from the Channel to the Atlantic'. And when Weygand spoke, after Churchill, to describe the actual military situation, holding out no

---

[1] Major-General Ismay.

[2] Unless reference is specifically made to the recollections of Eden, Spears, Reynaud or Ismay, references to what was discussed at this Council are taken from: Supreme War Council, 14th Meeting of 1939–1940, 'Record of the Fourteenth Meeting of the Supreme War Council held at GOG Briare, on Tuesday, 11th June, at 7 p.m.', 'Secret': Cabinet papers, 99/3, folios 91–4.

hope of halting the German advance on Paris, or beyond it, Spears 'looked round', as he later wrote, 'and read consternation on all the English faces. My own mouth was so dry that I could not swallow.'

As Weygand's survey continued, Spears noted down the French Commander-in-Chief's exact words, as he 'rapped out: "I am helpless, I cannot intervene for I have no reserves, there are no reserves. C'est la dislocation"—the break up.'

No one spoke; Churchill, 'hunched over the table' as Spears recalled, 'his face flushed, was watching Weygand intently. His expression was not benevolent.' But Weygand was now speaking, not of the military situation, but of his personal belief that 'those responsible'—the French politicians—had 'embarked upon the war very lightly and without any conception of the power of German armaments'.

Both Churchill and Eden intervened to return to the situation of that day, and to speak again of the arrival of the Canadians on French soil. But they were only successful, Spears recalled, 'in diverting the Commander-in-Chief back to his tale of woe'. And when Weygand had finished describing the weakness of his forces, their inability to continue sustained fighting, and their lack of reserves, Churchill 'did not even speak', as Spears wrote, 'he just looked at the ceiling, crossly making the gesture of one brushing away a fly'.

Throughout his survey, Weygand had produced no idea or suggestion for regrouping or reviving the fortunes of the French troops. Not only did Churchill say nothing to him, he did not even look at him again. Indeed, he asked that General Georges should be summoned, and while waiting for his friend of earlier, easier days, 'sat flushed and pre-occupied, playing with his ring'. But he did look several times at de Gaulle, a hard, quizzical stare, giving Spears the impression 'that he had detected in him the thing he was looking for'.

After several minutes, General Georges entered the conference room. But his message was the same as Weygand's. Of 103 Allied divisions in the line on May 10, thirty-five had been lost by the beginning of the German offensive of June 5, 'including the bulk of their mechanised forces and at least one armoured division'. Furthermore, the infantry divisions that had been lost 'were certainly among the best the Allies possessed'. The essential movement of French reserves had been 'impeded by the rapidity of the German advance and the activity of the enemies' bombers'. Since June 5, in six continuous days of battle, some eight or ten French divisions had been reduced 'to 2 battalions and a few guns'. As a result, half-trained troops 'had been put in to fill the gaps'. Now, Georges warned, 'there was nothing left to put in, and the line was held by nothing more than a light screen of reduced and weary divisions, with no reserves behind them'.

Churchill appreciated the truth and urgency of Georges' report: 'precarious' and 'menacing' were the adjectives Georges had used to sum up his survey. 'And the troops from Narvik?' Churchill asked, seeking to create hope through expectation of more troops. 'They only represent a small unit,' Georges replied. The French army was 'not in a position' to oppose a powerful German thrust.

'I was watching Churchill,' Spears noted, 'as we all were. It was evident that Georges' description had shaken him far more than had that of Weygand, for he trusted Georges and knew he would neither lie nor mislead. He was clearly horrified. But he would not surrender to the atmosphere of calamity that hung like miasma in the room.'

Churchill tried to break that atmosphere, 'doggedly', as Spears recalled, enumerating once more the troops that Britain would soon be able to send to France; the Canadian Division, 'of very fine troops' being landed that night, and a regular division withdrawn from Dunkirk would begin disembarkation on June 20. These two divisions were the limit of Britain's ability. There were no more troops ready to send, Churchill reiterated. There were, he warned, at that moment, 'no fully equipped forces anywhere in the British Isles', although Britain had at least twenty divisions in active training, 'awaiting equipment'.

General Georges now spoke again. The Allies were facing 'a preponderance of something like three to one'. Following the entry of Italy into the war, the French had only some 175 fighters left on the northern front.

The bleak picture seemed to have no redeeming feature in it. Yet Churchill saw as his task the revival of the will-power of the French leaders. If the French will to fight were gone, then the fall of Paris, and the fall of France, was inevitable. 'His mouth had been working,' Spears wrote, 'an indication that he was pouring an idea into the mould of words.' His voice when he spoke 'was warm and deep, an admirable medium for giving utterance to his generous ideas'.

When Churchill finally spoke, it was to express Britain's 'immense admiration' for the way in which the French armies were defending their territory, and 'her grief at finding that she could give so little help at such a moment'. Had the British Expeditionary Force not 'come out of Flanders literally naked', he said, there would now be thirteen or fourteen British divisions 'fighting by the side of the French'.

Such, Spears reflected when going over his own notes of the meeting, 'was the gist of his words, but they conveyed far more; the longing of the British people to help their friends in distress, their determination to do so the moment they could, and his evocation of the disaster in the north, whilst conveying no hint of reproach, nevertheless did recall facts that explained Britain's momentary helplessness'.

Churchill now turned to what he hoped would prove a wider and more encouraging perspective, telling Reynaud, Weygand and de Gaulle, as the official minutes recorded:

> He would venture to express the opinion that the German armies also were now in a state of extreme exhaustion, and that with their immensely long lines of communication they also must be feeling the strain greatly. If the line could be held for the next few days, he hoped that it would be possible to organize a counter-attack with the help of the British forces that would then be in position, eg, in the Rouen area.
>
> If the line held for another three or four weeks, moreover, there would be a substantial British force available to attack the enemy's flank. He was convinced that Germany was feeling her losses acutely; there was no sign of a victorious spirit within Germany.
>
> Every hour, every day gained was a step further.

General Weygand was not convinced. It was 'a question of hours', he said, not of days or weeks. The Germans were advancing up to fifty kilometres in one day. Immense reserves were needed if such advances were to be halted. But France had 'no reserves whatever'.

Weygand's voice was 'impatient, tinged with exasperation', recalled Spears. But Dill, 'grasping the Prime Minister's purpose' and 'anxious to support him', spoke directly to Weygand, soldier to soldier, making it clear, as the minutes recorded, that Weygand was 'entirely free' to make use of the British units now landing in whatever manner he considered most useful. There was no thought in the War Office's mind that the 52nd Division 'must be used as a complete unit or not at all'.

Dill's intervention created what Spears described as 'a new atmosphere', of which Churchill immediately sought to take advantage. By a strange coincidence, it was Churchill himself in March 1918 who had urged President Wilson and General Pershing to allow the same dispersal among French units of American troops then reaching the western front. Then, it had taken several weeks to convince the Americans. Dill's offer was spontaneous, and immediate.

Churchill now, as he himself recalled, 'appealed to Pétain, reminding him of Beauvais 1918'.[1] No record of this appears in the official minutes.

---

[1] Marginal note on his own copy of the Supreme War Council Minutes: Churchill papers, 23/2. The note was made after the war, when Churchill was writing his war memoirs.

But, as Spears later recalled, basing himself on his own detailed notes, Churchill had followed Dill 'like a ship of the line under full sail seizing the opportunity afforded by a change of wind to strike'. Churchill's 'broadsides', Spears wrote, 'were formidable. The tide might turn at any moment.' It had done so in the First World War, first on the Marne in 1914, and again in March 1918. Churchill then told the Supreme War Council, as Spears noted, 'of the days that had followed March 21st, 1918. Bowing courteously to Pétain, he said he recalled meeting the Marshal at Beauvais during that terrible time. I could see,' Spears added, 'he was gathering his immense reserves of moral strength in an attempt to carry the French with him away and out of the slough of despondency into which they had fallen.'

Churchill spoke of the need for the French to fight on, even in Paris itself. A great city, he said, if stubbornly defended, absorbed immense armies. The pageant of history, Spears recalled, 'the lurid glow of burning cities, some as beautiful as Paris, collapsing on garrisons who refused to accept defeat, arose before our eyes. The French perceptibly froze at this.'

Unknown to Churchill, Weygand had decided that very day to declare Paris an open, undefended city, and he was to confirm this order by telephone to the Military Governor of Paris on the following day. Nor was Pétain convinced by Churchill's friendly recollection, pointing out, as the official minutes recorded, 'that in the worst days of 1918, when a breach had been made in the front held by the 5th Army, he had been able to rush 20 divisions to the rescue, followed shortly afterwards with an equally large second reserve'. Pétain also said, as Spears recorded: 'To make Paris into a city of ruins will not affect the issue.'

It was Eden who now tried to reverse the tide of pessimism; a pessimism which for the French was imminent reality. The official minutes recorded his intervention. That very morning, Eden said, the British Government had received a report 'from a very reliable source', which showed that Germany's losses in the recent weeks 'had been exceedingly heavy and were causing great anxiety'. But now it was Reynaud's turn to reinforce what both Weygand and Pétain had said, telling the British, as the official minutes recorded, that 'the enemy was now almost at the gates of Paris; he had crossed the Seine and the Marne; the French troops were worn out through lack of sleep and shattered by the action of the enemy bombers. There was no hope of relief anywhere.'

It was Weygand who now challenged the hopes that Churchill had sought to rouse of a possible continuing French resistance. As Ismay later recalled:

Weygand started off by giving a picture of the plight of the French Army. It was at its last gasp. Unless it was immediately provided with a considerable reinforcement of air support, the end would come very soon. He insisted that it was a cardinal principle of strategy to concentrate all available forces at the decisive point. 'Here,' he exclaimed, 'is the decisive point. Now is the decisive moment. The British ought not to keep a single fighter in England. They should all be sent to France.'

There was an awful pause, and my heart stood still. The Prime Minister and the Cabinet had only recently been solemnly warned by Air Chief Marshal Dowding, Commander-in-Chief Fighter Command, that if any more fighter squadrons were sent to France, he could not guarantee the defence of the British Isles. That was clear enough.

It was a terrible position for a man like Churchill—generous, warm-hearted, courageous and with a pronounced streak of optimism, and I was terrified lest he might be so moved as to promise that he would ask his Government to send some additional air support. Thank God my fears were groundless.

After a pause, and speaking very slowly, he said, 'This is not the decisive point. This is not the decisive moment. The decisive moment will come when Hitler hurls his Luftwaffe against Britain. If we can keep command of the air over our own island—that is all I ask—we will win it all back for you.'

After another long pause, he continued magnificently, 'Of course if it is best for France in her agony that her Army should capitulate, let there be no hesitation on our account. Whatever happens here, we are resolved to fight on and on for ever and ever and ever.'

Reynaud, obviously moved, said: 'If we capitulate, all the great might of Germany will be concentrated upon invading England. And then what will you do?' Whereupon Churchill, with his jaw thrust well forward, rejoined that he had not thought that out very carefully, but that broadly speaking he would propose to drown as many as possible of them on the way over, and then to 'frapper sur la tête' anyone who managed to crawl ashore.

The French anguish about air support was paramount; and Churchill had to point out, as the official minutes recorded, that six or eight British squadrons took part in the battle of France every day, refuelling from French bases. The British Advanced Air Force under Air Marshal Barratt was likewise being kept up to full strength. He would again, Churchill assured the French, 'examine whether anything could be done' on the following day. But he hoped, as the minutes recorded, 'that the French representatives would understand that this was not a matter of selfishness on the part of the British. It was merely their deep conviction that if they broke up their fighter defence then they would be unable to carry on the war.' The British fighter force, he added, 'was the only weapon with which they could hope—and he was confident that they would succeed—to break the might of Germany, when the time came, that is, when the onslaught against the British Isles began'.

Spears has recorded the 'obvious relief' among the English present, at Churchill's words. They had, he wrote, 'been watching him intently and perhaps with some fear that French eloquence and the magnitude of the French disaster, which had so obviously awakened his deepest sympathy, might cause him to give way'.[1] But it was not to be; and this was confirmed with Churchill's final words, as recorded in the official minutes, that he could 'affirm truthfully that he longed to give France this further aid, but that the giving of it might in his view destroy the last hope the Allies had of breaking the back of Germany's might'.

In an attempt to lessen the force of the British blow, Churchill again stressed the continuing role of the British Advanced Air Force, and promised that Air Marshal Barratt and his command would remain in France 'at the complete disposal' of the French High Command, 'and would obey the latter's every request'.[2]

This promise could not mask the fact that Britain now saw herself as virtually alone, and Spears' notes graphically recorded Churchill's final words, essentially to that effect. Whatever happened, Churchill told Reynaud, Britain 'would fight on and on and on, *toujours*, all the time, everywhere, *partout, pas de grâce*, no mercy. *Puis la victoire!*'[3]

De Gaulle now spoke, for the first and only time at this meeting of the Supreme War Council. Basing himself on what he had just seen in England, he proposed, as the official minutes recorded, associating or amalgamating the British Armoured Division then in France, equipped as it was with 'light and thinly protected' tanks, to the French armoured forces, which themselves lacked 'lighter vehicles for reconnaissance duties'. The result, said de Gaulle, would be 'a much higher effectiveness'.

This was the first practical suggestion of the meeting, in immediate contrast to Weygand's pessimism and Pétain's aloofness. It was a suggestion, replied Churchill, which would be 'examined at once'. But Weygand now spoke again, at length, about the impossibility, if the

[1] Major General Sir Edward Spears, *Assignment to Catastrophe*, volume 2, London 1954, page 149.

[2] Supreme War Council Minutes: Cabinet papers, 99/3, folios 91–4.

[3] Major-General Sir Edward Spears, *Assignment to Catastrophe*, volume 2, London 1954, page 150.

existing last line of defence broke, of constituting another line. 'Not only Paris,' he said, 'but every large town would be occupied.' He found it difficult to imagine, if that happened, how France 'would carry on with the war'.

Nearly two hours had passed. Churchill now raised, in the dwindling circle of possibilities, one potentially effective strategy, that the British and French forces make plans, whatever the German successes in the centre or south, to hold 'one or more bridgeheads' on the Atlantic seaboard. Through these bridgeheads, British divisions would, he said, 'gradually and with increasing tempo be put in'. More than that, the United States 'would, he felt certain, also soon be taking their share'.[1]

Reynaud replied first to Churchill's plan, speaking, as Spears recorded 'without conviction', and quickly handing over the discussion to Weygand, who 'proceeded finally to demolish the project'.[2] As the official minutes recorded, Weygand gave three reasons for rejecting Churchill's proposal. Strategically, 'it would be a most difficult task to continue the fight and at the same time to bring forces back into the Redoubt in Brittany'. From the supply aspect, Britanny had 'no industries whatever', and any French forces there would be 'wholly dependent' upon the United Kingdom. From the German point of view, the continuance of any such military resistance would lead to the Germans seeking revenge by 'systematically destroying every town, village and factory in the occupied parts of France'. For these reasons, Weygand warned, Churchill's suggestion was 'a most grievous prospect to contemplate'.

Churchill now produced a final suggestion, in the event of the breakdown of 'co-ordinated defence'. There would be immense advantage, he said, in conducting 'what he might describe as guerrilla warfare on a gigantic scale throughout France', and he went on to explain, with further reference to his Redoubt plan:

The difficulties of the enemy would be tremendous, with his units scattered, his lines of communication immensely extended and precarious, and opponents on the watch for him at every turn. He felt confident that provided some effective means of dealing with the German tanks could be devised, and provided some secure bridgehead could be held on the Atlantic sea-board, such tactics might well save the situation during the few months that still would have to elapse before Britain's strength increased at a tremendous pace and before the United States came in on a full scale.[3]

[1] Supreme War Council Minutes, 11 June 1940: Cabinet papers, 99/3, folio 92.
[2] Major-General Sir Edward Spears, *Assignment to Catastrophe*, volume 2, London 1954, page 155.
[3] Supreme War Council Minutes: Cabinet papers, 99/3, folio 92.

Churchill was at the end of a desperate and unsuccessful attempt to persuade the French to see at least some alternatives to defeat. He had failed. This last offer of support, Spears later wrote, however generously meant, 'simply irritated the French'. Weygand showed 'ill-concealed scorn' and Pétain 'anger', telling Churchill: 'It would mean the destruction of the country.' Even Spears was surprised by the intensity of Pétain's feeling: 'Real wrath rumbled behind his words.' Nor did Reynaud dissent from his colleague's negative, and indeed hostile reaction.

Night had come. Darkness, rather than light, wrote Spears, 'was being shed from the now lighted chandeliers. A miasma of despond had fallen on the conference like a fog. No one appeared able to see his way.'[1]

Churchill then spoke with great intensity of feeling. As the minutes of the meeting recorded:

He realised, of course, that the prospect for France would be a terrible one. The United Kingdom had not yet suffered as France had suffered. Britain was, however, ready and willing to face the same horrors. She was indeed anxious to draw on to herself the full malice of the Nazis' tyranny and, however tremendous the German fury might prove to be, she would never give in.

The alternative of France accepting defeat was equally terrible. If it came, Great Britain would nevertheless carry on, if necessary for years. Her difficulties would be immensely increased, but he still felt that if she could survive the next three or four months then she would be in a position to wage war for as long as was necessary to smash the German domination.

She would fight in the air, she would fight with her unbeaten navy, and she would fight with the blockade weapon.

It might well become a war of Continents and although the collapse of France opened up the most distressing picture yet he felt certain that even then Germany could at last be brought to her knees.[2]

Churchill continued, with words recorded by Spears but not recorded in the official minutes: 'It is possible that the Nazis may dominate Europe, but it will be a Europe in revolt, and in the end it is certain that a regime whose victories are in the main due to its machines will collapse. Machines will one day beat machines.'

Churchill's words were electric. 'I was glad to see,' wrote Spears, 'that Reynaud was moved and as much affected as the British perceptibly were.' But not so Pétain, at whom Reynaud glanced, and whose

---

[1] Major-General Sir Edmund Spears, *Assignment to Catastrophe*, volume 2, London 1954, pages 155–6.
[2] Supreme War Council Minutes, 11 June 1940: Cabinet papers, 99/3, folio 92.

face 'might have been a mask of white plaster'. As for Weygand, if he had been 'warmed and moved by that fire', Spears wrote, 'he certainly did not show it'.

Anthony Eden was also watching 'the expressions opposite' as Churchill made his emotional appeal. 'Reynaud was inscrutable,' was his recollection, 'and Weygand polite, concealing with difficulty his scepticism.' Pétain was 'mockingly incredulous. Though he said nothing, his attitude was obviously *C'est de la blague.*' Once during the discussion, Eden added, Churchill, 'in his eagerness to convey his meaning, broke into French, at the same time looking earnestly at Reynaud. Since Reynaud spoke good English, the manoeuvre was of doubtful effect, but it led to a moment of some confusion when, at the end of one such passage, Reynaud murmured absently: *"Traduction".*' [1]

Briefly, Churchill then asked what the French Navy would do, if the French armies were forced 'temporarily to suspend fighting in France'. But before anyone could reply, he brushed any answer aside with the comment that these were 'nightmare questions'.[2] He hoped however, as the minutes recorded, 'that the disaster of a French collapse would never happen'.[3]

The discussion, as Spears recalled, 'now seemed to trail off'. Churchill was, as Spears saw, 'evidently haunted and tortured at watching the martyrdom of the people he liked so well, and in whom he had placed such implicit military trust'.[4]

Churchill now sought to express that trust, as something still not lost, telling Reynaud that Great Britain had 'the utmost confidence' in the French High Command. 'Every Englishman,' he added, 'was profoundly grieved that further military help could not be given to France in this grave hour.' But, and here his search for optimism returned, 'they were not far now from the time of harvest both of effectives and weapons'. He therefore suggested that Weygand and Dill 'should at once discuss the possibility of organising a counter-attack with the help of the strong and fresh British divisions now on the way'.[5]

The arrival of 'five or six new divisions', as Spears recalled, was the hope which Churchill now held out, and to which he linked the prospect of a counter-attack. He also asked that the 'Brittany bridgehead'

---

[1] The Earl of Avon, *The Eden Memoirs: The Reckoning*, London 1965, page 115.

[2] Major-General Sir Edward Spears, *Assignment to Catastrophe*, volume 2, London 1954, page 157.

[3] Supreme War Council Minutes: Cabinet papers, 99/3, folio 93.

[4] Major-General Sir Edward Spears, *Assignment to Catastrophe*, volume 2, London 1954, page 158.

[5] Supreme War Council Minutes: Cabinet papers, 99/3, folio 94.

plan should be studied,[1] and Reynaud noted that a French General, the younger Altmeyer, had been appointed by Weygand to draw up a plan, and that he was 'already actively engaged in this task'. Although the 'technical difficulties' were, as Reynaud phrased it, 'immense', the political advantages were, in his view, 'equally great'.[2]

Reflecting nine years later on his own advocacy of the idea of a Redoubt in Brittany, or elsewhere, Churchill wrote:

. . . the plan, for what it was worth, never reached the domain of action. In itself the idea was sound, but there were no facts to clothe it with reality. Once the main French armies were broken or destroyed, this bridgehead, precious though it was, could not have been held for long against concentrated German attack.

But even a few weeks' resistance here would have maintained contact with Britain and enabled large French withdrawals to Africa from other parts of the immense front, now torn to shreds. If the battle in France was to continue, it could be only in the Brest peninsula and in wooded or mountainous regions like the Vosges. The alternative for the French was surrender.

Let none, therefore, mock at the conception of a bridgehead in Brittany. The Allied armies under Eisenhower, then an unknown American colonel, bought it back for us later at a high price.[3]

As the minutes of the Supreme War Council recorded, Churchill had expressed his 'pleasure' at the appointment of General Altmeyer to study the Brittany plan.[4] It was after nine o'clock in the evening, and the Council meeting was about to end. Its deliberations had revealed what Churchill later described as 'real agony of mind and soul'.[5] The minutes record his final remarks. 'This was indeed,' he said, 'the darkest hour for the Allied cause, but he could only repeat that he had in no way lost confidence in the ultimate smashing of a regime created and kept in being by a small group of evil men.'

After Reynaud had said that he was 'equally confident',[6] the Supreme War Council adjourned, and while the participants washed their hands, a meal was brought to the conference table. Churchill, however, as Ismay recalled, 'insisted that he must have a bath and a change before dinner', so that dinner did not in fact begin until about ten o'clock.[7]

---

[1] Major-General Sir Edward Spears, *Assignment to Catastrophe*, volume 2, London 1954, page 158.
[2] Supreme War Council Minutes: Cabinet papers, 99/3, folio 94.
[3] Winston S. Churchill, *The Second World War*, volume 2, London 1949, page 169.
[4] Supreme War Council Minutes: Cabinet papers, 99/3, folio 94.
[5] Winston S. Churchill, *The Second World War*, volume 2, London 1949, page 138.
[6] Supreme War Council Minutes, page 7: Cabinet papers, 99/3, folio 94.
[7] *The Memoirs of General The Lord Ismay*, London 1960, page 140.

Before sitting down to dinner, Churchill had a few minutes private talk with General Georges, suggesting to him first the continuance of fighting everywhere on the home front in France, together with a 'prolonged guerilla' in the mountainous areas, and second 'the move to Africa', which a week before Churchill himself had regarded as a 'defeatist' measure. 'My respected friend,' he later recalled, 'who, although charged with much direct responsibility had never had a free hand to lead the French armies, did not seem to think there was much hope in either of these.'[1]

Even sitting down to dinner had a moment of drama. 'As we were taking our places,' Anthony Eden recalled, 'a tall and somewhat angular figure in uniform walked by on my side of the table. This was General Charles de Gaulle, Under-Secretary for Defence, whom I had met only once before. Weygand invited him pleasantly to take a place on his left. De Gaulle replied, curtly as I thought, that he had instructions to sit next to the British Prime Minister. Weygand flushed up, but made no comment, and so the meal began.'[2]

As dinner began, an atmosphere of calm was restored. 'There was soup,' Churchill later recalled, 'an omelette or something, coffee and light wine. Even at this point in our awful tribulation under the German scourge, we were quite friendly.' But as the dinner progressed, 'there was a jarring interlude'.[3] As Ismay recalled:

... before I had finished my soup I was summoned to the telephone to speak to Air Marshal A. S. Barratt, the RAF commander in France. He was in a rage. 'The local French authorities will not allow my bombers at Salon to take off against Italy,' he complained.

I told him that in addition to the Prime Minister, Eden, Dill, Reynaud and Weygand were all close at hand and that I would report to them and give him a reply as quickly as I could. I begged him not to let go of the telephone at his end, because the only instrument available to me was in the 'Gents' and there was little hope of making contact again if we were cut off.

I reported to the Prime Minister, and four or five of the principals left the table and discussed the matter in a small group in the passage.[4] The upshot was that Reynaud undertook to send orders that the British bombers were to be allowed to proceed. I duly telephoned the good news to Barratt, and hoped for the best.

But I was woken up at 4 a.m. next morning by a message from him to say

[1] Winston S. Churchill, *The Second World War*, volume 2, London 1949, page 138.
[2] The Earl of Avon, *The Eden Memoirs: The Reckoning*, London 1965, page 116.
[3] Winston S. Churchill, *The Second World War*, volume 2, London 1949, page 138.
[4] These 'principals' were Churchill, Dill, Eden, Reynaud and Weygand (Ismay to Churchill, 18 March 1948: Churchill papers, 4/44).

that the French had driven farm carts on to the airfield and that it had been physically impossible for our bombers to get into the air.[1]

Before going to bed at the Château du Muguet on the night of June 11, Churchill had taken coffee and brandy at a table with Reynaud. There, Reynaud gave Churchill the disquieting news that Marshal Pétain 'had informed him that it would be necessary to seek an armistice'.

Pétain had written a paper on the subject, but was, said Reynaud, so 'ashamed' of his proposal that he had not yet produced it. 'He ought also,' Churchill later wrote, 'to have been ashamed to support even tacitly Weygand's demand for our last twenty-five squadrons of fighters, when he had made up his mind that all was lost and that France should give in.'[2]

While Churchill slept that night in the Château de Muguet, an event was taking place in a United States port for which he had long worked and hoped: the first military supplies began to be loaded on to British and French merchant ships, for transit across the Atlantic. The port was the army docks at Raritan, New Jersey. The cargoes had been brought there in six hundred railway freight cars. The contents of the cars, authorized by Roosevelt himself ten days before, consisted of half a million rifles, manufactured in 1917 and 1918 and stored since then in grease, together with 250 cartridges each; 900 field guns with a million rounds of ammunition; and 80,000 machine guns. In listing these supplies, and their transfer, in his war memoirs, Churchill added: 'All this reads easily now, but at that time it was a supreme act of faith and leadership for the United States to deprive themselves of this very considerable mass of arms for the sake of a country which many deemed already beaten.'[3]

The man who, more than any other, had worked to secure this new and essential trans-Atlantic lifeline was the British-born explosives expert, and Canadian industrialist, described by Churchill in his memoirs as 'our agent, the highly competent and devoted Mr Purvis'.[4] Maintaining the close contact which he had already established with the Secretary of the Treasury, Henry Morgenthau, and meeting frequently with the Chief of Staff, General Marshall, Arthur Purvis received almost daily from London the telegraphic details of British

[1] *The Memoirs of General The Lord Ismay*, London 1960, page 140. The bombers sent to Salon, to bomb Italy, were given the code name 'Haddock Force'.

[2] Winston S. Churchill, *The Second World War*, volume 2, London 1949, page 140.

[3] Winston S. Churchill, *The Second World War*, volume 2, London 1949, page 129.

[4] Winston S. Churchill, *The Second World War*, volume 2, London 1949, page 23.

needs. He then transmitted these needs to those in Washington who could supply them, followed up each request with tenacity, and smoothed over the many difficulties which arose with skill and tact. His, it was later said, was 'the most frictionless mind'.[1]

Secrecy, which was essential if the isolationists were not to be stirred to protest, or the German U-boats to retaliation, was maintained; only Purvis's secret 'Purco' telegrams from Washington to London revealed, to the small circle of those who needed to know, the extent of what was being despatched. 'It is desired to keep the discussions secret and informal,' Purvis had explained to Monnet when their work began, 'and the stage will be so set in order to avoid trouble with isolationist groups.'[2]

It was a secret telegram from Purvis on June 15 which informed the Ministry of Supply, the War Cabinet and the Prime Minister that the first merchant ship of the new supply scheme, *Eastern Prince*, had sailed from the United States two days earlier with its cargo of essential munitions, including 37,284,960 ball cartridges, 15,259 Lewis machine guns, 14,900 leather gun-slings for Enfield rifles, 4,100 Browning automatic rifles, 392 Marlin machine guns and 48 seventy-five millimetre field guns and carriages.[3]

Following two further shipments on June 21 and June 22, Churchill was to receive a daily report of all munitions despatched from the United States.[4] From these reports, the difficulties which Purvis encountered, and surmounted, became clear. 'Unfortunately,' Churchill was told on June 26, 'there has been a hold-up in the release from the United States stocks of 250,000 Lee Enfield rifles, 400 Thomson submachine guns with 1 million rounds of ammunition and 4,093 Browning automatic rifles. Mr Purvis is working in the hope that the difficulty may be surmounted and the releases re-instated . . .'[5]

Churchill monitored each American shipment with considerable concern. 'I wish to draw the attention of the Admiralty,' he minuted to A. V. Alexander and Dudley Pound on the night of June 19, 'to the immense importance of the French ship which is bringing us 275,000 rifles. Her safety should be one of the first charges of the Navy.' The

---

[1] Blaikie Purvis, conversation with the author, Montreal, 13 November 1982.

[2] Washington Telegram No. 991, 31 December 1939: Cabinet papers, 85/14, folio 16.

[3] 'Purco' No. 205, 'Most Secret', 'Most Immediate', 15 June 1940: Premier papers, 3/372/1, folio 97.

[4] 'Field Guns and Rifles from the United States, Daily Report No. 1' was sent to Churchill by the Anglo-French Co-ordinating Committee on 24 June 1940: Premier papers, 3/372/1, folio 73.

[5] 'Field Guns and Rifles from the United States, Daily Report No. 3', 26 June 1940: Premier papers, 3/372/1, folio 69.

ships carrying the 75-millimetre guns, he added, 'are also important'.[1] Three further ships followed within the next three weeks: the *Cameronia*, which left New York for Glasgow on June 30 with sixteen Northrope aeroplanes aboard, the *Britannic*, which sailed from New York to Liverpool on July 3 with munitions, and the *Western Prince* which sailed on July 9 with 'a considerable quantity of special cargo on board'. So fast was this third ship that her speed was greater than that of any of the escort vessels.[2] All three, as well as the French ship, crossed the Atlantic unmolested.

At Briare, Churchill woke late on the morning of June 12. His detective, W. H. Thompson, who would normally have ensured that all the Prime Minister's domestic needs were attended to, had slept some distance away, in Reynaud's train. After Churchill had woken up, Thompson was much missed, for as Spears later learned:

Two French officers were finishing their *café au lait* in the conference room, which was also the dining room, when the big double door burst open and they beheld an astonishing sight. An apparition which they said resembled an angry Japanese genie, in long, flowing red silk kimono over other similar but white garments, girdled with a white belt of like material, stood there, sparse hair on end, and said with every sign of anger: '*Uh ay ma bain?*'

They were not used to seeing the Prime Minister in his night attire, so their fright and astonishment may be excused. But as usual he made his meaning perfectly clear even in French, and his needs were attended to.[3]

His bath over, Churchill began dressing. Even as he did so, he had a visitor. This was Air Marshal Barratt, who had driven through the night to report to Churchill about the French obstructions placed on the airfield to prevent British bombers taking off from Salon to bomb Italy. Barratt, as Ismay later wrote to Churchill, 'arrived at about 7 a.m. in a white heat of rage, and he and I came to see you while you were dressing'. But Churchill, as Ismay recalled, 'decided that the

---

[1] Minute of 0.45 a.m., 20 June 1940: Premier papers, 3/372/1, folio 136.

[2] 'Armament Programmes, Prime Minister's Inquiries': Cabinet papers, 115/70.

[3] Major-General Sir Edward Spears, *Assignment to Catastrophe*, volume 2, London 1954, page 161. Spears added at this point, as a footnote: 'Years later I reminded him of the incident one night after dinner. His expression was one of startled concern, as if an inaccurate quotation in a parliamentary debate had been alleged against him, and he said in a slightly guilty voice, in which rang a note of enquiry: "I suppose I ought to have said, 'Uh ay MONG bain?'" and he chuckled.'

French agony was too great to have any recriminations about this incident'.[1]

While Churchill was at breakfast, Spears reached the Château to discuss the forthcoming morning meeting with Reynaud. He would not, said Churchill, raise the question of the French obstruction of the airfield at Salon, with the resultant failure of the British bomber force to carry out its first attack of the war on Italian targets. Recriminations, Churchill told Spears, 'would not help in the frightful predicament we were in'. The British ground crews, Churchill added, 'had asked permission to shoot the obstructions off the airfield, but this was refused'. Once upon a time, Churchill reflected, at Crécy, 'the French cavalry cut their way through the Genoese members of their own army who obstructed them, to attack the English. Times had changed.'

As to Spears' own future role in France, Churchill was emphatic. 'Go on reiterating that we shall carry on, whatever they do,' he told his emissary and friend. 'If they have lost faith in themselves let them develop faith in us and in our determination. We will carry them, as well as everything else, or,' Churchill added, 'we will carry those who will let themselves be carried.'

The time had come to return to the conference room. 'Churchill said nothing as he went downstairs,' Spears recalled, 'but he looked very stern, with the expression of deep concentration he always wears when he is utterly absorbed in the contemplation of a problem.'[2]

Vexation as well as contemplation was the dominant mood among the British that morning. 'The French refusal to allow us to bomb Italy had been the last straw,' recalled Ismay. 'Not content with being unable or unwilling to fight themselves, they seemed to want to stop us fighting.'[3] Before the meeting began, Churchill stood with Eden on the porch of the Château, in the bright sunshine. Reynaud, as Eden later recalled, 'was canvassing with regret the decision he had felt compelled to take to put Pétain into the Government. At that moment the Marshal appeared, walking towards us across the grass. "He looks buoyant this morning," commented Reynaud. "There must be some bad news (*des nouvelles néfastes*)." There was.'[4]

Both at Briare and in London the news was indeed grim; 'darker', as

[1] Letter of 18 March 1948: Churchill papers, 4/44. In his memoirs Ismay wrote (page 140) 'I expected an explosion, but he took the news philosophically.'

[2] Major-General Sir Edward Spears, *Assignment to Catastrophe*, volume 2, London 1954, pages 163–4.

[3] *The Memoirs of General The Lord Ismay*, London 1960, page 141.

[4] The Earl of Avon, *The Eden Memoirs: The Reckoning*, London 1965, page 117.

Colville noted, 'than it has yet been', and he added, summarizing the news as it had been received in Whitehall that morning: 'General Haining says Paris will fall in twenty-four hours. Reynaud is prepared to fight to the end, Pétain is willing to make peace. The French troops are already flying the white flag.'[1]

The fifteenth meeting of the Supreme War Council began at 8 o'clock on the morning of June 12. Pétain did not attend, a fact which seemed proof to Spears that he disapproved of the continuing British belief that France should fight on. General Georges had returned to his headquarters. De Gaulle had gone to Brittany to investigate how the matter of the proposed bridgehead stood. In their place was Admiral Darlan, and General Vuillemin, whose ill-phrased request for further British fighters had caused so much offence a week earlier, and whose refusal to allow the British bombers to take off from Salon on the previous night had caused the British representatives so much frustration and anger.

It was Weygand who spoke first. There was now nothing, he said, to prevent the Germans getting to Paris by advancing south of the Seine. The artillery situation was grave: four of his divisions had 'no guns at all'. If the Germans continued to advance, resistance could only be carried out by 'isolated columns'. What of Brittany?, asked Churchill, who was told that de Gaulle was on his way there to make enquiries.

Weygand ended his survey with the declaration: 'it is I who read the armistice terms to the Germans twenty years ago, you can imagine what I feel'. Those who heard these words, wrote Spears, felt that there was 'more of weakness than of tragedy' in them, and 'shuddered inwardly at the abyss of surrender they implied'.[2]

In one last effort to persuade the French that all might not be lost, Churchill spoke of Britain's continuing air support. There were six squadrons of bombers and five squadrons of fighters under Air Marshal Barratt's command in France.[3] The best way of helping France, Churchill said, 'was to keep these squadrons right up to strength as far as possible'.

Reynaud again asked for more British fighter squadrons, specifying five squadrons as the number needed. The morale of the French troops

[1] Colville diary, 12 June 1940: Colville papers.

[2] Major-General Sir Edward Spears, *Assignment to Catastrophe*, volume 2, London 1954, pages 164–5.

[3] Air Marshal Barratt explained to the Supreme War Council that this meant 50 to 60 fighters and 70 to 80 bombers 'fit for operations' (Supreme War Council Minutes, 12 June 1940, 8 a.m.).

on the Front 'would be very high', he said, 'if they did not feel that they were dominated in the air'. Churchill did not dismiss Reynaud's request out of hand. It would, he said, be examined 'carefully and sympathetically' by the War Cabinet on his return. At the same time, Churchill pointed out, it should be borne in mind that there were already two British bomber forces operating over the German front and lines of communication: Barratt's force, and the bombers of Bomber Command. Barratt himself then intervened to point out that the Bomber Command forces were operating against objectives 'suggested by General Weygand'. Even as they spoke, 'a force of up to a hundred British bombers' was attacking German lines of communication, according to specific French requests.[1]

Both Eden and Dill then stressed the speed with which British and Canadian troops were being made available. The 52nd Division was being deployed about Le Mans, while the Canadian landing had already begun. The French, said Dill, repeating his offer of the previous evening, might, if they wished, 'engage the British forces unit by unit'. This meant, as they became available, and as and where they were needed.

The French, as Spears recalled, 'listened to all this in silence'.[2]

Reynaud then defended, and supported, General Vuillemin's decision not to take any air offensive against Italy. Great Britain could do 'whatever she wanted', said Reynaud, provided, he added ominously, 'these attacks were based on England'. Churchill had no option but to agree. It was Eden who intervened to point out that it was 'most unfortunate' that Vuillemin had not explained his views 'before so much time and trouble had been wasted'.

Churchill was still reluctant to bow to the tone and implication of the French position. There were, he said, four questions that he wished to ask. These were:

(i)   Will not the mass of Paris and its suburbs present an obstacle dividing and delaying the enemy as in 1914, or like Madrid?

(ii) May this not in his fatigue enable a counter-stroke to be organised with British and French forces across the Lower Seine?

(iii) If the period of co-ordinated war ends, will that not mean an almost equal dispersion of the enemy forces? Would not a war of columns and upon the enemy communications be possible? Are the enemy resources sufficient to hold down all the countries at present conquered as well as a large part of France, while they are fighting the French Army and Great Britain?

---

[1] Supreme War Council Minutes, 12 June 1940, 8 a.m.: Cabinet papers, 99/3, folios 95–6.

[2] Major-General Sir Edward Spears, *Assignment to Catastrophe*, volume 2, London 1954, pages 166–7.

(iv) Is it not possible thus to prolong the resistance until the United States come in?

Reynaud made no reply. Instead, Weygand spoke in an entirely opposite and negative sense. Neither the 1914 nor the Madrid analogies were apposite. It was not intended to hold Paris. Orders had already been given that if the outer defences fell, 'the city was to be declared an open one'.[1]

As to Churchill's second question, Spears recalled how Weygand said, with considerable sarcasm, that he fully agreed with the suggestion for a counter-attack on the lower Seine, 'if ten divisions, complete with artillery and provided of course with air support, were placed at his disposal'.

Spears' account continued:

Churchill was looking at the middle of the table, his lips slightly pursed. It was a pure guess, but it seemed to me that he had written off Weygand as a total loss in the grim balance sheet he was casting, and was working out a plan on a quite different set of values. But Weygand had not finished. He added a postscript. Answering Churchill's last question, he said he thought that Germany had ample forces to hold down all the subjugated nations and pursue the struggle against what was left of the Allied forces.

Chiming in to support Weygand's last point, Reynaud said that Germany had raised fifty-five divisions and built from four to five thousand tanks since the outbreak of the war. 'Our only hope,' he said, employing the expressive French gesture of raised shoulders, combined with open hands, palms upwards, the whole emphasised with a sigh, 'is in the industrial resources of the USA.'

'We are in the closest touch with the United States,' said Churchill, 'and will continue to impress on their Government the gravity of the situation and the urgency of our needs. . . .'

Churchill then promised Reynaud to send a special message to Roosevelt. But now, in a voice which Spears recalled of 'tremendous, slow emphasis', Churchill had a matter of importance to put to the French which 'overshadows all others'.[2] The official minutes recorded that final question. If there were 'any change in the situation', Churchill said, the French Government must let the British know about it 'at once', in order that they might come back once more to see the French leaders 'at any convenient spot', before the French took any final decisions 'which would govern their action in the second phase of the war'.

Thus was the end of the road for the Franco-British Alliance clearly

---

[1] Supreme War Council Minutes: Cabinet papers, 99/3.

[2] Major-General Sir Edward Spears, *Assignment to Catastrophe*, volume 2, London 1954, page 170.

marked out. The minutes went on to record that Churchill repeated
his request 'in the most formal manner'. Reynaud then agreed to it.[1]
The conference was over.

Before leaving the room, Churchill went up to Admiral Darlan, and,
speaking to him alone, said: 'Darlan, I hope you will never surrender
the Fleet.' To this, Darlan replied: 'There is no question of doing so; it
would be contrary to our naval tradition and honour.'[2]

Churchill then spoke to General Georges, who had come to the
Château to say goodbye to him. It was 'all but over' with the French
Army, Georges told him, and in his opinion 'an armistice would soon
be inevitable'. On the steps of the Château, Churchill reported this
forecast to Spears.[3] Then he got into his car, and was driven to the
airfield.

The Briare meetings were over. Churchill's hopes in a sustained
Anglo-French campaign, of checking the German mastery of Europe,
of holding the democracies in a painful yet self-preserving unity, were
crashing down. His beloved France was cracking. And yet, when Ismay
spoke bitterly during the drive to the airport of French perfidy, Churchill impressed on him just how 'niggardly' the British contribution to
the battle had been. The French had suffered nine-tenths of the casualties, and endured 'ninety-nine hundredths of the suffering'. As for
their demand for British fighter aircraft, 'was there not a perfectly
natural reason? They were continentals, who had no idea of amphibious
strategy, and no notion of the priceless twenty miles of salt-water which
separated us from the Continent.' In the French view, Churchill explained to Ismay, the result of the war could be decided in France. If
that was lost, all was lost. The battle for Britain would merely prolong
the agony: it would not affect the result.

During the Briare discussions Weygand had said to Reynaud that
Britain would have 'her neck wrung like a chicken'. Many of the
French leaders believed this. Why not, then, from the French perspective, adhere to the cardinal principles of strategy and concentrate
everything at the decisive point in France? 'But anyway,' Ismay wrote,
'it was unworthy to judge too harshly a friend who had fought with us
so loyally, and lost over one and a half million of the flower of her
manhood in 1914–18.'[4]

[1] Supreme War Council Minutes: Cabinet papers, 99/3.

[2] Quoted by Darlan in a letter to Churchill on 4 December 1942 (sent by Eisenhower to
Churchill, by telegram, 14 December 1942): Churchill papers, 4/351A.

[3] Major-General Sir Edward Spears, *Assignment to Catastrophe*, volume 2, London 1954, page
171.

[4] *The Memoirs of General The Lord Ismay*, London 1960, page 142.

The memories of 1914–18 were shared equally by the British and French leaders. Eden had fought in the trenches throughout the bloody battles of the western front, and two of his brothers had been killed in action. Churchill had followed the wartime battles from day to day, first as a member of Asquith's War Council, then as a battalion commander, and finally as Minister of Munitions in Lloyd George's Coalition Government. He had been at the front at the moment of the German breakthrough in March 1918. He had travelled with Clemenceau from shattered unit to shattered unit. He had seen the broken limbs and bleeding bodies, the incurable wounds and desperate scenes of casualty clearing stations and field hospitals. He had spoken in Parliament of how, every twenty-four hours, nearly a thousand men, 'Englishmen, Britishers, men of our own race, are knocked into bundles of bloody rags. . . .'[1] He knew also what the French had suffered in those four years. After the Armistice, he had believed in the French ability to defend themselves if war were to return. Now, with that belief in ruins, he prepared to return to England, and to Britain's own glaring weaknesses, without fear, and without reproach.

---

[1] *Hansard*, 23 May 1916. In a letter to Victor Cazalet on 25 March 1917 Churchill wrote: 'You know how much my mind is hostile to these costly offensives,' and on 23 October 1917, during the Passchendaele offensive, he referred to 'the bloody & blasted squalor of the battlefield'. Commenting in this same letter on a battalion which had recently lost 420 men out of 550, Churchill told Cazalet: 'I shd feel vy proud if I had gone through such a cataclysm.' (Cazalet papers: I am grateful to Thelma Cazalet-Keir for copies of these two letters.)

26

Tours: 'the darkest hour'

——

I T was during the mid-morning on Wednesday June 12 that Churchill returned by air from Briare in his Flamingo, accompanied by
Ismay. Eden and Dill flew in a second aircraft. Spears remained in
France. Because it was a cloudy morning, it proved impossible for the
twelve Hurricanes which had escorted them to France to escort them
back. As the Flamingo flew, unescorted, the cloud cleared, and they
saw below, from 8,000 feet, the port of Le Havre, burning. 'The smoke,'
Churchill later recalled, 'drifted away eastward.'

Suddenly the pilot of the Flamingo saw two German aircraft below
them, 'firing at fishing-boats'. The Flamingo at once dived down to a
hundred feet, just above the sea. The German pilots did not give chase.
Perhaps they had not seen the manoeuvre, and once so close to the
surface of the water, aircraft, as Churchill himself noted, 'are often
invisible'.[1] A new escort met the Flamingo off the English coast, and
flew back with it to Hendon.

At the War Cabinet at five o'clock that afternoon, Churchill gave
his impressions of Reynaud, Pétain and Weygand. 'They had been
studiously polite and dignified,' he said, 'but it was clear that France
was near the end of organized resistance.'

Churchill then gave an account of the Briare meeting, and of Weygand's pessimistic survey. There was, however, he went on, 'General
de Gaulle, who was sitting with M. Reynaud,' and who was 'all in
favour of carrying on a guerilla warfare'. De Gaulle, Churchill told the
War Cabinet, 'was young and energetic and had made a very favourable impression. He did not believe in a "war of fronts" and thought
that new methods must be adopted.' It seemed probable that, if the
present line collapsed, 'M. Reynaud would turn to General de Gaulle
to take command'.

[1] Winston S. Churchill, *The Second World War*, volume 2, London 1949, page 141.

As for Marshal Pétain, Churchill reported, he was without doubt 'a dangerous man' at that moment, and, Churchill commented, 'had always been a defeatist, even in the last war'.

During the discussion that followed, Neville Chamberlain asked whether, 'if we had thrown in the whole of our fighter resources regardless of our own safety, the battle would thereby have been won'. But Dill, replying, was 'emphatic that this was not so'. A good deal of the French feeling that Britain had not given them enough air support was, he added, 'in the nature of an excuse to cover themselves'.

Eden then quoted Reynaud and Weygand to the effect that a 'great attack' by the Allied air forces 'might even now turn the scale'. But Churchill commented 'that he could not believe that this was so', even though Britain would not lessen 'in any way' the amount of air support hitherto given.

Summing up the lessons of his French visit, and of the military situation that evening, Churchill told the War Cabinet that he thought that 'a chapter in the war was now closing. The French might continue the struggle; there might be two French Governments, one which made peace, and one which organized resistance in the Colonies and with the Fleet, and carried on a guerrilla warfare—it was too early to tell; but effective resistance as a great land Power was coming to an end.' As for Britain, Churchill said, everything must be concentrated on the defence of the Island, even if 'for a period' a measure of support might have to be sent to France. He viewed the new phase 'with confidence'. A declaration that Britain was firmly resolved to continue the war 'would prove the best invitation to the United States of America to lend us their support'. Britain should, meanwhile, maintain the blockade of Germany, 'and win through', though at the cost of what he described as 'ruin and starvation throughout Europe'. Meanwhile, he said, 'the flow of our forces to France must continue, and the Air Staff must consider how great an effort we could put in during the following two or three days to support the battle'.

The War Cabinet then invited Churchill to send a message to Roosevelt giving him 'a full picture' of the existing situation 'and possible developments', and took note that Churchill would draft a message for despatch to the French Government 'designed to sustain their determination, and to assure them of our unwavering support in all circumstances'.[1]

Following the War Cabinet meeting, Churchill telegraphed to Roosevelt, as the War Cabinet had invited him to. 'The aged Marshal

[1] War Cabinet No. 163 of 1940, 12 June 1940, 5 p.m.: Cabinet papers, 65/7.

Pétain,' he told the President, 'who was none too good in April and July 1918, is, I fear, ready to lend his name and prestige to a treaty of peace for France. Reynaud, on the other hand, is for fighting on, and he has a young General de Gaulle, who believes much can be done.'

Churchill's message to Roosevelt ended:

It seems to me that there must be many elements in France who will wish to continue the struggle either in France or in the French Colonies, or in both. This therefore is the moment for you to strengthen Reynaud the utmost you can, and try to tip the balance in favour of the best and longest possible French resistance. I venture to put this point before you, although I know you must understand it as well as I do.

Of course I made it clear to the French that we should continue whatever happened, and that we thought Hitler could not win the war or the mastery of the world until he had disposed of us, which has not been found easy in the past, and which perhaps will not be found easy now. I made it clear to the French that we had good hopes of victory, and anyhow had no doubts whatever of what our duty was. If there is anything you can say publicly or privately to the French, now is the time.[1]

Churchill's second task on the evening of June 12 was to draft a message for Reynaud and Weygand. In it, he reported that the Royal Air Force would make a further and 'increased' effort 'to render assistance to your valiant hard-pressed forces', both on the following day, 'and onwards'. During the daylight hours of June 13, 'all available Blenheims', some sixty in all, would be ready to attack targets indicated by General Georges. In addition, ten squadrons of fighters would work from England 'within the limits of their range'. On the night of June 13 a total of 182 heavy bombers would be available to attack targets 'as desired by General Georges'. A further six bomber and five fighter Squadrons under Air Marshal Barratt's orders, would remain in France, and special instructions had been issued 'to ensure that these squadrons are kept up to full strength in aircraft, pilots and crews'.[2]

As Churchill had made clear to the War Cabinet, General de Gaulle had made a considerable impact upon him at Briare. Little though de Gaulle had spoken or been asked to speak by his own superiors, there had been no doubt about his personal determination. 'There is apparently,' Colville noted in his diary, 'a young French General called de Gaulle of whom Winston thinks a great deal and perhaps he might organize further resistance in Brittany or on the Atlantic sea-board, to which our divisions could be sent.'

[1] Telegram of 12 June 1940: Premier papers, 3/468, folios 115-16.
[2] Final draft, 12 June 1940: Premier papers, 3/188/1, folio 8.

Of the other French leaders, Churchill told Colville: 'Reynaud is as indomitable as Pétain is defeatist.' And of the aim of the telegram to Roosevelt, Colville noted: 'he seems to hope that America will come in now—at any rate as a non-belligerent ally'.[1]

The military news during the evening of June 12 was dominated by the fate of the 51st Division, commanded by General Fortune. This Division, which had been driven back by the Germans to the Channel fishing port of St Valéry-en-Caux, planned to fight on, and then to evacuate by sea. But the local French commander, General Ihler, wished to surrender to the Germans. On the previous night, fog had made any naval evacuations impossible from the port itself, although, at the eastern end of St Valéry bridgehead, 2,137 British troops and 1,184 French troops had been safely evacuated.[2] Then, German air bombing, and the installation of German artillery covering the beach, prevented even this escape route being continued, and the Division was forced to capitulate. When the news of the surrender reached Churchill's entourage, Colville described it in his diary as 'the most brutal disaster which we have yet suffered'.[3] The 51st Division had surrendered to the commander of the Seventh Panzer Division, General Rommel.

General Fortune surrendered with his men. On the same day as his surrender, the commander-designate of all British forces still fighting south of the Seine, General Brooke, arrived in France.

That night there was 'great activity' at Admiralty House, as Colville noted. Those who had joined Churchill included Lord Beaverbrook, who was making 'a great deal of noise, apparently hoping to cheer people up thereby'. But the day ended, as it had begun, with confirmation of Britain's inability to give the French the air support they sought. 'The effective range of our fighters,' noted Colville, 'will not enable them to go far up the Seine, but it would be suicidal to send them to aerodromes in France, where they will be destroyed on the ground.'

As midnight passed, and Churchill prepared to go to bed, there was a telephone call from Reynaud. At first all was confusion; the line was so bad Churchill could not hear what Reynaud was trying to say to

---

[1] Colville diary, 12 June 1940: Colville papers.

[2] This was the second part of the operation code named 'Cycle', the planned evacuations by sea from Le Havre and St Valéry.

[3] Colville diary, 12 June 1940: Colville papers.

him. Eventually Colville managed to speak with some semblance of sense to Roland de Margerie. The message from France was ominous. Reynaud had moved westward from Briare to Tours, and wanted Churchill to meet him there early that same afternoon. 'This looks,' noted Colville, 'as if the French mean to give in.'

As the conversation proceeded, 'Winston was furious,' Colville wrote, 'because Reynaud would talk of his hour of arrival and the destination on an open line. He thought it very dangerous and spent a long time trying to deceive the Germans who must be listening in. At one moment he wanted me, through de Margerie, to say untruthfully he wasn't going to go. This would have caused chaos at the other end. At the risk of having my head bitten off, I dissuaded him.'

Churchill was thus to return to France. Colville noted, with the optimism of one who had seen the full force of the Prime Minister's personality: 'Perhaps Winston will be able to persuade them to carry on the war west of Paris on a guerrilla basis. The Germans will be exhausted and their lines of communication immense.'[1]

After sleeping at Admiralty House, Churchill prepared for his fifth visit to France since the outbreak of war, driving to Hendon airport with a member of his Defence Secretariat, Colonel Hollis. 'I remember the morning well,' Hollis later wrote. 'It was a warm day with the sun shining. I marvelled at the calmness and serenity everywhere, and then realized with a shock that hardly anyone in the crowds of people out in the sunshine—the clerks, the typists in their summer frocks, the shoppers—realized what fearful danger faced Britain. I was already so used to living near calamity that I had imagined others felt as I did.'

On reaching Hendon at eleven o'clock, Churchill learned that bad weather was forecast for later that day. Because of this, the Air Staff advised that the flight should be postponed. 'To hell with that,' Churchill told Hollis. 'I'm going, whatever happens! This is too serious a situation to bother about the *weather!*'[2]

Awaiting Churchill at Hendon were Beaverbrook, Ismay, Halifax, Cadogan and the interpreter, Captain Berkeley. Flying in two aircraft, the British mission flew over the Channel from Weymouth to the Channel Islands, and then on to Tours. 'Thunderstorm and rain as we arrived on pock-marked aerodrome,' Cadogan noted in his diary,[3] and Ismay later recalled how:

[1] Colville diary, 12 June 1940: Colville papers.

[2] Quoted in James Leasor, *War at the Top* (based on the experiences of General Sir Leslie Hollis, KCB, KBE), London 1959, page 85.

[3] Cadogan diary, 13 June 1940: David Dilks (editor), *The Diaries of Sir Alexander Cadogan, OM, 1938–1945*, London 1971, page 297.

Tours airfield had been heavily bombed the night before; but we landed safely and taxied around the craters in search of someone to help us. There was no sign of life, except for groups of French airmen lounging about by the hangars. They did not know who we were, and cared less. The Prime Minister got out and introduced himself. He said, in his best French, that his name was Churchill, that he was Prime Minister of Great Britain, and that he would be grateful for a '*voiture*'.

They lent us a small touring car, which took us to the *Préfecture* in considerable discomfort. The party included Halifax, who had very long legs, and Churchill took up more than his share of the room. No one at the *Préfecture* recognised or took the slightest notice of us, and we wandered through the dreary building, jostled by swarms of refugees.

Evidently the members of the French Government had not yet arrived, but fortunately a staff officer—blessings on his head—espied us and escorted us to a near-by restaurant. The manager cleared a small private room, and we sat down to a welcome meal of cold chicken, cheese and Vouvray wine.[1]

Reynaud's Secretary of the War Cabinet, Paul Baudouin, arrived during the luncheon and engaged Churchill in conversation. 'He began at once,' Churchill later recalled, 'in his soft, silky manner about the hopelessness of French resistance.' If the United States were to declare war on Germany, Baudouin told Churchill, it might then be possible 'for France to continue'. What did Churchill think about this, he asked. Churchill later recalled how 'I did not discuss the question further than to say that I hoped America would come in and that we should certainly fight on. He afterwards, I was told, spread it about that I had agreed that France should surrender unless the United States came in.'[2]

Baudouin's pessimistic talk was an ill-omen. And yet, as Colonel Hollis' biographer later recorded: 'Churchill paid no attention to this Niagara of doom; he might have been hearing an actor declaiming the decline of hope in some stage tragedy. His mind was made up; the defeatism of others could not change his intention.'[3]

As soon as their luncheon was over, the British group returned to the *Préfecture*. Reynaud had not yet arrived, nor did anyone seem to know where he was. Churchill waited, his time at Tours limited because he had to take off again for England in daylight. As the airfield had no lights, the pock-marked condition of the runway made a take-off after dark impossible.

---

[1] *The Memoirs of General The Lord Ismay*, London 1960, pages 143–4.

[2] Winston S. Churchill, *The Second World War*, volume 2, London 1949, page 159.

[3] James Leasor, *War at the Top (based on the experiences of General Sir Leslie Hollis, KCB, KBE)*, London 1959, pages 87–8.

Eventually, Reynaud arrived, as did two more Englishmen, Sir Ronald Campbell, the Ambassador, and General Spears. Campbell told Spears 'that he, like myself, had had no idea the Prime Minister was coming, was expected, or had been asked to come'. As the group went up the stairs to the meeting, Churchill hung back, until he could ask Spears about Baudouin. 'I told him,' Spears later recalled, 'that he was now doing his damnedest to persuade Reynaud to throw in the sponge.' He was 'working on behalf of Weygand and Pétain'. Churchill then 'growled that he had gathered as much, and that Baudouin had ruined our already inadequate meal by seasoning it with an outpouring of oily defeatism'.

The English and French representatives were shown into a room on the first floor, 'furnished inconveniently', as Spears recalled, 'with a few deep, light-coloured chairs and some straight chairs'.[1] There was no table, but a desk at which sat Georges Mandel, now Minister of the Interior. Of this meeting with Mandel, General Ismay later wrote to Churchill: 'When we found him in his office at the *Préfecture* after our lunch at the hotel, he was energy and defiance personified. His lunch, uneaten, was on a tray in front of him, and he had a telephone in each hand and was snapping out decisive orders in every direction. He was the only ray of sunshine—except when you inspired Reynaud to courage—that we ever saw on the French side.'[2]

Churchill was pleased to see Mandel, his friend of the inter-war years. But Mandel was not a member of the Supreme War Council, and almost immediately withdrew. Reynaud then took Mandel's place at the desk. Only two Frenchmen were present as the meeting began, Reynaud and Baudouin, facing eight Englishmen. But it was not the fact that the Englishmen were more numerous, Spears later wrote, that was striking; rather that the eight Englishmen constituted 'a solid mass, a steel buoy firmly moored in the eddying, whirling dark flood sweeping over France'.[3]

Reynaud opened the Council meeting with a grim report of how, according to General Weygand, the French armies were 'at their last gasp', so much so that it would 'soon be necessary to plead for armistice to save the soil and structure of France'.

---

[1] Major-General Sir Edward Spears, *Assignment to Catastrophe*, volume 2, London 1954, page 199.

[2] 'The Meeting at the Prefecture, Tours, on 13th June at 3.30 p.m.,' note by Ismay for Churchill, 20 May 1946: Churchill papers, 4/44.

[3] Major-General Sir Edward Spears, *Assignment to Catastrophe*, volume 2, London 1954, page 200.

Reynaud did not, however, 'consider the situation yet desperate'. Great losses had been inflicted on the Germans. If the French armies could fight on 'yet awhile', help would, he believed, 'soon come from Great Britain and from the United States'. The imperative need was to have 'definite proof' that America would enter the war 'with sufficient speed and force'. He therefore proposed, if the British agreed, to send a message to Roosevelt 'saying that the last hour had come, and that the fate of the Allied cause lay in America's hands'.

These were relatively fighting words, but Reynaud went on to explain that he would be 'unable to carry on' unless Roosevelt's reply conveyed 'a firm assurance of immediate aid'. If it did not do so, his colleagues would reply, 'why carry on with the certain result of an occupation of the whole of France, accompanied by systematic corruption and adulteration by Hitler's propaganda machine of the spirit and essence of the French people'.

Such might be the argument of Reynaud's colleagues. For his part, he said, the plan was to 'retreat and carry on'. But the French population would remain, and would be 'subtly but thoroughly transformed, and France would cease to exist'. There thus arose the alternative 'of armistice or peace'.

These were terrible words, yet Reynaud had not finished. He had been asked, he said, by his Council of Ministers, to find out what Britain's attitude would be 'should the worst come'. They realized that there was a solemn pledge that no separate peace would be entered into by either Ally. But Weygand and others in the Council of Ministers had pointed out that France 'had already sacrificed everything in the common cause'. She had 'nothing left', but had succeeded in weakening the Germans, the 'common foe'. In these circumstances it would be a 'shock', said Reynaud, if Britain 'failed to concede' that France was physically unable to carry on, or if France 'was still expected to fight on and thus deliver up her people to the certainty of corruption and evil transformation at the hands of ruthless specialists in the art of bringing conquered peoples to heel'.

That was the question which Reynaud wished to put to the British delegates: would Britain 'realize the hard facts with which France was faced?'

Stunned by the collapse of French resolve, Churchill spoke with dignity and compassion. Great Britain, he said, realized how much France had suffered 'and was suffering'. Britain's own turn would come, 'and she was ready'. At the same time, Britain 'grieved to find that her contribution to the land struggle was at present so small, owing to the reverses that had been met with'—and here he harked back to Dunkirk and to the Weygand plan—'as a result of applying an agreed strategy in the North'. His remarks continued, as the official minutes recorded:

The British had not yet felt the German lash but were aware of its force. They nevertheless had but one thought: to win the war and destroy Hitlerism. Everything was subordinate to that aim; no difficulties, no regrets could stand in the way. He was well assured of their capacity for enduring and persisting, for striking back till the foe was beaten.

They would therefore hope that France would carry on, fighting South of Paris down to the sea, and, if need be, from North Africa. At all costs time must be gained. The period of waiting was not limitless: a pledge from the United States would make it quite short.

The alternative course meant destruction for France quite as certainly. Hitler would abide by no pledges. If, on the other hand, France remained in the struggle with her fine Navy, her great Empire, her Army still able to carry on guerrilla warfare on a gigantic scale, and if Germany failed to destroy England, which she must do or go under, if then her might in the air was broken, then the whole hateful edifice of Nazidom would topple over. Given immediate help from America, perhaps even a declaration of war, victory was not so far off.

At all events, Churchill concluded, 'England would fight on. She had not and would not alter her resolve: no terms, no surrender.' The alternatives for Britain were death or victory. 'That was his answer to M. Reynaud's question.'

For Reynaud, Churchill's defiance was no answer, even if it represented, as clearly it did, the defiance of his colleagues and the defiance of Britain. He had 'never doubted England's determination', he replied, but what he asked was, would Britain realize that France might have either to ask for an armistice, or to make peace. It might be impossible to fight on. A future French Government, his or another's, might say, 'we know you will carry on. We would also, if we saw any hope of a victory soon enough to enable us to recreate France as she was and desires to be. But we see no sufficient hopes of any early victory,' no certainty of help from the United States, 'no light at the end of the tunnel'. The French people could not then be abandoned 'to indefinite German domination. We must come to terms. We have no choice.'

Such a decision, Reynaud conceded, would be a 'most grave' one for a French Government to take. 'But it might be the only one.' It was now 'too late', he said, to organize the redoubt in Brittany. Nowhere would a French Government have a hope of escaping capture on French soil, 'and Hitler's puppet Government would at once begin its task of undermining and corruption'. He therefore asked once more, would Britain acknowledge that France had given 'her best, her youth, her lifeblood: that she can do no more; and that she is entitled, having nothing further to contribute to the common cause, to enter into a separate peace. . . .'

The words 'separate peace' cut like a knife into each of the eight Englishmen present. Each one felt a sense of betrayal. Yet Reynaud went on, as if trying to make even the breach of the pledge less terrifying, that a separate peace could be made, while still, as he phrased it, 'maintaining the solidarity implicit in the solemn agreement entered into three months previously'.

Churchill replied at once. Britain, he said, would waste no time and energy in 'reproaches and recriminations'. But that did not mean that she would consent to action 'contrary to the recent agreement'. Such was his answer to Reynaud's question. But Churchill went on to suggest means of postponing, and perhaps avoiding altogether the moment of decision and of defeat. The first step, he said, ought to be for Reynaud to put the position 'squarely' to Roosevelt. The French Government should await Roosevelt's answer 'before considering anything else'. If Reynaud were to put the position to Roosevelt 'in the strongest terms', he, Churchill, would 'back up that message with another'. Meanwhile, Churchill declared, Reynaud could 'rest assured that there would be no reproaches whatever happened, that England would continue to cherish the cause of France, and that if she herself triumphed, France would be restored in her greatness'.

Reynaud appeared momentarily stirred by Churchill's suggestion, agreeing to it at once, and then outlining the contents of the message he would address to Roosevelt. Would American forces come to France's aid, he would ask, 'or would they await their turn to be destroyed piecemeal?' The Allies had committed 'grievous errors'. It was Hitler's hope to annihilate them one by one, 'including America', once Britain had been 'disposed of'. Would any United States citizen 'dare to hold his head high' if both France and England were overwhelmed, 'and his country did nothing?'

With these sentiments Churchill had no quarrel. A 'firm promise from America', he told Reynaud, would introduce 'a tremendous new factor' for France. Meanwhile, the French Government should also base its decision to fight on, or to surrender, on other factors, even if Roosevelt's answer were negative. As Churchill saw the future:

The war would certainly continue. The blockade if need be of the whole of Europe, would become increasingly effective. Famine and desperate suffering would ensue. These were very terrible, but inescapable prospects. France, if she were occupied by the Germans, could not hope to be spared, unless England, too, fell. There might arise bitter antagonism between the French and English peoples.

There would, in fact, be many matters to be considered if President Roosevelt's reply was of a negative character.

Meanwhile, he was anxious to know how long France could hope to hold out before General Weygand found himself obliged to sue for armistice. Was another week possible, or less?

Reynaud made no answer to Churchill's question. Instead, he dwelt on the consequences of a French collapse, telling the Englishmen present:

... that he viewed with horror the prospect that Great Britain might inflict the immense suffering of an effective blockade upon the French people. He was convinced that a separation of the two countries would be a great disaster, and that neither could hope for independence thereafter. Even if the worst came, if President Roosevelt's reply held out insufficient hope, if he himself was compelled to abandon the position to which he was desperately clinging, he hoped that Great Britain would, in recognition of the untold sacrifices of French men and women, make some gesture that would obviate the risk of an antagonism, the later consequences of which he considered fatal.

The future relations of the two countries would, Churchill replied, have to be examined with many other questions 'if France decided to enter into an armistice and Treaty'. The immediate issue, 'today', was to put the position before Roosevelt 'in its full brutal reality'.[1]

While Reynaud had been speaking earlier of the possibility of a separate peace, Spears had become alarmed that the French Government's intention was not honourable, and that danger lay in the request to maintain Anglo-French 'solidarity' even in the event of a separate peace. Of this remark by Reynaud, Spears later noted: 'It sounded uncommonly as if he were hinting that, should we not give some impossible promise not to injure France, she would consider joining the enemy.' Reynaud had said nothing of continuing the fight in North Africa. 'It was as disquieting as it was incomprehensible.'

Recalling similar moments of confusion at the Paris Peace Conference of 1919, Spears passed a note to Churchill, reminding him of Lloyd George's habit of asking for an adjournment to consult his col-

[1] Supreme War Council, 16th meeting of 1939–40, Tours, 13 June 1940, 3.30 p.m.: Cabinet papers, 99/3, folios 97–9.

leagues. Churchill read the note, reiterated his point about the need to appeal to Roosevelt, and then glancing out of the window, asked Reynaud if he could confer with his British colleagues '*dans le jardin*'.

Alone and bewildered, the eight Englishmen paced up and down the narrow garden, trying to avoid both the many puddles underfoot, and the wet, overhanging branches of the laurel bushes brushing their faces. Beaverbrook and Halifax, as Spears later recalled, 'at once expressed complete support of Churchill', and he added: 'I believe that everyone was too stunned to speak. I certainly was. I felt completely at sea, rather savage and greatly bewildered as well as frustrated and useless, being unable to cast any light on Reynaud's mood, or even guess at an explanation of what seemed a new and defeatist policy on his part. All I could say was that Reynaud had been completely different that morning when he had described how at the Cabinet meeting the night before he had resisted the "armisticers" and been supported by most of his colleagues in opposing Weygand's peace offensive.'

As the eight men paced round and round the 'hideous rectangle', as Spears described it, Churchill questioned now one, now the other, as to the meaning of what he had heard. He was particularly anxious to know the views of the Ambassador, Sir Ronald Campbell, and of Spears, both of whom had spoken to Reynaud at length earlier that same day. Churchill also asked Spears about de Gaulle. 'I told him,' Spears later wrote, 'I was certain he was completely staunch.' By contrast, Spears added, Weygand regarded everyone who wished to fight on 'as an enemy'.

After nearly twenty minutes of pacing and discussing, the general feeling among the eight Englishmen was that Reynaud would have liked to fight on, first in France and then in North Africa, but that he had so far failed to gather around himself a majority of Ministers likewise determined to continue the battle. 'It must be realized,' Spears later reflected, 'how very difficult was the task of civilians assailed by doubts as to their competence in face of the strong, the violent, opinion of the soldiers in favour of peace.' Although Reynaud was President of the Council, it was the voice of Weygand, the absent Commander-in-Chief, that threatened to prevail, and with it, the dreaded separate peace, following which Britain would find herself vulnerable and alone.

Then, suddenly, Beaverbrook spoke. 'His dynamism was immediately felt,' Spears later recalled, and he summarized the words of this controversial Canadian, Churchill's friend of more than three decades:

There is nothing to do but to repeat what you have already said, Winston. Telegraph to Roosevelt and await the answer. Tell Reynaud that we have nothing to say or discuss until Roosevelt's answer is received. Don't commit yourself to anything. We shall gain a little time and see how those Frenchmen sort themselves out. We are doing no good here. In fact, listening to these declarations of Reynaud's only does harm. Let's get along home.

Simple words, but advice that the other seven felt to be 'the voice of common sense'.[1] Their talk over, they returned to the conference room. While they had been gone, Reynaud had given an account of the Council meeting to the Presidents of the Senate and the Chamber, Jules Jeanneney and Edouard Herriot, as well as to Mandel. According to Baudouin, who was also present, the two Presidents had issued 'violent protests' against Reynaud having allowed it to be understood 'that one day France would decide on a separate armistice'. Both reproached Reynaud for his 'softness', and Herriot's 'wasted countenance', as Baudouin revealed, 'was bathed with tears'.[2]

At the reconvened meeting of the Supreme War Council, a third Frenchman was present, General de Gaulle. At the outset, Churchill told Reynaud that discussion with his colleagues 'had not altered his views, which were certainly shared by the whole British Government'. There could be no separate peace. The need now was to appeal to Roosevelt.

Reynaud replied with a new resolve, reading his proposed message to Roosevelt, urging the President 'to declare war if you can, but in any event to send us every form of help short of an expeditionary force'. If the United States were to take 'a further step forward', Reynaud declared, then, with America's 'full help', Britain and France would be able 'to march on to victory'.

Churchill responded eagerly to Reynaud's mood, saying that he also would telegraph to Roosevelt. 'All this might occupy one day or two.' Then he and Reynaud could consider the replies and 'what decisions were called for'. If America came into the war, Churchill assured Reynaud, 'they could be certain of victory; but if she did not and the French people had for a while to suffer Nazi domination, he felt convinced that their spirit would not break and that they would not grow to love Hitler's works however strong the effects of the German propaganda machine'.

Reynaud now spoke again, confident that when they next met it

[1] Major-General Sir Edward Spears, *Assignment to Catastrophe*, volume 2, London 1954, pages 213–15.

[2] *The Private Diaries (March 1940 to January 1941) of Paul Baudouin*, London 1948, pages 105–6.

would be to discuss 'ways and means of continuing their joint war effort'.[1] 'It was here,' General Ismay wrote to Churchill after the war, 'that you drew M. Reynaud's attention to the fact that several hundreds of German pilots were held prisoner in France, many of whom had been shot down by the Royal Air Force; and you asked that they should be despatched to England as a matter of urgency where they would be kept out of harm's way.' Reynaud replied that he would 'take action forthwith'.[2]

The mood as the Supreme War Council came to an end was one of renewed hope. The official minutes recorded the final exchanges of the two leaders:

Mr CHURCHILL said until their next meeting the British programme of disembarkations in France would continue as arranged.

M. REYNAUD expressed gratitude for this assurance. Everything that he had discussed earlier in the meeting was, of course, only a hypothesis which would arise if President Roosevelt's final answer was of a negative character.

Mr CHURCHILL said that this was certainly the darkest hour for the Allied cause. Nevertheless, his confidence that Hitlerism would be smashed and that Nazidom could not and would not over-rule Europe remained absolutely unshaken.

M. REYNAUD said that his confidence remained equally firm; else he could not endure to go on living.[3]

The Supreme War Council was over. It was never to reconvene. Churchill and Reynaud went downstairs where, in a ground floor room, Jeanneney and Herriot were waiting. 'Both these French patriots,' Churchill later recalled, 'spoke with passionate emotion about fighting on to the death.' His account continued: 'As we went down the crowded passage into the courtyard I saw General de Gaulle standing stolid and expressionless at the doorway. Greeting him, I said in a low tone, in French: "*L'homme du destin*". He remained impassive. In the courtyard there must have been more than a hundred leading Frenchmen in frightful misery. Clemenceau's son, was brought up to me. I wrung his hand.'[4]

At this moment, as Colonel Hollis later recalled, the Comtesse de

[1] Supreme War Council Minutes, 13 June 1940: Cabinet papers, 99/3, folios 97–9.
[2] 'The Meeting at the Prefecture, Tours, on 13th June at 3.30 p.m.,' note by Ismay for Churchill, 20 May 1946: Churchill papers, 4/44.
[3] Supreme War Council Minutes, 13 June 1940: Cabinet papers, 99/3, folios 97–9.
[4] Winston S. Churchill, *The Second World War*, volume 2, London 1949, page 162.

Portes, Reynaud's mistress, pushed forward from the throng. 'Mr Churchill,' she cried out, 'my country is bleeding to death. I have a story to tell and you *must* hear me. You must hear my side of it. You must!' But Churchill affected not to have seen or heard her, shut the car door behind him, and was driven to the airfield, repeating again and again to Reynaud, who was beside him: *'Don't* give in, don't go over to the enemy. Fight on!'

From the airport, Reynaud returned to Tours, and also, as Churchill later remarked to his Ministers, to the Comtesse de Portes. 'She had comfort to give him,' he commented, 'that was not mine to offer.'[1]

While Churchill was being driven to Tours airport, de Gaulle had gone up to Spears in the doorway of the Préfecture, and told him, as Spears later recalled, 'that Baudouin was putting it about to all and sundry, notably to journalists, that Churchill had shown complete comprehension of the French situation and would understand if France concluded an armistice and a separate peace'.

Had Churchill really said that, asked de Gaulle; and he went on to warn Spears that any such attitude would be 'most unfortunate', giving as it would to the defeatists among Reynaud's ministers the right to say: 'What is the good of fighting on even when the English do not expect us to?'

Spears sought to put de Gaulle's mind at rest, assuring him that what Churchill had said, when Reynaud had raised the idea of a separate peace, 'was "*Je comprends*" (I understand) in the sense of "I understand what you say", not in the sense of "I agree" '. But de Gaulle reiterated that Baudouin was already 'putting it about that France is now released from her engagement to England'.

Spears decided to try to catch Churchill at the airport, and to tell him about de Gaulle's concern. 'At the aerodrome,' he later recalled, 'all the planes were revving up against the dismal background of smashed hangars and a bomb-pitted runway.' His account continued:

I told Churchill of Baudouin's effort, and got from him absolute and categorical confirmation that at no time had he given to anyone the least indication of his consenting to the French concluding a separate armistice. 'When I said "*Je comprends*", that meant I understand. *Comprendre* means understand in French, doesn't it? Well,' said Winston, 'when for once I use exactly the right word in their own language, it is going rather far to assume that I intended it to

[1] Quoted in James Leasor, *War at the Top* (*based on the experiences of General Sir Leslie Hollis, KCB, KBE*), London 1959, page 91.

mean something quite different. Tell them my French is not so bad as that.'[1]

He beamed. 'Shay——' But I did not hear the rest, lost in the roar of the engine. He clutched his hat, bent his head to the draught of the propellers, waved his stick, and the precious, lovable man was off. I gazed upward, in a moment the Flamingo and its escort had disappeared.[2]

As Churchill and the English delegation flew back to England, making a wide detour to avoid the battle zone just to the north of Paris, Reynaud drove to the Château de Cangey, 22 miles east of Tours, for a Cabinet meeting. The French Ministers were at their moment of decision: to fight on, or to make peace. On the previous day, before the meeting at Tours, they had been assured by Reynaud that he would bring Churchill to speak to them when he was next in France. Now Churchill had come and gone. But Reynaud had not even mentioned to Churchill that the French Ministers wished to hear him. When the Ministers learned that Churchill had already left for England, some, as Mandel told Spears, 'were taken aback, others were aggrieved, none were pleased'.

Spears assured Mandel that had Churchill had 'the faintest idea' that the French Ministers had wished to speak to him, 'he would have grasped the vital importance of meeting them and stayed on'. Perhaps, Spears later reflected, Reynaud felt that he could convey Churchill's message to them without Churchill himself having to be present. 'I knew that if this was true,' Spears wrote, 'a terrible mistake had been made,' and he added:

I sensed that all these Frenchmen were looking to Churchill for a lead. I knew the formidable impact his eloquence and will always had on his auditors. I felt he might have carried them with him in his determination to fight on. He was the leader they really recognised and looked to. They would have feared his scorn and been glad to lay some at least of the responsibility they found so irksome on his broad shoulders.

Something perhaps irreparable had happened. An opportunity that might not recur had been missed.[3]

This was also Mandel's view. As Spears reported it:

The bad impression and the ill-temper caused by the disappointment of not

---

[1] Spears added at this point, as a footnote in his memoirs, of the discussion at Tours: 'Several times while Reynaud was speaking the Prime Minister had nodded or said "*Je comprends*", indicating his understanding of the words before they were translated.'

[2] Major-General Sir Edward Spears, *Assignment to Catastrophe*, volume 2, London 1954, pages 218–20.

[3] Major-General Sir Edward Spears, *Assignment to Catastrophe*, volume 2, London 1954, pages 225–6.

seeing Churchill had been the background of the discussion and undoubtedly played its part in swaying the majority of the Cabinet towards surrender. To these bewildered men the picture of Churchill flying off to his own country without seeing them gave them a feeling of being abandoned. Churchill would not confer with them, left them to their own devices? What could they do, when there was nothing left to fight with in France, and their most eminent soldiers advised surrender? It took a stout heart to opt for continued resistance now that the impression had been gained that Britain was cutting adrift. To be responsible, yet to be in flight, the forerunners of a flying army, with nothing solid on which to build either a plan or a hope, was dreadful indeed.[1]

After strong speeches by both Pétain and Weygand on the hopelessness of the situation, the French Cabinet Ministers assembled at the Château de Cangey decided to give up all idea of a fighting redoubt in Brittany, as favoured by both Churchill and de Gaulle, and to retire instead to Bordeaux. Churchill meanwhile was on his way back to London, unaware of this meeting at Cangey, or of the apparently demoralizing effect of his own absence on those French Ministers who still wished to continue the war. Later he wrote, in his war memoirs, of how, at Cangey, Reynaud's Cabinet had been 'vexed that I and my colleagues had not come there to join them. We should,' he added, 'have been very willing to do so, no matter how late we had to fly home. But we were never invited; nor did we know there was to be a French Cabinet meeting.'[2]

Churchill was often to reflect on Reynaud's failure to invite him to Cangey, and of the repercussions of that failure. In an unpublished reflection, intended for his war memoirs but deleted before they were published, Churchill gave unexpected support to Reynaud's decision, writing:

Perhaps the harassed Premier did not think I should be stern enough. In this fierce French quarrel I might well have done more harm than good. There was too much in my memory for me to be a harsh claimant. I lay under the impression of twenty years of history—the United States withdrawal from the League of Nations; the MacDonald efforts to reduce the French army to equality with Germany; our inadequate contribution to the awful battle. All these burdens would have hampered my advocacy.[3]

At 8.30 that evening, 13 June 1940, Churchill's Flamingo landed at

---

[1] Major-General Sir Edward Spears, *Assignment to Catastrophe*, volume 2, London 1954, page 227.
[2] Winston S. Churchill, *The Second World War*, volume 2, London 1948, page 162.
[3] Churchill papers, 4/155.

Hendon airport, after a two-and-a-half hour flight from Tours. The War Cabinet was summoned at once, for 10.15 that same night to hear his report. During the intervening hour and three quarters Joseph Kennedy brought Churchill the text of Roosevelt's answer to an earlier French message, of June 10, from Reynaud to the President.

Churchill was excited by Roosevelt's reply, which seemed to bode well for the further French appeal agreed upon at Tours. The American Government, Roosevelt informed Reynaud, was doing 'everything in its power to make available to the Allied Governments the material they so urgently require, and our efforts to do still more are being redoubled'. Roosevelt was particularly impressed, he added, by Reynaud's declaration 'that France will continue to fight on behalf of democracy, even if it means slow withdrawal, even to North Africa and the Atlantic'.[1]

This American message, Churchill told the War Cabinet that night, 'came as near as possible to a declaration of war and probably as much as the President could do without Congress'. The President, Churchill told his colleagues, 'could hardly urge the French to continue the struggle, and to undergo further torture, if he did not intend to enter the war to support them'. If not 'disavowed' by his own country, it was 'clear', Churchill said, that Roosevelt would bring the Americans into the war 'on our side' in the near future. The fact that Roosevelt's reply had come in advance of Reynaud's final appeal made the effect of that reply 'even more striking'.

For the War Cabinet at a crisis hour, it seemed as if this was the turning point. 'It was now inevitable,' Lord Beaverbrook asserted, 'that the United States of America would declare war.' Leaving the meeting for a few moments to see Joseph Kennedy, Churchill returned with the information, vouchsafed by the American Ambassador, that Roosevelt 'must have authorized' the publication of his message to Reynaud, even if no such authorization had been formally received.

The War Cabinet's discussion of Roosevelt's intentions concerned the virtual certainty of an American declaration of war. No Head of State could send such a message to France, it was argued, 'urging her to continue her agony, unless he was certain that his country was coming to her aid'. It was therefore agreed, at Churchill's suggestion, to tell Reynaud that Roosevelt's message 'fulfilled every hope and could only mean that the United States intended to enter the war on our side'. Churchill told his colleagues:

[1] 'Secret and Personal' telegram of 13 June 1940, War Cabinet of 13 June 1940, Annex 1: Cabinet papers, 65/7.

If the French continued the struggle, Hitler would enter Paris within a day or so, but he would find the capital a mere empty shell. Though he might occupy much of her country, the soul of France would have gone beyond his reach. No doubt he would offer very spacious terms to the French, but these we could not permit them to accept. When Hitler found that he could get no peace in this way, his only course would be to try and smash this island. He would probably make the attempt very quickly, perhaps within a fortnight; but before that the United States of America would be in the war on our side.

It was Clement Attlee who then spoke in favour of issuing 'a statement in dramatic terms', one which would 'hearten the people of France'. It was not enough, argued the Labour leader, to send 'messages of encouragement' to the French Government; and after Churchill had reiterated that he had made it quite clear at Tours that Britain would 'never quit the struggle until France had been fully restored', there was what the minutes described as 'general agreement' that an announcement should be issued 'in dramatic terms' stressing the solidarity of the two countries with the message that 'France and Great Britain were one'.

Much seemed now to depend upon Roosevelt's willingness to make public his message to Reynaud. Once more, Churchill left the War Cabinet to speak to the American Ambassador. Kennedy had spoken to the President on the telephone and, as Churchill told the War Cabinet, Roosevelt had been 'agreeable' to the publication of his message, but the Secretary of State, Cordell Hull 'was opposed to it'. It also seemed, Churchill reported, that Roosevelt 'did not realise how critical the situation was'.[1]

Churchill sought to remedy this situation at once, drafting a message to Roosevelt, which the War Cabinet approved, and which was given to Kennedy shortly after midnight. At Tours, Churchill warned, the French were 'very nearly gone'. The only possibility of continuing French resistance was if Reynaud could give his people the hope of ultimate victory. Such a hope 'could only be kindled by American intervention up to the extreme limit open to you'. The publication of Roosevelt's reply to Reynaud would be the decisive factor in this regard.

The British Cabinet, Churchill explained to Roosevelt, had been 'profoundly impressed' by the message, 'but Mr President', Churchill continued, 'I must tell you that it seems to me absolutely vital that this message should be published tomorrow 14th June in order that it may

[1] War Cabinet No. 165 of 1940, 13 June 1940, 10.15 p.m.: Cabinet papers, 65/7, folios 291–7.

play the decisive part in turning the course of world history'. Publication of the Roosevelt message, Churchill added:

... will I am sure decide the French to deny Hitler a patched-up peace with France. He needs this peace in order to destroy us and take a long step forward to world mastery. All the far-reaching plans, strategic, economic, political and moral which your message expounds, may be still-born if the French cut out now. Therefore I urge that the message should be published now. We realise fully that the moment Hitler finds he cannot dictate a Nazi peace in Paris he will turn his fury on to us.

Britain would do its 'best', Churchill told Roosevelt, to withstand that fury, and if she succeeded, 'wide new doors are opened upon the future and all will come out even at the end of the day'.[1]

In the light of Roosevelt's message, and with German troops not yet inside Paris, a decisive American act was envisaged from hour to hour. 'It seemed to us,' Halifax telegraphed to Sir Ronald Campbell on the following morning, 'that it would have been impossible for the President to send such a message unless he meant it to be published, and it seemed very near to the definite step of a declaration of war.'[2]

Immediately after the War Cabinet on the night of June 13, a further telegram, also drafted by Churchill and approved by the War Cabinet, was sent to Reynaud. If France were to remain in the war, Churchill declared, 'we feel that the United States is committed beyond recall to take the only remaining step, namely, becoming a belligerent in form as she has already constituted herself in fact'. If France continued to resist, Churchill added, an American declaration of war 'must inevitably follow'. Churchill's message ended: 'I do beg you and your colleagues, whose resolution we so much admired today, not to miss this sovereign opportunity of bringing about the world-wide oceanic and economic coalition which must be fatal to Nazi domination.' We see before us, Churchill ended, 'a definite plan of campaign, and the light which you spoke of shines at the end of the tunnel'.[3]

There remained one final message to be sent on June 13, the message on which Attlee had been emphatic, not just to the French Government but to the French people, stressing, as the War Cabinet minutes had

---

[1] 'Handed to Kennedy for despatch', 1.15 a.m., 14 June 1940: Premier papers, 3/468, folios 157–8; sent also as telegram No. 1106, 'Immediate', 'Secret and Personal', to the Marquess of Lothian (Washington), 2.15 a.m., 14 June 1940: Cabinet papers, 65/13, folio 299.

[2] Telegram No. 1154, C 7263/G, 'Secret', to Sir R. Campbell (France), 14 June 1940: Cabinet papers, 21/952, folios 69–70.

[3] Telegram to Tours, 'Most Immediate', 13 June 1940, War Cabinet No. 165 of 1940, Annex II: Cabinet papers, 65/7.

phrased it, that 'France and Great Britain were one'. Drafted by Churchill, the message read in full:

In this solemn hour for the British and French nations, and for the cause of freedom and Democracy to which they have vowed themselves, His Majesty's Government desire to pay to the Government of the French Republic the tribute which is due to the heroic fortitude and constancy of the French armies in battle against enormous odds. Their effort is worthy of the most glorious traditions of France and has inflicted deep and long-lasting injury upon the enemy's strength. Great Britain will continue to give the utmost aid in her power. We take this opportunity of proclaiming the indissoluble union of our two peoples and of our two Empires. We cannot measure the various forms of tribulation which will fall upon our peoples in the near future. We are sure that the ordeal by fire will only fuse them together into one unconquerable whole. We renew to the French Republic our pledge and resolve to continue the struggle at all costs in France, in this Island, upon the oceans and in the air, wherever it may lead us, using all our resources to the utmost limit and sharing together the burden of repairing the ravages of war. We shall never turn from the conflict until France stands safe and erect in all her grandeur, until the wronged and enslaved States and peoples have been liberated and until civilisation is freed from the nightmare of Nazidom.

'That this day will dawn,' the message ended, 'we are more sure than ever. It may dawn sooner than we now have the right to expect.'[1]

These were the passionate tones of the night of June 13. They were to be deflated, and then shattered, during the twenty-four hours that followed. Dawn on June 14 brought the first bad news, when Roosevelt's reply reached 10 Downing Street. It was conveyed in a telephone call from Joseph Kennedy, refusing permission to publish the President's message to Reynaud. 'It seems,' noted Colville, 'the Prime Minister's expectations last night of immediate American help were exaggerated.' The United States, Colville added, 'has been caught napping militarily and industrially. She may be really useful to us in a year but we are living from hour to hour.'[2]

In conveying Roosevelt's negative message, Kennedy asked Churchill to 'explain the position' to Reynaud. But, as Churchill told the War Cabinet later that morning, he had declined to do so, and had 'stressed strongly' to the Ambassador that if Roosevelt 'now appeared to be holding back, this would have a disastrous effect on French resistance'.[3]

The one factor under British control, through which it seemed to the

---

[1] Message of 13 June 1940, War Cabinet No. 165 of 1940, Annex III: Cabinet papers, 65/7.
[2] Colville diary, 14 June 1940: Colville papers.
[3] War Cabinet No. 166 of 1940, 12.30 p.m., 14 June 1940: Cabinet papers, 65/7.

War Cabinet that French resistance might still be encouraged, was the existence of more than 150,000 British troops south of the Somme, under General Brooke's command. For some days one section of this force, the second and third Brigades of the 52nd Division, commanded by Major-General Drew, had been moving up towards the front, while the 2nd Brigade Group of the Canadian Division were landing that very day at Cherbourg to augment the force.[1]

At the War Cabinet on June 14 Churchill approved the despatch from Britain of 'fresh troops' in an effort to 'keep alive' French resistance, telling the War Cabinet that such troops could continue to be sent for as long as French resistance was in fact continuing. But it was essential at the same time, he said, to go ahead with the 'wholesale withdrawal' of British Lines of Communication personnel at the bases. Churchill feared that French resistance might 'crumble' with a German attack on Le Mans, and a subsequent German advance to Nantes, whereupon the British position in western France would be 'serious'.[2]

Even while the War Cabinet was meeting in London, the Germans were securing their greatest triumph of the war so far, the conquest of Paris. In order to protect the capital from bombardment or street fighting, Weygand had agreed to German conditions for making it an open city: all French troops were to withdraw not only from the city itself, but from all its suburbs. Thus it was that during the morning of June 14, German troops, unopposed, entered Paris, the sixth capital to fall under their rule in nine months.[3]

With Paris lost, the sole remaining prospect of maintaining the battle in France seemed to be, as Colville noted in his diary, a defensive perimeter in Brittany. 'We must now fall back on the Atlantic,' he wrote, establishing 'new lines of Torres Vedras'—as in the Peninsular War against Napoleon—using 'British divisions and American supplies, and guerilla warfare on German Lines of Communication'.[4]

Such were the plans at 10 Downing Street on the afternoon of June 14. But, even as they were being discussed, the Chief of the Imperial

---

[1] Other non-French forces still on French soil included some 25,000 Polish, 5,000 Czech and 200 Belgian troops. The British troops included 8,837 men evacuated from Le Havre on and before June 13, and taken by sea round the coast to Cherbourg to continue the fight.

[2] War Cabinet No. 166 of 1940, 12.30 p.m., 14 June 1940, Confidential Annex, Minute 2: Cabinet papers, 65/13.

[3] German troops had entered Warsaw in September 1939, Copenhagen and Oslo in April 1940, The Hague and Brussels in May 1940.

[4] Colville diary, 14 June 1940: Colville papers. Two days later Lord Hamilton of Dalzell wrote to Churchill from Scotland: 'My dear Winston, For God's sake make a Torres Vedras line from Nantes to Caen. Brittany is the only bit of France that matters a damn to us' (letter of 16 June 1940: Churchill papers, 2/395).

General Staff arrived with a telegram from General Brooke. Its content was ominous: Weygand had told him that 'organised resistance' had come to an end, and that the French Army was 'disintegrating' into 'disconnected groups'. Both Weygand and Georges had stressed to Brooke the 'military impossibility' of holding Brittany, and Brooke added his own agreement with this. 'Strongly recommend decision should be reconsidered,' he wrote, 'as it can only lead to further losses of British troops without hope of result.'[1]

In fact, no decision to hold a redoubt in Brittany had yet been made. But Brooke's telegram was decisive. 'In these circumstances,' Churchill telegraphed to Reynaud, now that organized French resistance had ceased, 'I feel sure you will agree that the Allied cause would best be served by our stopping the disembarkation of any further British Forces in France till the situation is more clear.' Orders had also been issued, Churchill added, to evacuate 'the very large' British Lines of Communication personnel between Rennes and Nantes, and for Brooke 'to retire with the French Tenth Army upon Le Mans'.[2]

At the Defence Committee meeting at 6.30 that evening it was agreed to send this message to Reynaud, in order, as the minutes recorded, to prevent him from declaring that the British forces were 'deserting' the French Army. At the same time, it was urged that instructions must be sent to General Brooke 'regarding the evacuation of British troops from France and his own retirement'.

Churchill had now to face the imminent defeat of France. But he still believed in a continued Anglo-French resistance, pointing out to the Chiefs of Staff and Vice-Chiefs[3] that the French were not yet suing for an armistice, but 'falling back further into the country and continuing to fight, although action was unco-ordinated'. It was therefore 'essential', he felt, that if the French Tenth Army was still fighting, General Brooke 'should co-operate with them as long as they were putting up any resistance at all'.

As the discussion continued, however, it emerged that Brooke was already withdrawing his two brigades from the Le Mans area to the ports. Both brigades, said Churchill, 'should be put into the battle' if the French were continuing to fight. The Canadians, however, who had only just disembarked, 'should be re-embarked at once'.

---

[1] Telegram No. 239, 'Most Immediate' 14 June 1940: Cabinet papers, 69/1, folio 94 (Annex 1 to Defence Committee meeting No. 16 of 1940, 14 June 1940).

[2] 'Most Secret', 14 June 1940: Cabinet papers 69/1, folio 95 (Annex III to Defence Committee meeting No. 16 of 1940, 14 June 1940).

[3] Air Chief Marshal Sir Cyril Newall, General Sir John Dill, Admiral of the Fleet Sir Dudley Pound; Air Marshal Peirse, Vice-Admiral Phillips and Lieutenant-General Haining.

It was 8.20 in the evening, and a telephone connection had just been made with General Brooke himself. When Brooke told Dill of his plans to withdraw both his divisions to Le Mans, Dill told him, as Brooke recalled: 'The Prime Minister does not want you to do that.' Brooke added:

... I think I answered: 'What the hell does he want?' At any rate, Dill's next reply was: 'He wants to speak to you', and he handed the receiver over to him. To my surprise, I found myself talking to Churchill on this very bad line of communication. I had never met him, I had never talked to him, but I had heard a good deal about him!

He asked me what I was doing with the 52nd Division, and, after I had informed him, he told me that that was not what he wanted. I had been sent to France to make the French feel that we were supporting them.

I replied that it was impossible to make a corpse feel, and that the French Army was, to all intents and purposes, dead, and certainly incapable of registering what was being done for it.

Brooke's account continued:

However, he insisted that we should make them feel that we were supporting them, and I insisted that this was quite impossible and would only result in throwing away good troops to no avail. He then asked me whether I had not got a gap in front of me. When I replied that this was correct, he asked whether the division could not be put into the gap.

I told him that, as the gap was some thirty to forty miles broad at that time, and would probably be some forty to sixty miles to-morrow, the remainder of the 52nd Division would be of little avail in trying to block this widening chasm. I said that it would again inevitably result in the throwing away of good troops with no hope of achieving any results.

Brooke ended his recollection:

Our talk lasted for close on half an hour, and on many occasions his arguments were so formed as to give me the impression that he considered that I was suffering from 'cold feet' because I did not wish to comply with his wishes. This was so infuriating that I was repeatedly on the verge of losing my temper. Fortunately, while I was talking to him I was looking through the window at Drew and Kennedy[1] sitting on a garden seat under a tree. Their presence there acted as a continual reminder of the human element of the 52nd Division and of the unwarrantable decision to sacrifice them with no attainable object in view.

At last, when I was in an exhausted condition, he said: 'All right, I agree with you.'[2]

[1] Commanding the Royal Artillery of the 52nd Division.
[2] Arthur Bryant, *The Turn of The Tide 1939–1943: A Study based on the Diaries and Autobiographical Notes of Field Marshal the Viscount Alanbrooke KG, OM*, London 1957, pages 172–3.

Churchill's hopes of a continued military resistance in France were at an end. Deferring to the opinion of the General in the field, orders were given to withdraw more than 150,000 British troops from France. That night, as British ships were ordered to Cherbourg, Brest, St Nazaire and St Malo, Brooke was told that Air Marshal Barratt, then at Rennes, would be instructed 'to concert arrangements with you for withdrawal and cover'.[1] That same night Barratt was informed by the Chief of the Air Staff: 'you should forthwith withdraw to ports and evacuate all surplus personnel and stores'.[2] Barratt's remaining bomber squadrons now flew back to England, leaving only four fighter squadrons, based on Nantes, to cover the withdrawal.

Among those in London on June 14 who were tormented by the imminent defeat of France was a member of the French Economic Mission to Britain, René Pleven. That evening, Pleven obtained an interview with the Chief Whip, David Margesson, to whom he explained a novel plan: the political Union of Britain and France, together with the evacuation of as many French troops as possible from western France to Britain. The two Governments would act as one. The two armies would fight as one.

Margesson spoke at once to Desmond Morton, who had already heard of the plan from Pleven's colleague, Jean Monnet. As Morton approved the idea of such a Union, Margesson went to expound it to Neville Chamberlain, who was at that moment dining at 11 Downing Street with Lord Halifax.

It emerged that others were also excited by the possibilities of such an Anglo-French Union, among them the Head of the Treasury, Sir Horace Wilson, and Brendan Bracken; and it was Bracken who, that same evening, immediately after dinner, persuaded Churchill to see Pleven at 10 Downing Street. The meeting took place in the Cabinet Room. Colville later wrote:

Churchill was interested in the idea of bringing French troops across the Channel so as 'to make the island stiff with soldiers' and increase the defences against invasion. He was less interested in the grandiose idea of a Franco-British union. Indeed, according to Margesson, he was 'bored and critical', although he did finally walk through to No. 11 to talk the matter over with Chamberlain.[3]

[1] Telegram to General Brooke, 14 June 1940: Cabinet papers 69/1, folio 96 (Annex IV to Defence Committee meeting No. 16 of 1940, 14 June 1940).
[2] Telegram X. 182, 14 June 1940, 'Most Immediate': Cabinet papers 69/1, folio 97 (Annex V to Defence Committee meeting No. 16 of 1940, 14 June 1940).
[3] John Colville, *Footprints in Time*, London 1976, pages 85–6.

Churchill now waited at 10 Downing Street for the full text of Roosevelt's reply to the request to make his message to Reynaud public. 'America's attitude is vital to French morale,' Colville noted in his diary, 'but America is the slowest to act of all the democracies.' Meanwhile, influenced by René Pleven's enthusiasms, three members of Churchill's inner circle, Morton, Bracken and Sandys, together with Margesson, talked over the 'passing hope', as Colville called it, 'that we might bring the French Army over here'.[1] Morton was optimistic, envisaging, as he minuted for Churchill, some 250,000 'or more' armed French soldiers reaching England as a fighting force for future operations.[2]

At one thirty that morning the full text of Roosevelt's reply was brought to 10 Downing Street. His most recent message to Reynaud, Roosevelt stated, 'was in no sense intended to commit and did not commit the Government to military participation in support of Allied governments'. Only Congress could make any such commitment. The message to Reynaud should not be published, Roosevelt stressed, 'since I believe it to be imperative that there be avoided any possible misunderstanding in regard to the facts. . . .' But although the President would not, apparently, even ask Congress to declare war, he had already asked 'as a first step' for the 'immediate furnishing of food and clothing to civilian refugees in France', and this recommendation the Senate had 'unanimously approved' on the previous day.[3]

The extent and the imminence of a French collapse was made clear in a telegram from Colonel Redman, sent to Ismay during the night of June 14. The 'impression' at French headquarters, Redman reported, 'is that armistice may be signed tomorrow'.[4]

Following Roosevelt's telegram, there could be no further doubt that the United States would not declare war on Germany in order to stiffen French resolve. The American negative, and General Brooke's reports, made it impossible for Churchill to hold out any further hopes for continued French resistance. That night he told Eden, as Colville noted, that 'he thought France would crack internally in a day or two'.[5]

The Churchills had moved during June 14 from Admiralty House to

[1] Colville diary, 14 June 1940: Colville papers.
[2] Minute of 14 June 1940: Premier papers, 7/2.
[3] Message received at 1.30 a.m., 15 June 1940: Premier papers, 3/468, folios 148–9.
[4] 'Most Immediate', telegram despatched at 11 p.m., 14 June 1940, received 2.30 a.m., 15 June 1940: Cabinet papers, 21/952, folio 63.
[5] Colville diary, 14 June 1940: Colville papers.

10 Downing Street. But that night Churchill 'thought it best', as Colville wrote in his diary, to sleep elsewhere, and chose for what was left of the night to go to Stornoway House, the London home of Lord Beaverbrook, whose staunchness the day before, at Tours, has been so decisive. The mood when Churchill left 10 Downing Street at half past two that morning was summed up by Colville, who wrote in his diary: 'If we can hold on until November we shall have won the war. But holding on is going to be a grim business: the chance of the whale to show his superiority to the elephant.'[1]

That night, unable to accept Roosevelt's negative response as final, Churchill drafted a further telegram to the President, reiterating his earlier warnings that 'this moment is supremely critical for France', and adding that a public declaration 'that the United States will if necessary enter the war might save France'. Failing that, Churchill warned, 'in a few days French resistance may have crumpled and we shall be left alone'.

Forcefully, but with a sense of foreboding, Churchill sought to put to Roosevelt the full extent of defeat, and of its possible disastrous outcome. His message read:

Although the present Government and I personally would never fail to send the Fleet across the Atlantic if resistance was beaten down here, a point may be reached in the struggle where the present Ministers no longer have control of affairs and when very easy terms could be obtained for the British Island by their becoming a vassal state of the Hitler Empire. A pro-German Government would certainly be called into being to make peace, and might present to a shattered or a starving nation an almost irresistible case for entire submission to the Nazi will.

The fate of the British Fleet, as I have already mentioned to you, would be decisive on the future of the United States, because if it were joined to the Fleets of Japan, France, and Italy and the great resources of German industry, overwhelming sea-power would be in Hitler's hands. He might of course use it with a merciful moderation. On the other hand, he might not. This revolution in sea-power might happen very quickly, and certainly long before the United States would be able to prepare against it.

If we go down you may have a United States of Europe under the Nazi command far more numerous, far stronger, far better armed than the New World.

[1] Colville diary, 14 June 1940: Colville papers. Five days later Harold Nicolson wrote in his diary: 'I think it practically certain that the Americans will enter the war in November, and if we can last till then, all is well' (Nicolson diary, 19 June 1940: Nigel Nicolson, editor, *Harold Nicolson, Diaries and Letters 1939–1945*, London 1967, pages 96–7). It was widely expected, and rightly, that Roosevelt would be re-elected to a third four-year term in the November 1940 Presidential Election.

Churchill's telegram continued: 'I know well, Mr President, that your eye will already have searched these depths, but I feel I have the right to place on record the vital manner in which American interests are at stake in our battle and that of France.'

Churchill's draft ended with a plea to Roosevelt for the immediate despatch of thirty-five American destroyers to 'bridge the gap' until Britain's new naval construction 'comes in at the end of the year'. Here, Churchill urged, was a 'definite, practical and possibly decisive step which can be taken at once, and I urge most earnestly that you will weigh my words'.[1]

Churchill's draft telegram was considered by the War Cabinet on the morning of June 15, when Churchill pointed out that events 'were now moving very fast' and that 'nothing short of a declaration of war by the United States would be likely to sustain the French much longer'. Nor did this idea seem fanciful; indeed, it was Neville Chamberlain who suggested that Churchill should 'stress the moral and psychological effect of an American declaration of war'.[2]

The War Cabinet approved Churchill's message to Roosevelt. They also agreed to a special message being sent to the Dominion Prime Ministers, and Churchill dictated this in the Cabinet Room itself. The message was typed out as he dictated it, and when it was ready, Churchill took it out to the garden where the Chief of the Air Staff, Air Marshal Newall, was waiting to scrutinize it. 'He was evidently moved,' Churchill later recalled, 'and presently said he agreed with every word.'[3]

In this message to the Dominion Prime Ministers Churchill set out his reasons for believing that, even if France fell, Britain would fight on, surmounting even the inevitable German air bombardments and 'wearing them out' after weeks or even months of air struggle. 'No doubt,' Churchill told the Dominion leaders, 'we must expect novel forms of attack and attempts to bring tanks across the sea. We are preparing ourselves to deal with these as far as we can foresee them. No one can predict or guarantee the course of a life-and-death struggle of this character, but we shall certainly enter upon it in good heart.' His message ended:

. . . there are solid reasons behind our resolve not to allow the fate of France,

[1] Telegram of 15 June 1940: Churchill papers, 20/14.
[2] War Cabinet No. 167 of 1940, 15 June 1940, 10 a.m., Confidential Annex, Minute 6: Cabinet papers, 65/13.
[3] Winston S. Churchill, *The Second World War*, volume 2, London 1949, page 174.

whatever it may be, to deter us from going on to the end. I personally believe that the spectacle of the fierce struggle and carnage in our Island will draw the United States into the war, and even if we should be beaten down through the superior numbers of the enemy's Air Force it will always be possible, as I indicated to the House of Commons in my last speech, to send our fleets across the oceans, where they will protect the Empire and enable it to continue the war and the blockade, I trust in conjunction with the United States, until the Hitler *régime* breaks under the strain.

'We shall let you know at every stage,' Churchill added, 'how you can help, being assured that you will do all in human power, as we, for our part, are entirely resolved to do.'[1]

Churchill now read this message over for one last time, and as he did so, 'felt', as he later recalled, 'a glow of sober confidence'.[2]

The War Cabinet now returned to the discussion of the immediate crisis in France, and to Churchill's proposal that once the British troops had been withdrawn from western France to Cherbourg, they should not be brought back to Britain, but remain at Cherbourg 'so that if a fresh opportunity arose they could be ordered to proceed elsewhere in France'.[3] It was Neville Chamberlain who then put forward the idea, which Margesson had put to him the previous evening, for what he described to the War Cabinet as 'real unity between Great Britain and France, dramatically expressed, and fully realised by the two peoples'.

Although Churchill had been critical of this idea when it had first been put to him, he did not dismiss it out of hand. 'If means were to be found,' he told the War Cabinet, 'to prepare a statement as to the British and French unity, in a dramatic form which would make a big appeal to the French, so much the better.' But the 'main point' at this moment, he said, was 'to secure the French Fleet', and, as the French Government was at that moment transferring from Tours to Bordeaux, he proposed 'to fly over to Bordeaux' with one or two members of the War Cabinet, to discuss such 'vitally important matters' as the French Fleet with the French Ministers.[4]

During luncheon that day at the Carlton Club, Churchill was told more about the project for an Anglo-French Union. At the luncheon were Desmond Morton, Sir Robert Vansittart, and the two senior

---

[1] Telegram drafted on 15 June 1940: Premier papers, 4/43B/1. The telegram was despatched at 3.15 a.m., 16 June 1940. Its recipients were the Prime Ministers of New Zealand, Australia, South Africa and Canada.

[2] Winston S. Churchill, *The Second World War*, volume 2, London 1949, page 174.

[3] War Cabinet No. 167 of 1940, 15 June 1940, 10 a.m.: Cabinet papers, 65/7.

[4] War Cabinet No. 167 of 1940, 15 June 1940, 10 a.m., Confidential Annex, Minute 6: Cabinet papers, 65/13.

members of the French Economic Mission in London, Jean Monnet and René Pleven. Vansittart explained that the aim was to give Reynaud what Churchill later described as 'some new fact of a vivid and stimulating nature' with which to persuade a majority of his Cabinet to carry on the war, if necessary in North Africa. 'My first reaction was unfavourable,' Churchill later recalled. 'I asked a number of questions of a critical character, and was by no means convinced.'[1]

As the luncheon ended, it was agreed to raise the question of Union with General de Gaulle, who had just arrived in London to give orders for the ship *Pasteur*, then on its way with a cargo of arms from the United States to France, to land its arms in Britain instead. De Gaulle was due to fly back to Bordeaux within twenty-four hours.[2] Churchill agreed that de Gaulle should help to draft a suitable proclamation to be submitted to the War Cabinet for its consideration. Meanwhile, having returned to 10 Downing Street, Churchill was shown a draft telegram, prepared by Admiral Phillips, setting out for Roosevelt the precise details of Britain's naval losses and naval needs.[3] Phillips' draft, which Churchill sent to Roosevelt unaltered, but as if from himself, ended:

We are now faced with the imminent collapse of French resistance and, if this occurs, the successful defence of this island will be the only hope of averting the collapse of civilisation as we define it.

We must ask, therefore, as a matter of life or death, to be reinforced with these destroyers. We will carry on the struggle whatever the odds, but it may well be beyond our resources unless we receive every reinforcement and particularly do we need this reinforcement on the sea.[4]

[1] Winston S. Churchill, *The Second World War*, volume 2, London 1949, page 180. This was in fact Churchill's second unfavourable response: on the previous evening he had shown himself 'bored and critical' of the idea (see page 546).

[2] De Gaulle sent Churchill an account of his mission when Churchill was writing his war memoirs (letter of 3 November 1948: Churchill papers, 4/22).

[3] The first two paragraphs read: 'Since beginning of war Britain and France have lost 32 destroyers, with displacement of 47,380 tons, which were complete losses. Out of these 25 with displacement of 37,637 tons, were lost since 1st February. There is always a large number of destroyers out of action for repairs to damages caused by enemy action and hard service. From outbreak of war up to Norwegian invasion approximately 30% of British destroyers in home waters were in this condition, but since then the percentage has greatly increased and for instance out of 133 destroyers in commission in home waters today only 68 are fit for service, which is lowest level since war started. In 1918 some 433 destroyers were in service.' Phillips added: 'Only 10 small type new construction destroyers are due to complete in next four months.'

[4] Admiral Phillips' draft, 15 June 1940: Premier papers, 3/468, folios 159–60. Phillips had written: 'but I must frankly state that it will be beyond our resources. . . .' Churchill altered this to: 'but it may well be beyond our resources. . . .' Otherwise these two paragraphs were sent as Phillips drafted them.

Hardly had Churchill sent this telegram across to the Foreign Office for despatch to Washington under his own name, when Campbell, the British Ambassador to France, relayed a message from Reynaud, stating that unless the United States came into the war 'at a very early date', France would be unable to continue the war, even from overseas. This message raised in acute form the spectre of the French Fleet being no longer attached to a resisting French Government, but passing instead to the Germans. In his earlier telegram to Roosevelt, Churchill had pointed out that Italy's entry into the war had already 'brought into the seas' an extra hundred hostile submarines, while German control of both the Norwegian and Channel ports had faced Britain 'with a prospect of invasion which has more hopes of success than we had ever conceived possible'.

In a second telegram to Roosevelt, Churchill warned that there was 'no getting away from the fact', as now insisted upon by Reynaud, that France would not be prepared even to continue the war from North Africa if the United States declined to enter the war. Churchill's telegram continued:

Indeed, the British Ambassador in Bordeaux tells me that if your reply does not contain the assurance asked for, the French will very quickly ask for an armistice, and I much doubt whether it will be possible in that event for us to keep the French Fleet out of German hands.

When I speak of the United States entering the war I am, of course, not thinking in terms of an expeditionary force, which I know is out of the question. What I have in mind is the tremendous moral effect that such an American decision would produce, not merely in France but also in all the democratic countries of the world, and, in the opposite sense, on the German and Italian peoples.[1]

This telegram sent, Churchill then read aloud to Colville his earlier telegram to the Dominion Prime Ministers, commenting wistfully to his young Private Secretary: 'If words counted, we should win this war.'[2]

Churchill left London early on the evening of June 15 to spend the weekend at Chequers. It was intended to be a quiet occasion, with his wife, his daughter Diana, his son-in-law Duncan Sandys, Colville as the duty Secretary, and Lindemann.

[1] Telegram sent at 10.45 p.m., 15 June 1940: Premier papers, 3/468, folios 126–7.
[2] Colville diary, 15 June 1940: Colville papers.

Amid the hourly messages foreshadowing disaster in France, Churchill had still to study the problem of future policy, particularly in connection with British air strength, and a possible German invasion of the United Kingdom. Before the war, Churchill and Lindemann had often discussed how Germany's air superiority could be challenged, especially by technical advances. One such advance was the possibility of a radar device carried inside an aeroplane, to enable it to find and to follow an enemy aeroplane at night. On June 13 Lindemann had been able to report to Churchill the first trial of an experimental Air Interception device, known as AI, codename 'Smeller'. This device, Lindemann explained, 'should greatly help in *maintaining* the pursuit which the enemy might otherwise elude owing to clouds etc'.[1]

Experiments were going ahead in blind interception techniques. These experiments could not be completed in time to help the battle over France. But by autumn this ought to be able to make an effective contribution to the war in the air.[2] 'Smeller', like the Purvis supplies from the United States, could not help Reynaud; but it did strengthen Churchill's cause for confidence in Britain's long-term capacity to survive.

Lindemann had also put to Churchill on June 13 his thoughts on the nature of a German parachute landing in Britain. The first action of parachutists or saboteurs, he wrote, 'is likely to be the cutting of telephone cables'. To monitor this Lindemann advised that all important lines of communication 'should be tested every hour or so by sending, from suitable centres, an impulse too feeble to ring a bell or disturb the recipient but strong enough to activate a sensitive detector at the testing centre'. This, Lindemann believed, would be a 'very useful precaution', and Churchill at once asked the Postmaster General, William Morrison, to take up Lindemann's suggestion. The result was a meeting between Lindemann and a senior member of Morrison's staff, and rapid progress in devising a system of testing.[3]

At Chequers, during the evening of June 15, as Lindemann and the Sandys were dining with Churchill and Clementine, Colville recorded in his diary news of the worsening situation in France. Before going into the dining room, Colville wrote: 'I learned by telephone that the

---

[1] Minute of 13 June 1940: Premier papers, 3/22/5, folio 287.

[2] On 22 July 1940 the First German aircraft was shot down by use of AI. On 19 August 1940 a German aircraft was followed at night for twenty minutes using AI. By 20 October 1940 there had been 200 separate attempts to use AI for interception, with a 75% success rate (Night Air Defence Report No. 1 of 1940, 21 October 1940).

[3] Minute of 13 June 1940, and notes: Premier papers, 3/222/1.

position was deteriorating fast and the request to be allowed to make a separate peace was being put in a more brutal form. I imparted this to Winston who was immediately very depressed.'[1]

The message which had been read to Colville on the telephone was a further telegram from Campbell in Bordeaux. 'My impression is,' Campbell reported, 'that things are slipping fast. It is becoming more and more difficult to obtain a straight answer, or a definite expression of opinion. Ministers seek refuge in talking about the impossibility for the French troops to stand firm in their present state of fatigue, and of the necessity of putting an end to the present conditions, and of avoiding anarchy.'[2]

Dinner, Colville recorded, 'began lugubriously', with Churchill 'every now and then firing some technical question to Lindemann, who was quietly consuming his vegetarian diet.' Colville's account continued:

The Sandys' and I sat silent, because our sporadic efforts at conversation were not well received. However, champagne, brandy and cigars did their work and we soon became talkative, even garrulous.

Winston, in order to cheer himself and us up, read aloud the messages he had received from the Dominions and the replies he had sent to them and to Roosevelt.

'The war is bound to become a bloody one for us now,' he said, 'but I hope our people will stand up to bombing and the Huns aren't liking what we are giving them. But what a tragedy that our victory in the last war should have been snatched from us by a lot of softies!'

Winston and Duncan Sandys paced up and down the rose-garden in the moonlight while Diana, Lindemann and I walked on the other side of the house. It was light and deliciously warm, but the sentries with tin helmets and fixed bayonets, who were placed all round the house, kept us alive to the horrors of reality. I spent much of the time telephoning, searching for Winston among the rose-bushes and listening to his comments on the war.[3]

It was one o'clock in the morning. Churchill, Lindemann, Sandys and Colville came in from the garden. The Prime Minister lay down on a sofa in the hall, 'discoursed', as Colville wrote in his diary, 'on the building up of British fighter strength, told a few dirty stories and said: "Goodnight my children".'[4]

[1] Colville diary, 15 June 1940: Colville papers.
[2] Telegram No. 406 DIPP, sent from Bordeaux 2.45 p.m., received in London 5.25 p.m., 15 June 1940: Premier papers, 3/468, folio 131.
[3] Colville diary, 15 June 1940: John Colville, *Footprints in Time*, London 1976, pages 86–7.
[4] Colville diary, 15 June 1940: Colville papers.

Churchill went to bed. The imminent collapse of France was his ever-present nightmare. Reflecting on this period six months later, he told Anthony Eden: 'Normally I wake up buoyant to face the new day. Then I woke up with dread in my heart.'[1]

---

[1] Eden diary, 19 December 1940: The Earl of Avon, *The Eden Memoirs*, *The Reckoning*, London 1965, page 182.

27

'Fight on!'

WHILE Churchill was still asleep at Chequers on the morning of Sunday June 16, a despatch rider arrived with a telegram from Sir Ronald Campbell in Bordeaux. At 7.30, hearing that Churchill was awake, Colville took the telegram to his room. Churchill was lying in bed 'looking just like a rather nice pig clad in a silk vest'.

The Bordeaux telegram was unequivocal: the French Government wished to know if it could enquire, through the United States Government, 'what armistice conditions would be offered to France by the enemy'.[1]

Churchill had intended to stay at Chequers, to lunch with de Gaulle, Eden and Dill. But on scrutinizing the French request, he cancelled his luncheon and summoned the War Cabinet for a meeting at Downing Street that same morning.

During the drive to London, in pouring rain, Churchill dictated a number of minutes to Kathleen Hill; enough work, Colville noted, 'to keep us busy during the morning'. Colville added: 'One of the great differences between Chamberlain and Churchill is that whereas the former in reading Cabinet papers seldom made any comments and only on questions of the highest priority, Churchill scrutinizes every document which has anything to do with the war and does not disdain to enquire into the most trivial point.'[2]

---

[1] Sir R. Campbell, telegram No. 420 DIPP, received 16 June 1940: Premier papers, 3/468.

[2] Colville diary, 16 June 1940: Colville papers. Among the minutes dictated in the car that morning was one to Ismay about the 'sticky' bomb and the 'great sloth' said to be being shown 'in pressing this forward'; and one to the Secretary of State for Colonies, Lord Lloyd, about the possibility of raising a West Indies Regiment 'to be available for Imperial Service; to give an outlet for the loyalty of the Negroes, and bring money into these poor Islands' (Minute of 16 June 1940: Churchill papers, 20/13). In January 1939 Clementine Churchill had visited the West Indies, and sent her husband several long accounts of conditions on the Islands.

The War Cabinet met at 10.15 that morning. Its decision, transmitted at once to Reynaud, was that France was released from its obligation not to enter into negotiations with Germany 'provided, but only provided, that the French Fleet is sailed forthwith for British harbours pending negotiations'.[1]

This message was eventually sent by telephone to Bordeaux at 12.35 p.m., and reflected the War Cabinet's overriding concern about the future of the French Fleet. This concern was first expressed to the War Cabinet by Neville Chamberlain, who stressed that if the French Fleet 'fell into the hands of Germany, our position would very seriously deteriorate', and then by Clement Attlee who urged that 'the essential point was to secure the French Fleet'. After a question by Churchill as to the view of the three Services, the same concern was expressed by Pound, Sinclair and Eden. All were in agreement: the French Fleet must not be allowed to fall into German hands. No other condition was to be imposed on France. But unless that condition were met Britain would not release France from its undertaking.

Some worries were expressed at the War Cabinet of June 16 that Britain might be trapped through any French Government negotiations with or through the United States. Churchill summed up this feeling when he warned his colleagues:

... one danger of invoking President Roosevelt was that he might give advice which was of application to the United Kingdom as well as to France. He might, for example, issue an appeal to all the belligerent Governments to call the war off. This might to some extent shake some sections of British public opinion, the whole of which was at present united and inflexible. At the present juncture all thoughts of coming to terms with the enemy must be dismissed so far as Britain was concerned. We were fighting for our lives and it was vital that we should allow no chink to appear in our armour.

The single hopeful item of news reported to the War Cabinet on the morning of June 16 concerned General de Gaulle's visit to London. As Eden told his colleagues, de Gaulle had agreed that all French war materials coming from the United States should be 'diverted' to Britain. He had also offered to send to Britain 'some 4,000 German prisoners', including the pilots and officers whom Reynaud had earlier promised to send. De Gaulle also suggested that Britain take in 'some 30,000 French mechanics and up to 60,000 armament craftsmen', and he

[1] Cypher Telegram No. 368 to Sir Ronald Campbell, by Telephone, DIPP, sent 12.35 p.m., 16 June 1940, War Cabinet No. 168 of 1940, Appendix 1: Cabinet papers, 65/13, folio 320.

had told Eden that over a quarter of a million French army recruits were to be sent over to North Africa for training.[1]

It was to meet de Gaulle that Churchill now repaired once more for luncheon at the Carlton Club. The others present were Eden, Sir John Dill and the French Ambassador, Charles Corbin. 'It was at this luncheon,' Colville later wrote, 'that de Gaulle reminded Churchill of the project for a political union of the two countries and begged him to consider it seriously.'[2] This was indeed so, and two hours later Churchill reported to the War Cabinet that de Gaulle had impressed upon him 'that some very dramatic move was essential'. Its purpose would be to give Reynaud 'the support which he needed' to keep the French Government in the war. De Gaulle had suggested 'that a proclamation of the indissoluble union of the French and British peoples' would serve this purpose. The French Ambassador had supported the Under-Secretary for National Defence, and had expressed his concern at the War Cabinet's telegram, sent to Reynaud scarcely an hour earlier, granting France the right to seek an armistice.

It suddenly seemed as if, by a declaration of Union, such an armistice could be averted. This hope seemed to be confirmed immediately after the luncheon when de Gaulle managed to contact Bordeaux by telephone and speak direct to Reynaud. Over the telephone, de Gaulle read Reynaud the draft of a specific declaration of Union.

As a result of Reynaud's reception of the idea of Union, it had seemed 'advisable', Churchill reported, 'to suspend action for the moment' on the telegram agreed that morning. Accordingly, a second telegram had been sent to Sir Ronald Campbell 'instructing him to suspend action' on the earlier message.[3]

Churchill reported these developments to the War Cabinet when it met again in special session at three o'clock that afternoon. Lord Halifax then told his colleagues that the draft of a formal Declaration of Union had been prepared that morning, at Halifax's own suggestion, by Sir Robert Vansittart 'in consultation' with de Gaulle, Monnet, Pleven and Desmond Morton. The aim, Halifax explained, had been to draft 'some dramatic announcement which might strengthen M. Reynaud's hand'. This had now been done, and de Gaulle had 'impressed' upon Halifax 'the need for publishing the document as quickly as possible'. Indeed, de Gaulle wished to take the draft back with him

[1] War Cabinet No. 168 of 1940, 10.15 a.m., 16 June 1940, Minute 1: Cabinet papers, 65/13, folios 313-19.

[2] John Colville, *Footprints in Time*, London 1976, page 88.

[3] Churchill's report of his luncheon with de Gaulle and its aftermath is in the Minutes of War Cabinet No. 169 of 1940, 16 June 1940, 3 p.m.: Cabinet papers, 65/7, folio 315.

to France that night, and had suggested that Churchill himself should return to France in order to meet Reynaud 'next day'.

The draft Declaration of Union was then passed around the War Cabinet and a discussion began in which the Declaration was scrutinized clause by clause. 'At this most fateful moment in the history of the modern world,' the draft began, 'the Governments of the United Kingdom and the French Republic desire to make a declaration of indissoluble union . . .'. There were no longer to be 'two nations', but in their place 'one Franco-British Union'. There would be 'joint organs' of defence, foreign, financial and economic policies. Every citizen of the one country would enjoy 'immediate citizenship' of the other. While the war lasted, all the forces of Britain and France, whether on land, sea or in the air, would be placed under the direction of 'a single War Cabinet'. The draft ended with brave words with which the War Cabinet had no quarrel. 'The Union,' it declared, 'will concentrate its whole energy against the power of the enemy, no matter where the battle may be. And thus we shall conquer.'

As the discussion continued, it was clear not only that the War Cabinet approved of these concepts of Union, but that the idea of such a Union coming into being was inspiring them to the hope of a miracle in France. His own 'first instinct', Churchill admitted, 'had been against the idea', but, he added, 'in this grave crisis we must not let ourselves be accused of a lack of imagination. Some dramatic announcement was clearly needed to keep the French going. The proposal could not be lightly brushed aside, and he was encouraged to find such a body of opinion in the War Cabinet in favour of it.'

The discussion had lasted an hour when, at 3.55 p.m., news was brought to the War Cabinet of a French wireless announcement that the Council of Ministers would meet at Bordeaux at 5 p.m. 'to decide whether further resistance was possible'. The War Cabinet was also told that de Gaulle had been informed by Reynaud on the telephone 'that if a favourable answer on the proposed proclamation of unity was received by 5 p.m. M. Reynaud felt that he would be able to hold the position'.[1]

This message was decisive. Sir Edward Bridges, the Cabinet Secretary, left the Cabinet room to dictate the formal wording of the Declaration of Union, according to the comments of the various War Cabinet members. In the room adjoining the Cabinet room, de Gaulle and Corbin were waiting, together with Vansittart and Morton. Bridges brought Churchill the draft, and he at once left the Cabinet room with

[1] War Cabinet No. 169 of 1940, 3 p.m., 16 June 1940: Cabinet papers, 65/7.

it, to show it to its begetters. The General, he later recalled, 'read it with an air of unwonted enthusiasm'.[1]

Churchill now returned once more to the Cabinet room, this time together with de Gaulle, as the final touches to the Declaration of Union were hammered out. The meeting, as Colville noted in his diary, 'turned into a sort of promenade', with, as he described the ensuing scene:

... Winston beginning a speech in the Cabinet Room and finishing it in some other room; and everybody has been slapping de Gaulle on the back and telling him he shall be Commander in Chief (Winston muttering: 'Je l'arrangerai').

Is he to be a new Napoleon? From what I hear, it seems that a lot of people think so. He treats Reynaud (whom he called 'ce poisson gelé' at one point) like dirt and discourses familiarly on what he will do in France: yet he is only a major-general just recently discovered.

Meanwhile the King does not know what is being done to his Empire. The Lord President[2] is going to see him and will break the news. We may yet see the Fleur de Lys restored to the Royal Standard ...[3]

By 4.30 p.m. the Declaration of Union was complete. The War Cabinet, which was still in session, at once authorized its immediate despatch to Reynaud 'by the hand of General de Gaulle'. It was also decided to telephone the text to Reynaud in time for the imminent meeting of the Council of Ministers. As insurance that the full impact of the proposed Union would be understood, the War Cabinet also invited Churchill, Attlee and Sinclair, as the senior representatives of the three principal British political parties, to go to France 'at the earliest possible moment' to meet Reynaud, and to discuss the 'draft Proclamation' with him.[4]

Before de Gaulle left for France, he had one further discussion with Churchill, together with Jean Monnet. It was Monnet who pressed, once again, for the despatch of Britain's remaining fighter squadrons to the battle in France. Churchill explained that no such order could be given, but Monnet insisted that this was 'the decisive battle', it was 'now or never', 'if France falls, all fall'.

Churchill had no authority to make any such change of the War Cabinet's decision not to send further air forces to France. Nor did he believe that such a move could, at this late stage, help either France or

---

[1] Winston S. Churchill, *The Second World War*, volume 2, London 1949, page 184.
[2] Neville Chamberlain.
[3] John Colville, *Footprints in Time*, London 1976, pages 88–9.
[4] War Cabinet No. 169 of 1940, 3 p.m., 16 June 1940, Cabinet papers, 65/7.

Britain. All now depended upon Reynaud being persuaded by the Declaration of Union not to seek an armistice. Churchill therefore told Monnet that no more aircraft could be sent. Then, as Churchill recalled, his two French visitors got up and moved towards the door, Monnet leading. As they reached the door, de Gaulle, 'who had hitherto scarcely uttered a single word, turned back, and, taking two or three paces towards me, said, in English: "I think you are quite right." ' [1]

De Gaulle left Downing Street for the airport and for France. As soon as he had gone, Churchill prepared for his own journey to France with Attlee and Sinclair. A special train was organized, ready to leave Waterloo at 9.30 that same evening, for Southampton. A cruiser, the *Galatea*, then at Southampton, was ordered to be ready by midnight to sail for Concarneau, or some other point off the coast of Brittany, with the aim of reaching the French coast by noon the following day, where Churchill and Reynaud would meet on board ship.

The three Chiefs of Staff were likewise to make the long journey to Brittany, as was General Ismay. Another senior official chosen to go on this desperate mission was Sir Alexander Cadogan, who noted in his diary that he had been somewhat mysteriously summoned to leave 'on a sea trip tonight'. [2]

There was to be no sea trip that night, nor any return to France for Churchill for another four years. 'We had taken our seats in the train,' Churchill later recalled. 'My wife had come to see me off. There was an odd delay in starting. Evidently some hitch had occurred.'

Churchill and his colleagues waited, puzzled, on board the train at Waterloo. Unknown to them, a message had reached Downing Street from Sir Ronald Campbell in Bordeaux to say that a Ministerial crisis had 'opened' in France, and that the meeting between Churchill and Reynaud was now 'impossible'. The train had been told not to start, and a Private Secretary hurried to Waterloo with Campbell's message. As soon as he read the message, Churchill returned to Downing Street 'with a heavy heart'. [3] The powers of national and personal persuasion were not to be put to the test. The Declaration of Union was no longer a factor in the fate of France.

That same day, in the United States, a decisive transfer of authority was taking place: an agreement between the French Government, still

[1] Winston S. Churchill, *The Second World War*, volume 2, London 1949, page 189.
[2] Cadogan diary, 16 June 1940: David Dilks (editor), *The Diaries of Sir Alexander Cadogan, OM, 1938–1945*, London 1971, page 303.
[3] Winston S. Churchill, *The Second World War*, volume 2, London 1949, page 186.

headed by Reynaud, and His Majesty's Government. The agreement was signed by J. Frédéric Bloch-Lainé, Vice-Chairman of the Anglo-French Purchasing Board, and Arthur Purvis, the Board's Chairman. As Director General of French Purchases overseas, Bloch-Lainé had the powers to sign, and through his signature to transfer all French contracts in the United States to full British control. The 132 principal contracts transferred included orders for aircraft engines, spares, essential parts, instruments, machine guns and 965 bombers. These contracts had a contracted value of more than ninety million dollars.[1] There was also a series of contracts for machine tools, worth more than eighty-six million dollars, and other contracts for substantial quantities of petrol, brass and zinc.[2]

At Purvis' insistence, the United States was also made a party to this transfer, with United States Treasury lawyers brought in to ensure, as Purvis' secretary later recalled, that the transfer was legal according to United States law. 'They were wandering about from room to room,' she added, 'trying to work out how to transfer the orders from France to England.'[3]

The Anglo-French agreement, signed by Bloch-Lainé and Purvis on June 16, gave Britain a substantial extra source of future military supplies in the United States, and influenced every aspect of Britain's war needs. Nine days later, Lindemann drafted for Churchill a note about the impact of the agreement on the supply of steel. Owing to the transfer to Britain of French contracts, he wrote, 'our programme of purchases for the coming month has more than doubled and that we are now buying at the rate of about 600,000 tons a month. This is satisfactory, and we should certainly get as much from the United States as we can.'

In sending this note to Herbert Morrison, Churchill added at the end of the final sentence: 'while we are able to'.[4]

The June 16 agreement with France had been signed not a day too soon. Indeed, as the evening of June 16 wore on, the news from France took a decisive turn for the worse. As one of Churchill's Private Secretaries, John Martin, noted in his diary late that night: 'Reynaud resigned. Pétain to form Government.'[5] A few hours later, Pétain asked the Germans for an armistice. Britain was alone.

[1] Agreement 16 June 1940: Cabinet papers, 92/27.
[2] 'Assignment of French Contracts', 16 June 1940: Cabinet papers, 115/735.
[3] E. Lucille Brady, conversation with the author, Montreal, 14 November 1982.
[4] Lindemann draft, 24 June 1940; Churchill addition, 25 June 1940: Premier papers, 3/412/1, folio 3. The note was sent to Morrison as if written entirely by Churchill.
[5] Martin diary, 16 June 1940: Martin papers.

That evening Churchill looked up a memorandum he had written four years earlier, in June 1936. In it he had asked the Ministers of the day to consider what might happen if 200 German troop carrying aircraft, each with fifty soldiers, together with a hundred aircraft with stores and ammunition, were to be located making 'towards (say) Newcastle'.

Reprinting this memorandum for the War Cabinet on June 16, Churchill commented, in a covering note: 'We are asked to consider many plans of possible invasion by Germany, some of these seem to me very absurd. I have, however, always had anxiety about the Tyne, and I should be glad if the points made in the attached paper . . . could be reviewed.' Although Churchill presumed that an attack on Newcastle could not now succeed, he would be glad, he said, if the Home Defence authorities 'would trace out what the reactions which would follow such an attempt would be, and how they would deal with it'.

Churchill's memorandum of 1936 had ended with a sentence which, four years later, still summed up one of his strongest convictions. 'Perhaps,' he had written then, 'if people were told of their dangers, they would consent to make the necessary sacrifices.'[1]

---

[1] 'Invasion by Air, note by the Right Hon. Winston S. Churchill, CH, MP, June 1936', 'Printed for the War Cabinet, 16 June 1940': Cabinet papers, 120/10.

28

The Fall of France

M ONDAY, 17 June 1940, Britain's first day 'alone', did not create the widespread panic that Hitler might have expected. As Dowding wrote that day to Churchill, from the Headquarters of Fighter Command: 'Well! now it is England against Germany, and I don't envy them their job.'[1] But the strain of events was formidable. From Bordeaux, Cherbourg, St Malo, Brest and St Nazaire, the evacuation of British, French, Belgian and Polish troops had begun. At the same time, all British Air Forces in the south of France were ordered to evacuate their bases and return home.

That morning, at the War Cabinet, there was 'general agreement' that 'now that the French Government under Marshal Pétain were suing for an armistice, we would be sacrificing our men to no purpose if we told them to fight on'.[2] These new evacuations had none of the public drama of those at Dunkirk. The little boats that crossed to Cherbourg and St Malo in operation 'Ariel' never obtained the public spotlight of 'Dynamo' at Dunkirk.[3] Nor did the British public learn of the tragedy of the liner *Lancastria* which, with five thousand soldiers and evacuees on board, was bombed just as she prepared to leave St Nazaire.

Nearly three thousand of those on board the *Lancastria* were killed, most of them by drowning. 'When this news came to me in the quiet Cabinet Room during the afternoon,' Churchill later wrote, 'I forbade its publication, saying: "The newspapers have got quite enough disaster for to-day at least." I had intended to release the news a few days

[1] Letter of 17 June 1940: Churchill papers, 2/393.
[2] War Cabinet No. 170 of 1940, 17 June 1940, 11 a.m.: Cabinet papers, 65/7.
[3] The evacuations from Cherbourg and St Malo were completed on the afternoon of 18 June 1940 ('Operation Ariel', Report of 19 June 1940: Admiralty papers, 1/10481).

later, but events crowded upon us so black and so quickly that I forgot
to lift the ban, and it was some time before the knowledge of this
horror became public.'[1]

From the moment that the French Government made it clear that it
would seek an armistice with Germany, the immediate worry, and
greatest danger, was the possibility of France's powerful Fleet becoming
an adjunct of the German war arsenal. For the next two weeks, British
efforts focused on how to prevent the French ships, especially those at
Oran, from being transferred to German control. At the War Cabinet
on the morning of June 17 Eden pointed out that the telegram to
Reynaud insisting that the French fleet 'sail forthwith to British harbours' had been suspended by the Declaration of Union. Sir Ronald
Campbell had now been instructed to deliver the telegram to Marshal
Pétain. At Churchill's suggestion, Eden agreed to send a further telegram, pointing out that if the French Government sought an armistice
'without fulfilling this condition, our consent would not be forthcoming'.[2]

British consent was now academic. Fears for the future of the French
Fleet, however, were widespread. 'Camrose telephoned me in some
agitation,' Harold Nicolson noted in his diary that day. 'He is very
much afraid that if the Germans get hold of the French fleet, we shall
have no chance at all.'[3] At Downing Street, a telegram from Pétain's
new Foreign Minister, Paul Baudouin, made it appear, however, as
Colville noted, that 'the surrender of the Fleet may be refused', and
there were a series of false hopes generated during the day. 'Perhaps,'
Colville wrote, 'the new Government will in the end accept the Declaration if they consider Germany's terms cannot honourably be
accepted.'

But despite this comment, Colville realized that all was indeed lost.
'If only the Declaration had been agreed 24 hours earlier,' he wrote,
'Reynaud, supported by Mandel and de Gaulle and who knows by a
whiff of grapeshot, might have saved the situation.'[4]

During June 17 the deposed Reynaud wrote direct to Churchill:
'The project of Franco-British Union is worthy of your imagination
and your daring. It is there that the future lies for our two countries.'
In leaving office, Reynaud added, 'I tell you once more of my faith in

[1] Winston S. Churchill, *The Second World War*, volume 2, London 1949, page 172. The truth
about the *Lancastria* was made public at the end of July (see page 685, note 2).
[2] War Cabinet No. 170 of 1940, 17 June 1940, 11 a.m.: Cabinet papers, 65/7.
[3] Nicolson diary, 17 June 1940: Nigel Nicolson (editor), *Harold Nicolson, Diaries and Letters,
1939-1945*, London 1967, page 96.
[4] Colville diary, 17 June 1940: Colville papers.

final victory, my unbreakable allegiance to the common cause, and my friendship.'[1]

While the War Cabinet of June 17 was still in session, a message was brought in reporting that French troops had ceased fire at 12.40. Nothing was said. But when the War Cabinet ended, as Colville noted in his diary, 'the PM paced backwards and forwards in the garden alone, his head bowed, his hands behind his back'. He was doubtless considering, Colville added, 'how best the French Fleet, the Air Force and the Colonies would be saved. He I am sure will remain undaunted.'[2]

That afternoon Churchill spoke for two minutes over the BBC, telling the nation:

The news from France is very bad, and I grieve for the gallant French people who have fallen into this terrible misfortune. Nothing will alter our feelings towards them or our faith that the genius of France will rise again. What has happened in France makes no difference to our actions and purpose. We have become the sole champions now in arms to defend the world cause. We shall do our best to be worthy of this high honour. We shall defend our Island home, and with the British Empire we shall fight on unconquerable until the curse of Hitler is lifted from the brows of mankind. We are sure that in the end all will come right.[3]

Churchill's vigilance, and his awareness of the wide-ranging details of war policy, were again evident in his minutes of June 17. Above all, he urged the Minister of Supply, Herbert Morrison, to push forward 'large scale production' of field guns in the United States, and to arrange for the manufacture of ammunition for these guns in the United Kingdom. 'There are objections,' he wrote, 'to having two types in one army, but we are not in a position to indulge them.' The plan must be the eventual arming of 55 divisions. 'Anything you can do to accelerate delivery will be of immense benefit. An immediate speed up of delivery is everything.'[4]

---

[1] Letter of 17 June 1940: Foreign Office papers, 800/362.

[2] Colville diary, 17 June 1940: Colville papers.

[3] Broadcast, 17 June 1940: BBC Written Archives. As we have already seen, the phrase 'all will come right' was one of Churchill's favourite ones, the motto of the Orange Free State President, Martinus Steyn. Churchill had first heard it in South Africa forty years before. In Afrikaans: 'Alle sal reg kom.'

[4] Minute to the Minister of Supply (Herbert Morrison), 17 June 1940. The two types were the 25 pounder (UK) and the 75 millimetre (USA): Churchill papers, 20/13. It was intended that the 55 divisions should be formed and equipped by June 1941 (Churchill to Desmond Morton, 19 June 1940: Churchill papers, 20/13).

There were also naval dispositions to be suggested, both to guard against an Italian invasion of Egypt, and to plan for the seizure of the Canary Islands, as Britain's reply to any possible Spanish declaration of war, with the consequent loss of Gibraltar. With the Canary Islands in British hands, Churchill wrote, it would not be necessary to 'quit the Eastern Mediterranean', even with Gibraltar gone.[1]

That night Churchill decided to appeal at once to the new French leader, and to Weygand, about the future of the French fleet. Sir Alexander Cadogan was summoned to advise. 'PM had a scorching message to Pétain and Weygand,' he noted in his diary. 'I tried to tone it down a bit, but failed. So sent it off.'[2] In this message, Churchill expressed what he called 'my profound conviction that the illustrious Marshal Pétain and the famous General Weygand, our comrades in two great wars, will not injure their ally by delivering over to the enemy the fine French fleet'. Such an act, Churchill added, 'would scarify their names for a thousand years of history'. Now was the time to cease 'frittering away these few precious hours' when the French fleet could still be sailed to British or United States ports 'carrying with it the hope of the future and the honour of France'.[3]

That same day, from Bordeaux airport, at General Spears' suggestion, General de Gaulle was brought back to Britain in the very aeroplane in which he had carried the Declaration of Union to France on the previous night.

It was one o'clock in the morning when Churchill's telegram to Pétain and Weygand was ready to be despatched. Britain's first day 'alone' had come to an end, and the members of Churchill's Private Secretariat prepared for a brief respite before the new dawn. Nor was their master oblivious of the strain which he, and events, put upon them. 'The PM gave me such a kind and human goodnight,' John Martin wrote home, 'when he went up to bed at 1 o'clock this morning—put his hand on my arm and said he was sorry there had been no time in all the rush of these days to get to know me.'[4]

That night Ironside noted in his diary: 'There is no doubt that Winston has any amount of courage and experience. Thrown with his

---

[1] Minute to the First Lord of the Admiralty (A. V. Alexander), 17 June 1940: Churchill papers, 20/13. The plan to seize the Canary Islands was given the code name 'Bugle'. Its parallel operations were to be against the Cape Verde Islands ('Shrapnel') and the Azores ('Alloy').

[2] Cadogan diary, 17 June 1940: David Dilks (editor), *The Diaries of Sir Alexander Cadogan OM, 1938–1945*, London 1971, page 304.

[3] Telegram to Sir R. Campbell (Bordeaux), 17 June 1940: Churchill papers, 20/14.

[4] Letter of 17 June 1940: Martin papers.

back to the wall, he may lose some of his lack of balance.' But, Ironside added, 'He is quite undismayed by the state of affairs.'[1]

In a further attempt to prevent the French Fleet from being transferred to German control, both A. V. Alexander and Dudley Pound flew to Bordeaux on June 18 to appeal directly to Admiral Darlan. Their mission did not seem in vain. If the armistice terms were 'dishonourable', Darlan told them, 'the Fleet would fight to the end and anything that escaped would go to a friendly country or be destroyed'.[2] These were encouraging words. In London meanwhile, Lord Beaverbrook was able to make an equally encouraging report about the British production of new aircraft, which, he informed the War Cabinet, had risen from 245 a week to 363 a week, and production of aircraft engines from 411 to 620 a week.[3]

Also during June 18, Churchill learned of the successful evacuation of more than 40,000 troops from Cherbourg, Brest, St Malo and St Nazaire, despite the twin setbacks of the *Lancastria* disaster and the advance of German forces to the Loire.[4]

It was the anniversary of Waterloo, a day which, 125 years earlier, had seen the end of more than fifteen years of danger. As had the younger Pitt in the early years of the Napoleonic wars, Churchill now contemplated invasion, and, in a minute to Ismay, asked for a meeting with several senior Army officers, including the Chief Staff Officer to the Commander-in-Chief, Home Forces, General Paget. He wished to discuss the state of Britain's coastal defences, the numbers of troops held in reserve, and tank supply.

Churchill also wondered whether something might not be gained by emulating the German 'Storm Troop' formations. 'We have always set our faces against this idea,' he told Ismay, 'but the Germans certainly gained in the last War by adopting it, and this time it has been a leading cause of their victory.' There ought, Churchill wrote, to be at least 20,000 British Storm Troops—or 'Leopards' as he wished to call them—'drawn from existing Units, ready to spring at the throat of any

[1] Ironside diary, 17 June 1940: Roderick Macleod and Denis Kelly (editors), *The Ironside Diaries, 1937–1940*, London 1962, pages 366–7.

[2] Report of a conversation between A. V. Alexander, Sir Dudley Pound and Admiral Darlan, 19 June 1940: Admiralty papers, 205/4.

[3] Report of 18 June 1940: A. J. P. Taylor, *Beaverbrook*, London 1972, page 442. The report was submitted on the following day: Cabinet papers, 66/8.

[4] War Cabinet Joint Intelligence Sub-Committee, Special Report No. 92, 18 June 1940: Premier papers, 3/175.

small landings or descents'. These officers and men should be armed with the latest equipment, 'tommy guns, grenades etc' and given 'great facilities' also in motor-cycles and armoured cars.[1]

The problem was not solely one of soldiers and weapons; there was also the question of criticism of the conduct of the war, and the pressure, voiced by the Press, for the pre-War Ministers to be replaced.

In a speech to Parliament on the afternoon of June 18, Churchill dealt first with this aspect of public feeling, insisting that during 'the battle in France' the British Government had sent 'every man we could', as fast as they could be re-equipped and transported. Re-crimination as to whether Britain had done enough, he warned, would be 'utterly futile and even harmful'. Britain had now to think 'of the future and not of the past'; not only abroad, but also at home. His speech continued:

There are many who would hold an inquest in the House of Commons on the conduct of the Governments—and of Parliaments, for they are in it, too—during the years which led up to this catastrophe. They seek to indict those who were responsible for the guidance of our affairs. This also would be a foolish and pernicious process. There are too many in it. Let each man search his conscience and search his speeches. I frequently search mine.

Of this I am quite sure, that if we open a quarrel between the past and the present, we shall find that we have lost the future. Therefore, I cannot accept the drawing of any distinctions between Members of the present Government. It was formed at a moment of crisis in order to unite all the parties and all sections of opinion. It has received the almost unanimous support of both Houses of Parliament. Its Members are going to stand together, and, subject to the authority of the House of Commons, we are going to govern the country and fight the war. It is absolutely necessary at a time like this that every Minister who tries each day to do his duty shall be respected, and their subordinates must know that their chiefs are not threatened men, men who are here to-day and gone to-morrow, but that their directions must be punctually and faithfully obeyed. Without this concentrated power we cannot face what lies before us.

Churchill then spoke with confidence of Britain's ability to meet an invading force, on land, at sea, and in the air. 'I look forward confidently,' he said, 'to the exploits of our fighter pilots, who will have the glory of saving their native land, their island home, and all they love, from the most deadly of all attacks.'

Anticipating the German bombing raids which, he said, 'will certainly be made very soon upon us', Churchill told the House:

[1] Minute of 18 June 1940: Churchill papers, 20/13.

I do not at all underrate the severity of the ordeal which lies before us, but I believe our countrymen will show themselves capable of standing up to it, like the brave men of Barcelona, and will be able to stand up to it, and carry on in spite of it, at least as well as any other people in the world. Much will depend upon this, and every man and every woman will have the chance to show the finest qualities of their race and render the highest service to their cause. For all of us at this time, whatever our sphere, our station, our occupation, our duties, it will be a help to remember the famous lines: 'He nothing common did or mean, Upon that memorable scene.'[1]

Churchill did not disguise those ways in which Britain's position had 'worsened' since the beginning of the war, above all the German control of a large part of the coastline of western Europe, which 'aggravates the possibilities of air attack and adds to our naval preoccupations'. But the German ability to draw on the resources of western Europe was paralleled, he said, by Britain's assurance of 'immense, continuous and increasing' supplies of arms for Britain from the United States, and also, 'especially of aeroplanes and pilots', from the Dominions, regions beyond the reach of German bombers. In addition, as a result of the air battles above Dunkirk and over northern France, Britain had learned 'what we had no right to assume at the beginning, namely, the individual superiority of our aircraft and pilots'. Therefore, Churchill declared, 'in casting up this dread balance-sheet, contemplating our dangers with a disillusioned eye, I see great reason for intense vigilance and exertion, but none whatever for panic or despair'.

Churchill had spoken for just over half an hour. He had set out his reasons for the ability of Britain to survive the fall of France. He had warned of the imminent danger of air attack and invasion. 'What General Weygand called the "Battle of France" is over,' he said. 'I expect that the battle of Britain is about to begin,' and he ended:

Upon this battle depends the survival of Christian civilisation. Upon it depends our own British life and the long continuity of our institutions and our Empire. The whole fury and might of the enemy must very soon be turned on us. Hitler knows that he will have to break us in this island or lose the war. If we can stand up to him, all Europe may be free, and the life of the world may move forward into broad, sunlit uplands; but if we fail, then the whole world, including the United States, and all that we have known and cared for, will

[1] John Colville wrote in his diary that night: 'I was amused that he brought in Marvell's line, because he has been repeating it consistently and often irrelevantly for the last fortnight. Last Saturday he came out with it several times in the course of the evening, and could not resist quoting it to the American Ambassador on the telephone while demanding assistance from the United States' (Colville diary, 18 June 1940: Colville papers).

sink into the abyss of a new dark age made more sinister, and perhaps more protracted, by the lights of a perverted science.

Let us therefore brace ourselves to our duty and so bear ourselves that if the British Empire and its Commonwealth lasts for a thousand years men will still say, 'This was their finest hour.'[1]

These were 'only words', Churchill later reflected. Foreigners who did not understand 'the temper of the British race all over the globe when its blood is up might have supposed that they were only a bold front, set up as a good prelude for peace negotiations'. He was himself fully aware that, as he phrased it, 'Rhetoric was no guarantee of survival.' Peace terms might have been offered for which many 'plausible excuses' could have been presented. Why, many might have asked, should Britain not join the 'spectators' in neutral Japan, the United States, Sweden and Spain, to watch with detached interest, 'or even relish a mutually destructive struggle between the Nazi and Communist Empires?'[2]

The answer lay in the sincerity of Churchill's sentiments, and in the response of the listeners. Yet of the speech which was to become a legend in Churchill's own lifetime, Colville, who heard him deliver it, wrote that night: 'He spoke less well than on the last occasion and referred more often to his notes.' But, Colville added, 'he ended magnificently'.[3]

Four hours later Churchill broadcast the same speech. This was the version heard and remembered by several million listeners. Harold Nicolson, Parliamentary Under-Secretary of State at the Ministry of Information, who heard both the Commons speech and the broadcast one, wrote to his wife:

How I wish Winston would not talk on the wireless unless he is feeling in good form. He hates the microphone, and when we bullied him into speaking last night, he just sulked and read his House of Commons speech over again. Now, as delivered in the House of Commons, that speech was magnificent, especially the concluding sentences. But it sounded ghastly on the wireless. All the great vigour he put into it seemed to evaporate.[4]

'It was too long,' Colville noted that night of the speech as broadcast, 'and he sounded tired.'[5]

---

[1] Speech began at 3.49 p.m., ended at 4.25 p.m.: *Hansard*, 18 June 1940, columns 51–61.

[2] Winston S. Churchill, *The Second World War*, volume 2, London 1949, page 199.

[3] Colville diary, 18 June 1940: Colville papers.

[4] Harold Nicolson to Vita Sackville-West, 19 June 1940: in Nigel Nicolson (editor), *Harold Nicolson, Diaries and Letters, 1939–1945*, London 1967, pages 96–7.

[5] Colville diary, 18 June 1940: Colville papers. In a letter home three days later John Martin

Between the speech and the broadcast Churchill had been given a telegram from Sir Ronald Campbell, reporting that the new French Government felt it would be 'dishonourable' to negotiate an armistice unless their armed forces were still intact, even though it seemed likely, Campbell added, that the French Fleet 'would be denied to the Germans'. On being brought this message, Churchill enquired: 'Another bloody country gone west?'[1]

Campell's telegram maintained the illusion that the French Fleet, especially those ships then at Oran, might not be transferred to German control, even by Pétain. At the suggestion of Jean Monnet, strongly backed by Corbin and Vansittart, Churchill agreed to send a third emissary to Darlan at Bordeaux, Lord Lloyd, to see if it might still be possible to save the French Fleet.

Yet another problem created by the disasters in France was the future of the Belgian Government and the Belgian Empire. Not only was the Belgian Government already on its way southward, in exile, through France towards the Pyrenees, but there was concern in London that it might, on going into a second exile in Spain, declare its neutrality, and the neutrality of the Belgian territories in Africa. 'The most strenuous efforts,' Churchill minuted to Cadogan, 'should be made to rally the Belgians to their duty. There can be no question of their going out of the war. If they do, we will wash our hands of their interests altogether, and they must clearly understand that their Colonies will not be allowed to form part of the German system as long as we can prevent this by sea action.' Had the Admiralty already taken steps, Churchill asked Cadogan, 'to lay forcible hands on all Belgian shipping within our reach', and he added: 'Will you very kindly put this all in motion.'[2]

During the night of June 18, some 120 German bombers attacked

---

noted: 'Back in the evening on Tuesday in time for the PM's broadcast. His halting delivery at the start seems to have struck people and we had e.g. a telegram from someone saying that he evidently had something wrong with his heart and ought to work in a recumbent position. The fact was, I gather, that he spoke with a cigar in his mouth.' (Letter of 21 June 1940: Martin papers.) As a result of this episode there was 'a proposal that such speeches should be broadcast direct from the House of Commons, and Churchill would have welcomed that relief; but, when he found that opinion in the House was opposed to such an innovation, he did not pursue it (Sir John Martin, letter to the author, 24 October 1982).

[1] Colville diary, 18 June 1940: Colville papers.
[2] Minute dated 18 June 1940: Premiers papers, 3/69A, folio 150.

eastern England. Nine people were killed in Cambridge and an oil fire started at Canvey Island. At the War Cabinet on the morning of June 19, there was puzzlement at the 'rather purposeless and half-hearted way' in which the raid had been carried out, and Churchill hoped that during future raids 'a careful watch would be kept' on the expenditure of anti-aircraft ammunition. There were first reports, also, of fighting on the Egyptian-Libyan frontier between British and Italian troops. Of 300 Italians 'encountered', at least 20 had been killed and the rest captured, including an Italian General.

Even as this discussion continued, good news of a more important kind was brought in by Sir Dudley Pound, who had just returned from his mission to Bordeaux, and who reported to the War Cabinet that Admiral Darlan, who had seemed 'calm and determined', had throughout their conversation 'steadfastly maintained that in no circumstances would the French Fleet be surrendered'.

There were several emergency decisions to be taken during that morning's War Cabinet, including a suggestion by the Secretary of State for Dominion Affairs, Viscount Caldecote—formerly, as Sir Thomas Inskip, Minister for the Co-ordination of Defence—that Britain seize four destroyers, built in Italy for neutral Sweden, and at that very moment on their way from Eire to the Faroe Islands; 'a pretty high-handed proceeding', as Halifax wrote to Sir Samuel Hoare in Madrid, 'but, as they have little chance of getting to Sweden, we had better have them. . . .'[1]

Another emergency concerned the Channel Islands, and here a decision had to be made. The Chiefs of Staff had concluded that the Islands could not be defended, and recommended their demilitarization as soon as their aerodromes were no longer required for the evacuations from France.[2] Churchill opposed this recommendation, feeling that with the proper use of British sea power an invasion of the Islands could be prevented. 'It was repugnant now,' he said, 'to abandon British territory which had been in the possession of the Crown since the Norman Conquest.'

The Chiefs of Staff defended their conclusion, pointing out that it was 'impossible' to provide either anti-aircraft guns or fighters for the defence of the Channel Islands. As for the Islands Government itself, reported the Home Secretary, Sir John Anderson, it felt 'bound to

---

[1] Personal and Confidential, letter of 19 June 1940: Foreign Office papers, 800/323/H/XXXIV/30. Hoare had been appointed Ambassador to Spain at the end of May.

[2] War Cabinet Memorandum No. 208 of 1940, 19 June 1940: Cabinet papers, 66/8.

acquiesce in the policy of abandoning active defence'. Churchill deferred to these arguments.[1]

Earlier that morning Churchill had accepted General Paget's argument that British Storm Troopers as such should not be created. In their place Paget proposed the formation of special 'Tank Hunting Platoons', independent companies, and 'Special Irregular Units' including American volunteers. He warned, however, that no effective counter-attacks could be carried out 'without the requisite weapons'.[2]

Within ten days, nine special 'Leopard' groups had been set up, and six more were in the course of formation. British pre-war rearmament had not been on a sufficient scale to permit such schemes on any larger scale, whether on land or in the air. This was galling to Churchill, and yet, as Dill wrote to him that day: 'Your stupendous burden of today must to some small extent be lightened by the knowledge that your conscience is clear regarding the complete lack of preparedness of this country for war with Germany.'[3] Dill ended his letter: 'May I take this opportunity of saying how greatly I admire your courage and vitality in these dark days.'[4]

That evening Churchill, Beaverbrook, Pound, Phillips and Cadogan spent an hour together discussing the naval and legal implications of seizing the Swedish destroyers, as Caldecote and Halifax had proposed. Churchill also took steps to ensure that the tens of thousands of Polish troops still fighting in France should be able to reach Britain, a request which had been put to him that morning by the Polish Commander-in-Chief, General Sikorski. The Admiralty, Churchill minuted to Ismay, 'shd be asked to make every effort to evacuate the Polish forces and personnel'.[5] Plans were also made to occupy the Irish ports in the event of a worsening of the naval situation.[6]

---

[1] War Cabinet No. 172, 19 June 1940, 12.30 p.m.: Cabinet papers, 65/7.

[2] Defence Committee No. 17 of 1940, 19 June 1940, 10 a.m.: Cabinet papers, 69/1.

[3] Dill was thanking Churchill for a copy of *Arms and the Covenant*, an edition of Churchill's pre-war speeches on rearmament, originally published in 1938, compiled by Randolph Churchill.

[4] Letter of 19 June 1940: Churchill papers, 2/393. Ironside shared Dill's feelings, noting, of that morning's Defence Committee: 'Winston in good form and gingering people up. His energy is unabated' (Ironside diary, 19 June 1940: Roderick Maclead and Denis Kelly, editors, *The Ironside Diaries, 1937–1940*, London 1962, page 367).

[5] Minute of 19 June 1940: Premier papers, 3/351/1. The arrangements were made, as Churchill had requested, and of 25,000 Polish soldiers then in France, a total of 19,541 were evacuated by the time of the Franco-German armistice three weeks later.

[6] These plans had been outlined on 14 June 1940 (code-name 'Alcohol'). On 19 June 1940 they were prepared in greater detail for both Berehaven (code-name 'Kummel') and Queenstown Harbour ('Julep').

29

'No-one is down-hearted here'

ON the morning of June 20, as Marshal Pétain's plenipotentiaries set out for the forest of Compiègne to receive the German armistice terms, General Ismay was able to report to Churchill the successful evacuation of 111,505 British personnel from France, leaving only 16,000 'unaccounted for'.[1] At a meeting of the Supply Committee that morning, Churchill heard of tank production targets for March 1941, made possible only by the production of certain essential parts, in the United States.[2] Aircraft production plans were less easy to determine. 'It is always very difficult to deal with the Air Ministry,' Churchill minuted to Ismay, 'because of the variety of the figures which they give,' and he urged Ismay to insist upon the current conflicting sets of figures 'being reconciled immediately, and the many discrepancies explained'.[3]

It was the problem of armaments supply which cast the darkest shadow over Britain's ability to resist an invading force. The next major problem was whether General Paget was able to make the necessary plans to repel an invader. 'Winston is goading the C-in-C Home Forces,' Colville noted in his diary, 'who seems to lack imagination, and is busy forming special anti-tank forces of mobile troops. He is also taking the question of supply very seriously and has meetings almost every morning now.' Colville added that Professor Lindemann was Churchill's 'right hand man in this'.[4]

When the War Cabinet met at noon, the First Lord, A. V. Alexan-

---

[1] 'Secret', 20 June 1940: Premier papers, 3/175, folio 2.
[2] Defence Committee (Supply) No. 6 of 1940, 10 a.m., 20 June 1940: Cabinet papers, 70/1. The responsibility for procuring these essential war materials was that of Arthur Purvis who, on the demise of the Anglo-French Purchasing Commission at midnight on 16 June 1940, had become Chairman of the British Purchasing Commission.
[3] Minute of 20 June 1940: Churchill papers, 20/13.
[4] Colville diary, 20 June 1940: Colville papers.

der, learned further news of the French Fleet, being told that Pétain himself had assured both Lloyd and Pound—who had emphasized Britain's 'heavy destroyer losses'—that he would 'never allow' French destroyers 'to fall into German hands'. Alexander also reported Darlan's 'firm purpose' that the French Fleet should not only go on fighting, but 'should be kept by any means possible from falling into the hands of the enemy'.

Fearing that the French might decide to scuttle their Fleet as an alternative to surrender, Churchill suggested that the French authorities might be persuaded to make 'greater efforts to get the vessels away' if the United States were to offer to buy them. The money could be used to maintain French refugees overseas, or for the rehabilitation of French territory after the war.

Another fear discussed at the War Cabinet, and at considerable length, was of a German invasion of Eire. Neville Chamberlain suggested a firm approach to de Valera, who should be urged to 'give the British Navy' the use of the Irish Atlantic ports, to allow British troops and air forces to enter Eire 'before the invasion occurs', and to forestall the fifth column danger by interning 'all the leaders of the IRA still at large' as well as 'any suspicious Germans and Italians'. But, when Chamberlain explained that in return for this Britain should declare its support for 'the establishment of a United Ireland', Churchill replied that the Government must avoid putting 'undue pressure' on the loyal province of Ulster, that he 'was not convinced' that the military threat to Eire was as serious as it has been represented, and that if the Germans did in fact land in Eire, 'our forces should be ready to pounce upon them'.[1]

In his diary, Cadogan noted that Churchill had opposed in a 'passionate speech' what looked like Chamberlain's advocacy of the 'coercion' of North Ireland.[2] Churchill was equally emphatic in opposing a Foreign Office suggestion to evacuate civilians from Iceland in order to protect them from possible air attack, minuting to Halifax that the Icelanders had 'a large island and plenty of places to run into'.[3]

That afternoon the House of Commons met for the first time in Secret Session, to hear a full report of the military situation. Churchill spoke at the end of the session. No verbatim record survives, but his speech notes began with praise for the 'Cool and robust' mood of the

[1] War Cabinet No. 173 of 1940, 20 June 1940, 12 noon: Cabinet papers, 65/7.
[2] Cadogan diary, 20 June 1940, quoted in: David Dilks (editor), *The Diaries of Sir Alexander Cadogan OM, 1938–1945*, London 1971, page 305.
[3] Minute of 20 June 1940: Churchill papers, 20/13.

House of Commons. According to these notes, Churchill went on to warn that, despite the small scale of the two air raids so far, it would be 'folly' to underrate the gravity of the attack 'impending'. The notes continued:

Learn to get used to it.
  Eels get used to skinning.

Steady continuous bombing,
  probably rising to great intensity occasionally,
    must be regular condition of our life.

It was of the utmost importance, Churchill told the House of Commons, to preserve public morale, 'especially in the night work of factories'. The bombing would be a test 'of our nerve against theirs', with British bombing more precise, 'and already more effective'. Churchill added:

No one can tell result.

This supreme battle depends upon
  the courage of the ordinary man and woman.

Whatever happened, it was essential to keep 'a stiff upper lip', and it was the duty of all Members of Parliament 'to uphold confidence and speed production'.

Churchill then spoke of the battle in France, and commented, on the question of forming a Torres-Vedras line in Brittany, that it would have been 'quite impossible' in view of the inevitable German air attacks on all French ports. One in three supply ships, he said, would have been sunk. Britain would continue to urge the French to go on fighting, 'but all depends', he declared, 'upon the battle of Britain'. Of this battle, he added, 'I have good confidence.' The essence of the defence of Britain was 'to attack the landed enemy at once', to 'leap at his throat, and keep the grip until the life is out of him'.

The speech notes continued:

If Hitler fails to invade
  or destroy Britain
    he has lost the war.

I do not consider only the severities
  of the winter in Europe.

I look to superiority in Air power
                in the future.

Transatlantic reinforcements.

If get through next 3 months
   get through next 3 years.

It may well be our fine Armies
   have not said goodbye to the Continent of Europe.

If enemy coastline extends from the Arctic
   to the Mediterranean

   and we retain sea-power
     and a growing Air power

   it is evident that Hitler
     master of a starving, agonized and
       surging Europe;

   will have his dangers as well as we.

But all depends upon winning this battle
   here in Britain, now this summer.

If we do, the prospects of the future
             will expand,

   and we may look forward
     and make our plans for 1941 and 1942

   and that is what we are doing.

Of the attitude of the United States, Churchill remarked: 'Nothing will stir them like fighting in England.' It was 'no good', he said, suggesting to the Americans that Britain was down and out. It was the 'heroic struggle' of Britain that offered the 'best chance of bringing them in'. Anyhow, they had promised Britain the 'fullest aid' in materials and munitions. If only Britain could hold out until after the American elections that November, 'I cannot doubt the whole English-speaking world will be in line together.' Hitler would then have against him 'the Oceans and the Air', and 'all the Continents except Europe'. Churchill's notes continued:

I do not see why we should not find our way through
   this time, as we did last.

Churchill went on to refer to a possible German invasion of Eire. It was much better, he said, that the Germans break Irish neutrality 'than we'. The imperative need now in Britain was for loyalty and union 'among men who have joined hands'. Otherwise, there was no means of standing 'the shocks and strains which are coming'. His notes ended:

        I have a right to depend loyalty
              to the administration
        and feel we have only one enemy to face,
              the foul foe who threatens
                 our freedom and our life,
        and bars the upward march of man.[1]

Colville was later told by several Members of Parliament that Churchill's speech had been a 'great success'.[2] But many Conservative back benchers were still not ready to suspend their suspicions of Churchill's motives. Henry Channon noted in his diary: 'Winston wound up with his usual brilliance and out-of-place levity. His command of English is magnificent; but strangely enough, although he makes me laugh, he leaves me unmoved. There is always the quite inescapable suspicion that he loves war, war which broke Neville Chamberlain's better heart!'[3]

That evening Churchill dined with his nephew Johnny and Randolph's wife Pamela. These family meals were almost his only relaxation and break from the pressures of work. Then, at 11.15, he saw Lord Lloyd, who had just returned from his mission to Bordeaux. Lloyd reported, as Colville noted in his diary, that 'things were much better and that continued resistance in North Africa and the departure of the Government from France were now almost certain'. In addition, according to Lloyd, Admiral Darlan was 'full of spirit'.[4]

Such was the report from Bordeaux, but at Compiègne on the morning of June 21, the inexorable process of surrender continued, as the French delegates were given Germany's armistice terms, in the same railway coach in which Marshal Foch had received the German surrender in November 1918.

On the morning of June 21 Churchill was asked to listen to yet another tale of imminent danger. This time, the tale was scientific. At Lindemann's suggestion, the Deputy Director of Intelligence Research at the Air Ministry, R. V. Jones, a young man of twenty-eight, was summoned to the Cabinet Room to explain his reasons for claiming the existence of a highly secret German device which used radio

---

[1] Speech notes, printed in: Charles Eade (editor), *Secret Session Speeches by the Right Hon Winston S. Churchill OM, CH, MP*, London 1946, pages 8–16. Churchill had replaced the word 'menace' by 'threatens'. In speaking from these notes, he will have said 'depend *on* loyalty', or, possibly, '*demand* loyalty'.

[2] Colville diary, 20 June 1940: Colville papers.

[3] Channon diary, 20 June 1940: Robert Rhodes James (editor), *'Chips', The Diaries of Sir Henry Channon*, London 1967, page 258. On the following day, Sir Samuel Hoare wrote to Lord Beaverbrook from Madrid that he had just received a letter from Chamberlain in which Chamberlain 'speaks in warm praise of Winston': Beaverbrook papers.

[4] Colville diary, 20 June 1940: Colville papers.

beams to direct German aircraft upon precise targets, throughout Britain.

The possibility of such beams existing was, however, doubted by Sir Henry Tizard, Chairman of the Aeronautical Research Committee.

Jones had been researching intensely into the nature of these mysterious beams for nearly a month. Having momentarily regarded his summons to the Cabinet Room as a prank, he arrived at 10 Downing Street to find the meeting already in progress. Those present were Churchill, Lindemann and Beaverbrook on one side of the Cabinet table, Sir Archibald Sinclair, Sir Cyril Newall, Sir Hugh Dowding, Sir Charles Portal, Sir Philip Joubert, Professor Tizard and Robert Watson-Watt on the other. As Jones later recalled:

> I listened for a time while some of those around the table made comments which suggested that they had not fully grasped the situation; only then did Churchill address a question to me on some point of detail. Instead of dealing with it, I said, 'Would it help, sir, if I told you the story right from the start?'
>
> Churchill seemed somewhat taken aback, but after a moment's hesitation said, 'Well, yes it would!' And so I told him the story. The fact that my call to the Cabinet Room had been so sudden had given me no time to rehearse, or even to become nervous. The few minutes of desultory discussion that had ensued after my entry showed me that nobody else there knew as much about the matter as I did myself and, although I was not conscious of my calmness at the time, the very gravity of the situation somehow seemed to generate the steady nerve for which it called. Although I was only 28, and everyone else round the table much my senior in every conventional way, the threat of the beams was too serious for our response to be spoilt by any nervousness on my part.[1]

Jones spoke for about twenty minutes, perhaps more. As Churchill listened to his 'quiet tones', some lines from the *Ingoldsby Legends* came into his mind:

> But now one Mr Jones
> Comes forth and depones
> That, fifteen years since, he had heard certain groans
> On his way to Stone Henge (to examine the stones
> Described in a work of the late Sir John Soane's),
> That he'd followed the moans,
> And led by their tones,
> Found a Raven a-picking a Drummer-boy's bones![2]

[1] R. V. Jones, *Most Secret War*, London 1978, page 101.

[2] The *Ingoldsby Legends*, by Richard Harris Barham, were first published in 1840; enormously popular on account of their wit and narrative power, they were republished frequently during the second half of the century, and during Churchill's youth.

When Jones had finished his account of the beams, there was, as Churchill recalled, 'a general air of incredulity', and in the discussion that followed, one 'high authority'—it was in fact Sir Henry Tizard—'asked why the Germans should use a beam, assuming that such a thing was possible, when they had at their disposal all the ordinary facilities of navigation. Above twenty thousand feet the stars were nearly always visible. All our own pilots were laboriously trained in navigation, and it was thought they found their way about and to their targets very well.'

Such was Tizard's scepticism. But others round the Cabinet table, Churchill recalled, 'appeared concerned'.[1]

In retrospect, Jones himself felt that Tizard 'had perhaps overdone his scepticism' about the existence of the beams. But Churchill was now thoroughly alerted to the danger, and, as Jones recalled, asked him 'what we could do':

I told him that the first thing was to confirm their existence by discovering and flying along the beams for ourselves, and that we could develop a variety of countermeasures ranging from putting in a false cross-beam to make the Germans drop their bombs early, or using forms of jamming ranging from crude to subtle. Churchill added all his weight to these suggestions. In addition, he said that if the Germans were to fly along beams, this would be the ideal case for our sowing fields of aerial mines, which he had been pressing on the Air Ministry for some years, adding as he angrily banged the table, 'All I get from the Air Ministry is files, files, files!'[2]

Aerial mines had long been one of Churchill's special projects, both during his years in opposition, and at the Admiralty, where they had been given the code name 'Egg-layer'.[3] 'He did get very angry,' Jones later recalled. 'He really tore a strip off the Air Staff. They all sat there very miserably.'[4] And with that episode, the meeting ended.

The aerial mines were only a momentary diversion, however; it was the beams that mattered, and whose existence now seemed certain. This was their story. Only a month earlier, Jones had sent Lindemann a most secret report that it was 'possible' that the Germans 'have developed a system of intersecting beams so that they can locate a target such as London with sufficient accuracy for indiscriminate bombing'.[5]

[1] Winston S. Churchill, *The Second World War*, London 1949, pages 339-41.
[2] R. V. Jones, *Most Secret War*, London 1978, page 102.
[3] First Lord's Personal Minute No. 262, 24 March 1940: Churchill papers, 19/6.
[4] Professor R. V. Jones, conversation with the author, 12 October 1982.
[5] Air Scientific Intelligence Report No. 5, 'Indications of New German Weapons to be Used Against England', 'Secret', 23 May 1940: Air Ministry papers, 20/1623.

Jones' report had been dated May 23. Within two weeks, on June 5, a German radio message—a 'most secret source'—had been intercepted in England. Once intercepted, it had taken four days to decypher it. But, once it had been decyphered, it revealed a map reference, sent from somewhere in Germany at 2.55 p.m. on June 5, and pinpointing an area near Retford. The intercepted message also made use of the code name 'Knickebein', the meaning of which was unknown, beyond its literal translation of Dog Leg, or crooked leg.

Those who studied this message on June 9 realized that two aerodromes near Retford had in fact been bombed on the night of June 5, some five or six hours after the coded Retford area map reference had been sent from Germany. Two days later a German prisoner-of-war who had been shot down in Norway revealed under interrogation that 'Knickebein' was a 'bomb dropping device involving two intersecting beams, which were picked up on one Lorenz receiver, and which released the bombs automatically'. This prisoner-of-war, his interrogator added, 'was anti-war and was willing to tell us all he knew'.[1]

As further details accumulated, the mysterious beams developed, as Jones wrote, 'from a conjecture to a certainty'. Hence the meeting in the Cabinet Room, and the importance of Churchill being convinced. 'If our good fortune holds,' Jones noted a week later, 'we may yet pull the Crooked Leg.'[2]

As a result of the Downing Street meeting, Jones was authorized to pursue his researches. Not only was the beam located, but, shortly after it began to operate, it was successfully 'bent'.[3]

Recalling the impact that Churchill had made on him, and Churchill's personal comment on this crucial meeting, Jones wrote:

Here was strength, resolution, humour, readiness to listen, to ask the searching question and, when convinced, to act. He was rarely complimentary

---

[1] The interrogator was Squadron-Leader Felkin.

[2] Air Scientific Intelligence Report No. 6, 'Most Secret', 28 June 1940: Air Ministry papers, 20/1623.

[3] In his memoirs, Churchill wrote: 'Being master, and not having to argue too much, once I was convinced about the principles of this queer and deadly game I gave all the necessary orders that very day in June for the existence of the beam to be assumed. The slightest reluctance or deviation in carrying out this policy was to be reported to me. With so much going on I did not trouble the Cabinet, or even the Chiefs of Staff. If I had encountered any serious obstruction I should of course have appealed and told a long story to these friendly tribunals. This however was not necessary, as in this limited and at that time almost occult circle obedience was forthcoming with alacrity, and on the fringes all obstructions could be swept away' (Winston S. Churchill, *The Second World War*, volume 2, London 1949, page 342). Churchill made no reference in his memoirs, at this point or elsewhere, to the nature of the 'most secret source' involved (see pages 609–13).

at the time, handsome though his compliments could be afterwards, for he had been brought up in sterner days. In 1940 it was compliment enough to be called in by him at the crisis; but to stand up to his questioning attack and then to convince him was the greatest exhilaration of all.

As I was speaking at the Knickebein meeting, I could sense the impression that I was making on him. One day after the war, when I was sitting at his bedside, he told me about it: having surveyed our position in the early weeks of June 1940, he thought that we ought just to be able to hold the Luftwaffe by day. And then, when this young man came in and told him that they could still bomb as accurately by night, when our nightfighters would still be almost powerless, it was for him one of the blackest moments of the war. But as the young man went on the load was once again lifted because he said that there could be ways of countering the beams and so preventing our most important targets being destroyed.[1]

Hardly had the scientific meeting broken up on the morning of June 21, than the Defence Committee convened, to discuss the urgent question of what to do if Spain entered the war against Britain, as could happen at any moment, and Gibraltar at once became 'unusable' as a naval base. One plan suggested by the Chiefs of Staff, was to seize the Canary Islands as a base.[2] If the 1,500 Germans on the island were to stiffen Spanish resistance, however, the Chiefs of Staff proposed that Casablanca or Oran, in French North Africa, might be possible alternatives, to be seized likewise, whichever way the French armistice negotiations were to turn.[3]

Churchill told the Defence Committee that it was important to work out plans 'to seize and hold any bases we might require'. The commanders should be appointed immediately, and no delay incurred 'in getting the troops trained and making arrangements for embarkation at short notice irrespective of a decision as to their destination'.[4]

An alternative proposal to the loss of Gibraltar was an offer to the Spanish Government to 'discuss' Gibraltar 'after the war', hoping thereby to avert a Spanish declaration of war. Churchill rejected this proposal, minuting to Lord Halifax: 'I am sure we shall gain nothing by offering to "discuss" Gibraltar at the end of the war. Spaniards will know that, if we win, discussion would not be fruitful; and if we lose, they would not be necessary. I do not believe mere verbiage of this kind will affect the Spanish decision. It only shows weakness and lack

[1] R. V. Jones, *Most Secret War*, London 1978, pages 107–8.
[2] This was the operation code name 'Bugle'.
[3] Chiefs of Staff Memorandum No. 480 of 1940, 21 June 1940: Cabinet papers, 80/13.
[4] Defence Committee No. 18 of 1940, 21 June 1940, 11 a.m.: Cabinet papers, 69/1.

of confidence in our victory, which will encourage them the more.'[1]
Colville later reflected that the proposal to discuss Gibraltar with Spain
'was the sort of typical nonsense that Winston was very good at stopping'. It would, he added, 'have been very bad for morale'.[2]

Churchill had already taken one important step to try to show the
Spaniards that Britain would not go down, and that they should therefore avoid joining Hitler, and should beware of any temptation to do
so. At the same time that Sir Samuel Hoare had gone to Madrid as
Ambassador at the end of May, Churchill had spoken at length to the
British Naval Attaché in Spain, Captain Alan Hillgarth, who was then
on leave in London. Hillgarth had returned to Spain with a mission of
considerable importance and delicacy: to use his own many contacts in
Spain in order to try to keep Spain out of the war for at least six
months.

Hillgarth was tireless in urging upon the many influential Spaniards
to whom he had access that Britain would weather the storm. He had
told Churchill in May that he believed 'we could hold Spain unless we
lost Egypt' and that he could convince his contacts that even the fall of
France would not be a fatal blow to Britain's survival.

Churchill followed Hillgarth's progress with considerable care, and
encouraged him to persevere in his efforts. 'I am finding Hillgarth a
great prop,' Hoare had written to Churchill on June 12. This was
especially so in Madrid, a city in which there were 'thousands of well-
organised Germans ready to make trouble'.[3]

When the War Cabinet met again at noon on June 21, a mixed
panorama was presented to it. The agreed military evacuation of the
Channel Islands had been carried out, despite Churchill's preference
for an act of resistance. The Swedish destroyers on their way to Stockholm had been seized at the Faroe Islands, despite Halifax's growing
worries as to the effect this would have on neutral States elsewhere.
When Halifax again protested two days later at the effect of the seizure
of the Swedish ships 'on neutral opinion in general', Churchill told the
War Cabinet: 'It might well be that all Europe, including Spain and
Sweden, would fall under German control in the near future. But it
might well be to our advantage that the Germans should have to hold
down all these intelligent and freedom-loving people; the task of this
holding down all Europe should prove beyond even the strength of the

---

[1] Minute of 21 June 1940: Churchill papers, 20/13. The proposal had been put forward in
Foreign Office telegram No. 410 from Madrid.
[2] Sir John Colville, conversation with the author, 20 May 1981.
[3] Letter of 12 June 1940: Premier papers, 4/21/1, folios 146–7.

Gestapo, provided England could retain her liberty.' If the Swedes resisted, Churchill added, 'so much the better, but it was very doubtful whether the present incident over the destroyers would materially affect either Swedish resistance or German intentions'.[1]

Italy's entry into the war had also cast its shadow upon the War Cabinet discussions on June 21, when it was reported that the floating dock at Malta had been badly damaged by an Italian air raid.[2]

Throughout Britain, Sir John Anderson told the War Cabinet of June 21, enemy aliens were being locked up 'as fast as accommodation could be provided'. But on this question of internment, it was Churchill who sounded a note of caution. 'Many enemy aliens had a great hatred of the Nazi regime,' he said, 'and it was unjust to treat our friends as foes.'[3] His idea was to form such anti-Nazi aliens into a Foreign Legion, for training, and eventual use overseas, for example, in Iceland.

The news from France continued to worsen without respite. During the War Cabinet of June 21 Halifax reported that whereas Lord Lloyd had brought with him from Bordeaux a letter from Herriot 'in very satisfactory terms' with regard to the French Fleet, 'he had now been asked that this letter should be treated as confidential and should be destroyed'. It looked therefore, Halifax warned, 'as though the position had changed for the worse'.[4]

The true position would not be known until the French armistice terms were reported. Churchill went that Friday night to Chequers, and remained there until Saturday afternoon, together with his wife and a few friends, Brendan Bracken, Desmond Morton, Oliver Lyttelton, Lord Beaverbrook and General Ismay. Also invited was General Alexander who had returned from Dunkirk with the last boat.

[1] War Cabinet No. 174 of 1940, 21 June 1940, 12 noon: Cabinet papers, 65/7, folio 367. On 8 July 1940, while being detained by the British at the Faroe Islands, the ships were bombed in error by British aircraft.

[2] Two days later Churchill telegraphed to the Officer Administering the Government of Malta: 'The Cabinet watch with constant attention the resolute defence which your garrison and the people of Malta are making of that famous fortress and Island. I have the conviction that you will make that defence glorious in British military history, and also in the history of Malta itself. You are well fitted to rouse and sustain the spirit of all in enduring severe and prolonged ordeals for a righteous cause' (Telegram of 23 June 1940: Churchill papers, 20/14).

[3] Among those already interned was the German-born Eugen Spier, resident in London from the 1920s, who from 1936 to 1939 had financed and helped to organise Churchill's private 'Focus' group of all-Party opposition to Neville Chamberlain's foreign policy. He was not released until January 1941. He wrote of his experiences as an internee in *The Protecting Power*, London 1951.

[4] War Cabinet No. 174 of 1940, 21 June 1940, 12 noon: Cabinet papers, 65/7.

Despite the uncertainty created by the French armistice negotiations, Jean Monnet had continued to order war materials for Britain from the United States. Monnet's authority in London derived from his Chairmanship of the Anglo-French Co-ordinating Committee. On June 21, when the question arose of the availability of wood pulp in the United States, Monnet telegraphed tersely to Purvis: 'British want this', and the consignment was purchased within the hour.[1] But when during June 21 Churchill asked Ismay for a list of all United States aircraft and munitions deliveries 'which have actually arrived in the country', Ismay answered in one word: 'Nil.' Nor was anything expected before the end of July.[2]

At Chequers that weekend, the slow pace of United States' supplies, the uncertainty of the future of France, and the extent of Britain's own weakness in the event of a German invasion, were causes of grave concern. The strain on everyone who knew the full extent of the dangers was considerable; it was greatest on Churchill, whose responsibilities, so recently acquired, were formidable, yet whose power, so long denied, might still prove insufficient to avert defeat. His own mood reflected the grimness of the hour, and affected even his personal behaviour, so much so that one of his friends complained that weekend to Clementine Churchill, and she set down in writing her report:

My Darling,
    I hope you will forgive me if I tell you something that I feel you ought to know.
    One of the men in your entourage (a devoted friend) has been to me & told me that there is a danger of your being generally disliked by your colleagues & subordinates because of your rough sarcastic & overbearing manner—It seems your Private Secretaries have agreed to behave like school boys & 'take what's coming to them' & then escape out of your presence shrugging their shoulders. Higher up, if an idea is suggested (say at a conference) you are supposed to be so contemptuous that presently no ideas, good or bad, will be forthcoming. I was astonished & upset because in all these years I have been accustomed to all those who have worked with & under you, loving you—I said this & I was told 'No doubt it's the strain'——
    My Darling Winston—I must confess that I have noticed a deterioration in your manner; & you are not so kind as you used to be.

[1] 'Purco' No. 160 of 21 June 1940: Cabinet papers, 85/13, folio 318.
[2] Churchill Minute of 21 June 1940, and Ismay's reply: Premier papers, 3/479, folios 85, 86. Ismay listed, as already 'handed over for shipment' at United States ports, 89 million rounds of rifle ammunition, 345,000 high explosive shells for 75-millimetre field guns, 192,600 rifles, 44,269 machine guns for aircraft, 5,325 mortar shells, 1,811 machine guns for tanks, 898 Lewis guns, 143 75-millimetre field guns and 126 Stokes 3-inch mortars. Of the field guns, Ismay added, 48 had been 'already shipped'.

It is for you to give the Orders & if they are bungled—except for the King, the Archbishop of Canterbury & the Speaker you can sack anyone & everyone. Therefore with this terrific power you must combine urbanity, kindness & if possible Olympic calm. You used to quote:—'On ne règne sur les âmes que par le calme'—I cannot bear that those who serve the country & yourself should not love you as well as admire and respect you.

Besides you won't get the best results by irascibility & rudeness. They *will* breed either dislike or a slave mentality—(Rebellion in War Time being out of the question!)

Please forgive your loving devoted & watchful

Clemmie

Clementine Churchill ended this letter with a sketch of a cat. Then she tore the letter up. Four days later she pieced it together again and gave it to her husband.[1]

The stresses on Churchill were widely understood. 'You must indeed,' wrote Sir Samuel Hoare from Madrid on June 27, 'have had a terrible time during the last fortnight.'[2]

From London, Churchill's secretariat kept him informed from hour to hour of the telegrams from France. These telegrams included the first details of the actual armistice terms, as reported by Sir Ronald Campbell, together with Pound's further 'most secret' signal to Darlan, sent just after midnight on Saturday, asking for assurance that the French warships would not be handed over to the Germans if this was one of the armistice terms, but 'sent to British ports', so that Britain could 'make certain that they will not fall into the hands of our enemies'.[3]

As the details of the armistice terms came in to Chequers, it became clear just how total the French surrender was to be: the occupation of Paris; the setting up of a broad German zone of control along the Channel and Atlantic coasts, from Dunkirk to the Pyrenees; the de-mobilization and disarming of the French army; the handing over intact to Germany of all arms, munitions, military stores, installations and machinery; payment by France for the cost of the German occupation; French prisoners-of-war to remain in German custody until the conclusion of peace and, in direct contravention of Reynaud's pledge to Churchill at the Supreme War Council meeting at Tours on June 13, the release of all German prisoners-of-war, including all German pilots, who were being held on French soil.

---

[1] Given to Churchill on 27 June 1940: Baroness Spencer-Churchill papers.
[2] Letter of 27 June 1940: Churchill papers, 20/9.
[3] Message sent at 01.25 hours, 23 June 1940: Admiralty papers, 205/4.

The return of these pilots to Germany, from where they could fly once more against British planes and targets, was a blow to Churchill and his advisers, and a cause of bitter reflection in the months to come. But it was Article 8 of the German terms that constituted, that day at Chequers, the greatest threat to Britain's immediate future. For as the details emerged, it became clear that Hitler had indeed insisted upon controlling the French Fleet.

Article 8 of the German terms demanded that all French warships be collected in specific ports, demobilized, and 'disarmed under German or Italian control'. In addition, all French ships outside French territorial waters 'must be recalled to France'.[1]

Churchill hurried to London for an emergency War Cabinet, summoned for 9.30 that Saturday night.

It was still unclear from the telegrams from Bordeaux whether or not Pétain's Government would agree to Hitler's demands concerning the French Fleet.[2] Pétain himself, so it appeared from two of the seven telegrams received, 'had renewed his assurance regarding the safety of the French Fleet'.[3] But whether these assurances could be believed, or honoured, was far from certain.

The War Cabinet then heard from Pound about the number of French ships involved in Article 8. These ships included two battleships, one of which, the *Richelieu*, was in Pound's words 'the most powerful battleship afloat in the world today', then on her way to Dakar. The second battleship, the *Jean Bart*, was as yet not complete and had 'no fighting value at all at present'. The *Jean Bart*, Pound said, was then on her way to Casablanca. In addition, Pound told the War Cabinet, the French were being told to disarm and hand over two battle-cruisers, the *Dunkerque* and the *Strasbourg* at Oran, and various other cruisers, some at Toulon. Two of the French cruisers, however, were at Alexandria 'under the control of the British Fleet'.

This was a formidable fighting force, and could, in any German naval operation or invasion scheme, constitute a considerable addition to German power. Yet it appeared, Pound said, that the French Admirals had been ordered by their Commander-in-Chief 'to fight to a finish', and 'not to accept any orders from a foreign Government',

---

[1] War Cabinet Paper No. 217 of 1940, 23 June 1940 (circulated by Lord Halifax): Premier papers, 3/174/1.
[2] Telegrams No. 517 and 518 DIPP, War Cabinet No. 176 of 1940, 22 June 1940, 9.30 p.m.: Cabinet papers, 65/7.
[3] Telegrams No. 517 and 518 DIPP, War Cabinet No. 176 of 1940, 22 June 1940, 9.30 p.m.: Cabinet papers, 65/7.

proof, Pound believed, that Darlan was taking 'all possible steps' to safeguard Britain's interests.

Churchill disagreed. In a matter 'so vital to the safety of the whole British Empire', he said, 'we could not afford to rely on the word of Admiral Darlan,' however good his intentions. The *Richelieu* and the *Jean Bart* must not be allowed to fall into German hands. *Strasbourg* and *Dunkerque* would 'certainly be a great nuisance if they fell into the hands of the enemy. But it was the two modern ships which might alter the whole course of the war.' Churchill's overriding fears concerned *Richelieu*. At all costs, he said, it 'must not be allowed to get loose'. A strong British naval force should be sent to deal with it. British ships should go alongside *Richelieu* in Dakar and *Jean Bart* in Casablanca 'in order to open a parley with their captains'. This would have been better done 'in the high seas' but should now be done in the harbours. If the French captains refused to parley, 'they must be treated as traitors to the Allied cause'. The ships, he added, 'might have to be bombed by aircraft from *Ark Royal* or they might be mined into their harbours and naval forces stationed outside to prevent the minefield being swept up'.

The War Cabinet decided that the Admiralty should 'assume responsibility' that *Richelieu* and *Jean Bart* did not leave Dakar and Casablanca, while at the same time A. V. Alexander and Pound would make a further personal appeal to Darlan. There was also a plan to send both Admiral Phillips and Lord Lloyd direct to Oran, to appeal to the French Admiral there, Admiral Estéva, not to allow *Strasbourg* and *Dunkerque* to fall into German hands.[1]

On the following morning, General de Gaulle wrote from his London headquarters to ask Churchill for recognition of a special Council of Liberation, and for permission to broadcast that night. 'General de Gaulle was a fine fighting soldier,' Churchill told the morning War Cabinet, 'with a good reputation and a strong personality, and might be the right man to set up such a Council.'[2]

There were problems, however; throughout June 23 British officials talked with the French Ambassador, Charles Corbin, who opposed any such move, and any broadcast by de Gaulle, who was, said Corbin, 'an unknown personality'.[3] It was finally agreed that de Gaulle should broadcast at ten that night, and that a British Government statement

---

[1] War Cabinet No. 176 of 1940, 22 June 1940, 9.30 p.m.: Cabinet papers, 65/13.

[2] War Cabinet No. 177 of 1940, 23 June 1940, 10 a.m.: Cabinet papers, 65/7.

[3] As reported by Lord Halifax, War Cabinet No. 178 of 1940, 24 June 1940, 12 noon: Cabinet papers, 65/7.

should simultaneously announce Britain's official support for de Gaulle's Council, known henceforth as the French National Committee.

Churchill hoped that this Committee would serve as a focal point for those French politicians and servicemen who wished to continue fighting. On the following day, June 24, he suggested that de Gaulle and his Committee should be the 'operative authority' for a clandestine organization to enable French officers, soldiers and technicians to make their way out of France, minuting to Ismay: 'A sort of "underground railway", as in the olden days of slavery, should be established and a Scarlet Pimpernel organization set up. I have no doubt,' he added, 'there will be a steady flow of determined men. . . .'[1]

The situation in Britain itself remained grave; as Anthony Eden had written to Churchill on June 23, after visiting the Army Corps responsible for the defence of Kent, Sussex and Surrey, where invasion could most be expected: 'There is no anti-tank regiment nor anti-tank gun in the whole of this Corps area.'[2] Aware that such facts could be interpreted as showing the hopelessness of Britain's position, Churchill telegraphed on June 24 to the Canadian Prime Minister, Mackenzie King: 'I shall myself never enter into any peace negotiations with Hitler, but obviously I cannot bind a future Government, which, if we were deserted by the United States and beaten down here, might very easily be a kind of Quisling affair ready to accept German overlordship and protection.' It would help, Churchill added, 'if you would impress this danger upon the President, as I have done in my telegrams to him'.[3]

Although still rejecting Britain's urgent plea for destroyers, the United States' Government had proposed, as a gesture of support, the opening of Anglo-American Staff talks. This, however, Churchill opposed, telling Halifax that the main topic of any such talks from the American side was bound to turn 'upon the transfer of the British Fleet to trans-Atlantic bases'. Any discussion of such a transfer, he warned, 'is bound to weaken confidence here at the moment when all must brace themselves for the supreme struggle'.[4]

*   *   *

[1] Minute of 24 June 1940: Churchill papers, 20/13.

[2] 'Impressions of a visit to XII Corps Area', 23 June 1940, copy in: Foreign Office papers, 800/326, folios 136–8.

[3] 'Personal & Private', telegram despatched at 8.05 p.m., 24 June 1940: Premier papers, 4/43B/1, folios 252–3.

[4] Minute of 24 June 1940: Premier papers, 3/457, folios 43–44.

As the issue of the French Fleet drew towards a climax, Churchill strove to finish the reorganization of his own Secretariat and advisory circle. His Private Office was now complete, with Eric Seal presiding over a closely knit team in which Bevir, Martin, Peck and Colville each had their duties. John Martin later commented: 'Our main function was to see that things went smoothly, to make sure that the Prime Minister saw all that he had to see, and to shield him from unnecessary involvement.'

Churchill's instinct was to see 'in the raw' the materials that were sent to him. But the amount of paper reaching Downing Street each day was formidable, and had to be checked and sifted. Then there were Churchill's comments, written and verbal, which had to be transmitted to the correct Ministry or Department of State. 'With all the irritableness of the PM,' Martin recalled, 'and the rather fierce messages he sent, it was necessary to see that things did not go sour.' On rare occasions members of the Private Office would even 'chance their arm', as Martin noted, in holding back some letter or minute which they judged to be too harsh, by suggesting that it be referred before despatch to some Cabinet Minister or colleague who might tone it down.[1]

The working of Churchill's Private Office gave him the confidence that the mass of materials which came before him and the range of individuals with whom he had to deal would be as manageable as possible. In the Defence Office, Ismay had ensured, since the first days of Churchill's Premiership, that Churchill's daily contact with the Chiefs of Staff, even when stormy, did not disrupt the steady evolution of war plans and policy. Ismay also supervised the work of the War Cabinet Secretariat, in which were serving a number of officers who, Ismay explained to Churchill, had acquired while with the Secretariat of the pre-war Committee of Imperial Defence, 'a wide knowledge of the machinery of Government', as well as close contacts with officers and officials in every Government department concerned with defence, and 'the complete confidence of all with whom they came in contact'. Ismay added: 'I submit that they are thus particularly qualified to give you a full and unbiased picture of those activities which you particularly wish to survey and direct, and to drive ahead with any project which you may entrust to them.'[2]

Ismay's team made the working of the War Cabinet Secretariat a

[1] Sir John Martin, conversation with the author, 8 December 1982.
[2] 'Secret', minute of 1 July 1940: Cabinet papers, 120/3. The names of these officers are listed on page 323, note 3, of this volume.

model of efficiency at times of unprecedented danger. At the Cabinet Office, Sir Edward Bridges, the Cabinet Secretary since 1938, likewise ensured a similar smooth passage of instructions, replies and queries elsewhere in Whitehall.

Outside these important and sustaining groups was another stalwart, Lindemann, who was not only head of Churchill's Statistical Office, but a friend of twenty years, as close to Churchill in thought, proximity and ideas as any other individual. Just as Lindemann had been the single most frequent guest at Chartwell in the 1930s, so, during the war itself, he was the most regular attendant at Chequers. Neither a Member of Parliament nor, until 1942, a Cabinet Minister, Lindemann was Churchill's watchdog and guide over a wide range of scientific and technical matters, from poison gas to manpower; he saw the most confidential documents, and was privy from the outset to the most secret source of British Intelligence.[1]

Many of Lindemann's ideas were put up by Churchill as his own. Many of Lindemann's draft letters were circulated unaltered over Churchill's signature. Not only was Lindemann's loyalty to Churchill unquestioned; his conviction that Germany must and could be defeated was paralleled by the same fear as Churchill's, that it was not Hitler's power, but Britain's mistakes, that would pose the gravest dangers.

The combination of Churchill's authority and Lindemann's vigilance was not seen outside the smallest of circles; but it was a combination which was constant and unbreakable.

Those who saw how close Lindemann was to Churchill were often prone to criticize that friendship. John Martin later recalled the 'irritation' which Lindemann could arouse in others when, having received some 'tiresome' minute from Churchill, they reacted by saying, sometimes rightly but often wrongly, that it was Lindemann who had in fact written it. Lindemann also had, as Martin recalled, 'an unfortunate rather sneering manner' which acted against any easy or widespread popularity.[2]

There was an example of Lindemann's influence towards the end of June, when, having read the May reports of the Divisional Controllers, he warned Churchill that there was not only a serious shortage of labour for the manufacture of munitions, but that he had received evidence from numerous sources that the Ministry of Labour 'does not appreciate the scale of expansion that will be required' and conse-

---

[1] See pages 609–13 of this volume.
[2] Sir John Martin, conversation with the author, 8 December 1982.

quently was 'still unwilling to use its new powers of compulsion either to supply labour where it is needed or to make adequate preparations for the impending demand'. It was said, Lindemann added, that the Ministry of Labour was 'still working on peace-time assumptions'.

On receiving this note, Churchill at once asked Lindemann and Eric Seal to draft a letter *'together*, for me to see'; and then got Beaverbrook to stiffen the letter up, before sending it to the Minister of Labour, Ernest Bevin. In the event, Bevin was so angered by the Prime Minister's complaint that after a month of charges and counter charges, Churchill had to turn to Attlee to deal with what he called 'this complicated and delicate affair'.[1]

In almost exact proportion to Lindemann's ability to antagonize was the ability of the Secretary to the Cabinet, Sir Edward Bridges, to mollify and smooth ruffled tempers and hurt pride. Throughout Churchill's premiership, Bridges exercised a powerful influence on the day to day conduct of the war: discreet, firm, and calm in judgment, a link between Churchill and the main civil and military departments of State just as Ismay was the link with the Chiefs of Staff and their various committees.

Bridges, the son of a poet laureate, was a product of Eton and Oxford and a Fellow of All Souls. In the First World War he had won the Military Cross. His professional life had been spent in the Treasury. John Martin, who saw Bridges at work throughout the war years, has written of him:

Clear-headed, practical and industrious, with a rocklike strength of character reflected in the strong lines of his face, he combined these qualities with an absence of parade and pomposity, describing himself as no more than 'a general factotum on the civil side'. His advice was honest and fearless and he was ready to stand up to Churchill if he disagreed with him. In return the Prime Minister came to place great reliance on his judgment and turned to him to ensure the execution of his policies. Thus, though not one of the boon companions, Bridges was constantly brought into oral consultation and was often on the guest list at Chequers.

Under Bridges, as Martin reflected, the War Cabinet Office 'became a sort of Prime Minister's Department, in which the Secretary held together the civil and military branches. This came about partly because of Bridges' great ability; partly because of the location of the military and some of the important civilian staffs in the same office;

---

[1] During the dispute, which Lindemann's minute had provoked, Bevin accused Beaverbrook of 'selfishness, arbitrariness and failure to co-operate', according to Lindemann. It was Lindemann who then suggested mediation (Premier papers, 3/259).

and partly because the divorce between Sir Horace Wilson and No. 10 after Churchill's arrival brought it about that Bridges exercised in a personal capacity many of the functions that had traditionally attached to the office of the Secretary of the Treasury.' Martin's account continued:

One of Bridges' contributions to the smooth working of the machine was his insistence that, as far as practicable, any meeting of Ministers that was more than a huddle should be attended by an officer of the War Cabinet Office to keep a record, especially of any conclusions reached. He himself was a master of the art of recording in clear, unambiguous terms the outcome of even the most rambling and apparently inconclusive meeting.

Bridges himself, Martin added, 'won the admiration and affection of all who worked with him. His geniality—characteristically expressed by a dig in the tummy—and his patience contributed much to the happiness of the ship. . . .'[1]

In the last week of June 1940 that ship was still a largely untested craft, cast, almost adrift, on the strong and unpredictable sea of war. In order to be able to deal with the growing mass of material pressed forward daily from each sphere of war policy, and much of it calling for quick decisions as a matter of military urgency, Churchill needed, and used to the full, the help which was provided for him by Lindemann, Bridges, Ismay, Seal and the Offices over which they presided. He also received, from Major Desmond Morton, a close friend of pre-war years and pre-war battles, help in maintaining relations between the Prime Minister's Office and the Foreign Office, with the Secret Service, and in all matters involving Fifth Column activities.[2] Morton also had the task of liaison with the various and growing number of Governments-in-Exile in London, and succeeded, very usefully for Churchill, in giving each of these Governments the impression that the Prime Minister was in touch with them, even when he was not. Each time an exiled politician saw Morton, he felt that it was a contact for him with Churchill himself.[3] As part of this task, Morton was also Churchill's principal liaison with General de Gaulle's newly created French National Committee, and as such was in daily, and at this time almost hourly contact with de Gaulle.

From France, each hour's budget of news, however fragmentary, made it clear, as Churchill told the War Cabinet on June 24, that the

[1] Sir John Martin, notes for the author, 24 October 1982.
[2] Minute of 24 June 1940: Cabinet papers, 120/3.
[3] Sir John Martin, in conversation with the author, 8 December 1982.

Pétain Government was now 'completely under the thumb of Germany' and would allow the resources of France to be used against her previous Allies. 'There was grave danger,' Churchill said, 'that the rot would spread from the top through the Fleet, the Army and the Air Force, and all the French Colonies.' As a result of German pressure, the Pétain Government 'would inevitably be drawn more and more into making common cause with Germany', and Britain would soon become the object of the 'deepest hatred'. The greatest physical danger lay in German control of the French Fleet. 'We must at all costs,' Churchill warned, 'ensure that these ships either came under our control or were put out of the way for good.'[1]

Yet still it appeared that restraining hands were at work in France itself, and that Darlan, as Pound reported to the War Cabinet, had given orders to Admiral Estéva at Oran that the French ships 'must in no circumstances' fall into German or Italian hands. Those orders might, of course, not be obeyed, and the War Cabinet noted specifically that 'no reliance could possibly be placed' on the French naval crews, in view of what the minutes called 'the known Communist tendency of the French Navy before the war'.[2]

The War Cabinet on June 24, which had met at midday, reassembled at six o'clock that same evening, and within a few moments was informed that an armistice had been signed between France and Italy. With this, the Franco-German armistice also came into effect, whereby the French Government was obliged to prevent the French Fleet from falling into British control. The situation was such, Churchill told his colleagues, that Britain must 'avoid recriminations', but at the same time act 'solely in accordance with the dictates of our own safety'.

The French ships at Alexandria and in harbours in the United Kingdom could be prevented from leaving port. The *Richelieu* at Dakar and the *Jean Bart* at Casablanca were, the War Cabinet was told, being closely watched and 'should give no trouble'. But two battle-cruisers, *Dunkerque* and *Strasbourg*, and four cruisers, were still in French hands at 'various places' in the Mediterranean, centred upon Oran. The harbour defences there were 'powerful' and the position of the ships in the harbour ensured that they could not be torpedoed from the air.

It was decided, at that six o'clock War Cabinet, to send an ultimatum to Pétain's Government, demanding that it scuttle the ships at Oran 'within a time to be specified', otherwise the British Government

[1] War Cabinet No. 178 of 1940, 24 June 1940, 12 noon: Cabinet papers, 65/7.
[2] War Cabinet No. 178 of 1940, 24 June 1940, 12 noon, Minute 6, Confidential Annex: Cabinet papers, 65/13.

'should be forced to take action by force against them'.[1] Before the plans for that action were completed, however, one last attempt was to be made to create a French governing authority in alliance with Britain.

At the third War Cabinet of that day, summoned for 10.30 p.m., Sinclair suggested that British Government representatives should be sent by flying boat to 'get in touch' with Reynaud, who, it was just learned, had reached the Moroccan city of Rabat. The journey could be made in ten hours non-stop by flying boat. The Minister of Information, Alfred Duff Cooper, who offered to go himself, was authorized to undertake the mission, accompanied by Lord Gort. Their task, they were told, was to urge Reynaud and those of his former Ministers who were still with him, 'to set up a French Government', if possible in North Africa, or in Syria, or 'in Britain itself'.[2]

The French politicians at Rabat had not been allowed ashore. Instead, they were confined on board the ship, the *Massiglia*, on which they had sailed from Bordeaux at the time of the Armistice. Among those being held virtual captive on board the *Massiglia* was Mandel, whom Churchill envisaged replacing Reynaud as a possible leader of a French Government in exile, or as maintaining a legitimate French Government, opposed to Pétain, in some French territory overseas. Also on board was Campinchi, the former Minister of Marine who had so impressed Churchill with his energy and determination.[3]

The late night War Cabinet of June 24 also discussed the means whereby the French warships at Oran could be 'eliminated'. They were now reported to be in 'a new harbour', the naval base at Mers el-Kebir, three miles to the west of Oran, under the protection of 6-inch shore batteries. This force could only really be destroyed, said Pound, 'in a surprise attack carried out at dawn and without any form of prior notification'.

During the discussion, and as midnight drew near, the minutes of the War Cabinet recorded that a decision 'to order the destruction of people who had only 48 hours before been Allies would be hard to make', enabling the French and German Governments to declare 'that England was making war on France' and probably losing the sympathy

---

[1] War Cabinet No. 179 of 1940, 24 June 1940, 6 p.m., Minute 3, Confidential Annex: Cabinet papers, 65/13.

[2] War Cabinet No. 180 of 1940, 24 June 1940, 10.30 p.m.: Cabinet papers, 65/7.

[3] Another prisoner on the *Massiglia* was Pierre Mendès France, then aged 33, and a Deputy since the age of 25. Later imprisoned by the Vichy authorities, he escaped to London in 1942 and joined the Free French Air Force. In 1944 he became Minister of Economic Affairs in de Gaulle's Provisional Government, and from June 1954 to February 1955 was Prime Minister of France, responsible for bringing to an end the war in Indo-China, and granting autonomy to Tunisia.

'of the entire French Empire'. Churchill himself sounded a note of considerable caution. The ships that 'mattered most', he said, were the *Jean Bart* in Casablanca and the *Richelieu* in Dakar, both of which were at present unarmed and would prove 'easy to secure' once they left the shelter of port. But an operation to destroy the warships at Mers el-Kebir 'would undoubtedly prove very costly and might not be successful'.[1]

Hardly had the War Cabinet ended, at about one o'clock in the morning, than the air raid sirens sounded. It was a 'Red Warning', the first since the first day of war.[2] Churchill was then in the garden talking to Brendan Bracken, who later told a friend how, despite the sirens, 'they remained there drinking'.[3]

Duff Cooper, on the eve of his mission to Rabat, took refuge in the Downing Street shelter, where, as he later recalled, 'Miss Mary Churchill was already asleep.' He had then to walk home, 'as there were no taxis available'. On the following morning, joined by Gort, he left Calshot by flying boat at 9 a.m., reaching Rabat shortly after 7 p.m.

The *Massiglia* was now at Casablanca, an hour and a half's drive by road from Rabat. But the Vichy authorities had given instructions that Duff Cooper and Gort were not to get in touch 'with any of the French ex-Ministers', and at one point Gort was informed that he could not leave the hotel. After sleeping on board the anchored flying boat as a security precaution, the two men flew off at dawn for Gibraltar.[4] The dominance of Vichy France in North Africa was complete, and the ex-Ministers remained reluctant captives.

On June 25 General Paget, Chief of Staff to the Commander-in-Chief, Home Forces, presented his plans to combat a German invasion of Britain. But there were still outsiders who doubted Britain's resolve to fight on, including the Swedish Ambassador in London, Bjorn Prytz, who had come to the conclusion, after a talk on June 17 with the Under-Secretary of State for Foreign Affairs, R. A. Butler, that Britain would be prepared to negotiate peace. During June 25 Churchill wrote direct to Butler's superior, Lord Halifax:

It is quite clear to me from these telegrams and others that Butler held odd language to the Swedish Minister and certainly the Swede derived a strong

---

[1] War Cabinet No. 180 of 1940, 24 June 1940, 10. 30 p.m., Minute 2, Confidential Annex: Cabinet papers, 65/13.

[2] Martin diary, 25 June 1940: Martin papers.

[3] Channon diary, 25 June 1940: Robert Rhodes James (editor), *'Chips', The Diaries of Sir Henry Channon*, London 1967, page 259.

[4] Memorandum by Alfred Duff Cooper, 21 May 1947: Churchill papers, 4/201.

impression of defeatism. In these circumstances would it not be well to find out from Butler actually what he did say. I was strongly pressed in the House of Commons in the Secret Session to give assurances that the present Government and all its Members were resolved to fight on to the death, and I did so taking personal responsibility for the resolve of all. I saw a silly rumour in a telegram from Belgrade or Bucharest and how promptly you stamped upon it, but any suspicion of lukewarmness in Butler will certainly subject us all to further annoyance of this kind.[1]

There was certainly no 'lukewarmness' in Churchill's letter that day to Stalin, the first he had ever sent to the Soviet leader. The occasion was the despatch of Sir Stafford Cripps to Moscow, as Ambassador. Although Germany had become 'your friend', Churchill wrote, 'almost at the same moment as she became our enemy', a new factor had arisen which made it desirable for Britain and the Soviet Union to 'reestablish our previous contact', the need to decide how to react 'towards the prospect of Germany establishing a hegemony over the Continent'.

Britain, Churchill explained to Stalin, had two objects, 'one, to save herself from German domination', the other 'to free the rest of Europe from the domination which Germany is now in process of imposing on it'. The Soviet Union, Churchill added, was 'alone in a position to judge whether Germany's present bid for the hegemony of Europe threatens the interests of the Soviet Union', but he wished to assure Stalin of Britain's readiness 'to discuss fully with the Soviet Government any of the vast problems created by Germany's present attempt to pursue in Europe a methodical process by successive stages of conquest and absorption'.[2]

On the afternoon of June 25 it was again the terms of the French

---

[1] On 26 June 1940 R. A. Butler wrote to Lord Halifax to explain that he had met Prytz 'in the Park and he came into the Office for only a few minutes; not being an arranged interview I did not keep a record'. Butler added: 'This instance of my private conversation can only be judged by the Swedish Minister, since no one else was present. I do not recognise myself or my conversation in the impression given.' Butler offered to resign, but Halifax rejected his offer. In his resignation offer, Butler wrote: 'Had I not been ready to subscribe to the Prime Minister's courageous lead in the House of Commons, I should have felt bound to inform you and to leave the administration' (Foreign Office papers, 800/322, folios 278–81). Butler remained at the Foreign Office until July 1941, when he became President of the Board of Education, and from August 1944 Minister of Education.

[2] Letter of 25 June 1940: Churchill papers, 20/14. The principal stages still remaining of German conquest were to be Yugoslavia and Greece (April 1941) and the Soviet Union itself (June 1941). Following Japan's attack on Pearl Harbour, Germany declared war on the United States of America (December 1941). In 1943, following the overthrow of Mussolini, German troops occupied Rome; in 1944 they took control of Hungary. Although never occupied by Germany, Slovakia, Rumania, Bulgaria and Finland were likewise drawn into the German orbit.

Armistice on which attention was focused, and in a statement in the House of Commons, Churchill spoke of how the safety of Britain and the British Empire was 'powerfully, though not decisively, affected' by what happened to the French Fleet, which, under Article 8 of the armistice terms, was obliged to be demobilized and disarmed. Churchill would not be expected, he said, 'to say anything about the future'. But he might well have 'more to say', should the House of Commons permit him to 'make a further statement next week'. Meanwhile, the House must believe 'that neither patience nor resolution' would be lacking in the measures the Government might think it right to take 'for the safety of the Empire'.[1]

Of Churchill's personal resolution there was no doubt; when two of his secretariat dined together that night, one of them, Eric Seal, Churchill's Principal Private Secretary, told his junior colleague, John Colville, how much Churchill had changed since becoming Prime Minister. 'He had sobered down,' Colville noted in his diary, 'becoming less violent, less wild and less impetuous.' Seal thought, as Colville added, 'that Winston believes in his mission to extricate this country from its present troubles, and he will certainly kill himself if necessary in order to achieve his object'.[2]

The immediate 'object' was to deny Hitler an easy invasion, first, by keeping the French Fleet from him, at whatever cost, and then by building up the most effective anti-invasion forces possible. Churchill's task was threefold; that of initiator, co-ordinator, and spur of effort. He intended to neglect no area of preparedness, material or moral, practical or psychological. When Herbert Morrison suggested that the recently formed 'Local Defence Volunteers' should have a more inspiring name, and suggested 'Civil Guard', Churchill himself proposed 'Home Guard', minuting to Eden: 'Don't hesitate to change on account of already having made armlets etc, if it is thought the title of "Home Guard" would be more compulsive.'[3]

Yet not all Churchill's suggestions went unchallenged, and in this instance Eden protested that the term 'LDV' had already 'passed into current jargon'. In addition, Eden argued, it was already 'woven into a million brassards, 600,000 of which have already been issued'. It had also been decided, Eden explained, that the Local Defence Volunteers would be known as 'Volunteer Battalions' of their respective County regiments, as the men were anxious for a Regimental association.

[1] Speech of 25 June 1940: *Hansard*, columns 301–7.
[2] Colville diary, 25 June 1940: Colville papers.
[3] Minute of 26 June 1940: Churchill papers, 20/13.

Churchill was not convinced. 'As you are making this change,' he informed Eden, 'it would surely be worth while to adopt the more simple and better name of Home Guard.'[1]

Eden gave way, and the name Home Guard was born.

Should the Germans invade, and make serious advances inland, secret plans were ready to transfer the Government out of London. Since May 1939, during Neville Chamberlain's peace-time premiership, a scheme, code name 'Black Move', had been prepared whereby the so-called 'Higher Control Party', consisting of the Prime Minister and the War Cabinet, together with 'Party D'—the War Cabinet Secretariat—would go to Hindlip Hall, near Worcester, while the Service Departments moved to Malvern, Droitwich and Worcester itself. Parliament was also to be evacuated in 'Black Move', to Stratford upon Avon. Churchill, his family and his Private Office would be living at Spetchley House, near Worcester, fifteen minutes drive from Hindlip Hall.

A comprehensive evacuation plan was worked out to the smallest detail. As far as Churchill was concerned, this plan envisaged him and his party travelling to Worcestershire in six cars, along a carefully pre-arranged route, with Colville and Charles Barker[2] taking the current Cabinet papers in their cars, with a three-ton lorry to follow with the remaining Cabinet and other secret papers.[3]

The cellar at Spetchley House had already been converted into an air raid shelter, with a gas-proof door, and emergency food supplies had been brought in. Rooms had been prepared at Spetchley for Churchill and his wife, for their daughter Mary, for Sawyers the valet and Mrs Landemare the cook, as well as for six others—Desmond Morton, Eric Seal, Anthony Bevir, Kathleen Hill, Professor Lindemann, and Lindemann's valet Mr Harvey. John Peck, John Martin, Charles Barker and John Colville were to go to lodgings in Worcester.[4]

The emergency retreat was ready; 'Black Move' awaited only the signal. Churchill meanwhile, convinced that if invasion took place the invading forces could be contained, fought and driven back, went on

[1] Eden Minute of 28 June 1940, and Churchill Note of 30 June 1940: Premier papers, 3/498/1 and 2, folios 43-4.

[2] In charge of the administrative side of Churchill's Secretariat.

[3] Plan of 26 June 1940.

[4] Premier papers, 4/70/1.

June 26 to see for himself the state of the defences, along the Kent and Essex coasts, recalling in his memoirs how, at St Margaret's Bay, near Dover, the brigadier in charge of the beach defences informed him that he had only three anti-tank guns in his whole brigade, covering four or five miles 'of this highly-menaced coastline'. The brigadier also told Churchill that he had only six rounds of ammunition for each of these guns, 'and he asked me', as Churchill wrote, 'with a slight air of challenge, whether he was justified in letting his men fire one single round for practice in order that they might at least know how the weapon worked'. Churchill replied, however, 'that we could not afford practice rounds' and that five should be held 'for the last moment at the closest range'.[1]

General Ismay, who accompanied Churchill on this visit, later recalled two incidents. 'I remember,' he wrote to Churchill after the war, 'that the first visit you made to the troops was to a Corps commanded by General Massy and that you made it by car. I well recall your wrath on this occasion at being taken into the Corps War Room and introduced to all the staff. You told me that you had not come to see this sort of thing but to see troops exercising.' Such was Churchill's moment of anger; but it was compensated for when, as Ismay recalled, 'we went down the front at some small seaside place, where practically every house was a boarding house which relied on the summer visitors for a living. It was a miserable rainy day, but all the old women who owned these boarding houses, and who had temporarily lost their livelihood, turned out and cheered you wildly and called God's blessing upon you.'[2]

Back at Downing Street, Churchill was shown a report from Switzerland stating, as Colville noted in diary, 'that the planned invasion has been postponed if not abandoned and that the Germans were surprised by the intelligent heroism of our troops in France'. Personally, Colville noted, 'I think a peace offensive is almost certain unless it has dawned on Hitler that we shall not stop fighting until we have won.' Once Hitler's peace terms had been rejected, Colville added, 'very heavy bombing is I suppose inevitable'.[3]

Churchill was anxious to ensure that exaggerated or ill-publicized news of such future bombing would not lead to a loss of civilian morale. He therefore minuted to Duff Cooper on June 26 that Press and radio coverage of air raids should be handled 'in a cool way' and on 'a

[1] Winston S. Churchill, *The Second World War*, volume 2, London 1949, page 148.
[2] Ismay to Churchill, letter of 20 September 1948 and enclosure: Churchill papers, 4/44.
[3] Colville diary, 26 June 1940: Colville papers.

diminishing tone of public interest'. It must be made clear, Churchill explained, 'that the vast majority of people are not at all affected by any single air raid', and would hardly sustain 'any evil impression' if it were not 'thrust before them'. Everyone should learn, Churchill added, to take air-raids and air-alarms 'as if they were no more than thunderstorms'.[1]

It was not only the British public towards whom Churchill felt the need to maintain what he saw as a sense of proportion. Even his friend of nearly forty years, the South African Prime Minister, General Smuts, had expressed hesitations at Britain's chances. Churchill hastened, as he told Ismay, 'to reassure him',[2] stressing in a long telegram to Smuts on June 27 that plans were already being made for 'large-scale offensive amphibious operations' in 1940 and 1941.

Churchill told Smuts that he did not expect the 'winter strain' on Hitler to be decisive. But he did believe that Hitler's need 'to try to hold all Europe down in a starving condition with only Gestapo and military occupation and no large theme appealing to masses is not an arrangement which can last long'.

The development of British air power, Churchill added, particularly in regions 'unaffected' by German bombing, should cause Hitler 'increasing difficulties, possibly decisive difficulties' in Germany, 'no matter what successes he has in Europe or Asia'.[3] After all, Churchill pointed out, 'Hitler has vast hungry areas to defend and we have command of the seas. Choice of objectives in Western Europe is therefore wide.'[4]

---

[1] Minute of 26 June 1940: Churchill papers, 20/13.

[2] Minute of 27 June 1940: Churchill papers, 20/13.

[3] That these 'decisive difficulties' for Germany might be caused by the extent of British bombing was widely believed. On 29 June 1940 a Foreign Office report, based on what was called a 'reliable source', stated: '(i) Enemy raids on Germany are creating havoc and causing panic among the civil population. Raids had been expected on certain key points and preparations made for them, but the system of attacking here one day and somewhere else the next had not been reckoned with, and consequently the population is living in a state of acute nervous tension. (ii) Sleepless nights are having their effect on industrial production, and the general alarm is in no way allayed by half-formulated rumours that the authorities have ceased to give warning of air-raids in order to avoid the dislocation of traffic and labour which they entail. (iii) Nerves are becoming frayed, and people have begun to imagine and take refuge from non-existent aircraft during the day, as well as at night.' The report also stated that in the German Air Force: '(v) The number of flying accidents as well as damage caused by unskilful handling of the machines, and in particular of the aero-engines, has increased rapidly since April, owing to the fact that the most highly-trained men were lost at the beginning of the campaign' ('Germany, Effect of RAF raids etc', No. 175, 29 June 1940: Copy No. 13, Cherwell papers).

[4] 'Most Secret', 'Personal and Secret', 26 June 1940; despatched 3 p.m., 27 June 1940: Premier papers, 4/43B/1, folios 373–4.

Such was Churchill's long term perspective and optimism. But in the short term, further news of French naval opinion brought to an abrupt end all hope of the fulfilment of Admiral Darlan's promise not to allow the French Fleet to pass under German control. For Darlan was no longer Commander-in-Chief of the French Navy, but Minister of Marine. As such, he felt that it was his duty to carry out the policy of the Government of which he had become a part, and to honour the armistice terms. Darlan now protested against the British decision not to allow those French warships at Alexandria to leave harbour. But Pound was emphatic, in an interview with the head of the French Naval Mission to London, Admiral Odend'hal, that if the French ships left Egyptian waters, 'they would be fired on'.[1]

That same day, Lord Beaverbrook wrote from London to Sir Samuel Hoare in Madrid: 'Winston, whose outlook was always closely bound up with the French alliance, does not take a vy cheerful view of the possibilities of continued French resistance outside Europe.' Britain was now faced, Beaverbrook wrote, with the prospect 'of an unfriendly France'.[2] In this prospect, the naval confrontation was proving the testing point; Britain's first decisive act being the detention of all French warships in British harbours.[3]

A decision had now to be made about the French ships at Oran.[4] At the War Cabinet on June 27, Pound, as Chief of the Naval Staff, gave July 3 as the date by which it would be possible for a superior British naval force to reach Oran.[5] Churchill commented that he thought the War Cabinet approved 'in principle' of July 3 as the date of the operation, and it was agreed that the planning of the operation should be 'taken in hand at once'.[6] The code name of the operation: 'Catapult.'

[1] Note of 27 June 1940: Admiralty papers, 205/4. The French warships at Alexandria consisted of 1 battleship, 4 cruisers and 4 light cruisers (Premier papers, 3/179/1).

[2] Letter of 27 June 1940: Beaverbrook papers.

[3] These warships were, at Portsmouth, 1 battleship, 2 light cruisers, 5 torpedo boats and 2 submarines; at Plymouth, 1 battleship, 2 light cruisers, 2 destroyers, 1 torpedo boat and 3 submarines. There was also 1 destroyer at Gibraltar, 1 submarine at Malta, and 1 cruiser at Singapore, all likewise detained. The seizure of French warships in British ports was given the code name 'Grasp'.

[4] The French warships were in fact at the naval base of Mers el-Kebir, three miles west of Oran across the bay. For the French, the events of 3 July 1940 are normally spoken of as 'Mers el-Kebir', for the British as 'Oran'.

[5] The British capital ships involved were *Hood, Nelson, Valiant, Resolution* and *Ark Royal*. The French naval force at Oran consisted of 4 battleships, 1 cruiser, 7 light cruisers, 2 destroyers and 4 submarines (Premier papers, 3/179/1).

[6] War Cabinet No. 184 of 1940, 27 June 1940, 12 noon, Minute 5, Confidential Annex: Cabinet papers, 65/13.

The last week of June 1940 saw new difficulties emerge in Britain's relations with the United States. On the morning of June 26, in Washington, Purvis had spoken to Morgenthau about various essential orders then in preparation. The discussion had been disheartening: 'As a result of an attack in Congress,' Purvis reported at once to London, 'United States Administration has backwatered on granting of priorities and President has issued statement that transfer'—of twenty motor torpedo boats then under construction in the United States—'is no longer valid'. Purvis added that the provisions of an Act of 1917 had been invoked by the Navy, and that the Attorney General 'has confirmed that the sale to a belligerent of an armed vessel is illegal'. This law, Purvis warned, 'also prevents the sale of destroyers', and he added: 'For the moment I feel nothing will be gained by pressing for reconsideration. When effects of recent Débacle have been digested and the British ability to resist has become more evident, the attack can be renewed.'[1]

Purvis did not exaggerate: on the following morning a telegram from Lord Lothian confirmed that it would now be 'impossible' for any destroyers or other ships belonging to the United States Navy 'to be sold or delivered' to Britain.[2]

'It seems years,' John Colville noted in his diary on June 27, 'since we had even a gleam of good news.' And he added: 'America is disheartening, inclined to blame us for the fall of France, and less eager to counter Japan in the Far East.'

That morning Colville was summoned to Churchill's room at 10 o'clock. 'He was lying in bed,' Colville wrote, 'in a red dressing gown, smoking a cigar, and dictating to Mrs Hill who sat with a typewriter at the foot of the bed. His box, half full of papers, stood open on his bed, and by his side a vast chromium-plated spittoon to throw his cigars into. His black cat Nelson, who had quite replaced our old No. 10 black cat, sprawled at the end of the bed.'[3]

Among the minutes which Churchill dictated that morning was a further protest to Sinclair, expressing the extent to which 'everyone is astonished at the failure of the Air Ministry to expand the Air Force on the outbreak of war, and recently at the proved failure to provide a proper supply of pilots when they have so long been crying out about the plethora of pilots. . . .' Churchill added: 'I do hope and pray that

[1] 'Purco', No. 256 of 26 June 1940: Cabinet papers, 85/14.
[2] 'Special Distribution and War Cabinet', Telegram No. 1129, despatched 11.42 a.m., 26 June 1940, received, 9.30 a.m., 27 June 1940: Cabinet papers, 115/83.
[3] Colville diary, 27 June 1940: Colville papers. Sir David Hunt notes: 'The "vast, chromium-plated spittoon" was really an ice-bucket from the Savoy Hotel. Hugh Wontner kept him supplied' (Letter to the author, 2 September 1982).

you will feel yourself able to effect radical reforms in what is, I am sure, a most cumbersome and ill-working administrative machine.' Churchill had felt, he wrote, 'that with your new eye you would have a chance far greater than that enjoyed by persons compromised with the past'.[1]

One pressure on June 27 came from South Africa, where General Smuts asked for British troops and aircraft to be sent to East or West Africa, in order to act as a buffer against any German or Italian thrust southward. This, Churchill wrote, 'would not be the moment' to send such a force, nor did he see 'how they could be used or maintained if they got there'. Churchill's telegram continued:

British Eastern Mediterranean fleet is well-placed to resist an attack on Egypt, as well as to cover east coast of Africa. We can also send forces from here by the Atlantic far quicker than any German force can traverse the immense land distances of Africa, if indeed they are traversable except by very small numbers. Possibility of air attack on South Africa appears remote at present time. We are attacking Germans ceaselessly and heavily in their homeland, and are also being attacked ourselves, so far in a very unskilled fashion.

'It would not be right,' Churchill ended, 'to make any considerable detachment of Air Forces from Great Britain until we see what happens in the main trial of air strength now impending here.'[2]

On June 28 one of Churchill's earlier suggestions for defence against invasion came into being: these were the 'Leopard' formations intended to be the British version of Germany's Storm Troops. As Churchill minuted that day for the Chiefs of Staff Committee:

The safety of the country depends on having a large number (now only nine, but should soon be fifteen) of 'Leopard' brigade groups which can be directed swiftly, i.e., within four hours, to the points of lodgment. Difficulties of landing on beaches are serious, even when the invader had reached them; but difficulties of nourishing a lodgment when exposed to heavy attack by land, air, and sea are far greater. All therefore depends on rapid, resolute engagement of any landed forces which may slip through the sea control. This should not be beyond our means provided the field troops are not consumed in beach defences, and are kept in a high condition of mobility, crouched and ready to spring.

Should the Germans capture a port, Churchill added, larger formations with artillery would be needed, and four or five 'good divisions' should be held in reserve 'to deal with such an improbable misfortune'.

---

[1] Minute dated 27 June 1940, Private and Personal: Foreign Office papers, 800/326/H/XL/72.
[2] 'Personal and Secret', 27 June 1940: Premier papers, 4/43B/1, folios 361–2.

The battle would be won or lost, Churchill believed, 'not on the beaches, but by the mobile brigades and the main reserve'.[1]

Reading of a proposal from the Papal Nuncio in Switzerland to encourage peace negotiations, Churchill minuted for Halifax: 'I hope it will be made clear to the Nuncio that we do not desire to make any enquiries as to terms of peace with Hitler, and that all our agents are strictly forbidden to entertain any such suggestion.'[2] When his American friend Bernard Baruch, sent good wishes for the coming struggle, Churchill replied: 'We shall be all right here but your people are not doing much,' and he added tersely: 'If things go wrong with us it will be bad for them.'[3]

The United States was much on Churchill's mind. In answer to a suggestion from Lord Lothian, that American public opinion was in need of the spur of a Churchill broadcast, Churchill replied on June 28: 'No doubt I will make some broadcast presently, but I don't think words count for much now.' Churchill's telegram continued:

Too much attention should not be paid to eddies of United States opinion. Only force of events can govern them. Up till April they were so sure the Allies would win that they did not think help necessary. Now they are so sure we shall lose that they do not think it possible. I feel good confidence we can repel invasion and keep alive in the air. Anyhow, we are going to try.

Never cease to impress on President and others that if this country were successfully invaded and largely occupied after heavy fighting some Quisling Government would be formed to make peace on the basis of our becoming a German Protectorate. In this case the British Fleet would be the solid contribution with which this Peace Government would buy terms. Feeling in England against United States would be similar to French bitterness against us now. We have really not had any help worth speaking of from the United States so far.

We know President is our best friend, but it is no use trying to dance attendance upon Republican and Democratic Conventions. What really matters is whether Hitler is master of Britain in three months or not. I think not. But this is a matter which cannot be argued beforehand.

'Your mood,' Churchill told Lothian, 'should be bland and phlegmatic. No-one is down-hearted.'[4]

---

[1] Minute dated 28 June 1940: Churchill papers, 20/13.

[2] Minute of 28 June 1940: Churchill papers, 20/13. The proposal had come through the British Embassy in Berne (telegram No. 281).

[3] Telegram of 28 June 1940: Bernard Baruch papers.

[4] Telegram of 28 June 1940: Churchill papers, 20/14.

30

Awaiting Invasion

A S June 1940 came to an end, the situation was grave in the
extreme; 'I doubt whether the people yet realise what they are
going to be up against soon!' Lord Davidson had written to Stanley
Baldwin on June 21.[1] A week later Lindemann commented for Churchill on the most recent secret estimate of German air strength: 'The
strength of the units is increasing as the German Air Force works itself
up for major offensive operations.' As to the air figures themselves,
Lindemann noted, it appeared that the United Kingdom's air strength,
including reserves, and totalling 4,732 aircraft, was still overshadowed
by the equivalent German figure of 11,600 aircraft, despite the much
heavier German casualty rate.[2]

The German air superiority which these figures seemed to reveal
was one essential pre-requisite for a German invasion. A small clue
which seemed to suggest that German preparations for invasion were
already well advanced reached Churchill that same day, June 28, from
a most secret source; a German air force instruction that detailed
maps of Britain should be delivered to German anti-aircraft units in
France.

The source of this information was an actual instruction issued to
the German Air Force. This, and similar instructions, sent by radio to
the German unit commanders in the field, had begun to be received
simultaneously in Britain, by listeners in the British Intelligence service.
Their receipt of these instructions was made possible because radio
listening posts in many parts of Britain were now intercepting messages
encyphered on a German electro-mechanical machine, the Enigma
machine, and were relaying these messages, still in cypher, to the

[1] Letter of 21 June 1940: Baldwin papers, 174, folios 278–9.
[2] Between 10 May and 28 June British aircraft losses were estimated at 1,393, German losses at
3,080: Cherwell papers, G.7.

Government Code and Cypher School at Bletchley Park, north of London.[1]

For the previous five weeks, since May 22, the Bletchley cryptographic centre had succeeded in breaking regularly the daily changing settings of the Enigma machine used by the German Air Force. Later it was to break with equal regularity the variants of the machine used by the German Navy, Army and other organizations, including the SS, the Abwehr—the German High Command's intelligence service—and the German State Railways.

Breaking the German Air Force Enigma permitted the Bletchley 'listeners' to read the instructions and other correspondence passing by radio between forward German Air Force units and their rear headquarters. In late May and early June 1940 these messages were not particularly numerous, and were to remain relatively limited for the rest of 1940. But they were to grow immensely in volume in later years. Sometimes these Air Force messages contained information about the German Army, including the location and strength of army units, immediate operational instructions, and clues as to future plans.[2] The only difference between British and German access to the contents of these messages was that the German units held the key to the daily changing cypher, while the Bletchley cryptographers had to rediscover the key every twenty-four hours.

The ability to read these German messages in the exact form in which they were sent out, and for the most part with little delay, was a major Intelligence victory. The work of deciphering these messages was so complex that it involved by early 1942 nearly a thousand men and women at Bletchley Park, backed up by thousands more at intercept stations throughout Britain. One limitation to the Enigma revelations was that the British had access only to the initially small proportion of the messages which went by radio, since most of the message traffic in German-occupied Europe could go by landline, and could not be read.

Yet it was the Enigma machine which had already provided Air Force Intelligence with the essential clue to the discovery of the German beam method of bombing. This was the method which R. V.

---

[1] The School was usually known by the abbreviation GC & CS. Since it had been set up in the 1920s it had come under MI6 (Military Intelligence, Secret Intelligence Service) which was itself answerable to the Foreign Office. Later it became independent of MI6, having acquired its own Director-General, Commander Sir Edward Travis RN.

[2] The German Naval Enigma was not broken regularly until June 1941; the U-Boats, however, changed to their own model of the Enigma machine in February 1942, and this was not broken until December 1942.

Jones had explained to Churchill at the Downing Street meeting on June 21.[1] Now, only a week later, it was Jones himself who sent Churchill a report of a further Enigma message which had been successfully decyphered at Bletchley. Jones' report read:

On 22.6.1940, an unimpeachable source (who had previously given the vital clue to the Knickebein solution) reported that he saw on 20.6.40, a request from Flakcorps I (AA Corps) for the following maps to be delivered, among others, immediately to their H.Q.:
    (1) 800 copies England and Ireland, scale 1/100,000 and 1/300,000
    (2) 300 copies France and England 1/1,000,000.

In sending this decyphered German message to Churchill, Jones added his own comment. 'It will be noticed,' he wrote, 'that this request is from a Flakcorps, and not from a Fliegercorps, possibly indicating an intention to land motorised AA units in both England and Ireland.'[2]

Churchill at once asked Lindemann to study this report, and sent a copy to Ismay for his scrutiny.[3] What neither Churchill, Lindemann nor Ismay could know was that this request for the distribution of maps was evidently an anticipation by the German Flakcorps Commander of Hitler's order, not issued until July 2, to prepare for the invasion of Britain. Flak, and later the paratroop formations, although both branches of army warfare, came under the German Air Force, and therefore used the German Air Force Enigma machine.

In the summer of 1940 a pattern soon emerged whereby Churchill was to be able to make the maximum possible use of this most secret source. As soon as a set of messages was decyphered at Bletchley, they were sent to the headquarters of MI6, at Broadway, London, together with interpretations. At Broadway, only five minutes from Downing Street, a selection was then made, and immediately sent by messenger, locked in a special buff-coloured box, to Churchill. Churchill alone at Downing Street had the key to the box.

To protect the source of these messages, the code name 'Boniface' was used, in the hope, successful as it proved, of suggesting to any uninitiated eye that the material came from an individual agent, presumably a British-run spy in Germany, whose personal code name was 'Boniface'.[4]

---

[1] See pages 580–4 of this volume.
[2] Office of the Minister of Defence, 'Intelligence', PM/413/1, Message of 28 June 1940: Cabinet papers, 120/744.
[3] Minute of 2 July 1940 ('Gen Ismay to see, WSC'): Cabinet papers, 120/744.
[4] Jones himself in his submission of June 28, used for this same reason the expressions 'a source *who* had' and '*he* saw'.

After a short while, the code name 'Boniface' was replaced by 'CX', the standard two letter symbol for a British-run secret agent in enemy territory.[1] In his own notes and telegrams, however, Churchill continued to refer to the Enigma messages as 'Boniface', and was later heard to refer to the decyphering staff at Bletchley as 'the geese who laid the golden eggs and never cackled'.[2] He also called them, more colloquially, his 'hens'.[3]

Within two years, the Enigma decrypts, as the decyphered messages were called, were supplemented by those from other cypher machines used by the Italians and Japanese, and later still from the secret German teleprinter, Geheimschreiber. Together, these decrypts became known as 'Ultra', a word in use from 1941. They in turn were supplemented by information obtained from the breaking of numerous codes of lesser difficulty, used by the German armed forces and police. All this, together with information from direction-finding, radar listening, and other devices which did not depend on cypher or code-breaking was known collectively as 'Signals Intelligence' or 'Sigint'. When interpreted against the background of other Intelligence information, provided by such sources as air reconnaissance, prisoner-of-war interrogation and secret agents, 'Sigint', with the Enigma decrypts as its pearl, provided Churchill and his senior advisers with insight into an incredibly wide range of German strategic, operational and tactical decisions, as well as into how the Germans understood their own situation.[4]

In June 1940, however, the Enigma messages were still difficult to decypher, nor was the decyphering and interpretation sufficiently mastered to be of help in the hour by hour process of operational decision-making. As the frequency and value of the Enigma decrypts grew, however, they became of overriding importance in many of the main military, air and naval decisions of the war.

By the end of 1940, Churchill's own daily study of the Enigma decrypts, and of the Intelligence interpretations which were submitted

[1] The two letters CX (known as a digraph) were followed by a further digraph, JQ, indicating 'Boniface'. From June 1941 the trigraph MSS (for 'Most Secret Source') was used. In sending these messages overseas, other digraphs were used, including, in 1941, OL and MK.

[2] Quoted in Ronald Lewin, *Ultra Goes to War, The Secret Story*, London 1978, page 64.

[3] Communication from a Bletchley 'hand'.

[4] Details of the work of the various organisations comprising the British intelligence service during the period covered by this volume, and an account of British cypher breaking in the Second World War is to be found in: F. H. Hinsley and others, *British Intelligence in the Second World War, Its Influence on Strategy and Operations*, volume 1, London 1979; volume 2, London 1981.

with them, was to give him considerable and immediate knowledge of German plans and actions as they evolved; knowledge only shared by some thirty people in the most secret circle of war direction: some half dozen of his thirty-five Ministers, the three Chiefs of Staff and their three Vice-Chiefs, and no more than perhaps ten or twelve others concerned with the evolution of war policy at the centre.[1] Even Churchill's Private Secretaries, who saw him every day and throughout the day, did not have access to the locked buff box in which 'Boniface' reached their master: he alone had, on his key ring, the key by which the box could be opened. Overseas, knowledge of the Enigma secret was limited to the Commanders-in-Chief in the field and their principal Intelligence officers.

During June 28 Churchill had to deal with a matter of considerable delicacy. Since the defeat of France, the Duke and Duchess of Windsor had been in Madrid, seeking to return to Britain; but, as Sir Samuel Hoare had reported to Churchill, the Duke was insisting on several conditions before agreeing to come back. On June 27 the Duke set out his principal condition in a telegram to Churchill, which reached Downing Street on the morning of June 28. 'In the light of past experience,' he said, 'my wife and myself must not risk finding ourselves once more regarded by the British public as in a different status to other members of my family.'[2]

Churchill reacted sharply to this plea for special treatment in time of war. 'Your Royal Highness has taken active military rank,' he minuted on the Duke's telegram, 'and refusal to obey direct orders of competent military authority would create a serious situation. I hope it will not be necessary for such orders to be sent.' Churchill added, in a sentence which he deleted before sending his reply: 'Already there is a great deal of doubt as to the circumstances in wh your Royal Highness left Paris.' Churchill's reply ended: 'I most strongly urge immediate compliance with wishes of the Government.'[3]

Churchill submitted this reply to Buckingham Palace, from where Sir Alexander Hardinge replied that same day: 'The King thinks that the Prime Minister's telegram would have a very salutary effect.' But

---

[1] Including Professor Lindemann.

[2] Sir S. Hoare (Madrid) No. 437, sent 9.30 p.m. 27 June 1940, received 4.30 a.m., 28 June 1940: Churchill papers, 20/9.

[3] Minute of 28 June 1940: Churchill papers, 20/9.

Hardinge himself suggested that as he could not see how it was possible for the Duke 'as an ex-King to perform any useful service in this country', he might be given 'some appointment on Wavell's staff in Egypt'.[1] This Churchill rejected, and the Duke was ordered back to Britain. Meanwhile, Hoare informed Churchill that the Duke had now dropped his condition about receiving some official post, 'and that it boiled down to both of them being received once only for quite a short meeting by the King and Queen, and notice of the fact appearing in the Court Circular'. All that was at issue, Hoare commented, was a 'once only' audience of 'a quarter of an hour'.[2]

Hoare's telegram reached London on the morning of June 29. On the previous evening, Friday, Churchill had gone to Chequers for the weekend, driving from London with Lindemann. The other overnight guest was Ismay. As well as Clementine Churchill, Mary Churchill and her cousin Judy Montagu were part of the family contingent, which also included Diana and Duncan Sandys. Colville, two secretaries, two detectives, and Sawyers the valet, accompanied them.

That Friday night, the guests for dinner were Sir Robert and Lady Vansittart, and Alexis Léger, former Secretary General of the French Foreign Ministry, whom Churchill had met a number of times before the war. During the evening, Churchill told Léger, as Colville noted in his diary, that he was 'speaking to his "Cercle Sacré" and must express himself frankly'. He saw the possibility of France declaring war on Britain and wanted to know 'how we could maintain the goodwill of the French people, for whose salvation we were the last hope, when we were obliged to starve them by blockade and destroy their towns by bombs'. How could Britain, Churchill asked, convince the French people 'that we were being cruel in order to be kind'. It was 'essential', he added, to keep the French people 'well-disposed to us', even if their Government went to war with Britain.

One suggestion made by Léger was for a British propaganda campaign in the United States. But Churchill saw no merit in this. 'Propaganda is all very well,' he said, 'but it is events that make the world. If we smash the Huns here, we shall need no propaganda in the United States.' Britain had reached 'the night before the battle. It may be long. Now we must live. Next year we shall be winning. The year after that we shall triumph. But if we can hold the Germans in this coming month of July, and deny this country to them, our position will be

---

[1] 'Private and Confidential', 28 June 1940: Churchill papers, 20/9.

[2] Sir S. Hoare (Madrid) No. 440, sent 6.45 p.m. 28 June 1940, received 3.30 a.m., 29 June 1940: Churchill papers, 20/9.

quite different from today,' and, Churchill added, 'a very different wind will be blowing in the world.'

Léger and Vansittart remained at Chequers until one o'clock on the morning of June 29. At one moment, reflecting on the fall of France, and on his own dramatic but brief visits to Paris, Briare and Tours, Churchill told his visitors: 'I wish now that I had stayed there ten days, and had left Neville to carry on at home.'[1]

After sleeping at Chequers, Churchill spent the morning of June 29 working in bed. In a minute to Lindemann he reflected his concern with the coming air battle, asking about the possibility of multiple projectors and rockets directed by radar 'irrespective of cloud or darkness', and with the proximity fuse[2] working 'effectively by day and to a lesser extent in moonlight or starlight'.[3] If this combination could be effected, Churchill wrote, the defence against air attack 'would become decisive'. Churchill added: 'We are not far from it in every respect, yet it seems to baffle us. Assemble your ideas and facts so that I may give extreme priority and impulse to this business.'

Churchill realized that aircraft factory output and other war production in Britain alone could 'get round the invasion danger' in the coming three months. 'But what about 1941?' he asked Lindemann. 'It seems to me that only immense American supplies can be of use in turning the corner.'[4]

Churchill's plans encompassed not only 1941, but even 1942, as he sought to prepare for future warfare, and for British initiatives, despite the day-by-day dangers of the summer of 1940. Pondering the long-term question of experimenting with and then building 'concrete' barges, whose method of construction would, he had been told, provide a saving of 60% on steel and iron, as compared to an all-steel vessel, Churchill minuted to A. V. Alexander: 'I trust there will be no slowing down on the work of the concrete ships, and that not only small barges but larger vessels will be constructed. We shall want these in 1942.'

Churchill went on to ask Alexander for a 'special report' on the research into concrete ships, and their construction, to be sent to him

---

[1] Colville diary, 28 June 1940: Colville papers.
[2] Known as the PE fuse.
[3] Radar was then known as RDF (Radio Direction-Finding). Its existence was not publicly acknowledged until 1941, when it was referred to as Radiolocation. 'Radar', an American term (Radio Direction and Ranging), was adopted as the name in 1943, as part of the effort to establish a joint Anglo-American nomenclature.
[4] Minute of 29 June 1940: Churchill papers, 20/13.

on the seventh of each month, covering results to the last day of the previous month.[1]

As Churchill dictated his minutes, Colville noted in his diary: 'Winston is perturbed.' With the naval blockade of Germany no longer effective, all that was left for any British pressure was air attack. Yet so many of the discussions concerned withdrawal and retreat, or the aftermath of withdrawal. One such problem was the future of food supplies which had been left in the Channel Islands after the British forces there had been withdrawn. In a moment of whimsy, Churchill told Colville: 'Tell the Ministry of Food to evaluate it, and the Admiralty to evacuate it.'

While he was at Chequers on June 29, Churchill received from the Home Secretary a list of 150 prominent people who had been arrested under Regulation 18B[2] and interned. Of the first three on the list, two were cousins by marriage of Clementine Churchill, 'a fact', Colville noted, 'which piqued Winston and caused much merriment among his children'.[3]

Among those children was Randolph, who had reached Chequers with his wife during the afternoon, and who was, as Colville recorded, 'anything but kind to Winston, who adores him'. At dinner, Colville found Randolph 'coarse and aggressive', and he added: 'I felt ashamed for Winston's sake.' Yet Churchill opposed Randolph's request to be sent on active service, telling those present that if Randolph were killed 'he wouldn't be able to carry on with his work'.[4]

That evening Churchill received a minute from Air Intelligence, based upon a study of decrypted Enigma messages, which stated that Germany's long-range bombers would have completed refitting at their home bases by July 8. Colville, not knowing the source of this report,

[1] Minute of 29 June 1940: Premier papers, 3/381/2, folio 128. The first concrete ship was completed in May 1941. By March 1942, 59 of the 80 being constructed had been delivered.

[2] Technically, an Order or amendment (IA) to Defence Regulation 18B, passed by Parliament on 22 May 1940. Under this Order, the Government could detain any members of any organisation if 'the persons in control of the organisation have or have had associations with persons concerned in the government of, or sympathies with the system of government of, any Power with which his Majesty is at war'. Those arrested under 18B (IA) were imprisoned without trial and for an unspecified period. On 11 December 1946 Lord Jowitt, then Lord Chancellor, said in the House of Lords: 'Let us be fair to those people who were imprisoned under Order 18B, and let us remember that they have never been accused of any crime; not only have they not been convicted of a crime, but they have not been accused of a crime. That should be remembered in all fairness to them.'

[3] The cousins were Sir Oswald Mosley and George Pitt-Rivers, the latter a staunch racist and believer in a conspiracy of Jews, Free Masons and Communists as the deliberate cause of the war. His published works on these themes included *The Clash of Culture and the Contact of Races* (1927), *Weeds in the Garden of Marriage* (1931) and *The Czech Conspiracy* (1938).

[4] Colville diary, 29 June 1940: Colville papers.

noted in his diary that the German bombers would be 'ready by July 8'.[1] What Colville did not record was the Air Intelligence conclusion, in the minute as received by Churchill, that, because a German air force unit had been ordered to bring into effect new wireless telegraph instructions from 10 p.m. on June 30, 'the opening of the Offensive against this country must be anticipated from July 1st onwards'.[2]

Like the earlier Enigma revelations of the beams on June 20, and the maps on June 28, this new Enigma revelation of June 29 gave Churchill and his senior advisers a remarkable general insight into German preparations, even though it could give no indication of the political decisions, or hesitations, in Berlin.

That evening a telephone call from the Air Ministry gave details of German aeroplanes which were even then passing north of Aylesbury, less than ten miles from Chequers. Churchill told Colville: 'I bet you a monkey to a mousetrap they don't hit the house'; and then, as Colville wrote in his diary, 'hurried excitedly out to see if he could see anything, shouting at the sentry, "Friend, Tofrek (the password), Prime Minister", a formula which entirely nonplussed the unfortunate soldier.'

One of those present, General Paget, observing this scene, commented to Colville: 'what a wonderful tonic he is'.[3]

On the morning of Sunday June 30 Churchill was awake by 7.30, and spent the morning in bed, dictating to Mrs Hill. With the Enigma decrypt as his warning signal that German preparations for a possible invasion were actively under way, he asked the Admiralty, through Ismay, to study charts of tides, and of the state of the moon, for the Humber, the Thames Estuary and Beachy Head, 'with a view to ascertaining on which days conditions will be most favourable to a seaborne landing'.[4]

Casting about that morning for some effective deterrent that might be used on the beaches themselves, Churchill also asked Ismay for a report on the amount of mustard gas 'or other variants' in store, and whether such gas could be used in air bombs as well as fired from guns. Whatever the output, Churchill added, it should be 'speeded up', and he went on to explain what he had in mind:

Supposing lodgments were effected on our coast, there could be no better points for application of mustard than these beaches and lodgments. In my

---

[1] Colville diary, 29 June 1940: Colville papers.
[2] Minute No. 47 of 28 June 1940, by Group-Captain F. F. Inglis: Air Ministry papers, 40/2321, folio 39.
[3] Colville diary, 29 June 1940: Colville papers.
[4] Minute of 30 June 1940: Churchill papers, 20/13.

view there would be no need to wait for the enemy to adopt such methods. He will certainly adopt them if he thinks it will pay. Home Defence should be consulted as to whether the prompt drenching of lodgments would not be a great help.

'Everything should be brought to the highest pitch of readiness,' Churchill added, 'but the question of actual employment must be studied by the Cabinet.'[1] On the following day Colville noted in his diary: 'The Prime Minister has instructed Ismay to investigate the question of drenching the beaches with mustard gas if the Germans land. He considers that gas warfare would be justified if the Germans land.' And to a visitor to lunch at Chequers that Sunday, Churchill remarked: 'I have no scruples, except not to do anything dishonourable.'[2]

Three days later, the War Office replied that it was desirable to have Britain's preparations complete, 'so that we could retaliate', or indeed, if the War Cabinet decided, 'to initiate' gas warfare.[3] The building up of stocks began at once; but when, two months later, Herbert Morrison, the Minister of Supply raised the question of the purchase of chemical materials from the United States, Churchill agreed that 'it would be better to leave the United States out of this particular line', while urging Morrison: 'Press on here.'[4]

On June 30 Churchill received from Ismay the list of war materials and aircraft already on their way from the United States. This was the material released from United States Army and Naval stocks as a result of the efforts of Arthur Purvis, and with the connivance of General Marshall: it included 521 operational aircraft and 420 training aircraft.[5] On receiving this list Churchill minuted to Lindemann: 'Analyse & keep for the record,' and he added: 'Give me your comments.'[6] In reply, Lindemann informed Churchill that the shipments expected before the end of July were 'very satisfactory', and were in fact in the region of 'the requirements of 10 divisions'.[7]

From Beaverbrook came encouraging news on June 30: there were now 1,040 operational aircraft ready for service awaiting 'the disposi-

[1] Minute of 30 June 1940: Premier papers, 3/88/3, folio 250.

[2] Colville diary, 1 July 1940: Colville papers. The visitor was Major-General Thorne.

[3] Minute of 2 July 1940: Chiefs of Staff Paper No. 582 of 1941, 30 September 1941 (summary of official correspondence, circulated by Churchill): Premier papers, 3/88/1, Annex I, A-Offensive Measures.

[4] Prime Minister's Personal Minute, M.50, 31 August 1940: Premier papers, 3/88/3, folio 241.

[5] 'War Material Released From United States Army and Navy Stocks', 23 June 1940: Premier papers, 3/479/1, folios 86–8.

[6] Note of 30 June 1940: Premier papers, 3/479/1, folio 84.

[7] Minute of 3 July 1940: Premier papers, 3/474/1, folio 78.

tions of the Government'.[1] As a measure of 'our development',
Beaverbrook added, 'I would remind you that there were 45 aircraft
ready for service when your Administration began.'[2] This was a
powerful reminder of the consequences of pre-war defence policies of
which Churchill had been so stern a critic. Yet when Randolph Churchill remarked that the leaders of the former Government ought to be
punished, Churchill replied: 'We don't want to punish anybody now,
except the enemy,' and Colville noted in his diary how Churchill 'never
countenances a word against Chamberlain.' The only moment of
somewhat caustic retrospect came when Colville told Churchill that
the Germans had bombed the Baldwin ironworks. 'Very ungrateful of
them' was Churchill's comment.[3]

Beaverbrook had ended his letter of June 30 by offering Churchill
his resignation. He could not work 'with the Air Ministry or the Air
Marshals', and anyhow 'my work is finished and my task is over'.
Another man could now take it over, and expect the support and sympathy 'which has been denied to me'. Churchill rejected his friend's
appeal, telling him frankly, but scarcely brusquely in view of the circumstances:

I have received your letter of June 30, and hasten to say that at a moment
like this when an invasion is reported to be imminent there can be no question
of any Ministerial resignations being accepted. I require you therefore to dismiss this matter from your mind, and to continue the magnificent work you
are doing on which to a large extent our safety depends. Meanwhile I am
patiently studying how to meet your needs in respect of control of the overlapping parts of your Department and that of the Air Ministry, and also to
assuage the unfortunate differences which have arisen.[4]

On the day that Churchill wrote this letter to Beaverbrook, he was
brought into a technical controversy between Beaverbrook and Sinclair. The issue was the efficiency of a new anti-aircraft device, the
Parachute and Cable rocket, whereby wires held up by parachute were
to be sent up by rocket around the perimeter of an aircraft factory or
aerodrome. If an enemy aeroplane ran into the wire, a second parachute opened, forming a fatal drag on the aeroplane wing.

On July 1 Beaverbrook told Churchill that the device was not suitable to defend his aircraft factories, despite Sinclair's insistence that the

[1] Including 235 Hurricanes and 104 Spitfires.
[2] Note of 30 June 1940: Premier papers, 3/38, folios 52–3.
[3] Colville diary, 30 June 1940: Colville papers.
[4] Letter of 1 July 1940, Churchill papers, 20/4. It was the historian A. J. P. Taylor who
described Churchill's answer as 'brusque' (A. J. P. Taylor, *Beaverbrook*, London 1972, page 443).

Air Staff were 'most anxious' to go on with the scheme. 'Surely,' Churchill minuted to Lindemann, 'this is our most important item?'[1]

Lindemann undertook to examine the question for Churchill; serving both as scientific guide, and as mediator between conflicting claims and personalities.[2]

In an attempt to understand the situation on the ground in each area where the Germans might invade, Churchill had minuted to Ismay on June 28: 'I want to see another General this week,' and had suggested that the General commanding the southern side of the Thames Estuary, 'whoever he is', might lunch with him at Chequers.[3] The General concerned was Major-General Thorne, who had commanded the 3rd Battalion Grenadier Guards for two years in the First World War, and had served as Military Attaché in Berlin during the first two years of Hitler's Chancellorship.

No official record was kept of Churchill's meeting with Thorne, but, as Colville recorded in his diary, the two men discussed what would happen if the Germans landed 80,000 men in the area under the General's Command, between Thanet and Pevensey. 'Winston is less pessimistic,' Colville noted, 'and thinks the Navy will have much to say to that.' But he was not sanguine 'about our ability to hold the whole expanse of beaches and he pointed out that a river line had never proved a real obstacle to an enemy'. It would not be difficult, Churchill thought, for the Germans to find 'soft passages into which they can probe'.

Thorne told Churchill that he was worried that the Germans, acting according to their past practice, would concentrate all their forces against one place. In reply, Churchill explained the reasons for his more general optimism. 'Winston says Hitler must be having to change his plans,' Colville recorded. 'He cannot have foreseen the collapse of France, and must have planned his strategy of invasion on the assumption that the French armies would be holding out on the Somme or at least on the Seine, and that the British Expeditionary Force would either be assisting them or else have been wiped out.'

[1] Minute dated 2 July 1940: Premier papers, 3/347, folio 77.

[2] It emerged that, despite the Air Staff's keenness on the Parachute and Cable rocket, Dowding, for whose aerodromes they were principally intended, described them as 'not of any value'—or so Beaverbrook reported directly to Churchill on 16 August 1940 (Premier papers, 3/347, folio 13).

[3] Minute of 28 June 1940: Churchill papers, 20/13.

With France no longer in the battle, there were of course many more opportunities for a German invasion; but Churchill pointed out that if the invading troops were to be escorted, it would be difficult for the invading ships to penetrate the Straits of Dover. At the same time the whole of the British Expeditionary Force was now back in Britain to defend the island.

Thorne did not challenge this wider survey. He did point out, however, that his own divisions were 'scarcely equipped and only partly trained'. He could, he felt, hold down the German left wing in the Ashdown Forest, but 'he did not see what could prevent the right wing advancing through Canterbury to London', especially as his only trained and equipped division, the Third, was about to be transferred to Northern Ireland.[1]

Churchill understood the General's concern, and promised him that 'this would not be done'.[2] Writing that night to Ismay, Churchill set out his reasons against the despatch of the Third Division to Northern Ireland. It was, he pointed out, one of only two fully-equipped British divisions, and although its transfer had been proposed by the Chiefs of Staff, it would, Churchill told Ismay, constitute an 'undue risk'. An alternative scheme should be made, Churchill wrote, to send if necessary 'two or three lightly-equipped brigades' to Northern Ireland, where he doubted the Germans would make a full scale naval landing with substantial artillery. 'Air-borne descents,' he noted, 'cannot carry much artillery,' and in any case, 'nothing that can happen in Ireland can be immediately decisive'.[3]

Churchill returned to London during the afternoon of June 30. 'I saw him this evening after his bath,' John Martin wrote home, 'wrapped only in a huge towel, looking like one of the later Roman Emperors.' Martin added: 'when I told Winston that six people had died of heart failure during the air raid warning, he said that *he* was more likely to die of over-eating, but he didn't want to die yet when so many interesting things were happening'.[4]

On the following day Eric Seal, Churchill's Principal Private Secretary, wrote home: 'There is practically no news about the war, except that we are all beginning to wonder when the invasion is due.' And he

---

[1] The plan to move the Third Division to Northern Ireland had been given the code name 'Tulip'.

[2] Colville diary, 30 June 1940: Colville papers.

[3] Minute of 30 June 1940: Churchill papers, 20/13. The War Cabinet approved the holding back of the Third Division on 2 July 1940 (Cabinet papers, 65/14, folio 11).

[4] Letter of 30 June 1940: Martin papers.

added: 'I expect we'll have some fun & games in the next few weeks.'[1]

It was the prospect of imminent invasion that concerned Churchill most at the War Cabinet on the morning of July 1. It was the very morning on which the Enigma decrypts had suggested a German bombing offensive might begin, or at least be possible. What was being done, Churchill asked, about digging trenches 'in big fields in order to prevent the landing of aircraft'.

Seven weeks earlier, Lindemann's very first letter to Churchill when he became Prime Minister, a letter written out in his own neat handwriting on May 12, had been on this subject. Parachute troops, Lindemann had written, 'are probably not a great danger unless they are rapidly re-inforced by troop carriers landed in large fields seized and guarded by the parachutists'. In his letter of May 12, Lindemann had proposed that trenches be dug across 'potential landing grounds', especially those 'near vulnerable targets'. The delay while German parachute troops filled in the trenches to enable the troop-carriers to land should, Lindemann had written, 'give us time to bring up the comparatively small forces needed to deal with them'.[2]

On June 30, with the danger of invasion a topic of daily concern, Churchill asked Lindemann to draft a report for the digging of trenches across 'all flat fields more than 400 yards long'. These trenches should be dug, Lindemann advised, by civilian labour under the orders of the Local Authorities. If this were done it would reduce the danger from air-borne troops, Lindemann wrote, 'to negligible proportions'.

Under Lindemann's proposal, fields under crops would be excepted, and he added: 'A few trenches wrongly placed would not matter; the vast majority would serve their purpose namely holding up the troop carriers until the parachutists had filled in the trenches which would give us time to attack the parachutists.'

Lindemann advised an appeal for voluntary labour to dig these trenches. 'Let this be done today,' Churchill minuted to Ismay on July 1. 'The appeal should be reinforced from the BBC.'[3]

It was Eric Seal who then suggested that even fields under crops should have trenches dug across them, 'if they are large enough for a troop carrier to land'. Churchill agreed, noting 'that fields under crops should *not* be excepted from this treatment'.[4]

---

[1] Letter of 1 July 1940: Seal papers.

[2] Letter of 12 May 1940: Premier papers, 3/222/5, folios 28–9.

[3] Lindemann minute of 30 June 1940 and Churchill note of 1 July 1940, 'Action This Day': Premier papers, 3/222/5, folio 17.

[4] Minute by J. H. Peck, 1 July 1940: Premier papers, 3/222/5, folio 16.

In his minute of July 1, Churchill had suggested to Ismay, 'perhaps certain areas should have priority'. That same day Ismay reported back to Churchill that enquiries showed that the Defence Services had already arranged for the ploughing of ditches across all possible landing grounds within a radius of five miles from important objectives. Ismay suggested that this radius might now be extended, as a matter of priority, to ten miles, using local voluntary labour. Churchill approved of this measure at once.[1]

During the War Cabinet of July 1 Churchill asked with some perturbation why the authorities in Britain were hesitant about welcoming French volunteers. 'This attitude,' he said, 'was most unfortunate, and must not be allowed to continue.'[2] Nor was he in favour of expanding the scheme whereby British children were being evacuated to Canada and the United States. 'A large movement of this kind,' he said, 'encouraged a defeatist spirit, which was contrary to the true facts of the position and should be sternly discouraged.'

The War Cabinet ended with a discussion of the growing mood of pessimism, as invasion rumours abounded, and invited Churchill to issue a circular to the heads of all Government departments, 'instructing them to take drastic steps to put a stop to defeatist talk'.[3] On July 2, in another effort to curb despondency, Churchill told the War Cabinet that he 'questioned the wisdom' of continuing to publish British merchant shipping losses. 'Although it was true,' he said, 'that the British public always insisted on being told adverse news, however serious, their thoughts at present were more directed towards the dangers of invasion than to dangers of starvation.'[4]

Not only the British, but also the Americans, were concerned about an imminent disaster. 'I saw the President this afternoon,' Lothian telegraphed to London on July 2. 'He agreed that it was very important to have technical discussions as soon as possible as to what the situation would be if the British Navy were forced to relinquish Gibraltar, if French Fleet passed into German hands, if Germans and Italians were able to base their blockade operations upon French Channel and Atlantic ports etc., so that if and when a crisis arose British and Ameri-

[1] 'Home Defence, Military, Invasion, Enemy Aircraft Landings, Deterrents Against', Office of the Minister of Defence: Cabinet papers, 120/442. Two days later Jacob wrote to Ismay in some anger: 'The Ministers of Agriculture and Home Security are putting all kinds of obstacles in the way—of action, not German aircraft!' (Minute of 3 July 1940: Cabinet papers, 120/442).

[2] On the following day Churchill told the War Cabinet that General de Gaulle 'had already formed three battalions in this country, and had collected 380 aviators, 1,000 young men anxious to serve, and a company of small tanks' (Cabinet papers, 65/8, folio 33).

[3] War Cabinet No. 189 of 1940, 1 July 1940, 11.30 a.m.: Cabinet papers, 65/8.

[4] War Cabinet No. 191 of 1940, 2 July 1940, 12 noon: Cabinet papers, 65/8.

can Governments could come to decisions based upon a similar estimate of facts.'

Roosevelt added, however, that it was 'imperative' that there should be 'no publicity, especially owing to election'.[1]

'Secret Service reports,' noted Colville on July 2, suggested that the German invasion would be launched from Norway.[2] That same day, Hitler did indeed order plans for the invasion of England to be prepared, 'provided that air superiority can be obtained'.[3] This decision was unknown in London. But aware that some such decision might well be imminent, Churchill was contemplating both defensive and offensive action, minuting to Ismay, about London itself: 'I have a very clear view that we should fight every inch of it, and it would devour quite a large invading army.' Having learned on July 2 that several hundred German troops had landed in the Channel Islands, Churchill told Ismay: 'plans should be studied to land secretly by night on the Islands to kill or capture the invaders'. Such a raid, he wrote, 'is exactly one of the exploits for which the Commandos would be suited'.[4]

That afternoon Churchill set off once more to inspect coastal defences. He was not entirely pleased with what he saw, and on the following morning sent Eden a minute, marked 'Action This Day', in which he declared:

I was disturbed to find the 3rd Division spread along thirty miles of coast, instead of being, as I had imagined, held back concentrated in reserve, ready to move against any serious head of invasion. But much more astonishing was the fact that the infantry of this division, which is otherwise fully mobile, are not provided with the buses necessary to move them to the point of action. This provision of buses, waiting always ready and close at hand, is essential to all mobile units, and to none more than the 3rd Division while spread about the coast.

I heard the same complaint from Portsmouth that the troops there had not got their transport ready and close at hand. Considering the great masses of transport, both buses and lorries, which there are in this country, and the large numbers of drivers brought back from the BEF, it should be possible to remedy these deficiencies at once.

'I hope at any rate,' Churchill added, 'that the GOC 3rd Division will be told to-day to take up, as he would like to do, the large number of

[1] Washington Telegram No. 1201, 'Most Secret', 2 July 1940: Premier papers, 3/457, folio 13. The American Elections were to take place on 5 November 1940.

[2] Colville diary, 2 July 1940: Colville papers.

[3] Directive of 2 July 1940: H. R. Trever-Roper (editor), Hitler's War Directives 1939–1945, London 1964, page 33.

[4] Minute of 2 July 1940: Churchill papers, 20/13.

buses which are even plying for pleasure traffic up and down the sea
front at Brighton.'[1]

The General Officer Commanding the 3rd Division was General
Bernard Montgomery. He had cause to remember Churchill's visit,
and the buses, writing in his memoirs:

I showed him all that was possible in the time. I took him to Lancing
College, inhabited by the Royal Ulster Rifles, and showed him a counter-
attack on the small airfield on the coast below which was assumed to have
been captured by the Germans; he was delighted, especially by the action of
the Bren-gun carrier platoon of the battalion. We then worked our way along
the coast, finishing up in Brighton at about 7.30 p.m. He suggested I should
have dinner with him and his party at the Royal Albion Hotel, and we talked
much during the meal. He asked me what I would drink at dinner and I
replied—water. This astonished him. I added that I neither drank nor smoked
and was 100 per cent fit. This story is often told with embellishments, but the
above is the true version.

From the window of the dining-room we could see a platoon of guardsmen
preparing a machine-gun post in a kiosk on Brighton pier, and he remarked
that when at school near there he used to go and see the performing fleas in
the kiosk. Then we talked about my problems. The main thing which seemed
curious to me was that my division was immobile. It was the only fully
equipped division in England, the only division fit to fight any enemy anywhere. And here we were in a static role, ordered to dig in on the south coast.
Some other troops should take on my task; my division should be given buses,
and be held in mobile reserve with a counter-attack role. Why was I left
immobile? There were thousands of buses in England; let them give me some,
and release me from this static role so that I could practise a mobile counter-
attack role. The Prime Minister thought this was the cat's whiskers.

'I do not know what the War Office thought,' Montgomery added,
'but I got my buses.'[2]

While Churchill was on his tour of inspection of the south coast, Seal
remained at Downing Street amid the myriad files and concerns of the
Private Office. 'We are wondering,' he wrote that day to his wife,
'whether Hitler will dare to try to invade us, & if so, what will happen.
The best opinion is that he will get the "heil of a bloody crack", &
that it may prove the turning point of the war. I really do wonder,'
Seal added, 'now we have so many troops in the country, whether he
will dare.'[3]

At the War Cabinet on the morning of July 3, with the imminence

[1] Minute of 3 July 1940: Churchill papers, 20/13.
[2] *The Memoirs of Field-Marshal the Viscount Montgomery of Alamein, KG*, London 1958, pages 69–70.
[3] Letter of 2 July 1940: Seal papers.

of a possible German invasion uppermost in his mind, Churchill argued against continuing bombing raids on German oil refineries, aerodromes and marshalling yards, aimed at crippling the German Air Force, and asked instead 'considering that the coming week might well be so critical from the point of view of invasion' that the emphasis should be transferred to 'the bombing of German ports'.[1] That same day he minuted to Sinclair: 'I hear from every side of the need for turning your main emphasis on bombing the ships and barges in all the ports under German control.'[2]

Warning of the possible imminence of invasion, the Director of Military Intelligence, General Beaumont-Nesbitt, told the Chiefs of Staff on July 3 that all the Intelligence indications seemed to suggest it. These indications, Beaumont-Nesbitt explained, included special reconnaissance which showed a hundred 'special rafts' in Kiel harbour, rafts which the Intelligence staff of the Air Ministry felt were 'intended for landing operations'. In addition, in German Air Force units in northern France, 'stocks of petrol and other stores were being built up', while a German fighter patrol was being 'continuously maintained' above Calais. In addition, Beaumont-Nesbitt reported, two German parachute regiments had been moved to Belgium, as well as 'special assault detachments drawn from troops which had done particularly good work on the western front'. All this, Beaumont-Nesbitt concluded, constituted 'a considerable body of evidence which pointed to an invasion of this country at an early date'.[3]

While the nation awaited invasion, the flow of armaments from the United States gained momentum, indicating to those at the centre of events the success of Purvis's purchasing mission. On July 3 Bridges informed Churchill that the steamship *Britannic* had left New York that day for Liverpool carrying on board more than ten million rounds of rifle ammunition, 50,000 Enfield rifles, and a hundred 75-millimetre field guns, as well as field gun spares and machine gun components.[4]

These were the weapons and munitions of war with which Britain intended to challenge any German invasion.

[1] War Cabinet No. 192 of 1940, 3 July 1940, 11.30 a.m., Minute 2, Confidential Annex: Cabinet papers, 65/14.
[2] Minute of 3 July 1940: Churchill papers, 20/13.
[3] Chiefs of Staff Committee No. 205 of 1940, 10.15 a.m., 3 July 1940: Cabinet papers, 79/5. Two of the Enigma decrypts which formed a part of the Intelligence on which this report was based had revealed both that German Air-Force units were resting and re-fitting at airports in the Low Countries and north-west France, and that there was now a concentration of German dive bombers in the same area (F. H. Hinsley and others, *British Intelligence in the Second World War, Its Influence on Strategy and Operations*, volume 1, London 1979, page 177).
[4] Minute of 3 July 1940: Premier papers, 3/372/1, folio 133.

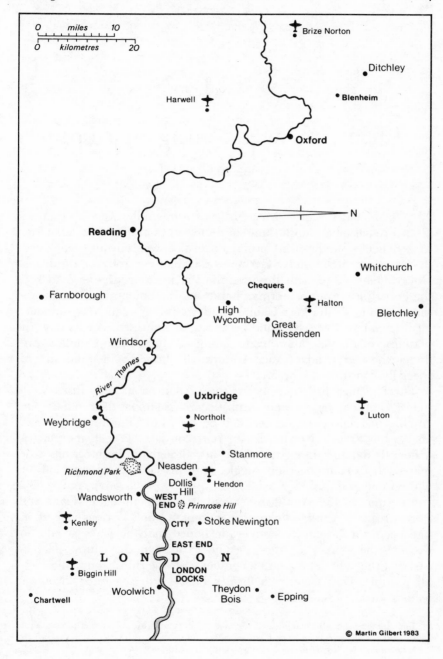

31

Oran: no weakening of resolve

A T the naval base of Mers el-Kebir, three miles west of Oran, the French naval authorities continued to maintain their adherence to Article 8 of the Franco-German Armistice, whereby all French war-ships were to come under German or Italian control. For the British Government, faced with the possibility of invasion, the need to keep the French Fleet out of German hands had become urgent; so much so that on June 27 the War Cabinet had set July 3 as the day on which all French naval vessels should be seized, or disarmed. For six days the planning of this operation, code name 'Catapult', had gone forward, under the command of Vice-Admiral Sir James Somerville and his specially constituted 'Force H'.

There seemed little doubt that the French naval authorities would indeed impose the German armistice terms upon their officers; an Intelligence report to this effect had been sent to Churchill on June 28. In all the French North African ports, it said, French morale was 'evidently deteriorating everywhere, and though diminishing minorities may wish to continue the struggle, it seems clear that senior officers will no longer do so'.[1]

On June 29 the War Cabinet had been told that the Naval Staff were already at work 'on plans for action at Oran'. Various suggestions had been put forward. Chamberlain hoped that the plans 'would not exclude the chance of effecting the capture of the ships'. Halifax 'stressed the value of obtaining contact with the ships' companies' if at all possible. Duff Cooper, a former First Lord, suggested 'dropping leaflets' on the French ships.[2]

---

[1] Joint Intelligence Sub-Committee Report No. 53, 28 June 1940 (information received up to 4.30 p.m.): Premier papers, 3/179/1, folios 42–5.

[2] War Cabinet No. 187 of 1940, 29 June 1940, 10 a.m., Minute 8, Confidential Annex: Cabinet papers, 65/13.

That same day, the Naval Staff sent Admiral Somerville details of the four choices he was to give to the French naval officers at Mers el-Kebir and Oran. The first choice was to bring their ships to British harbours 'and fight with us'. The second choice was to steam their ships into a British port, and hand them over to British crews. This choice, Churchill noted in a minute to Alexander and Pound, should be supplemented by a promise 'to repatriate the crews, to restore the ships at peace, and to pay full compensation for any loss or damage during the war'.[1] The third choice was 'to demilitarise their ships to our satisfaction'. The fourth choice was French action to sink their own ships. If none of these choices were accepted, then the British Admiral was 'to endeavour to destroy ships at Mers el-Kebir but particularly *Dunkerque* and *Strasbourg*', using, as he was informed on June 30, 'all means at your disposal'. Any French warships at nearby Oran were also to be destroyed 'if this will not entail any considerable loss of civilian life'.[2]

On June 30 the War Cabinet agreed that when 'Catapult' was put into operation it should simultaneously cover 'other French men-of-war', not only at Mers el-Kebir and Oran, but in the eastern Mediterranean and in British ports.[3] It was also agreed that the Operation would be 'enhanced' if it were made clear to the French Admiral at Oran that Britain was determined 'to continue the war against Germany', and that the interests of France, no less than those of Britain, 'depended on our victory'.[4]

That evening the three Chiefs of Staff and their Vice-Chiefs discussed the implications of taking action against the French Fleet at Oran. They concluded that 'on balance the operations contemplated should be carried out'. In the light of 'recent events', they wrote, 'we can no longer place any faith in French assurances, nor could we be certain that any measures, which we were given to understand the French would take to render their ships unserviceable before reaching French metropolitan ports, would be carried out'. Once French ships did reach

[1] 'Action this Day' Minute to A. V. Alexander and Sir Dudley Pound, 29 June 1940: Premier papers, 3/179/1, folio 38.

[2] Immediate signal to Force H, sent 1.03 a.m., 2 July 1940. Unless otherwise indicated, this, and all subsequent naval signals sent to or from Oran are from: Premier papers, 3/179/1.

[3] On 1 July 1940 Churchill minuted to Ismay: 'During the night of 2nd–3rd all necessary measures should be taken at Portsmouth and Plymouth, at Alexandria, and if possible at Martinique, on the same lines as "Catapult". The reaction to these events at Dakar and Casablanca must be considered, and every precaution taken to prevent the escape of valuable units' (Churchill papers, 20/13).

[4] War Cabinet No. 188 of 1940, 30 June 1940, 7 p.m., minute 1, Confidential Annex: Cabinet papers, 65/13.

those ports, it was certain that 'sooner or later, the Germans will employ them against us'.

The 'over-riding consideration' for the Chiefs of Staff was then set out. It was the need to ensure as far as possible the concentration of the maximum possible British naval strength in home waters 'to meet the imminent threat of invasion'. In view of these 'grave issues' at home, it was 'of paramount importance that the uncertainty regarding the French Fleet should be dissipated as soon as possible in order that the ships now shadowing the French Fleet can be released for operations elsewhere'.

In conclusion, the Chiefs of Staff and the Vice-Chiefs stated that 'from the military point of view', 'Catapult' should be carried out 'as soon as possible'.[1]

At the same moment when 'Catapult' was approved, a second proposed operation against Vichy France was rejected. This was 'Susan', originally called 'Catapult II', a would-be military landing in French Morocco which the Inter Services Planning Staff had drawn up, 'on the instructions of the Prime Minister'.[2] Its aim was to form 'a rallying point' around which a French administration 'sympathetic to the Allied cause' could be built up, and the port of Casablanca secured for British use. 'Susan' envisaged as many as 25,000 troops, British, French and Polish, landing at Fedala 'under cover of considerable naval fire', or a landing at Rabat or Port Lyautey, with the troops transferred overland the fifty or sixty miles to Casablanca. Two Royal Air Force fighter squadrons would also be needed for this operation. According to the Planning Staff, the first landings of 'Susan' could be made thirty-seven days after the War Cabinet gave its decision to go ahead.[3]

With their hopes on the urgent need to deny the French Fleet to Germany, the Chiefs of Staff advised 'most strongly' against the despatch of troops to North Africa, a plan, they insisted, that was 'not essential to the prosecution of the war'. Above all, they wrote, Britain's ability 'to continue the war' depended upon making both Britain and Eire 'secure against attack'. They were are present 'by no means secure.

[1] Chiefs of Staff Paper No. 510 of 1940, 'Implications of Action Contemplated in Respect of Certain French Ships. Aide Mémoire', 30 June 1940: Cabinet papers, 80/14.

[2] Churchill's initiation of 'Susan' was mentioned by the Chiefs of Staff at their meeting on 3 July 1940 (Cabinet papers, 79/5).

[3] 'Operation "Susan",' 1 July 1940: Premier papers, 3/416, folios 3–7 (Signed R. G. Onslow, W. L. Dawson, R. N. Gale). Gale, then a Lieutenant-Colonel, subsequently raised and commanded the 1st Parachute Brigade, was commander of the 6th British Airborne Division and, in 1945, as Lieutenant-General, was Deputy Commander of the 1st Allied Airborne Army.

We cannot therefore undertake unprofitable commitments which would prejudice their security.' To organize and equip in Britain the Polish forces needed for 'Susan' was not, the Chiefs of Staff added, 'a practicable military proposition', while to maintain the expedition once it had landed in North Africa would be 'an unacceptable drain on our resources'.[1]

Churchill was reluctant to accept this advice, regarding 'Susan' as precisely the type of operation the aim and scale of which seemed essential if, as he wrote to Halifax, Britain was effectively to pursue the policy 'of aiding General de Gaulle to which we are publicly and earnestly committed'. As Churchill explained to Halifax:

The attempt to set up a French Government in Morocco, and to obtain control of the *Jean Bart* and other vessels, and to open up a campaign in Morocco, with a base on the Atlantic, is in my opinion vital. It was most cordially adopted by the Cabinet in principle and apart from technical details, I should find very great difficulty in becoming a party to its abandonment, and to our consequent relegation to the negative defensive which has so long proved ruinous to our interests.

In an effort to reverse the Chiefs of Staff's decision, Churchill proposed to Halifax two days later that the Cabinet should 'sit in private at the opening of business at 11.30', and only summon the 'other colleagues' and Departmental advisers 'after we have had a talk among ourselves'.[2]

Undeterred by Churchill's support for 'Susan', or by his tactic of delay, the Chiefs of Staff stood by their conviction that there was 'nothing' in the operation that would cause them 'to modify their previous opinion that the proposed operation was unsound on military grounds'.[3] Churchill accepted this second rebuff, and 'Susan' was abandoned.

With plans for 'Catapult', however, moving steadily forward, Churchill still saw an opportunity, as he minuted to Ismay on July 1, at least 'to cut out and carry off the ships with the French politicians on board'[4] at Casablanca. But even this much more limited operation proved impracticable.

*   *   *

---

[1] 'Operation (Catapult II), Revised Draft Report', Chiefs of Staff Committee Paper No. 508 (Draft) of 1940, 1 July 1940: Premier papers, 3/416, folios 8–10.
[2] Letter of 3 July 1940, 'sent to S of S Foreign, 10.15 a.m., 3/7': Churchill papers, 4/201.
[3] Chiefs of Staff meeting No. 205 of 1940, 10.15 a.m., 3 July 1940: Cabinet papers, 79/5.
[4] Minute of 1 July 1940: Churchill papers, 20/13.

The Chiefs of Staff and the Vice-Chiefs had given 'Catapult' their approval. But during July 1 a signal reached London from Admiral Somerville, in which he reported the serious doubts of several of his officers, including Captain Holland, until recently the British Naval Attaché in Paris. After talking to Holland 'and others', Somerville reported, he was 'impressed with their view that the use of force should be avoided at all costs'. According to Holland, 'offensive action on our part would alienate all French wherever they are'.[1] But in reply that evening, the Admiralty reiterated that if the French would not accept any of Somerville's alternatives, 'they are to be destroyed'.[2]

At ten o'clock that night, Churchill and Pound had a final meeting to discuss the exact wording of Somerville's instructions. Then, in the very early hours of July 2, the Admiral was sent the final text of the message he was to deliver to the French Admiral at Oran, Marcel Gensoul. The message explained that Britain, committed as she was to restore 'the greatness and territory of France', must ensure that 'the best ships' of the French Navy were not used against her 'by the common foe'. Four choices were again set out. The first two were: to sail with Britain 'and continue to fight for victory against the Germans and Italians'; or to sail with reduced crews to a British port, after which the crews would be repatriated 'at the earliest moment'. In both these cases the ships would be restored to France at the end of the war, with full compensation to be paid if they were damaged. The third choice was to sail to some French port in the West Indies, 'Martinique for instance', and accept either demilitarization or be 'entrusted' to the United States, the crews being repatriated. If these 'fair offers' were refused, Somerville would 'with profound regret, require you to sink your ships within six hours'. Failing the above, 'I have the orders of His Majesty's Government to use whatever force may be necessary to prevent your ships from falling into German or Italian hands'.[3]

At the War Cabinet on the morning of July 2, Churchill reiterated that it was British policy 'to encourage any French sailors, who were willing to continue to fight for us, to do so'.[4] Throughout the day, Somerville prepared for the negotiations, and possible action, that he would have to take. That night, Pound telegraphed to Somerville: 'The War Cabinet will be impatiently awaiting news of "Catapult". I hope therefore you will be able to send short messages at intervals such as

[1] Signal sent at 12.20 p.m., 1 July 1940.
[2] Signal sent at 6.20 p.m., 1 July 1940.
[3] Signal sent at 1.08 a.m., 2 July 1940.
[4] War Cabinet No. 191 of 1940, 2 July 1940, 12 noon: Cabinet papers 65/8.

"Emissary has made contact". "French ships in harbour", etc.' Pound's signal ended: 'You are charged with one of the most disagreeable and difficult tasks that a British Admiral has ever been faced with, but we have complete confidence in you and rely on you to carry it out relentlessly.'[1]

Within an hour of midnight on July 2, the Admiralty signalled to HMS *Dorsetshire* at Dakar and HMS *Velox* at Casablanca that action was about to be taken at Oran and Alexandria to ensure that the French ships there 'cannot fall into enemy hands intact', and that 'similar action' against *Jean Bart* and *Richelieu* 'will probably follow'. It was therefore 'of first importance' that these ships should be shadowed, should they sail from Dakar or Casablanca on hearing of the Oran and Alexandria action.[2]

The first signal from the Admiralty to Oran on July 3 reached Somerville during the night. Operations, it said, must be completed in the daylight.[3] At 8.37 a.m. Somerville reported that the French warships were still at Oran, and that Captain Holland, in the destroyer *Foxhound*, was entering the harbour.[4] At 9.32 a.m. Holland himself reported that he was off Oran, and was signalling to the French the first option, that they should 'come and join us'.[5] The immediate response was unclear, for after only five minutes Holland signalled again: Admiral Gensoul was 'endeavouring not to be contacted', but was sending his Chief of Staff. At the same time, 'awnings were being furled' by the French battleships, a possible preliminary to seeking to leave harbour.[6]

For nearly an hour Holland waited off the boom. Then he reported that Gensoul refused to see him. He had therefore left *Foxhound* in a motor boat for the harbour boom, and had handed Britain's conditions to Gensoul's Flag Lieutenant, and was awaiting the reply, which was being 'brought out by barge'.[7]

In London, the War Cabinet met at 11.30 that morning. The first news was from Portsmouth, where the French ships had been taken over 'without bloodshed', and where many of the French sailors had said they wanted 'to become British subjects and to continue the fight on our side'. At Plymouth, however, there had been resistance, and in a scuffle on board the French submarine *Surcouf*, one British sailor and

[1] Signal sent at 10.55 p.m., 2 July 1940.
[2] Signal sent at 00.53 a.m., 3 July 1940: Premier papers, 3/179/4.
[3] Signal sent from London, 12.52 a.m.
[4] Signal sent at 8.37 a.m.
[5] Signal sent from Oran, 9.32 a.m.
[6] Signal sent from Oran, 9.37 a.m.
[7] Signal sent from Oran, 10.10 a.m.

one French officer had been killed: the first casualties of 'Catapult'.

From Alexandria, it appeared that the French Admiral would agree to accept the immobilization of his ships by discharging their oil.[1] Only at Oran was the response so far a negative one. The French, Holland reported, 'say they fight if force used'.[2]

Someone at the War Cabinet pointed out that the Admiral at Oran had not been given demilitarization as one of his choices, but it was decided not to offer it now, 'as this would look like weakening'. It was also agreed to signal Somerville that if he considered that the French Fleet were preparing to leave harbour, as one signal had suggested, he should 'inform them that if they move you must open fire'.[3] This signal crossed with one from Somerville: 'Am awaiting reply to letter before opening fire.'[4]

While the War Cabinet remained in session, a further message was brought in from Captain Holland. Gensoul, while repeating 'previous assurances' that his ships would not be allowed to fall intact into German or Italian hands, had refused all Britain's conditions and 'states he will fight'. Somerville, for his part, was prepared 'to open fire' at 1.30 p.m.[5]

There seemed no way in which a conflict could be avoided, especially as the War Cabinet were then told of Darlan's instructions to the French Admiral at Dakar 'calling upon him and his men to pay no attention to British demands and to show themselves worthy of being Frenchmen'. What had been sent to Dakar had presumably also been sent to Oran.[6] Somerville, meanwhile, had arrived off Oran with Force H, 'and proceeded to steam to and fro across the Bay'.[7] A signal was

[1] Signal received in London at 9.39 a.m., confirmed by signal received in London at 3.09 p.m.; oil being discharged reported by signal received in London at 5.17 p.m.

[2] Signal sent from Oran, 11.51 a.m., received in London, 12.16 p.m.

[3] Signal sent from London, 12.32 p.m.

[4] Signal sent from Oran, 12.09 p.m., received in London, 12.34 p.m.

[5] Signal sent from Oran, 12.31 p.m., received in London, 1.10 p.m.

[6] Twenty-eight years after 'Oran', Admiral Gensoul wrote, of his reasons for refusing the British demands: '1. Orders received from the French Admiralty at the time of the Armistice, particularly their telegram of 24 June 1940: Secret orders concerning scuttling to prevent enemy *or foreign powers* forcibly taking over a ship for their own use. 2. My submission to the British ultimatum would automatically have broken the Armistice agreement with the German government, which would have been disastrous for France. I had no right to bring about a new catastrophe. 3. Honour of the flag forbade me to submit to an ultimatum presented at gunpoint, even from former allies, and if stains there were on any flag that day, there were certainly none on ours. Lastly and on reflection after the event, it is obvious that Mr Churchill was well aware that his ultimatum was unacceptable since on that same morning of 3 July 1940 he had traitorously and forcibly seized all French ships then in British ports and which had in fact done what I was being asked to do' (Letter to Nicholas Piers Eadon, 14 September 1968: Eadon papers).

[7] 'Mers el-Kebir (Oran), 3rd July 1940' (narrative compiled in 1946 by Commodore G. R. G. Allen): Churchill papers, 4/196.

then sent to Gensoul that the French ships would not be allowed to leave the harbour unless the British terms were accepted, and to emphasize that this point was not a bluff, five magnetic mines were laid by British aircraft in the harbour entrance.[1]

As the War Cabinet discussions continued, it was agreed that some naval action was also needed at Casablanca, where the British Government should, as the minutes recorded, 'certainly take steps' to bring to Britain those former French Ministers who were being held on board the *Massiglia* in Casablanca harbour. The War Cabinet also discussed the appeal by the former French Prime Minister, Edouard Daladier, who had asked to be brought to Britain from Casablanca by flying boat or destroyer. But the arrival in Britain of Daladier 'alone' was deprecated by Halifax as 'embarrassing politically'. In the event, neither the prisoners on board the *Massiglia*, nor Daladier, were to reach Britain.[2]

There was also news during the War Cabinet of July 3 of President Roosevelt's attitude, for Lothian reported that he had asked the President whether American opinion 'would support forcible seizure of these ships'. Roosevelt had replied 'certainly', and had gone on to tell Lothian that the Americans would expect the French ships 'to be seized' rather than that they should 'fall into German hands'.[3]

Shortly after noon, Somerville signalled to London that as the French ships at Mers el-Kebir showed 'no further signs' of leaving harbour, he was giving them until 3 p.m. to reply to the British terms.[4] Then, within an hour, came news of what Somerville called a 'slight sign of weakening' on the part of Gensoul, who had said that he had 'no intention' of leaving harbour. Somerville was therefore giving the French Admiral an extra half hour, until 3.30 p.m., to accept the British conditions, or, he told the Admiralty and Gensoul: 'I shall open fire.'[5]

[1] The Admiralty had signalled to Somerville at 10.45 a.m. that he could lay magnetic mines to prevent the French warships from leaving harbour.

[2] Taken back to France after three weeks in Casablanca, Reynaud and Daladier, and also Léon Blum, were subsequently put on trial at Riom by the Vichy authorities, and then held as 'prominent' prisoner-hostages at various concentration camps and prison camps in Germany until May 1945, when they were liberated by Allied forces. Georges Mandel, however, was handed over during the war by the Germans to the Vichy militia, who executed him near Paris, on 7 July 1944, a month after the Allied landings in Normandy.

[3] Roosevelt also told Lothian that before the fall of the Reynaud Government 'he had offered to buy the Fleet from the French' but that 'there was nobody from whom he could buy it today' (Washington Telegram No. 1206, read to War Cabinet 192 of 1940, 3 July 1940, 11.30 a.m., Minute 5, Confidential Annex: Cabinet papers, 65/14).

[4] Signal sent from Oran at 1.47 p.m., received in London at 2.35 p.m.

[5] Signal sent from Oran at 2.40 p.m., received in London at 3.39 p.m.

Further hope that conflict could be avoided by Somerville's firmness reached London three minutes later. Gensoul had now agreed to receive Holland 'personally' on board the *Dunkerque*. In view of this, Somerville reported, he was 'postponing action', and he added: 'I think they are weakening.'[1]

It was Captain Holland's hope and belief that this was so, based, as he wrote in his report to London, 'on my appreciation of the French character since I have often found that an initial flat refusal will gradually come round to an acquiescence'. He had always felt, Holland added, that the threat of force 'even as a last extreme was fatal to the attainment of our object and I was thus using every endeavour to bring about a peaceful solution'.[2]

Even as Holland was nourishing these hopes, British Intelligence had intercepted the French Admiralty's orders to Gensoul. From this message it seemed to those in London that Gensoul's willingness to receive Holland was part of a tactic of delay. The French Admiralty's message, signed by Darlan's Chief of Staff, Rear-Admiral Le Luc, read: 'You will inform British Representatives that the C-in-C has given orders to all French naval Forces in the Mediterranean to join you immediately in fighting order. You are empowered to give orders to these forces. You are to answer force with force. Call in the submarines and air force if necessary.' The message ended: 'The Armistice Commission has been informed.'[3]

From this message it seemed clear that Pétain's Government, and Darlan, his Minister of Marine, intended to abide by Article 8 of the Armistice. One minute after sending the French message on to Somerville, the Admiralty telegraphed to him again: 'Settle the matter quickly or you may have French reinforcements to deal with.'[4]

Somerville could do nothing, for Holland was still on his mission to the *Dunkerque*, having reached the French warship at 4.15 p.m. Somerville therefore informed London: 'Am awaiting return of delegate whose entry and return delayed by minefield.'[5]

On board the *Dunkerque*, Holland was still talking to Gensoul. Throughout their talk, he wrote in his report to London, 'I thought we had won through and that he would accept one or other of the proposals.'[6] Yet on reaching the *Dunkerque* Holland had noticed that

---

[1] Signal sent from Oran at 2.59 p.m., received in London at 3.42 p.m.
[2] Captain Holland, 'Narrative of the Third June': Admiralty papers, 205/6.
[3] Signal timed at 1.30 p.m., sent from London to Oran at 4.13 p.m.
[4] Signal sent from London at 4.14 p.m.
[5] Signal sent from Oran at 4.37 p.m., received in London at 5.35 p.m.
[6] Captain Holland, 'Narrative of the Third June': Admiralty papers, 205/6.

all the French ships were in 'an advanced state of readiness for sea', that all control positions visible were manned, and that all but the *Strasbourg's* direction range finders 'were trained in direction of our fleet'.[1]

As Holland sought to persuade Gensoul to accept the British terms, Churchill waited in the Cabinet Room, in continual contact by telephone with Alexander and Pound in the Admiralty building across Horse Guards Parade.

Events at Oran were coming to a climax. Gensoul rejected the British terms, commenting that 'the first shot fired would alienate our two navies and do untold harm to us, and that he would reply to force by force'. At 5.15 p.m., while this conversation was in progress, a message reached the *Dunkerque* from Somerville, for Gensoul, that unless the terms were accepted by 5.30 'he would sink his ships'. Holland then signalled by projector that the talks had failed and prepared to return to *Foxhound*. 'Our leave taking was friendly,' he wrote in his report to London a few days later, 'and from the Admiral more friendly than our reception.' Even at that stage, Holland added, 'I do not believe that he thought that fire would be opened.' Holland's account continued:

We left *Dunkerque* at 17.25, and at the same time 'Action stations' were sounded off. Very little effort seemed to be being made to go to Action stations, and as we passed, large numbers of the crew were still on the upper decks of the battleships. The Officer of the Watch on board *Bretagne* saluted smartly as we passed.

We transferred to our motor boat at 17.35, and were clear of the net defences and about one mile to seaward when fire was opened . . .[2]

It was at 5.55 p.m. that Somerville gave the order to open fire, and within five minutes was himself heavily engaged. At 6.04 p.m. he ordered the cease fire in order to give the French crews the opportunity to leave their ships. The battle had lasted nine minutes. The *Bretagne* had blown up. The *Dunkerque* had run aground. The *Provence* was beached. And in those few minutes, more than 1,250 French sailors had been killed.[3]

Before anything was known in London of the bombardment at Oran, a further signal was sent from the Admiralty to Somerville. It read: 'French ships must comply with our terms or sink themselves or be

---

[1] Captain Holland, 'Interview with Admiral Gensoul': Admiralty papers, 205/6.

[2] Captain Holland, 'Narrative of the Third June': Admiralty papers, 205/6.

[3] Principally 1,012 on the *Bretagne* and a further 210 on the *Dunkerque*. The British casualties were one officer and one rating 'slightly wounded' (War Cabinet, Chiefs of Staff Committee, Weekly Résumé No. 44: Churchill papers, 23/5).

sunk by you before dark.'[1] There had been no weakening of resolve in London.

When the British bombardment had ceased, the scene inside the harbour had been covered in thick smoke. As the smoke cleared, *Strasbourg* and two destroyers were seen to be clear of the harbour, sailing eastward. They were at once subjected to a torpedo attack by six Swordfish aircraft which were already in the air, and two further attacks were mounted in the ensuing hours. But the French warships managed nevertheless, under cover of darkness, to reach Toulon.

At 10.50 p.m. Gensoul reported that all his ships remaining at Oran were out of action, and had been evacuated by their crews. Somerville, signalling the Admiralty that weather conditions were unsuitable for an air attack on the ships at Oran, set sail for Gibraltar.

The full extent of the loss of life at Oran was not yet known in London. Off the west coast of Ireland a further tragic loss of life had taken place, news of which reached the War Cabinet during July 3. On the previous morning a German U-boat had torpedoed the *Arandora Star*, a steamship carrying 1,190 enemy aliens under armed guard to Canada.[2] Among the deportees were 473 German nationals, many of them Nazi sympathizers, but including several Jewish refugees who were still technically enemy aliens, and more than a hundred German merchant seamen who had been captured at sea. Also on board were more than 700 Italians judged to have been in the 'dangerous character' category. In all, 714 of the deportees, 37 of their guards, and 4 crewmen were drowned; there were 868 survivors. 'The case of the brave German who is said to have saved so many,' Churchill minuted on reading the report of the sinking, 'raises the question of his special treatment—by parole or otherwise'.[3] Unfortunately, there was no evidence of his identity.

When the Defence Committee met at Downing Street at eleven o'clock on the night of July 3 to hear the first reports of the action at Oran, there was concern lest Britain's action might provoke the Bordeaux Government into a declaration of war, and those present were told that 'we had been referred to in one French message as "the enemy" '. It was then agreed to send a message to each of the Dominion

[1] Signal sent from London at 6.26 p.m.

[2] The sending of internees to Canada had been decided upon on June 19, code name 'Hedgehog'. Following the sinking of the *Arandora Star*, it was decided to send the internees to Australia ('Warthog').

[3] Minute of 5 July 1940: Premier papers, 3/49/1.

Governments based upon the situation that would arise in the event of a French declaration of war upon Britain. The Defence Committee also discussed the need for ensuring, even by further naval action, that the damaged French ships at Oran 'were completely out of action'.[1]

All those who were with Churchill at Downing Street were filled with conflicting thoughts and emotions. Colville, who was among those on duty that evening, noted in his diary Dill's remark that he had 'never seen anything comparable' to the two nations who had so recently been Allies now fighting, 'while the barbarians sat back and laughed'. Colville also recorded Churchill's bitter comment to A. V. Alexander that 'the French were now fighting with all their vigour for the first time since war broke out'. Nor did Churchill see how Britain could avoid being 'at war with France tomorrow'.[2]

In an attempt to combat fears inside Britain of imminent invasion and possible defeat, and to challenge the defeatism born of fear, the War Cabinet on July 1 had decided to issue some form of exhortation to each of the three fighting services, and to the Civil Departments. On July 3, as various drafts and methods of delivery of the exhortation were being discussed, Churchill decided that a simple message would be best and, as he minuted to Bridges, 'I should make this one admonition myself.'[3]

The need for such an 'admonition' was made clear to the War Cabinet that morning, when reference was made to the fears created by Press reports of the death of eleven civilians, and the injuring of 109, as a result of an air raid on the Newcastle area on the previous day. To publish the 'exact number' of such air raid casualties would not only give the Germans information that ought to be withheld from them, but might, as the War Cabinet minutes recorded, 'have a demoralising effect in this country'.[4]

---

[1] Defence Committee (Operations) No. 19 of 1940, 3 July 1940, 11 p.m.: Cabinet papers, 69/1. Those present were Churchill, A. V. Alexander, Sir Dudley Pound, Sir Edward Bridges, Sir John Dill, General Ismay, Lord Beaverbrook and Osbert Peake, Parliamentary Under-Secretary of State at the Home Office.

[2] Colville diary, 3 July 1940: Colville papers. In case 'under German pressure' France were to declare war on Britain, Sir Horace Wilson asked all non-military Government departments on July 4 to submit statements of the 'action deemed necessary' in the event of war with France ('French War Book, No. 1 of 1940, 4 July 1940: Cabinet papers, 107/1). Other than one French air raid on Gibraltar, as a reprisal for Oran, no Anglo-French hostilities broke out.

[3] Minute of 3 July 1940: Churchill papers, 20/13.

[4] War Cabinet No. 192 of 1940, 3 July 1940, 11.30 a.m., Minute 3: Cabinet papers, 65/8.

It was agreed that Churchill himself should draft and sign a single and emphatic message, and that this message should be sent out above a reproduction of his actual signature. Churchill's draft, approved that same day, was at once printed for distribution early on the following morning. That night, even as the printers reproduced hundreds of copies of the message for circulation to all Members of Parliament, all Peers, all Lord Lieutenants, all Lord Mayors and all Privy Councillors, the Defence Committee were told of a Joint Intelligence Sub-Committee report which stated starkly, on the basis of a study of many fragments of Intelligence, including 'Enigma', that 'invasion was imminent'.[1]

Churchill's message read:

On what may be the eve of an attempted invasion or battle for our native land, the Prime Minister desires to impress upon all persons holding responsible positions in the Government, in the Fighting Services, or in the Civil Departments, their duty to maintain a spirit of alert and confident energy. While every precaution must be taken that time and means afford, there are no grounds for supposing that more German troops can be landed in this country, either from the air or across the sea, than can be destroyed or captured by the strong forces at present under arms. The Royal Air Force is in excellent order and at the highest strength it has yet attained. The German Navy was never so weak, nor the British Army at home so strong as now. The Prime Minister expects all His Majesty's servants in high places to set an example of steadiness and resolution. They should check and rebuke expressions of loose and ill-digested opinion in their circles, or by their subordinates. They should not hesitate to report, or if necessary remove, any officers or officials who are found to be consciously exercising a disturbing or depressing influence, and whose talk is calculated to spread alarm and despondency. Thus alone will they be worthy of the fighting men, who in the air, on the sea, and on land, have already met the enemy without any sense of being outmatched in martial qualities.[2]

At the War Cabinet on the morning of July 4 it emerged that Admiral Godfroy's ships in Alexandria harbour had not yet agreed to Britain's conditions. Yet it was impossible for British ships to fire on Godfroy's force, as this would seriously damage Britain's own naval installations in the harbour. One suggestion was 'to starve them into surrender'. But Churchill deprecated this, and went on to explain that the 'spectacle' of deadlock in the harbour, would, in his view, 'do great harm to Egyptian opinion'.

---

[1] Defence Committee (Operations) No. 19 of 1940, 3 July 1940, 11 p.m.: Cabinet papers, 69/1.
[2] Premier papers, 4/68/9, folio 937.

With Alexandria unresolved, and the fate of the *Richelieu* at Dakar still not known, Churchill went that afternoon to the House of Commons to explain the reasons for the battle at Oran. Had the French Fleet been handed over to Germany, he said, 'mortal injury' might have been done to Britain by the Bordeaux Government. Churchill spoke also of the 'callous and perhaps even malevolent' treatment Britain had received when over 400 German air pilots who were prisoners in France, and whom Reynaud had promised to send to Britain 'for safe keeping', had been sent back to Germany. It had been 'particularly odious', Churchill said, to have handed over 400 skilled men 'with the sure knowledge that they would be used to bomb this country, and thus force our airmen to shoot them down for the second time over'. Such 'wrongful deeds' would not be 'condoned by history'.

Churchill then gave a summary of the events at Oran on the previous day. Throughout July 3, he explained, 'the parleys' had continued, 'and we had hoped until the afternoon that our terms would be accepted without bloodshed'. When the conflict opened, 'I need hardly say that the French ships were fought, albeit in this unnatural cause, with the characteristic courage of the French Navy'.

As to the judgment of Britain's action, Churchill left it, he said, 'with confidence, to Parliament'. 'I leave it also,' he added, 'to the nation, and I leave it to the United States. I leave it to the world and to history.'

Churchill then turned to the possibility of a German invasion of Britain 'before very long', of the 'imminent danger' that all should realize, and of the preparations which were being made 'occupying our toil from morn till night, and far into the night'. Britain appealed now to all British subjects, to her Allies and to 'well-wishers, and they are not a few, all over the world, on both sides of the Atlantic', to give their utmost aid. For Britain was moving through a period 'of extreme danger and of splendid hope, when every virtue of our race will be tested, and all that we have and are will be freely staked'. This was no time, Churchill said, 'for doubt or weakness. It is the supreme hour to which we have been called.'

Churchill then read out to the House of Commons the message he had sent that morning to all senior civil servants, and he offered also to send a copy to every Member of Parliament, 'not that such exhortations are needed'. Churchill then ended his speech with an appeal for the House to support the Government:

I feel that we are entitled to the confidence of the House and that we shall not fail in our duty, however painful. The action we have already taken should be, in itself, sufficient to dispose once and for all of the lies and rumours which have been so industriously spread by German propaganda and Fifth Column activities that we have the slightest intention of entering into negotiations in any form and through any channel with the German and Italian Governments. We shall, on the contrary, prosecute the war with the utmost vigour by all the means that are open to us until the righteous purposes for which we entered upon it have been fulfilled.[1]

Churchill had spoken for just under half an hour. As he ended, the whole House rose to its feet, cheering and waving Order Papers, 'as I have so often seen them do for Neville', one MP noted. 'Only it was not little Neville's turn now.' And he added: 'Winston suddenly wept.'[2]

John Martin later recalled: 'I was in the House for the Oran statement, when all (except, I think, the ILP members) rose and cheered for several minutes. There had been nothing like it, people said, since Munich. Churchill himself was quite overcome and his eyes filled with tears.'[3]

Nine years later, Churchill himself recalled this emotional scene, 'a scene unique', he wrote, 'in my experience'. Everybody 'seemed to stand up all around, cheering, for what seemed a long time'. Up till that moment, Churchill added, 'the Conservative Party had treated me with some reserve, and it was from the Labour benches that I received the warmest welcome when I entered the House or rose on serious occasions. But now all joined in solemn stentorian accord.'[4]

In a private letter home on the following day, Eric Seal wrote to his wife of Churchill's speech:

It was a tremendous success. The scene at the end was quite awe-inspiring —the whole crowded House rose, & cheered for a full two minutes. I had been nodding in the box—I always do—I know the speech by heart; but I was quite startled by the sudden burst of noise.

The PM was quite upset. He went pink, & there were certainly tears in his eyes. What it was all about I still really don't know. The speech was good, but

---

[1] *Hansard*, 4 July 1940, columns 1043–51, speech begun at 3.54 p.m., ended at 4.23 p.m.

[2] Channon diary, 4 July 1940: Robert Rhodes James (editor), *Chips, The Diaries of Sir Henry Channon*, London 1967, page 260. Harold Nicolson likewise noted of Churchill's speech: 'The grand finale ends in an ovation, with Winston sitting there with tears pouring down his cheeks.' Nicolson diary, 4 July 1940: Nigel Nicolson (editor), *Harold Nicolson: Diaries and Letters 1939–1945*, London 1967, page 100.

[3] Sir John Martin, letter to the author, 8 July 1982.

[4] Winston S. Churchill, *The Second World War*, volume 2, London 1949, page 211.

no better than the others; & the occasion—the outbreak of hostilities with our old ally—hardly one for rejoicing. I think that there had been a great deal more anxiety than we realised about the French Fleet, & there was general relief that such vigorous action had been taken.

Somerville, the Admiral, is an old friend of mine. It must have been a terrible order to give—to open fire on the French Fleet. But I think it was the only course to take. The reception in America seems to have been good, too.

What anxious & difficult times we do live in!

As Churchill left the Chamber, with Britain's action at Oran still uppermost in his mind, he turned to Leslie Hore-Belisha with the words: 'This is heartbreaking for me.'[1]

Churchill's colleagues saw his distress. When Leo Amery received a telegram from the Viceroy of India, reporting that Indian public opinion had seen in Britain's action 'proof of vigour and decision on our part', he sent the report to Churchill with the note: 'This should cheer you.' Tersely, Churchill noted in the margin: 'Good.'[2] There was also evidence from Spain of the positive impact of the events of July 3. 'I entirely approve of the action at Oran,' Samuel Hoare wrote to Churchill from Madrid, and went on to explain that, 'Apart from the grave risk to the balance of naval power, it was in my view essential to show strength. Everyone here is so completely dominated by the idea of German invincibility that they have scarcely been able to imagine any counter-action on our part.'[3]

The destruction of French ships and the loss of French life at Oran was a moment of grief for Churchill and the British leaders. Never before had Britain made war upon a beaten ally. It was this circumstance, as much as the scale of the deaths, that was so stunning. On the previous day, 755 men and women, the majority of them unarmed civilians, had died as a result of a German torpedo attack on the *Arandora Star*. Two weeks earlier, nearly three times the number of those killed at Oran had died as a result of a German bombing attack on the *Lancastria*. But these acts, however cruel, were acts of war between enemies, or at least acts of a particular method of war. Oran was the action of a recent ally, supporter and friend.

Seven months after Oran, in January 1941, Roosevelt's personal emissary to Churchill, Harry Hopkins, was a guest at Chequers. At one point, in conversation with Colville, he spoke of Oran. It was Oran, he said, that had convinced Roosevelt that, in spite of Ambassador Ken-

[1] Colville diary, 4 July 1940: Colville papers.
[2] Amery Minute of 6 July 1940, Churchill note of 9 July 1940: Premier papers, 3/179/1, folio 2.
[3] Letter of 5 July 1940: Premier papers, 4/21/1, folio 142.

nedy's defeatist opinions, Britain would continue the fight, as Churchill had promised, if necessary for years and alone.[1]

Churchill had been Prime Minister for fifty-five days. They had been the most demanding and most dramatic days of his life thus far. Yet by his own determination, by the support of his War Cabinet colleagues and senior Service advisers, by the final approval of the House of Commons, Britain had avoided that collapse of morale and division of counsel which had so hastened the fall of France. Now the ultimate challenge remained, that of invasion. It was a challenge which France, confronted by German military supremacy, had been unable to match. After Oran, as Churchill himself later recalled, 'there was no more talk about Britain giving in. The only question was, would she be invaded and conquered? That was the issue which was now to be put to the proof.'[2]

Personally, Churchill had no doubts as to what the outcome would be. At 7 p.m. on July 3, after the final orders had been sent to Oran for action, he had received a visit from the Soviet Ambassador, Ivan Maisky. 'The interview,' Churchill informed the Foreign Office, 'resolved itself into a talk about the war and our chances of winning, which I thought were good.'[3] 'At any rate,' Churchill reflected seven years later, the British action at Oran 'showed where we stood unmistakably and convinced the world that Germany had to face an indefinitely long war'.[4]

[1] Quoted in Warren Tute, *The Deadly Stroke*, London 1973, page 17 (introductory essay by John Colville).

[2] Winston S. Churchill, *The Second World War*, volume 2, London 1949, page 212.

[3] Minute of 9 July 1940: Premier papers, 3/395/1, folio 6.

[4] Note by Churchill for F. W. Deakin, 19 May 1947: Churchill papers, 4/198.

17. Cabinet reconstruction (see page 820). The three Labour Party members of the War Cabinet, Ernest Bevin, Clement Attlee and Arthur Greenwood, leave 10 Downing Street with Churchill on their way to the underground Central War Room, at midday on 4 October 1940. Five days later, Churchill accepted the Leadership of the Conservative Party (pages 835–8)

18. Major-General Sir Hastings Ismay, Chief of Staff to the Minister of Defence, and Churchill's representative on the Chiefs of Staff Committee

19. Churchill's dining room at the reinforced 'No 10 Annexe', Storey's Gate

20. The Cabinet room below ground level at the reinforced Central War Room (also known as the Cabinet War Room), Storey's Gate

21. Churchill in the Cabinet Room at 10 Downing Street, a photograph taken by Cecil Beaton on the morning of 20 November 1940 (see page 919)

22. Harry Hopkins, Brendan Bracken and Churchill, 10 January 1941 (see page 981)

23. Churchill signing the 'destroyers for bases' agreement, 27 March 1941 (see page 1044). On his right is the United States Ambassador, John G. Winant, and on his left the Canadian High Commissioner, Vincent Massey

24. Churchill at Bristol, 12 April 1941, in his University Chancellor's robes, for the honorary degree ceremony. On his right, the Australian Prime Minister, Robert Menzies; on his left, John G. Winant, the United States Ambassador

25. Bristol, 12 April 1941, Churchill talking to a woman who had only just been extricated from the ruins of her home (see page 1059)

26. Churchill and Averell Harriman talk to a worker in a naval establishment at Plymouth, 2 May 1941 (see page 1077)

27. Watching an anti-aircraft demonstration, 6 June 1941: Professor Lindemann, Air Chief Marshal Sir Charles Portal (Chief of the Air Staff), Admiral Sir Dudley Pound (First Sea Lord), Churchill and Major-General Loch (Director of Anti-Aircraft and Civil Defence) (see page 1103 n.6). Ismay is behind Pound and Churchill, pipe in mouth

28. Churchill watches the arrival of one of the first Boeing B-17 'Flying Fortresses' from the United States, 6 June 1941 (see page 1103 n.6)

29. Churchill at work during a train journey, June 1941. Facing him, the silent typewriter. On his lap, the folders beginning 'Top of the Box' (see pages 891–4)

30. Churchill fires a Sten gun, 17 June 1941 (see page 1103 n.6). Behind him, in bowler hat, is David Margesson, Secretary of State for War

© Martin Gilbert 1983

Part Three
Britain Alone

SCOTLAND

Clyde

Tyne

N o r t h

S e a

Belfast

ISLE OF
MAN

Hull

Manchester

Liverpool

ANGLESEY

Mersey

Retford

Derby

W A L E S

Yarmouth

NORFOLK

Lowestoft

Castle Bromwich

Birmingham

Coventry

Fishguard

SUFFOLK

Felixstowe

Llanelly

Swansea

Cardiff

Bristol

Frome

Canvey
Island

London

West Malling

Manston

THANET

Walmer

KENT

Dover

Canterbury

Barnstaple

Padstow

Southampton

Brighton

Eastbourne

Tangmere

Thorney

Portsmouth

ISLE OF WIGHT

St.Ives

Teignmouth

Poole

Studland Bay

PURBECK

Looe

Fowey

Dartmouth

Penzance

miles 75

kilometres 100

© Martin Gilbert 1983

32

'The great invasion scare'

THE crisis at Oran had riveted public attention on the western Mediterranean. But despite the drama and tragedy of Oran, Churchill's main focus of concern remained the Channel and the North Sea. Since the fall of France two weeks earlier, his paramount task had been to safeguard Britain against invasion, and to try with his advisers to anticipate every aspect of the danger. From the second week of June he had been much concerned, having seen the French failure to deny their oil supplies to the advancing Germans, with the need to make immediate plans to prevent Britain's own oil stores, especially those in coastal towns, being seized intact by the invader. 'Special arrangements must be made,' he had written to Ismay on June 9, 'for the destruction of the oil plants on the East Coast, and trustworthy persons should be stationed constantly to fire the charges or otherwise destroy.'[1]

When, on the following day, General Headquarters, Home Forces, reported that the existing plan was to 'immobilize' the oil plants by rapid action on the spot as the invaders approached, and only to destroy the stock later 'by air bombardment',[2] Churchill reiterated that petrol supplies were to be destroyed totally, and in advance, if their 'permanent seizure by the enemy was imminent'. It was 'essential', he added, 'that all preparations should be made'.[3]

Unknown to Churchill, or to British Intelligence through which his most secret knowledge came, Hitler had as yet not even ordered preparations to be made for a possible invasion of Britain, nor was he to do so until mid-July.

[1] Chiefs of Staff Paper No. 393 of 1940, 9 June 1940: Cabinet papers, 120/441.
[2] Major-General A. I. Macdougall to Lieutenant-Colonel E. I. C. Jacob, 10 June 1940, 'Secret', 1/2542: Cabinet papers, 120/441.
[3] Minute of 16 June 1940: Cabinet papers, 120/441.

A week before Oran, during his tour of the Kent and Essex coasts on June 26, Churchill had asked for a chart of 'tides and moons' for the next six weeks, until mid-August.[1] Two days later he had been given charts of the Humber area, the Thames estuary and Beachy Head. 'These should be studied,' he minuted on June 30, 'with a view to ascertaining on which days conditions will be most favourable to a seaborne landing.'[2]

Churchill's enquiry about the tides, moons and landing places was sent to the Director of Navigation at the Admiralty, Captain Morgan.[3] Replying on July 1, Morgan informed Churchill that the most likely time for a German seaborne landing was at high water, near dawn, on nights with no moon. 'Under these circumstances,' Morgan wrote, 'the enemy would have the best chance of approaching undetected and the landing would be carried out under the best conditions.' The specific days of such 'best conditions', Morgan informed Churchill, were 'within a day or two' either side of July 2 at Plymouth, July 3 at Hartlepool, July 8 at Harwich, July 11 at Dover and Portsmouth, July 12 at Yarmouth, July 14 at Cromer, and July 15 at the Wash.[4]

These were the days in July when a German invasion could most readily be expected. Churchill immediately instructed Ismay to communicate these dates to the local commanders and defence forces in each of the areas concerned.[5] At the same time, worried by the possibility that German troops, once ashore, might operate in British uniforms, Churchill asked the Chiefs of Staff to make immediate plans so that real British troops would be identifiable.[6]

Churchill's request had been discussed by the Chiefs of Staff on June 29. Five days later General Paget informed Ismay, for Churchill, that following a German invasion of Britain all British troops would have 'a sheet of cloth dyed a special yellow and attached to the gas mask container', while all British tanks would have a white circle painted on the top for recognition as friendly by British aircraft.[7]

In a further discussion on anti-invasion plans, Churchill, A. V. Alexander, Pound and Phillips had considered the possibility of laying

---

[1] Lieutenant-Colonel E. I. C. Jacob to Paymaster Captain R. V. Brockman, Admiralty, 'Secret', 27 June 1940: Cabinet papers, 120/444.

[2] Minute of 30 June 1940: Cabinet papers, 120/444.

[3] It was Morgan who, in 1938, as Captain of HMS *Enterprise*, had conveyed the Emperor of Abyssinia, after his abdication, from Jibuti to Haifa. In 1941 he commanded HMS *Valiant* at the battle of Matapan.

[4] Memorandum of 1 July 1940: Cabinet papers, 120/444.

[5] Minute of 1 July 1940: Cabinet papers, 120/444.

[6] Chiefs of Staff Paper No. 498 of 1940, 28 June 1940: Cabinet papers, 120/445.

[7] Home Forces No. 1/1147, 'Secret', 4 July 1940: Cabinet papers, 120/445.

mines in a large semi-circle around any successful German sea landing. The aim of these mines would be to hem in the German military lodgment from the sea, with or without 'a seaborne counter attack'. But Churchill, who had suggested this measure, was told that any such minefields would have to be 'of enormous size', as well as having the disadvantage of hampering Britain's own counter movements. The idea was abandoned.[1]

During this anti-invasion meeting, held on the afternoon of June 30, Churchill had commented that he had been 'unpleasantly surprised' to learn of the shortage of forces between the Tyne and Dover, for he was convinced that 'the enemy would go for London and attempt a knock-out blow'.

During the meeting the Vice-Admiral, Dover, commented that Dover 'was very weakly held', while the Commander-in-Chief Portsmouth questioned whether the army was 'really ready for an immediate and sudden move of their rescue brigades'.[2]

Churchill took up this complaint with his Defence Office, but they were not unduly alarmed by it. 'It has been explained *ad nauseam* to the PM', Colonel Jacob noted for Ismay on July 2, 'that transport for mobile reserves is held ready, and we really must leave the C-in-C to make his own plans.'[3]

There were other plans which needed Churchill's initiative to bring them into effect with greater speed. It was essential, he wrote to Ismay on July 4, for measures to be put 'actively in operation from today' to enable those who wished to remain in threatened sea ports during an invasion to do so. They should therefore have the best possible advice and materials as to preparing their cellars, including the ability 'to

---

[1] But Churchill returned to it, nevertheless, three weeks later, minuting to A. V. Alexander, Pound and Phillips: 'I cannot help feeling that there is more in the plan of laying mines behind an invader's landing than the Naval Staff felt when I mentioned the matter three weeks ago. In the interval, I sent a reminder asking that it should be further considered. If an invader lands during the night or morning, the flotillas will attack him in rear during the day, and these flotillas will be heavily bombarded from the Air, as part of the Air battles which will be going on. If, however, when night falls a curtain or fender of mines can be laid close inshore, so as to cut off the landing-place from reinforcements of any kind, these mines, once laid, will not have to be guarded from Air attack and, consequently, will relieve the flotilla from the need of coming back on the second day, thus avoiding losses from the Air and Air protection. At any rate, I think it improvident not to provide for the option whether to seal off the hostile landing by attack of flotillas or mines. There may be several landings, and you may want to leave one sealed off with mines in order to attack another. Of course, all the above will apply still more if the landing had got hold of a port instead of merely a beach.' ('Action this Day', 25 July 1940: Churchill papers, 20/13.)

[2] Upper War Room Meeting, 'Summarized notes . . .', 'Most Secret', 5 p.m., 30 June 1940: Cabinet papers, 120/443. The Vice-Admiral was Sir Bertram Ramsay.

[3] Minute of 2 July 1940: Cabinet papers, 120/443.

prop up the building overhead'. All this, Churchill added, 'must be put actively in operation from day to day'.[1] As to who should remain in the East Coast ports, from which more than 170,000 had already been evacuated, Churchill minuted to Ismay on July 5: 'Only those who are trustworthy should be allowed to stay. All doubtful elements should be removed.'[2]

Churchill envisaged an invading force being challenged and fought at every step. But there were many who felt, or feared, that no such resistance would take place. The Labour MP Josiah Wedgwood had written to Churchill to ask for a public or private assurance 'that London will never be declared an open city like Paris, and that we shall, if need be, fight in the streets'.[3] Churchill sent Wedgwood's letter to Ismay with the note: 'what is the position about London? I have a very clear view that we should fight every inch of it, and that it would devour quite a large invading army.'[4]

Ismay replied to Churchill's query on July 3. 'I am sure,' he wrote, 'that all military opinion would wholeheartedly endorse your opinion.'[5] On receiving Ismay's note, Churchill wrote at once to Wedgwood: 'you may rest assured that we should fight every street of London and its suburbs'. London, Churchill believed, 'would devour an invading army, assuming one ever got so far. We hope however to drown the bulk of them in the salt sea.'[6]

During the first week of July Churchill noted that Ministers not in the War Cabinet were 'depressed at not knowing more of what is going forward in the military sphere'. He therefore asked Sinclair, Eden and A. V. Alexander to take it in turns to talk to these Ministers once a week, answering questions and explaining the general position, provided such talks were not 'too heavy a burden upon you'.[7]

Churchill's leadership was being discussed that day by Lord Halifax and Victor Cazalet, who noted in his diary: 'We are disturbed some-what about Winston. He is getting very arrogant and hates criticism of any kind.' According to Cazalet, Halifax told him that it was 'almost impossible' to get five minutes conversation with Churchill.[8] But

[1] 'Action this Day', 4 July 1940: Premier papers, 3/222/3, folio 4.

[2] 'Action this Day', 5 July 1940: Premier papers, 3/222/3, folios 5–6.

[3] Letter of 30 June 1940: Cabinet papers, 120/453.

[4] Minute of 2 July 1940: Cabinet papers, 120/453.

[5] Minute of 3 July 1940: Cabinet papers, 120/453.

[6] Letter of 3 July 1940: Wedgwood papers.

[7] Minutes of 5 July 1940 to Sir Archibald Sinclair, Anthony Eden and A. V. Alexander: Churchill papers, 20/13.

[8] Diary entry for 5 July 1940, quoted in: Robert Rhodes James (editor), *Victor Cazalet, a Portrait*, London 1976, page 231.

Churchill was burdened by the hour by hour problems which the threatened invasion posed. On July 6 he asked Colonel Jacob for a 'careful report today' of 'any further indication of enemy preparations for raid or invasion'. Churchill added: 'Let me have this tonight. Thereafter I wish for daily reports till further notice.'[1]

During July 5 Churchill drafted a further telegram to Roosevelt. In it he stressed, as Colville noted in his diary, Britain's 'dire need' for destroyers, and stated that the United States would bear a 'grievous responsibility if she failed Britain now'. But, as Colville added, 'he has not sent it off owing to objections from Halifax to certain parts'.[2]

Halifax had objected to two particular passages. In one, Churchill had intended to write that de Valera and the Government of Eire were on the verge of 'throwing in their lot with the Germans *who they think are bound to win*'. Halifax urged the deletion of the italicized phrase. He also wished to delete the italicized phrases '*It seems to me very hard to understand why* this modest aid *is not given at the time when it* could be perhaps decisively effective.' Given these objections, Churchill decided not to send the message.[3]

Late that evening, Churchill went to the Central War Room, together with Beaverbrook, to see Ironside's 'work map'. Both men were 'pleased', Ironside noted in his diary, and he added: 'One cannot help Winston enough, although he seems to have enough courage for everybody.'[4]

On the following day Ironside was Churchill's guide during a visit to military exercises in Kent, together with Clementine Churchill. The troops involved were the Canadian Brigade and a Territorial Brigade of the 45th Division. 'Winston was in great form,' Ironside noted in his diary, 'and gave us lunch at Chartwell in his cottage. Very wet, but nobody minded it at all.'[5] Also present on this tour of inspection was Eric Seal, who wrote home:

We went off early on Saturday to visit troops. It was raining miserably, & was altogether a beast of a morning. We went down to Limpsfield, & duly found the rendezvous but no one was there to meet us! So we had a drink, & then went out to try & find the General who was supposed to meet us. He unfortunately had gone the other way. However, after a very long wait in the

[1] Minute of 6 July 1940: Churchill papers, 20/13.
[2] Colville diary, 5 July 1940: Colville papers.
[3] Premier papers, 3/462/2/3, folios 156–7.
[4] Ironside diary, 5 July 1940: Roderick MacLeod and Denis Kelly, *The Ironside Diaries 1937–1940*, London 1962, page 380. For the Central War Room, see pages 685–6.
[5] Ironside diary, 6 July 1940: Roderick MacLeod and Denis Kelly, *The Ironside Diaries 1937–1940*, London 1962, page 382.

rain, a junction was at length effected, & we went off & inspected some troops.

Then they said the column we had inspected would move off past us: so we took up our stand at a convenient spot, & waited. It was *very* wet; & we waited & waited & waited. The troops had gone off down another road! However, after that we did see them doing some evolutions, rounding up imaginary parachutists & invaders, & things went somewhat better. Also after lunch the weather cleared up.

The only real excitement was a Hun aeroplane overhead. No one seemed to worry about it, & it didn't worry about us, so even that wasn't too thrilling.

In the evening the PM, Mrs C & I went off to Chartwell, his house near Westerham. It is a wonderful spot, at the head of a private valley, with views from the house over the valley, & down it over the Weald. The gardens are lovely—not very well kept now, naturally—but designed as wild & natural gardens on the side of the hill, so that they don't look at all bad even if not fully maintained at concert pitch. One of the features of the place is a whole series of ponds, which are stocked with immense gold-fish—really a variety of carp. Some of them are well over a foot long; & there are hundreds of them. The PM loves feeding them: & we walked round with a bag of food on Sunday morning, watching them come to the surface & eat it up. One of his most amiable qualities is his obvious love of animals—he calls them all darlings, & shouts to the cat, & even the birds. The old swan on the lake knew his call, & answered back![1]

At Alexandria, the French ships detained under 'Catapult' were seeking to make some bargain whereby they might sail from Egypt, and thereby leave British jurisdiction. Churchill opposed this. 'Now that we have got them in our power,' he minuted on July 7, after his return to London from Chartwell, 'we must certainly not let them go.'[2] In Northern Ireland, plans were being made by the Chiefs of Staff to prepare the Royal Marine Brigade for operations against Portuguese islands in the Atlantic, should such operations be approved. But Churchill cautioned that the Brigade 'shd also remain available for service in Southern Ireland: eg Queenstown or Berehaven'. And he added, in a note to Ismay: 'Make sure this is understood.'[3]

Churchill had one cause for confidence on July 6, but one which he could not divulge outside the most secret circles of war direction. This was the admission by the Air Ministry, on the basis of Lindemann's

[1] Eric Seal, letter of 6 July 1940: Seal papers.

[2] Minute of 7 July 1940: Premier papers, 3/179/4, folio 136.

[3] Note of 7 July 1940: Premier papers, 3/361/1, folio 76. When, on July 9, Halifax expressed his opposition to the 'Atlantic Islands Project', Churchill replied: 'Nothing must be done without a Cabinet decision' (Minute of 10 July 1940: Premier papers, 3/361/1, folio 80). The Islands were the Azores (operational code name 'Accordion', and the Cape Verde Islands 'Sackbut').

scrutiny of Enigma decrypts, that Air Intelligence had overestimated the growth of German first-line bomber strength. In June this strength had been estimated at 2,500, with a daily bomb delivery capacity of 4,800 tons. As a result of Lindemann's scrutiny, these figures were scaled down to 1,250 bombers and 1,800 tons of bombs.

The Enigma decrypts on which this scaling down was based were described by the Air Staff as 'heaven-sent' and 'apparently sure'. The situation could now be viewed, the Air Staff conceded, 'much more confidently than was possible a month ago'.[1]

On July 7 Churchill advised that the Canadian troops, whose exercise he had watched, should be used for anti-invasion work in England rather than for their original task, the defence of Iceland. Churchill also gave instructions for the unloading of the first convoy of rifles from the United States, due to arrive during July 9. At least 100,000 of these rifles, he minuted to Eden, 'ought to reach the troops that very night, or in the small hours of the following morning', using trains to distribute them.[2] There was also a question for the Minister of Supply about Britain's offensive capacity. 'What is being done,' Churchill asked, 'about designing and planning vessels to transport tanks across the sea for a British attack on enemy countries?'[3]

Churchill was much encouraged by his new found knowledge of the reduced scale of German bomber strength, and in a minute to Beaverbrook on July 8, while agreeing that the production of fighter planes must be the 'prime consideration' until Germany's own air offensive was broken, he set out what he believed to be the only possible means of winning the war: a British bomber offensive. When 'I look round', Churchill wrote, 'to see how we can win the war I see that there is only one sure path', and he went on to explain:

We have no continental army which can defeat the German military power. The blockade is broken and Hitler has Asia and probably Africa to draw from. Should he be repulsed here or not try invasion, he will recoil eastward,

[1] Minute of 6 July 1940: Air Ministry papers, 40/2321. Lindemann's intervention on this occasion is described in F. H. Hinsley and others, *British Intelligence in the Second World War, Its Influence on Strategy and Operations*, volume 1, London 1979, pages 177-8, where it is confirmed, as Churchill had alleged repeatedly in 1934 and 1935, that the Air Ministry had, before the war, underestimated the figures of German air strength.

[2] Minute of 7 July 1940 (copies to A. V. Alexander and Sir Dudley Pound): Premier papers, 3/372/1, folio 131. The rifles arrived on July 9 on the *Tilsington Court*. 'Difficulties are,' Eden explained, 'that packing on the American side has been very haphazard, and cases have occurred of the bolts being packed separately from the rifles. Moreover, the solid, hard grease in the barrels is not easy to remove' (Minute of 9 July 1940: Premier papers, 3/372/1, folio 130).

[3] Minute to Herbert Morrison, 7 July 1940: Churchill papers, 20/13.

and we have nothing to stop him. But there is one thing that will bring him back and bring him down, and that is an absolutely devastating, exterminating attack by very heavy bombers from this country upon the Nazi homeland.[1]

Unless the Germans could be overwhelmed by aerial bombardment, Churchill added, 'I do not see a way through.'

Churchill ended his minute by telling Beaverbrook: 'We cannot accept any lower aim than air mastery. When can it be obtained?'[2]

On July 9 British and Italian warships came into brief contact in the Mediterranean. But, before any fighting could ensue, the Italian ships withdrew behind a smoke screen. That same day, the War Cabinet learned that the French battleship *Richelieu*, steaming off Dakar, had been attacked by depth charges and aerial torpedoes from the British aircraft carrier *Hermes*, and had been put out of action. There were now seven French capital ships out of service, Churchill pointed out, which could no longer fall into German hands. Churchill also expressed his hope that the *Jean Bart*, at Casablanca, could be 'put out of action' as a result of discussions between the British and French naval officers on the spot, 'without our having to carry out Fleet operations such as had been necessary at Oran'.[3]

One effect of the action at Oran, as the Chiefs of Staff and Vice-Chiefs had foreseen on June 30, was that the British warships were free to deploy in Home waters to challenge an invasion force. The War Cabinet now discussed the specific location of individual ships, and Churchill gave a survey of the anti-invasion deployment at sea. The Fleet as disposed, he told his colleagues on the morning of July 9:

... should be able to deal with what remained of the German Fleet if it endeavoured to escort an invading force. If any unescorted convoys endeavoured to make landings in this country, we should have sufficient small craft to deal with them. All round the coasts were some hundreds of armed trawlers,

[1] The future Commander-in-Chief of Bomber Command (1942–1945), Marshal of the Royal Air Force Sir Arthur Harris, commented on this Minute: 'It was the origin of the idea of bombing the enemy out of the war. I should have been proud of it. But it originated with Winston' (Sir Arthur Harris, conversation with the author, 21 October 1982).

[2] Secret, Minute of 8 July 1940: Churchill papers, 20/13. As to British Bomber losses, three days later Churchill minuted to Sir Archibald Sinclair: 'Generally speaking, the losses in the Bomber force seem unduly heavy, and the Bremen raid, from which only one out of six returned, is most grievous. At the present time a very heavy price may be paid (a) for information by reconnaissance of the conditions in the German ports and German-controlled ports and river-mouths, (b) for the bombing of barges or assemblies of ships thus detected. Apart from this, the long-range bombing of Germany should be conducted with a desire to save the machines and personnel as much as possible while keeping up a steady attack. It is very important to build up the numbers of the Bomber force, which is very low at the present time' (Churchill papers, 20/13).

[3] War Cabinet No. 198 of 1940, 9 July 1940, 12 noon: Cabinet papers, 65/14.

motor-torpedo boats and mine-sweepers which could take part in the mêlée, if invasion were attempted. In addition, the Admiralty had, with great speed, erected around the coast some 150 six-inch guns, in emplacements which would protect them from attacks by dive-bombers. These guns were manned by some 7,000 Naval ratings and marines. A number of land torpedo-tubes had also been fixed.

Another deterrent, Churchill told the War Cabinet, would be the minefield in the Straits of Dover which was being 'refreshed' by the addition of further mines.[1]

In an attempt to prevent any invading force from obtaining too great an initial advantage, Churchill decided that whereas the beach areas would continue to be defended, the principal battles would have to take place inland. In view of the army's still limited resources, there was little else that he could do. 'The Prime Minister has sent down an order,' Ironside noted in his diary, 'or what is practically an order, to withdraw two divisions from the beach-line. I have sent in to say I can withdraw one in a few days.' Ironside added: 'It is difficult to tackle Winston when he is in one of his go-getter humours.'

Ironside had expected the German invasion to take place on July 9, a Tuesday.[2] Colville, who was on duty that day at Downing Street, noted in his diary: 'invasion said to be on Thursday'.[3] But it was not invasion that proved the immediate danger. Instead, on the night of Wednesday July 10, a formation of 120 German bombers and fighters assembled behind Calais and attempted to attack a British convoy between Dover and Dungeness. At the same time, 70 German aircraft raided South Wales, bombing dockyards: the first large-scale bombing attack on Britain.[4]

To challenge these new and large-scale air attacks, British fighters moved with skill and daring, and with inevitable loss. But pressure had already mounted against the head of Fighter Command, Sir Hugh Dowding, and only a few days before the increased German air activity had begun, Sir Archibald Sinclair told Churchill that he had been considering removing Dowding from his Command, at the latest after four months. Churchill opposed Sinclair's decision, writing to him on July 10:

[1] War Cabinet No. 198 of 1940, 9 July 1940, 12 noon, Minute 3, Confidential Annex: Cabinet papers, 65/14.
[2] Ironside diary, 9 July 1940: Roderick MacLeod and Denis Kelly (editors), *The Ironside Diaries 1937-1940*, London 1962, page 383.
[3] Colville diary, 9 July 1940: Colville papers.
[4] War Cabinet, Chiefs of Staff Committee, Weekly Résumé No. 45: Churchill papers, 23/5.

Personally, I think he is one of the very best men you have got, and I say this after having been in contact with him for about two years. I have greatly admired the whole of his work in the Fighter Command, and especially in resisting the clamour for numerous air raid warnings, and the immense pressure to dissipate the Fighter strength during the great French battle. In fact he has my full confidence. I think it is a pity for an officer so gifted and so trusted to be working on such a short tenure as four months, and I hope you will consider whether it is not in the public interest that his appointment should be indefinitely prolonged while the war lasts. This would not of course exclude his being moved to a higher position, if that were thought necessary.

Churchill added that he was 'much averse' to making changes or putting in new men who would have to learn the work all over again, 'except where there is some proved failure or inadequacy'.[1]

Churchill's support for Dowding was paralleled by his criticism of Dill, especially when Dill opposed the War Cabinet's general injunction to get as many French soldiers as possible to stay in Britain, rather than be repatriated to Casablanca. 'I do not think,' Churchill wrote to Eden, 'we are having the help from General Dill which we hoped for at the time of his appointment, and he strikes me as being very tired, disheartened, and over-impressed with the might of Germany.'[2]

As soon as news reached Downing Street of the air battle above the Channel coast, Churchill made plans to visit Dover and Deal, travelling to Dover by train immediately after lunch on July 11. 'We hoped for an air raid,' Colville noted in his diary, and from the Admiral's room looked out 'across the sunlit Channel' to France. It was too clear and cloudless for German planes to come over again, and Churchill was 'disappointed' to see nothing. They did see, however, a 14-inch gun being prepared to fire across the Channel to France. This gun, Colville noted, was there 'owing to a caprice of Winston's', and could fire for only a hundred rounds. Three cranes were needed to put it into place, and the military authorities called it a 'pure stunt'.[3]

Four days after returning to London, Churchill minuted to Ismay: 'Make sure that over-head cover against bombing attack is provided for the 14-inch gun.' A structure of steel girders, he suggested, should be put up 'to carry sand-bag cover similar to that over the 6-inch guns which are mounted along the coast. All should be camouflaged. You will be told that it will be necessary to change the guns after 120 rounds. In that case the structure will have to be taken to pieces and

---

[1] 'Private and Confidential', 10 July 1940: Churchill papers, 20/2.
[2] 'Strictly Private & Confidential', 10 July 1940: Churchill papers, 20/1.
[3] Colville diary, 11 July 1940: Colville papers.

put up again after the gun is changed.' There should, Churchill added, 'be no difficulty in this'.[1]

During his tour of the south coast on July 11, Churchill 'enjoyed', as he told Colville on the following day, 'a real Hun hate' with one of the Generals. 'I never hated the Hun in the last war,' he remarked, 'but now, I hate them like an earwig.'[2]

Among those accompanying Churchill on this journey was Colonel Jacob, who commented, in a talk with Colville, that it was their former master, Neville Chamberlain, who bore a 'heavy responsibility for our present state of unpreparedness. He had starved the fighting forces.' Jacob added that their new master, Churchill, was 'the only man who could hold the country united'. If Churchill had a fault, Jacob added, 'it was to go too much into detail'.[3]

There was a fine divide between too much detail and too little. Throughout the 1930s Churchill had maintained his criticisms of Government defence preparedness, especially in the air, only by absorbing an immense amount of detail, some of it extremely technical. Throughout his earlier Ministerial career, as President of the Board of Trade, Home Secretary, First Lord of the Admiralty, Minister of Munitions, Secretary of State for War and Air, Colonial Secretary, and Chancellor of the Exchequer, he had been fascinated by the details which each of these seven Ministries had spanned, and had sought to master them. Now, as Prime Minister, the habit remained whereby everything he saw became a source of scrutiny, comment and exhortation. As Jacob later recalled: 'he pushed and pushed and pushed, which was all to the good—the admirable wish for the offensive—provided he had people to keep him on the rails'. At the Admiralty, Jacob reflected, no such restraints had been present, and for this reason, from September 1939 to May 1940, Churchill had 'dominated' the Board of Admiralty. But as Prime Minister the restraints were there: 'that' Jacob reflected, 'is one of the reasons why we won the war'.[4]

In balancing the forecasts of disaster and survival, Churchill had continually to assess an enormous range of information reaching him daily, and to give instructions for action where he felt his own authority

[1] Minute of 15 July 1940: Churchill papers, 20/13. Three weeks later Churchill minuted to A. V. Alexander: 'I am impressed by the speed and efficiency with which the emplacement for the 14-inch gun at Dover has been prepared and the gun itself mounted. Will you tell all those who have helped in this achievement how much I appreciate the sterling effort they have made' (Minute of 9 August 1940: Churchill papers, 20/13).
[2] Colville diary, 12 July 1940: Colville papers.
[3] Colville diary, 11 July 1940: Colville papers.
[4] Lieutenant-General Sir Ian Jacob: conversation with the author, 1 July 1982.

was needed as a spur or safeguard. One of the most important daily budgets of news to reach him, and one of the utmost secrecy, concerned the arrival of arms and munitions from the United States. Under Jacob's supervision a daily report was prepared to show Churchill exactly what supplies had arrived and were due to arrive from New York, on what ships, and in what convoys.

Churchill scrutinized each chart, urging larger escorts where he felt they were needed, or proposing the earlier despatch of warships to meet unescorted vessels. Brief notes from his Defence Office and Private Secretariat kept him informed of the safe arrival of individual ships.[1] On July 10 Jacob was able to report the arrival that day of more than a quarter of a million rifles and 77 million rounds of ammunition, as well as more than three hundred 75-millimetre field guns and nearly half a million rounds of high explosive 75-millimetre shells.[2] Within forty-eight hours, Eden had ensured that this cargo was distributed by train and lorry to where the guns and rifles were most needed.[3]

Learning from Jacob's charts of the sailing of the *Western Prince*, which had left New York unescorted on account of her high speed, and of other munitions ships already in mid-Atlantic in convoy, Churchill minuted to Ismay on July 13: 'Draw Admiralty attention to the importance of all these ships, especially *Western Prince*. What is her speed? It would be a disaster if we lost 50,000 rifles.' His minute continued: 'Draw attention also to the immense consequence of the convoy leaving New York between July 8 and 12. When will these various convoys be in the danger zone? When will they arrive?'

'Let me have a report on the measures to be taken,' Churchill added.[4] On the following day he received his answers. *Western Prince* was sailing 'independently' from New York to Liverpool at 14 knots, due at Liverpool on July 20; the ships leaving New York between July 8 and 12 would join the Halifax convoy on July 13 and reach Liverpool on July 30. Churchill was also told that these ships had 'an Ocean Escort, HMS *Ranpura*'. He minuted at once: 'Not enough.' As for the unescorted *Western Prince*, he asked: 'Can she be met far out?'[5]

---

[1] Thus on 22 July 1940, a note from Colville read: 'PM, The consignment of arms due today from the United States has arrived safely.' Churchill noted, 'Good.' (Premier papers, 3/372/1, folio 26.)

[2] 'Field Guns and Rifles from the United States, Daily Report No. 17', 10 July 1940: Premier papers, 3/372/1, folio 50.

[3] 'Progress Report on Distribution of American Rifles', 12 July 1940: Premier papers, 3/372/1, folios 128-9. These rifle reports were prepared by William Gorell Barnes of the War Cabinet Office.

[4] 'Action this Day', 'Most Secret', 13 July 1940: Premier papers, 3/372/1, folio 127.

[5] War Cabinet Office note of 14 July 1940, and Churchill comments: Premier papers, 3/372/1, folio 126.

This process of examining, questioning and suggesting action involved Churchill in constant visits to the places and personnel on whom Britain's survival depended. On July 12 it was to Kenley aerodrome, to inspect a Hurricane Squadron, where Churchill saw both men and machines in pouring rain, before flying to Northolt in a Flamingo aircraft, and on to Chequers for the weekend. Two Generals, Auchinleck and Paget, had been invited to Chequers, 'very much finer soldiers', noted Colville, 'than Ironside or Dill'.

Colville also recorded in his diary how, that Friday evening, Churchill reflected that he could not see 'much hope of a decision' before 1942. In the next three months, he told Auchinleck and Paget, Britain must fight 'for the negative purpose of preventing invasion and defeating it if it comes'. The winter would be terrible for Europe. Hitler would take 'the other children's candy'. But in 1941 Britain would have fifty-five divisions under arms, and was already preparing a series of 'butcher and bolt' raids on the Continent. She was also planning to obtain air superiority.

The rumour that weekend was of a German invasion launched from Norway. This Churchill thought 'ridiculous'. But wherever invasion came from, he considered it essential not to disperse the British troops along the beaches, but to hold the main British forces in complete divisions behind which 'a highly mobile reserve' could move quickly to wherever required. Meanwhile, Churchill told his guests, 'the great invasion scare, which we only ceased to deride six weeks ago, is serving a most useful purpose, and is well on the way to providing us with the finest offensive army we have ever possessed', keeping every man and woman 'tuned to a high pitch of readiness'.

He did not wish the 'scare' to abate, Churchill said, and although he personally doubted that invasion would take place, he intended in his next broadcast 'to give the impression of long and dangerous vigils'.

Discussing how the populace would respond in the event of invasion, General Paget said he wanted the public to stay at home. Auchinleck said they 'would not' do so, Churchill that they 'ought not' to do so. What was needed, said Churchill, was for every citizen 'to fight desperately'. This they would do, in his view, 'if they thought they were to be massacred'. The Home Guard must therefore be armed. If necessary, even women must be 'allowed to fight'.[1]

In the air, the German bombing offensive had continued, with an attack on the Aberdeen ironworks and shipyard on July 12, leading to 'considerable casualties'. In one week eighty-eight people had been

[1] Colville diary, 12 July 1940: Colville papers.

killed. These figures were circulated to the War Cabinet. But they were not made public, as a result of a War Cabinet decision, brought into effect on July 5, that Government Communiqués were henceforth to make no reference to the number of casualties. Churchill was anxious to ensure that this decision had been carried out. 'The Censors have now been informed of this new arrangement,' his Defence Office were told that same day, and it would be put into effect immediately.[1]

In reply to the German bombardment, Fighter Command had flown 3,288 sorties over Britain. At a cost of seventeen fighters lost, thirty-seven German aircraft had been destroyed.[2] Churchill was certainly buoyed up by this news of British fighter success in the air. On July 13 he telegraphed to Harold L. Ickes, the United States Secretary of the Interior, in reply to a letter of encouragement: 'We are doing our best.'[3]

That weekend, Colville noted, Churchill showed 'greater animation and exuberance than I have ever seen before'. Human beings did not require rest, Churchill declared, 'what they require is change, or else they become bloody minded', and he went on 'to praise brass bands, and to curse Hore-Belisha for abolishing them'.[4]

On the previous day Churchill had minuted to Eden: 'I am delighted at the action you have taken about bands, but when are we going to hear them playing about the streets?' Even quite small parade marches, Churchill added, 'are highly beneficial, especially in towns like Liverpool and Glasgow, in fact wherever there are troops and leisure for it there should be an attempt at military display'.[5]

That weekend, Colville wrote, Churchill felt 'more cheerful than at any time since he took office' and had spoken of the 'armoured panther springs' which Britain's mechanized divisions would make on the Continent in 1941, and of the 'superiority' which British bombers would obtain. 'Even if That Man reached the Caspian,' Churchill forecast, 'he would return to find a fire in his backyard'; indeed, 'it would avail him nothing if he reached the Great Wall of China'.

It was Britain's very superiority by 1941, Churchill commented,

---

[1] Norman Brook (Ministry of Home Security) to Ismay, 5 July 1940: Cabinet papers, 120/464. A member of the Cabinet Secretariat from 1941 to 1946, Brook was Secretary to the Cabinet from 1947 to 1962, including the years of Churchill's second Premiership.

[2] War Cabinet, Chiefs of Staff Committee, Weekly Résumé No. 46: Churchill papers, 23/5.

[3] Telegram of 13 July 1940: Churchill papers, 20/5.

[4] Colville diary, 13 July 1940: Colville papers.

[5] Minute of 12 July 1940: Churchill papers, 20/13.

which would tempt Hitler to invade. For this reason Britain's vigil might in fact be 'long and trying', and the nation would have to remain on guard against surprise attack. At any time in the year to come, Churchill warned, 'we could be brought to the greatest test'.

That Saturday evening Sir Hugh Dowding dined at Chequers. The last four days, Churchill told him, 'had been the most glorious in the history of the Royal Air Force'. These days 'had been the test', he added. 'The enemy had come, and had lost five to one. We could now be confident of our superiority.'[1]

Churchill's confidence was reflected in his private conversation. Commenting at Chequers that Sunday on the much anticipated invasion, he said that he thought it 'highly unlikely', and added: 'Hitler must invade or fail. If he fails he is bound to go east, and fail he will.' Churchill was also 'very good', as Colville noted, at relaxing, and 'taking his mind off invasion' by listening at luncheon to a discourse by the Liberal MP James de Rothschild on the beauty of the paintings at Chequers, and going 'into ecstasy' on a small Rubens painting in the dining room.[2]

That afternoon Churchill visited the Royal Air Force Station at Halton. He also dictated a letter to Lord Woolton on the absurdity of excessive food rationing. 'Almost all the food faddists I have ever known,' he wrote, 'nut-eaters and the like, have died young after a long period of senile decay. The British soldier is far more likely to be right than the scientists. All he cares about is beef.' Churchill's letter ended: 'The way to lose the war is to try to force the British public into a diet of milk, oatmeal, potatoes etc, washed down on gala occasions with a little lime juice.'[3]

That Sunday evening Churchill broadcast to the nation. His first words were of France. 'Today is the fourteenth of July,' he said, 'the national festival of France. A year ago in Paris I watched the stately parade down the Champs-Elysées of the French Army and the French Empire. Who can foresee what the course of other years can bring?

[1] Colville diary, 13 July 1940: Colville papers.

[2] Colville diary, 14 July 1940: Colville papers. The others present at luncheon were Clementine Churchill, Mrs de Rothschild, Horatia Seymour, Sir Henry Strakosch and Professor Lindemann. (Chequers Visitors Book.)

[3] Letter of 14 July 1940: Churchill papers, 20/2. On 15 July 1940 Lindemann supported Churchill's opposition to tea rationing with the comment: 'It is the only luxury of the working woman, whose morale should not be jeopardized.' (Churchill papers, 20/13.)

Faith is given to us to help and comfort us when we stand in awe before the unfurling scroll of human destiny. And I proclaim my faith that some of us will live to see a fourteenth of July when a liberated France will once again rejoice in her greatness and her glory. . . .'

Churchill spoke emotionally of those Frenchmen and Frenchwomen who 'in the darkest hour did not despair of the Republic', and urged his listeners not to waste their breath nor to cumber their thought with reproaches. 'When you have a friend and comrade,' he said, 'at whose side you have faced tremendous struggles, and your friend is smitten down by a stunning blow, it may be necessary to make sure that the weapon that has fallen from his hand shall not be added to the resources of your common enemy. But you need not bear malice because of your friend's cries of delirium and gestures of agony.'

Later in his speech, in a reference to Oran, Churchill spoke of the bond uniting and sustaining the Government in the public regard, 'namely (as is increasingly becoming known), that we are prepared to proceed to all extremities, to endure them and to enforce them'; that, he added, was the 'bond of union in His Majesty's Government tonight'. And yet, although Britain was fighting '*by* ourselves alone', she was not fighting '*for* ourselves alone'.

Churchill also spoke of the impending invasion, telling his listeners:

Here in this strong City of Refuge which enshrines the title-deeds of human progress and is of deep consequence to Christian civilization; here, girt about by the seas and oceans where the Navy reigns; shielded from above by the prowess and devotion of our airmen—we await undismayed the impending assault. Perhaps it will come tonight. Perhaps it will come next week. Perhaps it will never come. We must show ourselves equally capable of meeting a sudden violent shock or—what is perhaps a harder test—a prolonged vigil. But be the ordeal sharp or long, or both, we shall seek no terms, we shall tolerate no parley; we may show mercy—we shall ask for none.

Many countries, Churchill noted, including France, had been 'rotted from within before they were smitten from without'. But the people of Britain were 'in good health and in good heart'. The men of the Home Guard had 'the strongest desire to attack and come to close quarters with the enemy wherever he may appear'. Should the invader come to Britain, there would be 'no placid lying down of the people in submission before him, as we have seen, alas, in other countries'. Britain would defend, he said, 'every village, every town, and every city'. As for the 'vast mass' of London, he said, this, 'fought street by street, could easily devour an entire hostile army; and we would rather see London laid in ruins and ashes than it should be tamely and abjectly enslaved'.[1]

All now depended, Churchill declared, upon the 'whole life-strength of the British race' throughout the world, 'and all our well-wishers in every land' doing their utmost night and day, 'giving all, daring all, enduring all—to the utmost—to the end'. His broadcast ended:

This is no war of chieftains or of princes, of dynasties or national ambition; it is a war of peoples and of causes. There are vast numbers, not only in this Island but in every land, who will render faithful service in this war, but whose names will never be known, whose deeds will never be recorded. This is a War of the Unknown Warrior; but let all strive without failing in faith or in duty, and the dark curse of Hitler will be lifted from our age.[2]

'I clapped when it was over,' Harold Nicolson wrote to his wife after listening at the Reform Club to Churchill's speech. 'But really he has got guts that man. Imagine the effect of his speech in the Empire and the USA. I felt a great army of men and women of resolution watching for the fight. And I felt that all the silly people were but black-beetles scurrying into holes.'[3]

'It seems to me very important,' Churchill minuted to Ismay on the night of his broadcast, 'that everybody should be made to look to their gas masks now,' and he added: 'I expect a great many of them require overhauling, and it may well be Hitler has some gas designs upon us.' Enquiries must be made about setting the necessary overhauls on foot. 'Action,' Churchill wrote, 'should be taken at once.'[4]

---

[1] On the following day Churchill minuted for the Chiefs of Staff and Home Defence Committees that although the 'heaviest attack' of any invasion force was 'likely to fall in the North', yet 'the sovereign importance of London and the narrowness of the seas in this quarter make the South the theatre where the greatest precautions must be taken'. (Minute of 15 July 1940: Churchill papers, 23/4.)

[2] Broadcast of 14 July 1940, 9 p.m.: His Master's Voice recording, ALP 1435. Two weeks later Sir Alexander Duckham wrote to Churchill: 'Listening to you on Sunday the 14th inspired and fortified us. Reading you the next day we missed the timbre, the pauses, the stressing of words, the courage—in fact the spell.' Duckham had therefore asked Alfred Clark of HMV to allow the record of the speech to be distributed at colleges, schools and works. (Letter of 27 July 1940: Churchill papers, 20/ 10.) A few weeks later Churchill agreed to a request from Freda Dudley Ward that all the profits from his recorded speeches should go to her charity, the Feathers Clubs, which, Bracken told Churchill, 'are feeding thousands of harassed Londoners'. (Note of 17 October 1940: Churchill papers, 20/10.) A note on the sleeve of ALP 1435 (and all other HMV recordings of Churchill's speeches) states: 'Royalties from these records are being paid to Charities nominated by Sir Winston Churchill.'

[3] Letter of 14 July 1940, quoted in: Nigel Nicolson (editor), *Harold Nicolson, Diaries and Letters 1939–1945*, London 1967, page 102. On 15 July 1940 Air Marshal Dowding wrote to Churchill of 'how profoundly moved I was by your Sunday broadcast. You said what we all think but are too inarticulate to express.' (Premier papers, 3/22/2, folio 161.)

[4] Minute of 14 July 1940: Churchill papers, 20/13. For Churchill's further instructions in the event of a German gas attack, see page 674.

Churchill did not confine his scrutiny to affairs in Britain; on July 14 he also commented, to Eden, of the 'dead-alive' way in which the Middle East campaign was being run, and warned that the 'storm' would break there presently 'and the disasters which may follow may be very serious'.[1]

Both the needs of Britain, and of Britain's forces in the Middle East, depended upon the arrival of supplies from the United States. The placing of orders in the United States for war materials had continued uninterrupted since the transfer of all French contracts to Britain on June 16. But with so many demands made upon the United States by different Government departments in Britain, there was overlapping and some chaos; so much so that on July 4 Sir Horace Wilson had proposed setting up a central organisation in London to co-ordinate the departmental demands that were being made on Arthur Purvis and the British Purchasing Commission in the United States. The organization, known as the North American Supply Committee, was attached to the Cabinet Secretariat. It began its work on July 6.[2] Two days later it was decided that the Committee should co-ordinate supplies from both the United States and Canada. The Ministry of Supply had already placed orders costing 90 million dollars in the United States, a sum which represented 'between 25 and 30% of the Ministry of Supply's entire programme for the items in question'.[3] Nine days later, after a discussion with the Director General of Requirements at the War Office, and at the request of the Ministry of Supply, Sir Arthur Salter telegraphed to Purvis that the urgent need was for rifles, the number available being the 'main limiting factor' of Britain's defence force in the next few months.[4]

At noon on July 16, speaking to the War Cabinet, Churchill referred to 'the very great progress which had been made in the past month in improving the defences of this country against invasion'.[5] But at a meeting of the Defence Committee at five o'clock that evening, to discuss anti-aircraft projectiles and their trials, it was stressed that the purchase of essential components for them had to be made in the United States.[6]

[1] Personal and Secret, minute of 14 July 1940: Churchill papers, 20/13.
[2] North American Supply Committee, Memorandum No. 1 of 1940, 9 July 1940: Cabinet papers, 92/27. The Chairman of the Committee was Sir Arthur Salter, its Secretary, William Gorell Barnes.
[3] Notes of an Inter-Departmental meeting held on 8 July 1940: Cabinet papers, 92/27.
[4] Sir Walter Layton to Sir Arthur Salter, 17 July 1940: Cabinet papers, 115/83.
[5] War Cabinet No. 205 of 1940, 16 July 1940, 12 noon: Cabinet papers, 65/8.
[6] Defence Committee (Supply) No. 10 of 1940, 16 July 1940, 5 p.m.: Cabinet papers, 70/1.

As soon as the War Cabinet ended, Churchill went to Buckingham Palace for an audience with the King. Back at Downing Street he had a fifteen-minute interview with Roger Keyes, to whom he offered the post of Director of Combined Operations. He then received Colonel Stewart Menzies, 'C', the Head of the British Secret Service.[1]

Menzies remained with Churchill for half an hour. His mission was almost certainly to discuss Churchill's plans for the gathering of Intelligence from German-occupied Europe, and from the unoccupied region of Vichy France.[2] These plans involved the setting up of a new secret organization, and that same night Churchill's 'usual nocturnal visitors', as Colville called them, included Hugh Dalton, the Minister of Economic Warfare.[3] During their meeting, Churchill invited Dalton to take charge of 'a new instrument of war', the Special Operations Executive, or SOE. The aim of SOE, as Dalton later wrote, was to co-ordinate all action by way of subversion and sabotage 'against the enemy overseas'; Churchill called it the 'Ministry of Ungentlemanly Warfare'. 'And now,' the Prime Minister told him, 'set Europe ablaze.'[4]

Among those seeking British support for their endeavours to challenge the German dominance of Europe was General de Gaulle, now resident in London at the head of a small but determined group of Frenchmen, implacably opposed to the Government at Vichy, and to its representatives in North Africa, including Weygand.[5]

On July 16 Churchill's liaison with de Gaulle, Desmond Morton, warned the Prime Minister that de Gaulle's cause was 'suffering considerably from lack of intelligent publicity'. Morton proposed that an attempt should be made as soon as possible 'to publicize' de Gaulle in

---

[1] Churchill Engagement Cards: Thompson papers.

[2] Churchill kept a close watch on this aspect of Colonel Menzies' work, minuting to Ismay on 5 August 1940: 'I await proposals from Colonel Menzies for improving and extending our information about France and for keeping a continued flow of agents moving to and fro. For this purpose Naval facilities can, if necessary, be invoked. So far as the Vichy Government is concerned, it is not creditable that we have so little information. To what extent are American, Swiss and Spanish agents being used? Colonel Menzies should submit a report on what he has done and is proposing to do.' (Churchill papers, 20/13.)

[3] Colville diary, 16 July 1940: Colville papers.

[4] Hugh Dalton, *The Fateful Years, Memoirs 1931–1945*, London 1957, pages 366–7. One of Dalton's personal assistants at SOE was to be Churchill's own former research assistant, F. W. Deakin, who was later parachuted behind German lines in Yugoslavia, to make contact with Tito and his partisans. At the beginning of 1941 Morton wrote to Churchill: 'Dr Dalton proposes to employ Deakin first of all in sorting out from the mass of information which he receives that which is likely to be most helpful in regard to any special operations which he has on hand.' (Minute of 11 February 1941, in reply to Prime Minister's Personal Minute D.M. 1/1 of 11 February 1941: Churchill papers, 20/57.)

[5] Appointed by Vichy to be Governor-General of Algeria.

Britain, in the United States, in South America and in the French Colonies 'where he has contacts'. Morton suggested the expenditure of £300 a month in order that a public relations expert, Richard Temple, the Publicity Agent to the Metal Market, could promote de Gaulle's cause. Temple had already done propaganda on behalf of Finland after the Soviet attack at the end of 1939; propaganda which, Morton noted, had been 'particularly successful in the USA'. Morton added: 'It seems better to us to employ this man who will be under our control, whereby at any moment we can stop or change the lines of propaganda, rather than to assist General de Gaulle himself to improve his own lines, which would not easily be subject to our control.'[1]

Morton also told Churchill that he had certain reservations about de Gaulle. 'I still wonder,' he wrote to Churchill on July 26, 'if we could not find a potential Napoleon from among the French armed forces. I doubt if de Gaulle is more than a Marshal Murat.'[2] With the balance of forces so uneven, however, no ally, and no potential ally, could be ignored.

Unknown to British Intelligence, on July 16 Hitler had taken his long postponed decision to issue a directive for preparations to be made 'for a landing operation against England', code name 'Sealion'. His directive began:

Since England, in spite of her hopeless military situation, shows no signs of being ready to come to an understanding, I have decided to prepare a landing operation against England and, if necessary, to carry it out.

The aim of this operation will be to eliminate the English homeland as a base for the prosecution of the war against Germany and, if necessary, to occupy it completely. . . .

Preparations for the 'entire operation', Hitler ordered, 'must be completed by the middle of August'. Meanwhile, the British Air Force 'must be so reduced morally and physically that it is unable to deliver any significant attack against the German crossing'.[3]

The Battle of Britain had already begun. As part of Hitler's pre-invasion strategy, Goering now sought the systematic destruction of Britain's fighter bases. But Sir Hugh Dowding, whose task was to combat these attacks, saw the bombing of civilians as the greater danger, warning Churchill on July 16 that although the German night

---

[1] Minute marked 'Top of box, PM to see', 5 July 1940: Premier papers, 7/2. Churchill approved Morton's suggestion on 16 July 1940.

[2] Minute of 26 July 1940: Premier papers, 7/2.

[3] 'Directive No. 16', 16 July 1940: quoted in full in H. A. Trevor-Roper (editor), *Hitler's War Directives, 1939–1945*, London 1964, pages 34–7.

bomber could now be detected, there was as yet no night fighter able to follow up that detection with effective interception; the danger to Britain, Dowding believed, was massive bombing of civilian areas and 'the test' of a possible collapse of civilian morale. Colville, who heard this report was 'rather depressed' by what Dowding said.[1] Churchill himself was angered on the morning of July 16 when, at a meeting of the Defence Committee, he learned of serious deficiencies in both mortar ammunition production and the production of anti-tank guns. Of the first he said 'that the present production of mortar ammunition was absurdly low, and would not justify the issue of the weapon to the troops. It would be necessary for the War Office and the Ministry of Supply to consult together, and see what could be done either to expand the output of ammunition, or else to restrict the output of mortars and to devote the capacity released to other more urgent work.' Of the anti-tank gun production he declared:

... that the total requirement appeared to be in the neighbourhood of 7,000 guns, which, at the present rate of progress, would take years to reach. This was one of the most important articles of Army equipment, and strenuous efforts should be made to increase production by every possible means. It was a lamentable state of affairs that, after ten months of war, we could only produce 120 of these small weapons per month.[2]

Seeking to find out what was being done in the invasion areas, on July 17 Churchill visited the naval Commander-in-Chief at Gosport and the troops of Southern Command, commanded by General Alan Brooke. Eric Seal, who accompanied Churchill on this inspection, wrote home on the following day:

We had a most interesting & enjoyable day yesterday—at Portsmouth in the morning up to lunch time, & thereafter visiting troops in Purbeck. We motored through to Sandbanks, Studland & Wareham from Gosport, via Cadnam. I felt quite sentimental at seeing so many of our old haunts! ... I saw the place by the roadside where we all ate ices near Southampton on our way back from Swanage; & we visited the bit of beach by Studland which we know so well, & had tea at the Hotel on the road from Studland to the Ferry.

The beach is all cleared of people, & covered with wire netting. There are absolutely no visitors. Troops & guns are everywhere in evidence. The country looks better than ever—you've no idea what an improvement it is not to have tourists all over the place. ('Tourist' = a visitor other than yourself!)

---

[1] Colville diary, 16 July 1940: Colville papers.

[2] Defence Committee (Supply) No. 9 of 1940, 16 July 1940, 11 a.m.: Cabinet papers, 70/1. Both Lindemann and Morton were present at this meeting, at which the only other Minister was Herbert Morrison, the Minister of Supply.

We saw some very interesting exercises, with soldiers, tanks, guns & what-not. We even had two sinister looking men in captured German uniform to impersonate the enemy! All ended well, with the defeat of the enemy, & a visit to the dressing station, with men on stretchers impersonating the wounded.[1]

In his diary General Brooke recorded his impression of Churchill during their four hour tour of inspection of the Hampshire and Dorset coasts. He had found the Prime Minister, he wrote, 'in wonderful spirits, and full of offensive plans for next summer'.[2] This mood was also noted by others. Brendan Bracken, who had known Churchill for nearly twenty years, told Harold Nicolson on the following day that he had never seen Churchill 'as fit as he is today', and that his responsibilities 'seem to have given him a new lease of life'.[3]

In the House of Commons on July 18, Churchill spoke sternly of the 'crop of alarmist and depressing rumours', detrimental to the interest of National Defence, which had followed in the wake of the Government's scheme for evacuating children to Canada and the United States. It was 'most undesirable', he believed, for anything in the nature of a 'large-scale exodus' from Britain to take place.[4]

The death toll from German air raids for the first seventeen days of July was 194, nearly five times the number killed in the previous seventeen-day period. These figures had been kept secret.[5] But as the scale of the bombing clearly increased, Canada did seem to offer a place of safety for children. One child, however, who had no intention of going to Canada was the eleven-year-old David Wedgwood Benn, youngest son of the Labour MP and former Secretary of State for India, William Wedgwood Benn. On July 4 *The Times* had published a letter from David Wedgwood Benn, opposing his despatch to Canada, 'I would rather be bombed to fragments' he wrote, 'than leave England.'[6] Brendan Bracken sent a copy of this letter to Churchill, who wrote in his own hand to Wedgwood Benn senior: 'A splendid letter from yr boy. We must all try to live up to this standard.'[7] Churchill also sent the young man himself a signed copy of *My Early Life*, for which gift he received the following reply, delivered by hand to Downing Street:

[1] Letter of 18 July 1940: Seal papers.
[2] General Brooke diary, 17 July 1940: Arthur Bryant, *The Turn of the Tide 1939–1943*, London 1957, page 195.
[3] Nicolson diary, 18 July 1940: Nigel Nicolson (editor), *Harold Nicolson Diaries and Letters 1939–1945*, London 1967, page 103.
[4] *Hansard*, 18 July 1940, columns 394–5.
[5] Cabinet papers, 120/464.
[6] *The Times*, 4 July 1940.
[7] Letter in the possession of David Wedgwood Benn.

Dear Prime Minister,

I was greatly honoured to receive your book, on my return from school. I have read thirty-eight pages and find it very fascinating.

It will be interesting in my later life to remember your kindness and to keep your book as a relic for ever.

The Fortresses of London in which we shall fight for our lives 'street by street' will also be worthy of remembrance.

I am very glad that I am not to be ushered into safety.[1]

Churchill continued to oppose the exodus to Canada, and in reply to the Home Secretary's request that he send a message with the 'senior child' on the next boat of a hundred children on their way to Canada, Churchill wrote in protest: 'I certainly do not propose to send a message by the senior child to Mr Mackenzie King, or by the junior child either. If I sent any message by anyone, it would be that I entirely deprecate any stampede from this country at the present time.'[2]

Examining British naval strength and dispositions, Churchill had already set his mind considerably at rest as far as invasion was concerned, and on July 18 he decided to circulate to the War Cabinet a minute which he had written eight days earlier, giving the reasons for his confidence. A German sea-borne invasion, he had written, would be 'a most hazardous and even suicidal operation', involving the Germans in the need to commit a large army 'to the accidents of the sea in the teeth of our very numerous armed patrolling forces'. There were more than a thousand British armed patrolling vessels, of which 'two or three hundred' were always at sea manned by 'competent sea-faring men'. Behind these craft were forty destroyers. The greater part of these were at sea every night, the rest in the day, able to reach any landing point or points between the Humber and Portsmouth in two or three hours, and with the fire power to 'break up the landing craft, interrupt the landing, and fire upon the landed troops', who, however lightly equipped, would still need to have some proportion of their ammunition and equipment 'carried on to the beaches from their boats'. As to the German ability to intervene at sea, 'as far as we know

---

[1] Churchill papers, 2/392. David Wedgwood Benn's eldest brother, Flight-Lieutenant Michael Wedgwood Benn, died of injuries received on operations, 23 June 1944. His middle brother, Anthony Wedgwood Benn, was later (in Harold Wilson's Governments) Minister of Technology and Minister of Power. David Wedgwood Benn later joined the BBC External Services, subsequently (in 1982) being in charge of the Yugoslav Section.

[2] Minute dated 18 July 1940: Churchill papers, 20/13. Sir John Colville writes: 'The King flatly refused to consider a Ministerial, though not Churchillian, proposal that the Princesses be sent to Canada.' (Notes for the author, 7 February 1983.)

at present', Churchill pointed out, 'they have no heavy ships not under long repair', except those at Trondheim 'which are closely watched by our very largely superior forces'.[1]

The other defence against invasion was something Churchill continued to work for with considerable energy, the material aid of the United States. Through Desmond Morton, he was to learn of Colonel Donovan's mission from Roosevelt in connection with British arms purchases.[2] But he was cautious of too great a dependence upon the United States, and when it was suggested that Britain share its anti-submarine and radar secrets with the United States, he minuted to Ismay:

Are we going to throw all our secrets into the American lap, and see what they give us in exchange? If so, I am against it. It would be very much better to go slow, as we have far more to give than they. If an exchange is to be arranged, I should like to carry it out piece by piece, i.e., if we give them our Asdics, they give us their Norden bomb-sight; if we give them our RDF, they give us their highly-developed short-wave gadgets.

Generally speaking, I am not in a hurry to give our secrets until the United States is much nearer to the war than she is now. I expect that anything given to the United States Services, in which there are necessarily so many Germans, goes pretty quickly to Berlin in time of peace.

'Once it is war,' Churchill added, 'very much better controls are operative.'[3]

On July 19, three days after his 'Sealion' directive to prepare for the invasion of Britain, Hitler addressed the Reichstag in Berlin, offering Britain the choice between peace with Germany, or 'unending suffering and misery'. Of course, Hitler mocked, Churchill himself would not be among those who would suffer, 'for he no doubt will already be in Canada, where the money and the children of those principally interested in the war already have been sent'.[4] When asked if he wished to reply to Hitler's offer of peace negotiations, Churchill commented: 'I do not propose to say anything in reply to Herr Hitler's speech, not being on speaking terms with him.'[5]

[1] Minute of 10 July 1940, circulated to the War Cabinet as War Cabinet Paper No. 264 of 1940, 18 July 1940: Churchill papers, 23/4.
[2] Minute of 21 July 1940: Premier papers, 7/1. Donovan had left Washington on 14 July 1940.
[3] Minute of 17 July 1940: Premier papers, 3/475/1, folio 33-4.
[4] Speech of 19 July 1940, text as printed in the New York Times of 20 July 1940.
[5] Colville diary, 24 July 1940: Colville papers.

On the day that Hitler's speech was published in the British and American Press, Churchill's thoughts were also on Berlin. If there were to be a German air raid on the centre of Government in London, he minuted to Sinclair, 'it seems very important to be able to return the compliment the next day upon Berlin'. But perhaps, he added, the nights were 'not yet long enough' for the 'respectable party' of Stirling bombers expected to be ready by the end of the month to go and return in darkness.[1]

Sinclair's answer gave Churchill confidence that, if necessary, Berlin could be bombed. For it transpired that, even with less than twenty-four hours notice, Bomber Command could drop eight tons of bombs each night for a week, while with twenty-four hours notice, fifteen tons of bombs could be dropped every second night without interfering with the existing bombing programme. Indeed, Sinclair explained, on or after August 2 the whole of Britain's heavy bomber force could be employed, and 65 to 70 tons of bombs dropped each night of the week, with only twelve hours notice, rising to 150 tons on alternate nights.[2]

These statistics gave Churchill the confidence that if London were attacked in force, the British public would not have to watch helpless while no counter-action took place.[3] At the same time he had to answer criticisms from four Members of Parliament from West Country constituencies that the defences against invasion in their part of Britain were inadequate.[4] On July 20 Churchill dictated his reply. 'You will of course appreciate,' he wrote, 'that it is not possible or desirable for us to maintain troops along all the hundreds of miles of coastline which are now within reach of the enemy's seaborne raids'. His letter continued:

[1] Minute of 20 July 1940: Premier papers, 3/14/2, folio 147.

[2] 'Possibility of Bombing Berlin. Result of detailed examination by Bomber Command': Premier papers, 4/37/4, folios 145-6. On 23 July 1940 Sinclair informed Churchill that these raids could take place using Blenheims on moonlit nights, Hampdens, Whitleys and Wellingtons on dark nights.

[3] In an effort to release trainee-pilots for bombing missions, Churchill wrote to Sinclair on July 18: 'I understand, for example, that most of the 2,000 pilots with Wings still undergoing instruction are intended for Bombing Squadrons, also that we habitually send 2 pilots away in each Bomber employed on active operations. Would it not be possible to train some of the newly-fledged pilots by employing them as second pilots in the operational Squadrons? Any such adjustment would produce a treble economy. It would release not only pilots under instruction but Instructors, and it would enable some of the machines of operational types now employed for instruction to be added to our operational strength.' Churchill added: 'I should be grateful if you would give this matter your earnest consideration. We must increase our numbers available.' (Churchill papers, 4/201.)

[4] The MPs were Mavis Tate (Conservative MP for the Frome division of Somerset), Vernon Bartlett (Bridgewater division of Somerset, Independent Progressive), Sir Richard Acland (Barnstable division of Devon, Liberal) and Captain N. A. Beechman (St Ives, Cornwall, Liberal National).

In order to make the most effective use of our military resources it is necessary that a large proportion of the more highly-trained units should be held in the rear as a mobile reserve, disposed over the country in such a way that powerful forces can be rapidly brought to bear on any portion of these islands upon which the enemy may effect a landing, whether by sea or air.

Whilst you will not expect me to disclose the location of troops, I see no harm in informing you that some of our most seasoned and well-equipped mobile formations are so situated as to be able to engage the enemy with strong land forces supported by aircraft in any part of the West Country within a very short space of time.

As the training and equipment of the Home Guard proceeds, these will provide a valuable addition to our regular troops, in particular along the coast, where they will be able to harass and impede the enemy at the critical moment of disembarkation.

In order to destroy or obstruct any seaborne expedition, heavy guns are being mounted and concrete defences and tank obstacles are being constructed in the vicinity of harbours and beaches in those parts of the island which are the most accessible to the enemy. Every effort is being made to expedite this work, and considering how recently these preparations were begun, the progress already achieved is most encouraging.

Furthermore, Churchill continued, 'in estimating the strength of our defences, you must not underrate the part played by the Navy. We have many hundreds of armed craft constantly patrolling the seas around our coasts, and in the event of an attempted invasion larger naval vessels would immediately be available to intercept the enemy on the sea, or to fire upon his rear during or after landing.'[1]

In an attempt to ensure that when invasion came the local civilians would not be more at risk than was necessary, Churchill continued to keep a close watch on preparations to deal with a German gas attack. 'It seems to me,' he wrote to Ismay on July 23, 'that further and repeated warnings must be given about gas. Every mask must be tested, and civilians enjoined to use them and carry them everywhere. Gas-proofing of shelters, in so far as it exists, must be made efficient.'[2]

Each Government department worked to perfect its anti-invasion plans. In late July a Royal Air Force scheme, code name 'Banquet', was set up, whereby, in the event of invasion, pilots teaching at training schools would at once be released to fly operationally. On July 23 'Banquet' was extended to Scotland, in the event of a German landing

---

[1] At Churchill's request, his reply was redrafted (by John Peck) in the third person, before being sent. Draft dated 20 July 1940: Premier papers, 4/37/4, folios 229–30.
[2] Minute of 23 July 1940: Cherwell papers.

north of the border.[1] Churchill approved these plans without comment, seeing his task as one of intervention only where he felt things were going wrong, or had been neglected.

Churchill had also to approve changes in the higher military commands, and after his tour of the south coast defences with General Brooke, gave his final consent to Brooke's appointment as Commander-in-Chief, Home Forces.[2] At the same time General Auchinleck, who had impressed Churchill at Chequers, succeeded Brooke as General Officer Commanding Southern Command. Not every senior officer met with Churchill's approval, however; after being told that Admiral Dudley North had been critical of the naval action at Oran he minuted to A. V. Alexander: 'It is evident that Admiral Dudley North has not got the root of the matter in him, and I should be very glad to see you replace him by a more resolute and clear-sighted officer.'[3] North, who commanded the North Atlantic Station, a shore appointment at Gibraltar, remained however at his command.

On July 22 Colville noted in his diary, after the morning dictation: 'The PM is in a cantankerous frame of mind, demanding papers which are not available.'[4] During the day Churchill received notification of an Enigma message which revealed Hitler's decision to cancel the victory parade planned for July 23 in Paris. 'The reason for the cancellation is not known,' reported Major H. P. Whitefoord, of MI 14, the German section of Military Intelligence, 'but the most probable explanation is considered to be inability of the Gestapo to guarantee the Fuhrer's safety at such a ceremony.'[5]

That night Churchill dined alone with General Brooke, who noted in his diary:

Just by ourselves at the end of a long day's work was rather trying. But he was very nice and I got a good insight into the way his brain is working. He is most interesting to listen to and full of the most marvellous courage considering the burden he is bearing. He is full of offensive thoughts, but I think he fully realises the difficulties he is up against. He said that he wondered if England

---

[1] Air Ministry papers, 20/5298.

[2] Brooke replaced Ironside, who noted in his diary: 'And so my military career comes to an end in the middle of a great war. I have had 41 years and one month's service, and have reached the very top. I can't complain. Cabinets have to make decisions in times of stress. I don't suppose that Winston liked doing it, for he is always loyal to his friends' (Ironside diary, 19 July 1940: Roderick Macleod and Denis Kelly, editors, *The Ironside Diaries, 1937–1940*, London 1962, page 387).

[3] Minute of 20 July 1940 to A. V. Alexander: Admiralty papers, 1/19177.

[4] Colville diary, 22 July 1940: Colville papers.

[5] 'Officer Only. Most Secret,' MI 14, 11 a.m., 22 July 1940: War Office papers, 199/911 A, B.19.

had ever been in such straits since the Armada days. He refers to Hitler always as 'that man'![1]

On July 23 Churchill elaborated, in a minute for Eden, how he envisaged the offensive of which he had spoken to Brooke. First he wrote of what he did not wish to see. It would be 'most unwise', he explained, to disturb the coasts of Europe 'by the kind of silly fiascos which were perpetrated at Boulogne and Guernsey.[2] The idea of working all these coasts up against us by pin-prick raids and fulsome communiqués is one strictly to be avoided.' The aim was to plan, under the newly appointed head of Combined Operations, Sir Roger Keyes, a series of 'medium raids' by between 5,000 and 10,000 troops. Two or three of these raids might be 'brought off' on the French coast during the winter. Detailed preparations could be made 'as soon as the invasion danger recedes or is resolved'. Once these medium raids had been done, there would be 'no objection', Churchill added, 'to stirring up the French coast by minor forays', while during the spring and summer of 1941 'large armoured irruptions must be contemplated'.[3]

Churchill's zeal for taking the offensive, and his ability to look forward to distant initiatives, communicated itself in the House of Commons at Question Time. 'Winston was in roaring spirits today,' wrote Henry Channon, 'and gave slashing answers, which he himself had drafted, to foolish Questions, and generally convulsed the House.' Channon added: 'He is at the very top of his form and the House is completely with him, as is the country, but he knows very little about foreign affairs.'[4]

However 'little' Churchill knew of foreign affairs, and it was a subject on which he had devoted many years of thought, he had still to deal with them. Where they were linked with the pressing demands of war, he had also to deal with them promptly. Thus on July 24, at the Defence Committee, he suggested that the Admiralty ought to examine the 'immediate action' Britain might take against Spain in the event of a Spanish move against Gibraltar, while at the same time

[1] Brooke diary, 22 July 1940: Arthur Bryant, *The Turn of the Tide 1939–1943*, London 1957, page 199.

[2] On 24 June 1940, 115 commandos had landed, briefly, at Boulogne; followed on 14 July 1940 by a raid on Guernsey, code name 'Anger' (reconnaissance) and 'Ambassador' (the raid itself) when 140 commandos landed and then returned. Four commandos were captured.

[3] 'Most Secret' Minute, 23 July 1940: Churchill papers, 20/13.

[4] Channon diary, 23 July 1940. On the following day Channon noted in his diary: 'Lloyd George, whose affection for Winston has noticeably cooled of late, predicts that after the PM's first great blunder, the country, now admittedly hysterically infatuated with him, will turn against him and only remember his mistakes. I wonder?' (Robert Rhodes James, editor, *Chips, The Diaries of Sir Henry Channon*, London 1967, page 262.)

considering 'whether to draw attention' to the Spanish Government of the 'dangers to which they would expose themselves' if they took any sudden action against Gibraltar.[1] In a minute to Lord Halifax, Churchill reiterated his earlier suggestion for the possible seizure of the Azores, even if Spain made no move against Gibraltar. 'Must we always wait until a disaster has occurred?' he asked, and he added:

I do not think it follows that our occupation temporarily, and to forestall the enemy, of the Azores, would *necessarily* precipitate German intervention in Spain and Portugal. It might have the reverse effect. The fact that we had an alternative fuelling base to Gibraltar might tell against German insistence that we should be attacked there, or anyhow reduce German incentive to have us attacked. Moreover once we have an alternative base to Gibraltar, how much do we care whether the Peninsula is overrun or not?[2]

This Azores plan was envisaged for a distant future, for on the day after Churchill's minute to Halifax, Sir John Dill instructed the Officer Commanding the 1st and 2nd Marine Brigades to prepare to 'move overseas to a tropical climate' on or after 23 May 1941, these troops being required, he explained, for two linked operations, 'Accordion'— the occupation of the Azores—and 'Sackbut', against the Cape Verde Islands.[3]

Turkey was another country where British plans had already been made for a future emergency. A German attack on Turkey from Bulgaria, the seizure of the Bosphorus and the Dardanelles, and a crossing into Asia Minor, would threaten Britain's militarily weak position in Palestine and at the Suez Canal. To meet this threat, the Chiefs of Staff had agreed in April 1940 to three plans. The first, code name 'Leopard', was for the setting up of fifteen British observer groups along the borders of European Turkey, and fifteen more in Asia Minor. The second plan, 'Tiger' was for three British fighter squadrons to operate in Asia Minor, one on the Asiatic shore of the Bosphorus, one at Chanak, and one at Izmir, backed up by a British-controlled air warning and anti-aircraft system. 'In no stage,' the Chiefs of Staff noted, 'will Turkish AA defences be solely relied upon.' The third plan, 'Bear', was for an expanded air defence pro-gramme if German pressure on Turkey mounted: the despatch to Turkey of five squadrons of ten aircraft each, capable of attacking German air bases, organization and lines of communication in Bulgaria,

---

[1] Defence Committee (Operations), 24 July 1940, 11 a.m.: Cabinet papers, 69/1.
[2] 'Secret', Minute of 24 July 1940: Churchill papers, 20/13.
[3] Letter of 25 July 1940: Admiralty papers, 202/349.

Southern Rumania and southern Yugoslavia, in order 'to neutralize enemy air forces'.[1]

Within two weeks of Churchill becoming Prime Minister, 'Leopard' had been put into operation, with fifteen observer posts being established on the Turkish side of the Turkish-Bulgarian border, each manned by six Royal Air Force personnel.[2]

Further plans to protect Britain against the consequences of a German attack on Turkey were made during July, including a British military defence for Turkish naval bases, code name 'Abbess', the despatch of an air striking force to Turkey, code name 'Igloo', and the movement of an armoured division and three other divisions to Izmir, code name 'Satchel'.[3] These contingency plans for Turkey were completed by July 10, and awaited only the agreement of the Turkish Government. This, however, was not forthcoming.

In Spain, Captain Hillgarth continued, with Churchill's personal authority, to persuade the Spanish Government to maintain its neutrality and to look to Britain for military support in resisting German demands for the free passage of troops through Spain to Gibraltar. In London, following requests from several of the Governments-in-Exile, and from de Gaulle, Churchill agreed to arm the various foreign corps then in Britain, giving priority to arming the Poles and the French. In a minute to Ismay, Churchill expressed his hope that these forces could be used 'for foreign service in the near future'. The Polish unit, Churchill added, 'should be ripened as much as possible', and even given 'American rifles direct', with priority for these rifles over the Home Guard.[4]

On July 25 encouraging news reached London about American aircraft supplies: news of the signing in Washington on the previous night of an agreement between Morgenthau and Purvis for the allocation of aeroplanes and aeroplane engines. Hitherto, Purvis had told the Americans, Britain had made every effort to husband its dollars. Now, however, she had decided 'to shoot the wad'.[5]

The new agreement covered the total British aircraft requirements for the next twenty-one months, up to April 1942. Calculating the

---

[1] 'Air Defence Plan' dated 5 April 1940: Air Ministry papers, 23/6935.

[2] 'HQ No. 252 Wing, "Leopard", Plans and Policy', 22 May 1940, S.46363, 'Most Secret': Air Ministry papers, 23/6934.

[3] Churchill papers, 4/96.

[4] Minute to Ismay, for the Chiefs of Staff, 25 July 1940: Churchill papers, 20/13. The principal foreign troops then in Britain were Poles (14,000), Czechs (4,000), 'Anti-Nazi Germans' (3,000), French (2,000), Dutch (1,000), Norwegians (1,000) and Belgians (500): War Cabinet Paper No. 281 of 1940.

[5] Quoted in William L. Langer and S. Everett Gleason, *The World Crisis and American Foreign Policy: The Challenge To Isolation 1937–1940*, London 1952, page 714.

joint American and British requirements at just over 33,000 aircraft, of which 19,092 were needed by the United States and 14,375 by the British, the agreement specified schedules of manufacture and delivery in the ratio of 19 to 14 between the two countries.[1] Negotiations were also in progress for a similar agreement with the United States for rifles, tanks, field guns, anti-tank guns, and their ammunition. This agreement would cover both '*quantity* to balance our requirements by the end of 1941', Herbert Morrison explained to Sir Arthur Salter, and '*capacity* as an "insurance" against possible loss of capacity in this country'.[2]

Churchill suggested two further important foreign policy initiatives on July 25. First, he proposed that, despite the policy of placating Japan by closing the Burma Road to supplies for China, Britain should tell Japan that a Japanese attack on the Dutch East Indies would mean 'war with us', since to allow the Japanese to attack the Dutch East Indies unopposed would amount to 'allowing ourselves to be cut off from Australia and New Zealand, and they would regard our acquiescence as desertion'.[3]

Second, Churchill argued in favour of an immediate attempt by Britain to come to an arrangement with Vichy France for the setting up of a pro-war Government in North Africa, led, he hoped, by Weygand, to whom he intended to send an emissary as soon as possible.[4]

The Vichy authorities should be told, he said, that once the French forces had been disarmed according to the armistice terms, not only Germany and Italy, but also Spain, might move against Vichy in North Africa. Churchill proposed telling the Vichy authorities that if there were a 'friendly' French Government in North Africa, and if that Government were then to ask Britain to send food to the blockaded masses under Vichy rule in metropolitan France, then, 'even though a bad French Government were in power in the homeland, we should be willing to meet their need'. But food would only be allowed into Vichy France, Churchill stressed, if there were a French Government in North Africa 'which is continuing the war'.

Such a plan, Churchill told Eden, should be put to the Vichy French 'now, without any delay, in order that it may work in their minds as the German and Italian ill-usage and the food shortage exert their pressures', and before the German–Italian Armistice Commission had

[1] Morgenthau diaries, conferences of 24 July 1940: Morgenthau papers.
[2] Herbert Morrison to Sir Arthur Salter, 26 July 1940: Cabinet papers, 115/32.
[3] Minute of 25 July 1940, to Ismay: Churchill papers, 20/13.
[4] Weygand was at Algiers, as Governor-General of Algeria.

completed the demilitarization of North Africa. His aim, Churchill explained, was to 'promote a kind of collusive conspiracy in the Vichy Government whereby certain members of that Government, perhaps with the consent of some of those who remain, will levant to North Africa in order to make a better bargain for France from the North African shore and from a position of independence'.[1]

Churchill was confident that, once scrutinized, debated and modified by the Chiefs of Staff, the Defence Committee, and the War Cabinet, something would surely emerge from his many ideas to move Britain further along the road to victory. His ability to produce schemes covering every aspect of war policy was well matched by the ability of his advisers to sift, mould, and if necessary to reject those schemes. But it was the spirit behind them that gave them their strength, and animated all who received them.

---

[1] 'Action this Day', Minute dated 25 July 1940: Churchill papers, 20/13. Six days later Lord Halifax noted for the War Cabinet that General de Gaulle had 'no objection' to the British Government maintaining contact with Vichy. (War Cabinet Paper No. 296, 31 July 1940: Cabinet papers, 66/10.)

33

'The glow of Mount Sinai'

D URING the crisis periods of the First World War, Churchill
had particularly admired Lloyd George's capacity to see beyond
the dilemma of the day to the possibility of tomorrow: to refuse to
accept that a setback might be final, or a single defeat fatal. To Churchill in July 1940, Britain's imminent defeat was likewise an illusion,
but only if action were taken to ensure that every gap in Britain's
defences was filled, at whatever cost. On July 26, after Pound had sent
him a list of urgent naval requirements, Churchill sent the list to Lothian with the following note:

> Need of American destroyers is more urgent than ever in view of losses and
> the need of coping with invasion threat as well as keeping Atlantic approaches
> open and dealing with Italy. All was clearly set out in my telegram of June
> 15. There is nothing that America can do at this moment that would be of
> greater help than to send fifty destroyers, except sending a hundred. The
> flying-boats also are of the greatest importance now in the next two months.
> As I have repeatedly explained, the difficulty is to bridge the gap until our
> new war-time production arrives in a flood.

He would also, Churchill added, be sending a personal message to
Roosevelt.[1]

In view of the extent of Britain's dependence upon immediate aid
from the United States, Churchill now agreed to the exchange of secrets
between the two countries, an exchange which he had long resisted.
'What is the urgency of this matter?' he had asked Ismay on July 17,
'who is making a fuss, and what happens if we do not give an immediate
decision?'[2] Eight days later, following several telegrams from Lothian

---

[1] 'Action this Day', Minute of 26 July 1940: Churchill papers, 20/13. On the following day,
Colville noted in his diary: 'Winston is now appealing eloquently to the President both directly
and through Lothian for destroyers': Colville diary, 27 July 1940, Colville papers.

[2] Minute of 17 July 1940: Premier papers, 3/475/1, folios 33–5.

urging the need for such an exchange to be authorized as quickly as possible, a special meeting of senior Ministers gave its approval to the exchange of secrets, and to a special mission, headed by Sir Henry Tizard, to set the exchange in motion.

On July 26 Sinclair sent Churchill a list of the information 'which we propose to impart, and hope to receive from America'.[1] Reading Sinclair's list, Churchill wrote to Ismay: 'The data of the three Services should be compiled and forwarded. When will the mission be formed. Let me know.'[2]

United States aid was one of several issues of overriding importance with which Churchill dealt on a daily basis. Other issues, less urgent by comparison, often tried his patience. To the Viceroy of India he drafted a reply concerning proposals for a major new statement of British policy to India. 'You must remember that we are here facing constant threat of invasion with many strange and novel features,' the draft began, 'and this is only held off and can only be mastered literally from day to day by the prowess of our Airmen at heavy odds and by the vigilance of the Royal Navy.' In these circumstances, Churchill added, 'immense constitutional departures cannot be effectively discussed in Parliament, and only by the Cabinet to the detriment of matters touching the final life and safety of the State'.[3]

That same day Colville noted that Churchill wanted to send this telegram without the India Office knowing about it. But the Secretary of State for India, L. S. Amery, found out about it, and went to see Churchill at Downing Street, where they had what Colville called 'a bloody row'. As a result, Churchill's original telegram was not sent, but in its place a reasoned reply which began: 'I was very glad to get your telegram, and I am sorry that intense pressure of business prevented me from entering into direct relations with you earlier. . . .'[4]

Sometimes one of Churchill's schemes went no further than the

---

[1] Sinclair wrote: 'We propose to give the Americans information on: 1: existing RDF gear in use in the Royal Air Force, 2: inter-communication between air-to-air and air-to-ground, 3: research now being conducted on centimetre waves. We should give full information on these three points. In return we should hope to receive information on: 1: research on centimetre waves, 2: American location of aircraft and detection systems, 3: research facilities available in the USA for the rapid development of these and other similar devices and the possibilities of co-operation in research, 4: Productive capacity for existing RDF equipment and in particular for English valves. 5: Productive capacity for communication equipment.' (Letter of 26 July 1940: Premier papers, 3/475/1, folio 26.)

[2] Minute of 27 July 1940: Premier papers, 3/475/1, folio 26.

[3] Draft telegram of 26 July 1940: Churchill papers, 20/14.

[4] Colville diary, 26 July 1940: Colville papers.

dinner table. One such was his idea for a military landing from the sea to capture the Italian Red Sea port of Massawa. He decided to broach the project to General James Marshall-Cornwall, who, after his return from France, had been appointed to command III Corps. On Friday July 26 Dill telephoned Marshall-Cornwall to say that he was to spend the following night with the Prime Minister at Chequers. Several years later Marshall-Cornwall recalled the 'Mad Hatter's Dinner Party' of which he found himself a part:

I reached Chequers about six o'clock and was told that the PM was resting. Two hours later we sat down to dinner. It was indeed a memorable meal. I was placed on the PM's right, and on my right was Professor Frederick Lindemann, Churchill's scientific adviser. The others around the oval table were Mrs Churchill, Duncan Sandys and his wife, 'Pug' Ismay, Jack Dill, Lord Beaverbrook, and one of the PM's private secretaries.

Churchill was bubbling over with enthusiasm and infectious gaiety. I marvelled how he could appear so carefree with the enormous load of anxieties on his shoulders, and I wish that I could remember some of the splendid sentences that rolled off his tongue.

As soon as the champagne was served he started to interrogate me about the condition of my Corps. I told him that when I had taken it over I had found all ranks obsessed with defensive tactical ideas, the main object of everyone being to get behind an anti-tank obstacle. I had issued orders that only offensive training exercises were to be practised, and that the III Corps motto was 'Hitting, not Sitting', which prefaced every operation order.

This went down tremendously well with the PM, who chuckled and chortled: 'Splendid! That's the spirit I want to see.' He continued: 'I assume then that your Corps is now ready to take the field?' 'Very far from it, Sir.' I replied; 'Our re-equipment is not nearly complete, and when it is we shall require another month or two of intensive training.'

Churchill looked at me incredulously and drew a sheaf of papers from the pocket of his dinner-jacket. 'Which are your two Divisions?' he demanded. 'The 53rd (Welsh) and the 2nd London' I replied. He pushed a podgy finger on the graph tables in front of him and said: 'There you are; 100 per cent complete in personnel, rifles and mortars; 50 per cent in field artillery, anti-tank rifles and machine-guns.' 'I beg your pardon, Sir,' I replied; 'That state may refer to the weapons which the ordnance depots are preparing to issue to my units, but they have not yet reached the troops in anything like those quantities.'

The PM's brow contracted; almost speechless with rage, he hurled the graphs across the dinner-table to Dill, saying: 'CIGS, have those papers checked and returned to me tomorrow.'

An awkward silence followed; a diversion seemed called for. The PM leant across me and addressed my neighbour on the other side: 'Prof! What have *you* got to tell me today?' The other civilians present were wearing dinner-jackets, but Professor Lindemann was attired in a morning-coat and striped trousers. He now slowly pushed his right hand into his tail-pocket and, like a conjuror, drew forth a Mills hand-grenade. An uneasy look appeared on the faces of his fellow-guests and the PM shouted: 'What's that you've got, Prof, what's that?' 'This, Prime Minister, is the inefficient Mills bomb, issued to the British infantry. It is made of twelve different components which have to be machined in separate processes. Now *I* have designed an improved grenade, which has fewer machined parts and contains a 50 per cent greater bursting charge.' 'Splendid! Splendid! That's what I like to hear. CIGS! Have the Mills bomb scrapped at once and replaced by the Lindemann grenade.'[1]

The unfortunate Dill was completely taken aback; he tried to explain that contracts had been placed in England and America for millions of Mills bombs, and that it would be impracticable to alter the design now, but the PM would not listen. To change the subject he pointed a finger at Beaverbrook across the table; 'Max! What have *you* been up to?' Beaverbrook replied: 'Prime Minister! Give me five minutes and you will have the latest figures.' He rose and went to a telephone box at the far end of the room; after a very few minutes he returned with a Puckish grin on his face. 'Prime Minister,' he said, 'In the last 48 hours we have increased our production of Hurricanes by 50 per cent.'[2]

The brandy and coffee had now circulated and the PM lit his cigar. 'I want the Generals to come with me,' he said, and stumped off to an adjoining room, followed by Dill, Ismay and myself. On a large table was a rolled-up map, which the PM proceeded to spread out. It was a large-scale map of the Red Sea.

The PM placed his finger on the Italian port of Massawa. 'Now, Marshall-Cornwall,' he said, 'We have command of the sea and the air; it is essential for us to capture that port; how would you do it?' I was in no way prepared to answer a snap conundrum of this kind, and indeed had no qualifications for doing so.

I saw Dill and Ismay watching me anxiously and felt that I was being drawn into some trap. I looked hard at the map for a minute and then answered: 'Well, Sir, I have never been to Massawa; I have only passed out of sight of it, going down the Red Sea. It is a defended port, protected by coast defence and anti-aircraft batteries. It must be a good 500 miles from Aden,

---

[1] The Mills bomb (or Mills grenade) remained in production until the end of the war, with only minor modifications, and was essentially the same design as it had been in the First World War. For Lindemann to have intended adding a greater bursting charge to the Mills bomb was unlikely, as one of its accepted failings was that it had too high an explosive charge. For some of the weapons in fact designed with Lindemann's encouragement, see pages 746–7.

[2] Sir James Marshall-Cornwall writes: 'When I repeated this story later to a distinguished Air Marshal, I was told that the Minister's claim was quite illusory; a temporary spurt in production had been made by cannibalizing machines awaiting other components and by delaying the output of bombers, but no real improvement had been achieved. In fact, during the month of July our production of fighter aircraft had risen from 446 to 496, but during August it fell to 476.'

and therefore beyond cover of our fighters. The harbour has a very narrow entrance channel, protected by coral reefs, and is certain to be mined, making an opposed landing impracticable. I should prefer to wait until General Wavell's offensive against Eritrea develops; he will capture it more easily from the land side.'

The PM gave me a withering look, rolled up the map and muttered peevishly: 'You soldiers are all alike: you have no imagination.'

We went to bed. I left the Wonderland of Chequers on the following afternoon, after a walk in the woods with Duncan Sandys, whom I have never found very communicative. On our way back to London Jack Dill said to me: 'I'm thankful, Jimmy, that you took the line you did last night. If you had shown the least enthusiasm for the project, I should have been given orders to embark your Corps for the Red Sea next week.'[1]

During this weekend at Chequers, Churchill studied the figures of air engagements and casualties for the previous week, during which twenty-six British fighters had been shot down. Eighteen British bomber aircraft had also been lost, over Germany, while in German raids on Britain thirty-three civilians had been killed, and 206 injured: these casualties included six German prisoners-of-war.[2]

In anticipation of a severe bombardment of London, special emergency underground quarters had been prepared in Whitehall for the Prime Minister, his principal advisers, the Chiefs of Staff and the War Cabinet. Known as the Central War Room, this complex of rooms and corridors was located in the basement of the Government Offices at Storey's Gate, opposite St James's Park. Selected for use in May 1938, and reinforced first with oak and then with steel strutting in the autumn and winter of 1938, these rooms had first been used experimentally by the War Cabinet shortly after the outbreak of war.[3]

By the end of July 1940, rooms had been prepared in the Central War Room for the War Cabinet and the Joint Planning Committee. There was also a Map Room, Signal and Cypher Rooms, rooms for typists and telephonists, and small bedrooms—known to their Royal

[1] Sir James Marshall-Cornwall, unpublished recollections: Marshall-Cornwall papers. Massawa eventually surrendered, on 8 April 1941, to a Free French detachment of General William Platt's troops under Wavell's command, approaching from the hinterland. Had Marshall-Cornwall shown enthusiasm for the Massawa plan, it would first of all have been the task of the Joint Planning Committee to propose a detailed scheme, and then of the Chiefs of Staff Committee (of which Dill was a member) to give its approval. Had the Chiefs of Staff Committee rejected the plan, it could not have gone forward, however keenly Churchill might have favoured it.

[2] War Cabinet, Chiefs of Staff Committee, Weekly Résumé No. 47: Churchill papers, 23/5. It was on July 26 that the Ministry of Information announced the loss of the *Lancastria*, sunk off St Nazaire on June 17 (see page 564). The announcement was made after *The Times* of July 25 had quoted a United States' newspaper report of the previous day, describing the sinking.

[3] At 11.30 a.m. on 21 October 1939. Churchill was present on that occasion.

Marine Reservist guards as cabins—for Churchill himself, as well as for Bridges, Ismay and their private secretaries.[1] Rooms had also been set aside for emergency use by the General Headquarters, Home Forces, in the event of invasion.[2]

Above these reinforced quarters, at ground level, and with windows overlooking St James's Park, a less cramped flat was being prepared for Churchill and his wife, together with offices for Churchill's Private Secretariat. This ground level area was known as 'No 10 Annexe'. At the end of July it was not yet ready for occupation; it too was to have a Map Room, laid out for Churchill by Captain Pim.

On Monday July 29 the Central War Room—which later came to be known as the Cabinet War Room—was used by the War Cabinet for the first time.[3] This was a trial meeting; the rooms were not to be used again until the first week of September.

At one point in the discussion Churchill spoke of the need for Britain to have a plan to go to war with Japan, in the event of a Japanese attack on the Dutch East Indies. It was Chamberlain's view, Churchill reported, that 'if the Dutch resisted Japanese aggression against the Dutch East Indies, we ought to go in with them and try to shame the United States into joining us. . . .' Churchill himself stressed 'the importance of playing for time', telling his colleagues: 'In a few months our position might well be much stronger.'[4]

In following the daily battle, Churchill followed also the fate of those young men whom he had met since the outbreak of war, and whose exploits had so excited his interest. At the end of July he learned that one of those young men, Commander Bickford, had been lost at sea.[5] He wrote at once, by hand, to Bickford's mother:

It was with vy great sorrow that I learned that yr brave & brilliant son was reported as Missing. I had the fortune to have two long talks with him after his famous exploits, & never do I remember meeting any young officer who

---

[1] Churchill is only recorded as having used the underground bedroom three times during the whole of the war years, on September 16, September 18 and October 28, 1940; but he did use the room as a study when the War Cabinet or the Chiefs of Staff Committee met underground.

[2] 'Secret', 27 July 1940: Ministry of Works papers, 28/36.

[3] 'PM's card', July 1940, entry for 29 July 1940: Churchill papers, 20/19.

[4] War Cabinet No. 214 of 1940, 11.30 a.m., 29 July 1940, Minute 7, Confidential Annex: Cabinet papers, 65/14.

[5] On 25 July 1940 'CBB' wrote in *The Times*, in an obituary of Bickford: 'The whole Service owes a greater debt to Bicky than they realize. At the time he did his famous patrols, people were getting discouraged by the constant patrols and no results, and some were beginning to wonder why our submarines were not doing their stuff. Then came his brilliant patrol followed by *Ursula's* success. This at once altered the whole attitude, and it was that start which gave all our submarines their lead and from which they have never looked back' (*The Times*, 25 July 1940).

seemed to embody all the finest attributes of mind & body in so excellent a degree. Yr loss is also your country's. I offer you my profound sympathy & that of my wife and daughter who also met yr son in all his splendour. May God help you to bear yr pain, & may He also bring comfort to a widow in her unspeakable grief & loneliness.[1]

Churchill had now been Prime Minister for more than two and a half months. No one could predict, nor could even the most secret Intelligence foretell, the pattern of events to come. But a system of work and response had emerged whereby Churchill was able to maintain a vigilant watch over the essentials of war direction. In this watch, the efforts of Churchill's Defence Office were indefatigable and essential. On July 28 Colonel Jacob, upon whom much of the organization of the work had fallen, sent Churchill charts of the tide and moon for August. It was these charts, prepared by Captain Morgan at the Admiralty, which had already shown the most likely points of a German invasion during July. The August dates were now on Churchill's desk: the south and west coasts of Ireland being at their most vulnerable for invasion on August 2, Berwick to Flamborough Head on August 4, Harwich to Dover on August 8, Dover to the Isle of Wight on August 10, the Isle of Wight to Portland, and Cromer to Harwich on August 12. For the third week of August, the danger dates were August 14 from Flamborough Head to Cromer, August 15 from Portland to Start Point, and August 16 from Start Point to Newquay.[2]

With these dates and vulnerable points in front of him, Churchill studied the growing number of decrypted German signals received from Bletchley. These signals provided information which, while seldom decisive at this stage, did enable those at the centre of policy making to form a much clearer view of German intentions than would have been possible without them. Thus, on July 29, Churchill learned that the German Air Force had been 'reminded of the order to avoid at all costs' the attacking of quays in harbours along the south coast. This implied, as interpreted by Military Intelligence, 'that the Germans intend to use certain of these quays in the invasion of this country'. Which quays were involved might also be found out: as it was clear from this order that a previous order had not been complied with, the German section of Military Intelligence was making

---

[1] I am grateful to Commander Bickford's widow, the late Valerie Maydwell, for the text of this letter: she and Bickford had been married on 13 May 1940. Bickford's mother, replying to Churchill's letter on 30 July 1940, wrote: 'Both he and I had long looked to you as the only one to bring England out of the darkness': Churchill papers, 2/392.

[2] Lieutenant-Colonel E. I. C. Jacob, note and enclosure, 28 July 1940: Cabinet papers, 120/444.

enquiries 'with regard to which port or ports on the coast have been bombed recently'.[1]

Churchill was anxious to see more reports than those already prepared for distribution and selected for him by Intelligence. Commenting, for example, on the information available from Vichy France, he expressed himself 'not satisfied' either with its volume or quality. 'I do not wish,' he minuted to Ismay on August 5, 'such reports as are received to be sifted and digested by the various Intelligence authorities. For the present Major Morton will inspect them for me and submit what he considers of major importance. He is to be shown everything,' Churchill added, 'and submit authentic documents to me in their original form.'[2]

The information acquired through Enigma, and sent to Churchill each day and every day, gave him knowledge which was shared by only a small number of those involved in policy making. Those not in the secret often had no inkling whatsoever of the reasons behind a decision. Almost daily, decisions, instructions and enquiries which seemed at the time irrational or absurd, derived from the knowledge obtained from Enigma. Yet often the Enigma decrypts did not lead to action, the knowledge derived from them being too fragmentary. Meanwhile, decisions had to be made under the pressure of continuing air attacks, and with British production of essential munitions still incomplete. These decisions, and the reasons leading up to them, could not always be based on the Intelligence needed to be certain that all relevant factors were understood. Again and again, time was the enemy of an ideal response; a close second in enmity was the lack of resources.

It was to augment those resources that Churchill drafted a personal telegram to Roosevelt on July 30, encouraged to do so by Lothian. According to Lothian, 'this is the moment to press the President about destroyers etc'. 'I am sure,' Churchill told Halifax, 'that this is the moment to plug it in, and it may well be that we were wise to hold back the previous draft. But pray let this go now.'[3]

In his telegram, Churchill began by noting that it was 'some time since I ventured to cable personally to you, and many things both good and bad have happened in between'. His telegram continued:

[1] 'Officer Only. Most Secret.' MI 14, 10.30 a.m., 29 July 1940: War Office papers, 199/911 A.

[2] Churchill also minuted to Ismay on 5 August 1940 that all secret service reports about affairs in 'other captive countries' were to be shown to Morton, who, he wrote, 'is responsible for keeping me informed'. This Minute ended: 'Make sure this instruction is obeyed.' (Churchill papers, 20/13.)

[3] Minute of 30 July 1940: Premier papers, 3/462/2/3, folio 134.

It has now become most urgent for you to give us the destroyers, motor boats and flying-boats for which we have asked. The Germans have the whole French coastline from which to launch U-Boat and dive-bomber attacks upon our trade and food, and in addition we must be constantly prepared to repel threatened invasion by sea action in the narrow waters, and also to deal with any break-out from Norway towards Ireland, Iceland, Shetlands and Faroes. Besides this we have to keep control of the exits from the Mediterranean, and if possible the command of that inland sea itself, and thus to prevent the war spreading seriously into Africa.

Britain had a 'large construction of destroyers and anti-U-boat craft' coming forward, Churchill told Roosevelt, but the next three or four months were 'the gap of which I have previously told you'. Churchill then stressed the extent to which recent German air attacks had become 'injurious'. In the previous ten days, he revealed, four British destroyers had been sunk and six damaged.[1] 'All this,' he pointed out, 'in the advent of any attempt which may be made at invasion.' Destroyers, Churchill added, 'are frightfully vulnerable to Air bombing, and yet they must be held in the Air bombing area to prevent sea-borne invasions'. His telegram continued:

We could not sustain the present rate of casualties for long, and if we cannot get a substantial reinforcement the whole fate of the war may be decided by this minor and easily-remediable factor.

This is a frank account of our present situation, and I am confident, now that you know exactly how we stand, that you will leave nothing undone to ensure that 50 or 60 of your oldest destroyers are sent to me at once.[2] I can fit them very quickly with Asdics and use them against U-boats on the Western Approaches and so keep the more modern and better-gunned craft for the Narrow Seas against invasion.

Mr President, with great respect I must tell you that in the long history of the world this is a thing to do *now*. Large construction is coming to me in 1941, but the crisis will be reached long before 1941. I know you will do all in your power, but I feel entitled and bound to put the gravity and urgency of the position before you.

'I am sure,' Churchill ended, 'that, with your comprehension of the sea affair, you will not let this crux of the battle go wrong for want of these destroyers.'[3]

[1] *Brazen* sunk by aircraft off Dover on July 20, *Codrington* bombed and sunk in Dover harbour on July 27, *Wren* bombed and sunk off Aldeburgh on July 27 and *Delight* bombed and sunk off Portland on July 29.

[2] In the first draft of this telegram dated 30 July 1940, this sentence had read: 'I cannot understand why, with the position as it is, you do not send me at least 50 or 60 of your oldest destroyers': Churchill papers, 20/13.

[3] Text of telegram as sent on 31 July 1940: Premier papers, 3/462/2/3, folios 135–8.

Britain's need for destroyers was acute. But in the United States there was hesitation as to what conditions ought to be imposed, or what bargain struck, in return. On August 3 Churchill telegraphed urgently to Lothian: 'Now is the time when we want the destroyers. We can fit them with Asdics in about ten days from the time they are in our hands, all preparation having been made. We should also be prepared to give a number of Asdic sets to the United States Navy and assist in their installation and explain their working.' Churchill's telegram ended: 'Go ahead on these lines full steam.'[1]

While Churchill pressed for destroyers, there were disappointing messages from the United States about Britain's other urgent need, tanks and field guns. Recent telegrams from Purvis, the Foreign Office had reported to Lothian on the evening of July 27, 'indicate at least a temporary deterioration in the situation' in as much as the Defence Advisory Board in Washington 'appear to be unwilling to consider adoption of our types of tanks and field guns and may make it difficult to secure them in America'.[2]

Churchill resented these American hesitations: so much so that when he was given details on August 1 of the imminent departure of the Tizard Mission on the exchange of secrets, he minuted to Ismay: 'But in view of the holding-back on the American side which has manifested itself in the last three days, the question of the date of the departure of the Mission should be reviewed.'[3] Just over a week later, Churchill relented. 'I am anxious that they shd start as soon as possible,' he minuted to Halifax, '& under the most favourable auspices.' The 'check of Aug 1', he added, 'was only temporary'.[4]

One important improvement in Anglo-American relations was Roosevelt's decision, in late July, to send to Britain a three-man military mission from the United States. The 'cover' for this mission, as Bridges explained to Churchill, was a technical discussion on the standardization of arms, and the title 'Standardization of Arms Committee' was to be used on all documents relating to it. But, Bridges wrote, the reality of the mission was the holding of the first 'Staff Conversations' between senior military personnel on both sides.[5]

To stress the stature and scope of the mission, Roosevelt had chosen three senior officers, Admiral Robert L. Ghormley, the Assistant to the

[1] Telegram No. 1776, 11.50 p.m., 3 August 1940, 'Most Immediate': Premier papers, 3/462/2/3, folios 118, 120.
[2] 'Immediate', 'Secret'. Telegram No. 1706, 27 July 1940, 10.45 p.m.: Premier papers, 3/457.
[3] Minute of 1 August 1940: Premier papers, 3/475/1, folio 24.
[4] Minute of 9 August 1940: Premier papers, 3/475/1, folio 15.
[5] 'Most Secret', Minute of 9 August 1940: Premier papers, 3/457, folio 32.

Chief of Naval Operations, Brigadier-General George V. Strong, the Deputy Chief of the General Staff, and General Delos C. Emmons, Commanding General, General Headquarters, Air Force. These three were to hold talks at the highest level, with the British Chiefs of Staff.

On July 28 the Chiefs of Staff themselves had suggested to Churchill that 'complete frankness' should be the basis for the discussion of strategical questions with the American trio: 'you', Ismay noted to Churchill eleven days later, 'approved this attitude for the conduct of the conversations'.[1] Churchill also sought to encourage the mission personally, minuting to Ismay on the eve of their arrival: 'What arrangements are being made to receive this important United States mission? I should see them almost as soon as they come, and I could give them a dinner at No. 10. Pray let me know in good time.'[2]

As invasion talk intensified, it was met by anti-invasion measures everywhere, including the centre of Government. On July 30 Ismay asked Churchill to approve the plan to defend Whitehall itself by means of 'posts and anti-tank obstacles' which would, as Ismay explained, be capable of being put in place 'in one hour'. As to the need for such plans, Churchill commented: 'Yes. I sh'd think 500 men with light equipment wd be a reasonable scale of attack.'[3] At the same time, plans were made to defend Chequers with a military guard. 'There is no question,' John Martin noted, 'since the war will continue throughout the coming winter if not further winters, permanent quarters are necessary', with running water, heating and telephones.[4] Within three weeks the Chequers guard originally envisaged as limited to 35 men, had been enlarged to a company, 150 strong, of Guardsmen, equipped with four anti-aircraft Bren guns and two rocket guns 'as protection against dive bombers'. At the same time an armoured car was being prepared in case Churchill had to travel from Chequers to London 'during an emergency'.[5]

---

[1] 'Secret', Minute of 9 August 1940: Premier papers, 3/457, folio 6.

[2] Minute of 10 August 1940: Premier papers, 3/457, folio 5. The American delegation dined at 10 Downing Street on Thursday 22 August 1940 ('PM's Card', August 1940: Churchill papers, 20/19).

[3] Minute of 31 July 1940: Premier papers, 3/263/1.

[4] Minute of 4 August 1940: Cabinet papers, 120/13.

[5] General Paget to Captain Sandys, 23 August 1940: Cabinet papers, 120/13. Whenever a guard was needed at Chequers, Southern Command would summon it by means of the code word 'Elephant'.

Studying these arrangements. Ismay noted that the proper policy for the Bren guns was to 'follow the movement of any aircraft' above Chequers, but not to open fire unless and until the aircraft 'took some definitely hostile action'. Such a restraint would help to avoid attracting attention to Chequers, 'or giving the enemy any idea that it is an important target'.[1]

In the event of a German invasion, the question of targets would be crucial: on July 31 Dill sent Churchill a note about the guarding of 'vulnerable points' throughout the British Isles. Some 1,500 such points had been listed before the war by the Home Defence Committee, and the list had been revised after the outbreak of war by a special Sub Committee of the Vice-Chiefs of Staff. These vulnerable points included army establishments, radar stations, aerodromes, wireless stations, railway junctions and oil installations.

Dill proposed the appointment of a Vulnerable Points Adviser, whose aim would be to replace the regular units at present guarding these points by Home Guard units, thus releasing all regular soldiers for Army defence tasks.[2] On the evening of July 31 both Eden and Dill went to see Churchill to urge him to such a course 'as early as possible'. The officer concerned, Eden explained to Churchill five days later, 'would have power and authority to decide priorities under my general direction. At present each Dept puts forward & presses its own.'[3]

Churchill approved this proposal, stressing that its aim was the withdrawing of 'all troops of the mobile army' from vulnerable points.[4] He also decided that the man appointed as Vulnerable Points Adviser, Lieutenant-General M. G. H. Barker, should 'work under me in my capacity as Minister of Defence'. As Churchill explained to Eden: 'Many Departments are closely concerned in the questions for which he will be responsible, and their interests are bound to be in conflict from time to time. It would therefore make for smooth working and expedition of business if General Barker were not attached to any of the interested parties.'[5]

Within a month of his appointment General Barker had proposed both to reduce the number of vulnerable points and, by careful use of

[1] General Ismay to Colonel R. C. A. McCalmont, CVO, DSO, 25 August 1940: Cabinet papers, 120/13.
[2] 'Note on guarding of vulnerable points', 31 July 1940: Premier papers, 3/498/1, folio 36.
[3] Letter of 5 August 1940: Premier papers, 3/498/1, folio 33.
[4] Letter of 6 August 1940: Premier papers, 3/498/1, folio 32.
[5] Letter of 18 August 1940: Premier papers, 3/498/1, folio 9.

Home Guard units, to release 9,000 soldiers for Army duties.[1] Churchill scrutinized Barker's proposals, minuting 'Proceed as proposed',[2] and subsequently endorsing without comment or complaint the General's dispositions.[3]

Those who expected Churchill to explode with anger at the slightest provocation were often disappointed. As the stress of events intensified, such explosions were more frequently feared. Yet Ismay has recalled an incident where a different response resulted. It was during a conference summoned to discuss invasion plans, and the problem under discussion was the part to be played by the Home Fleet in the event of invasion. The Commander-in-Chief, Home Fleet, Admiral Forbes, asked that it should be clearly understood that his heavy ships could not, in any circumstances, operate south of the Wash.

'Everyone expected an explosion from Mr Churchill,' Ismay later wrote, 'and his reaction was surprising. He said, with an indulgent smile, that he never took much notice of what the Royal Navy said that they would, or would not, do in advance of an event, since they invariably undertook the apparently impossible without a moment's hesitation whenever the situation so demanded.' If, for example, Churchill went on to explain, 'two or three nurses were wrecked on a desert island, the Navy would rush to their rescue, through typhoons and uncharted seas; and he had not a shadow of doubt that if the Germans invaded the south coast of Britain we would see every available battleship storming through the Straits of Dover'.[4]

On August 1, unknown to anyone in Britain, even from the most secret sources, Hitler issued his Directive No. 17, aimed at establishing 'the necessary conditions for the final conquest of England'. To this end, the Directive ordered the intensification of air and sea warfare 'against the English homeland'. The German Air Force was to 'overpower the English Air Force with all the forces at its command, in the shortest possible time'. The directive continued:

The attacks are to be directed primarily against flying units, their ground installations, and their supply organisations, but also against the aircraft industry, including that manufacturing anti-aircraft equipment.

After achieving temporary or local air superiority the air war is to be con-

---

[1] 'Progress Report, 23rd September 1940', 'Secret' Premier papers, 3/498/1, folio 17.

[2] Minute of 10 November 1940: Premier papers, 3/498/1, folio 3.

[3] From 1936 to 1938 Barker had been Director of Recruiting and Organisation at the War Office; in 1939 General Officer Commanding the British Forces in Palestine and Transjordan; and in 1940 General Officer Commanding-in-Chief, Aldershot. In 1941 he was appointed Deputy Regional Commissioner for Civil Defence, London Region.

[4] *The Memoirs of General The Lord Ismay*, London 1960, pages 188–9.

tinued against ports, in particular against stores of food, and also against stores of provisions in the interior of the country.

Attacks on the south coast ports, however, were to be made 'on the smallest possible scale, in view of our own forthcoming operations'.

The 'intensification of the air war', Hitler added, was to begin 'on or after 5th August'.[1]

Although Hitler's actual directive remained a secret to those at the centre of policymaking in Britain, the general drift of his intentions was quite widely known, so much so that on August 2 Joseph Kennedy reported to Washington that, if the Germans possessed the air power which they claimed, they could certainly put the Royal Air Force 'out of commission', after which a British surrender 'would be inevitable'.[2]

Writing to Roosevelt that same day, the Secretary of the Interior, Harold L. Ickes, appealed to the President to act; if Britain went down, Ickes argued, the American people would want to know why American destroyers had not been sent to help prevent an invasion. 'It seems to me,' he added, 'that we Americans are like the householder who refuses to lend or sell his fire extinguisher to help put out the fire in the house that is next door, although that house is all ablaze and the wind is blowing from that direction.'[3]

The atmosphere of imminent invasion affected even the European neutrals: on August 1 the King of Sweden wrote to King George VI to propose a conference 'to examine the possibilities of making peace'.[4] In London, the Foreign Office prepared a draft reply, which Halifax sent to Churchill for his comments. Churchill had his own idea, however, of how to answer the peace move. 'I should reply as follows,' he wrote to Halifax, and then set out the answer he would like to give:

On October 12th, 1939, His Majesty's Government defined at length their position towards German peace offers in a maturely considered statement made by the then Prime Minister, Mr Chamberlain, and by the present Foreign Secretary, in their respective Houses of Parliament.

Since then a number of new hideous crimes have been committed by Nazi Germany against the smaller States upon her borders. Norway has been overrun, and is now occupied by a German invading army. Denmark has been seized and pillaged. Belgium and Holland, after all their efforts to placate

[1] Directive No. 17, 1 August 1940: quoted in full in H. A. Trevor-Roper (editor), *Hitler's War Directives 1939–1945*, London 1964, pages 37–8.

[2] Telegram of 2 August 1940: cited in William L. Langer and S. Everett Gleason, *The World Crisis and American Foreign Policy: The Challenge to Isolation 1937–1940*, London 1952, page 744.

[3] Letter of 2 August 1940: Roosevelt papers, Secretary's File, Box 58. See also page 970.

[4] Letter of 1 August 1940: Premier papers, 4/100/3, folio 134.

Herr Hitler, and in spite of all the assurances given to them by the German Government that their neutrality would be respected, have been conquered and subjugated. In Holland particularly, acts of long-prepared treachery and brutality culminated in the massacre of Rotterdam, where many thousands of Dutchmen were slaughtered, and an important part of the city destroyed.

These horrible events have darkened the pages of European history with an indelible stain. His Majesty's Government see in them not the slightest cause to recede in any way from their principles and resolves as set forth in October 1939. On the contrary, their intention to prosecute the war against Germany by every means in their power until Hitlerism is finally broken, and the world relieved from the curse which a wicked man has brought upon it, has been strengthened to such a point that they would rather all perish in the common ruin than fail or falter in their duty. They firmly believe, however, that with the help of God they will not lack the means to discharge their task. This task may be long; but it will always be possible for Germany to ask for an armistice, as she did in 1918, or to publish her proposals for peace.

Before, however, any such requests or proposals could even be considered, it would be necessary that effective guarantees by deeds, not words, should be forthcoming from Germany which would ensure the restoration of the free and independent life of Czechoslovakia, Poland, Norway, Denmark, Holland, Belgium and, above all, France, as well as the effectual security of Great Britain and the British Empire in a general peace.

As for the Foreign Office's more routine answer, this, Churchill noted, appeared to him 'to err in trying to be too clever, and to enter into refinements of policy unsuited to the tragic simplicity and grandeur of the times and the issues at stake'.[1] At that moment, Churchill added, when Britain had 'no sort of success' to show, 'the slightest opening will be misjudged. Indeed, a firm reply of the kind I have outlined is the only chance of extorting from Germany any offers which are not fantastic.'

Churchill had one final comment to make, about the author of the peace proposal, telling Halifax: 'I might add that the intrusion of the ignominious King of Sweden as a peace-maker, after his desertion of Finland and Norway, and while he is absolutely in the German grip, though not without its encouraging aspects, is singularly distasteful.'[2]

As July came to an end, British civilian deaths from German air attacks reached 258 for the month. In North Africa, against the

---

[1] The Foreign Office draft reply had been prepared by Sir Robert Vansittart and Sir Orme Sargent.

[2] Minute of 3 August 1940: Premier papers, 4/100/3, folios 129–32.

Italians, 25 British soldiers had been killed or were missing opposite the Egyptian frontier post of Sollum, before General Wavell decided to withdraw behind the Egyptian frontier. At a second Secret Session of the House of Commons on July 30, Churchill again spoke of the dangers and setbacks still to be encountered: forty minutes, as Henry Channon noted, 'of magnificent oratory and artistry, but he gave away no secrets'.[1] 'Winston surpassed even himself,' wrote Harold Nicolson,[2] and George Lambert, who had entered the House of Commons in 1891, thanked Churchill for treating MPs 'as responsible individuals and not as irresponsible nobodies'. Lambert went on to praise Churchill's leadership as 'incomparably the most brilliant that I can remember, save perhaps that of Mr Gladstone'.[3]

Churchill could now rest with confidence upon the support of the House of Commons. This was a remarkable turnabout from the suspicions and doubts of even three months earlier. 'Winston Churchill continues to be the man of the hour,' the Archbishop of Canterbury wrote in his diary. 'All his colleagues testify to his qualities of drive and courage, and his powers of glowing speech are a great public asset.' Most of the 'team' Churchill had collected, the Archbishop added, 'seem to be doing well, not least the two Labour men, Morrison and Bevin'.[4]

Churchill's secret knowledge of the possibility of invasion drove him increasingly to inspect every area of British defences. The urgency could not be denied. On July 31 Morton told Colville that the head of the Secret Service, Colonel Menzies, 'has had news of imminent invasion from over 260 sources'.[5]

In the last week of July Churchill had inspected an armoured brigade in Northamptonshire. 'I wish Hitler could have heard us at dinner,' one of those who had travelled with him, Roger Keyes, wrote to a friend. 'WC was in boisterous form. I must say he is a great fellow! He said to me apropos of his getting me a job, "You have a great many detractors." I said, "So had you, but you are now there in spite

---

[1] Channon diary, 30 July 1940, quoted in Robert Rhodes James, *Chips, The Diaries of Sir Henry Channon*, London 1967, page 263.

[2] Letter of 31 July 1940, to his wife, quoted in: Nigel Nicolson (editor), *Harold Nicolson, Diaries and Letters, 1939–1945*, London 1965, page 104.

[3] Letter of 31 July 1940: Churchill papers, 2/396. Churchill replied on 4 August 1940 by telegram: 'Greatly cheered by your letter. Thank you so much. Winston.' Lambert had been Civil Lord of the Admiralty when Churchill was First Lord from 1911 to 1915. He was Chairman of the Liberal Parliamentary Party from 1919 to 1921.

[4] Cosmo Gordon Lang, diary entry for 29 July 1940: J. G. Lockhart, *Cosmo Gordon Lang*, London 1949, pages 428–9.

[5] Colville diary, 31 July 1940: Colville papers.

of it." He replied, "There are no competitors for my job now. I didn't get it until they had got into a mess." '[1]

During one of his tours of coastal defences, Churchill had spent an hour in a shipyard in the North-East. As news of his visit spread, wives of shipyard workers gathered at the gates. Churchill, 'impressed by the warmth of his welcome', as *The Times* reported, 'shouted "Are we downhearted?" The women-folk responded with a roar, "No".'[2] Yet on the day that this news item appeared in *The Times* Colville noted, of the Censorship Reports reaching Downing Street: 'It is already being said in the Provinces that Churchill is played out and must go.'[3] The need for Churchill's personal inspiration could not be denied, however, and when General Pakenham-Walsh prepared to leave for the United States on an arms purchase mission of the highest urgency, Sir James Grigg urged Churchill to see him before he left, 'in order that he may have the glow of Mount Sinai still on him when he reaches Washington'.[4]

[1] Sir Roger Keyes, letter of 29 July 1940: Tomkinson papers.
[2] *The Times*, 1 August 1940.
[3] Colville diary, 1 August 1940: Colville papers.
[4] Minute of 31 July 1940: Premier papers, 3/493, folio 30. Churchill invited both Grigg and Pakenham-Walsh to dinner on 1 August 1940. Grigg, then Permanent Under-Secretary of State for War had been Churchill's Principal Private Secretary at the Exchequer from 1924 to 1929.

34

Royal Interlude

THROUGHOUT the daily tensions and dilemmas of July 1940, Churchill had been closely involved in an issue of extreme sensitivity, the future of the Duke and Duchess of Windsor. On July 1, with the approval of King George VI, Churchill had sent his telegram ordering the Duke to return to England from Spain, and reminding the Duke that he was still technically on active service.[1] The telegram read: 'Your Royal Highness has taken active military rank and refusal to obey direct orders of competent military authority would create a serious situation. I hope it will not be necessary for such orders to be sent. I most strongly urge immediate compliance with wishes of the Government.'[2]

The reference to the Duke having taken 'active military rank' referred to the fact that, at the outbreak of war, the Duke had been appointed liaison officer with No. 1 British Military Mission to French General Headquarters, with the rank of Major-General. After the fall of Paris he had been seconded to the Armée des Alpes, and shortly afterwards had attached himself to the French Command at Nice. He had left France on June 20, reaching Madrid three days later, and on July 2, after two weeks in Madrid, had travelled with the Duchess to Lisbon, reaching the Portuguese capital on the evening of July 3, ten days after his forty-sixth birthday.[3]

On reaching Lisbon, the Duke was given Churchill's telegram of July 1, which had been sent to the British Embassy in Madrid, had missed him there, and been sent on to the British Embassy in Lisbon. That same evening, in London, Churchill had been received by the

---

[1] For the background to this telegram, see pages 613–14.

[2] Telegram No. 458, 'Secret and Personal', 1 July 1940: Churchill papers, 20/9.

[3] For a detailed account of the Duke's movements and activities following the German invasion of France, see Michael Bloch, *The Duke of Windsor's War*, London 1982, pages 64–103.

King.[1] No report of what they discussed is available, but later that same night, at Downing Street, Churchill told Beaverbrook that the Duke was to be offered an appointment as Governor and Commander-in-Chief of the Bahamas.[2] Eleven days later the Colonial Secretary, Lord Lloyd, dined with his friend Sir Ronald Storrs, who noted in his diary that Lloyd had told him that the Duke of Windsor's appointment in the Bahamas was the King's own idea, 'to keep him at all costs out of England'.[3]

Colville, who was present during Churchill's discussion with Beaverbrook, noted in his diary that Churchill himself took the credit for the idea of sending the Duke to the Bahamas. 'I think it a very good suggestion of mine,' Churchill told Beaverbrook, and went on to ask: 'Max, do you think he'll take it?' 'He'll find it a great relief,' Beaverbrook replied, at which Churchill commented: 'Not half as much as his brother will.'[4]

The Bahamas appointment was in every way extraordinary. No member of the British royal family had ever served as Governor of a Crown Colony, while within the Colonial Service itself the Bahamas was among the least important of the thirty-five territories under control of the Colonial Office. Even within the nine colonies under the West Indian Department of the Colonial Office, the Bahamas stood last but one in importance.

On July 4 Churchill telegraphed to the Duke, formally offering him the Bahamas appointment. 'Personally,' Churchill added, 'I feel sure it is the best open in the grievous situation in which we all stand. At any rate I have done my best.'[5]

Before receiving Churchill's telegram the Duke had already made plans to comply with Churchill's earlier order of July 1, that he return to Britain. The Duke 'will leave Lisbon tonight by air for England', a Foreign Office official noted on the morning of July 4,[6] while the British Air Attaché in Lisbon had already telegraphed to the Air Ministry on the night of July 3 with the flight details. The Duke would leave Lisbon at 11.40 p.m. on July 4, reaching Poole at 5.50 a.m. on July 5.[7]

[1] Churchill's audience with the King was at 6.30 p.m., 'PM's card', July 1940: Churchill papers, 20/19.

[2] Colville diary, 3 July 1940: Colville papers.

[3] Storrs diary, 14 July 1940: Storrs papers.

[4] Colville diary, 3 July 1940: Colville papers.

[5] Foreign Office Telegram No. 356 to Lisbon, 'Most Immediate', 9.10 a.m., 4 July 1940: Churchill papers, 20/9.

[6] Foreign Office papers, 371/24249.

[7] Air Attaché, Lisbon to Air Ministry, London, 'Most Immediate', A.51, Serial No. X.1992, received 11.55 p.m., 3 July 1940: Churchill papers, 20/9.

The Duke's plans to fly back to London on July 4 were changed by the Bahamas offer; but before it became known in London whether the Duke would accept it or not, the Colonial Secretary, Lord Lloyd, had drafted a telegram which he wanted Churchill to send to the Prime Ministers of Canada, Australia, New Zealand and South Africa. The draft read, as if written by Churchill himself:

The activities of the Duke of Windsor on the Continent in recent months have been causing HM and myself grave uneasiness as his inclinations are well known to be pro-Nazi and he may become a centre of intrigue. We regard it as a real danger that he should move freely on the Continent. Even if he were willing to return to this country his presence here would be most embarrassing both to HM and to the Government.

In all the circumstances it has been felt necessary to try to tie him down in some appointment which might appeal to him and his wife and I have decided with HM's approval to offer him the Governorship of the Bahamas. I do not know yet whether he will accept. Despite the obvious objections to this solution we feel that it is the least of possible evils.[1]

Churchill did not accept this draft, and in his own handwriting, redrafted the telegram in quite a different sense, stressing the Duke's 'unimpeachable' loyalties. Meanwhile the Duke had accepted the appointment, and telegraphed to Churchill on the evening of July 4: 'I am sure you have done your best for me in a difficult situation.'[2]

In the light of the Duke's acceptance, the already much less strident telegram was now sent to the Dominions. It read, as redrafted by Churchill:

The position of the Duke of Windsor on the Continent in recent months has been causing His Majesty and His Majesty's Government embarrassment, as, though his loyalties are unimpeachable, there is always a backwash of Nazi intrigue which seeks to make trouble about him. The Continent is now in enemy hands. There are personal and family difficulties about his return to this country.

In all the circumstances it has been felt that an appointment abroad might appeal to him and his wife, and I have, with His Majesty's cordial approval, offered him the Governorship of the Bahamas. His Royal Highness has intimated that he will accept the appointment. I think he may render useful service and find a suitable occupation there.

I wished you to have the earliest possible advance information of this. You

---

[1] 'Most Secret and Personal', 'Decypher yourself', draft telegram, 3 July 1940: Churchill papers, 20/9.

[2] Lisbon Telegram No. 369, 'Most Immediate', 6.21 p.m., 4 July 1940: Churchill papers, 20/9.

will appreciate how necessary it is to preserve complete secrecy. We here are, of course, doing all we can to ensure this.[1]

News of the Duke's appointment was to be made public on July 10. Three days earlier Eric Seal discussed with Sir Alexander Hardinge, the King's Private Secretary, 'the question of preparing the Press'. The two men agreed, Seal reported to Churchill, 'that all that is necessary is to let them know that this appointment is a natural extension of the Duke's recent appointment in Paris and that there is nothing whatsoever about it deserving of special comment or handling'. He would, however, Seal added, consult 'first thing in the morning' with James Stuart 'about the best way of handling the Press'.[2]

Churchill agreed with Seal's proposal, adding that the Ministry of Information 'shd be warned & asked to cooperate'.[3]

On July 8, two days before the public announcement was to be made, Lord Lloyd suggested that as the Bahamas were so close to the United States, Churchill should inform Roosevelt of the Duke's appointment. But as Eric Seal wrote to Lloyd that same day, the Prime Minister 'does not think it either necessary or desirable to send a special message to Washington about the Duke's appointment'.[4] Churchill did agree, however, to the Colonial Office sending the President a similar text to that which had been sent to the Dominion Prime Ministers four days earlier, but deleting the sentence: 'I think he may render useful service and find a suitable occupation there.' The Prime Minister, the message to Roosevelt ended, 'wished the President to have the earliest possible advance information of this decision which has only just arrived'.[5]

The Duke's appointment was duly announced, leaked out in fact on the evening of July 9, but being received, Churchill telegraphed to the Duke in Lisbon, 'with general satisfaction here and with delight in the Bahamas'.[6] But the 'general satisfaction' was tempered in some quarters by secret information about the Duchess' activities in Lisbon. 'As I told

[1] Telegram of 4 July 1940: Churchill papers, 20/14.

[2] 'Top of box', 7 July 1940: Churchill papers, 20/9. James Stuart was a Government Whip.

[3] Note by Churchill, undated: Churchill papers, 20/9.

[4] E. A. Seal to Lord Lloyd, 8 July 1940: Churchill papers, 20/9.

[5] Foreign Office Telegram No. 1447, 9 July 1940. Lord Lothian, to whom this telegram was addressed, replied a week later: 'Owing to this telegram arriving in undecypherable form it was unfortunately impossible for me to communicate the information to the President before the evening of July 9th by which time news had been published in London. I explained that the Prime Minister had wished to give the President advance information and the latter has now written expressing appreciation of the Prime Minister's courtesy.' (Washington Telegram No. 1362, A.3580/434/45: Churchill papers, 20/9.)

[6] Telegram of 13 July 1940: Churchill papers, 20/14.

you once before,' the King's Private Secretary wrote from Buckingham Palace to Eric Seal at Downing Street, 'this is not the first time that this lady has come under suspicion for her anti-British activities and as long as we never forget the power that she can exert over him in her efforts to avenge herself on this country we shall be all right.'[1]

The appointment having been made public, Churchill expected to hear no more of the matter, but within a few days he found himself at the centre of a small but embarrassing difficulty. The Duke's travel arrangements, which the Duke had been asked to make for himself, involved crossing the Atlantic by sea to New York, en route to the Bahamas. The Foreign Office, Eric Seal wrote to Churchill on July 16, 'are strongly opposed to allowing the Duke of Windsor to go to New York, which he apparently wishes to do, on his way to Nassau'. It seemed to Seal 'silly to start off by crabbing him in this way'.[2] But the Foreign Office was adamant, as was Lord Lothian, who telegraphed from Washington that if the Duke were to visit New York the inevitable publicity there 'will be of an icy character'.[3] Churchill deferred to these opinions; but he rejected a Colonial Office draft, to be sent under his own signature to the Duke of Windsor, that 'all things considered I think it would be more convenient if your Royal Highness could go direct to the Bahamas and very much hope you will agree to this'.[4] Instead Churchill simply telegraphed, again on the basis of a Colonial Office draft, that an America Export Line ship would leave Lisbon on August 1, make a special call at Bermuda, and then connect with a Canadian National steamship due to call at Bermuda on its way to the Bahamas.[5]

The diversion to Bermuda was to be paid for by the British Government, at a cost of 7,500 dollars.[6]

At first, the Duke rejected these arrangements, urging Churchill to let him 'go direct to New York, as I had originally arranged', and telling Churchill with some anguish: 'Feel sure you do not know red tape we are up against as regards new appointment.'[7] But Churchill was firmly of the view, as one of his Private Secretaries, John Peck,

[1] Letter of 9 July 1940: Churchill papers, 20/9.

[2] 'Top of box', 16 July 1940: Churchill papers, 20/9.

[3] Washington Telegram No. 1373, 'Immediate', 'Personal', 17 July 1940: Churchill papers, 20/9.

[4] Draft submitted by Christopher Eastwood, Colonial Office, and intended to be sent 'for Duke of Windsor from Prime Minister' to the British Embassy in Lisbon: Churchill papers, 20/9.

[5] Foreign Office Telegram No. 442, A.3580, 18 July 1940: Churchill papers, 20/9.

[6] Washington Telegram No. 1484, A.3580/434/45, 23 July 1940: Churchill papers, 20/9. Three days later a State Department official, Thomas Burke, informed Sumner Welles that there might be a further 10,000 dollars 'or more' to be paid for the war risk insurance charge. (Thomas Burke, memorandum for Sumner Welles, 26 July 1940: National Archives, Washington.)

[7] Lisbon Telegram No. 448, 19 July 1940: Churchill papers, 20/9.

noted, that the Duke 'should not be allowed to go' to the United States.[1] Before he could reply to the Duke, however, there was one final hitch. On July 20, after Peck had spoken on the telephone to Lord Lloyd, he informed Churchill:

There has been trouble about two men-servants whom the Duke wishes to take with him and who are of military age. In a telegram to the Duke wishing him good luck and hoping he would enjoy the job, Lord Lloyd expressed the hope that he would not press for these two men, and quoted the precedent of Lord Athlone who had agreed not to take men of military age to Canada. Hence in the Duke's telegram about red tape.

Lord Lloyd also informed Churchill that a few days earlier he had seen the King, 'whose line was "tell him to do what he is told"'. Eden had also seen the King on the previous day 'and confirmed that it was what the King wished'.

The Duchess was as angry as the Duke about the order to avoid New York, and the refusal to let her husband take two men of military age as his soldier servants. Sir Walter Monckton, who had earlier been the Duke's legal adviser, now, in his wartime capacity as Director-General of the Press and Censorship Bureau, had received an intercept of a telegram from the Duchess protesting against the 'obstacles' being put in her husband's way.[2]

Churchill was unwilling to give way over the two men of military age. But a further telephone message from Lord Lloyd urged a compromise. As Peck informed Churchill:

I have just spoken to Lord Lloyd on the telephone. He asked me to let you know as soon as possible that he entirely agreed that we should remain adamant on the subject of his going to New York. On the point of the servants he wanted you to appreciate that Lord Lascelles[3] and Sir Walter Monckton both agreed that HRH had to be treated as a petulant baby, and that there was a by no means remote possibility that he was prepared to face a break on this subject, and that he was unable to appreciate how ludicrous the affair would appear when made public. Consequently Lord Lloyd suggested that you should relent on this point.[4]

That same day, Churchill telegraphed to the Duke of Windsor to

---

[1] J. H. Peck to E. A. Seal, 22 July 1940: Churchill papers, 20/9.

[2] 'Message from Lord Lloyd': Churchill papers, 20/9. Monckton was then Director-General of the Press and Censorship Bureau. He had been Attorney General to the Prince of Wales from 1932 to 1936, and the King's legal adviser throughout the Abdication crisis.

[3] In fact, *Sir* Alan Lascelles, the King's Assistant Private Secretary, and Lord Lloyd's brother-in-law; successively Assistant Private Secretary to King George V and King Edward VIII, and Principal Private Secretary to King George VI and Queen Elizabeth II.

[4] Minute by J. H. Peck, 20 July 1940: Churchill papers 20/9.

explain his point of view. 'I regret,' he said, 'there can be no question of releasing men from the Army to act as servants to your Royal Highness. Such a step would be viewed with general disapprobation in times like these and I should ill-serve your Royal Highness by countenancing it.'[1]

Churchill had no desire for an open clash with the Duke, who had been his friend for many years, and in whose cause in 1936 he had risked his own political future to support. To try to calm matters down, he persuaded the War Office to allow one of the men of military age whom the Duke had requested to be released for service in the Bahamas. But on the question of the stop-over in New York he informed the Duke on July 23: 'His Majesty's Government cannot agree to Your Royal Highness landing in the United States at this juncture. This decision must be accepted. It should be possible to arrange, if necessary, for the Duchess either to proceed from Bermuda to New York for medical reasons, or, alternatively, it will always be easy for her to go there from Nassau by sea or land.'[2]

The Duke now accepted the arrangements proposed, to sail direct to the Bahamas. But he asked if he could delay his departure for one week. In reply, Lord Lloyd urged the Duke to sail on August 1 as arranged.[3] Churchill supported Lloyd's request with a further telegram. 'I do very much hope,' he wrote, 'that you will be able to fall in with this proposal.' As to the Duke's wish that once he had been in the Bahamas for a while he might be able to visit the United States, 'we should naturally wish', Churchill wrote in this same telegram, 'to fall in with Your Royal Highness's wishes'. It was 'difficult', Churchill added, 'to see far ahead these days, but in accordance with the standing Royal instructions to Colonial Governors, which you already have, you would no doubt consult the Secretary of State for the Colonies before leaving the Colony, when we should naturally do our best to suit Your Royal Highness's convenience'.[4]

That same day Churchill sent the Duke a letter, by hand of Walter Monckton, who was flying out to Lisbon at Churchill's request, and

---

[1] 'Prime Minister to the Duke of Windsor', Telegram No. 453 to Lisbon, 20 July 1940: Churchill papers, 20/9.

[2] Foreign Office Telegram No. 478, 'Prime Minister to Duke of Windsor' 'Secret', 23 July 1940: Churchill papers, 20/9.

[3] Foreign Office Telegram No. 498, 'Immediate', 27 July 1940: Churchill papers, 20/9.

[4] Foreign Office Telegram No. 497, 27 July 1940: Churchill papers, 20/9. Sent to Churchill by the Colonial Office, Instruction XXXI of the Royal Instructions to the Governor of the Bahamas read: 'The Governor shall not, on any pretence whatever, quit the Islands without first having obtained leave from Us for so doing under Our Sign Manual and Signet, or through one of Our Principal Secretaries of State.' (Churchill papers, 20/9.)

would, as Churchill explained, 'talk over various matters on which you should be verbally informed'. Churchill's letter continued:

I am very glad to have been able to arrange for your Royal Highness and the Duchess a suitable sphere of activity and public service during this terrible time when the whole world is lapped in danger and confusion. I know Nassau, having stayed a month there recovering from my accident in New York,[1] and except for a few months in the year it has one of the most agreeable climates. Moreover, through its proximity to the United States, it presents a ceaseless flow of interesting people. I am sure that your Royal Highness and the Duchess will lend a distinction and dignity to the Governorship which will be in the best interests of the Island and its group, and may well have other results favourable to British interests.

It would of course be natural that from time to time your Royal Highness should ask for leave to visit the United States, or other Islands, or the United Kingdom. At the present time I do not think that a visit to the United States would be desirable, because as your Royal Highness sees, the Presidential Election and the critical character of the war here have created abnormal conditions. But you may surely rely upon me, as long as I hold my present position, to do all within my power to serve your Royal Highness' true interests, and to study your wishes.

Sir, may I venture upon a word of serious counsel. It will be necessary for the Governor of the Bahamas to express views about the war and the general situation which are not out of harmony with those of His Majesty's Government. The freedom of conversation which is natural to anyone in an unofficial position, or indeed to a Major-General, is not possible in any direct representative of the Crown. Many sharp and unfriendly ears will be pricked up to catch any suggestion that your Royal Highness takes a view about the war, or about the Germans, or about Hitlerism, which is different from that adopted by the British nation and Parliament. Many malicious tongues will carry tales in every direction. Even while you have been staying at Lisbon, conversations have been reported by telegraph through various channels which might have been used to your Royal Highness' disadvantage. In particular, there will be danger of use being made of anything you say in the United States to do you injury, and to suggest divergence between you and the British Government. I am so anxious that mischief should not be made which might mar the success which I feel sure will attend your mission. We are all passing through times of immense stress and dire peril, and every step has to be watched with care.

I thought your Royal Highness would not mind these words of caution from

> Your faithful and devoted servant,
> Winston S. Churchill[2]

---

[1] In December 1931, see volume 5 of this biography, pages 423–4.
[2] 'Secret', 27 July 1940: Churchill papers, 20/9.

Churchill's comment to the Duke that 'conversations have been reported by telegraph through various channels' may give the clue to the 'various matters' which Monckton was to discuss verbally with the Duke. On July 23 a telegram from the German Ambassador in Madrid to the Foreign Ministry in Berlin had given what were said to be details of conversations held in Lisbon between the Duke and a Spanish friend of his. According to a version of these conversations, which were reported by the friend to the Spanish Minister of the Interior and by him to the German Ambassador, 'Politically the Duke has moved further and further away from the King and from the present British Government,' and was 'toying with the idea of dissociating himself from the present tendency of British policy by a public declaration and breaking with his brother.'[1]

In a further telegram to Berlin, sent on July 25, the German Ambassador in Madrid reported that when the Duke's Spanish friend had suggested to the Duke that he 'might yet be destined to play a large part in British politics and possibly ascend British throne', both the Duke and Duchess 'appeared to be surprised'. Both of them, the friend commented, 'seemed to be completely bound up in formalistic ways of thought, since they replied that according to British constitution this was not possible after Abdication'.[2]

Although Churchill after the war opposed the publication of these telegrams on the grounds that they represented 'a Nazi-German intrigue to entangle and compromise a Royal Prince' and were based on 'the assertions of German and pro-German officials in making the most of anything they could pick up',[3] there is little doubt that their content was such as to make it essential for the Duke to be warned of the danger, so long as he remained in Europe, of the Germans using him in some way for their own purposes. As early as July 11 the German Foreign Minister, von Ribbentrop, had telegraphed to the German Ambassador in Spain that the Duke must be brought back from Portugal to Spain, 'persuaded or forced to remain on Spanish soil', and then 'informed at the appropriate time in Spain that Germany on her side wishes for peace with the British people, that the Churchill clique

---

[1] Madrid Telegram No. 2474, 'Urgent', 'Top Secret', German Ambassador, Madrid to German Foreign Minister, printed after the war for the British Cabinet in: 'Top Secret', C. (53), 'Publication of Captured German Documents', 12 August 1953, Annex A: Beaverbrook papers.

[2] Madrid Telegram No. 2495, 'Strictly Confidential', German Ambassador, Madrid for German Foreign Minister, 25 July 1940: Printed after the war for the British Cabinet in: 'Top Secret', C. (53), 'Publication of Captured German Documents', 12 August 1953, Annex A: Beaverbrook papers.

[3] 'Secret and Personal', 27 June 1953 (Churchill to Eisenhower), 'Top Secret', C. (53), 'Publication of Captured German Documents', 12 August 1953, Annex B: Beaverbrook papers.

is standing in the way of this, and that it would be a good thing if the Duke were to hold himself in readiness for further developments'.[1] Perhaps even Ribbentrop's absurd hopes had been read by eyes other than those of the German Ambassador after their arrival in Spain.

'I certainly told the Duke and Duchess' Monckton later recalled, 'that the Germans might be plotting to keep him in Europe, and if possible get hold of him, and that it would be the view of the German Government that if they had possession of him, he could be used to endeavour to destroy the unity of the British.'[2]

According to the Duchess of Windsor's recollections, Monckton said to her and her husband: 'Winston is convinced that Hitler is crazy enough to be tempted, in the event of a successful invasion of Britain, to try to put the Duke back on the throne in the belief that this would divide and confuse the people and weaken their will to resist further.'[3]

In view of this extraordinary Intelligence, there seemed evident danger to the Duke should he remain even a week longer on European soil. Yet even this bizarre aspect was to have a further twist. The Duke asked Monckton to talk to his Spanish friend about rumours of a *British* plot to kidnap him when he reached the Bahamas. These rumours had clearly been put about on German instigation in order to frighten the Duke from leaving Portugal, and implied that the Germans did indeed have plans to abduct him to Spain and keep him there. Monckton was able to put the Duke's mind at rest, but not easily. As he later recalled: 'The Duke was not satisfied until I had secured by telegram the attendance of a detective from Scotland Yard to accompany them and look after them.'[4] Thus it was that on the afternoon of July 29 Monckton telegraphed to Lloyd: 'For reasons which I cannot now disclose, I consider it essential that responsible CID detective be sent to accompany our friends for voyage to destination and to remain as long as necessary.'[5]

Churchill minuted in this telegram 'Action please if possible,'[6] and a detective was sent by flying boat to Lisbon on the July 31 flight.

[1] 'Urgent', 'Top Secret', 11 July 1940: Printed after the war for the British Cabinet in: 'Top Secret', C. (53), 'Publication of Captured German Documents', 12 August 1953, Annex A: Beaverbrook papers.

[2] Sir Walter Monckton to Sir George Allen, 4 May 1956: Duchess of Windsor papers.

[3] The Memoirs of the Duchess of Windsor, *The Heart Has Its Reasons*, London 1956, pages 342–3.

[4] Monckton's notes: Lord Birkenhead, *Walter Monckton*, London 1969, pages 180–2. The Duke's Spanish friend throughout the events described in this chapter was Miguel Primo de Rivera Marqués de Estella, son of the former Spanish Dictator Primo de Rivera.

[5] Lisbon Telegram No. 495, sent 2.24 p.m., 29 July 1940, 'Immediate': Churchill papers, 20/9.

[6] Churchill papers, 20/9.

Meanwhile, the Duke telegraphed direct to Churchill: 'Monckton has arrived and I agree to sail August 1st as you have arranged.'[1]

Before the Duke's agreement to leave on August 1 had been communicated to Washington, the State Department had become agitated at the prospect of delaying the departure of the Export Line ship for a whole week. 'This,' Lothian had telegraphed on July 29, 'would obviously cause great inconvenience and expense' to the shipping company, and Sumner Welles had told him that he assumed the British Government would not therefore support this proposal, for which a substantial extra charge would clearly have to be made. Welles had indeed told the Line, Lothian reported, 'to insist on sailing on August 1st'.

Lothian ended his telegram: 'Please confirm urgently that sailing date should remain August 1st.'[2] 'Yes,' Churchill noted.[3]

On July 31 the Duke wrote to Churchill to confirm once more that he would leave as asked on the following day, although, he explained, it was 'not too convenient' to sail without 'many of our things that we shall need in the Bahamas and which we are trying to recover from France'. The Duke's letter continued:

I naturally do not consider my appointment as one of first class importance, nor would you expect me to. On the other hand, since it is evident that the King and Queen do not wish to bring our family differences to an end, without which I could not accept a post in Great Britain, it is at least a temporary solution to the problem of my employment in this time of war.

While I of course see the wisdom of avoiding all risks of being in any way drawn into the controversies of the coming Presidential Elections in the United States, I can see by your letter that you perfectly appreciate how impossible it would be for me to be anchored indefinitely within the limits of the Bahamas. After November, I can surely take occasional periods of leave to visit America, my property in Canada and adjacent islands of the West Indies, without detriment to the public interest, and I thank you for your assurance of help in this respect.

I shall bear your word of counsel in mind, and hope that from time to time, you will let me know your views on the trend of events.

The Duchess joins me in sending you our best wishes, and believe me,

Yours very sincerely,
Edward[4]

---

[1] Lisbon Telegram No. 496, sent 3.24 p.m., 29 July 1940: 'Immediate': Churchill papers, 20/9.
[2] Washington Telegram No. 1545, A.3580/434/45, 29 July 1940 (sent 12.42 a.m., received 8.45 a.m. 30 July 1940): Churchill papers, 20/9. Copies of this telegram were sent to the Colonial Office, Sir Alexander Hardinge, the Ministry of Shipping, and the Admiralty.
[3] Note of 30 July 1940: Churchill papers, 20/9.
[4] Letter on British Embassy, Lisbon, notepaper, 31 July 1940: Churchill papers, 20/9.

The last of the telegrams to reach Churchill was short and welcome. Dated August 2, and sent from the British Embassy in Lisbon, it read simply: 'Duke and Duchess of Windsor sailed last night.'[1]

The voyage passed without incident, despite rumours of a German commerce raider in the Atlantic. Eight days earlier Churchill had asked the Admiralty if they could provide a cruiser escort to 'convoy' the Duke across the Atlantic. But Admiral Phillips had replied that 'we are very short of cruisers on every station', especially because of the need to retain 'a number of cruisers in the UK for anti-invasion purposes'. It was 'consequently very undesirable', Phillips added, 'that a cruiser should be used if any other method of transport can be found'.[2]

From the Bahamas, the Duke was repeatedly to press Churchill for permission to travel to the United States. But his European adventures were over, and whatever dangers did or did not exist in Lisbon were at an end.

Seven months later the Duke sought Churchill's permission to visit the United States. 'After much consideration and enquiry,' Churchill replied, 'I have reached conclusion that your Royal Highness's proposed visit to United States would not be in the public interest, nor, indeed, in your own at the present time. I trust, therefore, that you will be willing to defer it until a less crucial stage in British and American relations has been reached.' Churchill also drew the Duke's attention to an interview in the American magazine *Liberty* 'of which it is said that the language, whatever was meant, will certainly be interpreted as defeatist and pro-Nazi, and by implication approving of the isolationist aim to keep America out of the war.' Churchill's telegram continued: 'I have obtained the best report possible of the interview, which has been republished here in the *Sunday Dispatch* of March 16, and I must say it seems to me that the views attributed to your Royal Highness have been unfortunately expressed by the journalist, Mr Oursler. I could wish, indeed, that your Royal Highness would seek advice before making public statements of this kind.' Churchill's telegram ended: 'I should always be ready to help as I used to in the past.'[3]

---

[1] Lisbon Telegram No. 508, 2 August 1940: Churchill papers, 20/9.
[2] Minute of 22 July 1940: Churchill papers, 20/9.
[3] 'Private and Personal', 17 March 1941: Churchill papers 20/49.

35

'A slender thread'

ON August 2 German bombers dropped leaflets over southern
England with copies of Hitler's peace proposals. 'It looks as if
the German military authorities are becoming doubtful about
their ability to invade us,' was Colville's comment.[1] Churchill had
already told the War Cabinet on the previous day that Britain's position
'was now considerably more secure' than in May, and had used this
fact to argue that it should now be possible 'to take a somewhat less
rigid attitude in regard to the internment of aliens'.[2] There was also a
report, which Churchill circulated to the War Cabinet, of the development of anti-aircraft rockets, recently tested at Dover, which 'may well
inaugurate a decisive change in the relations of ground and Air, particularly in respect of ships and ports exposed to dive-bombing
attack'.[3]

These hopeful signs were known in Downing Street, and to the inner
circle of Churchill's Ministers, advisers and secretariat. But Churchill
also knew the dangers of complacency, and at Chequers on August 3
he drafted a statement for the Sunday morning papers. 'The Prime
Minister wishes it to be known,' the statement read, 'that the possibility
of German attempts at invasion has by no means passed away. The
fact that the Germans are now putting about rumours that they do not
intend an invasion, should be regarded with a double dose of the suspicion which attaches to all their utterances.' Britain's sense of 'growing
strength and preparedness', he added, 'must not lead to the slightest
relaxation of vigilance or moral alertness'.[4]

On the afternoon of August 3 Churchill visited Fighter Command

---

[1] Colville diary, 2 August 1940; Colville papers.
[2] War Cabinet No. 217 of 1940, 1 August 1940: Cabinet papers, 65/14.
[3] War Cabinet Paper No. 303 of 1940: Cabinet papers, 66/10.
[4] Statement of 3 August 1940: Premier papers, 4/68/9, folio 432.

headquarters at Stanmore. That evening, at Chequers, he dined with Lord Gort, Sir Hugh Dowding, Lindemann and Duncan Sandys.[1] At one o'clock that night, German bombers flew over Chequers itself, dropping their bombs four miles away, at Great Missenden.[2] 'Whether this was a personal compliment or not is uncertain,' Churchill wrote to Neville Chamberlain, who was in hospital after an operation for cancer.[3]

The search for the offensive continued without respite. On August 4 Churchill asked Sinclair and Newall to examine the possibility of 'heavy attacks' on the *Scharnhorst* and *Gneisenau* at Kiel, the *Bismarck* at Hamburg and the *Tirpitz* at Wilhelmshaven, 'all targets of supreme importance'.[4] On August 5 the War Cabinet approved operation 'Razzle', the dropping of incendiary pellets intended to start fires in German forests.[5] But, as Colville noted in his diary, 'only a fraction are within our range'.[6] In addition, as Newall had reported to Churchill, the Black Forest, originally envisaged as one of the principal targets, 'is not easily "fired" as its trees are mainly deciduous'.[7]

Preparations for meeting a German invasion continued, and instructions were issued as to what should be done in the event of a German occupation of any particular locality. On August 1 Lord Mottistone, who as J. E. B. Seely had been Secretary of State for War before the First World War, had telephoned Churchill to point out a police regulation to the effect that, once the Germans had overrun an area, the police would hand over their arms to the 'enemy' and then 'place themselves at the disposal of the enemy'.[8] A police order which Mottistone sent Churchill on the following day stated explicitly that the senior police officer of any overrun area 'should offer the assistance of the police in maintaining order'.[9]

Having studied this order, Churchill sent it to Clement Attlee and Sir John Anderson with the comment: 'The attached raises a very difficult question, and one that must be speedily settled. We cannot

---

[1] Churchill's engagement book: Churchill papers, 2/413.

[2] Martin diary, 3 August 1940: Martin papers.

[3] Churchill papers, 2/393. Churchill also told Chamberlain that he had added Lord Beaverbrook to the War Cabinet 'in order to get more help in the supply side of the Defence Ministry'. This would require 'delicate development', he noted, as Herbert Morrison, the Minister of Supply, was 'sensitive about his domain'.

[4] Minute of 4 August 1940: Cabinet papers, 120/300, folio 67.

[5] War Cabinet No. 219 of 1940, 5 August 1940: Cabinet papers, 65/14.

[6] Colville diary, 5 August 1940: Colville papers.

[7] Minute of 31 July 1940: Premier papers, 3/11/1, folio 32.

[8] 'Secret and Personal' note of 2 August 1942: Premier papers, 3/359, folios 15–16.

[9] 'Duties of the Police in Case of Invasion': Premier papers, 3/359, folios 18–19.

surely make ourselves responsible for a system where the police will prevent the people resisting the enemy, and will lay down their arms and become the enemy's servant in any invaded area.' Churchill's minute continued:

I confess I do not see my way quite clearly to the amendments required in the regulations. In principle, however, it would seem that the police should withdraw from any invaded area with the last of His Majesty's troops. This would also apply to the ARP and the Fire Brigades, etc. Their services will be used in other districts. Perhaps on invasion being declared the police, ARP, Fire Brigades, etc should automatically become a part of the military forces.[1]

After considerable discussion, it became clear that there was a division of opinion among Cabinet Ministers, and some confusion of council as to what ought to be the behaviour of individuals after the Germans had taken over an area. The issue was settled by Churchill himself, in a minute to Sir John Anderson:

We do not contemplate or encourage fighting by persons not in the armed forces, but we do not forbid it. The police, and as soon as possible, the ARP services, are to be divided into combatant and non-combatant, armed and unarmed; the armed will cooperate actively in fighting with the Home Guard and Regulars in their neighbourhood, and will withdraw with them if necessary; the unarmed will actively assist in the 'stay put' policy for civilians. Should they fall into an area effectively occupied by the enemy, they may surrender and submit with the rest of the inhabitants, but must not in those circumstances give any aid to the enemy in maintaining order, or in any other way. They may however assist the civil population as far as possible.[2]

As Britain awaited invasion, a hundred different problems confronted Churchill, who was shown daily a mass of plans and documentation. But, as with the establishment of the Vulnerable Points Adviser, once he had given his approval, he was often content with the action carried out, and made no further intervention. Many important decisions were made by his Ministers without his involvement in any way: they informed him of what had been done, and he accepted their actions without comment. One such decision, approved by Sinclair, was to set up decoy lighting systems, to persuade German bombers to drop their bombs in open fields. Near Sheffield, the 'Sheffield decoy', extending for some miles, simulated at two-thirds scale a row of furnaces, two stretches of factory roadway and four marshalling yards. The 'Chesterfield decoy' copied a marshalling yard and a factory road.

[1] 'Action this Day', 3 August 1940: Premier papers, 3/359, folio 14.
[2] Minute of 12 August 1940: Premier papers, 3/359, folio 4.

Throughout eastern England, the Air Ministry had experimented with decoy aerodromes: these, Churchill was told on August 5, 'have already attracted a large number of bombs'. An inter-departmental conference on decoy policy had made recommendations to the Deputy Chiefs of Staff Committee for further decoy systems. Under these recommendations, the Air Ministry would act as co-ordinator of decoy policy between the departments concerned.[1] 'So far,' Sinclair and Anderson informed Churchill on August 5, fifty-two German bombing attacks on existing Air Ministry decoys had been made on thirty different decoy sites, with not a single civilian casualty.[2]

Churchill approved the decoy lighting scheme, and gave it the full weight of his authority. 'There must be no delay', he minuted to Ismay on August 10. If any 'complaint' was made by the Ministry of Agriculture about the use of agricultural land, he added, it must of course be reported to the Cabinet. 'Meanwhile,' however, 'work must proceed.'[3]

Churchill saw no reason to question the decoy lighting plans in any way. Nor did he have any changes to suggest in the Air Staff's anti-invasion scheme, code name 'Banquet'. According to this scheme the aircraft and air crews at the disposal of Bomber Command would, in the event of invasion, be augmented immediately both by aircraft and crews hitherto with the Fleet Air Arm, and by officers engaged in giving instruction at Officer Training schools. At the same time it was agreed by the Air Staff, also without dissent by Churchill, that it would be the responsibility of the Commander-in-Chief, Home Forces, to indicate whenever British bomber attacks were required against targets in German-occupied areas of Britain.[4]

In two other matters relating to anti-invasion plans, Churchill received urgent recommendations from his advisers during August. On August 7 Lindemann had asked him to authorize the 'highest priority and all facilities' for experiments, 'which Dowding was so anxious to press forward', for a radar system to direct searchlights on to night flying aeroplanes.[5] Churchill gave his approval immediately.[6] Two

[1] Deputy Chiefs of Staff Committee, Memorandum No. 94 of 1940.
[2] 'Decoy Lighting', Joint Memorandum by the Secretary of State for Air and the Minister of Home Security, Civil Defence Committee Memorandum No. 40 of 1940, 5 August 1940: Premier papers, 3/93/1, folios 5–7.
[3] Minute of 10 August 1940: Premier papers, 3/93/1, folio 3.
[4] 'Royal Air Force Organisation for Air Action against Invasion of Britain', 'Secret', 18 August 1940: Air Ministry papers, 20/5298.
[5] This was the SLC-Yagi radar system. SLC = Searchlight Control. Yagi was the Japanese Nobel prizewinner and physicist whose aerial was an essential part of the system.
[6] Lindemann report of 7 August 1940 and draft Minute to Ismay of 8 August 1940: Cabinet papers, 120/385.

weeks later, Ismay told Churchill that the work of Anti-Aircraft Command was 'not adequately covered by your Defence Secretariat' and proposed that Duncan Sandys, who was an anti-aircraft gunner himself, should undertake anti-aircraft liaison with the Defence Secretariat as he already did with the Commander in Chief Home Forces.[1] Again Churchill gave his immediate approval, as did the Commander of Anti-Aircraft Command, General Pile, who wrote to Ismay: 'I personally will welcome anything that will help to get more Germans killed.'[2]

One decision of considerable importance both for immediate and long-term preparations against invasion, as well as for the defence of Egypt, was the opening in August of the Atlantic Ferry Operation, 'Atfero'. Under this scheme, aircraft manufactured for Britain in the United States and Canada were to be flown by Ferry pilots across the Atlantic, some to Britain, others to Takoradi on the Atlantic coast of Africa. Based at Dorval airport, near Montreal, 'Atfero' was operated both by Canadian and British service personnel, and by United States civilians: it quickly became an essential, if unspectacular arm of Britain's defence capability.[3]

Churchill gave his full authority to the development of the Atlantic Ferry scheme, as also to the setting up of the overland route from Takoradi to Egypt. This route, passing through Nigeria at Kano and the Sudan at Khartoum, covered a total distance of 3,700 miles. 'The Prime Minister wishes to have a report as soon as possible on the progress of the Air Route from Takoradi,' Ismay wrote to the Chief of the Air Staff on August 4. 'When will it be ready to use, and can anything be done to expedite it?'[4]

The answer came on the following day. By the end of August, Newall reported, the first operating party would reach Takoradi. By the first week of September six Hurricanes and six Blenheims would arrive from Britain, crated, by sea, together with an erecting party, and twenty-five Ferry pilots. Within twenty-four hours, thirty more Hurricanes would reach Takoradi on board the carrier Argus. No time would be lost in putting the route into practice, and on September 20 the first delivery flight of six Blenheims and thirty-six Hurricanes would leave

[1] Ismay Minute of 22 August 1940: Cabinet papers, 120/244.
[2] Letter of 31 August 1940: Cabinet papers, 120/244.
[3] By July 1941 'Atfero' employed 944 people, 758 in Montreal, 52 at Gander (Newfoundland) and 5 in the United States, including 187 service personnel (Royal Air Force and Royal Canadian Air Force), 30 British Overseas Airways Corporation personnel, and 62 United States civilians (Air Ministry papers, 20/6154). In addition, 60 Polish and 24 Czech pilots participated in the ferrying (Air Ministry papers, 20/6087).
[4] Minute of 4 August 1940: Cabinet papers, 120/300.

Takoradi, flown by the Ferry pilots, and reaching Khartoum four days later.[1]

There was now a method whereby the British forces in Egypt could receive aircraft reinforcements without the risk of Italian or German attack in the Mediterranean.

On August 5 Churchill asked Ismay to look into another aspect of trans-Atlantic supplies. 'What,' he asked, 'is the theme upon which munitions imports are now being regulated and how far has it been concerted with shipping possibilities.'[2] In reply, Sir Arthur Salter reported that all possible priority was being given in North Atlantic shipment to imports of steel, pig iron, scrap and other metals deemed essential by the Ministry of Supply. It was the difficulties of finding space to ship aircraft, Salter explained, that made it important that as many bombers and reconnaissance planes as possible 'should be flown over here'.[3]

Salter also sent Churchill a schedule of Atlantic Ferry flights to Britain. Several had already arrived. The first twenty-six of a total order of 238 Glenn Martin reconnaissance aircraft had reached Britain in July, the next fifty were due in August. The first eight of fifty Hudson reconnaissance aircraft to be flown over would come in August. The first two flying boats, of ninety already ordered, were expected in October; the first of 150 four-engined bombers were due to be delivered in February 1941.[4]

Even as the Atlantic Ferry system was being put into operation, and the Takoradi air route given its final plans, there were doubts in the United States about Britain's ability to survive a German assault, and on August 6 Churchill was perturbed by a telegram from Roosevelt, wanting reassurance that, if Britain were overrun, the British Fleet would continue to fight, and would neither be surrendered nor sunk. Nor was Churchill pleased by a plan to transfer British ships to Canada in the event of defeat. 'Winston is in a nervous and irritable frame of mind,' Colville noted. 'He refuses to consider even giving Canada a lien on our cruisers, and brands any such proposal as defeatism.' The only situation in which Churchill would give an undertaking to transfer British ships, Colville added, was 'in return for an Anglo-US alliance'.

---

[1] 'Air Route from Takoradi to Middle East', note by Newall for Churchill, 5 August 1940: Cabinet papers, 120/333. The despatch of Hurricanes to Takoradi was given the code name 'Stripe'.

[2] Minute of 5 August 1940: Cabinet papers, 115/70.

[3] 'Munitions Imports: New Programmes', 14 August 1940: Cabinet papers, 115/70.

[4] 'Programme for Flying Aircraft from North America', 'Most Secret', 10 August 1940: Cabinet papers, 115/70.

But Churchill did see the possibility of one quid pro quo with the United States, the lease of British naval bases in the West Indies 'to encourage a strong United States defence line in the western Atlantic'.[1]

At the Defence Committee that same day, Churchill spoke critically of 'the deplorable position' regarding the supply of ammunition for trench mortars, and was promised by the Minister of Supply, Herbert Morrison, that 'steps had been taken to prevent a repetition of such mistakes', by ensuring in future 'a closer association' between the design and production staffs.[2]

On August 6 Churchill lunched with F. W. Deakin, his devoted research assistant of the pre-war years. But moments of relaxation were few, and Roosevelt's hesitation and demands had much upset him. 'We must not discuss the question of what to do with the Fleet in the event of invasion,' he minuted to Halifax on August 7.[3] The question of the American destroyers must be decided 'solely' on the quid pro quo of West Indian bases. And to Lord Lothian he telegraphed that same day: 'Pray make it clear at once that we could never agree to the slightest compromising of our full liberty of action, nor tolerate any such defeatist announcement, the effect of which would be disastrous.'[4]

That night news came in of a troopship sunk off the coast of Ireland. This news, Colville noted, 'has depressed Winston greatly'. Only when it was learned that losses were relatively light did Churchill recover his equanimity.[5]

Amid all these pressures and problems, Churchill made regular visits to Buckingham Palace to report on the progress of the war to King George VI and Queen Elizabeth, both of whom, Colville noted, 'appreciate Churchill's qualities'. But both, he added, were 'a little ruffled by the offhand way he treats them—says he will come at six puts if off until 6.30 by telephone, then comes at seven'.[6]

On August 8 Intelligence reports brought news of various developments. The Foreign Office Weekly Intelligence Summary stated, as Colville noted, that as a result of the German failure to invade Britain

---

[1] Colville diary, 6 August 1940: Colville papers.

[2] Defence Committee (Supply) No. 14 of 1940, 6 August 1940, 10.30 a.m.: Cabinet papers, 70/1.

[3] Minute of 7 August 1940: Churchill papers, 20/13.

[4] Telegram of 7 August 1940: Churchill papers, 20/13.

[5] Colville diary, 7 August 1940: Colville papers. The ship was the SS *Mohamed Ali el-Kebir*, 7,527 tons, with 732 military and naval personnel on board. 600 survivors were rescued. (War Cabinet Chiefs of Staff Committee, Weekly Résumé No. 49.)

[6] Colville diary, 7 August 1940: Colville papers.

'a small cloud of doubt as to Germany's invincibility has arisen on the European horizon'.[1]

As the air battle continued there were mounting British losses: at the War Cabinet of August 9 Churchill learned of eighteen British aircraft shot down on the previous day, when 300 German aircraft had been intercepted over the Isle of Wight.[2] During the day, as every day, he scrutinized the charts and documents put before him. On August 9 they concerned aircraft losses and aircraft production, pilot recruitment and training, ammunition supply, the equipment of foreign troops in Britain, the equipment of British troops in the Middle East, the design of vessels capable of transporting armoured vehicles by sea and landing them on beaches, the clashes with Italy in north and east Africa and the Italian advance into British Somaliland, policy towards neutral Spain, plans for possible offensives against Crete and the Azores, and Intelligence reports from Germany based on Enigma decrypts and other secret sources.[3] These and many other issues involved a mass of paperwork, demanding Churchill's close attention and leading to much thought, discussion and correspondence.

It was during August 9 that Churchill decided to seek greater clarity in the way in which the problems were set before him. That day the War Cabinet were circulated with a directive entitled 'Brevity', which Sir Edward Bridges had drafted for Churchill, urging the need for 'short, crisp paragraphs' in Ministerial reports. 'Let us not shrink,' the directive added, 'from using the short, expressive phrase, even if it is controversial.'[4]

---

[1] Colville diary, 8 August 1940: Colville papers.

[2] War Cabinet No. 223 of 1940, 12.30 p.m., 9 August 1940: Cabinet papers, 65/8.

[3] Including a Combined Intelligence Committee report 'voicing the suspicion that unseen invasion preparations might be in train in the Baltic'. (F. H. Hinsley and others, *British Intelligence in the Second World War, Its Influence on Strategy and Operations*, volume 1, London 1979, page 183.)

[4] War Cabinet Paper No. 211 of 1940, 'Secret', 9 August 1940: Churchill papers, 23/4. Five months later Churchill wrote to Eden: 'You spoke to me the other day about the length of telegrams. I feel that this is an evil which ought to be checked. Ministers and Ambassadors abroad seem to think that the bigger the volume of their reports home the better is their task discharged. All kinds of gossip and rumours are sent regardless of credibility. The idea seems to be to keep up a continued chat which no one ever tries to shorten. I suggest that you should issue a general injunction, but that in addition telegrams which are unduly verbose or trivial should be criticised as such, and their authors told "this telegram was needlessly long". It is sheer laziness not compressing thought into a reasonable space. I try to read all these telegrams, and I think the volume grows from day to day. Please let me know what you think can be done.' (Prime Minister's Personal Minute, M.42/1, 11 January 1941: Churchill papers, 20/36.)

Churchill's own scrutiny of intricate documents and reports was without respite. On the day of his 'Brevity' directive he complained to Ismay that he was 'not getting the War Office telegrams as I should', and gave instructions that henceforth all important Naval, Air and Military telegrams should go to the Defence Office 'immediately', there to be sifted by Ismay's Staff, 'and anything of interest or importance marked to me'.[1]

That Friday evening Churchill went to Chequers, where he dined with Eden, Dill, Pound, Ismay and Wavell, the General Officer Commanding-in-Chief, Middle East. Colville, who was also present, recorded in his diary the view of Eden and Ismay that France's 'shame' was so great 'that she could never rise again'. But Churchill, he noted, 'profoundly disagrees'. The discussion turned to the German air attacks on British shipping in the Channel. For some days, coastal vessels had been used as 'bait', a plan which Churchill wished to see continued. But, Colville noted, 'he admits the surviving bait are getting a little fed up'.

That Britain was 'winning the air battles' seemed clear to Churchill. If the Germans were as powerful in the air as had been supposed, he said, 'they would be bombing our ports incessantly'. If they 'still hoped to starve us out', they did not realize the importance of the small convoys. Meanwhile, the British forward planning must go on. 'Fancy,' he mused, 'next year we shall have ten armoured divisions.' When Eden and Dill protested that they would not have the weapons for these divisions, Churchill replied: 'If you produce the men, I will see you get the weapons. Then we shall be able to undertake formidable raids on the continent.' That very autumn, he added, 'we shall land small forces of 10,000 men'.

Churchill went on to tell his guests how all the Generals seemed 'keen', both on the idea of the offensive, and on giving training by means of these actions to men who would form 'the core of future operations'. Britain had 'much open' to her: a landing in Holland followed by a 'destructive raid' into the Ruhr, or the seizure of the Cherbourg Peninsula, or an invasion of Italy; these were three of the offensive possibilities which Churchill mentioned. A fourth was suggested by Wavell: the invasion of Norway. 'We shall need skis for that,' Churchill commented. 'We don't want to go and get Namsos-ed again. We've had enough of that.' Then Eden suggested Sicily as the 'soft spot' in Italy's armour, as the Sicilians had 'always been anti-Fascist'.[2]

---

[1] Minute of 9 August 1940, 'Action this Day': Churchill papers, 20/13.

[2] The idea of the occupation of Sicily was later developed as operation 'Workshop', but subsequently abandoned, see pages 925–6, 933–4, 962–3, 987 and 1001.

As the discussion continued, Churchill told Wavell that he promised 'he would not ask him to effect a landing in enemy territory until we could clear the air over the place of disembarkation'.[1]

After dinner Churchill and his guests adjourned to a conference in the Hawtrey Room, where Churchill asked Wavell for a list of his military needs. This list, submitted in the following week to the War Cabinet, was approved in full.[2]

As the conference drew to its conclusion, a German raider flew overhead, and, as Colville noted, 'we all went out to look'.[3]

Even as the Prime Minister and his guests were at Chequers discussing possible long-term offensives, a less ambitious but more immediate offensive operation was nearing fruition in London. Its code name was 'Scipio', and its origins went back three and a half weeks to the War Cabinet of 5 July 1940. On that day Halifax had drawn his colleagues' attention to a telegram from the British Consul-General at Dakar, in French West Africa, stating that the French Mayor of Dakar 'considered that a show of force should be made by the British Fleet if possible by 10th July', in order to stimulate a coup d'état against the Bordeaux authorities there by 'French European patriots'. At this War Cabinet, Churchill had announced that General Spears would be meeting de Gaulle that morning to see whether de Gaulle was prepared to be put ashore 'somewhere behind Dakar with a view to rallying French forces in that neighbourhood'.[4]

Churchill believed the Mayor of Dakar's message to be of the 'utmost importance', and that it would be possible for the British Fleet 'to make contact almost by the day mentioned'.[5] The Mayor had warned that 'later on' the situation might be more difficult without 'consider-

[1] Colville diary, 9 August 1940: Colville papers.

[2] The list included 2 tank battalions (of 102 tanks in all), 1 light tank regiment (of 52 tanks), 48 anti-tank guns, 48 field guns, 500 bren guns, 20 light anti-aircraft guns and 250 anti-tank rifles. On 10 August 1940 Churchill asked Ismay if Wavell could also be furnished 'with some fast reconnaisance machines, also a good machine for him to get about in'. Churchill added: 'It occurred to me that the King's machine would be very suitable, being armed and fast, if, as I understand it, HM has decided not to use it.' (Churchill papers, 20/13.)

[3] Colville diary, 9 August 1940: Colville papers. At one moment during the evening's discussion Churchill had reflected on the brilliance of the German strategy in May 1940 in advancing through Abbeville to Calais, thus forcing the British into the Dunkirk perimeter. The British troops at Calais, he told his guests, were 'the bit of grit that saved us', by stopping the Germans as Sir Sidney Smith had stopped Napoleon at Acre.

[4] War Cabinet No. 194 of 1940, 5 July 1940, 12 noon: Cabinet papers, 65/14.

[5] Minute to Ismay, 5 July 1940: Premier papers, 3/276, folio 284.

able loss of life', whereas a British arrival in force by July 10 'might have the desired effect without much bloodshed'.[1]

Asked for his comments, de Gaulle stated that the situation in North Africa had so 'deteriorated' since Oran that 'even a very large force would be received with hostility',[2] while Admiral Somerville commented that the Consul-General's telegram 'should be taken with a grain of salt, and that any attempt at a coup d'état would certainly be strongly resisted'.[3] The whole issue, Churchill minuted on July 7, was 'not now so urgent', but, he added, 'Gen de Gaulle's preparation for installing himself in W Africa must be aided in every way.'[4]

On July 21 the Chiefs of Staff had warned that if the Germans were free to operate from Dakar 'the effect would be so serious that it would be essential to take action to deny him the use of the base', and recommending that plans be drawn up to destroy the base facilities at Dakar by naval bombardment.[5] Consideration of a 'show of force' in the French West African colonies was also recommended by Sir Robert Vansittart's Committee on French Resistance in its report of July 22.[6] Three days later Churchill saw de Gaulle again, with a view, as he told the War Cabinet, 'of his forming a rallying point in North Africa',[7] and on August 3, after lunching with de Gaulle at Chequers,[8] he sent de Gaulle his general approval to the plan, 'evolved' by Spears and Morton, to land Free French forces in West Africa.[9]

To the Colonial Secretary, Lord Lloyd, Churchill wrote that same day: 'the matter will be brought before Cabinet on Monday, but meanwhile, no time must be lost in preparation', and de Gaulle must be given immediate facilities 'of telegraphing through British channels to his agents' to avoid his telegrams being held up, as hitherto, sometimes 'for several days'. The 'utmost importance and urgency', Churchill noted, 'should be attached to the proposed operation'.[10] At the same time, Churchill had asked Sir Archibald Sinclair to 'find a flying

---

[1] Churchill papers, 20/13.
[2] Most Secret, Report by General Spears, 5 July 1940: Premier papers, 3/276, folios 286–8.
[3] Most Secret, Ismay to Churchill, 5 July 1940: Premier papers, 3/276, folios 281/2.
[4] Minute to Ismay, 7 July 1940: Premier papers, 3/276, folio 282.
[5] Report of 21 July 1940: Cabinet papers, 66/9.
[6] Report of 22 July 1940: Foreign Office papers, 371/24384.
[7] War Cabinet No. 212 of 1940, 25 July 1940, 11.30 a.m., Minute 4, Confidential Annex: Cabinet papers, 65/14.
[8] Chequers Visitors Book. Also present were Spears and Morton.
[9] 'The Dakar Operation', 'Secret', narrative printed for the War Cabinet, 5 February 1941: Churchill papers, 4/170.
[10] Minute of 3 August 1940: Churchill papers, 20/13.

boat' to fly three of de Gaulle's emissaries to Accra on a matter 'of the highest importance'. He also asked Eden to ensure the quickest possible completion of the equipment of de Gaulle's three battalions, and to 'accelerate this action by every means in your power'. To A. V. Alexander, Churchill wrote that same day: 'They may have to start within ten days.'[1]

Detailed plans for 'Scipio' were now evolved, and on August 4 the Joint Planning Sub-Committee submitted its report to the Chiefs of Staff Committee, which agreed that the expedition was to consist only of Free French forces, with British involvement limited to escorting and conveying them by sea to their point of landing. This landing was to be in any French West African port, provided that a port could be found where a landing could take place without opposition.[2] On the morning of August 5 the War Cabinet approved this plan, and instructed that it should be 'pressed forward' by the Departments concerned.[3]

Following this decision to proceed on the basis of no direct British involvement to fight, Pound, Phillips, Spears and Morton discussed the operation in detail with de Gaulle. The 'ideal situation', according to the Englishmen, would be for British warships to remain 'out of sight' while the de Gaulle expedition landed. But even after de Gaulle had landed, and even if the Colony had 'placed itself under his direction', there would remain 'the danger of a Vichy sea-borne expedition to recapture the colony', and de Gaulle wished to know what Britain's attitude would be 'towards intercepting such an expedition and in general protecting de Gaulle's rear from the sea'.[4]

On learning of the possibility of this wider involvement, and possible clash with Vichy forces, the Chiefs of Staff protested to Churchill, who on August 6 again saw de Gaulle, in the presence of Phillips, to evolve a new plan satisfactory to the Free French, but still avoiding direct British involvement in any military action against Vichy forces.

The new plan involved landing a force of Free French infantrymen either on a beach near Dakar, or at Conakry and thence overland to Dakar, or at Freetown and thence overland. At this meeting de Gaulle assured Churchill that he would not be a party 'to a fight between

---

[1] Minutes of 3 August 1940: Churchill papers, 20/13.
[2] War Cabinet Paper No. 304 of 1940, 4 August 1940: Cabinet papers, 66/9.
[3] War Cabinet No. 219 of 1940, 5 August 1940, 11.30 a.m., Minute 5, Confidential Annex: Cabinet papers, 65/14.
[4] Morton to Churchill, 'Secret. Top of Box', 5 August 1940: Premier papers, 3/276, folios 268–9.

Frenchmen', and again that afternoon he stressed in conversation with Spears and Phillips that his object was to take possession of 'friendly territory': if he met military opposition from the French in West Africa 'he would not consider going on with the operation'.

On the afternoon of August 7, the Chiefs of Staff Committee met to discuss de Gaulle's plan.[1] Recent reports, they noted, made it clear that 'considerable sections' of the population of French West Africa 'are friendly towards us and anti-Vichy'. Support for de Gaulle had been expressed in the Cameroons, Chad and French Equatorial Africa, but without any active breach with Vichy. For Britain, a hostile Vichy authority in West Africa could be 'extremely serious'. But a 'friendly and belligerent' French presence would bring 'obvious' military advantages and 'added security' to Britain's own West African possessions. The danger was to accept 'an unlimited liability in a theatre which is not vital to the prosecution of the war'.

The Chiefs of Staff concluded, and so informed Churchill, that, if further reports showed 'reasonable prospects of success', and provided de Gaulle's plan did not involve Britain in a 'considerable military commitment', they recommended 'that the expedition should be undertaken'. But if the reports were 'unfavourable', or it looked as if Britain would be involved in considerable military commitment, 'we recommend that the expedition should not be launched', but that Britain should seek a *'modus vivendi'* with the local French administration in each Colony, 'and endeavour to avoid an open breach with the Vichy Government on the Colonial issue'.[2]

This was not the decisive support for action for which Churchill had hoped, and when at eleven o'clock that night, he presided over a meeting of the Chiefs of Staff Committee,[3] the dissension was open. While the meeting was in progress, Colville arrived at Downing Street to find, as he noted in his diary, Churchill 'rending the Chiefs of Staff, who are being unsympathetic about Operation Scipio'. Colville added: 'He is rather determined to help the Free French.'[4]

'After a full discussion,' the War Cabinet's historical survey noted

---

[1] Those present were Newall, Pound, and Dill, as well as representatives of the Admiralty (Captain G. A. French), the Air Ministry (Wing-Commander W. L. Dawson) and the War Office (Major G. K. Bourne).

[2] Chiefs of Staff, 252nd Meeting of 1940, 7 August 1940, 3.30 p.m., Annex II, 'Operations in West Africa, Minute to the Prime Minister from the Chiefs of Staff': Cabinet papers, 79/6, folios 26–31.

[3] As well as Churchill, Newall, Dill, Phillips and Ismay. Lord Beaverbrook was also present at this meeting.

[4] Colville diary, 7 August 1940: Colville papers.

briefly, 'it was agreed that the only really effective place to land General de Gaulle's force was Dakar.'[1] During the meeting, Churchill had given as his considered opinion that, despite the earlier War Cabinet caveat, the expedition 'should have sufficient backing by British forces to ensure its success'.[2]

Yet another plan was now to be prepared, with British military as well as naval involvement, and in the early hours of August 8 Churchill set out for the Chiefs of Staff Committee the scope of the new plan as he saw it, and the reasons for this greater British involvement. There was, he pointed out, evidence of 'the danger of German influence spreading quickly' through French West Africa, 'with the connivance or aid of the Vichy Government'. Unless Britain were to act 'with celerity and vigour', Churchill warned, 'we may find effective U-boat bases, supported by German aviation, all down this coast, and it will become barred to us but available for the Germans in the same way as the Western coast of Europe'.

For this reason, Churchill argued, it seemed 'extremely important to British interests' that de Gaulle should take Dakar 'at the earliest possible moment', if peaceably 'so much the better', but if by fighting, then with an 'adequate' force of both Polish and British, as well as Free French troops. De Gaulle should be used, he explained, 'to impart a French character' to the expedition, 'and of course, once successful, his administration will rule'.

A plan should be prepared 'forthwith', Churchill wrote, and dates arranged. But he went on to stress the limitations of the operation as far as ultimate British involvement was concerned, telling the Chiefs of Staff:

It is not intended, after Dakar is taken, that we shall hold it with British forces. General de Gaulle's administration would be set up, and would have to maintain itself, British assistance being limited to supplies on a moderate scale, and of course preventing any seaborne expedition from Germanized France. Should de Gaulle be unable to maintain himself permanently against Air attack or air-borne troops, we will take him off again after destroying all harbour facilities. We should of course in any case take over under the French flag *Richelieu* and have her repaired. The Poles and the Belgians would also have their gold recovered for them.[3]

[1] War Cabinet, 'The Dakar Operation', 'Secret', Hist. (A)1. (Revise), 5 February 1941: Premier papers, 3/276.
[2] Chiefs of Staff, 253rd Meeting of 1940, 7 August 1940, 11 p.m.: Cabinet papers, 79/6, folios 32-3.
[3] This gold had been taken to France for safety during the fall of Poland and of Belgium respectively, and had been transferred for safety to Dakar as France herself fell.

In working out the Dakar plan, Churchill added, 'time is vital'. Too much had been lost already. As for the risk of a declaration of war by Vichy France, this was 'reserved for the Cabinet'.[1]

A hopeful signal had reached London on August 8 from the Commander-in-Chief South Atlantic, who reported that the British Military Liaison Officer with the Fleet had 'indications' that the demobilisation of the Dakar garrison had taken place, that supplies were getting short, and that 'if the fort was silenced there is every possibility a determined attack by smaller force would be successful'.[2] Having studied this message, and Churchill's minute, the Chiefs of Staff instructed the Joint Planning Sub-Committee to prepare a plan of the new operation. This plan was submitted to the Chiefs of Staff on the afternoon of August 9.[3] An 'assault by destroyers', Pound told his colleagues, was 'worth trying' in order to eliminate resistance from the *Richelieu*. As for using British troops, the Chiefs of Staff wished 'to emphasise the point' that the operation 'must be carried out by highly trained British forces', while de Gaulle's force 'must be kept below the horizon until our forces have taken control of the town and he can enter the harbour unopposed'. The expedition should be under British command. Undertaking it would temporarily rule out seizing the Azores, as Britain had 'neither the trained forces nor the equipment for both'.

Churchill's hopes had now been approved. Only on one detail did the Chiefs of Staff enter a caveat: they opposed the inclusion of Polish forces in the expedition, as they 'could not be trained in time', as it was politically 'undesirable to mix the French and Poles', and as it was understood that General de Gaulle 'does not want to have the Poles associated with his project'.[4]

Britain's first sea-borne invasion of the war was now in preparation; an offensive action such as Churchill had so wanted to see. Operation 'Menace', as the enlarged and extended 'Scipio' became, was from August 9 an authorized operation of war. It was to be based upon the landing of six separate parties at dawn—after about a month's prepara-

---

[1] Minute to Ismay from the Chiefs of Staff Committee, 8 August 1940: Cabinet papers, 79/6, folios 34-5.

[2] Signal No. 1324 of 8 August 1940, sent 1.24 p.m., received 8.58 p.m.: Cabinet papers, 79/6, folio 58.

[3] Those present were Newall (in the Chair), Pound, Major-General R. H. Dewing (representing the Chief of the Imperial General Staff), and Ismay. Also present were Captain G. A. French (Admiralty), Wing-Commander W. L. Dawson (Air Ministry) and Lieutenant-Colonel R. N. Gale (War Office).

[4] Chiefs of Staff Committee No. 257 of 1940, 9 August 1940, 4.30 p.m.: Cabinet papers, 79/6, folios 54-6.

tion—and was intended to achieve its success by thus dispersing the efforts of the defenders. Both the naval and military commanders, Vice-Admiral J. H. D. Cunningham and Major-General N. M. S. Irwin, were chosen on August 10, and the War Cabinet's approval was given three days later, when Churchill stressed the 'immense advantage' of getting de Gaulle 'firmly installed on French territory'.

During the War Cabinet, Attlee raised the question of 'the next step', and asked whether, if Dakar was taken, Britain might not then 'send the Expedition on and try to get control of the Cameroons'. This might indeed be 'the next step', said Churchill, or de Gaulle might hope 'to get a footing in Algiers'.[1]

The new plan was now approved. But few were to be allowed to know of its extended scope. As Churchill had minuted to Ismay and Bridges on August 11: 'The plan Scipio as originally conceived, namely, of de Gaulle getting at it by peaceable means from behind, is the sole plan which is to be imparted to any others but the War Cabinet and the Service Ministers and Chiefs. Knowledge of later developments is to be confined exclusively to the above, neither Minister of Information, nor Dominions Secretary nor Home Secretary being burdened with it.'[2] These Ministers were Duff Cooper, Lord Caldecote and Sir John Anderson.

From the moment that the expanded Dakar plan had been approved by the Chiefs of Staff, Churchill's mood became more buoyant. On August 10, while still at Chequers, and three days before the War Cabinet was to give its formal agreement, Churchill drafted a message for the Prime Ministers of Australia and New Zealand, to assure them that if Japan, 'contrary to prudence and self-interest', were to embark on an invasion of Australia or New Zealand 'on a large scale', then 'I have the explicit authority of the Cabinet to assure you that we should then cut our losses in the Mediterranean and sacrifice every interest, except only the defence and feeding of this Island, on which all depends, and would proceed in good time to your aid with a fleet able to give battle to any Japanese force which could be placed in Australian waters, and able to parry any invading force, or certainly cut its communications with Japan'.

Churchill then set out for the Australian and New Zealand Prime

[1] War Cabinet No. 225 of 1940, 13 August 1940, 12 noon, Minute 6, Confidential Annex: Cabinet papers, 65/14.
[2] Minute of 11 August 1940: Churchill papers, 20/13.

Ministers the strength, as he saw it, of Britain's position. The Royal Air Force had continued to show its 'individual superiority over the enemy'. Lord Beaverbrook had made 'astounding progress' in the production of 'the best machines'. Britain's fighter and bomber strength was 'nearly double' what it had been in mid-July. 'I do not think,' Churchill added, 'the German Air Force has the numbers or quality to overpower our air defences.' The Royal Navy was increasing in strength each month. The German Navy was 'weaker than it has ever been'. For Hitler to try to transport his army successfully to meet Britain's 'powerful force' on shore, and to maintain his own army with munitions and stores, would be 'a very unreasonable act'. Britain possessed 'several armoured divisions or brigades ready to strike in counter-attack at the head of any successful lodgments'. Yet if Hitler failed to invade and conquer Britain before the weather broke, 'he has received his first and probably fatal check'.[1]

This optimistic panorama ended on a note of confidence. 'We therefore feel,' Churchill wrote, 'a sober and growing conviction of our power to defend ourselves successfully, and to persevere through the year or two that may be necessary to gain victory.'[2]

It was to take more than four and a half years to gain that victory. Churchill had no illusions about the difficulties ahead, however confident in tone his telegrams to distant lands. 'It seems to me,' he minuted on a paper by Stafford Cripps on August 10 at Chequers, 'that the ideas set forth by Sir S. Cripps upon the post-war position of the British Empire are far too airy and speculative to be useful at the present moment, when we have to win the war in order to survive.' At lunch that day Churchill told his guests that there was 'only one aim, to destroy Hitler'.[3]

The most recent Intelligence reports, including the gleanings from Enigma, made it clear that a German invasion was unlikely in the next two weeks.[4] Not surprisingly, that Saturday at Chequers, Churchill

---

[1] Reading this sentence, Eden wrote to Churchill, of his 'very stimulating message': 'I do not wish to be pernickety, but I am rather apprehensive lest the account we are giving of our military reserves in this country should lead Australia and New Zealand to think that we are stronger than the facts warrant. You speak, for instance, of several armoured divisions or brigades ready to strike in counter attack. We have not, unhappily, one complete armoured division in this country, though we might say with some truth that we have several armoured formations. I would not like Australia and New Zealand to feel that we are unduly selfish in keeping so much of this great armoured power at home.' (Letter of 13 August 1940: Premier papers, 4/43B/1, folio 215.)

[2] Telegram drafted on 10 August 1940, despatched on the following day: Premier papers, 4/43B/1, folios 219–25.

[3] Colville diary, 10 August 1940: Colville papers.

[4] Sir Alexander Cadogan noted in his diary that same day, 10 August 1940, that Colonel

was 'in the best of humours', as Colville noted, talking brilliantly 'on every topic from Ruskin to Lord Baldwin'. Among the guests that night were two Generals, Gordon-Finlayson and Pownall, as well as Professor Lindemann, and Colonel Jacob. Churchill's mood was still, as Colville wrote, 'very friendly and garrulous', as he compared himself 'to a farmer driving pigs along a road, who always had to be prodding them on and preventing them from straying'.

That evening Churchill praised 'the splendid sang froid and morale' of the British people, 'and could not quite see', as Colville wrote, 'why he was so popular'. After all, Churchill told his guests, in the three months since he had come to power 'everything had gone wrong, and he had nothing but disasters to pronounce'. His platform, Churchill added, 'was only blood, sweat and tears'.[1]

Later that evening Churchill held a three hour conference with Pownall and Gordon-Finlayson—the newly appointed General Officer Commanding Western Command—on the problems and tasks of the Home Guard in the event of invasion.[2] Then, as evening turned into night, he studied the latest production charts of new aircraft, calling on Lindemann for frequent explanations, and commenting, as the scale of the increase in the supply of new aircraft became clear, that Beaver-brook, the man responsible, 'had genius, and also brutal ruthlessness'.

It was nearly midnight: 'we walked up and down beneath the stars, a habit which Winston has formed', Colville noted in his diary.[3] But Churchill's energies had not yet been exhausted, and the presence of Gordon-Finlayson, who had recently returned from commanding the troops in Egypt, gave Churchill the opportunity to obtain a first-hand account of the problems of the Western Desert, and the defence of Egypt. Colonel Jacob later wrote of this, his first visit to Chequers, that at 2.30 a.m., after an 'interesting discussion of all this', Churchill asked Gordon-Finlayson 'to put his views down on paper'. Then Churchill went to bed. Jacob's account continued:

We walked upstairs and dispersed. Almost immediately the General sought me out and asked whether I had a map of the Western Desert, as he couldn't

---

Menzies 'came in for a talk' at the Foreign Office, and 'says his "best source" expects nothing this month' (David Dilks, editor, *The Diaries of Sir Alexander Cadogan, OM, 1938–1945*, London 1971, page 320). Cadogan was aware of Enigma (see page 896 n.2).

[1] Colville diary, 10 August 1940: Colville papers.
[2] Minute to Eden, 11 August 1940: Churchill papers, 20/13.
[3] Colville diary, 10 August 1940: Colville papers.

write what he wanted to do without one. I said I hadn't, but that I would get the War Office to send one down first thing in the morning. I then groped my way downstairs again to the Private Secretaries' room to telephone to the War Office. There were a good many telephones there, and it was rather dark. Eventually I picked one up and unfortunately pressed the central knob. Almost at once a voice said, 'What is that? Is there any news?' I realised that it was the Prime Minister and apologised. He said, 'Well, please don't do it again, I was just dropping off.'

It cannot have been 'more than five minutes', Jacob noted, since Churchill had left his guests downstairs to go to bed. Yet he was already nearly asleep.[1]

There were a number of inter-departmental disputes to be dealt with while Churchill was at Chequers, including the conflict of authority between Bevin as Minister of Labour and two other Ministers, the First Lord, A. V. Alexander, and Beaverbrook, the Minister of Aircraft Production. Bevin had sought the main authority for the allocation of labour, and wished for a formal document to this effect. Both Alexander and Beaverbrook had protested. Churchill's advice to Bevin, sent on August 10, explained that there would be 'great difficulties' in any 'rigid rules' such as Bevin had suggested. The Ministry of Aircraft Production was unlikely to agree, Churchill explained, while the Admiralty could never allow themselves 'to be cut off from all right to deal with the great staffs they control'. Churchill's letter continued: 'Naturally your office takes the lead, and you would be the chief authority. If, however, the other Departments demur, the matter could only be settled by the Cabinet.'[2] The Cabinet, not Churchill, would have to be the final arbiter.

A further issue in Churchill's box that weekend concerned the possibility of labour unrest among coal miners confronted with a drastic fall in demand. This matter was being dealt with by the Minister of Mines, David Grenfell, a senior Labour Party figure, and himself a former miner, who had written to Churchill of the problems, and of the miners' response. Churchill replied to Grenfell from Chequers:

The tremendous upset in your plans due to the collapse of France and the loss of three-quarters of our export markets must have put a great strain on

---

[1] Essay by Lieutenant-General Sir Ian Jacob: Sir John Wheeler-Bennett (editor), *Action This Day, Working with Churchill*, London 1968, page 180.

[2] 'Private', 10 August 1940: Churchill papers, 4/201.

your Department. It must be very difficult after all your efforts to increase production to explain the sudden slump, but I have no doubt the men will understand.

'Indeed,' Churchill added, 'what you tell me about the fortitude of the Kent miners is an encouraging sign of the spirit which I believe informs all the working men in this country.'[1]

Churchill remained at Chequers on Sunday August 11. During that day, another German air raid was reported, the first for three days, and Colville was instructed to telephone continuously to London for the 'score'. Churchill, as he noted in his diary, was 'very excited', commenting that 'the swine had needed three days in which to lick their wounds before they came again'. He was much relieved to feel that Germany's air superiority was 'less than we had feared'.

That afternoon Churchill left Chequers briefly for a nearby rifle range, firing a rifle at 200, 300 and 400 yards, and also firing a revolver 'with considerable accuracy' as Colville noted, 'while smoking a cigar'. He also gave his view that the 'best way of killing Huns' was to use snub-nosed bullets. Randolph, who was present, protested that such bullets were illegal in war, but Churchill commented that as the Germans would make 'very short shrift' of him if they caught him, he did not see why he should have 'any mercy on them'.

That night both Beaverbrook and Bevin dined at Chequers, and stayed the night. Churchill was again in genial mood, telling Colville that Bevin was 'a good old thing, with the right stuff in him and no defeatist tendencies'. Reflecting on the day's air battle, during which seventy[2] German aircraft had been reported shot down over the Channel, Churchill expatiated 'on the debt we owed to our airmen' and claimed that the life of Britain depended on their intrepid spirit. 'What a slender thread,' he then exclaimed, his voice tremulous with emotion, 'the greatest of things can hang by.'[3]

Churchill returned to London from Chequers on the morning of August 12. That same day a German Military Intelligence Officer, Paul Thümmel, who had been an agent of Czech Intelligence before the war, and who now reported direct to London, sent a message that there would be no German invasion of Britain for at least two weeks,

[1] Letter of 11 August 1940: Churchill papers, 4/201. Grenfell, a Labour MP since 1922, had worked underground from the age of twelve to the age of thirty-five.

[2] Later amended to 62 (War Cabinet of 12 August 1940).

[3] Colville diary, 11 August 1940: Colville papers. One of Churchill's favourite quotations on this theme was Byron's haunting refrain, 'A thousand years scarce serve to form a State, an hour can lay it in the dust.'

and that it might 'even be three weeks' before the expeditionary forces assembled in Paris, Brussels and the Hague could be ready at their ports and airfields.[1] Also on August 12, an Enigma decrypt revealed that thirty men 'with a perfect knowledge of English' were being transferred to a particular German Air Force commander who had been active in providing close support during the conquest of France.[2]

Invasion was clearly still a possibility, and every day's delay was a day gained for further preparations. Small arms ammunition, General Brooke was able to report on August 12, had now been issued on a considerably increased scale for training purposes, and this 'should have a reassuring psychological effect on the men in the front line'.[3]

At the War Cabinet on August 12, Churchill and his colleagues learned that the 62 German aircraft shot down that Sunday had involved 25 British losses. Even as this report was made, a further air battle was in progress over Portsmouth.[4] That evening, at a meeting of the Defence Committee, Churchill pressed for the production of anti-aircraft weapons 'in large numbers' and for a review of the whole anti-aircraft weapon production programme, to ensure that the weapons easiest to supply quickly were given priority. New developments should be put into production, the Committee agreed, without waiting for 'unessential improvements' in design.[5]

At ten o'clock that night Churchill met again in conference with Wavell, together with Eden, A. V. Alexander, Dill, Newall, Pound and Ismay, in the Cabinet room at Downing Street. 'A very long and exhausting sitting,' Eden noted in his diary after the meeting broke up at 2 a.m.[6] The subject was the despatch of reinforcements to the Middle East. Wavell wished to have them sent around the Cape, to avoid the dangers of the Mediterranean. He was supported by Pound, who believed the chances of a convoy getting through the Mediterranean unscathed were 'remote'. Not only might the supply ships be lost, but

[1] Air Ministry papers, 40/1637. Thümmel was probably the only German Intelligence Officer who collaborated directly with the Allied Intelligence organisations. His code name was A.54.

[2] Both the Enigma decrypt and Paul Thümmel are referred to in: F. H. Hinsley and others, *British Intelligence in the Second World War, Its Influence on Strategy and Operations*, volume one, London 1975, pages 58, 183 and 184.

[3] Chiefs of Staff Committee No. 260 of 1940, 12 August 1940, 10.15 a.m.: Cabinet papers, 79/6.

[4] War Cabinet No. 225 of 1940, 12 August 1940, 12.30 p.m.: Cabinet papers, 65/8.

[5] Defence Committee (Supply) No. 15 of 1940, 12 August 1940, 7 p.m.: Cabinet papers, 70/1. The three Ministers present were Churchill (in the Chair), Beaverbrook (Aircraft Production), and Herbert Morrison (Supply). Others present included Lindemann, Morton and Jacob (the Committee's Secretary), as well as senior officers from the Ministry of Supply, War Office and Admiralty.

[6] Diary entry for 12 August 1940, quoted in: The Earl of Avon, *The Eden Memoirs, The Reckoning*, London 1965, page 131.

the warships convoying them would 'sustain damage'. The risk of losing his supplies, said Wavell, would not justify the 'gain in time' of the shorter route. Churchill's instinct was to challenge what he called the Admiralty's 'unduly pessimistic view of the risks involved'. In his opinion, 'it should be possible to pass a convoy of three fast ships through to Egypt without great difficulty'. Such a move should even act as a 'bait' to draw Italian naval units and thus give the British their 'desired opportunity to inflict serious damage upon the Italian Navy'.

Having expressed his hopes, Churchill deferred to the Admiralty view, feeling 'bound', as he expressed it, 'to accept the opinion of the Naval Staff although he was not in agreement with it'.[1] But this acquiesence did not last long, for on the following morning Churchill told the War Cabinet that he was now 'trying to persuade' the Chiefs of Staff 'to change their view on this matter'.[2] During August 13 Churchill also pondered what he considered to be Wavell's undue caution, not merely on the issue of the convoy, but of style and character. 'I am favourably impressed with General Wavell in many ways,' Churchill wrote to Eden on August 13, 'but I do not feel in him that sense of mental vigour and resolve to overcome obstacles, which is indispensable to successful war.' Instead, Churchill added, he found 'tame acceptance of a variety of local circumstances in different theatres, which is leading to a lamentable lack of concentration upon the decisive point'.

For Churchill, that decisive point was the defence of Egypt against the 'impending' Italian attack. 'Pray do not forget,' he told Eden, 'that the loss of Alexandria means the end of British sea power in the Eastern Mediterranean, with all its consequences.'[3]

Eden defended Wavell's caution, pointing out with much specific detail the General's considerable shortage of 'all the weapons which go to make up a modern force'. Eden added, in a handwritten note at the end of his letter:

Dill and I were much perturbed at your judgment of Wavell. Neither of us know of any General Officer in the army better qualified to fill this very difficult post at this critical time. As you know, we have made changes in almost every command, and I am sure that you will believe me when I write that I should not hesitate for a moment to ask you to agree if I thought that a change was called for in the Middle East. I still hope that our conversation

[1] Defence Committee (Operations) No. 25 of 1940, 12 August 1940, 10 p.m.: Cabinet papers, 69/1.
[2] War Cabinet No. 225 of 1940, 13 August 1940, 12 noon, Minute 7, Confidential Annex: Cabinet papers, 65/14.
[3] 'Secret and Personal', 13 August 1940: Churchill papers, 20/2.

tomorrow will enable you finally to remove any lack of confidence you may have felt in Wavell.

Eden and Dill saw Churchill again that evening, to try to impress upon him 'that equipment rather than man-power was the key to the situation', and to support Wavell's specific plans. But Churchill took the view, Eden noted, that Wavell was 'a good average colonel', who would make a 'good chairman of a Tory association'.[1]

As the dispute over Wavell continued, Colville noted in his diary that Churchill was 'very much on edge', concerned as he was with the 'quickest methods of sending reinforcements to the Near East before the expected attack on Egypt'. At the same time, not having had his usual afternoon sleep, he was not in the 'best' of tempers. Nor was Wavell the only cause for his anger. It was very difficult, he told Colville on their way back from the Admiralty War Room that afternoon, 'to make these fellows be sensible about sending troops through the Mediterranean. They were so confoundedly cautious.'[2]

The news on August 14 combined hope and danger. In the air seventy-eight German aircraft had been 'destroyed for certain', for the loss of only three British pilots. But from Africa came news of a military 'disaster' in Somaliland, where Italian forces had defeated the British, making it certain, as Colville noted, that 'the blow against Egypt can hardly be long delayed'.[3] That same evening, however, there was one item of news that transcended all others; a personal message from Roosevelt, to Churchill, agreeing to send the British Government at least fifty destroyers, motor torpedo boats and aircraft, as 'immediate assistance'.[4]

Roosevelt set out two conditions to the deal, which Churchill explained to the War Cabinet that evening. If the waters around Britain became 'untenable', the ships must not be turned over to Germany, or sunk, but sent to other parts of the Empire; and Britain must authorize the use of Newfoundland, Bermuda, the Bahamas, certain West Indian islands and British Guiana as naval and air bases by the United States in the event of an attack on the American hemisphere 'by any non-American nation'.

[1] Eden to Churchill, 13 August 1940, and Eden diary, entry for 13 August 1940, quoted in: The Earl of Avon, *The Eden Memoirs, The Reckoning*, London 1965, pages 131–2.
[2] On 15 August 1940 that caution was turned into policy, and finally accepted by Churchill, when the War Cabinet agreed with Dill and Wavell that an Italian attack was not imminent, and that therefore the convoys with Wavell's reinforcements should go around the Cape (War Cabinet No. 228 of 1940, 15 August 1940, 12 noon, Confidential Annex: Cabinet papers, 65/14).
[3] Colville diary, 14 August 1940: Colville papers.
[4] Telegram sent at 6 p.m., 13 August 1940: Premier papers, 3/468.

These conditions were both acceptable, in view of what was at stake. Once the destroyer deal went through, Churchill told the War Cabinet, the United States would have made 'a long step towards coming into the war on our side'.[1]

This had always been, and was to remain, Churchill's hope of victory. However fierce the air battle, however imminent invasion, however weak the British military position in Egypt, however bad the news from Somaliland or any other distant theatre of war, however risky any particular proposed operation, whether the sending of supplies through the Mediterranean or the Dakar landing, this United States commitment, so urgently pressed for and so long awaited, was the ultimate triumph of British policy. When Colville, the junior Private Secretary, commented critically that Roosevelt's condition for the deal 'rather smacks of Russian demands on Finland', Churchill replied: 'The worth of every Destroyer is measured in rubies.'[2] Churchill repeated this phrase on the following day, in thanking Roosevelt for his 'untiring efforts to give us all possible help'. Yet even at this moment of euphoria, Churchill continued to press for yet more help. Flying boats and rifles were also urgently needed, he told Roosevelt, and he added: 'We have a million men waiting for rifles.'[3]

There was additional cause for anxiety, from the trans-Atlantic perspective, as General Pakenham-Walsh found during the first days of his mission to the United States in search of urgent supplies of heavy guns and tanks. Pakenham-Walsh had arrived in Washington on August 12, his arm in a sling as a result of his wound at Dunkirk, only to discover 'a doubt in the capability of Britain to survive', and the United States 'shy of starting production of weapons for a country which might "go under" at any moment'.[4]

---

[1] War Cabinet No. 227 of 1940, 14 August 1940, 6.30 p.m.: Cabinet papers, 65/8.

[2] Colville diary, 14 August 1940: Colville papers. But Churchill realized, all too well, as he telegraphed to Lord Lothian, that any public announcement of these conditions would have a 'disastrous effect' on British morale. (Telegram of 14 August 1940: Premier papers, 3/462/2/3.)

[3] Telegram sent at 1 a.m., 15 August 1940: Premier papers, 3/462/2/3.

[4] Premier papers, 3/493.

36

'Never in the field of human conflict . . .'

D URING the second week of August 1,419 civilians had been killed during German air raids, 1,286 of them in London. These figures, circulated to the War Cabinet, were withheld from the public according to the War Cabinet's decision.[1]

On August 14 German aircraft attacked Southampton and Hastings. That same day three Blenheims and a Spitfire were destroyed on the ground.[2] During the morning Churchill learned that 526 Biritish pilots had been killed in action in June and July. A total of 4,596 young men were at that very moment training to be pilots. The urgent need now was for aircraft on which pilots could be trained.[3]

In the air, the battle intensified. On August 15 a hundred German bombers attacked shipping, ports, aerodromes, aircraft factories and Air Force installations throughout Tyneside, while a further eight hundred German aircraft sought to pin down Britain's fighters in the South. Yet Britain's confidence in surviving was 'enormously and legitimately strengthened', Churchill had informed Roosevelt in his telegram sent in the early hours of August 15, 'by the severe air fighting in the past week'. The 'spirit of our people', Churchill declared, 'is splendid. Never have they been so determined.'[4]

---

[1] Cabinet papers, 120/464. On September 15 Churchill asked Colonel Jacob how many service personnel had been among those killed during these air raids. Jacob replied two days later that 79 service personnel were among the 1,286 dead (Minute of 17 September 1940: Cabinet papers, 120/464).

[2] In all, more than a hundred British aircraft were destroyed on the ground in ten days ('RAF aircraft destroyed on the ground as a result of enemy action in the United Kingdom from 8th to 18th August, 1940', 'Most Secret': Cherwell papers, G.9).

[3] Defence Committee (Operations), 14 August 1940, 10.15 a.m.: Cabinet papers, 69/1.

[4] Telegram of 15 August 1940: Premier papers, 3/462/2, 3.

At the risk of a substantial increase in stress and danger in the South, Sir Hugh Dowding had, on his own strategic insight, earlier transferred seven squadrons of fighters from the South to the North. Now, in the battle above Tyneside, this courageous decision was rewarded, as thirty German bombers were shot down, for a cost of only two injured British pilots. In the South, all twenty-two British squadrons were engaged in the diversionary battle. Forty-six German aircraft were shot down, for a loss of twenty-four British fighters. That evening, as news of the different engagements came in to Downing Street, Churchill was 'consumed with excitement', Colville noted in his diary.[1] The details of the battle were still unclear. Eden, who had been to see Churchill about the Middle East, later recalled how:

... our business over, I sat on in the Cabinet room with him while reports came in of the air battle which was developing. Squadron after squadron of the Royal Air Force went up to engage the enemy and still the Luftwaffe kept coming. The news was scrappy at first and still more squadrons were called for, until it seemed that they had all been committed. As we listened and conjectured, things looked very stern, with the odds heavy against us.[2]

Churchill now decided to go himself to Fighter Command headquarters at Stanmore. On his return to Downing Street he reported 'over a hundred' German aircraft shot down,[3] and instructed Colville to telephone Neville Chamberlain to tell him the news. Chamberlain, at first 'somewhat cold at being disturbed at dinner', was 'overcome with joy' when he heard the news, and 'very touched' at the Prime Minister thinking of him. Colville noted: 'It is typical of Winston to do a small thing like this which could give such pleasure.'

'The Lord President is very grateful to you,' Colville reported.

'So he ought to be,' Churchill replied, 'it is one of the greatest days in history.'

That evening Churchill dictated a minute to Eden and Dill on the forthcoming operations in the Middle East; 'the first time', Colville noted, 'I have seen his long experience as a strategist and student of war put into effect with such rapidity and confidence'.[4] The theme of Churchill's minute, intended as a directive for Wavell, was that the defence of Egypt was paramount. Even the Somaliland evacuation could be put to good use, Churchill believed, by sending the evacuated troops to where they were most needed. Polish and French troops

[1] Colville diary, 15 August 1940: Colville papers.
[2] The Earl of Avon, *The Eden Memoirs, The Reckoning*, London 1965, page 137.
[3] In fact, 76, in itself a staggering total.
[4] Colville diary, 15 August 1940: Colville papers. For the directive as finally sent to Wavell eight days later, see pages 755–6.

should be sent from the Nile Delta to Palestine, for 'internal security', thus liberating six battalions of Australian troops then in Palestine for service in Egypt. With other deployments which he listed, including troops from South Africa and New Zealand, Churchill envisaged an 'Army of the Delta' made up of a total of 56,000 men and 212 heavy guns, in place by October 1 'at the latest' for the defence of Egypt. The Delta must meanwhile be fortified, he wrote, and inundations prepared, to 'await the Italian invasion'.[1]

As the air battle intensified, Churchill's 'favourite port of call', as Ismay later wrote, was the Operations Room of No. 11 Group, Fighter Command, the 'nerve centre from which he could follow the whole course of the air battle'. It was here that he went on August 16, when both Chatham and Kenley were hit. As Ismay recalled:

There had been heavy fighting throughout the afternoon; and at one moment every single squadron in the Group was engaged; there was nothing in reserve, and the map table showed new waves of attackers crossing the coast. I felt sick with fear. As the evening closed in the fighting died down, and we left by car for Chequers. Churchill's first words were: 'Don't speak to me; I have never been so moved.' After about five minutes he leaned forward and said, 'Never in the field of human conflict has so much been owed by so many to so few.' The words burned into my brain and I repeated them to my wife when I got home.

'Churchill too,' Ismay reflected, 'had evidently photographed them in his mind.'[2]

During the day, forty-seven British aircraft, including seven heavy bombers, had been destroyed on the ground at Brize Norton, six at Tangmere, three at Harwell, three at Thorney and one at West Malling.[3] At the same time, as Colville noted, Beaverbrook had seemed 'a

[1] Prime Minister's Minute to Eden and Dill, M.15, 15 August 1940, 'General Directive for Commander-in-Chief, Middle East': Churchill papers, 20/13. On the following night Sir John Reith dined with Dill, noting in his diary: 'He sees no hope in the Middle East and is afraid Egypt will be overrun also. There are 250,000 white Italian troops in those parts and 50,000 British. "Does it make sense?" he said, and it does not. He clearly was in favour of making friends with Germany years ago, as I have always been. How right. And equally wrong therefore the present PM who urged preparations for war against Germany. Churchill now cashes in on this whereas it is all part of the wrongness. There is no doubt what Dill feels about Churchill and the present regime or rather *galère*.' (Reith diary, 16 August 1940: Charles Stuart, editor, *The Reith Diaries*, London 1975, page 261.)

[2] *The Memoirs of General the Lord Ismay*, London 1960, pages 179-80.

[3] Cherwell papers. On the following day Churchill minuted to Newall: 'While our eyes are concentrated on the results of the air fighting over this country we must not overlook the serious losses occurring in the Bomber Command. Seven heavy bombers last night and also 21 aircraft destroyed now on the ground—the bulk at Tangmere—Total 28. These 28, added to the 22 fighters, makes our loss 50 on the day, and very much alters the picture presented by the

little blue', telling Churchill that the Germans 'were concentrating on his aircraft factories'.[1]

Churchill was also concerned about defences beyond the battle zone, minuting to Ismay on August 17: 'What is the condition of the Northern Aerodromes?'[2] It was Colonel Hollis who at once followed up this question, reporting back that each of the northern aerodromes had a small military guard, a Royal Air Force guard, and other Royal Air Force personnel 'trained as riflemen available in emergency and armed with a proportion of rifles'. In addition, there were 'in all cases' units of Home Forces 'within easy reach of the aerodromes and available for counter attack'. But two aerodromes were as yet not 'adequately protected': at these, Hollis assured Churchill, defence personnel and rifles were 'being increased'.[3]

Churchill knew that he could rely upon the staff of his Defence Office not only to follow up each of his queries, but to act upon them where action was needed. In this instance, as in so many others, no further intervention from him was needed: the smooth and effective working of the machine was already a central factor of his control, and of action.

That weekend, at Chequers, John Martin noted in his diary: 'Another hot, bright weekend. Ismay and Lindemann also here. Also at dinner Duncan and Diana Sandys, Lord Beaverbrook, Air Marshal Portal and Brendan Bracken,' and he added: 'German plane overhead after midnight.'[4]

One hopeful message to reach Churchill during this Chequers weekend came from Sir Arthur Salter, who reported a trans-Atlantic telephone conversation that evening with Arthur Purvis. According to Purvis, if the destroyer negotiations 'were going well from our side', he thought it 'highly opportune and highly important', as Salter reported, 'that we should simultaneously (a) revive our request for the additional 250,000 rifles which we just failed to get in June (b) revive our requests for motor torpedo-boats and flying boats, and should increase the numbers asked for'. Britain had asked for twenty torpedo boats, Salter recalled, 'for which the prospect seemed good till we encountered the

---

German loss of 75.' (Prime Minister's Personal Minute, M.18, 17 August 1940: Churchill papers, 20/13.)

[1] Colville diary, 16 August 1940: Colville papers.

[2] Prime Minister's Personal Minute, D.8, 17 August 1940: Premier papers, 3/4/1, folio 269.

[3] 'Secret', 24 August 1940: Premier papers, 3/4/1, folio 268. The two aerodromes needing extra protection were Edzell and Evanton.

[4] Martin diary, 17 August 1940: Martin papers.

same obstacle as in the case of the destroyers', and for 100 flying boats. Salter added: 'Mr Purvis is in intimate association with the highest authorities concerned in the American Administration and his advice certainly means that if we *immediately* make the further requests he suggests, we have an excellent chance of succeeding.'

In a second trans-Altantic call later that same evening, Purvis had added that, 'if the 200 Curtis P.40 fighters which we tried to get before are regarded as absolutely vital, it might perhaps be worth while to add them to our request'. Purvis warned, however, 'that they would prove much more difficult and he thought we should not go for them unless we consider them really vital—and not in any case rely on getting them'.[1]

From Chequers, having studied these two messages, Churchill minuted to Bridges: 'Pray have a telegram drafted after this question has been discussed with the Service authorities concerned.' Churchill added: 'I see no reason why we should not ask for all we want, provided there is a reasonable chance of getting it.'[2]

The United States connection was both vital and fragile: there was therefore welcome news in a second minute from Salter on the following day, reporting a further item of his telephone conversation with Purvis. As Salter reported, 'Mr Purvis also asked me to let you know that Colonel Donovan was most impressed with the welcome which was accorded to him here, and particularly with the extent to which we had disclosed secret information to him.' As a result of this, Purvis declared, 'Colonel Donovan was working with great energy in our interest. We now had a firm friend in the Republican camp and this was proving of immense value.' Donovan had also asked Purvis to let Churchill know 'how deeply he appreciated the way in which he had been treated here'.[3]

While at Chequers, Churchill also studied an Air Ministry request for the manufacture of 8,000 Parachute and Cable Defence rockets a month, for airfield defence. Sinclair had broached this requirement to Beaverbrook, stressing that it was a substantial reduction from the 60,000 a month originally requested of this 'distress' type rocket, with its wire and parachute suspension.

Churchill questioned the need for even the reduced number. 'I am very doubtful about the PAC rockets,' he minuted to Sinclair on August 17, and he went on to explain: 'They are one of many suggestions which we took up at the Admiralty at the time when our small ships

---

[1] Minute of 16 August 1940: Cabinet papers, 115/83.
[2] Prime Minister's Personal Minute, C.2, 17 August 1940: Cabinet papers, 115/83.
[3] 'Secret', 17 August 1940: Cabinet papers, 115/83.

were being attacked on the East Coast, and we had nothing to put in them. I do not think they would be suitable for regular use; certainly it would be a great mistake to use up the wire which is needed for the aerial mines.' Even the figure of 8,000 a month 'appears to me', Churchill wrote, 'to be altogether excessive'. The supply of this particular rocket, Churchill added, should be 'brought to a close in the course of the next month or six weeks, with a minimum waste of material already assigned to it'.[1]

Sinclair defended the Air Ministry's use of these rockets, and within a week Churchill had arranged to see a demonstration, after which he rescinded his original request to bring the production of the rocket to a close. As he later minuted to Sinclair, in giving way to the Air Ministry's decision:

I visited Kenley on Thursday,[2] saw the gunner in question and had a rocket fired off. Moreover it was the Admiralty Committee over which I presided early in the year which produced the idea of using these distress rockets. I am therefore well acquainted with the subject.

The Air Ministry, not for the first time, spread itself into very large demands and using its priority barged in heavily into other forms of not less important production.

I agree that PAC rockets may be a good interim defence against low-flying attack, but they have to take their place in the general scheme. I thought myself about 5,000 a month would be sufficient but I am willing to agree to 1,500 a week or 6,000 a month. . . .

Even this figure, Churchill wrote, could be 'somewhat extended', if projects to recover the rockets' wire were to be further developed, and 'proved an effective economy'.[3]

Churchill remained at Chequers throughout Sunday August 18. Among the guests at luncheon were de Gaulle, Ismay, Morton, Spears, Lindemann and Halifax.[4] Dinner was a quieter occasion, with Clementine and Sarah Churchill, Duncan and Diana Sandys, Lindemann and John Martin.[5] Throughout the day, as wave after wave of German bombers attacked again Britain's ports, factories and airfields, seventy-one German aircraft had been destroyed. Two days earlier, the Combined Intelligence Committee had repeated its conclusion that Germany would take no final decision to invade until the result of the

[1] Prime Minister's Personal Minute, M.16, 17 August 1940, marked by Churchill, 'Lord Beaverbrook to see & return': Premier papers, 3/347, folio 1.

[2] Thursday, 22 August 1940.

[3] Prime Minister's Personal Minute, M.34, 25 August 1940: Premier papers, 3/347, folio 2.

[4] Churchill engagement diary: Churchill papers, 2/413.

[5] Chequers Dinner List for 18 August 1940: Chequers archive.

struggle for air superiority was clear.[1] British losses on August 18 were 22 fighters shot down, 16 pilots lost, and 15 aircraft destroyed on the ground, including ten at Kenley.

Britain's own offensive against Germany also continued, despite heavy losses. But for the first time since the outbreak of war, on August 19 the number of Bomber crews available exceeded the number of aircraft.[2] In his minutes that day, Churchill voiced two particular concerns relating to morale and propaganda. The first was his distress at the Admiralty's assertion that Britain had only destroyed twenty-five U-boats since the war began. 'Considering,' he wrote, 'that the Germans have got twenty of ours, this would be a lamentable reflection upon all our flotillas and hunting-craft, as well as upon the Asdic method.' Surely, he asked, the number must be higher, and the Anti-submarine Warfare Department at the Admiralty was 'rendering a poor service by the line they take of declaring futile all the efforts of our hunting craft'.[3] The second concern was British propaganda in the United States. Emery Reves, the man who before the war had arranged the syndication of Churchill's articles throughout the European Press, and beyond, had put up a scheme for 'one central organisation' power-ful enough to fight the German propaganda machine across the Atlan-tic. This proposal had been sent on by Churchill to the Ministry of Information. 'I hope,' Churchill minuted to Duff Cooper, 'you will not allow it to be weakened by official caution.'[4]

During the weekend at Chequers, and throughout Monday August 19, Churchill worked on his coming Parliamentary speech. The Prime Minister, noted Colville, 'fertilizes a line of poetry or a phrase for weeks'. One such phrase was: 'Hitler's reputation for veracity will be seriously impaired.' Another: 'Even if Hitler is at the *Caspian*. . . .'

---

[1] F. H. Hinsley and others, *British Intelligence in the Second World War, Its Influence on Strategy and Operations*, London 1979, page 183. The Combined Intelligence Committee (CIC) was an ad-hoc inter-Service committee set up to meet daily in the Admiralty and to examine evidence of German invasion intentions. The highest Intelligence appreciation and administration body was the Joint Intelligence Committee (JIC), which formed part of the Chiefs of Staff machinery, and was headed throughout the war by Victor Cavendish-Bentinck (later Duke of Portland).

[2] Churchill to Vice Chief of the Air Staff, Minute M.22A of 19 August 1940: Churchill papers, 20/13.

[3] Prime Minister's Personal Minute, M.20, 19 August 1940: Churchill papers, 20/13. The Admiralty was right and Churchill was wrong.

[4] Prime Minister's Personal Minute, M.22, 19 August 1940: Churchill papers, 20/13. Having sought sympathetic action on behalf of Reves' idea, Churchill again minuted to Duff Cooper six days later, when further criticism arose of it: 'I had, of course, not read Mr Reves's scheme and I am in no way wedded to it. Is it true, however, that Mr Harcourt Johnstone, Dr Dalton etc were, in principle, in favour of something on these lines, and also Mr Attlee was said to be in favour.' (Prime Minister's Personal Minute, M.23, 25 August 1940: Churchill papers, 20/13.)

On the night of August 19 Churchill went to bed shortly after midnight, 'which is early by his standards', wrote Colville. That night there was no German air raid. 'They are making a big mistake,' Churchill remarked, 'in giving us a respite.'[1]

As Churchill finished preparing his speech on the morning of August 20, Neville Chamberlain was writing to encourage him, having no doubt 'it will be a strong one with such material as you know how to use to the utmost'.[2] That same afternoon, Churchill spoke for nearly fifty minutes, giving a survey of the 'dark, wide field'. This war, he said, was not the 'prodigious slaughter' of the First World War, but 'a conflict of strategy, of organisation, of technical apparatus, of science, mechanics and morale'. From the moment the Germans 'drove the Jews out', and thereby lowered their own 'technical standards', Churchill commented, 'our science is definitely ahead of theirs', while Britain's geographical position, her 'command of the sea', and her friendship with the United States, enabled her 'to draw resources from the whole world and to manufacture weapons of war of every kind, but especially of the superfine kinds, on a scale hitherto practised only by Nazi Germany'.

Britain must now prepare, Churchill declared, 'resolutely and methodically', for the campaigns of 1941 and 1942. Being the 'sole champions' of the liberties of all Europe, 'we must not grudge these years as we toil and struggle through them'. Many opportunities might lie open to amphibious power 'and we must be ready to take advantage of them'. Whether the road to victory was 'long or short, rough or smooth, we mean to reach our journey's end'.

Churchill then spoke of Britain's military and naval preparedness. 'The whole Island,' he declared, 'bristles against invaders, from the sea or from the air.' The increased production and rapid repair of aircraft and engines had been achieved by Lord Beaverbrook's 'genius' of organization and drive, Churchill said, which, 'looks like magic', and which was enabling Britain 'to continue the air struggle indefinitely and as long as the enemy pleases'. The longer the struggle continued, the more rapid would be Britain's approach, 'first towards that parity, and then into that superiority in the air, upon which in a large measure the decision of the war depends'.

Churchill then spoke of the British airmen involved in the battle. 'The gratitude,' he said, 'of every home in our Island, in our Empire,

---

[1] Colville diary, 19 August 1940: Colville papers.
[2] 'Private', 20 August 1940: Churchill papers, 20/1. Chamberlain was then in Hampshire, recuperating from an operation for cancer.

and indeed throughout the world, except in the abodes of the guilty, goes out to the British airmen who, undaunted by odds, unwearied in their constant challenge and mortal danger, are turning the tide of war by their prowess and by their devotion.' Churchill went on to say, in the phrase which had so impressed Ismay a week earlier: 'Never in the field of human conflict was so much owed by so many to so few.'[1]

All hearts went out, Churchill continued, to the fighter pilots 'whose brilliant actions we see with our own eyes day after day'. But no one should forget, he said, 'that all the time, night after night, month after month, our bomber squadrons travel far into Germany, find their targets in the darkness by the highest navigational skill, aim their attacks, often under the heaviest fire, often with serious loss, with deliberate, careful discrimination, and inflict shattering blows upon the whole of the technical and war-making structure of the Nazi Power'. On no part of the Royal Air Force, Churchill added, did the 'weight of the war' fall more heavily 'than on the daylight bombers who will play a valuable part in the case of invasion, and whose unflinching zeal it has been necessary in the meanwhile on numerous occasions to restrain'.

Churchill was confident that Britain's own bombing of German military industries and communications, as well as the air bases and storage depots 'from which we are attacked', would continue 'upon an ever-increasing scale until the end of the war, and may in another year attain dimensions hitherto undreamed of'. This was the 'most certain', if not the shortest 'of all the roads to victory'. 'Even if,' Churchill forecast, 'Nazi legions stood triumphant on the Black Sea, or indeed the Caspian, even if Hitler were at the gates of India, it would profit him nothing if at the same time the entire economic and scientific apparatus of German war power lay shattered and pulverized at home.'

Churchill spoke next of the post-war world, and of the need, before beginning the task of rebuilding, to be convinced 'ourselves', and to convince 'all other countries', that 'the Nazi tyranny is finally going to be broken'. The right to guide the course of world history 'is the noblest prize of victory'. Meanwhile, the task ahead was 'more practical, more simple and more stern' than peacemaking. 'I hope—indeed I pray,' Churchill went on, 'that we shall not be found unworthy of our victory

[1] Three weeks later Lady Violet Bonham Carter, Asquith's daughter, wrote to Churchill: 'Your sentence about the Air-war—"Never in the history of human conflict has so much been owed by so many to so few"—will live as long as words are spoken and remembered. Nothing so simple, so majestic & so true has been said in so great a moment of human history. You have beaten your old enemies "the Classics" into a cocked hat! Even my Father would have admitted that. How *he* would have loved it!' (Letter of 10 September 1940: Churchill papers, 2/392.)

if after toil and tribulation it is granted to us. For the rest, we have to gain the victory. That is our task.'[1]

Churchill's final words were of the Destroyers for Bases deal with the United States. The sovereignty of the British bases, he explained, was not to be transferred. Instead, a 99 years' lease would be granted to the United States. 'Undoubtedly,' he said, 'this process means that these two great organisations of the English-speaking democracies, the British Empire and the United States, will have to be somewhat mixed up together in some of their affairs for mutual and general advantage.' He did not view that process 'with any misgivings'. And he ended: 'I could not stop it if I wished; no one can stop it. Like the Mississippi, it just keeps rolling along. Let it roll. Let it roll on full flood, inexorable, irresistible, benignant, to broader lands and better days.'[2]

His speech over, Churchill returned to Downing Street with Colville, who noted: 'he sang Ole Man River in the car all the way back'.[3]

Important though American opinion was, Churchill baulked at a proposal to allow United States newspaper correspondents to check Britain's figures of German aircraft shot down. 'I must say,' he minuted to Sinclair, 'I am a little impatient about the American scepticism. The event is what will decide all.' His minute set out clearly a view he had long held, and had asserted for more than forty years in his different public offices. As he explained to Sinclair:

The important thing is to bring the German aircraft down and to win the battle, and the rate at which American correspondents and the American public are convinced that we are winning, and that our figures are true, stands in a much lower plane. They will find out quite soon enough when the German air attack is plainly shown to be repulsed. It would be a pity to tease the Fighter Command at the present time when the battle is going on from hour to hour and continuous decisions have to be taken about air raid warnings, &c. I confess I should be more inclined to let the facts speak for themselves. There is something rather obnoxious in bringing correspondents down

[1] On 23 August 1940 Churchill told the War Cabinet that he favoured 'some kind of Council of Europe' after the war, made up of four groupings, the five Great Powers of Europe, and three confederations of Northern Europe, Middle Europe, and the Balkans. 'There should be a Court,' he said, 'to which all justiciable disputes should be referred, with an international air force.' There must also be a scheme 'for a fair distribution of raw materials'. It was also important, Churchill added, 'that there should be no attempt at a vindictive settlement after the war'. (War Cabinet No. 223 of 1940, 23 August 1940, 11.30 a.m.: Cabinet papers, 65/8.)

[2] *Hansard*, 20 August 1940, columns 1159–1171, 3.52 p.m. to 4.40 p.m. Churchill's friend Sir Terence O'Connor, KC, MP, wrote after the speech: 'You must have been inspired by the reception which the House gave you,' and he added: 'May you feel fortified by the regard & confidence which all feel in your courage & imagination.' (Churchill papers, 2/397.)

[3] Colville diary, 20 August 1940: Colville papers.

to air squadrons in order that they may assure the American public that the fighter pilots are not bragging and lying about their figures.

Churchill added: 'We can I think afford to be a bit cool and calm about all this.'[1]

Despite the sceptical tone of this minute, Churchill's personal contact with at least one American journalist was friendly and constructive. During the week before his 'Mississippi' speech he had given lunch to the twenty-eight-year-old Whitelaw Reid, London correspondent of the *New York Herald Tribune*, who wrote to Churchill on August 21:

The tribute you paid the work of the Herald Tribune was most heartening and should inspire it to ever greater heights, I only hope it can succeed in inspiring those destroyers!

It is extraordinary that you should have time to ferret me out in the midst of your busy day—and I want you to know how deeply I appreciated both your kindness to me and the generous things you said about Mother. Meeting you in your distinguished home was a great privilege and this takes with it much gratefulness and cheers for your superb speech yesterday.

'May your Mississippi roll on,' Whitelaw Reid ended, 'until it floods the nation!'[2]

In order to take the propaganda war across the Atlantic to the Americans, Churchill had already given Emery Reves his blessing to go to the United States; there Reves worked for the rest of the war to propagate, not merely the policies, but also the ideals of the British cause.[3]

During the third week of August the intensity of the German air attacks on Britain began to slacken, despite bombing raids on August 20 on the City of London and the West India Docks. Churchill did not allow the reduction in the number of raids to lull him into complacency. 'I do not think,' he telegraphed to Roosevelt on August 22, 'that bad

---

[1] 'Action this Day', Prime Minister's Personal Minute, M.24, 21 August 1940: Churchill papers, 20/13.

[2] Letter of 21 August 1940: Churchill papers, 2/398. Reid's mother, Mrs Ogden Reid, had visited Churchill at Chartwell in the summer of 1939. From 1947 to 1955 Whitelaw Reid was editor of the *New York Herald Tribune*. The 'most striking aspect' of the luncheon discussions, Whitelaw Reid later recalled, 'was the relaxed way in which they were carried on, despite reports that were brought in from time to time on nearby bombings'. (Letter to the author, 11 January 1983.)

[3] In 1942 Reves published *A Democratic Manifesto* and in 1945 *The Anatomy of Peace*. The theme of his arguments in the United States, as expressed in the first of his books, and in innumerable lectures was: 'Only if we put force at the service of justice can we hope that it will not be used against justice.'

man has yet struck his full blow,' and he added that Britain was suffering 'considerable losses' in merchant ships in the North-Western Approaches.[1]

The extent to which Britain ought to become financially indebted to the United States was discussed by the War Cabinet on August 22. The French contracts in the United States which Britain had taken over two months earlier were proving an onerous financial burden. In the previous six weeks, Britain's gold reserves had fallen from £380 million to £290 million. Yet the United States Treasury was unwilling to consider measures to lessen the burden of Britain's debt. 'As usual,' Neville Chamberlain wrote to Churchill, 'the difficulty arises out of the American election and the problem is to hold on till that is run without unduly depleting our resources.'[2]

So serious did the situation seem, that the Chancellor of the Exchequer, Sir Kingsley Wood, suggested the possible requisitioning of wedding rings and gold ornaments, although this measure was not expected to raise more than £20 million. Such action, Churchill told the War Cabinet, should only be adopted at a later stage, 'if we wished to make some striking gesture for the purpose of shaming the Americans'.[3]

Three days later, in a direct appeal to Roosevelt, Churchill set out at length various Treasury suggestions for an amelioration of Britain's mounting gold losses. He ended on a personal note: 'I am so grateful to you for all the trouble you have been taking,' he wrote, 'and I am so sorry to add to your burdens, knowing what a good friend you have been to us.'[4] Once more, the need to retain the best possible links and confidence with Roosevelt himself was a main theme of Churchill's work, despite any particular setback or dispute.

One successful result of Churchill's work was apparent in the question of British tank production in the United States. On August 19 General Pakenham-Walsh telegraphed from New York that, whereas it would be difficult to secure 'any extensive American adoption of British types', the American authorities were willing to accept the British designed turret, fighting compartment and armour in the mass pro-

[1] Telegram of 22 August 1940: Churchill papers, 20/14. In the week ending 22 August 1940 German U-boats sunk 5 British, 2 Swedish and 1 Belgian ship in the North-Western Approaches. During the first seventeen days of August, 53,400 tons of cargo destined for Britain had been sunk, the equivalent of one ton sunk for every 36.6 tons safely landed from ships in convoy. (War Cabinet, Chiefs of Staff Committee, Weekly Résumé No. 51: Churchill papers, 23/6.)

[2] Letter of 21 August 1940: Churchill papers, 20/4.

[3] War Cabinet No. 232 of 1940, 22 August 1940, 12 noon, Minute 3, Confidential Annex: Cabinet papers, 65/14.

[4] Telegram of 25 August 1940: Premier papers, 3/462/2, 3.

duction of their own M2 tank, and to modify it accordingly. The production of the chassis and turret of this modified tank, the M3, was promised in eight months, Pakenham-Walsh reported, and the Americans were prepared 'to allot firms for production if we order an agreed type at once'.[1]

Eden and the War Office were keen to take up the American offer without delay, and drafted a reply, ordering 1,000 of the effectively Anglo-American M3 tank. The War Office were careful, however, not to order more, in view of the 'immediate limitations' of American productive capacity, and in order not to make it more difficult in future to persuade the Americans to produce an all-British tank. 'For this reason,' Pakenham-Walsh was told, 'we think it wise to limit our initial order for M3 to 1,000.'

This order was shown at once to the Minister of Supply, Herbert Morrison, and, at Churchill's request, to Beaverbrook and Lindemann. 'The War Office are anxious to send it off at the earliest opportunity,' John Peck explained to Lindemann.[2] The Professor had no objection. Nor did the Ministry of Aircraft Production, which informed Eric Seal the same day that Beaverbrook, having considered the War Office draft 'on behalf of the Prime Minister', approved its 'immediate dispatch'.[3] The order was sent at once, forging yet another link in the chain of United States commitment and supply.

The modification and purchase of tanks was an urgent problem. At the same time Churchill also kept a close watch over the development of weapons which might be of importance in the years to come, not only for defence, but for offence. Towards the end of August he decided to increase the authority of Major Jefferis, the officer in charge of the army's experimental establishment, whose abilities had much struck him both in the winter of 1939, during the planning for mining of the Rhine, and in April 1940, when Jefferis had blown up key railway bridges behind German lines in Norway. 'I regard this officer,' Churchill minuted on August 24, 'as a singularly capable and forceful man who should be brought forward to a higher position. He ought certainly to be promoted Lieutenant-Colonel as it will give him more authority.'[4]

At first the army resisted Jefferis' advancement in rank before his time. He was '150th on the list' of Royal Engineer Majors, Dill

[1] Telegram No. 1, New York No. 397, 10.40 p.m., 18 August 1940, received 8.15 a.m., 19 August 1940: Premier papers, 3/493, folio 29.
[2] 'Secret', J. H. Peck to Professor Lindemann, 21 August 1940: Premier papers, 3/493, folio 24.
[3] F. M. Smith to E. A. Seal, 21 August 1940: Premier papers, 3/493, folio 26.
[4] Minute of 24 August 1940: Cabinet papers, 120/379.

informed Ismay on August 27.[1] But Churchill persisted in his view. 'Surely,' he wrote directly to Dill four days later, 'it is important to bring able men forward in war time, instead of deferring entirely to seniority.'[2]

To ensure that Jefferis was given the necessary powers, Churchill transferred the experimental establishment from the War Office to the Ministry of Supply, with the added safeguard that Jefferis should also report direct to Lindemann. A year later, Churchill brought the establishment directly under the Minister of Defence.[3] Known as MDI, and based just outside Whitchurch in Buckinghamshire, only ten miles from Chequers, Jefferis' establishment was the scene of intensive rocket and bomb research throughout the war. Lindemann visited it once every two weeks to watch experiments, and from time to time the rockets or bombs were taken across to Chequers itself for demonstrations there.[4]

In this way, Churchill sought to lay the groundwork for future military strength. But from day to day there were setbacks which could not easily be overcome. As preparations for the Dakar expedition went ahead, several setbacks threatened to impede it. On August 14 Churchill had informed General Irwin and Admiral Cunningham, in separate but identical telegrams, that their task was 'to install General de Gaulle and his Free French Force in Dakar in order that he may rally the French in West Africa to his cause'.[5] But only five days later Churchill was angered to learn that Cunningham had reported that 'the only suitable day' for carrying out 'Menace' was September 12, on account of the favourable tide and moon, and that if this date was missed owing to storms, no other days would be possible until September 27.

[1] 'Most Secret', 27 August 1940: Cabinet papers, 120/379. In this letter Dill informed Ismay that among the appliances designed by Jefferis' section were the Light Camouflet Set, Pull Switches, Pressure Switches, Striker Pattern Delays and Limpets; among the appliances in the process of being designed were Scatter Bombs, an Untouchable Device, Clam, an anti-tank Mortar and a 'new design of easily produced machine guns'. Clam was a magnetic explosive device to attach to tanks, or to the side of ships. Jefferis and his section subsequently also designed the 'PIAT' (Projector Infantry Anti-Tank) a hand held infantry anti-tank rocket.

[2] Minute of 1 September 1940: Cabinet papers, 120/379.

[3] Prime Minister's Personal Minute, C.70/1, 8 September 1941: Cabinet papers, 120/379.

[4] In 1942 Jefferis was promoted Brigadier. In 1945 Churchill wrote to Eden of 'the remarkable work done by Brigadier Jefferis in producing various weapons of war'. (Prime Minister's Personal Minute, M.509/5, 21 May 1945: Cabinet papers, 120/379.) In 1945 Jefferis was promoted Major-General and received the KBE. The weapons which he had designed and developed during his first year under Churchill's authority included the Sticky Bomb (1½ million produced), the Bombard (1¾ million), the Puff Ball (50,000) and the Long Delay Fuse (250,000).

[5] Churchill to Vice-Admiral J. H. D. Cunningham, Naval Commander of Operation 'Menace' and Major-General N. M. S. Irwin, Military Commander of Operation 'Menace', 14 August 1940: Churchill papers, 20/14.

Learning this, Churchill minuted to Ismay: 'All this raises most grave questions. The Admiral cannot take up a position that only in ideal conditions of tide and moon can the operation be begun. It has got to be begun as soon as possible, as long as the conditions are practicable, even though they be not the best. People have to fight in war on all sorts of days, and under all sorts of conditions.' It would be a 'great misfortune', Churchill added, if there were any delay beyond the first week of September.[1]

Churchill's protest came too late. On August 18 Cunningham and Irwin, who were still in London, had asked to see the Chiefs of Staff 'at once' to say, as Ismay reported, that they no longer believed it would be possible, if surprise failed, 'to transform the operation from being a peaceful penetration into a violent assault'.

Reporting on this development to Churchill, in a letter on August 20, Ismay also told Churchill that the Vice-Chiefs of Staff had held 'three long meetings' to consider how best to install General de Gaulle at Dakar 'at the earliest possible moment', and had been 'unable to find a satisfactory answer', other than to 'fall back' on the 'original' project of a landing at Conakry, and an overland march to Dakar.[2] The Vice Chiefs of Staff had, on the previous day, reported fully in this sense, urging that it might be best to install de Gaulle at Conakry 'as a first step to the raising of his standard in West Africa'. To land at Conakry, they concluded, 'would be a relatively simple operation which could be carried out without delay'.[3]

Ismay proposed a discussion between the Chiefs of Staff Committee and Churchill on the evening of August 20, and this Churchill agreed to at once. The meeting was held at 10.30 p.m., with de Gaulle present throughout, together with Spears and Morton. Churchill now proposed that while the Dakar operation should go ahead, it should be in a much modified form, with de Gaulle trying first to enter Dakar by negotiations. Only if these failed would British warships open fire on the French gun positions, but they should do so, Churchill urged 'with the utmost restraint'. If determined opposition was met with, however, the British forces 'would use all means to break down resistance'. In 'any event', Churchill stressed, 'it was essential that by nightfall General de Gaulle should be master of Dakar'.[4]

---

[1] Prime Minister's Personal Minute, D.12, 19 August 1940: Churchill papers, 20/13.

[2] 'Secret', 20 August 1940: Premier papers, 3/276, folios 232–3.

[3] 'Operation "Menace" Report' signed by R. E. C. Peirse (VCAS), T. S. V. Phillips (VCNS) and R. H. Haining (VCGS) 'Secret', Chiefs of Staff paper No. 643 of 1940, 19 August 1940: Premier papers, 3/276, folios 234–6.

[4] Chiefs of Staff Committee No. 275 of 1940, 20 August 1940, 10.30 p.m.: Cabinet papers, 79/6.

De Gaulle accepted Churchill's proposal, as did the Vice-Chiefs, who on August 21, met to work out further details with de Gaulle, Cunningham and Irwin. They feared, however, 'that it might not be possible', as Churchill had hoped, for de Gaulle 'to be completely master of Dakar by nightfall of the first day'.[1] That evening, at a meeting of the Defence Committee, however, Sir Richard Peirse reported that the two Commanders and de Gaulle 'had expressed their general agreement that the Operation as now conceived was feasible and an improvement on the previous conception'.[2]

On the night of August 21 Churchill discussed the new 'Menace' with Eden and Sir Roger Keyes, coming to the conclusion, as he minuted to Ismay on August 22, 'that the operation "Menace" had best be entrusted to a smaller number of more highly mobile trained troops than is now proposed'. Churchill's minute continued:

It is a mistake to treat the Marine Brigades as trained for this purpose. They consist almost entirely of recruits brought in since the war and are only now beginning boat-work or manoeuvre. For training and mobility they cannot compete with many battalions of the Regular Army. Moreover, they can do very good work here, while they are maturing. One regular Battalion and one Battalion of Marines may be sent as reserve.

The Director of Combined Operations, Sir Roger Keyes, will in three days furnish 1,500 men from his Companies and commands, and these, with the reserve aforesaid, will constitute the fighting force of the expedition, apart from the French troops. Pray let me have your dates for the whole programme. There must be no delay.[3]

'Menace' was to go ahead, amended in its scope, questioned in its details, and yet judged by all who studied it to be a feasible and important operation of war. Intelligence reports seemed to bear out the feasibility of the attack: on September 8 the Colonial Office was informed by telegram from the Gambia that a former French airman recently returned to Dakar 'found 40% of the people he met pro-British, 50% wavering and 10% pro-Vichy', while the 'commercial

---

The Chiefs of Staff were represented by Peirse, Haining, Phillips and Ismay. Churchill was in the Chair.

[1] Chiefs of Staff Committee No. 276 of 1940, 21 August 1940, 10 a.m.: Cabinet papers, 79/6. Those present were Peirse (in the Chair), Phillips, Haining, Ismay, Cunningham, Irwin, Spears, Morton and de Gaulle.

[2] Defence Committee (Operations) No. 28 of 1940, 21 August 1940, 6.15 p.m.: Cabinet papers, 69/1. Those present were Churchill (in the Chair), A. V. Alexander, Eden, Phillips, Haining, Peirse and Ismay.

[3] Prime Minister's Personal Minute, D.18, 22 August 1940: Churchill papers, 20/13.

people' were '100% pro-British'. At Dakar, people were also 'very anti-German', while in the nearby air base of Thies there were 'many pro-British among aviators'. Were the landing at Dakar to be made by Free French forces and not British, the airman reported, 'there would be no firing'.

Having read this report, Churchill noted on it: 'This shd be reported to "Menace"'; and it was at once sent by Desmond Morton to the Joint Intelligence Committee, for dispatch to Cunningham, Irwin and de Gaulle.[1]

Churchill's pleasure at this Intelligence report was offset by his knowledge that a member of de Gaulle's entourage had revealed, in public, the destination of the Dakar expedition. On the instructions of the Chiefs of Staff, the Inter-Service Security Committee later investigated this breach of security and reported 'that the leakage of information had undoubtedly taken place through French sources'. General de Gaulle himself, the enquiry established, 'when purchasing a large quantity of tropical equipment at "Simpson's" in Piccadilly, remarked in public this his destination was West Africa', while at a dinner in a restaurant in Liverpool 'French Officers had toasted "Dakar"', and Dakar 'was also common talk amongst the French troops'. As far as British troops were concerned, however, 'only Major-General Irwin and two or three of his officers whom he had told were in possession of the true facts and there was no leakage through them'.[2]

Alerted to this breach of security in the third week of August, Churchill commented in a minute to Ismay that Halifax had told him that a Polish exile source had also revealed the expedition's destination. Churchill continued:

> The operation 'Scipio' was necessarily much talked about. Being entirely a French project no doubt many in General de Gaulle's circle had to be consulted. The Poles, who were at one time to assist in manning de Gaulle's artillery, have also got to know. . . .
>
> Inside 'Scipio' another operation of a different kind has developed called 'Menace'. Although few people know the scope and character of 'Menace' yet one may be sure that General de Gaulle will have been forced to consult his principal lieutenants, and, anyhow, there is bound to be a lot of talk centring on the place in question among the foreigners involved. This is shown by the General's wish to postpone repatriation of any Frenchmen from here pending events. . . .

[1] Telegram No. 247 from the Gambia, 'Most Secret', received 7 September 1940, 1.50 p.m.: Premier papers, 3/276, folios 196–8.

[2] Report to the War Cabinet, 25 September 1940, quoted in 'The Dakar Operation', 5 February 1941, Annex III: Premier papers, 3/276.

Churchill did not, however, consider that 'the chances of the operation would be prejudiced', unless the Germans were to fly 'a hundred or so of their people to the spot'. These, in conjunction with Vichy supporters in Dakar, 'might make trouble'. 'Anyhow,' Churchill added, 'we must accept that risk.' His minute continued: 'The question is whether we can assign some other purpose to the expedition as a blind. Perhaps Martinique might be used in talk. Let me have suggestions.'

General de Gaulle, Churchill added, 'should be warned in due course about his entourage. It does not look worse than pure indiscretion.'[1]

Churchill's suggestion for the use of Martinique as a cover for 'Menace' was examined by Colonel Hollis, who pointed out that there already was a 'bogus' operation, code name 'Reflex', aimed at pretending that Egypt was the actual destination of the Free French forces. To give 'Reflex' credibility, camp sites had been marked out in the Canal Zone for the impending French contingent, while the senior British naval officer in the Indian Ocean had been sufficiently deceived as to have made enquiries 'why he had not been consulted about it'.

Were Martinique to be given out as the destination, Hollis warned, it would mean that Britain was going to use French troops against their French 'co-nationals', and this 'would not be very good for General de Gaulle's shares'.[2] There was 'no apparent reason' otherwise for such an operation.

After a reference to the '£60 millions of gold' then in Martinique as an 'apparent reason' for the cover operation, Churchill deferred to his Defence Office, his confidence in the original 'Reflex' cover being revived when Desmond Morton reported that 'two well known agents of the Vichy Government are now under the impression that General de Gaulle is about to sail round the Cape to Egypt'. Morton added: 'In collaboration with the Chiefs of Staffs we have taken other action calculated to confuse the enemy.'[3]

On August 29, the afternoon of Morton's note, de Gaulle and Churchill met at 10 Downing Street. Spears and Morton were the only others present. A note of what was said was given later that day by Morton to Colonel Hollis, who sent copies to the Chiefs of Staff and to Ismay.

At the meeting, as Hollis reported, de Gaulle asked Churchill 'what

[1] Prime Minister's Personal Minute, D.19, 24 August 1940: Churchill papers, 20/13.

[2] '"Blind" for Operation "Menace"', 'Secret', 28 August 1940, and Churchill's note: Premier papers, 3/276, folio 204.

[3] Minute of 29 August 1940 (initialled by Churchill, 30 August 1940): Premier papers, 3/276, folio 214.

assistance would be afforded by His Majesty's Government if French territory which had rallied to the de Gaulle standard were attacked by sea'. Churchill then gave de Gaulle 'a most formal undertaking that His Majesty's Government would, in the common cause, assume responsibility for the defence from the sea of any French Colonies which might declare their intention of continuing the fight under the de Gaulle standard, or might be forced to do so by a coup d'état, this undertaking including the defence against any attempted attack or landing organised by the Vichy Government'.

This undertaking, Hollis noted, 'was given orally', but Morton had informed him 'that it was none the less categorical and binding'.[1]

Despite the security leak, Churchill had made de Gaulle a pledge of substantial British support. But there were other ominous signs: on August 29 a naval Lieutenant, R. T. Paget, who had been given command of a section of assault landing craft in the expedition, wrote to A. V. Alexander: 'The Germans must know by now of the existence and composition of the expedition and they must further know that its destination is in the tropics and an assault landing is contemplated somewhere. They may or may not know of our precise destination. I do; not because I have been let into the secret but because I have picked up sufficient clues to enable me to identify the place.' Even before this, Paget added, 'I was told of our destination by a man on the Liverpool docks.'[2]

Before the war, as Labour candidate for Northampton, Paget had spoken on the same platform as Alexander; hence his most irregular letter for a serving officer. Alexander showed it to Churchill. 'No action is possible,' Churchill minuted on September 4, 'except to make sure the faults do not recur next time,' and he added: 'The writer is granted protection by me, & must not be proceeded against in any way.'[3]

With the 'Menace' security leaks already in his mind, on August 25 Churchill had drafted a general directive on secrecy, to be addressed both to the Service Ministers and to all those Government Departments likely to be affected by plans for future operations. The draft, as sent to Sir Edward Bridges for action, read:

We shall soon be engaged in preparing plans for offensive operations next Spring, the success of which will depend to an exceptional degree on surprise.

[1] 'Secret', 29 August 1940: Cabinet papers, 79/7, folio 73.

[2] Letter of 29 August 1940: Admiralty papers, 199/1931.

[3] Minute of 4 September 1940: Admiralty papers, 199/1931. Aged 32 at the time of the Dakar expedition, an old Etonian and a Barrister, Paget was later Labour MP for Northampton (1945–1974), became a QC in 1947, and was created a Life Peer in 1974.

But surprise will be impossible of attainment if future plans are made known to a large number of officers who, in turn, pass them on and discuss them with their colleagues. In this way, what should be a closely guarded secret, becomes in a short time a matter of common knowledge and gossip throughout Whitehall and the Clubs of Pall Mall.

I have given instructions that the circulation of papers dealing with future plans shall be rigidly restricted to the Departments directly concerned. But this precaution will be of no avail unless each Minister takes steps to ensure that knowledge of future operations is only imparted to those individuals who must be acquainted with them, and only to the extent that is necessary to enable action to be taken.

For this to be effective, a change of outlook is wanted. No one, in whatever position, should regard it as in any sense a reflection on his prudence, if a plan is only communicated to him partially, or not at all. Everyone must be able to realise that the only way to keep a secret is to insist ruthlessly on the rule that only those are told who must be told.

'Everyone should take pride,' Churchill ended, 'not in how much knowledge of future plans he can acquire, but in carrying on with his work without asking unnecessary questions, or expecting to be told more than is required for the task he is called on to perform.'[1]

The instructions which Churchill mentioned in this directive had been issued on the same day. Papers dealing with future plans, Churchill minuted, were to be circulated only to members of the Defence Committee and to the Joint Planning Committee. If such plans called for action by departments other than the Service Departments, 'no more of the plan should be communicated' to them than was necessary. 'All papers connected with future plans,' Churchill added, 'are to be circulated under the arrangements appropriate to lock and key papers, *i.e.*, in sealed envelopes in locked boxes.' Documents relating to future operations, he stressed, were only to be communicated to those officers who had to be acquainted with their contents.[2]

With his thoughts very much on future plans, Churchill had set out, in a minute for Ismay and Bridges, the future status of the Joint Planning Committee. These 'Joint Planners' were no longer to be a part of the Cabinet Secretariat system, but were to 'work directly under the orders of the Minister of Defence'—Churchill himself—becoming a part of the Minister of Defence's Office. Churchill went on to explain:

They will retain their present positions in and contacts with the three Service Departments. They will work out the details of such plans as are com-

---

[1] Prime Minister's Personal Minute, C.4, 25 August 1940: Churchill papers, 20/13.
[2] Prime Minister's Personal Minute, C.3, 25 August 1940: Churchill papers, 20/13.

municated to them by the Minister of Defence. They may initiate plans of their own after reference to General Ismay. They will of course be at the service of the Chiefs of Staff Committee for the elaboration of any matters sent to them.

All plans produced by the Joint Planning Committee, or elaborated by them under Churchill's instructions, would be referred to the Chiefs of Staff Committee 'for their observations'. Thereafter, Churchill added, 'should doubts and differences exist, or in important cases, all plans will be reviewed by the Defence Committee of the War Cabinet which will consist of the Prime Minister, the Lord Privy Seal[1] and Lord Beaverbrook, and the three Service Ministers; the three Chiefs of the Staff with General Ismay being in attendance'.[2]

This instruction was issued on August 24, a Saturday. It was to come into effect, Churchill told Ismay and Bridges, on the following Monday, August 26. A week later, Eden forwarded to Churchill the comments of a reluctant Dill, who feared an erosion of his own authority as Chief of the Imperial General Staff if the Joint Planning Committee submitted military advice 'direct' to the Prime Minister.[3] Answering this criticism, Churchill wrote to Eden: 'There is no question of the Joint Planning Committee "submitting military advice to me". They are merely to work out plans in accordance with directions which I shall give,' and he commented: 'I have found it necessary to have direct access to and control of the Joint Planning Staffs because after a year of war I cannot recall a single plan initiated by the existing machinery.' He felt 'sure', Churchill added, that he could count upon Eden and the other two Service Ministers 'to help me in giving a vigorous and positive direction to the conduct of the war, and in overcoming the dead weight of inertia and delay which has so far led us to being forestalled on every occasion by the enemy'.[4]

[1] Clement Attlee.

[2] Prime Minister's Personal Minute, D.21, 24 August 1940: Premier papers, 3/119/10, folios 23–4.

[3] 'Memorandum by the CIGS, Joint Planning Arrangements', 28 August 1940: Premier papers, 3/119/10, folio 35.

[4] Prime Minister's Personal Minute, M.52, 31 August 1940: Premier papers, 3/119/10, folios 30–31.

37

'Strength for Battle'

I N the third week of August the situation in Africa was much on
Churchill's mind as Italian troops drove the British out of British
Somaliland, and prepared in the western desert to take advantage of
Britain's weakness. In July a Ministerial committee headed by Eden,
and in early August staff conversations, had both concluded that substantial reinforcements must be sent to Egypt. 'The decision to give
this blood transfusion,' Churchill later wrote, 'while we braced ourselves to meet a mortal danger, was at once awful and right.'[1]

On August 23, in the directive which he had first dictated eight days
earlier, and which had now been approved both by Eden and the
Chiefs of Staff, Churchill warned Wavell that a 'major invasion of
Egypt from Libya must be expected at any time now'. It was therefore
necessary, Churchill directed, 'to assemble and deploy the largest possible army' on and towards the Egyptian–Libyan frontier. Further
south, British troops being evacuated from the Somaliland would be
sent to Aden, the Sudan or Egypt 'as may be thought best'. Kenya
could be reinforced only if the Italians were seen to be about to attack
in force.

The principal need was to defend Egypt; to this end, Churchill
informed Wavell, an 'army of the Delta' would have to be established
within the next five weeks, made up of some 56,000 men and 212
heavy guns.[2] Ideally, the aim of this army was to 'destroy Italian forces
in the desert' but, if this were impossible, then 'as a last resort' it would
have to hold the line of the Delta 'at all costs'.

The campaign for the 'Defence of Egypt', Churchill added, might

---

[1] Winston S. Churchill, *The Second World War*, volume 2, London 1949, page 379.

[2] Including fifteen British Regular Infantry Battalions, the New Zealand Brigade, the Australian
Brigade from Palestine, part of the Union Brigade from East Africa, the Polish Brigade and the
French Volunteer Unit.

'as a last resort, resolve itself into: strong defence with the left arm from Alexandria inland, and a reaching out with the right hand', using British sea power to attack and harass the Italian lines of communication.

If the Italians allowed time for the defence of Egypt to be built up as proposed, well and good. If not, Churchill warned, 'we must do what we can'. All trained or Regular units, whether fully equipped or not, 'must be used in the defence of Egypt against invasion'. But within five weeks there would be a spectacular reinforcement, the despatch of three regiments of tanks from England, together with a considerable armament.[1] 'The arrival of this force,' Churchill noted, 'by the earliest possible date must be considered so important as to justify a considerable risk in their transportation.'[2]

The removal of these armoured troops from Britain to Egypt, at the very moment when Britain herself seemed so vulnerable, was a decision of courage by all concerned, principally Churchill, Eden and the Chiefs of Staff; constituting, as John Martin has written, the despatch 'of precious troops and arms, including nearly half our best tanks. . . .'[3]

Churchill failed, however, in his attempts to persuade Pound or the Chiefs of Staff to send these armaments through the Mediterranean. The risk of Italian air attack on the convoys was, said Pound, too great, and despite Churchill's vigorous protest the tanks had to proceed on the far longer voyage around the Cape. 'I was both grieved and vexed at this,' Churchill later recalled. 'Though my friendship for Admiral Pound and confidence in his judgement were never affected, sharp argument was maintained.'

Pound was supported in his arguments by Dill, who doubted that an Italian attack on Wavell's forces was imminent, as Churchill feared. Following Dill's entry into the debate, Churchill accepted 'with regret' that the Cape route must be the route of Egypt's reinforcement.[4]

On August 24 the first German bombs fell by day in central London, damaging the church of St Giles, Cripplegate. Also, from August 24,

---

[1] Sent from Britain were 154 tanks, 48 anti-tank guns, 20 Bofors light AA guns, 48 25-pounder field guns, 500 bren guns and 250 anti-tank rifles, together with their ammunition.

[2] 'General Directive from Commander-in-Chief, Middle East', 23 August 1940: Premier papers, 3/309/1, folios 3–5.

[3] Sir John Martin, in Sir John Wheeler-Bennett (editor), Action this Day: Working with Churchill, London 1968, page 149.

[4] Winston S. Churchill, The Second World War, volume 2, London 1949, pages 397–8.

the German air attacks on the airfields of South and South-East England gained in intensity and effectiveness. On the coast of Kent two airfields, Manston and Lympne, were made unfit for several days for operating fighter aircraft. The outlook for Fighter Command was bleak, nor was the danger compensated for by British successes elsewhere. By the end of August, British scientists succeeded in bending the German beam on which the accuracy of the German night bomber offensive depended. This was a triumph for the persistence of R. V. Jones, and for Churchill's own willingness to believe in the beam, and to give authority to those who insisted it could be countered. Even so, while four-fifths of the German bombs were deflected away from their city targets, the fifth that fell in built-up areas wrought considerable destruction. A further British success came on the night of August 25 when more than eighty British bombers struck for the first time at Berlin.[1]

But it was the defence of the airfields upon which all depended. Churchill and his advisers knew that the German operation against the airfields was Hitler's prelude to a sea-borne attack. On August 27 the Combined Intelligence Committee reiterated with greater emphasis than hitherto, on the basis of its scrutiny of all its secret sources, that on the success of the German air attacks on airfields and aircraft factories 'will depend the decision as to invasion'.[2]

Churchill's concern about the seriousness of the situation was not apparent to those who met him socially. When the editor of The Times, Geoffrey Dawson, lunched at Downing Street on August 26, he found Churchill 'in excellent form, fit and confident, and full of Beaverbrook's achievements in production'.[3]

As lunch came to an end, the air raid sirens sounded, the first of the expected retaliation raids following the British raid twelve hours earlier on Berlin. Churchill at once ordered guests and staff to the shelters. On learning that the next British bomber target was Leipzig, and not Berlin, he minuted to the Chief of the Air Staff: 'Now that they have begun to molest the capital, I want you to hit them hard, and Berlin is the place to hit them.'[4]

That night the German bomber forces again struck at London.

---

[1] Their objectives were military targets. But bad weather prevented most of the bombers from locating their targets.

[2] F. H. Hinsley and others, British Intelligence in the Second World War, Its Influence on Strategy and Operations, London 1979, page 183.

[3] Diary entry for 26 August 1940, quoted in: Evelyn Wrench, Geoffrey Dawson and our Times, London 1955, page 425. The other luncheon guests were the Archbishop of Canterbury (Cosmo Gordon Lang), and Sir Henry Strakosch.

[4] Quoted in Colville diary, 26 August 1940: Colville papers.

Having once more sent family and staff into the shelters, Churchill watched the raid from the garden of 10 Downing Street, with Sir Archibald Sinclair, Air Marshal Courtney, Herbert Morrison, Peck and Colville. After 'pacing the lawn for some time', Colville noted, Churchill, 'tin hat in hand', retired to sleep in the Downing Street shelter.[1] For the first time since the bombing had begun, the alert lasted throughout the night.

The Destroyers for Bases deal had become caught up in a series of snags and delays, and by August 27 no actual agreement had yet been signed. 'The American attitude simply infuriates me,' Neville Chamberlain wrote to Churchill from Hampshire, 'but we can't win as we would wish without their help and I think your handling is admirable.'[2] Churchill had already decided to telegraph direct to Roosevelt, in an attempt to cut across the tangle of negotiations. The destroyers had become urgent, he explained, because of Mussolini's recent 'menace' to Greece.[3] 'If our business is put through on big lines.' Churchill wrote, 'and in the highest spirit of goodwill, it might even now save that small historic country from invasion', and Churchill added: 'Even the next forty-eight hours are important.'[4]

On the following day Churchill asked Newall and Ismay for proposals to move four heavy bombing squadrons to Egypt to 'operate from advanced bases in Greece as far as may be convenient should Greece be forced into the war by Italy'. The bombers would then be able to refuel in Greece 'before attacking Italy', and he added: 'Many of the finest targets, including the Italian Fleet, will be open to such attacks.'[5]

But it was in the skies above Britain, not in the waters of the Aegean, that the decisive contest now took place, with at least six hundred German aircraft massing in attack each day between August 24 and September 6. Throughout each day numerous questions were brought to Churchill for decision. He was also expected to be the arbiter of many an inter-departmental dispute. Responsible at the end of the day for every facet of war policy, he was conscious of how little any one man could do. 'Each night,' he told Colville, 'I try myself by

---

[1] Colville diary, 26 August 1940: Colville papers.

[2] Letter dated 29 August 1940: Churchill papers, 2/393.

[3] On 14 August 1940 the Greek light cruiser *Elli* was sunk by the Italians at Tinos.

[4] Telegram of 27 August 1940: Premier papers 3/462/2, 3.

[5] 'Action this Day', Prime Minister's Personal Minute No. D.31, 28 August 1940: Churchill papers, 20/13.

Court Martial to see if I have done anything effective during the day. I don't mean just pawing the ground, anyone can go through the motions, but something really effective.'[1]

There were many long term decisions made. One of them, the scheme for training British pilots in Canada, which had been initiated by the Air Ministry, was challenged by the Ministry of Aircraft Production: and this conflict between Sinclair and Beaverbrook, like so many others, was brought to Churchill for resolution. Churchill wrote to Beaverbrook, in an attempt to persuade his friend to allow the scheme to go ahead:

My dear Max,

I feel great difficulty in overruling the Air Ministry on the subject of moving training schools to Canada. They are the Department responsible, and they are all united. It is not usual to overrule Service Departments upon an essential part of the policy for which they are responsible. I cannot think that the Admiralty would ever have put up with such a thing from any less authority than the Cabinet. The Cabinet must of course consider the question, and I have marked it for Thursday next. Will you please write your arguments from the Supply angle, i.e. the waste of spare parts, etc. We shall have to reach a decision that day.

Churchill also offered Beaverbrook a private meeting with Sinclair and himself 'to try to reach a settlement'.[2] Beaverbrook agreed to allow the Canadian training scheme to go ahead. But at the same time he continued to urge the impossibility of providing the Navigational Schools in Britain with the aircraft and materials they needed. Once more, Churchill resorted to a stern rebuke:

It is absolutely necessary to meet these facts. The reason why our aircraft are able to bomb Germany accurately by night is because they have superior navigational training. I do not see how we can possibly adopt the attitude that these Navigation Schools are to be brought to a standstill. I attach the greatest importance to your opinion, but you must either face the facts and answer them effectively and with a positive plan or allow the opinion of those who are responsible to prevail.[3]

'I have,' Churchill noted three days later, 'become increasingly anxious about the violent interruptions & restrictions of training, especially Navigators, wh is the present state.'[4]

[1] Colville diary, 27 August 1940: Colville papers.
[2] 'Private', 24 August 1940: Churchill papers, 4/201.
[3] 'Private', 27 August 1940: Churchill papers, 4/201.
[4] Churchill's manuscript note, date 30 August 1940 and marked 'not to be sent': Premier papers, 3/24/5, folio 60A.

In his search for the highest possible number of operational pilots and machines, Churchill was impartial in his criticism between his two friends, both of whom he had known since before the First World War, whose company he enjoyed, and whose new and onerous responsibilities since May 1940 derived entirely from him. In the third week of August, while his criticism of Beaverbrook over the Navigational Schools was at its height, Churchill had asked Sinclair why so many communication squadrons were being maintained for non-operational purposes. When Sinclair's reply failed to satisfy him, Churchill wrote, on August 25:

My dear Archie,
    I feel unhappy about your answers on the attached paper. I cannot feel you are justified in maintaining the present scale of communication squadrons when we are fighting so heavily. The sole end should surely be to increase the reserve and operational strength of our fighting squadrons and to meet the problem of trainer aircraft.
    Surely your dominant idea should be STRENGTH FOR BATTLE. Everything should be keyed on to this, and administrative convenience or local vested interests must be made to give way. In your place I should comb and re-comb. I have been shocked to see the enormous numbers at Hendon, and I would far rather give up flying on inspections altogether for Members of the Government than that this should be made an excuse for keeping these forces out of the fight.
    I should have thought that Hendon could provide at least two good squadrons of fighter or bomber aircraft of the reserve category, and that they should have the machines issued to them and practice on them as occasion serves. Then they could be thrown in when an emergency came.
    Ought you not every day to call in question in your own mind every non-military aspect of the Air Force. The tendency of every Station Commander is naturally to keep as much in his hands as possible. The Admirals do exactly the same. Even when you have had a thorough search if you look around a few weeks later you will see more fat has gathered.

'I hope,' Churchill added, 'you will be able to give some consideration to these wishes of your old friend.'[1]
    As the German air raids intensified, Churchill was concerned by their effect on the population. At eleven in the evening of August 28, after a visit to the South-East coast defences at Dover and Ramsgate, he returned to Downing Street 'much affected', Colville noted, 'by the plight of those whose houses have been destroyed or badly damaged by raids'. Churchill told Colville that he was 'determined' that those whose houses had been destroyed or badly damaged 'should receive full com-

---

[1] 'Private', 25 August 1940: Churchill papers, 4/201.

pensation', up to £2,000, and he 'made a note to the effect that he would browbeat the Chancellor of the Exchequer next day'.[1]

Other directives also followed Churchill's South-East visit of August 28. 'I was much concerned on visiting Manston aerodrome yesterday', he minuted to Sinclair, Newall and Ismay, 'to find that, although more than four clear days have passed since it was last raided, the greater part of the craters on the landing ground remain unfilled, and the aerodrome was barely serviceable.' His minute continued:

When you remember what the Germans did at the Stavanger aerodrome, and the enormous rapidity with which craters were filled, I must protest emphatically against this feeble method of repairing damage. Altogether there were 150 people available to work, including those that could be provided from the Air Force personnel. These were doing their best. No effective appliances were available, and the whole process appeared disproportionate to the value of maintaining this fighting vantage ground.

Churchill then set out what he felt ought now to be done:

All craters should be filled in within 24 hours at most, and every case where a crater is unfilled for a longer period should be reported to higher authorities. In order to secure this better service it will be necessary to form some crater-filling companies. You might begin with, say, two of 250 each for the South of England, which is under this intensive attack. These companies should be equipped with all helpful appliances and be highly mobile, so that in a few hours they can be at work on any site which has been cratered. Meanwhile, at every aerodrome in the attack-area, and later elsewhere, there must be accumulated by local contractors stocks of gravel, rubble and other appropriate materials sufficient to fill without replenishment at least 100 craters. Thus the mobile air-field repair companies would arrive to find all the material all ready on the spot.

After the craters had been refilled, Churchill added, 'camouflage efforts might be made to pretend they had not been', although this, he wrote, 'is a refinement'.[2]

Spurred and inspired by all that he had seen on the Kentish promontory, Churchill cast about for further means of defending that vulnerable coastline from sea-borne attack, and in a further minute he set out for the Chiefs of Staff Committee his ideas for finding and using various heavy guns. If British ships could not use the Straits of Dover, he wrote, 'the enemy must not be able to', and he went on to suggest that some of Britain's 18-inch howitzers and 9.2-inch guns 'should be planted in positions wherever they can deny the ports and landings to

---

[1] Colville diary, 28 August 1940: Colville papers. When the question of compensation was put to Kingsley Wood on the following day, he proved to be, Colville noted, 'the perfect yes man'.

[2] Prime Minister's Personal Minute No. M.47, 29 August 1940: Churchill papers, 20/13.

the enemy', as well as support the counter-attack 'which would be launched against any attempted bridgehead'. Churchill added: 'Much of this mass of artillery I saved from the last war has done nothing, and has been under reconditioning for a whole year.'[1]

Another anti-invasion weapon continually in Churchill's mind was poison gas, to be used only if used first by the Germans, but a definite weapon in Britain's defence armoury once German troops were on the beaches. 'I am very glad to know,' Churchill minuted to Herbert Morrison on August 31, 'that the stocks are piling up in this country. Let me know what the total now amounts to.' The necessary containers, Churchill added, 'should be brought level with supply'.[2]

Churchill also envisaged help from the United States in Britain's anti-invasion preparations. He had taken two Americans with him on the journey to Kent,[3] and had raised the question with Brigadier-General Strong, head of the recently arrived American Mission.[4] As Churchill had explained in his minute for the Chiefs of Staff on August 30, he hoped to obtain from the United States 'at least a pair of their 16-inch coast defence weapons', and he added:

> These fire 45,000 yards, throwing a ton and a quarter, without being supercharged. They should therefore be very accurate. General Strong, United States Army, mentioned this to me as a promising line. He thought, without committing his Government, that the United States Army might be prepared to take a couple of these guns and their carriages away from some of their twin batteries.

The negotiations for, and transport of these guns, Churchill wrote, might take about three months, just the time in which it 'ought to be possible' to make their concrete foundations.[5]

The 'general weakness' of the defence of Dover itself in heavy guns was, Churchill minuted, two days later, 'a matter of great seriousness. We must not simply look at dangers piling up without any attempt to

---

[1] Prime Minister's Personal Minute, D.33, 30 August 1940: Churchill papers, 20/13.

[2] Minute of 31 August 1940: Churchill papers, 3/88/3, folio 241.

[3] The Military Attaché, Raymond E. Lee, and Admiral Ghormley. On return to London, Lee wrote to Churchill: 'Dover and the Channel are rapidly becoming the Verdun of this war, staunch and impassable,' and he added: 'there is no one of my countrymen who more fervently wishes you the full measure of success.' (Churchill papers, 2/396.) On 4 September 1940 Ghormley thanked Churchill for sending him an autographed set of his four Marlborough volumes. (Churchill papers, 2/394.) A set was also sent to General Strong.

[4] Admiral Ghormley, in thanking Churchill for 'the trip to and from Dover' added: 'To me this is an occasion which will never be forgotten, not only for the enjoyable trip, but because a man loaded with responsibility can at the same time be the genial host which you were.' (Letter of 29 August 1940: Churchill papers, 2/394.)

[5] Prime Minister's Personal Minute No. D.33, 30 August 1940: Churchill papers, 20/13.

forestall them.'[1] But the air danger was more immediate. The German fighters, he reported to the War Cabinet on August 30, 'were now heavily armoured', and the losses on the two sides 'were tending to approximate'. Britain, he warned, was 'getting through' her reserves of aircraft 'at a dangerous rate'.[2]

That weekend Churchill was again at Chequers. He had invited the three members of the Joint Planning Committee, Air Commodore Slessor, Brigadier Playfair and Captain Daniel, Director of Plans at the Admiralty. Ismay was also present, and at dinner on the Friday night, 'fortified', as Colville noted, 'by 1911 Champagne', Churchill began by expressing his two immediate worries, that in the shipping losses in the North Western Approaches 'lay the seeds of something that might be mortal if allowed to get out of hand', and that in the German gun batteries at Cap Gris Nez lay the danger that Dover 'might be laid in ashes'. To avoid this second danger, Churchill proposed destroying the batteries from the sea. Captain Daniel suggested landing troops, on the French coast to destroy the batteries.

The discussion then turned to wider strategies. He had invited the Joint Planning Committee, Churchill explained, to give them his general idea, 'which they could elaborate' of the 'campaign of 1941'. He would not look as far as 1942, Colville noted, as 1942 'would be the child of 1941'. But he would like to discuss the offensive action Britain should be able to take during 1941 'in order to turn the tables on the Germans and make them wonder for a change where they were going to be struck next'. The 'essential prerequisite' was the command of the Air over the beaches on which British troops and armoured forces might be disembarked. There were a large number of weapons 'well on the road to development', Churchill added, 'which could help us in this', including the AI Air Interception night radar, which was to be used for the first time in flight on the following night, 'to discomfort the enemy night prowlers', as Churchill phrased it. Two other new devices were 'Elsie', the radar and wireless controlled searchlight using the Yagi aerial, and the Photo-Electric proximity fuse.[3] Once these weapons were available, and the likelihood of being 'Namsos-ed' again had 'passed away', British forces could land on the Continent.

Churchill then gave the Joint Planning Committee his own ideas,

---

[1] Prime Minister's Personal Minute No. M.53, 1 September 1940: Churchill papers, 20/13.

[2] War Cabinet No. 238 of 30 August 1940, 11.30 a.m., Minute 1, Confidential Annex: Cabinet papers, 65/14.

[3] This fuse, known as the PE fuse, was later handed over to the Americans, who mass produced it. In 1944 it was to play a crucial part in shooting down the V1, and thus in preserving London.

'*just* to study', of four possible future operations. These were, as Colville noted them down with Churchill's comments, one, the capture of Oslo and the consequent undoing 'of Hitler's first great achievement'; two, the invasion of Italy by sea; three, the cutting off of the Cherbourg peninsula, which might be used as a feint, as he did not wish 'to frighten France'; and four, 'the most attractive of all', a landing in the Low Countries, followed by the seizure of the Ruhr, or at any rate some North German territory, 'so that the enemy might be made to experience war in his own land'.

For such tasks Churchill envisaged the use of between 100,000 and 120,000 men. 'If successful,' he said, 'who could tell to what they might lead.'[1] That same weekend, Desmond Morton wrote to Churchill from London to propose 'a bolder policy' in the Middle East. What he had in mind, he explained, was the possibility of an anti-Vichy coup d'état in Syria. Churchill responded with alacrity, replying at once: 'We must be ready to profit by any favourable reactions from "Hats" and "Menace".'[2]

The casualty figures from air bombardment for the week that had just ended were higher than in any previous week: a total of 296 killed and 565 seriously injured.[3] Churchill also received news on August 31 that one of the ships taking children to the United States had been sunk. 'This disturbed him particularly,' Colville noted.[4] Colville also recorded Churchill's musings during the rest of the weekend. 'It was curious,' he told his guests, 'but in this war he had had no success, and had received nothing but praise, whereas in the last war he had done several things which he thought were good, and had got nothing but abuse.' As to the United States, he commented, it was 'very good in applauding the valiant deeds done by others'.

---

[1] Colville diary, 30 August 1940: Colville papers. Colville later commented: 'Winston wasn't trying to force this idea of the offensive down, but to play it over.' (Conversation with the author, 10 March 1981.)

[2] Minute of 30 August 1940: Premier papers, 7/1. 'Hats' was a trial operation to send ships across the Mediterranean from Gibraltar to Malta without interception. It succeeded, and was followed by the sending of ships to Alexandria. 'Menace' was the Dakar operation.

[3] War Cabinet, Chiefs of Staff Committee, Weekly Résumé No. 52: Churchill papers, 23/6. Of those killed, 80 had been at Portsmouth and 25 at Ramsgate on 24 August 1940, 33 in Birmingham and 10 in London. During August 1940, 1,075 civilians had been killed in the United Kingdom from air bombardment.

[4] The ship, the 15,434 ton Dutch liner *Volendam*, although torpedoed by a U-boat on August 30, had not been sunk. All 884 passengers, including 317 children, were rescued. At the same time a second liner, the *Duchess of Bedford*, reached Quebec from Liverpool with several hundred children on board, among them the author, then aged 3¾. A third ship, the *City of Benares*, was sunk on 18 September 1940, and 77 children drowned. The evacuation of children was then halted (see page 793).

There was further talk that weekend with the Joint Planning Committee, joined on the Saturday by the director of Combined Operations, Sir Roger Keyes. 'I make myself detestable to everybody,' Churchill commented wistfully, 'except Roger, whose dupe I am.' Keyes was keen to take the Channel Islands, and also to seize Casablanca after the completion of operation 'Menace' and the capture of Dakar. Churchill was impressed with this idea, minuting to Ismay on the following day:

I presume you will be thinking about what is to happen should 'Menace' succeed, with little or no bloodshed. It would seem that as soon as de Gaulle has established himself there and in the place a little to the north, he should try to get a footing in Morocco, and our ships and troops could be used to repeat the process of 'Menace', if it has been found to work, immediately and in a more important theatre.

This operation, Churchill added, 'may be called "Threat"'.[1]

As with each of Churchill's proposals for a military operation, the Morocco landing was first put to the Joint Planning Committee for their suggestions as to how it could be carried out, and then to the Chiefs of Staff Committee for their scrutiny. As a result of this process, 'Threat' was elaborated, examined, but in the end rejected. 'We do not consider,' the Chiefs of Staff Committee concluded on September 12, 'that the forces allotted to Operation "Menace", even if reinforced, could succeed in operation "Threat" in the face of organized resistance on a serious scale.' If a choice had to be made, the Chiefs of Staff wrote, they would prefer to carry out the operation to seize the Azores, assuming that Germany decided to occupy Spain once the Allies had taken Dakar.[2]

Those who rejected Churchill's ideas, and who frequently exercised their authority to do so, understood as he did the need for the offensive, and appreciated his search for a worthwhile initiative. On September 1 Colville noted in his diary: 'Ismay's admiration for the PM as a man who has himself experienced the warfare he now directs, knows no bounds.'[3]

On the afternoon of Saturday, August 31, Churchill went to Uxbridge, the Headquarters of No. 11 Group, controlling all the fighter squadrons of the South East. There he witnessed the substantial air

---

[1] Prime Minister's Personal Minute, D.41, 1 September 1940: Premier papers, 3/431, folio 13.

[2] 'Operation "Threat" Report', Chiefs of Staff paper No. 3 (O) of 1940, 12 September 1940 (signed by Newall, Phillips and Haining): Premier papers, 3/431.

[3] Colville diary, 1 September 1940: Colville papers.

battle then in progress above the airfield itself, and was 'deeply moved', as Colville noted, by what he saw. It had, he said, 'brought the war home to him'.[1] He found it 'very instructive', he told the War Cabinet two days later, 'to watch the Officers of the Fighter Command deploying their forces and building up a front at the threatened points'.[2]

From Uxbridge, Churchill returned to Chequers with Sir Hugh Dowding, who, in discussing the German invasion tactics, argued that pilots escaping by parachute should be shot as they came down. But Churchill opposed this, arguing that 'it was like a drowning sailor'.

That night the First Lord, A. V. Alexander, telephoned Chequers to tell Churchill that German ships were at that very moment steering west from the Dutch island of Terschelling. 'Invasion may be imminent,' Colville noted. 'If these German ships came on, they would reach the coast of Norfolk tomorrow morning.'

No further messages of imminent invasion reached Chequers during the night, but there was nevertheless much concern, while, in the battle for the airfields, the news that night was bad. Although at least eighty-five German planes had been shot down that day, British losses were high, with thirty-seven fighters lost and twelve pilots killed. The reason for these increased losses, Churchill was told, was that the Germans were now 'armouring their planes from behind'.[3]

On August 31 Churchill made a final effort to settle the Destroyers for Bases deal with the United States. He was now prepared to give Roosevelt the assurances on which the President had been so insistent. His telegram read:

You ask, Mr President, whether my statement in Parliament on June 4, 1940, about Great Britain never surrendering or scuttling her Fleet, 'represents the settled policy of His Majesty's Government'. It certainly does. I must however observe that these hypothetical contingencies seem more likely to concern the German Fleet, or what is left of it, than our own.[4]

Churchill's last message on August 31 was to Neville Chamberlain, whose 'counsel and assistance', he told him, he would have greatly welcomed on several topics, among them 'more generous treatment of individuals whose houses are smashed in those battered regions' on the coast, as well as on general policy. Churchill's letter continued:

---

[1] Colville diary, 31 August 1940: Colville papers.
[2] War Cabinet No. 239 of 1940, 2 September 1940, 12 noon: Cabinet papers, 65/9.
[3] Colville diary, 31 August 1940: Colville papers.
[4] 'Prime Minister to President', 31 August 1940: Premier papers, 3/462/2, 3, folio 18.

However we are fairly well on top of our job, and everyone was most deter-mined not to allow you to come back until you are fit; and we beg you not to hesitate to take another week besides this one if you feel you will thereby gather more reserve. After operations of this kind, as I know from my own experience, one very quickly recovers enough energy to do half a day's work but it takes some time to get to full efficiency. The great thing is not to try to start too soon and then have a set-back.

We are having fewer Cabinets now and the business often does not take more than an hour. This is not because many things are not going forward, but because we have got into a groove in which much action is outside our control.

A change seems to be coming over the air attack. For some days they sent no dive bombers, and fewer bombers, and were trying to beat our fighters with their newly armoured craft. This tends somewhat to diminish our pro-portion of prizes, but we are all ready with our strong development of cannon guns, against which no armour will be any protection, and hope we shall be cutting into them pretty sharply in the near future. Yesterday they sent the bombers out again and the results were again good for us. We also hope that AI[1] will be ready quite soon for the night prowlers.

There is a certain menace of invasion in the shipping gathering at Kiel and Emden, which we are looking after; but the new focus is upon the North Western Approaches where losses have become very heavy.[2] I have been reading the Riot Act at intervals for the last ten days to the Admiralty, and I am satisfied they are exerting their full strength and ingenuity. I have never known them fail. The fifty American destroyers will be a godsend, and our own new construction is at last beginning to flow.

The spirit of the people is wonderful, but my heart bleeds for the little watering-places which are first impoverished and then badgered and battered.

'However,' Churchill ended, 'when all is said and done I must say I feel pretty good about this war. It will be a long pull if we are to get a thoroughly good result.'[3]

On the morning of Sunday September 1 there was relief at Chequers when the expected invasion 'proved to be nothing', as Colville noted. That afternoon Churchill returned to the Headquarters of No. 11 Group at Uxbridge, together with Ismay, Lindemann and Colville. 'He is full of admiration of the pilots,' Colville noted, 'but said, "It is terrible, terrible, that the British Empire should have gambled on this."' It was, Churchill added, 'one of the most unnecessary wars, and it will probably be one of the most terrible'.

[1] Air Interception, code name 'Smeller', the radar set being installed in British aircraft.

[2] Between August 25 and August 31, fifteen British merchant ships had been sunk by German submarines, and three by German aircraft, including the *Cape York*, torpedoed only ten miles off Kinnaird's Head.

[3] Letter of 31 August 1940: Churchill papers, 2/393.

While at Uxbridge, Churchill watched radar reports coming in on a map 'in the bowels of the earth', fifty feet underground, and discussed the situation with Air Marshal Park, commenting after the visit: 'the Admiralty is now the weak spot. The Air is all right.'

That night Park dined at Chequers, while Lindemann, Churchill's constant companion, described some of the new weapons being designed, and their prospects of success. 'This,' said Churchill, 'was a war of science, a war which could be won with new weapons.'[1]

That night Churchill minuted, for Ismay, about the experimental Searchlight control radar sets with their 'Yagi' aerials: 'Some must be in action during the next moon phase. Report to me how this will be achieved. Use all necessary authority.'[2] Two days later Colonel Jacob informed Churchill that 'all are agreed' that the first twelve sets then being produced should be tried out 'as soon as possible' and that all the necessary work 'will be pushed forward as fast as possible'.[3]

If this was a war which could be 'won with new weapons', it was also a war which could only be won with a sufficiency of weapons, and on September 2 the Treasury gave its approval to considerable added expenditure in the United States. A new emissary, Sir Walter Layton, was sent to join Purvis, in order to seek American agreement that all capital expenditure incurred in preparing the plant and machine tools needed to fulfil Britain's orders would be met 'in part or wholly' by the American administration. But these negotiations were 'not permitted', Sir Richard Hopkins told Layton, 'to interfere with the rapidity of the execution of the contracts for war material upon which we depend for the success of our effort'. It was for Purvis and Layton, Hopkins added, to reach a solution 'favourable to us'.[4]

Censorship reports reaching Downing Street that morning showed that public morale was 'extremely high', Colville noted.[5] But the public was sheltered from the daily fragments of information which brought a less encouraging picture. On September 2 Group Captain Inglis, the

---

[1] Colville diary, 1 September 1940: Colville papers.

[2] Minute of 1 September 1940: Cabinet papers, 120/385.

[3] Minute of 3 September 1940: Cabinet papers, 120/385. On 13 September 1940 the Sixth Weekly Progress Report stated that the first SLC (Yagi) set would be ready on September 16, the second on September 18, four more by September 26, and then two a day, up to a total of twenty-four sets. Then, 'if justified', production could begin 'in quantity' (SLC No. 6, report dated 13 September 1940: Cabinet papers, 120/385).

[4] Treasury letter No. S.47257, 2 September 1940: Cabinet papers, 115/32. Hopkins was Second Secretary at the Treasury; Layton was Director-General of Programmes at the Ministry of Supply (Layton had worked under Churchill at the Ministry of Munitions in 1918, Hopkins under Churchill at the Treasury from 1924 to 1929).

[5] Colville diary, 2 September 1940: Colville papers.

Deputy-Director of Air Ministry Intelligence, noted that the most recent information available, in fact a series of Enigma decrypts, showed that accommodation and supplies were being prepared at fifteen aerodromes between the mouth of the Somme and Dunkirk, for German dive bomber and fighter units, and that all these aerodromes were to be occupied from September 4. In addition, five other aerodromes along the coast were to be prepared as advanced landing-grounds, and supplies of 500-kilogramme bombs were to be distributed among them. Inglis noted:

This congregation of Dive-Bomber Units in a small area opposite the Straits of Dover is significant in view of the fact that Units of this type have not been employed since the 18th August. It may indicate their re-employment on a large scale in preparation for an invasion of the South and South-East Coasts.[1]

Such reports were a continual cause for concern and scrutiny. But Churchill never allowed himself to be carried by the Enigma decrypts into too alarmist a view. Others, unaware of the daily revelations of the most secret source, shared his hopeful outlook. 'There are of course many sources of anxiety in front of us,' Neville Chamberlain wrote from Hampshire on the anniversary of Britain's declaration of war on Germany, 'but like you I feel a growing confidence in the future'. Chamberlain added: 'I can't see why, if Hitler thinks he can smash us, he hasn't done so.'[2]

On Tuesday September 3 the underground Central War Room was used by the War Cabinet for the second time.[3] It was at this War Cabinet that Churchill's Ramsgate experience was effective in a matter of domestic policy, when he obtained his colleagues' approval for compensation for war damage of up to £2,000 for each house destroyed by German bombs.

On that first anniversary of the outbreak of war, Churchill's mind was focused on the needs and offensives of 1941. Whereas only the fighters could be Britain's 'salvation' in the current battle for air mastery over Britain, it was 'the bombers alone' that would provide the means of victory. With that in mind, he wrote in a memorandum for the War Cabinet:

[1] Minute 10, 2 September 1940: Air Ministry papers, 40/2321.
[2] Letter of 3 September 1940: Churchill papers, 20/1.
[3] Further meetings held underground in the Central War Room during September, with Churchill present, were held on September 8 (Chiefs of Staff Committee, 5 p.m.), September 16 (Air Raid Warning Committee, 5 p.m.), September 17 (War Cabinet, 12 noon), September 19 (Chiefs of Staff Committee, 5 p.m.), September 23 (Chiefs of Staff Committee, Forces for India, 9.30 p.m.), September 24 (Chiefs of Staff Committee, Bombing Targets, 9.30 p.m.) and September 26 (War Cabinet, 12 noon). ('PM's Card', September 1940: Churchill papers, 20/19).

We must therefore develop the power to carry an ever-increasing volume of explosives to Germany, so as to pulverise the entire industry and scientific structure on which the war effort and economic life of the enemy depend, while holding him at arm's length from our Island. In no other way at present visible can we hope to overcome the immense military power of Germany, and to nullify the further German victories which may be apprehended as the weight of their force is brought to bear upon African or Oriental theatres.

After the Air priority, Churchill wrote, came the Army's needs. It was 'lamentable' to be told that no more than half a million rifles could be manufactured in Britain before the end of 1941. Home defence would be needed on a 'far greater scale' as large numbers of Regular Army troops were sent abroad, primarily to the defence of the Middle East. Of the nature of Home Defence needs, Churchill commented:

The danger of invasion will not disappear with the coming of winter, and may confront us with novel possibilities in the coming year. The enemy's need to strike down this country will naturally increase as the war progresses, and all kinds of appliances for crossing the seas that do not now exist may be devised. Actual invasion must be regarded as perpetually threatened, but unlikely to materialise as long as strong forces stand in this Island.

With scientific advances, Churchill wrote, both the Air and Naval situations 'will be profoundly altered', and Britain's power to take 'offensive action' would be increased. Churchill added: 'The multiplication of the high-class scientific personnel, as well as the training of those who will handle the new weapons and research work connected with them, should be the very spear-point of our thought and effort.'[1]

Science was the hope, but in the response of some of his officials Churchill saw other factors at work. When he was shown a report drawn up in the Admiralty, stating that the bombardment of German guns at Cap Gris Nez by guns at Dover would not be effective, and giving details of the Dardanelles bombardment of 1915 to confirm this, he minuted angrily to Pound that the account in this report of what happened at the Dardanelles was far from correct. It showed, Churchill wrote, 'a great deal of the prejudice which was so largely responsible for the lamentable passivity to which the Navy was reduced'. His minute continued: 'I trust the same prejudice has not animated the earlier pages. Very fine arguments are always given for doing nothing. The Admiralty will not have helped us very much if they allow these

---

[1] War Cabinet Paper No. 352 of 1940, 'The Munitions Situation', 'Secret', 3 September 1940: Cabinet papers, 66/11, folios 127-8.

powerful batteries to come into existence at Gris Nez without any effort even being made to prevent their being erected.'[1]

That afternoon, in the House of Commons, Churchill surveyed the course of the air battle, outlining the compensation plans for those whose houses were bombed, and reporting, of the Destroyers for Bases deal, that British naval crews were already meeting the Destroyers 'at the various ports where they are being delivered'.[2] But 'no one must suppose', he said, 'that the danger of invasion has passed', even after September 15, 'or whatever is Hitler's latest date'. Even then Britain would not be free 'from the menace of deadly attack from overseas; because winter, with its storms, its fogs, its darkness, may alter the conditions', although some of those changes 'cut both ways'.[3]

Churchill gave the House no information about British losses in the air, which had mounted considerably during the previous week. These details were circulated to the Chiefs of Staff Committee at the weekend: 157 British fighters and 15 bombers had been destroyed, nine of the fighters while on the ground. More than 50 of the fighter pilots had also been killed. In addition, 469 civilians had been killed, and 906 seriously wounded; the dead included sixty-one workers at the Armstrong Vickers aircraft factory at Weybridge during a daylight raid on the afternoon of September 4, fifty-nine civilians killed at Luton, forty-eight at Orpington, thirty-three in Swansea and thirty-two in Liverpool. 'Systematic machine-gunning of civilians' was also reported from Wareham and also from the Scilly Islands. In the first four days of September, twelve merchant ships, nine of them British, had been sunk by mines, torpedo or air attack.[4]

Against these losses could be set several successes, among them four further British air raids on industrial targets in the Berlin area, the safe arrival in Britain of 11,200 Canadian troops on September 2, and the completion on September 3 of Operation 'Hats', in which four ships, *Valiant, Coventry, Calcutta* and *Illustrious*, took anti-aircraft guns and other stores through the Straits of Gibraltar to Malta, which had been under almost uninterrupted air attack from Italy. The success of 'Hats', Churchill minuted to Pound, showed that it would have been 'quite easy to have transported the armoured brigade through the Malta

[1] Prime Minister's Personal Minute, M.67, 5 September 1940: Admiralty papers, 205/6.

[2] Although Churchill did not say so, the port was Halifax, Nova Scotia, where the first group of eight of the destroyers arrived on 6 September 1940. Some 1,680 British officers and ratings had been sent as an advanced party. Halifax was the only port, Churchill's public reference to 'various ports' being a deliberate deception.

[3] *Hansard*, 5 September 1940, columns 39–49.

[4] War Cabinet, Chiefs of Staff Committee, Weekly Résumé No. 53: Churchill papers, 23/6.

channel, and that it would now have been in Egypt, instead of more than three weeks away'. Churchill added: 'I am not impressed by the fact that Admiral Cunningham reiterates his views. Naturally they all stand together like doctors in a case which has gone wrong. The fact remains that an exaggerated fear of Italian aircraft has been allowed to hamper operations.'[1]

On September 6, as a counter measure to the German bombing raids, Churchill suggested to Peirse that a series of 'minor, unexpected, widespread attacks', should be made on two or three nights in a month, on 'the smaller German centres'. Churchill went on to tell Peirse: 'You must remember that these people are never told the truth, and that, wherever the Air Force has not been, they are probably told that the German defences are impregnable.'[2]

Peirse passed on Churchill's suggestion to the Commander-in-Chief, Bomber Command, Air Vice-Marshal Portal, who submitted on September 11, a list of twenty large German towns which he felt should be bombed, and their names broadcast in advance to the Germans 'together with a statement that as a reprisal for each night of indiscriminate bombing by the enemy, one of these towns would be selected for indiscriminate bombing by the RAF'. Portal favoured striking at military objectives in towns where it would be clear 'that the normal spread of such a heavy attack would inevitably cause a high degree of devastation in the town'.[3]

The news from the United States on Saturday September 7 was of Roosevelt's personal efforts to help overcome the continuing difficulties in war supplies from America. On the previous evening Lord Lothian had asked Roosevelt 'when Britain could expect delivery of the 20 motor torpedo boats, the five flying boats and five Flying Fortresses, and the rifles'. Roosevelt had replied, as Lothian reported to London shortly after midnight, 'that he understood that the rifles were already ready but that the Attorney General's opinion made it impossible for him to secure delivery of any of the motor torpedo boats before January'. Lothian then asked Roosevelt 'whether he could secure for early de-

[1] Prime Minister's Personal Minute, M.74, 'Secret and Personal', 6 September 1940: Churchill papers, 20/13.
[2] Prime Minister's Personal Minute, M.72, 6 September 1940: Cabinet papers, 120/300 (PM/406/7).
[3] Portal to Harold Balfour (Under Secretary of State for Air), 11 September 1940: Air Ministry papers, 14/1925.

livery additional flying boats in lieu of motor boats and he authorised me to ask Morgenthau in conjunction with Purvis to put through as soon as possible an alternative programme which would best meet your needs'.

To expedite this, Lothian added, Purvis would see Morgenthau as soon as the Secretary of the Treasury returned to Washington on the coming Monday.[1]

While Churchill was at Chequers on Saturday, September 7, a series of reports were being studied by the Joint Intelligence Committee in London, pointing to the probability of a German invasion beginning within twenty-four hours. These alarming reports came in part from two particularly reliable sources. The first was photographic Intelligence, which showed 'a striking increase' of barges in the Ostend area, and a gradual movement of barges westward. On August 31 there had been 18 barges at Ostend; by September 7 the number had increased to 270.

Meanwhile, on the previous day, September 6, the second principal source of the alarm, an Enigma decrypt, revealed that the transfer of dive-bombers from Norway to France, ordered in the first days of September, had taken place. A report had also been received that all German army leave was to be stopped from September 8, while on September 7, the day of the Joint Intelligence Committee's concern, the Photographic Reconnaissance Unit warned that a 'large-scale and disciplined' movement of barges was taking place to forward bases in the Channel.

The Joint Intelligence Committee judged that the Germans would not bring the barges within range of British air attack unless invasion was imminent. The Committee also noted that the conditions of moon and tide on the south-east coast would be 'particularly favourable' for landings between September 8 and September 10.

Such were the Intelligence indications: photographic, decrypted, and tidal.[2] After they had been assembled during Saturday September 7, an emergency meeting of the Chiefs of Staff was summoned in London, for half past five that afternoon. Churchill was still at Chequers.

At the Chiefs of Staff meeting, the Director of Military Intelligence, Major-General F. G. Beaumont-Nesbitt, explained that Intelligence reports indicated that the German invasion was 'imminent'. It might

---

[1] Washington Telegram No. 1935, sent 1.06 a.m., received 9.55 a.m., 7 September 1940: Premier papers, 3/462/2, 3, folio 11.

[2] These indications were first published in F. H. Hinsley and others, *British Intelligence in the Second World War: Its Influence on Strategy and Operations*, volume 1, London 1979, pages 184–5.

even be launched that Sunday. The Chiefs of Staff therefore decided to order all defence forces in the United Kingdom to 'standby at immediate notice'.[1]

Less than two hours later, at 8.07 p.m., General Headquarters, Home Forces, issued on its own initiative the code word 'Cromwell', bringing all home defence forces to 'immediate action'.

It was a false alarm. Hitler had not yet even set a date for the invasion of Britain, nor had his planners fixed the precise landing places, in the event of a decision to invade. 'Neither I nor the Chiefs of Staff were aware,' Churchill later wrote 'that the decisive code-word "Cromwell" had been used, and the next morning instructions were given to devise intermediate stages by which vigilance could be increased on future occasions without declaring an invasion imminent'. As may be imagined, Churchill added, 'this incident caused a great deal of talk and stir, but no mention of it was made in the newspapers or in Parliament. It served as a useful tonic and rehearsal for all concerned.'[2]

Not an invasion force by sea, but a new assault in the air, was in preparation during the afternoon and evening of September 7. It was an assault that was to bring the whole of Germany's bomber strength against British cities and civilians. That night more than two hundred German bombers struck at London.

---

[1] Chiefs of Staff Committee No. 300 of 1940, 7 September 1940, 5.30 p.m.: Cabinet papers, 79/6. The Chiefs of Staff were represented by Pound, Dill, Peirse (Vice-Chief of the Air Staff), and Ismay.

[2] Winston S. Churchill, *The Second World War*, volume 2, London 1949, page 276.

38

8th to 15th September 1940:
The Blitz begins

T HE Blitz had begun: and when that first night's bombardment was over at dawn on September 8, more than 300 Londoners had been killed, and 1,337 seriously injured. At midday on September 8 Churchill set off with his brother Jack, his son-in-law Duncan Sandys, and Ismay, to visit the worst hit area, the East End of London and the London Docks. As Ismay later wrote to Churchill, recalling that visit:

One of the first places to which you were taken was an air raid shelter which had had a direct hit. About 40 of the inmates has been killed and a very large number wounded. The place was full of people searching for their lost belongings when you arrived. They stormed you, as you got out of the car with cries of 'It was good of you to come Winnie. We thought you'd come. We can take it. Give it 'em back.'

It was a most moving scene. You broke down completely and I nearly did, and as I was trying to get to you through the press of bodies, I heard an old woman say 'You see, he really cares, he's crying.'

Later in the day, as Ismay recalled, 'we found many pathetic little Union Jacks flying on piles of masonry that had once been the homes of these poor people'.

The visit to the bombed area had lasted all afternoon and into the hours of darkness. Fires were still burning in many of the stricken buildings, and, Ismay remembered, 'the Luftwaffe returned to this blaze of light before you left the docks'. The Prime Minister's car had 'a long job', Ismay added, 'getting out through narrow streets, many of which were blocked by houses having been blown across them'.[1]

Even while Churchill was on his visit to the bombed areas, a digest

[1] 'Mr Churchill's Visits During the Blitz, 1. London Docks', notes enclosed with a letter from Ismay to Churchill of 26 November 1946: Churchill papers, 4/198.

of recent Enigma decrypts on German invasion preparations in the French ports brought welcome news to those who were in the secret. The report, circulated by the head of MI 14, Lieutenant-Colonel Kenneth Strong, concluded 'that the training is not complete and there is no indication of any hard and fast decision to take action in any particular direction'.[1]

Counter-invasion preparations, as well as offensive action, could benefit from such knowledge, and at the War Cabinet at noon on September 9, Churchill 'emphasised the importance', as the minutes recorded, 'of attacking ports such as Calais or Boulogne'. Such attacks, he said, 'would affect the morale of German troops assembled to invade this country'.[2] Churchill was able to send Neville Chamberlain, who had just returned to 11 Downing Street, 'a very good report' from No. 11 Group, Fighter Command, that the 400 German aircraft which had crossed the coast that evening 'were met by at least 200 of our fighters who broke them up into small parties, which fled after pursuit'. The losses were 'not yet known', Churchill wrote, but 'I thought you would like to know', and he added, on a personal note: 'I am so glad you are back to share our experiences. I have told them to see to the air conditioning of yr shelter.'[3]

On September 10 the War Cabinet were told that the bombing of London had been 'quite indiscriminate', and it was agreed, as an act of retaliation, that British bombers over Germany should be instructed 'not to return home with their bombs if they failed to locate the targets which they were detailed to attack'.[4]

For three nights, the German bombers over London had been unopposed. On the night of September 10 the anti-aircraft barrage opened, accompanied, as Churchill himself later recalled, 'by a blaze of searchlights'. This 'roaring cannonade', he noted, 'did not do much harm to the enemy, but gave enormous satisfaction to the population. Everyone was cheered by the feeling that we were hitting back.'[5] Churchill's own minutes reflected the needs of the hour; on September 11 he asked Ismay and his Private Office:

'Please call for reports on whether any serious effects are being produced by the air attacks on—

[1] 'Officer Only', 'Most Secret', MI14, 1 p.m., 8 September 1940: War Office papers, 199/911A, B.44.
[2] War Cabinet No. 245 of 1940, 9 September 1940, 12.30 p.m.: Cabinet papers, 65/9.
[3] 'Private', 9 September 1940: Churchill papers, 2/393.
[4] War Cabinet No. 246 of 1940, 10 September 1940, 12.30 p.m.: Cabinet papers, 65/9.
[5] Winston S. Churchill, *The Second World War*, volume 2, London 1949, page 303.

(*a*) food supplies and distribution;
(*b*) numbers of homeless, and provision therefor;
(*c*) exhaustion of Fire Brigade personnel;
(*d*) sewage in London area;
(*e*) gas and electricity;
(*f*) water supplies in London area.'

Churchill added that Ismay should find out the 'practical effect' of the bombing on munitions production at Woolwich.[1]

Public concern was focused on the Blitz. But in the secret circle attention was continually drawn to the prospect of invasion. On September 11 an Enigma decrypt of an order issued by the German Air Force Command headquarters in Western France referred to the need 'drastically' to curtail the transport of individual troops and units during what was described as 'the current movement of armament and of engineer units connected therewith'. Although no definite conclusion could be drawn from this, commented MI 14, 'it cannot be overlooked that it may be in connection with the movement of troops and armament for invasion purposes'.[2]

Churchill reported on other German invasion moves when the War Cabinet met on the morning of September 11. The 'enemy', he said, 'was continuing to pass convoys of ships westward down the French coast', despite a successful British air attack on a small number of ships off Ostend on the previous night. A 'powerful armada', he warned, 'was thus being deployed along the coasts of France opposite this country'. But he added, as the minutes recorded, 'he thought it was by no means impossible that the Germans would in the end decide not to launch an attack on this country because they were unable to obtain the domination over our fighter force'.[3]

This was also Churchill's theme when he broadcast that evening. The German effort to secure 'daylight mastery' of the air over England, he said, was 'the crux of the whole war'. So far, it had 'failed conspicuously', and had cost the Germans 'very dear'. A German invasion attempt without having secured air mastery would be 'a very hazardous undertaking'. Yet invasion preparations 'on a great scale' were steadily going forward: several hundreds of self-propelled barges were 'moving down the coasts of Europe' from the German and Dutch harbours to

[1] Prime Minister's Personal Minute, D.51, 11 September 1940: Churchill papers, 20/13.
[2] 'Most Secret', 'Officer Only', MI14, 11 September 1940: War Office papers, 199/911A, B.45.
[3] War Cabinet No. 247 of 1940, 11 September 1940, 12.30 p.m., minute 3, Confidential Annex: Cabinet papers, 65/15.

the Bay of Biscay, with convoys of merchant ships 'in tens and dozens' moving into the Channel and 'dodging along from port to port', and behind 'clusters' of ships or barges were very large numbers of German troops 'awaiting the order to go on board and set out on their very dangerous and uncertain voyage across the seas'. Churchill continued:

We cannot tell when they will try to come; we cannot be sure that in fact they will try at all; but no one should blind himself to the fact that a heavy, full-scale invasion of this Island is being prepared with all the usual German thoroughness and method, and that it may be launched at any time now— upon England, upon Scotland, or upon Ireland, or upon all three.

If this invasion is going to be tried at all, it does not seem that it can be long delayed. The weather may break at any time. Besides this, it is difficult for the enemy to keep these gatherings of ships waiting about indefinitely, while they are bombed every night by our bombers, and very often shelled by our warships which are waiting for them outside.

Therefore, we must regard the next week or so as a very important week for us in our history. It ranks with the days when the Spanish Armada was ap- proaching the Channel, and Drake was finishing his game of bowls; or when Nelson stood between us and Napoleon's Grand Army at Boulogne. We have read all about this in the history books; but what is happening now is on a far greater scale and of far more consequence to the life and future of the world and its civilization than these brave old days of the past.

'Every man and every woman,' Churchill declared, 'will therefore prepare himself to do his duty, whatever it may be, with special pride and care,' and he emphasized that the Royal Air Force was at the highest strength it had ever reached, conscious also 'of its proved supe- riority, not indeed in numbers, but in men and machines'. Britain's shores were 'well fortified and strongly manned'. The British Army was far larger and better equipped 'then we have ever had before', and besides this were more than a million and a half men of the Home Guard, 'who are just as much soldiers of the Regular Army in status as the Grenadier Guards, and who are determined to fight for every inch of the ground in every village and in every street'. It was 'with some confidence', Churchill added, 'that I say, "Let God defend the right"'.

Churchill then spoke of the Blitz, telling his listeners:

These cruel, wanton, indiscriminate bombings of London are, of course, a part of Hitler's invasion plans. He hopes, by killing large numbers of civilians, and women and children, that he will terrorize and cow the people of this mighty imperial city, and make them a burden and anxiety to the Government and thus distract our attention unduly from the ferocious onslaught he is preparing. Little does he know the spirit of the British nation, or the tough

fibre of the Londoners, whose forebears played a leading part in the establishment of Parliamentary institutions and who have been bred to value freedom
far above their lives.

This wicked man, the repository and embodiment of many forms of soul-
destroying hatreds, this monstrous product of former wrongs and shame, has
now resolved to try to break our famous Island race by a process of indiscriminate slaughter and destruction. What he has done is to kindle a fire in British
hearts, here and all over the world, which will glow long after all traces of the
conflagration he has caused in London have been removed. He has lighted a
fire which will burn with a steady and consuming flame until the last vestiges
of Nazi tyranny have been *burnt* out of Europe, and until the Old World—
and the New—can join hands to rebuild the temples of man's freedom and
man's honour, upon foundations which will not soon or easily be overthrown.

It was a time, Churchill said, 'for everyone to hold together and to
stand firm, as they are doing'. The 'composure and fortitude' of the
citizens of London would constitute a 'message of good cheer' from the
capital city to the soldiers, sailors and airmen, proof that behind the
waiting forces were a people 'who will not flinch or weary of the struggle, hard and protracted though it will be', but 'that we shall rather
draw from the heart of suffering itself the means of inspiration and
survival, and of a victory, won not only for ourselves, but for all; a
victory won not only for our own time, but for the long and better days
that are to come'.[1]

That day, eighty-nine German raiders were shot down, at a cost of
twenty-eight British fighters, and during the night a third of the
German bomber force bound for London was turned back before
reaching the capital, driven off by a much increased anti-aircraft barrage. No German aircraft were shot down that night, but the damage
to London was correspondingly less. In the week ending September 11,
however, the death toll from bombing had reached a height never
before known. A total of 1,211 civilians had been killed, 976 in the
London area.[2]

For Churchill and his senior advisers, impending invasion caused
even greater alarm than the heavy death toll; on September 12 Chur-
chill visited the area which, on the previous day, he had told the War
Cabinet was the most vulnerable to invasion, Dungeness and North
Foreland. With him were A. V. Alexander, Pound, Dill, Ismay and
Brooke. That same day, an Enigma decrypt revealed that the Com-

---

[1] Broadcast of 11 September 1940: 'Every Man to his Post', His Master's Voice recording ALP
1436. The emphasis was Churchill's, as he spoke.
[2] War Cabinet, Chiefs of Staff Committee, Weekly Résumé No. 54: Churchill papers, 23/6.

mander-in-Chief of the German Army, Field Marshal Walter von Brauchitsch, was attending Engineer exercises that day south of Etaples, and that special anti-aircraft protection was being provided.[1] A further decrypt, circulated by Lieutenant-Colonel Strong, gave details of German Air Force officers appointed on the previous day to 'embarkation staffs' at Antwerp, Ostend, Dunkirk and Calais. 'This information,' Strong noted, 'suggests invasion preparations', although it was 'possible' that it related, not to invasion, but to the movement of German Air Force stores by coastal shipping.[2]

These indications could give no precise answer to the invasion plan, or date. Churchill spent the day examining coastal defences, lunching at Dover. 'After lunch,' General Brooke recorded in his diary, 'PM wanted to watch air-fight but there was none to see.' Brooke added: 'PM was very pleasant and as usual most refreshing and entertaining. His popularity is astounding, everywhere crowds rush up to see him and cheer him wildly, encouraging him with shouts of "Stick it!"'[3]

That night, the German bombers came again, and in their wake brought a new problem. Unexploded and delayed action bombs forced the evacuation of thousands of people, and delayed the repair of railway lines and marshalling yards. Unexploded bombs caused in places as much disruption as the bombs themselves: the War Cabinet learnt that in one area, of 29 unexploded bombs reported after a raid, 28 had proved to be 'incorrect' reports.[4] On the night of September 12, Churchill spoke by telephone to the Minister of Transport, Sir John Reith, about railway dislocation, and then telephoned Eden to report that, as a result of unexploded bombs in London, the congestion in the marshalling yards was becoming 'acute', and that clearance parties should be brought both from the North and the West. The existing organization, Churchill added in a minute on the following morning, must be expanded as rapidly as possible, 'to cope with this nuisance, which may soon wear a graver aspect'.[5]

On account of the ferocity of the bombing, which on the night of September 12 had damaged the Ministry of Transport among other buildings, the War Cabinet met on September 13 in the recently reinforced Central War Room, underground. During the meeting, a mes-

[1] 'Most Secret', 'Officer Only', 12 September 1940: War Office papers, 199/911A, B.48.
[2] 'Officer Only', 'Most Secret', 12 September 1940, 6.50 p.m.: War Office papers, 199/911A, B.49.
[3] Diary entry for 12 September 1940, quoted in: Arthur Bryant, *The Turn of the Tide 1939–1943*, London 1957, pages 215–16.
[4] War Cabinet, Chiefs of Staff Committee, Weekly Résumé No. 54: Churchill papers, 23/6.
[5] Prime Minister's Personal Minute, M.91: Churchill papers, 20/13.

sage was handed to Churchill to say that Buckingham Palace had been dive-bombed, but that the King and Queen were safe. This, said Churchill, indicated that the Germans 'meant business'.[1] That afternoon Churchill drove to Chequers, stopping briefly at No. 11 Fighter Group Headquarters at Uxbridge, and at Dollis Hill, where emergency headquarters had been prepared in case the Government had to leave central London. He had already visited Dollis Hill on September 8 and approved the accommodation selected at Neville's Court for his personal use.

The Dollis Hill centre was known by the codeword 'Paddock'. Its principal focus, the substitute War Rooms, were in an underground section of the General Post Office's research centre, and had been built as part of the GPO's own emergency preparations before the war.

On the morning of September 14, after a further night of intense bombing, Churchill decided that plans must be made to evacuate certain civil servants. He was asked whether this included 'yellow' civil servants, those carrying out essential tasks, and 'black', those doing less essential work, as well as Ministers and their senior staffs. His answer was unequivocal. 'I have not at any time,' he minuted, 'contemplated wholesale movement from London of black or yellow Civil Servants. Anything of this nature is so detrimental that it could only be forced upon us by Central London becoming practically uninhabitable. Moreover, new resorts of Civil Servants would soon be identified and harassed, and there is more shelter in London than anywhere else.'

Churchill did see, however, the Dollis Hill centre in use fairly soon by senior officials and Ministers, explaining to Bridges, Ismay and Jacob:

The movement of the high control from the Whitehall area to 'Paddock' or other citadels stands on a different footing. We must make sure that the centre of Government functions harmoniously and vigorously. This would not be possible under conditions of almost continuous air raids. A movement to 'Paddock' by echelons of the War Cabinet, War Cabinet Secretariat, Chiefs of Staff Committee, and Home Forces GHQ must now be planned, and may even begin in some minor respects. War Cabinet Ministers should visit their quarters in 'Paddock' and be ready to move there at short notice. They should be encouraged to sleep there if they want quiet nights. Secrecy cannot be expected, but publicity must be forbidden.

Churchill went on to explain, writing from Downing Street:

[1] Sir John Reith, diary entry for 13 September 1940, quoted in: Charles Smith (editor), *The Reith Diaries*, London 1975, page 263.

We must expect that the Whitehall-Westminster area will be the subject of intensive air attack any time now. The German method is to make the disruption of the Central Government a vital prelude to any major assault upon the country. They have done this everywhere. They will certainly do it here, where the landscape can be so easily recognised, and the river and its high buildings afford a sure guide, both by day and night.

'We must forestall this disruption of central Government,' Churchill warned, and went on to say that he envisaged some two or three hundred 'principal persons' being moved to Dollis Hill. Plans for the first transfers should be made within forty-eight hours, he wrote, and should include those concerned at the Air Ministry, the War Office, and the Home Forces headquarters. The Admiralty was to be located half a mile from 'Paddock', the Air Ministry at another nearby citadel, and the Prime Minister himself in Neville's Court.[1] These plans were made at once; from the Air Ministry, six hundred people were to move in six hours. Those going to Dollis Hill, Bridges told Churchill, 'could move out and occupy "Paddock" at an hour or two's notice, if necessary'.[2] But on September 16 Churchill minuted to Bridges: 'The time has not yet come to move.'[3]

In these minutes about 'Paddock', Churchill made no reference to himself; but his own safety was very much the concern of others. On September 15 Sir Archibald Sinclair, who had been his second-in-command on the western front in 1916, where he had watched Churchill fortify and re-fortify their battalion headquarters of Laurence Farm, wrote from the Air Ministry:

Winston,

One thing worries me these days—that you stay at Downing Street without a proper shelter. This is sad backsliding since we last made war together, when you insisted on battalion headquarters having the best shelter that was available at Laurence Farm! You were right then but you *must* apply the same principle now & go and live in the War Room or somewhere where reasonable protection exists. You are making us ridiculous if you insist on us living in basements & refuse to do it yourself! Whether the country would agree about the rest of us I am not sure—but I am quite sure that they would be angry as well as amazed if they knew that you were not sleeping in reasonable safety.[4]

[1] Prime Minister's Personal Minute, C.5A, 14 September 1940: Premier papers, 4/69/1.
[2] 'Most Secret', 'Arrangements for Move to Paddock', 15 September 1940: Premier papers, 4/69/1, folios 203–7. Paddock's twenty-five rooms were to provide offices for Churchill, the other members of the War Cabinet, their Secretaries, a Cabinet Room, the Staff of Advanced GHQ Home Forces, the headquarters of GHQ Reconnaissance Unit, the War Office staff, a Map Room and a Dominions Liaison Officer.
[3] Minute of 16 September 1940: Premier papers, 4/69/1.
[4] 'Personal', 15 September 1940: Churchill papers, 20/8.

By mid-September arrangements had been completed for Churchill's working headquarters and bedroom to be transferred to the specially prepared rooms at nearby Storey's Gate, known as the No. 10 Annexe, above the underground Central War Room. It was in this Annexe that Churchill and his wife were now to live for the rest of the war, protected, as John Martin later recalled, 'with steel shutters which could be closed over the windows during raids'.[1]

This ground floor flat was made up of two rooms formerly used by Government typists, and now turned into a bedroom and a sitting room. Churchill and his wife moved there on September 16, when 10 Downing Street was reported to be unsafe. Another plan, recorded by Colville that same day, was to move away from the confines of White-hall, possibly to Church House, Westminster.[2] But this further move never came into effect, and it was the Annexe, as John Peck later wrote, which henceforth was to be Churchill's 'real residential base'. Even so, Peck added, although 10 Downing Street remained 'totally insecure' from bombs, and later from flying bombs and rockets, 'Churchill insisted on using No. 10 itself whenever it was reasonably safe to do so, and the sudden changes of venue for meals & meetings produced hair-raising escapes from chaos'.[3]

On Sunday September 15, while Churchill was at Chequers, with his thoughts on Britain's future offensive operations for 1941 and beyond, he minuted to Dudley Pound: 'Great efforts should be made to produce the landing craft as soon as possible.'[4] Then, together with his wife and John Martin, he was driven the sixteen miles to Uxbridge, to watch the Staff control and direction of the day's air battle at No. 11 Fighter Group Headquarters. Twenty-five squadrons reported, and received instructions, from this one point, under the control of Air Vice-Marshal Park.

Churchill, his wife and John Martin were taken down to the bomb-proof Operations Rooms, fifty feet below ground. Nine years later Churchill recalled the events that followed:

The Group Operations Room was like a small theatre, about sixty feet across, and with two storeys. We took our seats in the Dress Circle. Below us

[1] Note attached to diary entry for 14 September 1940: Martin papers.
[2] Colville diary, 16 September 1940: Colville papers.
[3] Sir John Peck, notes for the author, 10 November 1982.
[4] 'Secret', 15 September 1940: Admiralty papers, 205/5.

was the large-scale map-table, around which perhaps twenty highly-trained young men and women, with their telephone assistants, were assembled. Opposite to us, covering the entire wall, where the theatre curtain would be, was a gigantic blackboard divided into six columns with electric bulbs, for the six fighter stations, each of their squadrons having a sub-column of its own, and also divided by lateral lines. Thus the lowest row of bulbs showed as they were lighted the squadrons which were 'Standing By' at two minutes' notice, the next row those at 'Readiness', five minutes, then at 'Available', twenty minutes, then those which had taken off, the next row those which had reported having seen the enemy, the next—with red lights—those which were in action, and the top row those which were returning home.

On the left-hand side, in a kind of glass stage-box, were the four or five officers whose duty it was to weigh and measure the information received from our Observer Corps, which at this time numbered upwards of fifty thousand men, women, and youths. Radar was still in its infancy, but it gave warning of raids approaching our coast, and the observers, with field-glasses and portable telephones, were our main source of information about raiders flying overland. Thousands of messages were therefore received during an action. Several roomfuls of experienced people in other parts of the underground headquarters sifted them with great rapidity, and transmitted the results from minute to minute directly to the plotters seated around the table on the floor and to the officer supervising from the glass stage-box.

On the right hand was another glass stage-box containing Army officers who reported the action of our anti-aircraft batteries, of which at this time in the Command there were two hundred. At night it was of vital importance to stop these batteries firing over certain areas in which our fighters would be closing with the enemy. I was not unacquainted with the general outlines of this system, having had it explained to me a year before the war by Dowding when I visited him at Stanmore. It had been shaped and refined in constant action, and all was now fused together into a most elaborate instrument of war, the like of which existed nowhere in the world.

'I don't know,' said Park, as we went down, 'whether anything will happen to-day. At present all is quiet.' However, after a quarter of an hour the raid-plotters began to move about. An attack of '40 plus' was reported to be coming from the German stations in the Dieppe area. The bulbs along the bottom of the wall display-panel began to glow as various squadrons came to 'Stand By'. Then in quick succession '20 plus', '40 plus' signals were received, and in another ten minutes it was evident that a serious battle impended. On both sides the air began to fill.

One after another signals came in, '40 plus', '60 plus'; there was even an '80 plus'. On the floor-table below us the movement of all the waves of attack was marked by pushing discs forward from minute to minute along different lines of approach, while on the blackboard facing us the rising lights showed our fighter squadrons getting into the air, till there were only four or five left 'At Readiness'.

These air battles, on which so much depended, lasted little more than an hour from the first encounter. The enemy had ample strength to send out new waves of attack, and our squadrons, having gone all out to gain the upper air, would have to refuel after seventy or eighty minutes, or land to rearm after a five-minute engagement. If at this moment of refuelling or rearming the enemy were able to arrive with fresh unchallenged squadrons some of our fighters could be destroyed on the ground. It was therefore one of our principal objects to direct our squadrons so as not to have too many on the ground refuelling or rearming simultaneously during daylight.

Presently the red bulbs showed that the majority of our squadrons were engaged. A subdued hum arose from the floor, where the busy plotters pushed their discs to and fro in accordance with the swiftly-changing situation. Air Vice-Marshal Park gave general directions for the disposition of his fighter force, which were translated into detailed orders to each Fighter Station by a youngish officer in the centre of the Dress Circle, at whose side I sat. Some years after I asked his name. He was Lord Willoughby de Broke. (I met him next in 1947, when the Jockey Club, of which he was a Steward, invited me to see the Derby. He was surprised that I remembered the occasion.) He now gave the orders for the individual squadrons to ascend and patrol as the result of the final information which appeared on the map-table.

The Air Marshal himself walked up and down behind, watching with vigilant eye every move in the game, supervising his junior executive hand, and only occasionally intervening with some decisive order, usually to reinforce a theatened area. In a little while all our squadrons were fighting, and some had already begun to return for fuel. All were in the air. The lower line of bulbs was out. There was not one squadron left in reserve.

At this moment Park spoke to Dowding at Stanmore, asking for three squadrons from No. 12 Group to be put at his disposal in case of another major attack while his squadrons were rearming and refuelling. This was done. They were specially needed to cover London and our fighter aerodromes, because No. 11 Group had already shot their bolt.

The young officer, to whom this seemed a matter of routine, continued to give his orders, in accordance with the general directions of his Group Commander, in a calm, low monotone, and the three reinforcing squadrons were soon absorbed. I became conscious of the anxiety of the Commander, who now stood still behind his subordinate's chair. Hitherto I had watched in silence. I now asked: 'What other reserves have we?' 'There are none,' said Air Vice-Marshal Park. In an account which he wrote about it afterwards he said that at this I 'looked grave'. Well I might. What losses should we not suffer if our refuelling planes were caught on the ground by further raids of '40 plus' or '50 plus'! The odds were great; our margins small; the stakes infinite.

Another five minutes passed, and most of our squadrons had now descended to refuel. In many cases our resources could not give them overhead protection. Then it appeared that the enemy were going home. The shifting of the discs on the table below showed a continuous eastward movement of German bombers and fighters. No new attack appeared. In another ten minutes the action was ended. We climbed again the stairways which led to the surface, and almost as we emerged the 'All Clear' sounded.

'We are very glad, sir, you have seen this,' said Park. 'Of course, during the last twenty minutes we were so choked with information that we couldn't handle it. This shows you the limitation of our present resources. They have been strained far beyond their limits to-day.' I asked whether any results had come to hand, and remarked that the attack appeared to have been repelled satisfactorily. Park replied that he was not satisfied that we had intercepted as many raiders as he had hoped we should. It was evident that the enemy had everywhere pierced our defences. Many scores of German bombers, with their fighter escort, had been reported over London. About a dozen had been brought down while I was below, but no picture of the results of the battle or of the damage or losses could be obtained.[1]

It was four o'clock in the afternoon. The results of the day's air battle would not be known for some hours. Churchill and his wife returned to Chequers. According to his habit, Churchill would now sleep for an hour or two, before embarking on the evening's work. But that afternoon his sleep was to be postponed, for alarming news awaited him. September 15 was the day on which Operation 'Menace' was to take place, with the landing of de Gaulle's troops at Dakar, under the protection of British naval guns, and if necessary with British military support. The hope had always been that this landing would be unopposed. But a series of misfortunes now endangered 'Menace'.

---

[1] Winston S. Churchill, *The Second World War*, volume 2, London 1949, pages 293–7. After the war Churchill asked Park to read this account in draft, and to check all its technical aspects. On 19 October 1946 Park wrote to Churchill: 'I have done as you suggested by writing my comments and amendments in pencil into the enclosed draft document. If my remarks are not clear or are not all you require I shall be very willing to supplement them in writing or to make a journey up to London to explain in person to you.' ('Private', 19 October 1946: Churchill papers, 4/198.) Most of the technical details in Churchill's account were taken from Park's comments. 'Thank you so much,' Churchill replied on 22 October 1946, 'for all the trouble you have taken in correcting my notes. It has so greatly helped me in telling this story.' (Letter of 22 October 1946, from 28 Hyde Park Gate: Churchill papers, 4/198.)

39

Menace Endangered

FRENCH and British troops had sailed for Dakar at the end of August and by early September were assembled well to the south of Dakar. But on September 9 a force of six French warships loyal to Vichy had left Toulon, sailed through the Straits of Gibraltar on the morning of September 11, and reached Casablanca unopposed.[1] The departure of these warships from Toulon had been reported from Madrid by the British Naval Attaché, Captain Hillgarth, who had been given the information by the Vichy Naval Attaché, Captain Delaye. The destination of the ships, Hillgarth added, was 'not known'.[2]

Hillgarth's signal was sent at 6.09 p.m. on September 10 both to London and Gibraltar, and relayed back to Gibraltar from London. The signal reached London that same night, ten minutes before midnight. It also reached Gibraltar, shortly after midnight, but was not acted upon by Admiral North, the Flag Officer Commanding the North Atlantic Station. A month later, on October 15, the Board of Admiralty removed North from his command. Captain R. H. Bevan, the Director of Operations (Foreign) at the Admiralty, who had delayed the message in London by his decision not to wake up Pound with it, but to add it to the regular 8 a.m. morning distribution pile, later received a letter expressing 'their Lordship's displeasure'.[3]

[1] The warships were the three cruisers *Georges Leygues*, *Gloire* and *Montcalm*, and the three light cruisers, *Le Malin*, *Le Fantasque* and *L'Audacieux*.

[2] Signal from the Naval Attaché, Madrid to Senior Officer (Intelligence) Gibraltar, repeated to the Director of Naval Intelligence, Admiralty, despatched 6.09 p.m., 10 September 1940: Churchill papers, 4/170.

[3] Letter of 20 September 1940. Churchill wanted Bevan placed on half pay, regarding the Board of Admiralty's 'displeasure' as a 'minor and altogether inadequate' punishment for what he described as 'a gross case of neglect of duty in a Staff Officer'. But Alexander and the Naval Staff stood by their decision, arguing that Churchill's proposal would be 'contrary to Naval Justice and civil practice'. In accepting this decision, Churchill minuted to Alexander and Pound: 'The

As soon as the seriousness of the situation was realized in London, a British naval force, led by the battleship *Renown*, was at once ordered to patrol southward off Casablanca 'to prevent these ships from entering Dakar'.[1] The British force waited in its war station from the morning of September 12 until the afternoon of September 13, while haze shrouded Casablanca and its vicinity; then, at 4.20 p.m. on September 13, *Renown* received an air reconnaisance report that there were no cruisers in Casablanca. They had in fact, under cover of the haze, sailed undetected to Dakar.

It was on his return to Chequers at 4.30 on the afternoon of September 15 that Churchill learned of the arrival of the French warships at Dakar.[2] Three-quarters of an hour later he telephoned to Desmond Morton at 10 Downing Street, instructing him to call an immediate meeting of the Chiefs of Staff or Vice-Chiefs, and to give orders for Operation 'Menace' to be 'cancelled'.

Churchill proposed to Morton that the British force should land instead at Conakry, in French Guinea, and make its way up the railway, towards Bamako, with the idea of cutting off Dakar by land, while Dakar was blockaded from the sea and all sea-borne communications with Vichy, or other sources of supply or reinforcement, cut off.

The land force which was to advance from Conakry to Dakar must, Churchill told Morton, be 'adequate', and must therefore include British Commandos. It was 'no longer essential to keep the operation wholly French', Churchill added. 'It is far more important that the operation should succeed.'[3]

The Chiefs of Staff Committee met at six that evening to consider Churchill's telephone message. They accepted that 'Menace' should be cancelled, but pointed out that Britain had insufficient naval forces to blockade Dakar, and at the same time deal with the invasion of Britain, and maintain a force strong enough at Gibraltar to prevent Vichy naval reinforcements again breaking out of the Mediterranean. At the same time they doubted the feasibility of British or French troops

---

premature infliction of a minor and altogether inadequate punishment is now held to bar proper disciplinary treatment of a gross case of neglect of duty in a Staff Officer. I greatly regret the result.' (Minutes of 19 to 27 October 1940: Premier papers, 3/71.)

[1] War Cabinet No. 248 of 1940, 12 September 1940, 12.30 p.m.: Cabinet papers, 65/9.

[2] Only two hours before Admiral Cunningham arrived off Dakar with *Ark Royal* and three cruisers, *Devonshire*, *Australia* and *Cumberland*.

[3] 'Most Secret', record of telephone conversation initialled by Desmond Morton, 15 September 1940: Premier papers, 3/276, folios 195–6.

advancing the 400 miles by rail and track from Conakry to Bamako, and then the further 230 miles by track to Dakar.

The Chiefs of Staff proposed another plan: de Gaulle should 'proceed at once' to Duala, which had declared itself for him, disembark there, 'and advance into Chad province'.[1]

Churchill accepted the Chiefs of Staff's advice, and was relieved that they too wished to cancel 'Menace'. That night he drafted a message to Admiral Cunningham and General Irwin which began: 'Arrival of Vichy cruisers possibly with troops on board seems to me to destroy hope of a bloodless capture of Dakar, and must make its storm a far more severe operation with evil political consequences. You should immediately reconsider the whole position with de Gaulle....'[2] On the following morning Churchill put the cancellation to the War Cabinet, giving as his opinion that to undertake 'Menace' now that the six French warships were at Dakar was 'out of the question, and in view of the fact that the French warships might have troops on board would, if attempted, end in bloodshed'.

A 'fiasco', Churchill added, 'had undoubtedly occurred', and it was to be hoped 'it would not too much engage public attention'.[3]

At 2 p.m. on September 16 Admiral Cunningham and General Irwin were informed by Churchill that the presence of French cruisers at Dakar rendered the Dakar Operation 'impracticable'.[4] But both men telegraphed direct to Churchill, urging that they be allowed to attempt a landing despite the cruisers. De Gaulle had likewise, as Hollis noted two weeks later, 'emphatically protested against the cancellation'.[5]

De Gaulle was supported in his protest by Spears, who argued in a telegram to Churchill that if de Gaulle were forced to give up the Dakar expedition, 'his power to influence either West Africa or any part of the French Empire would be gone for ever'.[6]

The War Cabinet discussed Spears' telegram and de Gaulle's own

---

[1] War Cabinet, Chiefs of Staff Committee, Operation 'Menace', Report, 15 September 1940, signed 'C. L. N. Newall, Dudley Pound, R. H. Haining for CIGS.': Premier papers, 3/276, folios 160-1.

[2] 'Secret and Personal', unsent, marked by Churchill 'Show me later': Premier papers, 3/276, folio 180.

[3] War Cabinet No. 250 of 1940, 16 September 1940, 12 noon. Minute 4, Confidential Annex: Cabinet papers 65/15.

[4] Prime Minister's Personal Minute, M.96, 'Most Immediate', 16 September 1940, 2 p.m.: Churchill papers, 4/170.

[5] 'Secret', memorandum of 30 September 1940: Premier papers, 3/276, folio 156.

[6] 'Secret', 'The Dakar Operation', prepared by the Naval Staff, 30 September 1940: Premier papers, 3/276, folios 112-20.

protest at its meeting on September 17. At this meeting Eden reiterated Spears' view, telling his colleagues 'that General de Gaulle had no political future if he did not carry out an operation more or less on the lines of "Menace"'. Eden added that in his view 'the right course was bold action against Dakar'. He was supported by Neville Chamberlain, who thought that 'the risk of not going on with the operation was greater than the risk of carrying it through'. If the operation were abandoned, Chamberlain said, 'it seemed to him that nothing could prevent the disintegration of the Free French forces in West Africa'.

Churchill adopted a cautious tone. The arrival of 'six medium sized warships', he agreed with Pound, 'was not very much', but he thought that they might nevertheless 'strengthen the determination of the pro-Vichy forces in Dakar'.[1]

The majority of those who spoke favoured the continuation of 'Menace', and on the following day the War Cabinet set September 23 as the new date for the landing.[2] 'As you know,' General Irwin telegraphed to Dill on the day of the War Cabinet's decision to defer to the opinion of the Commanders on the spot, 'I have already accepted risks in this operation to be fully justified on purely military grounds. New information possibly increases these risks, but I consider them worth accepting in view of obvious results of success.' Irwin added that de Gaulle 'has also committed himself to complete co-operation with British troops in case of need and has not shirked responsibility of fighting between Frenchmen'.[3]

Churchill's caution of September 15 had been eclipsed by the enthusiasm of others. Soon, he too was to regain his earlier hopes for a successful action. But his first reaction on learning of the arrival of the Vichy warships had been to bring 'Menace' to an end.

---

[1] War Cabinet No. 252 of 1940, 17 September 1940, Confidential Annex: Cabinet papers, 65/15.

[2] War Cabinet No. 253 of 1940, 18 September 1940, 12 noon, Confidential Annex: Cabinet papers, 65/15.

[3] Telegram despatched at 4.48 a.m., and received 8.30 a.m., 18 September 1940, 'Most Immediate', 'Personal', printed in War Cabinet, 'The Dakar Operation', 'Secret', Hist. (A) 1. (Revise), 5 February 1941: Premier papers, 3/276, Annex V, 12.

40

'Never maltreat the enemy
by halves'

A T 5.15 p.m. on September 15, having given the order to cancel
the Dakar operation, Churchill had taken a belated afternoon
sleep. Tired by his visits to No. 11 Fighter Group Headquarters that
afternoon, and by the dramatic news from Dakar, he slept until eight
in the evening. Waking, he rang for John Martin, who was on duty at
Chequers that weekend. As Churchill later recalled, Martin then came
in with the evening budget of news from all over the world. 'It was
repellent,' Churchill wrote. 'This had gone wrong here; that had been
delayed there; an unsatisfactory answer had been received from so-
and-so; there had been bad sinkings in the Atlantic.[1] "However," said
Martin, as he finished this account, "all is redeemed by the air. We
have shot down one hundred and eighty-three for a loss of under
forty." '[2] Two days later Churchill told the House of Commons:
'Sunday's action was the most brilliant and fruitful of any fought upon
a large scale up to that date by the fighters of the Royal Air Force,'
and he added: 'We may await the decision of this prolonged air battle
with sober but increasing confidence.'[3]

Churchill had been considerably alarmed by a report, sent to him
by Pound two days earlier, on the possibility of the Germans deciding
to launch their invasion in fog.[4] This was precisely the sort of surprise
against which plans would have to be made well in advance; perhaps,

[1] Two British and a Norwegian merchant ship sunk on September 14, a British and a Greek
merchant ship (both bringing timber from Canada) on September 15.

[2] Winston S. Churchill, *The Second World War*, volume 2, London 1949, page 297. After the war
the German losses were put at 56. British losses were 25, with 14 pilots killed.

[3] *Hansard*, 17 September 1940; columns 135–8, speech begun at 4.20 p.m.

[4] 'Possibility of attempted invasion in fog or weather of low visibility', 'Most Secret', 14 September 1940: Premier papers, 3/222/4, folios 8–9.

Churchill felt, *the* surprise. During September 16 he asked Colonel Jacob to send Pound's report to the Commander-in-Chief Home Forces, through the Chiefs of Staff, together with his own comment:

I consider that fog is the gravest danger, as it throws both Air Forces out of action, baffles our artillery, prevents organized Naval attack, and specially favours the infiltration tactics by which the enemy will most probably seek to secure his lodgments. Should conditions of fog prevail, the strongest possible Air barrage must be put down upon the invasion ports during the night and early morning. I should be glad to be advised of the proposed Naval action by our flotillas, both in darkness and at dawn: (a) if the fog lies more on the English than the French side of the Channel; (b) if it is uniform on both sides.

Are we proposing to use radio aids to navigation?

Prolonged conditions of stand-by under frequent British air bombardment would, Churchill wrote, 'be exhausting to the enemy'. None the less, he added, 'fog is our foe'.[1]

This was Churchill's private, secret worry; for the public, it was the scale of deaths by bombing that was causing the greatest alarm. During his speech on September 17, Churchill told the House of Commons that during the first half of September, 2,000 civilians had been killed, and about 8,000 wounded by air bombardment, four-fifths in London; and he went on to warn that 'we must expect that very much more intense forms of air fighting will be experienced in future than we have yet seen'.[2] Harold Nicolson commented in his diary: 'I must say that he does not try to cheer us up with vain promises.'[3]

The House of Commons was under no illusions as to the reality of the bombardment. Even before Churchill spoke, the air raid sirens had sounded, and MPs had gone down into the cellars until the all-clear. After Churchill's short statement, the House went into Secret Session, and Churchill outlined plans to keep the dates of the public Sessions as secret as possible, to protect the Houses of Parliament from becoming too tempting a target. 'We ought not to flatter ourselves,' he said, 'by imagining that we are irreplaceable, but at the same time it cannot be denied that two or three hundred by-elections would be a quite needless complication of our affairs at this particular juncture.' Sessions would begin at eleven and end at four, to avoid the now 'nightly air raiding'.

The next few weeks, Churchill warned, were 'grave and anxious'. Upward of 1,700 self-propelled barges and more than 200 sea-going

---

[1] Prime Minister's Personal Minute, D.58, 16 September 1940: Premier papers, 3/222/4, folio 5.

[2] *Hansard*, 17 September 1940, columns 135-8, speech begun at 4.20 p.m.

[3] Diary entry for 17 September 1940, quoted in: Nigel Nicolson (editor), *Harold Nicolson, Diaries and Letters 1939-1945*, London 1967, page 114.

ships, some very large, were 'already gathered' at the many invasion ports in German occupation. Churchill then told his fellow MPs:

If this is all a pretence and stratagem to pin us down here, it has been executed with surprising thoroughness and on a gigantic scale. Some of these ships and barges, when struck by our bombing counter-attack and preventive attack, have blown up with tremendous explosions, showing that they are fully loaded with all the munitions needed for the invading armies to beat us down and subjugate us utterly.

The shipping available and now assembled is sufficient to carry in one voyage nearly half a million men. We should, of course, expect to drown a great many on the way over, and to destroy a large proportion of their vessels.

But when you reflect upon the many points from which they could start, and upon the fact that even the most likely sector of invasion, i.e. the sector in which enemy fighter support is available for their bombers and dive bombers, extending from the Wash to the Isle of Wight, is nearly as long as the whole front in France from the Alps to the sea, and also upon the dangers of fog or artificial fog, one must expect many lodgments or attempted lodgments to be made on our island simultaneously.

These we shall hope to deal with as they occur, and also to cut off the supply across the sea by which the enemy will seek to nourish his lodgments.

The difficulties of the invader are not ended when he sets foot on shore. A new chapter of perils opens upon him. I am confident that we shall succeed in defeating and largely destroying this most tremendous onslaught by which we are now threatened, and anyhow, whatever happens, we will all go down fighting to the end.

'I feel as sure as the sun will rise tomorrow,' Churchill added, 'that we shall be victorious.'[1]

Despite Churchill's confidence in the long-term prospects, bad news continued to crowd in upon him and his advisers. After his speech in the House of Commons on September 17 he had returned to Downing Street, to learn that Italian troops had crossed the Egyptian frontier and were advancing on Sidi Barrani, sixty miles inside it. He also learned that in the Atlantic a German submarine had torpedoed the *City of Benares*, and that 77 children being evacuated to Canada had been drowned, together with 72 adults accompanying them, and members of the crew.[2] Nor had the danger of invasion through fog receded, and

[1] Speech of 17 September 1940: full text in Charles Eade (editor), *Secret Session Speeches by the Right Hon. Winston S. Churchill, OM, CH, MP*, London 1946, pages 17–23.

[2] Only 15 children and 18 women were saved (as reported to War Cabinet No. 254 of 1940, 19 September 1940, 12 noon: Cabinet papers, 65/9). On 23 September 1940 Churchill told the Defence Committee 'that in view of the recent disaster to the ship carrying women and children to Canada, the further evacuation overseas of children must cease'. There was no dissent. (Cabinet papers, 79/6, folio 323.)

'Cromwell', invasion Alert No. 1, was still in force, sustained by an Intelligence assessment by the Naval Section at Bletchley that as far as German invasion preparations were concerned 'everything was ready'.[1]

Early on the following morning, Churchill asked Ismay to enquire from the Chiefs of Staff Committee 'whether in view of the rough weather, Alert No. 1 might not be discreetly relaxed to the next grade'.[2] That same day, in lighter mood, he wrote to the First Lord of the Admiralty: 'Surely you can run to a new Admiralty flag. It grieves me to see the present dingy object every morning.'[3]

Further intercepted signals implied that preparations were still continuing, and Alert No. 1 remained in force. Realizing that he could not relax his vigilance, on September 18 Churchill asked Ismay to inquire if there was any way 'in which a sheet of flaming oil cannot be spread over one or more of the invasion harbours', rather as, he wrote, at the time of the Armada 'a fire-ship had been used' against the Spanish ships off Dunkirk.[4] 'The Admiralty can surely think of something,' Churchill added.[5]

On September 18 Wavell's forces to the south of Sidi Barrani were keeping the Italians under observation as they advanced along the coastal plain. Churchill telegraphed to the Commander-in-Chief: 'On the eve of what may prove to be one of the memorable battles of history I send you every wish for good fortune and my assurance that all acts or decisions of valour and violence against the enemy will, whatever their upshot, receive the resolute support of His Majesty's Government.'[6] Even as this telegram was on its way to Cairo, the Italians arrived in the area of Sidi Barrani, eighty miles west of Wavell's main preparations for battle at Mersa Matruh. The British were now holding a line more than a hundred and forty miles inside Egypt, and less than a hundred and forty-five miles from Alexandria. The Italians, under Graziani, came on no further.

On September 19 a War Office Intelligence Summary reported that the increased number of merchant vessels at Brest, Cherbourg and Le

[1] Report of 13 September 1940, quoted in F. H. Hinsley and others, *British Intelligence in the Second World War, Its Influence on Strategy and Operations*, volume 1, London 1979, page 186. This particular assessment had been made by Hinsley himself.

[2] Prime Minister's Personal Minute, D.61, 'Action this Day', 18 September 1940: Churchill papers, 20/13.

[3] Prime Minister's Personal Minute, M.99, 18 September 1940: Churchill papers, 20/13.

[4] In fact *eight* fire-ships, off *Calais*.

[5] Prime Minister's Personal Minute, D.62, 'Action this Day', 18 September 1940: Premier papers, 3/264, folio 13.

[6] Telegram of 18 September 1940: Premier papers, 3/309/1, folio 5.

Havre 'has extended the invasion threat to the West of England and Eire'.[1] But suddenly a new facet of the Blitz became the dominant cause for concern, when, on the morning of September 19, German aircraft dropped at least thirty-six large mines by parachute. These were indiscriminate bombings, of a type new to aerial warfare. Churchill's initial reaction was, as he told Colville, to say that 'we must drop two for every one of theirs'.[2] That same morning Churchill minuted to Ismay, for the Chiefs of Staff Committee:

1. It was not solely on moral grounds that we decided against retaliation upon Germany. It pays us better to concentrate upon limited high-class military objectives. Moreover in the indiscriminate warfare the enemy's lack of skill in navigation, etc., does not tell against him so much.

2. However, the dropping of large mines by parachute proclaims the enemy's entire abandonment of all pretence of aiming at military objectives. At five thousand feet he cannot have the slightest idea what he is going to hit. This therefore proves the 'act of terror' intention against the civil population. We must consider whether his morale would stand up to this as well as ours. Here is a simple war thought.

3. My inclination is to say that we will drop a heavy parachute mine on German cities for every one he drops on ours; and it might be an intriguing idea to mention a list of cities that would be black-listed for this purpose. I do not think they would like it, and there is no reason why they should not have a period of suspense. . . .

The retaliation he favoured, Churchill added, was to 'act by parachute mines upon a number of German towns not hitherto touched', and he wished to know by the night of September 21 'what is the worst form of retaliation, i.e. equal retaliation, that we can inflict upon ordinary German cities for what they are now doing to us by means of the parachute mine'.[3]

Later that same morning, Churchill told the Chiefs of Staff Committee 'that we should retaliate in like manner on the enemy', and asked for a report on what steps could be taken 'to produce similar or equally destructive types of explosives for dropping on Germany'.[4] That evening Harold Nicolson wrote in his diary: 'The only solution I can see at present are reprisals, which we are both unable and unwilling to exert.

[1] War Office Weekly Intelligence Commentary No. 57, 'Secret', to 12 Noon on 19 September 1940: Churchill papers, 20/16.
[2] Colville diary, 19 September 1940: Colville papers.
[3] Prime Minister's Personal Minute, D.66, 19 September 1940: Premier papers, 3/314/2, folios 67–9.
[4] Chiefs of Staff Committee No. 316 of 1940, 19 September 1940, 10 a.m.: Cabinet papers, 79/6.

If we are saved, we shall be saved by our optimism. Few people really believe that this ordeal can be continued for ever. They hope that "something may turn up".'[1]

The Chiefs of Staff replied to Churchill's request for retaliation bombing with support for a resumption of the bombing of Germany 'in such a form as to combine a further taste of their own medicine for the German population with the continuance of our strategic offensive'.[2]

A crisis had arisen in the second week of September with the realization in London that certain essential war supplies due from the United States were not arriving. 'He had been assured,' Churchill told Sir Alexander Cadogan, 'that this material had been promised to us, and could not but feel growing disappointment at its failure to materialize.'

On Churchill's instructions, Cadogan telephoned Lord Lothian on the afternoon of September 20, 'to ask where we stood' in regard to these essential materials. That same day Cadogan sent Churchill an account of the conversation, in which it became apparent that in many areas of essential supply there were problems and delays. As Cadogan reported:

Lord Lothian said that, as we knew, owing to a ruling of the American Attorney-General, the motor torpedo boats could not be transferred before January. As regards the rest of the material, the 250,000 rifles were arranged for and ready for shipment.

I told him that I understood there had been some difficulty owing to the requirements of our own people in the matter of packing and I asked him to look into that matter and to do everything possible to expedite shipment.

The Ambassador also said that the Flying Fortresses were arranged for, but that only one of these was at present ready. . . .

I again impressed upon him that the Prime Minister regarded this as a matter of the greatest urgency and importance. He promised to do everything possible to expedite matters.[3]

Churchill decided that he must intervene personally to instil the necessary sense of priority, and to obtain the facts. On the night of September 22 he spoke on the trans-Atlantic telephone to Purvis, explaining the 'relative urgency' of Britain's various needs, and asking

---

[1] Diary entry for 19 September 1940, quoted in: Nigel Nicolson (editor), *Harold Nicolson, Diaries and Letters 1939–1945*, London 1967, page 115.

[2] 'Secret', 'Bombing Targets', 21 September 1940: Premier papers, 3/314/2, folios 64–5.

[3] 'Most Secret', 20 September 1940: Cabinet papers, 115/70.

Purvis to telegraph daily a report on the position of his negotiations regarding munitions releases and shipping arrangements.

Purvis' first telegram was sent at four minutes past midnight on the night of his talk with Churchill, and read:

Releases.
Daily report No. 1.
Rifles. The 250,000 just released are at Rock Island Arsenal, Illinois, 24 hours by express from New York and are now being made ready for shipment. First 50,000 expected to leave Arsenal Monday; balance it is hoped by Thursday evening. United States Administration hopes to use United States Steel Export Corporation as before as intermediary legally required and the arrangements for this will probably be completed tomorrow Monday. Meanwhile are making sure quickest arrival methods will be used.[1]

Henceforth, Churchill was able, by a scrutiny of these daily telegraphic reports from Purvis, to see exactly where delays or difficulties might occur. On September 23 Sir Arthur Salter promised Churchill that these reports would be sent to him 'at once on their arrival'. Salter added that he would personally ensure that other important Purvis telegrams were also 'brought to your notice without delay'.[2]

Even as Purvis was preparing his second daily report for Churchill, the Prime Minister had to deal with a crisis which had arisen in the administrative aspect of Britain's relations with the United States, and which involved Purvis at its centre. For some weeks there had been growing resentment in Washington at the number of British missions, and their apparently overlapping functions; the United States Administration, reported the British Embassy, while continuing to 'extend the spheres in which it helps us', was 'a little bewildered by some of our missions, which seemed to overlap'.[3] 'Let me have a complete list,' Churchill minuted to Bridges on September 21, 'of the Missions which we have sent to the United States which are at work there.'[4]

In reply, a list of eleven missions was compiled. The first mission on the list was the British Purchasing Commission headed by Purvis. The second was the Layton Mission, which had reached Washington on September 19, was working closely with Purvis, and was intended to be temporary. There were three military missions,[5] an Air Com-

---

[1] 'Pursa' No. 107, 'Most Immediate', sent 12.04 a.m., received 10 a.m., 23 September 1940: Cabinet papers, 115/70.
[2] 'Secret', 23 September 1940: Cabinet papers, 115/70.
[3] 'Weekly Political Summary', Washington Telegram No. 2109: Cabinet papers, 115/70.
[4] Prime Minister's Personal Minute, 'Secret', 21 September 1940: Cabinet papers, 115/70.
[5] Brigadier Pratt (tanks), General Pakenham-Walsh and Colonel Campion (guns) and Lieutenant-Colonel Smith (other Service vehicles).

mission,[1] an Admiralty Technical Mission,[2] a shipbuilding mission sent by the Admiralty to investigate the possibility of the purchase of merchant ships,[3] an economic warfare mission attached to the British Embassy in Washington,[4] an Oil mission under Sir Andrew Agnew and a Scientific Research mission under Sir Henry Tizard.

Most of these missions, Bridges pointed out, were in close touch with the Purchasing Commission. Many had intended to be of only short duration. Sir Andrew Agnew's mission, for example, 'was originally to last a week but he has now been in America a month'.[5]

Reading of these various missions, Churchill minuted to Bridges: 'Let me have your criticisms on the systems which have grown up piecemeal, and may require to be reduced to order.' The Layton mission 'in particular', Churchill added, 'seems very vague. When is he coming back?'[6]

The importance of strenghening Purvis' authority was quickly recognized. 'In a matter of this kind,' Bridges told Churchill, 'personalities count tremendously. As you know, Purvis is on very intimate terms with Morgenthau, who is such an important means of approach to the President.'[7] But Bridges made no suggestions in his minute for any changes, and Churchill wrote again: 'I am sorry you are not able to make me a more clear-cut proposal about these missions. I cannot feel that "all is for the best in the best of all possible worlds".'

Churchill suggested to Bridges that Sir Arthur Salter should be consulted 'with a view to outlining proposals for a considerable tidying up'. Meanwhile, Sir Walter Layton should be asked through the Ministry of Supply 'to expedite his return' and the War Office should be asked to 'do the same by Pakenham-Walsh'. When, Churchill asked, could the Admiralty mission 'be wound up', or placed 'under the general control of Mr Purvis?' Churchill's minute ended: 'When is Sir Henry Tizard's mission coming to an end, and why does Sir Andrew Agnew delay his return?'[8]

It was finally decided, at Churchill's suggestion, to seek further advice on the matter. 'Nothing can be settled,' Churchill minuted three

---

[1] Sir Henry Self (on behalf of the Ministry of Aircraft Production).

[2] Vice Admiral A. E. Evans (headquarters in Ottawa; a liaison officer in New York).

[3] R. Cyril Thompson.

[4] Mr Stopford and Mr Marris.

[5] 'British Missions in the United States', Memorandum 'sent by Sir E. Bridges to the Prime Minister': Cabinet papers, 115/70.

[6] Prime Minister's Personal Minute, C.9, 26 September 1940: Premier papers, 3/477/1, folio 20.

[7] 'Secret', 28 September 1940: Cabinet papers, 115/70.

[8] Minute of 29 September 1940: Cabinet papers, 115/70.

weeks later, 'till Sir W. Layton and Mr Purvis are here.'[1] Two days later, Bridges informed Churchill that Purvis was bringing with him to London a scheme 'for the reorganization of our missions'.[2] No more could be done until his arrival. But it was clear, from remarks which Roosevelt had made to Layton on September 27, that some drastic rearrangements were needed. Roosevelt had been particularly emphatic about the need for 'weekly information' from Britain about the changes in British requirements 'so that very early knowledge of a changing situation should be available to the Administration'. Roosevelt also asked that, in order 'to prevent the crossing of wires', Purvis should remain 'the channel of communication' and Morgenthau 'the clearing house' for all British requests.

On the question of the strategy for winning the war, Layton reported how, in his talk with Roosevelt:

I then suggested that in view of Germany's preponderance we had to consider a strategic plan by which Germany could be beaten. The President interrupted with the remark 'Starve them out'. The Germans, he said, were not like 'us'; they would hold out to a certain point and then break down completely, whereas 'we' would give way only gradually.

Roosevelt also told Layton that he 'had always urged that we should bomb the Germans everywhere, not merely at a few major points'.[3]

On Friday September 20 Churchill returned once more to Chequers. On the drive, with his son Randolph and John Colville, he stopped at the Dollis Hill underground headquarters and inspected the flat which he would move into if Operation 'Paddock' were to be put into effect. 'Safe but forbidding,' Colville noted. 'We should become troglodytes'— or 'trogs' as Churchill called them.

At Chequers, the discussion turned to the possible use by the Germans of poison gas. Both Churchill and Ismay, who was also present, were 'confident', as Colville noted, 'that nothing new or more devilish than mustard gas is available'. Churchill added that he was 'doubtful whether invasion will be tried in the near future', even though there was no doubt 'that every preparation' had been made.

---

[1] Minute of 17 November 1940: Premier papers, 3/477/1, folio 2.
[2] Minute of 19 November 1940: Premier papers, 3/477/1, folio 7.
[3] 'Notes on points mentioned in conversation with the President—Friday September 27, 1940': Cabinet papers, 115/32.

That week, Churchill had driven to Wandsworth, one of the worst bombed parts of London. The sights of devastation had shaken and angered him. 'He is becoming less and less benevolent towards the Germans,' Colville noted, 'having been much moved by the examples of their frightfulness in Wandsworth which he has been to see, and talks about castrating the lot!'

As midnight came and went, Churchill relaxed, reminiscing about the Boer War, 'the last enjoyable war' he called it, and recalling the beauties of the Veldt. Colville noted: 'His thirst for talking military strategy is unquenchable.'[1] But Churchill also had time for the civilian side of policy; that very morning he had told his War Cabinet colleagues that streets and shops should be brightly lit 'for people going to cinemas and theatres'.[2] And, learning that Neville Chamberlain had suffered a relapse, he had also suggested that he and his wife return to Hampshire, if only to be able to sleep at nights free from sirens, shelters and the explosion of bombs. Anne Chamberlain accepted this suggestion. 'Neville asks me to add,' she wrote, 'how very deeply he appreciates your consideration.'[3] Churchill replied on September 20:

My dear Mrs Neville,

I am most obliged to you for taking my advice. I can't bear to think of Neville, while still recovering from a major operation, being under this continued bombardment in London. He must give himself a decent chance to recover full efficiency.

I have been very much worried about you both during the last ten days, though I have not ventured to interfere.

I should like to let you know that I do not think much will be left of Downing Street after a few weeks. I am having all the Government pictures and the few odd daubs we possess dumped in the vaults of the National Gallery, and all but the smallest personal effects of ours are being removed tomorrow. I propose to lead a troglodyte existence with several 'trogs'.[4]

In the event, Dollis Hill was never used, and 'Paddock' joined the many other wartime contingency plans for which preparations were made, but action deferred. For the rest of the Blitz, and beyond, the underground Central War Rooms below Storey's Gate proved adequate protection for the Government, while Churchill lived at the 'Annexe' at ground level. But for the population of London, the existing

---

[1] Colville diary, 20 September 1940: Colville papers.
[2] Quoted in Sir John Reith, diary entry for 20 September 1940: Charles Smith (editor), *The Reith Diaries*, London 1975, page 264.
[3] Letter of 19 September 1940, from 11 Downing Street: Churchill papers, 2/393.
[4] 'Private', 20 September 1940: Churchill papers, 2/393.

shelters seemed quite inadequate, and towards the end of September there was considerable pressure to open the London Underground for shelter purposes, using the Tubes as dormitories.

Churchill had already asked the War Cabinet why the Tubes could not be used as air raid shelters, 'even at the expense of transport facilities'. But he was told that after a careful review, it had been decided that using the Tubes was 'most undesirable'. He was therefore puzzled to learn that the Aldwych Tube was to be used as a shelter. 'Pray let me have more information about this,' he minuted to the Home Secretary and to the Minister of Transport on September 21, 'and what has happened to supersede the former decisive arguments.' His minute continued:

I still remain in favour of a widespread utilisation of the Tubes, by which I mean not only the stations but the railway lines, and I should like a short report on one sheet of paper showing the numbers that could be accommodated on various sections and the structural changes that would be required to fit these sections for their new use. Is it true, for instance, that 750,000 people could be accommodated in the Aldwych section alone? We may well have to balance the relative demands of transport and shelter.

3. I am awaiting the report of the Home Secretary on the forward policy of—
   (a) Making more shelters.
   (b) Strengthening existing basements.
   (c) Making empty basements and premises available.
   (d) Most important. Assigning fixed places by tickets to a large proportion of the people, thus keeping them where we want them, and avoiding crowding.[1]

At Chequers that evening, with Gort and Dowding, the discussion turned to the German use of parachute mines. As these could not be aimed, like bombs, they led inevitably to indiscriminate slaughter, and Churchill again proposed retaliation: one British parachute mine dropped on an open German town for every one dropped on Britain. This, said Gort, was 'the only language they understood', at which Churchill commented: 'When we've abolished Germany, we'll establish Poland—and make the Poles a permanent thing in Europe.'

Unknown to Churchill's guests, or to Colville who recorded the evening's discussion in his diary, Paul Thümmel, the Allied agent inside the Abwehr—the Intelligence arm of the German Supreme Command—had recently sent details of the German invasion plans. Not

[1] Prime Minister's Personal Minute, M.116, 21 September 1940: Churchill papers, 20/13. The Aldwych Tube was a dead-end, not essential for the system.

dates, but destinations; the landings, Thümmel reported, were to be in the Brighton to Ramsgate area. On September 21 Thümmel gave Dover as the main point of attack.[1] Colville noted that evening: 'PM thinks if there is an invasion, North Foreland to Dungeness is the danger area,' and that 'the most dangerous condition' would be fog. Colville added: 'The PM seems rather more apprehensive than I had realised about the possibility of invasion in the immediate future, and he keeps on ringing up the Admiralty and asking about the weather in the Channel.'[2]

On the morning of Sunday September 22 Churchill received a message from Roosevelt, stating that the German invasion of Britain would take place that very day, at 3 p.m. But Churchill was 'thoroughly sceptical', Colville noted, while Clementine Churchill and their daughter Mary 'treated the whole matter as a most entertaining joke'.[3] If the Germans did manage to land, Churchill told his luncheon guests, 'we shall show them no quarter'.[4]

On receiving this news, Churchill telephoned Eden, who was spending the weekend on the south coast. Eden's comment was that 'it was wet and blowing' and that he 'felt quite safe'. Then, after going to the top of a nearby hill and looking towards France, Eden sent Churchill a further message: 'it was so rough', he said, 'that any German who attempted to cross the Channel would be very sea-sick'.[5]

It emerged that the message from Roosevelt had been garbled. Not Britain, but French Indo-China, was the country about to be invaded. That afternoon Japanese forces occupied Saigon. The German troops remained at Calais, across the stormy Channel from Dover.

At Chequers on the following day Churchill was in reflective mood, expressing his surprise at the speed with which Britain had been able to 'reorientate' itself to the fall of France, 'the collapse of an Ally upon whose support so much seemed to be staked'. He was also 'full of confidence', as Colville noted, on the outcome of the battle against the Italians in North Africa, 'unless', Churchill remarked, 'our men behave like skunks and the Italians like heroes'. Returning to London, Churchill travelled in the same car as Gort, 'whom he seems to like' Colville

[1] F. H. Hinsley and others, *British Intelligence in the Second World War, Its Influence on Strategy and Operations*, volume 1, London 1979, page 187, note. Thümmel was identified in these reports only as Agent A.54.

[2] Colville diary, 21 September 1940: Colville papers.

[3] Colville diary, 22 September 1940: Colville papers.

[4] Recalled by one of those present, General Sir Frederick Pile, General Officer Commanding-in-Chief Anti-Aircraft Command: *Ack-Ack: Britain's Defence Against Air Attack during the Second World War*, London 1949, page 168.

[5] The Earl of Avon, *The Eden Memoirs, The Reckoning*, London 1965, page 138.

noted, and on seeing Gort's bombed flat, Churchill was 'most compassionate'.[1]

When the War Cabinet met at 5 p.m. that evening, the Chief of the Air Staff reported that he had given orders for 100 heavy bombers to attack Berlin, and 45 medium and 5 heavy bombers to attack German barges and other installations in the Channel ports.[2] Churchill's comment, to Colville: 'Let 'em have it. Remember this. Never maltreat the enemy by halves. Once the battle is joined, let 'em have it.'[3]

[1] Colville diary, 23 September 1940: Colville papers.
[2] War Cabinet No. 256 of 1940, 23 September 1940, 5 p.m.: Cabinet papers, 65/9.
[3] Colville diary, 23 September 1940: Colville papers.

41

'Menace': 'the heart made sick'

ON Monday, September 23, battle was joined at Dakar. Six days earlier, from Sierra Leone, General de Gaulle had appealed by telegram to Churchill: 'I wish to insist to you personally and formally that plan for reconquest of French Africa through Dakar should be upheld and carried out.'[1] Both Admiral Cunningham and General Irwin, the two British commanders, also argued in favour of an offensive, and at a meeting of the War Cabinet on the evening of September 17, Churchill also spoke in favour of allowing 'Menace' to go ahead.

The War Cabinet, Churchill pointed out, 'had lived to bless the day on which they had decided upon the "Oran" Operation'. Churchill added that in his view insufficient attention had been paid to the moral effects of a failure of Operation 'Menace'. 'If our expedition came back with its tail between its legs,' he declared, 'we could hardly hope that the fact would escape notice.'[2]

The War Cabinet had agreed that night to allow the commanders on the spot to go ahead as they wished. 'We cannot judge relative advantages of alternate schemes from here,' Churchill had telegraphed to them both on September 18. 'We give you full authority to go ahead and do what you think is best, in order to give effect to the original purpose of the expedition.'[3] If de Gaulle were to establish himself in Dakar, and become 'master of Western and Central Africa', Churchill wrote to Sir Samuel Hoare, 'Morocco is next on the list.'[4]

The words 'Morocco is next on the list' were changed at the suggestion of the Foreign Office to 'a spontaneous & successful Free French

---

[1] 'Most Immediate', S.27, sent 6.26 a.m., received 11.55 a.m., 17 September 1940, Annex to War Cabinet No. 252 of 17 September 1940: Cabinet papers, 65/15, folio 23.

[2] War Cabinet No. 252 of 1940, 17 September 1940, 9 p.m., Minute 1, Confidential Annex: Cabinet papers, 65/15.

[3] 'Most Immediate': Admiralty papers, 205/6.

[4] Prime Minister's Personal Minute, D.65, 18 September 1940: Churchill papers, 20/13.

movement in Morocco may automatically follow, which neither HMG nor Gen de Gaulle could check'.[1]

On the afternoon of September 22, through Lord Lothian, Churchill sent Roosevelt an account of the Dakar plan. 'The following message,' Lothian was informed, 'is of the highest degree of secrecy and is for the personal information of the President only.' There was a 'reasonable chance', Churchill told Roosevelt, of the operation being carried out 'without heavy casualties on either side'. In view of the 'far reaching political and strategical advantages', he explained, 'which would follow from establishment of Free French flag at this place, we have decided to accept the risk (which we hope is not a grave one) of such action leading to declaration of war by Vichy France.'[2]

Lothian read Churchill's telegram to Roosevelt that same night. 'He was delighted,' Lothian reported, 'and repeatedly said "splendid". At the end he said he was "happy" about it.' Roosevelt even asked what Churchill would think 'of his sending a cruiser and a couple of destroyers to Monrovia, touching at Freetown and if possible at Dakar on the way purely as a friendly move'. Roosevelt was also prepared, he told Lothian, to announce that a declaration of war by Vichy on Britain 'would be derogatory to Franco-American relations' and would 'inevitably mean a loss to Vichy' of French possessions in the West Indies and the Pacific.[3]

To General Smuts, Churchill had already set out on the evening of September 21 the reasons for the Dakar action, telling the South African Prime Minister that if Dakar were to fall under German control and become a U-boat base 'the consequences to the Cape route would be deadly'. Churchill's message continued:

Naturally the risk of a bloody collision with the French sailors and part of the garrison is not a light one. On the whole I think the odds are heavily against any serious resistance, having regard to the low morale and unhappy plight of this French colony, and the ruin and starvation which faces them through our sea control. Still, no one can be sure till we try.

The argument that such a risk ought not to be run at a time when French opinion, encouraged by British resistance, is veering towards us even at Vichy, and that anything like a second Oran would be a great set-back, has weighed heavily with us. Nevertheless we came to the united conclusion that this objection might not turn out to be valid, and must in any case be surpassed

[1] Premier papers, 3/276, folio 192.
[2] Telegram No. 2344, 'Immediate', 'Most Secret', 4 p.m., 22 September 1940: Premier papers, 3/468, folio 109.
[3] Washington Telegram No. 2076, 'Immediate', 'Most Secret', sent 11.15 p.m., 22 September 1940, received 8.45 a.m., 23 September 1940: Premier papers, 3/468, folio 108.

by the dangers of doing nothing and of allowing Vichy to prevail against de Gaulle.

If Vichy did not declare war after Oran, or under the pressure of our blockade, there is no reason why they should do so if there is a fight at Dakar. Besides the strategical importance of Dakar and political effects of its capture by de Gaulle, there are sixty or seventy millions of Belgian and Polish gold wrongfully held in the interior, and the great battleship *Richelieu*, by no means permanently disabled, would indirectly come into our hands.

'Anyhow,' Churchill added, 'the die is cast.'[1]

Six thousand Royal Marines and French Foreign Legionaries awaited the moment of landing. Two British battleships, *Barham* and *Resolution*, and the aircraft carrier *Ark Royal*, together with three 8-inch cruisers, were to be their shield. The *Richelieu*, which had 'never yet' fired her guns, was said to be 'in an incomplete state'.[2]

'Menace' opened in the early hours of September 23. Fog, which Churchill had feared so much as the cover for a German invasion of Britain, proved the initial downfall of the attackers' hopes. Nor did the local welcome which the Free French expected materialise. When de Gaulle's two aeroplanes landed on the Dakar airfield, their pilots were arrested. Emissaries, sent in by boat under protection of the white flag, were fired on, and two were wounded. The batteries at Dakar then opened fire, and to the consternation of the attackers, the *Richelieu* opened fire with its 15-inch guns, never before fired in combat.

The first news to reach London did not reflect the ill-omen of these events. As Churchill told his War Cabinet colleagues at noon, 'the first messages had stated that General de Gaulle's emissaries had been received, and that our aircraft had landed at the aerodromes'. A later message had indicated 'sporadic and formal resistance', so that the British and Free French forces 'would have to interfere and open fire'. The cruiser *Cumberland* had been hit amidships from a shot from one of the Vichy batteries 'and was out of action'.

While the War Cabinet was still in session, a message was received, timed at 1.58 p.m., stating that de Gaulle 'was attempting a landing' under cover of fog, ten miles east of Dakar, at Rufisque: Operation 'Charles'. It was also known, the War Cabinet were told, that de Gaulle had delivered an ultimatum to the Vichy forces, and that these forces 'had been ordered to resist'.[3]

---

[1] Telegram No. 560, 'Most Secret and Personal', sent at 1 a.m., 22 September 1940: Premier papers, 3/276, folios 182–3.

[2] Report by Sir Dudley Pound to the War Cabinet, 17 September 1940, 9 p.m.: Cabinet papers, 65/15, folio 24.

[3] War Cabinet No. 256 of 1940, 23 September 1940, 12.30 p.m.: Cabinet papers, 65/9.

Because of the fog, the British and Free French naval forces had withdrawn from the Dakar shore at 11.30 a.m. Also, because of dense fog and the resultant chaos, de Gaulle abandoned his landing at Rufisque. At 7.19 p.m. a signal reached London that the British military and naval commanders had decided to withdraw the troop-ships, and to resume 'Menace' only on the following day. Churchill signalled in reply: 'Having begun, we must go on to the end.' His message ended: 'Stop at nothing.'[1]

That night Churchill telegraphed to Roosevelt:

I was encouraged by your reception of information conveyed by Lord Lothian about Dakar. It would be against our joint interests if strong German submarine and aircraft bases were established there. It looks as if there might be a stiff fight. Perhaps not but anyhow orders have been given to ram it through.

Churchill's telegram continued, in answer to Roosevelt's own offer to send United States warships to the region:

We should be delighted if you would send some American warships to Monrovia and Freetown and I hope by that time to have Dakar ready for your call. But what really matters now is that you should put it across the French Government that a war declaration would be very bad indeed for them in all that concerns United States. If Vichy declares war that is the same thing as Germany, and Vichy possessions in the Western Hemisphere must be considered potentially German possessions.

Reverting briefly to the continuing possibility of a German invasion of Britain, Churchill told Roosevelt: 'We are all ready for them,' and he added: 'I am very glad to hear about the rifles.'[2]

These rifles were 250,000 Enfields, released by Roosevelt to Purvis. 'I am informed,' Roosevelt telegraphed to Churchill, that evening, 'that the rifles are already under way to New York for shipment.'[3] Churchill replied at once: 'We will use them well.'[4]

As the battle continued off Dakar during September 24, the prospects of success receded. 'Reduction of defences, and neutralization of French

[1] 'Most Immediate', signal timed at 10.14 p.m., 23 September 1940: Premier papers, 3/276, folio 60.

[2] Telegram No. 2352, 'Most Immediate and Secret', 2.30 a.m., 24 September 1940: Premier papers, 3/468, folio 107.

[3] Telegram of 24 September 1940, sent from Washington at 7 p.m.: I have taken the text of this telegram from Warren Kimball (editor), *Churchill and Roosevelt: The Complete Correspondence in Three Volumes*, volume 1, 'The Alliance Emerging', Princeton 1983.

[4] Telegram of 25 September 1940: Premier papers, 3/276, folio 167.

battleship *Richelieu* and French cruisers', Admiral Cunningham signalled to London shortly after midday, 'present an impossible project for
available forces in prevailing visibility and a most difficult operation
for any force in any weather while morale of defenders remains as high
as at present'.[1] Churchill realized that the original hopes for 'Menace'
were now almost certainly at an end, telling Colville: 'A rapid and
bloodless fait accompli for which we all hoped would have been
accepted in France. This hard fighting may have different
results.'[2]

At 8.15 on the morning of September 25, a signal from General
Spears reached Churchill in London. It began: 'General de Gaulle
agrees with commanders it would be unwise to attempt landing now in
face of unexpectedly determined opposition.' The French troops landed
at Rufisque had had to be re-embarked owing to the presence of two
Vichy cruisers 'in fog' off the shore. Had the cruisers discovered the
French transports, the transports 'could have been instantly destroyed'.
De Gaulle now proposed to abandon the assault on Dakar, and to go
to Bathurst, to the safety of a British colony.[3]

Churchill's instinct on receiving this signal was to press for renewed
action, and after a meeting with the Chiefs of Staff he signalled to
Cunningham and Irwin:

> We do not understand conditions under which bombardment proceeded for
> some hours at 10,000 yards without grave damage to ships or fort unless
> visibility was so bad as to make targets invisible. Also if visibility bad, why is
> it not possible to force a landing at beaches near Rufisque in spite of fire from
> Goree Island.
>
> Without this fuller information we can only ask why you do not land
> in force by night or in the fog or both on beaches near Rufisque and take
> Rufisque for a start, observing that enemy cannot be heart-whole and
> force at Rufisque is comprised largely of native troops. At the same time if the
> weather clears you could hold down batteries on Goree Island in daylight by
> long-range sea-fire, and if there is fog you would not need to do so. It should
> be possible to feed the force, once ashore, by night. This force, once landed,
> ought to be able to advance on Dakar.

More ammunition, Churchill added, was being sent from Gibraltar.
But there was not 'unlimited time': not only French but probably
German submarines might arrive 'in six or seven days'. The signal

---

[1] Signal sent at 2.17 p.m., received at 6.50 p.m., 24 September 1940: Premier papers, 3/276,
folio 174.

[2] Colville diary, 24 September 1940: Colville papers.

[3] Signal sent at 8.51 p.m., 24 September 1940; received 8.15 a.m., 25 September 1940: Premier
papers, 3/276, folios 175-6.

continued: 'Pray act as you think best, but meanwhile give reasoned answers to these points.' Churchill ended: 'Matter must be pushed to conclusion without undue delay.'[1]

Reporting to the War Cabinet later that morning, Churchill told his colleagues that *Cumberland* had suffered damage from the guns of the fortress. British air reconnaisance had been hampered by anti-aircraft fire. De Gaulle's men had withdrawn from Rufisque. The resistance of the Vichy defenders 'remained unimpaired and morale seemed to be high'. After all this bad news had been received, Churchill added, a further signal had arrived to say that *Resolution* had been hit, and was withdrawing.[2]

The situation, Churchill concluded, was 'obscure and unsatisfactory'. In such circumstances, to continue with 'Menace' would, he warned, 'undoubtedly commit us to a great effort and great risks'. But to abandon the operation would equally undoubtedly mean 'that we should suffer a serious rebuff', and would enhance the position of the Vichy Government, which had begun to deteriorate.

Churchill came to no conclusion. But his Ministers were emphatic in theirs. In view of the 'unexpectedly stiff' Vichy resistance at Dakar, Clement Attlee proposed 'calling the operation off and cutting our losses'. He was supported in this by Lord Halifax, Arthur Greenwood, A. V. Alexander—because of the damage to *Resolution*—Anthony Eden and Lord Lloyd.[3] Churchill thereupon withdrew from the meeting, to dictate to Mrs Hill a telegram to Admiral Cunningham and General Irwin, that 'Menace' should be brought to an end.[4] 'On all the information now before us,' the telegram read, 'including damage to *Resolution*, we have decided that the enterprise against Dakar should be abandoned . . .'[5]

That night Churchill telegraphed to Roosevelt: 'Very much regret we had to abandon Dakar enterprise. Vichy got in before us and animated defence with partisans and gunnery experts. All friendly elements were gripped and held down.' In addition, Churchill told the President, several of the British ships had been hit, 'and to persist with landing in force would have tied us to an undue commitment when

[1] Prime Minister to Combined Command, Dakar Force, 25 September 1940: Premier papers, 3/276, folios 168–9.

[2] *Resolution* had been hit by a torpedo fired from a Vichy submarine shortly after 9 a.m.

[3] War Cabinet No. 258 of 1940, 25 September 1940, 11.30 a.m., Minute 2, Confidential Annex: Cabinet papers, 65/15.

[4] Colville diary, 25 September 1940: Colville papers.

[5] Signal sent at 1.27 p.m., 25 September 1940: Churchill papers, 4/170.

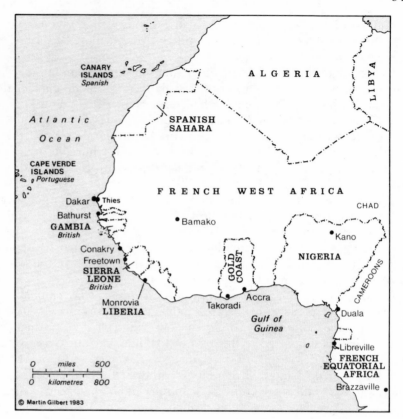

you think of what we have on our hands already'.[1] 'I am afraid Dakar has not gone too well,' Neville Chamberlain wrote to Churchill that night, 'but I hope we shall succeed in capturing it. I am sure it was right to go for it.'[2] For Clementine Churchill, looking back on Dakar after the war, it was 'the progressive & sickening disappointment' that she remembered most. It was, she wrote, 'a classic example of Hope deferred making the Heart sick'.[3]

[1] 'Personal and Secret', 'Former Naval Person to President', 25 September 1940: Premier papers, 3/276, folio 167.
[2] 'Personal', 25 September 1940: Churchill papers, 20/1.
[3] Notes by Clementine Churchill in the margin of Churchill's draft war memoirs: Churchill papers, 4/170.

42

The invasion dilemma:
'An autumn nip in the air'

THROUGHOUT the last week of September the German air raids continued, with a heavy bombardment of London on the night of September 25. There were also 'heavy blows', as Churchill described them, to aircraft factories at Bristol, Weybridge and Southampton. In view of this, Churchill urged Sinclair to grant Beaverbrook the right to surplus stocks in the Air Ministry controlled Universal Equipment Depots. 'I really could not endure another bickering over this,' he wrote, 'considering the gravity of the situation.'[1]

Intelligence indications still pointed to the possibility of invasion, and with 'heavy barge concentrations at the invasion ports', as Churchill wrote to Lord Trenchard on September 26, there had to be diversion of bombing efforts from Berlin to the ports. 'You are probably aware,' Churchill added, 'that we are under conditions of Alert No. 1.' Nevertheless, he noted, 'the weight of the heavy Bombers is kept in Germany in the main'.[2] That same day, an Intelligence summary noted: 'The threat of invasion to this country cannot be said to have lessened.'[3]

On September 24, an Enigma decrypt revealed that arrangements had just been made setting out the responsibility for German 'air rescue vessels' in several French, Dutch and Norwegian ports.[4] An MI 6 telephone message on September 26, to MI 14, raised once more the possibility of an immediate German assault. It read: 'Ships ready to sail

[1] Prime Minister's Personal Minute, M.142, 26 September 1940: Churchill papers, 20/13.
[2] 'Secret', 26 September 1940: Churchill papers, 20/2.
[3] War Office Weekly Intelligence Commentary, No. 58, to 12 noon, 26 September 1940: Churchill papers, 20/16.
[4] 'Officers Only', 'Most Secret', MI 14, 5.55 p.m., 24 September 1940: War Office papers, 199/911A, B.56.

from Schiehaven (Rotterdam?).'[1] Once more, Enigma was the source.

Whatever these fragments implied about invasion, there could be no dispute about the intensity of the Blitz. During the week ending at noon on September 26, more than 1,500 civilians had been killed in Britain, 1,300 of them in London. Three major fires had been caused at the Woolwich Arsenal. Several railway stations had been damaged, and unexploded bombs at pumping stations had reduced some districts 'uncomfortably near to a water famine'. Many hospitals had been hit, and several stores and shops in Oxford Street, Bond Street and Regent Street damaged. The increased use of parachute mines had caused 'wide havoc and dislocation'. There were also signs, according to Intelligence reports, 'of increased hatred of Germany', and demands for reprisals were 'numerous'.[2] 'The present conditions of bombardment are vexatious,' Churchill had written to Chamberlain on September 24, 'but I do not think that they will continue at their present height for many weeks.' Churchill added: 'I have greatly admired your nerve and stamina under the cruel physical burden which you bear. Let us go on together through the storm. These are great days.'[3]

The failure at Dakar had led to suggestions that relations with Vichy might be repaired. At first, Churchill opposed this. 'It would be a great mistake,' he minuted on September 28, 'to fall into a mood of being afraid of offending Vichy, or trying to "kiss and make friends",' and he supported the proposal to allow de Gaulle to try to set up his authority at Duala, in the Cameroons, and later elsewhere in French Equatorial Africa.[4] At the War Cabinet three days later, however, when Halifax argued that the failure of the Dakar expedition would make it possible to open new negotiations with Vichy, Churchill did not disagree, he said, with the 'principle' of negotiations, 'but only on the emphasis to be laid on them'. The present moment was not however, he felt, 'a golden opportunity to come to an understanding'. Support must still be given to de Gaulle. If, from Duala in the Cameroons, de Gaulle then wished, as Churchill told the War Cabinet, 'to make an expedition to some French colonial territory which had not yet declared for him', he should be 'allowed to do so'. Halifax was dubious. But Churchill went on to ask: 'How could we refuse to back up General de

---

[1] Telephone message from MI 14 to GHQ (I), 7 p.m., 26 September 1940: War Office papers, 199/911A, B.57.

[2] War Cabinet, Chiefs of Staff Committee, Weekly Résumé No. 56: Churchill papers, 23/6.

[3] 'Personal', 24 September 1940: Churchill paper, 20/1. The 'cruel physical burden' was cancer.

[4] Prime Minister's Personal Minute to General Ismay, for the Chiefs of Staff Committee, D.74, 28 September 1940: Churchill papers, 20/13.

Gaulle' if he decided to try to gain control of some further French African territory.[1]

On September 27 a ten-year pact was signed in Berlin between Germany, Italy and Japan, recognizing a 'New Order' in Europe and the Far East. When Colville took the news in to Churchill, the Prime Minister looked 'pensive', Colville noted. Churchill also feared that the coming United States elections would 'paralyse' the American war effort. But he could still look ahead to action and success. 'Personally,' he told Colville, 'I should like to wage war on a great scale in the Middle East. By next spring I hope we shall have sufficient forces there.' Colville noted: 'He has been taking tremendous pains lately about the despatch of re-inforcements to Egypt.'[2] The route from Cairo to Khartoum, Churchill was able to report to Eden that day, 'is being opened up for Takoradi' and the Ferry pilots with their precious aircraft reinforcements, could now fly to Takoradi, on the Gold Coast, from Britain or the United States, and then across Nigeria, Chad and the Sudan, to Egypt.[3]

At Chequers that weekend, Churchill again discussed possible future campaigns with the Joint Planning Committee.[4] The news of the arrival of the first United States destroyers was welcome. But a further series of Enigma decrypts, which Churchill saw that weekend, set out various German measures connected with invasion, including the appointment of German Air Force officers to the embarkation Staffs at certain ports, and instructions issued to a German air formation headquarters making arrangements to settle details 'of loading units and equipment into ships'. It was also known that the ground personnel of certain German dive-bomber units had been allotted to a third crossing point. There was no shadow of doubt, Military Intelligence concluded, 'that preparations are being pressed forward for a sea-borne expedition'. The 'cessation of movement of shipping', far from being a hopeful sign, 'tends to show that an advanced state of preparedness has been reached'. As for the actual date of the invasion, one 'known fact' was that the move of certain Italian air units to bases in Holland and Belgium would not be completed before the end of September, in two days time.[5]

---

[1] War Cabinet No. 263, 1 October 1940: Cabinet papers, 65/15.

[2] Colville diary, 27 September 1940: Colville papers.

[3] Prime Minister's Personal Minute, M.143, 27 September 1940: Cabinet papers, 120/333.

[4] Captain Daniel, RN, Brigadier Playfair and Group-Captain Slessor. The other guests included Ismay, Bevin, Oliver Lyttelton, Sir Kingsley Wood, Sir Roger Keyes, and Lindemann. John Peck was the duty Private Secretary.

[5] 'Officers Only', 'Most Secret', 'German Preparations for Invasion', MI 14, 28 September 1940: War Office papers, 199/911A, B.58.

This Intelligence, coming as it did from the most secret source, could indicate invasion on any date from October 1. Meanwhile, the Blitz continued, with more than 200 deaths in London alone on the night of September 28. On the following morning Churchill gave orders for 'Paddock' to be 'broken in', and for the War Cabinet to meet at the Dollis Hill underground fortress on the following Thursday, October 3. At the same time, he minuted for Bridges and Ismay, 'other Departments should be encouraged to try a preliminary move of a skeleton staff'.[1]

By the end of September 1940 the success achieved by the decrypting staff at Bletchley was such that the daily flow of Enigma messages and interpretations was now substantial, so much so that Churchill decided to institute a regular system whereby he would receive his 'golden eggs'. From 'now on', Eric Seal minuted for Churchill's Private Office on September 28, 'boxes will come regularly every day from "C" marked "only to be opened by the Prime Minister in person"'. This marking, Seal stressed, 'is not mere camouflage and is to be taken seriously'. The boxes thus marked were to be put on Churchill's desk 'and left for him to re-lock'. Once re-locked Seal added: 'They will be returned to "C".'[2]

Sometimes 'C' himself would bring a box across from MI 6 headquarters at Broadway to Downing Street, sending a note across to the Private Secretaries to say that he was 'on his way'.[3]

The Enigma decrypts provided a window, albeit at this time a somewhat opaque one, into German intentions. They also stimulated the search for counter-measures. Against the bombers themselves, a series of beam bending devices, known by the code name 'Headache', were in the process of development. At the same time, radar sets were being developed both for anti-aircraft gun directional finding (GL), code name 'George', and for search-light control (SLC), code name 'Elsie'. Reading a report of technical setbacks in the development of the search-light control system known as 'Yagi' Churchill asked Lindemann on September 23: 'What has happened: & what can be done.'[4]

Hearing that production of the GL system was being hampered by a dispute between the Minister of Supply, Herbert Morrison, and the

---

[1] Prime Minister's Personal Minute, C.11, 29 September 1940.
[2] Note of 28 September 1940: Premier papers, 4/80/3, folio 673.
[3] Private communication to the author, 15 December 1982.
[4] Minute of 23 September 1940, on SLC (Yagi) system, Report of 31 August 1940: Premier papers, 3/200/1.

Minister of Labour, Ernest Bevin, Churchill transferred the authority for production of both GL and 'Yagi' to Beaverbrook and the Ministry of Aircraft Production. By an oversight, on September 20 Beaverbrook had taken with him from Downing Street the original manuscript minute transferring the GL production authority to the Ministry of Aircraft Production. As a result, no copies of this minute could be made by Churchill's secretariat in order to inform the other two Ministries. As Seal explained to Churchill on September 27: 'Lord Beaverbrook, by walking off with the manuscript minute in his pocket, made it impossible for the machine to work.'[1] The result was chaos for several days.

Reflecting six years later on Beaverbrook's work at this time, Churchill wrote: 'Lord Beaverbrook rendered signal service. This was the hour of his life. His energy, contrivance, personal force & genius swept aside many obstacles. Everything in the supply "pipe-lines" was drawn forward to the battle.' Aeroplanes, Churchill added, 'streamed forward to the fighter squadrons in numbers never known before'.[2]

At the end of June, Desmond Morton had told Churchill of the possibility of sending fire ships into German-controlled French ports to 'scatter burning oil all over the harbour, possibly with most pleasing results'.[3] With Lindemann's approval, and the Ministerial help of Geoffrey Lloyd, experiments had gone forward throughout July, August and early September. On September 19 all was set for a first venture seven days later, on the night of September 26. The ships, however, broke down, and the operation, code name 'Lucid', was postponed. It was to have a dismal history: on October 4 two fire ships were sent against Calais and one against Boulogne, but the wind was blowing in the wrong direction for the burning oil to be squirted out successfully. During a second attempt three days later the escorting destroyer struck a mine, and the ships had to be recalled. 'Lucid' was in disarray, although the fireships were to remain for many months 'at 7 days notice for operations'.[4]

With invasion fears still uppermost, Churchill continued to worry during the last two weeks of September about the use of fog as a cover for a German attack. The Admiralty were confident, however, that

[1] Premier papers, 3/200/3, folio 50. On October 15 Churchill confirmed that Beaverbrook would have 'an overriding responsibility for the co-ordination of the work' on the GL and 'Yagi' appliances. (Premier papers, 3/200/3, folios 34–5.)

[2] Notes prepared by Churchill in 1946: Churchill papers, 4/162.

[3] Note of 27 June 1940: Premier papers, 3/264, folio 14.

[4] Notes and plans, June 1940 to February 1941: Premier papers, 3/264. On October 10 the fire ship scheme received its code names. These were 'Anemone' (an attack on Le Havre), 'Barnacle' (Zeebrugge), 'Dewberry' (Boulogne), 'Flounders' (Flushing), 'Greengage' (Cherbourg), 'Hyacinth' (St Malo) and 'Juniper' (Antwerp): Churchill papers, 4/96. Churchill only learned of these, as of all other code names, after they had been chosen, see pages 966–7.

during foggy periods they could pick up the directional beams by which the German barges would be guided towards the landing beaches. In a minute to Ismay on September 23, however, Churchill questioned the validity of such reasoning. 'It is pointed out,' he minuted, 'that in a fog the enemy can point his beams very easily at one part of the coast, and switch off at the last stage to another. Also, could he not point at one part, and could his ships not steer so many degrees to the right or left of the beam?' If this were so, Churchill added, 'it would seem that this security is not as good as is supposed, and also there would be danger in making concentrations in consequence of beam indications which are the easiest feints in the world to make'.[1]

Were the Germans to invade, and to use poison gas, Churchill was determined to be in a position to retaliate. On September 28 he pressed Ismay to ensure that Britain's stocks of gas were being maintained. 'We should never begin,' Churchill noted, 'but we must be able to reply. Speed is vital here. The highest priority must be given,' and he added: 'I regard the danger as very great.'[2]

Every aspect of war policy crowded in upon Churchill for decision or comment: not only anti-invasion measures, and operational matters on land, at sea and in the air, but a host of diplomatic problems. When Halifax wrote to him at the end of September, suggesting that Spain should be excluded from some of the rigours of the blockade, Churchill agreed, being conscious of the need for Britain to encourage and if necessary to sustain Spanish neutrality. This should be done, he told Halifax, 'by economic favours, and other favours', rather than by the 'promise of giving up Gibraltar after we have won the war'. British territory should not be used as a bargaining counter to keep Spain neutral. But French territory could be, for, Churchill explained to Halifax:

I do not mind if the Spaniards go into French Morocco. The letters exchanged with de Gaulle do not commit us to any exact restoration of the territories of France, and the attitude of the Vichy Government towards us and towards him has undoubtedly justified a harder feeling towards France than existed at the time of her collapse.

I would far rather see the Spaniards in Morocco than the Germans, and if the French have to pay for their abject attitude, it is better that they should pay in Africa to Spain than in Europe to either of the guilty Powers. Indeed, I think you should let them know that we shall be no obstacle to their Moroccan ambitions, provided they preserve their neutrality in the war.[3]

[1] Prime Minister's Personal Minute, D.71, 23 September 1940: Premier papers, 3/222/4, folio 4.
[2] Minute of 28 September 1940: Premier papers, 3/88/3, folios 219–20.
[3] Prime Minister's Personal Minute, M.154, 29 September 1940: Premier papers, 4/21/1, folios 113–14.

Churchill accepted the pressures and uncertainties of events philosophically. His motto was, as he was later to exhort John Martin, in an inscription in 1944 in one of the volumes of his war speeches: 'Keep jogging along.'[1]

At the end of September Neville Chamberlain asked Churchill if he could resign as Lord President of the Council and return to private life. Churchill accepted Chamberlain's resignation, telling him how grieved he had been to learn from Halifax 'how hard you had found the struggle to do your work under the severe conditions which prevail in London, and will certainly become more marked as the dark hours lengthen'. Churchill added:

... let me express to you my admiration for the heroic effort you have made to do your duty and to see this grim business through, and my sincere sorrow that, with nerve unshaken and mental prowess unimpaired, your physical strength no longer bears you up in a public station. I trust indeed that having put down this burden you find life more endurable, and that a real improvement will set in.

I have greatly valued our comradeship and your aid and counsel during these five violent months, and I beg you to believe me your sincere friend.

Yours ever,
Winston S. Churchill[2]

Five days later Chamberlain's doctor, Lord Horder, wrote to Churchill from Harley Street: 'My dear Winston, Your letter to Neville has so touched my heart that I am impelled to tell you so. And I add that your gentle and skilful handling of a sick comrade during the vagaries through which his mind has been passing has put even me to shame! You have greatly softened the blow and I want to thank you.'[3]

Although his partnership with Chamberlain had been short, Churchill wrote to Halifax of how 'it has travelled through the storms, and it is with sincere regret that I view its ending'. Churchill then suggested to Halifax that Eden should go to the Foreign Office, and Halifax become Lord President, 'the second position in the Government'; or, if Halifax wished to remain where he was, that Eden should become Lord President. If Halifax chose the Lord Presidency, Churchill added, 'I should hope you would come and live at No. 11 (as long as it stands!)'

---

[1] Sir John Martin, letter to the author, 8 February 1983.
[2] 29 September 1940: Churchill papers, 2/393.
[3] Letter of 4 October 1940: Churchill papers, 2/395.

and also lead the House of Lords.[1] But Halifax wished to remain at the Foreign Office, while at the same time suggesting that Sir John Anderson would be better as Lord President than Eden, having 'that sort of orderly mind which Neville had—and which I don't think Anthony has'.[2] Churchill accepted this advice.

Among the other changes that were made, Herbert Morrison left the Ministry of Supply to become Home Secretary and Minister of Home Security in Anderson's place, leaving Churchill free to appoint Lord Beaverbrook as Minister of Supply. On the evening of September 30 Churchill urged Beaverbrook to accept. But the same night Beaverbrook wrote to Churchill that his asthma, which had long troubled him and indeed almost crippled him, 'drives me to the unhappy conclusion that the cold weather & sharp winds bring my labours to nothing'. He had tried 'many devices', but still 'nights pass in procession without any sleep for me'.[3]

That evening Eden went to see Churchill at Downing Street. 'I am in your hands,' Eden had written from the War Office earlier that afternoon, 'and will take any office that you consider will lighten your burden—or none.' If the matter were left to his personal choice, Eden added, 'I am content to stay here.'[4]

At the beginning of the day, Churchill had hoped to send Eden to the Foreign Office, but Halifax had not wished to move. Then he had hoped to give him the Lord Presidency, but this Halifax had deprecated, and Eden himself, apparently, did not wish to work entirely in the domestic sphere. Now the issue had to be resolved. Eden has left an account of their meeting in his diary:

Found him depressed because Max is suffering from asthma and will not take on Supply which is in a mess. This was holding up all his arrangements. I told him that if he wished for help in defence I was ready to do anything I could, even to give up War Office to be Lord President. I would then sit with Chiefs of Staff and him on Defence Committee, and could perhaps relieve him of much. Winston appeared to like this. He reiterated that he was now an old man, that he would not make Lloyd George's mistake of carrying on after the war, that the succession must be mine. John Anderson could clearly not 'be in the way' in this respect.[5]

[1] 'Private', 29 September 1940: Churchill papers, 2/395.

[2] Letter of 30 September 1940: Churchill papers, 2/395.

[3] Letter of 30 September 1940: Churchill papers, 2/392.

[4] Letter of 30 September 1940: Churchill papers, 2/394.

[5] Eden diary, 30 September 1940: The Earl of Avon, *The Eden Memoirs, The Reckoning*, London 1965, page 145.

Churchill said he would think over Eden's suggestion to help him on the defence side. But twenty-four hours passed and, as Eden recorded in his diary: 'not having heard from Winston all day and having gone to bed, I was fetched round after midnight in pyjamas. I protested that I was in bed, but W said he must talk over his list with me.' Eden arrived at Downing Street where, as he wrote:

Winston said that he had thought over my defence suggestion and had reluctantly decided to turn it down. It would make too many cogs in the machine and I should be in an uncomfortable position, which is perfectly true. He referred to my two letters, the latter written late Monday night after our talk. 'Your two very sweet letters, generous and worthy of the occasion.'

He lamented that he could not give me Foreign Office and thus bring me into War Cabinet and seemed distressed at this. 'It is not what I want,' he repeated many times. He thought at Foreign Office I could help much with USA. I begged him not to worry about all this. Said with truth that I was happier where I was. He said: 'We shall work this war together, and began to talk of future projects. . . .'[1]

On the night of September 30, Churchill had written to Neville Chamberlain, asking if he could submit his name to the King for the Garter. 'Austen had it,' Churchill wrote, 'and was proud to wear it. Unless you forbid me this will be done.'[2] Chamberlain replied on the following day:

It is kind of you to think of putting me forward for so great an honour as the Garter, but you will, I think, not misunderstand me when I say that I prefer to die plain 'Mr Chamberlain' like my father before me, unadorned by any title. This applies to the Garter just as much as to a peerage which you once before suggested to me.

'I shall continue,' Chamberlain added, 'to watch your conduct of affairs with anxious solicitude & the most earnest wishes for your success.'[3]

Cabinet reconstruction continued as September 1940 came to an end. In that one month, 6,954 British civilians had been killed in air attacks, most of them in London. In Europe, German rule had brought increasing hardship to millions of subject peoples. 'Be of good cheer,' Churchill broadcast on September 30 to the people of Czechoslovakia. 'The hour of your deliverance will come. The soul of freedom is deathless; it cannot, and will not, perish.'[4]

[1] Eden diary, 1 October 1940: The Earl of Avon, *The Eden Memoirs, The Reckoning*, London 1965, page 145.
[2] Letter of 30 September 1940: Churchill papers, 2/393.
[3] 'Personal', 1 October 1940: Churchill papers, 2/393.
[4] Broadcast of 30 September 1940: Churchill papers, 9/144.

Churchill's concern with anti-invasion preparations was continuous. Earlier that week, Eden had shown him a list of equipment that had 'been sent' to the Independent Companies and Commandos. Churchill had one of the Commandos, No 7 at Felixstowe, 'rung up as a sample', and, as he wrote to Eden, found that it had 'no Bren guns, no Anti-Tank rifles, and though it has some Tommy guns, they have no ammunition'. Churchill ended his letter: 'I am sorry to be insistent upon these small points, but they have an alarming aspect.'[1]

The Cabinet changes were finalized on October 2. 'We have had a great day of interviews in connection with the reconstruction of the Government,' John Martin wrote home, and he added: 'It must be wearing for the PM; but he is still in particularly good form.'[2]

Despite Churchill's wish to have Eden as his Foreign Secretary, Halifax and Eden remained in their existing posts, while Sir John Anderson succeeded Chamberlain as Lord President of the Council, presiding, as Chamberlain had done, over the Cabinet's Home Affairs Committee, to which substantial authority was delegated over the whole sphere of domestic policy.[3]

There were also, Colville noted, to be changes in the Chiefs of Staff, who were 'sound but slow', and in the Navy, which was 'certainly called for' as a result of the continuing heavy losses of merchant ships.[4] Sir Charles Portal succeeded Sir Cyril Newall as Chief of the Air Staff.[5] But Pound and Dill remained at their posts.

On October 2 there was good news from West Africa, where a small Free French detachment succeeded, without bloodshed, in winning control of Duala, and in obtaining the adherence of the French Cameroons to the anti-Vichy flag.[6] This news prompted Churchill to

---

[1] Letter of 30 September 1940: Churchill papers, 20/1.

[2] Letter of 2 October 1940: Martin papers.

[3] Among other changes, Sir Andrew Duncan became Minister of Supply, Oliver Lyttelton President of the Board of Trade, and J. Moore-Brabazon Minister of Transport. Ernest Bevin, remaining Minister of Labour and National Service, now entered the War Cabinet, as did the Chancellor of the Exchequer, Sir Kingsley Wood. All changes were effective from 3 October 1940. Of Duncan's appointment, Beaverbrook wrote to Churchill: 'The choice of Sir Andrew Duncan is admirable, if I may be allowed to say so. He knows the job and he will deliver the goods. Now that he is in Office you will have no difficulty about Priorities.' (Letter of 2 October 1940: Churchill papers, 2/392.)

[4] Colville diary, 2 October 1940: Colville papers.

[5] Newall had been appointed Governor-General of New Zealand. The change took place on 25 October 1940.

[6] General de Gaulle himself reached Duala on 7 October 1940. On learning of this Churchill telegraphed: 'I send my best wishes to you and to all other Frenchmen who are resolved to fight on with us. We shall stand resolutely together until all obstacles have been overcome and we share in the triumph of our cause.' (Telegram of 7 October 1940: Churchill papers, 20/14.)

reply with considerable anger to a message from the Australian Prime Minister, Robert Menzies, sent to Churchill on September 29, and criticizing the Dakar Operation for having been undertaken without there having been in advance what Menzies called 'overwhelming chances of success'. Menzies had also told Churchill that it had been 'humiliating' for the Australian Government to learn of the events of Dakar from the newspapers, and he went on to urge Churchill to ensure a 'clear-cut victory' in the Middle East, where the difficulties seemed to have been 'underestimated'.[1]

Churchill replied:

I am very sorry to receive your message of September 29, because I feel that the great exertions we have made deserve a broad and generous measure of indulgence, should any particular minor operation miscarry. You already have the information contained in my message of September 27, which is far more explicit than anything given to the British Parliament up to the present. A full secret report will be cabled to you when we ourselves hear the details from the Commanders on the spot.

The situation at Dakar was revolutionised by arrival of French ships from Toulon with Vichy personnel and the manning of the batteries by the hostile French Navy. Although every effort was made, the British Navy was not able to stop these ships on their way. After strongly testing the defences, and sustaining the losses I have already reported to you, the naval and military Commanders did not consider they had the strength to effect and support a landing, and I think they were quite right not to get us committed to a shore operation which could not, like the naval attack, be broken off at any moment, and might have become a serious entanglement.

With regard to your criticisms, if it is to be laid down that no attempt is to be made which has not 'overwhelming chances of success', you will find that a complete defensive would be imposed upon us. In dealing with unknown factors like the degree of French resistance, it is impossible to avoid uncertainty and hazard. For instance, Duala, and with it the Cameroons, were taken by twenty-five Frenchmen after their Senegalese troops had refused to march. Ought we to have moved in this case without having overwhelming force at hand?

Secondly, I cannot accept the reproach of making 'a half-hearted attack'. I hoped that you had not sustained the impression from these last five months of struggle which has excited the admiration of the whole world that we were 'a half-hearted Government' or that I am half-hearted in the endeavours it is my duty to make. I thought, indeed, that from the way my name was used in the Election that quite a good opinion was entertained in Australia of these efforts.

[1] Telegram of 29 September 1940: Premier papers, 4/43B/1, folio 144.

Every care will always be made to keep you informed before news is published, but we could not prevent the German and Vichy wireless from proclaiming the course of events as they occurred at Dakar before we had received any information from our Commanders.

With regard to what you say about the Middle East, I do not think the difficulties have been underestimated, but, of course, our forces are much smaller than those which the Italians have in Libya and Abyssinia, and the Germans may always help them. The defection of France has thrown the whole Middle East into jeopardy and severed our communications through the Mediterranean.

We have had to face the threat of invasion here and the full strength of Germany's air bombing attack on our cities, factories and harbours. Nevertheless, we have steadfastly reinforced the Middle East, and in spite of all our perils at home and scanty resources have sent over 30,000 men, nearly half our best tanks, many anti-aircraft guns needed to protect our vital aircraft factories, two of the finest units in the Fleet, the *Illustrious* and *Valiant*, and a considerable number of Hurricane fighters and Wellington bombers.

We have done this in the face of an accumulation across the Channel and the North Sea of barges and shipping sufficient to carry half a million men to these shores at a single voyage and in a single night. Therefore, if the Middle East difficulties and dangers have not been fully met, it is not because the Mother Country has shirked her share of perils and sacrifice. At present the situation in Egypt and the Sudan looks better than we feared some time ago.

Still, my dear Prime Minister and friend, as you have allowed me to deem you, I cannot guarantee 'clear-cut victory' in the Middle East, or that Cairo, Khartoum, the Suez Canal and Palestine may not fall into Italian or German hands. We do not think they will, and we are trying our utmost to resist the attacks which are massing against us. But I can make no promises at all of victory, nor can I make any promises that regrettable and lamentable incidents will not occur, or that there will not be disappointments and blunders. On the contrary, I think the only certainty is that we have very bad times indeed to go through before we emerge from the mortal perils by which we are surrounded.

'I felt it due to your great position,' Churchill ended, 'and the extremely severe tone of your message to reply with equal frankness.'[1]

Churchill was to remember his rebuke of Menzies three months later when the Secretary of State for the Dominions, Lord Cranborne, suggested consulting the Dominions in advance of decisions such as the ending of the Dakar attack. One way of ensuring Dominion goodwill, Cranborne suggested, was to have a Dominion representative present at the War Cabinet. But Churchill was opposed to any such course, minuting to Cranborne: 'It would certainly not be possible to consult the Dominions before breaking off an action such as that at Dakar, nor

[1] Telegram of 2 October 1940: Premier papers, 4/43B/1, folios 136–8.

indeed about any direct military operation, even where their own troops were liable to be engaged. . . .' The safety of the troops themselves required 'unity and secrecy in the command'. Churchill added: 'I could not for a moment admit the right of the Dominions to have a representative at every meeting of the War Cabinet, or, to reverse the statement, that His Majesty's Servants may never meet without supervision.'[1]

The one exception which Churchill had made to his rule was in telling General Smuts about the Dakar operation. This had been at Ismay's suggestion; but even Ismay had advised that it would be 'clearly understandable' that any communication to Smuts, or to any other Dominion Prime Minister, should not 'give the impression that we were inviting their comments on the project'.[2] Churchill had agreed to send a telegram to Smuts, but in doing so had instructed Ismay: 'It is not necessary to tell all the others. We cannot carry on the war, if every secret operation has to be proclaimed to every Dominion.'[3]

On October 3 the Dollis Hill centre of Government was used for the first and last time. As Churchill later recalled: 'We held a Cabinet meeting at "Paddock" far from the light of day, and each Minister was requested to inspect and satisfy himself about his sleeping and working apartments. We celebrated this occasion by a vivacious luncheon, and then returned to Whitehall.'[4] In Churchill's absence, as Colville noted in his diary, 'John Martin and I remained alone at No. 10 dealing placidly with our business', unhampered by bells, visitors 'and the general atmosphere of rush which surrounds the PM'.[5]

Churchill's Private Secretariat did not limit their interventions to drafting messages and organizing Churchill's work load, and schedules. On October 3 Eric Seal, after a talk with Lindemann, wrote to Churchill that 'both of us feel' that more could be done to counteract the 'menace of night bombing'. Even with decent shelters, Seal warned, the people of London could not spend 4.30 p.m. to 7 a.m. in them every night 'without serious results', yet that 'is what soon will be happening'. Seal added:

[1] Prime Minister's Personal Minute, M.10/1, 3 January 1941: Churchill papers, 20/36.
[2] 'Secret', 29 August 1940: Premier papers, 3/276, folio 213.
[3] Note of 30 August 1940: Premier papers, 3/276, folio 213.
[4] Winston S. Churchill, *The Second World War*, volume 2, London 1949, page 324.
[5] Colville diary, 3 October 1940: Colville papers.

I feel you ought to adopt the same tactics with the Fighter and Anti-Aircraft Commands as you did with the Naval Staff at the beginning of the war, when we were so successful in combating the early U-boat attacks, and above all the magnetic mine. That is to say, that you should send for the responsible officers, and probe deeply into the details of what they are doing, and ask for day to day reports of progress. Dowding has the reputation of being very conservative, and of not being receptive to new ideas.

The Admiralty too, Seal felt, needed 'galvanizing' about the anti-submarine campaign. 'I do hope,' he ended, 'that you will forgive this note, but I always said that I would speak plainly when I felt strongly.'[1]

These concerns were well based; in the week ending October 2, eleven merchant ships had been torpedoed and sunk, most of them in the Atlantic west of Ireland. During that same week, 2,000 civilians had been killed and 2,800 wounded in air raids; of the dead, 1,700 were killed in London.[2] This scale of killing had led to repeated calls for a more massive bombing campaign against Germany, even, as one Labour MP, J. J. Tinker, had written to Churchill, at the expense of bombing the invasion barges in the Channel ports. 'I know,' Churchill replied on October 4, 'there are others who favour the very bold strategy you mention.' But he went on to point out that 'the bulk' of Britain's air effort was already against Germany. 'He would be a very dangerous guide,' Churchill added, 'who deliberately courted an invasion of this Island because we felt sure of being able to defeat it. They will not come unless they think they can make good, and we must not lay our country open to miseries from which we can shield them.'[3]

That those miseries might be imminent was suggested on that same day, when seven Enigma messages to German commanders indicated to those at Bletchley and Broadway an acceleration and perfecting of plans for the German invasion. In the opinion of the General Staff, noted Colonel Strong, 'there can remain no doubt that preparations are continuing for a sea-borne expedition'. The inclusion of an 'aerodrome construction unit' in the second crossing of transport, Strong noted, 'would seem to indicate that they are to be required at an early stage to make an aerodrome ready to receive German aircraft'. All

---

[1] E. A. Seal, Minute, 3 October 1940: Premier papers, 3/22/1, folios 116-17.

[2] War Cabinet, Chiefs of Staff Committee, Weekly Résumé No. 57: Churchill papers, 23/6.

[3] 'Secret', 4 October 1940: Churchill papers, 20/8. In the Labour Government of 1924, Tinker had been Parliamentary Private Secretary to the Secretary of State for War.

that was not known, Strong added, was the date on which the invasion would be launched.[1]

Despite its knowledge of German invasion preparations, the War Cabinet decided on October 4 to risk conflict with Japan by letting the Burma road be re-opened for supplies to China. The road would open again on October 17, when the current three-month closure period expired. 'I know how difficult it is for you,' Churchill telegraphed that day to Roosevelt, 'to say anything which would commit the United States to any hypothetical course of action in the Pacific. But I venture to ask whether at this time a simple action might not speak louder than words. Would it not be possible for you to send an American squadron, the bigger the better, to pay a friendly visit to Singapore . . .'

Churchill also suggested to Roosevelt that advantage might be taken of the arrival of an American squadron at Singapore 'for a technical discussion of Naval and Military problems in those and Philippine waters', with the Dutch East Indies Government 'invited to join'. As Churchill explained: 'Anything in this direction would have a marked deterrent effect upon a Japanese declaration of war upon us over the Burma Road opening. I should be very grateful if you would consider action along these lines as it might play an important part in preventing the spreading of the war.'

Churchill also gave Roosevelt a survey of European attitudes to events since Dakar, telling the President:

In spite of the Dakar fiasco the Vichy Government is endeavouring to enter into relations with us, which shows how the tides are flowing in France now that they feel the German weight and see we are able to hold our own.

Although our position in the air is growing steadily stronger both actually and relatively our need for aircraft is urgent. Several important factories have been seriously injured and the rate of production is hampered by air alarms. On the other hand our losses in pilots have been less than we expected because in fighting over our own soil a very large proportion get down safely or only wounded. When your officers were over here we were talking in terms of pilots. We are now beginning to think that aeroplanes will be the limiting factor so far as the immediate future is concerned.

'I cannot feel that the invasion danger is past,' Churchill added. 'The gent has taken off his clothes and put on his bathing suit, but the water is getting colder and there is an autumn nip in the air.' Churchill's telegram ended: 'We are maintaining the utmost vigilance.'[2]

[1] 'Officer Only', 'Most Secret', 'German Preparations for Invasion', MI 14, 4 October 1940: War Office papers, 199/911A, B.59.
[2] Telegram despatched on 4 October 1940: Premier papers, 3/468, folios 94–5.

43

Amid bombardment

INVASION and Blitz were the daily anxiety of those with access to some inside knowledge of German plans, and aware of the full scale of German bombing effectiveness. But Churchill maintained his optimism, telling Robert Menzies, who had sent a placatory reply to Churchill's angry telegram, that in accepting his 'generous message' he felt 'confident that the act of mass terror which Hitler has attempted will fail, like his magnetic mines and other deadly schemes'.[1]

Churchill's confidence was based in part on a daily scrutiny of British war production. Noting that the earlier fall in the manufacture of bullets was over, he wrote to Herbert Morrison, the outgoing Minister of Supply: 'I am very glad you have been able to achieve a recovery in production in the teeth of the enemy's attack.'[2] Other problems required more vigorous exhortations, as when, on October 6, he discovered that a War Cabinet decision of a year earlier, on the supply of material for chemical warfare, had not been implemented. 'Have you no machinery,' he minuted to Bridges and Ismay, 'for seeing that orders are carried out?'[3]

Not only orders, but actual defence measures, were at times difficult to implement. On the morning of October 7 Churchill presided over an emergency meeting summoned to consider the urgent problems of Night Air Defence. As well as Sinclair, Beaverbrook, Lindemann and Bridges, twelve senior officers and officials concerned with the problem of locating and shooting down the German raiders were present.[4] The

[1] Telegram, 6 October 1940, 2.15 p.m.: Premier papers, 4/43B/1, folios 125–6.
[2] Letter of 4 October 1940: Churchill papers, 4/201.
[3] Prime Minister's Personal Minute, D.81, 6 October 1940: Churchill papers, 20/13. The unimplemented War Cabinet decision was dated 13 October 1939.
[4] Sir Cyril Newall (Chief of the Air Staff), Sir John Salmond (Ministry of Aircraft Production), Sir Hugh Dowding (Air Officer Commanding-in-Chief, Fighter Command), Sir P. B. Joubert de la Ferté (Air Ministry), Air Vice Marshal W. S. Douglas (Deputy Chief of the Air Staff), Robert

meeting heard that as a result of German action the production of Beaufighters had been 'completely stopped', but that the use of radar sets carried by fighters, and gun-laying radar sets on anti-aircraft guns was to go ahead, despite technical and manning problems.[1]

It was these problems to which the meeting now addressed itself, scrutinizing every aspect of night interception of German aircraft, both over land and sea. So urgent was this interception that it was decided that the use of anti-aircraft rocket batteries 'must not be delayed on the grounds that the falling projectile might cause damage or injury'.[2]

The meeting then discussed the 'urgent necessity' of retrieving all trained anti-aircraft persons from the Field Army, and re-transferring them to the Air Defence of Great Britain, in view of the highly technical character which anti-aircraft gunnery was assuming. Steps were also to be taken to 'press forward' with the areas of interception over the sea, and to ensure a 'substantial increase' in the number of technical personnel capable of maintaining and operating radar equipment. Experiments were also in progress with the short-wave AI radar sets to enable pilots 'to aim and fire at an unseen target'.[3]

Each of the technical matters discussed at this meeting was considered that same evening by the technical and service experts of the Committee, with Newall in the Chair. Their report was approved by Churchill, who directed 'that action shall be taken in accordance with it'.[4] The Night Air Defence Committee, as it became known, met twice more with Churchill in the Chair, to ensure that the necessary priorities of production and personnel were being directed towards countermeasures to meet the nightly German air assault.[5] 'Soon,' Ismay later recalled, as a result of the Committee's work, 'there was progressive increase in the number of aircraft destroyed, and those that survived were kept at a respectful height by the improved efficiency of the AA guns.'[6]

Watson-Watt (Air Ministry), Sir Frederick Pile (General Officer Commanding-in-Chief, Anti-Aircraft Command), Major General K. M. Loch (Director of Coast Defence, War Office), Vice-Admiral B. A. Fraser (Third Sea Lord), Commander H. F. Lawson (Naval Ordnance Department, Admiralty) and Sir F. E. Smith (Ministry of Supply).

[1] The airborne sets were the AI sets (Air Interception). The anti-aircraft gun sets were GL sets (Gun Laying).

[2] These were the UP (Unrotating Projectile) rockets.

[3] Meeting of 7 October 1940, 11.45 a.m. (Night Air Defence Committee No. 1): Cabinet papers, 81/22.

[4] Night Air Defence Committee, Report No. 1, 7 October 1940: Cabinet papers, 81/22.

[5] The second Night Air Defence Committee meeting was held in the Central War Room October 21, the third on November 19; both with Churchill in the Chair. The fourth meeting was held on December 9, with Beaverbrook in the Chair.

[6] The Memoirs of General the Lord Ismay, London 1960, page 183.

The responsibility for carrying out these anti-aircraft measures lay with Anti-Aircraft Command under General Pile. 'It was extremely interesting,' Colonel Jacob had reported to Ismay on October 2, after a visit to the 1st Anti-Aircraft Division, 'to see that at least one-third of the enemy raiders wouldn't face the inner artillery zone.' The German technique, Jacob added, appeared to be to approach the zone, 'perhaps more than once, as if looking for a hole, and then finally turn away and go home'.

Jacob suggested that Churchill himself might like to visit the headquarters of the 1st Anti-Aircraft Division, and see their work.[1] Churchill agreed to do so, and to watch a demonstration both of the UP rocket, and of the new radar sets for controlling searchlights.[2] He decided to go to the experimental searchlight rocket site north of Redhill, travelling by car with General Pile, with whom he first visited the anti-aircraft guns in Richmond Park. Night had come, and with it the first wave of German bombers. At the Park a barrage was in progress as bombs exploded in the distance and the sky was lit up with flashes of light from the bombs, and from the anti-aircraft fire. Churchill was at first reluctant to leave the Park for his next destination, commenting, as Pile later recalled: 'This exhilarates me. The sound of these cannon gives me a tremendous feeling.'[3]

From Richmond Park, Churchill and Pile were driven to Biggin Hill, where Churchill was shown the Air Force Operations Room. Then they went on to the experimental searchlight and rocket site north of Redhill, where they were met by the commanding officer of the 31st Anti-Aircraft Battalion, Lieutenant-Colonel Harvie-Watt, a Conservative MP and Assistant Government Whip. As they arrived, Pile told Harvie-Watt that Churchill was 'frozen and in a bad temper' and suggested that the Prime Minister be brought 'a strong whisky and soda'. Harvie-Watt sent a despatch rider to find one. 'Meanwhile,' he later recalled, 'everything was going from bad to worse. The field was almost waterlogged and the rain poured down. Everything I tried to show the Prime Minister he had seen before.' The searchlight control radar set, which had worked on the previous night, failed to function.

Churchill and Harvie-Watt soon turned, inevitably, to political talk.

---

[1] Letter to Ismay of 2 October 1940: Cabinet papers, 120/244.

[2] These were the SLC (Searchlight Control) sets, code name 'Elsie', with their 'Yagi' aerials.

[3] General Sir Frederick Pile, *Ack-Ack, Britain's Defence Against Air Attack During The Second World War*, London 1949, page 169.

A few days earlier it had been announced that because of ill-health Chamberlain would resign as Leader of the Conservative Party. The question being much debated was whether or not Churchill should succeed Chamberlain as Leader. 'I said it would be fatal if he did not lead the Conservative Party,' Harvie-Watt recalled, 'as the bulk of the party was anxious that he should be the Leader now we were at war.' Churchill, however, 'was still suspicious of them and of their attitude to him before the war. I said it was only a small section of the party that took that line and that the mass of the party was with him. My strongest argument, however, and I felt this very much, was that it was essential for the PM to have his own party—a strong one with allies attracted from the main groups and especially the Opposition parties. But essentially he must have a majority and I was sure this majority could only come from the Conservative Party.'

Not wishing to miss an opportunity of advice from a member of the Whips Office, Churchill questioned Harvie-Watt about 'the strength of Ministers and what influence they wielded'. Harvie-Watt replied: 'if you have a strong army of MP's under you, Ministers would be won over or crushed, if necessary.' Churchill, he noted, 'seemed to appreciate my arguments and thanked me very much. Then he began to feel the cold again and agitated to get away.'

At this moment the despatch rider arrived with the whisky, and Harvie-Watt poured one for the freezing Prime Minister. Churchill swallowed a half-tumbler, then cried out at the taste of the neat whisky: 'You have poisoned me.'[1]

Churchill and Pile left Redhill for London. As they approached the capital, bombs were still falling. As Pile later recorded:

> By now it was about 4.30, and the Prime Minister suddenly said to me: 'Do you like Bōvril?' (the 'o' pronounced as in 'Hove'). I said I did. He pondered for a bit, and then he said: 'Bōvril and sardines are very good together.' I had never tried them, but I was ready to try anything at that time of morning. 'Well,' he said, 'we will see what the commissariat can do for us as soon as we get back to No. 10.'

> Very shortly afterwards we drew up in front of the door. The Prime Minister had a walking-stick with him with which he rapped the door sharply: When the butler opened it the Prime Minister said: 'Goering and Goebbels coming to report,' and added: '*I* am not Goebbels.' And so we went in. He tried to persuade me to stay the night, on account of the dangers outside, but as soon

[1] G. S. Harvie-Watt, *Most of My Life*, London 1980, pages 37–9. Harvie-Watt later wrote: 'I thought I had done my cause no good.' But nine months later Churchill appointed him Parliamentary Private Secretary, in which position he served Churchill until 1945.

as I had had my Bovril and sardines I felt that honour was more than satisfied, and left.[1]

The failure of 'Elsie' to perform that night did not inhibit her subsequent progress. By the end of November 'users reports', Churchill was told, 'have been more encouraging', and new sets were being designed with an extended range of 14,000 yards.[2]

One small but effective anti-aircraft scheme initiated by Churchill during October was the firing of blank charges in anti-aircraft guns, the aim being to 'confuse the enemy by the flashing on the ground, and tend to make him less aware of our attacking fighters'. The blanks would also help, Churchill explained to Sinclair and Newall, 'to avoid discouraging silence for the population'.[3]

During the first week of October there had been Press criticism in Britain of the Dakar expedition. At the War Cabinet on October 7, Churchill mentioned in particular two *Sunday Pictorial* articles of September 29 and October 6, the latter of which had contained criticisms by H. G. Wells to the effect that until the Army was better led, 'we stood no chance of beating the Germans'. There had, Churchill said, been 'scurrilous' attacks on several members of the Government in both the *Sunday Pictorial* and the *Daily Mirror*, and he wanted to consider a criminal prosecution against the two papers, telling the War Cabinet on October 7:

The immediate purpose of these articles seemed to be to affect the discipline of the Army, to attempt to shake the stability of the Government, and to make trouble between the Government and organised labour. In his considered judgement there was far more behind these articles than disgruntlement or frayed nerves. They stood for something most dangerous and sinister, namely, an attempt to bring about a situation in which the country would be ready for a surrender peace.

It was not right that anyone bearing his heavy responsibilities should have to submit to attacks of this nature upon his Government. It was intolerable

---

[1] General Sir Frederick Pile, *Ack-Ack, Britain's Defence Against Air Attack During The Second World War*, London 1949, page 171.

[2] 'SLC No. 15' (fifteenth progress report), to 29 November 1940: Cabinet papers, 120/385. In all, 76 Searchlight Control sets were ordered for the end of February 1941 and a further 100 sets for mid-April 1941. Quantity production was planned to begin in May 1941. (SLC No. 18, to 18 January 1941: Cabinet papers, 120/385.)

[3] Prime Minister's Personal Minute, M.208, 20 October 1940: Cabinet papers, 120/244.

that any newspaper should indulge in criticism and abuse, far beyond what was tolerated in times of acute Party strife, in a time of great national peril.

Despite Churchill's strong feelings, the War Cabinet concluded that it might do 'more harm than good' to prosecute the papers, but it should be made clear to the Proprietors that these 'malicious articles' would not be tolerated.[1] It was decided that Attlee should speak to Cecil King, editor of the *Sunday Pictorial*, and Guy Bartholomew, editorial director of the *Daily Mirror*. 'Attlee was critical,' King noted in his diary, 'but so vague and evasive as to be quite meaningless. We got the impression that the fuss was really Churchill's. . . .'[2]

In one of the uncontested wartime by-elections, Randolph Churchill had been returned for Preston,[3] and on October 8 was introduced to the Commons, amid applause, by his father, and by the Chief Whip, David Margesson. 'The applause, needless to say, was for Winston,' Colville noted in his diary, 'whose popularity in the House, as in the country, remains untarnished.'[4]

In his own speech, Churchill spoke of the homes destroyed in the Blitz. 'We will rebuild them,' he said, 'more to our credit than some of them were before.' London, Liverpool, Manchester and Birmingham 'may have much more to suffer, but they will rise from their ruins, more healthy and, I hope, more beautiful'. One must not exaggerate, Churchill added, the material damage which had been done. The papers were full of pictures of demolished houses, 'but naturally they do not fill their restricted space with the numbers that are left standing'. If one went, he was told, to the top of Primrose Hill, 'or any of the other eminences of London, and look around, you would not know that any harm had been done to our city'.

At the present rate, Churchill noted, it would take ten years for half of the houses of London to be demolished. After that, the progress of demolition would be much slower. But 'quite a lot of things are going to happen to Herr Hitler and the Nazi regime before 10 years are up'. He had visited the scenes of destruction himself, and, he said:

---

[1] War Cabinet No. 267 of 1940, 7 October 1940, 5 p.m.: Cabinet papers, 65/9. Two days later Lord Beaverbrook told the War Cabinet that the *Sunday Pictorial* and *Daily Mirror* 'were conducted in a manner which was damaging to the repute of newspapers generally' (War Cabinet No. 268).

[2] Cecil King diary, 12 October 1940: William Armstrong (editor), *With Malice Towards None, a War Diary by Cecil H. King*, London 1970, pages 80–4.

[3] On 25 September 1940, following the death of A. C. Moreing, the Conservative MP. Preston was a two member constituency. In 1945 both Randolph Churchill, and the second Conservative candidate Julian Amery, were defeated at the General Election.

[4] Colville diary, 8 October 1940: Colville papers.

In all my life, I have never been treated with so much kindness as by the people who have suffered most. One would think one had brought some great benefit to them, instead of the blood and tears, the toil and sweat which is all I have ever promised. On every side, there is the cry, 'We can take it,' but, with it, there is also the cry, 'Give it 'em back.'

On the question of reprisals, for which so many people had pressed, Churchill was insistent that only military targets should be attacked. These would do Germany the most injury, he said, and would most speedily lessen their power to strike at Britain. 'Is that a reprisal?' he went on to ask. 'It seems to me very like one. At any rate, it is all we have time for now.'[1]

Speaking of the German invasion 'which we have been promised every month and almost every week since the beginning of July', Churchill said:

Do not let us be lured into supposing that the danger is past. On the contrary, unwearying vigilance and the swift and steady strengthening of our forces by land, sea and air which is in progress must be at all costs maintained. Now that we are in October, however, the weather becomes very uncertain, and there are not many lucid intervals of two or three days together in which river barges can cross the narrow seas and land upon our beaches. Still, those intervals may occur. Fogs may aid the foe. . . .

Churchill also spoke of aid to Britain from the United States. 'If it were not for the resources of the New World,' he said, 'which are becoming increasingly available, it would be a long time before we should be able to do much more than hold our own.' Of the failure at Dakar he declared: 'His Majesty's Government have no intention whatever of abandoning the cause of General de Gaulle until it is merged, as merged it will be, in the larger cause of France.' After describing in outline the course of events at Dakar, Churchill reflected:

What an irony of fate it is that this fine French Navy, which Admiral Darlan shaped for so many years to fight in the common cause against German aggression, should now be the principal obstacle to the liberation of France and her Empire from the German yoke, and should be employed as the tool of German and Italian masters whose policy contemplates not merely the defeat

---

[1] Five days later, in opposing an International Red Cross suggestion to monitor bombing raids in both Britain and Germany, Churchill minuted to Halifax: 'It would simply result in a Committee under German influence or fear, reporting at the very best that it was six of one and half-a-dozen of the other. It is even very likely they would report that we had committed the major breaches. Anyhow, we do not want these people thrusting themselves in, as even if Germany offered to stop the bombing now, we should not consent to it. Bombing of military objectives, increasingly widely interpreted, seems at present our main road home.' (Prime Minister's Personal Minute, M.182, 13 October 1940: Cabinet papers, 120/300.)

and mutilation of France, but her final destruction as a great nation. The Dakar incident reminds us of what often happens when a drowning man casts his arms around the strong swimmer who comes to his rescue and seeks in his agony to drag him down into the depths.

Of Press criticism of Dakar, which had been discussed by the War Cabinet on the previous day, Churchill commented that it was 'so vicious and malignant that it would be almost indecent if applied to the enemy'. It was important if one's nerves were 'frayed by the stresses of the war' not to give vent to feelings that could 'weaken the national resistance and blunt our sword'.

Churchill then spoke of Britain's earlier agreement with Japan to close the Burma Road to supplies to China. Japan had continued in its struggle 'to subjugate the Chinese race', he said, 'with all its attendant miseries', and in the circumstances the agreement to close the Burma Road would not be renewed once it has run its course in nine days time. He also spoke of Spain, telling the House of Commons that the 'wide compass' of the British blockade would not lap Spain, provided she did not become 'a channel of supply to our mortal foes'.

Britain's 'giant, enduring, resilient strength' was now recognized by friends and foes, Churchill declared. But this should not 'dull for one moment the sense of the awful hazards' in which Britain still stood. 'Do not let us lose the conviction,' he warned, 'that it is only by supreme and superb exertions, unwearying and indomitable, that we shall save our souls alive.' His speech ended:

No one can predict, no one can even imagine, how this terrible war against German and Nazi aggression will run its course or how far it will spread or how long it will last. Long, dark months of trials and tribulations lie before us. Not only great dangers, but many more misfortunes, many shortcomings, many mistakes, many disappointments will surely be our lot. Death and sorrow will be the companions of our journey; hardship our garment: constancy and valour our only shield. We must be united, we must be undaunted, we must be inflexible. Our qualities and deeds must burn and glow through the gloom of Europe until they become the veritable beacon of its salvation.[1]

This peroration, Colville noted, 'was eloquently spoken and enthusiastically received'. That night Churchill dined with Eden in his new dining-room in the basement of 10 Downing Street, the former typists' room, 'now redecorated and reinforced'. In relaxed mood, Churchill wore his blue siren-suit. 'He was in great form,' Colville noted, 'and amused Eden and me very much by his conversation with Nelson, the

[1] *Hansard*, 8 October 1940, columns 289–303.

black cat, whom he chided for being afraid of the guns and unworthy of the name he bore.' 'Try to remember,' Churchill said to Nelson reprovingly, 'what those boys in the RAF are doing.'[1]

During the evening of October 8, Enigma decrypts of German Air Force movement plans, and of cloud reports sent to the reception areas, were interpreted as indicating 'that units of German Air Force are still making final arrangements for the operation *Seelöwe*[2] (understood to be the invasion of the United Kingdom)' and that adjustments were being made as to the different echelons in which their sub-units would move.[3]

A further Enigma decrypt on October 9 was a request from the headquarters of the 2nd German Airfleet for provision at Rotterdam and Antwerp of two tankers, each filled with approximately 250,000 gallons of aviation fuel 'to be held in readiness for S + 3 day'. This, commented MI 14, was 'presumably the third day of invasion operations against UK'.[4]

The preparations were clearly continuing. But the date on which the invasion was to be launched, if it were indeed to be launched, was unknown. That night German bombers struck again at London, and a high-explosive bomb plunged through the roof of St Paul's.[5] Even as this air raid was in progress, British naval forces, as part of the increased activity against the invasion ports, bombarded German barges and port facilities in Cherbourg harbour.[6] Evidence was 'still accumulating', Churchill told the War Cabinet on October 10, 'that preparations for invasion were still going forward and that it would be premature to dismiss the possibility of an attempt being made'. Nevertheless, 'we should have to consider in the near future the extent to which we could afford to reinforce the Middle East at the expense of this country'.[7] The British Naval Attaché in Belgrade, Churchill had told the War Cabinet on the previous day, had reported an un-

---

[1] Colville diary, 8 October 1940: Colville papers.

[2] Sealion. Also known as 'Operation Smith'.

[3] 'Officer Only', 'Most Secret', MI 14, 8 October 1940, 6 p.m.: War Office papers, 199/911A, B.60.

[4] 'Officer Only', 'Most Secret', MI 14, 9 October 1940, 1 p.m.: War Office papers, 199/911A, B.61.

[5] Plunging through the roof of the choir, the bomb exploded when it struck the crown of the stone arch just above the high altar, tearing a hole in the vault 'and momentarily lifting the roof timbers from their seatings. It brought down tons of masonry and the upper part of the marble reredos.' (J. M. Richards, 'Night Watch at St. Paul's', *Country Life*, 30 July 1981, pages 363–7.)

[6] This was the operation, code name 'Medium', during which *Revenge* fired 120 rounds of 15-inch shell in eighteen minutes, at ranges of between fourteen and sixteen thousand yards, the 5th Destroyer Flotilla joining in for the first four minutes when they fired 801 rounds of 4.7-inch high explosive shell.

[7] War Cabinet No. 269 of 1940, 10 October 1940, 12 noon: Cabinet papers, 65/9.

confirmed story to the effect that two 'German Air Divisions' were about to leave for Libya.[1]

Since the announcement of Neville Chamberlain's resignation as Leader of the Conservative Party, Churchill had been urged by many to accept the Party leadership, as he had been by Harvie-Watt during his visit to the anti-aircraft battery near Redhill. But Clementine Churchill was against acceptance, arguing 'with passionate conviction', as her daughter Mary has written:

... that Winston had been called by the voice of the whole nation, irrespective of party, at a time of grave national emergency to head a National Government, and that, although he might feel his position to be stronger in Parliament by accepting the Conservative Leadership, he would affront a large body of opinion in the country. Clementine put her view with vehemence, and all her latent hostility towards the Tory Party boiled over; there were several good ding-dong arguments between them. But Winston's view prevailed: he accepted the Leadership of the Conservative Party, and felt sustained through some tough times by the assurance of their solid support.

True to her custom, Clementine accepted her defeat without recriminations. But she never altered her opinion that this step was a mistake, and that it alienated much of the support which Winston derived from the working-classes through the vindication of his pre-war prophecies and his record as a war leader. When about a year later she was invited to head the Red Cross Aid to Russia Fund, she accepted with alacrity, not only because of her wish to do something for the Russians, but also because she felt that in some way this might help to redress the balance.[2]

Churchill's leadership of the Conservative Party marked an historic and poignant moment for him. He had first joined the Conservative Party during the reign of Queen Victoria, left it in the reign of King Edward VII to become a Liberal, and had joined it again, on being appointed Chancellor of the Exchequer in the reign of King George V. 'I hate the Tory Party, their men, their words & their methods,' he had written thirty-seven years earlier;[3] and in January 1939 he had written to his wife of 'these dirty Tory hacks who would like to drive me out of the Party' as a result of his criticisms of Chamberlain and

---

[1] War Cabinet No. 268 of 1940, 9 October 1940, 12 noon, minute 4, Confidential Annex: Cabinet papers, 65/15.

[2] Mary Soames, *Clementine Churchill*, London 1979, pages 299–300.

[3] Letter of 3 November 1903, to Lord Hugh Cecil, quoted in volume 2 of this biography.

appeasement.[1] Now he was to lead the Party which his father had hoped, in vain, to lead. During the course of his speech of acceptance, Churchill had asked himself this question, he said, before accepting:

Am I by temperament and conviction able sincerely to identify myself with the main historical conceptions of Toryism, and can I do justice to them and give expression to them spontaneously in speech and action?

My life, such as it has been, has been lived for forty years in the public eye, and very varying opinions are entertained about it—and about particular phases in it.

I shall attempt no justification, but this I will venture most humbly to submit and also to declare, because it springs most deeply from the convictions of my heart: that at all times according to my lights and throughout the changing scenes through which we are all hurried I have always faithfully served two public causes which I think stand supreme—the maintenance of the enduring greatness of Britain and her Empire and the historical continuity of our Island life.

Churchill then elaborated on the central aspect of his personal and political philosophy, the result of more than four decades of thought and participation in the principal events of his country and his age:

Alone among the nations of the world we have found the means to combine Empire and liberty. Alone among the peoples we have reconciled democracy and tradition; for long generations, nay, over several centuries, no mortal clash or religious or political gulf has opened in our midst. Alone we have found the way to carry forward the glories of the past through all the storms, domestic and foreign, that have surged about us, and thus to bring the labours of our forebears as a splendid inheritance for modern progressive democracy to enjoy.

It is this interplay and interweaving of past and present which in this fearful ordeal has revealed to a wondering world the unconquerable strength of a united nation. It is that which has been the source of our strength. In that achievement, all living Parties—Conservative, Liberal, Labour and other Parties, like the Whigs, who have passed away all have borne a part. . . .

Sacrifices of Party interest, and of Party feeling, Churchill added, would have to be made to defend 'the grand human causes' now under attack; it was because he felt that both he and the Conservatives shared 'these deep conceptions lying far beneath the superficial current of Party politics and the baffling of accidental events' that he had accepted

[1] Letter of 8 January 1939, to Clementine Churchill, quoted in volume 5 of this biography.

the trust and duty of Party Leadership, 'solemnly, but also buoy-antly'.[1]

Among the letters of congratulation which Churchill received was one from Sir Samuel Hoare in Madrid. When Hoare had entered the House of Commons in 1906 as a Conservative, Churchill was already a Liberal. But they had found common ground in Churchill's anti-Bol-shevik days in 1919, before coming into bitter dispute during the India Bill controversy in the mid-1930s. Through all these storms, their per-sonal friendship had survived. Hoare's letter read:

I feel that as one of the oldest Conservative MPs I must write a line to congratulate you upon becoming leader of the Conservative Party. From many points of view I am glad that the choice has now been made. You will yourself be much stronger with the Party machine behind you. This means that there need be no repetition of the LG collapse after the last war. Besides this, it seems to me vital to the Party itself that it should have at once a popular leader at its head.

The Party is still the greatest political instrument for the maintenance of the Empire and the preservation of its traditions. Without it the country will drift into the shallow waters of the ideologues. Both during the war and after it we must stop this drift and you with your personality and prestige will be able to stop it.

Naturally, having myself been connected with Cabinet changes over a period of many years, I felt greatly isolated here whilst these last were being made. I daresay that you had the same kind of feelings when you were out of office after 1929. I do not believe that in either of our cases this feeling is chiefly due to personal ambition. We have both had our share of Government posts and the commendable desire to obtain them cannot be as keen as it was. It is rather, I think, a desire to play a part in the great events and the fear of frustration that makes us cling to public life. . . .[2]

There were some Conservatives who could not quite reconcile them-selves to the enemy of former years, nor could Churchill quite come to terms with them. As Henry Channon wrote in his diary on October 10: 'I ran into Winston in the House: I wonder why he always bows and withdraws into himself when he is aware of hostility? When he shakes hands with someone he dislikes, he seems to contract, suddenly to look smaller and his famous charm is overclouded by an angry taurine look.'[3]

[1] Speech of 9 October 1940: Churchill papers, 9/145.
[2] 'Private & Personal', 10 October 1940, Subject file, Political (16a) Conservative Party: 10 Downing Street papers.
[3] Channon diary, 10 October 1940: Robert Rhodes James (editor), *Chips, The Diaries of Sir Henry Channon*, London 1967, page 269.

On Friday October 11 Churchill went for the weekend to Chequers, where a formidable series of guests was to join him.[1] The youngest was his new grandson Winston, Randolph's son, who had been born at Chequers on the previous day.[2] Colville, who was on duty that weekend, found Churchill 'cheerful, despite the fact that our air results today and yesterday have been bad'.

On October 9 a flight of aircraft had been destroyed on the ground at Hendon. But the number of civilians killed in the week ending October 11 was down from more than two thousand in the previous week to 711. Churchill commented on the news: 'That Man's effort is flagging.'

During the weekend the question arose of the vulnerability of Chequers from the air. 'Probably,' said Churchill, 'they don't think I am so foolish as to come here. But I stand to lose a lot. Three generations at a swoop.'[3]

That Friday night Dill and Brooke were up until 2 a.m. discussing, as Brooke noted in his diary, 'the probable course of the war, likelihood of German moves in Mediterranean, also reason for failure of Dakar expedition'. When the discussion ended, Brooke wrote in his diary of Churchill: 'He has a wonderful vitality and bears his heavy burden remarkably well. It would be impossible to find a man to fill his place at present.'[4]

While Churchill was at Chequers came yet more indications from the Enigma decrypts that the Germans were still proceeding with their invasion preparations. The German air formation headquarters in charge of equipment in Belgium and Northern France had asked 'what distance the troops would have to march to reach their port of embarkation'.[5] The same headquarters had also asked 'When will the arrangements for showing screened lights on the R Scheldt be completed?' and what 'S' days, or Sealion days, were to be allotted for '(i) taking over stores; (ii) the beginning of loading of packed vehicles, and (iii) the embarkation of troops?' An 'early reply' had been requested,

---

[1] Among those at Chequers at different moments that weekend, either for meals, or to stay overnight, were five Generals (Ismay, Brooke, Pile, Hobart and Dill), Air Chief Marshal Dowding, Air Marshal Portal, Admiral of the Fleet Sir Dudley Pound, Attlee, Lindemann, Alistair Forbes (a young friend of the family just returned from Dakar), Randolph, Diana, Mary and Pamela Churchill, and Colville.

[2] Winston Spencer Churchill, who in 1970 was elected Conservative MP for Stretford. From 1976 to 1978 he was Conservative Party front-bench spokesman on Defence.

[3] Colville diary, 11 October 1940: Colville papers.

[4] Brooke diary, 11 October 1940: Arthur Bryant, *The Turn of the Tide, 1939–1943*, London 1957, page 253.

[5] 'Officer Only', 'Most Secret', MI 14, 11 October 1940: War Office papers, 199/911A, B.62.

and had been sent that same day. Stores were to be assembled at S minus 9, that is, nine days before Sealion; the loading of packed vehicles was to begin from eight to five days before, and troops were to be embarked from four days to one day before.

MI 14 noted that this report 'once again' confirmed 'that preparations for invasion are being actively pursued'. Taking October 11 as the first day of these final moves, S minus 9 would give October 20 as 'the earliest possible zero day'. But, MI 14 added, 'in all probability it will be after that date'.

'S' day, reiterated Military Intelligence, was 'considered to be the zero day of the invasion operations again UK and/or Eire'.[1]

While Military Intelligence pondered the date of the German invasion, British anti-invasion measures continued, among them Operation 'Medium', the night-time naval bombardment of German gun positions on the French coast. Following the starting of fires in the target area by the Royal Air Force, HMS *Revenge* had opened fire with her heaviest guns. Many salvoes, she reported on the afternoon of Friday October 11, were seen to burst in the target area, and 'volumes of dense smoke were observed, with flames rising several hundred feet in the air'.[2]

Reading this report at Chequers, Churchill noted a paragraph which described how, as *Revenge* and her attendant destroyers were retiring, a battery of heavy German guns had opened fire with such accuracy that, as *Revenge* reported, 'it would appear' some form of radar had been used for ranging. This development of radar in conjunction with coastal batteries, Churchill noted, was serious. 'We have for a long time been on the track of this device,' he noted for Ismay, 'and I drew attention to it some weeks ago. I was then told that it had to have a low priority because of other even more urgent needs.' Perhaps, Churchill suggested, it would be possible to bring it forward. 'Evidently,' he added, 'it will turn night into day so far as defence against sea bombardment is concerned.'

'Pray see,' Churchill ended, 'if some proposals can be made without injury to other radio projects.'[3]

Churchill had indeed asked Ismay, in the second week of September, to examine reports of German batteries firing by radar 'without illuminants'. 'We have had this idea for a long time,' Churchill had noted,

[1] 'Officer Only', 'Most Secret', 'German Preparations for Invasion', MI14, 10 p.m., 11 October 1940: War Office papers, 199/911A, B.63.
[2] Signal No. 791, sent 2.23 p.m., 11 October 1940: Premier papers, 3/369/1, folio 8.
[3] Prime Minister's Personal Minute, D.84, 12 October 1940: Premier papers, 3/369/1, folio 7.

'but what has happened about it, and what progress has been made?'[1] Ismay had asked Colonel Jacob to arrange for Churchill to be sent a report 'after trials in October'.[2] The answer both to Churchill's first minute of September 11, and to his reminder of October 12, came two weeks later, when Ismay reported to Churchill that the Inter Services radar Committee, under the presidency of Air Marshal Joubert, had been trying for some time to find a means of 'speeding up' the project 'as you desire', but that 'the result, I am afraid, is not very favourable'.

All available radio capacity, Ismay explained, was taken up with the 'urgent needs' of producing the anti-aircraft gun GL sets and their offshoots, the PE proximity fuse, and the SLC searchlight control sets. There was therefore 'little or no prospect' of Coast Defence fire control sets being produced in any quantity before August 1941. Pilot trials would, however, take place during November, and preparations for production made. As far as the British guns on the Straits of Dover were concerned, Ismay wrote, 'something can be improvised very soon', and it was hoped that the first radar control apparatus would be installed on a Dover gun about the end of November.[3]

Churchill remained at Chequers throughout Saturday October 12. After lunch, 'sitting in his siren suit and smoking an immense cigar', Colville noted, 'he said he thought this was the sort of war which would suit the English people once they got used to it. They would prefer all to be in the front line taking part in the battle of London than to look on hopelessly at mass slaughters like Passchendaele.' Of the Fifth Column danger Churchill commented that he 'much disliked locking people up and the suspension of Habeas Corpus'. The 'filthy Communists', he added, were 'just as dangerous' as the fascists.[4]

During October 12 there was a further Enigma decrypt of orders to a German anti-aircraft regiment to carry out 'embarkation and disembarkation exercises' at the Channel port of Gravelines on the following day, October 13. These exercises were to include the passing of

---

[1] Prime Minister's Personal Minute, D.50, 11 September 1940, Premier papers, 3/369/1, folio 10.

[2] Minute of 22 September 1940: Premier papers, 3/369/1, folio 9.

[3] Minute of 31 October 1940, 'Secret': Premier papers, 3/361/1, folios 5–6. The first Coast Defence fire control trial took place on December 6, and two sets, type 284, were made available at the end of December to work with two gun batteries, a 6-inch battery at Dover and a 9·2-inch battery at South Foreland.

[4] Colville diary, 12 October 1940: Colville papers.

barges through locks and the approach to the shore, 'as well as actual landing'. MI 14 commented: 'Evidence is thus still accumulating that invasion preparations are actively proceeding.'[1]

Still 'obviously worried' about a German air raid on Chequers, Churchill told Attlee and Dill that Saturday evening, as Colville noted, that 'he does not object to chance, but feels it a mistake to be the victim of design'.[2]

During the evening discussion, Churchill told Attlee that he had learnt 'one great lesson from his father—never to be afraid of British Democracy'.

The news that night was bad; in a raid over London, German bombers had scored direct hits on the War Office and the National Gallery. Churchill was, 'much disturbed', Colville noted,[3] but he still refused to neglect the search for British initiatives, and in a minute for the Chiefs of Staff Committee on the morning of Sunday October 13, he set down his suggestions for the immediate reinforcement of Malta and the protection of Duala from a counter-stroke by the French cruisers at Dakar. 'It should be possible also,' Churchill wrote, 'to provide by the end of July a striking force for amphibious warfare of six divisions, of which two should be armoured.' The various alternative plans for the employment of such a force, he added, were already being studied.[4]

That Sunday at lunch, Churchill commented to his guests: 'A Hun alive is a war in prospect.'[5]

During this weekend, Churchill studied the reports on defensive measures being undertaken against invasion, and on the production of the much-needed small arms and ammunition, minuting to Colonel Jacob: 'Let me know whether any further action or decisions are required from me.'[6] There was a sense of relief at Chequers that Sunday when Dowding reported that the German air attacks, despite the heavy casualties and damage caused, were 'lacking in purpose'. The Germans, he said, 'do not concentrate on one target, or on a small area first with

---

[1] 'Officer Only', 'Most Secret', 'German Preparations for Invasion', MI 14, 4.15 p.m., 12 October 1940: War Office papers, 199/911A, B.64.

[2] Shortly after this, Churchill decided to spend the weekends nearest to the full moon at Ditchley Park, Ronald Tree's house on the Oxford–Stratford road, further from London, and more protected by trees. The broad gravel drives at Chequers looked, from the air, almost like an arrow cut in the lawn and pointing at the house.

[3] Colville diary, 12 October 1940: Colville papers.

[4] 'Most Secret', 13 October 1940: Churchill papers, 20/13. Circulated on 15 October 1940 as War Cabinet paper No. 42 of 1940 (Churchill papers, 23/4).

[5] Colville diary, 13 October 1940: Colville papers.

[6] Prime Minister's Personal Minute, D.85, 13 October 1940: Churchill papers, 20/13.

incendiary and then with high explosives'. In saying goodnight to Dowding and Portal that Sunday night, Churchill told them, Colville noted, that he 'felt sure we were going to win the war, but he confessed he did not see clearly how it was to be achieved'.[1]

On October 14 an Enigma decrypt set out the list of air force supplies which were to be 'loaded into the ship of the army', along with the ground personnel of the squadron, for use in 'the first 20 days' of operation Sealion. These supplies and personnel were to constitute the air component of the German 16th Army. A second Enigma decrypt showed that the third 'wave' of the invasion would take with it the ground party for 160 dive-bombers, to be despatched from Rotterdam.[2]

That night, German bombers struck again at London. 'I expect you have heard that this district suffered last night,' Mrs Hill wrote from 10 Downing Street on the following morning, to one of Churchill's former literary helpers, 'but we are now cleaning and patching up as best we can.'[3] Bombs had fallen throughout Whitehall and Pall Mall, and on Downing Street itself. 'So many thanks for a lively dinner,' the newly appointed Minister of Transport, J. T. C. Moore-Brabazon, wrote to Churchill on the following morning, 'bombs and all!!',[4] and John Martin, who was on duty that night, wrote home two days later:

A high explosive bomb fell a few yards from No. 10. I was upstairs and dashed down to the shelter as I heard it fall, to the accompaniment of the most terrific explosion. It is difficult to remember exactly what happened; but I seemed to fly down with a rush of 'blast', the air full of dust and the crash and clatter of glass breaking behind. There was a rush of several of us into the shelter and we tumbled on top of one another in a good deal of confusion. Afterwards it was several minutes before the air cleared and, with the clouds of dust and the acrid, sooty smell, we thought that the house or the Treasury next door was on fire. Fortunately that was not so and by the light of torches we were able to survey the damage. The mess in the house was indescribable—

---

[1] Colville diary, 13 October 1940: Colville papers.

[2] 'Most Secret', 14 October 1940: War Office papers, 199/911A, B.60.

[3] Letter of 15 October 1940, to C. C. Wood: Churchill papers, 2/411.

[4] Letter of 15 October 1940: Churchill papers, 20/4. Moore-Brabazon also sent Churchill the secret report of the effect of the bombing at Stoke Newington. The report read: 'At 2031 hours a heavy calibre bomb struck a block of flats and caused them to collapse completely. Many of the occupants were in the basement shelter which was divided into three compartments, two of which were buried by the debris. The third became flooded and although about 50 persons escaped it is believed that many were drowned. It is feared that rather more than 200 people have been buried in the other two compartments and that there is little chance of their being rescued alive. These casualty figures take no account of any persons who may have been in the demolished flats.'

windows smashed in all directions, everything covered with grime, doors off hinges and curtains and furniture tossed about in a confused mass.

Fortunately the PM has been using the basement and was dining there at the time at the opposite side of the house, with steel shutters closed, so was none the worse. Meanwhile incendiaries and HE were being dropped whole-sale in the West End and there was a line of fire along the Pall Mall and Piccadilly direction. The Carlton Club was wrecked and burnt. The Reform Club had a fire, but was not (as far as I could see today) too badly damaged, though we can't use it. (During the night, I telephoned the hall porter at the Reform and asked how things were. A calm voice replied 'The Club is burning, Sir.') St James's Club in Piccadilly was burnt out. A big house in St James's Square was reduced to a heap of rubble—and so on. The hut of the soldiers who guard Downing Street was completely demolished: fortunately they had taken refuge elsewhere.[1]

Nine years later Churchill also recalled this scene. As well as Moore-Brabazon, his dinner guests had been Sir Archibald Sinclair, and Oliver Lyttelton, the newly appointed President of the Board of Trade. After a bomb had fallen some hundred yards away on Horse Guards Parade, Churchill had ordered his butler, cook and servants to leave the meal in the dining room, leave their kitchen, and go into the basement. Then, only about three minutes later, had come the second bomb. As Churchill recalled:

My detective came into the room and said much damage had been done. The kitchen, the pantry, and the offices on the Treasury side were shattered.

We went into the kitchen to view the scene. The devastation was complete. The bomb had fallen fifty yards away on the Treasury, and the blast had smitten the large, tidy kitchen, with all its bright saucepans and crockery, into a heap of black dust and rubble. The big plate-glass window had been hurled in fragments and splinters across the room, and would of course have cut its occupants, if there had been any, to pieces. But my fortunate inspiration, which I might so easily have neglected, had come in the nick of time.

The bomb on the Treasury had killed one civil servant and wounded two. After the explosion, Churchill had gone up with Sinclair to the roof above the Annexe. His account continued:

The night was clear and there was a wide view of London. It seemed that the greater part of Pall Mall was in flames. At least five fierce fires were burning there, and others in St James's Street and Piccadilly. Farther back over the river in the opposite direction there were many conflagrations. But Pall Mall was the vivid flame-picture. Gradually the attack died down, and presently the 'All Clear' sounded, leaving only the blazing fires.[2]

[1] Letter of 16 October 1940: Martin papers.
[2] Winston S. Churchill, *The Second World War*, volume 2, London 1949, pages 305–6.

The morning after the raid was John Martin's thirty-sixth birthday. As he wrote home:

... my birthday treat was to visit the ruins of the Carlton Club with the PM, who stumped in and wandered about amongst the wreckage, regardless of the impending roof. The dining room was like a bit of Pompeii, with unfinished meals and decanters of wine on the tables. At a bedroom door we found the Chief Whip David Margesson's bedroom slippers awaiting him. At the entrance steps the Prime Minister pointed to a piece of marble statuary half buried in rubble. Lifted up it was seen to be the head of Pitt.[1]

On the afternoon of October 15 the War Cabinet discussed the intensification of the air bombardment. Fear was expressed that there might be an 'unfortunate effect on our war effort' if feeling were allowed to grow that Britain was not 'hitting back hard enough at Germany in our bombing'. It would take two to three months to improve the means of countering night bombing substantially, Churchill warned. Meanwhile, 'we were retaliating as effectively as we could on Germany'. But Britain's bomber force was 'much smaller' than that of Germany, and had to make much longer flights to reach its targets. The people of Britain, he said, 'must stick it out'.[2]

---

[1] Letter of 16 October 1940: Martin papers. That same month, in an introduction to the third edition of Pitt's speeches published by the Oxford University Press, Churchill wrote: 'No historical analogies can be exact, and in one respect our situation is very different from what it was in Pitt's day. A Nazi victory would be an immeasurably worse disaster for us and for all mankind than Napoleon's victory could ever have been. As modern France, and not France only, knows, Napoleon could construct as well as destroy. There can be no comparison, indeed, in the scale of civilization between the Nazi system and that of the Napoleonic Empire; nor could the humane, free-spirited French people ever have become the docile instruments of such barbarism as now issues from Berlin. All the firmer, therefore, must be our determination to fight on, as Pitt and his successors fought on, till we in our turn achieve our Waterloo'. (Foreword dated October 1940: R. Coupland, editor, *The War Speeches of William Pitt the Younger*, Oxford 1940.)

[2] War Cabinet No. 271 of 1940, 15 October 1940, 5 p.m.: Cabinet papers, 65/9. In the week ending 17 October 1940 Bomber Command flew a total of 764 sorties on the Channel Ports and Germany. Berlin had been bombed on two nights, and Krupp's Works at Essen on three nights. In addition, the gasometer at Gelsenkirchen, 'the largest on the Continent', had been 'hit and rendered useless'. (War Cabinet, Chiefs of Staff Committee, Weekly Résumé No. 59: Churchill papers, 23/7.)

44

Priorities

I T was with his thoughts on 1941 and 1942 that Churchill had decided, during his Chequers weekend, to set out in detail the priorities which he felt ought now to be put into effect. On October 15, in a note for the War Cabinet, he wrote: the 'very highest priority' in personnel and material must be assigned to 'the Radio sphere' of preparations; that is, to radar. This was the area of invention and research with which Churchill had been involved, through the Cabinet's pre-war Air Defence Research sub-committee, from 1935 to 1939: his sole official link with pre-war policy, at its most secret level. In 1936 he had given personal encouragement to Robert Watson-Watt, at a time when the Air Ministry had been reluctant to give radar research the fullest priority.[1]

Now that his own authority was paramount, Churchill emphasized, of the 'Radio sphere': 'This demands Scientists, Wireless Experts, and many classes of highly-skilled labour and high-grade material.' His note continued: 'On the progress made, much of the winning of the war and our future strategy, especially Naval, depends. We must impart a far greater accuracy to the AA guns, and a far better protection to our warships and harbours. Not only research and experiments, but production must be pushed hopefully forward from many directions, and after repeated disappointments we shall achieve success.'

Churchill then set out what he considered to be the next, or IA, priority: aircraft production, for the purpose 'of executing approved Target programmes'. It was essential for the Ministry of Aircraft Production, he wrote, to 'continue by every conceivable means' not to let

---

[1] 'It was clear to me,' Watson-Watt wrote in June 1936, 'that the Ministry wished to avoid setting up emergency machinery in place of the accelerated normal machinery. Even after acceleration, this normal machinery has held down my rate of advance.' ('Secret', 12 June 1936: Churchill papers, 25/10.)

this priority be 'abused and needlessly hampered by other vital Departments'. Yet at the same time the labour and materials required for aircraft production should be specified quarter by quarter or, if practicable, month by month, so that all surplus could then be made available for others 'immediately'. Nor was the priority for aircraft production to be exercised, Churchill warned, 'in the sense that Aircraft Production is completely to monopolise the supplies of any limited commodity'. Indeed, where the Ministry of Aircraft Production's demands were such as to absorb the total supply, a 'special allocation must be made', he insisted, 'even at prejudice to Aircraft Production, to provide the minimum essential needs' of other departments and branches.

Churchill now surveyed the priority situation with regard to the Army's needs in a year's time, for the end of 1941. The paramount need was for Armoured Fighting Vehicles. Large purchases of motor transport would have to be made in the United States. For the Home Army, 'Improvisation and makeshift must be their guides. A Staff Officer renders no service to the country who aims at ideal standards, and thereafter simply adds and multiplies until impossible totals are reached.' Any attempt, Churchill added, 'to make heavy weather out of this problem is a failure to aid us in our need'.

Wherever possible, Churchill continued, horse transport should be used to supplement motor transport. 'We improvidently sold a great many of our horses to the Germans,' he noted, 'but there are still a good many in Ireland.'

Churchill then wrote of the need to give 'special aid' and occasional 'temporary priorities' to what he described as 'the Laggard elements': rifle production, and the manufacture of small arms ammunition. For these, he wrote, 'intense efforts' must be made to bring the new factories into production. The fact that 'scarcely any improvement is now expected until the end of the year, i.e. 16 months after the outbreak of war, is a grave reflection on those concerned. Twelve months should suffice for a cartridge factory.' Britain had been 'mercifully spared from the worst consequences of this failure', he wrote, 'through the Armies not being in action as was anticipated'. Trench mortar ammunition and anti-tank gun ammunition were also in 'a shocking plight, and must be helped'.

To ensure his own continued scrutiny of these areas of production, Churchill added: 'All these Laggards must be the subject of weekly reports to the Production Council and to me.'

In the sphere of naval construction, Churchill wished priority to be given to small craft and anti-U boat building, as well as to merchant shipbuilding and 'craft for landing operations'. Delay must be accepted upon all larger vessels that could not be finished by the end of 1941. To ensure no setback in the pace of production, the 'utmost possible steel and armour-plate' must be ordered in the United States.[1]

As a result of his work that weekend at Chequers, Churchill also sent the War Cabinet on October 15 a directive on future strategy in the Mediterranean. First in urgency was the reinforcement of Malta. Where tanks could not be sent, Churchill wrote, 'mock-up tanks might be exhibited where they could be detected from the Air'. Aircraft, troops, and 'the largest anti-aircraft outfit possible', should also be sent. Occasional visits to Malta by the whole Battle Fleet could, he added, be an 'immense deterrent to hostile attack', and while the visit lasted could also be a threat to Italy's communications with Libya.

In his directive of October 15, Churchill also set out his thoughts on Britain's relations with Vichy:

We cannot accept the position that we must yield to the wishes of Vichy out of fear lest they make Air raids upon Gibraltar; for there would be no end to that. We must reassert our blockade of the Straits, dealing with vessels whether escorted or unescorted, though without violating Spanish Territorial waters. We should assemble a sufficient force at Gibraltar for this purpose at the earliest date possible. Meanwhile, we must maintain as good a blockade of Dakar as possible, and protect Duala, &c., from a counter-stroke by the French cruisers in Dakar.

Churchill's directive continued:

The conversations with Vichy, if they take place, may reach a *modus vivendi*, falling somewhat short of these desiderata. Of course, if we could be assured that Vichy, or part of Vichy, were genuinely moving in our direction, we could ease up on them to a very large extent. It seems probably that they will be increasingly inclined to move as we desire, and I personally do not believe that hard pressure from us will prevent this favourable movement.

It was becoming 'more difficult every day', Churchill believed, for Vichy 'to lead France into war with us', and he added: 'We must not be too much afraid of checking this process, because the tide in our favour will master and overwhelm the disturbing eddies of the blockade, de Gaulle, and possible sea incidents.' Churchill doubted that the

[1] 'Priorities, Note by the Prime Minister', War Cabinet Paper No. 416 of 1940, 'Secret', 15 October 1940: Cabinet papers, 120/10.

Vichy authorities would seek to stop the impending reinforcements for Malta. 'The chance is there,' he noted, 'but it is remote and might be faced.'

Churchill's directive then examined Britain's bombing policy. It was the disabling of the *Bismarck* and the *Tirpitz*, he continued, that constituted 'the greatest prize' open to Bomber Command. Were the *Bismarck* set back for three or four months, the *King George V* could play a decisive part in the 'reoccupation' of Malta by the Fleet, an event which would 'speedily transform' the strategic situation in the Mediterranean.

Should October pass without invasion, Churchill concluded—a fact 'which cannot be assumed'—then Britain should begin to reinforce the Middle East by the Cape route 'to the utmost extent our shipping permits', sending up to five British divisions to Egypt by March 1941, as well as a 'further strong reinforcement' of bombers and fighters at once, and two flotillas of destroyers by the end of the year.

Whatever reinforcements were sent to Egypt, Churchill added, in Britain a minimum of twelve mobile divisions of the Home Army 'must lie in reserve, apart from troops in the trenches, at any time'.[1]

Colville noted in his diary: 'I told the PM how much I admired this review. He replied it was by no means in a finished state. He had just written down what was in his head.' But Colville felt that the paper showed 'breadth and vision'.[2]

By six in the morning of October 16, the figure of those killed by air raids during the previous week was estimated at 1,567, of whom 1,388 were killed in London.[3] During the day, an analysis of Enigma decrypts confirmed, as Colonel Strong reported, 'the fact that invasion preparations are actively proceeding or indeed becoming intensified'.[4] Studying the circulation list of these decrypts, Churchill minuted that same day to Ismay:

[1] War Cabinet paper No. 421 of 1940, 'The Mediterranean', 15 October 1940: Churchill papers, 23/4.

[2] Colville diary, 13 October 1940: Colville papers. Of Churchill's directives, Colville later reflected: 'They were in a sense the basis of our strategy,' and he added: 'They are not taken seriously enough by historians.' (Sir John Colville, conversation with the author: 21 January 1981.) This historian, however, has sought to give them their due weight.

[3] War Cabinet, Chiefs of Staff Committee, Weekly Résumé No. 59: Churchill papers, 23/7.

[4] 'Officer Only', 'Most Secret', 'German Preparation for Invasion': War Office papers, 199/911A, B.67.

I am astounded at the vast congregation who are invited to study these matters. The Air Ministry is the worst offender and I have marked a number who should be struck off at once, unless after careful consideration in each individual case it is found indispensable that they should be informed. I have added the First Lord, who of course must know everything known to his subordinates, and also the Secretary of State for War.

A machinery should be constructed which makes other parties acquainted with such information as is necessary to them for the discharge of their particular duties. I await your proposals.

As well as A. V. Alexander and Eden, there were two other names Churchill wished to add to the list, the Commander-in-Chief Fighter Command, Sir Hugh Dowding, and the newly appointed Commander-in-Chief Bomber Command, Sir Richard Peirse, 'it being clearly understood', he wrote, 'that they shall not impart them to any person working under them or allow the boxes to be opened by anyone save themselves'.[1]

During the morning of October 16 Churchill learned that considerable damage had been done during the night by land mines, dropped by parachute.[2] He wrote at once to Sinclair and Portal: 'Let me have your proposals forthwith for effective retaliation upon Germany.' His minute continued:

I am informed that it is quite possible to carry similar mines or large bombs to Germany, and that the Squadrons wish to use them, but that the Air Ministry are refusing permission. I trust that due consideration will be given to my views and wishes. It is now about three weeks since I began pressing for similar treatment of German military objectives to that which they are meting out to us.

'Who,' Churchill asked, 'is responsible for paralysing action?'[3]

In reply, Sinclair pointed out that use of the mines still awaited a War Cabinet decision, but that at present the Hampdens, the only aircraft equipped to carry the mine to 'the heart of Germany', were fully engaged attacking the heavy German naval units in Kiel, Hamburg and Wilhelmshaven, 'a task in which these squadrons have specialized'. More effective than the mine, Sinclair suggested, might be the 130 American demolition bombs 'now in the country', and specially

---

[1] Prime Minister's Personal Minute, D.92, 16 October 1940: Churchill papers, 20/13.

[2] The extent of the parachute mine damage was kept secret. An official note to the Air Ministry, War Office, Ministry of Home Security and Ministry of Information stated: 'No disclosure should be made of the severity of effect, in the public estimation, of these mines. From their size it would be apparent that they constituted a severe attack, but the added danger of their magnetic properties and the widespread destruction of house property they caused should not appear.' ('Land Mines on London', TO 7405/40, 23 October 1940: Premier papers, 3/314/2, folios 53-4.)

[3] Prime Minister's Personal Minute, M.193A, 16 October 1940: Cabinet papers 120/300.

designed 'for their blast effect'. The Air Staff did wish, however, to make a 'limited trial' of the mines against 'one of the large industrial targets', and this would be done as soon as the present moon-phase, ideal for more precision bombing, had passed.[1]

After receiving this minute, Churchill discussed the question of retaliating by parachute land mines on Germany with Sir Richard Peirse. 'I have come to the conclusion,' Churchill minuted to Sinclair and Portal after this discussion, 'that it would at the present time be an improvident use of our bomb-carrying capacity, except as a purely experimental, psychological feature, as proposed by you.' His minute continued:

While I am convinced that *Bismarck* and *Tirpitz* are at the present moment targets of supreme importance, I should not suggest they should be bombed night after night by considerable forces. Could not the treatment be varied? A close range dive-bombing attack by three or four machines would be a feat of arms of the highest merit. Perhaps this might be considered.

Churchill then told Sinclair and Portal of his view that the use 'of the heaviest 1,000-pound and 2,000-pound bombs on Berlin is much to be desired'. Would it not be well, he asked, 'to save up for this, merely disturbing them meanwhile?'

Churchill's minute continued with a highly critical paragraph:

I am deeply concerned with the non-expansion, and indeed contraction, of our Bomber Force which must be expected between now and April or May next, according to present policy. Surely an effort should be made to increase our bomb-dropping capacity during this period. In moonlight periods the present arrangements for bombing are the best possible, and the only difficulty is our small numbers compared to the many attractive military targets.

Churchill's minute continued: on 'no account should the limited Bomber Force be diverted from accurate bombing of military objectives reaching far into Germany'. But, never a believer in giving rebuke without having some recommendation to give as well, he added:

. . . is it not possible to organize a Second Line Bomber Force which, especially in the dark of the moon, would discharge bombs from a considerable and safe height upon the nearest large built-up areas of Germany, which contain military targets in abundance. The Ruhr of course is obviously indicated. The object would be to find easy targets, short runs and safe conditions.

How is such a Second Line or Auxiliary Bomber Force to be improvised during the winter months? Could not crews from the Training Schools do occasional runs? Are none of the Lysander and Reconnaissance pilots capable

[1] Minute of 17 October 1940: Premier papers, 3/314/2, folios 26–28.

of doing some of this simpler bombing, observing that the Army is not likely to be in action unless invasion occurs?

'I ask,' Churchill ended, 'that a whole-hearted effort shall be made to cart a large number of bombs into Germany by a Second Line organization such as I have suggested, and under conditions in which admittedly no special accuracy would be obtained. Pray let me have the best suggestions possible, and we can then see whether they are practical or not.'[1]

In his reply, Sinclair sought to reassure Churchill as to the pace and scale of bomber developments. But Sinclair went on to explain that the need to re-equip some of the Medium Squadrons 'now using obsolescent aircraft such as the "Battle",' would mean 'a temporary reduction in the actual number of front line aircraft'. Once the changeover was made, Sinclair added, there would be 'a considerable improvement in our striking power'.[2]

During the night of October 16 another bomb fell in the yard at Downing Street. 'A large part of the Treasury demolished,' noted John Martin, 'and four people killed in the basement.'[3] It could only be a 'question of days', Colville and Bracken agreed, before 10 Downing Street 'fell a victim' to the bombing.[4]

During October 17 Churchill was present at a meeting of Ministers and civil defence experts to discuss the fall in morale in London because of 'bad handling of transport' after air raids.[5] The demand for reprisal raids on Germany was also mounting, as Churchill learned when he went briefly to the Smoking Room of the House of Commons that same day. Harold Nicolson recorded in his diary:

He sits there sipping a glass of port and welcoming anyone who comes in. 'How are you?' he calls gaily to the most obscure Member. It is not a pose. It is just that for a few moments he likes to get away from being Prime Minister and feel himself back in the smoking-room. His very presence gives us all gaiety and courage.

People gather round his table completely unawed. They ask him questions. Robert Cary makes a long dissertation about how the public demand the unrestricted bombardment of Germany as reprisals for the raids on London. Winston takes a long sip at his port gazing over the glass at Cary. 'My dear

---

[1] Minute of 20 October 1940: Premier papers, 3/314/2, folios 20–3. This minute, without the section about the *Bismarck* and the *Tirpitz*, which he asked to be deleted after it had been sent, became Prime Minister's Personal Minute M.207, 20 October 1940: Cabinet papers, 120/300.

[2] Minute of 25 October 1940: Premier papers, 3/314/2, folios 9–12.

[3] Martin diary, 17 October 1940: Martin papers.

[4] Colville diary, 17 October 1940: Colville papers.

[5] Colville diary, 17 October 1940: Colville papers.

sir,' he says, 'this is a military and not a civilian war. You and others may desire to kill women and children. We desire (and have succeeded in our desire) to destroy German military objectives. I quite appreciate your point. But my motto is "Business before Pleasure".'

'We all drift out of the room,' Nicolson added, 'thinking, "That was a man"'.[1]

Enigma decrypts studied on October 17 showed that German preparations for invasion had been 'still continuing' four days earlier, and were now 'almost complete'. The temptation to take a decision to invade, an Intelligence summary noted, 'will be great when preparations are complete and conditions appear favourable'. These conditions would involve 'a calm sea and restricted visibility', so that German forces could 'get to grips' with British forces 'without suffering too heavily from sea and air attack'.[2]

On October 18 a further analysis of all Enigma decrypts about Sealion confirmed five 'embarkation points' in the area of operations of the 2nd Airfleet: Antwerp, Ostend, Dunkirk, Calais and Rotterdam.[3] At a Chiefs of Staff Committee meeting that day, a Joint Intelligence Committee analysis was discussed, which gave some date after October 19 as the most likely when moon, tides, fog and Hitler's horoscope were all favourable.[4]

That night news of an unexploded bomb in St James's Park reached Downing Street. Churchill refused to leave No. 10, however, and was 'chiefly worried', Colville noted, 'about the fate of "those poor little birds" in the lake'.[5]

Concern for Churchill himself was widespread. 'Please do take every care of yourself in these trying days,' F. W. Deakin wrote to him on October 18,[6] and Neville Chamberlain wrote on the following day

[1] Diary entry for 17 October 1940: Nigel Nicolson (editor), Harold Nicolson, *Diaries and Letters, 1939–1945*, London 1967, pages 121–2.

[2] 'Most Secret', 'Invasion of England' (Operation Smith), A.I. 3.b. (HD), 17 October 1940: War Office papers, 199/911A.

[3] 'Officer Only', 'Most Secret', 'Invasion of U.K. and/or Eire (Seelöwe–Sealion Question), MI 14, 5.30 p.m., 18 October 1940: War Office papers, 199/911A.

[4] Chiefs of Staff Committee No. 353 of 1940, 18 October 1940: Cabinet papers, 79/7. Those present were Newall, Dill, Phillips, Ismay, and for the secretariat, Colonel Hollis and Major Anthony Head.

[5] Colville diary, 18 October 1940: Colville papers.

[6] Letter of 18 October 1940: Churchill papers, 2/393.

from Hampshire: 'My thoughts are constantly with you in these anxious days. I hope you are taking some care for your own health.'[1] There was another friendly gesture in the gift presented to him by his friends of the Other Club, a silver-gilt snuff box that had belonged to Nelson.[2]

That weekend Churchill was at Chequers.[3] From there he wrote to Moore-Brabazon suggesting a plan to improve public morale by short-ening bus queues. 'Get 20,000 unused motor cars,' he wrote, 'to ply in the rush-hours and not only in these hours, but staggered, and organise them into a regular corps.' There were, he pointed out, thousands of motor cars without petrol 'reposing in garages or back-yards', with thousands of men and women drivers 'who would be enchanted to come in and carry off this painful accumulation of hard-working folk'. If Moore-Brabazon were to fail, he wrote, 'there will be no great harm. But if you succeed there will be great help in our need.'[4]

Another area in which Churchill believed an effort ought to be made was Britain's relations with Vichy France. In Spain, Sir Samuel Hoare and Captain Hillgarth had maintained close contacts with their Vichy opposite numbers, receiving information and giving encouragement to attitudes of independence. 'I hope,' Churchill telegraphed to Hoare on October 20, 'you will manage to convey to Vichy through the French Ambassador two root ideas.' These were: 'First, that we will let bygones go and work with anyone who convinces us of his resolution to defeat the common foes. Secondly that as we are fighting for our lives as well as for a victory which will relieve simultaneously all the captive states, we shall stop at nothing.'

Churchill's message to Hoare continued:

Try to make Vichy feel what we here all take for certain, namely that we have got Hitler beat and though he may ravage the Continent and the war may last a long time, his doom is certain. It passes my comprehension why no French leaders secede to Africa where they would have an Empire, the com-mand of the seas and all the frozen French gold in the United States. If this had

[1] Letter of 19 October 1940: Churchill papers, 2/402.
[2] More than sixty members of the Other Club, founded by Churchill and his friend F. E. Smith in 1911, paid £1 each towards the gift. The donors included Maurice Baring, Robert Boothby, Lord Camrose, Lord Chatfield, Alfred Duff Cooper, J. L. Garvin, David Lloyd George, Lord Gort, J. M. Keynes, Sir Edwin Lutyens, Sir Edward Marsh, Lord Moyne, James de Rothschild, Sir Archibald Sinclair, Lord Trenchard, Lord Tyrrell, Sir Robert Vansittart, H. G. Wells, and the Duke of Westminster. (Camrose papers.)
[3] Those present at luncheon on Saturday October 19 were Churchill, his wife, his daughter Diana, Ismay, Mrs Romilly (Clementine Churchill's sister) and the duty Private Secretary, John Peck. That night Sir Richard Peirse was the only extra dinner guest. Professor Lindemann arrived for lunch on the Sunday.
[4] Prime Minister's Personal Minute, M.201, 19 October 1940: Churchill papers, 20/13.

been done at the beginning we might well have knocked Italy out by now. But surely the opportunity is the most splendid ever offered to daring men.

'Naturally,' Churchill ended, 'one would not expect precise responses to such suggestions, but try to put it in their heads if you see any opening.'[1]

Churchill's faith in the future was reflected in a letter which he sent that same day to Neville Chamberlain, with news and suggestions:

My dear Neville,

I do hope you are getting on and finding relief in repose. The weeks in London have become very hard now with the press of business and our numerous meetings having to be arranged under continued Alerts and Alarms. We have had two very near misses with big HE bombs at No. 10. They fell in the little yard by the Treasury passage, one in the corner and the other on the Treasury, the first killing one and wounding two, and the second killing four, including two principal clerks serving in the Home Guard. The effect of these explosions has been to shatter all our windows, doors, etc. on the exposed side, and render the greater part of the house uninhabitable. However, the Cabinet Room is intact, and I am carrying on for the present in the downstairs rooms formerly used by the secretaries who dealt with correspondence.

Churchill's letter continued:

I have moved everybody I can away, for really it is like living at a Brigade Headquarters in France. We shall have to find some safer quarters soon. But where? For Edward told me about your five cows being killed, and the windows being sucked out at your house in the country. However, as I heard one of the Home Guard remark the other night, 'It's a grand life, if we don't weaken.'[2]

Churchill then told Chamberlain of what he believed to be Hitler's most serious error; an error which confirmed Churchill's confidence in eventual victory. 'The Germans,' he wrote, 'have made a tremendous mistake in concentrating on London to the relief of our factories, and in trying to intimidate a people whom they have only infuriated. I feel very hopeful about the future, and that we shall wear them down and break them up. But it will take a long time.'

Churchill added:

It has occurred to me that while you are, I am sure, glad to be relieved of the mass of Papers which War Cabinet Ministers have to wade through, you

---

[1] Cypher telegram No. 910, sent 6.55 a.m., 20 October 1940, 'Personal and Private': Premier papers, 3/186A/2, folio 48.

[2] Churchill repeated this story, and this phrase, when he spoke in the House of Commons on 5 November 1940 (see page 888).

might like to see occasional Papers or Telegrams on some points of special interest. In case you should feel any scruple about what is, perhaps, a somewhat unorthodox arrangement, I mentioned my intention to make this arrangement to the King the other day, and he most cordially approved it. I am telling Bridges to send you occasional Papers on matters which he thinks are likely to interest you especially, without sending so much as to become a burden.

Pray give my kindest regards to Mrs Neville. . . .

In a postscript Churchill added: 'Very bad news has just come in about our convoys in NW Approaches. But we shall be stronger there in a month or so.'[1] The bad news was that from two merchant shipping convoys, both from Halifax, Nova Scotia, one had lost seventeen ships, the other fourteen, as a result of the Germans using radar equipment captured in France. Colville noted on the following day: 'This preys on the PM's mind greatly.'[2]

Still much exercised also by the future of Vichy France, and by the extent to which Laval and even Darlan might ensure the domination of the pro-German faction in the Government, Churchill decided to broadcast to France, in French. The decision had come to him suddenly, one evening at Chequers. The broadcast was made first in French, then in English. Both versions went out live, recorded on the evening of October 21, as bombs fell over London. The broadcast in French began: 'Français! C'est moi, Churchill, qui vous parle.'[3] In the English version, Churchill began: 'Frenchmen! For more than thirty years in peace and war I have marched with *you*, and I am marching still along the same road.' A few moments later he declared: 'When good people get into trouble because they are attacked and heavily smitten by the vile and wicked, they must be very careful not to get at loggerheads with one another. The common enemy is always trying to bring this about, and, of course, in bad luck a lot of things happen which play into the enemy's hands. We must just make the best of things as they come along.'

In London, Churchill went on, 'we are waiting for the long-promised invasion. So are the fishes.' What Hitler sought, he warned, was not the defeat of France, but the 'complete obliteration' of its religion,

---

[1] Letter of 20 October 1940: Premier papers, 4/7/8, folios 744–6.

[2] Colville diary, 21 October 1940: Colville papers. Two days later the Chiefs of Staff Committee were told that British merchant shipping tonnage lost since September 1939 'now exceeds two million tons'. (War Cabinet, Chiefs of Staff Committee, Weekly Résumé No. 59: Churchill papers, 23/7.) This was a total of 501 ships. German losses for the same period were 314 ships, totalling 1½ million tons.

[3] Broadcast of 21 October 1940: BBC Written Archives.

laws, language, culture, institutions, history and traditions, and he went on to declare:

Frenchmen—rearm your spirits before it is too late. Remember how Napoleon said before one of his battles:[1] 'These same Prussians who are so boastful today were three to one at Jena, and six to one at Montmirail.' Never will I believe that the soul of France is dead. Never will I believe that her place amongst the greatest nations of the world has been lost for *ever*. All these schemes and crimes of Herr Hitler are bringing upon him and upon all who belong to his system a retribution which many of us will live to see. The story is not yet finished, but it will not be so long. We are on his track, and so are our friends across the Atlantic Ocean, and *your* friends across the Atlantic Ocean. If he cannot destroy us, we will surely destroy him and all his gang, and all their works. Therefore, have hope and faith, for all will come right.

Presently, Churchill told all those in occupied France, 'you will be able to weight the arm that strikes *for* you, and you ought to do so'. But even now 'we trust that Frenchmen, wherever they may be, feel their hearts warm, and a proud blood tingle in their veins, when we have some success in the air or on the sea, or presently—for that will come—upon the land'. Britain sought no control over French ships or colonies, as the German-controlled wireless claimed. 'We seek,' he said, 'to beat the life and soul out of Hitler and Hitlerism. That alone, that all the time, that to the end. We do not covet anything from any nation except their respect.'

Churchill wished to say to those Frenchmen in occupied France, who were under 'the sharp discipline, oppression and spying of the Hun', the words 'which Gambetta, that great Frenchman, uttered after 1870 about the future of France and what was to come: "Think of it always: speak of it never,"' and Churchill ended his own broadcast:

Good night, then: *sleep* to gather strength for the morning. For the morning will come. Brightly will it shine on the brave and true, kindly on all who suffer for the cause, glorious upon the tombs of heroes. Thus will shine the dawn. *Vive la France!* Long live also the forward march of the common people in all the lands towards their just and true inheritance, and towards the broader and fuller age.[2]

One of Churchill's closest French friends, the painter Paul Maze, who had managed to escape through Bordeaux in June 1940, bringing

---

[1] The battle was Waterloo; tactfully, Churchill did not name it.

[2] Broadcast of 21 October 1940: His Master's Voice, ALP 1555. The italics are of words stressed by Churchill in the broadcast.

with him a convoy of orphans, and who was then serving in the Home
Guard in Hampshire, wrote to Churchill that same night: 'Every word
you said was like every drop of blood in a transfusion.'[1]

Neville Chamberlain had also been among the listeners to Churchill's
broadcast, which would, he wrote, 'have done a lot to encourage our
friends everywhere'.[2] As a first selection of documents, Churchill
had sent Chamberlain the recently prepared secret account of the
Dakar Expedition, the telegrams being received from Eden during
his current visit to Egypt, and what were described as 'any Foreign
Office telegrams of special interest'.[3] After receiving the first selection, Chamberlain wrote to Churchill: 'It was just like you to think
of sending me some of the Cabinet reports and since you have
already informed the King I confess I should be very glad to see
them.'[4]

Churchill received a pleasing report in the third week of October,
when he learnt that the AI Air Interception radar apparatus, code
name 'Smeller', had been tried on a total of two hundred night en-
counters, and that in three quarters of the attempts to use it, it had
led to an effective interception. Experiments were in progress, supervised by Robert Watson-Watt, to increase still further the success
rate.[5]

The progress of 'Smeller' was among several anti-aircraft activities
reported to the second meeting of the Night Air Defence Committee,
held on October 21 with Churchill in the chair.[6] Some of the reports
were less encouraging, at least in the short term. German bombers, it
was reported, could fly and bomb 'in weather when our Fighters are
unable to leave the ground'. But the Lorenz blind landing apparatus
could not be carried in the British single-seater fighters because its
weight would affect the centre of gravity of the aircraft 'and necessitate
a flat and dangerous landing approach with the flaps down'. There
was also the danger, where the blind landing apparatus was used in
the Beaufighter night fighter—which was wired to carry it—of the

---

[1] Letter of 21 October 1940: Churchill papers, 2/396.

[2] Letter of 23 October 1940: Premier papers, 4/7/8, folios 742–3.

[3] Note by Sir Edward Bridges for Anthony Bevir, 18 October 1940: Premier papers, 4/7/8, folio
754.

[4] Letter of 23 October 1940: Premier papers, 4/7/8, folios 742–3.

[5] Night Air Defence Committee, Report No. 1, 21 October 1940: Premier papers, 3/22/5.

[6] In his capacity as Minister of Defence. The other Ministers present were Sinclair and Beaverbrook. The officials present included Newall, Portal, Dowding, Watson-Watt, Ismay, Bridges
and Lindemann, as well as Lieutenant-General Sir Frederick Pile (General Officer Commanding-
in-Chief, Anti-Aircraft Command), Major-General K. M. Loch (Director of Coast Defence, War
Office) and Sir Frank Smith (Ministry of Aircraft Production).

Germans making use of it themselves by tuning in to its frequency 'to guide them to our aerodromes'.

There was better news from Sir Frederick Pile, who reported that thirty-five out of the sixty anti-aircraft guns equipped with radar control had already been calibrated, 'and that the calibration was improving daily'.[1] A team of scientists had been formed to train anti-aircraft crews in the use of radar equipment, and it was expected that sixty qualified technical experts would shortly be attached to the batteries.

Pile also reported progress with searchlights working 'in clumps of six', thereby providing 'a pillar of illumination which served as a pointer to fighters to the area where they should search for the enemy'. At the same time, twenty-four sets of radar control for searchlights had been installed in the Tangmere sector, and some of these were already working.[2] Although giving promising results, these searchlight control sets, which were hand-made, were 'faulty, and were apt to be affected by rain and damp weather'.[3] Seventy-six more sets had been ordered; of an improved pattern, they would be delivered by the end of November. Their design, however, had not yet been approved, Sir Frank Smith reported, whereupon Churchill directed 'that this point should be settled and production pressed forward'.

The discussion turned to the two types of fuses, both of which were used in the UP weapon,[4] but many of which had exploded 'prematurely' during trials at Manorbier. There should, Churchill said, be further trials on October 30 'which he hoped to attend'.

The Committee heard one item of considerable cheer, that of the success of the Government's scientists 'in jamming and bending enemy beams', and the Chief of the Air Staff was asked to consider the advisability of a British bomber attack on the stations operating the beams.[5]

The bending of the beams could protect smaller towns, or those not readily identified from the air. London, so clearly identified from the air by the Thames estuary, remained particularly vulnerable, and during October the Germans bombed London without respite. Bombing of the capital, Churchill wrote to Sir Edward Bridges on October 22, was likely to continue to be 'severe and protracted', so much so that it was 'probable indeed that the bombing of Whitehall and the

---

[1] These were the GL sets, code name 'George'.

[2] These were the SLC (searchlight control) sets, code name 'Elsie'.

[3] As Churchill himself had discovered during his visit to the anti-aircraft research site earlier that month (see page 828).

[4] UP = Unrotated Projectile (rocket).

[5] Night Air Defence Committee No. 2 of 1940, 21 October 1940, 11.30 a.m.: Cabinet papers, 81/22.

centre of Government will be continuous until all old or insecure buildings have been demolished'. Churchill's minute continued:

It is therefore necessary to provide as soon as possible accommodation in the strongest houses and buildings that exist, or are capable of being fortified, for the large nucleus staffs and personnel connected with the Governing machine and the essential Ministers and Departments concerned in the conduct of the war. This becomes inevitable as a consequence of our decision not to be beaten out of London, and to release to the War Office or other Departments the accommodation hitherto reserved in the West of England for the Black Move.[1] We must do one thing or the other, and having made our decision, carry it out thoroughly.

Churchill then told Bridges of his attitude to, and decision about the Dollis Hill refuge, code name 'Paddock'. His minute continued:

The accommodation at 'Paddock' is quite unsuited to the conditions which have arisen. The War Cabinet cannot live and work there for weeks on end, while leaving the great part of their staffs less well provided for than they are now in Whitehall. Apart from the Citadel[2] there is no adequate accommodation or shelter, and anyone living in Neville Court would have to be running to and fro on every Jim Crow warning. 'Paddock' should be treated as a last resort to Citadel, and in the meantime should be used by some Department not needed in the very centre of London.

Churchill then turned his attention to the centre of London:

Nearly all the Government buildings and shelters beneath them are either wholly unsafe, or incapable of resisting a direct hit. The older buildings, like the Treasury, fall to pieces as we have seen, and the shelters beneath them offer no trustworthy protection. The Foreign Office and Board of Trade blocks on either side of King Charles Street, are strongly built and give a considerable measure of protection in their basements.

It was in the basement of the Board of Trade building, in the Central War Room, that the War Cabinet and several of its Committees had held many of its meetings since the beginning of September. Churchill now planned to strengthen these premises against the possibility of an even heavier bombardment. As he told Bridges: 'I have approved the provision of a substantial measure of overhead cover above the War Room and Central War Room offices, and Home Forces location in the Board of Trade building. This will take a month or six weeks with perpetual hammering. We must press on with this. But even when finished, it will not be proof.'

[1] For details of the Black Move, see page 601.
[2] The main building of 'Paddock', with substantial accomodation below ground.

Essential work being done in the various War Cabinet Committee rooms in Richmond Terrace, Churchill added, 'suffers from conditions prevailing there'. The Board of Trade should therefore move to new premises 'out of London', to enable most of the essential war policy bodies to move into the Board of Trade building. Churchill himself was now to move from Downing Street to the 'No. 10 Annexe' above the Central War Room, where work was in progress to make the rooms as blast proof as possible, and suitable for the Prime Minister and his staff.

Other Ministers had also to find more secure accommodation. Churchill's minute continued:

There are several strong modern buildings in London, of steel and cement construction, built with an eye to air raid conditions. These should immediately be prepared to receive the War Cabinet and its Secretariat, and also to provide safe living accommodation for the essential Ministers. We need not be afraid of having too much proof accommodation, as increasing numbers will certainly have to be provided for. It is essential that the central work of the Government should proceed under conditions which ensure its efficiency.

The final section of Churchill's minute to Bridges concerned the House of Commons and the House of Lords. As he wrote:

I have already asked for alternative accommodation for Parliament, but no satisfactory plan has yet been made. The danger to both Houses during their Sessions is serious, and it is only a question of time before these buildings and chambers are struck. We must hope they will be struck when not occupied by their Members. The protection provided below the Houses of Parliament is totally inadequate against a direct hit. The Palace of Westminster and the Whitehall area is an obvious prime target of the enemy, and I daresay already more than fifty heavy bombs have fallen in the neighbourhood. The Cabinet has already favoured the idea of a trial trip being made by the Houses of Parliament in some alternative accommodation. I propose to ask for an Adjournment from Thursday next for a fortnight, by which time it is hoped some plan can be made in London for their meeting. . . .[1]

Having set out these thoughts, and given Lord Beaverbrook the responsibility for implementing them, Churchill left London for Scotland, to inspect the Polish forces under General Sikorski. With him on the train north were his wife, General Brooke, Ismay and the British liaison officer with Sikorski, Victor Cazalet. The Private Secretary on the journey, Colville, recorded in his diary Churchill's remark that 'people

[1] Prime Minister's Personal Minute, C.19, 22 October 1940: Premier papers, 4/69/1, folios 172–6.

talked a lot of nonsense when they said nothing was ever settled by war. Nothing in history was ever settled *except* by wars.'[1]

In his own diary, Victor Cazalet, a Conservative MP whom Churchill had known for many years, noted how, on the journey north, Churchill 'quoted poetry and as always as the evening got later he got more jovial and genial'.

The train reached Coupar, in Fife, on the morning of October 23. 'Generals galore to meet us,' Cazalet wrote, and he added:

> W, who had just ordered an iced soda water and started a cigar, went out to review the guard of honour. Afterwards he came back to get his cigar and drink his soda, but the train moved off with both, and Dill's raincoat. Eventually we started off for a camp. Everything went very well. We had to limit the National Anthem as it was raining and W would have got his head wet. He was very impressed with the men. After their march past which they do with a kind of goose step he had tears in his eyes saying—'magnificent, magnificent'. Clemmie Churchill was with us and was delightful to everyone. W very anxious she would see everything.[2]

After lunching with Sikorski in the train, Churchill travelled to Rosyth for a tour of the battleship *King George V*, 'squeezing', as Colville noted, 'into the tiny hole of a 14-inch turret', and getting stuck. Later he addressed the ship's company, before continuing by train to Dalmeny, and showing himself 'obviously delighted', as Colville wrote, 'by the stirring reception given to him by all the people, civilians and others, who had seen him that day'. But he was aggrieved at Brooke and Dill's hostility to one of his proposed military promotions, the return of General Hobart to high command. 'Remember,' he told Dill, 'it isn't only the good boys who help to win wars. It is the sneaks and stinkers as well.'[3]

In March 1940, on the decision of the Selection Board, Hobart had been retired.[4] Dill, understandably reluctant to re-employ him, asked Churchill to 'read a short account of the circumstances which had led

---

[1] Colville diary, 22 October 1940: Colville papers. During the journey Ismay told Colville that at the time of the Munich crisis of 1938 (when Ismay was Secretary to the Committee of Imperial Defence) 'there was no thought of waiting until we were better prepared. The sole object was to avert war, not to postpone it.'

[2] Cazalet diary, 23 October 1940: Robert Rhodes James, *Victor Cazalet, A Portrait*, London 1976, pages 242–3. To Halifax, Cazalet wrote on the following day: 'The PM's visit was *huge success*. Heaven knows what PM promised him [Sikorski] now & after the War!' (Foreign Office papers, 800/321/H/XXVII/35.)

[3] Colville diary, 23 October 1940: Colville papers.

[4] 'Statement in the case of Major-General P. C. S. Hobart, CB, DSO, OBE, MC, psc, (Retired)', 'Confidential', 15 October 1940: Premier papers, 3/220, folios 48–9.

to his retirement'. This account, which Dill was having prepared that same day,[1] stated that Hobart had been on 'various occasions' in his military career 'impatient, quick-tempered, hot-headed, intolerant and inclined to see things as he wished them to be instead of as they were'. In spite 'of his very hard work, his wide technical knowledge and of his ideas and drive', his judgments remained, according to his commanding General in May 1939, 'impetuous and inconsistent, and therefore did not inspire confidence'.[2] In November 1939 Hobart's new commanding General had reported that Hobart 'had so lost the confidence of those under him that the efficiency of the force would suffer gravely in the event of war'.[3]

Two weeks earlier Churchill had said to General Brooke, about Hobart: 'you cannot expect to have the genius type with a conventional copy book style'.[4] But undeterred by Dill's critical account, Churchill minuted to Dill on October 19:

. . . I am not at all impressed by the prejudices against him in certain quarters. Such prejudices attach frequently to persons of strong personality and original view. In this case General Hobart's original views have been only too tragically borne out. The neglect by the General Staff even to devise proper patterns of tanks before the war has robbed us of all the fruits of this invention. These fruits have been reaped by the enemy, with terrible consequences. We should therefore remember that this was an officer who had the root of the matter in him, and also vision.

Churchill's minute continued:

We are now at war, fighting for our lives, and we cannot afford to confine Army appointments to persons who have excited no hostile comment in their career. The catalogue of General Hobart's qualities and defects might almost exactly have been attributed to most of the great commanders of British history. Marlborough was very much not the conventional soldier, carrying with him the goodwill of the Service. Cromwell, Wolfe, Clive, Gordon, and in a different sphere Lawrence, all had very close resemblance to the characteristics set down as defects. They had other qualities as well, and so I am led to believe has General Hobart.

This was a time, Churchill added, 'to try men of force and vision and

---

[1] Minute of 15 October 1940: Premier papers, 3/220, folio 50.
[2] The officer was General Sir Robert Gordon-Finlayson, then General Officer Commanding-in-Chief, Egypt.
[3] This second officer was Lieutenant-General Sir Henry Maitland Wilson.
[4] Colville diary, 11 October 1940: Colville papers.

not to be exclusively confined to those who are judged thoroughly safe by conventional standards'.[1]

As Churchill wished, Hobart was re-employed.[2]

It was not only the War Office that had incurred Churchill's displeasure. Returning to London on October 24, he told Colville that the Foreign Office needed 'a substantial application of the boot'. In reflective mood, Churchill commented, of his own popularity with the public: 'I represent to them something that they wholeheartedly support: the determination to win. For a year or two they will cheer me.'

Britain was not yet a nation in arms; it took four years, Churchill explained to Colville, for a State to reach a peak in war production. Germany had already reached that maximum strength. Britain was only at the end of the second year of her effort.[3]

Churchill went to bed that night in the relative security of 'The Barn', the converted Down Street Underground station in Piccadilly put at his disposal by the London Transport Executive.[4] At four in the morning, while he was asleep at Down Street, two telegrams reached Downing Street from Sir Samuel Hoare in Madrid. The news was urgent: at noon that same day the Vichy Government would hand over Toulon to the Germans. A telegram from the King to Marshal Pétain, Hoare urged, might turn the scales, as Pétain, and also Weygand, were known to be against the decision, which Laval and Darlan supported. Colville, who was handed the message at No. 10 shortly before six o'clock that morning, at once telephoned to Cadogan, who spoke to Halifax. It was decided not to wake Churchill until 7.30.

When, at 7.30 Churchill was told the news, he returned at once to Downing Street. There he went to bed again, and from his bed drafted the message for the King to send to Pétain. As the telegram was being dictated, the air raid sirens sounded, whereupon Churchill got out of bed again, and went down to his own basement shelter.[5] The telegram,

[1] Prime Minister's Personal Minute, M.202, 19 October 1940: Premier papers, 3/220, folio 43.
[2] Raising first the 11th Armoured Division, and then the 79th (specialized) Armoured Division, which he commanded through North-West Europe, 1944–5; he was knighted in 1943.
[3] Colville diary, 24 October 1940: Colville papers.
[4] Churchill had gone to 'The Barn', while No. 10 was being shored up as a result of the earlier bomb damage, and rooms were being prepared for him in the more bomb-proof Annexe at Storey's Gate, on the ground floor of the Board of Trade building. As John Martin wrote home at the end of the week: 'All week we seem to have lived in a madhouse at the office, with the din of builders and carpenters added to the confusion of translation from No. 10 to the Annexe.' Martin added: 'Nelson, the PM's cat, has been evacuated to Chequers under the evacuation scheme; but Treasury Bill, alias the Munich Mouser, still prowls about the ruins of his home.' (Letter of 27 October 1940: Martin papers.)
[5] Colville diary, 25 October 1940: Colville papers.

approved by the King, expressed confidence that Pétain would not bring 'dishonour to France and grave damage to a late ally'. As for Britain, 'We are resolved to fight on to the end, and we are sure that the end will be a complete British victory over Hitler and his régime.'[1]

Three days earlier a French Canadian Professor, Louis Rougier, had reached London from Vichy, having spoken at length to Pétain and Baudouin about Vichy's future relations with both Britain and de Gaulle. Rougier saw Churchill and Halifax on October 25, and suggested to them the possibility of an 'agreement' between Churchill and Pétain, whereby Vichy would agree not to attack any French Colony that had declared itself for de Gaulle, while for his part de Gaulle, at Britain's urging, would not attack any colony loyal to Vichy. Churchill warned Rougier, however, that under any such quid pro quo, if a colony were to rally to de Gaulle spontaneously, 'we could not disavow General de Gaulle'.

Churchill also told Rougier that if Vichy would 'resist German threats and blandishments', and at the same time organize 'a sphere of resistance' in North Africa, Britain would for her part 'certainly consider relaxing the blockade'.[2]

While Churchill and Halifax were talking to Rougier, details were published in the British newspapers of a meeting at Montoire between Pétain and Hitler, with rumours of an agreement, as already reported by Hoare, for the transfer of French warships and naval bases to Germany. The rumours were false, but this Churchill could not know. That evening he minuted to the Chiefs of Staff Committee:

I see rumours in the papers that they may cede the use of their bases or some of them to Germany and Italy. If anything like this were to come from Vichy, immediate action would have to be taken. Let the Joint Planning Committee set to work at once upon a plan to capture Dakar as an important and purely British operation.

I should think myself that a landing by fifty or sixty tanks out of range of the guns of the fortress would very quickly bring about a decision. It must be recognized as quite intolerable that Dakar should become a strong German U-boat base. Time is very precious, and the sooner a plan is made the better. We can go into ways and means after.[3]

[1] Cypher telegram No. 935, sent 25 October 1940, 1.20 p.m.: Premier papers, 3/186A/2, folio 37.

[2] Minutes of a conversation between Churchill and Rougier (with Halifax also present), 25 October 1940: Foreign Office papers, 371/24361.

[3] Joint Planning Committee paper No. 577 (E) of 1940, 25 October 1940: Cabinet papers, 84/21.

That evening the London evening newspapers published rumours of an actual peace treaty signed at Montoire between Pétain and Hitler. When Rougier returned to see Churchill on the following day Churchill 'shouted at him', Rougier later recalled: 'I will send the Royal Air Force to bomb Vichy. I will broadcast to the people of France to tell them of my resolve to pursue their government of traitors wherever they go.'

Rougier begged Churchill not to take these rumours seriously, but to proceed with the scheme they had discussed on the previous day. Following this second talk, a draft agreement was prepared whereby the Vichy authorities would promise neither to attack any colony that had declared for de Gaulle, nor to surrender the forts of Provence, or the bases of French North Africa, Morocco or French West Africa to Germany. To prevent French warships being taken over by the Germans or Italians, the Vichy authorities would scuttle them. For her part, Britain would take no military action against a colony still loyal to Vichy, the BBC would cease its attacks on Pétain, and the British blockade would be relaxed 'if France were to assist, either actively or passively, in a British victory'.

The document also made clear that if the Vichy Government were to surrender 'any air or naval bases to the totalitarian powers', Britain 'could no longer give any guarantees as to the future of France and of her empire'. Churchill added, according to Rougier, that in the event of such a surrender by Vichy, 'Great Britain would do everything in her power to strike at a government which had been guilty of so base a betrayal.' Churchill also wrote across the top of the document: 'If General Weygand[1] will raise the standard in North Africa, he can count on the renewal of the whole-hearted collaboration of the governments and peoples of the British Empire, and on a share of the assistance afforded by the US.'

In an effort to tempt Weygand to action, Churchill sent him a personal message, asking him to send an officer to Tangier, and thence to Gibraltar, to tell the British what equipment he would need to take up arms once more against German and Italian forces.[2]

Neither the Rougier-Churchill discussions, nor Churchill's appeal to Weygand, had any immediate result. Aware, however, of just how these two initiatives might appear to de Gaulle if he heard of them indirectly, Churchill minuted to Eden on October 26: 'Surely something should be said to General de Gaulle apprising him of the course

[1] Weygand was at that time Governor-General of Algeria.
[2] Louis Rougier, *Mission secrète à Londres*, Montreal 1946, pages 72–82.

we have taken, and of the fact we have communicated with General Weygand, or tried to. In view of our relations with de Gaulle, and engagements signed, he has a right to feel assured we are not throwing him over.'

Britain was already committed to protecting de Gaulle's forces in Libreville from an attack by pro-Vichy forces from Dakar. Such British action would be impossible were the Churchill–Rougier quid pro quo to come into effect. In order not to destroy its chances, such as they were, Churchill told Eden:

I have spoken to the First Sea Lord, and neither at Libreville nor in the Straits will any forcible action be taken for the next few days, or without definite prior sanction from here. *Devonshire* and *Delhi* are, however, ostentatiously showing themselves off Libreville to prevent reinforcements from Dakar being sent thither. The Admiral knows we do not want an incident, and I have little doubt that should reinforcements be intercepted they will be turned back by peaceful persuasion. The remote chance of a collision must, I think, be accepted in this particular theatre, as it is the French who would be seeking to alter the *status quo*.[1]

On November 1, discussing Vichy policy, the War Cabinet agreed not to give de Gaulle the same measure of support for an attack on Libreville as they had done for his landing in Duala. 'De Gaulle is definitely an embarrassment to us in our dealings with Vichy and the French people,' Colville recorded Churchill as saying on November 1.[2] Yet at the War Cabinet that morning Churchill warned his colleagues that 'we must not allow ourselves to become obsessed with the idea that we must never in any circumstances offer provocation to the Vichy Government'. That idea, he said, 'might bring great dangers in its train'.[3]

On the previous day, in a private conversation with Halifax and Attlee in the Central War Room, Churchill had urged, as he had already told Rougier, that Britain should make it clear 'in any communication that we might make to the Vichy Government, that in the event of any act of hostility on their part we should immediately retaliate by bombing the seat of the Vichy Government, wherever it might be'.[4]

---

[1] Prime Minister's Personal Minute, M.229, 26 October 1940: Churchill papers, 20/13.

[2] Colville diary, 1 November 1940: Colville papers. On 1 November 1940 Hoare wrote to Halifax: 'It is an excellent thing that you and Winston have seen Rougier in London and still more important if he now sees Weygand.' (Foreign Office papers, 800/323.)

[3] War Cabinet No. 281 of 1940, 1 November 1940, 12 noon, minute 3, Confidential Annex: Cabinet papers, 65/16.

[4] 'Most Secret', 12.30 p.m., 31 October 1940 (note dictated by Ismay): Cabinet papers, 127/14.

Yet Churchill still hesitated to embark on any open measures that might alienate Vichy, commenting a week later, on a suggestion that de Gaulle might go to Cairo, that 'he feared that, if he went there, that might arouse the antagonism of General Weygand', and he would prefer de Gaulle to come to London instead.[1] That same day Churchill wrote to both Halifax and the Chiefs of Staff to question 'the wisdom of de Gaulle flying to Cairo'. His argument was that de Gaulle's presence in Egypt:

... will bring all the collision between Weygand France—of which I still have some hopes—and Free France, to a head. It would be much better for General de Gaulle to come home here as soon as the Libreville situation is cleared up. We must put frankly before him the facts which are developing, and the position of his Movement in relation to them.

It is a good thing for him to have captured this Western African and Equatorial domain and every effort must be made by us to hold it for him. But he and his Movement may now become an obstacle to a very considerable hiving off of the French Empire to our side. There is no doubt that men like Weygand and Noguès[2] when searching their souls about their own misdeeds harden themselves against us by dwelling on the insubordination of de Gaulle. It will be much easier to point all these things out to de Gaulle at close quarters than when he is a distant potentate.

After capturing Libreville, Churchill added, de Gaulle should be 'urged' to return to London immediately, 'without going to Egypt'.[3]

On October 27, in an attempt to assert the primacy of his own movement, de Gaulle, who was then in Brazzaville, had announced the setting up of an Empire Defence Council. This 'Brazzaville declaration', about which the British had not been consulted, seemed to the British Foreign Office a virtual declaration of war on Vichy. 'I hope we may play down de Gaulle,' Cadogan noted in his diary, adding that de Gaulle was, he thought, 'a loser'.[4] But Churchill was impressed by the Brazzaville declaration, minuting to Eden: 'this is a very remarkable document, and it is bound to have a great effect on the minds of Frenchmen on account both of its scope and its logic. It shows de Gaulle in a light very different from that of an ordinary military man.'[5]

---

[1] War Cabinet No. 285 of 1940, 8 November 1940, 11.30 a.m.: Cabinet papers, 65/10.

[2] General A. P. Noguès, French Resident General in Morocco, and, like Weygand in Algeria, maintaining allegiance to Vichy.

[3] Prime Minister's Personal Minute, M.279, 8 November 1940: Churchill papers, 20/13. De Gaulle's forces entered Libreville five days later.

[4] Cadogan diary, 5 November 1940: David Dilks (editor), *The Diaries of Sir Alexander Cadogan OM, 1938–1945*, London 1971, page 334.

[5] Prime Minister's Personal Minute, M.326, 20 November 1940: Churchill papers, 20/13.

The Brazzaville declaration was certainly outspoken: 'the body that has its seat at Vichy,' it declared, 'and claims to bear that name, is unconstitutional and in subjection to the invader. In its state of servitude, this body can only be, and is in fact only, an instrument used by the enemies of France against the honour and interests of the country.' The declaration also sought, in Churchillian tones, to bind the Allies to de Gaulle's cause:

I call to war, that is to say to combat or to sacrifice, all the men and all the women of the French territories which have rallied to me. In close union with our Allies, who proclaim their determination to contribute towards restoring the independence and greatness of France, our task is to defend against the enemy or against his auxiliaries a part of the national patrimony which is in our hands, to attack the enemy wherever it shall be possible, to mobilize all our military, economic and moral resources, to maintain public order and to make justice reign.[1]

Impressed by de Gaulle's declaration, but determined not to close the door on any possible future arrangement either with Pétain in Vichy or with Weygand in Algiers, Churchill telegraphed to de Gaulle at Libreville, where the Free French Forces were in the final phase of establishing their control:

Situation between France and Britain has changed remarkably since you left. A very strong feeling has grown throughout France in our favour, as it is seen that we cannot be conquered and that war will go on. We know Vichy government is deeply alarmed by the very stern pressure administered to them by United States. On the other hand, Laval and revengeful Darlan are trying to force French declaration of war against us and rejoice in provoking minor naval incidents. We have hopes of Weygand in Africa, and no one must underrate advantage that would follow if he were rallied.

'We are trying,' Churchill explained, 'to arrive at some *modus vivendi* with Vichy which will minimize the risk of incidents and will enable favourable forces in France to develop.' But, Churchill added: 'We have told them plainly that if they bomb Gibraltar or take other aggressive action we shall bomb Vichy, and pursue the Vichy Government wherever it chooses to go.'[2]

In the inner circle of Ministers, there was a growing feeling that the

[1] Declaration of 27 October 1940: text in François Kersaudy, *Churchill and de Gaulle*, New York 1982, page 115, note 1.
[2] Telegram of 10 November 1940: Churchill papers, 20/13.

invasion danger was subsiding. 'Though Hitler has enough shipping in the Channel,' Halifax had told Hoare on October 24, 'to put half a million men on to salt water—or into it, as Winston said the other day—it really does seem as if the invasion of England has been postponed for the present.'[1] To Roosevelt, Churchill telegraphed two days later: 'In spite of the invasion threats and Air attacks of the last five months, we have maintained a continuous flow of reinforcements round the Cape to Middle East, as well as sending modern aircraft and major Units of the Fleet. I do not think the invasion danger is yet at an end, but we are now augmenting our Eastern transferences.' The strain was 'very great' in both theatres, Churchill added, 'and all contributions will be thankfully received'. Churchill also warned Roosevelt that if Pétain succumbed to German pressure, the French Moroccan bases on the Atlantic 'in bad hands' would be 'a menace to you and grievous embarrassment to us'. American pressure on Vichy France was therefore essential, to prevent 'the betrayal of bases'.[2]

During October another aspect of United States help had become urgent, following a telegram on October 3 from Arthur Purvis and his two most senior colleagues on the British Purchasing Commission, Morris Wilson and Jean Monnet. The Commission had telegraphed to London to warn of criticism from both Major General Strong[3] and Colonel Spotts, on their return from Britain. Both men were saying that the British need was 'for pilots, not for aeroplanes' and that Britain's own aircraft production programme had overtaken the pilot training programme. In consequence, any aeroplanes shipped from the United States 'would merely be stocked unused for a long time, with the danger of being bombed'.

Morgenthau, who had passed on this complaint to the British Purchasing Commission, added, as the Commission reported, that:

The Army representatives substantiated these statements with figures which they stated had been furnished to them confidentially in London by the various Services. Army representatives also took the position that their information from UK showed that the UK for the purpose of building up large stocks had been in the habit of somewhat indiscriminately multiplying its needs, not only for aeroplanes but also for engines and machine tools.

The Purchasing Commission's report continued:

Mr Morgenthau was not able to answer these statements nor were we able

---

[1] Letter of 24 October 1940: Foreign Office papers, 800/323.
[2] Telegram of 26 October 1940: Premier papers, 3/468, folios 79–80.
[3] Director of the Planning Division, General Staff.

to give him counter figures and felt that he had the ground partially cut from under his feet and was put in a difficult position at the very moment when he was fighting to prevent the Army from taking from us the French engines and machine tools and when he was trying to arrange plane releases and an acceleration of aeroplane deliveries.

The need was urgent, as the Commission's leaders explained:

Mr Morgenthau wanted it clearly understood that the co-operation we expected from this country could only be given adequately if we gave the US the complete facts as to our situation and that this applied particularly to the position of plane production synchronized with pilot availability. He said that he realised how secret some of this information might be and therefore the American Govt would undertake that such information would be confined to the President, Mr Stimson, Col. Knox and himself.[1]

The need, stressed the Commission, was twofold: first, for 'the fullest general statement now' for use in the current negotiations, and second, for 'continuous information' in the future in order to satisfy Roosevelt 'that the expansion of America's Air Force is not being unnecessarily delayed' by superfluous British orders.

Morgenthau had urged the Purchasing Commission to prepare 'as documented a statement as possible' of the anticipated production of aircraft for Britain, both in Britain and in America, over the next nine months, 'and of our pilot training plan over the same period', this statement to be supplemented 'by regular statements of production, training results, losses and progress in squadron formation'.

Morgenthau had also suggested that, in order 'to open up this channel of information on a high level', Air Vice-Marshal Portal should visit the United States.[2] But Portal was now Chief of the Air Staff designate, and could not go. In his place, Sinclair suggested to Churchill that the Director of Plans at the Air Ministry, Air Commodore Slessor, should undertake this sensitive task.[3]

On October 26 Churchill discussed the Slessor mission with Sinclair and, as John Martin noted, 'after Ld Lothian had confirmed urgency from Mr Purvis by telephone it was agreed that Air Commodore shd leave for USA immediately'.[4]

As Slessor prepared to leave, an Air Ministry survey of Britain's needs was made ready for him. Britain's hope was to form 100 new

---

[1] Stimson was Secretary for War, Knox for the Navy.

[2] 'Pursa', No. 128, 3 October 1940: Premier papers, 3/483/1, folios 33–4. (Copies to be passed to Churchill, Beaverbrook and Sinclair: Premier papers, 3/483/2, folios 108–9.)

[3] Minute of 24 October 1940: Premier papers, 3/483/1, folios 29–30.

[4] Note by John Martin, 27 October 1940: Premier papers, 3/483/1, folio 29.

squadrons in the next nine months. By July 1941 some 13,600 operational aircraft were expected from the Ministry of Aircraft production.[1] The number that would have to be made up from the United States was 3,530 'operational type machines'.

The Air Ministry survey then set out in detail the monthly wastage rate of aircraft, and the monthly loss of pilots, of whom more than 400 were lost each month, either killed, wounded or taken prisoner-of-war, and of whom there was a 'present deficiency' of 350 in operational and training units. The note explained that it was intended to train a further 9,300 pilots, to meet the expanded programme. These figures, it was noted, 'make no allowance for unforeseen difficulties due to enemy action etc, i.e. it is assumed the situation will not deteriorate'.[2]

Churchill agreed that Slessor should take this note with him to the United States, minuting to Sinclair and Portal on October 29:

This paper makes it easy for anyone to understand exactly what we are doing and what we want. It would therefore be of particular value for the purposes of Air Commodore Slessor's mission, as the American Ministers concerned will be able to take it in quickly. The whole movement of the argument leads up to the conclusion that we need the planes from them to carry out a carefully worked out plan, and that we have very nicely adjusted the balance between the pilots and the machines. It may be that some alterations in numbers or phrasing are necessary, but it would be a great pity if the movement and sequence of this orderly argument were in any way deranged.

That afternoon, at 5 p.m., Churchill went through the Air Ministry note with Sinclair and Portal in the Central War Room, adding to it, as he suggested in his minute, 'something to show how steeply the expansion will rise after June 1941'.[3] The note was duly sent to Washington, but only after Churchill had added the caveat, to Sinclair, 'keep it simple and do not try to tell everything, and safeguard yourself at every point'. No one would read it, Churchill added, 'unless it is short and clear'.[4]

In a further effort to sustain and augment Britain's war effort, the British Purchasing Commission had been holding a series of talks with the United States army chiefs. As a result of these talks, as Sir Walter Layton reported to Churchill on the evening of October 25, the United States administration had agreed 'to equip fully and maintain' ten

---

[1] Bombers, 5,075; Fighters, 7,640; General Reconnaissance, 235; Army Co-operation, 645.

[2] 'Most Secret', 'Output and Requirements of Operational Type Aircraft and Pilots during the period October 1940 to June 1941', undated: Premier papers, 3/483/1, folios 23–8.

[3] Minute of 29 October 1940: Premier papers, 3/483/1, folio 22.

[4] Minute of 13 November 1940: Premier papers, 3/483/1, folio 4.

additional divisions of British and British Empire forces, using American types of weapons, and equipping these divisions in time for the 'campaign of 1942'.

In his telegram to Churchill, Layton pointed out that it was a scheme 'which of course assumes no involvement of United States in war', but which had the particular advantage for the United States that it would enable American production to be maintained at a higher output than was possible for the American army under its current programme. Layton's telegram continued:

If United States become involved in circumstances which lead to sending of an American expeditionary force, War Department will have already placed its orders on the basis of X plus 10 instead of X divisions. If on the other hand America remains bound by undertakings not to send American armies overseas, scheme means that first call on America's new armament production will be made available practically in full for British Empire divisions.

I have pointed out that such a scheme means that United States would in fact be equipping an expeditionary force equal in size to British expeditionary force of May last, but with its supply base in United States and that British General Staff could only make plans on such a basis if there were the clearest undertaking (a) that amount of armament involved would be forthcoming at the times indicated, (b) that a force so equipped, whenever it might be operative, must be continuously provisioned from United States, (c) that in allocating output between United States Army and such a force, the latter must have absolute priority to fullest extent of its military needs.

At a meeting on October 24, Layton reported, General Marshall had given his approval to these conditions, which were likewise agreed to by Stimson, the Secretary for War, as well as by the Chief of Ordnance and the Deputy-Chief of Ordnance.

As a result of this agreement, Layton informed Churchill, the United States was now committed to 'handing over' to Britain substantially 'all new equipment' coming out during 1942, 'and doing so in spite of pressures that might be brought to bear to issue new type weapons to America's own army'. Layton added: 'The Army Chiefs are apparently satisfied that a modest share of new weapons would be sufficient for instruction of their own Army and that public opinion would be gratified if American arms were being used by a British expeditionary force'.

The Layton–Marshall agreement of October 24 had considerable scope. Ten British divisions were to be equipped with American types of rifles, machine guns, field guns, anti-tank guns and ammunition by 31 December 1941, with additional supplies 'to establish reserves and provide full battle wastage' by 1 March 1942. The United States

Administration also agreed to 'ensure priority' in the allocation of United States output 'where required' to maintain this ten division Field Force, the scheme to be 'in supplement to and *not* in substitution' for orders already placed in the United States in order to maintain the 'present British Army programme'. Both Stimson and the army chiefs, Layton added, 'would like to see their work effective in hastening offensive power of British army'.

Layton asked Churchill whether he approved in principle of this arrangement. 'Yes,' minuted Churchill in the margin of the telegram.[1] Churchill then sent Layton's telegram to Dill, who commented that it would be 'sound' from a military point of view to accept it. 'It will be an insurance,' Dill wrote, 'against dislocation of our own production by bombing. It is better to have American equipment than none.' It would also help to release any surplus British stock to satisfy 'demands for war material which we cannot meet—from Iraq, Ireland, Turkey, Greece etc.'[2]

Churchill minuted on Dill's letter: 'This is splendid. We shd at once accept offer. Action accordingly.'[3]

The Layton–Marshall agreement of October 24, for the equipping of an extra ten divisions, involved financing by the United States Treasury of the capital costs necessary to prepare the special plant needed in order to manufacture these equipments. Discussions with the General Staff Defence Council, Arthur Purvis reported on October 26, had 'met with real success' in preparing the ground. What was now needed was some new impetus in order to ensure that quick action would follow. The 'initial moment has arrived', Purvis informed Sir Arthur Salter, 'for action from the highest quarters'. But if action were delayed, it was 'equally clear that in a few days time lethargy will supervene'.

Following a United States Cabinet meeting that afternoon, Purvis explained, Roosevelt had decided that he would have to intervene personally 'to achieve rapid progress'. He had also asked Morgenthau for confirmation from the British Government by telegram of the programmes which it desired to place in the United States, 'stressing their urgency'. Roosevelt would use this telegram, Purvis explained, 'as a means of sweeping away any opposition to swift action'.[4]

[1] Washington Telegram No. 2408, 'Most Immediate', sent 6.58 p.m., 25 October 1940, received 4.40 a.m., 26 October 1940: Premier papers, 3/483/2, folios 96–9.

[2] Letter of 26 October 1940: Premier papers, 3/483/2, folio 94.

[3] Minute of 28 October 1940: Premier papers, 3/483/2, folio 94.

[4] 'Pursa' No. 180, 26 October 1940, copies sent to members of the War Cabinet: Premier papers, 3/483/2, folios 101–2.

At the technical level, Purvis' appeal for action was answered at once, and a comprehensive list of Britain's needs, and priorities, sent direct to Roosevelt. This list was then studied by the President's Co-ordinating Committee, which drafted a statement for Roosevelt's speech, and then amended the statement after a talk with Purvis, Sir Henry Self [1] and Sir Walter Layton. 'It will be seen,' Layton reported to the War Cabinet, 'that this statement committed the President in advance to a practical approval of the programmes put forward.' [2] Roosevelt's statement read:

The British have now asked for permission to negotiate again with American manufacturers for another 12,000 additional planes. I have directed the request to be given most sympathetic consideration by the Priorities Board consisting of William S. Knudsen, Edward R. Stettinius Jr, and Leon Henderson. When these additional orders are approved, it will bring Britain's present orders for military planes from the United States to more than 26,000, and require extra plant facilities so that the present programme of building planes for military purposes, both for the United States and Great Britain, will not be interrupted.

Also large additional orders are being negotiated for artillery, machine guns, rifles and tanks, with equipment and ammunition. The plant capacity necessary to produce all of this military equipment will be available to serve the needs of the United States in any emergency. [3]

Roosevelt's statement gave an important safeguard to Britain's orders in the United States. Those more recently submitted, only four days before Roosevelt's speech, included 250 aircraft engines, 205,750 ball bearings and roller bearings, 78 million rifle cartridges, 78 million cartridges suitable for the Thompson machine gun, 27 million automatic pistol cartridges, more than a million 75-millimetre cartridge cases, and more than two and a half million gallons of explosives. [4]

These were substantial orders. But the need to respond at the highest level still remained. It was this response 'from the highest quarters' that Purvis had urged on October 26. Now, on the afternoon of October 27, Churchill's own appeal was ready. It began by reiterating the existing, and growing dangers. These were, he said, a hostile Vichy, with Oran and Bizerta becoming German–Italian air and submarine bases,

[1] Director-General of the British Air Commission in Washington.

[2] 'Visit to the United States, Report by Sir Walter Layton', North American Supply Committee Memorandum No. 3 of 1941, 1 January 1941: Cabinet papers, 115/32.

[3] North American Supply Committee Memorandum No. 3 of 1941, 1 January 1941, Annex II: Cabinet papers, 115/32.

[4] British Purchasing Commission, 'Weekly Summary Reports on Preliminary Negotiations', 'Submitted during week ended 26th October, 1940': Cabinet papers, 92/27.

the probability of the war in the Middle East widening in 1941 to include both Turkey and Greece and leaving Britain in a position of even greater weakness in the Eastern Mediterranean, the continuing need to maintain an anti-invasion force on British soil, and the German U-boat and air attacks on 'our only remaining life-line', the North-Western Approaches. These attacks, Churchill told Roosevelt, could only be repelled 'by the strongest concentration of our flotillas'. His appeal continued:

You will see, therefore, Mr President, how very great are our problems and dangers. We feel, however, confident of our ability, if we are given the necessary supplies, to carry the war to a successful conclusion, and anyhow we are going to try our best.

You will, however, allow me to impress upon you the extreme urgency of accelerating the delivery of the programme of aircraft and other munitions which has already been laid before you by Layton and Purvis.

So far as aircraft is concerned, would it be possible to speed up the deliveries of the existing orders so that the numbers coming to our support next year will be considerably increased?

Furthermore, can the new orders for the expanded programme also be placed so promptly that deliveries may come out in the middle of 1941? The equipment of our Armies, both for Home Defence and Overseas, is progressing, but we depend upon American deliveries to complete our existing programme, which will certainly be delayed and impeded by the bombing of factories and the disturbance of work.

A Memorandum on technical details is being furnished you through the proper channels, and having placed all the facts before you, I feel confident that everything humanly possible will be done.

Churchill ended: 'The World Cause is in your hands.'[1]

---

[1] 'Message for President from Former Naval Person, to be communicated through Mr Purvis & Mr Morgenthau', sent to the Cabinet Office for transmission, 4.15 p.m., 27 October 1940: Premier papers, 3/468, folios 64–8 and 3/483/2, folios 87–91.

45

'How are we to win the war?'

O N the morning of October 28 Churchill was woken by bad news, an Italian ultimatum to Greece; and within a short while Colville informed him that Italian planes had bombed Athens. 'Then we must bomb Rome,' was Churchill's reply.[1] At the Chiefs of Staff Committee at ten that morning, it was agreed that British bombers should attack towns in Northern Italy that same night, while the Chief of the Air Staff should submit a plan to Churchill for operating bombers from Malta 'against Rome and other targets in Southern Italy'.[2] Explaining the proposal to bomb Rome to the War Cabinet that afternoon, Churchill told his colleagues: 'It was of course most important to avoid bombs falling on the Vatican City.'[3] All bombing of Italy from bases in Greece, however, which Churchill urged, was turned down by the Joint Planning Committee, and Churchill 'bowed', at least temporarily, before what he described to Ismay as 'the difficulties so industriously assembled' and the 'general attitude of negation'.[4]

Throughout October 29 plans were made both to help Greece militarily, and to try to prevent Crete from falling under Italian control. Considerable efforts were to be made, despite the shortage of British troops and military supplies in the Middle East, to come to the aid of Greece. The reinforcements of British troops in the Middle East, Churchill warned the War Cabinet that day, 'had also to be balanced with the strength of the forces which must be retained in this country'. Already 72,000 reinforcements had been sent to the Middle East, and

[1] Colville diary, 28 October 1940: Colville papers.

[2] Chiefs of Staff Committee No. 362 of 1940, 28 October 1940, 10 a.m.: Cabinet papers, 79/7.

[3] War Cabinet No. 278 of 1940, 28 October 1940, 5 p.m., minute 2, Confidential Annex: Cabinet papers, 65/15.

[4] Prime Minister's Personal Minute, D.113, 7 November 1940: Churchill papers, 20/13.

another 53,000 were to be sent out by the end of the year. But the War Cabinet should be 'under no illusion' as to the extent of help Britain could give Greece.[1]

Churchill also warned against too ready a compliance with Morgenthau's plea, through Purvis, for fullest details of Britain's military needs. In view of the apparent continuing hesitations of the United States, Churchill told the Defence Committee that afternoon, he was 'inclined towards a stiffer attitude' as far as giving the United States details of Britain's expansion schemes. Britain, he said, 'should not give detailed figures of the kind demanded'.[2] Churchill was also concerned about the security aspect of telegrams to the United States, minuting to Eden two days later, on a telegram sent to Washington describing the effect of German air bombardment: 'ought all this to have been sent to America? It will almost certainly get back to Germany through indiscretion or some lurking enemy.'[3]

'I am so sorry that everything nowadays is so worrying for you,' King George VI wrote by hand from Windsor Castle on October 29; 'there is not a bright spot anywhere. But I am sure something bright will turn up one day.'[4]

The King's sympathetic words were not mistimed; on October 29 the week's losses in Allied shipping totalled 198,000 tons, the heaviest since the outbreak of war. That same day, more than 450 German fighters attacked strategic targets in the south-eastern counties, and the London area. Twenty-eight were shot down, with the loss of seven British fighters, and two pilots killed. That night, 250 German bombers attacked London, Birmingham and Coventry. In London, several public air raid shelters were hit, fifty people being killed at the Druid Street railway arch shelter in Bermondsey and eighteen in St Peter's Crypt, Southwark. By six o'clock on the morning of October 30, a total of 829 civilians had been killed in Britain that week, 519 of them in London and 149 in Birmingham.[5]

This war, Churchill told Herbert Morrison on October 30, was the 'most unnecessary war in history', a war 'far harder to win than to avoid'.[6] With Greece now under attack for the third successive day,

---

[1] War Cabinet No. 279 of 1940, 29 October 1940, 12 noon, minute 1, Confidential Annex: Cabinet papers, 65/15.
[2] Defence Committee (Operations) No. 38 of 1940, 29 October 1940, 5.30 p.m.: Cabinet papers, 69/1.
[3] Prime Minister's Personal Minute. M.247, 31 October 1940: Churchill papers, 20/13.
[4] Letter of 29 October 1940: Churchill papers, 20/1.
[5] War Cabinet, Chiefs of Staff Committee, Weekly Résumé No. 61: Churchill papers, 23/7.
[6] Colville diary, 30 October 1940: Colville papers.

aid to Greece became a major concern of British policy. But at a meeting with Attlee and Halifax in the Central War Room shortly after midday, in response to a series of telegraphic appeals from the Greeks, Churchill warned 'that it would be wrong and foolish to make them promises which we could not fulfil'. Halifax hoped, however, that it would be possible for Britain 'to put a few aeroplanes in Greece itself at once', and Churchill said that this idea was under 'active consideration' by Sir Charles Portal, the new Chief of the Air Staff.[1] As for the bombing targets to be chosen in future air attacks against Italy, Churchill noted for Portal on October 31 'that the morale of the Italian population may for the time being be considered a military objective'.[2] Sinclair opposed this, however, noting for Churchill that same day, in a reference to the German bombing of Britain, that 'in so far as the Germans may have been led away by their theories of the total war into attacking our civilian population instead of concentrating upon our aircraft and air engine factories, it is very lucky for us'.[3]

Britain was indeed 'lucky', despite a civilian death toll as of October 31 of 6,334 for the month of October, that the vital air factories had been given a respite. Indeed, arising out of Germany's failure to destroy Britain's fighter power or to cripple the pace of aircraft production, the long-awaited, repeatedly forecast invasion at last seemed to have been indefinitely postponed; the first Enigma decrypt to hint at this had been circulated on October 27. It was a message that the troops concerned in 'Sealion' were 'to continue their training according to plan'. From this, commented the interpreters of MI 14, 'it appears that the Invasion of UK and/or Eire is not imminent'.[4] This single indication that training and not action were the German order of the day was not conclusive. But it did seem to be confirmed on the following day by a Combined Intelligence Committee assessment. This stated,

---

[1] 'Most Secret', 'Note of an Informal Meeting . . .', 31 October 1940, 12.30 p.m.: Cabinet papers, 127/14.

[2] Prime Minister's Personal Minute, M.245, 31 October 1940: Cabinet papers, 120/300. Three days later, after criticism from Sinclair and Portal, Churchill minuted to both: 'I do not dissent from the general principles and statements which your minute contains. In view, however, of the consensus of opinion among authorities on German and Italian morale, it is felt that a temporary diversion should be made to less precise objectives, especially in the case of Italy. This diversion is in the nature of an experiment. We have seen what inconvenience the attack on the British civilian population has caused us, and there is no reason why the enemy should be freed from all such embarrassments. Unless the results are seen to be good within a comparatively short time, the emphasis should be thrown again on to the precise objectives.' (Prime Minister's Personal Minute, M.256, 2 November 1940: Foreign Office papers, 800/326, folio 167.)

[3] Minute of 31 October 1940: Foreign Office papers, 800/326/War (General), folios 161–3.

[4] 'Officer Only', 'Most Secret', MI 14, 27 October 1940: War Office papers, 199/911A.

on the basis of photographic reconnaissance which had detected the
first considerable movement of shipping eastwards out of the Channel,
that this eastward movement, 'if maintained, could reduce the risk of
invasion'.[1]

The 'plain fact', Churchill told the House of Commons eight days
later, 'that an invasion, planned on so vast a scale, has not been
attempted in spite of the very great need of the enemy to destroy us in
our citadel, and that all these anxious months, when we stood alone
and the whole world wondered, have passed safely away—that fact
constitutes in itself one of the historic victories of the British Isles and is
a monumental milestone on our onward march'.[2]

The Defence Committee met on the morning of October 31 to discuss
the implications of the end of the threat of imminent invasion. It was a
meeting of supreme importance for the future conduct of the war.[3] On
the matter of invasion, which had hitherto been so open a question
and so imminent a danger, it was pointed out that it was 'unlikely that
any attempt would be made' to tow barges across the Channel during
the winter months, and 'it was believed' that little or no training had
been carried out 'in this difficult operation'. The only real danger of
invasion by barge would be foggy conditions, but such conditions would
prevail on average only four days a month in the vulnerable Dungeness
area.

The receding danger of invasion led at once to two possible areas of
future strategy: greater anti-submarine activity in the North Western
Approaches, and a more intense bombing of Germany. As the minutes
of the Defence Committee recorded:

The threat to our trade in the North Western Approaches made it essential
to reduce to a minimum the light naval forces allotted to anti-invasion duties.
At the same time, it was desirable to concentrate our bomber force on objectives in Germany and Italy in order to reduce their war potential and under-

[1] Quoted in F. H. Hinsley, *British Intelligence in the Second World War: Its Influence on Strategy and
Operations*, volume 1, London 1979, page 189.

[2] *Hansard*, 5 November 1940, column 1246.

[3] The seven members of the Defence Committee present were Churchill, A. V. Alexander and
Sinclair (War Cabinet Ministers), Pound, Dill and Portal (Chiefs of Staff) and Ismay (Offices of
the War Cabinet). Also present were Admirals Drax (C-in-C Nore), Tovey (C-in-C Home Fleet),
James (C-in-C Portsmouth), Dunbar-Nasmith (C-in-C Western Approaches), Ramsey (C-in-C
Rosyth), Ramsay (Vice Admiral, Dover), Phillips (Vice Chief of the Naval Staff) and Rawlings
(Chief of Staff, the Nore); Generals Brooke (C-in-C Home Forces), Pile (C-in-C Anti-Aircraft
Command), Pownall (GOC British troops in Ireland), and Haining (Vice Chief of the Imperial
General Staff). The airmen present were Dowding (C-in-C Fighter Command), Peirse (C-in-C
Bomber Command), Bowhill (C-in-C Coastal Command), Carr (AOC Northern Ireland) and
Douglas (Deputy Chief of the Air Staff).

mine the morale of their people. Consequently our bombers should not be
diverted to invasion ports unless it seemed certain that an invasion was about
to be attempted.

A few moments later Churchill told the Committee that the danger
of invasion would 'remain relatively remote', provided that 'we maintained our vigilance, and did not permit over-confidence in the country'.
As well as the North Western Approaches and the bombing of Germany, the 'march of events' in South East Europe, dominated by the
Italian invasion of Greece, 'compelled us to accept the risk of sending
reinforcements to the Middle East to the limit of shipping capacity'.[1]

In view of the new situation, Churchill set out for the Defence Committee the future course of the war as he saw it. The previous five
months had shown Britain's ability 'to continue the war indefinitely'.
There seemed little possibility of a 'major' British offensive in the remaining two months of 1940 or in 1941, but by 1942 'we should have
overtaken the lag in munitions production' and with the United States
'to help us', Britain might possibly reach peak production at the end of
the third, rather than the fourth year: that was, by the end of 1941
rather than by the end of 1942.

In Europe, Germany was now 'the master' and the German army
could move 'where it pleased'. During 1941, if they wished, the Germans had 'ample forces' for simultaneous campaigns in Spain, and
against Turkey 'and Russia'. At the same time, they could help Italy
with both men and munitions. The Germans, Churchill foresaw, 'would
inevitably turn their eyes to the Caspian and the prize of the Baku oil
fields'. In that event, he added, 'Russia would have to fight, as without
oil for her agriculture, her people would starve'.

The Germans might also seek to drive through Turkey to the Suez
Canal, and a Turkish resistance 'might greatly delay the German advance'; hence Britain should back up Turkey 'with all that we could
send'. Britain's aim was an army of 55 divisions 'ready by the end of
1941', with equipment supplied as a result of the recent offer by the
United States to equip 'an additional 10'.[2] Some twenty-five to thirty
of these British divisions would be in the Middle East.

---

[1] Defence Committee (Operations) No. 39 of 1940, 31 October 1940, 11 a.m.: Cabinet papers,
69/1, folios 226–34.

[2] But there was no intention of using the equipment for new divisions, rather for the planned
fifty-five total. As Churchill minuted to Dill five days later, 'Say nothing to make the Americans
suppose we are not going to raise the additional ten Divisions. We shall certainly need all the
equipment. Do nothing to put them off giving it to us. Accept the American offer in the best
possible way.' (Prime Minister's Personal Minute, M.269, 5 November 1940: Premier papers,
3/483/2, folios 32–3.)

In the Air, Churchill told the Defence Committee, Britain hoped to add a hundred squadrons by June 1941, after which the rate of increase 'would rise very steeply'. He added: 'We must bomb Germany and Italy to the greatest extent possible,' and his remarks continued:

The question might be asked 'How are we to win the war?' This question was frequently posed in the years 1914–1918, but not even those at the centre of things could have possibly given a reply as late as August of the last year of the war.

For the moment, all that we could do was to bank on the pressure of the blockade accompanied by the remorseless bombing of Germany and Italy. By 1941, however, we would be in a position to take on medium operations of an amphibious nature; and by 1942, we should be able to deliver very heavy overseas attacks.

Our power of survival depended on the maintenance of the life of this island. This postulated continued superiority in air defence and, in particular, the successful countering of night bombing. That we must keep our sea communications open went without saying. There had been a serious recrudescence of submarine warfare, and recent losses had been heavy. The United States destroyers were coming in, however, and a welcome amount of new construction would be available before the end of the year. It had been decided to bring up the destroyer strength in the Western Approaches to 60 by the 15th November.

The use of naval and air bases in Eire would greatly simplify our problems, but it would be most unwise to coerce Ireland until the danger was mortal. The United States might help us there, however; and after the Presidential elections it might be possible to persuade the Americans to send warships to Eire.[1]

In the early hours of November 1, British bombers struck at military targets in both Berlin and Naples. During the day, Churchill urged Sinclair and Portal to make further efforts 'to expand' Britain's bomber force. It was 'a scandal', he wrote, 'that so little use is made of the immense masses of material provided'. Churchill added: 'The discharge of bombs on Germany is pitifully small,'[2] and to Portal alone he wrote with asperity of his 'extreme regret' that the new Chief of the Air Staff would not meet his wish for an expansion of Bomber Command. Churchill's minute continued:

[1] 'Most Secret', Defence Committee (Operations), 31 October 1940, Confidential Annex: Cabinet papers, 69/1, folios 235–6.
[2] Prime Minister's Personal Minute, M.254, 1 November 1940: Premier papers, 3/25/1.

The first offensive object of the Royal Air Force is the delivery of bombs overseas, and particularly on Germany. It is the rising scale of delivery of bombs which must be taken as the measure of the success of our policy. It is deplorable that so few Bombers are available even on good nights. I have made various suggestions for increasing the Bomber Force. If, instead of simply turning all these down, you and the Secretary of State recognised the need of increasing the bomb delivery, and set to work to contrive the means of doing so, it would be a very great help.

'I beg you,' Churchill added, 'to let me have some further proposals of a constructive character.'[1] And in a second minute to Portal that same day he stressed the need to 'increase the bomb-dropping tonnage upon Germany', a tonnage, he wrote, which was not only 'lamentably small', but constituted 'a serious reproach to the organisation of the RAF that only such limited results can be shown for so much money & material'. Churchill's minute ended: 'I wish I cd persuade you to realise that there is a gt failure in *quantitative delivery*: No one shd be content with the present delivery.'[2]

Churchill was as concerned with the Near East and with Greece as he was with the bombing of Germany. 'You have taken a very bold and wise decision,' he telegraphed to Air Marshal Longmore, Air Officer Commanding-in-Chief, Middle East, who had just despatched a Blenheim Mark I Squadron to Greece, and he added: 'I hope to reinforce you as soon as possible.'[3] And in his search for reinforcements to the Middle East, Churchill minuted on Eden's request for 100,000 rifles, Eden then being in Cairo: 'Can we not supply these out of the American packet, or is there any small parcel of rifles anywhere in the world to be picked up?'[4]

Ismay passed on Churchill's request to Hollis. Two days later Hollis informed Churchill that 10,000 Mauser rifles with 500 rounds per rifle, as well as 10,000 American rifles 'taken from the Home Guard' together with ten million rounds of ammunition, had been despatched to the Middle East in the liner *Stirling Castle*, via the Cape.[5] These rifles were due to arrive in the Middle East in about mid-December.

As the pressures mounted, Churchill's mental and physical stamina was formidable. Yet the strains of decision-making on a man ap-

[1] Prime Minister's Personal Minute, M.251, 1 November 1940: Churchill papers, 20/13.
[2] Prime Minister's Personal Minute, M.253, 1 November 1940: Premier papers, 3/25/1, folio 131.
[3] Telegram of 1 November 1940: Premier papers, 3/309/1, No. 5.
[4] Minute to Ismay, for Chiefs of Staff Committee, Prime Minister's Personal Minute, D.108, 1 November 1940: Premier papers, 3/373/2, folio 144.
[5] 'Secret', 3 November 1940: Premier papers, 3/372/2, folio 143.

proaching his sixty-sixth birthday were considerable. 'The PM felt ill,' Colville noted on October 31, 'was sick, and went off to Down Street where he had no dinner.'[1] On the following evening, however, driving to Chequers after a hard working day, and visiting RAF Northolt on the way, Churchill revived, and after a spirited rendering of *Under the Spreading Chestnut Tree* turned to Colville with the words: 'I should now like to have dinner at Monte Carlo, and then go on to the Casino. . . .'[2]

At Chequers that weekend Churchill spoke of the new situation. 'He now thinks invasion is off,' Colville noted, 'but that can only be because of our constant vigilance. If we relaxed that, invasion would be an imminent danger. But that meant keeping great forces immobilized at home.' As to Vichy, Churchill commented scathingly: 'Owing to our unexpected resistance, they have been able to market their treachery at a slightly higher rate than would otherwise have been possible.' He could understand people being wicked, Churchill added, but he could not understand them being 'so contemptible'.

Churchill was also 'determined', Colville noted, 'that all possible by land, sea and air should be done for Greece', and as Dill drove away from Chequers that weekend Churchill's last words to him were: 'Don't forget, the maximum possible for Greece.'[3]

But aid to Greece was to bring immediate protest from Eden, who was still in the Middle East, and from Wavell, and an acrimonious exchange of messages ensued. On November 1 Eden telegraphed to Churchill from Cairo: 'We cannot from Middle East resources send sufficient air or land reinforcements to have any decisive influence upon course of fighting in Greece.' To send forces from Egypt, or to divert reinforcements on their way to Egypt, or approved for Egypt, would, Eden stressed, 'imperil our whole position in the Middle East and jeopardize plans for offensive operations now being laid in more than one theatre'. It would, Eden added, be 'bad strategy' to be diverted from the Middle East plans, 'and unwise to employ our forces in fragments in a theatre of war where they cannot be decisive'.[4]

Replying to Eden on November 2, Churchill telegraphed: 'Greek situation must be held to dominate others now. We are well aware of

---

[1] Colville diary, 31 October 1940: Premier papers. The nature of the illness was unclear. Two days later the doctor whom Churchill had consulted, H. Beckett Overy, wrote to him: 'I wanted you to take the castor oil for I felt it was an opportunity to clear out whatever was irritating you.' (Letter of 2 November 1940: Churchill papers, 2/392.)

[2] Colville diary, 1 November 1940: Colville papers.

[3] Colville diary, 2 November 1940: Colville papers.

[4] Telegram AE, 45A, 1 November 1940: Premier papers, 3/309/1, No. 6.

our slender resources. Aid to Greece must be attentively studied lest whole Turkish position is lost through proof that England never tries to keep her guarantees.'[1]

The guarantees to Greece and Turkey had both been given by Neville Chamberlain, following Hitler's occupation of Prague in March 1939. Churchill had approved them then, but had warned at the same time of the need to ensure that they could be implemented. Now it was he, as Chamberlain's successor, who was caught in the vice of inadequate means. 'If Greece was overwhelmed,' he told the War Cabinet on November 4, 'it would be said that in spite of our guarantees we had allowed one more small ally to be swallowed up.' It was possible, he said, to argue that the guarantee had been a joint Anglo-French one, and that plans for implementing it were in the hands of General Weygand, 'but no answer would really help if another small ally was overwhelmed'.[2]

Churchill had already asked Portal, on November 2, for four bomber squadrons to fly to Crete or Greece via Malta, their personnel and ground stores to be 'carried through by cruiser'. His minute ended: 'Perhaps you will say that all I propose is impossible. If so, I shall be very sorry, because a great opportunity will have been missed, and we shall have to pay heavily thereafter for it.' Churchill ended, as so often: 'Please try your best.'[3]

For more than four decades, one of Churchill's favourite maxims had been: 'Neglect no means.' Yet now the means were slender, and could not match the need. At Chequers that weekend, Churchill's thoughts ranged forward to the years of the offensive, as he showed his guests some of the albums of aircraft production which had been prepared for him by Lindemann.

Lindemann's albums were a regular feature of the Chequers weekends. Two months later Eric Seal gave instructions to all Private Secretaries to arrange for 'a copious supply' of these albums 'even when the Professor is not about'. Seal added: 'Last night the Prime Minister wanted to show them to the Canadians and they were not here. His annoyance was justified!'[4]

Among those who were shown the Lindemann albums were two

---

[1] Telegram of 2 November 1940: Churchill papers, 20/14.

[2] War Cabinet No. 282 of 1940, 4 November 1940, 4 p.m., minute 2, Confidential Annex: Cabinet papers, 65/16. During this meeting Lord Halifax, as the minutes recorded, 'welcomed the decisions taken by the Prime Minister. To have sent no help to Greece would have undermined the will to resist of other Balkan countries.'

[3] Prime Minister's Personal Minute, M.258, 2 November 1940: Churchill papers, 20/13.

[4] Minute of 22 December 1940: Premier papers, 4/80/3, folio 663.

young pilots, Squadron-Leader Kayll and Flight-Lieutenant Gaynor.[1] Kayll, the Commanding Officer of 615 Squadron, of which Churchill had been honorary Air Commodore since before the war, later recalled:

> We talked about the Hurricane aircraft and especially about the supply of bullet proof petrol tanks. These were causing great concern to pilots as one incendiary bullet in the main tank, which was just in front of the pilot, was usually fatal. As far as I can remember it was a few months after this that I was sent to RAF Farnborough to see a demonstration of a bullet proof petrol tank which shortly after was put into production.[2]

During this Chequers weekend Churchill remarked, Colville noted in his diary, that he hoped that Britain would, by the end of 1941, be bombing 'every Hun corner' of Europe, and doing so every night. But, Churchill cautioned Sir Richard Peirse that same weekend, 'we must be very careful not to bomb the Pope. He has a lot of influential friends!'[3]

On the morning of Sunday November 3, while still at Chequers, Churchill dictated a long telegram to Eden, in which he argued that the collapse of Greece 'without any effort by us' would have a 'deadly effect' on Turkey, and on the future of the war. No one, Churchill added, 'will thank us for sitting tight in Egypt with ever growing forces' while the Greek situation 'and all that hangs on it is cast away'. His final exhortation read: 'Trust you will grasp situation firmly, abandoning negative and passive policies and seizing opportunity which has come into our hands. "Safety First" is the road to ruin in war, even if

---

[1] Colville later recalled: 'He was always very good with young men. He always treated them as if they were frightfully important, and contemporaries.' (Sir John Colville, conversation with the author, 21 January 1981.) On November 6 Kayll wrote to Churchill: 'I had hoped that before I wrote to thank you, we would have been able to add to our score, but we have had no luck. We chased two lots of 109s yesterday but were unable to catch them unfortunately.' (Churchill papers, 2/395.)

[2] Wing Commander J. R. Kayll, letter to the author, 31 July 1982. Awarded the DSO and DFC in 1940, Kayll was shot down over France on 6 July 1941, near St Omer, and taken as a prisoner-of-war to Germany. In late 1942 he and some 300 other RAF prisoners-of-war were sent to a camp in Poland. In 1945 he was liberated by the British Army at Lübeck.

[3] Colville diary, 2 November 1940: Colville papers. The visitors at Chequers that weekend included Ismay, Lindemann, A. V. Alexander, Pound, Portal, Dill and Peirse (Chequers Visitors Book). Convinced that striking Italy by air would not involve bombing Rome, the British Minister to the Vatican, D'Arcy Osborne, had proposed that Britain gain credit with the Italian people and the Catholic world by letting it become known 'that we have deferred to the Pope's request to spare Rome on account of its Christian tradition. . . .' In this way 'the credit' for sparing Rome could be divided between the Pope and Britain. Reading this proposal, Churchill minuted in the margin: 'It will be unwise to try to make this point because we shall soon be bombing Rome.' (Telegram No. 10, via Berne No. 1295, received 12 November 1940, and minute of 13 November 1940: Premier papers, 3/14/3, folios 463, 464.)

you had the safety, which you have not. Send me your proposals earliest, or say you have none to make.'[1]

Colville, who was present when Churchill dictated this telegram to
Mrs Hill, recorded in his diary:

He lay there in his four-post bed with its flowery chintz hangings, his bed-
table by his side. Mrs Hill sat patiently opposite while he chewed his cigar,
drunk frequent sips of iced soda-water, fidgeted his toes beneath the bed-
clothes and muttered stertorously under his breath what he contemplated
saying.

To watch him compose some telegram or minute for dictation is to make
one feel that one is present at the birth of a child, so tense is his expression, so
restless his turnings from side to side, so curious the noises he emits under his
breath.

Then comes out some masterly sentence and finally with a 'Gimme' he
takes the sheet of typewritten paper and initials it, or alters it with his fountain-
pen, which he holds most awkwardly half way up the holder.[2]

That Sunday night, the first British troops landed on Greek soil.
Above Britain, German air losses in the previous three months battles
reached 2,433 machines destroyed, and 6,000 German airmen killed or
taken prisoner. At the same time, November 3 was the first night for
nearly two months that no German war planes came over London, no
alarm sounded, and no one was victim of bomb or aerial mine. 'The
Prime Minister is much impressed by the slackening of the air attack,'
Colville noted in his diary on November 4. 'He says it is not all due to
the weather. The Germans have to continue their attacks in order to
try to hide their defeat. But evidently they do not like the reception
they got here, or the retaliation on Berlin.'

There was, however, Colville noted, 'depressing news from the sea'.[3]
Two armed merchant cruisers, the *Laurentic* and the *Patroclus*, had been
sunk by U-boats. 'Dangers in the air,' Churchill was to tell the House
of Commons on the following day, 'are sudden and might have become
catastrophic, but the dangers to our sea-borne traffic mature much
more slowly.' They are, he added, 'none the less formidable, however,
and if in any way neglected, they would touch the life of the
State.'[4]

Having discussed the question of aid to Greece with Churchill on
the evening of November 3, the Chiefs of Staff telegraphed to the mili-

[1] Letter of 3 November 1940: Churchill papers, 20/14.
[2] Colville diary, 3 November 1940: Colville papers.
[3] Colville diary, 4 November 1940: Colville papers.
[4] *Hansard*, 5 November 1940, column 1244.

tary, naval and air Commanders-in-Chief, Middle East, on the following morning that 'the greatest possible material and moral support'
was to be given to Greece 'at the earliest possible moment', even though
this would 'leave Egypt very thin for a period'. But everything would
be done to replace supplies sent to Greece from Britain, 'as soon as
possible'.[1] How early these replacements would in fact be ready was
made doubtful only an hour later, when Churchill told the Defence
Committee that, having studied the most recent tank production
figures, he was 'extremely concerned to find so great a failure in the
realisation of the tank programme'. Designs had been changed three
times in less than a year, and it was this 'continual introduction of
fresh ideas into established programmes', he added, 'which was one of
the main causes for our present deplorable situation'. He was also
'shocked to hear', and this affected all his plans for the future offensives,
'that there would be so great a deficiency in tank production by the
end of March 1941, in comparison with the forecasts which had been
given'.[2] To the War Cabinet two days later, Churchill recognized
that this falling off of tank production was, in fact 'largely, but not he
thought, wholly, attributable to the effect of air raids'.[3]

On November 5 Churchill went to the House of Commons to speak
on the war situation. Two diarists were among the MPs in the Commons
that morning. Each gave his perspective of Churchill's appearance and
mood. The first, the National Labour MP Harold Nicolson, noted in
his diary:

> The Prime Minister makes a statement after Question-time. He is rather
> grim. He brings home to the House as never before the gravity of our shipping
> losses and the danger of our position in the Eastern Mediterranean. It has a
> good effect. By putting the grim side foremost he impresses us with his ability
> to face the worst. He rubs the palms of his hands with five fingers extended up
> and down the front of his coat, searching for the right phrase, indicating
> cautious selection, conveying almost medicinal poise. If Chamberlain had

[1] Telegram No. 22, Annex 1, Chiefs of Staff Committee No. 372 of 1940, 4 November 1940,
10.30 a.m.: Cabinet papers, 79/7. At a Chiefs of Staff Committee meeting on the following day 'it
was pointed out that the plan approved by the Prime Minister for assisting the Greeks was in
general accordance with the conclusions reached by the Joint Planning Staff'. (Chiefs of Staff
Committee No. 374 of 1940, 5 November 1940, 10.30 a.m.: Cabinet papers, 79/7.)
[2] Defence Committee (Supply) No. 16 of 1940, 4 November 1940, 11.45 a.m.: Cabinet papers,
70/1.
[3] War Cabinet No. 283 of 1940, 6 November 1940, 12 noon: Cabinet papers, 65/10.

spoken glum words such as these the impression would have been one of despair and lack of confidence. Churchill can say them and we all feel, 'Thank God that we have a man like that!' I have never admired him more.

'Thereafter,' Nicolson added, 'he slouches into the smoking-room and reads the *Evening News* intently, as if it were the only source of information available to him.'[1]

The second diarist was the Conservative MP, Henry Channon, whose dislike of Churchill had been a feature of the previous decade; he wrote: 'I admire the PM's pluck, his courageous energy and magnificent English: his humour, too, although often in doubtful taste, is immense.' But, Channon added:

This morning one of his secretaries rushed up to me in the House, and asked me if I had seen him? He was apparently due to lunch at the Palace, and it was already 1.15. Luckily I had just seen him 'boozing' in the Smoking Room, and so I volunteered to remind him. I went up to him politely, but unsmilingly, and he got up ungraciously, after grunting at me. He can be very unattractive when he is in a bad temper.[2]

During his speech Churchill told the House of Commons that 14,000 civilians had been killed in the Blitz. On active service, in those same two months, 300 soldiers had been killed. As he was 'going home the other night' he had asked a group of steel-helmeted men who stood about the door, 'what was going on', and a deep voice in the background had said: 'It's a grand life, if we don't weaken.' There, said Churchill, 'is the British watchword for the winter of 1940. We will think of something else by the winter of 1941.'[3]

Churchill could give no account of Britain's war plans. 'If I were to set them high,' he said, 'I might raise false hopes; if I set them low, I might cause undue despondency and alarm; and if I stated exactly what they were, that would be exactly what the enemy would like to know.' What then did the British Government intend? 'We shall do our best,' he said, 'That is all I can say. To that decision and declaration, generously and faithfully interpreted, I invoke with confidence the approval of the House.'[4]

---

[1] Nicolson diary, 5 November 1940: Nigel Nicolson (editor), *Harold Nicolson, Diaries and Letters, 1939–1945*, London 1967, page 125.

[2] Channon diary, 5 November 1940. On the following day Channon noted, 'Members are complaining openly that Winston trades on his position, on his immense following in the country, though his popularity is on the decline: but it is still high. Yet the country does not want a dictator.' Robert Rhodes James (editor), *Chips, The Diaries of Sir Henry Channon*, London 1967, page 272.

[3] *Hansard*, 5 November 1940, columns 1241–2.

[4] *Hansard*, 5 November 1940, column 1250.

On the afternoon of November 5, at a meeting of the Defence Committee, Churchill, his senior colleagues and advisers addressed themselves to the problem of what would happen if Greece, and then Turkey, and then Syria, were to come under German pressure, or control.[1] The Chiefs of Staff wanted Britain to do all in its power to encourage and to assist Turkey to resist any German advance. But this resistance might fail, and plans should therefore also be made for 'the demolition of Turkish communications', and for 'the destruction of Iraqi oil wells, and of oil pipe lines in Iraq, Syria and Palestine'.[2]

The necessary plans were at once prepared.[3] Meanwhile, in the United States, the way to greater help for Britain had been opened on November 2, with the re-election of President Roosevelt to a third term of office. Roosevelt would now be President for at least four more years, and Churchill saw at once a pointer of hope for Britain. 'I did not think it right,' he telegraphed to Roosevelt on November 6, 'for me as a foreigner to express my opinion upon American politics while the election was on, but now I feel you will not mind my saying that I prayed for your success and that I am truly thankful for it.' Churchill added:

Things are afoot which will be remembered as long as the English language is spoken in any quarter of the globe, and in expressing the comfort I feel that the people of the United States have once again cast these great burdens upon you I must avow my sure faith that the lights by which we steer will bring us all safely to anchor.[4]

That evening, an Enigma decrypt revealed that the Headquarters of

[1] The instructions issued by Air Chief Marshal Longmore for the newly appointed commander of the British Air Forces in Greece, Air Commodore J. H. D'Albiac, included the paragraph: 'The future trend of events in Greece cannot be appreciated but the possibility of a sudden and complete collapse of Greece must not be lost sight of when making your decisions in the location of the squadrons.' ('Most Secret', O.45575/Plans, 5 November 1940: Air Ministry papers, 23/6370.)

[2] Defence Committee (Operations) No. 40 of 1940, 5 November 1940, 5.30 p.m.: Cabinet papers, 69/1.

[3] These plans received the code names 'Bilge' (destruction of oil plant in Syria), 'Boatswain' (destruction of the oil terminal in the Lebanese port of Tripoli), 'Brass' (destruction of the oil plant at Kirkuk in Iraq), 'Bullion' (destruction of the oil plant at Haifa) and 'Clump' (destruction of the oil pipe line from Iraq across Transjordan to Palestine).

[4] Telegram of 6 November 1940: Premier papers, 3/468, folio 63. Two and a half weeks later, having received no answer to his telegram, Churchill telegraphed to Lord Lothian: 'Would you kindly find out for me most discreetly whether President received my personal telegram congratulating him on re-election. It may have been swept up in electioneering congratulations. If not I wonder whether there was anything in it which could have caused offence or been embarrassing for him to receive. Should welcome your advice.' ('Personal and Private', 26 November 1940: Premier papers, 4/17/1, folios 139–40.) Roosevelt never replied to Churchill's congratulations.

the German 16th Army had given instructions that a part of the apparatus for equipping invasion barges, lighters and ferries in Belgium
and Northern France 'should be returned to store', leaving only apparatus sufficient for 'exercises'.[1] There was also news on November 6
of the death toll from bombing during the week ending that morning
having fallen once more, this time to 399, of whom 253 were in London.
This represented a second substantial decline. The number of unexploded bombs had likewise fallen, to below three thousand for the
first time in two months.[2]

[1] 'Officer Only', 'Most Secret', 'German Preparations for Invasion', MI 14, 5.30 p.m., 6
November 1940: War Office papers, 199/911A.
[2] War Cabinet, Chiefs of Staff Committee, Weekly Résumé, No. 62: Churchill papers, 23/7.

46

'The intolerable shackles
of the defensive'

T H E invasion danger was now much reduced, perhaps averted altogether. With this daily and dreadful pressure relaxed for the first time since the fall of France, Churchill was able to streamline the organization of his Private Office and his daily work. It was a workload that did not diminish however. In some areas it had increased. 'The amount of paper in the Prime Minister's box,' noted Colville on November 7, 'is becoming unwieldy'; a 'farrago', Colville described it, of operational, civil, political and scientific matters.[1]

But a system had been devised to draw Churchill's attention to this mass of paper in some sequential way, based upon its urgency and importance. That system centred upon Churchill's box: a box which went with him wherever he went, whether at 10 Downing Street or the Annexe, the Central War Room, Chequers, or any of the journeys by train or car to army, navy or air force units, to factories, or to research establishments.

The arrangement of the box, John Peck has written, 'was peculiarly Winston's own, and it was in a sense the nerve centre of his war effort'. It was a black despatch box, to which only Churchill and his personal staff carried the keys. In it were a series of foolscap-size numbered cardboard folders, into which his Private Secretaries would place all Churchill's work. The usual headings, as Peck recalled, were:

Top of the Box
Foreign Office Telegrams
Service Telegrams
Periodical returns

[1] Colville diary, 7 November 1940: Colville papers.

Parliamentary questions
For signature
To see
General Ismay (reports from Chiefs of Staff)
Answers other (than from Gen. Ismay)
Ecclesiastical
R Week-end

'Top of the Box,' Peck noted, 'contained the material culled from the other folders which the senior Private Secretary on duty considered to be really urgent. Selecting the right items could be hazardous. If the system was not to defeat itself, "Top of the Box" had to be kept small, and urgency had to be measured not only by objective standards of importance, deadlines, and so on, but in part subjectively by the degree of the Prime Minister's personal interest at the time. So we had to see and understand what was in his mind, and he relied on us to be able to do this.'

The folder, 'Periodical Returns', Peck wrote, was the key to an important part of Churchill's method: 'He was keenly interested in the development of new equipment. He was also much concerned about the absolute necessity for speed and punctuality in delivery despite bombing, breakdowns, and other causes of delay.' Now that he had the power he had earlier lacked, Churchill 'was going to make sure', Peck wrote, 'that there were no disasters due to lack of zeal or direction in the back rooms'. He, and equally Lindemann, wanted to know 'what was going on'. Churchill therefore sent out to his Ministers 'a stream of written requests for monthly, fortnightly, weekly, or even daily returns on production, technical developments, manpower, training, tank and aircraft strengths, which he would then scrutinize with care'.

Producing these returns, Peck added, 'was understandably unpopular, but it put all concerned on notice that Winston was on the warpath, and a Minister might be instructed at any time to bring with him the official concerned to explain the figures in person'. Where delays or other unsatisfactory situations were disclosed, they were often due to priorities or procedures operating elsewhere, and an adjustment decided with Churchill's personal authority would, Peck noted, 'solve or ease the problems' of the department or official concerned. Consequently Peck wrote, 'there was no part of the war effort so obscure that it might not suddenly be picked up in the glare of an intense and highly penetrating searchlight'.

The folder, 'To see', contained routine work which Churchill might either initial to indicate he had seen it, or decide to annotate with some question or instruction. The folder, 'R Week-end', contained only those files which Churchill himself had marked in this way. 'It meant,' wrote Peck, 'that he was deferring the consideration of them until the comparative calm of the following weekend at Chequers, but by the time the weekend came guests would have been invited, some crisis or planning meeting would occur, and the "R Week-end" file would sit for another week.'

This file contained two types of paper, the ones, Peck recalled, 'that Winston was interested in and really intended to study at leisure and pronounce upon', and others, 'indigestible or uninteresting', which were often the result of some initiative of Churchill's own 'which he had decided to abandon'. But, Peck noted, as Churchill 'was never prepared to admit that he was dropping anything that he had started, much ingenuity was required on our part, in the way of submitting draft instructions to Ministers or proposals for disposing of the subject by other means, to enable him to get rid of the thing without loss of face'.[1]

Each of the folders in the box was carefully prepared by the Private Secretariat. 'We read right through the Foreign Office telegrams,' Colville later recalled, 'and selected those that would interest him, or ought to interest him. We took out about two-thirds.' Churchill himself, Colville later recalled, used to mark many of the Service telegrams 'Ismay to explain'.[2] Technical papers, statistical returns, and many military, naval and air force documents would be marked 'Prof L to see' or 'Prof L to advise', and often Lindemann would submit draft replies, written as if by Churchill, which Churchill would accept unaltered, and send as if they were his own.

From Churchill's reading of the contents of his box, there flowed a stream of minutes and instructions. This was a deliberate attempt to prevent the chaos that had so often resulted during the First World War following some verbal remark by Asquith, or Lloyd George, upon which actions were initiated, and then challenged by the Prime Minister as not being what he had asked for. To avoid any such confusion,

[1] Sir John Peck, article in *The Atlantic Monthly*, March 1965. There was also the problem of 'dead matter' in the 'R Week-end' file, as Eric Seal minuted to the Private Secretaries. 'All dead matter,' he wrote, 'should be pruned from it regularly, and either buried or brought to the Prime Minister's notice as appropriate.' The Private Secretary on duty each weekend, Seal added, 'should regard it as his business to bring the papers in the file to the Prime Minister's notice', and he went on to warn: 'These files must be recognised as a serious responsibility and put under the supervision of a responsible member of the staff. Perhaps Mr Martin would keep a special eye on them.' (Minute of 24 November 1940: Premier papers, 4/80/3, folio 664.)

[2] Sir John Colville: conversation with the author, 21 January 1981. Or, on one occasion, 'elucidate' (author).

Churchill had laid down the following rule, which was rigidly and successfully observed: 'Let it be clearly understood,' he had minuted to Ismay, Bridges and Dill in the summer of 1940, 'that all directions emanating from me are made in writing, or should be immediately afterwards confirmed in writing, and that I do not accept any responsibility for matters relating to national defence, on which I am alleged to have given decisions, unless they are recorded in writing.'

On Churchill's instructions, this ruling was shown to Seal, Bevir, Martin, Peck and Colville.[1]

The mass of secret and official documents which Churchill saw as Prime Minister and Minister of Defence did not prevent him from continuing his pre-war habit of reading almost every morning newspaper, and even seeking the news before it was generally available. Before the war, at Chartwell, once Clementine Churchill was in bed, he used, as Mrs Hill later recalled, to telephone the *Daily Mail* news department to find out the news, 'at midnight or later'.[2] During his visit to the Maginot Line in August 1939 he had arranged for a set of London newspapers to be flown out to him each day via Paris. This habit of looking at the whole range of morning newspapers had continued when he went to the Admiralty in September 1939, and on through his Premiership.

While he was Prime Minister, Churchill would normally see the newspapers twice: once at midnight or after, when they would be brought to him by Despatch rider, and then again in the morning. 'With breakfast,' John Peck has written, 'he would always examine the daily newspapers, at least nine in number. He always did this himself and never relied on any press reader or system of clipping or marking. He was an expert skimmer.'[3]

Often this reading of the newspapers would lead to some immediate response, as when Churchill read, in the *Daily Express* on November 23, of a sentence of five years' penal servitude for looting imposed on each of six London Auxiliary Fire Service men. The men had stolen £11 of whisky after going to a fire in a public house near St Paul's. The article also gave details of a six months' prison sentence on a labourer who had stolen two pairs of net lace curtains.[4]

Reading of these sentences, Churchill at once dictated a minute to the Home Secretary, Herbert Morrison:

[1] Minute of 19 July 1940: Premier papers, 4/68/9, folio 933.
[2] Kathleen Hill, conversation with the author, 15 October 1982.
[3] Sir John Peck, typescript 'Bull and Benediction', page 112.
[4] 'You have disgraced your uniform': *Daily Express*, 23 November 1940.

There seems to be great disparity in these sentences, and I wonder whether any attempt is being made to standardize the punishments inflicted for this very odious crime. Five Years' penal servitude for stealing whisky for immediate consumption seems out of proportion when compared with sentences of three or six months for stealing valuables. Exemplary discipline is no doubt necessary as people must be made to feel that looting is stealing. Still I should be glad to know that these kind of cases are being reviewed and levelled out.[1]

Morrison replied by explaining that there had been 'many cases of looting which though not of the gravest kind must be regarded seriously', and that in the case of the firemen the judge had apparently taken into consideration 'not only the amount of loot, which was large, but the fact that the men concerned had taken advantage of their position as members of a public service'. 'I personally,' Morrison added, 'feel that the sentence was heavy.'[2] So did Churchill, nor did he forget it. 'I still think,' he minuted to Morrison six months later, on being sent details of further looting sentences, 'the case of the firemen stands out as utterly disproportionate to all the others.'[3]

Newspapers, official papers in the black box, Enigma decrypts in the buff box: sometimes even Churchill could find the mass of materials unnecessarily vast. On November 12, in a minute to both Ismay and Bridges in protest at the 'mass of stuff' which had reached him 'in a single morning', much of it Central War Room Reports and Joint Intelligence Committee Summaries, the contents of which he had already seen in the Service and Foreign Office telegrams, Churchill wrote: 'More and more people must be banking up behind these different papers, the bulk of which defeats their purpose,' and he added: 'Try now and simplify, shorten and reduce.'[4]

Of predominant concern to Churchill throughout his Premiership was the need to curtail the circulation of secret papers, principal among them those derived from the Enigma decrypts, and containing inter-

[1] Prime Minister's Personal Minute, M.335, 23 November 1940: Premier papers, 4/40/19, folio 993.

[2] Minute of 10 December 1940: Premier papers, 4/40/19, folios 991–2.

[3] Prime Minister's Personal Minute, M.626/1, 4 June 1941: Premier papers, 4/40/19, folio 975. In July 1941 Churchill reacted critically to a sentence of five years' penal servitude on Miss Elsie Orrin, for saying to two soldiers 'that Hitler was a good ruler, a better man than Mr Churchill'. In a minute to the Home Secretary, Herbert Morrison, Churchill wrote on July 19: 'I should like to have my opinion put on record that this sentence is far too heavy for expressions of opinion, however pernicious, which are not accompanied by conspiracy. Nothing in the internal state of the country justifies such unreasonable and unnatural severity.' Such 'excessive action', Churchill added, 'defeats its own ends'. (Prime Ministers's Personal Minute, M.751/1, 19 July 1941: Churchill papers, 20/36.)

[4] Prime Minister's Personal Minute, C.24, 12 November 1940: Churchill papers, 20/13.

pretations based upon the Enigma messages. He himself, at the end of September, had instructed 'C' to send him 'daily all Enigma messages'.[1]

On November 8 a list was drawn up for Churchill of all those in receipt of this most secret of secret sources. There were thirty-one recipients in all.[2]

Other reports, in which Enigma material appeared in a disguised form, were likewise the object of Churchill's scrutiny. Of one such, a copy of which was being shown to General Lee, the Military Attaché at the United States Embassy, Churchill minuted to Bridges later that month: 'This report and others like it should be steadily damped down, and its circulation restricted as far as possible.' The reports given to the American Attaché, he added, 'should not be broken off suddenly but should become less informative and padding used to maintain bulk.' This was not through any 'lack of confidence' in the Attaché himself, Churchill explained, 'but because the wild scattering of secret information must be curbed'.[3]

Secrets relating to British future war plans and operations had likewise to be guarded with vigilance; here also Churchill's scrutiny was continuous. As soon as he read a telegram sent to the Dominion Prime Ministers, giving details of British aid to Greece, including Naval movements, he minuted to Ismay and Bridges: 'Who is responsible for drawing it up and sending it out? No one is entitled to be informed of impending movements of British ships. . . .'

It was 'intolerable', Churchill added, 'that all these secret matters connected with operations should be scattered round the world'. It might sometimes be necessary where Dominion forces were involved to give 'specific details', but more usually 'general statements' should suffice. 'I had no idea,' Churchill added, 'such information was being *circularized*. Not only the lives of troops and sailors, but the success of operations are involved. In future no such statements are to be issued without my approval.'[4]

---

[1] Quoted in F. H. Hinsley and others, *British Intelligence in the Second World War: Its Influence on Strategy and Operations*, volume 1, London 1979, page 295.

[2] 'Distribution List of the Secret Situation Report as from 8th November, 1940': Cabinet papers, 120/744. The thirty-one were, in the order listed: Churchill, Bridges, Ismay, Halifax, Vansittart, Cadogan, Orme Sargent, 'C', A. V. Alexander, Pound, Phillips, the Director of Naval Intelligence, Eden, Dill, Haining, the Director of Military Intelligence, Sinclair, Portal, Freeman, the Director of Air Intelligence, Sir John Anderson, Attlee, Greenwood, Beaverbrook, Bevin, Kingsley Wood, Sir Alexander Hardinge (for the King), the Secretary of the Joint Intelligence Committee (Colonel Capel Dunn), the officer in charge of 'Secret Records', the Duty Officer at the Central War Room, and Professor N. F. Hall, Ministry of Economic Warfare.

[3] Minute of 22 November 1940: Cabinet papers, 120/744.

[4] Prime Minister's Personal Minute, D.115, 9 November 1940: Premier papers, 4/43B/1, folio 91.

In reply, Ismay pointed out that this telegram, having been sent only to the four Dominion Prime Ministers, could hardly be said to have been circularized; and that it had been sent in accordance with a War Cabinet instruction to inform these four Prime Ministers 'in strict confidence' of the decisions which had been taken 'to run certain risks in Egypt for the time being' and to reassure them that the air squadrons being sent to Greece from Egypt 'were being replaced as quickly as possible'.[1] The naval details, Ismay added, had been included in the telegram 'at the request of the Naval Staff'.

Ismay now asked if, in future, Churchill's approval was needed for all telegrams 'which relate to future operations'. At the same time, he inquired if telegrams concerning future operations should no longer give 'very specific information of dispositions and impending operations'.[2] 'Yes,' Churchill replied to both questions, and he added: 'Nothing relating to future operations is to go forth without my permission in each case.'[3]

Churchill's vigilance extended to the speeches of his Government Ministers. Reading of remarks by the Secretary of State for India, Leo Amery, about future British policy in the eastern Mediterranean, he wrote at once:

My dear Leo,
It was a pity that in your Speech you dealt with strategy and military policy, which are altogether outside the scope of your Department. Although it sounds quite harmless to say that when we have disposed of the Italians in Egypt, we shall transfer our forces to Greece or the Balkan Peninsula (I have not the actual words), this might have unfortunate results. If the Germans thought we were establishing a land front in Greece, they would certainly be inclined to intervene against Greece. The longer this can be put off the better.

There are great dangers in speaking of these matters when one is not fully informed. We do not want to tell the enemy everything.

Not wishing to upset Amery too much, before sending this letter

---

[1] War Cabinet No. 282 of 1940, 4 November 1940.

[2] Minute of 12 November 1940: Premier papers, 4/43B/1, folios 88–90.

[3] Minute of 13 November 1940: Premier papers, 4/43B1, folio 90. With such a mass of secret material at both 10 Downing Street and the Annexe, it was not surprising that vigilance was being continually urged upon his Private Office. One such minute was sent out by Eric Seal early in 1941. It read: 'I asked the other day that secret papers should not be left lying on desks. As I nevertheless still find that papers are left in my "in tray" when I am not in the room I think it is better that there should be a written rule. The Prime Minister is very concerned that every care should be taken to safeguard the security of secret matters. The rule should be that they are kept in a locked box or some other equally secure place unless they are actually in use, being sorted etc.' (Minute of 6 January 1941: Premier papers, 4/80/3, folio 601.)

Churchill deleted the last paragraph, and the phrase 'which are altogether outside the scope of your Department'.[1]

As Greek and Italian forces clashed in mainland Greece, and British help to Greece was sent from Egypt, Churchill had been drawn into the problems posed by the need to defend Crete against a possible Italian attack. On November 4 the British Military Mission in Athens had telegraphed to London and Cairo with details of a Greek request for British troops to be sent to Crete, since they urgently needed to transfer two thirds of the Greek Fifth Division from Crete to the Epirus front.[2] It would be 'difficult to deny' the Greeks the use of their own troops, Churchill wrote to Dill, but 'perhaps the Polish Brigade might go there', as well as 'some of the British details, or some of the less trained Australians'. It was important, Churchill added, that the Germans should think 'that we are landing considerable numbers'. The area to be watched was 'very extensive', and the consequences of a counter-attack 'would be disastrous'.[3]

On November 6 the Greeks repeated their request for their own troops to be transferred from Crete to Epirus.[4] 'We shall render poor service to Greece,' Churchill told Dill, 'if in consequence of our using Crete for our own purposes we deny them the use of two-thirds of their own Fifth Division.' The defence of Crete, Churchill noted, 'depends on the Navy, but nevertheless there must be a certain deterrent force of troops on shore'. It was for Wavell to provide, from Egypt, 'in meal or in malt', three of four thousand additional British troops and 'a dozen guns'. He must provide these troops 'from forces which he will not be using in the possibly impending battle'. Churchill's minute continued:

Every effort should be made to rush arms or equipment to enable a Reserve Division of Greeks to be formed in Crete. Rifles and machine guns are quite sufficient in this case. To keep a Greek Division out of the battle on the Epirus front would be very bad and to lose Crete because we had not sufficient bulk of forces there would be a crime.[5]

For Wavell, the demands of Crete, however small, were nevertheless

---

[1] 'Personal and Secret', 3 December 1940: Churchill papers, 20/3.
[2] British Military Mission, Athens, Telegram No. 6, 4 November 1940.
[3] Prime Minister's Personal Minute, M.273, 6 November 1940: Premier papers, 3/109, folio 163.
[4] British Military Mission, Athens, Telegram No. 7, 6 November 1940.
[5] Prime Minister's Personal Minute, M.275, 7 November 1940: Premier papers, 3/109, folios 161–2. No Reserve Cretan Division was formed. Nor was a third of the Fifth Division retained on Crete.

unwelcome. 'I have already had to withdraw a badly needed field company from Western Desert for Crete,' he telegraphed to Dill on November 7, as well as 'a considerable number' of administrative units to service the Royal Air Force squadrons sent to Greece. He was prepared to send the Black Watch to Crete, 'but no more, and that reluctantly'. His telegram ended: 'If we allow the Greek and Cretan commitments to grow any further at expense of Egypt we shall risk our whole position here.'[1]

Churchill's desire to reinforce Crete and Wavell's concern for his own strength in Egypt could not be reconciled.

November 8 brought better news from Greece: the Italian advance was being checked, and Greek troops had trapped a whole Italian division. That evening, while Churchill was working in the Down Street underground shelter, Eden returned from his visit to the Middle East, and together with Dill, went to report to Churchill on his mission. As Churchill later wrote:

He brought with him the carefully-guarded secret which I wished I had known earlier. Nevertheless no harm had been done. Mr Eden unfolded in considerable detail to a select circle, including the CIGS and General Ismay, the offensive plan which General Wavell and General Wilson[2] had conceived and prepared. No longer were we to await in our fortified lines at Mersa Matruh an Italian assault, for which defensive battle such long and artful preparations had been made. On the contrary, within a month or so we were ourselves to attack. The operation was to be called 'Compass'.

Wavell's plan, Churchill noted, while it involved 'a serious risk', also offered 'a glittering prize'. His account continued: 'Here, then, was the deadly secret which the Generals had talked over with their Secretary of State. This was what they had not wished to telegraph. We were all delighted. I purred like six cats.'[3]

Ismay, who was present as Eden unfolded the details of Wavell's planned offensive, later recalled, of Churchill's 'cat' simile: 'That is putting it mildly. He was rapturously happy. "At long last we are going to throw off the intolerable shackles of the defensive," he declaimed. "Wars are won by superior will-power. Now we will wrest the initiative from the enemy and impose our will on him." '[4]

On November 9 Churchill spoke at the Mansion House of the task ahead. 'People sometimes wonder,' he said, 'why we are unable to take

[1] Telegram No. 0/25034, 7 November 1940: Premier papers, 3/109, folios 160–1.
[2] Sir Henry Maitland Wilson, General Officer Commanding-in-Chief, Egypt.
[3] Winston S. Churchill, *The Second World War*, Volume 2, London 1949, pages 479–80.
[4] *The Memoirs of General the Lord Ismay*, London 1960, page 195.

the offensive against the enemy, and always have to wait for some new blow which he will strike against us.' But Britain's munitions production would eventually give the strength needed for the offensive. It would be 'a long and arduous road' to travel, he warned, and yet, he declared, 'I do not doubt that we shall succeed.'[1]

After his Mansion House speech Churchill went, for the first time, to his weekend retreat at Ditchley, north of Oxford.[2] Here, as the guest of Ronald Tree and his wife Nancy, at their beautiful and secluded house, Churchill was to spend many of the weekends when the moon was full, and Chequers thought to be most vulnerable to a German air raid. While he was at Ditchley, Churchill was sent some inquiries about the defence of Chequers, replying to Sinclair that the carriage drive there was being turfed to make it less visible from the air. In answer to Sinclair's suggestion that he should be protected while at Chequers by Bofors anti-aircraft guns, Churchill wrote: 'This is also desirable, but I cannot bear to divert Bofors from the fighting positions. What about trying a few rockets, which are at present only in an experimental stage?' Churchill noted: 'I am trying to vary my movements a little during the moonlight intervals,' and he added: 'It is very good of you and your Ministry to concern yourselves with my safety.'[3]

During Churchill's stay at Ditchley, he and Eden discussed Wavell's plans for the offensive. After their discussion Churchill telegraphed direct to Wavell to tell him that Eden 'has given me full account of your plans and projects'. Churchill added: 'We here fully appreciate limitations placed on your actions by many calls upon you. You may, however, be assured that you will have our full support at all times in any offensive action you may be able to take against the enemy.' Whether the outcome would be 'well or ill', Churchill promised, 'we will sustain you in any well considered operation you may launch against the enemy'.[4]

While Churchill was still at Ditchley, news came that Neville Chamberlain had died. Churchill wrote at once to his widow, Anne:

[1] *The Times*, 10 November 1940.

[2] The other guests at Ditchley included Lothian, Bracken, Eden, Lindemann, Clementine and Mary Churchill, and that weekend's duty Private Secretary, Eric Seal. (Ditchley Visitors Book.)

[3] Prime Minister's Personal Minute, M.292, 10 November 1940: Cabinet papers, 120/13. Four months later Churchill agreed that Bofors guns could be sent 'to any house' at which he might be staying for the weekend. (Ismay to Sir Frederick Pile, 'Secret & Personal', 28 March 1941: Cabinet papers, 120/13.)

[4] Telegram No. 88500, 11 November 1940: Premier papers, 3/288/1, folios 38–9. This telegram, in draft, is in Eden's handwriting, on Ditchley Park writing paper.

My dear Mrs Neville,

I heard the news of Neville's death and your grievous loss with deep sorrow.

During these long violent months of war we had come closer together than at any time in our twenty years of friendly relationship amid the ups and downs of politics. I greatly admired his fortitude and firmness of spirit. I felt when I served under him that he would never give in: and I knew when our positions were reversed that I could count upon the aid of a loyal and unflinching comrade.

I feel keenly for you in your grief, for I know what you were to one another, and I offer respectfully my most profound sympathy.[1]

'Neville shared your sense of comradeship,' Anne Chamberlain replied, '& felt secure in the knowledge that you too would never give in.'[2]

Churchill returned to London from Ditchley on November 11. While he was having his afternoon sleep at Downing Street, he had to be wakened on account of a German air raid. Going to the shelter, he again went to bed. But once more he was disturbed, as Colville noted, 'by the shriek of bombs nearby'. Colville added: 'He soon got tired of the shelter and returned to his room.'[3]

The loss of Neville Chamberlain, Churchill told the War Cabinet that evening, 'would be felt most deeply by all those who had worked with him'. They had all admired the 'great courage' he had shown in continuing work for a fortnight 'in failing health, after his severe operation'. Perhaps, Churchill said, Chamberlain's 'great grief' in leaving life had been 'that he had not lived to see the end of the struggle in which we were engaged. But maybe he had lived long enough to feel confident as to the outcome.'[4]

That night news reached Downing Street that more German raiders than usual had been shot down, as well as eight Italian pilots. 'The Prime Minister gave a whoop of joy when I told him,' Colville wrote.[5] Also on November 11, British naval air forces struck at the Italian fleet at Taranto: three of Italy's six battleships, including the new *Littorio*, were torpedoed from the air, and half the remaining ships put out of action for six months, a triumph aided by photographic reconnaissance carried out by a squadron of Glenn Martin reconnaissance aircraft newly arrived in Malta from the United States.[6]

---

[1] Letter of 10 November 1940: Churchill papers, 2/393.

[2] Letter of 12 November 1940: Churchill papers, 2/393.

[3] Colville diary, 11 November 1940: Colville papers.

[4] War Cabinet No. 286 of 1940, 11 November 1940, 5.30 p.m.: Cabinet papers, 65/10.

[5] Colville diary, 11 November 1940: Colville papers.

[6] 'Notes on Action at Taranto for President Roosevelt' (prepared by Admiral Phillips for Churchill), 16 November 1940: Premier papers, 3/468, folio 23.

At 9.30 that same evening, at a meeting of the Defence Committee, Churchill and his advisers discussed the reluctance of the Middle East commanders to provide the aid for Greece which London had requested. It was 'only natural', said Churchill, that they should feel they were being 'unduly weakened'.[1] The lack of war supplies was felt throughout the Services; on the previous day Colville had noted in his diary Churchill's comment: 'We are still paying for our failure to rearm in good time'.[2]

Churchill's criticisms of Chamberlain's pre-war conduct of affairs were based upon more than the memory of pre-war conflicts. From the moment war had begun, Churchill had seen from the vantage point of a War Cabinet Minister just how short Britain was of essential war materials, especially for the Army and Air Force. The first six months of his own Premiership had in part been dominated by the struggle to make good those shortages. But now, as he prepared his public oration on Chamberlain, Churchill brooded over deeper issues than those of policy and performance.

Late in the evening of November 11, after the Defence Committee, Churchill had gone to the underground War Rooms. 'He was so tired,' Mrs Hill later recalled. 'He said "I *must* have ten minutes sleep." He flung himself on the bed.' Ten minutes later Churchill was up, dictating his tribute. As Mrs Hill, who took the dictation, later recalled: 'Then he showed it to Mrs Churchill. She said, "It is very good." "Well," he replied with a twinkle in his eye, "of course I could have done it the other way round." '[3]

Eric Seal had already gone to bed before dictation took place. 'Fetch the Seal from his ice floe,' Churchill asked, 'and let him read this.' Seal later commented: 'He was proud of it and with good reason. There is not an unjust or unkind word, nor the slightest attempt at dissimulation.'[4]

As Churchill spoke—about Chamberlain—not in the House of Commons but in Church House, to which MPs had moved for safety in case the Chamber were struck by German bombs, his words were dignified, grave and moving. The 'fierce and bitter controversies', he began, 'which hung around him in recent times, were hushed by the news of his illness, and are silenced by his death'. In paying tribute, no one

---

[1] Defence Committee (Operations) No. 41 of 1940, 11 November 1940, 9.30 p.m.: Cabinet papers, 69/1.
[2] Colville diary, 10 November 1940: Colville papers.
[3] Kathleen Hill, conversation with the author, 15 October 1982.
[4] Sir Eric Seal, typescript 'The Unifying Theme', folio 235.

was obliged 'to alter the opinions he has formed or expressed upon issues which have become a part of history'. But, he added:

... at the Lychgate we may all pass our own conduct and our own judgements under a searching review. It is not given to human beings, happily for them, for otherwise life would be intolerable, to foresee or to predict to any large extent the unfolding course of events. In one phase men seem to have been right, in another they seem to have been wrong. Then again, a few years later, when the perspective of time has lengthened, all stands in a different setting. There is a new proportion. There is another scale of values. History with its flickering lamp stumbles along the trail of the past, trying to reconstruct its scenes, to revive its echoes, and kindle with pale gleams the passion of former days. What is the worth of all this? The only guide to a man is his conscience; the only shield to his memory is the rectitude and sincerity of his actions. It is very imprudent to walk through life without this shield, because we are so often mocked by the failure of our hopes, and the upsetting of our calculations; but with this shield, however the fates may play, we march always in the ranks of honour.

Churchill's tribute continued:

It fell to Neville Chamberlain in one of the supreme crises of the world to be contradicted by events, to be disappointed in his hopes, and to be deceived and cheated by a wicked man. But what were these hopes in which he was disappointed? What were these wishes in which he was frustrated? What was that faith that was abused? They were surely among the most noble and benevolent instincts of the human heart—the love of peace, the toil for peace, the strife for peace, the pursuit of peace, even at great peril and certainly to the utter disdain of popularity or clamour.

Whatever else history may or may not say about these terrible, tremendous years, we can be sure that Neville Chamberlain acted with perfect sincerity according to his lights and strove to the utmost of his capacity and authority, which were powerful, to save the world from the awful, devastating struggle in which we are now engaged.

Churchill went on to note that Hitler 'protests with frantic words and gestures that he has only desired peace', and he went on to ask: 'What do these ravings and outpourings count before the silence of Neville Chamberlain's tomb?'[1]

Throughout the first and second weeks of November, appeals had been reaching London from Greece, for substantial military aid against the Italian forces threatening Greece from Albania. 'Long lists of

[1] *Hansard*, 12 November 1940, columns 1617-19.

demands are coming in by telegram,' Bridges had told Churchill on November 7, and at Bridges' suggestion, supported by Ismay, Lord Hankey was put in charge of making sure that the questions of supplies to Greece moved forward 'without delays', with matters for decision being brought before the Defence Committee or the War Cabinet. 'So proceed,' Churchill noted,[1] and on November 9 Dill arranged for fifty anti-tank rifles with 5,000 rounds of ammunition, and 20,000 American rifles with five million rounds of ammunition to be shipped to Greece on a special Mediterranean convoy.[2]

Churchill sent this information to Hankey, to whom he wrote on November 12: 'I am awaiting your proposals for assisting Greece with munitions. When you have made up the best packet you can, let me know, but not later than Friday next, so that I can then take up the question of transportation with the Admiralty.'[3]

During November 12 the Chiefs of Staff suggested that, although the Greeks were 'in hopes' of receiving military supplies from the United States, the Russians 'might be prepared to sell equipment to Greece'. Soviet arms would, at least, arrive in Greece 'very much quicker'.[4] But this was no substitute for the aid which the Greeks had requested from Britain. Also on November 12 the War Office telegraphed to the British Military Mission in Athens a list of British Military supplies available for despatch. Many of the Greek requirements could not be met.[5] Lindemann wrote to Churchill: 'The munitions which it is proposed to send to Greece seem very meagre. Briefly we seem only ready to spare about 1% of the totals we have available here, if indeed we are ready to send anything.' The 8 anti-tank guns to be sent were 'out of our total of 1,100 in this country'; the 12 Bofors guns were out of 700 in England 'with a monthly output of 100'.[6]

---

[1] Bridges' minute and Churchill's note, 7 November 1940: Premier papers, 3/214, folios 133–4.

[2] 'Most Secret', 9 November 1940: Premier papers, 3/214, folio 131.

[3] Prime Minister's Personal Minute, M.296, 12 November 1940: Premier papers, 3/214, folio 128.

[4] Chiefs of Staff Committee No. 386, 12 November 1940, 10.30 a.m.: Cabinet papers, 79/7.

[5] No anti-tank guns could be provided 'until deliveries from the United States of America begin to come forward'. Of the three-ton lorries required, only 200 could be supplied; the rest would have to be bought in the United States through Purvis and the British Purchasing Commission. No motorcycles with side-cars were available. No binoculars were available. No pistols were available. Only 8 anti-aircraft guns and 12 Bofors guns could be sent. Of the 100,000 field dressings requested, only 20,000 could be supplied at once, a further 40,000 in December and the remaining 40,000 in January 1941. Other items could be sent more readily, including 2,000,000 sand bags from the Middle East, 12,000 sets of hospital clothing, 100 field telephones, 100 motor ambulances, 100,000 pairs of boots, 40 tons of gelignite, 50,000 fuses a month for making Molotov Cocktails, 5 torpedoes every fortnight, 1,000 machine guns, 1,000 automatic rifles, and 100,000 hand grenades a month. (Telegram No. 884 to Athens, 4 p.m., 12 November 1940: Premier papers, 3/214, folios 122–4).

[6] Minute of 20 November 1940: Premier papers, 3/214, folios 112–13.

Churchill had Lindemann's criticisms retyped, and sent under his own initials to Hankey and Ismay.[1] He also studied a proposal from Hankey to send the Greeks an oil device to help supplement the lack of anti-tank weapons: oil, barrels and detonators were all available. If the War Office thought this advisable, Churchill noted, 'I approve.' But, he added, 'shipping space *through* the Meditn is precious'.[2]

As a result of Churchill having sent on Lindemann's criticisms, the Chiefs of Staff agreed to send Greece, in addition to the original list, 24 field guns and ammunition, 20 anti-tank rifles, 10 light tanks 'which are only used for training purposes but should be of value in Greece', 100 Vickers machine guns, 100 American trench mortars and ammunition, 16 heavy and 24 light anti-aircraft guns, and 20 Hurricane fighters. The fighters were already in Malta.[3]

Churchill accepted these increases, but added one cautionary note. 'I cannot approve the 20 Hurricanes going to Greece,' he minuted to Ismay. 'They are all needed to augment our own force in ME. They must be disembarked in Egypt.'[4] At the same time, the local inhabitants of each region must do their part. 'I hope to be assured,' Churchill minuted to Ismay on December 1, in a note about British air assistance for Crete, 'that many hundreds of Cretans are working at strengthening the defences and lengthening and improving the Aerodromes.'[5]

Churchill had to balance the needs of Greece and the needs of Egypt. As in this note about the Hurricanes going to Egypt and not to Greece, he accepted that there was a limit to how much could be taken away from Wavell and Longmore. Not everyone understood, however, just how minutely these conflicting needs were examined, or how closely involved were the War Cabinet, the Defence Committee and the Chiefs of Staff in every decision. On November 12 Churchill had read a telegram from the British Ambassador to Egypt, Sir Miles Lampson, describing the sending of British military supplies from Egypt to Greece as 'completely crazy'. Churchill replied:

Your private and personal telegram to Mr Eden was laid before me as soon as it had been decoded in the Foreign Office. You should not telegraph at Government expense such an expression as 'completely crazy' when applied

[1] Prime Minister's Personal Minute, M.329, 21 November 1940: Premier papers, 3/214, folio 110.

[2] Minute of 22 November 1940: Premier papers, 3/214, folio 107.

[3] Hollis to Churchill, 24 November 1940: Premier papers, 3/214, folios 93–5.

[4] Minute of 25 November 1940: Premier papers, 3/214, folio 95.

[5] Prime Minister's Personal Minute, D.132, 1 December 1940: Premier papers, 3/205, folio 30. British air support sent to Crete included troops, anti-aircraft guns and radar sets.

by you to grave decisions of policy taken by the Defence Committee and the War Cabinet after considering an altogether wider range of requirements and assets than you can possibly be aware of.[1]

Churchill sent this telegram to the Foreign Office, to be despatched to Cairo. But Lord Halifax held it up, writing to Churchill on the following day that he would be 'much relieved' if the telegram were not sent. Lampson, he explained, had marked his original message to Eden 'Most Personal'. Only through an error was a copy sent to Churchill. It would, in these circumstances, be 'unfair', Halifax wrote, to penalise Lampson for a phrase 'used in the heat of the moment in what was a purely private message to someone who happens to be an old friend as well as a Minister. . . .'.[2]

Churchill was not convinced. 'Nothing,' he wrote on the bottom of Halifax's letter, 'cd be milder or more well merited than my rebuke,' and he added: 'I expect to be protected from this kind of insolence. I request that my telegram may be sent. Indeed I thought it would have gone by now.'[3] The telegram was despatched that day.

On the night of November 12, German bombers had again attacked London. During the raid Sloane Square underground station received a direct hit, and some thirty people were killed. There was little enough good news to compensate for the continuing air attacks, attacks on convoys, and the shortage of weaponry in the Middle East. When, on November 13, Churchill spoke of the naval victory at Taranto, his description of the action as 'this glorious episode'[4] was greeted by the House of Commons, as Colville noted, 'with enthusiastic cheers from an assembly hungry for something cheerful'.[5] As he entered the Chamber, Churchill had muttered, with a smile to Channon: 'We've got some sugar for the birds this time.' During question time, few had realized what was to come. 'Questions seemed interminable,' Channon noted, 'but finally Winston rose and gave the electrified House the wonderful Nelsonian news.'[6]

The victory over the Italians was a cause for considerable public rejoicing. But in private Churchill remained much troubled by the situation in Egypt. 'I am grieved,' he telegraphed on November 13 to Air Marshal Longmore in Cairo, 'that the imperative demands of the

[1] 12 November 1940: Churchill papers, 20/6.
[2] 13 November 1940: Churchill papers, 20/6.
[3] 14 November 1940: Churchill papers, 20/6.
[4] *Hansard*, 13 November 1940, column 1713.
[5] Colville diary, 13 November 1940: Colville papers.
[6] Channon diary, 13 November 1940: Robert Rhodes James (editor), *Chips, The Diaries of Sir Henry Channon*, London 1967, page 276.

Greek situation and its vital importance to the Middle East should have disturbed your arrangements at this exceptionally critical time.' Churchill had also been perturbed by the apparent unused surplus of British aircraft and personnel in the Middle East, as reported in the official returns, telling Longmore:

I was astonished to find that you have nearly 1,000 (one thousand) aircraft and 1,000 (one thousand) Pilots and 16,000 (sixteen thousand) Air Personnel in the Middle East excluding Kenya. I am most anxious to re-equip you with modern machines at the earliest moment; but surely out of all this establishment you ought to be able if the machines are forthcoming to produce a substantially larger number of modern aircraft operationally fit? Pray report through the Air Ministry any steps you may be able to take to obtain more fighting value from the immense mass of material and men under your Command.[1]

In reply, Longmore was able to put Churchill's mind at rest, explaining that the high figures which had been quoted in the official returns contained a large proportion of non-operational aircraft and ancillary personnel. 'Please rest assured,' he added, 'I will continue to operate all available aircraft of types which will contribute to further depression of Italians, whilst not providing their numerous and quite efficient fighters with too easy prey.'

Longmore's main worry, he explained, was that deliveries of aircraft to Egypt from the United States, the Curtis fighter and the Glenn Martin reconnaissance aircraft, had been delayed from their original November estimate, and 'will not begin to filter through until January'.[2]

These American supplies for Greece and the Middle East were only a small part of the total supplies Britain was seeking; indeed, the plans for a 55 division Army by the middle of 1942 depended for their completion on America's factories and arsenals. On November 7 Arthur Purvis had discussed these programmes with Roosevelt and Morgenthau. Three important points emerged. First, Roosevelt said that as far as conflicting British and American military needs were concerned, 'his rule of thumb' was to make available to the United Kingdom arms and munitions 'on a fifty fifty basis'.

[1] Telegram No. X.10, 13 November 1940: Premier papers, 3/309/1, No. 15.
[2] Telegram No. A.500, 15 November 1940: Premier papers, 3/309/1, No. 17. It was the Glenn Martins based on Malta which had already, on 11 November 1940, been of decisive importance in the Battle of Taranto.

Roosevelt's second point was the growing danger of the German U-boat sinkings of British merchant ships, a problem regarding which, Purvis noted, 'he is obviously anxious'.[1] Roosevelt then 'indicated', as Purvis reported to London, 'that United States might have to make a major effort in this field. In subsequent discussion this was crystallized into a possible United States effort (a) to re-condition 70 last war boats now laid up. (b) to build some 300 new merchant vessels.'

Roosevelt's third point was the most important, novel and far-reaching of all. It concerned the method by which Britain might pay for this swelling stream of production. The problem of Britain's 'dollar resources', he told Purvis, was 'some six months off'. Nevertheless, his solution as far as any American shipping effort was concerned would be, as Purvis telegraphed, 'to build such ships and rent them to the United Kingdom with the understanding that insurance would be carried by the United Kingdom. He indicated that this system might be extended to cover certain other similar items.'[2]

To build, and to rent: in this concept was borne the solution eventually adopted, Lend-Lease. But the crisis in payment was to come sooner than Roosevelt had imagined, as Britain's needs grew with every week of war.

The Germans had failed to destroy Britain's fighter force, or to weaken significantly British aircraft production. The fighter pilots, and their Commander, Sir Hugh Dowding, had won the Battle of Britain. They had been aided considerably by radar, and at times by German radio signals, in less secure codes than Enigma, but which nevertheless revealed, sometimes sufficiently in advance to act upon them, the precise German targets. But these signals had been no more than a bonus. The victory was that of Fighter Command, aided at all stages by their radar devices, and the personnel so recently trained in radar techniques.

At the same time, the strain on Dowding had been formidable, and it was decided, by the Secretary of State for Air and his senior advisers

---

[1] During October, 63 British merchant ships had been sunk (with a total weight of 301,892 tons), including the 42,000 ton *Empress of Britain*, bombed and machine gunned by a German Focke Wolfe while returning from the Middle East with 643 passengers (including 150 naval and military personnel). Fifty of the passengers had been killed.

[2] 'Pursa' No. 218, 'Most Immediate', 'Most Secret', sent 9.47 p.m., 10 November 1940, received 5.35 a.m., 11 November 1940 (advance copies to Churchill, Eden, Sir Andrew Duncan, Bridges and Kingsley Wood): Cabinet papers, 115/83.

on the Air Staff, that Dowding must go.[1] Churchill accepted this advice, and Dowding was offered a post as head of a mission to the United States. Dowding was reluctant to accept. But on the morning of November 14 Churchill explained to him 'the importance of getting American war aviation developed on the right lines'. Dowding expressed 'great doubts' as to his ability to fulfil the mission, but, Churchill told Sinclair, 'on my telling him I wished him to undertake it in the public interest, of which I was the judge, he accepted the task, subject to the condition that, if he wrote to me saying he was not getting on with it over there, he should be allowed to go home'.

'Personally,' Churchill told Sinclair, 'I think he will perform the task very well,' and he added: 'I have a very great regard for this Officer, and admiration for his qualities and achievements.'[2]

At noon on November 14 Churchill was at Westminster Abbey for Neville Chamberlain's funeral. The windows of the Abbey had been shattered by bomb blast. Churchill was among the pall bearers. The Service had been kept secret, announced to the House of Commons two days earlier at a secret session. 'There had been some uneasiness,' Henry Channon noted, 'lest the Germans would stage a raid and get Winston and the entire Government with one bomb.' Channon added: 'There in the Abbey, and it angered me to see them, were all the little men who had torpedoed poor Neville's heroic efforts to preserve peace, and made his life a misery: some seemed to be gloating. Winston, followed by the War Cabinet, however, had the decency to cry as he stood by the coffin. . . .'[3]

Immediately after Chamberlain's funeral, Churchill returned to Downing Street, where, at a meeting of the Defence Committee, the discussion centred on the possibility of an offensive against Italy in North Africa. Churchill urged that 'limitations of shipping' must not be allowed 'to interfere with the urgent military necessity' of concentrating such forces as were needed, even if sacrifices had to be made, as the Minister of Shipping warned, 'in our imports of food and other

[1] On 6 November 1940 Sir Reginald Clarry, having chaired a meeting of the Executive of the 1922 Conservative Private Members Committee, wrote to Churchill: 'I was requested to represent to you the lack of confidence in which Sir Hugh Dowding is held in certain quarters of the personnel of the Force, and the grave concern felt by my Executive.' (Letter of 6 November 1940: Premier papers, 4/3/6, folio 216.)

[2] Prime Minister's Personal Minute, M.305, 14 November 1940: Premier papers, 3/466, folio 21.

[3] Channon diary, 14 November 1940: Robert Rhodes James, *Chips, The Diaries of Sir Henry Channon*, London 1967, page 276. Colville, who was also present, wrote in his diary: 'I noticed the look of disdain in Duff Cooper's face, the boredom of Bevin.' (Colville diary, 14 November 1940: Colville papers.)

commodities'.[1] Then, in a telegram to Wavell, Churchill pointed out that, with Italy's check on the Greek front, the British naval success at Taranto, the 'poor showing' made by Italian airmen over Britain, and 'above all the general political situation', it had become 'very desirable' to undertake operation Compass, of which Wavell himself had spoken to Eden. 'It is unlikely,' Churchill added, 'that Germany will leave her flagging ally unsupported indefinitely. Consequently it seems that now is the time to take risks and strike the Italians by land, sea and air.'[2]

At the end of November, Churchill was in dispute with Wavell over Palestine. Earlier that month, 1,771 Jewish refugees reached Palestine from Europe on two ships the *Milos* and the *Pacific*. As 'illegal' immigrants they were at once transferred by the British authorities to a French liner, the *Patria*, for deportation to the Indian Ocean island of Mauritius. While the *Patria* was still in Haifa Bay, explosives, by which the Haganah[3] hoped to immobilize the ship, blew it up more forcefully than intended, and within fifteen minutes of the explosion the *Patria* had sunk. More than two hundred and fifty of the refugees on board were drowned.

In the view of the scale of the tragedy, the British Government announced that the surviving 'illegals' on board the *Patria* would not be deported, but allowed to stay in Palestine. Wavell at once protested, in a telegram to Eden, that such a decision would be disastrous 'from the military point of view', particularly, Wavell warned, on Arab opinion in Syria, Egypt and Iraq; so much so that he did not feel he could now open the strategically vital Basra-Baghdad-Haifa road, as he had earlier recommended.[4] It was Churchill himself who replied to Wavell:

Secretary of State has shown me your telegram about Patria. Cabinet feel that, in view of the suffering of the immigrants, and perils to which they had been subjected through the sinking of their ship, that it would be necessary on compassionate grounds not to subject them again immediately to the hazards of the sea.

Personally, I hold it would be an act of inhumanity unworthy of British name to force them to re-embark. On the other hand Cabinet agreed that

---

[1] Defence Committee (Operations) No. 43 of 1940, 14 November 1940, 12.45 p.m.: Cabinet papers, 69/1. The Minister of Shipping was R. H. Cross. In his diary that day, Colville noted that Cross had been invited to lunch after the Defence Committee and that 'Winston rushed over to me. "What is the name of the Minister off Shipping?" "Cross". "What is his Christian name?"' (Colville diary, 14 November 1940.) His Christian name was Ronald; he had been Conservative MP for Rossendale since 1931, and a Government Whip from 1935 to 1937.

[2] Telegram No 88842, 14 November 1940: Premier papers, 3/288/1, folio 28.

[3] The defence force of the Jewish Agency for Palestine.

[4] Cairo Telegram No. 0/27581 of 26 November 1940: Premier papers, 4/51/2.

future consignments of illegal immigrants should be sent to Mauritius provided that tolerable conditions can be arranged for them there.

Churchill's telegram continued:

I wonder whether the effect on the Arab world will be as bad as you suggest. If their attachment to our cause is so slender as to be determined by a mere act of charity of this kind it is clear that our policy of conciliating them has not borne much fruit so far. What I think would influence them much more would be any kind of British military success. I therefore suggest that you should reconsider your statement about Basra-Baghdad-Haifa road when we see which way the compass points.

I am sorry you should be worrying yourself with such matters at this particular time and I hope at least you will believe that the views I have just expressed are not dictated by fear of violence.[1]

Churchill's telegram was decisive, and Wavell withdrew his protest. The *Patria* deportees were allowed to remain in Palestine, first in an internment camp, and within a year at liberty. Nor was Churchill's judgement of the effect of this decision at fault; on December 14 a military Intelligence report concluded that the effect on Arab opinion of letting the *Patria* refugees remain in Palestine had been 'remarkably small'.[2]

[1] Telegraam of 2 December 1940: Premier papers, 4/51/2.
[2] Military Intelligence Report, 14 December 1940: Colonial Office papers, 733/430. (I am grateful to Dr Ronald W. Zweig for this reference).

47

Coventry, 'Compass' and the United States

FOLLOWING the Defence Committee of November 14, Churchill lunched with the Minister of Shipping and others at Downing Street. Then, accompanied by John Martin, he set off by car for his second weekend at Ditchley Park. 'As the cars were about to leave from the garden gate,' Martin later wrote, 'I handed him a top secret message which had just been received.' Martin knew nothing of the contents of the message he had just given to Churchill. A few minutes after the car had set off, Churchill began reading it. 'We had then reached Kensington Gardens,' Martin wrote, 'and he immediately told his driver to return to Downing Street.'

On their return, Churchill explained to Martin 'that the German "beam" indicated the prospect of a heavy raid on London and that he was not going to spend the night peacefully in the country while the metropolis was under heavy attack'.[1]

This operation, Colville noted in his diary that night, 'is known from the contents of those mysterious buff boxes which the PM alone opens, sent every day by Brigadier Menzies'. Of that particular night's raid, Colville added: 'its exact destination the Air Ministry say they find it difficult to determine'.

Churchill, and those who received the Enigma decrypts, had been told two days before, on November 12, that a major German bombing attack was in the offing. Even its code name had been read in the decrypts: 'Moonlight Sonata'. It would be an operation 'of very considerable dimensions', Air Intelligence reported. As they intercepted it on November 12, several different target areas seemed to have been

[1] Sir John Martin, letter to *The Times* of 26 August 1976, published in *The Times* on 28 August 1976.

mentioned as possibilities in the intercepted German signals instructions. On November 12 these were interpreted by Air Intelligence as being either central London, Greater London, the Thames Valley, Kent or the Essex coast.[1]

Other Intelligence information, derived from a German pilot who had been shot down on November 9, suggested that Coventry and Birmingham would be the towns attacked in 'a colossal' raid between the full moon night of November 15 and November 20, and that 'every bomber' would be engaged. This information was sent to the Director of Air Intelligence on November 12, but with a note that the senior Air Intelligence Liaison Officer at Bletchley, Squadron Leader Humphreys, 'has pretty definite information that the attack is to be against London and the Home Counties', probably in retaliation for a recent British bombing raid on Munich. Thus the captured pilot's information as to Coventry and Birmingham being the objectives should be regarded as 'doubtful', as probably Humphreys' information was 'later'.[2]

The Air Staff had sent Churchill its own summary of these reports later on the morning of November 14, while Churchill was at Chamberlain's funeral, telling him that the date of 'Moonlight Sonata' was still not known, but that counter-measures, code name 'Cold Water', had been prepared early that morning, and that the target area would be 'probably in the vicinity of London'. If, however, they added, 'further information' were to indicate 'Coventry, Birmingham or elsewhere', it was hoped that instructions for counter-measures could be got out in time.

The first indication that 'Moonlight Sonata' would be carried out that night came from intercepted German messages at one o'clock that same afternoon, while Churchill was at the Defence Committee. An executive order to implement the 'Cold Water' counter-measures was issued at once. But still the target was not known. It was only at about three o'clock, as Churchill was preparing to leave for Ditchley, that it was learned by Air Ministry Intelligence that the radio beams for the raid were intersecting over Coventry. All Royal Air Force Commands were at once informed, as were the Home Security and Home Forces chiefs.

It was as he opened his buff box in the car as it sped past Kensington Gardens, that Churchill had read one of the messages about the night's attack, and ordered his car to turn back to Downing Street, determined not to be out of the capital, if he could help it, during a serious air bombardment. It is probable that the message he read was the first

[1] AI 1(w), Memorandum to Directorate of Home Operations, 12 November 1940: Air Ministry papers, 2/5238.

[2] AI 1(k), Memorandum to Director of Air Intelligence, 12 November 1940: Air Ministry papers, 2/5238.

one, stating merely that the 'Moonlight Sonata' attack would be that night, and not the second message, that Coventry would be the target. Those who had been alerted to the actual target, Coventry, hurried to protect the city as best they could, directed to do so by the order to carry out the 'Cold Water' measures. No thought of protecting the source of the knowledge of the target inhibited these defensive measures.

Back at Downing Street, Churchill awaited what for him seems to have been the expected attack on London. As he waited, he sent two of his duty Private Secretaries, John Colville and John Peck, to the Down Street underground shelter with the words: 'You are too young to die.' In his diary, Colville recorded that Churchill then went to the Central War Room, but 'became so impatient that he spent most of the time on the Air Ministry roof waiting for the Moonlight Sonata to begin'.[1]

At 7.20 that night, while Churchill scanned, with Ismay, the empty skies above London, three hundred German bombers struck at Coventry. In an attempt to lessen the magnitude of the attack, the Air Staff, alerted three and a half hours earlier, by the identification of the beams, had sent eight British bombers 'to attack the enemy aerodromes from which the bombers had been expected to take off'. From this counter-measure, Portal told the War Cabinet on the following morning, 'fairly good results had been obtained', while in addition, 'also thanks to the beams' warning, 'a continuous fighter patrol had been maintained over Coventry itself'. But only one 'inconclusive' engagement had taken place between the British and German attackers.

Coventry had been massively bombed, 'the heaviest raid yet experienced, on a munition centre', Sir John Anderson told the same War Cabinet.[2] Yet the ground defences, alerted by the warning, had, as the Chiefs of Staff later noted, kept the attacking aircraft 'very high', the fire-density of the anti-aircraft barrage 'being greater than any put up on any one night by the London defences'. Nevertheless, fires started in the centre of the city by incendiary bombs had illuminated the target for the attack by high explosive bombs and parachute mines.[3]

Coventry had already been a target for German air raids.[4] Indeed,

[1] Colville diary, 14 November 1940: Colville papers. Sir John Martin writes: 'it might confirm Churchill's expectation of a raid on London to mention that he gave instructions for the women members of staff to be sent home'. (Letter to the author, 24 February 1983.)
[2] War Cabinet No. 289 of 1940, 15 November 1940: Cabinet papers, 65/10.
[3] 'Secret', War Cabinet, Chiefs of Staff Committee, Weekly Résumé No. 64, 21 November 1940: Churchill papers, 23/80.
[4] On 8 November 1940 a Chiefs of Staff paper (No. 922 of 1940) entitled 'Defence of the City of Coventry' had noted that between October 1 and November 8 there had been 73 German air raids on London, 29 on Dover, 18 on Eastbourne and Brighton, 16 on Coventry and 13 on

as a result of the personal complaint by Ernest Bevin to Churchill on November 7 as to 'the undefended state of the town' before a previous raid on November 2, Churchill had referred this 'very difficult, urgent and serious matter' to the Vice-Chiefs of Staff, with the result that instructions had been given to strengthen Coventry's anti-aircraft defences and preparations.[1] These instructions had been carried out by the morning of November 14. Although they could mitigate, they could not avert the scale of the destruction that night. Indeed, Sir Archibald Sinclair was furious at the episode, writing to Churchill on the following day: 'The result of last night's battle was thoroughly unsatisfactory. 300 German aircraft converged upon a previously known target. Round that target were five times as many guns per head of population as there are around London. 100 British fighters were airborne. Yet the only German casualty is claimed neither by the fighters nor by the guns.'[2]

The British casualties at Coventry were on a major scale, with 507 civilians killed and more than 420 seriously injured.[3] In the days that followed, other targets were struck with similar ferocity, and by the following weekend 484 civilians had been killed in London, and 228 in Birmingham. As well as the destruction of Coventry Cathedral during the raid of November 14, other buildings hit during the following week included seven London hospitals, while more than twenty soldiers were killed by a parachute mine at Theydon Bois.[4]

Ten months after the raid on Coventry, Herbert Morrison, then Home Secretary, opposed raising the status of the Mayors of Coventry, Swansea and Southampton to that of Lord Mayors. 'I am sorry to see your negative minute of October 1,' Churchill replied. 'It is during the

---

Liverpool, with 5,090 killed in London in that same period, and 545 killed in the Birmingham–Coventry area. The paper also reported: 'The morale of the workers in Coventry has unquestionably deteriorated as a result of enemy air attacks. War production has attracted a large population from other parts of the country. These people naturally are not imbued with the same civic patriotism, and consequently do not have the same anchors, as the long-established inhabitants of other provincial towns or of London. Coventry moreover is a small town and the effect of bombing is therefore more concentrated than in the case of large towns.' (Premier papers, 3/108, folios 39–43.)

[1] Bevin to Churchill, 'Urgent', 7 November 1940: Premier papers, 3/108, folios 47–8; Churchill to Ismay for Chiefs of Staff Committee, 'Action this Day', Prime Minister's Personal Minute, D.114, 8 November 1940: Premier papers, 3/108, folio 45.

[2] Sinclair to Churchill, 'Personal and Secret', 15 November 1940: Premier papers, 3/22/3, folio 199.

[3] J. H. Peck Minute, 26 November 1940: Premier papers, 3/108, folio 9.

[4] 'Secret', War Cabinet, Chiefs of Staff Committee, Weekly Résumé No. 64, 21 November 1940: Churchill papers, 23/8.

war-time, while wounds are fresh, that these compliments are valued. All these three towns, Coventry, Southampton and Swansea, thoroughly deserve this honour. But Coventry, with the largest population and the origin of the German expression "Coventrated", certainly deserves it most.' 'I cannot see,' Churchill added, 'what harm would be done by the conferring of this distinction. You give me no reasons whatever in your minute. What harm could possibly result from these people having comfort and honour in their distress?'[1]

Churchill's concern for those under bombardment was again shown on November 12 when he minuted to the Home Secretary, Herbert Morrison: 'How are you getting on with the comfort of the shelters in the winter—flooring, drainage and the like? What is being done to bring them inside the houses?' Churchill added: 'I attach the greatest importance to gramophones and wireless in the shelters. How is that going forward? Would not this perhaps be a very good subject for the Lord Mayor's Fund?'[2]

The German Enigma used by the beam units continued to divulge its secret, and a major raid on Birmingham on November 19 was known sufficiently in advance to alert the anti-aircraft and fighter defences, as those on Coventry had been. The bombing was not a one-way traffic; more than a hundred British bombers had struck at Berlin on November 14, during which raid eleven bombers were lost. During a further raid on Hamburg on November 16, when cloud and severe icing prevented as accurate an attack on military targets as had been hoped, 233 German civilians were killed.

[1] Prime Minister's Personal Minute, M.972/1, 6 October 1941: Churchill papers, 20/36. Reading the Home Office note of November 1940, against a Lord Mayor for Coventry, Churchill minuted: 'This note achieves its negative purpose by breaking down successively every separate argument in favour of the honour. Antiquity is no guide. Population cannot be trusted. Air raid damage is novel and invidious. One might agree that each of these in itself could form no foundation. The case for Coventry is that all three come together in a peculiarly high degree. Coventry has been a city, as the Home Office note says, "from time immemorial". It has a population of 237,000, which places it well in the list of population claims. Finally it has suffered the most spectacular bombing and has been selected as the special victim of German malice. It is the conjunction of these three claims which gives Coventry its unique position at the present time. No other city can show the same combination, and there should be no difficulty in resisting other claims, if it were desired to do so.' Churchill added: 'I should myself have liked to see both Southampton and Swansea similarly honoured, but I feel that Coventry stands by itself.' (Prime Minister's Personal Minute, M.1020/1, 29 October 1941: Churchill papers, 20/36.) Coventry's Mayor did not become a Lord Mayor until the Coronation in May 1953, during Churchill's second Premiership.

[2] Prime Minister's Personal Minute, M.295, 12 November 1940: Churchill papers, 20/13.

Reading of the loss of the eleven British bombers on the night of November 14, Churchill minuted to Sinclair and Portal:

I said the other day by minute that the operations were not to be pressed unduly during these very adverse weather conditions. We cannot afford to have losses of this kind in view of your very low replacements. If you go on like this, you will break the Bomber Force down to below a minimum for grave emergencies. No results have been achieved which would in any way justify or compensate for these losses.

Churchill added: 'I consider the loss of 11 aircraft out of 130, i.e. about 8 per cent., a very grievous disaster at this stage of our Bomber development.'[1]

As Churchill studied reports of the damage done by these British air raids, he was not impressed. Two months later he told the Defence Committee that he was 'sceptical of these cut and dried calculations which showed infallibly how the war could be won' by bombing. 'In the early days of the war,' he continued, 'it had been said that if the Royal Air Force were allowed to launch an attack upon the Ruhr, they would, with preciseness and certitude, shatter the German industry. Careful calculations had been made to show that this could be done. After anxious thought, the attack was eventually made when the Germans invaded the Low Countries, but there had only been a fractional interruption of work in the industries of the Ruhr.'[2]

Intelligence reports during November 18 showed considerable Greek successes against the Italians. Working, as was now their habit, at the Annexe, Colville watched as Churchill put red ink circles around the names of the Greek towns in the reports, 'chortling when he thought of the discomfiture of the Italians'. That evening, Colville wrote, 'when I was desperately coping with the mountainous papers on my desk, the PM appeared, and bidding me bring a torch, he led me away to look at girders in the basement intended to support the building'. With 'astonishing agility', Colville added, 'he climbed over girders, balanced himself on their upturned edges, some five feet above the ground, leapt from one to the other without any sign of undue effort extraordinary in a man of almost sixty-six who never takes exercise of any sort'.[3]

[1] Prime Minister's Personal Minute, M.312, 15 November 1940: Cabinet papers, 120/300.
[2] Defence Committee (Operations) No. 4 of 1941, 9.30 p.m., 13 January 1941: Cabinet papers, 69/2.
[3] Colville diary, 18 November 1940: Colville papers.

That night, to the Prime Minister of New Zealand, who had expressed his concern at Parliamentary and Press criticisms of the conduct of the war, Churchill telegraphed: 'We dwell under a drizzle of carping criticism from a few members and from writers in certain organs of the Press. This has an irritating effect and would not be tolerated in any other country exposed to our present stresses. On the other hand, it is a good thing that any Government should be kept keen and made aware of any shortcomings in time to remedy them.' 'You must not suppose everything is perfect,' Churchill ended, 'but we are all trying our best, and the war effort is enormous and morale admirable.'[1]

One area of criticism had been voiced by the Conservative MP, Vyvyan Adams, who protested in Parliament that David Margesson, Chamberlain's Chief Whip at the time of 'Munich', was still Chief Whip under Churchill. When Vyvyan Adams wrote to Churchill direct to apologize for his criticisms, Churchill replied that the appointment of Margesson as Chief Whip was 'my unfettered decision', and he went on:

It has been my deliberate policy to try to rally all the forces for the life and death struggle in which we are plunged, and to let bygones be bygones. I am quite sure that Margesson will treat me with the loyalty he has given to my predecessors.

The fault alleged against him which tells the most is that he has done his duty only too well. I do not think there is anyone who could advise me better about all those elements in the Tory Party which were so hostile to us in recent years. I have to think of unity, and I need all the strength I can get.

Moreover I ought to tell you that even during the bitterest times I have always had very good personal relations with Margesson, and knowing what his duties were I never had any serious occasion to complain. Several times when I heard the Whips were putting stories about which were not true I spoke to him plainly and he stopped them. The Liberal and Labour Whips have the very highest opinion of his integrity and good faith in all House of Commons relations, and there is no doubt that he is the most efficient servant who could be found for these functions in a Three-Party Government.

Finally I may tell you in confidence that I have long had a very high opinion of Margesson's administrative and executive abilities, and that when I formed the new Government I offered him a Secretaryship of State. He declined this but offered in the frankest manner to go out altogether. I can assure you he has been a great help to me on many occasions since I became Prime Minister, and I am absolutely sure he will go on to the bitter end.[2]

On the morning of November 20 Churchill breakfasted in the Cabi-

[1] Telegram of 18 November 1940: Churchill papers, 20/14.
[2] 'Private and Confidential', 16 November 1940: Churchill papers, 20/3.

net room. Then, after showing, as Colville noted, 'great reluctance' to being photographed by Cecil Beaton, he welcomed Beaton and was photographed at the Cabinet table. Then he dictated a minute about financial help to Greece.[1] The minute, sent that day to the Chancellor of the Exchequer, read:

It seems most necessary that as we can hardly give any other help, financial assistance should be given to Greece in the manner most likely to help them. I do hope that this will not be an occasion for the Treasury to do one of their regular Departmental grimaces, which no doubt are very necessary in ordinary circumstances, but would be very much out of place now. I gathered that you were in full agreement with the Cabinet wish that the Greeks should have prompt, effectual and adequate financial assistance.

'Remember,' Churchill added, 'that we can only give them a handful of aeroplanes and no troops.'[2]

During November 20, Churchill gave sherry to those Ministers not in the War Cabinet, and their Junior Ministers, to discuss the forthcoming King's Speech. Among those present was Harold Nicolson, Parliamentary Secretary at the Ministry of Information, who had first entered Parliament in 1935, but whom Churchill had long known before then both as a diplomat and a writer. Nicolson noted in his diary:

He seems better in health than he has ever seemed. That pale and globular look about his cheeks has gone. He is more solid about the face and thinner. But there is something odd about his eyes. The lids are not in the least weary, nor are there any pouches or black lines. But the eyes themselves are glaucous, vigilant, angry, combative, visionary and tragic. In a way they are the eyes of a man who is much preoccupied and is unable to rivet his attention on minor things (such as me).

'But in another sense,' Nicolson wrote, 'they are the eyes of a man

---

[1] Colville diary, 20 November 1940: Colville papers.

[2] Prime Minister's Personal Minute, M.325, 20 November 1940: Premier papers, 3/207, folio 9. At the Chiefs of Staff Committee three days later, at which Pound, Dill, Portal and Phillips were present, as well as Major General G. N. Macready, Assistant Chief of the Imperial General Staff, it was recommended that the Greeks should be sent 100 Vickers machine guns, 100 American Stokes Mortars, 24 Bofors guns (without predictors or personnel), 24 75-millimetre Field Guns, 20 Hurricanes, 20 anti-tank rifles, 16 3.7 inch anti-aircraft guns and 10 British Light Tanks (Vickers). (Chiefs of Staff Committee No. 399 of 1940, 23 November 1940, 10.30 a.m.: Cabinet papers, 79/7.) Nine days later Churchill minuted: 'I did not approve the sending of Hurricanes to the Greek Air Force. They must be used for the rearmament of our own Air Force first'; and he added: 'Beware of sending them plans by aeroplanes which may fall into enemy hands.' (Prime Minister's Personal Minute, 'Action this Day', M.349, 29 November 1940: Churchill papers, 20/13).

faced by an ordeal or tragedy, and combining vision, truculence, resolution and great unhappiness.'[1]

In his speech at the opening of the new Parliamentary Session on
November 21, Churchill again spoke bluntly of the difficulties. 'We
have a long road to travel,' he said. He had never concealed from the
nation or the House of Commons 'the darker side of our dangers and
burdens', but, he said, 'it is there', and he added, 'I know that it is in
adversity that British qualities shine the brightest, and it is under these
extraordinary tests that the character of our slowly wrought institutions
reveals its latent, invincible strength.'

Up to the present, Churchill said, the war had been waged between
'a fully-armed Germany and a quarter- or half-armed British Empire'.
Even so, 'We have not done so badly,' and he looked forward with
confidence to a time 'when we ourselves shall be as well armed as our antagonists', and if need be beyond that, when 'the arsenals and training
grounds and science of the New World and of the British Empire' would
give Britain that material superiority which, 'added to the loyalty of
constant hearts, will surely bring victory and deliverance to mankind'.[2]

On the morning of November 22 Churchill received encouraging
news from the Balkans and the Middle East. On the Greek front, ten
Gladiators of the Australian Air Force had shot down five enemy fighters, on November 19. On the ground, despite 'intense enemy air activity' which made further advance impossible, the Greeks had captured
'large quantities of supplies', including 35 anti-tank guns with ammunition and 20 mountain guns. Over Germany, hits had been scored
and fires started at naval stores and marshalling yards in Berlin, at oil
plants in Hamburg, at the docks and shipyards in Kiel, and in the
Skoda armaments works at Pilsen.[3]

Elsewhere overseas, alerted by Samuel Hoare to the growing hunger
in Spain, Churchill telegraphed to Roosevelt to allow food in to Spain
in order to prevent a collapse of morale and with it a switch of loyalty
to Germany, 'An offer by you,' Churchill told Roosevelt, 'to dole out
food month by month, so long as they keep out of the war might be
decisive.' His telegram continued: 'Small things do not count now, and
this is a time for very plain talk to them. The occupation by Germany
of both sides of the Straits would be a grievous addition to our naval
strain already severe.' The Germans would soon have batteries working

---

[1] Nicolson diary, 20 November 1940: Nigel Nicolson (editor), *Harold Nicolson, Diaries and Letters,
1939–1945*, London 1967, pages 127–8.

[2] *Hansard*, 21 November 1940, columns 24–7.

[3] Cabinet War Room Record No. 445, to 7 a.m., 21 November 1940: Cabinet papers, 120/744.

by radar which would close the Straits 'both by night and day'. With a major campaign developing in the Eastern Mediterranean and the need 'to reinforce and supply our Armies there all round the Cape we could not contemplate any military action on the mainland Straits. The Rock of Gibraltar will stand a long siege, but what is the good of that if we cannot use the harbour or pass the Straits?' Once in Morocco the Germans would 'work south', and German submarines and aircraft would soon be operating 'freely' from Casablanca and Dakar. 'I need not, Mr President, enlarge upon the trouble this will cause to us,' Churchill added, 'or the approach of trouble to the Western Hemisphere.' Churchill's telegram ended: 'We must gain as much time as possible.'[1]

Churchill's other fear was based upon a reading of Enigma decrypts showing the build-up of German troop concentrations and other warlike preparations in Rumania and Bulgaria.[2] These preparations suggested a future German attack into Turkey. This would force Britain to defend the Suez canal from Palestine and the North. The timing of 'Compass'—Wavell's offensive into Libya—seemed urgent. 'A British victory in Libya,' Churchill minuted to Eden and Dill on November 22, would probably 'turn the scale' in Turkey's decision to come in to the war as Britain's ally. But Turkey would demand, as the price of coming in, 'immediate assistance in arms, men and ships'. After a victory over the Italians in Libya, Britain could 'shift our forces to the new theatre'. How long would it be, Churchill asked, before the Germans 'could strike at Greece through Bulgaria?' There might 'just be time', he added, 'for Wavell to act in Libya before the pressure becomes decisive'. Anyhow, Churchill ended, 'all his troops, except the barest defensive minimum, will be drawn out of him before long'.[3]

To Wavell, Churchill telegraphed setting out these same views, but with a caveat about the lack of Air Force cover which might make it impossible even to embark upon 'Compass'. Churchill's telegram to Wavell ended:

Importance of getting Turkey in and perhaps Jugoslavia would far outweigh any Libyan operation, and you would be relegated to the very minimum defensive role in Egypt. If, however, you could do Compass in the first fort-

---

[1] Telegram despatched 23 November 1940: Premier papers, 3/468, folios 26–7. 'If you think well,' Churchill minuted to Halifax on November 23, 'pray send off the attached message.'

[2] In particular, the Enigma decrypt CX/JQ 417 of 1 November 1940, confirming the German intention to install an aircraft warning system in Rumania and Bulgaria. (F. H. Hinsley and others, *British Intelligence in the Second World War: Its Influence on Strategy and Operations*, volume 1, London 1979, page 350.)

[3] Prime Minister's Personal Minute, M.330, 22 November 1940: Premier papers, 3/288/1, folios 33–4.

night of December a new and very important event would occur rendering more favourable alternatives possible. On the other hand, I do not wish to press you into precipitate action without the Air Force, which your judgement requires. We may be forced to abandon Compass altogether, or there may be time to work it in before other things develop. I must, however, know what you are going to do, and when it would happen.[1]

Wavell replied to Churchill at once, with assurances that the 'importance of Compass' was not only realized, but had already led to the decision to undertake the operation 'in spite of risks involved'. As to the possibility of landing troops and stores on the coast, which Churchill had urged, 'neither the Navy nor myself', Wavell reported, 'are very hopeful of results'. Conditions were not favourable 'to this form of action'. All the commanders concerned in the operation were however 'alive to necessity for fullest exploitation of any success and plans are being prepared'. Wavell added: 'We share your apprehension of German stroke through Bulgaria and need for support to Turkey which we have been considering for some time.'[2]

On Saturday November 23 Churchill was at Chequers, with Eric Seal as the duty Private Secretary. That night was a 'Naval night', with A. V. Alexander, Pound, Phillips and Fraser as the principal guests. After dinner, as Seal wrote to his wife, 'Alexander & Winston had a long & friendly discussion about socialism—the Prime Minister just scintillating on these occasions, & is full of fascinating sayings & anecdotes. All tremendous fun. But afterwards work went on until 2 am!'[3]

In the last week of November, Intelligence reports seemed to indicate an imminent German attack on Yugoslavia and Greece. To counter this, the Chiefs of Staff had suggested the immediate seizure of the Dodecanese; the Italian islands just off Turkey's south-western coast of which Rhodes, Leros and Kos were the largest. This operation, given

[1] Telegram No. 90494, 'Personal and Secret', 22 November 1940: Premier papers, 3/288/1, folios 35–6.
[2] Telegram No. 0/27661, 'Most Secret', 27 November 1940: Premier papers, 3/309/1, No. 25.
[3] Letter of Sunday 24 November 1940: Seal papers. In another letter Seal wrote of how the laughter in the 'Annexe' Mess 'must have penetrated to poor Winston, dining alone with his thoughts & Clemmie in the room below. Anyway, at 9.30 he was discovered, morose and unhappy, stalking up & down the passage, exclaiming that no one was looking after him, & that he had been deserted!! As he had only to send a marine up one flight of stairs to have anybody or anything he wanted this was a trifle hard; but later on he warmed up, & became quite happy again. He really is fond of congenial companions, & a fearful babe.' (Seal papers.)

the code name 'Mandibles', was supported by Halifax, who hoped that the islands 'may in one way or another be taken from the Italians in the early future'.[1] But Churchill deprecated such action 'for the present', telling Eden that not only would the capture of these islands be a 'big operation', but that Greece and Turkey 'would quarrel over the prize if we won it'.

The urgent need, Churchill told Eden, was to 'firm up' Turkey and Yugoslavia against the expected German attack. 'The impending fort-night,' he added, 'is momentous.'[2] But, writing to Dill immediately after Eden, Churchill queried the Intelligence reports on which the alarm had been based. 'I thought myself,' he wrote, 'that this estimate,' of five full German divisions assembled in Rumania, 'was altogether too pessimistic, and credited the enemy with a rapidity of movement and a degree of preparedness which were perhaps more serious than the facts.' Not a fortnight, but 'perhaps a month' might elapse, Chur-chill added, before 'anything serious' could happen on the Greek fron-tier, and his minute ended: 'The great thing is to get the true picture, whatever it is.'[3]

That night Churchill and Eden dined alone, 'champagne and oysters in his bedroom', Eden noted in his diary. The talk was of Wavell's impending offensive and, as Eden wrote:

I told him that if 'Compass' went reasonably well, we should need to deter-mine future dispositions, after discussion with C.-in-Cs. on the spot and Greeks and possibly Turks. We could not leave an army inactive in Africa. Should we reinforce Greeks, if so where, Salonica? And what could these men achieve? I suggested I should pay another visit. We must continue to hammer Italians, either in Africa, or Europe or both. Winston agreed generally. He felt that 'Compass' might influence attitude of all these countries.

This was 'true', Eden added, 'though one must not place the high hopes on "Compass", which is at present a limited operation'.[4]

[1] 'The Dodecanese', Memorandum by Lord Halifax, 'Secret', War Cabinet Paper No. 464 of 1940, 27 November 1940: Premier papers, 3/124/2, folio 49.

[2] 'Secret', Prime Minister's Personal Minute, M.341, 24 November 1940: Churchill papers, 20/13.

[3] Prime Minister's Personal Minute, M.342, 24 November 1940: Churchill papers, 20/13. Churchill's disbelief was justified by the Enigma decrypts, which first reached him from the Balkans in the last week of October 1940, following the arrival of a German Air Force Mission in Rumania. Throughout November the Mission's messages, sent through Enigma, dealt mainly with routine matters like weather reporting. But on 1 November 1940 one such message had confirmed the German intention to install an aircraft warning system in Rumania and Bulgaria (see page 909 n.2).

[4] Eden diary, 25 November 1940: The Earl of Avon, *The Eden Memoirs, The Reckoning*, London

One result of Churchill's talk with Eden was a telegram from Churchill to Wavell that 'risks inseparable from great deeds are fully justified', as the success of 'Compass' could affect the outcome of the whole war, with the attitude of Spain 'now trembling on the brink' and Italy 'in grievous straits'. From the tactical perspective, Churchill wished to be 'assured' that the possibility of following up success on land by 'long hops' along the coast by sea and the establishment of new supply bases, had been 'weighed, explored, and as far as possible prepared'. Whatever the result, Churchill told Wavell, 'we shall stand by you and Wilson[1] in any well-conceived action, irrespective of result, because no one can guarantee success in war, but only deserve it'.[2]

Churchill also sought to encourage Turkey 'to come into the war as soon as possible', and in a draft telegram to the British Ambassador in Turkey, approved by the Chiefs of Staff Committee on the evening of November 26, Churchill suggested warning the Turks that if they did not fight 'there and then' to stop German troops crossing Bulgaria on their way to Greece, Turkey would find herself 'absolutely alone, the Balkans will have been eaten up one by one, and it will be beyond our power to help her'. The Turks should also be told that by the summer of 1941 Britain hoped to have at least 15 divisions operating in the Middle East, and by the end of 1941, nearly 25. 'We do not doubt,' Churchill added, 'our ability to defeat Italy in Africa.'[3]

The possibility of a German attack on Greece, Turkey or even Spain, led Churchill to see a series of moves that might follow Wavell's success in North Africa. As he minuted to Ismay on November 26:

... it may be that once 'Compass' has been decisively successful, we shall be

---

1965, page 175. Two days later, the Chiefs of Staff (Pound, Dill and Portal) noted for Churchill that they had found 'considerable difficulty' in making a study of the exploitation of 'Compass', as Churchill wished, as Wavell 'has very rightly kept secret all the detailed information on which a study of this kind must be based', not informing them, for example, of 'the strength and disposition of the forces which are to be employed in the attack, nor the strength and location of the reserves'. In fact, the Chiefs of Staff added, 'we find ourselves in the position of a playwright who sets out to conceive the last scene of a drama without any precise knowledge of the opening acts'. (Premier papers, 3/288/1, folios 9–10.)

[1] General Sir Henry Maitland Wilson, General Officer Commanding-in-Chief, Egypt (or, as Churchill had expressed it, commander of the 'Army of the Nile' or 'Army of the Delta').

[2] Telegram No. 90494, 26 November 1940: Premier papers, 3/228/1, folios 29–30.

[3] 'Action this Day', Prime Minister's Personal Minute, M.344, 26 November 1940: Churchill papers, 20/14.

called upon to go to the aid of Greece or Turkey, and that the centre of
gravity will shift from Cairo to Constantinople, and that the Fleet will have
some elements in the Black Sea.

There is no need to decide which course will be best, or whether there will
not be time to come to a final decision in Libya before having to move into
Greece and Thrace, but both courses should be thoroughly explored, so that
our minds may be prepared for the decisions which may be required in the
near future.

A plan should also be made for landing a British Army of not less than 4
Divisions on the African shore of the Straits of Gibraltar, with a view to
occupying Ceuta and the defences of the Straits. . . .[1]

With such offensive plans in mind, Churchill was vexed to learn on
November 26 that a planned advance against Italian troops who had
crossed into Kenya was to be postponed until May or June 1941. 'The
proposal to keep the brigade and not to fight,' he minuted to Ismay, 'is
most depressing.'[2] That night, in the continuing bombing offensive
against Germany, British bombers struck at military targets in Cologne,
which they attacked again on November 27.[3] Another initiative
proposed by Churchill on November 27 was the bombing of Rumanian
oil fields 'from air bases in Greece',[4] while plans also went ahead, in
case of final approval of the Chiefs of Staff, for 'Workshop', a landing
on the Italian island of Pantelleria.

Learning through the distribution list of an Admiralty telegram[5] of
the widening number of people who had been told of 'Workshop',
Churchill minuted to A. V. Alexander, Pound and Ismay on November
25: 'it is terrifying to read the enormous list of people in the Admiralty
alone who must be told the actual name of the Island. I suppose it will
now be published to even wider circles throughout the three Services
in the Middle East. There was no necessity to have allowed the name
ever to have been breathed except to the highest authorities. Any Island

[1] Prime Minister's Personal Minute, D.128, 26 November 1940: Premier papers, 3/288/1, folios
12–13.

[2] 'Action this Day', Prime Minister's Personal Minute, M.343A, 26 November 1940: Churchill
papers, 20/14. On 2 December 1940, after a conference in Cairo, Wavell reported that postponing
until May or June the move to recapture Kismayu was essential, to avoid being caught by the
spring rains.

[3] German bombers had also struck several times at British cities, Birmingham being their target
on November 22, Southampton on November 23 and Bristol on both November 24 and November
26.

[4] War Cabinet No. 297 of 1940, 27 November 1940, Minute 1, 'Confidential Annex: Cabinet
papers, 65/16. On the same day, the Iron Guard in Rumania admitted the execution of 64
political figures, including the ex-Prime Minister, Professor Jorga. In London, the Rumanian
Minister, V. V. Tilea, resigned.

[5] Admiralty Telegram No. 507, sent to General Headquarters Middle East.

would have sufficed to explain the bulk of the preparations to subordinates concerned.'[1]

On November 25 Sir Arthur Salter noted that Churchill had 'on
several occasions' during the previous few weeks expressed his concern
regarding the number of British missions operating in the United States
on supply matters. The position of these missions, he had asked, should
be reviewed 'with the greatest urgency'.[2] To assist in this work, Arthur
Purvis was asked to come to Britain, and had reached London that
same day, November 25. Churchill saw Purvis on the morning of
November 27, writing to Eden on the following day: 'I had a long talk
with Purvis yesterday, and thought him very able and zealous. I think
you should have a talk with him . . .'.[3]

As a result of their talk, Churchill and Purvis established a common
ground for action. 'Some way must be found,' Purvis told Churchill,
'to dramatize our remaining requirements from the United States.'[4]
Churchill had been working for some weeks on a letter to Roosevelt in
this sense. 'I am still struggling with my letter to President,' he had
telegraphed to Lothian on November 26, 'but hope to cable it to you
in a few days.'[5] Churchill now showed Purvis his draft letter to Roosevelt, and asked Purvis to redraft it for him. 'As requested yesterday,'
Purvis wrote to Churchill on November 28, 'I have prepared the
attached preliminary re-draft of your letter to the President. I suggest
you bear in mind that the value of its wording is such that the President
can show it confidentially to Members of his Cabinet and possibly a
few other key people.' Churchill's suggestion in the original letter that
the United States should establish bases in Eire 'might give a handle',

---

[1] 'Action this Day', Prime Minister's Personal Minute, M.349, 29 November 1940: Churchill
papers, 20/13. On the same day, Churchill telegraphed to Wavell: 'Actual place of Operation
"Workshop" must be kept utterly secret. Even high Staff Officers should only be told it is for an
Operation on the Sicilian shore, and actual town in Sicily should never be mentioned. Alternatively, expedition might quite well go to Dodecanese, and if this leaked out it would not matter
much. Pray make sure that Admiralty telegram 507 does not pass out of your personal control,
and is not circulated to any branches. Fact should be confused and buried.' (29 November 1940:
Churchill papers, 20/14.)

[2] North American Supply Committee Memorandum No. 38 of 1940, 25 November 1940: Cabinet papers, 92/27.

[3] Prime Minister's Personal Minute, M.353, 30 November 1940: Premier papers, 3/483/2, folio
60.

[4] Memorandum of 28 November 1940: Cabinet papers, 115/14.

[5] 'Personal and Private', Sent to Foreign Office for despatch, 26 November 1940: Premier
papers, 4/17/1, folios 139–40.

Purvis warned, 'to isolationist opposition'. When Morgenthau returned to his office on December 1, Purvis added, 'then is the time to strike'.[1]

In an acccompanying memorandum, Purvis suggested to Churchill that a specially prepared 'Balance Sheet' of British needs, be prepared by Purvis' office, in order to stimulate the United States authorities to the further productive effort needed 'to meet the joint UK and US defence needs'. In the past, Purvis pointed out, Britain had suffered by having fed her requirements to the United States 'piece-meal'. The urgent need now was to present Roosevelt 'personally' with a 'comprehensive picture'. Both Morgenthau and Roosevelt, Purvis added, had intimated to him that Roosevelt would welcome this.[2]

Churchill accepted Purvis' advice, and re-wrote his letter to Roosevelt accordingly. The 'Balance Sheet' was also drawn up, revealing a mass of orders and priorities.[3]

On December 12 the War Cabinet decided to set up a British Supply Council in North America. As Churchill wished, Purvis was to be its Chairman, with Morris Wilson of the Ministry of Aircraft Production as his deputy. Their task as set out by the War Cabinet, was 'to deal with all issues of policy concerning supply', including 'all representations' made to the United States Administration by the different British authorities.[4]

The Supply Council's London link was to be a new Supply Committee, under the chairmanship of Sir Andrew Duncan, the recently appointed Minister of Supply, with Beaverbrook and A. V. Alexander as his fellow committee members. The existing North American Supply Committee was thus 'superseded'.[5]

Saturday November 30 was Churchill's sixty-sixth birthday. He celebrated it at Chequers, and also the christening of his grandson Winston. During the day Britain's links with the United States were much on his mind. In view of the continued serious shipping position,[6] he had been

---

[1] Letter of 28 November 1940: Cabinet papers, 115/14.

[2] Memorandum of 28 November 1940: Cabinet papers, 115/14.

[3] The British Purchasing Commission had placed priority orders for 324 Curtiss P.40, 170 Lockheed P.38, 170 Bell P. 39 and 106 other aircraft and aircraft engines. The Commission had also secured release from United States stock for purchase by Britain of 145,648,787 rounds of small arms and pistol ammunition; 26,793,000 pounds of cannon powder and TNT; 1,175,000 rounds of shell and mortar bombs; 918,978 machine guns, rifles and pistols; 5,908 aircraft bombs; 1,213 field guns and mortars; 100,000 ammunition belts; 3,333 belt-filling machine and 1,350 75-millimetre caissons and limbers. (List as of 5 November 1940: Cabinet papers, 115/4.)

[4] War Cabinet No. 304 of 1940, 12 December 1940.

[5] North American Supply Committee Memorandum No. 48 of 1940, 'Re-constitution of the Committee', 24 December 1940: Cabinet papers, 115/1.

[6] In November 1940 seventy-five British merchant ships were sunk by German torpedo, mine,

re-drafting and strengthening the letter to Roosevelt which Arthur Purvis had scrutinized for him three days earlier. Purvis had been invited to Chequers to help with the final version. It was now almost ready, with the exception of one paragraph which the Chancellor of the Exchequer, Sir Kingsley Wood, opposed. The disputed paragraph read:

While we will do our utmost, and shrink from no proper sacrifice to make payments across the Exchange, I should not myself be willing, even in the height of this struggle, to divest Great Britain of every conceivable saleable asset, so that after the victory was won with our blood and sweat, and civilization saved and the time gained for the United States to be fully armed against all eventualities, we should stand stripped to the bone.

'Such a course,' Churchill added, 'would not be in the moral or economic interests of either of our countries.'[1]

When a schedule of Britain's munitions production was prepared for the United States, in order to show exactly how essential American help would be, Churchill warned the War Cabinet 'that if the picture was painted too darkly, elements in the United States would say that it was useless to help us, for such help would be wasted and thrown away. If too bright a picture was painted, then there might be a tendency to withhold assistance.' Churchill had been 'rather chilled', he told his colleagues, 'by the attitude of the United States since the Election', although it 'might well be' that Roosevelt was waiting for the election atmosphere to 'disperse' before taking any 'striking action'.[2]

'Amid all your anxieties,' Sir Archibald Sinclair wrote to Churchill on November 30, 'you have much to gladden your heart this birthday —the successes against Italy, for example, which owe so much to your own judgement and action. . . .'[3] And Sinclair's deputy at the Air Ministry, Harold Balfour, wrote: 'The lower members of your team do get a view of the load you have to carry. If we can lift it to any extent by our efforts, then we are lucky in our opportunity, for at times I cannot help wondering how the human brain cells can accept, sift, and expel the thoughts of not only one man's brain but the thoughts brought to it by so many things you have to deal with'.[4] Anthony Eden wrote that same day:

---

ship or air attack. 'The recent trend of German military policy,' the Deputy Director of Air Ministry Intelligence had minuted on November 11, 'leaves little doubt that it is directed to the severance of our communications with America.' (Minute No. 33, 11 November 1940: Air Ministry papers, 40/2321.)

[1] Diary entry for 30 November 1940, Colville diary: Colville papers.
[2] War Cabinet No. 299 of 1940, 2 December 1940: Cabinet papers, 65/10.
[3] Letter of 30 November 1940: Churchill papers, 1/355.
[4] Letter of 30 November 1940: Churchill papers, 2/392.

My dear Winston,

Many and happier returns of the day. Very few men in all history have had to bear such a burden as you have carried in the last six months. It is really wonderful that at the end of it you are fitter & more vigorous, and better able than ever to guide & inspire us all.

You do not know how you heartened me on Monday night by your comment that never in your life had you felt more equal to your work. All the same, take care of yourself.

I have just read in a telegram a rumour that Italians in Libya are short of water & generally in trouble, and I feel better. So do we clutch at straws.

Bless you; thank you for all your kindness to me, and may we yet celebrate the last stage of a long hard road travelled together, 'la main dans la main'.

Yours ever
Anthony [1]

'Thank you so much dear Anthony,' Churchill replied that same day. 'I am truly grateful for your help and kindness.' [2]

That night, after a further German air raid, British deaths from air bombardment during November reached 4,588. Five and a half months earlier, as German troops had entered Paris, Colville had written in his diary: 'If we can hold on until November we shall have won the war.' Holding on, Colville added, 'is going to be a grim business'. [3] To the amazement of many, it had been done. The Battle of Britain had been fought and won. The severity of the Blitz had failed to undermine the morale of the British people. The reinforcements sent to the Middle East had not proved a fatal mistake. No German troops had attempted to land on British soil. November, despite the continuing severity of German submarine sinkings, had passed without catastrophe.

---

[1] Letter of 30 November 1940: Churchill papers, 2/394.
[2] Letter of 30 November 1940: Churchill papers, 2/394.
[3] Colville diary, 14 June 1940: Colville papers.

Part Four
World War

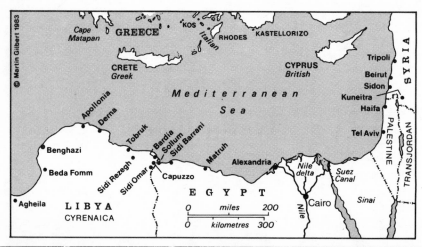

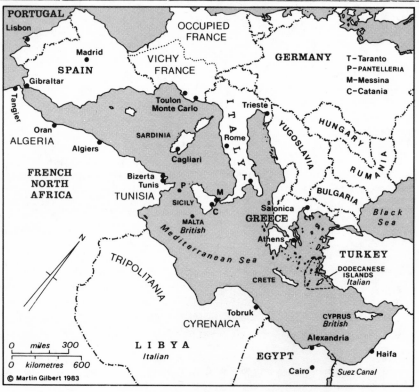

48

December 1940: 'More sure
of the future . . .'

O N December 1 Churchill set out for the Chiefs of Staff Committee his thoughts as to what Britain ought to do, were 'Compass' to have any 'considerable' success. He would, he wrote, ask the
War Cabinet to agree to the launching of 'Brisk' and 'Shrapnel' against
the Azores and Cape Verde Islands 'hot foot upon it'. Both should be
ready at forty-eight hours notice from the third or fourth of December.
The Staff study of 'Counterpoise', the seizure of Ceuta, must also be
ready for his scrutiny 'early' that week. 'I take it as settled,' he added,
that 'Workshop'—against Pantelleria—'goes forward leaving here
18th.'

Reflecting on the setting up of British air and naval bases in Crete,[1]
Churchill concluded:

The fact that we now have established ourselves at Suda Bay, entitles us to
feel much easier about Malta. While the Fleet is or may be at Suda, it will be
most unlikely that any large landing would be attempted at Malta, which we
have already reinforced by tanks and guns. Therefore it is not necessary to
send the remaining two Battalions from ME. On the contrary, Malta can
easily spare one Battalion to hold 'Workshop', if needed.

'The possession of Suda Bay,' Churchill ended, 'has made an enormous
change in the Eastern Mediterranean.'[2]

In reply, Wavell stressed that he was already committed to the seizure of the Italian Dodecanese Islands,[3] and that this would be the
limit of his future resources. 'General Wavell will have over a quarter

---

[1] The establishment of air bases on Crete was given the code name 'Index'; the setting up of the
naval base at Suda Bay was code named 'Drink'. (Code names for 29 October 1940: Churchill
papers, 4/96.)
[2] Prime Minister's Personal Minute, D.133, 'Most Secret': Premier papers, 3/288/1, folios 3–5.
[3] Operation 'Mandibles'.

of a million men under his command by the end of the year,' Churchill
minuted to Ismay on December 4. 'Does he really suppose that action
against the Dodecanese will be sufficient employment for these great
armies, assuming that success attends the defence of Egypt?'[1] That
same day, after a meeting of the Defence Committee, Eden noted in
his diary: 'W asked for news of "Compass" and was indignant that I
had not asked date. He was also critical of army and generals. "High
time army did something", etc.[2] I made it plain that I did not believe
in fussing Wavell with questions. I knew his plan, he knew our view,
he had best be left to get on with it. This did not suit W.' Sir John Dill,
Eden added, 'was very angry' at Churchill's attitude.[3] Churchill had
telegraphed to Wavell, urging him to have faith in the ability of Sir
Roger Keyes to carry out a successful attack on Pantelleria, operation
'Workshop', and reminding Wavell of Keyes' first world war attack on
the German submarine base at Zeebrugge:

> Capture of 'Workshop' no doubt a hazard, but Zeebrugge would never
> have got past scrutiny bestowed on this. Commandos very highly trained,
> carefully picked volunteers for this kind of work. Weather and fixed date of
> convoy may of course prevent attempt, in which case whole outfit will go to
> Malta or Suda for other enterprises. If conditions favourable nothing will be
> stinted. . . .

Churchill's telegram continued:

> On strategic grounds 'Workshop' gives good air command of most used line
> of enemy communications with Libyan army, and also increased measure air
> protection for our convoys and transports passing so-called Narrows. Joint
> Staffs here consider very high value attaches to removal of this obstruction to
> our East and West communications. Besides all this, we need to show ourselves
> capable of vehement offensive amphibious action.

'I shall call upon you therefore,' Churchill added, 'to use your utmost
endeavours to procure success should conditions be favourable at the

---

[1] 'Action this Day', Prime Minister's Personal Minute, D.137, 4 December 1940: Churchill
papers, 20/13.

[2] The anger which at times pervaded Churchill's thoughts and minutes was born of immediate
pressures. But he could also be magnanimous. When the former military correspondent of *The
Times*, Captain Basil Liddell-Hart, submitted what Colville described as 'a curious document',
advocating 'peace with Germany' as war could only lead to stalemate or defeat, A. V. Alexander
had been concerned about the treason aspect, describing Liddell-Hart's article as 'pregnant with
defeat'. (Colville diary, 3 December 1940: Colville papers.) But Churchill commented on the
document, 'It is now out of date,' and stopped further action against Liddell-Hart with the
words: 'he seems more a candidate for a mental home than for more serious action.' (Minute of 2
December 1940: Churchill papers, 20/26.)

[3] Eden diary, 4 December 1940: The Earl of Avon, *The Eden Memoirs, The Reckoning*, London
1965, page 178.

zero hour.'[1] But at the Defence Committee meeting on December 5 Sir Dudley Pound, speaking for the Chiefs of Staff, told Churchill that Pantelleria could not be seized unless naval forces essential to its capture were diverted from convoy duty in the Channel and Western Approaches, while Eden commented that Wavell regarded Pantelleria as 'an insufficient prize'.

Churchill, as the official minutes recorded, 'regretted' the Chiefs of Staff opposition to 'Workshop', telling the Committee:

. . . There was, of course, no absolute guarantee of success in war nor was it ever possible during a campaign to provide what could be regarded as fully adequate forces for any particular battle or operation. Many of the greatest battles of history had been won with forces which, before the event, would have been considered hopelessly inadequate. It was quite out of the question to denude Home Waters to the extent contemplated and, at the most, two additional destroyers might be added to the eight already proposed.

Later in the discussion, Pound said that, if it was 'so important to score a success' with the capture of Pantelleria, and if the risks of carrying out the operation with insufficient forces were accepted, then the Chiefs of Staff would make 'every endeavour to see that the forces available were put to the best use and given every assistance possible'. But the Committee finally agreed, 'in the face of the arguments put forward by the Chiefs of Staff', that the existing plan for the seizure of the island 'cannot be accepted'. It was decided that the Chiefs of Staff should see whether the plan could be 'improved', to an extent that would 'justify them' in recommending its adoption by the Defence Committee, on the basis that no essential naval craft be denuded from 'vital' areas.[2]

Wavell's main offensive, Operation 'Compass', was now imminent, yet Churchill was still worried that opportunities would be missed. 'If,' he wrote to Dill, 'with the situation as it is, General Wavell is only playing small, and is not hurling in his whole available forces with furious energy, he will have failed to rise to the height of circumstances,' and Churchill added: 'I never "worry" about action, but only about inaction.'[3]

[1] 'Personal and Most Secret', drafted on 3 December 1940, sent on 11 December 1940: Premier papers, 3/124/2, folios 89–91.

[2] Defence Committee (Operatives) No. 48 of 1940, 5 December 1940, 9.30 p.m.: Cabinet papers, 69/1. Those present were Churchill (in the Chair), A. V. Alexander, Eden, Sinclair, Pound, Dill, Portal and Ismay.

[3] 'Secret', Prime Minister's Personal Minute, M.384A, 7 December 1940: Premier papers, 3/288/1, folio 24.

United States' 'inaction' was another of Churchill's worries, and on Sunday December 8 he sent Roosevelt the letter on which he had been working for so many days, stressing that it was Britain's duty 'in the common interest, as also for our survival, to hold the front and grapple with the Nazi power until the preparations of the United States are complete'. The past five months had witnessed 'a strong and perhaps unexpected recovery' by Great Britain, fighting alone, 'but with the invaluable aid in munitions and in destroyers placed at our disposal by the great Republic of which you are for the third time the chosen Chief'.

Although the danger of defeat by 'a swift, overwhelming blow' had for the time being greatly receded, a less sudden 'but equally deadly' danger was the 'steady and increasing diminution of sea tonnage'. As Churchill explained: 'We can endure the shattering of our dwellings and the slaughter of our civil population by indiscriminate air attacks, and we hope to parry these increasingly as our science develops, and to repay them upon military objectives in Germany as our Air Force more nearly approaches the strength of the enemy.' But, he went on to warn Roosevelt:

... The decision for 1941 lies upon the seas. Unless we can establish our ability to feed this Island, to import the munitions of all kinds which we need, unless we can move our armies to the various theatres where Hitler and his confederate Mussolini must be met, and maintain them there, and do all this with the assurance of being able to carry it on till the spirit of the Continental Dictators is broken, we may fall by the way, and the time needed by the United States to complete her defensive preparations may not be forthcoming.

Churchill then set out in detail Britain's shipping losses, and naval building programme, and the continuing threat that the naval forces of Vichy France would join the Axis, taking control of West Africa 'with the gravest consequences' to Britain's sea communications between the north and south Atlantic. The Far East was also a danger point, for, as Churchill wrote:

... Here it seems clear that Japan is thrusting southward through Indo-China to Saigon and other naval and air bases, thus bringing them within a comparatively short distance of Singapore and the Dutch East Indies. It is reported that the Japanese are preparing five good divisions for possible use as an overseas expeditionary force.

'We have today,' Churchill warned, 'no forces in the Far East capable of dealing with this situation should it develop.'

Churchill then set out his requests: a reassertion by the United States of the doctrine of the freedom of the seas 'from illegal and barbarous methods of warfare' backed up by United States destroyer protection for all lawful trading on the high seas and the use by the United States for this convoy purpose of 'bases in Eire for the duration of the war'. Failing this, Churchill wanted Roosevelt to agree to 'the gift, loan, or supply of a large number of American vessels of war', above all destroyers, to enable Britain to maintain the Atlantic route. At the same time, he wanted the United States to extend its naval control on the American side of the Atlantic 'so as to prevent molestation by enemy vessels' of the approaches to the new American bases being established in British islands in the West Indies.

'To ensure final victory,' Churchill told Roosevelt, not less than three million tons of additional merchant shipping capacity would have to be built. 'Only the United States can supply this need.' In the military sphere, manufacture of machine tools and the release of certain equipment from stock in the United States remained essential if the British were to be able to equip fifty Divisions in 1941. As for Finance, Churchill wrote:

The moment approaches when we shall no longer be able to pay cash for shipping and other supplies. While we will do our utmost, and shrink from no proper sacrifice to make payments across the Exchange, I believe you will agree that it would be wrong in principle and mutually disadvantageous in effect if at the height of this struggle Great Britain were to be divested of all saleable assets, so that after the victory was won with our blood, civilisation saved, and the time gained for the United States to be fully armed against all eventualities, we should stand stripped to the bone. Such a course would not be in the moral or economic interests of either of our countries. We here should be unable, after the war, to purchase the large balance of imports from the United States over and above the volume of our exports which is agreeable to your tariffs and industrial economy. Not only should we in Great Britain suffer cruel privations, but widespread unemployment in the United States would follow the curtailment of American exporting power.

Moreover, I do not believe that the Government and people of the United States would find it in accordance with the principles which guide them to confine the help which they have so generously promised only to such munitions of war and commodites as could be immediately paid for.

This was a massive set of requests political, naval, military, diplomatic and economic: but Roosevelt would not regard it, Churchill ended, 'as an appeal for aid, but as a statement of the minimum action necessary to achieve our common purpose'.[1]

[1] War Cabinet Paper No. 466 (Final Revise) of 1940, 8 December 1940: Churchill papers, 23/4.

Churchill's letter did not lead to United States warships protecting British convoys, neither to United States bases in Eire, nor to United States pressure on Eire.[1] But it did lead to Roosevelt seeking a closer link with Churchill, by means of a personal emissary, his friend and political adviser, Harry Hopkins.

His letter to Roosevelt having been completed, Churchill remained at Chequers for the rest of the weekend. Among those present at dinner on the Sunday night was a Lieutenant in the Life Guards, Michael Francis Eden, whose mother was a cousin of Clementine Churchill. After listening to the after-dinner conversation between Churchill, Sholto Douglas and Lord Louis Mountbatten, the young Lieutenant reported home that the new United States destroyers 'aren't much good—or won't be till the Spring as they are badly built. They roll 70° and there was apparently a domestic scandal about them in America & the naval Under-Secretary & designer were sacked & the ships were never put into commission'. Michael Eden added: 'Winston looked full of vigour and bright of eye and seemed to be in a cheerful & confident frame of mind.'[2]

During December the Blitz continued in all its ferocity. In a heavy German bombing raid on the night of Sunday December 8, eighty-five civilians were killed in London and seventeen elsewhere. The House of Commons was among the many buildings which were damaged. On the following day Churchill visited the scene of the destruction. Henry Channon, who was also there, noted in his diary:

I went into what was the Members' cloakroom and saw a scene of devastation; confusion, wreckage, broken glass everywhere, and the loveliest, oldest part of

---

[1] On 13 December 1940 Churchill telegraphed to Roosevelt again: '... we are so hard pressed at sea that we cannot undertake to carry any longer the 400,000 tons of feeding-stuffs and fertilizers which we have hitherto convoyed to Eire through all the attacks of the enemy. We need this tonnage for our own supply and we do not need the food which Eire has been sending us...' His telegram ended: 'I should like to know quite privately what your reactions would be if and when we are forced to concentrate our own tonnage upon the supply of Great Britain. We also do not feel able in present circumstances to continue the heavy subsidies we have hitherto been paying to the Irish Agricultural Producers. You will realise also that our merchant seamen, as well as public opinion generally, take it much amiss that we should have to carry Irish supplies through Air and U-boat attacks and subsidise them handsomely when de Valera is quite content to sit happy and see us strangled.' (Premier papers, 3/468.)

[2] Letter of 15 December 1940: Baron Henley papers. In 1962 Michael Eden succeeded his father as 7th Baron Henley. From 1966 to 1967 he was President of the Liberal Party, then Chairman until his death in 1977.

the vast building a shambles. Suddenly I came upon Winston Churchill wearing a fur-collared coat, and smoking a cigar; he was led by a policeman and followed by Seal, his secretary. 'It's horrible' he remarked to me without removing his cigar; and I saw that he was much moved, for he loves Westminster; I walked with him. 'They would hit the best bit' I said. 'Where Cromwell signed King Charles's death warrant,' he grunted.

Channon also sensed 'the historic significance of the scene', as he watched Churchill 'surveying the destruction he had long predicted, of a place he loved'.[1]

That same day, Churchill instructed the Minister of Works and Buildings, John Reith, to give special attention to the repair of buildings which were only slightly damaged, minuting on December 9:

Sometimes I see a whole row of houses whose windows are blown out, but are not otherwise damaged, standing for weeks deserted and neglected. Active measures should be taken to replace the tiles and to close up the windows with fabric, with one small pane for light, and to make such repairs as make the houses fit for habitation. In dealing with house casualties, the least serious should claim priority. You ought to have a regular corps of workmen who would get this job done so that the people may get back into their homes, which are unlikely to be hit a second time. Branches of this corps should exist in all the great cities.

'Not a day should be lost,' Churchill ended. 'How the expense is met or divided can be settled with the Treasury. But this question must be no impediment on action.'[2] When Reith sent Churchill details of 'the nucleus of an emergency organisation' which he was even then in the process of setting up, Churchill minuted approvingly: 'Press on.'[3]

Since the night of December 7, British troops commanded by General O'Connor had been advancing against the Italian strong points in the

[1] Diary entry, 9 December 1940: Robert Rhodes James (editor), *Chips, The Diaries of Sir Henry Channon*, London 1967, page 278.

[2] 'Action this Day', Prime Minister's Personal Minute, M.395, 9 December 1940: Premier papers, 3/18/1, folios 117–18. On the following day, after Clementine Churchill had visited air raid shelters in London, Churchill wrote to Herbert Morrison and Malcolm MacDonald: 'I should be so much obliged if you could read these notes which my wife has made on her visits to the shelters, so that we could talk them over tomorrow night.' Churchill's minutes ended: 'I would like very much to give you all the help in my power.' (10 December 1940: Churchill papers, 20/2.)

[3] Letter of 10 December 1940 and note of 11 December 1940: Premier papers, 3/18/1, folio 116. Four weeks later Churchill minuted to Reith: 'I continue to see great numbers of houses where the walls and roofs are all right, but the windows have not been repaired, and which are consequently uninhabitable. At present I regard this as your No. 1 war task.' Churchill added: 'Do not let spacious plans for a new world divert your energies from saving what is left of the old.' (Prime Minister's Personal Minute, M.22/1, 6 January 1941: Churchill papers, 20/36.)

western desert. Operation 'Compass' had begun, and, at dawn on December 9 British forces reached their first objectives, having met no 'hindrance'.[1] On December 10 Churchill told the House of Commons that south of Sidi Barrani, in the first defended area 'which was assaulted and over-run', 500 Italian prisoners had been taken, and the Italian General killed in action.[2] A signal from Wavell later that afternoon reported 'between 4,000 and 5,000' prisoners, with 28 Italian medium tanks captured at Nibeiwa, and effective British air and naval support throughout the advance.[3]

On the afternoon of December 11 news reached the War Office that the whole Sidi Barrani position had been overrun, and three Italian generals captured. 'Rang Winston,' Eden noted in his diary, 'who congratulated me warmly on a great victory.'[4] That night, Wavell reported a total of 7,000 prisoners already counted, and further large numbers still being brought in.[5] In reporting on the battle by telephone that evening to the King, Churchill told him: 'My humble congratulations to you, Sir, on a great Imperial victory.'[6]

'I am sure you will be glad about Libya,' Churchill telegraphed to Mackenzie King on December 12. 'We must be doubly thankful when we remember where we were four months ago. I am very glad we ran the risk in the teeth of the invasion menace of sending our best tanks to this distant battlefield.' The consequences of the victory, Churchill added, 'may be far reaching. We must be worthy of them.'[7] Churchill also telegraphed after Sidi Barrani to the Prime Minister of Australia, Robert Menzies. 'Remember,' he said, 'that I could not guarantee a few months ago even a successful defence of the Delta and Canal.'[8]

'One has a growing feeling,' Churchill telegraphed to Smuts on December 13, 'that wickedness is not going to reign', and he went on

---

[1] War Cabinet No. 302 of 1940, 9 December 1940, 5 p.m., Minute 1, Confidential Annex: Cabinet papers, 65/16. In making his report of the action to the War Cabinet, Churchill explained that in view of the secrecy of the operation, 'he had only sought the approval of the Defence Committee (Operations)' and not of the War Cabinet.

[2] *Hansard*, 10 December 1940, columns 797–9.

[3] 'Most Immediate', O/29443, despatched 11.50 a.m. received 14.45 p.m., 10 December 1940: Premier papers, 3/288/1.

[4] Eden diary, 11 December 1940: The Earl of Avon, *The Eden Memoirs, The Reckoning*, London 1965, page 181.

[5] 'Most Immediate', O/29744, despatched 10.18 p.m., received 11.20 p.m., 11 December 1940: Premier papers, 3/288/1.

[6] Colville diary, 11 December 1940: Colville papers.

[7] 'Personal and Secret', 12 December 1940: Premier papers, 3/483/2, folio 10.

[8] 'Personal and Secret', 12 December 1940: Premier papers, 4/43B/1, folio 25.

to comment, of the Italian troops: 'It looks as if these people were corn ripe for the sickle,' and he added: 'let us gather the harvest.'[1] In private, however, Churchill chafed at what he feared was to be a lack of real urgency in Wavell's 'Compass' plans. As Eden noted in his diary on the following day:

Winston rang up early in morning and complained that we were not pursuing enemy and had much to say about missed opportunities. After an angry riposte from me, it emerged that he had not seen telegram that appeared during night giving details of further plans. But this is all symptomatic of his distrust of local leaders which to my disappointment is not abated at all. He even went so far as to say when I saw him later that this showed we should have held Somaliland. I replied: 'That is most ungenerous at this moment, you know that we had not a gun there.' 'Whose fault was that?' Winston retorted.

'Our talk,' Eden commented, 'was less cordial than usual.'[2]

At home, censorship reports submitted to Churchill revealed a certain criticism of the war as being engineered for financial reasons and in the interests of the upper classes. Reading this, Churchill circled it in red, telling Colville: 'It is difficult to think politically or socially —in classes—any more. There is a kind of warmth pervading England.'[3]

Churchill's understanding of popular feeling gave him a strength of willpower which he could not have had, or maintained, if his instincts had been out of true with the mood of the British public. But there were times when it seemed that he himself did not fully grasp just how important his own personal leadership had become. As Ismay later recalled:

. . . I was walking with him in the garden at Chequers, after dinner. London was under bombardment, and we could see the glow of the fires from afar. Churchill was sad at all the suffering and said that he wished that he could do more 'for the poor people'. I reminded him that whatever the future held, nothing could rob him of the credit of having inspired the country by his speeches. 'Not at all,' he retorted, almost angrily. 'It was given to me to express what was in the hearts of the British people. If I had said anything else, they would have hurled me from office.'

[1] 'Personal and Private', 13 December 1940: Premier papers, 4/43B/1, folio 38. Recalling two mutual friends, Sir Abe Bailey and the first Earl of Birkenhead, Churchill ended on a personal note: 'I remain always your faithful friend and I wish Abe and Freddie could rejoice with us tonight.'

[2] Eden diary, 12 December 1940: The Earl of Avon, *The Eden Memoirs*, *The Reckoning*, London 1965, page 181.

[3] Colville diary, 11 December 1940: Colville papers.

Ismay reflected on Churchill's remark:

I had never attributed to him the quality of humility, and it struck me as odd that he failed to realise that the upsurge of the national spirit was largely his own creation. The great qualities of the British race had seemed almost dormant until he had aroused them. The people then saw themselves as he portrayed them. They put their trust in him. They were ready to do anything that he asked, make any sacrifice that he demanded, and follow wherever he led.[1]

On December 12 it was learned in London that Lord Lothian, Britain's Ambassador in Washington, had died. 'We have lost a good friend and high Interpreter,' Churchill telegraphed to Roosevelt[2] and, as Colville noted, 'lamented' Lothian's death.[3] Churchill had now to consider, as a matter of urgency, who should be Lothian's successor in this main diplomatic post. 'He would like to try Lloyd George,' Colville wrote, 'if he could trust him.' Colville himself suggested either Lord Cranborne, who had resigned from the Government at the time of Eden's resignation in February 1938, or Sir Robert Vansittart, who had been removed from his post as Permanent Under-Secretary of State at the Foreign Office a few weeks before Eden's resignation.[4] Churchill had already thought of both. But Lloyd George seemed favoured, even by Cranborne, who argued that 'his knowledge of munitions problems and his fiery personality marked him out'.

Churchill's first idea was to make Lloyd George a member of the War Cabinet, so that he would not feel 'under' the Foreign Secretary, Lord Halifax: a colleague rather than a subordinate. 'He believed,' Colville added, 'that LG would be loyal to him. If not, he could always sack him.'

Another suggestion was to move Sir Stafford Cripps from Moscow to Washington, but Churchill commented to Colville: 'He is a lunatic in a country of lunatics. It would be a shame to move him.'

---

[1] *The Memoirs of General the Lord Ismay*, London 1960, page 155.

[2] Telegram, 13 December 1940: Premier papers, 3/468.

[3] Of Lothian's decision as a Christian Scientist not to be operated on, Churchill commented: 'What a monstrous thing that Lothian should not have allowed a doctor to be called.' (Colville diary, 13 December 1940: Colville papers.)

[4] On 17 December 1940 Churchill defended Vansittart in the House of Commons against charges of 'humiliating' the German people in recent radio broadcasts. In his defence Churchill described Vansittart as 'a man who has had the root of the matter in his hands throughout this great controversy' (*Hansard*, 17 December 1940, columns 1101-2).

That evening at Chequers, Churchill was concerned with matters other than the Washington appointment. As Colville wrote in his diary that night, 'He spoke of the defeat of the Italians, who possessed every requisite for Empire except courage, and of the terrible miscalculation they had made about us.' Churchill also reflected that Britain 'had had a wonderful escape in these last months', and it was already difficult to remember 'what we had been through'. Colville's account of Churchill's conversation continued:

Talking of the future he sketched the European Confederation that would have to be formed ('with their Diets of Worms') and shuddered as he thought of the intricate currency problems etc. He did not understand such things and he would be out of it.

He did not wish to lead a party struggle or a class struggle against the Labour leaders who were now serving him so well. He would retire to Chartwell and write a book on the war, which he already had mapped out in his mind chapter by chapter. This was the moment for him: he was determined not to prolong his career into the period of reconstruction. I said I thought he would be demanded by the people: there was no other leader.

After a few slashes at Baldwin for not making better use of the Sanctions period against Italy, he moved from the dining-room, with his multi-coloured dressing gown over his siren-suit, rang up Gwilym Lloyd George[1] to sound him about his father, and then stood beaming in front of the fire in the Great Hall.

He asked if I had heard LG during the debate in which Chamberlain fell. I said I had, and deplored Chamberlain's mistake in saying 'I have my friends'; to the hostile minority in the House. The PM said it had been a wonderful opportunity for him: the stars in their courses had fought at his side. He had been able to defend his Chief to the utmost and only to win esteem and support in so doing. No one could say he had been disloyal or had intrigued against Chamberlain: 'and I never have done that sort of thing'.[2]

Churchill was in discursive mood, talking of his ideas of the future of Europe, and setting out his feelings of what Europe might become once Nazism were defeated. Once more, Colville recorded Churchill's thoughts:

. . . We had got to admit that Germany should remain in the European family: 'Germany existed before the Gestapo'. When we had won the war he visualised five great European nations: Great Britain, France, Italy, Spain and Prussia. In addition there would be four confederations: the Northern, with its capital at The Hague; the Middle European with its capital at Warsaw or Prague; the Danubian including Bavaria, Württemberg, Baden, Austria and Hungary,

---

[1] Parliamentary Secretary, Board of Trade, from 1939 to 1941. From 1942 to 1945 he was Minister of Fuel and Power.

[2] Colville diary, 12 December 1940: Colville papers.

with its capital at Vienna; and the Balkan with Turkey at its head and Constantinople as its capital. These nine powers would meet in a Council of Europe, which would have a Supreme Judiciary and Economic Council, and each would contribute men to a Supranational Air Cohort. None might have its own air force, but each would be allowed its own militia, since democracy must be secured on a people's army and not left to the mercy of oligarchs or a secret police. Prussia alone would, for a hundred years, be denied all armaments apart from her share in the Supranational Air Cohort.

Britain would be part of Europe, but she would also be part of the English-speaking world which, as the reward for victory, would alone control the seas, though bound by covenant to respect the commerce and colonial rights of all peoples. Russia would fit into an Eastern Confederation and the whole problem of Asia would have to be faced; but as far as Europe was concerned a system of confederation was necessary to allow the small powers to continue to exist and to avoid balkanisation. There must be no war debts, no reparations and no demands on Prussia. Certain territories might have to be ceded, and exchanges of population would have to take place on the lines of that so successfully achieved by Greece and Turkey after the First World War. But there must be no pariahs, and Prussia, though unarmed, should be secured by the guarantee of the Council of Europe.

Only the Nazis, Churchill said, 'the murderers of 30 June 1934 and the Gestapo, would be made to suffer for their misdeeds'.[1]

That night, the German bombers returned, their target Sheffield. Churchill meanwhile, had decided to press Wavell to follow up the victory of Sidi Barrani by a further attack, and, being aware of Wavell's love of poetry, he telegraphed on December 13, congratulating Wavell on, his 'splendid victory' and adding:

The poet Walt Whitman says that from every fruition of success, however full, comes forth something to make a greater struggle necessary. Naturally, pursuit will hold the first place in your thoughts. It is at the moment when the victor is most exhausted that the greatest forfeit can be exacted from the vanquished. Nothing would shake Mussolini more than a disaster in Libya itself. No doubt you have considered taking some harbour in Italian territory to which the Fleet can bring all your stuff and which will give you a new jumping-off point to hunt them along the coast until you come up against real resistance. It looks as if these people were corn ripe for the sickle.

'I shall be glad to hear from you,' Churchill added, 'your thoughts and plans at earliest.' Meanwhile, Egypt, he felt, should declare war on Italy: 'Now is the appointed time.'

[1] Colville diary, 12 December 1940: Colville papers.

Once the British troops had come 'to a full-stop' on the African coast, Churchill told Wavell, 'several attractive choices will open'.[1] To his guests at Chequers, Lindemann, Ismay and Admiral Phillips, Churchill confided his fears that 'Compass' itself might never have come to pass. 'The Prime Minister said he had been living in hopes of it for five weeks,' Colville noted in his diary, 'and had been terrified some sandstorm would give the men on the spot a chance to back out.' It had, Churchill added, 'been well-planned and brilliantly executed, unlike Narvik, which of all the fiascos for which he had had any responsibilities, had been the worst—except for Dakar.'[2]

As the talk of Wavell's victory continued, Churchill told his guests, as Colville recorded on the following day:

. . . we had taken the right course: we had risked sending troops and material to Egypt when still under the threat of invasion at home, and we had sent substantial air assistance to Greece in spite of the fact that we were preparing for a 'Spring of the Lion' in North Africa. But if events had taken a different course, as they might have, what would history have said?

He quoted dramatically from a mythical history book of the future, denouncing the criminal gambler who sent the divisions which might have turned the scale against the German invasion at home, or the vacillators who sent to Greece the aeroplanes which could have turned the North African campaign into a success.[3]

Among those lunching at Chequers that weekend was General de Gaulle, who felt, as Colville noted in his diary, that Britain ought to 'make more' of the fact that she was 'standing alone'. Were she to do so, he said, 'Oran would seem natural, merely because the world was at stake.'

The discussion then turned, as Colville noted, to Intelligence indications of an imminent German move, codenamed 'Felix' which, Colville recorded, 'seemed aimed either at Ireland or Spain'. Churchill thought it would be Spain: 'he would go that way if he were Hitler'. As the speculation continued, a German invasion of Switzerland, and even of Italy, were also being mentioned.[4] Meanwhile, a despatch rider brought to Chequers telegrams from Tangier, where Spain was occupying the International Zone, suggesting that Spain would as a result

---

[1] Telegram No. 92792, 13 December 1940: Premier papers, 3/309/1, No. 27.

[2] Colville diary, 13 December 1940: Colville papers.

[3] Colville diary, 14 December 1940: Colville papers.

[4] 'Felix' was in fact the code name for a German attack on Gibraltar, after ensuring Spanish cooperation. Britain had, since August, a counter-operation, 'Apathetic', for use if German and Italian forces entered Spain, 'Spain not resisting' (Code name for 30 August 1940: Churchill papers, 4/96.)

of this action become an active ally of Germany. If true, Churchill warned, this 'would entail a drastic reorganisation of four or five of our own projected operations', as it would be undesirable 'to have our forces and our transports sprawled about the world at such a moment.[1]

From Chequers, Churchill was driven to Ditchley, where, on December 14, he studied Lindemann's graphs of British aircraft production, held a conference with Pound, Portal, Haining, Phillips and Ismay, mocked at the Italians 'whose civilisation and achievements he greatly admires but of whom he finds it easy, indeed irresistible, to make fun', and saw Charlie Chaplin's new film *The Great Dictator*, which had not yet been released in Britain. After the film, Churchill dictated a short telegram to Roosevelt, 'asking if Lloyd George would be acceptable as Ambassador'.[2]

On Sunday December 15, at Chequers, after watching the film *Gone with the Wind*, he had sat from two until three in the morning discussing the campaign in North Africa with Eden.[3] As they talked, the total number of Italian prisoners of war captured by Wavell's army reached 35,000.[4]

As a result of his conversation with Eden, Churchill telegraphed to Wavell on the following day, praising his 'memorable victories' and the 'glorious service' of what he called 'the army of the Nile'. Churchill's telegram continued:

Your first objective now must be to maul the Italian Army and rip them off the African shore to the utmost possible extent. We were very glad to learn your intentions against Bardia and Tobruk, and now to hear of the latest captures of Sollum and Capuzzo. I feel convinced that it is only after you have made sure that you can get no farther that you will relinquish the main hope in favour of secondary action in the Sudan or Dodecanese. The Sudan is of prime importance, and eminently desirable, and it may be that the two Indian brigades can be spared without prejudice to the Libyan pursuit battle.[5]

[1] Colville diary, 13 December 1940: Colville papers. The operations listed by Colville as being at risk included 'Brisk', 'Shrapnel', 'Excess' and 'Challenger'. 'Excess' was the proposed convoy of stores from Gibraltar to Egypt. 'Shrapnel' and 'Brisk' were moves to secure British air and refuelling bases in Portuguese West Africa and on the Cape Verde Islands. 'Challenger' was the occupation of Ceuta, a Spanish enclave on the North African coast opposite Gibraltar.

[2] Colville diary, 14 December 1940: Colville papers.

[3] Colville diary, 15 December 1940: Colville papers.

[4] The final figure of Italian prisoners, announced on 23 December 1940, was 35,949. There were 133 British and Allied deaths during the campaign.

[5] Anticipating Churchill's suggestion Wavell had already, on the day after the victory, removed the two Indian brigades and sent them to the Sudan.

Wavell's 'supreme task', Churchill added, was to inflict 'further defeats' upon the main Italian army, and his telegram continued:

I cannot of course pretend to judge special conditions from here, but Napoleon's maxim, 'Frappez la masse et tout le reste vient par surcroît,' seems to ring in one's ears. I must recur to the suggestion made in my previous telegram about amphibious operations and landings behind the enemy's front to cut off hostile detachments and to carry forward supplies and troops by sea.[1]

Two days later, in an effort to encourage Wavell to persevere with offensive plans, Churchill telegraphed the single reference: 'St Matthew, Chapter 7, Verse 7.'[2]

Although the dangers of immediate invasion had receded, Churchill was still concerned with anti-invasion measures. In this regard he continued to urge preparations for defensive gas warfare, while still 'deeply anxious', as he told the Chiefs of Staff Committee on December 26, that gas warfare 'should not be adopted at the present time' but that every precaution 'must be kept in order' and every effort made to increase Britain's 'retaliatory power'. His minute continued:

Sometimes I have wondered whether it would be any deterrent on the enemy if I were to say that we should never use gas ourselves unless it had first been used against us, but that we had actually in store many thousands of tons of various types of deadly gas with their necessary containers, and that we should immediate retaliate upon Germany. On the whole, I think it is perhaps better to say nothing unless or until we have evidence that the attack is imminent.

There would, Churchill commented, 'be too much bluff in any such statement.' 'If anyone is of a different opinion,' Churchill added, 'I shall be glad to know.' The subject, he reiterated, 'causes me much anxiety'.[3]

That anxiety was reflected in Churchill's constant questionings of Britain's own defences against gas attack. Early in the New Year he pressed both the Chiefs of Staff Committee and Herbert Morrison, the Home Secretary: 'to examine carefully the condition of gas masks

[1] Telegram No. 93181, drafted 16 December 1940, despatched 17 December 1940: Premier papers, 3/309/1, No. 29.

[2] Telegram No. 93374, 18 December 1940: Premier papers, 3/309/1, No. 31. The reference was to the verse: 'Ask, and it shall be given you; seek, and ye shall find; knock, and it shall be opened unto you.' On the following day Wavell replied by telegram: 'St James, Chapter 1, Verse 17.' This read: 'Every good gift and every perfect gift is from above . . . and cometh down from the Father of lights, with whom is no variableness, neither shadow of turning.' Wavell added: 'More aircraft are our immediate need and these you are providing. Additional anti-aircraft also much required.' (Telegram No. 0/30879, 19 December 1940: Premier papers, 3/309/1, No. 32.)

[3] Prime Minister's Personal Minute, D.154, 'Secret', 26 December 1940: Churchill papers, 20/13.

among the civilian population', and asked: 'have they been overhauled regularly?' Churchill also noted that 'very few people carry masks nowadays', adding: 'is there any active system of gas training?'

Churchill went on to stress that the question of protection against gas had become extremely urgent following increasing indications pointing to the use of gas. His minute ended:

Finally, it is important that nothing should appear in the newspapers, or be spoken on the BBC, which suggests that we are making a fuss about anti-gas arrangements, because the enemy will only use this as part of his excuse, saying that we are about to use it on him. I am of opinion, nevertheless, that a nation-wide effort must be made.[1]

One further anti-invasion measure had been under investigation for several months, the use of an oil-based sea flame barrage. As the Germans prepared to land, it was intended to set alight oil on the surface of the sea at the point where the troops would have to wade ashore. By December 20 sufficient progress had been made to carry out an experiment. The site chosen was Studland Bay. But the test was disappointing in the extreme. The smoke given off by the burning oil was likely, General Brooke reported, 'to be a considerable hindrance to the defence'. In addition, the sea being choppy, the flames were extinguished 'where the waves broke'. Nor did the flaming pools of oil join up as intended, since the oil 'tended to drift straight to the shore'. One final reason for abandoning the scheme: the smoke blown *inland* from the burning oil 'would have blinded everybody for half a mile inland'.[2]

In mid-December Churchill enjoyed a brief respite from war direction. In the autumn of 1940 the headmaster of Harrow School had asked Colville, who like Churchill was an Old Harrovian, if the Prime Minister could visit the School. 'I enquired,' Colville later wrote, 'and received a curtly negative reply.' A second approach, made by an old Harrovian Cabinet Minister, Leo Amery, was equally unsuccessful. Then Harrow was bombed and, Colville recalled, 'the Prime Minister, who had never spoken of the School except with dislike, volunteered

---

[1] 'Action this Day', Prime Minister's Personal Minute, D.17/1, 'Secret', 19 January 1941: Churchill papers, 20/36.

[2] Home Forces 2832/ops, report of 26 December 1940: Admiralty papers, 1/11214. The originator of this scheme was Jan Le Witt, a painter, who had come to Britain from Poland in 1937, and who had first submitted it both to the French and British Governments on 11 June 1940 at the time of the fall of France. (Le Witt papers.)

the statement that it was courageous to remain on the Hill and not to emigrate to more peaceful pastures'.

Colville's account continued:

Several days later an important telegram arrived from President Roosevelt just before dinner. I took it upstairs to the Prime Minister who was in his bath, with the door wide open, and singing 'St Joles' at the top of his voice. After reading the telegram (still in his bath) and giving instructions about it, he continued cheerfully with 'St Joles' and then proceeded to tell me what an inspiration the Harrow Songs had been to him throughout his life. Indeed, he said, he was immensely grateful to Harrow on two accounts: the Songs and the fact that he had been well taught the beauties of the English language.

He added, as an afterthought, that if the boys would sing him the songs he liked best—and he must be allowed to choose—he would after all go down to Harrow, where they were showing such courage under bombardment, even though he had long ago resolved never to set foot in the place again.

I asked why he had so resolved and (still in the bath) he told me the following story. In 1910 or 1911, when party passions were aroused over Irish Home Rule and the Parliament Bill to a degree which seems almost incomprehensible now, Mr Churchill, a member of the Liberal Cabinet, was motoring not far from Harrow with his personal friend but political opponent, F. E. Smith. It suddenly occurred to him to divert the car and take 'FE' to see his old School. When they arrived Bill was in progress and the boys waiting in the yard recognised Winston Churchill. They booed him as loud and long as they could, so that even Churchill, who was seldom disconcerted, felt ashamed and humiliated. Above all he felt angry at being so boorishly received in the presence of his friend, and he turned on his heel vowing never to have anything more to do with Harrow. He sent his son to Eton and for thirty years he thought of the School, if he thought of it at all, with distaste and contempt.[1]

The visit to Harrow took place on December 18, and, as Colville noted, Churchill 'thoroughly enjoyed himself'. He was accompanied by his wife, and by six old Harrovians: his brother Jack, Leo Amery, Colonel Moore-Brabazon, Geoffrey Lloyd, David Margesson and Colville. During a short speech, Churchill told the boys:

Hitler, in one of his recent discourses, declared that the fight was between those who have been through the Adolf Hitler Schools and those who have been at Eton.[2] Hitler has forgotten Harrow, and he has also overlooked the

[1] J. R. Colville, 'St Joles in the Bath', *The Harrovian*, 30 January 1965. Churchill had in fact offered his son the choice of Eton and Harrow, and had taken Randolph, then at prep school, to visit both establishments. Randolph chose Eton.

[2] In offering a barony to his friend Lord Hugh Cecil, Provost of Eton, Churchill wrote: 'It would be good to have you in the House of Lords to repel the onset of the Adolph Hitler schools,

vast majority of the youth of this country who have never had the advantage of attending such schools, but who are standing staunchly together in the nation's cause and whose skill and prowess is the envy of the whole world.

When this war is won by this nation, as it surely will be, it must be one of our aims to work to establish a state of society where the advantage and privileges which hitherto have been enjoyed only by the few shall be far more widely shared by the many and the youth of the nation as a whole.

The boys of Harrow, Churchill noted, had already 'had the honour of being under the fire of the enemy', and had, acquitted themselves 'with befitting courage and decorum'.[1]

One of those whom Churchill had taken with him to Harrow, Geoffrey Lloyd, later recalled the visit and its sequel:

It was, for all of us, I think, and certainly for me, an occasion with an emotional impact it was quite impossible to resist. Here was Winston Churchill, the Prime Minister, who was leading our country in a desperate effort to survive the mortal danger with which it was faced, taking time off to visit his old school and bring with him a small number of Old Harrovians who were also members of his Government. Suddenly to be taken away from one's hard Ministerial work and constant anxieties and to have before one several hundred of the rising generation, seeming in a way, as they sang, so fresh and vulnerable, yet so full of vitality and singing the boisterous Harrow Songs—this was indeed a sudden and delightful interlude of emotion and hope.[2]

For the boys of Harrow the visit has been long remembered.[3] The fifteen-year-old Michael Thomas later recalled the 'excitement and

---

to sustain the aristocratic morale, and to chide the Bishops when they err,' and, Churchill added, 'now that I read in the newspapers that the Eton flogging block is destroyed by enemy action, you may have more leisure and strength'. ('Private', 21 December 1940: Quickswood papers. Hugh Cecil accepted Churchill's offer, becoming Baron Quickswood.)

[1] *The Harrovian*, 24 December 1940. On the morning after this speech, Leo Amery wrote to Churchill: 'Your little speech to the boys couldn't have been bettered. As I listened I half wished I were one of the boys to carry it with me on my start in life. There will be some of them whose whole future will be shaped by it.' (Personal', 19 December 1940: Churchill papers, 2/392.)

[2] Lord Geoffrey-Lloyd, letter to the author, 30 September 1982.

[3] Among the boys at Harrow in November 1940 were Peter Green (who in 1944 served in the Russian convoys), later Chairman of Lloyds; L. J. Verney, later a Circuit Judge; Anthony Royle, later Parliamentary Under-Secretary of State for Foreign and Commonwealth Affairs (1970–74); Robert Farquarson, later Ambassador to Yugoslavia (1977–81); Roger Dudley North, the son of Admiral North; John Lumsden, a member of the British Pentathlon team in the 1948 London Olympic Games; and Alastair McCorquodale, the fastest white man in the 1948 Olympics (he came fourth in the 100 yards, after three black runners). Other boys at the school in November 1940 included Ronald Mutter, later Lieutenant, Scots Guards, killed in action in Germany on 27 April 1945; Humphrey Bridgeman, killed in action in Italy on 28 May 1944; and Duncan Davidson, died of wounds in Burma, on 2 March 1945.

anticipation' of Churchill's arrival in Speech Room—'almost 500 boys chattering away, then a deadly hush as we realised that he was at the door and then cheering—the sort of noise that only small boys can generate—that seemed to go on for ever'. The songs were sung 'as never before', Thomas added, 'the words reflecting his own fighting spirit and defence of our country and way of life'. When 'The Silver Arrow' was sung 'a large handkerchief appeared': the Prime Minister was in tears.[1] The songs over, Churchill had then spoken—'almost too briefly for some of us'—and left the hall. The boys then returned to their houses 'exhausted but exhilarated'.[2]

Among the songs sung was *Stet Fortuna Domus*, for which a new verse had been introduced:

> Nor less we praise in darker[3] days
> The leader of our nation,
> And Churchill's name shall win aclaim
> From each new generation.
> While in this fight to guard the Right
> Our country you defend, Sir,
> Here grim and gay we mean to stay,
> And stick it to the end, Sir.[4]

On the afternoon following his visit to Harrow, Churchill spoke in the House of Commons of the desert victory, praising the commanders and their men.[5] 'Vigilance must be unceasing,' he declared.[6] That night, 'tired but cheerful', as Eden noted in his diary, the two men recalled earlier moments of the struggle. 'We spoke of the dark days of the summer,' Eden wrote, 'I told him that Portal and I had confessed to each other that in our hearts we had both despaired at one time. Winston said "Yes. Normally I wake up buoyant to face the new day. Then I awoke with dread in my heart." '[7]

[1] Sir Anthony Royle recalls: 'Winston wept copiously throughout the singing, which amused all of us small boys.' (Sir Anthony Royle, letter to the author, 12 January 1983.) Royle was then 13 years old.

[2] Sir Michael Thomas, letter to the author, 7 January 1983. Thomas' father, Sir Godfrey Thomas, 10th Baronet, was from 1919 to 1936 Private Secretary to the Prince of Wales, and from 1937 to 1957 to the Duke of Gloucester.

[3] In his speech to the boys, Churchill deprecated the word 'darker'. He said that 'sterner' would be more appropriate, and 'sterner' has been sung ever since.

[4] 'The Prime Minister's Visit', *The Harrovian*, 24 December 1940.

[5] One phrase in Churchill's speech was cause for wry smiles. 'I certainly deprecate any comparison between Herr Hitler and Napoleon; I do not wish to insult the dead.'

[6] *Hansard*, 19 December 1940, columns 1398–1407.

[7] Eden diary, 19 December 1940: The Earl of Avon, *The Eden Memoirs, The Reckoning*, London 1965, page 182.

49

'A *busy* Christmas . . .'

A S Christmas approached, Churchill had still to find a new Ambassador for the United States. The choice of Lloyd George for Washington had proved a controversial one among those aware of it. Nevile Butler, the Chargé d'Affaires at the British Embassy in Washington, was emphatic. 'I am fully alive,' he telegraphed to Halifax on December 16, 'to the importance of new Ambassador's being an individual of outstanding personality and on close personal terms with Prime Minister. I am also fully conscious of the advantages which would be derived from Lloyd George's experience, aptitude, genius and lion-hearted courage. But I feel that I ought to point out certain— to my mind very real—disadvantages . . .' 'Rightly or wrongly,' Butler added, 'Lloyd George is, I think, regarded in this country as an appeaser and as not unwilling to consider making terms with Germany.'[1]

This telegram of protest against Lloyd George's possible appointment as Ambassador was sent from Washington one minute after a telegram from Roosevelt to Churchill, approving of Lloyd George for the post. Roosevelt's telegram began: 'Choice will be entirely agreeable. I knew him in world war.' Roosevelt added: 'I assume that over here he will in no way play into the hands of the appeasers.'[2] Lloyd George, however, declined the appointment on medical grounds, his doctor, Lord Horder, having advised that he was too old.[3] Churchill now pondered the possibility of sending Oliver Lyttelton. Finally he decided upon Halifax, the Foreign Secretary himself, telling Colville that Halifax

[1] Washington Telegram No. 3108, 'Most Immediate', 'Personal and Secret', 'To be decyphered by Private Secretary', 8.56 p.m., 15 December 1940: Foreign Office papers, 954/29, folio 95.

[2] Washington Telegram No. 3109, 'Most Immediate', 'Personal and Secret', 'Following from President for Prime Minister', 8.55 p.m., 15 December 1940: Foreign Office papers, 954/29, folio 96.

[3] Lloyd George was to be seventy-eight in January. He died in 1945.

'would never live down his reputation for appeasement which he and the Foreign Office had won themselves here. He had no future in this country. On the other hand he had a glorious opportunity in America, for, unless the United States came into the war, we could not win, or at least we could not win a really satisfactory peace.' If Halifax were to succeed in the United States, Churchill added, 'he would come home on the crest of the wave'.

Churchill's decision, Colville noted, had been influenced by the monthly censorship reports, which showed that Halifax was 'unpopular here because of his association with Neville Chamberlain'.[1] Reluctantly, Halifax accepted the Washington appointment. Eden became Foreign Secretary, with David Margesson succeeding Eden at the War Office.

During December the Enigma decrypts revealed massive German troop movements, with air support, into the Balkans. The Intelligence did not reveal the goal of these forces, but the interpreters, and all who saw the decrypts, felt certain that a German attack on Turkey was imminent, and once Turkey fell, Syria and Iraq were vulnerable, Palestine exposed, and Egypt effectively besieged from both the Sinai and western deserts.

One idea to counter such a German advance was the occupation of the Italian Dodecanese Islands, in the eastern Aegean, off the southwestern coast of Anatolia. This was the proposal sent to London by the three Commanders-in-Chief in the Middle East, Wavell, Longmore and Cunningham.[2] 'Let models be made of Rhodes and Leros,' Churchill had asked Ismay on December 11, with the added note: 'Report when they will be ready.'[3]

The models were made, based in part upon special air reconnaissance carried out for the purpose. On December 20 the Chiefs of Staff Committee reported on the scheme, stating that it had been 'impressed by the force of arguments' of the Middle East Commanders-in-Chief, and asking the Foreign Office 'what we propose to do with the Islands after

[1] Colville diary, 20 December 1940: Colville papers.

[2] The planned capture of the Dodecanese Islands was given the code name 'Mandibles'. The code names chosen for operations against the individual Islands were 'Cordite' (Rhodes), 'Allowance' (Leros), 'Consumption' (Stampalia), 'Armature' (Karpathos), 'Blunt' (Kasos), 'Beneath' (Kos), 'Commandeer' (Patmos), 'Border' (Lipsos) and 'Abstention' (Kastellorizo).

[3] Prime Minister's Personal Minute, D.147, 11 December 1940, 'Secret': Premier papers, 3/124/2, folio 36.

their capture'.[1] Two days later, Colonel Hollis pointed out to Churchill that the Commanders-in-Chief favoured a plan whereby the first phase of the operation would be to seize 'some of the smaller islands on the outer ring', in the hope that the more heavily defended places, such as Rhodes and Leros, 'would fall easily through starvation or a general lowering of morale'.[2]

Churchill was uncertain about this aspect of the plan, minuting for the Chiefs of Staff Committee: 'I do not think it would be wise to attack these smaller islands. They are no use in themselves, they are not necessary for the attack upon the larger islands now that we hold Crete. Stirring up this quarter will put the enemy on their guard, and will bring about the disagreement between Greece and Turkey which has become only too apparent as we have explored tentatively this subject.' Churchill also noted that the Defence Committee 'have not approved these operations'.[3] But the Commanders-in-Chief in the Middle East were concerned with several eventualities, principal of which was the threat posed by Italian naval and air forces operating from the Dodecanese to the 'main lines of supply' to both Greece and Turkey 'if and when major operations take place in the Spring'.[4]

It was to protect British interests during any German spring offensive in the Balkans or Turkey that plans were being made to establish British aerodromes both in Greece and Turkey. Several of those in Greece were already in use by British squadrons helping Greek forces against the Italians. The Air Staff now wanted these prepared and extended to enable their possible use against German troops and targets in Rumania. On December 22 Churchill wrote to Portal: 'It is not our interest to draw down German vengeance upon Greece. In any case the Greeks would have to be the final authority as to the use made of their aerodromes.'[5]

At Churchill's request, the Air Ministry provided him with a fortnightly report on the development of the work being done on Greek aerodromes to enable them to take British bombers and fighters. 'It is

[1] Chiefs of Staff Committee No. 1051 of 1940, 'The Dodecanese', 20 December 1940: Premier papers, 3/124/2, folio 70.

[2] 'Secret', 23 December 1940: Premier papers, 3/124/2, folios 71–2.

[3] Prime Minister's Personal Minute, D.14/1, 13 January 1941: Premier papers, 3/124/2, folio 43.

[4] Note by Colonel Hollis of the arguments of the Commanders-in-Chief, 23 December 1940: Premier papers, 3/124/2, folio 71.

[5] Prime Minister's Personal Minute, M.446, 22 December 1940: Premier papers, 3/205, folios 22–3.

quite clear to me,' Churchill had minuted to Portal on December 15, 'that this is going to be most important in the near future, and we must try not to be taken by surprise by events.'[1]

At the very moment when, on Churchill's instructions, the Chiefs of Staff were building up British air support and ground facilities in Greece and planning for similar facilities in Turkey, Churchill was presented with yet another proposal for action. On the afternoon of December 28 Dudley Pound told Churchill of a plan which was being prepared for occupying Sicily, code name 'Influx'. Later that same day, Hollis sent Churchill a brief summary of the plan, prepared by the Directors of Plans, and told him that 'Influx' was to be considered in detail by the Chiefs of Staff in two days time. 'I mention the code name,' Hollis added, 'because I do not think you have been made aware of it.'[2]

As explained by the Joint Planning Committee, 'Influx' was intended to anticipate any German move into Italy by a British initiative, and to 'do all we can' to interfere with communications from Central to Southern Italy. It envisaged the initial use of two infantry brigades for the capture first of Catania and then of Messina.[3] On December 31 the Chiefs of Staff gave 'Influx' their approval, informing the Commanders-in-Chief, Middle East, that if Sicily turned 'against the Axis and Fascist Government' forces might be landed 'without opposition'. Forces might also be landed if 'a limited degree of resistance' were expected.[4] Three weeks later the Chiefs of Staff telegraphed again about 'Influx' to the Commanders-in-Chief, Middle East, instructing them to 'prepare plans and nominate commanders and forces'.[5]

Churchill was unhappy about all these plans and orders, and on reading a telegram from the Admiralty to the Commander-in-Chief Mediterranean about the need to prepare plans for the naval forces involved in seizing Sicily, Churchill minuted for the Chiefs of Staff Committee:

Surely this is burdening the Middle East Command with too much. Wavell will have to use all his spare strength to help Turkey and/or Greece. How can he possibly develop a large-scale operation of this character? I do not think this telegram should have been sent without previous reference to me, and I

[1] Prime Minister's Personal Minute, M.423, 'Secret' 15 December 1940: Premier papers, 3/205, folio 27.

[2] 'Most Secret', 28 December 1940: Premier papers, 3/234, folio 5.

[3] 'Secret', 27 December 1940: Premier papers, 3/234, folio 6.

[4] Chiefs of Staff Telegram No. 38, 31 December 1940, 'Hush. Most Secret': Premier papers, 3/234, folio 7.

[5] Chiefs of Staff Telegram No. 50, 24 January 1941, 'Hush. Most Secret': Premier papers, 3/234, folio 6.

would then have decided whether reference to the Defence Committee were necessary.[1]

The problems confronting Churchill and his advisers as 1940 ended were particularly complex. One of these problems was the possibility of Spain allowing the Germans to cross the Iberian peninsula to attack Gibraltar.[2] Another was Britain's attitude towards Vichy France. Churchill might despise those who had created Vichy. He might wish to persevere with Britain's commitment to de Gaulle. He might place his hopes on Roosevelt's continuing pressure to prevent any anti-British naval move on the part of Vichy. But in the background was the tantalizing prospect that the Vichy Government might decide to abandon its subservience to the Reich, if German pressures increased, or if British blandishments were sufficiently persuasive.

On November 26 Churchill discussed with de Gaulle the possibility of General Weygand being prepared, from his base in North Africa, to declare himself against the Vichy authorities. In any future development, de Gaulle told Churchill, 'he thought General Weygand might play a very leading part'. But, as Churchill told Halifax on the following day, de Gaulle 'did not say' that he would serve under Weygand.[3]

In his talk with de Gaulle, Churchill agreed to provide British naval help to enable de Gaulle to capture Jibuti from the Vichy-controlled garrison there.[4] 'This would be a very agreeable development,' Churchill told the Chiefs of Staff Committee, 'and is very much the best thing de Gaulle could do at the present time. It should be studied attentively and in conjunction with General de Gaulle.'[5]

At the same time as Churchill's efforts to help de Gaulle, the messages from Vichy continued to imply the possibility of some accommodation, including an acceptance of de Gaulle's ascendancy in French Equatorial Africa, at least until the end of the war. On December 5 Professor Rougier informed Churchill, by letter, of three specific assurances given, he said, by Pétain personally:

---

[1] Prime Minister's Personal Minute, D.22/1, 25 January 1941: Premier papers, 3/234.

[2] With the possibility of a German occupation of Spain, the Defence Committee on December 16 discussed two new plans: Operation 'Grind' for the landing of a British force in Tangier, and Operation 'Humour', to land a small force in Morocco at the invitation of the local Spaniards, 'to help stiffen their resistance'. But such an operation, Churchill feared, 'would hardly be sufficient', as the Spaniards would no doubt expect Britain to help them in their resistance against Germany 'in Spain itself', and preparations should be made for such an operation. (Defence Committee (Operations) No. 50 of 1940, 16 December 1940, 9.30 p.m.: Cabinet papers, 69/1.)

[3] 'Conversations', 27 November 1940: Foreign Office papers, 800/362, H/XIV/477.

[4] The Jibuti operation was given the code name 'Marie'.

[5] Prime Minister's Personal Minute, D.131, 1 December 1940: Churchill papers, 20/13.

1. France would not sign a separate peace with the Axis before the end of hostilities between Great Britain and Germany.
2. France would not cede naval or air bases or the fleet to the Axis and would resist any attempt by Spain, Germany or Italy to seize the French colonies in North Africa.
3. France accepted the submission of French Equatorial Africa to General de Gaulle as a *fait accompli* till the end of the war on the understanding that the territories would then be restored to France and that meanwhile no attack would be directed against French West Africa, North Africa or Morocco.[1]

On Saturday December 21 Churchill gave dinner at Chequers to the Canadian Government's representative at Vichy, Pierre Dupuy, who had just returned from Vichy. Dupuy reported that Pétain, Darlan, and the Minister of War, General Huntziger 'had spoken to him about the possibility of co-operation in North Africa and Continental France' provided that 'the present atmosphere of tension' between Britain and Vichy, could be maintained 'as a smoke screen, behind which contacts could be made and information exchanged'.

Churchill told Dupuy, according to the official record of their talk, that 'he was ready to enter into a procedure along the lines suggested above' and that he would like Dupuy 'to inform the French Government of his readiness to send divisions to North Africa in case the French Government should decide to abandon the metropolitan territory or considered it opportune to receive British support in North Africa'. Churchill added that 'it was important that the question should be examined as soon as possible in order to avoid experiences similar to those of Norway, the Netherlands and Belgium'.

At the end of their meeting, Churchill entrusted Dupuy 'with the mission of presenting his point of view to the interested Department of the French Government, as well as to the French military authorities in North Africa'.[2]

The secret discussions between Britain and Vichy were suddenly made public, on December 24, by the *Chicago Daily News* correspondent in London, Helen Kirkpatrick, who sent to Chicago details of Professor Rougier's earlier visit to London and added that a further 'confirmatory message' had been brought to London from Vichy by Pierre Dupuy, including 'a personal message from Marshal Pétain and Admiral Darlan'.[3]

---

[1] Letter of 5 December 1940: Foreign Office papers, 371/24361.

[2] 'Conversation between Mr Winston Churchill and M. Pierre Dupuy on Saturday, 21st December, 1940', 'Canadian Legation, London', 26 December 1940: Admiralty papers, 199/1928.

[3] 'Petain tells Britain Vichy will not aid Nazi Attack', 'Special cable to the Chicago Daily News Foreign Service', London, 24 December 1940.

Reading this despatch, Churchill minuted: 'Miss Helen Kirkpatrick should be shipped out of the country at the earliest moment. It is very undesirable to have a person of this kind scouting about private houses for copy regardless of British interests.'[1]

Dupuy went back to Vichy, reporting to the Canadian Prime Minister, Mackenzie King, that Pétain was 'still alert and hoping for a British victory', that 'secret collaboration' between France and the British Commonwealth would be possible behind a smokescreen of continued Anglo-French tension, and that the French military authorities, who were preparing in both occupied and unoccupied France 'for any eventuality', would apply for British support in material and men 'at a later stage'. Dupuy noted that the expulsion of Laval from the Cabinet was 'proof' that Pétain is ready to resist as far as possible any German interference in his Government policy', while the appointment of Flandin, 'although not ideal should be considered an improvement'.[2]

Dupuy's report to Ottawa was forwarded to London.[3] To Eden, Dupuy reported direct three days later that Pétain, Darlan and Huntziger had suggested opening negotiations between Britain and Vichy, ostensibly on commercial matters, but 'with the hope that such negotiations might lead to closer collaboration between the two countries'.[4]

Churchill understood the delicacy and difficulties of Dupuy's mission. 'We are greatly indebted to Monsieur Dupuy,' he told Eden, 'for what he has done.' His efforts to detach Vichy France from Germany should continue. 'The sooner he can get back to Vichy or North Africa the better. Vichy would be better, in view of the turn events are taking but we must leave it to him.'[5]

Churchill meanwhile had prepared a note for Dupuy for his use in

[1] Prime Minister's Personal Minute, M.2/1, 1 January 1941: Churchill papers, 20/36. After Brendan Bracken had assured Churchill that Helen Kirkpatrick was a stoutly loyal and pro-Allied American, Churchill agreed to let her remain in the country minuting on the file in which her accidental indiscretions were described: 'O Lor!' (Premier papers, 3/126/1.) Helen Kirkpatrick writes, of Rougier and Dupuy: 'I never met either one. I know that I first learned of their presence in London from Eve Curie, and I suspect that more details of their reports came from Desmond Morton whom I saw regularly. . . .' (Helen Robbins Milbank, letter to the author, 24 June 1979.)

[2] Laval had been Foreign Minister of Vichy France since October 28 (in succession to Baudouin). On December 15 he was replaced by Flandin (who was himself succeeded by Darlan in February 1941. Laval returned to the post in April 1942.)

[3] 'Copy of telegram sent to External, Ottawa, on 24th December, 1940': Admiralty papers, 199/1928.

[4] Letter of 27 December 1940, C.13953: Foreign Office papers, 371/24296.

[5] Prime Minister's Personal Minute, M.480, 29 December 1940: Admiralty papers, 199/1928.

North Africa when he went to see Weygand and Noguès.[1] This note set out in measured argument why the French authorities in North Africa should abandon Vichy, and what Britain was prepared to do should they do so. Churchill's note read:

Should you see Generals Weygand or Noguès, you should explain that we now have a large, well-equipped Army in England, and have considerable spare forces already well trained and rapidly improving, apart from what are needed to repel invasion.

The situation in the Middle East is also becoming good. If at any time in the near future the French Government decide to resume the war in Africa against Italy and Germany, we would send a strong and well-equipped Expeditionary Force to aid the defence of Morocco, Algiers and Tunis. These divisions could sail as fast as shipping and landing facilities were available. The British Air Force has now begun its expansion, and would also be able to give important assistance. The Command of the Mediterranean would be assured by the reunion of the British and French Fleets, and by our joint use of Moroccan and North African bases. We are willing to enter into Staff talks of the most secret character with General Weygand, or any officers nominated by him.

Churchill then stressed the need for urgency, if Weygand was to take up this offer of direct talks with Britain. Delay, Churchill warned, 'is dangerous', and he went on to explain:

At any time the Germans may, by force or favour, come down through Spain, render unusable the anchorage at Gibraltar, take effective charge of the batteries on both sides of the Straits, and also establish their Air Forces in the aerodromes. It is their habit to strike swiftly, and if they establish themselves at Casablanca the door would be shut on all projects. We are quite ready to wait for a certain time, provided that there is a good hope of bold action, and that plans are being made. But the situation may deteriorate any day and prospects be ruined.

It was 'most important', Churchill concluded, 'that the Government of Marshal Pétain should realise that we are able and willing to give powerful and growing aid. But this may presently pass beyond our power.'[2]

Eight days later, Dupuy himself took this message to Pétain, and a copy was sent by emissary to Weygand, at Algiers.[3] Neither Pétain nor

---

[1] The French (Vichy) Government's Resident-General in Morocco.

[2] Prime Minister's Personal Minute, D.153, 23 December 1940, 'Most Secret': Churchill papers, 20/13.

[3] The emissary was Colonel Mittelman, code name 'Lancelot'. It was 'most important', Churchill minuted to Eden, 'that a copy of my telegram to Pétain should reach Weygand by any channel, and not necessarily wait for Mittelman to deliver it'. Prime Minister's Personal Minute, M.36/1, 9 January 1941: Churchill papers, 20/36.

Weygand replied direct, but in his report on his mission three weeks later Dupuy said, as Colville noted in his diary, that he had found Pétain 'much more alert than we had supposed, and anxious for a British victory'. General Huntziger was doing 'excellent work behind the scenes, in preparation for the day of liberation', and even Darlan, so Dupuy reported, 'was determined not to let his personal animosity against the Admiralty make him work against a British victory'.[1]

That same day, Eden told the War Cabinet that 'distinctly encouraging' messages had been received from Weygand, while Churchill commented 'that he conceived Marshal Pétain's main object to be to keep the Germans out of Unoccupied France by threatening that if they came in, the Fleet, and North Africa would join this country'. It remained to be seen, Churchill added, 'how long he could keep the Germans in play'.[2]

With his thoughts focused on the many dangers in the Aegean and Mediterranean, Churchill broadcast on the evening of December 23 to the Italian people. He spoke from the Central War Room, deploring the fact that Britain and Italy were at war, 'condemned to work each other's ruin'. The cause for this, he said, lay with 'one man, and one man alone', Mussolini. 'That he is a great man I do not deny, but that after eighteen years of unbridled power he has led your country to the horrid verge of ruin can be denied by none.'

Churchill then read out his exchange of letters with Mussolini the previous May, when he had appealed to the Italian leader not to range Britain and Italy against each other 'in mortal strife'. After reading out the text of his letter, and of Mussolini's reply, Churchill ended his broadcast with the words:

Anyone can see who it was wanted peace, and who it was that meant to have war. One man, and one man only, was resolved to plunge Italy after all these years of strain and effort into the whirlpool of war. And what is the position of Italy today? Where is it that the Duce has led his trusting people after eighteen years of dictatorial power? What hard choice is open to him now? It is to stand up to the battery of the whole British Empire on sea, in the air, and in Africa, and the vigorous counter-attack of the Greek nation; or, on the other hand, to call in Attila over the Brenner Pass with his hordes of ravenous

[1] Colville diary, 20 January 1941: Colville papers.
[2] War Cabinet No. 8 of 1941, 20 January 1941, Minute 3, Confidential Annex: Cabinet papers, 65/21.

soldiery and his gangs of Gestapo policemen to occupy, hold down and protect the Italian people, for whom he and his Nazi followers cherish the most bitter and outspoken contempt that is on record between races.

There is where one man, and one man only, has led you; and there I leave this unfolding story until the day comes—as come it will—when the Italian nation will once more take a hand in shaping its own fortunes.[1]

After this broadcast, Harold Nicolson noted in his diary that some of the United States Press correspondents in London had told him 'that they think it is the best thing that Winston has ever done'.[2]

From London, Churchill planned to go to Chequers for Christmas. It was to be a family gathering: Clementine Churchill, Mary Churchill, Diana and Duncan Sandys, Randolph Churchill and his wife, Vic Oliver and Sarah, and Clementine Churchill's cousin Marriot Whyte.[3] The only non-family members present over the holiday were Lindemann, Sir Wilfrid Freeman,[4] Lord Woolton, and, as duty Private Secretary, John Martin. Before leaving for Chequers, Churchill despatched two presents to the Palace, a Siren Suit for the King, whom he had helped with the text of his Christmas broadcast, and Fowler's *Dictionary of Modern English Usage* for the Queen.[5] Wishing his staff 'a *busy* Christmas and a *frantic* New Year', he was gone.[6]

To Eric Seal, who had suggested that he should arrange short periods of leave during the recess, he replied: 'No holidays can be given at Christmas, but every endeavour should be made to allow members of the Staff to attend Divine Service either here or in London on Christmas Day, either in the morning or afternoon. My own plans will be to work either here'—at Chequers—'or in London continuously.' He would however approve, he added, of one week's holiday for each member of his Private Office 'being worked in and well spread between now and March 31'.[7]

---

[1] 'To the Peoples of Italy', 23 December 1940: His Master's Voice recording, ALP 1555.

[2] Diary entry, 23 December 1940: Nigel Nicolson (editor), Harold Nicolson, *Diaries and Letters, 1939–1945*, London 1967, page 131.

[3] Chequers Visitors' Book. On 26 December 1940 the man who in 1921 had given Chequers to the nation, Lord Lee of Fareham, replying to Churchill's thanks for 'the inspiration which moved you to make this splendid gift to the nation', declared: 'For the house of ancient memories this is its finest hour.' (Churchill papers, 2/396.)

[4] The new Vice-Chief of the Air Staff, and Portal's confidant.

[5] Replying to the Queen's letter of thanks, Churchill wrote: 'I am very glad that Your Majesty found Fowler's Dictionary entertaining. He is a real master of his subject, always sensible, lucid and practical, and above all never a pedant. He liberated me from many errors and doubts, e.g. "I should have liked to have been there" instead of the simple "I sh'd have liked to be there."' (Letter of 3 February 1941: Churchill papers, 20/29.)

[6] Colville diary, 24 December 1949: Colville papers.

[7] Martin papers.

Churchill's exhortation to spend 'a *busy* Christmas' was not only for those working for him. He adhered to it himself, dictating a series of minutes on December 25, among them minutes on the need to restrict the circulation of secret papers, to keep the Dominions informed fully of the progress of the war, to establish a single authority to take charge of the needs of those in shelters, and to remedy the 'grave situation' created by congestion in the Liverpool docks.[1] John Martin, the duty Private Secretary who witnessed this activity, and its aftermath, wrote home:

The Prime Minister has made a great point of working as usual over the holiday and yesterday morning was like almost any other here, with the usual letters and telephone calls and of course many Christmas greeting messages thrown in. His present to me was an inscribed copy of 'Great Contemporaries'.

From lunch time on, less work was done and we had a festive family Christmas, with the three daughters, two sons-in-law and one daughter-in-law and no official visitors. For lunch we had the largest turkey I have ever seen, a present from Lord Rothermere's farm, sent in accordance with one of his last wishes before he died.[2]

Afterwards we listened to The King's speech and Vic Oliver played the piano and Sarah sang. It was the same after dinner. For once the shorthand writer was dismissed and we had a sort of sing-song until after midnight.

The PM sang lustily, if not always in tune, and when Vic played Viennese waltzes he danced a remarkably frisky measure of his own in the middle of the room. He then would sit up and talk till 2 a.m.; but I found him as brisk as ever this morning, cheerfully munching one of Lloyd George's apples from Churt.[3]

'We have been very peaceful here over Christmas,' Churchill wrote to Halifax on Boxing Day. 'No one but the family, and oddly enough the whole of it.'[4]

Returning to London on December 28, Churchill emphasized his keenness to seize Pantelleria. 'Constant reflection,' he minuted to Ismay for the Chiefs of Staff Committee, 'has made me feel the very high value of "Workshop", provided,' he added, that a 'thoroughly good plan' could be worked out and 'given a chance.' His minute ended:

The effect of 'Workshop', if successful, would be electrifying, and would greatly

---

[1] Prime Minister's Personal Minutes, M.454 to M.457: Churchill papers, 20/13.
[2] The 1st Viscount Rothermere, Churchill's friend for more than two decades, had died on 26 November 1940. Two of his three sons had been killed in the First World War.
[3] Letter of 26 December 1940: Martin papers.
[4] Letter of 26 December 1940: Churchill papers, 20/2.

increase our strategic hold upon the Central Mediterranean. It is also a most important step to opening the Narrows to the passage of trade and troop convoys, whereby so great an easement to our shipping could be obtained.

Urgency is supplied by the danger that the Germans, if they take over Italy, will take over 'Workshop' island and make it a very difficult proposition both for nuisance value and against assault.'[1]

On the night of Sunday December 29, in a heavy incendiary raid on the City of London, German bombers struck at the railway stations and docks, in which eight Wren churches were among hundreds of buildings destroyed or damaged. This raid brought the total number of civilian deaths from bombing in December to 3,793, with a further five thousand injured. On the following evening Churchill telegraphed to Roosevelt:

They burned a large part of the City of London last night, and the scenes of widespread destruction here and in our provincial centres are shocking; but when I visited the still-burning ruins to-day the spirit of the Londoners was as high as in the first days of the indiscriminate bombing in September, four months ago.[2]

On the advice of the British Embassy in Washington, this paragraph was not sent to Roosevelt, for fear that it 'might revive the defeatist impression of some months ago'.

While reading the mass of material put before him each day, Churchill always kept in mind the security aspect, repeatedly, pressing his advisers to let him see the lists of officials and departments to whom particular telegrams had been distributed, and seeking to cut down on any needlessly large circulation. On Christmas day 1940, he had minuted to Bridges and Ismay, his principal advisers on all matters concerning security:

With the new year, a fresh effort must be made to restrict the circulation of secret matters in Service and other Departments. All the markings of papers in the Service Departments, Foreign Office, Colonial and Dominions Offices, &c., should be reviewed with a view to striking off as many recipients as possible.

The official concerned in roneo-ing the various circulations should be consulted, and a return made for me showing how many are struck off of different secret documents.

Pray report to me how this object can be achieved.[3]

On New Year's day 1941, in his first minute of the new year, Chur-

---

[1] Prime Minister's Personal Minutes, D.159, 28 December 1940: Churchill papers, 20/13.
[2] Premier papers, 4/17/1, folio 88 (see pages 974–7).
[3] Prime Minister's Personal Minute, C.34, 25 December 1940: Churchill papers, 20/13.

chill instructed Bridges and Ismay to make 'a new intense drive' in order to 'secure greater secrecy in all matters relating to the conduct of the war'. Each Government department was to be asked to submit proposals 'for restricting the circulation of papers', a restriction which was 'all the more important', Churchill stressed, 'on account of the ever increasing elaboration of Government departments and the Whitehall population'. Churchill's minute continued:

The use of boxes with snap locks is to be enforced for all documents of a secret character. Ministers and their private secretaries should have snap-lock boxes on their desks, and should never leave confidential documents in trays when they are out of the room. Boxes should always be snapped to when not immediately in use. Access to rooms in which confidential secretaries and Ministers are working should be restricted wherever possible, and ante-rooms provided into which visitors can be shown. A small red star label should be devised to be placed on most secret papers—i.e., those dealing with operations and the strength of the armed forces. It is not necessary for all the private secretaries in the office to read these starred documents. They should always be circulated in locked boxes, and transferred immediately to other locked boxes for my use and for the use of the Ministers.

Churchill also warned in this minute against the habit which had grown up of mentioning a particular future operation together with its code name. 'All such documents which contain the name of the place and the code word,' Churchill directed, 'should be collected and either destroyed by fire or put in a safe.' Churchill's minute continued:

The wide circulation of Intelligence Reports and the general tendency to multiply reports of all kinds must be curtailed. Each department connected with the war should be asked to submit a report showing what further restrictions and curtailments they propose to introduce in the New Year. Some time ago the late Cabinet decided that Ministers not in the War Cabinet should submit beforehand speeches on the war, or references in speeches to the war, to the Minister of Information. This has apparently fallen into disuse.

Let me have a report as to what is happening. A more convenient method might be that Ministers wishing to refer to these subjects should consult General Ismay as representing the Minister of Defence beforehand. No officials who have, for instance, been on missions abroad should make public statements concerning their work without previous Ministerial approval.[1]

By the end of February Bridges prepared a new system of Departmental security. Churchill's proposal for a small red star label would not work, he said, having the 'disadvantage of drawing attention unduly to the fact that the Paper belongs to the most secret class'. But

[1] Prime Minister's Personal Minute, C.1/1, 1 January 1941: Churchill papers, 20/36.

Bridges was able to assure Churchill that the circulation lists for Intelligence reports and other secret papers had recently been 'overhauled', and the circulation lists 'drastically cut'.[1]

On May 27 the Bridges memorandum was to be issued officially with a covering note by Churchill which began: 'An intense effort should be made to achieve greater security in matters where secrecy is of fundamental importance to the conduct of the war.'[2] The memorandum itself dealt with the mailing, distribution, handling and filing of security papers, as well as the protection of code names and a general warning against 'the dangers of gossip on confidential matters'. The note also warned that a 'constant check must be kept to see that Secret waste does not go into the ordinary wastepaper basket to which unauthorised persons have access'.[3]

In a further effort to tighten security in Whitehall, Churchill noted that the scrambler telephone at present 'works unhandily but those concerned must get used to it', and it should be made to work 'easily and effectively'. As for telephone conversations on the special Green Line telephone circuit this, Churchill minuted, 'ought not to be used for any precise discussion about very secret matters, especially future operations. Should this become indispensable, guarded terms and synonyms should be used, care always being taken that the conversation would not be intelligible to anyone not in the swim.'[4]

Churchill's concern for security was paramount. Seeing, on one occasion, a document which included details from a most secret source he asked Ismay and Bridges: 'how many copies were struck, in what Department is the duplicating machine which struck it off, and who gave the orders for it to go in this form'. Meanwhile, he added, 'withdraw every copy and substitute the amended version. The copies circulated are to be destroyed by fire under the supervision of the Defence Committee.' The circulation of this material, Churchill ended, 'is a very good example of what not to do'.[5]

On another occasion, in his scrutiny of circulated materials, Churchill noted that one of the regular Secret Situation Reports contained a paragraph which followed closely the Enigma decrypt from which it was drawn, and that the dates given in the decrypt were repeated in

---

[1] 'Secret', 'Security', 25 April 1941: Cabinet papers 120/76.
[2] War Cabinet paper (G) No. 43 of 1941, 'Security' 27 May 1941: Churchill papers, 23/9.
[3] 'Memorandum', 27 May 1941: Churchill papers, 23/9.
[4] 'Action this Day', 'Please implement', Prime Minister's Personal Minute C.41/1 (to Ismay and Bridges): Churchill papers, 20/36.
[5] Prime Minister's Personal Minute, D.56/1, 17 February 1941: Cabinet papers, 120/744.

the Report. He at once asked 'C' why this had happened. 'The dates given in the special message,' replied 'C' to Ismay, 'were repeated in the Report as it was thought desirable that the highly select circle to which these reports are sent for perusal and immediate destruction should be informed of these significant dates.' Orders had been issued, 'C' assured Churchill, 'to ensure that in future these special messages will be carefully paraphrased'.[1]

The secrecy of code names was another aspect of security on which Churchill sought information, asking Ismay at the beginning of 1941 for a list of all the code names of operations then in force.[2] In his reply Ismay explained to Churchill that the issuing and coordinating of code names was done by the Inter-Services Security Board working under the direction of the Joint Intelligence Committee. It was the Security Board that allotted to different Government Departments blocks of suitable words. These words were kept on central indexes available to each of the three Service Ministers. At the same time, a book was being prepared which would list some 9,000 words available for use as code names, for future operations.

The blocks of words already allotted as code names, and the code names chosen for future operations, were kept on a card index system, but never typed out as a complete list. Access to the card index was restricted 'by the most stringent regulations'.[3]

'I am glad to see that the matter is being organised so well,' Churchill wrote to Ismay on receiving this account. 'It is essential,' he added, 'that there should be *no book*. Each section may have its own small circle, but only one list of the whole should be kept, and that in the office of the Minister of Defence. Whatever you do, do not let the official printing presses go and blether out these secrets, as they do so many others.'[4]

Two weeks later Churchill received, in a sealed envelope, a list of the code names allotted to him, as Minister of Defence, by the Inter-Services Security Board. These were thirty-two names on the list, which Churchill was welcome to use at random for any future operation needing a code name. The fourth name on the list was 'Battleaxe'.[5]

---

[1] Minute of 24 February 1941: Cabinet papers 120/744.
[2] Prime Minister's Personal Minute D.4/1, 3 January 1941: Cabinet Papers 120/413.
[3] 'Secret', 5 January 1941: Cabinet Papers 120/413.
[4] Prime Minister's Personal Minute D.10/1, 7 January 1941: Cabinet papers 120/413.
[5] 'Code Names Allotted to the Minister of Defence', 22 January 1941: Cabinet papers 120/413. The code name 'Battleaxe' was eventually given to Wavell's offensive against Rommel in the Western Desert, launched on 15 June 1941. Anxious to maintain the secrecy of convoys, Churchill

The last day of 1940, Tuesday December 31, was spent in the shadow of the German air raid of Sunday night and Monday morning. 'Winston is in mellow mood,' Colville noted. That day, while inspecting two of Herbert Morrison's new domestic shelters, he was able to 'demonstrate his technical knowledge as a builder', as he spoke in the technical terms and with detailed comments on the 'stresses and strains' to which building material could be subjected.[1]

As 1940 ended, many of Churchill's hopes for 1941 were based on the United States: its material and its moral support, and its possible direct participation in the war. But even as the courtesies of the season were being exchanged, a crisis of confidence, and of cash, threatened to disrupt the progress that had been made in Anglo-American relations during the first seven months of his Premiership, and to jeopardize the economic and material assistance from the United States on which Britain was so dependent.

------

later minuted to the Ministers concerned: 'where so much is visible and must be known, the continued fabrication and dissemination of false information is a necessary part of security. All kinds of Münchhausen tales can be spread about to confuse and baffle the truth. Sun helmets or winter clothing should be hawked about and calculated leakages made of false and sometimes true intentions.' (Prime Minister's Personal Minute, M.492/1, 30 April 1941: Churchill papers, 20/36.)

[1] Colville diary, 31 December 1940: Colville papers.

50

Crisis with America: 'We do not know what you have in mind'

E VEN after Roosevelt's re-election in November, the feeling had persisted in the United States, not merely among Isolationists, that Britain did not wish to make the necessary financial sacrifices to secure the mass of supplies needed to continue the war. In Washington, a senior Treasury official, Sir Frederick Phillips, worked to resolve these difficulties.[1]

On December 10 Phillips informed London that the total figure of all British orders placed or to be placed up to the end of August 1941 'amounted to about 9 billion dollars'. This sum was 'so large', Morgenthau had told Phillips on the previous day, that Roosevelt needed time 'to make up his mind' how to present the problem to Congress. Meanwhile, the 10 Division Army Programme—Army Programme B— of 957 million dollars, was to be contracted for at once, with 257 million payable in advance, and 100 million of capital expenditure financed by the United States.[2]

In a second telegram that same day. Phillips pointed out that against Britain's proposed expenditure in the United States for the coming December, January and February alone was about 1,000 million dollars, against which Britain had only 574 million dollars in gold and United States dollar balances combined. The only way to obtain the 'necessary assistance' from the United States Administration in advance

---

[1] Phillips was Joint Second Secretary at the Treasury, and Treasury Representative in the United States from 1940 until his death in 1943. During Churchill's Chancellorship he had been Principal Assistant Secretary.

[2] Washington Telegram No. 3005, 'Most Immediate', 'Most Secret', 10 December 1940: Premier papers, 4/17/1, folio 137.

of Congressional action, Phillips warned, was to 'make use' of Allied, Dominion and French gold 'or prove to their satisfaction there are overwhelming reasons why we cannot do this'.[1]

In a telegram on December 11, Phillips reported Morgenthau's expectation that Britain would 'take' and use all French gold then held in Canada. 'It is the United States suspicion,' Phillips wrote, 'that we are not seriously trying to realize what assets we can that is causing the whole difficulty.' American officials believed that Britain was 'withholding information' about her assets, Phillips added, and the 'absence of information' about direct investments in the United States, was 'at present prejudicing the administration's goodwill'. If the crisis were not resolved soon, 'the Administration will wash its hands of us', Phillips warned.[2]

Churchill, Halifax, Eden and Kingsley Wood met on the morning of December 16 in the Cabinet Room at 10 Downing Street to discuss these telegrams. After the meeting, Churchill drafted a personal appeal to Roosevelt. The appeal read:

Am much puzzled by deadlock about programmes. We were told that we could have an extra ten divisions' equipment on American types and that our acceptance would enable American plants to be planned on a larger and more provident scale. Certainly this equipment would have enabled us to act and bleed on the front of another 200,000 men in 1942. We should welcome this opportunity, but we could not take it at the expense of the far-more urgent programmes needed for '41.

We are now told that unless we accept the additional ten Divisions equipment and pay 257 millions of our rapidly-dwindling dollars as advance cover 'the Administration will wash its hands of us'.

I feel sure there must be some misunderstanding and should be grateful for your advice. We could not sacrifice programme A to programme B, still less could we use for programme B nearly half of the cash which is left to us without knowing broadly what you are going to give us over and above what we can pay for.

If you were to 'wash your hands of us' i.e. give us nothing we cannot pay for with suitable advances, we should certainly not give in, and I believe we could save ourselves and our own National interests for the time being. But we should certainly not be able to beat the Nazi tyranny and gain you the time you require for your re-armament.

You may be absolutely sure that whatever you do or do not feel able to do, we shall go on to the utmost limits of our resources and strength, but that

[1] Washington Telegram No. 3009, 'Most Immediate', 'Most Secret', 10 December 1940: Premier papers, 4/17/1, folio 136.

[2] Washington Telegram No. 3035, 'Most Immediate', 'Most Secret', 11 December 1940: Premier papers, 4/17/1, folio 132.

strength unaided will not be sufficient to produce a world-result of a satisfactory and lasting character.[1]

In anticipation of a public statement by Roosevelt that same day, Churchill decided to hold back this telegram, and as soon as he read the statement, he cancelled the telegram. For Roosevelt had announced that the United States could take over British munitions orders and 'enter into some kind of arrangement for their use by the British on the grounds that it was the best thing for American defence, with the understanding that when the show was over, we would get repaid sometime in kind, thereby leaving out the dollar mark'—and 'substituting it for a gentleman's obligation to repay in kind'. Roosevelt added, by way of explanation of this plan, that if his neighbour wanted to borrow his garden hose to put out a fire, he would not say ' "Neighbour, my garden hose cost me $15; you have to pay me $15 for it." ' It was not the $15 he wanted, but 'my garden hose back after the fire is over.'[2]

Roosevelt's remarks encouraged Churchill to await an American initiative on the now evolving Lend-Lease concept. But he still felt that it was necessary to correct the American suspicion that Britain had not been able to man the American destroyers whose despatch had been described as so urgent. On December 21 Churchill asked Pound to let him have details of when the destroyers had arrived, and when and where they had been in action. He wanted the answer to this 'at the earliest moment', as well as details of 'defects that had to be remedied', improvements made, numbers brought into action, how long they were at sea and 'what happened to each'. He needed these facts, Churchill told Pound, 'as I want to send a cable to the President'.[3]

Two days later, while Pound was still preparing these naval facts and figures, Churchill learnt from Kingsley Wood that there had still been no response from the American Administration 'to our claim to their help in overcoming the temporary difficulty due to the exhaustion next week of our dollars and gold located in America'.[4]

On the very day Kingsley Wood sent this minute to Churchill, Sir Frederick Phillips reported from Washington that, as the British gold reserves in the United States were about to run out in the coming week, Roosevelt had arranged for a United States battleship or cruiser

[1] 'Prime Minister to President', 'Personal', 'Secret', draft of 17 December 1940: Premier papers, 4/17/1, folios 121–2.
[2] *The Times*, 18 December 1940.
[3] Minute of 21 December 1940: Premier papers, 3/462/1, folio 29.
[4] Minute of 23 December 1940: Premier papers, 4/17/1, folio 114.

to call in South Africa to collect the fifty million pounds of British gold held there. There was 'nothing for it', Phillips added, 'but to acquiesce'.

Phillips also reported that he had been pressed 'strongly' by Morgenthau, 'from the President, to take some action with regard to direct investment'. The sale 'of even one business', he wrote, 'or the presence in New York of an agent known to be willing to sell, would help them enormously with Congress'.[1]

As soon as Churchill read this telegram, on Christmas Day, he minuted to Kingsley Wood: 'What about the latest developments? I do not like it.'[2] Nor did the Treasury. 'Further reflection about the South African ship proposal,' Phillips was informed that evening, 'makes us dislike it the more and we should prefer to leave this in abeyance until we have exhausted other alternatives.'[3]

Lord Beaverbrook was among those who had been angered by the American demand for Britain's South African gold. 'It should be made amply clear,' he protested to Churchill on Boxing Day, 'that we are not prepared to relinquish any more gold here or in South Africa and that we must retain any interest we possess in gold in the Dominions. These are the last resources of the British people and should be held intact to provide us with essential means in the case of a compelling necessity to obtain foodstuffs for our people.'[4]

Kingsley Wood was likewise worried. If Roosevelt failed to obtain 'very early Congress approval' of the Lend-Lease scheme, he minuted to Churchill that same day, 'we are liable to be stripped bare in the interval while Congress is debating'. Churchill's own intervention with Roosevelt should therefore be, not on the issue of the gold, but on the need for Roosevelt either to use 'his utmost endeavours' to secure Congress's approval, 'or else act in advance of it'.[5]

Churchill, meanwhile, was still working to counter the damage done by allegations that Britain had not had sufficient sailors to man the American destroyers, America's first material contribution to the battle. On December 16 he sent Roosevelt a memorandum on the use of the ships, explaining that the ships had needed refitting, together with a covering telegram in which he admitted: 'We have of course been dis-

[1] Washington Telegram No. 3241, 'Most Immediate', 'Most Secret', 23 December 1940: Premier papers, 4/17/1, folio 112.

[2] Minute of 25 December 1940: Premier papers, 4/17/1, folio 114.

[3] Telegram No. 3719, 'Most Immediate', 'Most Secret', 8.15 p.m., 25 December 1940: Premier papers, 4/17/1, folio 102.

[4] Minute of 26 December 1940: Premier papers, 4/17/1, folios 104–7.

[5] Minute of 26 December 1940: Premier papers, 4/17/1, folios 98–99.

appointed in the small number we have yet been able to get into service.' It was not 'through want of trying', he added, 'as our need can prove'.[1]

On the gold issue, Kingsley Wood suggested that in order to meet Roosevelt's wishes 'as far as possible', Britain should offer to load ten million pounds worth of British gold in South Africa on board the warship which Roosevelt had despatched. 'As you propose,' Churchill noted in the margin of the draft telegram to Phillips, instructing him to pass on this compromise.[2] But Phillips was convinced that this was a mistake, telegraphing back to London on December 27:

I am terrified of effect of your attitude on the President. You did ask him urgently for help and as a favour to us, he is doing most unusual thing in sending a Cruiser. He knows there is some fifty million pounds in South Africa. Effect of our decision not to ship more than ten million pounds will be deplorable, the more so, as we want his help again almost immediately in a dozen directions. It will be impossible to enlist his help hereafter in the form of immediate cash assistance, which you recognise that we surely want before Congress has acted, if you do not make full use of the help in the form in which it has already been offered.

When we are asking and expecting to receive help without interest to the extent of 800 million pounds a year and upwards, an unsympathetic attitude by the President will cost us very many times anything we may now risk at sea.

'Most strongly recommend,' Phillips ended, 'you send at very least bulk of gold at Capetown.'[3]

Churchill now intervened directly to try to resolve the gold crisis, and on December 28 drafted a personal telegram of considerable force and anguish. As first drafted, it read:

We are very anxious to tide over the interval of payments until you have declared policy of United States to Congress. But I am much puzzled and even perturbed by the proposal now made to send a United States battleship to collect whatever gold there may be in Capetown. This would inevitably become known to the world, and it would wear the aspect of a sheriff collecting the last assets of a helpless debtor. I cannot tell what the effect would be on the public opinion here, or what encouragement it would give to enemy coun-

---

[1] Foreign Office Telegram No. 3758, 'Former Naval Person for President' 'Personal & Secret', drafted 26 December 1940, sent 7.17 p.m., 28 December 1940: Premier papers, 3/462/1, folios 26 (draft), and 7 (as sent).

[2] Draft Telegram, 'Most Immediate', 'Most Secret', and Churchill note, 26 December 1940: Premier papers, 4/17/1, folio 100.

[3] Washington Telegram No. 3286, 'Most Immediate', 'Most Secret', 27 December 1940: Premier papers, 4/17/1, folio 95.

tries to know that our relations had reached this point. I therefore venture to draw your attention to paragraphs 17, 18 and 19 of my letter to you of December 8.[1] Remember, Mr President, we do not know what you have in mind, or what the United States is going to do, and we are fighting for our lives. But we have so far received no word upon that or in answer to my letter of December 8.

It is not fitting that any nation should put itself wholly in the hands of another, least of all a nation which is fighting under increasingly severe conditions for what is proclaimed to be a cause of general concern. If I have some word from you showing us where we stand, and that the United States is going to supply us with the thousands of millions of dollars worth of munitions which we shall need in 1941 and 1942 if Nazi-ism is to be beat, I will gladly give directions for any gold in Capetown to be put on board any warships you may send or do anything else that may be just and fair. I feel however that I should not be discharging my responsibilities to the people of the British Empire if, without the slightest indication of how our fate was to be settled in Washington, I were to part with this last reserve, from which alone we might buy a few months' food.

Whatever happens we shall certainly not give in, and I believe we can save ourselves and our own national interests for the time being. But you will not, I am sure, mind my saying that if you are not able to stand by us in all measures apart from war, we cannot guarantee to beat the Nazi tyranny and gain you the time you require for your rearmament. You may be absolutely sure that whatever you do or do not feel able to do, we shall go on to the utmost limit of our resources and strength. But I gravely fear that that strength unaided will not be sufficient to produce a world result of a satisfactory and lasting character.[2]

Churchill revised this draft several times, modifying its tone; then he decided, as he had done with his previous telegram, to wait until Roosevelt's forthcoming broadcast on the following day, 'and see what he says'.[3] This was a wise precaution. Roosevelt's broadcast, one of his

---

[1] Parts of paragraphs 17 and 18 are printed on pages 936–7 of this volume. The rest of paragraph 18 read: 'You may be certain that we shall prove ourselves ready to suffer and sacrifice to the utmost for the Cause, and that we glory in being its champions. The rest we leave with confidence to you and to your people, being sure that ways and means will be found which future generations on both sides of the Atlantic will approve and admire.' Paragraph 19 read: 'If, as I believe, you are convinced, Mr President, that the defeat of the Nazi and Fascist tyranny is a matter of high consequence to the people of the United States and to the Western Hemisphere, you will regard this letter not as an appeal for aid, but as a statement of the minimum action necessary to achieve our common purpose.' (War Cabinet Paper No. 466 (Final Revise) of 1940, 'Most Secret', 8 December 1940: Churchill papers, 23/4.)

[2] 'Prime Minister to President', 'Personal and Private', 28 December 1940: Premier papers, 4/17/1, folios 89–91.

[3] Prime Minister's Personal Minute, M.473, 28 December 1940 (to Kingsley Wood): Premier papers, 4/17/1, folio 86.

annual end of the year Fireside Chats, was a plea to the people of the United States to give all aid to Britain short of war. Should Britain be defeated, he said, 'all of us, in all the Americas, would be living at the point of a gun—a gun loaded with explosive bullets economic as well as military. . . .'

'Frankly and definitely,' Roosevelt told the American people, 'there is danger ahead—danger against which we must prepare. But we well know that we cannot escape danger, or the fear of danger, by crawling into bed and pulling the covers over our heads. We,' Roosevelt told his listeners, 'must be the great arsenal of democracy.'[1]

As a result of Roosevelt's speech, Churchill decided still to hold back his telegram about Britain's gold. But he did send a further telegram to Roosevelt about the destroyers. 'I believe,' he wrote, 'you know that we have not yet been able to bring many of your destroyers into action. As I have seen it stated that this is due to our inability to man them I should like to tell you that this is not the case.' Indeed, Churchill continued, 'we could man another 30 destroyers from America from April next onwards, besides your first fifty'. Churchill's telegram ended:

The main reason for delay has been the necessity for carrying out considerable dockyard work to fit them for service in the arduous conditions of the north western approaches. Extensive re-conditioning is, of course inevitable in the case of ships laid up for long periods, and the Admiralty is giving your Naval Attaché here details of the work we have found necessary, as it may be valuable for you to have them in case you want to work up any of the destroyers lying in your yards.[2]

This second telegram about the American destroyers went, as did the first, through the British Embassy in Washington. But there, the British Chargé d'Affaires, Nevile Butler, had already held back the first telegram. 'I venture to suggest,' he had telegraphed to Eden on December 30, 'that it would be undesirable to send in the Prime Minister's message to the President today directly after the President's broadcast address last night.' The President, Butler warned, might feel that to deliver the destroyer message just at that moment was 'rather ungrateful' and it might have 'an unfortunate effect on him'.

Nevile Butler suggested delaying the destroyer message for a few days, until at least January 2, and he added that Arthur Purvis 'shares

---

[1] *The Times*, 30 December 1940.
[2] Foreign Office Telegram No. 3795, 'Immediate', 2.30 p.m., 31 December 1940: Premier papers, 3/462/1, folio 3.

this view fully'.[1] Churchill at once deferred to their joint démarche. Butler's telegram had reached London at 9.20 on the evening of December 30; an hour after midnight Churchill sent his reply. 'Message about destroyers is not urgent,' he telegraphed to Butler, 'and you should let me know when an opportune moment arrives for imparting these facts. Any time in the next fortnight will do.'[2]

Twelve hours later, Eden telegraphed to Butler again to say that 'on reconsideration' it had been decided not to send Roosevelt the information 'about the shortcomings of the destroyers', but to pass it on instead to the United States Naval Attaché in London. Butler should await, however, the very next telegram from London, which contained 'the text of a message from the Prime Minister to the President which you should deliver at the first suitable opportunity'.[3]

Colville, who was present while Churchill dictated this telegram, helped by Eden, Kingsley Wood and Beaverbrook, noted in his diary:

Sombre though the telegram was, with its warning that only by American financial help could Hitlerism be 'extirpated from Europe, Africa and Asia', the PM seemed to enjoy drafting it and his 'obiter dicta' to Kingsley Wood who sat perched on the edge of his armchair, were not particularly depressing. But he obviously fears that the Americans' love of doing good business may lead them to denude us of all our realisable resources before they shew any inclination to be the Good Samaritan.[4]

Churchill's telegram began, as Sir Frederick Phillips had urged it should, with an approving reference to Roosevelt's Fireside Chat:

We are deeply grateful for all you said yesterday. We welcome especially the outline of your plans for giving us the aid, without which Hitlerism cannot be extirpated from Europe and Asia. We can readily guess why you have not been able to give a precise account of how your proposals will be worked out.

'Meanwhile,' Churchill told the President, 'some things make me anxious.' These were:

First, sending the warship to Capetown to take the gold lying there may produce embarrassing effects. It is almost certain to become known. This will disturb public opinion here and throughout the Dominions and encourage the enemy, who will proclaim that you are sending for our last reserves. If you

---

[1] Washington Telegram No. 3324, 'Most Immediate', received 9.20 p.m., 30 December 1940: Premier papers, 3/461/1, folio 6.

[2] Foreign Office Telegram No. 3785, 'Most Immediate', 1 a.m., 31 December 1940: Premier papers, 3/461/1, folio 5.

[3] Foreign Office Telegram No. 3794, 'Immediate', 1.40 p.m., December 1940: Premier papers, 3/462/1, folio 4.

[4] Colville diary, 1 January 1941: Colville papers.

feel this is the only way, directions will be given for the available Capetown gold to be loaded on the ship. But we should avoid it if we can. Could we, for instance, by a technical operation, exchange gold in South Africa for gold held for others at Ottawa and make the latter available for movement to New York? We must know soon because the ship is on its way.

Churchill's telegram continued:

My second anxiety is because we do not know how long Congress will debate your proposals and how we should be enabled to place orders for armaments and pay our way if this time became protracted. Remember, Mr President, we do not know what you have in mind, or exactly what the United States is going to do, and we are fighting for our lives. What would be the effect upon the world situation if we had to default in payments to your contractors, who have their workmen to pay? Would not this be exploited by the enemy as a complete breakdown in Anglo-American co-operation? Yet, a few weeks' delay might well bring this upon us.

The next point which Churchill made concerned the broader aspect of Britain's indebtedness. 'Thirdly,' he wrote:

... apart from the interim period, there arises a group of problems about the scope of your plan after being approved by Congress. What is to be done about the immense heavy payments still due to be made under existing orders before delivery is completed? Substantial advance payments on these same orders have already denuded our resources. We have continued need for various American commodities not definitely weapons: for instance, raw materials and oil. Canada and other Dominions, Greece and refugee Allies have clamant dollar needs to keep their war effort alive. I do not seek to know immediately how you will solve these later questions. We shall be entirely ready, for our part, to lay bare to you all our resources and our liabilities around the world, and we shall seek no more help than the common cause demands. We naturally wish to feel sure that the powers with which you propose to arm yourself will be sufficiently wide to deal with these larger matters, subject to all proper examination.

Churchill went on to tell Roosevelt that Sir Frederick Phillips was already discussing these matters with Morgenthau, and would explain 'the war commitments we have in many parts of the world for which we could not ask your direct help, but for which gold and dollars are necessary'. This also applied to the Dutch and Belgian gold which Britain might 'in due course' become under an obligation to return.

After telling Roosevelt about the previous night's blitz on London, and the high 'spirit of the Londoners',[1] Churchill added, in further reference to Roosevelt's Fireside Chat: 'I thank you for testifying before

[1] See page 963.

all the world that the future safety and greatness of the American Union are intimately concerned with the upholding and the effective arming of that indomitable spirit.'

'All my heartiest good wishes to you,' Churchill ended, 'in the New Year of storm that is opening upon us.'[1]

On 3 January 1941 there was a renewed offensive against the Italians in Libya. Australian troops, with British tanks leading the assault, had by the afternoon of January 4 broken into the defensive perimeter of Bardia. A day later, they overcame the remaining resistance, capturing in all more than 45,000 prisoners and a total of 462 guns. At sea, however, German submarines continued to sink British merchant ships, and in a collision between two ships in convoy, one, the *City of Bedford*, was sunk with the loss of seven and a half million cartridges from the United States: 'a grievous blow' as Churchill described it.[2] But other news from the United States early in January gave Churchill comfort, the imminent arrival in Britain of American pilot and aircrew volunteers. 'This is a project I have long cherished,' he wrote to Sinclair.[3]

On January 3, in an attempt to placate Roosevelt, Churchill agreed to break the British blockade of German controlled Europe in order to allow United States supplies of milk, vitamin concentrate, and clothing to be sent to children in Vichy France. In any announcement of the scheme in the United States, Churchill added, 'we should like our part in the transaction to be presented in as favourable a light as possible'. While it would be made clear that the step had been taken on Roosevelt's initiative, 'we would like it stated that the relief goods are available only by goodwill of His Majesty's Government', creating the impression 'of Anglo-American co-operation for humanitarian ends'.[4]

On January 6, Roosevelt spoke in Washington of the 'four freedoms' which the United States was pledged to defend, and of his determination to provide Britain with the weapons she needed to defend democracy. That same day, Wavell's Western Desert Force, called by Churchill in his speech 'the Army of the Nile', reached the outskirts of Tobruk.

Concerned about the need to husband military resources for the

---

[1] Foreign Office Telegram No. 3787 to Washington, 'Most Immediate', 'Most Secret', 'Following for the President from Former Naval Person', 'Personal—Private', 3.45 a.m. (by telephone), 31 December 1940: Premier papers, 4/17/1, folios 77–8.

[2] To A. V. Alexander and Sir Dudley Pound, Prime Minister's Personal Minute, M.14/1, 3 January 1941: Churchill papers, 20/36.

[3] Prime Minister's Personal Minute, M.32/1, 7 January 1941: Churchill papers, 20/36. Sinclair's mother, like Churchill's, was an American.

[4] Telegram of 3 January 1941: Churchill papers, 20/49.

campaign of 1941, Churchill telegraphed to Wavell on January 7: 'I am sorry to jar the hour of your splendid victory by awkward matters of housekeeping. If your demands for non-fighting services are maintained on the present scale the whole scope and character of our effort in the Middle East will have to be reviewed. Shipping has now become the dominant factor and will remain so certainly for six months.' In Britain, Churchill pointed out, the rations of workers in heavy munitions factories were being 'cut down to levels of which British armies, except in actual operations, have never dreamed'. The main war effort of the nation, Churchill warned, 'may be compromised', and Wavell must therefore cut back his 'rearward services'. Churchill added:

I have a right to ask you to make sure that the rearward services do not trench too largely upon the effective fighting strength, that you have less fat and more muscle, that you have a smaller tail and larger teeth. You have well over 350,000 troops on your ration strength, and the number of units which are fighting or capable of fighting appears to me disproportionately small. It is distressing to see convoys sent by the heart's blood of the nation's effort consisting so largely of rearward services of all kinds.

Churchill did not dispute, he told Wavell, the validity of the arguments in favour of the ideal establishments, 'drawn up by staff officers and pushed out to us as essential minima'. But, his telegram ended: 'I beg you to convince me that you will continually comb, scrub and purge all rearward services in a hard unrelenting manner, as Kitchener did.' This conviction would enable him 'to impose the severe sacrifices required upon the British nation, and to secure for the campaign of 1941 in the Middle East the opportunities which may await it under your direction'.[1]

For some days, the Enigma decrypts had told an alarming tale, and together with other Intelligence reports suggested that two German armoured divisions, supported by 200 German dive bombers then in Rumania, would cross Bulgaria and invade Greece 'about 20th January'. If a winter campaign seemed folly, the Intelligence was nevertheless emphatic.[2] The Norwegian campaign, Churchill told the Defence Committee on January 8, 'had shown that Germany was not deterred by snow'. There was no other course open to Britain, he added,

---

[1] 'Private and personal', telegram of 7 January 1941: Churchill papers, 20/49.

[2] Defence Committees No. 1 and No. 2 of 1940, 8 and 9 January 1940: Cabinet papers, 69/1. A crucial Enigma decrypt on January 9 gave the news that German Air Force personnel were moving into Bulgaria to lay down telephone and teleprinter lines to the Bulgarian-Greek border along the main axis of advance towards Salonica. (F. H. Hinsley and others, *British Intelligence in the Second World War. Its Influence on Strategy and Operations*, Volume 1, London 1979, page 353.)

'but to make certain that we had spared no effort to help the Greeks, who had shown themselves so worthy'.[1]

Eden, who had also seen the Intelligence reports, agreed with Churchill, emphasizing 'the importance of our action in Greece as a deciding factor in the attitude of Turkey', while Churchill told his colleagues:

... the prosecution of the campaign in Libya must now take second place. We should naturally continue to advance if resistance was feeble, and if it could be overcome with the small forces now operating. From the political point of view, it was imperative to help the Greeks against the Germans . . .[2]

From Egypt, Wavell protested that the reported imminent German move into the Balkans was a 'move in the war of nerves' designed to help Italy by 'upsetting Greek nerves' and to induce Britain 'to stop our advance in Libya and disperse our forces in the Middle East'. Wavell wanted the Chiefs of Staff to reconsider 'whether the enemy's move is not bluff'.[3] But the Chiefs of Staff in London concurred with Churchill's reply that there was 'a mass of detail indicating that a large-scale movement through Bulgaria towards the Greek frontier' would begin 'before the end of the month', and that while nothing must 'hamper the capture of Tobruk', thereafter all operations in Libya were 'subordinated to aiding Greece'. Churchill's telegram contained also the sentence: 'We expect and require prompt and active compliance with our decisions, for which we bear full responsibility.'[4]

At Churchill's urging, Wavell prepared to fly to Athens with Longmore to consult with the Greek leaders. Prince Paul of Yugoslavia, fearful, Eden told the War Cabinet, of provoking a German attack, urged Britain not to send Wavell to Athens.[5] Churchill was not impressed by Prince Paul's views. 'They leave me unchanged,' he minuted. 'It is for the Greeks to say whether they want Wavell to visit Athens or not. It is the Greeks who must be the judges of the German reactions.' His minute continued:

... if the Germans are coming south they will not require pretexts. They are, it would seem, already acting in pursuance of a carefully thought-out plan which one can hardly assume will be hurried or delayed in consequence of

---

[1] Defence Committee No. 1 of 1941, 8 January 1941, 9.30 p.m.: Cabinet papers, 69/2.

[2] Prime Minister's Personal Minute, D.6/1, 6 January 1941: Churchill papers, 20/36.

[3] Telegram No. 42 of 10 January 1941: Cabinet papers, 105/1.

[4] Draft telegram, Prime Minister's Personal Minute, D.11/1, 10 January 1941 (enclosure) to Ismay for the Chiefs of Staff: Churchill papers, 20/36; text as sent, Telegram No. 44 of 11 January 1941: Cabinet papers, 105/1.

[5] As reported by Eden at War Cabinet No. 6 of 1941, 14 January 1941, Minute 2, Confidential Annex: Cabinet papers, 65/12.

any minor movements of ours. The evidence in our possession of the German movements seems overwhelming. In the face of it Prince Paul's attitude looks like that of an unfortunate man in the cage with a tiger, hoping not to provoke him while steadily dinner-time approaches.[1]

It emerged during Wavell's visit, however, that the Greeks did not want a British military reinforcement. Wavell was instructed to continue his advance in the desert, to try to capture Benghazi, to seize as soon as possible the island of Rhodes in order to forestall a German air base on the island, and to form a strategic reserve of four divisions to be ready to help both Greece and Turkey, should German troops move across their borders. 'Turkey, Yugoslavia, Russia, all perhaps favourably influenced,' Churchill had telegraphed to General Smuts at the height of the Enigma indications, 'by evidence of British support of Greece.'[2]

---

[1] Prime Minister's Personal Minute M.55/1, 14 January 1941: Churchill papers, 20/36. Six days later, Churchill told the War Cabinet 'that it seemed clear that Prince Paul had told the Greek Government that if they allowed any British land forces to enter Greece, the Yugo-Slav Government would allow the Germans to attack Greece through Yugo-Slavia'. There was no doubt, Churchill added, that Prince Paul 'had then tried to curry favour with the Germans by telling them that he had kept British units out of Greece'. (War Cabinet No. 8 of 1941, 20 January 1941, Minute 2, Confidential Annex: Cabinet papers, 65/21.)

[2] 'Most Secret and Personal', 12 January 1941: Churchill papers, 20/49.

51

January 1941: The Hopkins Visit

THE danger of economic conflict with the United States had now to be averted, and the lines of communication between Churchill and Roosevelt put on a sounder and more personal basis. On January 8 Harry Hopkins arrived in Britain as Roosevelt's emissary. The letter he carried with him from Roosevelt to King George VI explained: 'Mr Hopkins is a very good friend of mine in whom I repose the utmost confidence.'[1]

On January 10 Churchill spent three hours alone with Hopkins at Downing Street, his desk diary noting the occasion thus: 'Mr Hopkins to lunch.'[2] Churchill and Hopkins were 'so greatly impressed with each other', Colville noted in his diary, 'that their tête-à-tête did not break up till nearly 4.0.'[3] In his report to Roosevelt, Hopkins described his first impressions of 10 Downing Street and Churchill:

His man Friday—Brendan Bracken—met me at the door—showed me about the old and delightful house that has been home of Prime Ministers of the Empire for two hundred years. Most of the windows are out—workmen over the place repairing the damage—Churchill told me it wouldn't stand a healthy bomb.

Bracken led me to a little dining-room in the basement—poured me some sherry and left me to wait for the Prime Minister. A rotund-smiling-red-faced gentleman appeared—extended a fat but none the less convincing hand and wished me welcome to England. A short black coat—striped trousers—a clear eye and a mushy voice was the impression of England's leader as he showed me with obvious pride the photographs of his beautiful daughter-in-law and grandchild. . . .[4]

[1] Letter dated 4 January 1941: Robert E. Sherwood, *The White House Papers of Harry L. Hopkins*, volume 1, London 1948, page 233.
[2] Churchill Engagement Cards, 10 January 1941: Thompson collection.
[3] Colville diary, 10 January 1941: Colville papers.
[4] Pamela Churchill and 'young' Winston.

In this report to Roosevelt, Hopkins described how, in their first talk together, he and Churchill had discussed 'the difficulty of communication with the President at long range'. There was 'no question', Hopkins added, 'but that he wants to meet the President—the sooner the better'. He was only sorry he could not see him in April in Bermuda—'go on a cruiser and by accident meet the President at the appointed place—and discuss our problems at leisure'.

Hopkins' report continued:

I told him there was a feeling in some quarters that he, Churchill, did not like America, Americans or Roosevelt. This set him off on a bitter though fairly constrained attack on Ambassador Kennedy, who he believes is responsible for this impression.[1] He denied it vigorously—sent for a secretary to show me a telegram which he had sent to the President immediately after his election in which he expressed his warm delight at the President's re-election.[2]

Several times during the lunch, as Hopkins told Roosevelt, Churchill had assured him 'that he would make every detail of information and opinion available to me', and had said that he hoped Hopkins would not leave England until he was 'fully' satisfied 'of the exact state of England's need and the urgent necessity of the exact material assistance Britain requires to win the war'.

Churchill had gone on to tell Hopkins that 'he did not *know* that England could withstand the onslaught after France fell—but he felt sure that it could—it did—and it will withstand the next one ...' Were the Germans to gain a foothold in England, Churchill declared, 'we shall drive them out'. If Hitler were to use poison gas, England would reply in kind 'killing man for man', for, Churchill told the President's emissary, 'we too have the deadliest gasses in the world'.

Surveying the European scene, Churchill told Hopkins that he did not think Hitler would attack Spain that winter 'but the Spring might tell a different story'. Hopkins added: 'He thinks Greece is lost—although he is now reinforcing the Greeks—and weakening his African Army.' Hitler would permit Mussolini to go 'only so far downhill' in Greece, and the Germans, Churchill told Hopkins, were 'now preparing for the attack which must bring its inevitable result'. Churchill went on to tell Hopkins that he knew the loss of Greece would be 'a blow to British prestige'. It seemed obvious to Hopkins that Churchill 'was considering ways and means of preparing the British public for it'.

[1] Two months earlier Churchill had written to Herbert Morrison to thank him for a speech during which he had answered 'Kennedy's vapourings'.

[2] This was the telegram Roosevelt had not acknowledged, and had almost certainly never seen (see page 889).

Churchill also told Hopkins that the 'debacle in Greece' would be overcome in part by the 'sure defeat of the Italians in Africa'. Hopkins' account continued:

He feels England can bring great military pressure on Italy—and fully intends to—Britain will control the Mediterranean and the Suez against Germany. He has offered Weygand six divisions—if the former strikes—he is in close touch with Pétain on this point—he spoke with no great assurance about it—but it is clear Churchill intends to hold Africa—clean out the Italians and co-operate with Weygand if the opportunity permits. He expressed the hope that we would not go too far in feeding any of the dominated countries. He feels that tough as it is, one of Hitler's great weaknesses is to be in control of territory inhabited by a dejected and despairing people.

After their lunch, which took place in the small downstairs dining room which had formerly been a secretarial room, Churchill took Hopkins up to the Cabinet room, showing him on a map the routes of the transatlantic convoys reaching Liverpool and Glasgow and 'the route the German bombers were taking from France to Norway to intercept them'.[1]

That afternoon Hopkins drove to Ditchley as one of the weekend guests there.[2] As Bracken and Colville, who were also invited, drove down together, Bracken told Colville that Hopkins, 'the confidant of Roosevelt, was the most important American visitor to this country we had ever had'. He had come in order to tell the President 'what we needed' and to form an opinion of the country's morale. He could influence Roosevelt, Bracken added, 'more than any living man'.[3]

Even as Churchill and Hopkins talked, the text of the Lend-Lease Bill was published, the first stage of its long passage into law. It was expected to go before the Senate in March.[4] From Ditchley, Churchill told Sir Kingsley Wood, in deprecating any appeal to Roosevelt about a possible British default on payments if the Bill's passage were prolonged, 'we must trust ourselves to him', as he felt 'sure' that Roosevelt

---

[1] Hopkins report, 10 January 1941: Robert E. Sherwood, *The White House Papers of Harry L. Hopkins*, volume 1, London, 1948, pages 239–40.

[2] The others were Clementine Churchill, Venetia Montagu, Oliver Lyttelton, Freda Casa Maury, Professor Lindemann, Brendan Bracken and the duty Private Secretary, John Colville. (Ditchley Park Visitors Book, 10–13 January 1941.)

[3] Colville diary, 10 January 1941: Colville papers.

[4] Bill No. 1776, 'An Act to promote the defence of the United States'. On 13 January 1941 it was referred to the Foreign Affairs Committee of the House of Representatives. The Bill's number, the year of the American Declaration of Independence, was deliberately chosen.

'will find some way of steering round such a breakdown'.[1] In allowing British warships to use United States ports, and in giving Roosevelt wide powers to grant Britain military assistance, the Bill was, according to a 'delighted' Churchill, 'tantamount to a declaration of war by the United States'; but by contrast Kingsley Wood had 'lamented' to Colville that the Bill would make it more difficult to resist the American tendency 'to strip us of everything we possess in payment for what we are about to receive'.

That weekend at Ditchley was to be decisive for the future of Anglo-American cooperation. Colville, who was present, noted in his diary the course of the conversation, and the almost immediate rapport between the President's emissary and the Prime Minister:

... at lunch we had no host or hostess, although the son of the house—a trooper in the Life Guards—came in towards the end. But Mr Hopkins arrived with Tommy Thompson and his quiet charm and dignity held the table. He said that the new Presidential bill would arouse loud controversy, but he felt sure it would succeed. He told us of the Duke of Windsor's recent visit to the President on his yacht when the former spoke very charmingly of the King (a fact which touched Winston), and he said that the Duke's entourage was very bad. Moreover HRH's recent yachting trip with a violently pro-Nazi Swede did not create a very good impression.[2] It was the astounding success of the King and Queen's visit to the US which had made America give up its partizanship of the Windsors.

Winston expressed the opinion, forcibly, that Socialism was bad, that jingoism was worse, and that the two combined, in a kind of debased Italian fascism, was the worst creed ever designed by man ...

At tea-time, Hopkins was driven to Blenheim by Brendan Bracken. During this visit, Hopkins told Bracken—as Bracken later told Colville—that his mission 'was to see what was needed so that we might get it, even if it meant transferring to us armaments belonging to the US forces'. Hopkins also told Bracken that Roosevelt 'was resolved that we should have the means of survival and of victory'.

Hopkins returned to Ditchley for dinner. Once more, Colville was a witness to the conversation:

[1] Prime Minister's Personal Minute, M.38/1, 11 January 1941: Churchill papers, 20/36.

[2] Churchill took steps to warn the Duke of Windsor about the Swede. 'There would be no objection,' he wrote, 'and indeed advantage if your Royal Highness cared to make a cruise about the West Indian Islands. It would be impossible, however, for His Majesty's Government to approve the use of Mr Wenner-Gren's yacht for such a purpose. This gentleman is, according to the reports I have received, regarded as a pro-German international financier, with strong leanings towards appeasement, and suspected of being in communication with the enemy. Your Royal Highness may not, perhaps, realise the intensity of feeling in the United States about people of this kind and the offence which is given to the Administration when any countenance is given to them.' (Private and Personal, 17 March 1941: Churchill papers, 20/49.)

When the ladies had gone, Mr Hopkins paid a graceful tribute to the PM's speeches which had, he said, produced the most stirring and revolutionary effect on all classes and districts in America. At an American Cabinet meeting the President had had a wireless-set brought in so that all might listen to the Prime Minister.

The PM was touched and gratified. He said that he hardly knew what he said in his speeches last summer; he had just been imbued with the feeling that 'it would be better for us to be destroyed than to see the triumph of such an impostor'. When, at the time of Dunkirk, he had addressed a meeting of Ministers 'below the line' he had realised that there was only one thing they wanted to hear him say: that whatever happened to our army we should still go on. He had said it.

Churchill then told Hopkins, as Colville noted, that after the war he could 'never lead a Party Government' against the Labour Opposition leaders 'who had cooperated so loyally'. His hope was for a National Government to continue for two or three years after the war 'so that the country might be undivided in its efforts to put into effect certain principles—or rather measures—of reconstruction'. Churchill then told Hopkins that the text of the Lend-Lease Bill, which he had read that morning, 'had made him feel that a new world had come into being'. Churchill then outlined the scheme of that new world, beginning by saying 'there must be a United States of Europe', and that he believed it should be built by the British: 'if the Russians built it', he told Hopkins, 'there would be Communism and squalor; if the Germans built it there would be tyranny and brute force.'[1]

Warming to his subject, Churchill told Hopkins, as one of the other guests present, Oliver Lyttelton, later recalled:

We seek no treasure, we seek no territorial gains, we seek only the right of man to be free; we seek his rights to worship his God, to lead his life in his own way, secure from persecution. As the humble labourer returns from his work when the day is done, and sees the smoke curling upwards from his cottage home in the serene evening sky, we wish him to know that no rat-a-tat-tat—here he rapped on the table—of the secret police upon his door will disturb his leisure or interrupt his rest. We seek government with the consent of the people, man's freedom to say what he will, and when he thinks himself injured, to find himself equal in the eyes of the law. But war aims other than these we have none.

Churchill paused. 'What will the President say to all this,' he asked. There was silence, and, as Lyttelton recalled:

[1] Colville diary, 11 January 1941: Colville papers.

Harry Hopkins did not reply for the best part of a minute—and how long that seems—and then, exaggerating his American drawl, he said, 'Well, Mr Prime Minister, I don't think the President will give a dam' for all that.' Heavens alive, it's gone wrong, thought I. There was another pause, and then Harry said, 'You see, we're only interested in seeing that that Goddam sonofabitch, Hitler, gets licked.'

There was loud laughter, and at that moment a friendship was cemented which no convulsion ever undermined.[1]

In his diary that night, Colville recorded how Hopkins then said:

. . . that there were two kinds of men: those who talked and those who acted. The President, like the Prime Minister, was one of the latter. Although Hopkins had heard him sketch out an idea very similar to the PM's, Roosevelt refused to listen to those who talked so much of war aims and was intent only upon one end: the destruction of Hitler. Winston hastily explained that he had been speaking very freely and was just anxious to let Hopkins realise that we were not all devoid of thoughts of the future: he would be the first to agree that the destruction of 'those foul swine' was the primary and over-riding objective.[2]

Hopkins remained at Ditchley with Churchill throughout Sunday January 12. During the day, Hopkins discussed Britain's shipping and import programmes with Lindemann, who told Hopkins 'that the minimum imports to meet essential war requirements were about 40 million tons (24 million supply, 16 million food) and that anything less than this would definitely have a deleterious effect on our war effort'.[3]

Unknown to Hopkins, during January 12 Churchill received encouraging news concerning Germany's plans for invasion. For on that day an Enigma decrypt revealed that German wireless stations on the circuit of the air formation headquarters responsible for German Air Force equipment in Belgium and Northern France were 'no longer to be manned as from 10 January'. At the same time, firing practices which could not be completed 'owing to frost' were to be transferred to southern France. This seemed clearly to reduce, at least until the frosts in northern France and Belgium were 'less severe', the prospect of an imminent invasion.[4]

At Ditchley that evening, after dinner, the discussion was largely about the United States, and, as Colville noted, 'in particular about the American principle of coping with unemployment by providing

---

[1] Oliver Lyttelton, Viscount Chandos, *The Memoirs of Lord Chandos*, London 1962, pages 165–6.

[2] Colville diary, 11 January 1941: Colville papers.

[3] Minutes of Sir Andrew Duncan, 'Secret', 22 January 1941: Cabinet papers, 21/999.

[4] 'Officer Only', 'Most Secret', 'Invasion of Great Britain', MI 14, 12 January 1941: War Office papers, 199/911A.

work instead of a dole', a plan which in England would cost four times as much as dole payments. During this discussion, Churchill asked, as Colville noted, 'what the Americans would do when they had accumulated all the gold in the world and the other countries then decided that gold was of no value except for filling teeth. "Well," ' replied Hopkins, ' "We shall be able to make use of our unemployed in guarding it!" '

From the dining room, the guests proceeded to the drawing room, where they saw several films, including *Night Train to Munich*. During the film show, news was telephoned from London that HMS *Southampton* had been sunk by German dive-bombers in the Mediterranean.[1] This led Churchill 'bitterly' to regret that he had been dissuaded from allowing operation 'Workshop', the seizure of Pantelleria Island, to go through. 'I flinched,' he said, 'and now I have cause to regret it.'

The possibility of German air bases in Sicily seemed to make even a revival of 'Workshop' worthwhile, for any such bases, as Churchill minuted to Ismay, for the Chiefs of Staff Committee, 'may be the beginning of evil developments in the Central Mediterranean', and he added:

I am very apprehensive of the Germans establishing themselves in Pantelleria, in which case with a strong force of dive-bombers they will close the Narrows. I fear this may be another example of the adage 'A stitch in time saves nine'.

It is necessary now that 'Workshop' should be reviewed. It has become far more urgent, and also at the same time more difficult, and once the Germans are installed there it will become more difficult still. I should be glad if revised and perfected plans could be ready by to-day week. Plans should also be made to find an opportunity at the earliest moment. The question to try it or not can only be settled after these matters of method and timing have been satisfactorily disposed of.

'I remain completely of the opinion,' Churchill's minute ended, 'that "Workshop" is cardinal.'[2]

That night at Ditchley Churchill was in a reflective mood, and, as Colville recorded in his diary, from midnight until about two in the morning:

... the PM, smoking a phenomenally large cigar, paced about in front of the fire at the far end of the Library and gave, for Hopkins' benefit, an apprecia-

---

[1] This was the first German naval appearance in the Mediterranean, and had been known to the Air Ministry in advance through Intelligence sources, partly Enigma and partly low-grade. By mischance, however, the information never reached either the Admiralty or Churchill.

[2] Prime Minister's Personal Minute, D.16/1, 13 January 1941: Churchill papers, 20/36.

tion of the war up to date. Ronnie Tree, Oliver Lyttelton, Prof., Tommy Thompson and I sat and goggled, while Hopkins occasionally made some short comment.

He began by discussing the future. The question of populations was important. Germany had 60 millions on whom she could count; the remainder were at least a drag and potentially a danger. The British Empire had more white inhabitants than that, and if the US were with us—as he seemed in this discourse to assume they actively would be—there would be another 120 millions. So we were not outmatched in numbers any more than we were in courage and resolution. He did not believe that Japan would come in against the threat of Anglo-American armed resistance and he thought it more than probable that the Germans would be obliged to occupy the whole of France, thus driving the French to take up arms again in North Africa. He later said he believed that if he had gone to Bordeaux in those last fateful days he would have been able to tip the balance in favour of further resistance overseas.

Turning to the past, he sketched the whole history of the war, Norway, the trap when we marched our men right up into Belgium, his visits to France, the air battles, Libya, and, above all, the threat of invasion. He believed that Oran had been the turning-point in our fortunes: it made the world realise that we were in earnest in our intentions to carry on. He sketched the possibilities of invasion, of 'lodgments', of the use of gas, but he said he now felt quite confident, even though it was wrong to say that we should actually welcome invasion as so many people were now feeling.

'I think,' Colville noted, 'Hopkins must have been impressed.'[1] Hopkins was indeed impressed, writing to Roosevelt: 'people here are amazing from Churchill down, and if courage alone can win—the result will be inevitable. But they need our help desperately, and I am sure you will permit nothing to stand in the way. Some of the ministers and underlings are a bit trying, but no more than some I have seen.' Hopkins continued: '*Churchill* is the gov't in every sense of the word—he controls the grand strategy and often the details—labour trusts him—the army, navy, air force are behind him to a man. The politicians and upper crust pretend to like him. I cannot emphasize too strongly that he is the one and only person over here with whom you need to have a full meeting of minds.'

Hopkins told Roosevelt that Churchill had again asked about meeting the President, but that Hopkins had explained Roosevelt's 'problem' until the Lend-Lease Bill was passed. Hopkins himself was 'convinced', however, that a meeting between Roosevelt and Churchill 'is essential—and soon—for the battering continues and Hitler does not wait for Congress'. Hopkins went on: 'I was with Churchill at 2 a.m.

[1] Colville diary, 12 January 1941: Colville papers.

31. Sir Dudley Pound, Sir John Dill, Churchill and Sir Wilfrid Freeman on board the *Prince of Wales* on their way to Argentia, August 1941. (See pages 1154–8)

32. Churchill and Harry Hopkins on board the *Prince of Wales*, August 1941

33. On board the *Prince of Wales* at Argentia, August 1941. In the front row: Sir Wilfrid Freeman, Sir Dudley Pound, Churchill, Sir John Dill, Sir Alexander Cadogan. Standing, far left, Lieutenant-Colonel Jacob. Colonel Hollis is standing behind Sir Dudley Pound, with Commander Thompson on his left, next to Professor Lindemann, Captain Pim and John Martin. On the far right is Captain Leach, Captain of the *Prince of Wales*

34. Churchill on board the *Prince of Wales* at Argentia

35. On board the battleship *Augusta*, Churchill hands Roosevelt a letter from King George VI, 9 August 1941 (see page 1158). Roosevelt is supported by his son Elliott

36. Divine Service on board the *Prince of Wales*, 10 August 1941 (see page 1159)

37. Churchill with Lord Beaverbrook at Argentia

38. Returning to London from Argentia, Churchill buys an Air Raid Distress Fund flag in Downing Street, 19 August 1941

39. John Colville, Clementine Churchill, and Churchill at Manston aerodrome, 25 September 1941 (see page 1201)

40. Churchill entertained to tea by the pilots of 615 Squadron, Manston aerodrome, 25 September 1941

41. The sherry party at 10 Downing Street on 29 September 1941, John Colville's last day (page 1206). Left to right: John Colville, Leslie Rowan, Churchill, John Peck, John Martin, Miss Watson, Commander C. R. Thompson, Anthony Bevir and Charles Barker

42. Churchill outside at 10 Downing Street on 21 November 1941, wearing a 'Thumbs up' badge sent to him by Mayor La Guardia of New York (see page 1238 n.4)

43. Churchill outside 10 Downing Street on 25 November 1941, two weeks before Pearl Harbour. On Churchill's right is Representative John B. Snyder, Chairman of the Military Appropriation Sub-Committee of the House of Representatives (see page 1238 n.4)

Sunday night when he got wind of the loss of the *Southampton*—the serious damage to the new aircraft carrier (*Illustrious*)—a second cruiser knocked about—but he never falters or displays the least despondence—till four o'clock he paced the floor telling me of his offensive and defensive plans.'

Hopkins continued:

I cannot believe that it is true that Churchill dislikes either you or America—it just doesn't make sense.

Churchill is prepared for a setback in Greece—the African campaign will proceed favourably—German bombers in the Mediterranean make the fleet's operation more difficult—convoys must all go around the Cape. An invasion, they feel sure, can be repelled—Churchill thinks it will not come soon, but Beaverbrook and others think it will come and soon.

It was clear from Hopkins' letter just how impressed he had been. 'This island needs our help now, Mr President,' he wrote, 'with everything we can give them.'[1]

Churchill had made plans to see Lord Halifax off to the United States from Scapa on board the most recently launched, and most powerfully armed of all Britain's battleships, the *King George V.* He asked Hopkins to accompany him on the train journey to Scotland. 'Hopkins and I spent the weekend together,' Churchill telegraphed to Roosevelt before the two men set off, 'and he is coming with me on a short tour of Fleet bases, so we shall have plenty of time to cover all points at leisure,' and he added: 'I am most grateful to you for sending so remarkable an envoy, who enjoys so high a measure of your intimacy and confidence.'[2]

The visit to Scotland was nearly postponed, at Clementine Churchill's insistence, for, as Churchill's doctor noted in his diary, when he called at the Annexe at Storey's Gate:

... the man at the door said that Mrs Churchill wanted to see me before I saw the Prime Minister. She said that he was going to Scapa. 'When?' 'Today at noon. There is a blizzard there, and Winston has a heavy cold. You must stop him.'

I went to his room and said my piece. He became very red in the face, and throwing off the bed-clothes, shouted, 'What damned nonsense! Of course I am going.'

I went back to Mrs Churchill to report progress. 'Well,' she said shortly, 'if you cannot stop him, the least you can do is to go with him.' I had nothing

[1] Report of 10 January 1941: Robert E. Sherwood, *The White House Papers of Harry L. Hopkins*, volume 1, London, 1948, pp. 239–40.

[2] Telegram of 13 January 1941, 'Personal and Private': Churchill papers, 20/49.

with me, but the PM lent me a greatcoat with a broad astrakhan collar. He said it would keep out the wind.[1]

Churchill and Hopkins left London by special train from Kings Cross on the night of January 14, together with Clementine Churchill, Churchill's doctor, Lord and Lady Halifax, Ismay, Commander Thompson and the duty Private Secretary, John Martin. Another development that day was Roosevelt's assurance to 'C's' representative in Washington, William Stephenson,' that United States naval Intelligence, being given to Britain 'could be trusted'.[2] This boded well for the increasing exchanges of Intelligence material.

On the morning of January 15 Churchill and Hopkins reached Caithness, in northern Scotland, waking up in the train, as John Martin wrote home, 'in the middle of a deserted heath, the ground white with snow and a blizzard howling at the windows'. From Thurso, to Scapa Flow, a night on board *King George V*, returning to Thurso in even stormier seas, and then, as Martin wrote:

... down through the night to Inverkeithing, for a visit to the dockyards, where the PM was received with immense enthusiasm. Thence to Edinburgh, where we picked up the Regional Commissioner, Tom Johnston, and his principal officer, Norman Duke, and gave them lunch in our train on the way to Glasgow.

The visit was supposed to be a secret; but a mob of hundreds if not thousands was waiting at Queen Street Station and we had quite to fight our way to our cars and then into the City Chambers. The PM had been asked to meet the Councillors and Baillies and say a few words to them; but to our horror we found a crowd of about 200, a platform and press reporters. The PM rose to the occasion however, though he had no prepared speech, and made a full length oration, which went down very well . . .[3]

In his speech, and in the presence of Hopkins, Churchill spoke to those assembled of how Roosevelt's emissary had come 'in order to put himself in closest relation with things here. He will soon return to report to his famous chief the impressions he has gathered in our islands.' Churchill added: 'We do not require in 1941 large armies from oversea. What we do require are weapons, ships and aeroplanes.'

Churchill ended his speech:

My one aim is to extirpate Hitlerism from Europe. The question is such a

---

[1] Lord Moran, *Winston Churchill, The Struggle for Survival 1940–1965*, London 1966, pages 5–6.

[2] Naval Attaché, Washington to Director of Naval Intelligence, 14 January 1941: Admiralty papers, 233/84.

[3] John Martin, letter of 15 January 1941: Martin papers.

simple one. Are we to move steadily forward and have freedom, or are we to be put back into the Middle Ages by a totalitarian system that crushes all forms of individual life and has for its aim little less than the subjugation of Europe and little more than the gratification of gangster appetites?

Do not suppose that we are at the end of the road. Yet, though long and hard it may be, I have absolutely no doubt that we shall win a complete and decisive victory over the forces of evil, and that victory itself will be only a stimulus to further efforts to conquer ourselves and to make our country as worthy in the days of peace as it is proving itself in the hours of war.[1]

All that Churchill had seen in Glasgow, both the warmth of his reception and the civil defence preparations, had much impressed him. 'I was struck by the evident keenness and efficiency of the various Civil Defence services,' he wrote to the Lord Provost some days later, 'and came away fortified by the assurance that, if the full force of the enemy's attack should be turned upon Glasgow, as upon so many cities in the South, her citizens will endure and surmount it.'[2]

That night Churchill and Hopkins were given dinner in Glasgow by the Regional Commissioner for Scotland, Tom Johnston, at the Station Hotel.[3] Churchill's doctor, who was among those present, recorded in his diary:

. . . I sat next to Harry Hopkins, an unkempt figure. After a time he got up and, turning to the PM, said:

'I suppose you wish to know what I am going to say to President Roosevelt on my return. Well, I'm going to quote you one verse from that Book of Books in the truth of which Mr Johnston's mother and my own Scottish mother were brought up: "Whither thou goest, I will go; and where thou lodgest, I will lodge: thy people shall be my people, and thy God my God." ' Then he added very quietly: 'Even to the end.'

I was surprised to find the PM in tears. He knew what it meant.

'Even to us,' the doctor added, 'the words seemed like a rope thrown to a drowning man.'[4]

From Glasgow, Churchill took Hopkins with him to Tyneside, and

---

[1] Speech of 17 January 1941: Churchill papers, 9/150. Two days later, reading the draft of a statement to be issued by Ernest Bevin, Churchill wrote to Bevin: 'You want about ten lines at the end, which I think might well express the determination of the working people of this country to eradicate the curse of Hitlerism from Europe, and the way in which they mean to go on whatever it costs.' (Letter of 19 January 1941: Churchill papers, 20/21.)

[2] Letter of 28 January 1941: Churchill papers, 20/21.

[3] On 4 February 1941 John Colville noted in his diary: '. . . saw Tom Johnston, who the PM thinks one of the best of the Labour Party. He is to be offered the Scottish Office' (Colville papers).

[4] Lord Moran, *Winston Churchill, The Struggle for Survival 1940–1965*, London 1966, page 6.

then, returning to London in a snowstorm on January 18, the two men went on to Chequers for the weekend.[1]

'We have staying with us over the weekend,' Eric Seal, who was duty Private Secretary at Chequers, wrote home on the Sunday, 'one Harry Hopkins, an American, who is a close confidant of the President's. He is really a very charming and interesting man. Winston has taken to him tremendously. Tonight (this is for your ear only) we rang up the President—and the Prime Minister spoke to him. He started off "Mr President—it's me—Winston speaking"!!'[2]

Even while Churchill and Hopkins were talking at Chequers, Britain's urgent needs were being telegraphed to the United States. On Saturday January 18 Beaverbrook and Sir Andrew Duncan informed Arthur Purvis and Morris Wilson that Britain needed more than 9,000 heavy bombers in 1941 and a further 17,000 in 1942. 'As you know,' Purvis and Wilson were told, 'we hope to get considerable proportion of these requirements from United States production.'[3]

In advance of Hopkins' discussions with various Ministers, Churchill had alerted them to his special status, minuting to Bridges on January 13: 'Mr Hopkins' relations are with the President alone and he does not want them complicated by an appearance of doing business on the Departmental level. Should it be necessary in spite of the above to make any reference I should be glad to be acquainted beforehand and see the draft telegrams.'[4]

On Friday January 24 Churchill took Harry Hopkins to Dover, to see the gun batteries there, and to look across the Channel to the cliffs of German-occupied France. That evening, Churchill and Hopkins reached Chequers, for the weekend.[5] Colville, who was present, recorded in his diary:

At dinner Hopkins said how impressed he had been to see, when dining with Bevin, Morrison and Sir Andrew Duncan, on what friendly and familiar terms a great industrialist could be with Labour leaders. Such a thing could not happen in America.

---

[1] The other guests on the weekend of Saturday 18 and Sunday 19 January 1941 included Ismay, Lindemann, Air Marshal Sholto Douglas, Sir Richard Peirse, Sir Dudley Pound, Mary Churchill, Randolph Churchill, Judy Montagu, Robin Maugham and Flight Lieutenant Coward. (Chequers Visitors Book.)

[2] Letter of 19 January 1941: Seal papers.

[3] 'Pursa' No. 15 'Most Secret', 18 January 1941: Cabinet papers, 115/4.

[4] Prime Minister's Personal Minute, C9/1, 13 January 1941: Cabinet papers, 21/999.

[5] Among those present as overnight guests or at meals were Clementine and Mary Churchill, Judy Montagu, John and Lady Gwendeline Churchill, the Duke and Duchess of Marlborough, Lindemann, Dill and Portal (Chequers List, Weekend 25 January 1941).

Hopkins told the PM that during the afternoon at Dover he had heard one workman say to another, as Winston passed, 'There goes the bloody British Empire.' Winston's face wreathed itself in smiles and turning to me he lisped: '*Very* nice.' I don't think anything has given him such pleasure for a long time.

The PM said he did not now see how invasion could be successful and he now woke up in the mornings, as he nearly always had, feeling as if he had a bottle of champagne inside him and glad that another day had come. In May and June, however, he had been sorry when the nights were over and he had often thought about death, not, he said, 'that I much believe in personal survival after death, at least not of the memory'. He was not, he said, much worried by the chance of being bombed—in this connexion he is fond of quoting M Poincaré's statement, 'I take refuge beneath the impenetrable arch of probability.'

Jack Churchill asked when we were going to recapture British Somaliland. The PM replied that we must concentrate on the major operation. As Napoleon said, 'Frappez la masse et le reste vient par surcroît.'

At midnight, Churchill took Hopkins into the Private Secretaries' office, and, as Colville recorded in his diary, spoke against any talk of a negotiated peace:

'Never give in,' said the PM, 'and you will never regret it.' A negotiated Peace would be a German victory and would leave open the way for another and final 'spring of the Tiger' in a few years time. Hopkins agreed and said that Lindbergh, and others in America who favoured a negotiated Peace, really desired a German victory. The PM wound up by saying that after the last war he had been asked to provide an inscription for a French War Memorial. His suggestion, which was rejected, had been: 'In war fury, in defeat defiance, in victory magnanimity, in peace goodwill.'[1]

While still at Chequers on January 25, Hopkins showed Churchill and Dill details of the American rearmament programme. 'It is clear that gigantic efforts are being made,' Colville noted, 'but the PM warned Hopkins that the results would not be expected for about 18 months.' Britain's own war factories, he explained, were only just beginning their full production, and, for example, in the previous week British ammunition output doubled.

The discussion then turned to invasion, and to 'Victor', a military exercise then taking place as practice against a German landing.[2] If,

---

[1] Colville diary, 24 January 1941: Colville papers.

[2] Four days later, General Brooke wrote to Churchill: 'I think that all the Services and Departments engaged have derived great value from the exercise by way of improving plans for Home Defence. Conferences are now being held to distil the main lessons. . . .' On February 1, Brooke sent Churchill a detailed account of the exercise, during which the 'German' invading forces had been checked after fifteen separate landings (the main ones on the Norfolk, Suffolk and Kent

said Churchill, he had to deliver a speech after a German invasion, he would end it: 'The hour has come; kill the Hun.'

During their talk, Hopkins wondered whether Britain would receive any warning of an invasion, but Churchill and Dill, as Colville recorded, 'seem confident that complete surprise is impossible'.[1] On the following evening a further discussion took place in the Great Hall, 'as interesting a discussion as I ever hope to hear', wrote Colville:

We sat in a circle, Portal, Hopkins, Jack Churchill, myself and Prof, while the PM stood with his back against the mantlepiece, a cigar between his teeth, his hands in the armpits of his waistcoat. Every few seconds he would start forward, trip over the marble grate, walk four or five paces, turn abruptly and resume his position against the mantlepiece. All the while a torrent of eloquence flowed from his lips, and he would fix one or another of us with his eye as he drove home some point. He talked of the past, the present and the future, and the subject matter of his talk was roughly as follows:

In recent history two men had been the most harmful influence in English politics, Joseph Chamberlain and Baldwin. The first had pushed us into the Boer War and, by setting Europe against us, had stimulated the Germans to build a fleet. The second had dominated the scene for 15 years. He had pushed out of public life the men with the greatest experience, LG, Birkenhead etc; and he had made possible the resurgence of Germany and the decay of our own strength. He was just sufficiently good to be suffering now acutely for what he had done.

This led to a digression about the 'Carthaginian peace' of Versailles: we had exacted a thousand millions in reparations; we and the US had contributed 2,000 millions in loans to set Germany on her feet again and rebuild her power. It was possible that in some 20 months we and the US would again have to make a peace settlement and there would once more be those who wished to help Germany on to her feet. 'Only one thing in history is certain: that mankind is unteachable.'

Churchill then spoke of currency problems, coming out strongly, as Colville noted, in favour of 'the commodity dollar', the rate of which would be fixed by the prices of a number of selected commodities. Churchill told Hopkins that the currency problem was similar to that of daylight saving; 'by a little tampering with the clock great benefits

---

coasts). In London, two 'German' brigades and thirty light tanks were 'landed' by parachute: 'They succeeded in seizing Neasden power station and the Metropolitan Water Works. Action was in progress against all parachute parties at the end of the exercise.' (HF3978/Ops, General Headquarters, Home Forces, 1 February 1941: Premier papers, 3/4696/2, folios 2–16.)

[1] Colville diary, 25 January 1941: Colville papers.

could be reaped, but by overdoing it in either direction all advantage must be lost'.

Hopkins told Churchill that Roosevelt was in favour of some such scheme as Churchill had just outlined, but that the 'opposition of Wall Street had been intense'. Churchill, speaking for once in favour of the financiers,[1] pointed out, as Colville noted, that 'today everybody wanted Credit but nobody had any patience with creditors!'

Churchill then spoke of the post-war world. As Colville noted in his diary:

The PM said that when the war was over there would be a short lull during which we had the opportunity to establish a few basic principles, of justice, of respect for the rights and property of other nations, and indeed of respect for private property so long as its owner was honest and its scope moderate. We could find nothing better than Christian Ethics on which to build and the more closely we followed the Sermon on the Mount, the more likely we were to succeed in our endeavours. But all this talk about war aims was absurd at the present time:[2] the Cabinet Committee to examine the question had produced a vague paper, four fifths of which was from the Sermon on the Mount and the remainder an Election Address!

Japan and the US was the next topic, and Hopkins expressed the belief that if America came into the war the incident would be with Japan. The PM said that the advantage of America as an ally to the disadvantage of Japan as an enemy was as 10 to 1. Why, look at their respective power of steel production— and 'modern war is waged with steel'. Besides Japan must have been greatly affected by the fate of the Italian navy, which on paper had been so strong. 'Fate holds terrible forfeits for those who gamble on certainties.'

Churchill then sat down, saying that he had talked 'too much' and asking Hopkins for his views. Once again, Colville recorded the opinion

---

[1] As Chancellor of the Exchequer fifteen years earlier, Churchill had written to one of his senior advisers: 'I do not pretend to see even "through a glass darkly" how the financial and credit policy of the country could be handled so as to bridge the gap between a dearth of goods and a surplus of labour; and well I realise the danger of experiment to that end. The seas of history are full of famous wrecks. Still if I could see a way, I would far rather follow it than any other. I would rather see Finance less proud and Industry more content.' (Companion Volume 5 of this biography: Part 1, 'The Exchequer Years', London 1979, pages 411–12.)

[2] Five weeks later, after reading the draft of a speech on war aims that Lord Halifax was about to make in Washington, Churchill telegraphed to the Ambassador: 'In paragraph 15 I do not understand how the whole world can be compelled to join together to bring the world back to health. We may call a conference of sixty or seventy nations, but it is very probable that most of them will be thinking of their own interests. All the thought in these four paragraphs suffers from being both hackneyed and loose. There is no teeth in it anywhere. I should strongly advise recasting on less ambitious lines. It is a pretty tough job to reshape human society in an after-dinner speech. Pray forgive me striking this note of caution, but, of course, I have no doubt the speech will work out all right.' (Telegram of 1 March 1941: Churchill papers, 20/49.)

of the man whose link between Churchill and Roosevelt was of such importance and urgency:

Speaking slowly but very emphatically, Hopkins stated that the President was not much concerned with the future. His preoccupation was with the next few months. As far as war aims were concerned, there were only very few people in America, liberal intellectuals, who cared about the matter; and they were nearly all on our side. He believed the same to be true of people in this country. All he would say of the future was that he believed the Anglo-Saxon peoples would have to do the rearrangement: the other nations would not be ripe for cooperation for a long time. He thought the problems of reconstruction would be very great, greater than the PM had implied, and we should have to send men to the conference table who were tough and not sentimental.

As far as the present was concerned, there were four divisions of public opinion in America: a small group of Nazis and Communists, sheltering behind Lindbergh, who declared for a negotiated peace and wanted a German victory; a group, represented by Joe Kennedy, which said 'Help Britain, but make damn sure you don't get into any danger of war'; a majority group which supported the President's determination to send the maximum assistance at whatever risk; and about 10% or 15% of the country, including Knox, Stimson and most of the armed forces, who were in favour of immediate war.

The important element in the situation was the boldness of the President, who would lead opinion and not follow it, who was convinced that if England lost, America, too, would be encircled and beaten. He would use his powers if necessary; he would not scruple to interpret existing laws for the furtherance of his aim; he would make people gape with surprise, as the British Foreign Office must have gaped when it saw the terms of the Lease and Lend Bill. The boldness of the President was a striking factor in the situation. He did not want war, indeed he looked upon America as an Arsenal which should provide the weapons for the conflict and not count the cost; but he would not shrink from war.

More than this, Churchill had never expected to hear; and this in itself was enough to lift his worries about Roosevelt's intentions. As he went to bed, it was other worries that he discussed with Colville, who found his Master 'most communicative and benign'. Colville added:

Nobody is more loveable than he when he is in this frame of mind. He recounted to me the difficulties in the way of an invader whose lines of communications would be cut and who could not dominate the air during the day-time. But, I said, the Germans must know this as well as we do and surely the implication is that they will not invade. 'To tell you the truth,' he said, 'that is what I think, and so does Portal. But the others don't think so.'

He said he would not feel so confident, remembering as he did Neville

Chamberlain's conviction a year ago that Germany would not invade Holland and Belgium, were it not for the fact that we had air superiority in the day and that we were not pinning our faith in the Maginot Line, 'a great China Wall', but in our troops *behind* the beaches who would attack any lodgment and make each separate one into a Sidi Barrani, a Bardia or a Tobruk.

He snuggled down beneath the bedclothes, I gave him his 'Boswell's Tour of the Hebrides', and smiling sweetly he wished me good-night.

Colville noted in his diary on the following day: 'the PM has throughout been at his most entertaining and shown the sunniest side of his disposition'. At dinner the previous evening he had said 'that he hated nobody and didn't feel he had any enemies—except the Huns, and that was professional!' Few men, Colville reflected, were as 'good natured' as Churchill, and he added: 'it is an interesting spot-light on No 10 last winter that he should have been regarded with such dislike and mistrust'.[1]

Eric Seal wrote home that weekend: 'Hopkins, the President's envoy, whom I told you about last week, was I think very impressed by the cheerfulness & optimism he found everywhere. I must confess that I am surprised at it myself!' Seal added: 'There is definitely a much more cheerful spirit than there was a year ago—don't you think? We really do feel we are getting on with the war, & that we haven't done so badly since France fell out.'[2]

In a telegram to Roosevelt, Hopkins gave a full account of his 'twelve evenings' with Churchill, during which, he explained, 'I have explored every aspect of our mutual problems with him.' He had been given 'complete access to all confidential material which is concerned with my mission here'. Hopkins went on to tell Roosevelt: 'Your "former Navy person" is not only the Prime Minister, he is the directing force behind the strategy and the conduct of the war in all its essentials. He has an amazing hold on the British people of all classes and groups. He has particularly strength both with the military establishments and the working people.'[3]

On Monday January 27, Staff Conversations opened in Washington, authorized by Churchill and Roosevelt to determine 'the best methods by which the armed forces of the United States and British Com-

[1] Colville diary, 25–7 January 1941: Colville papers. On 8 February 1941 Colville's grandfather, the Marquess of Crewe, who had been a senior Cabinet Minister in the Liberal Governments of 1905 to 1915, told his grandson that Churchill 'had greatly mellowed of recent years and had, he thought, lost the sudden fits of unreasonable temper to which he had once been subject'.

[2] Letter of 25 January 1941: Seal papers.

[3] Telegram quoted in Robert E. Sherwood, *The White House Papers of Harry L. Hopkins*, London 1948, volume 1, pages 256–7.

monwealth, with its present Allies, could defeat Germany and the Powers allied with her, should the United States be compelled to resort to war', and to seek agreement on the methods and nature of Anglo-American military cooperation, strategy, strength of forces and eventual 'unity of field command in cases of strategic or tactical joint operations'.[1]

On the day that these Staff Conversations began in Washington, Churchill lunched in London with Roosevelt's recent opponent for the Presidency, Wendell Willkie, who brought Churchill a letter from Roosevelt. The letter read:

Dear Churchill,

Wendell Willkie will give you this. He is truly helping to keep politics out over here.

I think this verse applies to your people as it does to us.

'Sail on, O Ship of State!
Sail on, O Union, strong and great!
Humanity with all its fears,
With all the hope of future years
Is hanging breathless on thy fate.'[2]
As ever yours,
Franklin D. Roosevelt[3]

'I received Willkie yesterday,' Churchill telegraphed to Roosevelt on January 28, 'and was deeply moved by the verse of Longfellow's which you had quoted. I shall have it framed as a souvenir of these tremendous days, and as a mark of our friendly relations, which have been built up telegraphically but also telepathically under all the stresses.' As to the President's emissary, Churchill added: 'It has been a great pleasure to me to make friends with Hopkins, who has been a great comfort and encouragement to everyone he has met. One can easily see why he is so close to you.'[4]

Hopkins remained one further week in Britain. An important feature

---

[1] 'United States–British Staff Conversations, Report', 27 March 1941, 'Secret', ABC-1: Premier papers, 3/489/2, folios 8–13. The British delegation consisted of Rear Admirals Bellairs and Danckwerts, Major-General Morris, Air Vice-Marshal Slessor and Captain A. W. Clarke, RN. The American delegation included Major-General S. D. Embick and Rear-Admiral Ghormley. (ABC = American–British Conversations.)

[2] Longfellow wrote 'hopes' in the fourth line, and opened the stanza: 'Thou too, sail on, O Ship of State.' (*Building of the Ship*.)

[3] Letter dated 20 January 1941, delivered 27 January 1941, reproduced in facsimile in Winston S. Churchill, *The Second World War*, volume 3, London 1950, page 24. Willkie had polled 22,305,198 votes to Roosevelt's 27,244,160, despite his firm backing for Roosevelt's war policy, which many Republicans wished him to oppose. Willkie died in October 1944, aged 52.

[4] 'Personal and Secret', 28 January 1941: Churchill papers, 20/49.

of his visit was his discussion at the Admiralty of items on which the United States and Britain could work together. These included transport of aircraft to Britain in United States' aircraft carriers 'in case of urgent need', and the pooling of Intelligence in 'enemy-occupied countries'.[1]

From January 31 to February 3, Hopkins was again at Chequers, together for one of the nights with Wendell Willkie.[2] Before going to Chequers, he was taken by Churchill to Southampton and Portsmouth, where recent bombing raids had led to further civilian deaths.[3]

'One cannot help feeling enormously encouraged,' Churchill told the citizens of Portsmouth, 'by the spirit of the ever-growing movement to aid Britain which we see laying hold of the mighty mass of the United States.'[4]

Eric Seal, who accompanied Churchill and Hopkins to visit the south coast ports, wrote to his wife that weekend: 'On Friday we went off to Southampton & Portsmouth, to look at the damage. It is a dismal sight, particularly at Portsmouth, where one whole street we went along has just ceased to exist. There is nothing but stacks of debris on either side of the road.' It was comparable, Seal wrote, 'only to the damage one saw in France in the last war. We did not see anything quite so bad at Southampton; but they say that it is even worse there in places. This damage is however surprisingly local—you go along a devastated street, and then suddenly find yourself in a normal town.' Seal's account, written from Chequers, continued:

We came straight back here by special train, Hopkins came with us all the way, & spent the night. It was quite a small party—PM, Mrs C, Hopkins, General Ismay, Commander Thompson (Tommy) & myself. PM was in great form. He gets on like a house afire with Hopkins, who is a dear, & is universally liked. As you know, he lives in the White House with Roosevelt, & is very much in his confidence.

After dinner Hopkins produced a big box of gramophone records, all American tunes or ones with an Anglo-American significance. We had these

---

[1] Notes of a discussion: Admiralty papers, 1/11168.

[2] Chequers Visitors Book. The other guests and visitors included Ismay, Beaverbrook, Attlee, Eden, Lindemann and Sir Alan Brooke, who wrote in his diary: 'After dinner, epidiascope was produced and I had to give a lecture on our recent Home Defence Exercise. They were all three very interested in it and the PM very flattering about the defensive measures that had been taken. But he would not acknowledge that an invasion of this country on that scale was possible in the face of partial sea-control and local air-control.' (Brooke diary, 2 February 1941: Arthur Bryant, *The Turn of the Tide*, London 1957, page 241.)

[3] In January 1941, 1,500 civilians were killed in Britain during German air raids, and over 2,000 injured.

[4] Speech of 31 January 1941: Churchill papers, 9/150.

until well after midnight, the PM walking about, sometimes dancing a pas-
seul, in time with the music. We all got a bit sentimental & Anglo-American,
under the influence of the good dinner & the music.

The PM kept on stopping in his walk, & commenting on the situation—
what a remarkable thing that the two nations should be drawing so much
together at this critical time, how much we had in common etc. He feels a
great bond of sympathy for America, & in particular for Roosevelt. He had
an American mother, as you know.

Seal's letter continued:

I feel sure that great things may come of this extraordinary feeling of close
relationship. It was at the time very pleasant & satisfying—but difficult to
convey in words, especially within the confines of a letter. Everyone present
knew & liked each other—it is quite extraordinary how Hopkins had endeared
himself to everyone here he has met.

Of Hopkins himself, Seal wrote that weekend:

He is a quaint, rather twisted little man, with a frail appearance and a whim-
sical look. I think you would like him—quite different from the ordinary
American go-getter. He lost his wife 4 years ago, and since then has been
seriously ill—he nearly died after an operation. But he is full of soul and wit, a
ready and amusing talker.

Harry Hopkins left Chequers that Saturday morning, and, as Seal
wrote, 'Willkie came in his stead, with two henchmen. . . .'

'The plain fact of the matter,' Seal ended, 'is that everyone is feeling
much happier, because we feel the war is getting on. No doubt there
will be a terrific crack soon—but we all feel that we have stood a
pretty hot one without flinching, and that we will be able to take it.
Also, that Hitler must get a decision soon, or bust!'[1]

---

[1] Letter of 2 February 1941: Seal papers.

52

The Balkans and
The Battle of the Atlantic:
'The strain is growing here'

O N January 18, at a conference at Chequers, Churchill had
agreed, reluctantly, to postpone Operation 'Workshop', the seizure of Pantelleria Island, for a month. Then, on January 20, he had
finally to give up his hopes for 'Workshop' altogether, for on that day,
at a meeting of the Defence Committee, the Chiefs of Staff opposed it
as too much of a risk, a conclusion, Churchill commented, that 'seemed
to lead to the minimum of aggressive action'.[1]

'He admits it cannot be carried out,' Eden noted in his diary after a
talk with Churchill, 'but is very irritated against Chiefs of Staff for not
having done it sooner.'[2] That same day, he told the Defence Committee
that he wanted a plan studied 'to capture Sardinia'. This was operation
'Yorker', studied by the Joint Planning Committee on the following
morning, and based upon the use of 40,000 troops, including 2,000
Free French troops from West Africa. If approved that day, Ismay told
Churchill, 'Yorker' could be put into effect within five weeks.[3]

[1] Defence Committee (Operations), 20 January 1941, 9.30 p.m.: Cabinet Papers, 69/2.

[2] Eden diary, 20 January 1941: The Earl of Avon, *The Eden Memoirs, The Reckoning*, London
1965, page 187. In his memoirs, written eight years later, Churchill reflected, on both sides of the
argument: 'Long before the month had passed the German Air Force arrived in Sicily, and all
wore a very different complexion. There is no doubt about the value of the prize we did not gain.
Had we been in occupation of Pantelleria in 1942 many fine ships that were lost in our convoys,
which we then fought through to Malta, might have been saved, and the enemy communications
with Tripoli still further impaired. On the other hand, we might well have been overpowered by
German air attack, lost our vantage, and complicated our defence of Malta in the interval.'
(Winston S. Churchill, *The Second World*, volume 3, London 1950, pages 52–3.)

[3] 'Operation "Yorker", preliminary examination', 20 January 1941: Premier papers, 3/509/1,
folio 26. Although Sir Roger Keyes gave his approval to 'Yorker' on January 25, it was first
postponed, then modified into the capture and holding of Cagliari alone (code name 'Garrotter')
using only 7,500 troops, and then abandoned.

A further operation which Churchill approved in January, after it had been proposed by Hugh Dalton and supported by the Chiefs of Staff, was 'Claymore'. This was a landing on the Norwegian Lofoten Islands, to destroy the fish-processing plant there, this being, as Dalton informed Churchill, the 'most important source' by which Germany obtained vitamins A and D.[1] Churchill approved, provided the Chiefs of Staff were satisfied that the plan would not 'stir up the Norwegian coast and lead to re-inforcements of the German forces in the Peninsula'.[2]

During the evening, news reached London that the Italians had withdrawn from Kassala, a necessary first step to their defeat in East Africa. But it was the Balkan situation that dominated the Defence Committee's deliberations. The danger to Turkey was such, Eden urged, as to make the capture of the Dodecanese 'even more important' than securing Benghazi,[3] while Churchill, in reference to the Greek refusal to accept a British force told the Committee that 'we could not force the Greeks to receive British help', and he added:

We were open to no reproach in the matter, and he did not regret the offer we had made; but he could not believe that General Metaxas was right in his theory that the Germans were limiting themselves to defensive action in the Balkans. All our information showed that preparations were well under way for the occupation of Bulgaria, with the connivance of the Bulgarian authorities. There would be no invasion; the country would be sapped from within like Roumania. The Turks would probably remain quiescent, and the Germans would gain a dominating position from which to threaten Salonica.

In these circumstances, Churchill commented, 'it was hopeless for us to imagine that we would fight for Salonica'.[4]

Still unable to shake off his cold, Churchill was cast down. Eden, who had drinks with him on the evening of January 21, noted in his diary that night, after a discussion of Australian Government demands to reinforce Malaya so as to protect Australia against a possible Japanese attack:

[1] 'Most Secret', SC/1589/6, 17 January 1941: Premier papers, 3/328/7, folio 212.

[2] Prime Minister's Personal Minute, D.20/1, 22 January 1941: Premier papers, 3/328/7, folio 211. In the first week of March, after 'Claymore' had been carried out, Churchill signalled to Admiral Tovey: 'I am so glad you were able to find the means of executing "Claymore". This admirable raid has done serious injury to the enemy and has given an immense amount of innocent pleasure at home.' (Signal of 7 March 1941: Premier papers, 3/328/7, folio 204.)

[3] On the evening of 27 January 1941 Churchill went to the underground Central War Room to 'inspect' models of the islands of Leros and Rhodes. (Churchill Engagement Book: Thompson papers.)

[4] Defence Committee (Operations), 20 January 1941, 9.30 p.m.: Cabinet papers, 69/2.

Winston was tired and depressed, for him. His cold is heavy on him. He was inclined to be fatalistic about the House, maintained that bulk of Tories hated him, that he had done all he could and would be only too happy to yield to another, that Malaya, Australian Government's intransigence and 'nagging' in House was more than any man could be expected to endure.[1]

This mood of fatalism had passed by the following afternoon, however, and when Churchill spoke in the House of Commons, Colville, who heard him speak, noted in his dairy:

He did so extremely well, explaining his reasons for the new Committee machinery[2] (which has been much criticized) with the utmost clearness and cogency.

The House was much entertained by his quips and his mastery of the art of anti-climax. He expounded the little understood facts about the slowness of changing from Peace to War production and the increased need of man-power, in industry rather than the forces, as that transfer takes place.

He answered the demand for a Dictator on the Home Front, to correspond with the Minister of Defence on the military side, by disparaging dictators in general and by pointing out that he could only maintain his ascendancy as Minister of Defence because he was also Prime Minister. In general he welcomed criticism even when, for the sake of emphasis, it parted company with reality![3]

Defending Parliamentary criticism of his policies, Churchill commented: 'I may be stunned by it, and I may resent it; I may even retort—but at any rate Debates on these large issues are of the very greatest value to the life-thrust of the nation, and they are of great assistance to His Majesty's Government.' At the end of his speech,

---

[1] Eden diary, 21 January 1941: The Earl of Avon, *The Eden Memoirs, The Reckoning*, London 1965, page 318.

[2] The new machinery was the setting up of the Production Executive in December 1940, of which Colonel Jacob later wrote: 'The Production Executive was a small body consisting of the three Supply Ministers, the Minister of Labour and the President of the Board of Trade, to ginger up production. The Minister of Labour was appointed as Chairman. The real object of this body was to replace the Production Council, which, under Mr Greenwood's Chairmanship, had been a large, amorphous and ineffective body, by a smaller and more compact organization. At the same time, the Import Executive was set up. This body comprised the three Supply Ministers, the President of the Board of Trade and the Minister of Food. The Minister of Supply was made Chairman. This body was set up to secure a more effective handling of the import programme, which had hitherto not been dealt with very effectively. It was also intended to secure a better co-ordination of the arrangements for (a) unloading, etc. at the ports, and (b) transport from the ports to destinations in this country.' ('Changes in Committee organisation made in December, 1940', 'The Jacob Document': Cabinet papers, 120/290.)

[3] Colville diary, 22 January 1941: Colville papers. Among Churchill's quips was the comment that the Chairman of the Imports Executive would be 'not *facile princeps* but *primus inter pares*', which, he added, 'for the benefit of any old Etonians present, I should, if very severely pressed, venture to translate'. (*Hansard*, 22 January 1941, column 263.)

Churchill spoke of the victories of Sidi Barrani and Bardia and that 'it may well be that while I am speaking Tobruk and all it contains are in our hands'.[1] His final words were of caution combined with confidence, as he told the House:

Far be it from me to paint a rosy picture of the future. Indeed, I do not think we should be justified in using any but the more sombre tones and colours while our people, our Empire and indeed the whole English-speaking world are passing through a dark and deadly valley.

But I should be failing in my duty if, on the other side, I were not to convey to the House the true impression, namely, that this great nation is getting into its war stride. It is accomplishing the transition from the days of peace and comfort to those of supreme, organised, indomitable exertion.

Still more should I fail in my duty were I to suggest that the future, with all its horrors, contains any element which justifies lassitude, despondency or despair . . .[2]

As January 1941 came to an end, Churchill's son Randolph set off for the Middle East, with No. 8 Commando. Before he left, his father's friend Robert Boothby defended himself against charges of financial impropriety in the House of Commons. Boothby's speech, Churchill told Randolph, 'was a remarkable Parliamentary performance, and perceptively affected the opinion of the House. I do not think he will have to resign his seat.'[3]

Two days later, in thanking his father for his letters of introduction to both Smuts and Wavell, Randolph added: 'I pray that all will go well with you & that success will continue to reward all your tremendous exertions.'[4]

Those exertions covered every sphere. On February 2 Churchill proposed a warning to the Rumanian dictator, General Antonescu, against committing what Colville described as 'sadistic atrocities unsurpassed in horror', such as taking 'hundreds of Jews to cattle slaughter-

---

[1] On 22 January 1941 Australian and British troops entered Tobruk, and five days later a total of 25,000 Italian prisoners and 50 tanks were in Allied hands. On the following day Churchill telegraphed to Wavell: 'I again send you my most heartfelt congratulations on the third of the brilliant victories which have in little more than six weeks transformed the situation in the Middle East, and have also sensibly affected the movement of the whole war. The daring and scope of the original conception, the perfection of Staff work and execution have raised the reputation of the British and Australian army and its leadership, and will long be regarded as models of the military art . . .' (Personal and Secret, 23 January 1941: Churchill papers, 20/49.)

[2] *Hansard*, 22 January 1941, columns 269/70.

[3] Letter of 28 January 1941: Churchill papers 1/362. Boothby did not resign his seat, but he had already had to give up a Junior Ministerial appointment at the Ministry of Food, nor did he receive any further Ministerial appointment. But he remained a Member of Parliament until 1958. At Churchill's submission he became a KBE in 1953 (in 1958 he was created a Life Peer).

[4] Letter of 30 January 1941: Churchill papers, 1/362.

houses and killing them according to the Jews' own ritual practices in slaughtering animals'.[1] Would it not be well, Churchill had already asked Eden, 'to tell General Antonescu that we will hold him and his immediate circle personally responsible in life and limb if such a vile act is perpetrated?' Perhaps Churchill added, 'you may think of something more diplomatic than this'.[2]

The future of Turkey also exercised Churchill's time and thought. On the last day of January he had sent a long letter to the President of Turkey, Ismet Inönü, stressing his 'sure information' that German officials were already 'establishing themselves' on Bulgarian aerodromes, and that very soon, perhaps within a few weeks, German troops and air squadrons would move into Bulgaria.[3] Then Churchill warned, 'unless you promise the Germans not to march against Bulgaria, or against their troops passing through Bulgaria, they will bomb Istanbul and Adrianople the same night, and also dive-bomb your troops in Thrace'. Churchill's forecast continued:

No doubt they would hope either to reach Salonica unopposed or to compel the Greeks to make peace with Italy and yield them air bases in Greece and in the islands, thus endangering the communications between our armies in Egypt and the Turkish Army. They would deny the use of Smyrna to our Navy, they would completely control the exits from the Dardanelles, and thus complete the encirclement of Turkey in Europe on three sides. This would also facilitate their attacks upon Alexandria and Egypt generally.

All this, Churchill told Inönü, 'may fall upon us in February or March'. To seek to forestall it, he proposed an Anglo-Turkish agreement, whereby at least ten squadrons of British fighters and bombers, apart from the five squadrons already in action in Greece, would be sent to Turkey 'at the earliest moment that accommodation can be provided'.[4] If Greece surrendered, or were 'beaten down', Britain

---

[1] Colville diary, 2 February 1941: Colville papers.

[2] Prime Minister's Personal Minute, M.109/1, 1 February 1941: Churchill papers, 20/36.

[3] An Enigma decrypt 18 January 1941 showed German Air Force hutments being sent to Bulgaria. A decrypt of 20 January 1941 showed that the German Air Force mission in Rumania was discussing long-term arrangements for the supply of German Air Force fuel to depots in Bulgaria (CX/JQ 603 and 605 quoted in F. H. Hinsley and other, *British Intelligence in the Second World War, Its Influence on Strategy and Operations*, volume 1, London 1979, page 355.)

[4] The proposal to send the ten squadrons of British aircraft to Turkey had come from the Chief of the Air Staff, Sir Charles Portal, to whom Churchill minuted a week after his letter to Inönü: 'Suppose they do accept, and after that Greece demands further aid beyond the five squadrons allotted, what are you going to do? I am afraid you have got to look at this very seriously. I am in it with you up to the neck. But have we not in fact promised to sell the same pig to two customers? We might have a legal quibble about the word "promise", but I think we have got to look into this matter rather more deeply than that. Let me know what you feel about it and what you think

would transfer her five air squadrons in Greece to Turkish airfields, and 'further, we will fight the air war from Turkish bases with ever-increasing air forces of the highest quality'.

Once British squadrons were on Turkish airfields, Churchill added, Turkey would be in a position to threaten to bombard the Rumanian oilfields unless the Germans withdrew from Bulgaria. And there was 'more to come', for, as Churchill went on to explain:

The attitude of Russia is uncertain, and it is our hope it may remain loyal and friendly. Nothing will more restrain Russia from aiding Germany, even indirectly, than the presence of powerful British bombing forces which could attack the oilfields of Baku. Russia is dependent upon the supply from these oilfields for a very large part of her agriculture, and far-reaching famine would follow their destruction.

Thus Turkey, once defended by air-power, would have the means perhaps of deterring Germany from overrunning Bulgaria and quelling Greece, and of counterbalancing the Russian fear of the German armies.

If this 'decisive position' were to be saved, Churchill wrote, 'there is not an hour to lose'. On receipt of Inönü's assent, British personnel, either in uniform or in plain clothes 'as you prefer' could start for Turkey, together with a hundred anti-aircraft guns complete with personnel 'either in uniform, if you so desire, or in the guise of instructors'. He had already, Churchill said, discussed these measures with Marshal Chakmak.[1]

When this message reached Ankara, Churchill told the War Cabinet four days later, it had been delivered to the Foreign Minister, who had viewed it 'with some dismay', regarding it as 'tantamount to a declaration of war on Germany, for which his country was not ready'. But, Churchill warned, if the 'German plan' for the Balkans was allowed to develop unhindered, there was 'every prospect' that South Eastern Europe would witness 'this spring' a repetition of last spring's events in Scandinavia and the Low Countries. Unless Turkey were to agree to Britain's proposals, Portal added, Britain would be unable to deliver a 'counter stroke' against the Rumanian oil fields.[2]

Four days later the British Ambassador in Ankara, Sir Hughe Knatch-

---

can be done. Nothing was said about time or priority, so we have that to veer and haul on.' ('Private, Secret', Prime Minister's Personal Minute, M.135/1, 6 February 1941: Churchill papers, 20/36.)

[1] Letter dated 31 January 1941: Premier papers, 3/309/1, No. 81.

[2] War Cabinet No. 12 of 1941, 3 February 1941, Minute 3, Confidential Annex: Cabinet papers, 65/21.

bull-Hugessen, telegraphed to Eden: 'I am convinced of extreme importance of increasing military supplies to Turkey without delay. President, who spoke still more strongly about this, said to me that, if Turkey had had all that we promised, we might have had a different answer.' It was 'quite clear', the Ambassador added, 'that the Turkish Government feel that their present state of inadequate preparation excludes the possibility of any action likely to be provocative'.[1]

With the Enigma decrypts giving clear indication of the German military build-up in the Balkans, Churchill now saw a series of German advances, if not imminent, then certainly in prospect. 'The information reaching me from every quarter,' he had telegraphed to Wavell on January 26, 'leaves me no doubt that the Germans are now already establishing themselves upon the Bulgarian aerodromes, and making every preparation for action against Greece. This infiltration may, indeed almost certainly will, attain decisive proportions before any clear cut issue of invasion has been presented to the Turks, who will then be told to keep out or have Constantinople bombed.' Churchill's telegram ended: 'We must expect a series of very heavy, disastrous blows in the Balkans and possibly a general submission there to German aims. The stronger the strategic reserve which you can build up in the Delta, and the more advanced your preparations to transfer it to the European shores, the better will be the chances of securing a favourable crystallization.'[2]

In the western desert, success for the British arms came in the first week of February, when General O'Connor, taking extreme risks, despatched a small armoured force by unknown desert routes to Beda Fomm. Here, the force cut the road running south from Benghazi along which the Italians were retreating. In fierce engagements on February 5 and 6 the Italians failed to break past the British force, and all the survivors were captured. In two months, eleven Italian Divisions had been destroyed, 400 tanks and 1,290 guns captured, and 130,000 Italian soldiers taken prisoner.

On Saturday February 8, as O'Connor's troops entered the border town of Agheila, completing the conquest of Cyrenaica, the House of Representatives in Washington passed the Lend-Lease Bill by 260 to 165 votes. It had still to pass the Senate, and be approved by the President. But a major hurdle had been surmounted.

Churchill was at Chequers that Saturday when he learned the welcome news that Lend-Lease had been approved by the House of Rep-

[1] Ankara Telegram No. 272, 7 February 1941: Premier papers, 3/309/1, No. 95.
[2] Telegram of 26 January 1941: Premier papers, 3/309/1.

resentatives. Shortly afterwards Harry Hopkins arrived for a farewell visit. Churchill was working on the speech he intended to broadcast on the following evening, 'with American public opinion' as Hopkins noted: 'the principle target'.[1]

Hopkins discussed with Churchill many of the points of the speech, staying at Chequers until late on the Saturday night, when he left for the first stage of his journey back to the United States, accompanied by a British security officer.[2]

Before leaving Chequers Hopkins wrote to Churchill:

My dear Mr Prime Minister, I shall never forget these days with you—your supreme confidence and will to victory—Britain I have ever liked—I like it the more.

As I leave for America tonight I wish you great and good luck—confusion to your enemies—victory for Britain.

Ever so cordially, Harry Hopkins.[3]

On the evening of February 9 Churchill broadcast to Britain and the Empire, his first broadcast for five months. Hopkins, who had reached Bournemouth, and was about to take the flying boat from Poole to Lisbon, listened to the speech in his hotel, with Brendan Bracken.

Speaking from Chequers, Churchill praised the civilians who had stood up to the German air bombardment, the Civil Defence Services who had helped them through 'this formidable ordeal', the growing success of the Royal Air Force against airborne acts 'of terror and torture against our people at home', and the victory of Generals Wavell and Wilson, helped by Air Chief Marshal Longmore,[4] against Mussolini, 'still smarting under the Greek lash in Albania'. Egypt and the

---

[1] Quoted in Robert E. Sherwood, *The White House Papers of Harry L. Hopkins*, London 1948, volume 1, pages 260–1.

[2] Lieutenant Anthony McComas, who travelled to Washington with Hopkins to carry and safeguard his voluminous papers, including some important technical secrets which Churchill had authorized Hopkins to transmit to the United States Armed Forces.

[3] Letter on Chequers notepaper: Premier papers, 4/25/3, folio 130.

[4] Two weeks later Churchill minuted to Portal that 'Longmore has shown himself very unappreciative of the immense efforts we are making to support him and to increase his forces. At every stage throughout this Libyan affair we have had to press him forward beyond his judgement or inclination, with results which should be very satisfactory to him as well as to the public interest. As you know, I have long been more than doubtful whether he is making efficient and effective use of the enormous Air personnel now at his disposal. He has been most pessimistic and unduly cautious at every stage. The programme of squadrons with which he proposes to support any action in Greece and/or Turkey is far below what is necessary.' (Prime Minister's Personal Minute, M.222/1, 22 February 1941: Churchill papers, 20/36.) On that same day (February 22), in Athens, Eden wrote in his diary: 'Longmore is much weaker than I had thought and much weaker than he should be.' (Eden diary, 22 February 1941: The Earl of Avon, *The Eden Memoirs: The Reckoning*, London 1965, page 204.)

Suez Canal were now safe, and the port, the base and the airfields of Benghazi constituted 'a strategic point of high consequence to the whole of the war in the Eastern Mediterranean'.

Churchill also spoke of the 'mighty tide' of United States sympathy, goodwill and effective aid which had 'begun to flow' across the Atlantic, and of the visits of Hopkins and Willkie. 'We may be sure,' he said, 'that they will both tell the truth about what they have seen over here, and more than that we do not ask.'

Of the German threat to the Balkans, Churchill declared: 'of course, if all the Balkan people stood together and acted together, aided by Britain and Turkey, it would be many months before a German army and air force of sufficient strength to overcome them could be assembled in the south east of Europe', and in those months, American aid to Britain would become effective, British air power would grow, Britain would become 'a well-armed nation' and the British armies in the East would increase in strength. But nothing was more certain, he warned, than that, if Bulgaria and the other countries of southeastern Europe allowed themselves 'to be pulled to pieces one by one', they would share the fate of Denmark, Holland and Belgium.[1]

In Britain, Churchill stressed, plans to combat and repel invasion were complete, and Britain 'incomparably stronger' than in the summer and autumn of 1940. But he must drop 'a word of caution', for, next to cowardice and treachery, 'overconfidence, leading to neglect or slothfulness, is the worst of martial crimes', and all must be prepared to meet gas attacks, parachute attacks and glider attacks 'with constancy, forethought and practical skill'.

Churchill then told his listeners:

In order to win the war Hitler must destroy Great Britain. He may carry havoc into the Balkan States; he may tear great provinces out of Russia, he may march to the Caspian; he may march to the gates of India. All this will avail him nothing. It may spread his curse more widely throughout Europe and Asia, but it will not avert his doom. With every month that passes the many proud and once happy countries he is now holding down by brute force and vile intrigue are learning to hate the Prussian yoke and the Nazi name as nothing has ever been hated so fiercely and so widely among men before. And all the time, masters of the sea and air, the British Empire—nay, in a certain sense, the whole English-speaking world—will be on his track, bearing with them the swords of justice.

[1] Bulgaria allowed German troops to enter her territory in March 1941, and participated in the German invasion of Greece and Yugoslavia in April 1941, occupying Thrace and Macedonia. On 26 August 1944 Bulgaria sued for peace with the western Allies. On 3 September 1944 Soviet troops entered Bulgaria.

Churchill ended his speech by quoting the verse from the Longfellow poem which Roosevelt had sent him in January, and he went on to ask:

What is the answer that I shall give, in your name, to this great man, the thrice-chosen head of a nation of a hundred and thirty millions? Here is the answer which I will give to President Roosevelt. Put your confidence in us. Give us your faith and your blessing and, under Providence, all will be well.

We shall not fail or falter; we shall not weaken or tire. Neither the sudden shock of battle, nor the longdrawn trials of vigilance and exertion will wear us down. Give us the tools, and we will finish the job.[1]

A 'first-rate broadcast,' Colville noted, 'triumphant yet not over-optimistic', addressed, he added, 'largely to American ears'.[2] And from General Smuts in South Africa came the message: 'Each broadcast is a battle.'[3]

At the Defence Committee on the evening of February 10 it was decided not to advance through Tripolitania to Tripoli, but to halt Wavell's army at Agheila, holding Cyrenaica, and focusing British efforts on building up in Egypt forces strong enough to come to the eventual aid of Greece. It would be 'wrong', Churchill told the Committee, 'to abandon the Greeks, who were putting up a magnificent fight, and who were prepared to fight the Germans, so that we could later help Turkey, who was shirking her responsibilities, and taking no action to prevent the Germans establishing themselves in a threatening position in Bulgaria'. But, he added, 'we could not blame the Greeks if they bowed to the superior force of the Germans, if we refused them help'.[4]

To Wavell, Churchill telegraphed on the following day, with the approval of the Defence Committee:

---

[1] Broadcast on 9 February 1941: His Master's Voice, ALP 1554. Among those who listened to the broadcast was Randolph Churchill, then on his way to Egypt via South Africa, and who telegraphed from on board ship: 'Greatly enjoyed your fine speech.' (Churchill papers, 1/362.)

[2] Colville diary, 9 February 1941: Colville papers. Churchill's perspective on the war had influenced his Private Secretary, who noted in his diary on the following day (it was shortly after his 26th birthday): 'I am confident we have won. We shall see much serious damage and undergo many trials and dangers; but with the certainty of American material help and the determination of the people, the ultimate issue cannot be in doubt. The aftermath is unforeseeable, but there is reason to hope that we have learnt enough from the experiences of the recent past to see the folly of allowing the ideal to part company from the practical.'

[3] Phrase repeated to Churchill by his son, 23 February 1941: Churchill papers, 1/362. On 9 April 1963, in proclaiming Churchill an honorary citizen of the United States, President John F. Kennedy declared: 'he mobilised the English language and sent it into battle'.

[4] Defence Committee (Operations) No. 7 of 1941, 10 February 1941, 9.30 p.m.: Cabinet papers, 68/2.

Our first thoughts must be for our ally Greece, which is actually fighting so well. If Greece is trampled down or forced to make a separate peace with Italy, yielding also Air and naval strategic points against us to Germany, effect on Turkey will be very bad. But if Greece with British aid can hold up for some months German advance, chances of Turkish intervention will be favoured. Therefore it would seem that we should try to get in a position to offer the Greeks the transfer to Greece of the fighting portion of the Army which has hitherto defended Egypt and make every plan for sending and reinforcing it to the limit with men and material.[1]

One further military move, General Cunningham's advance into Italian East Africa from the south, was to continue. It had begun on February 10, and four days later Cunningham captured the port of Kismayu in Italian Somaliland.[2] At sea, however, on the night of February 10 and 11, there was a reminder of the continuing fragility of Britain's overseas links, when German bombers attacked a convoy off the Azores, sinking five ships.

The conquest of Cyrenaica led Churchill to broach the idea of turning the region into 'the beginning of a Free Italy', proclaiming to the world 'that we were holding it in trust for Italy' and calling upon Italian volunteers to 'join our efforts to overthrow Fascist tyranny'.[3] And to Ismay, for the Chiefs of Staff Committee, he explained his idea in greater detail:

Volunteers might be called for from the hundred thousand prisoners we have taken. There must be a great many who hate fascism. We might even rule Cyrenaica under the Free-Italian flag and treat it in the same way as de Gaulle's colonies are being treated, subject to our military control. Anyhow, I wish Cyrenaica to be petted and made extremely comfortable and prosperous, more money being spent upon them than they are intrinsically worth. Can we not make this place a base for starting a real split in Italy and the source of anti-Mussolini propaganda? We might make it a model of British rule, hold it in trust for the Italian people, and have four or five thousand Italian troops sworn to the liberation of Italy from the German and Mussolini yoke.

'This could be run,' Churchill added, 'as world propaganda.'[4]

These plans were to be frustrated however, not by Italian but by

---

[1] Defence Committee (Operations) No. 8 of 1941, 11 February 1941, 6 p.m., Annex 1, telegram marked 'Most Secret and Personal': Cabinet papers, 69/2. The telegram was sent to Wavell on 12 February 1941.

[2] On 17 February 1941 a War Office communiqué stated: 'No Italians remain on the soil of Egypt, the Sudan or Kenya except as prisoners.'

[3] Defence Committee (Operations) No. 8 of 1941, 11 February 1941, 6. p.m.: Cabinet papers 69/2.

[4] Prime Minister's Personal Minute, D.36/1, 11 February 1941: Churchill papers, 20/36.

German action, for on February 12 a German General, Erwin Rommel, arrived in Tripoli with his personal staff to take command of the growing German forces in Tripolitania. By chance, also on February 12, Eden and Dill prepared to set out for Cairo and Athens, to report at first hand on Greek needs and Britain's ability to meet them. 'Request you will take all possible precautions,' Churchill telegraphed to Wavell, and to the British Ambassador in Greece, 'for safety of our two Envoys, having regard to nasty habits of Wops and Huns.'[1]

Eden and Dill set out for the eastern Mediterranean. A week later, in a minute to Cadogan, Churchill commented that if Greece resolved to resist the expected German advance 'we shall have to help them with whatever troops we can get there in time. They will not, I fear,' Churchill added, 'be very numerous.' The alternative to such military aid would be 'to invite Greece to make a separate peace with Italy at German dictation with the consequences of the German occupation of all Greek airfields'. Should this happen, 'we must save what we can from the wreck', and, Churchill warned, 'it may well happen'.[2]

On the morning of February 20, Churchill told the War Cabinet that it was possible that before the Germans advanced into Greece, they would offer the Greeks 'such attractive terms' that the Greeks would feel 'bound' to make peace. Churchill continued:

In that case we could not very well blame them, nor should we take such a decision on the part of the Greeks too tragically. We should have done our duty and should then have to content ourselves by making our position in the Greek Islands as strong as possible.

From the Islands, Churchill told his colleagues, 'we could wage air war against Germany, which might eventually turn in our favour'.

Churchill also 'hoped', as he told the War Cabinet on February 20, that it would not be necessary to put 'any large part' of the British army into Greece. 'In fact,' he said, 'it was unlikely that it would be possible for a large British force to get there before the Germans.'[3]

Despite Churchill's instinctive hesitations about Britain becoming too involved militarily in Greece, his principal advisers were emphatic in their urgings to the contrary. From Cairo, Eden, having discussed

[1] Telegram of 12 February 1941: Churchill papers, 20/49. Eden and Dill flew from Britain on the evening of 16 February 1941, having been held up at Portsmouth by bad weather. The first clash between British and German troops on the border of Cyrenaica and Tripolitania took place on 27 February 1941.

[2] Prime Minister's Personal Minute, M.208/1, 19 February 1941: Churchill papers, 20/36.

[3] War Cabinet No. 19 of 1941, 20 February 1941, 12 noon, Minute 1, Confidential Annex: Cabinet papers, 65/21.

the question of aid to Greece with Wavell and Dill, telegraphed to Churchill in London that all three were agreed 'we should do everything in our power to bring the fullest measure of help to Greeks at earliest possible moment'. If the British offer were accepted by the Greeks, Eden reported, 'we believe that there is a fair chance of halting a German advance and preventing Greece from being overrun'.

Only the limitations of British air resources, Eden added, prevented help being given to Turkey at the same time, if Greece were to be supported 'on an effective scale'.[1] On the following day Eden telegraphed to Churchill that, despite the 'gamble' of sending British forces to mainland Greece to fight the Germans, it was his view that if 'we fail to help the Greeks there is no hope of action by Yugoslavia, and the future of Turkey may easily be compromised'. He, Wavell and Dill were therefore agreed 'that this attempt to help Greece should be made'.

In a telegram to Eden on February 20, Churchill stated emphatically, for Eden's guidance and his own: 'Do not consider yourselves obligated to a Greek enterprise if in your hearts you feel it will only be another Norwegian fiasco. If no good plan can be made please say so. But of course you know how valuable success would be.'[2]

Eden, Wavell and Dill then flew to Athens, where they were told that the Greeks would defend their national territory against any German attack, 'even if she has to do so alone'.[3]

Following these discussions in Athens, Eden, Wavell and Dill advised Churchill to despatch the 'maximum' British military and air support to Greece which was available, and to do so at the 'earliest possible moment'.[4] That same afternoon, the War Cabinet met to discuss this advice, and reach its decision. General Wavell, Churchill pointed out, 'was in favour of the operation, although he was inclined to understatement, and so far had always promised less than he had performed, and was a man who wished to be better than his word'. His support for action in Greece, given his obvious 'first wish' to complete the campaign in North Africa, must therefore have 'considerable weight'. Dill also, Churchill noted, had telegraphed to the Vice Chief of the Imperial General Staff 'that he considered, by sending our forces to Greece, we had a reasonable chance of resisting a German advance'.

[1] Telegram of 20 February 1941: Cabinet papers, 65/2.
[2] 'Personal and Secret', 20 February 1941: Churchill papers, 20/49.
[3] Telegram dated 21 February 1941, and written declaration by the President of the Council, 22 February 1941: Premier papers, 3/294/1.
[4] Telegram dated 24 February 1941: Cabinet papers, 65/21.

Swayed from his earlier judgement, by Eden's telegram, Churchill told the War Cabinet that he was 'in favour of going to the rescue of Greece, one of the results of which might be to bring in Turkey and Yugoslavia, and to force the Germans to bring more troops from Germany'. The reaction of the United States, he added, 'would also be favourable'.

Churchill then invited each of the Ministers present to express their views.[1] The views then expressed, as the official minutes recorded, were, 'without exception, in favour of sending military assistance to Greece'.[2] 'Therefore,' Churchill telegraphed to Eden as soon as the War Cabinet was over, 'while being under no illusions, we all send you the order "Full Steam ahead".'[3]

On the night of February 24 a British raiding party of two hundred Commandos landed on the outlying Dodecanese island of Kastellorizo. This was the first phase of operation 'Abstention'. Before the larger force waiting offshore could land, the Italians struck back, first by air and then by sea, causing havoc to the British plans. What was to have been a permanent occupation of the island was abruptly abandoned.[4] Sixty of the troops already ashore surrendered. The rest were taken off, and the expedition returned to Crete. 'No communiqué,' Churchill was informed, 'has or will be issued.' The withdrawal must be treated 'as though the intention was to carry out a raid only'.[5]

Reading this, Churchill telegraphed at once to Eden: 'I am perplexed and somewhat unsettled by accounts which have so far reached me about Castelorizzo.' His telegram continued:

How was it that enemy could be reinforced by sea observing we had supposed we had local command of the sea. What was the Naval and Military force which relieved and reinforced. Where did they come from; how did they get there. How was it that after island reported captured it was only discovered during evacuation that a considerable enemy ship was in the inner harbour. Did we ever take the inner harbour or the defences around it. Anxiety also

[1] The War Cabinet Ministers present were: Attlee, Greenwood, Kingsley Wood, Sir John Anderson, Beaverbrook and Bevin.
[2] War Cabinet No. 20 of 1941, 24 February 1941, Minute 4, Confidential Annex: Cabinet papers, 65/21.
[3] Telegram dated 24 February 1941: Churchill papers, 20/49.
[4] 'Report on "Abstention"', 12 March 1941, 'Most Secret': Admiralty papers, 1/11056.
[5] Signal from C. in C. Mediterranean, 9.44 a.m., 28 February 1941: Premier papers, 3/124/1, folio 14.

arises from severity of air attack. Was this foreseen. Where did it come from. Was it Italian or German. Please ascertain all these details.

Churchill saw the Kastellorizo disaster as boding ill for the wider Dodecanese operation, 'Mandibles'. As he told Eden, without the 'certainty that we can take and hold main "Mandibles" whole question of communications of larger scheme seems challenged'.[1] The 'larger scheme' was aid for Greece.

As details of the landing at Kastellorizo were sent to Churchill it became clear that there had been a series of misunderstandings between the naval and military wing of the operation. 'It is necessary to clear this up,' Churchill minuted to Ismay, 'on account of impending and more important operations,' and he added: 'One does not want to worry people who are doing so well for us in many ways and are at full extension, and yet it is indispensable for our success that muddles of this kind should not be repeated.'[2]

Hearing of Eden's visit to Greece, Sir Stafford Cripps suggested that Eden go on to see Stalin. But Churchill replied to this suggestion, deprecating such a visit, and telling Eden:

Best way of gaining Russians is a good throw in Balkans. A mere visit would do no good. They might simply trade it off to Germany. I would hardly trust them for your personal safety or liberty. Of course, if they thought we would win, all would be well, but then your visit would be unnecessary and they would come to us.

It is no good running after these people. Events alone will convince them and they would be glad to be convinced. If Stalin likes to invite you to meet him at Odessa that is a serious proposition, but why should he do that while odds seem heavily against us in Greece.

As for British aid to Greece, Churchill added: 'Half-measures are vain.'[3]

On February 25 South African troops captured Mogadishu, in Italian Somaliland. On the following night, British bombers struck at Cologne.[4] But shortly after midnight on February 26 came news of a

---

[1] 'Personal and Secret', 'to be decyphered by Mr Eden or his Personal Assistant', 12.30 a.m., 1 March 1941: Premier papers, 3/124/1, folios 12–13.

[2] Prime Minister's Personal Minute, D.83/1, 9 March 1941: Premier papers, 3/124/1, folio 9. On March 21 Churchill minuted to A. V. Alexander and Pound: 'What disciplinary or other measures are going to be taken upon this deplorable piece of mis-management occurring after we have had already eighteen months' experience of war?' (Prime Minister's Personal Minute, M.322/1, 21 March 1941: Churchill papers, 20/36.)

[3] Telegram dated 23 February 1941: Churchill papers, 20/49.

[4] As for the Italians, Churchill minuted to Sinclair on February 28, 'let them have a good dose where it will hurt them most'. (Prime Minister's Personal Minute, M.248/1, 28 February 1941: Premier papers, 3/14/3, folio 459.)

different nature. Colville, who was on duty that night, noted in his diary:

In the early hours news came from the Admiralty of another serious disaster to a convoy. Brendan and I commented gloomily on the great threat to our life-line which is developing and will continue to develop. He suggested I should not tell the PM tonight as it would prevent him sleeping. But at 3.0 a.m. he asked me point-blank if there was any news from the Admiralty and I had to tell him. He became very pensive.

'It is very distressing,' I said weakly.

'Distressing!' he replied, 'it is terrifying. If it goes on it will be the end of us.'[1]

Churchill was working into the early hours on a speech for the following day, in which he explained to the House of Commons why Members of Parliament who were given diplomatic or political appointments abroad, such as Cripps in Moscow, Hoare in Madrid, and Malcolm MacDonald in Ottawa, would retain their seats, despite a possible absence from Parliament of several years.[2]

The debate took place on February 27, Churchill scoring, Seal wrote to his wife, 'a resounding Parliamentary success, with far greater knowledge of his subject and depth of argument than any of his opponents'.[3] Seal added: 'It sounds ridiculous that we should do such a thing in the middle of a war—but it was really a sort of holiday for him, & he was quite braced up as a result, like anyone who can do something supremely well, & enjoys the sensation of a perfect piece of work!'[4]

In an attempt to relieve the shipping difficulties, Churchill spent the following morning presiding over the Import Executive, where he had invited the Minister of Shipping, Ronald Cross, to prepare a draft

[1] Colville diary, 26 February 1941: Colville papers.

[2] Following the death of Lord Lloyd on 2 February 1941, several Cabinet changes had taken place. Lord Moyne had been appointed Secretary of the State for the Colonies, and Malcolm MacDonald was replaced by Ernest Brown as Minister of Health. Tom Johnston, who had so impressed Churchill at Glasgow during the Hopkins visit, became Secretary of State for Scotland. The Duke of Norfolk became Under-Secretary for Agriculture. 'The PM told me he was delighted with the "lay-out",' Colville noted in his diary, 'which includes the Editor of "Forward" (Tom Johnston) and the Premier Duke (Under Sec. for Agriculture) and thus shews the breadth of the Administration.' (Colville diary, 6 February 1941: Colville papers.)

[3] That night Victor Cazalet wrote in his diary: 'To hear Winston—55 mins. Saw him in Smoking Room afterwards. He was exhausted. Tears in his eyes. He had worked till 3 a.m. to prepare it. He makes a mistake at end, and his peroration was badly interrupted by Aneurin Bevan. How difficult to say anything not to upset him in this mood.' Cazalet diary, 27 February 1941: Robert Rhodes James, editor, *Victor Cazalet, A Portrait*, London 1976, pages 254–5.

[4] Letter of 27 February 1941: Seal papers.

telegram for him to send to President Roosevelt, 'asking for his assistance in obtaining the use of enemy shipping in USA ports and in
particular of Danish ships'. Cross told the meeting that he hoped to
discuss shortly with representatives of the United States Maritime
Commission 'the employment of USA ships outside the danger zone so
as to relieve the burden on British shipping'.[1] 'PM very gloomy on
shipping situation,' Cadogan noted in his diary after the War Cabinet
of February 27, 'which is murky enough (and an argument against this
Balkan expedition).'[2]

Fears of further German attacks on war supplies coming from the
United States led Churchill to scrutinize the table and charts of the
Import Executive. This led, on February 28, to a minute to A. V.
Alexander and Dudley Pound about the *City of Calcutta*, due at Loch
Ewe in Scotland on March 2, and reported to be proceeding from
there to Hull. 'This ship must on no account be sent to the East Coast,'
Churchill wrote. 'It contains 1,700 machine guns, 44 aeroplane engines,
and no fewer than 14,000,000 cartridges. These cartridges are absolutely vital to the defence of Great Britain, which has been so largely
confided by the Navy to the Army and the Air.' That it should be
proposed to send such a ship round to the East Coast, 'with all the
additional risk', was, he wrote, 'abominable'.

Another ship 'now of great importance', Churchill noted, was the
Euriades, due at Liverpool on March 3, with over 9,000,000 cartridges
on board.

'I shall be glad to receive special reports,' Churchill added, 'as to
what will be done about both ships.'[3] That same day, Churchill telegraphed to Harry Hopkins, who had just returned to Washington:

The packet[4] of rifles and ammunition which we owe to your intercession

[1] Import Executive, meeting held at 5.00 p.m., 26 February 1941: Cabinet papers, 86/1. Those
present were Churchill (in the Chair), Sir Andrew Duncan (Minister of Supply and Chairman of
the Import Executive), A. V. Alexander, Oliver Lyttelton, Lord Woolton, J. T. C. Moore-
Brabazon, Cross and Lindemann.

[2] Cadogan diary, 27 February 1941: David Dilks (editor), *The Diaries of Sir Alexander Cadogan
OM, 1938–1945*, London 1971, page 359. On the following day, Churchill minuted to A. V.
Alexander and Dudley Pound: 'While I am personally convinced of the soundness of the convoy
system, I nevertheless wish that it should be continually subjected to unprejudiced judgement in
the light of ascertained facts. The question of lowering the speed-limit for ships routed independently is, as you know, being raised by the Import Executive' (Prime Minister's Personal Minute,
M.241/1, 28 February 1941: Churchill papers, 20/36).

[3] 'Action this Day', Prime Minister's Personal Minute, M.238/1, 28 February 1941: Churchill
papers, 20/36.

[4] The 'packet' was 250,000 rifles and 50 million rounds of ammunition. They reached Britain
with a Canadian troop convoy. 'I now hope,' Churchill wrote to David Margesson, 'you will
make a rapid evolution of this windfall, so that the weapons are in the hands of those who need

has safely arrived, and is a great addition to our security. I am, however, increasingly anxious about high rate of shipping losses in North-Western Approaches and shrinkage in tonnage entering Britain. This has darkened since I saw you. Let me know when Bill will be through. The strain is growing here.[1]

The news of the shipping losses continued to reach Churchill wherever he was. At Chequers on Saturday March 1, one of his guests, the Australian Prime Minister Robert Menzies, noted in his diary: 'The PM in conversation will steep himself (and you) in gloom on some grim aspect of the war, tonight shipping losses to Focke Wulf planes and U-boats—the supreme menace of the war, and which, with Dudley Pound, First Sea Lord, we have had much talk—only to proceed to "fight his way out" while he is pacing the floor with the light of battle in his eyes.'

At one point Churchill said to Menzies: 'Why do people regard a period like this as "years lost out of our lives" when beyond question it is the most interesting period of them? Why do we regard history as of the past and forget we are making it?'[2] On the following night, while still at Chequers, Menzies wrote in his diary: 'Churchill grows on me,' and he added:

He has amazing grasp of detail and by daily contact with the Services' HQs knows of dispositions and establishments quite accurately.

But I fear that (though experience of supreme office has clearly improved and steadied him) his real tyrant is the glittering phrase—so attractive to his mind that awkward facts have to give way. But this is the defect of his quality. Reasoning to a pre-determined point is mere advocacy, but it becomes something much better when the conclusion is that you are going to win a war and that you're damned if anything will stand in your way.

'Churchill's course is set,' Menzies added. 'There is no defeat in his heart.'[3]

The Lend-Lease Bill was still working its way through the American political process, having still to be voted on in the Senate. Meanwhile,

---

them at the earliest moment.' (Prime Minister's Personal Minute, M.249/1, 1 March 1941: Churchill papers, 20/36.)

[1] Foreign Office Telegram No. 1124, 2.35 p.m., 28 February 1941, 'Personal and Secret': Foreign Office papers, 954/29, folio 124. In a telegram to Hopkins five days earlier, aimed at challenging American suspicions that Britain herself was not making sufficient efforts, Churchill set out details of the substantial increases in taxation since the outbreak of war. Income tax for a married man with two children earning £2,000 a year had increased from £359 to £600. The tax on a bottle of whisky had increased from 8/5½d to 11/4¼d. Tax on a packet of twenty cigarettes had doubled.

[2] Menzies diary, 1 March 1941: Menzies papers.

[3] Menzies diary, 2 March 1941: Menzies papers.

a dispute had arisen as to the extent of United States control in the Caribbean bases to be leased under the destroyer for bases deal. After dining with the new American Ambassador, John Winant,[1] and his deputy, Herschel Johnson, Churchill minuted to the Colonial and Dominions Secretaries, Lord Moyne and Lord Cranborne: 'You can easily have a first-class row with the United States about these matters, and this will be particularly vexatious at a time when the Lease and Lend Bill is on its passage. I am anxious, therefore, by one means or another to keep this business as quiet as possible till the Bill is through. We shall then have only the President to deal with, and not be in danger of giving ammunition to our enemies in the Senate.'[2] To Lord Halifax, who wished to take up the difficulties in Washington, Churchill telegraphed that same day: 'Do not act on these for the moment. I am hoping to get matters smoothed out and clarified here with Mr Winant before troubling the President and Mr Hull.'[3]

Churchill saw the four men principally concerned in London— Moyne, Cranborne, Herschel Johnson and Winant—in the Cabinet Room at 10 Downing Street on March 5. The West Indian Colonies, 'the oldest of the Crown', Colville noted, were 'resentful' and their feelings were shared 'by many people here in view of the conditions which the Americans have demanded and which amount to Capitulations'. Colville added:

Both sides are haggling and ill-feeling has arisen. Bridges thinks that if the Government accepted all the American desiderata they would be defeated in the House of Commons. The Colonial Office are frightened that in the heat of conflict we shall cede much that will afterwards be most regrettable. Lord Cranborne sees in the American attitude a dangerous emphasis on hemisphere defence: an inclination to make special concessions to Canada because she is an American nation; a tendency which might well lead to Western hemisphere isolationism after the war.

But the PM is ill-satisfied with the point of view expressed by his colleagues. He believes that the safety of the state is at stake, that America is providing us with credits that will enable us to win the war which we could not otherwise do, and that we cannot afford to risk the major issue in order to maintain our pride and to preserve the dignity of a few small islands.

[1] When Winant's appointment had been made known, R. A. Butler wrote: 'His picture of England will depend upon his personal contacts, which incline to be erratic. He is not a trained diplomat and will not give scientific appreciations. He is passionately interested in seeing our triumph over the Axis and will react well to exhibitions of resolution. His personal relations are apt to be on the "hit or miss" principle. He is satisfied to go all out if he feels there is a community of view.' (Minute of 24 January 1941: Foreign Office papers, 371/26224.)

[2] 'Secret', Prime Minister's Personal Minute, 4 March 1941: Churchill papers, 20/36.

[3] Telegram of 4 March 1941: Churchill papers, 20/49.

'I think,' Colville added, 'his view is statesmanlike, but America, if she persists, is going to arouse a lot of bitterness in England.'[1]

In Washington, Roosevelt acted to follow up the Hopkins mission by an appointment that might help to bridge the gulfs of distance and misunderstanding. In the third week of February he had said to the 49-year-old banker and businessman Averell Harriman: 'I want you to go over to London and recommend everything that we can do, short of war, to keep the British Isles afloat,' and on March 6 he instructed Harriman to proceed to Britain 'there to act as my Special Representative, with the rank of Minister, in regard to all matters relating to the facilitation of material aid to the British Empire'. Harriman was also instructed to take 'all appropriate measures to expedite the provision of such assistance by the United States'.

On March 7 Harriman lunched with Roosevelt, and suggested, as a first measure, the provision of American naval escorts for British convoys from American ports as far as Iceland. Roosevelt, however, 'stressed the difficulties of convoying'. He was ready, he told Harriman, to go 'as far as American public opinion would permit'. But it would, he said, 'do the British no good if, as a result of a clash between an American ship and a German submarine, Hitler were to decide that he was in a state of war with the United States and thus free to attack American vessels anywhere on the seven seas'.[2]

It was indeed at sea that the greatest danger to Britain seemed to lie. By the beginning of March, the Import Executive's figures showed more than 1,700,000 tons of shipping immobilized by the need of repairs, and a further 930,000 tons undergoing repair while loading cargoes. 'How willingly,' Churchill later wrote, 'would I have exchanged a full-scale invasion for this shapeless, measureless peril, ex-

---

[1] Colville diary, 5 March 1941: Colville papers. Winant himself later recalled: 'I had never seen Mr Churchill at work before, and I was deeply impressed not only with his grasp of the values involved and his appreciation of the defense needs of the United States, but also with his knowledge of the detail of the negotiations with which he had familiarised himself on such short notice. I became quickly conscious of his vast experience in public matters which he had acquired during more than forty years of active participation in public life.' Winant added: 'There was no detail of the problem before us which was not alive to him and on which his knowledge of the past did not throw light as well as constructive criticism.' (John G. Winant, *A Letter from Grosvenor Square, An Account of a Stewardship*, London 1947, pages 24–5.)

[2] W. Averell Harriman and Elie Abel, *Special Envoy to Churchill and Stalin, 1941–1946*, London 1976, pages 18–19. The first American ship to be in action against a German submarine was the destroyer *Greer*, which on 4 September 1941 replied with depth charges to an attack by U.652. The first American ship to be torpedoed and sunk was the destroyer *Kearney*, on 17 October 1941. On 31 October 1941 the *Reuben James* was sunk while escorting the British trans-Atlantic convoy HX 156 from Halifax. But Hitler did not, as Roosevelt feared, make this the prelude to a general war at sea against the United States.

pressed in charts, curves, and statistics!'[1] In the coming three months, a further 500,000 tons of merchant shipping were to be sunk by German air attack, mostly in coastal waters, and another 40,000 tons in two air attacks on the Liverpool docks in May. This 'mortal danger to our life-lines', Churchill later wrote 'gnawed my bowels'.[2]

On March 6, Churchill set out his concerns in a Directive entitled 'The Battle of the Atlantic'. In it, he wrote that the coming four months 'should enable us to defeat the attempt to strangle our food supplies and our connection with the United States'. But this could only be done by taking the offensive against the U-boat and the Focke-Wulf 'wherever we can and whenever we can'. The ports 'on which we specially rely' must be provided with 'a maximum defence' against air attack. Every form of 'simplification and acceleration of repairs' must be applied, 'even at some risk', to reduce 'the terrible slowness' of the turn-round of merchant ships in British ports. A conference of port officers should be convened, 'where all difficulties could be expressed and ideas interchanged'.[3]

On March 9, in a telegram to Halifax, Churchill wrote: 'With much suffering and stringency we ought to get through this year in spite of heavy shipping losses, but there is little hope of victory and none of the United States being armed for her own security till the end of 1942.' Churchill added: 'We cannot get through 1942 without several million tons of United States new construction of merchant ships whether by Hog Island plan or some other. Salter will be excellent in keeping all this alive. You should rub it in all you can, drawing attention to what I wrote in my long letter sent to President at Lothian's request.'[4]

Churchill's reference to Salter was to the Parliamentary Under-Secretary of State for Shipping, Sir Arthur Salter, whom he had just appointed to be the head of a Shipping Mission to the United States. Churchill and Salter lunched together at Downing Street on March 8, when Churchill gave Salter his instructions. 'The Battle of the Atlantic has begun,' he told him in his letter of appointment three days later. 'The issue may well depend on the speed with which our resources to combat the menace to our communications with the Western Hemisphere are supplemented by those of the USA. I look to you to bring

[1] Winston S. Churchill, *The Second World War*, volume 3, London 1950, pages 100–1.
[2] Winston S. Churchill, *The Second World War*, volume 3, London 1950, page 106.
[3] 'Most Secret', 'The Battle of the Atlantic', Directive by the Minister of Defence', 6 March 1941: Cabinet papers, 120/10.
[4] Foreign Office Telegram No. 1289, 9 March 1941: Premier papers, 3/487/1.

this fact home to the US Administration and to convince them that they must act accordingly.'[1]

During their lunch together, Churchill quoted to Salter some lines by the poet Arthur Clough—lines which he had first heard, and learned by heart, before the First World War. The stanza which most impressed Salter read:

> And not by Eastern windows only,
> When daylight comes, comes in the light.
> In front the sun climbs slow, how slowly!
> But westward, look, the land is bright.[2]

---

[1] 'Confidential', 12 March 1941: Churchill papers, 20/21.
[2] Arthur Salter, *Slave of the Lamp, a public servant's notebook*, London 1967, page 155.

53

March 1941: 'very anxious decisions'

O N March 1 Bulgaria formally joined the Axis, and on the next day the Bulgarian Parliament approved, by 150 votes to 20, the presence of German troops in Sofia and Varna. Churchill remained convinced, through Intelligence and intuition, of the growing dangers to each of the Balkan States. 'Your main appeal,' he telegraphed to Eden in Athens, 'should now be made to Yugoslavia.' A 'sudden' Yugoslav military move south in support of Greece would, he urged, produce an Italian disaster 'of the first magnitude', possibly decisive on the whole Balkan situation. His telegram continued:

If at the same moment Turkey declared war the enemy could not gather sufficient forces for many months, during which our air strength will grow. I am absolutely ready to go in on a serious hazard if there is reasonable chance of success, at any rate for a few months, and all preparations should go forward at fullest speed.

If, however, Churchill added, Eden felt that there was 'not even a reasonable hope' of Yugoslavia and Turkey joining Greece, then he should retain the power 'to liberate Greeks from any bargain and at the same time liberate ourselves'.[1]

It quickly became clear that the 'reasonable hope' was a chimera. Turkey declined to become a belligerent, and the Yugoslav Regent, Prince Paul, sought safety in closer relations with Berlin, promising Hitler orally, while at Berchtesgaden on March 4, to follow the example of Bulgaria in allowing German troops and aircraft to be based in his country.

'Very anxious decisions have been in the air,' Colville noted in his diary on March 7, 'making the PM impatient, the atmosphere electric

[1] Telegram of 1 March 1941: Churchill papers, 20/49.

and the pace tremendous.'[1] Three days earlier Operation 'Lustre', the movement of British troops to help Greece, had begun. The plan, which had been agreed by Eden, Dill and Wavell in Athens on February 27, was for Empire troops—most of the infantry being Australians and New Zealanders—to hold the Aliakhmon Line against any German advance, and to hold it together with Greek troops pulled back to the Line from the Macedonian border further north. The plan envisaged the British 1st Armoured Brigade leaving Egypt on March 7 and reaching the Line by March 27. The first British troops to embark in Egypt consisted of anti-aircraft and administrative units which left Egypt on March 4, bound for Piraeus.[2]

But in Athens on that same day, March 4, Eden, having returned from Turkey, reported to London that General Papagos, whose 'attitude and spirit' had been so impressive a week before, was now, 'unaccommodating and defeatist'. The atmosphere in Athens, Eden and Dill telegraphed to Churchill that night, was 'changed and disturbing'. General Papagos now argued that instead of Greek and British forces making their first defence on the Aliakhmon Line, with Greek troops falling back from the Macedonian border to hold the Line, the Macedonian border should be held, although he admitted 'they could not hold out for long', and British troops should be sent up to the Macedonian border piecemeal as they reached Greece.

This was a major blow to the planning and prospects of 'Lustre'. Yet Eden and Dill ended their telegram by stating that whereas the operation was clearly going to be 'more hazardous than it seemed a week ago', it was 'still not by any means hopeless'.[3]

In London, this telegram had caused considerable perturbation to, among others, the Secretary of State for War, David Margesson. On the following day Colville noted in his diary:

Last night David Margesson told me how much he disliked the whole venture upon which we are about to embark. Many others feel the same. It was thrust upon us partly because, in the first place, the PM felt that our prestige, in France, in Spain and in the US, could not stand our desertion of Greece;

[1] Colville diary, 7 March 1941: Colville papers. Churchill was still suffering from a cold. As Seal wrote to his wife: 'His Doctor came down to see him, & spent the night, bringing with him a nasal specialist, who pronounced that the cold was due to snuff, wh the PM was taking in the vain hope that it would ward off a cold!! Anyway, snuff has been eschewed, & the cold is much better.' But two days later Seal wrote again: 'Winston is very active, & not in too good a humour. I think his cold is getting him down a bit.' (Letters of 4 and 6 March 1941: Seal papers.)

[2] Telegram 0/45461 of 3 March 1941, Wavell to War Office: Cabinet papers, 65/22.

[3] Telegram No. 313, 'Personal and Secret', 'Most Immediate', 'Most Secret', 5 March 1941, despatched 4.05 a.m., received 7.55 a.m.: Cabinet papers, 65/22.

partly because Eden, Dill, Wavell and Cunningham (who has now tele-graphed to point out the extreme length to which his resources are stretched) recommended it so strongly. But the danger of another Norway, Dunkirk and Dakar rolled into one looms threateningly before us.

Colville's diary continued:

After his afternoon sleep, the PM, emerging from beneath the bedclothes and yawning, said, voicing his waking thought: 'The poor Chiefs of the Staff will get very much out of breath in their desire to run away.' I shewed him a telegram from Eden urging that a high decoration for General Papagos would help matters. 'Too cheap,' he commented with a disgusted gesture.[1]

At the War Cabinet that afternoon it was noted that Papagos, having been deprived of the guidance of Metaxas—who had died at the end of January—'seemed to have lost confidence' in the forthcoming strug-gle with Germany. He now wished Britain to 'double up' its forces piecemeal to the Macedonian frontier, but he offered only 16 to 23 Greek battalions for the Aliakhmon Line, instead of the 35 Greek bat-talions 'which we had been led to expect'.

In cautionary tone, Churchill then raised two 'new factors' that had just 'come into play': the British landing on the Dodecanese Island of Kastellorizo had 'been a fiasco', and it had also become evident 'that the air menace to the Suez Canal had in no way been mastered'.[2] Nevertheless, Churchill told his colleagues, he had received a personal telegram from Eden to say that neither he nor his advisers 'saw any alternative' in Greece 'to doing our best to see it through'.

The Parliamentary Under-Secretary of State for Foreign Affairs, R. A. Butler, then spoke in favour of action, warning that 'if we abandoned Greece, this might have a bad effect on the position in Spain which was uncertain, and in North Africa where German infiltration was increasing'. Churchill disagreed; the effect in Spain and North Africa, he said, 'would be worse if we landed in Greece and were driven out, than if we remained masters of the Delta and seized the Dodecanese'. Papagos had said that he would not withdraw Greek troops from the Albanian front for the Aliakhmon Line since they were 'exhausted and greatly outnumbered'. Might not this mean that his troops could not face 'being put up against German forces?' Might not Greece 'collapse in the face of a German ultimatum?'

[1] Colville diary, 5 March 1941: Colville papers.

[2] On 3 March 1941, the day on which the Suez Canal was to have been cleared of mines, the Germans had put in ten more mines, and the Canal, 'now completely closed' was not likely to be clear until March 11. ('Aide Memoire' by the Chiefs of Staff', 5 March 1941, Cabinet papers, 65/22.)

It was decided to tell Eden of the War Cabinet's doubts 'as to the wisdom of proceeding with the enterprise',[1] and that night the Defence Committee met to discuss what form the message to Eden should take. Churchill told his colleagues that he was worried that, 'in the face of a German ultimatum', the Greeks would find it 'impossible to carry on the struggle', and that there was 'little or nothing which we could do to assist them in time'. But the Defence Committee was also told that both Eden and Dill remained convinced 'that there was still a good chance of successfully holding up the German advance'.[2]

That night, with the approval of the Defence Committee, Churchill telegraphed to Eden to express the Committee's doubts, and those of the wider War Cabinet, as to whether 'we now have any power to avert the fate of Greece unless Turkey and/or Yugoslavia came in, which seems improbable', especially in view of Eden's report of General Papagos' new mood and proposals. Britain must be careful, Churchill warned, not to urge Greece against her better judgement 'into a hopeless resistance alone, when we have only handfuls of troops which can reach the scene in time'. The loss of Greece and the Balkans, Churchill added, was 'by no means a major catastrophe for us provided Turkey remains honestly neutral'.

Churchill now feared a disaster in Greece with wide repercussions. 'We are advised from many quarters,' he told Eden, 'that our ignominious ejection from Greece would do us more harm in Spain and Vichy than the fact of submission of Balkans which with our scanty forces alone we have never been expected to prevent.' If necessary, Churchill added, Eden should not be afraid of 'liberating the Greeks' from feeling that they were 'bound to reject' a German ultimatum.[3]

Churchill also sent Eden that night the Chiefs of Staff commentary on the situation, which concluded that 'despite our misgivings and the recognition of a worsening of the general situation, we are not as yet in a position to question the military advice of those on the spot'—that is, Eden himself and Dill—'who in their latest telegram, describe the enterprise as not by any means hopeless'.[4]

That night a second telegram reached Churchill from Eden and Dill, warning of a possible German attack 'during the next six or seven

[1] War Cabinet No. 24 of 1941, 5 March 1941, 5 p.m., Confidential Annex: Cabinet papers, 65/22.
[2] Defence Committee (Operations) No. 9 of 1941, 5 March 1941, 10 p.m.: Cabinet papers, 69/2.
[3] Telegram No. 607, 'Most Secret', 'Most Immediate', despatched 2.20 a.m., 6 March 1941, Defence Committee (Operations) No. 9 of 1941, Annex 1: Cabinet papers, 69/2.
[4] Telegram No. 608, 'Aide Memoire by the Chiefs of Staff': Cabinet papers, 65/22.

days'. The Greeks, however, wanted no bombing of German communications, in order to avoid 'retaliation'. The telegram ended: 'Thus the margin is narrow and the risk is considerable. Nevertheless as we stated in our telegram No. 313 March 4th this risk appears to us the least dangerous of the three possibilities with which we were faced.'[1]

The first telegram to reach London from Athens on the morning of March 7 was the text of an agreement signed on March 4 between Dill and Papagos. Three Greek divisions would remain in Macedonia to defend the northern frontier, on the Nestos–Rupel line. Three further divisions, and seven battalions would concentrate on the Aliakhmon position. The British forces would be despatched to Piraeus and Volos 'as rapidly as shipping will permit', and 'will concentrate on Aliakhmon position on which it is intended the Graeco-British forces should be able to battle'.[2]

Eden, commented Alexander Cadogan that morning, 'has evidently committed us up to the hilt'.[3] But it was not Eden alone who felt that Operation 'Lustre' should go ahead. That same morning the British Ambassador to Athens, Sir Michael Palairet, telegraphed to Eden, who was then on his way back to Cairo:

... How can we possibly abandon the King of Greece after the assurances given him by the Commander-in-Chief and Chief of the Imperial General Staff as to reasonable chances of success? This seems to me quite unthinkable. We shall be pilloried by the Greeks and the world in general as going back on our word.

There is no question of 'liberating the Greeks from feeling bound to reject the ultimatum'. They have decided to fight Germany alone if necessary. The question is whether we help or abandon them.[4]

In Cairo, Eden and Dill found that Wavell, Longmore and Cunningham were as emphatic as the Ambassador in feeling that 'Lustre' should go ahead. But news of their opinion had not yet reached London

---

[1] Telegram No. 314, 'Most Immediate', 'Personal', despatched 7.30 p.m., received 10.40 p.m., 5 March 1941: Cabinet papers, 65/22.

[2] Telegram No. 326, 'Immediate', 'Most Secret' (Eden and Dill to Churchill), despatched 1.50 a.m., received 7.10 a.m., 6 March 1941: Cabinet papers, 65/22.

[3] Cadogan diary, 6 March 1941: David Dilks (editor), *The Diaries of Sir Alexander Cadogan OM, 1938–1945*, London 1971, page 361.

[4] Telegram No. 327, 'Most Immediate', 'Personal', 6 March 1941, despatched from Athens, 12.25 p.m., received in London, 2.35 p.m.: Cabinet papers, 65/22. Palairet also reported (Telegram No. 330, sent 11.30 a.m., received 3.30 p.m., 6 March 1941) that the King of Greece had spoken 'today' to the British Air Attaché in Athens with 'absolute determination to carry out agreed plan of action against German attack'. Palairet added: 'He has every confidence in the chances for success and is satisfied that this confidence is shared by General Papagos and his Government.'

when the War Cabinet met at six o'clock on the evening of March 6. It was 'inconceivable', said Churchill, that Dill would have signed the agreement of March 4 with Papagos 'if he regarded the chances of success in the operation as hopeless'.[1] But no decision was reached, and it was agreed only that Churchill should telegraph to Eden that the War Cabinet 'are taking no decision until we receive your reply'.[2]

Eden's reply reached London shortly after ten o'clock that evening. It was unambiguous in its support of the Dill–Papagos agreement, and of British action in Greece. As Eden told Churchill:

Chief of Imperial General Staff and I, in consultation with the three Commanders-in-Chief, have this afternoon re-examined the question. We are unanimously agreed that, despite the heavy commitments and grave risks which are undoubtedly involved, especially in view of our limited naval and air resources, the right decision was taken in Athens. Palairet's telegrams Nos 89 and 90 to Cairo[3] show the position from Greek angle.

This message, Eden added, 'is merely to indicate to you how our minds are working while we await Cabinet view. . . .'[4]

That night General Wavell explained to the Australian and New Zealand commanders who would be going to Greece, Generals Blamey and Freyberg, the 'additional risks' that would be involved in the Greek campaign. That same night, Dill reported from Cairo, to Margesson in London, that both Blamey and Freyberg 'have expressed their willingness to undertake operations under new conditions'. And Dill added: 'You will no doubt inform Prime Minister.'[5]

The War Cabinet met at noon on March 7 for what was to be one of its most difficult, and fateful, decisions of the war.[6]

In front of the Ministers were all the telegrams cited in the previous pages of this chapter. But the decisive telegram was that just received

[1] War Cabinet No. 25 of 1941, 6 March 1941, 6 p.m., Confidential Annex: Cabinet papers, 65/22.
[2] Telegram No. 621, despatched 8 p.m., 6 March 1941, 'Most Immediate', 'Secret': Cabinet papers, 65/22.
[3] Palairet's Nos 327 and 330 to London.
[4] Telegram No. 455, 'Most Immediate', 'Most Secret', 'Personal', despatched from Cairo, 8.55 p.m., received in London, 10.10 p.m., 6 March 1941: Cabinet papers, 65/22.
[5] Telegram No. 46261, 'Immediate', 'Personal', 'Most Secret', 'Officers Only', despatched 00.45 a.m., received 3.45 a.m., 7 March 1941: Cabinet papers, 65/22.
[6] The War Cabinet Ministers present were Churchill (in the Chair), Clement Attlee, Arthur Greenwood, Sir Kingsley Wood, Sir John Anderson, Lord Beaverbrook and Ernest Bevin. Seven other Cabinet Ministers were also present: Herbert Morrison, Lord Moyne, David Margesson, Viscount Cranborne, Sir Archibald Sinclair, A. V. Alexander and Alfred Duff Cooper, as well as R. A. Butler, Sir Dudley Pound, Sir Alexander Cadogan, Sir Charles Portal and Sir Robert Haining.

from Eden, giving Churchill 'the views of your envoys', and strongly urging action. The whole position, said Eden, had been reviewed both with the Commander-in-Chief, and with General Smuts, who had just reached Cairo from South Africa. All were agreed, Eden wrote, that:

Collapse of Greece without further effort on our part to save her by intervention on land, after the Libyan victories had, as all the world knows, made forces available, would be the greatest calamity. Yugoslavia would then certainly be lost; nor can we feel confident that even Turkey would have the strength to remain steadfast if the Germans and Italians were established in Greece without effort on our part to resist them.

No doubt our prestige will suffer if we are ignominiously ejected, but in any event to have fought and suffered in Greece would be less damaging to us than to have left Greece to her fate. . . .

In the existing situation, Eden added, 'we are all agreed that the course advocated should be followed and help given to Greece'. They also 'devoutly' trusted that 'no difficulties will arise with regard to the dispatch of Dominions forces as arranged', nor that there would be any delay in supplementing 'the various serious gaps in our forces, particularly in the air'. Air weakness was 'our chief anxiety in this theatre of war'. If Britain's air force Commander-in-Chief in the Middle East, Longmore, 'can hold his own', then, Eden declared, 'most of the dangers and difficulties of this enterprise will disappear'.[1]

According to the War Cabinet minutes, two points were 'dominant' during the ensuing discussion. These were:

First, we must not take on our shoulders the responsibility of urging the Greeks against their better judgement to fight a hopeless battle.

Secondly, it happened that most of the troops who would be involved at the start would be the New Zealand Division and, after March, the Australians. We must be able to tell the Australian and New Zealand Governments that the campaign was undertaken, not because of any commitment entered into by a British Cabinet Minister in Athens, but because the Chief of the Imperial General Staff and the Commanders-in-Chief in the Middle East were convinced that there was a reasonable fighting chance.

'So far,' the minutes added, 'few facts or reasons had been supplied which could be represented to these Dominions as justifying the operation on any grounds but *noblesse oblige*.' A precise military appreciation was 'indispensable'.

It was Ernest Bevin, the Minister of Labour and National Service,

---

[1] Telegram No. 455 from Cairo (submitted to the War Cabinet of 7 March 1941): Cabinet papers, 65/22.

who pointed out that the advice from the Commanders-in-Chief in Cairo, Wavell, Longmore and Cunningham, 'gained greatly in value for the reason that it had not been given under political pressure'. Indeed, Bevin added, the political pressure had been 'in the opposite direction'.

Churchill now put forward five considerations which 'seemed to him to be of importance'. These were, as set out in the minutes, that:

(a) We had a fair prospect of reaching the Aliakhmon line in time to check the German advance. If so there might be a pause while the enemy brought up new forces.
(b) The Yugoslavs were adopting a cryptic attitude, but we need not despair entirely of their entry into the war on our side.
(c) If the Anglo-Greek forces were compelled to retire from the Aliakhmon line, they would be retiring down a narrowing peninsula, which contained a number of strong defensive positions.
(d) We should shortly have strong air forces in Greece. They would be out-numbered by the enemy's air forces but the odds would not be greater than they had been on many occasions.
(e) Our policy had been so developed that nobody could represent us as having forced a hopeless resistance on the Greeks.

His own view, Churchill said, was that 'we should go forward with a good heart'.

There was no dissent. Even the Australian Prime Minister, Robert Menzies, who was present at the meeting, 'found himself', as the minutes recorded, 'in agreement with the Prime Minister'. Yet he commented, somewhat wryly, that, while the decision was being taken in virtue of the trust reposed in the judgement of Eden, Dill and the three Commanders-in-Chief, 'the arguments with which they had supplied us told against, rather than in favour of, their advice'.[1]

'The time had now come,' Churchill told his colleagues, 'for taking a decision.' In his view, 'it was our duty to go forward', and in its formal conclusion, the War Cabinet 'confirmed the decision to give military assistance to Greece, and agreed that all the arrangements to this end should proceed'.[2] By this conclusion, Churchill telegraphed to Eden, 'Cabinet accepts for itself the fullest responsibility.'[3]

Late that night, Churchill drove to Chequers. Ismay, Bridges and

---

[1] War Cabinet No. 26 of 1941, 7 March 1941, 12 noon, Confidential Annex: Cabinet papers, 65/22.
[2] War Cabinet No. 26 of 1941, 7 March 1941, 12 noon, Confidential Annex: Cabinet papers, 65/22.
[3] Telegram of 7 March 1941: Churchill papers, 20/49.

Colville were also there. 'The PM was much happier,' Colville noted. 'His mind is relieved now that a great decision has been irrevocably taken. He was witty and entertaining.'[1] That night, while Churchill slept, Hopkins telephoned from New York to say that the Lend-Lease Bill had passed the Senate by 60 votes to 31. All that remained was the final vote in the House of Representatives, and Presidential assent. That same night, in a renewed air attack on London, many were killed when bombs fell on the Café de Paris.[2]

At Chequers that weekend, Churchill's son-in-law Duncan Sandys was, as Colville noted, 'very bloodthirsty', arguing in favour of a severely punitive treatment of Germany after the war. Churchill opposed this, telling those present, who now included de Gaulle, Menzies and Spears,[3] that:

He did not believe in pariah nations, and he saw no alternative to the acceptance of Germany as part of the family of Europe. In the event of invasion he would not even approve of the civil population murdering the Germans quartered on them. Still less would he condone atrocities against the German civil population if we were in a position to commit them. He cited an incident in Ancient Greece when the Athenians spared a city which had massacred some of their citizens, not because its inhabitants were men, but 'because of the nature of man'.[4]

The passage of the Lend-Lease Bill was the main cause for pleasure that weekend. 'Thank God for your news,' Churchill telegraphed to Hopkins, but he added, of the shipping situation: 'Strain is serious.'[5] To Roosevelt, who was to give his formal assent to the Bill two days later, Churchill telegraphed on March 9: 'Our blessings from the whole British Empire go out to you and the American nation for this very present help in time of trouble.'[6]

[1] Colville diary, 7 March 1941: Colville papers.

[2] Among the dead were many young officers, and also the popular Caribbean jazz band leader, Ken 'Snakehips' Johnson. Among those who survived was Stanley Baldwin's daughter, Betty, who was badly cut about the head. Since the Café de Paris was underground, it was believed to be safe, and had been advertised as 'London's safest restaurant'. (Constantine FitzGibbon, *The Blitz*, London 1957, pages 244–65.)

[3] On 31 March 1941 Churchill wrote to the Secretary of State for the Colonies, about the Governor-General of the Sudan: 'you should inform Sir B. Bourdillon that General Spears has my full confidence, and that he and General de Gaulle are working satisfactorily together. You should tell him that the description of General Spears as "an unscrupulous politician with no military knowledge at all" is highly offensive and untrue. Very few people saw more of the Great War from the High Staff and front line than General Spears.' (Prime Minister's Personal Minute, M.378/1, 31 March 1941: Churchill papers, 20/36.)

[4] Colville diary, 8 March 1941: Colville papers.

[5] Telegram of 9 March 1941: Premier papers, 3/224/1, folio 3.

[6] Telegram of 9 March 1941: Churchill papers, 20/49. That night Menzies wrote in his diary:

The extent of that 'trouble' was clear enough. The existing American shipbuilding programme, Churchill explained to the Minister of Food on March 10, 'is less than half what we need'.[1] And to David Margesson he wrote that it was of 'the utmost importance that a clear and consistent picture of our requirements should be presented to the United States Administration, and that their efforts on our behalf should not be hampered by any doubts as to our vital needs and their order of priority'.[2]

For the first time since he had become Prime Minister, Churchill was too ill to return to London for the Monday War Cabinet. His persistent cold had turned into bronchitis. And yet, Colville noted, 'his capacity for work is totally unimpaired and his temper is scarcely ruffled'.[3] It was the continued German sinkings of merchant ships that caused Churchill greatest concern. 'Nothing is of more importance,' he wrote from Chequers to the Minister of Shipping, Ronald Cross, 'than the shipping problem, and the key to its solution lies largely in America.'[4] Re-iterating his earlier remarks to Hopkins, Churchill telegraphed to Roosevelt that same day: 'The sinkings are bad and the strain is increasing at sea.'[5]

On March 11 the Lend-Lease Bill was approved by the House of Representatives by 317 votes to 71, and signed by Roosevelt: 'so great an event', Churchill wrote to Winant, 'in the history of our two nations'.[6] That day, despite his bronchitis, Churchill 'insisted on returning to London', as Colville noted, for his weekly Tuesday lunch with the King.[7] During the night, German bombers struck at Portsmouth.

'Winston is completely certain of America's full help, of her participation in a Japanese war, and of Roosevelt's passionate determination to stamp out the Nazi menace from the earth. Is he right? I cannot say.' (Menzies diary, 9 March 1941: Menzies papers. The Australian Prime Minister added: 'If the PM was a better listener and less disposed to dispense with all expert or local opinion, I might feel a little easier about it—he's a holy terror. I went to bed tired.')

[1] Prime Minister's Personal Minute, M.281/1, 10 March 1941: Churchill papers, 20/36.

[2] Prime Minister's Personal Minute, M.282/1, 10 March 1941: Churchill papers, 20/36. Similar minutes were sent to A. V. Alexander, Sir Archibald Sinclair, Sir Andrew Duncan and Lord Beaverbrook.

[3] Colville diary, 10 March 1941: Colville papers.

[4] Letter of 10 March 1941: Churchill papers, 20/21.

[5] 'Personal and Most Secret', 10 March 1941: Churchill papers, 20/49.

[6] Letter of 11 March 1941: Churchill papers 20/21. Under the Lend-Lease Act, seven billion dollars were appropriated 'to carry out national policy of giving every possible material assistance to the countries resisting aggression'. The first appropriation, up to 31 August 1941, was set at 5,295 million US dollars, out of which Britain would be able to draw on 4,736 million. The second biggest sum, 320 million, was for China. ('Second Report under the Act of March 11, 1941—Lend-Lease Act', copy in Cabinet papers, 115/436.)

[7] Colville diary, 11 March 1941: Colville papers.

In the House of Commons on March 12, Churchill described the Lend-Lease Bill as a 'monument of generous and far-seeing statesmanship', a declaration by 'the most powerful Democracy' that it would devote its 'overwhelming' industrial and financial strength to ensure 'the defeat of Nazism in order that nations, great and small, may live in security, tolerance and freedom'.[1]

Of immediate concern was America's continuing aid to Vichy France, breaking, with Britain's earlier assent, the close blockade of German-controlled ports. On March 12 Churchill drew Roosevelt's attention to a French ship, the *Bangkok*, with 3,000 tons of rubber on board, 'which is certainly not all for the teats of babies' bottles'. There were 'abundant cases of all kinds', Churchill added, of valuable munitions materials which were going 'straight to Germany or Italy'. Even if only food were going to Vichy France, it would be 'a great pity', Churchill wrote, 'if any large number of ships, which are all needed for our life and the war effort, were used up in food carrying', and he went on to appeal to Roosevelt:

I do not want the people here, who, apart from heavy bombardment likely to be renewed soon, are having to tighten their belts and restrain their few remaining comforts, to feel that I am not doing my best against the enemy. Nevertheless, if it were not unwelcome I would gladly invite you to act as intermediary and make the best plan you can to beat Hitler.

'We have supreme confidence in you,' Churchill ended, 'and would receive with profound respect what you thought best to be done.'[2]

Two days later, Roosevelt's new envoy, Averell Harriman, was Churchill's guest at Chequers for the first time.[3] Harriman's relations, Purvis informed the Supply Committee in London, 'will be with various supply departments here, but mainly with Hopkins and President'.

---

[1] *Hansard*, 12 March 1941.

[2] 'Personal and Secret', 12 March 1941: Churchill papers, 20/49. Two days later Churchill minuted to Cadogan, A. V. Alexander, Pound and Dalton (the Minister of Economic Warfare): 'It may be necessary for us to ease up on food for unoccupied France, but surely this should only be part of a much stricter enforcement of blockade on non-foodstuffs, of the war materials type like the rubber. This point does not seem to me to be sufficiently brought out in our communications to America up to the present.' (Prime Minister's Personal Minute, M.288/1, 14 March 1941: Churchill papers, 20/36.)

[3] Chequers Visitors Book, week ending 15 March 1941. The other guests included Winant, Bracken, Lindemann and Dupuy.

Purvis added: 'We all consider him an excellent appointment and are convinced that his heart is in his job.'[1]

'The Prime Minister welcomed me most warmly,' Harriman later recalled, and he told his biographer of how:

He remembered our first meeting, when I called on him at Cannes in 1927 to get his advice about Russia, and he talked about our meeting in New York two years later, when he was staying with Bernie Baruch at the time of the Wall Street crash. He freely admitted having caught the speculative fever of the time and lost the money he had just received from the publication of a new book.

I was surprised to see how grateful Mrs Churchill was for a small bag of tangerines I had brought her from Lisbon. Her unfeigned delight brought home to me the restrictions of the dreary British wartime diet, imposed by the sharp reduction of imports, even in the Prime Minister's house.

After dinner Churchill took me aside and began to describe in considerable detail the problems of the war and what the United States might do to help. I forgot all about presenting my letter from Roosevelt. There was no need for formal introductions. As soon as I could I explained to the Prime Minister that Washington would need a lot more information about Britain's war plans and prospects if there was to be a large increase in assistance under the new Lend-Lease law. I warned him that the demands of our own Army and Navy were so great, and the immediately available resources so pitifully limited, that it would be a struggle unless our military chiefs were persuaded that Britain could make better use of the matériel.

My own usefulness in pleading Britain's case, I told him bluntly, would depend entirely upon the extent of my knowledge and understanding of her position and needs. I was greatly reassured by his response.

'You shall be informed,' Churchill said. 'We accept you as a friend. Nothing will be kept from you.'[2]

Churchill confirmed this frankness when he minuted to Bridges: 'I am all for trusting Mr Harriman fully and working with him on the most intimate terms.' But, Churchill added, with a sense of caution, 'at the same time we must keep the power of private correspondence with Pursa'—Arthur Purvis and the British Purchasing Commission. 'It should not be difficult,' Churchill noted, 'to devise methods for a secret series of this kind.'[3]

In mid-March friction arose over the method of Britain's payment for Lend-Lease. 'I am clear,' Churchill telegraphed to Halifax on

[1] 'Pursa' No. 173, 13 March 1941: Cabinet papers, 115/83.

[2] W. Averell Harriman and Elie Abel, *Special Envoy to Churchill and Stalin 1941–1946*, London 1976, pages 21–2.

[3] Prime Minister's Personal Minute, C.34/1, 26 March 1941: Churchill papers, 20/36.

March 15, 'that this is no time for us to be driven from pillar to post.' A breakdown, deadlock or crash, Churchill added, 'might clear the air'. Churchill's telegram continued:

Remember that although they may not all realise it their lives are now in this business too. We cannot always be playing up to minor political exigencies of Congress politics. Morgenthau may have a bad time before his Committee but Liverpool and Glasgow are having a bad time now. Much more evil is coming to us quite soon. Don't you think there has been too much telegraphing on the Treasury File and that it would be good to make a break of two or three days and see what happens.

'As far as I am concerned,' Churchill ended, 'I refuse altogether to be hustled and rattled. God knows that we are doing our bit.'[1]

In the air, the Blitz and counter-bombing continued. On March 12 British bombers struck at Berlin, Hamburg and Bremen, while German bombers attacked the docks at Merseyside. On March 12 Merseyside was attacked again, and on March 13 the Clyde. But Britain's air defences now mitigated the full horror of earlier night attacks, and on March 14 Churchill telegraphed to Eden, who was still in Cairo: 'we have begun to claw the Huns down in the moonlight to some purpose'.[2] That night, and again on March 15, British bombers struck again at military targets in Germany, this time in Düsseldorf.[3]

In Egypt, preparations went ahead for the Greek campaign, and men and stores were already on their way from Alexandria and Port Said to Piraeus. It was 'very fortunate', Wavell wrote to Churchill from Cairo on March 13, that Eden and Dill had been in Cairo 'when some difficult and dangerous decisions had to be taken', and he added: 'I am sure the decisions were the right ones, though they will bring us new hazards and anxieties.'[4]

---

[1] 'Personal and Secret', 15 March 1941: Premier papers, 4/17/2, folios 166–7. Kingsley Wood approved this telegram, but when that same day he suggested a direct appeal from Churchill to Morgenthau, Churchill replied: 'I am very doubtful whether I should open up a correspondence in detail with Morgenthau. I do not know whether the President would like me to address particular American Departmental Ministers directly. I could of course send a purely personal message of thanks for favours to come.' (Prime Minister's Personal Minute, M.302/1A, 15 March 1941: Premier papers, 4/17/2, folio 176.)

[2] Telegram No. 722, 14 March 1941, 9.45 p.m., 'Personal and Secret': Cabinet papers, 65/22. In the Merseyside raids, twelve merchant ships were damaged, but only two were expected to be a 'total loss' (Premier papers, 3/18/2, folio 102).

[3] Part of Operation 'Abigail', a series of reprisal raids, but not publicly revealed as such, and including Düsseldorf, code name 'Delilah'; Bremen, code name 'Jezebel' and Mannheim, code name 'Rachel'. The Air Ministry's instructions to Bomber Command for these raids included the sentence: 'With object causing widespread uncontrollable fires suggest first ten sorties carry incendiary bombs only. . . .' (Telegram X.629, 2 December 1940: Air Ministry papers, 20/5195.)

[4] Letter of 13 March 1941: Churchill papers, 2/423.

The movement of British troops to Greece continued. But Turkey, for whom this effort was in part envisaged, insisted on maintaining a strict neutrality. 'We are working on the Turks to the best of our ability,' Churchill telegraphed to Cripps in Moscow, 'but they are unresponsive through fear.'[1] Three days later Churchill telegraphed to Eden, who was still in the Middle East: 'Try to bring Yugoslavia home in the bag.'[2] And on the following day Churchill telegraphed again, as Eden tried to bring Turkish and Yugoslav policy into harmony: 'Attitude of Yugo outweighs everything else.'[3] But neither Turkey nor Yugoslavia would commit themselves against Germany, despite Churchill's telegram to Smuts on March 20 that 'Hope is broadening in the Balkans.'[4]

At Chequers and in London, Churchill was in daily contact with his new American emissary, Averell Harriman, and with John G. Winant, the new American Ambassador, telling the War Cabinet on March 17 that he had been 'greatly encouraged' by their attitude. As Churchill went on to explain:

These two gentlemen were apparently longing for Germany to commit some overt act that would relieve the President of his election and pre-election declaration regarding keeping out of the war. Mr Harriman had said that the United States might be prepared to escort their own ships outside the prohibited area. He was working out a scheme whereby United States ships would take over the long hauls, leaving us with the short hauls. They were also planning a very big merchant shipbuilding programme, which would mature in 1942.

Churchill warned the War Cabinet that the shipping difficulties 'were the blackest cloud which we had to face'. But 'we must remember', he added, 'that we had dealt with, and overcome, equal perils in the past.'[5]

Churchill's efforts to build upon United States aid and support had reached a critical point, nor did he hide from Winant, Harriman, or the new American Ambassador to the Governments-in-exile in London, Anthony Biddle, the extent of Britain's weakness. In a speech on March 18, formally welcoming Winant to Britain, he spoke of Britain's shipping losses as 'this potentially mortal challenge'. It would be met, how-

---

[1] 'Personal', 16 March 1941: Churchill papers, 20/49.
[2] 'Personal and Secret', 19 March 1941: Churchill papers, 20/49.
[3] Telegram, 20 March 1941: Churchill papers, 20/49.
[4] Telegram, 20 March 1941: Churchill papers, 20/49.
[5] War Cabinet No. 29 of 1941, 17 March 1941, 5 p.m., Minute 1, Confidential Annex: Cabinet papers, 65/18.

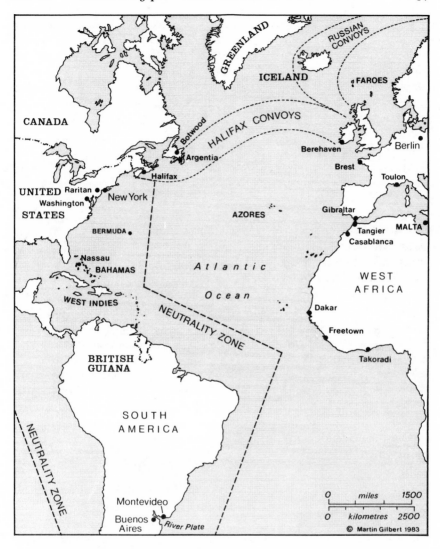

ever, he declared, by a naval and air strength that were growing 'every week', and with that strength came the 'words and acts' of the President and people of the United States, 'like a draught of life, and they tell us by an ocean-borne trumpet call that we are no longer alone'.[1]

[1] Luncheon speech, Pilgrims' Society Luncheon, London, 18 March 1941, broadcast live from the Savoy Hotel: *The Times*, 19 March 1941.

54

'Take the rough with the smooth'

O N the night of March 19 Churchill gave dinner at Downing
Street to Harriman and Biddle. While they were dining, there
was a heavy air raid on London, whereupon 'he took his guests', as
Colville noted, 'and his whole private office, up to the roof of the Air
Ministry to watch the fun'.[1] As they watched the fires and explosions,
Churchill quoted to his guests Tennyson's lines on aerial warfare.[2] The
American emissaries were then shown the Central War Room, and
given a survey of Britain's military, air and naval activities over-
seas.

It was Biddle's first week in London. Four days later he wrote to
Churchill: 'On the roof I gained an impressive picture of the effective
strides achieved here, both by the air and ground organizations (civil
as well as military). It is a great tribute to your courageous intelligence
and inspiring leadership and to the magnificent spirit of your brave
countrymen. Then too I was so grateful for the opportunity of going
with you "below"—for it was so interesting to see what you have done
there, and to gain a "first-hand" clear perspective of the many activities
as you so kindly pointed them out on the maps. It was grand being
with you. . . .'[3]

[1] Five days later the War Cabinet was told that the casualties in London on the night of March
19 'had been heavier than at first reported': 504 killed and 1,511 injured. Two nights later, 150
civilians were killed and 230 seriously injured during a German air raid on Plymouth. (War
Cabinet No. 31 of 1941, 5 p.m., Minute 4: Cabinet papers, 65/18.)
[2] Colville diary, 19 March 1941. Colville papers. The lines were:

> 'Hear the heavens fill with shouting,
>   and there rain'd a ghastly dew
> From the nations' airy navies
>   grappling in the central blue.' (*Locksley Hall.*)

[3] Letter of 23 March 1941: Churchill papers, 2/416.

Seal, who was present that evening, wrote home to his wife of how, while the 'pretty bad Blitz' was still in progress, 'the PM insisted on taking two Americans—Biddle (an Ambassador) & Harriman, onto the roof, & a fantastic climb it was—up ladders, a long circular stairway, & a tiny manhole right at the top of a tower. No bombs fell whilst we were up—although fire engines were continually passing, & the guns were firing all the time, with planes droning overhead.'

On returning to the Central War Room Seal learned that the flat of a friend of his had been bombed. 'So I asked the Prime Minister if I could borrow the armoured car to send him home.' Churchill agreed, with the resultant 'great excitement amongst the Americans', Seal noted, 'who felt they were at last in the war!'[1]

That same night, Churchill telegraphed to Roosevelt about German raiders now using the Central Atlantic as their centre of operations against British merchant shipping. This was 'almost unknown water' to Britain, because few vessels could be spared from convoy duty to search it or to 'round up' German supply ships there. 'It would be a great help,' Churchill wrote, 'if some American warships and aircraft could cruise about in this area, as they have a perfect right to do, without any prejudice to neutrality.' The mere presence of American ships, Churchill noted, 'might be decisive', as the German raiders 'would fear they might report what they saw and we could then despatch an adequate force to try to engage them.'[2]

On March 19 Churchill took the chair at a specially constituted War Cabinet Committee, the Battle of the Atlantic Committee. Immediately after the war, in a note describing the administrative organization of Churchill's premiership, Ian Jacob recalled that the meetings of this Committee had begun mainly dealing with operational matters, but that 'later on everything which had a bearing on our import programme was brought up at these meetings'. The subjects with which the Battle of the Atlantic Committee dealt, as a matter of urgency, included, Jacob noted, 'the defensive measures for protecting our convoys—the measures to secure a quicker turn round of ships—steps to increase manpower on ship repairs so as to enable repairs to be overtaken— progress with inland sorting depots; and even on occasion, the allocation of imports between the supply programme and the food programme'.[3]

At the very first meeting of the Committee, on March 19, Churchill 'emphasised', as the minutes recorded, 'the vital need' for reducing the

[1] Letter of 19 March 1941: Seal papers.
[2] 'Personal and Private', 19 March 1941: Churchill papers, 20/49.
[3] 'The Jacob Document': Cabinet papers, 120/290.

time of the turn around of ships in port by up to fifteen days. 'Every effort,' he said, 'must be directed to this end.'[1]

The worries about the Atlantic were now paramount. 'I'm not afraid of the Air,' Churchill told his War Cabinet colleagues on March 20, 'I'm not afraid of invasion, I'm less afraid of the Balkans—but—I'm anxious about the Atlantic.'[2] And it was to safeguard the Atlantic that American help was essential.

Churchill persevered with patience and determination in his efforts to prise an ever greater commitment from the Americans, both in shipping and other spheres.[3] But there were many setbacks, especially in the economic sphere, where Lend-Lease hid a host of hard, and, as Britain saw it, often ruthless bargaining. On March 20 Churchill wrote angrily to the Chancellor of the Exchequer, Sir Kingsley Wood:

Are we going to get our advances for building up factories in the United States repaid to us to enable us to finance our American affairs outside the Lease and Lend Bill provision? If not, how can we carry on? Anyhow, if we do not get any accommodation in this way, we must clearly hold on to all our remaining assets and gold yields. I am sure we shall have to come to a 'showdown'; but I would precede it by a 'lie-down' and appear dumb and immobile. Let the difficulties mount up, and let things have a small crash.

As far as *I* can make out we are not only to be skinned, but flayed to the bone.[4] I would like to get them hooked a little firmer, but they are pretty well on now. The power of the debtor is in the ascendant, especially when he is doing all the fighting.

'Keep this to yourself,' Churchill ended, 'but let me have your views.'[5]

---

[1] Battle of the Atlantic Committee, 1st Meeting, 5 p.m., 19 March 1941: Cabinet papers, 86/1. The Ministers present were Beaverbrook, Bevin, A. V. Alexander, Sinclair, Moore-Brabazon, Margesson, Sir Andrew Duncan and Lord Woolton.

[2] Cadogan diary, 20 March 1941: David Dilks (editor), *The Diaries of Sir Alexander Cadogan OM, 1938–1945*, London 1971, page 364.

[3] Under the Atlantic Ferry Operation, more than 150 aircraft a month were now being flown by Ferry Pilots from the United States across the Atlantic to Takoradi. On March 17 Churchill had resolved a long-standing dispute between Sinclair and Beaverbrook by giving Beaverbrook control of the Atlantic Service. Following a meeting between Churchill and Beaverbrook, Air Vice Marshal Dawson was put in charge of the Service. By the end of June, 200 aircraft a month were being flown across. (Air Ministry papers, 20/6087.) Churchill subsequently hoped to use the changes involved in Dawson's appointment to give Dowding command of Army Co-operation Command in Britain. 'I hope you will be able to do this,' he minuted to Sinclair, 'as I am sure nothing but good will come of it.' But Sinclair declined to re-employ Dowding in an operational command, even though Churchill argued it would 'give confidence to the Army'. (Prime Minister's Personal Minute, M.620/1, 2 June 1941: Premier papers, 3/9.)

[4] Churchill had originally written: 'As far as I can make out we are not only to be thin-skinned but super-skinned.'

[5] 'Most Secret', Prime Minister's Personal Minute, M.325/1, 20 March 1941: Premier papers, 4/17/2, folio 156.

The pressure at sea remained severe. One hopeful sign, however, was Roosevelt's agreement to repair HMS *Malaya* in an American yard. Another was his decision to put ten Revenue Cutters at Britain's disposal for convoy duties.[1] But the sense of imminent peril was almost simultaneously heightened with the mid-Atlantic depredations of the German battle cruisers *Scharnhorst* and *Gneisenau*, which, as Churchill telegraphed to Roosevelt, 'has forced us to disperse our whole battle fleet'. As the Germans knew of Britain's fleet dispersal, Churchill added, 'it has had its bearing on invasion. There are, however, no signs that this is imminent.' But three trans-Atlantic convoys in succession had been 'headed off' by the two warships. 'The strain on our resources,' Churchill warned, 'is extreme.'[2] On the following day, Churchill learned that the British, Allied and neutral merchant shipping losses for the previous week totalled nearly 60,000 tons. That night, British bombers again struck at military targets near Berlin, Kiel and Hanover. But these were mere pin-pricks of battle.[3] 'The issue of the war,' Churchill telegraphed on March 24 to Mackenzie King, 'will clearly depend on our being able to maintain the traffic across the Atlantic.'[4]

Hope still persisted in London that the Balkan situation would improve before any German attack on Greece, by some Turkish or Yugoslav commitment, even if it fell short of active alliance. 'At any time,' Churchill wrote to the Minister of Supply on March 23, 'we may have Allies or neutrals to arm.'[5] He had already appealed to the Yugoslav Prime Minister, Dr Cvetkovic, in what Colville called the 'diplomatic battle for the Soul of Yugoslavia', now reaching its height and swaying 'either way with vertiginous speed'.[6] Churchill's telegram was as powerful an appeal as could be put into words. 'The eventual total defeat of Hitler and Mussolini is certain,' it began. No 'prudent and far-seeing man' could doubt this, in view of the 'respective declared

---

[1] 'The ten cutters will be a Godsend,' Churchill telegraphed to Roosevelt on 30 March 1941. 'I cannot conceal from you,' Churchill added, 'that rate of loss due to inadequate escorts is terribly costly.' ('Personal and Secret', 30 March 1941: Premier papers, 3/324/10, folios 194–5.)

[2] 'Personal and Most Secret', 22 March 1941: Churchill papers, 20/49.

[3] The War Cabinet were told, of this raid on Berlin: 'weather conditions had been unfavourable, and only about half our machines had reached their targets. Good results had, however, been obtained at Kiel and Hanover.' (War Cabinet No. 31 of 1941, 24 March, 5 p.m., Minute 1: Cabinet papers, 65/18.)

[4] Telegram of 24 March 1941: Churchill papers, 20/49.

[5] Prime Minister's Personal Minute, M.347/1, 23 March 1941: Churchill papers, 20/36.

[6] Colville diary, 22 March 1941: Colville papers.

resolves' of the British and American democracies. Furthermore, Churchill told Cvetkovic:

There are only 65,000,000 malignant Huns, most of whom are already engaged in holding down Austrians, Czechs, Poles, and many other ancient races they now bully and pillage. The peoples of the British Empire and of the United States number nearly 200,000,000 in their homelands and British Dominions alone.

We possess the unchallengeable command of the oceans, and with American help will soon obtain decisive superiority in the air. The British Empire and the United States have more wealth and more technical resources and they make more steel than the whole of the rest of the world put together. They are determined that the cause of freedom shall not be trampled down nor the tide of world progress turned backwards by the criminal dictators, one of whom has already been irretrievably punctured.

We know that the hearts of all true Serbs, Croats and Slovenes beat for the freedom, integrity, and independence of their country, and that they share the forward outlook of the English-speaking world. If Yugoslavia were at this time to stoop to the fate of Roumania, or commit the crime of Bulgaria and become accomplice in an attempted assassination of Greece, her ruin will be certain and irreparable. She will not escape, but only postpone, the ordeal of war, and her brave armies will then fight alone after being surrounded and cut off from hope and succour.

On the other hand, the history of war has seldom shown a finer opportunity than is open to the Yugoslav armies if they seize it while time remains. If Yugoslavia and Turkey stand together with Greece, and with all the aid which the British Empire can give, the German curse will be stayed and final victory will be won as surely and as decisively as it was last time.

'I trust,' Churchill ended, 'your Excellency may rise to the height of world events.'[1]

Churchill's appeal failed. Two days later Cvetkovic, and his Foreign Minister Dr Cincar-Markovic, travelled by train to Vienna and, to the alarm and anguish of many Yugoslav patriots, signed a pact with Hitler. But still Churchill did not despair. He knew of the divisions in Yugoslav society, and of the strong pro-British feeling there. Within 24 hours of learning of Cvetkovic's mission to Vienna, he telegraphed to the British Ambassador in Belgrade, Ronald Campbell, urging him not to allow 'any gap' to grow between the British Embassy, the Regent Prince Paul—whom Churchill had often derided as 'Prince Palsy'—and those Ministers known to be hostile to Germany. Churchill's telegram continued:

[1] Telegram dated 22 March 1941: Churchill papers, 20/49.

Continue to pester, nag and bite. Demand audiences. Don't take NO for an answer. Cling on to them, pointing out Germans are already taking the subjugation of the country for granted. This is no time for reproaches or dignified farewells. Meanwhile, at the same time, do not neglect any alternative to which we may have to resort if we find present Government have gone beyond recall. Greatly admire all you have done so far.

'Keep it up,' Churchill added, 'by every means that occur to you.'[1]

That night, in Belgrade, the anti-German forces seized the ascendancy, arresting Dr Cvetkovic, dissolving the Council of Regency, proclaiming Peter II King and dethroning Prince Paul.[2] The leader of the coup, General Simovic, became Prime Minister on March 27, and the pact with Hitler was declared void. 'PM very elated,' noted Cadogan, who had suggested to Churchill the phrase which Churchill used that same day: 'Yugoslavia has found its soul.'[3] The events in Belgrade, Churchill told the Conservative Central Council, which he was addressing that day for the first time as Leader of the Party, arose 'from the wrath of a valiant and warlike race at the betrayal of their country . . .'[4] and at a meeting of the Defence Committee that night, at which Churchill presided, it was agreed 'that an expression of appreciation should be conveyed to Doctor Dalton for the part played by his Organisation[5] in bringing about the coup d'état in Yugoslavia'.[6]

Churchill now sought to follow up Yugoslavia's transformation by drawing Turkey in to the web of States opposed to Germany. 'Your Excellency,' he telegraphed to President Inönü on March 27, 'the dramatic events which are occurring in Belgrade and throughout Yugoslavia may offer the best chance of preventing the German invasion of the Balkan peninsula. Surely now is the time to make a common front which Germany will hardly dare assail.'[7]

---

[1] Telegram of 26 March 1941: Churchill papers, 20/49.

[2] Prince Paul had become Regent in 1934, following the assassination of his cousin King Alexander at Marseilles; Peter was then ten years old. In April 1941 Peter was evacuated to Athens, then to Egypt, and came to London in June 1941, where he was educated at Clare College, Cambridge. After the Yugoslav monarchy was abolished in November 1945, he went to America. He died in Denver, Colorado in 1970. In April 1941 Prince Paul went from Athens to Kenya, where he was interned, then to South Africa. After the war he lived in Paris, where he died in 1976.

[3] Cadogan diary, 27 March 1941: David Dilks (editor), *The Diaries of Sir Alexander Cadogan OM, 1938–1945*, London 1971, pages 366–7.

[4] Speech of 27 March 1941: Charles Eade (compiler), *The Unrelenting Struggle, War Speeches by the Right Hon. Winston S. Churchill CH MP*, London 1942, pages 183–188.

[5] SOE.

[6] Defence Committee (Operations) No. 10 of 1941, 27 March 1941, 9.45 p.m., Minute 3: Cabinet papers, 69/2.

[7] Telegram of 27 March 1941: Churchill papers, 20/49.

The events of March 27 were recorded by Eric Seal in a letter to his wife. 'The news from Yugo is good,' he wrote, 'we are all very cheered.' Seal had been with Churchill throughout the day, including at a luncheon to Winant given by the Trades Union Congress. His letter continued:

The PM made a very fine impromptu speech; & driving away in the car together I said to him that I thought he got on better with the Trades Union people than with the Tories—he said yes, they have a certain native virility—although he found himself in sympathy with the Tories on theoretical matters like free enterprise & the rights of property. I said they (the Trades Unionists) were essentially conservative & not much of the pale intellectual about them, & he agreed.

When we got back to No 10 the Bases Agreement with the Americans was signed—in the glare of arc lights & cameras.[1]

Churchill's confidence was boosted on March 27 by the completion in Washington of the United States–British Staff Conversations, which had culminated in 'Joint Basic War Plan Number One' of the United States and the British Commonwealth 'for war against the Axis Powers'. This plan, which was comprehensive in its scope, covered the detailed disposition of the land, sea and air forces of both Britain and the United States, from the moment that America entered the war.[2]

Further encouraging news of the strengthening of Anglo-American links came a week later, when Sinclair informed Churchill that as part of these Staff Conversations, decisions had been reached concerning 'the allocation of air equipment before and after United States intervention' and that 'specially secret material on the air expansion programme is included'. Air Vice-Marshal Slessor, who had conducted these air negotiations for Britain, warned however 'that any delay' in placing Britain's aircraft orders in accordance with the Staff decisions 'may give an opportunity for the development of opposition on the part of certain sections of the US Naval Staff'.[3]

There was a further area of British concern in which active American help seemed essential—the Far East. As he followed reports of the travels of the Japanese Foreign Minister, Yosuke Matsuoka, Churchill was convinced that Japan could be deterred from aggressive action only by the active pressures of American policy. A month earlier, on February 20, he had telegraphed to Roosevelt: 'I have better news about

---

[1] Letter of 27 March 1941: Seal papers.
[2] Britain–United States (J) No. 30 of 1941, 27 March 1941, 'Secret': Premier papers, 3/489/1. Also known as 'Defence Plan No. 1'.
[3] 'Secret', 4 April 1941: Premier papers, 3/488/2.

Japan. Apparently Matsuoka is visiting Berlin, Rome and Moscow in the near future. This may well be a diplomatic sop to cover absence of action against Great Britain. If Japanese attack which seemed imminent is now postponed, this is largely due to fear of United States. The more these fears can be played upon the better. . . .'[1]

At the end of February, Matsuoka had begun his travels, visiting Berlin, Rome and Moscow. Churchill shared the Foreign Office's concern lest Matsuoka persuade his various hosts that the time had come for a Japanese attack on Britain in the Far East, and obtain their acquiescence in such a move. Shortly before Matsuoka set off to the Axis and Soviet capitals, Churchill spoke in London to Shigemitsu, the Japanese Ambassador: 'What a pity it would be,' Churchill said, if at this stage Japan 'when she already had China on her hands', got into a war with Britain and the United States.[2]

Matsuoka now embarked upon his diplomatic journey. In Berlin, Ribbentrop pressed him, on Hitler's authority, to attack British possessions in the Far East as soon as possible. A quick attack on Singapore, said the German Foreign Minister, would be a decisive factor in the speedy overthrow of England. Aware, through Intelligence sources, of the nature of German pressure on Matsuoka, Churchill sent the Japanese Foreign Minister a message to be read during his return journey to Japan through Moscow and on the Trans-Siberian railway. The message contained eight terse questions, which seemed, Churchill wrote to Matsuoka, to 'deserve the attention' of the Japanese Government and people. Each question was designed to give the Japanese pause before committing their fleets and armies against Britain. The questions read:

1. Will Germany, without the command of the sea or the command of the British daylight air, be able to invade and conquer Great Britain in the spring, summer or autumn of 1941? Will Germany try to do so? Would it not be in the interests of Japan to wait until these questions have answered themselves?

2. Will the German attack on British shipping be strong enough to prevent American aid from reaching British shores with Great Britain and the United States transforming their whole industry to war purposes?

3. Did Japan's accession to the Triple Pact make it more likely or less likely that the United States would come into the present war?

4. If the United States entered the war at the side of Great Britain, and Japan ranged herself with the Axis Powers, would not the naval superiority of

---

[1] Prime Minister's Personal Minute, M.210/1, 19 February 1941: Churchill papers, 20/36.

[2] 'Secret', Prime Minister's Personal Minute, M.192/1, 17 February 1941: Churchill papers, 20/36.

the two English-speaking nations enable them to dispose of the Axis Powers in Europe before turning their united strength upon Japan?

5. Is Italy a strength or a burden to Germany? Is the Italian Fleet as good at sea as on paper? Is it as good on paper as it used to be?

6. Will the British Air Force be stronger than the German Air Force before the end of 1941 and far stronger before the end of 1942?

7. Will the many countries which are being held down by the German Army and Gestapo learn to like the Germans more or will they like them less as the years pass by?

8. Is it true that the production of steel in the United States during 1941 will be 75 million tons, and in Great Britain about 12½, making a total of nearly 90 million tons? If Germany should happen to be defeated, as she was last time, would not the 7 million tons steel production of Japan be inadequate for a single-handed war?

'From the answers to these questions,' Churchill's telegram ended, 'may spring the avoidance by Japan of a serious catastrophe, and a marked improvement in the relations between Japan and the two great sea Powers of the West.'[1]

As an added inducement to caution, Portal had already given instructions, as he informed Churchill, 'that a heavy attack should be made on Berlin on the night that we expect Matsuoka to be there'.[2]

Churchill was under no illusions about Japanese intentions. 'Let me have a report,' he was to minute to Ismay on May 4, 'on the efficiency of the gunners and personnel managing the 15-inch batteries and searchlights at Singapore.' Were they, he asked, fitted with radar?[3]

The defences in place at Singapore were to be made efficient, but no new forces were to be sent out. This was made clear by the Defence Committee in answer to a memorandum by Menzies, urging the immediate despatch of British naval and air reinforcements to Singapore.[4] To send Hurricanes to Singapore, Sinclair had told the Defence Committee on April 9, 'would be a mistake'. But, as Churchill stated, in the event of a 'serious, major attack' by Japan on Australia 'we would abandon everything to come to their help'; that, however, 'did not

---

[1] Prime Minister's Personal Telegram, T.29, 2 April 1941: Premier papers, 3/252/2, folios 33–5. Five months later, after Matsuoka had been replaced, Churchill minuted to Eden: 'Will you telegraph to Craigie at Tokio asking him to make sure that the new Foreign Secretary has a chance of reading the warning letter I sent to Matsuoka. It will read better now than it did then.' (Prime Minister's Personal Minute, M.891/1, 12 September 1941: Premier papers, 3/252/2, folio 2.)

[2] 'Secret', Minute of 19 March 1941: Premier papers, 3/14/2, folio 126. Churchill approved these instructions on 21 March 1941.

[3] Prime Minister's Personal Minute, D.152/1, 4 May 1941: Churchill papers. 20/36.

[4] Chiefs of Staff Paper No. 230 of 1941.

mean that we would give up our great interests in the Middle East on account of a few raids by Japanese cruisers'. As Churchill had already told Menzies, it was the painstaking building up of Britain's military strength in the Middle East that was paramount, and could not be jeopardized.

The Defence Committee of April 9 had also discussed whether or not Britain should 'automatically' declare war on Japan if she were to attack the Dutch East Indies. Such a course was favoured by Amery, Cranborne and Sinclair, who argued that it would be 'morally indefensible not to go to the immediate assistance of an Ally who was fighting on our side over here if she were attacked by Japan'. Both Dudley Pound and Churchill sounded a note of caution, telling the Defence Committee as the minutes recorded:

Although we might decide to go to war with Japan if she attacked the Netherlands East Indies, it would be wrong to tie ourselves down to do so beforehand. There was little or no help which we could give to the Netherlands East Indies if the Americans did not join with us; and it might therefore pay us when the time came to delay a declaration of war until a more suitable moment.

All our action must be judged from its effect on our power to win the war against Germany. If, when the moment came, the right way to win the war against Germany were thought to be to declare war on Japan, then we should do so. If, on the other hand, it appeared at the time that it would pay us to keep out of war with Japan, we should not hesitate to do so.

We ought to wait to see what the United States of America would do. The Americans would be in a bad position to criticise us if they were to hang back when we, who already had our hands full with Germany and Italy, did not go to war with Japan.[1]

In the last week of March, in East Africa, two armies achieved success: General Platt's with the capture of Keren in Eritrea,[2] and General

---

[1] Defence Committee (Operations) No. 12 of 1941, 9 April 1941, 9.45 p.m.: Cabinet papers, 69/2.

[2] A week later Churchill telegraphed to the Viceroy of India: 'The whole Empire has been stirred by the achievement of the Indian forces in Eritrea. For me the story of the ardour and perseverance with which they scaled and finally conquered the precipitous heights of Keren recalls memories of the North-West Frontier of long years ago, and it is as one who has had the honour to serve in the field with Indian soldiers from all parts of Hindustan, as well as in the name of His Majesty's Government, that I ask Your Excellency to convey to them and to the whole Indian Army the pride and admiration with which we have followed their heroic exploits.' (Prime Minister's Personal Telegram, T.53, 7 April 1941: Churchill papers, 20/49.)

Cunningham's with the capture of Harar in Ethiopia. 'Yesterday was a grand day,' Churchill telegraphed to Harry Hopkins on March 28, 'Belgrade, Keren, Harar,' but he added: 'The strain at sea on our naval resources is too great for us to provide adequate hunting groups, and this leads to a continuance of heavy disastrous losses inflicted on our immense traffic and convoys. We simply have not got enough escorts to go round and fight at the same time.'

Churchill's telegram to Hopkins ended: 'Am in closest touch with Harriman. Kindest regards from all here.'[1]

There was, however, a victory at sea that very night, when three Italian heavy cruisers and two modern destroyers were sunk off Cape Matapan, with only two British aircraft, and no ships, lost. 'How lucky the Italians came in,' Churchill said to Colville when the news reached him.[2] The victory was made possible in part because of decrypts of high grade Italian cypher messages; in part also because the British aircraft had been able to operate from airfields in Greece.[3] This boded well for 'Lustre', as did the Belgrade coup d'état. On March 30 Churchill telegraphed to the acting Prime Minister of Australia:

When a month ago we decided upon 'Lustre' it looked a rather bleak military adventure dictated by *noblesse oblige*. Thursday's events in Belgrade show far-reaching effects of this and other measures we have taken on whole Balkan situation. German plans have been upset and we may cherish renewed hopes of forming a Balkan front with Turkey comprising about 70 Allied divisions from the four Powers concerned. This is, of course, by no means certain yet. But even now it puts 'Lustre' in its true setting, not as an isolated military act, but as a prime mover in large design. Whatever outcome may be, everything that has happened since 'Lustre' decision taken justifies it. Delay also will enable full concentration to be made on Greek front instead of piecemeal engagement of our forces.

'Result unknowable,' Churchill added, 'but prize has increased and risks have somewhat lessened.'[4]

Churchill's hopes were now considerable. 'Together,' he telegraphed to Eden, who had returned to Athens, 'Yugoslavia, Greece, Turkey

[1] Foreign Office Telegram No. 1704, 28 March 1941: Premier papers, 3/224/1, folio 2.

[2] Colville diary, 30 March 1941: Colville papers. Among those who fought at Matapan was Prince Philip, later Duke of Edinburgh and husband of Queen Elizabeth II.

[3] The Italian Enigma machine involved had first been used by the Italians during the Spanish Civil War. It passed into disuse in May 1941 and was overtaken by a new machine which was also decrypted at Bletchley on a regular basis, and was to exercise a profound effect on the North African campaigns, including the battle of El Alamein, by depriving Rommel of his essential supplies. (Edward Thomas, notes for the author, 3 December 1982.)

[4] 'Most Secret', 30 March 1941: Churchill papers, 20/49.

and ourselves have seventy divisions mobilized in this theatre. Germans have not yet got more than thirty.' These seventy ought to be able to say to the thirty: 'If you attack any of us you will be at war with all.' This was Turkey's 'best chance of avoiding war'; by 'doing nothing', as Churchill phrased it, Turkey ran 'the greatest danger of having everything concentrated upon her'. What was needed was a 'firm, united declaration'.[1] But no such declaration was forthcoming.

Churchill still urged the Turks to make common cause with Yugoslavia, Greece and Britain, and believed that they might do so. Even without Turkey, the combination was impressive. 'Lustre,' Churchill telegraphed to Wavell on March 30, 'abundantly justified already as part of much larger and still hopeful combination.'[2] And to A. V. Alexander and Dudley Pound he minuted on the following day; 'We ought to tell the Turks that if they enter the war we will make sure they have the command of the Black Sea.' To this end, he noted, Britain should 'give aid by means of a Submarine Flotilla', as it was 'no use leaving the Black Sea entirely to the Turkish Navy . . .'[3]

The accelerated pace of events, and with them both military and naval victories, and diplomatic expectations, affected all those in Churchill's circle, despite the sinking in the Mediterranean of the cruisers HMS *York* on March 30 and HMS *Bonaventure* on the following day.[4] 'This has been a wonderful weekend,' Colville wrote in his diary on March 31, 'the culmination of a week of victories.' Churchill, he added, had been 'elated by the naval victory following so close on the Yugoslav revolution, the fall of Keren and the capture of Harar. He emphasizes the effect it will have on Japan—this "tearing up of the paper fleet of Italy". . . .' In addition, Colville wrote:

The PM told me he was now sure Germany would attack Yugoslavia before Greece or Turkey and he is very hopeful on that front.

The naval news has stirred him to compose several brilliant telegrams, to Roosevelt etc., and he has spent much of the weekend pacing—or rather tripping—up and down the Great Hall to the sound of the gramophone (play-

---

[1] 'Private and Secret', 28 March 1941: Churchill papers, 20/49.

[2] Telegram of 30 March 1941: Churchill papers, 20/49.

[3] 'Action this Day', Prime Minister's Personal Minute, M.380/1, 31 March 1941: Cabinet papers, 120/713.

[4] There was also an increase in civilian deaths from German air raids in March 1941, when 4,259 civilians were killed during the month. But neither these figures, nor news of the loss of the two cruisers, reached Churchill until after the weekend of celebration.

ing martial airs, waltzes and the most vulgar kind of brass-band songs) deep in thought all the while.[1]

One reason for Churchill being 'deep in thought' was his scrutiny of Intelligence reports of German troop movements. An Enigma decrypt had shown, on March 26 that, following the Yugoslav Pact with Germany and Italy, but before the Yugoslav coup, substantial German military trains had been ordered to move from the Yugoslav border to Southern Poland. The instructions had been to transport three out of the five Panzer divisions then in Rumania towards the German-Soviet border. A further Enigma decrypt immediately after the coup, however, showed that these orders had been cancelled. The import of the two decrypts was clear: it was towards Germany's Russian border that these substantial forces had originally been ordered, being no longer needed, so it had seemed, to coerce Yugoslavia.

On March 30 Churchill telegraphed to Eden that, as a result of the Yugoslav coup and 'my reading of the Intelligence', it looked as if 'Bear will be kept waiting a bit'. But the order and counter-order which Enigma had revealed had made clear to Churchill what he called Germany's 'magnitude of design' against both the Balkans, and, eventually, Russia.[2] On the previous night, after studying the crucial decrypts, Churchill had given Colville 'a short lecture on the various invaders of Russia, especially Charles XII'.[3]

A new area of war was on the horizon, far beyond the Balkans. As Churchill studied the Enigma decrypts, he took a decision of risk, but calculated risk, and sent a personal message to Stalin, through Sir Stafford Cripps, disguising his source, but not its evidence. His message read:

I have sure information from a trusted agent that when the Germans thought they had got Yugoslavia in the net, that is to say, after March 20, they began to move three out of the five Panzer Divisions from Roumania to Southern Poland. The moment they heard of the Serbian revolution this movement was countermanded. Your Excellency will readily appreciate the significance of these facts.[4]

At first, Cripps refused to deliver this message, fearing that it might somehow provoke Soviet–German hostilities. When Churchill learnt of Cripps' hesitations he wrote to Eden, on April 16: 'I set special import-

[1] Colville diary, 31 March 1941: Colville papers.
[2] 'Most Secret', 30 March 1941: Churchill papers, 20/49.
[3] Colville diary, 29 March 1941: Colville papers.
[4] Prime Minister's Personal Telegram, T.18 (Foreign Office Telegram No. 278 to Moscow), 3 April 1941: Premier papers, 3/170/1, No. 1.

ance on the delivery of this message from me to Stalin. I cannot understand why it should be resisted. The Ambassador is not alive to the military significance of the facts. Pray oblige me.'[1]

After yet further delays, Cripps agreed to deliver the message, which he handed to the Soviet Foreign Minister, Vyshinski, on April 19. Four days later, Vyshinski informed Cripps that the message 'had been conveyed to M. Stalin'.[2] Stalin made no reply, however.

Although, as we now know, Stalin had received information about Germany's planned attack from many other sources, and had chosen to ignore it, Churchill was furious at Cripps' action. His sense of outrage was heightened in October 1941 when Stalin spoke to Beaverbrook in Moscow about 'not remembering when he was warned'. On hearing of this remark Churchill wrote, to both Eden and Beaverbrook about his warning message of April 3:

This was the only message before the attack that I sent Stalin direct. It had to be somewhat cryptic, in view of the deadly character of the information contained. Its brevity, the exceptional character of the communication, the fact that it came from the Head of the Government and was to be delivered personally to the Head of the Russian Government by the Ambassador were all intended to give it special significance and arrest Stalin's attention.

It was astonishing that the Ambassador should have had the effrontery to delay this message for sixteen days, and then merely to hand it to Vyshinski. It may very well never have reached Stalin at all, or merely have been put casually before him.

That Sir Stafford Cripps should think the fact that he had been writing a long personal letter about the war to Vyshinski, and that this would be more likely to make an impression than a direct message from me, only shows his lack of sense of proportion.

Churchill went on to argue that Cripps had 'a great responsibility for his obstinate, obstructive handling of this matter'. It was not so much the Intelligence aspect by which Churchill was perturbed, but because he felt that had Cripps 'obeyed his instructions, it is more than possible that some kind of relationship would have been constructed between me and Stalin'.[3]

---

[1] Prime Minister's Personal Minute, M.490/1, 16 April 1941: Churchill papers, 23/9.
[2] Eden to Churchill, 30 April 1941: Churchill papers, 23/9.
[3] Prime Minister's Personal Minute M.993/1, 14 October 1941: Churchill papers, 20/49. In reply Eden wrote, 'It should be borne in mind that at this time the Russians were most reluctant to receive messages of any kind; and, even if Stalin did receive your message, he now probably prefers to forget the fact. Only thus, to some extent, can he exonerate himself. The same attitude was adopted towards the later messages which, with your permission, I gave to Maisky, beginning several weeks before the attack. These have never been acknowledged or referred to, to this day.' (Minute of 14 October 1941: Churchill papers, 20/49.)

As London awaited news of a German attack upon Yugoslavia, Greece or even Turkey, German forces moved towards British front line positions in Cyrenaica, and within a few days it looked as if the territory so recently captured from the Italians would be again a battlefield. 'It seems most desirable,' Churchill telegraphed to Wavell on April 2, 'to stop the German advance against Cyrenaica.' Any 'rebuff' to the Germans, he added, would have 'far-reaching prestige effects'. Ground could be given up for the purposes of manoeuvre, 'but any serious withdrawal from Benghazi would appear most melancholy'.[1]

On the day that Churchill sent this telegram, the superior armour of Rommel's forces was overrunning and disorganizing Wavell's front line positions, causing serious losses. As a result, Wavell ordered the 7th Australian Division, then near Cairo, and about to embark for Greece, to move to the western desert instead. The seizure of Rhodes, another feature of Britain's Aegean policy, had likewise to be abandoned. Rommel's first victory was Greece's first defeat.

Even before the news of the switch of the Australians became known, Churchill saw the implications of Rommel's advance, telegraphing to Eden, who was in Athens:

> Far more important than the loss of ground is the idea that we cannot face the Germans and that their appearance is enough to drive us back many scores of miles. This may react most evilly throughout Balkans and Turkey. Pray go back to Cairo and go into all this. Sooner or later we shall have to fight the Huns. By all means make the best plan of manoeuvre, but anyhow fight.

Could nothing be done, Churchill asked, to cut the coastal road by a 'sea-borne descent' behind the German forces, 'even if it means putting off Rhodes?'[2]

During April 3 news reached London that Wavell had decided to evacuate Benghazi. 'The PM is greatly worried,' Colville noted in his diary.[3] But on the following day, encouraged by Ismay, who refused to 'take it too tragically', Churchill telegraphed to Wavell: 'I warned the country a week ago that they must not expect continuance of unbroken successes and take the rough with the smooth.' Therefore, Churchill added, 'be quite sure that we shall back you up in adversity even better than in good fortune'.[4]

---

[1] 'Personal and Secret', 'Most Immediate', Telegram 002, despatched 6.30 p.m., 2 April 1941, Prime Minister's Personal Telegram, T.8: Churchill papers, 20/39.

[2] Prime Minister's Personal Telegram, T.24, 'Personal, Private and Secret', 3 April 1941, 10.30 p.m., Defence Committee (Operations) No. 11 of 1941, Annex IV: Cabinet papers, 69/2.

[3] Colville diary, 3 April 1941: Colville papers.

[4] Prime Minister's Personal Telegram, T.32, 4 April 1941, 11.15 p.m.: Churchill papers, 20/37.

Wavell replied two days later that while the situation in Cyrenaica seemed 'somewhat easier', nevertheless, in view of the 'weakness of our armoured forces', a withdrawal towards Derna would be necessary.[1] Late that night, Eden, who had returned from Athens to Cairo, telegraphed to Churchill: 'You know of our two chief weaknesses which are on modern types of aircraft needed here and in Greece, and armoured vehicles.' The latter, especially the cruiser tanks which had arrived with the 2nd Armoured Division, 'seem to have a disturbingly high percentage of breakdowns in recent operations'.[2]

Since March 26 decrypting of German Air Force Enigma messages had enabled Churchill and his advisers to follow each phase of the Balkan crisis. The forces that had been halted in the Balkans on that day, it was known, included three armoured divisions and the SS division Adolf Hitler. Further divisions had, within forty-eight hours, been sent as reinforcements by rail from Germany to the Rumanian–Yugoslav border area. Various German Air Force movements had also been reported through this most secret source, and on April 4 the date of April 6 was given for a planned operation, code name 'Retribution'.[3]

This was clearly the operation to attack Yugoslavia. On reading these decrypts, Churchill hastened to inform the leader of the coup, General Simovic, of the situation as he knew it, including what he described, in order to protect Enigma, as 'large movements of air forces reported to us from France by our agents there', and of German bombers even withdrawn from Tripoli, 'according to our African Army Intelligence'.

Churchill urged Simovic to use what little time he had left to attack the 'demoralised and rotten' Italian forces in Albania, catching them

[1] Telegram o/54358, despatched 12,47 p.m., received 4.15 p.m., 5 April 1941: Churchill papers, 20/37.

[2] Telegram No. 855, despatched 3,02 a.m., received 4.15 a.m., 6 April 1941: Churchill papers, 20/37. Three months later, when he studied a detailed report of the withdrawal from Cyrenaica, Churchill commented: 'The whole of this account shows how well and faithfully the troops of all units acquitted themselves in the midst of so much order, counter-order and disorder.' (War Cabinet Paper No. 159 of 1941, 'Most Secret', 11 July 1941: Premier papers, 3/283.)

[3] Enigma decrypts CX/JQ 803, 808, 821, 825 and 849 (military movements) and 823 and 829 (air preparations), summarized in F. H. Hinsley and others, *British Intelligence in the Second World War, Its Influence on Strategy and Operations*, volume 1, London 1979, page 371–2.

in the rear of their Greek front, and making use of the 'masses of equipment that would fall into your hands'. The 'one supreme stroke for victory and safety', Churchill wrote, 'is to win a decisive forestalling victory in Albania. . . .'[1]

It was all too late; fearful of provoking the pro-German Croats inside Yugoslavia, Simovic had refused even to receive Eden in Belgrade, or to sign any military agreement with Dill, whose mission to the capital on April 3 was fruitless. At dawn on Sunday April 6—Palm Sunday—the Germans launched operation 'Retribution', a massive air attack on the Yugoslav capital. After two days of intense bombardment, more than 17,000 of the citizens of Belgrade had been killed.[2] Also on April 6, German warplanes struck at the Greek port of Piraeus, where at that very moment units of the British Expeditionary Force were disembarking. Six ships with military cargoes were sunk, before the port itself was devastated when a British ship, Clan Fraser, hit by German bombs, blew up with 200 tons of high explosives on board.

As German troops pushed across the Yugoslav borders, they were joined by Hungarian units. Within twenty-four hours, the Yugoslav border defences were broken.

'Every one here has taken the new German invasion with calm fortitude,' Randolph Churchill wrote to his father from Cairo on April 6. 'No one seems at all rattled. We are all hoping now that there will be plenty of fighting for all of us.'[3] 'We have a hard struggle before us,' Churchill telegraphed that night to Roosevelt, 'both in Greece and Libya but will do our best according to our resources.'[4]

That same night, six Royal Air Force Wellington bombers struck at the railway yards of the Bulgarian capital, Sofia, hoping thereby to delay the movement of German military supplies to the Yugoslav front.[5] In Greece, the New Zealand Division, the 6th Australian Division and one armoured Brigade were on their way to the Aliakhmon line. In the Aegean, the island of Lemnos had been occupied with one battalion. But the sinking of a second ship, the Northern Prince, in the eastern

[1] Prime Minister's Personal Telegram, T.37, Foreign Office No. 500 to Belgrade, 4 April 1941, 9.45 p.m.: Churchill papers, 20/37.
[2] Some six per cent of the population; but the city was crowded with many Yugoslavs from other towns and villages, who had come into the city for Palm Sunday.
[3] Letter of 6 April 1941: Churchill papers, 1/362.
[4] Prime Minister's Personal Telegram, T.45, Foreign Office No. 1875 of 6 April 1941, despatched 2.55 a.m., 7 April 1941: Churchill papers, 20/37.
[5] The bombing of military targets in Germany also continued, with raids on Kiel on the nights of April 7–8, 8–9, 15–16, 24–25 and 30 April–1 May.

Mediterranean, was, as Churchill told the War Cabinet on April 7, a 'serious loss', as the ship had contained material badly needed by the Greek explosives factory.[1]

The War Cabinet also had before them a telegram from Wavell, reporting that the situation in the western desert had 'greatly deterioriated', with further German advances and further vehicle losses in the 2nd Armoured Division 'by mechanical breakdown and air bombardment'.[2] That evening Churchill confided to Colville 'that he thought Wavell etc had been very silly in north Africa and should have been prepared to meet an attack there',[3] while to Wavell himself Churchill telegraphed that night that Tobruk, with its 'permanent Italian defences' now at Britain's disposal, 'seems to be a place to be held to the death without thought of retirement'. Churchill added that there was 'more complaint' in London about Wavell's communiqué 'belittling the value of Benghazi' than there had been about the loss of the town. 'London,' Churchill warned, 'is the place where opinion has to be held.'[4]

Intent on following the defence of Tobruk as closely as possible, Churchill asked Ismay to prepare both a large-scale plan and a model for him, and, meanwhile, 'the best photographs available, both from the air and from the ground'.[5] Forced also to remain vigilant as to any possible German invasion of Britain while the Balkans were ablaze, Churchill instructed Bridges to ensure that there was 'no serious break' in Ministerial work over Easter. Ministers, he wrote, 'are responsible for being on the telephone at the shortest notice', and should take their holidays in rotation. 'I am told,' Churchill added, 'that Easter is a very good time for invasion.'[6]

There had been a further German air raid on Coventry on April 8,

---

[1] War Cabinet No. 36 of 1941, 7 April 1941, 5 p.m., Minute 1, Confidential Annex: Cabinet papers, 65/22.

[2] Telegram 0/54815, despatched 1,02 p.m., received 3.15 p.m., 7 April 1941: Cabinet papers, 65/22.

[3] Colville diary, 7 April 1941: Colville papers.

[4] Prime Minister's Personal Telegram, T.54, despatched 00.27 a.m., 8 April 1941: Churchill papers, 20/37.

[5] Prime Minister's Personal Minute, D.123/1, 8 April 1941: Churchill papers, 20/36.

[6] Prime Minister's Personal Minute, C.38/1, 8 April 1941: Churchill papers, 20/36. On the previous day Churchill had minuted to David Margesson, the Secretary of State for War: 'It has been suggested that it might be useful in case of invasion to have ready a number of official-looking labels in German which could be used as required, e.g. to misdirect the troops, or mislead about mined bridges and contaminated petrol. Being in German they would not mislead our men. Some idea of the appearance of such labels could probably be obtained from people returned from France.' (Prime Minister's Personal Minute, M.414/1, 7 April 1941: Churchill papers, 20/36.) Italy had invaded Albania on 7 April 1939, Good Friday.

and on the following day it was announced that 29,856 British civilians had died as a result of air bombardment since the outbreak of war.[1]

There had been some progress, however, in the use of decoy fires. In March German bombers had struck for up to six hours at decoy sites near Cardiff and Bristol. At Portsmouth on April 17 more than 75 per cent of the bombs dropped were to fall on the decoy area.[2]

In the House of Commons on April 9, Churchill gave a survey of the war situation. His speech had originally been planned, and had been announced as a motion congratulating the fighting services on their victories. 'These victories,' Harold Nicolson noted in his diary, 'are now dust and ashes.' His account continued:

The PM comes in at 11.56 and is greeted with cheers. He sits between Greenwood and Attlee, scowls at the notes in his hand, pulls out a gold pencil and scribbles an addition to the last sheet. He then gets up to speak in a grim and obstinate voice. He throws out news incidentally. We have taken Massawa.[3] The Germans entered Salonica at 4 a.m. this morning. At this news there is a silent wince of pain throughout the House. He discloses that the USA have given us their revenue cutters. His peroration implies that we are done without American help.[4]

At the end of his speech, referring to the continued possibility of a German invasion of Britain, Churchill commented: 'That is an ordeal from which we shall not shrink.' But there were 'many signs', he said, which pointed to 'a Nazi attempt to secure the granary of the Ukraine and the oil fields of the Caucasus. . . .' as a means of gaining the resources needed 'to wear down the English-speaking world'. All this was of course, he said, 'speculation'. But once more the image of a German attack on Russia had been projected.

Churchill's survey ended with a declaration that, once the Battle of the Atlantic was gained, and Britain was certain 'of the constant flow of American supplies which is being prepared for us', then, however far Hitler might go, 'or whatever new millions or scores of millions he

[1] In the Coventry raid serious damage was done to three aircraft factories, and, as Beaverbrook wrote to Churchill, at Daimler No. 1 Shadow Factory all magnesium, raw materials, steel and aluminium had been destroyed in ten bays. But, Beaverbrook added, 'we will escape complete disaster by reason of the dispersal plans which were carried out last year'. (Minute of 9 April 1941: Premier papers, 3/18/2, folio 98.)

[2] Reports by Sir Archibald Sinclair to Churchill of 25 March 1941 and 23 April 1941: Premier papers, 3/118, folios 3, 6 & 7.

[3] The principal port of Italian Eritrea, it had surrendered on 8 April 1941, when more than 10,000 Italian soldiers were taken prisoner.

[4] Nicolson diary, 9 April 1941: Nigel Nicolson (editor), *Harold Nicolson, Diaries and Letters, 1939–1945*, London 1967, page 161.

may lap in misery, he may be sure that, armed with the sword of retributive justice, we shall be on his track'.[1]

On the following day Averell Harriman wrote to Roosevelt: 'England's strength is bleeding. In our own interest, I trust that our Navy can be directly employed before our partner is too weak.'[2]

[1] *Hansard*, 9 April 1941, columns 1587–98.

[2] Letter of 10 April 1941: W. Averell Harriman and Elie Abel, *Special Envoy to Churchill and Stalin, 1941–1946*, London 1976, page 31.

55

Greece and Crete: 'hard times, but the end will repay'

DURING the second week of April there was bad news from every front. At Derna, in Libya, two thousand British troops had been captured by Rommel's forces.[1] In Yugoslavia, German troops had driven a wedge between the Greek and Yugoslav armies. In less than three days, 31,000 tons of British merchant shipping had been sunk at sea.[2]

On April 11 there was another German air raid on Coventry, with further serious damage to the aircraft factories there. 'The effect upon production,' Beaverbrook warned, 'will be felt for some time to come.'[3]

That night Churchill had travelled to Bristol with Ambassador Winant and Robert Menzies, who were to receive honorary degrees from Churchill, the University's Chancellor. Clementine Churchill, Mary Churchill and Averell Harriman went with them. That night Churchill, family and guests slept in a special train just outside the city. While they slept, German bombers struck at Bristol docks. Woken by the sirens and the bombardment, they watched and listened to the distant raid. Next morning, amid scenes of destruction and still-smouldering fires, Churchill saw something of the damaged city: 'devastation', noted Colville, who was with them, 'such as I had never thought possible'.

As Churchill drove for an hour through the ruined city the people, Colville noted, 'looked bewildered but, as at Swansea, were brave and

---

[1] Captured well south of Derna, which they had left some time before travelling in one car, were two Generals, O'Connor and Neame, and Brigadier Combe. The Generals escaped from captivity at the time of the Italian armistice in 1943, Combe in 1944.

[2] War Cabinet No. 38 of 1941, 10 April 1941, 12 Noon: Cabinet papers, 65/18.

[3] Minute of 12 April 1941: Premier papers, 3/18/2, folio 96–7.

were thrilled at the sight of Winston who drove about sitting on the hood of an open car and waving his hat'.[1]

Next to the University, a building was still in flames. 'That you should gather in this way,' Churchill told his University audience, 'is a mark of fortitude and phlegm, of a courage and detachment from material affairs worthy of all that we have learned to believe of ancient Rome or of modern Greece.'[2]

Mary Churchill later recalled the scene: 'It was quite extraordinary. People kept on arriving late with grime on their faces half washed off. They had their ceremonial robes on, over their fire fighting clothes which were still wet.'[3]

That afternoon, Churchill again inspected the ruins. Five and a half years later Ismay recalled the scene in a letter to Churchill:

People were still being dug out, but there was no sign of a faltering anywhere. Only efficiency and resolution. At one of the rest centres at which you called, there was a poor old woman who had lost all her belongings sobbing her heart out. But as you entered, she took her handkerchief from her eyes and waved it madly shouting 'Hooray, hooray.'[4]

As Churchill's train pulled out of Bristol station, and the last of the cheering crowds were gone, Averell Harriman noticed that tears filled the Prime Minister's eyes, and he picked up a newspaper to hide his face from those who were with him, choking, through his emotion: 'They have such confidence. It is a grave responsibility.'[5]

Returning to Chequers by train, Churchill was sunk deep in thought. Then, 'quite suddenly' as Winant later recalled, he turned to the American Ambassador and said 'I am going to see to it that the necessary tonnage is allotted for foodstuffs to protect them (the civil population) from the strain and stresses that they may be subjected to in this period of great emergency.'

Winant commented:

In allotting more tonnage for foodstuffs I realised that Mr Churchill had been deeply moved by what he had seen on this trip of the people's needs. At this desperate time there was always the temptation to cut down on food because of the compelling need for steel and armaments. When I wrote to the

[1] Colville diary, 12 April 1941: Colville papers.
[2] Speech of 12 April 1941.
[3] Lady Soames, conversation with the author, 19 October 1982.
[4] Letter of 28 November 1946: Churchill papers, 4/198.
[5] Quoted in Averell Harriman and Elie Abel, *Special Envoy to Churchill and Stalin, 1941–1946*, London 1976, pages 29–30.

President of the Prime Minister's few words on the train I told him that I felt deeply that this policy of protection was necessary. I knew that he would fully understand.[1]

That evening Churchill dined at Chequers, 'a hectic night', Colville noted, 'starting in gloom and ending in glad momentous news from the USA'[2] During the evening Ambassador Winant who was dining at Chequers, received a telegram from President Roosevelt, for Churchill, announcing that the United States would extend her security zone and patrol areas in the Atlantic as far east as the 25th meridian. The United States, the telegram read, would want 'in great secrecy' notification of movement of British convoys so that American patrol units 'can seek out any ships or planes of aggressor nations operating west of the new line of the security zone'. America would then 'immediately make public to you' the location of such 'aggressor ships or planes'.[3]

Churchill at once dictated a reply to Roosevelt, expressing deep gratitude 'for your momentous cable'. United States patrols to the 25th meridian were, he said, 'a long step towards salvation'.[4] This was all that Churchill had asked, and more than he had hoped. 'I transmitted this telegram to the Admiralty,' he later wrote, 'with a deep sense of relief.'[5]

Amid momentous events, Churchill had time to concern himself with the reputation of a man who could no longer speak for himself. On April 5 he had been sent an Air Ministry booklet, the *Battle of Britain*. It was, he replied at once, an 'admirable' booklet, but he added, 'I can not help regretting that Sir Hugh Dowding, the Commander-in-Chief in this great battle, is not mentioned in it.'[6] On April 12, after his return from Bristol, he made his protest direct to Sinclair. 'This is not a good story,' he wrote, and continued:

[1] John G. Winant, *A Letter from Grosvenor Square, An Account of a Stewardship*, London 1947, pages 48–9.
[2] Colville diary, 12 April 1941: Colville papers.
[3] 'Message to the Former Naval Person from the President', 11 April 1941: Premier papers, 3/460/2. When, at Chequers, Colville asked Averell Harriman if Roosevelt's decision 'might mean war with Germany', Harriman replied: 'That's what I hope.' (Colville diary, 13 April 1941: Colville papers.)
[4] Prime Minister's Personal Telegram, T.68, Foreign Office Telegram No. 2003, 13 April 1941, despatched 4.40 a.m.: Premier papers, 3/460/2.
[5] Winston S. Churchill, *The Second World War*, volume 3, London 1950, page 116.
[6] Letter to H. A. St G. Saunders, 5 April 1941: Churchill papers, 2/422.

The jealousies and cliquism which have led the committing of this offence are a discredit to the Air Ministry, and I do not think any other Service Department would have been guilty of such a piece of work. What would have been said if the War Office had produced the story of the Battle of Libya and had managed to exclude General Wavell's name, or if the Admiralty had told the tale of Trafalgar and left Lord Nelson out of it!

It grieves me very much that you should associate yourself with such behaviour. I am sure you were not consulted beforehand on the point, and your natural loyalty to everything done in your Department can alone have led you to condone what nine out of ten men would unhesitatingly condemn.[1]

On April 13 German troops entered Belgrade. In Greece, British, Australian and New Zealand troops prepared to defend the Aliakhmon line. In Iraq, a new scene of conflict, a pro-German coup d'état by Rashid Ali threatened Britain's oil and strategic supply lines throughout the Middle East.[2] In Libya, Rommel's forces had captured Bardia and were encircling Tobruk, opening up the prospect, as Churchill told the Defence Committee that morning, of driving Britain, not only out of Cyrenaica, but out of Egypt 'altogether'. Churchill added:

It was true that even if the Canal were lost, the Mediterranean Fleet, together with such merchant shipping as happened to be in the Mediterranean at the time, would undoubtedly fight its way out westwards, but we should lose our whole army of about half a million men and all their equipment. This would not mean losing the war, but it was unthinkable that we should suffer a disaster of such magnitude without making a supreme effort to avert it.

The Royal Navy, Churchill urged, should bombard Tripoli, and if thereby sufficient damage were caused to delay the German advance by two or three months, the loss of one or two capital ships 'would be amply justified'. It was, Churchill declared, 'unthinkable that we should sit idle and allow a terrible misfortune to overtake us without having taken serious risks to avert it'. The 'honour of the Navy' was involved.[3]

---

[1] Prime Minister's Personal Minute, M.432/1, 12 April 1941: Churchill papers, 20/36.

[2] Plans were at once drawn up to send reinforcements from India to Iraq. At first these plans met with Churchill's disapproval. But two weeks later he telegraphed to General Auchinleck, the Commander-in-Chief, India: 'We are greatly obliged to you for the alacrity with which you have improved on your previous arrangements.' (Prime Minister's Personal Telegram, T.119, War Office No. 63891, 28 April 1941: Churchill papers, 20/38.)

[3] British naval forces bombarded Tripoli at dawn on 21 April 1941. The British force, Churchill told the House of Commons on 22 April 1941, 'was not seriously molested and suffered no loss in ships'. (*Hansard*, 22 April 1941.) On 22 April 1941 Admiral Cunningham informed the Admiralty

At this same meeting, the Defence Committee authorised the despatch of air- and sea-borne troops from India to Iraq, and pressed upon the Government of India, in whose sphere the Iraq operations lay, the need for an 'Air demonstration' over Baghdad.[1]

The fortunes of battle changed with every hour; and on April 14, Easter Monday, six battles were in progress; in Yugoslavia, in Greece, in Cyrenaica, in Iraq, on the Atlantic Ocean and above Britain.[2]

From London, Churchill and his advisers read and discussed each day the dozens of important telegrams describing distant, unclear and yet vital events. Setbacks were succeeded by triumphs, triumphs overtaken by disaster. 'Bravo Tobruk,' Churchill telegraphed to Wavell on April 14, when he learned that the German assault had been thrown back, six out of twenty of the attacking German tanks captured, 12 out of the fifty dive-bombers shot down, and more than 200 German prisoners taken.[3] In a directive that same day to the Chiefs of Staff, Churchill set out various suggestions for regaining the initiative, particularly at sea, and stating:

> It is above all necessary that General Wavell should regain unit ascendancy over the enemy and destroy his small raiding parties, instead of our being harassed and hunted by them. Enemy patrols must be attacked on every occasion, and our own patrols should be used with audacity. Small British parties in armoured cars, or mounted on motor-cycles, or, if occasion offers, infantry, should not hesitate to attack individual tanks with bombs and bombards, as is planned for the defence of Britain.

It was important, Churchill added, 'to engage the enemy even in small affairs in order to make him fire off his gun ammunition, of which the

---

that he did not wish to repeat the attack as he doubted if he could achieve surprise again, and that in carrying out the attack the Fleet had already run 'unjustifiable risks'. (Signal 118, 'Hush, Most Secret', 2.36 p.m., 22 April 1941: Churchill papers, 4/351B.)

[1] Defence Committee No. 13 of 1941, 11.15 a.m., 13 April 1941: Cabinet papers, 69/2.

[2] Following the Coventry and Bristol raids of April 8 and 11, the dockyards at Belfast were bombed on the night of April 15, London on April 16 and Portsmouth on April 17 and 27. The April 16 raid was one of the heaviest raids of the war on the capital, with 450 German war planes taking part. On the following morning Colville noted in his diary: 'London looks bleary-eyed and disfigured. There is a great gash in the Admiralty. St Peter's, Eaton Square, has been hit (and Mr Austin Thompson killed), Chelsea Old Church is demolished, Jermyn Street is wrecked. Mayfair has suffered badly. After breakfast Eric Seal and I walked in the sun on the Horse Guards' parade and found Pamela Churchill and Averell Harriman also examining the devastation. The streets were soon full of people intent on sight-seeing. The roads everywhere were covered with glass.' (Colville diary, 17 April 1941: Colville papers.) During April 1941, civilian deaths in Britain from German air raids totalled 6,065.

[3] Prime Minister's Personal Telegram, T.73, 14 April 1941: despatched as War Office No. 61627, 15 April 1941, 3.40 a.m.: Cabinet papers, 69/2.

supply must be very difficult'.[1] 'All this,' Churchill reflected nine years later, 'was easier to say than do.'[2]

To Air Chief Marshal Longmore, whose aircraft were now in action both in the western desert and Greece, Churchill telegraphed on April 15 his praise for the Air Force's 'vigorous reactions', adding: 'Now is the time to strike.' The Government, Churchill assured Longmore, 'were crowding everything we can out to you, and stream is now beginning to flow'.[3]

Longmore responded to Churchill's encouragement, which was, he said, 'greatly appreciated', and he reported confidently: 'The game is plentiful both in the air and on the ground and we are taking heavy toll of Germans both in Libya and Greece.'[4] In Libya, at least, the situation seemed to be improving, despite the loss of almost the whole of Cyrenaica. Tobruk, Churchill told Wavell on April 17, 'is your offensive hook, and has called their bluff to some purpose already'. Churchill added, with a veiled reference to the most recent Enigma decrypts: 'All our best information shows they are frightfully short of everything. It would be a fine thing to cop the lot. This is certainly possible if we can cut off their supplies and wear them down.'[5]

On April 14, aware from the Enigma decrypts of the extent to which German war material was now being poured into Libya, Churchill issued a directive in which he wrote: 'If the Germans can continue to nourish their invasion of Cyrenaica and Egypt through the port of Tripoli and along the coastal road they can certainly bring superior armoured forces to bear upon us with consequences of the most serious character.' If, on the other hand, their communications from Italy and Sicily with Tripoli were cut, 'and those along the coastal road between Tripoli and Agheila constantly harassed, there is no reason why they should not themselves sustain a major defeat'. Churchill added that to stop the sea-borne traffic 'heavy losses in battleships, cruisers and destroyers, must if necessary be accepted'. Every German convoy that got through, he warned, 'must be considered a serious naval failure'.[6]

---

[1] 'The War in the Mediterranean', 'Most Secret', 14 April 1941: Cabinet papers, 120/10.

[2] Winston S. Churchill, *The Second World War*, volume 3, London 1950, page 188.

[3] Prime Minister's Personal Telegram, T.80, Air Ministry No. X.624, 15 April 1941: Churchill papers, 20/37.

[4] No. X.5105, 'Immediate', 15 April 1941, received 5 p.m.: Churchill papers, 20/37. 'We do not feel at all outmatched at present in the air,' Churchill telegraphed to Roosevelt on April 16, 'and are growing stronger constantly.' (Prime Minister's Personal Telegram, T.78, Foreign Office No. 2057, 16 April 1941, despatched 17 April 1941, 2 a.m.: Churchill papers, 20/37.)

[5] Prime Minister's Personal Telegram, T.84, War Office No. 004, despatched 8.30 p.m., 17 April 1941: Churchill papers, 20/37.

[6] 'The War in the Mediterranean', 'Most Secret', 14 April 1941: Cabinet papers, 120/10.

Two days after Churchill issued this directive, British warships sank a German–Italian convoy of two supply ships and three escorting Italian destroyers between Sicily and Tripoli. These supply ships were carrying units of the 15 Panzer Division to Africa. Although a British destroyer, the *Mohawk*, was sunk, the engagement constituted the first significant victory for the German Air Force Enigma decrypts in the Mediterranean shipping war, and took the cutting edge off the knife of danger on which Churchill's directive had focused. Henceforth, and with increasing impact, German and Italian high grade decrypts were to contribute significantly to the sinking of Axis supply ships.[1]

On April 16, at the Battle of the Atlantic Committee, Churchill was also able to report 'a considerable improvement' in the rate of discharge of bulk cargoes in their British ports of arrival. Averell Harriman had likewise reported 'a considerable improvement in recent weeks'.

Churchill then proposed a further saving in the round voyage timings, if the loading of ships in Britain 'were cut out, exports being sacrificed', and the ships sent back to the United States unloaded or only partly loaded to collect their next cargo of vital war supplies.[2]

At the Defence Committee later that evening, Churchill told his colleagues that it should be explained to the Press, which was concerned about the danger of British troops being 'cut off' in Greece, that Britain was 'in a dilemma'. If the Government announced that 'everything was going well' in Greece, and then bad news came, it would be 'accused of concealing the truth'. If it announced that the situation was very serious and likely to deteriorate, it would 'discourage those taking part in the operations and particularly the Greeks'. Emphasis should at least be laid, he said, on the 'heroic struggle' of the Greeks 'and of the great sufferings they had endured for the cause'.

The note to strike about Egypt, Churchill told the Defence Committee, 'was one of subdued confidence'. The Press must not, however, lose sight of the fact that the Battle of the Atlantic and the attitude of the United States of America 'were the decisive factors in the war'.[3]

*   *   *

[1] F. H. Hinsley and others, *British Intelligence in the Second World War, Its Influence on Strategy and Operations*, volume 1, London 1979, pages 394 and 400. This Enigma success, one of the official historians, Edward Thomas, has written, 'set the pattern for a most important development', the setting up of 'Force K'. As Thomas noted, Churchill had 'immediately grasped the significance' of this Enigma success. (Edward Thomas, notes for the author, 3 December 1982.) For the story of 'Force K' see page 1172.

[2] Battle of the Atlantic Committee No. 5 of 1941, 5 p.m., 16 April 1941: Cabinet papers, 86/1.

[3] Defence Committee (Operations) No. 16 of 1941, 16 April 1941, 9.45 p.m.: Cabinet papers, 69/2.

In Greece, German troops were driving southwards with such force through the Greek and British positions that on April 16 General Papagos suggested that British troops should be re-embarked, and leave Greece altogether, in order to 'save Greece from devastation'.[1] At the Defence Committee in London that night, it was decided that if such a withdrawal did take place, the troops should be sent to Crete, and Crete 'held in force' against the Germans.[2] 'We shall aid and maintain defence of Crete to the utmost,' Churchill telegraphed to Wavell, in the early hours of April 17, with the approval of the Defence Committee.[3]

On April 17 the Yugoslav army surrendered to its overwhelmingly stronger German attackers, and King Peter was flown to safety by a Royal Air Force flying boat which picked him up on the Dalmatian coast. On April 18 the Greek Prime Minister committed suicide. That afternoon Churchill saw the Press editors 'to prepare their minds', as Colville noted, 'for grave possibilities in Greece'.[4] And in answer to a request from Longmore as to which of the war zones should receive priority, given the shortage of aircraft to fight adequately in each, Churchill telegraphed, with the approval of the Chiefs of Staff Committee: 'Libya counts first, evacuation of troops from Greece second, Tobruk shipping unless indispensable to victory must be fitted in as convenient, Iraq can be ignored and Crete worked up later.'[5]

On April 18, in a radio broadcast, the German Government warned that both Athens and Cairo might soon be bombed, as reprisal against a British bombing raid on Berlin on the previous night, April 17. Churchill at once issued a statement from Downing Street which began: 'In view of the German threats to bomb Athens and Cairo, His Majesty's Government wish it to be understood that if either of these two cities is molested, they will commence a systematic bombing of Rome. Once this has begun, it will continue as convenient till the end of the war.' The 'greatest care' Churchill added, 'will be taken not to bomb the Vatican city, and the strictest orders to that effect have been issued'.[6]

---

[1] Report of a conversation between General Wilson and Papagos, sent by Wilson to Cairo at 5 p.m. on 16 April 1941, and passed on to London by Wavell in his telegram 0/57341 of 16 April 1941, despatched 7.15 p.m., received in London 10.50 p.m.: Cabinet papers, 65/18.

[2] Decision reported to the War Cabinet on the morning of 17 April 1941, War Cabinet No. 41 of 1941, 17 April 1941, 12 Noon, Minute 2, Confidential Annex: Cabinet papers, 65/22.

[3] Telegram No. 836, despatched 3.25 a.m., 17 April 1941: Churchill papers, 20/37.

[4] Colville diary, 18 April 1941: Colville papers.

[5] Prime Minister's Personal Telegram, T.87, 18 April 1941: Churchill papers, 20/37.

[6] 'Telephoned to BBC, 5.20 p.m.', 18 April 1941: Premier papers, 3/14/3, folios 451–2.

On April 19 Churchill took 'an afternoon off', as John Martin described it, visiting the Czech President in Exile, Eduard Beneš, and inspecting the Czech forces. He was accompanied by Clementine Churchill, Winant, Harriman and Biddle. Martin wrote home:

I thought it rather moving—all those poor exiles, the tiny remnant of an army and they were so pleased to be visited and eager in their welcome. We had tea in the officers' mess—a band, a singer, their own special cakes and neat whiskey handed round in small glasses. As the PM left a choir of soldiers sang Rule Britannia with great enthusiasm. We also had that sad National Anthem. They showered on the Churchills all sorts of gifts of their own making—drawings, coloured woodwork, embroidery, etc.

It is again quite an American party, with three of Roosevelt's envoys. We also have the Chief of the Air Staff (Sir Charles Portal) and Lord Rothermere.[1]

On April 20 Churchill learned from Wavell that the British forces in Egypt were dangerously short of tanks, and from the Enigma decrypts that Rommel was likely to be reinforced by a German armoured division. It was Sunday. Churchill was at Ditchley Park. Believing in the urgent reinforcement of Wavell's army, he summoned Ismay to Ditchley. The Chiefs of Staff, he instructed Ismay, must meet at once.[2]

The Chiefs of Staff met that evening, and, despite their initial hesitations, agreed by noon the following day to Churchill's plan to send Wavell immediate reinforcements 'at all costs'. The result was operation 'Tiger'.[3] 'The risks of losing the vehicles,' Churchill minuted to Ismay, 'or part of them, must be accepted. Even if half got through, the situation would be restored.' The personnel for the tanks would travel on the longer, but far safer route via the Cape. As for the tanks themselves, 'the enemy's dive-bombers have many other objectives, and they will not know what the convoy contains'. Planning must be started at once. 'Speed is vital. Every day's delay must be avoided.' To ensure the maximum secrecy possible, 'no one outside the highest circles need know of the intention to turn off at Gibraltar. Everyone on board the convoys must think they are going round the Cape.'[4]

---

[1] Letter of 20 April 1941: Martin papers. Lord Rothermere was the 2nd Viscount, son of Churchill's friend Esmond Rothermere who had died three months earlier.

[2] The Memoirs of General the Lord Ismay, London 1960, page 202.

[3] Not to be confused with the earlier 'Tiger' of July 1940, the proposal to send fighter squadrons to Turkey, see page 677.

[4] Prime Minister's Personal Minute, D.130/1, 'Most Secret', to Ismay for the Chiefs of Staff Committee, 20 April 1941: Premier papers, 3/432, folios 39–41. In the event, secrecy was maintained, and only one of the ships in the convoy was sunk. Of the 295 tanks sent through the Mediterranean, 238 reached Wavell safely before the end of May.

'A momentous decision was taken today,' Colville noted. 'Operation "Tiger" was adopted.'[1]

The problem was not only shipping the vital tanks to Egypt, but substantially increasing tank production in Britain to fill the gap. To this end, on April 21, Churchill authorised Ismay to set up 'a conference on tank questions and future developments'.[2] Two weeks later this came into being as the 'Tank Parliament', in which the Ministers concerned, senior civil servants and technical experts discussed as a matter of urgency, the necessary measures to accelerate production.[3]

One area of possible material aid for Britain was, apparently, the Soviet Union, neutral for the past nineteen months, her resources untouched and untapped. The British Ambassador in Moscow, Sir Stafford Cripps, favoured an approach to the Soviet authorities, and some sort of exchange of goods needed by the Soviets, possibly from the United States, for goods needed by Britain. Telegrams had already been sent to this effect by Cripps to the Foreign Office, and from the Foreign Office to Washington.[4]

Churchill deprecated any such move, telling Eden on Aprill 22 that the Soviets 'know perfectly well their dangers and also that we need their aid. You will get much more out of them by letting these forces work than by frantic efforts to assure them of your love. This only looks like weakness and encourages them to believe they are stronger than they are.' Churchill added: 'Now is the moment for a sombre restraint on our part, and let them do the worrying.' Above all, he wrote, 'we ought not to fret the Americans about it'.[5]

When the War Cabinet met on the afternoon of April 21, it had to consider a telegram from Wavell, sent only an hour earlier from Athens, advising the immediate evacuation of all British forces from Greece, or, as Wavell phrased it, 'such portion of his army as he could'.[6]

The evacuation from Greece began at once. 'In the execution of this

---

[1] Colville diary, 21 April 1941: Colville papers. Late that night Churchill telegraphed to Wavell: 'I have been working hard for you in the last few days. . . .' (Prime Minister's Personal Telegram, T.100, 'Personal and Most Secret', despatched at 1.10 a.m., 22 April 1941: Churchill papers, 20/49.)

[2] Prime Minister's Personal Minute, D.132/1, 21 April 1941: Cabinet papers, 120/52.

[3] The first Tank Parliament met on 5 May 1941, the fourth and last on 19 June 1941.

[4] Moscow Telegrams No. 387 and 388 and Foreign Office Telegram No. 2111 to Washington.

[5] 'Action this Day', Prime Minister's Personal Minute, M.461/1, 22 April 1941: Churchill papers, 20/36.

[6] Wavell, Wilson and Palairet had seen the King of Greece in Athens on the morning of 21 April 1941. Wavell's report of the meeting, and of his proposal to end the Greek campaign, was sent from Athens at 2.40 p.m., reaching London at 4 p.m., that same day, Telegram No. 772, War Cabinet No. 42 of 1941, 21 April 1941, 5 p.m., Minute 2, Confidential Annex: Cabinet papers, 65/22.

policy,' Churchill telegraphed to Wavell shortly before midnight on April 21, 'you will no doubt not worry about vehicles or stores but get the men away. We can re-arm them later.'[1]

During the nights of April 24 and April 25 a total of 17,000 men were brought away from the coves and beaches of Greece. During April 26 German forces seized Corinth, the Corinth Isthmus and the vital bridge over the Corinth Canal, driving on through the Peloponnese towards the southernmost beaches. The Aliakhmon line, of which much had been hoped, was broken up. At Thermopylae, Allied troops fought a desperate action on the scene of ancient heroism. But German air power overwhelmed them, and during April 26 Athens itself came within range of the German artillery. That same day, General Papagos resigned as Commander-in-Chief of the Greek Army.

On the night of April 26, more than 19,000 further troops were evacuated from the beaches, but under intense air bombardment. In a series of German dive bomber attacks, 700 survivors of the sunken transport *Slamat*, who had been rescued by the destroyers *Diamond* and *Wryneck*, were again dive bombed, and 650 of them were killed. By April 30 more than 50,000 soldiers and airmen had been evacuated: British, Australians, New Zealanders, Cypriots, Greeks, Yugoslavs and Palestinian Jews. But over 11,500 men had been taken prisoner. 'I am afraid you have been having a very worrying time lately,' Princess Elizabeth wrote to Churchill on April 23—in thanking him for 'the lovely roses you sent me for my birthday'—and she added: 'but I am sure things will begin to look up again soon'.[2]

During the course of the week-long evacuation, twenty-six Allied ships were sunk by air attack, including five hospital ships. At midnight on April 24, as the evacuation from Greece had begun, the American Atlantic Fleet took up its new positions in the western Atlantic, to establish its extended Security Zone two thousand miles out from the east coast of the United States: an act unheralded by the headlines, but of cardinal significance for the war, and for British morale. 'We are deeply impressed,' Churchill telegraphed to Roosevelt, 'by the rapidity with which it is being brought into play.' The 'action you have taken', he added, 'may well decide the battle of the Atlantic in a favourable sense'.[3] These hopes, however, like the earlier hopes for Cyrenaica, were premature.

---

[1] Prime Minister's Personal Telegram, T.99, Foreign Office No. 772, 'Personal and Secret', 'Most Immediate', despatched at 1.10 a.m., 22 April 1941: Churchill papers, 20/37.

[2] Letter from Windsor Castle, 23 April 1941: Churchill papers, 20/29. Princess Elizabeth celebrated her fifteenth birthday on 21 April 1941.

[3] Prime Minister's Personal Telegram, T.111, Foreign Office No. 2204 to Washington, de-

Churchill now set off for a tour of Liverpool, Manchester and Merseyside, accompanied by Averell Harriman, and the most recent of Roosevelt's emissaries, James Forrestal, with whom he had already had 'long talks' at Ditchley. Their purpose, Churchill telegraphed to Roosevelt, was 'to study the position in the Mersey area, so important to the North-Western Approaches'.[1]

Two days later, in an evening broadcast from Chequers, Churchill spoke of the 'exaltation of spirit' he had seen in his recent tours of Britain's bombed cities, of the earlier triumphs of General Wavell 'whom we cheered in good days and will back through bad', of the Greek appeal for British help—'Strained as were our own resources, we could not say them nay'—of the Yugoslav revolution, of Yugoslavia 'struck down by the ruthless and highly-mechanized Hun', of the 'vexatious and damaging defeat' in Libya, of the Egyptian front held by 'the fortress of Tobruk', and of Greece 'overwhelmed'.

One thing was certain about war, Churchill told his listeners, 'that it is full of disappointments and also of mistakes'. The Germans might have made a mistake in making 'a river of blood and hate between themselves and the Greek and Yugoslav peoples'. The war might spread to Spain or Morocco, to Turkey or Russia. 'The Huns may lay their hands for a time upon the granaries of the Ukraine and the oil wells of the Caucasus. They may dominate the Black Sea. They may dominate the Caspian. Who can tell?' But one thing was certain, to win the war, Hitler must either conquer Britain by invasion, 'or he must cut the ocean life-line which joins us to the United States'.

Churchill then spoke of Roosevelt's commitments to Britain, of American munitions production for British needs, and of the new patrol zone. The war had entered 'a more grim but at the same time a far more favourable phase'. The United States were 'very closely bound up with us now'. In the 'awful struggle' there could be 'no drawing back'. But his faith in victory was absolute, as he explained:

No prudent and far-seeing man can doubt that the eventual and total defeat of Hitler and Mussolini is certain, in view of the respective declared resolves of

---

spatched 3.30 p.m., 25 April 1941: Premier papers, 3/460/1, folio 3. Three days later Churchill telegraphed to Lord Halifax in Washington: 'Do not discourage the President from posing his questions direct to me or allow any of the Naval Staff to do so. My personal relations with him are of importance, and it would be a pity if they were superseded by ordinary staff routine.' (Prime Minister's Personal Telegram, T.116, 28 April 1941: Foreign Office papers, 954/29, folio 160.)

[1] Prime Minister's Personal Telegram, T.106, Foreign Office No. 2186 to Washington, despatched 2.45 p.m., 24 April 1941: Churchill papers, 20/38.

the British and American democracies. There are less than seventy million malignant Huns—some of whom are curable and others killable[1]—many of whom are already engaged in holding down Austrians, Czechs, Poles, French and the many other ancient races they now bully and pillage.

The peoples of the British Empire and of the United States number nearly two hundred millions in their homelands and in the British Dominions alone. They possess the unchallengeable command of the oceans, and will soon obtain decisive superiority in the air. They have more wealth, more technical resources, and they make more steel, than the whole of the rest of the world put together. They are determined that the cause of freedom shall not be trampled down, nor the tide of world progress turned backwards, by the criminal Dictators.

However much one viewed with 'sorrow and anxiety' many of the events happening in Europe and in Africa, and events which 'may happen in Asia', one must not, Churchill told his listeners, lose a sense of proportion 'and thus become discouraged or alarmed'. Nothing that was happening now was 'comparable in gravity' with the dangers through which Britain had passed in 1940.

Churchill ended with the poem he had recited to Arthur Salter before sending him on his Shipping Mission to the United States. They were lines, he said, 'apt and appropriate to our fortunes tonight' and would be so judged 'wherever the English language is spoken or the flag of freedom flies'. The lines were, as Churchill spoke them:

> For while the tired waves, vainly breaking,
> Seem here no painful inch to gain,
> Far back, through creeks and inlets making,
> Comes silent, flooding in, the main.
>
> And not by eastern windows only,
> When daylight comes, comes in the light;
> In front the sun climbs slow, how slowly!
> But westward, look, the land is bright.[2]

His broadcast over, Churchill dined with Sir Alan Brooke, Commander-in-Chief of Home Forces, Major-General Kennedy, the Director of Military Operations, David Margesson, the Secretary of State

---

[1] This phrase from 'malignant Huns' to 'killable', led Corder Catchpool, veteran pacifist and first world war conscientious objector, to publish an open letter to Churchill in which he declared: 'I think that such a wholesale indictment is not in accordance with truth, and that the spirit it breathes is a pagan spirit, the opposite of what Jesus taught as to the Christian attitude towards sinful mankind. I make bold to prophesy that if this spirit predominates in the minds of our Government and People, then the present generation will pass away without any hope of realising that new and better world for which men are agonising now.' (Letter dated 3 May 1941: Catchpool papers.)

[2] Broadcast, 27 April 1941: Churchill papers, 9/150.

for War, Ismay and Lindemann.[1] The talk continued until 3.30 a.m., and was summarised by Brooke in his diary. When Kennedy contemplated 'a fairly free evacuation of Egypt', Churchill was so 'infuriated' that, as Brooke noted, 'we had some trouble calming him down'.[2]

Churchill had been upset to learn from General Kennedy, for the first time, that plans had been prepared 'in certain eventualities for the evacuation of Egypt'.[3] Kennedy defended the existence of these plans, and argued that they might indeed have to be implemented. 'I cannot get out of my mind,' Kennedy wrote to Churchill on the following day, 'that you may still think I was being defeatist in my discussion with you last night,' and he added: 'I would rather give up my post than hold it upon such a basis. I have never believed, and never will, that we can lose this war. No one under your leadership could believe such a thing.' There was, however, Kennedy argued, 'a limit to the price we can safely pay' for victory in the Middle East.[4]

Despite Churchill's clash with Kennedy, Alan Brooke, for whom it had all been deeply embarrassing, noted that once dinner was over, and the men retired to the Great Hall, 'I had good opportunities discussing my troubles,' in the preparation of Home Defences, troubles which included 'shortage of man-power, loss of tanks transferred to Egypt, danger of concentrating authority for destruction of petrol, danger of forming multitude of detachments from main effort for such efforts as fire-fighting, clearing of houses, agriculture, etc., which can equally well be done by civilians.' Brooke also stressed to Churchill what he called the 'very unsatisfactory air situation at home'.[5]

*　　　*　　　*

[1] But before dining, Churchill telephoned Violet Bonham Carter and to her amazement asked: 'Did you hear my broadcast,' 'Of course I did Winston' she replied, 'Everybody in England listens when you speak.' 'Did you not recognise the poem?' he went on to ask her. Violet Bonham Carter did; thirty-five years earlier she had read it to him, noticing then how struck he had been by it, and staggered now that he should not only remember that poetry reading of so long ago, but also telephone her about it. (Baroness Asquith of Yarnbury, conversation with the author, 25 August 1964.)

[2] Brooke diary, 27 April 1941: Arthur Bryant, *The Turn of the Tide, 1939–43*, London 1957, page 254.

[3] Prime Minister's Personal Minute, M.479/1, 'Most Secret' (to Sir John Dill), 28 April 1941: Churchill papers, 20/36.

[4] Letter of 28 April 1941: Churchill papers, 20/26. Churchill replied on the following day: 'My dear General, Our conversation was purely informal and private. I am very glad to read what you say about it. I do not agree with your views, but you were perfectly entitled to express them.' (Letter of 29 April 1941: Churchill papers, 20/26.)

[5] Brooke diary, 27 April 1941: Arthur Bryant, *The Turn of the Tide, 1939–1943*, London 1957, page 254. On the following day Brooke wrote to Churchill: 'This is just a short line to thank you again for your great kindness in inviting me periodically to Chequers, and of thus giving me an opportunity of discussing the problems of the Defence of this Country with you, and of putting some of my difficulties before you. These informal talks are of the very greatest help to me, & I do hope you realize how grateful I am to you for your kindness.' (Churchill papers, 20/24.)

On April 28 Enigma decrypts revealed an imminent German attack on Crete by sea and air. Churchill telegraphed to Wavell: 'It seems clear from our information that a heavy airborne attack by German troops and bombers will soon be made on Crete.[1] Let me know what forces you have in the island and what your plans are. It ought to be a fine opportunity for killing the parachute troops.' The island, Churchill added, 'must be stubbornly defended'.[2] But to the War Cabinet that evening he told those present that he was 'somewhat doubtful of our ability to hold Crete against a prolonged attack'.

Had Britain not sent troops to Greece, Churchill commented, 'Yugoslavia would not now be an open enemy of Germany. Further, the Greek war had caused a marked change of attitude in the United States.' Now, throughout the eastern Mediterranean, and including Egypt, the 'air menace', he said, 'was the greatest menace which we had to face'.[3] On the following day, during an afternoon 'of busy operational discussions', Colville noted the overriding theme: 'we must save Egypt and Suez at all costs'.[4]

The loss of Egypt and the Middle East, Churchill warned in a War Cabinet directive on April 28, 'would be a disaster of the first magnitude to Great Britain, second only to successful invasion and final conquest'. His directive continued:

Every effort is to be made to reinforce General Wavell with military and Air forces, and if Admiral Cunningham requires more ships, the Admiralty will make proposals for supplying them. It is to be impressed upon all ranks, especially the highest, that the life and honour of Great Britain depends upon the successful defence of Egypt.

It is not to be expected that the British forces of the land, sea and air in the Mediterranean would wish to survive so vast and shameful a defeat as would be entailed by our expulsion from Egypt, having regard to the difficulties of the enemy and his comparatively small numbers. Not only must Egypt be defended, but the Germans have to be beaten and thrown out of Cyrenaica.

---

[1] The 'information' to which Churchill referred was that contained in the most recent Enigma decrypts, also available in summary form, but not in the original, to Wavell.

[2] Prime Minister's Personal Telegram, T.117, War Office No. 63822, telephoned from Chequers, 11.30 a.m., despatched from London 4.10 p.m., 28 April 1941: Premier papers, 3/109, folio 152.

[3] War Cabinet No. 44 of 1941, 28 April 1941, 5 p.m., Minute 2, Confidential Annex: Cabinet papers, 65/22.

[4] Colville diary, 29 April 1941: Colville papers. On the same day Churchill minuted bitterly to Ismay: 'Is it not rather strange that, when we announced that the port of Benghazi while in our occupation was of no use, and, secondly, that on our evacuation we had completely blocked it, the enemy are using it freely?' (Prime Minister's Personal Minute, D.144/1: Churchill papers, 20/36.)

'This offensive objective,' Churchill added, 'must be set before the troops.'

To prevent any loss of morale should Britain's contingency plans become known, Churchill ordered that:

All plans for evacuation of Egypt or for closing or destroying the Suez Canal are to be called in and kept under the strict personal control of Headquarters. No whisper of such plans is to be allowed. No surrenders by officers and men will be considered tolerable unless at least 50 per cent casualties are sustained by the Unit or force in question. According to Napoleon's maxim, 'when a man is caught alone and unarmed, a surrender may be made'. But Generals and Staff Officers surprised by the enemy are to use their pistols in self defence. The honour of a wounded man is safe.

'Anyone who can kill a Hun or even an Italian,' Churchill continued, 'has rendered a good service,' and he went on: 'The Army of the Nile is to fight with no thought of retreat or withdrawal. This task is enforced upon it by physical facts, for it will be utterly impossible to find the shipping for moving a tithe of the immense masses of men and stores which have been gathered in the Nile Valley.'[1]

Many other fears pressed in upon Churchill as he contemplated a victorious German army and air force in control of Greece. Upon Turkey, he told Roosevelt, 'dangerous demands' might be made, and Britain would be 'content if Turkey remained an unmolested pad, protecting, albeit passively, our Eastern flank in Egypt'. A 'far more imminent' danger was Syria, where German air-borne troops might land, after refuelling at Rhodes. Such forces, once installed in Syria, would soon 'penetrate and poison' both Iran and Iraq, and threaten Palestine.[2] 'We have also to fight for Crete, which may, according to our information, soon be attacked.'[3]

[1] 'Most Secret', 'Directive by the Prime Minister and Minister of Defence', 28 April 1941: Premier papers, 3/156/6, folios 138–9.

[2] In the last week of April 1941 Professor Lindemann had suggested to Churchill that plans should be made to destroy the oil wells of Iran. On reading Lindemann's note, Churchill minuted for Ismay and the Chiefs of Staff: 'If any preparations are made, they would have to be made secretly, and at the same time we should have to have a substantial armed force in plain clothes on the spot. We must expect that, if the Shah falls under the German influence or menace, he will soon be looking after his wells for them. What has been done about this?' (Prime Minister's Personal Minute, D.145/1, 29 April 1941: Churchill papers, 20/36.)

[3] Although 'our evidence points the other way', Churchill minuted to Ismay for the Chiefs of Staff Committee on April 29, 'we must not exclude the possibility that Crete is a blind, and Syria or Cyprus the quarry'. (Prime Minister's Personal Minute, D.147/1, 29 April 1941: Churchill papers, 20/36.) 'It may be,' Churchill telegraphed to Peter Fraser, Prime Minister of New Zealand, on 3 May 1941, 'that the enemy is only feinting at Crete, and will be going further east.' (Prime Minister's Personal Telegram, T.136, 'Most Secret' 8 p.m., 3 May 1941: Premier papers, 3/109, folios 139–40.)

In the western Mediterranean, Churchill told Roosevelt, the Spanish situation was 'most critical' and Hitler, if he obtained control of the Spanish batteries dominating Gibraltar, could establish German control, and the German air force, in Morocco, after which 'it will not be long before Dakar becomes a German U-boat base'.

It was up to Roosevelt, Churchill urged, to put 'the most extreme pressure' on Vichy France to break with Germany if the Germans 'violate Syria, Morocco, Algeria or Tunis'. Important areas would be lost if America did not act to exert this pressure, and if at 'a later period' the United States became a belligerent, 'we should all have a much longer journey to take'.

Churchill's telegram ended: 'I feel Hitler may quite easily now gain vast advantage very cheaply, and we are so fully engaged that we can do little—nothing to stop him spreading himself.'[1]

Each day, Churchill worked for greater United States involvement. But the Foreign Office had opposed an American request for British warships to help escort United States troops to Iceland. Such an escort would be needed, the Americans explained, in the event of an American occupation of Iceland if war were ever imminent between Germany and the United States. The Foreign Office argument, made on behalf of the War Office and the Admiralty, was that to provide any such British escort would inconvenience British shipping schedules, and a telegram to this effect was sent to Washington. 'I would rather,' Churchill minuted to Eden, A. V. Alexander and Margesson, 'that telegrams of this kind should not be sent without my seeing them first. What does the convenience of our shipping mean compared to engaging the Americans in the war? A negative answer like this is chilling and ill-suited to our present purpose.'[2]

A second cause for anger was the discovery a few days later that the head of the British naval mission in Washington, Admiral Danckwerts, had declined an official United States suggestion to move a substantial portion of the American Pacific Fleet to the Atlantic. 'Our chance of victory,' Churchill told the Defence Committee on May 1, 'was almost

[1] Prime Minister's Personal Telegram, T.123, 29 April 1941: Premier papers, 3/187, folios 100–2. Yet another fear was expressed by Beaverbrook, in conversation with his fellow Press proprietor, Lord Camrose, who noted that after lunch on 1 May 1941 'Beaverbrook took me aside and said that the war was assuming a very ugly shape, that the Germans would launch a very full attack against us with all their resources in the next few days. It was a very serious position indeed and he emphasized that we would have to bear the brunt of a tremendous attack by the Germans immediately. He emphasized again "in a few days". He added—"In my opinion invasion is imminent. Although I know some people do not agree with me, I am sure I am right." ' (Memorandum dated 1 May 1941: Camrose papers.)

[2] Prime Minister's Personal Minute, M.486/1, 29 April 1941: Premier papers, 3/230/1, folio 44.

certainly bound up with American participation; and within the last
two or three days he had thought it right to send a personal telegram
to Mr Roosevelt begging him to do his utmost to get the United States
of America into the war as soon as possible.' It was therefore 'disturbing' Churchill added, 'to find that when two of the President's principal
colleagues had suggested an advance into the Atlantic, the suggestion
had been received with a cold douche'.[1]

This 'cold douche' was doubly vexing since Churchill had learned,
at the Battle of the Atlantic Committee on the previous afternoon,
'that after a period of very few sinkings in the North West Approaches
there had been a successful U-boat attack on a convoy in daylight on
the previous day. This was the first attack in daylight on an escorted
convoy for six months.'[2]

On April 30 Iraqi troops attacked British forces and civilians in the
Habbaniya air base. 'So you've got another war on your hands
tonight,' Churchill remarked during the day to Sir Alexander Cadogan.[3] A German air raid on Plymouth had caused further devastation
to docks and homes.[4] At sea, the sinking of British, Allied and neutral
merchant shipping had risen to a total of 581,251 tons sunk in April
alone, of which 187,054 tons had been sunk in Greek ports during the
evacuation.

As a matter of urgency, Churchill now set up an air equivalent of
the 'Tiger' operation, whereby tanks were to be sent across the Mediterranean to Egypt. Two earlier operations, 'Winch' and 'Dunlop',
had been used to carry fighter planes in convoy through the danger
zones of the Mediterranean. Under this further operation, a total of
140 fighters would be convoyed by the end of May on board the aircraft
carriers *Ark Royal*, *Argus*, *Furious* and *Victorious*. The codename of this
vital dash was to be 'Jaguar'. On April 30 Churchill minuted to Ismay,
A. V. Alexander, Pound and Beaverbrook:

All concerned are reminded that we have in the Middle East an army of
nearly half a million men, whose whole fighting value may be frustrated and

---

[1] Defence Committee No. 22 of 1941, 1 May 1941, 1 p.m.: Cabinet papers, 69/2.

[2] Battle of the Atlantic Committee No. 7 of 1941, 5 p.m., 30 April 1941: Cabinet papers, 86/1.

[3] Cadogan diary, 30 April 1941: David Dilks (editor), *The Diaries of Sir Alexander Cadogan OM,
1938–1945*, London 1971, page 375. On 2 May 1941, in reply to the Iraqi attack on Habbaniya,
British forces occupied Basra.

[4] Churchill visited Plymouth on the morning of 2 May 1941. During the nights of May 1, 2 and
3, Liverpool was the target for German night raids, the last two nights being particularly severe.

even destroyed by a temporary hostile superiority in tanks and aircraft. The failure to win the battle of Egypt would be a disaster of the first magnitude to Great Britain. It might well determine the decisions of Turkey, Spain and Vichy. It might strike the United States the wrong way, i.e., they might think we are no good.

'Thus,' Churchill ended, 'a true sense of proportion must rule, and the necessary accommodations must be made and the inevitable risks run.'[1]

On 1 May 1941 Lord Beaverbrook was appointed Minister of State, with Colonel Moore-Brabazon replacing him as Minister of Aircraft Production. Lord Leathers succeeded Ronald Cross as Minister of Shipping. Beaverbrook's new position included a watching brief, and powers, 'in respect of Priorities'.[2]

Events now superseded plans, as the General Officer Commanding the New Zealand Division on Crete, General Freyberg, telegraphed to Wavell: 'Forces at my disposal are totally inadequate to meet attack envisaged.'[3] But that same day, with the approval of the Chiefs of Staff and the Defence Committee, Churchill telegraphed to Wavell: 'It is now necessary to fight hard for Crete, which seems soon to be heavily attacked.'[4]

From Crete came worse news on May 2, a telegram from New Zealand reporting a message from General Freyberg that the Germans 'can bring to bear upward of 800 planes' while British air strength on the island 'consists of only six Hurricanes and 17 obsolete aircraft'.[5] This ominous telegram crossed with one from Churchill personally to Freyberg, whom he had known and admired since their early meetings during the First World War.[6] 'Congratulate you on your vitally im-

---

[1] 'Most Secret', Prime Minister's Personal Minute, D.149/1, 30 April 1941: Churchill papers, 20/36. 'We are making extreme efforts to re-inforce you from the Air' Churchill telegraphed to Wavell on 1 May 1940. (Prime Minister's Personal Telegram, T.127, 1 May 1941: Churchill papers, 20/38.)

[2] Prime Minister's Personal Minute, C.46/1 (to Sir Edward Bridges, Sir Horace Wilson and Eric Seal): Churchill papers, 20/36.

[3] 'Most Secret and Immediate', 1 May 1941: Churchill papers, 4/217.

[4] Prime Minister's Personal Telegram, T.127, War Office No. 64484, 9.35 p.m., 1 May 1941: Churchill papers, 20/38.

[5] 'Most Secret and Personal', Government of New Zealand to Churchill, Telegram No. 164, received 11.40 a.m., 2 May 1941: Churchill papers, 20/38. Freyberg's telegram had been sent to New Zealand on 1 May 1941.

[6] In the First World War, at Gallipoli and on the western front, Freyberg had been three times gravely wounded, had twenty-seven other wound scars, and had been awarded the Victoria Cross, and the DSO with two bars.

portant command,' Churchill wrote. 'Feel confident your fine troops will destroy parachutists man to man at close quarters. Every good wish.'[1]

During the night of May 1, Churchill had travelled by sleeper to Plymouth, reaching a Devonshire siding at dawn, and drawing into Plymouth Station at 9.30 in the morning. He was accompanied by his wife, Harriman, Pound, Ismay, 'Tommy' Thompson and Colville, who recorded in his diary the day's events, beginning with a tour of the Royal Naval Dockyard:

The PM arrived in a launch and we then walked for miles, along quays, through workshops, over ships. We saw *Centurion*, now a decoy ship made to look like one of the KG V class. Just before lunch we reached the RN barracks, where bombs had killed a number of sailors. There was a gruesome sight in the Gymnasium: beds in which some 40 slightly injured men lay, separated only by a low curtain from some coffins which were being nailed down. The hammering must have been horrible to the injured men, but such has been the damage that there was nowhere else it could be done.

The men lunched in the barracks, in a room decorated with a frieze of wooden ships representing the Armada, designed by Wylie. We had a revolting lunch (tepid brown Windsor soup, etc.!) and then returned to Admiralty House so that the PM might sleep.

At 3.30 we drove around Plymouth. It has suffered five heavy raids in nine nights and scarcely a house seems to be habitable. It is far worse than Bristol: the whole City is wrecked except, characteristically, the important parts of the naval establishment. Mount Edgecumbe, where we used to land from the sea, is burnt out as well. In Plymouth itself I saw a bus which had been carried bodily, by the force of an explosion, on to the roof of a building some 150 yards from where it had been standing.

We had tea at Lady Astor's house, where I had a long talk with the wife of the Regional Commissioner, Lady Elles.

At 6.30 we left the scene of horror and desolation on the return journey to Chequers, where we arrived at midnight.

On entering Chequers, Churchill was confronted with news which made him, as Colville recorded, 'gravely depressed'. It was, indeed, depressing news, from four quite separate spheres. As Colville explained, Churchill had then to read:

A long telegram from Roosevelt explaining that the US could not cooperate with us in preventing Germany from seizing the Azores and Cape Verde Islands; news that one of the ships containing many tanks for the reinforcement of Wavell (Operation Tiger) had developed serious engine trouble; a signal that HMS *Jersey*, one of Lord Louis Mountbatten's destroyers, had

---

[1] Prime Minister's Personal Telegram, T.134, 2 May 1941: Premier papers, 3/109, folio 135.

sunk at Malta blocking the Grand Harbour; and finally the fact that the Iraqis, who opened fire on our troops this morning (two hours before we had intended firing on them!) were fighting well and were not proving to be the rabble we expected.

The Prime Minister, Colville noted, was 'in the worst gloom that I had ever seen him', and at once dictated a telegram to Roosevelt 'drawing a sombre picture of what a collapse in the Middle East would entail'. Churchill then sketched out, for Harriman, Ismay and Colville, 'a world in which Hitler dominated all Europe, Asia and Africa, and left the US and ourselves no option but an unwilling peace'.[1]

Churchill's telegram to Roosevelt was a cry of anguish and an appeal for help: help in the form of the entry of the United States into the war, echoing, but with an even greater appeal than at the time of the fall of France ten and a half months earlier. The message read:

We must not be too sure that the consequences of the loss of Egypt and the Middle East would not be grave. It would seriously increase the hazards of the Atlantic and the Pacific, and could hardly fail to prolong the war, with all the suffering and military dangers that this would entail. We shall fight on whatever happens, but please remember that the attitude of Spain, Vichy, Turkey, and Japan may be finally determined by the outcome of the struggle in this theatre of war.

I cannot take the view that the loss of Egypt and the Middle East would be a mere preliminary to the successful maintenance of a prolonged oceanic war. If all Europe, the greater part of Asia and Africa, became, either by conquest or agreement under duress, a part of the Axis system, a war maintained by the British Isles, United States, Canada, and Australasia against this mighty agglomeration would be a hard, long, and bleak proposition. Therefore, if you cannot take more advanced positions now, or very soon, the vast balances may be tilted heavily to our disadvantage.

Mr President, I am sure that you will not misunderstand me if I speak to you exactly what is in my mind. The one decisive counterweight I can see to balance the growing pessimism in Turkey, the Near East, and in Spain would be if United States were immediately to range herself with us as a belligerent Power. If this were possible I have little doubt that we could hold the situation in the Mediterranean until the weight of your munitions gained the day.

We are determined to fight to the last inch and ounce for Egypt, including its outposts of Tobruk and Crete. Very considerable risks are being run by us for that, and personally I think we shall win, in spite of the physical difficulties of reinforcing by tanks and air. But I adjure you, Mr President, not to underrate the gravity of the consequences which may follow from a Middle Eastern

[1] Colville diary, 2 May 1941: Colville papers.

collapse. In this war every post is a winning-post, and how many more are we going to lose?

The United States alone, Churchill added, could put pressure on Vichy not to give way entirely before German demands of active military support. 'You alone,' he said, 'can forestall the Germans in Morocco. . . .'[1]

After preparing this telegram to Roosevelt, Churchill found, as Colville noted, 'a less dark mood', telling his three listeners, Harriman, Ismay and Colville that 'this moment is decisive: it is being established not whether we shall win or lose, but whether the duration of the war will be long or short. With Hitler in control of Iraq oil and Ukrainian wheat, not all the staunchness of "our Plymouth Brethren" will shorten the ordeal.'

'I think,' Colville added, 'it is largely Plymouth that has caused him such melancholy—he keeps on repeating: "I've never seen the like." '[2] That night, to his predecessor at the Admiralty, Lord Stanhope, one of whose homes had been destroyed in the Blitz, Churchill wrote, after sympathising with his plight: 'Hard times: but the end will repay!'[3]

Three days later, in a message for the annual meeting of the American Booksellers Association, Churchill spoke of what had been described 'as the mighty power of the spirit in the word'. This power, he said, 'has been taken away from many nations by Nazi tyrants. Not easily will it be taken from English speaking peoples, who from writers living and dead gather courage and constancy to strengthen us in the trials we must undergo.' When the minds of nations could be 'cowed by the will of one man', Churchill added, 'civilization is broken irreparably', and he went on to tell the booksellers:

A one-man state is no state. It is an enslavement of the soul, the mind, the body of mankind. The brute will of Germany's fleeting dictator has exiled or imprisoned the best of her writers. Their fault is that they stand for a free way of life. It is a life that is death to meteoric tyrants. So be it. And so it will be.'[4]

---

[1] Prime Minister's Personal Telegram, T.139, sent 4 May 1941: Churchill papers, 20/38.

[2] Colville diary, 2 May 1941: Colville papers. At a Civil Defence Committee meeting in the Cabinet Offices on 7 May 1941, Herbert Morrison was, as Harold Nicolson noted, 'worried about the effect of the provincial raids on morale. He keeps on underlining the fact that the people cannot stand this intensive bombing indefinitely and that sooner or later the morale of other towns will go, even as Plymouth's has gone.' (Nicolson diary, 7 May 1941, Nigel Nicolson, editor, *Harold Nicolson, Diaries and Letters, 1939–1945*, London 1967, page 164.)

[3] Letter of 2 May 1941: Churchill papers, 20/21.

[4] Foreign Office Telegram No. 2413 to Washington, 5 May 1941: Churchill papers, 20/38.

56

May 1941: Crete—'the worst days'

THE imminent battles in Crete, Cyrenaica and Iraq, and the consequent threat to Egypt and the Middle East, were cause for grave concern in the first week of May 1941. The continuing Blitz over Britain, and the mounting merchant shipping toll in the Atlantic, added to the distress of all those who knew the full extent of Britain's weakness.[1] Yet Churchill now learned through the Enigma decrypts that Rommel's forces were in a seriously weakened position, unable to advance through lack of supplies, and that Egypt might yet be saved.

Colville, who knew nothing of this secret information, noted in his diary on May 3, 'the PM, some of whose worries have been relieved and who is inspired by the fact that a real fight is taking place at Tobruk, was very mellow and stayed up till 3.30 laughing, chaffing, and alternating business with conversation'. To Colville, Churchill commented, that evening at Chequers, that 'Tobruk was playing the same part as Acre did against Napoleon. It was a speck of sand in the desert which might ruin all Hitler's calculations.'[2]

The information from Enigma revealed the full extent to which Rommel's Africa Corps was running out of supplies. Sending this information on to Wavell, who was already receiving it independently, the General Staff stressed that the Germans were 'thoroughly exhausted'. But Wavell made no forward move. On May 4 Churchill telegraphed to him direct: 'Presume you realise authoritative character of information?'[3] Until the 15th Panzer Division reached him, Rommel

---

[1] Following the Plymouth air raid which had so distressed Churchill, Belfast was severely bombed on the night of May 4.

[2] Colville diary, 3 May 1941: Colville papers. Just how close Colville got to the secret is revealed in his diary that same day: 'Meanwhile,' he wrote, 'the PM, tempted by the warmth, sat in the garden working and glancing at me with suspicion from time to time in the (unwarranted) belief that I was trying to read the contents of his special buff boxes.'

[3] Since March 1941 Wavell had been receiving Enigma decrypts direct from Bletchley Park;

was unable 'to do more than hold ground gained'. Churchill's telegram continued:

This condition of enemy only bears out what you believed would be brought upon him by supply difficulty and his premature audacious advance. Severe fighting which has attended his attacks on Tobruk imposes utmost strain on troops in this plight. It would seem to me, judging from here, most important not to allow fighting round Tobruk to die down, but to compel enemy to fire his ammunition and use up his strength by counter-attack. For this purpose trust you will consider reinforcing Tobruk as well as harrying enemy about Sollum. It seems to me that if you leave him quiet he will gather supplies and strength for a forward move. But if continuously engaged now, his recovery will be delayed and perhaps prevented.

'I trust,' Churchill added, 'no respite will be given to enemy. . . .'

Churchill's hope was that, as operations 'Jaguar' and 'Tiger' proceeded, and even before they were completed, the resultant reinforcements of both aircraft and tanks would provide an early stimulus to even more ambitious action. For Enigma made it clear that Rommel's reinforcements would be substantial. 'If you wait till you are quite ready,' Churchill warned Wavell, 'enemy may well be ready too, and victory which is now not far off may recede indefinitely.' [1]

At the first meeting of the Tank Parliament, on May 5, Churchill urged those present to consider 'not only 1941 and 1942, but also 1943'. Even in the midst of crisis, he could not neglect long-term planning. If British military operations 'could land really powerful forces of tanks', he said, 'at various places in the enemy's enormous coastline', then, he believed, 'we could reckon on the uprising populations to assist us'. [2]

Thus, even while Russia and the United States were still neutral, and Britain's immediate prospects in the Middle East and the Aegean were grim, Churchill characteristically looked ahead, and gathered together those who would have to plan for a military challenge to Germany on continental Europe. Three days later, in confirming to the Battle of the Atlantic Committee that the defence of ships 'now

---

Churchill, who scrutinized every day the telegrams sent to Cairo, as well as the original decrypts on which the messages to Wavell were based, often objected to the wording of a telegram to Wavell on the grounds that it did not convey 'the atmosphere' of the original decrypt. (Private Communication.)

[1] Prime Minister's Personal Telegram, T.141, 7 May 1941: Churchill papers, 20/49.

[2] Tank Parliament No. 1 of 1941, 11.15 a.m. 5 May 1941: Cabinet papers 120/52. Three Ministers were present: Beaverbrook, Margesson and Sir Andrew Duncan. Others present included: senior representatives of the Ministry of Supply and the War Office, General Brooke, and Professor Lindemann. Lieutenant Colonel E. I. C. Jacob was the Tank Parliament Secretary.

had first priority', Churchill added the caveat: 'This however did not mean that all the weapons available should be allotted to that purpose.' Under the 'present system', he explained, 'priority and allocation went hand in hand'.[1]

A further call on materials and manpower was discussed on May 12 at the Night Air Defence Committee, when Churchill invited Beaverbrook 'to report whether the advantages of smoke-screens justified the calls made for materials and man-power, and generally as to the scale on which smoke-screen units should be provided'. Churchill also pointed out that he had 'made suggestions some time back that smoke-screens should be provided at Malta and Tobruk. He asked to be informed what action had been taken on this matter.'[2]

Churchill also sought to divert some of Wavell's resources to Syria. 'A supreme effort must be made,' he minuted to Ismay on May 8, 'to prevent the Germans getting a footing in Syria with small forces and then using Syria as a jumping-off ground for Air domination of Iraq and Persia. It is no use General Wavell being vexed at this disturbance on his eastern flanks.'[3]

In Crete, on May 5, General Freyberg, commanding the New Zealand forces there, was appointed Commander-in-Chief of all Allied Forces on the island. Even as he prepared for the battle, a victory in East Africa was announced with the entry of British troops into Addis Ababa, and the return of Haile Selassie into the capital from which he had been driven by the Italians five years before. At the same time, in Iraq, the siege of Habbaniya was lifted, and all British women and children evacuated to British-occupied Basra.[4] Over Germany, British bombers made the first of three night raids on Mannheim. But the German bombers also found their targets, on Clydeside on May 5 and May 6, and on Merseyside on May 7. On May 8, in a particularly successful effort at bending the German 'beam', German bombers, striking as they thought at the Rolls-Royce works at Derby, dropped 235 high-explosive bombs on empty fields many miles away in the Vale of Belvoir. But the bombing raids still took a steady toll: at Hull,

---

[1] Battle of the Atlantic Committee No. 8 of 1941, 8 p.m. 8 May 1941: Cabinet papers, 86/1. Both Harriman and Lindemann were present at this meeting.

[2] Night Air Defence Meeting No. 3 of 1941, 11.30 a.m., 12 May 1941: Cabinet papers, 8/22. Both Lindemann and Robert Watson-Watt were present at this meeting. The Secretary was Major A. H. Head (later Secretary of State for War in Churchill's 1951 administration).

[3] Prime Minister's Personal Minute, D.161/1, 8 May 1941: Churchill papers, 20/36.

[4] 'Your vigorous and splendid action has largely restored the situation,' Churchill telegraphed to the Air Officer Commanding Iraq, on 7 May 1941. 'We are all watching the grand fight you are making. All possible aid will be sent. Keep it up.' (Prime Minister's Personal Telegram, T.150. Air Ministry No. X.864, 7 May 1941, 8.55 p.m.: Churchill papers, 20/38.)

Manchester and Bristol 'serious fires' had been started on the night of May 7, with extensive damage to the Merseyside docks, already much damaged over the past four days.[1] In the raid on Clydeside, 57 civilians had been killed.

The fall of Greece and the loss of Cyrenaica had led to an upsurge of Parliamentary criticism. 'This sudden darkening of the landscape,' Churchill had told the House of Commons on May 7, in answer to strongly critical speeches by Hore-Belisha, Lloyd George and others, 'after we had been cheered by a long succession of victories over the Italians, is particularly painful.' He had watched the fate of Greece 'with agony'. For Hore-Belisha to have urged the importance of accurate Intelligence of enemy movements and intentions was 'one of those glimpses of the obvious and the obsolete with which his powerful speech abounded': the Government had received 'long and ample warning of what was in prospect' in the Balkans.[2]

Some people, Churchill said, compared Hitler's conquests with those of Napoleon. 'It may be,' he added, 'that Spain and Russia will shortly furnish new chapters to that theme.'[3] Nor should it be forgotten that Napoleon's empire 'with all its faults, and all its glories, fell and flushed away like snow at Easter till nothing remained but His Majesty's ship *Bellerophon* which awaited its suppliant refugees'.

Churchill went on to assure the House of Commons that, in the decisions of war policy, no 'violence' had been done to expert military opinion, either in the Chiefs of Staff Committee at home or in the generals commanding in the field. But, as head of the Government, he must 'obviously' assume the ultimate responsibility in certain circumstances and emergencies: 'It follows therefore, when all is said and done, that I am the one whose head should be cut off if we do not win the war.'

He had never underrated the dangers, Churchill said. 'I feel that we are fighting for life and survival from day to day and hour to hour. But believe me, Herr Hitler has his problems too. . . .' Little did Hitler know, in Britain's 'dark hour' in June 1940, when he received the capitulation of France, and expected to be master of Europe in a few

[1] Thirteen merchant ships had been bombed and sunk at Liverpool docks on May 3, one on May 4, one on May 5, two on May 7 and three on May 8.

[2] Churchill could make no reference to, nor did the House of Commons or Hore-Belisha know of, the existence of the Enigma decrypts.

[3] In an attempt to forestall a German occupation of Spain, Operation 'Puma' involving a British military landing, had been devised, but, as Churchill told the Defence Committee on 14 May 1941, in postponing 'Puma', 'we should have to face the possibility that we might be forestalled in the Iberian Peninsula by German action'. (Defence Committee, Operations, No. 29 of 1941, 14 May 1941, 5 p.m.: Cabinet papers, 69/2.)

months, and of the world in a few years, 'that 10 months later, in May 1941, he would be appealing to the much-tried German people to prepare themselves for the war of 1942', and Churchill ended:

When I look back on the perils which have been overcome, upon the great mountain waves in which the gallant ship has driven, when I remember all that has gone wrong, and remember also all that has gone right, I feel sure we have no need to fear the tempest. Let it roar, and let it rage. We shall come through.[1]

Churchill's speech was followed by a Division, in which the Government received a vote of confidence of 447 to three.[2] As Churchill went out of the Chamber towards the Members' Lobby there was, as Harold Nicolson noted, 'a spontaneous burst of cheering which is taken up outside', and he added: 'He looks pleased.' Later, he reflected: 'I am happy about the House today. Members are a bit defeatist. But Winston cheers them up. Yesterday it was rather like a hen-coop of wet hens: today they all strutted like bantams.'[3]

'The PM went early to bed, elated by his forensic success,' Colville noted in his diary, and he added: 'Tonight we shot down more night-raiders than ever before: at least 23 fell to guns and fighters.'[4]

Constantly seeking means of making the war machinery more effective, on May 8 Churchill established a Ministry of War Transport, unifying the Ministries of Shipping and of Transport under a single Minister, and choosing for the task 'Ted' Leathers, on whom a Peerage was conferred. A major part of Leathers' work, was the links he built up with his American opposite number, Lewis Douglas, of the United States Shipping Board.[5] On the day after Leathers' appointment, the

---

[1] *Hansard*, 7 May 1941: columns 927–946.

[2] To the new Chief Whip, James Stuart, Churchill wrote on the following day: 'As yesterday was your first big day in the House, I must thank you and congratulate you upon the most remarkable Lobby that resulted from your care and exertions. I am sure the country will be strengthened and its interests advanced by the remarkable vote of confidence at a moment when many things are difficult.' (Letter of 8 May 1941: Churchill papers, 20/29.)

[3] Nicolson diary, 7 May 1941: Nigel Nicolson (editor), *Harold Nicolson, Diaries and Letters, 1939–1945*, London 1967, pages 164–5. A week later Lord Beaverbrook wrote to Sir Samuel Hoare: 'In the House of Commons' debate the other day, Winston at once brought the whole House under his control. If democracy means the sort of Parliament that he is handling, then in making war there is no evil in democracy. But, in truth it is only a sham of a Parliament. The Front Bench is part of the sham. There Attlee and Greenwood, a sparrow and a jackdaw, are perched on either side of the glittering bird of paradise.' (Beaverbrook papers.)

[4] Colville diary, 7 May 1941: Colville papers. The main German air attack that night was on Humberside.

[5] Churchill wrote in his war memoirs: 'Leathers was an immense help to me in the conduct of the war. It was very rarely that he was unable to accomplish the hard tasks I set. Several times when all staff and departmental processes had failed to solve the problems of moving an extra

Battle of the Atlantic Committee of the War Cabinet were told that British merchant shipping losses in April had amounted to 500,000 tons sunk and 285,000 damaged, two-thirds in the Atlantic, one third in the Mediterranean. Churchill at once telegraphed to Hopkins, who was in Washington:

> Besides the loss in ships sunk and damaged at sea we are losing very heavily in the bombing of our western ports when cargoes are destroyed or damaged. I have had to take labour off long-term new construction of merchant ships in order to keep pace with repairs. I send you the full list of monthly losses sunk since the beginning of the war, and also the last few months' monthly total of damaged ships under repair.
>
> Harriman, who attends my weekly meetings of the Battle of the Atlantic Committee, will tell you what efforts we are making, and with success, to reduce the arrears of repairs. It is this general aspect of our tonnage losses and enforced concentration on repairs which constitutes the crux of the Battle of the Atlantic.
>
> The case is not only the loss of particular cargoes of weapons, for these we can often guard specially, but also the loss of food cargoes and steel and the constant diminution of our available tonnage, and the still greater diminution of our importing capacity, which is now less than half what it was in peace.[1]

On the afternoon of May 9, Churchill learned that operation 'Tiger' had begun, and within twenty-four hours the tanks had reached Alexandria. But one ship of the five struck a minefield off Malta and sank: 'The poor tiger,' Churchill told Colville, 'has already lost one claw and another is damaged; but still I would close on what is left.'[2]

On May 10 Churchill contemplated a desperate course, to save Crete. The Enigma decrypts were providing a complete picture of exactly where the Germans intended to land in Crete. One feature of these plans was the seizure of airfields by glider and airborne landings.

Studying these decrypts, Churchill thought of a plan, to send the 'actual texts of all the messages' to Freyberg, 'by special officer, by air', so that Freyberg could be shown 'personally' all the German messages relating to the seizure of airfields. 'These messages could then be destroyed by fire.' The officer taking them out, Churchill continued, 'would be answerable for their destruction in the event of engine failure

---

division or trans-shipping it from British to American ships, or of meeting some other need, I made a personal appeal to him, and the difficulties seemed to disappear as if by magic (Winston S. Churchill, *The Second World War*, volume 3, London 1950, page 132).

[1] Prime Minister's Personal Telegram, T.155, Foreign Office No.2468 to Washington, 9 May 1941, 3.55 p.m.: Churchill papers, 20/38.

[2] Colville diary, 9 May 1941: Colville papers. The ship sunk was *Empire Song*.

en route. No-one should be informed but the General who would give his orders to his subordinates without explaining his full reasons.'

Once Freyberg knew the precise German plans, Churchill explained to Pound, Dill and Portal, then, the German glider landings or airborne landings having begun, 'tanks and special assault parties in concealment nearby, could advance and destroy the intruders'.[1]

This bold plan was presumably judged far too dangerous: had the Germans learnt that Britain was decrypting the Enigma messages, the single most important British advantage of the war would have been irretrievably lost.

As was his custom, Churchill kept the King and Queen closely informed of the progress of the war. 'The Queen thanks Mr Churchill *most gratefully,*' wrote Queen Elizabeth from Windsor on May 12, 'for his kindness in sending news of the progress and safe arrival of Tiger. Even though he lacks a claw or two, it is to be hoped that he will still be able to chew up a few enemies,' and she added: 'Any risk was well worth taking.'[2] When, however, a few days later, the Admiralty resisted a repeat performance of 'Tiger', on the grounds of risk, Churchill, despite his determination to reinforce Wavell by the quickest possible route, deferred to their judgement, and the second convoy of tanks, 'Tiger No. 2', sailed round the Cape, reaching Egypt only in July.[3]

On May 10 the worst, and in fact final attack of the Blitz of 1941 was made on London. The debating Chamber of the House of Commons, empty at the time, was among the buildings destroyed. Five docks and more than thirty factories were destroyed, and for three nights the glow of the fires lit the London sky.[4] On the same night,

---

[1] Prime Minister's Personal Minute, D.164/1, 'Most Secret', 10 May 1941; Premier papers, 3/109, folios 120–1. The *substance* of these Enigma messages was already being passed to Freyberg, giving, in factual outline, details of German plans and preparations.

[2] Letter of 12 May 1941: Churchill papers, 1/361.

[3] Wavell was determined to take the offensive, with or without the 'Tiger' tanks, informing Churchill on May 13, that without waiting for 'Tiger' he had ordered 'all available tanks' to join General Gott's force 'to attack enemy Sollum area'. (Telegram No.0/64018: Churchill papers, 20/38.)

[4] Among the buildings burning on the night of May 10 were Westminster Abbey, Westminster School and St Thomas' Hospital. 'Don't be distressed at the ruins,' Josiah Wedgwood wrote to Churchill on May 11. 'Such ruins are good assets—all round the globe, and especially in America!' (Churchill papers, 20/30.) During one night of bombing, more than 1,400 civilians were killed, 5,000 houses destroyed and 12,000 people made homeless. As several German bomber units had already been transferred eastward, many of the bomber crews had to fly double sorties. In all, 541 sorties were made. Only 14 bombers failed to return. (Alfred Price, *Blitz on Britain, 1939–1945*, London 1977, pages 123–4.)

Churchill learned of a hitch in the 'splendid offer' of the United States Army Air Force General, Henry H. Arnold, whom he had seen earlier in London, to make available to British pilots one third of the United States' pilot training capacity. 'We have made active preparations,' Churchill told Roosevelt, 'and the first 550 of our young men are now ready to leave'; yet there now seemed to be some legal difficulties. Churchill appealed direct to Roosevelt to overcome any remaining obstacles. 'Such ready-made capacity of aircraft, airfields and instructors all in balance,' Churchill explained, 'we could not obtain to the same extent and in the same time by any other means. It will greatly accelerate our effort in the air.'[1]

On the evening of May 11, while Churchill was at Ditchley, a telephone call from Scotland revealed the astounding news that Hitler's deputy, Rudolf Hess, had flown to Britain, arriving on British soil by parachute, near Glasgow. Hess's flight, Churchill told the House of Commons on May 13, 'is one of these cases where imagination is sometimes baffled by the facts as they present themselves'.[2] Following the questioning of Hess by a Foreign Office German expert, Ivone Kirkpatrick, who had served in Berlin and knew Hess, it emerged, as Colville noted in his diary, that Hess genuinely believed that he could 'persuade us that we cannot win', and that a compromise peace was obtainable. Hess's 'essential prerequisite', Colville added, 'is the fall of the Churchill Government.'[3]

The impact of Hess' flight was relevant to British policy in one important area. 'The most serious result,' reported the British Consul-General in New York, Gerald Campbell, 'has been the introduction into the minds of some industrialists of doubts as to the advisability of vast plant expansion lest this rumoured peace negotiation should prove a reality.' Campbell continued: 'While most of this rumour and speculation is only circulated by private conversation there is undoubtedly

[1] Prime Minister's Personal Telegram, T.164, 10 May 1941: Churchill's papers, 20/38. Ten days later Roosevelt replied: 'All plans discussed with you by Arnold for training pilots have been approved here. There are no legal difficulties in the way and the training can begin promptly.' Roosevelt added: 'We are rushing six additional small aircraft carriers for you. First three should be available in three or four months.' (Churchill papers: 20/39.) Churchill replied on 27 May 1941: 'All this will be most helpful.' (Foreign Office Telegram No. 2858 to Washington, 27 May 1941: Foreign Office papers, 954/29, folio 189.)

[2] *Hansard*, 12 May 1941, column 1085.

[3] Colville diary, 13 May 1941: Colville papers. Kirkpatrick's report was shown only to Churchill, Eden, Attlee and Beaverbrook.

abroad an undefinable but widely-held feeling of apprehension and uncertainty which fertilizes the soil for German propaganda.'[1]

Hess himself, imprisoned and alone, had similar delusions. 'He firmly believes,' Desmond Morton reported to Churchill in July, 'that the Government will one day wish to send him back to Germany with an offer of peace terms.'[2]

Hess' delusions were perhaps encouraged by the speed and extent of the German conquests in Yugoslavia and Greece, which had cast a pall of gloom upon many observers in London. Churchill sought, as usual, to draw from the disaster some positive reflections, minuting to Dill on May 13:

I wonder whether the German action in the Balkans can be cited as an example of 'their capacity for overcoming the most formidable difficulties'. As a mere exercise in historical perspective, I should have thought the opposite was true. They were allowed to accumulate unresisted, overwhelming forces to attack Yugoslavia before it was mobilized, and when it had been betrayed by its pre-war Government, Greece was exhausted and held by the Italian Army, and we were left practically alone with only one-fifth the armoured vehicles, and practically no Air, to resist their overwhelming onslaught.

The fact that with all these advantages so cheaply gained, the Germans were unable to impede seriously the masterly extrication and re-embarkation of our forces, inspires me with confidence and not with apprehension.[3]

On May 14 Enigma decrypts gave the precise German order of battle for an attack on Crete. 'Everything seems to be moving in concert for that,' Churchill telegraphed to Wavell, 'and with great elaboration.' The German assault might begin 'any day after 17th'. But, Churchill continued: 'It may well be that in so huge and complicated a plan zero date will be delayed. Therefore reinforcements sent now might well arrive in time and certainly for the second round should enemy gain a footing.'

Churchill went on to tell Wavell: 'I should particularly welcome chance for our high-class troops to come to close grips with those people under conditions where enemy has not got his usual mechanical advantages, and where we can surely re-inforce much easier than he can.'[4]

[1] New York Telegram, No. 56, 19 June 1941: Premier papers, 3/219/1, folio 43.

[2] Minute of 28 July 1941: Premier papers, 3/219/2, folio 5.

[3] 'Secret and Personal', Prime Minister's Personal Minute, M.536/1, 13 May 1941: War Office papers, 216/5.

[4] Prime Minister's Personal Telegram, T.176, 14 May 1941: Premier Papers, 3/109, folio 117.

Further Enigma decrypts on May 15 made it clear that the defence of Crete, code name 'Colorado', was going to be a difficult operation against a German airborne assault. 'I am increasingly impressed,' Churchill telegraphed that day to Wavell, 'with the weight of attack impending. . . .'[1] In reply, Wavell assured Churchill that he had done his best 'to equip "Colorado" against beetle pest', including reinforcements of six tanks, sixteen light tanks and eighteen anti-aircraft guns. There was however a 'problem', he reported, in landing these reinforcements. The defence of Crete, Wavell added, was not an 'easy commitment, and German blitzes usually take some stopping. But we have stout-hearted troops, keen and ready for fight, under resolute commander, and I hope enemy will find their "scorcher" red-hot proposition.'[2]

'Scorcher' was the British code name for the impending German attack. In Crete itself, General Freyberg did not entirely despair of success. 'I do not wish to be overconfident,' he wrote, 'but I feel that at least we will give an excellent account of ourselves. With the help of the Royal Navy,' he added, 'I trust Crete will be held.'[3] On the following day, in a more distant war zone, the Duke of Aosta, Commander-in-Chief of Italian East Africa, and since 1937 Governor of Ethiopia, surrendered, with five Generals and 7,000 men, to the Allied forces. That same day, in the western desert, General Gott's forces advanced thirty miles against Rommel's Africa Corps, capturing Sollum, and taking 500 German prisoners. But it was a victory in Crete, Churchill telegraphed to Freyberg on May 18, which would 'powerfully affect world situation'.[4] And to Admiral Cunningham, Churchill telegraphed that same day: 'May you have God's blessing in this memorable and fateful operation which will react in every theatre of the war.'[5]

On May 20 the German attack on Crete began, as 1,500 German troops, landing by parachute, fought to capture Maleme aerodrome. That same day, news reached London that German aircraft had landed

[1] Prime Minister's Personal Telegram, T.179, War Office No.002 of 15 May 1941: Churchill papers, 20/38.

[2] Telegram No. 0/64501, 15 May 1941: Churchill papers, 20/38.

[3] Message of 16 May 1941, enclosed in Telegram No. 0/65072 (Wavell to Churchill) of 17 May 1941: Churchill papers, 20/38.

[4] Prime Minister's Personal Telegram, T.190, 18 May 1941, despatched 5.45 p.m.: Churchill papers, 20/38.

[5] Prime Minister's Personal Telegram, T.189, 18 May 1941, despatched 4.54 p.m., 'Hush—Most Secret': Churchill papers, 20/38. Cunningham replied on the following day: 'We fully realise the importance of success in this venture and will do our best.' (Signal No. 426, 'Hush—Most Secret' received 4.13 a.m., 19 May 1941: Churchill papers, 20/38.)

in Syria. Churchill, who was given this news while in his car on the way back from the House of Commons, turned to Colville with the words, 'We must go in,'[1] and an hour later, having summoned the Defence Committee, it was agreed to allow Free French troops under General Catroux to move into Syria from Transjordan, with British logistic, military and air support. The opportunity, the Committee noted, was 'too good to miss and the advance must be regarded as a political coup, in which time is all important, rather than a military operation'.[2] Not only a Free French declaration of independence for Syria, but also for the Lebanon, the Committee agreed, was now a British aim.[3]

Another British aim, Churchill wrote for the War Cabinet, was to negotiate with Ibn Saud of Saudi Arabia a 'Jewish State of "Western Palestine", which might form an Independent Federal Unit in the Arab Caliphate'. Churchill added: 'This Jewish State would have to have the fullest rights of self-government, including immigration and development, and provision for expansion in the desert regions to the southward, which they would gradually reclaim.'[4]

On May 20 a message was found in the pocket of one of the siren suits which had been made to order for Churchill. 'May God grant you the very best of health and strength,' it read, 'to carry us through our Greatest Ordeal in History to keep the British Empire Free.' The note was signed, simply, 'From British Workers.'[5]

During the afternoon of May 20, a further 3,000 German parachutists were dropped in several parts of Crete.[6] Even as the battle raged, Churchill was troubled by a conflict that had developed in a far distant region, in the United States, as to what Britain's real needs were, and whether the United States ought to be more cautious as far as its commitments were concerned. 'It is impossible,' Harriman wrote to a friend, 'for one to understand the ostrich-like attitude of America.

[1] Colville diary, 20 May 1941: Colville papers.

[2] But military operation it became, code name 'Exporter'.

[3] Telegram to Wavell, Defence Committee (Operations) No. 32 of 1941, 20 May 1941, 1 p.m., Annex: Cabinet papers, 69/2.

[4] 'Syrian Policy, Note by the Prime Minister and Minister of Defence', 'Most Secret', 19 May 1941: Cabinet papers, 120/10. The area of 'Western Palestine' extended from the Mediterranean to the river Jordan.

[5] Churchill papers, 2/415.

[6] The Suda Bay, Heraklion and Retimo areas.

Either we have an interest in the outcome of the war, or we have not.'[1] Every day that America delayed using its own Navy and Air Force in the struggle, Harriman added, 'we are taking an extreme risk that either the war will be lost or the difficulty of winning it multiplied, for each week we delay'.[2]

Churchill's own sense of frustration, and of fear, in regard to the intentions of the United States, was expressed in two telegrams that he drafted on May 21, the first, for Wendell Willkie, was sent to Roosevelt but then cancelled. Its central message was to have read:

> I have never said that the British Empire cannot make its way out of this war without American belligerence, but no peace that is any use to you or which will liberate Europe can be obtained without American belligerence, towards which convoys is a decisive step. Every day's delay adds to the length of the war and the difficulties to be encountered. West Africa, Spain, Vichy, Turkey, the Arab world, all hang in the balance. Japan hangs in the balance. Wait three months and all this may be piled up against us in adverse sense, thus lengthening the war to periods no man can pretend to know about, and increasing immensely the danger and burden to be borne by someone before Hitler is beat. How easy now—how hard a year hence will be the task.
>
> At present rate, in next twelve months we shall lose four and a half million tons of shipping. The United States, by a prodigy of generous constructive effort, will build perhaps three and a half and we build the other million. Where have we got to then? Just marking time and swimming level with the bank against the stream. Whereas co-operation of even a third of the American Navy would save at least one-half of the tonnage beforehand and give that mastery which alone can abridge the torments of mankind.[3]

To Roosevelt, Churchill telegraphed that same day:

> I hope you will forgive me if I say there is anxiety here. We are at a climacteric of the war, when enormous crystallisations are in suspense but

[1] On 1 June 1941, Churchill was sent a copy of a letter written by Frazier Jelke of New York, a stockbroker whom he had known before the war; the letter stated, of the Duke and Duchess of Windsor: 'I was in Nassau for over three months during the past winter where I had a house. During this time I became thoroughly saturated with the English point of view and propaganda, with regard to their winning the war and the repeated successes of her victorious armies in Northern Africa. However, I was later amazed upon dining at Government House and meeting the Duke and Duchess intimately on a number of other occasions to be told by each of them personally and separately that they were opposed to America entering the war, as it was too late to do any good. When I said to His Royal Highness, "Sir, you are certainly not a wishful thinker," he replied, "No, I have always been a great realist and it is too late for America to save Democracy in Europe. She had better save it in America for herself."' (Churchill papers, 20/31.)

[2] Letter of 21 May 1941: W. Averell Harriman and Elie Abel, *Special Envoy to Churchill and Stalin, 1941–1946*, London 1976, pages 32–3.

[3] Foreign Office Telegram No. 2721 to Washington, 'submitted to President but cancelled', Prime Minister's Personal Telegram, T.202, 21 May 1941: Foreign Office papers, 954/29, folio 184.

imminent. Battle for Crete has opened well. I had steps taken to reinforce Egypt in a manner which gives me good confidence about the Western Desert. Should Winant come home, he will explain to you what was done. We now have to launch out into Syria with the Free French in the name of Syrian and Lebanon independence. Spain, Vichy and Turkey are a riveted audience.

At heavy cost in other waters we have been doing better in Battle of the Atlantic lately, but as I send this message Admiralty tell me that eight ships have been sunk in a convoy as far out as the fortieth meridian west longitude. You will see from my cancelled message to Willkie how grievous I feel it that the United States should build 3 or 4 million tons of shipping and watch their equivalent being sunk beforehand.

'Let me once again express my gratitude,' Churchill ended, 'and that of the British Empire, for all you have done for us.'[1]

Churchill's private anguish in regard to the United States came on a day of worsening news from Crete. 'It is a most strange and a grim battle that is being fought,' he told the House of Commons on the following day. 'Our side have no air, because they have no aerodromes and not because they have no aeroplanes, and the other side have very little or no artillery or tanks. Neither side have any means of retreat. It is a desperate, grim battle.'[2] German air bases in Greece, he telegraphed to Wavell, 'make our hold of Crete precarious', and he went on to warn that if the Germans were to secure air bases in Crete, Cyprus, Cyrenaica and Syria, it would make 'our hold on Egypt difficult'. 'We have some very difficult months ahead,' he added, 'but will not lose heart.'[3] Later that same night Churchill telegraphed again to Wavell: 'Crete battle must be won. Even if enemy secure good lodgments, fighting must be maintained indefinitely in the island, thus keeping enemy main striking force tied down to the task,' and giving Wavell himself time to mobilize the tanks of operation 'Tiger'—his 'Tiger-cubs'—in order to 'dominate' the situation in the western desert.[4]

On the evening of Friday, May 23, Churchill drove to Chequers for the weekend.[5] 'The PM laments very strongly,' Colville noted in his diary, 'that the tanks which he asked Wavell to send to Crete were not sent. They might have made the whole difference to the battle.' But the lament for Crete turned to expectations elsewhere as news reached

[1] Foreign Office Telegram No. 2723 to Washington, Prime Minister's Personal Telegram, T.204, 21 May 1941, 'Personal and Secret' Foreign Office papers, 954/29, folio 186.

[2] Hansard, 22 May 1941, column 1680.

[3] Telegram 0/66385, despatched 4.20 p.m., 22 May 1941: Churchill papers, 20/39.

[4] Prime Minister's Personal Telegram, T.211, War Office No. 030, despatched 4.30 a.m., 23 May 1941: Churchill papers, 20/39.

[5] The overnight guests included Captain Margesson, General Pownall, General Ismay and Averell Harriman (Chequers List).

Chequers that the new German battleship, the *Bismarck*, together with the new 8-inch cruiser, the *Prinz Eugen*, was near Iceland, on its way to attack British merchant shipping in the Atlantic, but 'hotly pursued' by the *Prince of Wales* and the *Hood*. 'There is an excellent chance,' Colville noted in his diary that night, 'of catching her at dawn in the Denmark Straits.'[1]

Even if the *Bismarck* evaded capture, Churchill knew he could rely upon the recent agreement with the United States, to report on the location of all German ships in the western half of the Atlantic. Telegraphing that evening to Roosevelt about the chase, he added: 'Should we fail to catch them going out your Navy should surely be able to mark them down for us.' British warships would be on their tracks. 'Give us the news and we will finish the job.'[2]

That night Churchill awaited news of further developments to be telephoned to him from the Admiralty. But no further news came. Five years later he recalled, in an early draft of his war memoirs, how, at 3 a.m.:

There was however nothing for me to do and I went to bed, asking not to be called on the naval affair until I rang. I was so well tired out with other work that I slept soundly. I had complete confidence in the First Sea Lord, Admiral Pound, and liked the way he was playing the hand.

I awoke in peaceful Chequers about 9 a.m. with all that strange thrill which one feels at the beginning of a day in which great news is expected, good, or bad. . . .[3]

General Ismay, who, with Averell Harriman, was among the guests at Chequers that Friday, later recalled:

The situation in Crete was critical, but the conversation at Chequers that night was confined almost exclusively to the impending clash at sea, and we sat up even later than usual, on the chance of getting some news. But none came, and at last we went to bed. I had only just dropped off to sleep— or so it seemed—when I heard the sounds of conversation in Averell's room, which was opposite mine. I jumped out of bed to see the Prime Minister's back view disappearing down the corridor. Averell's door was ajar and I went in. He looked puzzled. 'Winston has just been in and told me that the *Hood* has blown up but that he reckons we have got the *Bismarck* for certain.'[4]

[1] Colville diary, 23 May 1941: Colville papers.
[2] Prime Minister's Personal Telegram, T.213, 23 May 1941: Churchill papers, 20/39.
[3] Unpublished note: Churchill papers, 4/219.
[4] *Memoirs of General the Lord Ismay*, London 1960, page 219.

The *Hood* was Britain's fastest warship. Her loss was a disaster in more ways than one. Only three of her crew survived: 1,500 were killed.

Churchill was in his bedroom at Chequers when he received the still secret news of the sinking of the *Hood* on the morning of May 24. Among those at Chequers that weekend was his son-in-law Vic Oliver, who later recalled how Churchill:

. . . came down from his study looking inexpressibly grim. We guessed that yet another disaster had occurred, though we knew it was no use to ask him what it was. Mrs Churchill quietly poured him a glass of port, and, thinking it would relieve the tension, suggested I play something on the piano. I was about to start on *Lily of Laguna*, but immediately checked myself, feeling that a popular song would be out of place; so after a few seconds' reflection I decided on Beethoven's *Appassionata* sonata, but I had played only a few bars when Mr Churchill rose to his feet and thundered: 'Stop! Don't play that!'

We were all surprised, for it was the first time he had raised his voice to me. I turned round, puzzled, and asked: 'What's the trouble—don't you like it?'

'Nobody plays the *Dead March* in my house,' he said. We all laughed. 'It's not the *Dead March*,' I said. 'It's the *Appassionata* sonata.'

Mr Churchill was notoriously unmusical. He glowered again. 'You can say what you like,' he said, 'I know it's the funeral march.'

I turned back to the piano. 'But surely, sir, you can tell the difference between this. . . .' and I struck a few chords of the *Appassionata*, 'and. . . .'

Before I had time to finish, Mr Churchill thundered again: 'Stop it! Stop it! I want no *Dead March*, I tell you.'

Sarah rushed over to the piano and told me to play his favourite song instead. I did so, and the moment passed. Next day it was announced that HMS *Hood* had been sunk with heavy loss of life.[1]

Churchill had gone to bed on the night of May 23 believing that the *Bismarck* would be caught and sunk within hours. But at about half past eight in the morning of May 24, one of his Private Secretaries entered his bedroom with, as Churchill recalled, 'a strained look' on his face. 'Have we got her?' Churchill asked. 'No,' the Private Secretary replied, adding that the *Prince of Wales* had 'broken off the action.'[2] This was, Churchill later wrote, 'a bitter disappointment and grief to me'.[3]

In Crete the battle continued. The Germans, Colville noted in his diary on May 24, 'are fighting with blind courage and have complete control of the air. The crux of the matter is how long the Navy can

---

[1] Vic Oliver, *Mr Showbusiness* (an autobiography), London 1954, pages 143–4.
[2] Winston S. Churchill, *The Second World War*, volume 3, London 1950, page 273.
[3] Unpublished note: Churchill papers, 4/219.

carry out its dangerous task of preventing sea-borne landings.'[1] Mean-while, in the Atlantic, the *Bismarck* escaped its pursuers during Saturday night, and at Chequers, on Sunday May 25, as Colville noted, 'a day of fearful gloom ensued'. His account continued:

The PM cannot understand why the Prince of Wales did not press home her attack yesterday and keeps on saying it is the worst thing since Troubridge turned away from the Goeben in 1914. He berated the First Lord and the First Sea Lord continuously, both on this account and because in the Mediter-ranean the navy shows, he thinks, a tendency to shirk its task of preventing a sea borne landing in Crete since Cunningham fears severe losses from bomb-ing.

The PM's line is that Cunningham must be made to take every risk: the loss of half the Mediterranean fleet would be worth while in order to save Crete.

Also vexed at Wavell for not managing to send the tank reinforce-ments into battle immediately they had arrived, Churchill told those present, Ismay, 'Tommy' Thompson, Lindemann and Colville, that if he could be 'put in command' in Wavell's place, he would gladly lay down the Premiership, 'yes, and even renounce cigars and alcohol!'. The past three days, Churchill remarked on going to bed, 'had been the worst yet'.[2]

Churchill's friends and colleagues sympathized with him in his dis-tress. 'My dear Winston,' Anthony Eden wrote to him on May 26, 'This is a bad day; but tomorrow—Baghdad will be entered, Bismarck sunk,' and Eden added: 'On some date the war will be won, and you will have done more than any man in history to win it.'[3]

During May 26 the *Bismarck* had been found again, steaming towards the shelter of the French coast, and at daylight on May 27 battle had been joined. 'I do not know the results of the bombardment', Churchill told the House of Commons, then meeting in Church House. But hardly had he sat down then he was handed a slip of paper brought in by Brendan Bracken, and passed on to him by John Peck. He rose again. 'I have just received news,' he said, 'that the *Bismarck* is sunk.'[4]

---

[1] Colville diary, 24 May 1941: Colville papers.

[2] Colville diary, 25 May 1941: Colville papers.

[3] Churchill papers, 20/26. Rashid Ali fled from Baghdad on 30 May 1941, together with Haj Amin el-Husseini, the former Mufti of Jerusalem, who had likewise allied himself to the Axis. Before he knew of Rashid Ali's flight, Churchill told Ismay, of the proposal by Morton and Lindemann to order the destruction of the Iraqi oil fields: 'There will be a fierce and justifiable outcry if we fail to destroy these oilfields before they fall into enemy hands.' (Prime Minister's Personal Minute, D.174/1, 30 May 1941: Churchill papers, 20/36.)

[4] *Hansard*, 27 May 1941, columns 1714–8. Among the telegrams of congratulations which Churchill received on the sinking of the *Bismarck* was one from General de Gaulle, sent from Cairo on 28 May 1941. (Churchill papers, 20/25.)

'The tension snapped and the House was overjoyed,' John Peck later recalled, and he added:

Facing Winston sat the two most persistent critics of his conduct of the war— Emanuel Shinwell and Aneurin Bevan. Shinwell looked across and caught Winston's eye, grinned broadly and gave him a friendly and encouraging nod. Bevan sat with shoulders hunched and hands in pockets; a black scowl on his face, unable to conceal his chagrin that Churchill should have a victory to record.[1]

After the sinking of the *Bismarck*, British warships had gone to the rescue of the German sailors milling about in the water, but scarcely had they begun their work of rescue when a German U-boat approached, forcing the British warships to withdraw. When later they were able to return only five more German sailors were found and rescued: nearly 2,000 had perished.[2]

All eyes now turned to Crete where, against increasing odds, and German air mastery, the battle continued, although, as Freyberg reported to Wavell on May 26, 'in my opinion the limit of endurance has been reached by the troops under my command here at Suda Bay'. Whatever decision was taken in Cairo, Freyberg added, 'our position is hopeless'.[3]

Before a copy of this message could reach him, Churchill telegraphed to Wavell: 'Victory in Crete is essential at this turning point in the war. Keep hurling in all aid you can.'[4] He also telegraphed direct to General Freyberg: 'Your glorious defence commands admiration in every land. We know enemy is hard pressed. All aid in our power is being sent.'[5] But on the morning of May 27, when the facts of the situation had reached him, he told the War Cabinet 'that all chances of winning the battle in Crete now appeared to have gone, and we should have to face the prospect of the loss of most of our forces there'. There was 'no action', he added, 'that we in this country could take in regard to the matter'.[6]

That night Churchill summoned the Defence Committee to discuss

---

[1] Sir John Peck, 'Bull and Benediction', typescript: Peck papers.

[2] In the final phase of the battle, after the sinking of the *Hood*, only 25 British sailors had been killed.

[3] Signal of 26 May 1941: Premier papers, 3/309/4.

[4] Prime Minister's Personal Telegram, T.223, 'Most Immediate'. War Office No. 68836, despatched 2 a.m., 27 May 1941: Premier papers, 3/109, folio 91.

[5] Prime Minister's Personal Telegram, T.222, War Office Telegram No. 68838, despatched from London at 1.35 a.m., 27 May 1941: Premier papers, 3/109, folio 90.

[6] War Cabinet No. 54 of 1941, 27 May 1941, 10.30 a.m., Minute 1, Confidential Annex: Cabinet papers, 65/22.

Crete, where, as Colville noted, the situation was 'deplorable'. It seems, he added, 'that we are finished there, owing to lack of air support'.[1] This was also Wavell's considered judgement: 'Crete is no longer tenable and the troops must be withdrawn as far as possible.' It had been impossible, Wavell added, 'to withstand weight of enemy air attack which has been on unprecedented scale and has been through force of circumstances practically unopposed'.[2]

Churchill and the Defence Committee had no choice but to accept Wavell's advice. In view of Wavell's report, Churchill minuted for the Chiefs of Staff Committee, 'he should be ordered to evacuate Crete forthwith. . . .'

Once Crete had been evacuated, Churchill advised, it should be possible to destroy the German force in Cyrenaica 'thus disengaging Tobruk', and then to 'peg out claims in Syria' for reinforcement after a Cyrenaican victory. This should be possible by mid-June. But until British aerodromes were established in Syria, Churchill added, no attempt should be made to hold Cyprus. 'We must not repeat in Cyprus,' he warned, 'the hard conditions of our fight in Crete.'[3]

With Crete's loss accepted, Churchill looked to three other areas for immediate action. The first was against Rommel in Cyrenaica. 'Hope you are preparing your desert stroke and that Tobruk will not be idle,' he telegraphed to Wavell,[4] and he added, on the following day: 'Now before the enemy has recovered from the violent exertions and heavy losses involved in his onslaught upon Crete, is the time to fight a decisive battle in Libya and go on day after day facing all necessary losses until you have beaten the life out of General Rommel's army.'[5] The proposed offensive, against Rommel, first code name 'Bruiser', subsequently 'Battleaxe', was to begin on June 15.

The second area Churchill looked to for action was in preparation for retaking in 1942 some of the Mediterranean islands 'so easily occupied by the enemy', and for which he wanted preparation of 5,000 parachutists and an Air-borne Division 'on the German model'. Reflecting on Britain's current total of 500 gliders, he commented to Ismay: 'Thus we are always found behind-hand by the enemy.'[6]

---

[1] Colville diary, 27 May 1941: Colville papers.

[2] Telegram o/67808, despatched 9.30 a.m., received 1.55 p.m., 27 May 1941: Churchill papers, 20/39.

[3] Prime Minister's Personal Minute, D.171/1, 27 May 1941: Churchill papers, 20/36.

[4] Prime Minister's Personal Telegram, T.221, 27 May 1941: Churchill papers, 20/49.

[5] Prime Minister's Personal Telegram, T.228, War Office No. 69157, 28 May 1941, 8.30 p.m.: Churchill papers, 20/39.

[6] Prime Minister's Personal Minute, D.169/1, 27 May 1941: Churchill papers, 20/36.

The third area of planning urged by Churchill on May 27 concerned the need for greater tank production. After a meeting that day of the Tank Parliament, General Brooke noted in his diary, of Churchill:

It is surprising how he maintains a light-hearted exterior in spite of the vast burden he is bearing. He is quite the most wonderful man I have ever met, and it is a source of never-ending interest, studying him and getting to realise that occasionally such human beings make their appearance on this earth— human beings who stand out head and shoulders above all others.[1]

[1] Brooke diary, 27 May 1941: Arthur Bryant, *The Turn of the Tide, 1939–1943*, London 1957, page 252.

57

June 1941: 'Battleaxe' and beyond

THE evacuation of Crete was begun on May 27, and by the morning of May 29 nearly 5,000 men had been taken off, under continual German air bombardment. During the night of May 29 a further 6,000 men were embarked.[1] As the evacuation continued, Wavell telegraphed to Churchill, warning 'that losses in Crete will be very heavy'. He also described his own Middle Eastern situation as 'likely to be critical for some months', requiring 'more reinforcements than at present in sight'.[2] Colville noted in his diary: 'PM is much upset by telegram from Wavell who shows some signs of defeatism. "He sounds a tired and disheartened man" said the PM.'[3]

At the Defence Committee that evening, it was decided that the evacuation of Crete should continue, despite the continued German air attacks on the evacuation ships.[4] On the following night, 4,000 troops were taken off and reached Alexandria in safety. But the anti-aircraft cruiser *Calcutta*, sent out to help them, was bombed and sunk on the way back.[5] A further 5,000 troops who remained on the island were authorized to surrender.[6] Churchill had wanted to 'overrule' Wavell,

[1] Among them David Hunt, subsequently Private Secretary to Attlee (1950–51) and Churchill (1951–54).

[2] Telegram O/68447, sent 3.47 p.m., received 5.15 p.m.: 29 May 1941: Churchill papers, 20/39.

[3] Colville diary, 29 May 1941: Colville papers.

[4] Defence Committee (Operations) No. 36 of 1941, 29 May 1941, 6 p.m.: Cabinet papers, 69/2. In his war memoirs Churchill wrote of how the Battle of Crete had broken 'the spear-point of the German lance', and constituted 'an event which brought us far-reaching relief at a hingeing moment'. (Winston S. Churchill, *The Second World War*, volume 3, London 1950, pages 253 and 268.)

[5] Earlier in the evacuation the cruisers *Fiji* and *Gloucester* had been sunk, as well as six destroyers.

[6] In all, 16,500 men were evacuated from Crete, and 13,000 killed, wounded or taken prisoner. German killed and wounded on Crete were in excess of 17,000. In the Atlantic, the British had lost 1,500 men on the *Hood*. During May, a further 5,394 civilians had been killed during German air raids on the United Kingdom.

as Eden noted in his diary on June 1, and to carry on the evacuation for another night, but, Churchill told Eden, 'he had found that Wavell had already issued orders to capitulate'.[1]

After the war Freyberg wrote to Churchill: 'We were broken, but only after some of the heaviest fighting of the war. There are over 4,000 German graves in the Suda Bay area alone and, I believe, a similar number of our own, a lot of them men blasted out with 500 lb bombs.'[2]

Amid the distressing news of the evacuation of Crete came news of a most welcome kind, Roosevelt's decision to take over from Britain the military and air bases in Iceland which had been for more than a year under British control. This, Churchill told Roosevelt with delight, 'will liberate a British division for defence against invasion or the Middle East', and would enable the British flying boats already in Iceland to concentrate on the North Western Approaches. If the decision could be implemented 'in the next three weeks or less, or even begun', Churchill added, 'it would have a moral effect even beyond its military importance'.[3]

In a further telegram to Roosevelt, sent from Chequers that weekend, Churchill pointed out that the capture of Crete would be exploited 'to the full' by German propaganda and that any open move Roosevelt could make, 'like sending even a Brigade to Iceland' could not come at a more 'timely' moment. 'See also,' Churchill added, 'second epistle to the Corinthians, chapter 6, verse 2.'[4]

Roosevelt now responded with increasing alacrity to Churchill's urgent requests, encouraged to do so by Harriman in London and Hopkins in Washington, and on June 4 Churchill was able to inform Wavell that 'in addition to the 30 ships under the American flag, another 44 vessels, which carry among other things, 200 additional Light Tanks from the United States Army Production', were on their way to him.[5]

[1] Diary entry, 1 June 1941: The Earl of Avon, *The Eden Memoirs, The Reckoning*, London 1965, page 244. On 2 June 1941 John Colville noted in his diary, of Churchill: 'He is much perturbed by the fact that the rear-guard, consisting of Royal Marines, was left behind on Crete. He blames the Navy and went so far as to describe it as a shameful episode' (Colville papers: Churchill was spending the evening at Chartwell).

[2] Letter of 23 February 1949: Churchill papers, 4/217.

[3] Prime Minister's Personal Telegram, T.237, Foreign Office telegram No. 2929 to Washington, 30 May 1941, 12.35 p.m.: Churchill papers, 20/39.

[4] Prime Minister's Personal Telegram, T.247, Foreign Office telegram No. 2983 to Washington, 31 May 1941, 7.55 p.m.: Churchill papers, 20/49. The verse reads: 'For he saith, I have heard thee in a time accepted, and in the day of salvation have I succoured thee; behold, now *is* the accepted time; behold, now *is* the day of salvation.'

[5] Prime Minister's Personal Telegram, T.256, 4 June 1941, War Office No. 70159: Churchill papers, 20/39. The extra items on their way also included 24 anti-aircraft guns, with 12,000

Among the guests at Chequers that weekend was Averell Harriman's daughter, Kathleen. To her sister she sent this account of the impression Churchill made on her, as they met for the first time:

The PM is much smaller than I expected and a lot less fat. He wears RAF blue jaeger one-piece suits (the only way to keep warm in that house), and looks rather like a kindly teddy bear.

He expresses himself wonderfully—continually comes out with delightful statements. I'd expected an overpowering, rather terrifying man. He's quite the opposite: very gracious, has a wonderful smile and isn't at all hard to talk to.[1]

In the aftermath of Crete, Churchill made a single change in command in the Middle East, replacing Air Chief Marshal Longmore, whom he appointed to be Inspector General of the Royal Air Force, by Air Vice-Marshal Tedder.[2]

In a telegram to Wavell on June 3, Churchill sent details of supplies on their way from across the Atlantic. President Roosevelt, he reported, 'is now sending, in addition to the 30 ships under the American flag, another 44 vessels, which carry, among other things, 200 additional Light Tanks from the United States Army Production, and many other important items of which I will furnish you a list'. Churchill added: 'It seems to me probable, and I am trying to arrange, that a great part of the supply of your armies shall come direct from the United States both by the Eastern and the Western routes.'

Churchill also told Wavell of the imminent arrival of Averell Harriman in Cairo. 'Mr Harriman enjoys my complete confidence,' Churchill wrote, 'and is in the most intimate relations with the President and with Mr Harry Hopkins. No one can do more for you.' It would, Churchill added, be 'disastrous' if large accumulations of American

---

rounds of three-inch shrapnel, 30 sets of small box girder bridges with transporters, 5 sets of heavy pontoons with transporters, 100 sets of water supply equipment, 700 ten-ton trucks and 490,000 rounds of 155 millimetre howitzer ammunition (Wavell to Churchill, 5 June 1941, 2.45 a.m., Prime Minister's Personal Telegram, T.259: Churchill papers, 20/39).

[1] Quoted in W. Averell Harriman and Elie Abel, *Special Envoy to Churchill and Stalin, 1941–1946*, London 1976, page 61.

[2] Churchill's first thought was to recall Sir Hugh Dowding to active service as Commander-in-Chief of the Middle East Air Forces. This, however, was resisted by Sinclair and the Chief of the Air Staff. On October 23 Churchill wrote in the third person, to Ismay, that 'the Prime Minister told the Secretary of State and the Chief of the Air Staff only six weeks ago that he thought it would be well that Sir Hugh Dowding should replace Air Marshal Tedder in the Middle East. However the Prime Minister deferred to the representations then made to him by the Secretary of State and the CAS'. (Premier papers, 4/68/9, folio 916.)

supplies were to reach Cairo 'without efficient measures for their reception and without large-scale planning for the future'. Large numbers
of American engineers and mechanics would also be arriving to service
and repair the American aircraft, tanks and motor vehicles reaching
Egypt.

Churchill's telegram to Wavell ended: 'I commend Mr Harriman to
your most attentive consideration. He will report both to us in Government and to me as Minister of Defence.'[1]

Churchill made no move to replace Wavell, although, as Colville
noted in his diary on June 3: 'He said some very harsh things about
Wavell, whose excessive caution and inclination to pessimism he finds
very antipathetic.'[2]

Churchill also contemplated asking Lord Beaverbrook, who was
serving as Deputy Chairman of the Defence Committee (Supply) to
take on a specific departmental task, either as Minister of Fuel, Power
and Light, or as Minister of Agriculture. 'You know that you will
always find me ready,' Churchill wrote, 'so long as I have any life left
in my carcass, to try to meet your wishes and harness your drive and
force of nature to our heavily-laden wagon.'[3] But in the event, he held
this letter back, and asked Beaverbrook to take, first the Ministry of
Food, which he rejected,[4] and then the Ministry of Supply, which he
accepted at the end of June. Once more, his friend had caused him
much time-consuming work and thought, and Colville noted in his
diary, about Beaverbrook: 'Brendan says that he takes up more of the
P.M.'s time than Hitler.'[5]

Criticism of the Crete campaign was also taking up much of Churchill's time in the first week of June. 'On all sides one hears increasing
criticism of Churchill,' Henry Channon wrote in his diary on June 6.
'He is undergoing a slump in popularity and many of his enemies, long

[1] 'Most Secret', Prime Minister's Personal Telegram, T.256, 3 June 1941: Cabinet papers
120/10.

[2] Colville diary, 3 June 1941: Colville papers. Colville had dined alone with Churchill, during
a rare wartime visit to Chartwell.

[3] Letter marked 'Hold': Churchill papers, 20/24.

[4] Beaverbrook wrote to Churchill: 'I do not know anything about food, and cannot grasp the
problem in a short time. Experience is needed. I have none. It is not even a production job. I
have energy and a sense of urgency. These are at your disposal if you can use them in face of
hostility from all those elements doing little and delaying much.' (Letter of 2 June 1941: Churchill
papers, 20/24.)

[5] Colville diary, 5 June 1941: Colville papers. Five days later, having tasted Beaverbrook's
present of five dozen bottles of Deidesheimer Hofstuck 1937, Churchill telegraphed, accepting
Mrs Hill's suggestion for his reply: 'Thank you so much for your exhilarating gift' (Churchill
papers, 2/416). On 12 June 1941, in the Honours List, Mrs Hill received an MBE (and Professor
Lindemann a barony: he became Lord Cherwell).

silenced by his personal popularity, are once more vocal.' Crete, added Channon, 'has been a great blow to him'.[1] At 2.30 in the morning Colville noted in his diary:

On late duty. The PM dictated his speech for next Tuesday, rather cantankerous in tone and likely, unless substantially toned down, to cause a good deal of unfavourable comment. Pug[2] says he thinks it is impossible to run a war efficiently if so much time has to be devoted to justifying one's actions in the House of Commons. At the risk of seeming smug he maintains that no error or misconception was made in the direction of the campaign from this end.

General Freyberg, Ismay told Colville, 'specifically said he was not afraid of the air'.[3]

On the morning of June 7 Churchill saw the editors of the main newspapers, 'with a view to damping down their criticisms and explaining the position'.[4] In a secret minute to Dill he also criticized Wavell's reluctance 'to undertake large scale offensive armoured operations', and urged that Wavell would be 'very well advised' to do just that 'while his fleeting authority remains'. If Wavell could 'destroy or cripple' the German armoured forces, Churchill added, and occupy 'the all-important airfields', then the German pressure against Egypt would be 'greatly retarded and reduced'.[5] With the second part of Operation 'Jaguar', fifty aircraft, reaching Egypt on the previous night, 'I cannot help being hopeful about the future,' Churchill telegraphed to Menzies on June 7.[6]

At two o'clock on the morning of June 8, British, Australian, Indian and Free French forces moved into Syria, north and east from Palestine and Transjordan. Operation 'Exporter' had begun. Its objectives, the

[1] Channon diary, 6 June 1941: Robert Rhodes James (editor), *Chips, The Diaries of Sir Henry Channon*, London 1967, page 307.

[2] Major-General Ismay.

[3] Colville diary, 6 June 1941: Colville papers.

[4] Colville diary, 7 June 1941: Colville papers.

[5] Prime Minister's Personal Minute, M.633/1, 7 June 1941: Churchill papers, 20/36. Two days later Churchill telegraphed to Wavell again: 'I venture once again to emphasize that the objective is not the reaching of particular positions, but the destruction by fighting of the armed force of the enemy wherever it may be found. As your force diminishes, so should his. He has a far longer line of communications than you and must be in greater difficulties about supply, especially of ammunition.' (Prime Minister's Personal Telegram, T.278, War Office No. 71086, 9 June 1941: Premier papers, 3/287/1.) 'So long as enemy can make considerable use of Benghazi, as he does at present,' Wavell replied, 'his communications are little more difficult than mine.' (Telegram O/71957, 10 June 1941: Churchill papers, 20/39.)

[6] Prime Minister's Personal Telegram, T.271, 7 June 1941: Churchill papers, 20/49. A day earlier Churchill had watched the arrival of the first 'Flying Fortresses' from the United States. He had also seen an anti-aircraft demonstration of new rocket types. Eleven days later he personally tested various weapons, including a Sten gun.

capture of Damascus and Beirut, were at first hampered by a successful Vichy tank counter-attack at Kuneitra, and an air attack on two British destroyers bombarding Sidon. Reinforcements had then to be sent from Egypt, further inhibiting any forward movement by Wavell against Rommel. It was not until June 20, after three days of severe fighting outside Damascus, that the Australian troops entered the Syrian capital.[1] At Ditchley, on the first day of the Syrian campaign, Churchill wrote to his son, serving in the western desert with the Commandos:

Darling Randolph,

Averell Harriman is travelling out to the Middle East, and I take the opportunity of sending you a line. There is so much to say, one hardly knows where to begin.

Harriman's daughter, who is charming, and Pamela have made friends and are going to take a small house together while he is away. It seems a pity that the house that was furnished at Ickleford is not available. Still, you are getting a very good rent.

A gigantic 4,000 pound bomb fell just outside the building of your flat in Westminster Gardens, obliterating the fountain and cracking the whole structure on one side. Unluckily it is the wrong side for you. The CIGS, who was sleeping quite close, in fact about twenty yards away, seems to have had a marvellous escape and is greatly exhilarated by the explosion. I am trying to get a similar stimulus applied in other quarters, but it is difficult to arrange.

The Annexe is now becoming a very strong place, but we have only once been below the armour during a raid. Your Mother is now insisting upon becoming a fire watcher on the roof, so it will look very odd if I take advantage of the securities provided. However, I suppose everybody must do their duty.

I sent you out an inquiry about the 60 men[2] because I heard a great deal of criticism here about these special troops surrendering in droves, and so on, and whatever other people may think, I am quite clear that these men ought to have fought till at least thirty per cent. were killed or wounded. Large, general capitulations are of a different character, but small parties are expected to put up a fight and not walk out of a cave with their hands up like a lot of ridiculous loons.

A young officer brought a letter from you hot-foot last week, but it was dated March 3, arriving on June 6. Much your best chance would be to post letters at the Embassy, and I daresay they would stretch a point to oblige you.

[1] In the course of 'Exporter', 4,600 Allied troops, and 6,500 Vichy troops, had been killed or wounded. Among the Allied forces was a unit of Palestinian Jews, one of whom, Moshe Dayan, lost an eye during the campaign.

[2] Sixty of the two hundred commandos who had landed at Kastellorizo on 24 February 1941 (see page 1014).

I see Pamela from time to time, and she gives me very good accounts of Winston. I have not seen him as he is living in Max's domains.

The Air attack has greatly lessened, and the Air Force are very disappointed that this moon-phase should have been spoiled by clouds, as they were hoping to make an impression upon the raiders. On the whole, I think the attack will not be so successful as it has been in the past, and at the moment we are having very little of it. Anyhow, I think the Baby is quite safe where he is.

You know Duncan had a frightful accident. He was going down in a car from London to Aberporth, and was lying down asleep with his shoes off. He had two drivers, but both fell asleep simultaneously. The car ran into a stone bridge which narrowed the road suddenly, and both his feet are smashed up, also some injury to his spine. For the time being he has had to give up his Command, but it is possible he may be able to return to his duties by hobbling about. He has done extraordinarily good work, and had become a Colonel. If he breaks down, there is always the House of Commons.

Our old House of Commons has been blown to smithereens. You never saw such a sight. Not one scrap was left of the Chamber except a few of the outer walls. The Huns obligingly chose a time when none of us were there. Oddly enough, on the last day but one before it happened I had a most successful Debate and wound up amid a great demonstration. They all got up and cheered as I left. I shall always remember this last scene.[1] Having lived so much of my forty years in this building, it seems very sad that its familiar aspect will not for a good many years be before me. Luckily we have the other place in good working order, so that Parliamentary institutions can function 'undaunted amid the storms'. We are now going to try the experiment of using the House of Lords. The Peers have very kindly moved on into the big Robing Room, and handed over their Debating Chamber to us. In about a fortnight I expect we shall be there. I never thought to make speeches from those red benches, but I daresay I shall take to it all right.

An Opposition is being formed out of the left-outs of all Parties,—LG, Hore-Belisha, Shinwell, Winterton, and some small fry, mostly National Liberals. They do their best to abuse us whenever the war news gives them an opportunity, but there is not the slightest sign that the House as a whole, or still less the country, will swerve from their purpose. I expect next Tuesday when I have to speak on Crete, we shall have Horeb[2] discanting upon the

---

[1] On 17 May 1941 the *Daily Telegraph* published an extract from a First World War reminiscence by A. MacCallum Scott, who had been in the House of Commons with Churchill one evening in March 1917. 'Just before we left the building,' MacCallum Scott recalled, 'he took me by the arm and steered me into the deserted Commons chamber. All was darkness, except from a ring of faint light from concealed lamps under the gallery. We could dimly discern the untidy litter of papers on the floor and the table, but the walls and the roof were invisible. "Look at it!" he said. "This little place is what makes the difference between us and Germany. It is in virtue of this that we muddle through to success, and for lack of this Germany's brilliant efficiency will lead her to final disaster. This little room is the shrine of the world's liberties."'

[2] Leslie Hore-Belisha, the former Secretary of State for War.

shortage of anti-aircraft guns. I am going to remind him of the Privilege case,[1] and a few other things which occur to me.

I hope you will try to see Averell Harriman when he arrives. I have made great friends with him, and have the greatest regard for him. He does all he can to help us.

By the time you get this, all sorts of things will have happened which I cannot refer to on paper. At the present time I am hopeful that we shall retrieve and restore the position. Meanwhile, in the larger sphere, not only are we gaining mastery over the Air attack, but making good progress in the Battle of the Atlantic. The United States are giving us more help every day, and longing for an opportunity to take the plunge. Whether they will do so or not remains an inscrutable mystery of American politics. The longer they wait, the longer and the more costly the job will be which they will have to do.

I am sending with this a copy of 'Into Battle'. It appears that this title was the name of Julian Grenfell's sonnet, and I got a note from Ettie Desborough saying how much she appreciated our having appropriated it. In order to put this right, I have, as you will see, had inserted in the new editions some of the best lines of his poem.[2]

We have a pleasant party here (Ditchley), and a very good film each night. I find this a great relief at week-ends, as it takes one away for a couple of hours from the war mill. Oliver Lyttelton is here with his wife. He has had a great success with a Bill to crush out all small businesses, and another to take all our clothes away from us. These very severe measures have proved extremely palatable to the nation, and the victims seem to have been all reduced to complacency. I also put, as you will have seen, Mr Leathers in a fine position. He is our Traffic Manager.[3] Pray God he delivers the goods.

Mr Brabner has just arrived with messages from you, and also news of the battle—fresh from Maleme Aerodrome; but as he left before the battle began, he was not quite so informative as I had hoped.

[1] On 17 June 1938 Duncan Sandys had sent Hore-Belisha the draft of a question which he wished to ask on London's air defences. As the question was clearly based on secret information, Hore-Belisha, with Churchill's approval, told Sandys to call on the Attorney-General, who told Sandys that unless he disclosed the name of his informant, he would be liable to prosecution under the Official Secrets Act. On June 29 Sandys informed the House that, in his capacity as a junior officer in the Territorial Army, he had received orders to appear in uniform before the Military Court of Inquiry. This he submitted, was a 'gross breach' of the privileges of the House. His submission was upheld, and a Committee of Privileges reported on the following day that a breach of privilege had indeed been committed. During the ensuing debate, Churchill commented caustically that an act devised to protect the national defence should not be used to shield Ministers who had neglected national defence.

[2] Two of Lady Desborough's three sons were killed on the western front, Julian, on 26 May 1915 and Gerald on 30 July 1915. Her third son died in 1926 as a result of a motor car accident.

[3] On 8 May 1941 Leathers had been appointed Minister of War Transport, a Ministry which he headed for the rest of the war, and in the 'Caretaker Government' from May to July 1945. He had been created Baron on 19 May 1941. In 1954, while Secretary of State for Co-ordination of Transport, Fuel and Power in Churchill's second Premiership, he was created Viscount.

Everything is very solid here, and I feel more sure than ever that we shall beat the life out of Hitler and his Nazi gang. We are waiting with much interest to know what fortunes have attended our entry into Syria. No one can tell which way the Vichy French cat will jump, and how far the consequences of this action will extend. It looks to me more and more likely that Hitler will go for Stalin. I cannot help it. All my sympathies are already fully engaged.

I am having this letter left for you at the Embassy, Cairo, and am asking them to tell you that it has arrived. I do not want it to go up to the line, and after you have received it, you should not take it there. Leave it at the Embassy, or burn it. Do not show it to strangers. I am glad that Lampson and his wife have been nice to you, and I am sure it is a comfort to have a good hot bath and a clean bed there when you come in from the Desert.

All good luck.

My very best wishes
Your loving father
Winston S. Churchill

PS. I send you a cheque for £100 which I expect you can get cashed in Cairo. I am telling Lloyds to notify some Bank or other there in case they have not a Branch, and will send you full advice about it.[1]

On June 10 Churchill made his House of Commons speech in answer to criticisms of the Crete campaign, 'a forceful speech', Colville noted, 'lasting $1\frac{1}{2}$ hours'.[2] In answering Hore-Belisha's criticisms of lack of anti-aircraft guns in Crete, Churchill declared that, after two years and seven months at the War Office, Hore-Belisha had left the army in a 'lamentable state'. Churchill also referred to one of his speeches, in March 1937, when he had warned that the Germans already possessed 1,500 mobile anti-aircraft guns in addition to the whole of their static artillery of anti-aircraft defence. He had given these warnings. But those whom he had warned, and who were now so vocal in criticism, had left a 'dismal' legacy.

What would have been said, Churchill wondered, 'if we had given up the island of Crete without firing a shot. We should have been told that this pusillanimous flight had surrendered to the enemy the key of the Eastern Mediterranean. . . .' Britain should not, he added, 'regret the Battle of Crete'. The fighting there had attained 'a severity and fierceness which the Germans have not previously encountered in their walk through Europe'.[3]

---

[1] Letter of 8 June 1941: Churchill papers, 1/362. *Into Battle*, a volume of Churchill's speeches from May 1938 to November 1941, had been edited by Randolph, and was published in February 1941.
[2] Colville diary, 10 June 1941: Colville papers.
[3] *Hansard*, 10 June 1941, columns 138–164.

On June 11 Churchill learned of Roosevelt's final agreement to send troops to help Britain with the garrisoning of Iceland.[1] On the following day he spoke to the representatives of the Dominions and of the 'Allied Countries'. A new secretary at No 10, Elizabeth Layton, kept a carbon copy of his speech notes, which included the lines:

> The prisons of the continent
>   no longer suffice.
>
> The concentration camps are crowded.
>
> Every dawn the G firing-parties
>   are at their work.
>
> Czechs, Poles, Dutchmen, Norwegians,
>   Serbs and Greeks, Frenchmen, Belgians,
>   Yugoslavs,
>   make the final sacrifice
>   for faith and country.
>
> A vile race of Quislings
>   —to use the new word wh will carry
>   the scorn of mankind
>   down the centuries—
>
> is hired to fawn upon the conqueror,
>   to 'collaborate' in his designs
>
> and to enforce his rule
>   upon their fellow-countrymen
>   while grovelling low themselves.
>
> Such is the plight of once glorious Europe,
>   and such are the atrocities
>   against wh we are in arms.[2]

Churchill ended his speech with a peroration which Oliver Lyttelton later described as 'among the highest flights in oratory'[3]

Hitler may turn and trample this way and that through tortured Europe. He may spread his course far and wide, and carry his curse with him: he may break into Africa or into Asia. But it is here, in this island fortress, that he will have to reckon in the end. We shall strive to resist by land and sea. We shall be on his track wherever he goes. Our airpower will continue to teach the German homeland that war is not all loot and triumph.

[1] Premier papers 3/230/1. Six days later, on 17 June 1941, Churchill minuted: 'The movement is most secret till completed,' and to preserve secrecy he referred to Iceland in a telegram to Roosevelt only as 'that cold place'.

[2] 'Speech to Allied Govts', 12 June 1941, speech notes: Nel papers.

[3] Oliver Lyttelton, Viscount Chandos, *The Memoirs of Lord Chandos*, London 1962, page 186.

We shall aid and stir the people of every conquered country to resistance and revolt. We shall break up and derange every effort which Hitler makes to systematise and consolidate his subjugation. He will find no peace, no rest, no halting-place, no parley. And if, driven to desperate hazards, he attempts the invasion of the British Isles, as well he may, we shall not flinch from the supreme trial. With the help of God, of which we must all feel daily conscious, we shall continue steadfast in faith and duty till our task is done.

This, then, is the message which we send forth today to all the States and nations bond or free, to all the men in all the lands who care for freedom's cause, to our allies and well-wishers in Europe, to our American friends and helpers drawing ever closer in their might across the ocean: this is the message—Lift up your hearts. All will come right. Out of the depths of sorrow and sacrifice will be born again the glory of mankind.[1]

Two days later, setting Churchill's mind at rest about earlier hesitations, Roosevelt announced publicly that he was freezing all German and Italian assets in the United States.

In a telegram to Roosevelt on June 14, Churchill reflected: 'People must have hope, to face the long haul that lies ahead.'[2]

That same day, Churchill broadcast to the United States. The occasion was his acceptance of an honorary degree from Rochester University. It was in the city of Rochester, Churchill had earlier written, 'where my Grandparents spent so many happy years'.[3] In his broadcast, Churchill spoke of that 'sense of kinship and unit' which he felt existed between the two peoples. His broadcast ended:

For more than a year we British have stood alone, uplifted by your sympathy and respect and sustained by our own unconquerable will-power and by the increasing growth and hopes of your massive aid. In these British Islands that look so small upon the map we stand, the faithful guardians of the rights and dearest hopes of a dozen States and nations now gripped and tormented in a base and cruel servitude. Whatever happens we shall endure to the end.

But what is the explanation of the enslavement of Europe by the German Nazi regime? How did they do it? It is but a few years ago since one united gesture by the peoples, great and small, who are now broken in the dust, would have warded off from mankind the fearful ordeal it has had to undergo. But there was no unity. There was no vision. The nations were pulled down one by one while the others gaped and chattered. One by one, each in his turn, they let themselves be caught. One after another they were felled by brutal violence or poisoned from within by subtle intrigue.

[1] Broadcast, 12 June 1941, typescript: Churchill papers, 9/151.

[2] Prime Minister's Personal Minute, T.295, 'Most Secret and Personal', Foreign Office Telegram No. 3281 to Washington, 14 June 1941 (sent 1.09 a.m., 15 June 1941): Premier papers, 3/230/1, folio 35.

[3] Foreign Office Telegram No. 2574 to Washington, 14 May 1941: Foreign Office papers, 371/26260. Lady Randolph Churchill's parents were Leonard and Clara Jerome.

And now the old lion with her lion cubs at her side stands alone against hunters who are armed with deadly weapons and impelled by desperate and destructive rage. Is the tragedy to repeat itself once more? Ah no! This is not the end of the tale. The stars in their courses proclaim the deliverance of mankind. Not so easily shall the onward progress of the peoples be barred. Not so easily shall the lights of freedom die.

But time is short. Every month that passes adds to the length and to the perils of the journey that will have to be made. United we stand. Divided we fall. Divided, the dark age returns. United, we can save and guide the world.[1]

On June 13 Churchill was given a first-hand account of the Crete campaign by Brigadier Inglis. As Inglis unfolded the details of all he had seen, Churchill was shocked to learn of severe deficiencies not only of supply, but also of preparation. 'I cannot feel,' he minuted for the Chiefs of Staff Committee on the following day, 'that there was any real grip shown by Middle East HQ upon this operation for the defence of Crete', and after setting out the details of the Brigadier's account, he added: 'The slowness in acting upon the precise intelligence with which they were furnished, and the general evidence of lack of drive and precision filled one with disquiet about this Middle East Staff.' It was 'evident', Churchill warned, 'that very far-reaching steps will have to be taken'.[2]

On June 15 Wavell launched 'Battleaxe', the much urged, long awaited offensive against Rommel. 'I naturally attach the very greatest importance to the venture,' Churchill telegraphed to Roosevelt on the eve of the attack.[3] But after an initial success, the attackers were forced to withdraw, with the loss of more than 100 tanks.[4] Churchill had gone down to Chartwell on the evening of June 17, wishing to be alone. But on his return Colville found him 'in good spirits, less perturbed than I had expected by the fiasco of "Battleaxe" ', and telling Colville 'that he was now busy considering where next we could take the offensive'.[5]

[1] Broadcast of 16 June 1941, recorded in the Central War Room: Text printed in full in *The Imperial Review*, No. 6, volume VIII, 28 June 1941.

[2] Prime Minister's Personal Minute, D.186/1, 'Most Secret', 14 June 1941: Churchill papers, 20/36.

[3] Prime Minister's Personal Telegram, T.295, 'Most Secret and Personal', Foreign Office No. 3281 to Washington, 1.09 a.m., 15 June 1941: Churchill papers, 20/39.

[4] A month later Churchill was told that 122 British troops had been killed during the four days of 'Battleaxe', 259 reported missing, and 558 wounded. (Note by Lieutenant-Colonel Jacob, 14 July 1941, 'Secret': Premier papers, 3/287/1, folio 2.)

[5] Colville diary, 18 June 1941: Colville papers.

For the 'time being', Churchill telegraphed to General Smuts, 'we have little hope of regaining the initiative'. But, referring to his dominant concern, he also told Smuts: 'I have increasingly good hopes of the United States,'[1] and on the following day he minuted to Eden, about the imminent arrival of more than four thousand American Marines in Iceland: 'As soon as the troops have arrived and begun to land, I should like the fullest publicity.'[2] When the news came out, Churchill told the War Cabinet, 'it was bound to create a great impression'.[3]

The severe merchant shipping losses; British, Allied and neutral, of 296,418 tons in April and 136,260 in May, were a spur to all Churchill's United States contacts, including Willkie, Hopkins and Harriman, to press continually for a wider American contribution to Britain's war effort, whether in shipping tonnage or weapons of war. Willkie in particular had stressed these shipping losses in public speeches designed to win the support of audiences throughout the United States. Acutely aware, from his experiences in the summer of 1940, of the dangers inherent in painting a black picture, however true, Churchill telegraphed to Willkie on June 20:

Please be careful my friend lest in trying to galvanise American opinion you disclose facts which dishearten our merchant seamen who have to go repeatedly to sea in the teeth of many dangers and at the same time lead the enemy to redouble his attacks. I am sure you will think of the effect on all the different audiences who will study your words.[4]

A further United States contribution was Roosevelt's agreement to establish a Ferry Service across the Atlantic from Brazil to West Africa, using American Army pilots, and the establishment of American manned staging posts with servicing facilities. The additional 'generous provision', Churchill telegraphed to Roosevelt on June 20, of twenty American transport aircraft on the route between Takoradi and Egypt, crossing Africa, 'will greatly ease our difficulty'.[5]

Seeking to create yet a further link between Britain and the United

---

[1] Prime Minister's Personal Telegram, T.302, No. 667 of 18 June 1941, sent 1.20 p.m., 'Personal and Most Secret': Premier papers, 3/287/2, folios 6–7.

[2] Prime Minister's Personal Minute, M.658/1, 19 June 1941: Churchill papers, 20/36.

[3] War Cabinet No. 61 of 1941, 19 June 1941, 12.30 p.m., Minute 3, Confidential Annex: Cabinet papers, 65/22.

[4] Prime Minister's Personal Telegram, T.313, 'of particular secrecy', Foreign Office No. 3432 to Washington, 20 June 1941: Churchill papers, 20/40. In June the merchant shipping tonnage sunk fell to 61,414.

[5] Prime Minister's Personal Telegram, T.310, 20 June 1941: Churchill papers, 20/40. At that very moment, Averell Harriman was on the Takoradi route, at Churchill's request, to give his advice on how to improve it.

States, on June 19 the Tank Parliament had approved Churchill's suggestion to 'propose the formation in America' of an Anglo-American Tank Board.[1] Churchill telegraphed to Roosevelt to ask for such a Board to be set up.[2] But Roosevelt replied that a 'joint British-American Tank Board' had already been in existence for some months'.[3] On reading Roosevelt's reply Churchill minuted to David Margesson, the Secretary of State for War: 'Surely I ought to have been told about this existing joint Tank Board, before I was asked to father a WO telegram to the President, asking for another.'[4]

Amid the grave problems and setbacks, signs of strain in Churchill were noted that day by two members of his own Secretariat, Peck and Colville, who watched the Prime Minister at closest quarters. 'John Peck and I agreeed,' Colville noted in his diary on June 19, 'that the PM does not help the Government machine to run smoothly and his inconsiderate treatment of the Service Departments would cause trouble were it not for the great personal loyalty of the Service Ministers to himself.' Colville added: 'He supplies drive and initiative but he often meddles where he would better leave things alone and the operational side of the war might profit if he gave it a respite and turned to grapple with Labour and Production.'[5] A week later, Anthony Eden's Private Secretary, Oliver Harvey, heard the same complaint from Eden, noting in his diary: 'He told me how difficult the PM was: in spite of splendid qualities as a popular leader, he had a devastating effect on planning.' Eden told Harvey the 'great need' was of a Minister of Defence 'independent of the PM'.[6]

On the following day Churchill went to Dover with Sinclair, Keyes,

---

[1] Tank Parliament No. 4 of 1941, 5 p.m., 19 June 1941: Cabinet papers, 120/52.

[2] The telegram was drafted in its entirety by the War Office.

[3] 'Secret', 11 July 1941: Premier papers, 3/426/3, folio 16.

[4] Minute of 11 July 1941: Premier papers, 3/426/3, folio 6.

[5] Colville diary, 19 June 1941: Colville papers. Six days later Churchill told the House of Commons, in Secret Session: 'I do not think, and my colleagues will bear me witness, any expression of scorn or severity which I have heard used by our critics, has come anywhere near the language I have been myself accustomed to use, not only orally, but in a continued stream of written minutes. In fact, I wonder that a great many of my colleagues are on speaking terms with me. They would not be if I had not complained of and criticised all evenly alike. But, bound together as we are by a common purpose, the men who have joined hands in this affair put up with a lot, and I hope they will put up with a lot more. It is the duty of the Prime Minister to use the power which Parliament and the nation have given him to drive others, and in a war like this that power has to be used irrespective of anyone's feelings. If we win, nobody will care. If we lose, there will be nobody to care.' (Charles Eade, compiler, *Secret Session Speeches by the Right Hon. Winston S. Churchill, OM, CH, MP*, London 1946, pages 34–5.)

[6] Harvey diary, 25 June 1941: John Harvey (editor), *The War Diaries of Oliver Harvey*, London 1978, page 15.

Dill, Morton, Colville and others, to inspect an 18-inch gun on its railway mounting, and to examine anti-aircraft defences on the South Coast. Then, when the others returned to London, Churchill left the train with Morton and Colville, to go once more to Chartwell, to which he sometimes went at times of crisis. 'There will be no weakening here,' Churchill had telegraphed to Roosevelt, earlier that day,[1] with Operation 'Battleaxe' at a halt, with Brigadier Inglis' account of the Crete disaster still very much on his mind.

That afternoon, at Chartwell, Churchill had slept for several hours, and then, as Colville noted, 'in a purple dressing-gown and grey felt hat, took me to see his goldfish'. He was ruminating, Colville wrote, 'about the fate of Tobruk since the failure of "Battleaxe" and contemplating means of resuming the offensive. He continued this train of thought in the cottage, conversing the while with the Yellow Cat and with Desmond about his garden.'[2]

Churchill had come to a decision of considerable moment: that Wavell must be replaced.[3] On June 20 he telegraphed to Lord Linlithgow, the Viceroy of India, explaining his decision, and proposing to replace Wavell by the Commander-in-Chief, India, General Auchinleck. Churchill's telegram read:

I have come to the conclusion that a change is needed in the command in the Middle East. Wavell has a glorious record, having completely destroyed the Italian Army and conquered the Italian Empire in Africa. He has also borne up well against the German attacks and has conducted war and policy in three or four directions simultaneously since the beginning of the struggle. I must regard him as our most distinguished General.

Nevertheless, I feel he is tired, and that a fresh eye and an unstrained hand is needed. I wish therefore to bring about a change-over for temporary war time conditions between him and Auchinleck.

I feel sure Auchinleck would infuse a new energy and precision into the defence of the Nile Valley, and that Wavell would make an admirable Commander-in-Chief in India, who would aid you in the whole of the great sphere which India is now assuming as our flank moves eastward.

[1] Prime Minister's Personal Telegram, T.310, 20 June 1941: Churchill papers, 20/40.

[2] Colville diary, 20 June 1941: Colville papers.

[3] Six weeks earlier, Eden noted in his diary, after a talk with Churchill on 10 May 1941: 'He was in favour of changing Auchinleck and Wavell about. Max agreed as Amery had already done. The other three of us were more doubtful. As I knew the men best, I found the advice not easy to give. I have no doubt that Archie has the better mind, but one does not know how he is bearing the strain and one cannot tell, though some of his recent reactions seem to indicate that he is flagging. In the end I weakly counselled delay and asked to wait for Crete result.' (Eden diary, 10 May 1941: The Earl of Avon, *The Eden Memoirs*, *The Reckoning*, London 1965, page 250.)

'Anyone can see arguments against such an exchange,' Churchill added, 'but I hope you will help me in bringing this about.'[1]

On June 21 Churchill telegraphed to Wavell:

I have come to the conclusion that the public interest will best be served by the appointment of General Auchinleck to relieve you in the Command of the armies of the Middle East. I have greatly admired your command and conduct of these armies both in success and adversity, and the victories which are associated with your name will be famous in the story of the British Army and are an important contribution to our final success in this obstinate war. I feel however that after the long strain you have borne a new eye and a new hand are required in this most seriously menaced theatre.

Churchill added that he was sure that Wavell was 'incomparably the best man and most distinguished officer to fill the vacancy of Commander in Chief in India'.[2]

In explaining his decision, Churchill told Ismay that to remain on the defensive in Cyrenaica, as Wavell had proposed, and to do so for the next three months, would mean the evacuation of Tobruk, 'with losses of 50 tanks, 100 guns, 1,000 vehicles and all stores, also the possibility of disaster'. Still, Churchill admitted, 'it might be done'. His explanation continued:

Further consequences are that the enemy will reinforce very strongly and build up his army for a main offensive against Egypt as soon as the weather cools, or perhaps sooner. The Admiral has abandoned all hopes of blocking Tripoli, and perhaps Benghazi also with *Anson*. Every single one of our plans has failed. The enemy has completely established himself in the Central Mediterranean. We are afraid of his dive-bombers at every point. Our ships cannot enforce any blockade between Italy and Cyrenaica or Greece and Cyrenaica, apart from submarines. The Air Force are plainly unable to stop them reinforcing.

Churchill ended: 'Have we really got to accept this?'[3]

At Chequers on the day of Wavell's dismissal, Churchill talked over with Colville what had been done, telling Colville it had been a 'very difficult' decision. Colville's account of the conversation continued: 'I wondered if Wavell might not sulk and refuse India,' but Churchill told him he had been 'afraid of just putting him on the shelf, as that would excite much comment and attention'. Colville suggested, as had

---

[1] Prime Minister's Personal Telegram, T.309, 'Most Urgent. Absolutely Secret and Personal', 20 June 1941: Churchill papers, 20/49.

[2] Prime Minister's Personal Telegram, T.320, 'Personal and Secret', 21 June 1941: Churchill papers, 20/40.

[3] Prime Minister's Personal Minute, D.196/1, 21 June 1941: Cabinet papers, 120/10.

Dill, that Wavell would 'use his pen' after the war to write up the episode, to which Churchill replied 'that he could use his too, and would bet he sold more copies!'[1]

On June 22 Wavell telegraphed from Cairo: 'I think you are wise to make change and get new ideas and action on many problems in Middle East and am sure Auchinleck will be successful choice.' Wavell added: 'I appreciate your generous references to my work and am honoured that you should consider me fitted to fill post of C-in-C India.'[2]

In telling Roosevelt of Wavell's dismissal Churchill wrote: 'I must regard him as our most distinguished General.' Nevertheless, he added, 'though this should not be stated publicly, we felt that, after the long strain he had borne, he was tired, and a fresh eye and an unstrained hand were needed in this most seriously menaced theatre'.[3]

The decision to replace Wavell was to remain a controversial issue during and after the war. Seven years later, looking back over these events, Churchill wrote to Ismay of Wavell's decision in February 1941, four months before 'Battleaxe', to send the remaining brigade of the 7th Armoured Division back to the Delta, 'wearing out its tanks by a 400-mile trek back to Cairo'. Churchill's letter continued:

He could easily have left these tanks in situ and refreshed their tired crews from his large surplus of tank men at the base. The 7th Armoured Division wore out its tanks in going home to be refitted, and did not come into action for nearly five months. Its tanks had enough kick in them to have beaten Rommel instead of trekking home. It was replaced by the 2nd Armoured Division, which was new to the game. These are explanations of why our left flank in the Desert was bashed in, with immense resulting disaster.[4]

As Ismay helped Churchill to prepare the war memoirs, he too reflected on Wavell's dismissal, writing to Churchill in December 1948:

The deciding episode that lives in my mind was that both Eden and Dill thought that Wavell had been tremendously affected by the breach of his desert flank by Rommel. His Intelligence had misinformed him and the thrust came as a complete surprise. I seem to remember Eden saying that Wavell had 'aged ten years in the night'. You yourself said that Rommel had torn the new won laurels from Wavell's brow and thrown them in the sand.

Apart from that particular episode, Ismay added, 'I think there was

---

[1] Colville diary, 21 June 1941: Colville papers.
[2] Telegram No. 75271, 22 June 194:. Churchill papers, 20/40.
[3] Premier papers, 3/469.
[4] Letter of 23 April 1948: Churchill papers, 4/208.

a very general impression in Whitehall that Wavell was very tired.'[1]
And six weeks later, Ismay wrote to Churchill again:

Some time ago you asked me whether I remembered the reasons that
impelled you to replace Wavell by Auchinleck, and I replied that you and all
of us in London got the feeling that Wavell was a tired man.

Ian Jacob reminded me last night of an episode which confirmed this view,
and which I now recollect very vividly. I can see you now, holding out both
your hands as though you had a fishing rod in each of them, and you said: 'I
feel that I have got a tired fish on this rod, and a very lively one on the other'.

'You were very pleased with Auchinleck at that time,' Ismay
recalled, 'because he had been so forward in the Iraq affair'.[2]

[1] Letter of 13 December 1948: Churchill papers, 4/220.
[2] Letter of 2 February 1949: Churchill papers, 4/220.

58

Russia: 'We shall do everything to help you . . .'

FOR some weeks the Enigma decrypts, and other Intelligence reports, had indicated the possibility of a German attack on Russia. 'It looks as if Hitler is massing against Russia,' Churchill had telegraphed to Smuts on May 16. 'A ceaseless movement of troops, armoured forces, and aircraft northwards from the Balkans and eastwards from France and Germany is in progress.'[1]

If Russia were to resist a German attack, Portal told the War Cabinet on June 9, 'we could then undertake to do all we could to draw off German air forces', by air action in the West. This proposal met with 'general approval'.[2]

On June 12 British Intelligence decrypted a message, which was dated June 4, sent from Berlin to Tokyo by the Japanese Ambassador to Germany. The Ambassador, Oshima, reported a conversation with Hitler, in which the Führer told him that Communist Russia must be 'eliminated'. Hitler added that if Japan 'lagged behind when Germany declared a state of war against Russia, it was quite open to her to do so'.

Neither Hitler, nor Ribbentrop, who was also present at the discussion, gave any date for this 'state of war'. But the Ambassador reported that the atmosphere of urgency during the conversation suggested that a German invasion of Russia was close at hand.[3]

Oshima's report to Tokyo was decrypted on the Purple machine.

[1] Prime Minister's Personal Telegram, T.183, 16 May 1941: Churchill papers, 20/39.
[2] War Cabinet No. 58 of 1941, 9 June 1941, 5 p.m., Confidential Annex: Cabinet papers, 65/22.
[3] Joint Intelligence Committee Report No. 252(O) of 1941, 12 June 1941: F. H. Hinsley and others, *British Intelligence in the Second World War, Its Influence on Strategy and Operations*, volume 1, page 478, London 1979.

Unlike Enigma, whose operational messages, essential in themselves, provided few clues of long-term or high level thinking, as opposed to imminent military moves, the Purple decrypts threw light on what was being said and decided at the highest level of policymaking in Germany. The combination of the Purple and Enigma decrypts was decisive. Three days later, on June 15, Churchill telegraphed to Roosevelt:

> From every source at my disposal, including some most trustworthy, it looks as if a vast German onslaught on Russia was imminent. Not only are the main German armies deployed from Finland to Roumania, but the final arrivals of air and armoured forces are being completed. The pocket battleship *Lützow*, which put her nose out of the Skagerrak yesterday and was promptly torpedoed by our coastal aircraft, was very likely going north to give naval strength on the Arctic flank.
>
> Should this new war break out, we shall of course give all encouragement and any help we can spare to the Russians following principle that Hitler is the foe we have to beat.

'I do not expect any class political reactions here,' Churchill added, 'and I trust a German–Russian conflict will not cause you any embarrassment.'[1]

On Saturday, June 21, Churchill lunched at Downing Street with Lord Louis Mountbatten, who had just returned from Crete, where he had commanded the destroyer *Kelly*. Mountbatten gave Churchill a dramatic account, which he then repeated to Colville, of how, when the *Kelly* had been sunk, 'the Germans machine-gunned him and his crew as they swam'. From Downing Street Churchill drove to Chequers, for the rest of the weekend. Eden, Winant and Sir Edward Bridges were among the guests. Colville, who was on duty that weekend, recorded in his diary:

> The PM says a German attack on Russia is certain and Russia will assuredly be defeated. He thinks that Hitler is counting on enlisting capitalist and right-wing sympathies in this country and the US. PM says he is wrong: he will go all out to help Russia. Winant asserts that same will be true in US.
>
> After dinner, when I was walking on the lawn with the PM, he elaborated this and I said that for him, the arch anti-communist, this was bowing down in the House of Rimmon.[2] He replied that he had only one single purpose—

---

[1] Prime Minister's Personal Minute, T295, 'Most Secret and Personal', Foreign Office Telegram No. 3281 to Washington, 14 June 1941 (sent 1.09 a.m., 15 June 1941): Premier papers, 3/230/1, folio 35.

[2] '... when my master goeth into the house of Rimmon to worship there, and he leaneth on my hand, and I bow myself in the house of Rimmon: when I bow down in the house of Rimmon, the Lord pardon thy servant in this thing'. (2 Kings 5, verse 18.)

the destruction of Hitler—and his life was much simplified thereby. If Hitler invaded Hell he would at least make a favourable reference to the Devil!

That night, while those at Chequers slept, Hitler's forces invaded Russia. The 'new war' had begun, and the first report of it was telephoned to Chequers shortly after four o'clock that morning. Colville, who was woken to receive the message, decided not to wake Churchill, who had given strict orders that he was never to be woken before 8 o'clock in the morning, unless Britain itself had been invaded. It was not therefore until 8 o'clock that Colville 'went a round of the bedrooms breaking the news'. Churchill's only comment to him was: 'Tell the BBC I will broadcast at 9 tonight.'[1]

Eden, who had spent the night at Chequers, later recalled how:

... at about half-past seven the Prime Minister's valet, Sawyers, came into my bedroom and said: 'The Prime Minister's compliments and the German armies have invaded Russia.' Thereupon he presented me with a large cigar on a silver salver.

I put on my dressing-gown and went along to the Prime Minister's bedroom. We savoured the relief, but not for me at that hour the cigar, and discussed what was immediately to do. Churchill said he would speak to the nation that night and tell them that we intended to treat the Russians as partners in the struggle against Hitler. . . .[2]

During the first hours of the 'new war', the American Ambassador, Winant, said that he suspected it might all be a 'put up job' between Hitler and Stalin. Later, Colville noted, both Churchill and Sir Stafford Cripps, who had been summoned at once to Chequers, 'laughed this to scorn'. Another of those brought into the discussion that morning was Lord Beaverbrook, who expressed, as he later recalled, 'faith in Russia's strength and power to resist'. But Cripps felt differently, and, with his knowledge of Russian weakness derived from the perspective of Moscow, dwelt, as Beaverbrook recalled, 'on the handicaps which Russia would face in striving to deal with this type of blitzkrieg, which had laid the great French army low within a single month'. Beaverbrook's account continued:

Mr Churchill listened, questioned, considered, all through the day. Occasionally he sat in the garden in the hot sunshine. Then again he would stride to his office, restless to a degree. But though he was restless he had in fact early made up his mind. He would broadcast that night his determination that Russia should be given all the aid in Britain's power.

It was a decision taken without calling his Cabinet together. There was no

[1] Colville diary, 22 June 1941: Colville papers.
[2] The Earl of Avon, *The Eden Memoirs, The Reckoning*, London 1965, page 270.

time to summon his colleagues. It was a decision taken in the likelihood that it would arouse a measure of hostility, albeit unspoken, among sections of his own Party. Nor could he have any guarantee either of the attitude of the British newspapers. . . .[1]

Churchill worked on his broadcast throughout the day. It was not yet ready half an hour before it was due, and 'gave me great anxiety', Colville noted, 'but even more so to Eden who wanted to vet the text and couldn't'.[2]

Another of those brought into the discussion, this time by telephone, was the new Minister of Aircraft Production, Colonel Moore-Brabazon. Six weeks later he wrote to Churchill of how 'you will remember that you rang me up the day the Germans marched on Russia about production matters and in concluding the talk, in that you were going to broadcast that night, you did say: "Do you not think we ought to help?" And I said "yes" enthusiastically.'[3]

Churchill's broadcast began with a survey of his own attitude to Communism since the Bolshevik revolution of 1917. The Nazi regime, he said, 'is indistinguishable from the worst features of Communism. It is devoid of all theme and principle except appetite and racial domination. It excels all forms of human wickedness in the efficiency of its cruelty and ferocious aggression.' His speech continued:

No one has been a more consistent opponent of Communism than I have for the last twenty-five years. I will unsay no word that I have spoken about it. But all this fades away before the spectacle which is now unfolding. The past, with its crimes, its follies, and its tragedies, flashes away.

I see the Russian soldiers standing on the threshold of their native land, guarding the fields which their fathers have tilled from time immemorial. I see them guarding their homes where mothers and wives pray—ah, yes, for there are times when all pray—for the safety of their loved ones, the return of the bread-winner, of their champion, of their protector. I see the ten thousand villages of Russia where the means of existence is wrung so hardly from the soil, but where there are still primordial human joys, where maidens laugh and children play.

I see advancing upon all this in hideous onslaught the Nazi war machine, with its clanking, heel-clicking, dandified Prussian officers, its crafty expert agents fresh from the cowing and tying down of a dozen countries. I see also the dull, drilled, docile, brutish masses of the Hun soldiery plodding on like a swarm of crawling locusts. I see the German bombers and fighters in the sky,

[1] 'The Second Front', a narrative prepared by Beaverbrook and David Farrer after the second world war: A. J. P. Taylor, *Beaverbrook*, London 1972, page 475.

[2] Colville diary, 22 June 1941: Colville papers.

[3] 'Private', 3 September 1941: Churchill papers, 20/24.

still smarting from many a British whipping, delighted to find what they believe is an easier and a safer prey.

Churchill then spoke of the need for an immediate British response,
telling his listeners:

I have to declare the decision of His Majesty's Government—and I feel
sure it is a decision in which the great Dominions will in due course concur—
for we must speak out now at once, without a day's delay.

I have to make the declaration, but can you doubt what our policy will be?
We have but one aim and one single, irrevocable purpose. We are resolved to
destroy Hitler and every vestige of the Nazi regime. From this nothing will
turn us—nothing.

We will never parley, we will never negotiate with Hitler or any of his
gang. We shall fight him by land, we shall fight him by sea, we shall fight him
in the air, until, with God's help, we have rid the earth of his shadow and liberated its peoples from his yoke. Any man or state who fights on against Nazidom will have our aid. Any man or state who marches with Hitler is our foe.

That is our policy and that is our declaration. It follows therefore that we
shall give whatever help we can to Russia and the Russian people. We shall
appeal to all our friends and allies in every part of the world to take the same
course and pursue it, as we shall, faithfully and steadfastly to the end. . . .

The German invasion of Russia, Churchill said, was 'no more than a
prelude' to an attempted invasion of Britain. Hitler hoped, no doubt,
to defeat Russia 'before the winter comes', and then to turn his forces
upon Britain, 'before the Fleet and air-power of the United States may
intervene'. By continuing to destroy his enemies one by one, a process
by which 'he has so long thrived and prospered', Hitler hoped the scene
would be clear 'for the final act', the subjugation of the Western Hemisphere 'to his will and system'. For this reason, Churchill continued:

The Russian danger is therefore our danger, and the danger of the United
States, just as the cause of any Russian fighting for his hearth and home is the
cause of free men and free peoples in every quarter of the globe. Let us learn
the lessons already taught by such cruel experience. Let us redouble our exertions and strike with united strength while life and power remain.[1]

'A masterpiece,' Harold Nicolson noted in his diary, commenting
that Churchill 'does not conceal that Russia may be beaten quickly,
but having indicated to us the approaching collapse of India and
China, and, in fact, of Europe, Asia and Africa, he somehow leaves us
with the impression that we are quite certain to win this war.'[2]

[1] Broadcast of 22 June 1941: His Master's Voice recording, ALP 1556.
[2] Nicolson diary, 22 June 1941: Nigel Nicolson (editor), *Harold Nicolson, Diaries with Letters,
1939–1945*, London 1967, page 174.

That night, at Chequers, there was an argument between Churchill and Eden, joined by Lord Cranborne, as to the wisdom of Churchill's declaration. The question at issue, Colville noted in his diary, was whether there should be an immediate debate in the House of Commons on Russia, and he recorded how:

Eden and Cranborne took the Tory standpoint that if there was it should be confined to the purely military aspect, as politically Russia was as bad as Germany and half the country would object to being associated with her too closely. The PM's view was that Russia was now at war; innocent peasants were being slaughtered; and we should forget about Soviet systems or the Comintern and extend our hand to fellow human-beings in distress. The argument was brilliant and extremely vehement. I have never spent a more enjoyable evening.

Later, the night being very warm, we all walked in the garden and I gossiped with Edward Bridges while the PM continued an onslaught, begun at dinner, on the people who had let us in for this most unnecessary of all wars. He was harsh about Chamberlain whom he called 'the narrowest, most ignorant, most ungenerous of men'. At dinner it had been Chatfield whom he belaboured and the people at the Admiralty and elsewhere whose desire for 'absurd self-abasement had brought us to the verge of annihilation'.[1]

On going to bed the PM kept on repeating how wonderful it was that Russia had come in against Germany when she might so easily have been with her. He is also very pleased with our daylight sorties by fighters which, today and yesterday, accounted for 58 enemy planes over France for the loss of 3 pilots. We seem to command the daylight air over enemy territory as well as our own.[2]

From the moment that Hitler invaded Russia, Churchill envisaged rapid British counter-action, suggesting to the Chiefs of Staff Committee on June 23 the possibility not only of a series of intensified bombing raids on German military and naval installations, but the launching of 'a large raid', under full Air protection, of 25 to 30 thousand men across the Channel to German-occupied France. The Commandos, plus one of the Canadian Divisions, might do this, he suggested, 'with considerable result'. 'Now the enemy is busy in Russia,' he added, 'is the

---

[1] When Lord Chatfield, former First Sea Lord, and Minister for Co-ordination of Defence in 1939, sought permission to use official records for his memoirs, Churchill minuted to Sir Edward Bridges: 'No man has more need to fear investigation of his record than Lord Chatfield, who shamefully failed to state the naval case against giving away the Irish bases. Moreover, he was a sailor who prolonged his official life after he had left the Navy by building up credit with the advocates of appeasement. If it comes to a fight, he is going to get pretty knocked about. But this is the very reason why a controversy of this kind should not be allowed.' (Prime Minister's Personal Minute C.95/1, 'Secret', 23 December 1941: Churchill papers 20/36.)

[2] Colville diary, 22 June 1941: Colville papers.

time to "Make hell while the sun shines."'[1] And in response to a suggestion from H. G. Wells to ignite German forests and crops, Churchill minuted for Sinclair and Portal: 'What is the position about bombing of the Black Forest this year? It ought to be possible to produce very fine results.'[2]

On June 23 the Soviet Ambassador in London went to see Eden. The activity of the Royal Air Force over France, Eden reported to Churchill had 'evidently given satisfaction to the Russians'. But Maisky went on to ask whether there was 'no other intervention Britain could do,' such as 'attempting any form of landing on any part of the German occupied coasts now that a large part of the German Air Force was away in the East'.

As Eden minuted to Churchill, he had been 'of course, non-committal, and only contented myself with pointing out the difficulties and emphasising that it was the German Air Force we were most anxious to draw off'. Nevertheless, Eden added, 'I know you share my conviction that this is the time for us to press the Germans in the West by any means in our power. Whether this can be extended from air action to land action I cannot judge but I thought Maisky's comments worth passing on.'[3]

On June 24 German forces struck deep into Russian-annexed Poland and the Baltic States, occupying Brest-Litovsk, Vilna, and Kovno. Each Soviet retreat raised the spectre of a German victory on the eastern front. The brunt of Hitler's armed power could then be thrown against Britain, either across the Channel, or in the Middle East. In order to meet this threat with the best possible chance of success, Churchill felt above all the need for a massive increase in British tank strength, telegraphing to Roosevelt on June 26:

Our common aim, you will agree, must be to design much better tanks than the Nazis, to be ahead in the race guns *versus* armour, and to produce them quicker than they can. This, I feel sure, can only be achieved by the closest co-operation in design as well as in production, and I think there is already ample evidence that we can learn a lot from your technicians on the mech-

---

[1] Prime Minister's Personal Minute, D.195/1, 23 June 1941: Churchill papers, 20/36.

[2] Prime Minister's Personal Minute, M.671/1, 23 June 1941: Premier papers, 3/11/1, folio 18. On 2 July 1941 Portal minuted to Churchill: 'crops will not burn, but forests will'. Bomber Command 'will therefore go for the forests'. What was needed, he explained, was 'a variant on the sticky bomb or Molotoff Cocktail which will scatter an inflammable mixture on the trees themselves' as there was no undergrowth under pine trees for a standard incendiary bomb to set fire to. A new bomb was therefore to be devised. (Premier papers, 3/11/1, folio 12.)

[3] Minute of 24 June 1941, PM/41/53, SU/41/18: Foreign Office papers, 954/24, folio 323.

anical side, whilst we can possibly give you valuable advice, obtained by newly-bought experience, as to the fighting requirements.[1]

In elaborating on his proposal in a telegram to Hopkins, Churchill also urged the maximum possible production in the United States of tanks for Britain over the coming six to nine months, when Britain might have to 'fight hard on land' in two areas, against a German attempt 'to capture Egypt and the vital oil areas of Iraq and Persia', and against an invasion attempt on Britain itself. 'A large number of tanks in both theatres is a necessity,' Churchill warned, 'if we are successfully to overcome these dangers.'[2]

Churchill also gave instructions, on the following day, for the manufacture of Beach Protection Vehicles for future British amphibious landings overseas. 'Report progress in one week,' he instructed,[3] and he then watched progress week by week through the charts that Colonel Hollis submitted to him.

On June 27 Churchill sought to lay plans for yet another aspect of Britain's future offensive power, the creation of sea-borne anti-aircraft batteries which could cover landing grounds against dive bombing attack[4] between 'the first landing' and the seizure of airfields from which British fighter squadrons could provide air protection 'It can only be done,' he wrote, 'by the provision of floating batteries which can take their stations in the dark hours of the first attack and be ready to protect the landing places from daylight onwards.'

Churchill's minute ended: 'pray let me have a report in one week, showing the proposed action and the timetable'.[5]

Strongly advised to do so by his son Randolph, on June 27 Churchill had also decided to set up a new Middle East authority, that of Minister of State in the Middle East, with powers to provide, as Randolph had suggested, 'day to day political and strategic direction'.[6] The position

[1] Prime Minister's Personal Telegram, T.342, 26 June 1941: Churchill papers, 20/49.
[2] Prime Minister's Personal Telegram, T.343, 26 June 1941: Churchill papers, 20/49.
[3] Prime Minister's Personal Minute, D198/1, 27 June 1941: Premier papers, 3/260/1.
[4] It was the lack of such cover that had led to the abandonment of the attempt to seize Kastellorizo, operation 'Abstention', see page 1014.
[5] Prime Minister's Personal Minute, D.198/1, to General Ismay and the Controller, Admiralty, 'Report Progress in One Week' (label), 27 June 1941: Premier papers, 3/260/1, folios 12–14. At the end of September, after the designs and first tests were completed, Churchill minuted: 'These vessels must be hurried forward with the highest priority and special exertions. The guns, crews and battery organizations should be assembled forthwith on shore and should be exercised in battery in a space conforming to the deck space and with every other circumstance necessary to resemble the conditions at sea. Thus when the vessels are ready, the crews will be integral units and largely worked-up. They should have plenty of target practice.' (Prime Minister's Personal Minute, to Colonel Hollis, D.271/1, 3 October 1941: Premier papers, 3/260/1, folio 6.)
[6] Randolph Churchill, telegram of 7 June 1941.

would involve responsibilities for supply, censorship, Intelligence and propaganda. The first incumbent, appointed on June 28, was Oliver Lyttelton, the President of the Board of Trade. As representative of the War Cabinet, the new Minister would, Churchill explained, give the local Commanders-in-Chief 'that political guidance which has not hitherto been available locally', as well as relieving the Commanders-in-Chief of such 'extraneous policies with which they have hitherto been burdened', such as relations with the Free French, the administration of occupied enemy territory, finance and economic warfare, and propaganda and subversive warfare.[1]

The Minister of State was to be Chairman of a Middle Eastern War Council, and of a smaller Middle Eastern Defence Committee. The Council was to include among its members the Prime Minister of South Africa, General Smuts.[2]

At the same time a second, military authority, that of Intendant-General, was set up, to prepare, together with Averell Harriman's watching support, the large scale organisation 'for the reception of American munitions', as well as improving the servicing arrangements for tanks, motor transport and aircraft. The officer chosen for this task was General Sir Robert Haining.[3]

These two changes were made in order to help prepare the Middle East for the possibly imminent German attack on Egypt and the Suez Canal, once Russia had been defeated.

To Menzies, Churchill telegraphed on June 29: 'We must be prepared here for an extraordinary assault, and I am having everything

---

[1] 'Functions of the Minister of State for the Middle East, Memorandum by the Prime Minister', War Cabinet paper 148 of 1941, 28 June 1941: Cabinet papers, 120/250.

[2] Other members of the thirteen-member Middle Eastern War Council were the British Ambassadors in Cairo and Baghdad, the High Commissioner for Palestine and the Governors of Cyprus and Aden. The Middle Eastern Defence Committee was to be limited to the Minister of State and the three Commanders-in-Chief, Admiral Sir Andrew Cunningham, Auchinleck and Tedder. (Cabinet papers, 120/250.)

[3] Prime Minister's Personal Telegram, T.348 (to the Prime Minister of Australia) 28 June 1941: Churchill papers, 20/40. Of Haining, Randolph Churchill wrote to his father on 5 July 1941, from Alexandria: 'I have taken a great liking to your Intendant-General. He has struck me as incomparably the ablest General I have ever met. Even judged by normal standards, he would be remarkable. It is immensely refreshing to find one man with red tabs whom one can talk to on level terms as an ordinary human being. It is also refreshing to find a General who has a private secretary. It makes it quite a pleasure to do business with him. One of the handicaps that Military people suffer from is that the first 20 years of their life they are never in a position to learn how to run an office or even to dictate a letter. By the time that such amenities are in their power, they are too set in their ways to change; as a result of which you can see Generals wandering round GHQ looking for bits of string and sealing wax. My solution for "Muddle East", as it is widely known, is to sack half of the people in the office and provide half the remainder with competent shorthand typists. It would treble the efficiency of the Army.' (Churchill papers, 20/33.)

brought to concert pitch by September 1. I shall broadcast a warning next Sunday. We must not overlook the needs of the main front.'

Informing Menzies of the imminent United States garrisoning of Iceland, Churchill described it as 'an immense advantage towards the war', but, he wrote, 'hope deferred maketh the heart sick'.[1]

While working so hard on American involvement, Churchill was greatly angered to read in a Foreign Office telegram from Washington of a proposal that American destroyers should, for strategic reasons, operate 'on their side of the Atlantic rather than upon ours'. Whoever had 'put this about', Churchill minuted to Eden, A. V. Alexander and Pound, 'has done great dis-service, and should be immediately removed from all American contacts'. Churchill added: 'No question of Naval strategy in the Atlantic is comparable with the importance of drawing the Americans to this side. May I ask that this should be accepted at once as a decision of policy. . . .'[2]

At the Battle of the Atlantic Committee three days later, Churchill asked 'what help has been derived' from the United States naval patrols in the western Atlantic.

The answer was disappointing: 'some little help had been received in regard to raiders', he was told, 'but virtually none at all in regard to U-boats'. He had it in mind, Churchill commented, 'to invite the US Government to let us have a greater number of escort vessels'.[3]

Asked that same day whether the imminent arrival of United States troops in Iceland meant that British troops could withdraw, Churchill minuted to Ismay: 'The only thing that matters is for the United States to arrive in Iceland, as soon and as many as possible. Whether we stay or go, in whole or in part, is altogether secondary: and indeed I think it preferable that the two forces should be in the Island together for some time to come.'[4]

Churchill had further cause for concern about the actual working of Anglo-American supply links when he received on July 3 a telegram from Averell Harriman, who had flown out to Cairo through Takoradi to see the workings of the Takoradi Air Ferry route and the use to

---

[1] Prime Minister's Personal Telegram, T.349, 29 June 1941: Churchill papers, 20/40.

[2] 'Action this Day', Prime Minister's Personal Minute, M.676/1, 28 June 1941: Churchill papers, 20/36.

[3] Battle of the Atlantic Committee No. 11 of 1941, 5 p.m., 2 July 1941: Cabinet papers, 86/1. Among those present were Lindemann and Harold Macmillan (Parliamentary Secretary, Ministry of Supply). At least three of the seventeen people present had American mothers: Churchill, Sinclair and Macmillan.

[4] Prime Minister's Personal Minute, D.207/1, 'Most Secret', 4 July 1941: Premier papers, 3/230/1, folio 23.

which United States supplies were being put. Harriman informed Churchill:

(a) There are no adequate arrangements for salvage of tanks—a deficiency which added materially to losses in recent Greek campaign.

(b) Little has been done to develop port facilities on the Red Sea against the contingency of the Canal being closed, although all agree this is more than a possibility.

(c) Although buildings have been erected, there are no tools or equipment to overhaul the American aircraft engines.

(d) There is no one person in charge of Takoradi-Cairo ferry service. Responsibility is divided in four jurisdictions. . . .

There was a 'general waste of equipment', Harriman added, 'in both air force and army through lack of supervision'.

Churchill minuted on receiving this telegram: 'A gt effort must be made to make up the ground lost.'[1]

Churchill's support for Harriman was total: he realized the extent to which Harriman was acting in Britain's interest. This realization was strengthened on July 5, when Randolph Churchill wrote from Alexandria:

It was indeed kind of you to suggest that I should be attached to the Harriman Mission. I have thereby not only obtained all the latest news of you and Pamela, and all my friends in London, but have also had a wonderful opportunity of learning about things out here.

I have been tremendously impressed by Harriman, and can well understand the regard which you have for him. In 10 very full and active days he has definitely become my favourite American. He seems to me to possess a quite extraordinary maturity of judgement that is almost on a par with FE's. He got down to work out here with amazing ease and sure footedness, and has won the confidence of everyone he met. I have become very intimate with him and he has admitted me to all the business he has transacted. I am sure you would do well to back his opinions on the situation out here to the limit.

Randolph added: 'It has been most cheering to hear from Harriman how well and vigorous you are. I am sure you know what a tremendous admiration he has for you. He clearly regards himself more as your servant than R's. I do hope you will keep him at your side, as I think he is the most objective and shrewd of all those who are around you.'[2]

Aid to Russia was clearly urgent. But it was proving difficult to find out precisely what Russia needed. 'Molotov will tell us nothing,' Col-

---

[1] Cairo Telegram No. 2085, sent 9.53 p.m., 2 July 1941, received 7.20 a.m. 3 July 1941, 'Personal and Secret', and Churchill minute: Premier papers, 3/217/2, folios 15–16.

[2] 'Private', 5 July 1941: Churchill papers, 20/33.

ville noted in his diary on June 30, 'beyond what is in the official communiqués. Now, in their hour of need, the Soviet Government—or at any rate Molotov—is as suspicious as when we were negotiating a Treaty in the summer of 1939.'[1]

At the War Cabinet on June 30 it was reported that, despite considerable German military and air losses, 'the Russian military position appeared to be grave'.[2] Churchill had already sought to ensure that, by September 1, Britain's anti-invasion preparations would be at a high point of readiness, fearing the rapid switch of German military power from a conquered East to an exposed and isolated Britain. On the previous day he had written to Margesson and Dill:

We have to contemplate the descent from the air of perhaps a quarter of a million parachutists, glider-borne or crash-landed aeroplane troops. Everyone in uniform, and anyone else who likes, must fall upon these wherever they find them and attack them with the utmost alacrity—

'Let every one
Kill a Hun.'[3]

This spirit must be inculcated ceaselessly into all ranks of HM forces—in particular military schools, training establishments, depots. All the rearward services must develop a quality of stern, individual resistance. No building occupied by troops should be surrendered without having to be stormed. Every man must have a weapon of some kind, be it only a mace or a pike. The spirit of intense individual resistance to this new form of sporadic invasion is a fundamental necessity.

'I have no doubt,' Churchill added, 'a great deal is being done.'[4]

That same day, Churchill wrote to Sinclair and Portal, in respect of the responsibility of the Air Force for the local and static defence of aerodromes, that every man in Air Force uniform 'ought to be armed with something—a rifle, a tommy-gun, a pistol, or a mace; and every

---

[1] Colville diary, 30 June 1941: Colville papers.

[2] War Cabinet No. 64 of 1941, 30 June 1941, 5 p.m.: Cabinet papers, 65/18.

[3] In 1919, at the height of the British intervention against Bolshevik Russia, Churchill's slogan had been:

'Kill the Bolshie
Kiss the Hun.'

[4] Prime Minister's Personal Minute, M.682/1, 29 June 1941: Churchill papers, 20/36. Two weeks later Churchill minuted to Brooke and Ismay: 'How do we stand at present on the strategies and tactical camouflaging of defences against enemy attacks on airfields?' and he went on to ask, with the fate of Crete still much in his mind: 'What body is studying the lessons of Maleme and the batteries thereabouts?' His own suggestion was for two or three dummy guns 'or even more' for every real gun, and a 'confusing variety' of anti-aircraft battery emplacements 'in which no one can tell the real from the sham'. (Prime Minister's Personal Minute, M.726/1 10 July 1941: Churchill papers, 20/36.)

one, without exception, should do at least one hour's drill and practice every day'.

Churchill added that every airman ought to have his place in the defence scheme, and at least once a week 'an alarm should be given as an exercise (stated clearly beforehand in the signal that it is an exercise), and every man should be at his post'. Ninety percent of the men, Churchill noted, 'should be at their fighting stations in five minutes at the most'. Churchill's minute continued:

It must be understood by all ranks that they are expected to fight and die in the defence of their airfields. Every building which fits in with the scheme of defence should be prepared, so that each has to be conquered one by one by the enemy's parachute or glider troops. Each of these posts should have its leader appointed. In two or three hours the troops will arrive; meanwhile every post should resist and must be maintained—be it only a cottage or a mess—so that the enemy has to master each one. This is a slow and expensive process for him.

Churchill went on to point out that the 'inherent difficulty' in the organization of the Royal Air Force was the 'enormous mass of non-combatant personnel who look after the very few heroic pilots, who alone in ordinary circumstances do all the fighting . . .'. In the defence of the airfields, Churchill believed, was the chance 'for this great mass to add a fighting quality to the necessary services they perform'. Every air field, he ended, 'should be a stronghold of fighting airgroundsmen, and not the abode of uniformed civilians in the prime of life protected by detachments of soldiers'.[1]

On June 30 Churchill visited Northolt aerodrome. 'It was a surprise visit,' Churchill's secretary Elizabeth Layton noted in her diary, 'to see how the men would take a sudden invasion scare, and they were fairly slow. He discovered some of them about half an hour later still in the canteen place, and sent them off with hives of bees in their bonnets.'[2]

On July 1 German forces captured Riga, and reached the Beresina river. As Churchill had suggested, in a minute to the Chiefs of Staff Committee on June 23, the Royal Air Force began a series of daily daylight bombing and fighter attacks over Northern France and the Channel, starting with Brest on July 1, and including Cherbourg, Lorient, Le Havre and the Seine shipyards. At the same time, a series

---

[1] Prime Minister's Personal Minute, M.683/1, 29 June 1941: Churchill papers, 20/36.

[2] Layton diary, 30 June 1941: Nel papers. Miss Layton ended her day's diary: 'Dictation that night, and he was most amiable. I had to sit for hours in the Cabinet Room opposite him, waiting (we are working at No. 10 at night now, he prefers it). General Ismay was there. It is funny to listen to old Big Ben chiming the quarters and hours, and the sound getting all mixed up with its own echo which comes across the Horse Guards from the Admiralty. . . .' (Nel papers.)

of night bomber raids were launched against Bremen, Cologne, the Rhineland and the Ruhr, beginning on July 3 with Bremen and the Ruhr. But the German advance into Russia was swift and relentless, and Churchill's fears intensified of a Russian defeat within two months, followed by a German invasion of Britain in September or October. In asking Roosevelt to accelerate still further the American merchant shipbuilding programme, and to increase the number of American escort vessels on the Transatlantic convoy routes, Churchill told the President: 'I am asking that everything here shall be at concert pitch for invasion from September 1.'[1]

Churchill scrutinized the charts, graphs, statistics and reports that were put before him daily. On July 3, when the lack of sufficient American escort vessels was made evident, he told the Defence Committee that he would draw American attention to 'the futility of a policy which, through lack of effective help, permitted sinkings to continue at a high rate and relied on making them good by future building'. At that same Defence Committee, commenting on the 'large mass of men' already available in the Middle East, he declared 'that there was mismanagement and disorganization and he did not feel at all inclined to press for extra shipping to carry further additions to the rearward services which were already much too large'.[2]

In the hope of remedying this situation, or at least of proposing a remedy, Churchill asked the War Office to give him a detailed list of equipment, formation by formation, already in the Middle East, and to provide, henceforth, a monthly statistical return. 'You are wrong,' Churchill minuted to Dill, when Dill opposed the request on the grounds of the extra work involved, 'in supposing that this return is needed for statistical purposes only.' His minute continued:

Without a clear up-to-date picture of the state of Middle East formations no view or major decisions can be taken by the Defence Committee or the War Cabinet. The alternative is to continue in the state of ignorance and confusion which is leading us towards disaster.

While I should be ready to agree to some small simplification of details, if you will propose it to me, I must insist upon knowing all the essential facts.[3]

On July 3 Churchill learned that most of the aid the Soviet Union

---

[1] Prime Minister's Personal Telegram, T.363, 'Personal and Secret', 1 July 1941: Churchill papers, 20/49.
[2] Defence Committee (Operations) No. 45 of 1941, 3 July 1941, 9.45 p.m.: Cabinet papers, 69/2.
[3] Prime Minister's Personal Minute, M.705/1A, 6 July 1941: Churchill papers, 20/36.

had requested in a message on June 30 could not be supplied.[1] The Chiefs of Staff did not intend to supply information about the AI Air Interception radar equipment.[2] 'We cannot afford to supply any 4,000 pound bombs' they informed the British Military Mission in Moscow. Modern fighter and bomber aircraft could not be provided 'as the intensive operations in progress are at present absorbing our full output'. No incendiary bombs could be supplied, only 'full particulars and drawings'. Nor could Britain supply 'any light anti-aircraft guns or flame throwers'.[3]

In a desperate attempt to help Russia, and also to forestall a German seizure of the Caucasus oil-fields, on July 4 Britain offered to destroy those oil-fields herself in order 'to deny oil to the enemy', and to help the Soviet Government replace the 'consequent deficiences' both in home supplies of oil and in machinery destroyed.[4] But when Churchill's earlier idea of helping Russia by a commando raid on northern France was elaborated by Sir Roger Keyes, who wished to land 320 men and six tanks near Le Touquet, clear the village of Germans, capture prisoners, 'beat up' an aerodrome and withdraw after an hour and a quarter on shore, Churchill rejected the plan. It was, he told the Defence Committee on July 4, 'inadequate and out of proportion to the whole war situation'. The results would be small, and only achieved with 'disproportionate loss'. Eden agreed, hoping that it would be possible to have an operation 'on a much larger scale'.[5]

The United States now prepared to make a further commitment in its Atlantic patrol policy. On July 4 Defence Plan No. 3 was ready for Presidential approval.[6] On that day Admiral Ghormley informed the Chiefs of Staff Committee: 'It is the policy of the United States to ensure the safe arrival at destination of all of the material being furnished by the United States to nations whose security is essential to the defense of the United States.' In pursuance of this policy, 'US naval

---

[1] The list, submitted by the Russian Chief of Staff to the British Military Mission in Moscow, included 3,000 'modern fighter aircraft with full equipment', 3,000 'ditto' bombers, as many of Britain's 'latest big bombs' as she could spare, 20,000 light anti-aircraft guns, and flame throwers. The Russians also asked for 'full information' regarding Britain's night-fighter equipment and air-borne radar, as well as 'one specimen aircraft of our latest night fighter, designed with full war equipment'. (Moscow Telegram No. 663, 29 June 1941: Premier papers, 3/401/1, No. 3.)

[2] Code name 'Smeller'.

[3] Foreign Office Telegram No. 710 to Moscow, 3 July 1941: Premier papers, 3/401/1, No. 4.

[4] Ministry of Economic Warfare to Moscow, Telegram No. 143, 4 July 1941: Cabinet papers, 65/18.

[5] Defence Committee (Operations) No. 46 of 1941, 4 July 1941: Cabinet papers, 69/2.

[6] Known officially as 'Western Hemisphere Defense Plan Number Three'.

forces will conduct operations for the protection of shipping employed in the transportation of such material while within the Western Hemisphere. Axis naval and air forces within the Western Hemisphere will be deemed potential threats to this shipping and will be attacked where ever found.' Ghormley added: 'It is intended that this action should be taken as a measure short of war and one that may not necessarily lead to existence of formal war between the United States and Axis powers.'[1]

'I was encouraged,' Churchill telegraphed to Roosevelt on July 7, 'to read the documents on Defence Plan No. 3.' Putting such a plan 'into immediate operation', he added, 'would give timely and needed aid. At present the strain upon our resources is far too great.'[2]

Within a week Roosevelt had decided to make a change in the plan, whereby a ship flying the American or Icelandic flag would be placed in all trans-Atlantic convoys. 'How much worse is this than we had hoped for,' Churchill asked Pound.[3] But Pound explained to Churchill that the flying of these flags in every convoy would, presumably, provide 'the political justification for the plan', and therefore constituted 'a great advance towards American belligerency, to our own advantage'. Circling the words 'a great advance', Churchill noted on the bottom of Pound's letter: 'Good.'[4]

On July 12 Churchill had received welcome news direct from Roosevelt: a planned increase in United States tank production from 600 to 1,000 tanks a month. 'Assuming these schedules are maintained,' Roosevelt wrote, 'and I believe they will be, it means that we can give you 800 to 1,000 light tanks and 800 to 1,000 medium tanks prior to January 1.' As of August 1, Roosevelt added, the United States could also start training 500 'of your tank corps men in this country, if you think that would be helpful'.[5]

*   *   *

[1] 'Secret', Serial 00176, 4 July 1941: Cabinet papers, 127/16. The United States Ocean Escort was to consist of 6 battleships, 5 heavy cruisers, 27 destroyers, 27 'old' destroyers and 48 patrol aircraft, plus British Commonwealth forces of escort vessels, plus Canadian aircraft. There was also a United States Striking Force of 3 aircraft carriers, 4 light cruisers, 12 destroyers and 12 patrol aircraft.

[2] Prime Minister's Personal Telegram, T.378, 'Personal and Secret', 7 July 1941: Premier papers, 3/460/2, folios 6–9.

[3] Prime Minister's Personal Minute M.734/1, 13 July 1941: Premier papers, 3/460/3, folio 6.

[4] Letter of 14 July 1941, note of 16 July 1941: Premier papers, 3/460/3, folios 4–5. Pound also told Churchill: 'It is interesting to note that American naval forces will have instructions to operate under War conditions including darkening ship at sea; and that they will take all proper measures for their own security and security of convoys both at sea and in port.'

[5] 'Secret', 12 July 1941: Premier papers, 3/469, folio 176.

In North Africa, German pressure was lessened as the German assault on Russia continued. Intelligence reports showed only Italian re-inforcements in Libya. 'However,' Churchill warned Auchinleck in his first telegram to the new Commander-in-Chief in the Middle East, 'a Russian collapse might soon alter this to your detriment', without, Churchill added, 'diminishing invasion menace here'.[1]

As the British bombing of French ports continued, Churchill questioned the need to send, as had been done on the night of July 6, 'no less than 108 bombers' against a single port, in that instance Brest. 'This is far too great an emphasis to put on Brest,' he minuted to Portal, 'at a time when the devastation of the German cities is urgently needed in order to take the weight off the Russians by bringing back aircraft.'[2] That same afternoon Churchill telegraphed to Stalin:

We shall do everything to help you that time, geography, and our growing resources allow. The longer the war lasts the more help we can give. We are making very heavy attacks, both by day and night with our Air Force, upon all German-occupied territory and all Germany within our reach.

About 400 daylight sorties were made overseas yesterday. On Saturday night over 200 heavy bombers attacked German towns, some carrying three tons apiece, and last night nearly 250 heavy bombers were operating.

This will go on. Thus we hope to force Hitler to bring back some of his air-power to the West and gradually take some of the strain off you.

Churchill added that he had hopes of 'a serious operation' to take place in the near future in the Arctic, followed by contact between the British and Russian navies. Meanwhile, he said, British warships operating along the Norwegian coast had intercepted 'various supply ships which were moving north against you'.

Churchill ended with his familiar refrain: 'We have only to go on fighting to beat the life out of these villains.'[3] Even as his telegram was being encyphered for despatch to Moscow, German troops were attacking Minsk, and pressing forward towards Pskov, on the road to Leningrad. At the same time, to Churchill's consternation, the new Commander-in-Chief in the Middle East, General Auchinleck, on whom he had set high hopes, made a public and widely reported

[1] Prime Minister's Personal Telegram, T.374, 'Susan' No. 064, 'Personal and Secret', 6 July 1941: Premier papers, 3/291/1.
[2] Prime Minister's Personal Minute, M.712/1, 'Action this Day', 7 July 1941: Churchill papers, 20/36.
[3] Prime Minister's Personal Telegram, T.377, Foreign Office No. 748 to Moscow, 'Personal and Most Secret', 7 July 1941: Premier papers, 3/401/1, No. 5.

speech stressing both the need for American man-power in the war against Germany, and doubting Russia's ability to stand up to the superior German war machine. Churchill telegraphed at once to Cairo:

At this particular moment when the President, having landed Marines in Iceland, is trying to obtain authority from Congress, where he has no certain majority, to allow United States Army troops to be dispatched overseas outside the Western Hemisphere, I fear your remarks will be exploited by the isolationists and will be an impediment to the end we all desire. The American Ambassador, Mr Winant, tells me that Wavell's references a few days ago on the same lines did harm, and that your observations will be unhelpful. They are also contrary to what I have said about our not needing an American Army this year or next year, or any year that I could foresee.

It is a mistake for Generals in High Command to make speeches or give interviews to Press correspondents. There are several other passages in your speech which I would rather you had left out. The very cool and almost disparaging reference to the Russian effort will give offence in some important quarters in this country, and I doubt the wisdom of revealing so many of your own thoughts, however sensible they may be, to the enemy. Now that you have broken the ice with the war correspondents, I trust you will not find it necessary to make any further public statements on political or strategic issues, or that if you wish to do so you will consult me beforehand.[1]

On the evening of July 9 the War Cabinet discussed a request from Stalin for a Treaty between the two countries. It was agreed that, not a Treaty, but certainly an 'agreed declaration' on war policy, should be made, and made in the terms Stalin wished.[2] Churchill immediately telegraphed to Stalin the proposed British declaration: the two Governments mutually undertook 'to render each other assistance of all kinds in the present war against Germany', and further undertook that 'during this war' they would neither negotiate nor conclude an Armistice or treaty of peace 'except by mutual agreement'.[3]

That evening, at Chequers, Churchill was in a relaxed and reflective mood, talking to Sinclair until 2 a.m. At one point, Colville, who was present, noted:

[1] Prime Minister's Personal Telegram, T.379, 8 July 1941: Churchill papers, 20/49. Eight days later Churchill telegraphed to Oliver Lyttelton: 'Have not had any acknowledgment from Auchinleck of telegram I was forced to send him about his speech. I should be sorry if he were hurt by the absolutely necessary warning which I had to give him about political speeches. My only desire is to help him in every way.' (Prime Minister's Personal Telegram, T.410, 'Private and Secret', 19 July 1941: Churchill papers, 20/41.)

[2] War Cabinet No. 67, of 1941, 9 July 1941, 6.30 p.m.: Cabinet papers, 65/19.

[3] Prime Minister's Personal Telegram, T.385, Foreign Office No. 764 to Moscow, 1 a.m., 10 July 1941: Premier papers, 3/170/1, No. 3.

They talked of what should be done with the enemy leaders after the war. The PM thought that when the war was over there should be an end to all bloodshed, though he would like to see Mussolini, the bogus mimic of Ancient Rome, strangled like Vercingetorix in old Roman fashion. Hitler and the Nazis he would segregate on some island, though he would not so desecrate St Helena.[1] But we still had a long way to go.

The PM inveighed against defeatism and said it would be better to make this island a sea of blood than to surrender if invasion came. He had been impressed by a letter from Reynaud to Pétain, sent some weeks ago, in which the former recalled how the Generals had said to him that after the Franco-German Armistice England would have 'her neck wrung like a chicken' in three weeks.[2] Reynaud had sent copies of this letter through the American Ambassador at Vichy to the PM and to the President.

The evening ended with Churchill and Sinclair agreeing, as they reflected on the events of June 1940, that, as Colville recorded, France 'had acted shamefully in demanding more fighter squadrons after they knew the battle was lost'.

As Churchill went to bed, he listened to a personal request from Colville to be allowed to leave the Private Office and join the Royal Air Force. Clementine Churchill supported Colville's request. 'I owe my release,' Colville noted, 'largely to Mrs C's spirited intervention on my behalf.' A Fighter Pilot, Churchill remarked that night, 'had greater excitement than a polo-player, big game shot and hunting-man rolled into one'.[3] But Churchill, who was always reluctant to take on new members of his Staff, finally agreed only at the end of September to let Colville go.

Help for the Russians now became, as help for the French had been a year before, a principal object of British war policy. For behind the defeat of Russia, as behind the defeat of France, there continued to lie the menace of an attempted invasion of Britain. On July 10 Churchill proposed a 'small mixed squadron of British ships in the Arctic to contact and operate with the Russian Naval forces, and he went on to explain:

[1] On 11 July 1941 Churchill's step father, Major George Cornwallis-West, wrote to him: 'My great wish is to be allowed to see the end of Hitler and his gang. Before execution they ought to be shewn round the Countries they have devastated in large iron cages!' (Churchill papers, 1/361.)

[2] Referring to this remark in a speech later in the war, on 30 December 1941, Churchill commented: 'Some chicken! Some neck!'

[3] Colville diary, 9 July 1941: Colville papers.

The effect upon the Russian Navy and upon the general resistance of the Russian Army of the arrival of what would be called a British fleet in the Arctic might be of enormous value and spare a lot of English blood.

The advantage we should reap if the Russians could keep the field and go on with the war, at any rate until the winter closes in, is measureless. A premature peace by Russia would be a terrible disappointment to great masses of people in our country. As long as they go on, it does not matter so much where the front lies. These people have shown themselves worth backing and we must make sacrifices and take risks even at inconvenience, which I realize, to maintain their morale.[1]

On July 12, in Moscow, the Anglo-Soviet agreement was signed, pledging 'mutual assistance' against Germany, and no separate peace. That same day, the Vichy forces in Syria surrendered to the Allied armies, and an armistice was signed at Acre.[2] Also in the eastern Mediterranean, Italian aircraft bombed the Suez Canal. On the previous night, in the north sea, British bombers struck at the German port installations of Wilhelmshaven, and, as a result of Churchill's request to Portal on July 7 for the 'devastation of the German cities', in an effort to draw German aircraft back from the Russian front,[3] the British bombing of German cities had intensifed; Hanover was bombed on July 14, 19 and 25; Hamburg on July 16 and 25, Frankfurt and Mannheim on July 21, 22 and 23 and Berlin itself on July 25.

On July 14 Churchill broadcast from County Hall, London. 'In the last few weeks alone,' he said, 'we have thrown upon Germany about half the tonnage of bombs thrown by the Germans upon our cities during the whole course of the war,' and he added: 'But this is only a beginning, and we hope by next July to multiply our deliveries manifold.' It was for this reason, he warned, 'that I must ask you to be prepared for vehement counter-action by the enemy'.[4]

The British raids did indeed provoke a counter-action. It was to come on the night of July 27, with a two hour German raid on London, the first such raid since May 10.

---

[1] Prime Minister's Personal Minute, 'Most Secret', 'Action this Day', M.722/1, 10 July 1941: Churchill papers, 20/36.

[2] 'If anyone had predicted,' Churchill told the House of Commons on July 15, 'that we should already, by the middle of July, have cleaned up the whole of the Levant and have re-established our authority there for the time being, such a prophet would have been considered most imprudent' (*Hansard*, 15 July 1941, column 465). British troops entered Beirut on 15 July 1941.

[3] Minute of 7 July 1941: Air Ministry papers, 20/2214.

[4] Broadcast of 14 July 1941: Churchill papers, 9/152.

59

Russia and the Middle East: 'we are at the utmost strain'

A S German forces continued their advance into Russia, occupying the Baltic States and pressing in upon Leningrad, the Finnish Government attacked Soviet positions to the north-east of Leningrad. 'In view of the obnoxious and aggressive attitude of Finland,' Churchill wrote to Eden on July 16, 'I trust we have already seized all the Finnish ships and subjected the Finns to every inconvenience in our power,' and he added: 'One cannot be on two sides at once.'[1] This was the same Finland whose resistance against Russia a year and a half earlier had been described by Churchill as 'heroic, nay, sublime'.

On July 16 German forces reached the outskirts of Smolensk. There, a fierce Russian defence held up their advance for another four weeks. In the Pskov area, the Red Army was still falling back towards Leningrad, but at a less precipitate pace. The Russians, Colville noted in his diary that day, 'though still retiring, are evidently taking severe toll of the Germans who, for the first time, are short of fighter support. Thus our daily raids on Northern France are serving their purpose even though,' Colville noted, 'they are not a sufficiently formidable diversion and we ought to do something more.' The attitude of the Chiefs of Staff, however, he added, 'is as negative as it could be'.[2]

Churchill had already asked the Chiefs of Staff to examine the possibility of British military action, either to link up with Russia in Norway, or to divert German forces away from Russia by means of an attack on France. On July 21 they reported to Churchill that, having examined the question in detail they saw no way of 'joining hands' with Russia through Norway. Any British force sent to northern Norway would,

[1] Prime Minister's Personal Minute, M.743/1, 16 July 1941: Churchill papers, 20/36.
[2] Colville diary, 16 July 1941: Colville papers.

they warned, 'be subjected to a considerable scale of air attack without any air cover'. In view of the 'recent events' in Greece and Crete, they added, 'we could not possibly afford to be "Namsosed"'.'

As for a landing in France, the Chiefs of Staff reported that they had examined the possibilities of raids on either Brest or Cherbourg, 'but they cannot recommend either of these operations'.[1]

Churchill's secretary, Elizabeth Layton, wrote of Churchill's reaction to the week's news: 'He was in a bad temper all this week and every time I went to him he used a new and worse swear word. However, he usually rounded it off by beaming goodnight at me, so one can't bear any malice or even let it worry one.'[2]

Churchill's bad temper was also affected by Auchinleck's continued reluctance to contemplate an early offensive in the Western Desert. At the Defence Committee on July 17 Churchill explained why he feared delaying such an offensive until mid-September, its earliest possible date in view of the impending despatch of 150 of the latest cruiser tanks from Britain. By then, he said, the situation in Russia 'might have changed drastically to our disadvantage and we might be faced with an imminent threat of invasion'. The tanks would then have to be brought back to Britain, or not be sent at all.

During the discussion, Attlee 'stressed', as the minutes recorded, that it was important to re-occupy Cyrenaica 'whilst the Germans were still engaged on the Russian front', and added that he thought Auchinleck had 'overstressed' the imminence of the threat of a German descent in September through Turkey, across Syria, and on to Palestine and Iraq. 'We should seize our chance,' Attlee declared, 'before the Germans were free to disengage their forces from their eastern front and send reinforcements to North Africa.'[3]

On the following day Stalin appealed to Churchill to establish two fronts 'against Hitler', one 'in the West—Northern France', and the other in 'the North—the Arctic'. A front in Northern France, Stalin added, would not only divert Hitler's forces from Russia, 'but at the same time would make it impossible for Hitler to invade Great Britain'.[4] In reply, Churchill explained the extent of Britain's lack of offensive capability, the nature of German fortifications in France, and the scale of Britain's Middle East and Atlantic commitments:

[1] 'Most Secret', Chiefs of Staff Report 145 (o) of 1941, signed by Pound, Dill and Freeman, 21 July 1941: Premier papers, 3/401/2, folios 3–5.

[2] Layton diary, 18 July 1941: Nel papers.

[3] Defence Committee No. 51 of 1941, 17 July 1941, 10.30 p.m.: Cabinet papers, 69/2.

[4] Telegram delivered by the Soviet Ambassador, 19 July 1941: Premier papers, 3/170/1, No. 4.

Anything sensible and effective that we can do to help will be done. I beg you however to realise limitations imposed upon us by our resources and geographical position. From the first day of the German attack upon Russia we have examined possibilities of attacking Occupied France and the Low Countries.

The Chiefs of Staff do not see any way of doing anything on a scale likely to be of the slightest use to you. The Germans have forty divisions in France alone, and the whole coast has been fortified with German diligence for more than a year, and bristles with cannon, wire, pill-boxes, and beach-mines. The only part where we could have even temporary air superiority and air fighter protection is from Dunkirk to Boulogne. This is one mass of fortifications, with scores of heavy guns commanding the sea approaches, many of which can fire right across the Straits. There is less than five hours' darkness, and even then the whole area is illuminated by searchlights.

To attempt a landing in force would be to encounter a bloody repulse, and petty raids would only lead to fiascos doing far more harm than good to both of us. It would all be over without their having to move or before they could move a single unit from your front.

You must remember that we have been fighting alone for more than a year, and that, though our resources are growing, and will grow fast from now on, we are at the utmost strain both at home and in the Middle East by land and air, and also that the Battle of the Atlantic, on which our life depends, and the movement of all our convoys in the teeth of the U-boat and Focke-Wulf blockade, strains our naval resources, great though they be, to the utmost limit.

In the north, Churchill told Stalin, Britain had already begun operational plans designed 'to destroy enemy power of transporting troops by sea to attack your Arctic flank'. At the same time, British warships would go to Spitzbergen to raid German shipping 'in concert with your naval forces'. A flotilla of British submarines was also on its way to intercept German traffic on the Arctic coast, although, owing to the perpetual daylight, 'this service is particularly dangerous'. In addition, a British minelayer was on its way to the Soviet Arctic port of Archangel 'with various supplies', and the possibility of basing some British fighter air squadrons at the White Sea port of Murmansk was also being considered.[1]

On July 21 Russian forces evacuated the province of Bessarabia, which they had annexed from Rumania in 1940, and crossed the Dniester river, Russia's pre-war western boundary. If Russia 'collapses soon', Lyttelton warned Churchill that same day, Auchinleck 'might

---

[1] Prime Minister's Personal Telegram, T.418, 'Personal and Secret', Foreign Office No. 856 to Moscow, 20 July 1941: Premier papers, 3/170/1, No. 5.

be obliged to fight defensive battles' in Syria or Palestine against a German attack, thus ending all chance of a western desert attack against Rommel, and the recapture of Cyrenaica.[1] To launch an offensive 'with the inadequate means at present at our disposal', Auchinleck himself telegraphed to Churchill on July 23, 'is not in my opinion a justifiable operation of war, and is almost certain to result in a further lengthy postponement of date on which we can assume offensive with reasonable chances of success'.[2]

'All your telegrams and ours,' Churchill had already telegraphed that same day, 'show that we should have a talk',[3] and on the following day, reporting Auchinleck's fear to the War Cabinet, he described a German attack through Turkish Anatolia in September as 'surely most unlikely'.[4]

Among United States policymakers, criticism had grown of Britain remaining in the Middle East at all, as the needs of that theatre absorbed so large a proportion of the United States war supplies to Britain. On the evening of July 24 five Americans broached this concern to Churchill at 10 Downing Street: Hopkins, Harriman, Admiral Ghormley, Major-General Chaney and Brigadier-General Lee. The Americans were worried that Britain's needs in the Middle East, even if purely defensive, would take away resources and energy from the Battle of the Atlantic which, in their view, would be the decisive battle of the war. Everything, therefore, should be concentrated on it.

The Chiefs of Staff, Pound, Portal and Dill, then spoke in turn of Britain's growing strength at sea, in the air and on land, and of Britain's ability to defend the Atlantic route and to prevent invasion. After each had spoken, Dill gave what Churchill later described as a 'powerful exposition' of the reasons which made it necessary for Britain to stay in the Middle East. 'My feeling at the end of our discussion,' Churchill recalled, 'was that our American friends were convinced by our statements and impressed by the solidarity among us.'[5]

These convictions had already been expressed in practical terms, a few hours earlier, at the first meeting of the War Cabinet's Technical Assistance from the United States of America Committee, with Bevin

[1] 'Most Secret and Personal', Cairo telegram No. 2283, 21 July 1941: Churchill papers, 20/41.
[2] Telegram No. 1535, 'Personal', 23 July 1941: Premier papers, 3/291/1.
[3] Prime Minister's Personal Telegram, T.432, War Office No. 070, 23 July 1941: Churchill papers, 20/41.
[4] War Cabinet No. 73 of 1941, 24 July 1941, 12 noon, Minute 2, Confidential Annex: Cabinet papers, 65/23.
[5] Winston S. Churchill, *The Second World War*, volume 3, London 1950, pages 377-9.

in the Chair, Cherwell[1] and Hankey[2] among the British representatives, and Hopkins, Harriman and Lee among the Americans. The Committee was able to report that the United States Government would arrange for American firms 'to undertake complete responsibility' of various specific areas of the manufacture of military equipment, tasks to be, if possible, the American representatives added, 'of the highest importance'.[3]

On the following day, Churchill took Chaney and Lee to see something of Britain's defence preparations, and also to see the 1st Armoured Division, which had just been deprived of 150 cruiser tanks, needed for the proposed offensive in the western desert. General Brooke, who was present during Churchill's visit, noted in his diary: 'Everywhere he has had an astounding reception. He drove in my car between troops lining both sides of the road, all of them cheering him as he went and shouting, "Good old Winnie!".' Churchill's popularity, Brooke added, 'is quite astonishing'.[4]

After two months experience of Churchill at close hand, Elizabeth Layton reflected in a letter to her parents:

You might think that seeing such a person at close quarters might lessen one's admiration and respect, or make him seem more commonplace. But not so in this case; he is just as amazing and *terrific* and full of character in his private life as he is over the radio or in the H of C.

He bullies his servants, but then completely makes up by giving a really charming smile. On the rare occasions when a brave soul has expostulated at his treatment he has been told 'Oh don't mind me, it's only my way'. So that is the way one has to look at it. Last week everything I did seemed to be wrong and there were some truly healthy swear-words flying. I felt a bit upset once, but he afterwards said goodnight so sweetly I couldn't bear any malice! And so he gets away with it![5]

*   *   *

[1] Professor Lindemann, who had just been created Baron Cherwell. Eleven days earlier Cherwell had sent Churchill a minute signed 'C' to replace his former initials, 'FAL'. Churchill noted: 'You had better sign yourself "Cherwell" as there is a "C" already in my circle.' (Minute of 10 July 1941: Premier papers, 3/22/4, folio 242.) The existing 'C' was Menzies, head of the Secret Intelligence Service.

[2] Formerly Chancellor of the Duchy of Lancaster, but since 20 July 1941, Paymaster General.

[3] Technical Assistance from the United States of America Committee, First meeting of 1941, 3 p.m., 24 July 1941: Cabinet papers, 99/36. The tasks suggested were for the maintenance and repair of aircraft, the assembly and overhaul of tanks, and the maintenance of shipping, both in Britain and in the Middle East.

[4] Brooke diary, 25 July 1941: Arthur Bryant, *The Turn of the Tide*, London 1957, page 251.

[5] Letter of 25 July 1941: Nel papers.

Continued concern that the Germans might move against Spain, or through Spain to Morocco, neutralizing Gibraltar, led the War Cabinet to decide, at the end of July, to plan for the seizure of the Canary Islands from Spain. This plan, at first codenamed 'Puma', then 'Pilgrim', was to take place before the end of August. A total of 20,000 men were to take part in it, commanded by General Alexander. Britain would be 'well advised', Churchill told the War Cabinet, to make certain of securing the islands, 'before we were anticipated by the enemy'.[1]

The ability to make such plans depended to a large extent upon the continuing supplies reaching Britain and the Middle East from the United States, and Roosevelt responded readily to Churchill's various requests for specific items or priorities. He also took initiatives of his own, suggesting, for example, towards the end of July, that British Tank Corps personnel should be trained in the United States. On July 25 Churchill telegraphed to Roosevelt:

We have been considering here our war plans, not only for the fighting of 1942, but also for 1943. After providing for the security of essential bases, it is necessary to plan on the largest scale the forces needed for victory. In broad outline, we must aim first at intensifying the blockade and propaganda. Then we must subject Germany and Italy to a ceaseless and ever-growing air bombardment. These measures may themselves produce an internal convulsion or collapse.

But plans ought also to be made for coming to the aid of the conquered populations by landing armies of liberation when opportunity is ripe. For this purpose it will be necessary not only to have great numbers of tanks, but also of vessels capable of carrying them and landing them direct on to beaches. It ought not to be difficult for you to make the necessary adaptation in some of the vast numbers of merchant vessels you are building so as to fit them for tank-landing fast ships.

No moment should be lost, Churchill added, for Britain and America to frame 'an agreed estimate of our joint requirements of the primary weapons of war', and to consider how these requirements were to be met 'by our joint production'.[2]

There was another call on British supplies which Churchill strove to meet: the Soviet needs. The War Cabinet had decided, as Churchill informed Stalin on July 25, to send Russia as soon as possible two hundred Tomahawk fighter aeroplanes, sixty of which would come from British supplies being manufactured in the United States. This

---

[1] War Cabinet No. 74 of 1941, 24 July 1941, 5.30 p.m., Confidential Annex: Cabinet papers, 65/23.

[2] Prime Minister's Personal Telegram, T.441, 25 July 1941: Churchill papers, 20/41.

would be done, Churchill explained, in spite of the fact that it 'will seriously deplete our fighter aircraft resources'. In addition, as requested by Stalin, between two and three million pairs of ankle boots would be available shortly for shipment from Britain to the Soviet Union, as well as 'large quantities' of rubber, tin, wool, woollen cloth, jute, lead and shellac. 'Where supplies are impossible or limited from here,' Churchill added, 'we are discussing with the United States of America.' His telegram ended: 'We are watching with admiration and emotion Russia's magnificent fight, and all our information shows the heavy losses and concern of the enemy. Our air attack on Germany will continue with increasing strength.'[1]

Could Russia avoid almost immediate defeat? On July 26 members of the Defence Committee were sent an Intelligence forecast that German troops might reach the Caucasus 'by mid-August', and be ready, after a month of organizing an air-striking force, to develop a 'large scale attack' on northern Iraq, or on Britain's 'whole position' at the head of the Persian Gulf.[2] Despite these possibilities, and in part hoping to forestall them, Churchill continued his search for the raw materials for which Stalin pressed. Rubber, in such short supply in Britain, would be sent, nevertheless, he told Stalin, either from Britain or the United States, 'by the best and quickest route'. It was for Stalin to say 'exactly what kind of rubber, and which way you wish it to come'. Preliminary orders had already been given.

Churchill also told Stalin that Harry Hopkins had asked Roosevelt to let him go to Moscow. In his telegram Churchill tried to impress on Stalin how important Hopkins' mission had been for Britain, and could be for Russia:

I must tell you that there is a flame in this man for democracy and to beat Hitler. He is the nearest personal representative of the President. A little while ago when I asked him for a quarter of a million rifles they came at once. The President has now sent him full instructions and he leaves my house to-night to go to you. You will be advised of his arrival through the proper channels. You can trust him absolutely. He is your friend and our friend. He will help you to plan for the future victory and for the long-term supply of Russia.

'You could talk to him also,' Churchill added, 'freely about policy, strategy and Japan.'

[1] Prime Minister's Personal Telegram, T.441, Foreign Office Telegram No. 887 to Moscow, 'Most Secret', 25 July 1941: Premier papers, 3/170/1, No. 6. German air attacks on Britain, although much diminished, still caused 501 civilian deaths in July 1941.
[2] Defence Committee (Operations) Paper No. 3 of 1941, 25 July 1941: Cabinet papers, 69/3.

Churchill's telegram to Stalin, his second in three days, ended with further words of encouragement, thanks and assurances.

The grand resistance of the Russian Army in defence of their soil unites us all. A terrible winter of bombing lies before Germany. No one has yet had what they are going to get. The naval operations mentioned in my last telegram to you are in progress. Thank you very much for your comprehension in the midst of your great fight of our difficulties in doing more. We will do our utmost.[1]

On July 27 Portal presented Churchill with the Air Ministry's plan to send two Hurricane squadrons to Murmansk, 'to operate in support of Russian operations' and to 'protect as far as possible' the Murmansk area.[2] 'So proceed,' Churchill noted. 'We must give what help is possible.'[3]

Britain's vast machinery of production was now at work providing Russia with the supplies she needed. Yet at this very moment there was criticism in the British Press, led by the *Daily Mirror*, alleging serious defects and bungling in the system of priorities and manufacture.

One senior Conservative MP, Sir John Wardlaw-Milne, speaking with all his authority as chairman of the Select Committee on National Expenditure, declared that British industry was working at 'not more than 75 per cent of our possible efficiency'.[4] Churchill had already begun preparation for a major defence of the Government's policy, minuting to Bridges on July 17: 'I have a feeling that Parliament does not at all understand the very great advance made in the refinement of priority questions through the development of the allocation principle. Let me have a note on this not exceeding one page.' Churchill added, that one heard 'very little about priorities now', and yet, he asked Bridges, 'am I not right in supposing that all is running smoothly?' Churchill's minute continued:

[1] Prime Minister's Personal Telegram, T.448, Foreign Office No. 904 to Moscow, 28 July 1941: Premier papers 3/170/1, No. 7. That same day Anthony Eden's Private Secretary, Oliver Harvey, noted in his diary: 'PM is developing a regular correspondence with Stalin by private telegraph—much to AE's concern. PM's style is becoming so sentimental and florid that Cripps has telegraphed privately to AE to try to restrain him. We fear that it will have the worst effect on Stalin who will think guff no substitute for guns.' Harvey added: 'It is worrying how little we apparently can do by way of military operations to help Russia—though we are sending her aircraft. The slowness and lack of imagination of our Chiefs of Staff are enough to frighten one.' (Harvey diary, 28 July 1941: John Harvey, editor, *The War Diaries of Oliver Harvey*, London 1978, page 24.)
[2] 'Outline Plan', 'Secret', 26 July 1941: Premier papers. 3/395/4, folio 93.
[3] Note of 27 July 1941: Premier papers, 3/395/4, folio 92.
[4] Reported in the *Manchester Guardian*, 22 July 1941.

See, for instance, how well the giving of 1A to the production of tanks on psychological grounds has been adjusted. Priorities now resolve themselves into the opening out of bottle-necks. No one has an absolute priority to the exclusion of all others. There have been no recent clashes.

'Comment freely on this,' Churchill added, 'by Friday.'[1]

To prepare his production speech, Churchill asked Lord Cherwell for 'comparisons of output under four or five large heads at the 22nd month of the last war and the 22nd month of this war'.[2] He also asked for, and received, detailed factual information from the Admiralty, the Air Ministry, the Ministry of Agriculture and Fisheries, the Ministry of Labour, the Ministry of Supply, the Board of Trade, Lord Woolton, Lord Beaverbrook, Ismay and Bridges.

The facts and figures having been assembled, Churchill spent the weekend at Chequers, and by the night of Friday August 1 he was ready to dictate his speech. Elizabeth Layton, the secretary to whom it was dictated, wrote home to her parents of how:

At about one a.m. we repaired to a lovely room, sort of library-cum-picture gallery, called the Hawtrey Room, and he shooed everyone else off saying 'Off to bed with all of you, leave me alone with Miss Layton'. I felt like a lamb being led to the slaughter!

He dictated until 4.30 without a break—shorthand this time—and really it was an education to take it down. Some of it was just plain statement, expounding '*production*' (it is for the Production Debate) but some of it was real rhetoric. All the gestures and intonations were there. I couldn't help feeling rather thrilled.

Once he stopped for about 5 minutes. Said 'Are you tired?' I assured him I wasn't. Said he 'We must go on and on, like the gun-horses, till we drop'. One phrase made me giggle '. . . and the whole can cry a dismal cacophonous chorus of stinking fish all round the world'. (Heaven knows what it means)— but you should have heard the fire with which it was delivered.

When we finished he went off and Mr Martin and I cleared up. We were so hungry I had to go and raid the kitchen, and we ended in the Great Hall about 4.45 eating some scones. . . .

'One thing about Mr C,' Miss Layton added '—he would never be one to take a dislike for no reason—he is a most warm-hearted person and infinitely loyal to his friends. And if one ever managed to gain his regard he'd stand by one to the death.'[3]

[1] Prime Minister's Personal Minute, C.60/1, 17 July 1941: Premier papers, 4/85/1, folio 116.

[2] Prime Minister's Personal Minute, S.26/1, 22 July 1941: Premier papers, 4/85/1, folio 344.

[3] Elizabeth Layton, letter of 1–3 August 1941: Nel papers. Sometimes Churchill had less time

In the debate on production, on Monday July 29, Churchill spoke in detail, and with confidence of the machinery of production, and set out at length what had been done to ensure the most effective production possible of arms and munitions. The work of all the organisations involved, he said, 'proceeds ceaselessly', while the strategic aspect of production was also continuously considered by the Chiefs of Staff Committee, 'which meets every day'.

'For more than a year,' Churchill ended, 'we have been all alone: all alone, we have had to guard the treasure of mankind.'[1] It was the hundredth week of the war. On July 31, at the War Cabinet, it was revealed that ten ships in a convoy in the South Atlantic had been sunk. Such attacks, Churchill warned, 'would almost certainly be followed by others'. But as soon as 'American plans matured', British destroyers could be brought back from the Canadian port of Halifax to protect the South Atlantic route.

Churchill had another reason for hoping that the German sinking of merchant ships in the Atlantic would now decline, and decline substantially. By the end of July, as a result of increasingly successful progress at Bletchley in breaking the German naval Enigma, all German U-boat instructions were being read, 'continuously and with little or

---

for preparing a speech. A few weeks later Miss Layton described a car journey from Chequers to the House of Commons: '. . . we started out at 10.30, me in the car with him. It was rather exciting. At first he just read things, and passed them to me to hold, and then he started in on his speech. It was difficult at first trying to write in the joggling car, and several times I almost landed on top of him with a bump. However, he was quite oblivious to any kind of interruption. His right hand was gesturing just as it would (I knew) when the speech was delivered, and his tones were gentle or rasping, according to what he was expressing—in fact the motions and tones were just as expressive as the words themselves. It was a fine speech—I don't think anyone after hearing Mr Churchill composing a speech could possibly doubt his utter single-mindedness and nobility of purpose. When we got up to town it must have been about 11.45, and he was due to reach the Mansion House at 1.15. He jumped out and said 'Now run in and type like *hell*,' which I did. A few minutes later, however, there was an urgent call 'go to the Cabinet Room with your notebook'. When I got in there were His Lordship and the Foreign Secretary, and HE said 'I want the FS to hear that bit about this time last year—just read it'. So I fumbled with my notebook, couldn't find the place and must have looked rather embarrassed, for he then said 'Just sit down and take your time. I don't want you to hurry'. (Layton diary: Nel papers.)

[1] *Hansard*, 29 July 1941, columns 1274–1300. Harold Nicolson described Churchill's speech as 'long and careful', but he added: 'It does not go very well. There is a sense of criticism in the air' (Nicolson diary, 29 July 1941: Nigel Nicolson, editor, *Harold Nicolson, Diaries and Letters 1939–1945*, London 1967, page 183). Henry Channon commented: 'The PM, sober, and determined, made an important speech. The theme was production, and it was meant to be a reply to his critics. He held the House which was interested certainly, but not enthusiastic, though there were few of his usual oratorical tricks. Someone has told him that we are weary of his eloquence.' (Channon diary, 29 July 1941: Robert Rhodes James, editor, *Chips, The Diaries of Sir Henry Channon*, London 1967, page 310.)

no delay'.[1] As a result, trans-Atlantic convoys could be routed away from the U-boat packs.

This Intelligence breakthrough came at the very moment when fears had intensified that the rate of sinking of merchant ships would soon overtake the rate of new construction.[2] Thanks to the decrypts of the naval Enigma, that nightmare was now over, and Churchill could be far more confident that the trans-Atlantic supplies would not be fatally interrupted. The Battle of the Atlantic Committee, which struggled so hard to find new construction and to accelerate the rate of turn-round of ships in port, could meet now in a less fearful atmosphere. For the rest of 1941, one area at least of Churchill's anguish could be reduced.[3] Within a month, the vital Enigma secret, and Purple, were augmented by yet another cryptographic success, the breaking of the Italian naval high grade cypher machine, 'C.38m'. The first Intelligence transmitted from Bletchley to the Middle East from this new source had been sent to Cairo on June 23, giving details of the sailing of four liners from Italy to Africa with Italian troops.[4]

In Russia, as July came to an end, German forces had suffered heavy casualties. In the north and centre, the front was stable. But south of Kiev, the War Cabinet were told on July 31, the Germans were making 'steady progress'.[5] That same day, in pursuance of the War Cabinet's policy to give Russia whatever help could be spared, or even not spared, Churchill telegraphed again to Stalin:

Following my personal intervention, arrangements are now complete for the dispatch of 10,000 tons of rubber from this country to one of your northern ports.

In view of the urgency of your requirements, we are taking the risk of depleting to this extent our metropolitan stocks, which are none too large and will take time to replace. British ships carrying this rubber, and certain other

[1] F. H. Hinsley and others, *British Intelligence in the Second World War, Its Influence on Strategy and Operations*, volume 2, London 1981, page 163.

[2] In April 1941 more than 70 British merchant ships had been sunk; in May 1941 more than 90; in June the number fell to just under 60 and in both July and August to under 30 a month.

[3] But only for another six months; at the end of February 1942 a new U-boat Enigma setting remained unbroken for another ten months, and the nightmare returned. From January 1943, however, the decrypting was restored, and safety again assured.

[4] F. H. Hinsley and others, *British Intelligence in the Second World War, Its Influence on Strategy and Operations*, volume 2, London 1981, page 283.

[5] War Cabinet No. 76 of 1941, 31 July 1941, 12.15 p.m.; Cabinet papers, 65/15.

supplies, will be loaded within a week, or at most ten days, and will sail to one of your northern ports as soon as the Admiralty can arrange convoy.

This 10,000 tons, Churchill explained, was additional to the 10,000 tons of rubber already allotted from Malaya.[1]

Before leaving for Moscow, Hopkins had been particularly concerned that the American policymakers did not understand Britain's continuing plans to attack the Germans in the Middle East, considering the losses and disasters which Britain had suffered in Greece and Crete. On July 24 Colville had noted in his diary: 'On late duty at No. 10 where future strategy in the Middle East was being discussed. First Harry Hopkins and then the PM spoke to President Roosevelt on the telephone, and the PM, forgetting he was not on the "scrambler", said some things about a certain rendezvous which he afterwards bitterly regretted!'[2]

On July 25 the King agreed to allow Churchill to leave Britain, and meet the President on board ship somewhere off Newfoundland. In seeking the King's permission to leave England, Churchill pointed out that 'I can of course return by flying-boat from Newfoundland in a few hours.' He could not foresee, however, 'any cause likely to make this necessary'.[3] 'I confess,' the King wrote in giving his assent, 'that I shall breathe a sigh of relief when you are safely back home again!'[4]

The Queen also sent Churchill her 'heartfelt good wishes and prayers for your voyage', adding, 'May God keep you and guide you and bring you safely home.'[5] 'I must say,' Churchill replied, 'I do not think our friend would have asked me to go so far, for what must be a meeting of world wide notice, unless he had in mind some further forward step.' In fact, Churchill reflected, 'the meeting will be a forward step in itself'.[6]

The meeting with Roosevelt was to take place on August 8, code name 'Riviera'. Churchill was to sail on the *Prince of Wales*, and was, noted Colville on August 1, 'as excited as a schoolboy on the last day of term',[7] planning, John Martin noted, all the details of Roosevelt's

[1] Prime Minister's Personal Telegram, T.452, Foreign Office Telegram No. 933 to Moscow, 31 July 1941: Premier papers, 3/170/1, No. 8.

[2] Colville diary, 24 July 1941: Colville papers.

[3] Letter of 25 July 1941, 'sent in sealed envelope and box to Buckingham Palace, 12.00 noon': Premier papers, 3/485/6, folios 59–60.

[4] Letter of 25 July 1941, from Windsor Castle: Churchill papers, 20/20.

[5] Letter of 2 August 1941, sent from Windsor Castle: Churchill papers, 20/20.

[6] Letter of 3 August 1941: Churchill papers, 20/20.

[7] Colville diary, 1 August 1941: Colville papers.

entertainment, 'ordering grouse, ordering turtle and ordering a band'.[1]

During August 1, Clementine Churchill wrote to her husband: 'I feel very strongly that on this all-important journey you should have a Doctor with you (The Ship's Doctor—no good—merely like Doctor Jones of the Enchantress). *Please* take Sir Charles Wilson.' Bracken, she added, 'agrees with me'.[2] Churchill deferred to his wife's judgement.

On the weekend before leaving for Newfoundland, Churchill and Auchinleck spent the weekend together at Chequers. Churchill hoped to persuade the General to agree to a September or October offensive in the western desert. Two weeks earlier, when Auchinleck was still in Cairo, Churchill had telegraphed to him, about Wavell's conduct in breaking off the Battle of Sollum on the third day:

> Our forces were defeated in detail by the arrival on the 3rd morning of all the enemy tanks from Tobruk, whose garrison meanwhile stood idle. It would have seemed more consistent with accepted principles of strategy and common sense to have engaged the Tobruk garrison in heavy and continuous action before or during the climax of the attack upon Sollum. There may, of course, be reasons of which we are not aware, which rendered these well-worn principles of war inapplicable. Neither can we judge from here on our present information whether it was right to break off the battle on the third day.

'There are always,' Churchill had added, 'excellent reasons in favour of retirements. Victory rewards those whose will-power overcomes these reasons.'[3]

On Friday August 1, before going to Chequers, Auchinleck was present at a meeting of the Defence Committee, telling the Committee that, while the 'necessity for action was obvious', the means of doing so were not so easy. Serious pressure could not be brought on the Germans in the western desert without using Britain's only brigade of Cruiser tanks. 'The risk of such a battle could be taken,' said Auchinleck, 'but it might prove annihilation of the brigade, and this would put back our ultimate major offensive perhaps for several months.'

The Defence Committee was then told that the tank forces of Britain and Germany were about equal: some 230 tanks each, 'comparable in power'. Yet all experience showed, warned Auchinleck, 'that a major offensive could hardly succeed without about a 2 to 1 superiority, which we should not have before the 1st of November'.

[1] Martin diary, 4 August 1941: Martin papers.
[2] Letter of 1 August 1941: Spencer-Churchill papers.
[3] Prime Minister's Personal Telegram, T.411, 19 July 1941: Premier papers, 3/291/1, folios 21–4.

It was Eden who stated the 'political aspect' for an earlier offensive. 'If the Russians held the Germans,' he said, 'they would be in a position to say that they had won the war for us at a period when we had been unable to take any offensive action. If the Russians failed, then not only would our chance of a successful offensive pass but we should be accused of having done nothing to save them.'[1]

Churchill then asked whether it might not be possible for 'more energetic steps' to be taken to bring the tanks which reached the Middle East into action 'earlier than at present forecast'. It seemed 'incredible', he said, 'that it should take a month for a brigade of the 1st Armoured Division to be fit for action after its arrival in the Middle East'. But Auchinleck was adamant that acceleration was impossible, stressing that the tanks had first to be unloaded then 'put through the shops to correct any defects and make them fit for the desert', then have 'short period' of desert training. 'He was advised,' Auchinleck concluded, 'that it would be most unwise to put the brigade of the 1st Armoured Division into action before the 1st of November.'

Clement Attlee then spoke in favour of an earlier offensive. How could Egypt be saved, he asked, 'if we waited till the Germans had ample time to re-inforce'. Churchill then told Auchinleck:

... the war could not be waged on the basis of waiting until everything was ready. He thought that it was a frightful prospect that nothing should be done for four and a half months at a time when a small German army was having the greatest difficulty in so much as existing. The army should establish closer contact with the enemy at Tobruk and in the Western Desert and set to work to make the enemy fight. He was ready to authorise quite exceptional measures if by any means a battle could be brought on earlier than November.

Eden now cautioned that, although 'politically he desired a battle', he did not want 'another one like the last'.[2]

On the following day Churchill had a long private talk with Auchinleck at Chequers. Aware that the General might not respond to Churchill's mood or methods, particularly as he had already been cross-examined by Churchill at the Defence Committee, Ismay decided to try to smoothe the discussion by telling Auchinleck:

---

[1] On 1 August 1941 General Mason-Macfarlane reported from Moscow what seemed to be the encouraging news that 'Stalin seems absolutely confident of being able to hold up the German attacks this autumn without losing either Leningrad, Moscow or Kiev. He does not think the Germans will penetrate anywhere to a depth of more than 100 kilometres from the present front.' (Letter of 1 August 1941: War Office papers, 216/124.)

[2] Defence Committee No. 53 of 1941 11 a.m., 1 August 1941: Premier papers, 3/286, folios 18–25.

Churchill could not be judged by ordinary standards; he was different from anyone we had ever met before, or were ever likely to meet again. As a war leader, he was head and shoulders above anyone that the British or any other nation could produce. He was indispensable and completely irreplaceable.

The idea that he was rude, arrogant, and self-seeking was entirely wrong. He was none of these things. He was certainly frank in speech and writing, but he expected others to be equally frank with him. To a young brigadier from Middle East Headquarters, who had asked if he might speak freely, he replied: 'Of course. We are not here to pay each other compliments.'

He was a child of nature. He venerated tradition, but ridiculed convention. When the occasion demanded, he could be the personification of dignity; when the spirit moved him, he could be a *gamin*. His courage, enthusiasm and industry were boundless, and his loyalty was absolute. No commander who engaged the enemy need ever fear that he would not be supported. His knowledge of military history was encyclopaedic, and his grasp of the broad sweep of strategy unrivalled.

At the same time, he did not fully realise the extent to which mechanisation had complicated administrative arrangements and revolutionised the problems of time and space; and he never ceased to cry out against the inordinate 'tail' which modern armies required. 'When I was a soldier,' he would say, 'infantry used to walk and cavalry used to ride. But now the infantry require motor-cars, and even the tanks have to have horse boxes to take them to battle.'

He had a considerable respect for the trained military mind, but refused to subscribe to the idea that generals were infallible or had any monopoly of the military art. He was not a gambler, but never shrank from taking a calculated risk if the situation so demanded. His whole heart and soul were in the battle, and he was an apostle of the offensive. Time and again he would quote from Nelson's Trafalgar memorandum: 'No captain can do very wrong if he places his ship alongside that of an enemy.'

He made a practice of bombarding commanders with telegrams on every kind of topic, many of which might seem irrelevant and superfluous. I begged Auchinleck not to allow himself to be irritated by these never-ending messages, but to remember that Churchill, as Prime Minister and Minister of Defence, bore the primary responsibility for ensuring that all available resources in shipping, man-power, equipment, oil, and the rest were apportioned between the Home Front and the various theatres of war, in the best interests of the war effort as a whole. Was it not reasonable that he should wish to know exactly how all these resources were being used before deciding on the allotment to be given to this or that theatre?

Ismay had gone on to tell Auchinleck that Churchill 'was not prone to harbouring grievances' and that it would be 'a mistake to take lasting umbrage if his criticisms were sometimes unduly harsh or even unjust'.

'If I had done so,' Ismay added, 'I should never have had a moment's happiness.'[1]

That Saturday, August 2, at Chequers, in an attempt to encourage Auchinleck to embark upon an earlier offensive, Churchill asked him if he would like an 'infusion of new blood' on his Staff. Was Haining 'suited to the task?'[2] Was Auchinleck 'satisfied with Middle East Intelligence, either its system or its Staff?' Could Harriman help at all with any of his 'interesting suggestions?'[3]

Auchinleck stood his ground: there could be no offensive until November 1. 'I have had a long talk with Auchinleck,' Churchill telegraphed to Lyttelton on August 3, adding that he had 'the greatest confidence' in him.[4] On the following day Churchill telegraphed to Smuts that while Auchinleck had 'at present' not committed himself to 'anything large' before November 1, 'when our armoured reinforcements will not only have arrived but become desert-worthy and desert-trained', he had nevertheless 'promised to try to accelerate by every possible means'. Anything Smuts could do in that direction, Churchill wrote, 'will be most welcome to me', and he added:

I dread the idea of this long delay, when, as we know for certain, the enemy is hard pressed for supplies and would be greatly embarrassed by making exertions. In war one cannot wait to have everything perfect, but must fight in relation to the enemy's strength and plight. I am appalled by the proposal to remain passive all this time, when the golden opportunity may be lost.

'But,' Churchill ended, 'you must hear the very strong practical arguments advanced from the other side.'[5]

The new offensive, codenamed 'Crusader', would take place in November, as Auchinleck wished, despite Churchill's personal preference for an earlier attack, and his fear that a great opportunity was being lost while Germany was embroiled in Russia.

---

[1] *The Memoirs of General the Lord Ismay*, London 1960, pages 269–70.

[2] Three weeks later Churchill minuted to Dill: 'I felt ill-used when I learned that General Haining had not been selected and recommended to me for this post because you thought he was the best man but because there was a desire to get him out of the War Office where he had made himself objectionable. I do not feel the public interest was sufficiently consulted in this matter. As you will remember, I asked definitely a second time whether you were satisfied he was the best man. Now that I have learned the truth, and am in presence of this report from the Minister of State, I feel we should look around for a successor. If you do not give me your very best man, and one thoroughly capable of doing the work, I will look for a civilian of the Eric Geddes type, and have him invested with the necessary military rank.' (Prime Minister's Personal Minute, M.815/1, 'Secret', Action this Day', 22 August 1941: Churchill papers 20/36.)

[3] 'Points for discussion with General Auchinleck', notes by Ismay, 2 August 1941: Premier papers, 3/286, folios 2–4.

[4] Prime Minister's Personal Telegram, T.463, 3 August 1941: Churchill papers, 20/41.

[5] Prime Minister's Personal Telegram, T.474, 4 August 1941: Churchill papers, 20/41.

SWEDEN

Baltic

Leningrad

Novgorod

Pskov

Riga

German front line 15 November 1940

Kovno

Danzig

Vilna

Moscow

GREATER GERMANY

Minsk

Smolensk

Brest
Litovsk

S O V I E T   U N I O N

Kursk

Kiev

HUNGARY

Kharkov

Don

Dnepropetrovsk

Zaporozhe

Taganrog

Odessa

Nikolaiev

Rostov on
Don

RUMANIA

Azov

CRIMEA

Simferopol

Kerch

BULGARIA

Yalta

B l a c k   S e a

Caucasus

Salonica

Istanbul

Batum

Ankara

Izmir

T U R K E Y

miles   200

A N A T O L I A

kilometres   300

© Martin Gilbert 1983

60

Meeting with Roosevelt

BEFORE leaving Britain, Churchill made plans for the Bletchley Park decrypts to reach him in Newfoundland. An 'assortment of "Boniface" ', he minuted to Bridges and Ismay on August 3, 'perhaps paraphrased', should be sent out to him by air. But the decrypts should be sent, he continued, 'in a weighted case, so that they will sink in the sea if anything happens to the aeroplane'.

Churchill added that 'competent people must make the assortments'.[1] Two days later the most recent recruit to his Private Office, Leslie Rowan, informed him that 'C' would be responsible for the selection of 'Boniface', while at the same time Desmond Morton should select the equally secret 'BJ' material.[2] This 'BJ' material was the decrypts of various diplomatic messages picked up regularly by British intercept stations.

At noon on August 3 Churchill was driven from Chequers to Wendover where, just after one o'clock in the afternoon, he boarded his special train on the first stage of his journey to meet Roosevelt. The Prime Minister, wrote Colville, who was to stay behind, 'left for the north with a retinue which Cardinal Wolsey might have envied'.[3]

The train reached Thurso in northern Scotland, on the morning of

[1] Prime Minister's Personal Minute, C. 62/1A, 'Secret', 3 August 1941: Premier papers, 3/485/6, folio 22.

[2] 'Note', 5 August 1941: Premier papers, 3/485/6, folio 18.

[3] Colville diary, 3 August 1941: Colville papers. The 'retinue' included Dill, Pound and Air Chief Marshal Sir Wilfrid Freeman; the newly ennobled Professor Lindemann (now Lord Cherwell), Sir Alexander Cadogan, Commander C. R. 'Tommy' Thompson, John Martin, and Detective Inspector W. H. Thompson; Colonel Hollis and Lieutenant-Colonel Jacob of the Office of the Minister of Defence, Captain Schofield (Director of the Trade Division, Admiralty), Commander Goodenough (Plans Division, Admiralty), Paymaster Captain Brockman, Brigadier Dykes (Director of Plans, War Office), Captain Nutting (Military Assistant to Sir John Dill), and Group Captain Yool (Staff Officer to the Vice Chief of the Air Staff, Sir Wilfred Freeman): Premier papers, 3/485/7, folio 81.

August 4. Churchill then crossed by destroyer to Scapa Flow, and by late afternoon, was steaming out of Scapa in the *Prince of Wales*.[1] On the battleship was Harry Hopkins, who had reached Scapa from Moscow two days before. From on board ship, Churchill signalled to Roosevelt that evening:

Harry returned dead-beat from Russia, but is lively again now. We shall get him in fine trim on the voyage. We are just off. It is twenty-seven years ago to-day that Huns began their last war. We must make good job of it this time. Twice ought to be enough. Look forward so much to our meeting. Kindest regards.[2]

'After dinner,' Lieutenant-Colonel Jacob noted in his diary, 'we had a cinematograph show in the Ward Room at which the Prime Minister was present wearing the Mess Dress of the Royal Yacht Squadron.' The film was 'Pimpernel Smith', 'which he quite obviously enjoyed very much. He had not done a stroke of work during the day and was in a thoroughly good temper. We all went to bed about midnight, and very soon afterwards the ship began to heave. . . .'[3]

Early on August 5, when heavy seas made it essential to slow down the *Prince of Wales* if the destroyer escort were to keep up with her, it was decided to drop the escort and proceed unprotected. Forced to maintain absolute radio silence, there was, as Churchill later noted, a 'lull in my daily routine and a strange sense of leisure which I had not known since the war began'. His account continued: 'Resting in my small but comfortable sea-cabin and bed on the bridge, I brooded on the future battle in the desert in the light of all the reports which I had studied of the spring fighting and achieved a memorandum for the Chiefs of Staff, with the first sentence of which I was much pleased. . . .'[4] The first sentence read: 'Renown awaits the Commander who first, in this war, restores the artillery to its prime importance upon the battlefield, from which it has been ousted by heavily armoured tanks.'[5]

[1] Commanded by Captain J. C. Leach, MVO, the *Prince of Wales* had been in action three months earlier against the *Bismarck* when the *Hood* had been sunk. The *Prince of Wales* had obtained the two hits which had slowed down the *Bismarck* and led to her ultimate destruction. Captain Leach was on the bridge when it was struck by a shell from the *Bismarck*; most of those standing with him were killed.

[2] Prime Minister's Personal Telegram, T.466, Tudor No. 1, 4 August 1941, 6.25 p.m.: Churchill papers, 20/41. Tudor No. 2 was a signal from Hopkins to Roosevelt, telling him to bring to the meeting with Churchill the full figures of monthly United States munitions production for 1942.

[3] Jacob diary, 4 August 1941: Jacob papers.

[4] Winston S. Churchill, *The Second World War*, volume 3, London 1950, page 382.

[5] 'Secret', 'A Note by the Minister of Defence', printed on 30 August 1941: Cabinet papers, 120/10.

Churchill's confidential secretary, Kathleen Hill, was not on board to take dictation of these efforts. It had been thought that a woman would not be able to manage the rigours of the journey. Churchill had therefore to find a shorthand writer to whom he could dictate this, and other memoranda, letters, telegrams and minutes while on board ship. When he rang the bell in his cabin, it was the Army sergeant selected for this task who entered. Without looking up, Churchill remarked: 'This is a melancholy story. . . .'

Sympathetically, the sergeant laid down his pencil. 'Oh dear! How unfortunate,' he said, thinking Churchill's comment was intended for him. 'Well,' Churchill shot back, *'take it down. . . .'*[1] The piece in question was a minute commenting on a report of deficiencies in aircraft carriers.[2]

By the end of the voyage the sergeant, Peter Kinna, had become an accepted member of Churchill's team. He was to remain so for the rest of the war.

At midday on August 5 the *Prince of Wales* altered course to avoid a U-boat reported ahead.[3] It was, John Martin noted, 'a comparatively idle day', with Churchill reading a novel.[4] As Churchill himself recorded, 'for the first time in many months I could read a book for pleasure'. The book he chose had been given to him by Oliver Lyttelton: it was *Captain Hornblower RN*, which, he recalled, 'I found vastly entertaining.'[5]

'Though still keen on hearing news,' Ian Jacob noted in his diary, 'the Prime Minister on board ship seems quite content to forget about what is going on elsewhere and simply to enjoy himself, so we have not been at all troubled.' That afternoon, Jacob added, Churchill joined the Chiefs of Staff at tea 'in very skittish form', asking them 'what they were doing' and commenting that 'it did him good to see them working'. He then went to the other end of the room with Hopkins to listen to the wireless.[6]

During August 6 the *Prince of Wales* was met and escorted onward by a British destroyer from Icelandic waters. Shortly afterwards Chur-

[1] Peter Kinna, conversation with the author, 24 August 1982.

[2] Prime Minister's Personal Minute, M.798/1, addressed to Pound, Sinclair and Moore-Brabazon: Churchill papers, 20/36. This Minute did indeed begin: 'This is a melancholy story. . . .'

[3] This was not as dangerous an incident as most of those on board imagined, since by August 1941 the daily decrypting of the German naval Engima, which included all patrol orders to U-boats, was enabling Allied shipping to be diverted clear of U-boats on a regular basis.

[4] John Martin diary, 6 August 1941: Martin papers.

[5] Winston S. Churchill, *The Second World War*, London 1950, page 382.

[6] Jacob diary, 5 August 1941: Jacob papers.

chill signalled to Attlee, who was presiding over the War Cabinet in his absence, that Eden must resist the Free French opposition to Britain's support for an eventually independent Syria. 'Tell Anthony to be very stiff with de Gaulle, Catroux and Free French,' he signalled. 'They can not be allowed to mess up our Syrian position and spoil our relations with Arabs.' The Free French 'pretensions', Churchill added, 'require to be sternly corrected, even use of force not being excluded'. His signal ended: 'It is important to let them realize in good time that they will be made to obey. I do not know how they can resist.'[1]

Ian Jacob's diary for August 7 recorded:

> The Germans, in their Transozean broadcast, gave a report, said to have emanated from Lisbon, that the Prime Minister and President Roosevelt were going to have a meeting in the near future somewhere in the Western Hemisphere. The Lord Privy Seal[2] asked what he was to do about it. The Prime Minister did not seem to worry in the least, and he is secretly hoping the 'Tirpitz' will come out and have a dart at him. . . .[3]

That same day, August 7, in Churchill's absence, the Defence Committee agreed to Stalin's request for a British naval landing at Spitzbergen, to evacuate some two thousand Russians working at the mining settlements and wireless and metereological stations. At the Defence Committee it was pointed out 'that the Spitzbergen expedition had been originally decided on for purely political reasons'. The Russians had asked 'for much that we could not do, e.g. an expedition of 22–25 divisions on the Continent, the supply of 5,000 fighters, 5,000 bombers and 10,000 anti-aircraft guns, and so forth'. It had, therefore, been decided 'to accede to the request that Spitzbergen and Bear Island should be occupied'.

The Russians hoped for a permanent British presence at Spitzbergen. But the Admiralty felt that such a permanent presence would serve 'no useful purpose'.[4]

That night Clementine Churchill wrote to Churchill from 10 Down-

---

[1] Tudor No. 3, 'Most Secret', 6 August 1941: Churchill papers, 20/48.

[2] Clement Attlee.

[3] Jacob diary, 7 August 1951: Jacob papers.

[4] Defence Committee (Operations) No. 55 of 1941 7 August 1941: Premier papers 3/410 folio 50. The landing took place on 25 August 1941, when the 2,000 Russians were taken by the *Empress of Canada* to Archangel. The British force then withdrew. Churchill minuted on 20 October 1941, after the Germans had landed a permanent force on the island: 'How was it that we did not think it worth while to remain in occupation of Spitzbergen when the Germans evidently do?' His Minute continued: 'Why was it necessary to burn all the valuable coal stores, and quit the Island? The whole Operation has a half-hearted air. What is it proposed to do about Spitzbergen now?' (Prime Minister's Personal Minute, D.284/1, 20 October 1941: Premier papers, 3/410, folio 17.)

ing Street that she had just received a message by despatch rider which said 'you had spent a day in complete idleness! I can scarcely believe this; but if it is so I hope you will continue to rest.' Her letter ended:

I do hope my Darling that this momentous journey besides being an impulse to American resolve will rest & refresh you.

How I would love to be with you in that beautiful ship. I hope you often sip the air on the Bridge.

Tender love my dearest

Clemmie[1]

August 8 dawned without fog, a fair morning with sun. But, as Cadogan noted in his dairy, the *Prince of Wales* had reduced its speed, as Pound 'is determined to oppose PM's wishes on this question of the time of arrival'. His account continued:

We had a rehearsal of the reception of the President on board, for which I was impressed to impersonate the President. We have lost a destroyer, in the fog of yesterday evening.

Film 'Lady Hamilton' after dinner. Excellent. PM, seeing it for the fifth time, still deeply moved. At the close, he addressed the ship's company: 'Gentlemen, I thought this film would interest you, showing great events similar to those in which you have been taking part.'

I left him and HH[2] playing backgammon. HH ended up a winner of seven guineas.[3]

On the morning of August 9, as the *Prince of Wales* entered Placentia Bay, Churchill and his advisers prepared for the meeting with Roosevelt on board the battleship *Augusta*. It was then discovered that the American ships were, as John Martin noted, 'keeping a zone time $1\frac{1}{2}$ hours ahead of Newfoundland summertime and we were turned round, to delay before coming in'.[4]

As he waited, Churchill sent a telegram to Oliver Lyttelton to thank him for his leisure reading. It read, simply: 'Hornblower admirable.'[5] This message, Churchill later recalled, 'caused perturbation in the Middle East Headquarters, where it was imagined that "Hornblower" was the code-word for some special operation of which they had not been told'.[6] Churchill also telegraphed that morning to the King. 'With

---

[1] Letter of 7 August 1941: Spencer-Churchill papers.

[2] Harry Hopkins.

[3] Cadogan diary, 8 August 1941: Churchill papers, 4/255. When Churchill was writing his war memoirs Cadogan sent him this and several other diary extracts cited here.

[4] Martin diary, 9 August 1941: Martin papers.

[5] Tudor No. 8, 9 August 1941: Churchill papers, 20/49.

[6] Winston S. Churchill, *The Second World War*, volume 3, London 1950, page 382.

humble duty, I have arrived safely and am visiting the President this morning.'[1]

The *Prince of Wales* entered Placentia Bay once more, and Churchill crossed by barge to the *Augusta*. Awaiting him on the upper deck was Roosevelt, supported on the arm of his son Elliott. Churchill handed Roosevelt a letter from King George VI. 'This is just a note,' it read, 'to bring you my best wishes, and to say how glad I am that you have an opportunity at last of getting to know my Prime Minister. I am sure that you will agree that he is a very remarkable man, and I have no doubt that your meeting will prove of great benefit to our two countries in the pursuit of our common goal.'[2]

Roosevelt then invited Churchill to a tour of *Augusta*, and to lunch, while their respective staffs met and mingled. 'The PM has been in his best form,' Averell Harriman wrote to his daughter Kathleen, and to Churchill's daughter-in-law Pamela. Roosevelt, he added, 'is intrigued and likes him enormously.'[3] On Sunday August 10 Roosevelt and Churchill attended Divine Service on board the *Prince of Wales*. John Martin wrote in his diary:

The PM had given much thought to the preparations for his Service (which he said should be fully choral and fully photographic), choosing the hymns (O God our Help in Ages Past, Onward Christian Soldiers and Eternal Father Strong to Save), and vetting the prayers (which I had to read to him while he dried after his bath). You would have had to be pretty hard-boiled not to be moved by it all—hundreds of men from both fleets all mingled together, one rough British sailor sharing his hymn sheet with one American ditto. It seemed a sort of marriage service between the two navies, already in spirit allies, though the bright peace-time paint and spit and polish of the American ships contrasted with the dull camouflage of the *Prince of Wales*, so recently in action against the *Bismarck*.[4]

After the ceremony, there was lunch in the Ward Room, followed by short speeches from Churchill and Roosevelt. The President then returned to the *Augusta* whereupon, Cadogan noted in his diary:

I changed and went ashore on a shingly bay with the PM (in his rompers), Harriman, the 'Prof', John Martin and Tommy Thompson.

[1] Tudor No. 11, 9 August 1941: Churchill papers, 20/49.

[2] Letter dated 3 August 1941: Roosevelt papers.

[3] Undated letter, quoted in W. Averell Harriman and Elie Abel, *Special Envoy to Churchill and Stalin, 1914–1946*, London 1976, page 75. In 1971 Harriman, then aged eighty, married Pamela Churchill (as his third wife). She was then the Hon. Mrs Leyland Hayward.

[4] Martin diary, 10 August 1941: Martin papers.

We clambered over some rocks, the PM like a schoolboy, getting a great kick out of rolling boulders down a cliff.

We soon re-embarked and landed on a spit further along, over which we walked and found a turf clearing—an ideal place for a picnic. But it clouded over and we were caught in a short, but extremely violent, shower.

Back about 5.45 and soon changed into a dinner jacket. We gave a dinner on board to American Generals and Admirals, and Sumner Welles. . . .[1]

Of the expedition ashore, John Martin recalled: 'We went about like the first discoverers, with not a soul to meet, the PM collecting a fistful of flowers.'[2]

On Monday, August 11, the Conference proceeded with three separate sets of talks in almost continuous and parallel session: the diplomatic talks between Cadogan and Sumner Welles, the military talks at the level of Chiefs of Staff,[3] and the talks between Churchill and Roosevelt. After hearing Hopkins' account of his talks with Stalin, Roosevelt agreed to give immediate aid to Russia 'on a gigantic scale', and, at Churchill's suggestion, to send an Anglo-American Mission to Moscow at the earliest possible moment to settle the nature and scale of munitions and other supplies to Russia by Britain and the United States 'conjointly'.[4]

In reporting progress on August 11, in a telegram to Attlee, Churchill was able to announce agreement on 'Naval Plan 4', whereby the United States Navy would take over all patrolling in the America to Iceland stretch of the Atlantic. Agreement was also reached that day, Churchill reported to Attlee, on the need to seek to restrain Japan from further aggression in the Far East, and in particular, 'to make no encroachment upon Siam', and to remove its military forces from Indo-China. Roosevelt also agreed, Churchill reported, to end his communication with Japan 'with a very severe warning, which I drafted'.[5]

In the course of their discussions, Churchill explained to Roosevelt the nature of operation 'Pilgrim', a British seizure of the Canary Islands in anticipation of a German descent upon Spain. For his part,

[1] Cadogan diary, 10 August 1941: Churchill papers, 4/225.

[2] Martin diary, 10 August 1941: Martin papers.

[3] The British Chiefs of Staff team consisted of Pound, Dill and Freeman; the American team consisted of Admiral Stark (Chief of Naval Operations), Admiral King (Commander-in-Chief, Atlantic Fleet), Rear-Admiral Turner (Chief of Naval War Plans), General Marshall (Chief of Staff) and Major-General Arnold (Army Air Corps).

[4] The Memoirs of General the Lord Ismay, London 1960, page 228.

[5] Tudor No. 15, 'Most Secret', despatched 1.51 p.m., 11 August 1941: Premier papers, 3/485/1, No. 11. The warning read: 'Any further encroachment by Japan in the South-West Pacific would produce a situation in which the United States Government would be compelled to take counter-measures, even though these might lead to war between the United States and Japan.'

Roosevelt agreed, as Churchill telegraphed to Eden on August 11, that 'Pilgrim' would be no barrier to an American protective occupation of the Azores, which the Portuguese Government had asked the United States to undertake in the event of a German invasion of Portugal. Indeed, Churchill informed Eden, the President was 'holding strong forces available' for the purpose of taking action in the Azores.[1]

Churchill and Roosevelt were agreed on these specific plans. But on the wider issue of the United States' entry into the war, it was clear throughout the talks that the United States had no intention of making any commitment, or of holding out even the remotest hope of one. The American Navy, Ian Jacob noted in his diary on August 11, 'seem to think that the war can be won by our simply not losing it at sea'. The American Army, Jacob added, 'sees no prospect of being able to do anything for a year or two, and is thus completely taken up with equipment problems'. Not 'a single American officer', Jacob wrote, 'has shown the slightest keenness to be in the war on our side. They are a charming lot of individuals but they appear to be living in a different world from ourselves. The war certainly seems very remote over here, even to us who are so desperately interested in it.'[2]

It was for one specific area of agreement that the Argentia meeting was to be best remembered: the 'Atlantic Charter'. This document had its origin in a telegram from Roosevelt to Churchill, sent to London nearly a month earlier, in which Roosevelt referred to a matter 'which might cause unpleasant repercussions over here'. This was the rumour that the British Government had begun to commit itself to various 'trades or deals' with some of the occupied countries. For example, Roosevelt wrote, 'the stupid story that you have promised to set up Yugoslavia[3] again as it formerly existed', and another story 'that you promised Trieste to Yugoslavia'.

There were, Roosevelt warned, 'certain racial groups' in the United States for whom such promises would cause 'dissention and argument', such as the Czechs and Slovaks or the Walloons and Flemings. 'You will remember,' Roosevelt added, 'that back in early 1919 there was serious trouble over actual and alleged promises to the Italians and to others.' Roosevelt's telegram continued: 'I am inclined to think that an overall statement on your part would be useful at this time, making it

---

[1] Tudor No. 18, 'Most Secret', despatched 6.52 p.m., 11 August 1941: Premier papers, 3/485/1, No. 13.

[2] Jacob diary, 11 August 1941: Jacob papers.

[3] Possibly a mistake for Czechoslovakia.

clear that no postwar peace commitments as to territories, populations or economies have been given. I could then back up your statement in very strong terms.'[1]

The subject of this 'overall statement' had been broached by Roosevelt at his first talk with Churchill on August 9. Churchill recognized at once the importance to Britain of a joint Anglo-American declaration of principles which would, despite continuing American neutrality, link in some public and striking way Britain's war aims with the aspirations of the United States. He therefore prepared a draft declaration which he handed to Roosevelt on August 10, immediately after Divine Service.[2]

During August 11, as the discussions of Churchill's draft continued, and an acceptable version began to emerge, it became clear that the War Cabinet's approval would be essential, and also urgent, if the declaration was to be made public at the end of the meeting. In his telegram to Attlee on August 11, Churchill sent the most up to date version of the draft. Of the paragraph pledging an 'effective international organization' to afford all States security 'within their own boundaries', 'without fear of lawless assault or the need to maintain burdensome armaments', Churchill told Attlee: 'The President undoubtedly contemplates the disarmament of the guilty nations, coupled with the maintenance of strong united British and American armament both by sea and air for a long indefinite period.' Churchill's telegram to Attlee continued:

It would be most imprudent on our part to raise unnecessary difficulties. We must regard this as an interim and partial statement of war aims designed to reassure all countries of our righteous purpose and not the complete structure which we should build after victory.

You should summon the full War Cabinet, with any others you may think necessary, to meet to-night, and please let me have your views without the slightest delay. . . .[3]

The War Cabinet met an hour and three-quarters after midnight, and approved both the idea and principal points of the proposed declaration. Their reply, sent from London at 4 a.m. London time, reached Argentia shortly after one o'clock Argentia time, in the early hours of

[1] Telegram received on 15 July 1941, 'Secret': Churchill papers, 20/41.

[2] The statement had been drafted by Sir Alexander Cadogan, at Churchill's request, following Churchill's first talk with Roosevelt on August 9. Cadogan, wrote in his dairy of how, after the hymns on August 10: 'Sat about on deck after. PM gave my drafts to the President.' (Cadogan diary, 10 August 1941: Churchill papers, 4/255.)

[3] Tudor No. 15, 'Secret', despatched 1.50 p.m., 11 August 1941: Premier papers, 3/485/1, No. 11.

August 12. When the message was brought to Churchill's room by Colonel Hollis, he was about to go to bed, talking animatedly with Lord Cherwell. 'Am I going to like it?' he asked Hollis apprehensively, looking, as Colonel Jacob noted in his diary, 'rather like a small boy about to take medicine.'[1]

In their reply, the War Cabinet asked for the insertion of a point on the need to secure after the war 'improved labour standards, economic advancement and social security' for all. This, both Churchill and Roosevelt approved. Also in the final draft was a sentence drafted by Churchill, envisaging 'a world at peace' after 'the final destruction of the Nazi tyranny'. This was a remarkable commitment by the United States while still a neutral power.

As Roosevelt had proposed in his telegram of mid-July, the two countries pledged themselves, first to 'no aggrandisement, territorial or other', as a result of the war, second, to no territorial changes 'that do not accord with the freely expressed wishes of the peoples concerned', the third—and this point became the crux and gravamen of the Charter for millions of repressed or captive peoples—Britain and the United States pledged themselves to: 'respect the right of all peoples to choose the form of government under which they will live; and they wish to see sovereign rights and self-government restored to those who have been forcibly deprived of them'.[2]

Churchill had reservations, however, about the application of this third pledge. Eight days after the Atlantic Charter had been signed, he wrote, in a minute to L. S. Amery, the Secretary of State for India, that in his view the application of this particular pledge 'would only arise in such cases when transference of territory or sovereignty arose'. It was surely not intended, he wrote, 'that the natives of Nigeria or of East Africa could by a majority vote choose the form of Government under which they live, or the Arabs by such a vote expel the Jews from Palestine'. It was 'evident', Churchill added, 'that prior obligations require to be considered and respected, and that circumstances alter cases.'[3]

A year later, when Roosevelt proposed a message to celebrate the anniversary of the Atlantic Charter, Churchill repeated these caveats, telegraphing to the President from Cairo, again with particular reference to the pledge of self-government:

---

[1] Jacob diary, 12 August 1941: Jacob papers.

[2] 'Joint Declaration by the President and the Prime Minister', 12 August 1941: Premier papers, 3/485/7, folio 73.

[3] Prime Minister's Personal Minute M. 812/1, 20 August 1941: Churchill papers, 20/36.

We considered the wording of that famous document line by line together and I should not be able, without mature consideration, to give it a wider interpretation than was agreed between us at the time. Its proposed application to Asia and Africa requires much thought. Grave embarrassment would be caused to the defence of India at the present time by such a statement as the Office of War Information has been forecasting. Here in the Middle East the Arabs might claim by majority they could expel the Jews from Palestine, or at any rate forbid all further immigration. I am wedded to the Zionist policy, of which I was one of the authors.

This Churchill added, was 'only one of the many unforeseen cases which will arise from new and further declarations'.[1]

The final act of Argentia was yet to be played, the setting up of the joint Anglo-American Mission to Moscow, to be headed by Beaverbrook and Harriman. To discuss the Soviet supply needs in relation to American production, Beaverbrook and Arthur Purvis set off at once from Scotland by air for Newfoundland, in separate planes only a few hours apart. Beaverbrook reached Newfoundland safely. Purvis and all those with him were killed when their plane flew into a hill within minutes of take-off.

The death of Purvis, Churchill later recalled, was 'a grievous loss, as he held so many British, American and Canadian threads in his hands, and had hitherto been the directing mind in their harmonious combination'. Churchill had been convinced that Beaverbrook and Purvis together would give Britain 'the best chance of coping with the painful splitting of supplies' between Britain and the Soviet Union.

When Beaverbrook reached the *Prince of Wales*, Churchill told him 'the shocking news' of Purvis' death. 'He was silent for a moment,' Churchill later recalled, 'but made no comment. It was war-time.'[2] The loss of Purvis, Churchill telegraphed to Halifax four days later, 'is most grievous'.[3]

The planning of the Anglo-American Mission to Russia went ahead. As Churchill explained to Attlee on August 12, the presence of Russia 'as a welcome guest at hungry table', and the need for a large supplementary programme both for British and American forces, 'makes review and expansion of US production imperative'. Churchill also explained to Attlee that he and Roosevelt had apprised Stalin of this

[1] Prime Minister's Personal Telegram, T.1097/2, 'Secret and Personal', Cairo Telegram No. 128, 11.55 p.m., 9 August 1942: Premier papers, 3/485/9, folio 34.

[2] Winston S. Churchill, *The Second World War*, volume 3, London 1950, pages 396–7.

[3] Prime Minister's Personal telegram, T. 488, Foreign Office No. 4584 to Washington, 16 August 1941: Churchill papers, 20/41.

plan.[1] 'We are at the moment cooperating,' they telegraphed jointly to Stalin on August 12, 'to provide you with very maximum supplies that you most urgently need. Already many shiploads have left our shores and more will leave in immediate future.' But the needs and demands of the Soviet, British and United States armed forces were such that a meeting in Moscow of 'high representatives' would alone enable 'speedy decisions' to be taken as to the apportionment 'of our great resources'. These resources, Churchill and Roosevelt stressed, 'though immense, are limited, and it must become a question as to where and when these resources can best be used to further to principal extent our common effort'. The telegram to Stalin ended:

We realise fully how vitally important to the defeat of Hitlerism is the brave and steadfast resistance of the Soviet Union, and we feel therefore that we must not in any circumstances fail to act quickly and immediately in this matter of planning the programme for the future allocation of our joint resources.[2]

As for United States aid to Britain, Churchill told Attlee that the Americans were sending Britain 'immediately' a further 150,000 rifles, and had promised improved 'allocations of merchant shipping' to carry bombers and tanks across the Atlantic, as well as delivering bombers both to Britain and West Africa 'by American pilots', many of whom would then 'stay for war training purposes with us'.[3]

These were important additional agreements, derived from the long hours of negotiations between the British and American Chiefs of Staff. As for Churchill's own achievement, and conclusion, 'I am sure,' he told Attlee, 'I have established warm and deep personal relations with our great friend.'[4]

*   *   *

[1] Tudor No. 23, 'Most Secret', despatched 4.39 p.m., 12 August 1941: Premier papers, 3/485/1, No. 24. Four days earlier Churchill had minuted to Eden that figures of the production of British war supplies in the United States should not be given to Russia. The Russians, he wrote, had been preparing for years, 'we still have a dangerous leeway to make up'. (Minute of 8 August 1941: Premier papers, 3/401/3.)

[2] Text in Tudor No. 21, 'Most Secret' (Churchill to Attlee), despatched 12 August 1941: Premier papers 3/485/1, No. 22.

[3] In a reciprocal move, Air Vice-Marshal Harris was sent to Washington for eight months as head of the Royal Air Force Delegation to the United States, as adviser to General Arnold, 'to help get his outfit war worthy'. (Sir Arthur Harris, conversation with the author, 21 October 1982.) On his return to Britain, Harris was appointed Commander-in-Chief, Bomber Command, a position which he held from 1942 to 1945.

[4] Tudor No. 23, 'Most Secret', despatched 4.29 p.m., 12 August 1941: Premier papers, 3/485/1, No. 24.

The relations established by Churchill and Roosevelt found an echo in those of their respective Chiefs of Staff, whose continuous meetings throughout those same four days had resulted in a considerable improvement in understanding of their respective needs and concerns. But it became clear also during these discussions that there was a gulf between the two Staffs which would not be easy to bridge.

Colonel Jacob's conclusion, after the 'Riviera' meeting, was:

The Americans have a long way to go before they can play any decisive part in the war. Their Navy is further ahead than their Army, both in thought and in resources. Both are standing like reluctant bathers on the brink, but the Navy are being forced to dip a toe at a time into the shark-infested water. Their ideas, however, have not got beyond how to avoid being bitten; they have not yet reached out to thoughts of how to get rid of the sharks. The President and his entourage are far ahead, and intend to keep pushing forward until the time comes when the Germans can no longer disregard American provocation. The sailors and soldiers only hope that moment won't come before they can gather together some respectably armed forces with which to fight.[1]

Several important inhibiting factors were raised by the American team: that America was 'far from being prepared for active operations on a war footing'; that American public opinion as well as the Chiefs of Staff themselves would 'insist' on a considerable measure of the new American equipment being allotted to their own 'new army and air force'; that the American Army Air Corps was 'still in embryo' and its shortage of equipment 'acute'; and that the British were not the 'only claimants' to war materials as 'Russian demands' as well as to a lesser degree 'the demands of other friends' such as China 'cannot be set aside'.

These were formidable caveats. The American Chiefs of Staff also thought that the British planners attached 'too much importance' to the bombing offensive and had given an 'unduly high priority' to the production of heavy bombers.

'We were successful, however,' the Chiefs of Staff told Churchill, 'in convincing the Americans of the correctness of our policy to fight in the Middle East,' but they still felt that Britain should not 'over-allot' equipment to the Middle East at the expense 'of other vital theatres'. In consequence, the Chiefs of Staff warned, 'we should be careful not to embark on a major extension of our effort in the Middle East which it might be impossible to sustain'.

[1] Jacob diary, 19 August 1941: Jacob papers.

The Chiefs of Staff ended their report to Churchill with both general and specific concerns:

To sum up, we neither expected nor achieved startling results. The American Chiefs of Staff are quite clearly thinking in terms of the defence of the Western Hemisphere and have so far not formulated any joint strategy for the defeat of Germany in the event of their entry into the war. Nevertheless, the personal contacts with our American colleagues will prove of the greatest value for our future collaboration. We have, we think, convinced the Americans that our policy in the Middle East is sound. They, in turn, have made us understand their difficulties. A most distressing revelation is the reduction in heavy bomber and Catalina[1] allocation to us. This we consider a serious matter. We are also concerned at the small number of Catalinas allocated to the United Kingdom during the next few months.[2]

Despite these secret caveats, the impact and outcome of the Argentia meeting were to affect the whole course of the war. Two indications in particular gave Churchill cause for optimism. The American naval officers present at the meeting, he told the War Cabinet on his return, 'had not concealed their keenness to enter the war',[3] and in a survey of Roosevelt's views and commitments, Churchill told his War Cabinet colleagues:

... he had got on intimate terms with the President. Of the six meals they had had together, five had been on the President's ship. The President had shown great activity, considering his physical disabilities, and on one occasion had walked (every step causing him pain) a considerable distance in front of Marines drawn up on parade, notwithstanding that his own people had advised him against doing this.

The Prime Minister said that the family influence on the President was great. Both his sons were in uniform and clearly urged him that American assistance in money and *matériel* was not enough.

Churchill also gave the War Cabinet his impression of Roosevelt's attitude towards the entry of the United States into the war, telling them, as the minutes recorded, that Roosevelt 'was obviously determined that they should come in'. Churchill's report continued:

On the other hand, the President had been extremely anxious about the Bill for further appropriations for Lease-Lend, which had only passed with a very narrow majority. Clearly he was skating on pretty thin ice in his relations with Congress, which, however, he did not regard as truly representative of

---

[1] The PBY twin-engined flying boat.

[2] 'British-American Chiefs of Staff Discussions', HMS *Prince of Wales*, 15 August 1941 (signed Dudley Pound, J. G. Dill, W. R. Freeman, VCAS): Premier papers, 3/485/7, 74–80.

[3] War Cabinet No. 84 of 1941, 19 August 1941, 11.30 a.m.: Cabinet papers, 65/19.

the country. If he were to put the issue of peace and war to Congress, they would debate it for three months.

Roosevelt had told Churchill, in conclusion, that 'he would wage war, but not declare it, and that he would become more and more provocative'. If the Germans 'did not like it', he said, 'they could attack American forces!'

Churchill then told the War Cabinet that, as a result of the Argentia discussions, each of Britain's North Atlantic convoys would be escorted by five United States destroyers, together with a capital ship or cruiser. The President's orders to these escorts were 'to attack any U-boat which showed itself, even if these were 200 or 300 miles away from the convoy'. Any Commander who sank a U-boat, Admiral Stark told Churchill, 'would have his action approved', and 'everything was to be done' to force an incident. This, Churchill told the War Cabinet:

... would put the enemy in the dilemma that either he could attack the convoys, in which case his U-boats would be attacked by American Naval forces, or, if he refrained from attack, this would be tantamount to giving us victory in the Battle of the Atlantic. It might suit us, in six or eight weeks' time, to provoke Hitler by taunting him with this difficult choice.

For as long as the Russian front 'remained in being', Churchill told the War Cabinet, 'we might have to make some sacrifices' as far as war supplies were concerned, but he had 'thought it right', he added, to give Roosevelt 'a warning', telling him:

... that he would not answer for the consequences if Russia was compelled to sue for peace and, say, by the Spring of next year, hope died in Britain that the United States were coming into the war. The President had taken this very well, and had made it clear that he would look for an 'incident' which would justify him in opening hostilities.[1]

On these secret commitments and declarations the British policy-makers and planners were to build their detailed preparations in the months to come, despite formidable obstacles of priority and production. For Churchill, it was the fact that he had established a personal relationship with the President, which constituted the main achievement of 'Riviera'.

---

[1] War Cabinet No. 84 of 1941, 19 August 1941, 11.30 a.m., 'Secretary's file only': Cabinet papers, 65/19.

61

Russia and the Middle East: 'Bleakest Times'

O N August 16, while Churchill was still returning from Argentia, an Anglo-Soviet agreement was signed in Moscow by Cripps and Molotov, giving the Soviet Union £10 million of British credit, at 3 per cent interest over five years, to replace lost war material from British stock. That night, in the continuing effort to divert German figher aircraft from the Russian front, British bombers struck again at Cologne and other Rhineland targets, and on August 17 at Bremen. But the cost of these attacks was heavy: between August 1 and August 18 a total of 107 British bombers had been shot down.

On August 16 the *Prince of Wales* reached Iceland, where Churchill inspected the British and American troops garrisoned there. He also addressed the sailors of the destroyer *Churchill*, one of the fifty American destroyers of the 'destroyers for bases' deal. *Churchill* was serving as a guide and escort to the Halifax convoys crossing the Atlantic on the northerly route. One of those on board later recalled how, the sailors having been fallen in on the destroyer's forecastle deck:

The Prime Minister appeared, stumping stolidly forward. He wore a Trinity House jacket and cap, and was followed by a US naval ensign who was Franklin Roosevelt junior. There was a flurry as he suddenly barked 'Bring me a soapbox'. A dais was found and he climbed on it.

He spoke to us for nearly a quarter of an hour, saying that the war would last another three years at least and that hard times lay ahead. He told us that we were carrying out one of the most vital jobs of the war in ensuring that the food and supplies without which Britain could not survive reached us from North America. He would not deny that this was one of the bleakest times in Britain's history, but he was confident that we would survive, and with right on our side and help from allies—a glance to the ensign here—we should win through to a great and glorious victory.

'Three cheers for the Prime Minister,' said the Captain. For the first time Winston smiled and with a wave of the hand stalked off the foredeck, followed by the officers. We were dismissed and rushed amidships to cheer him on his way as the launch left the ship's side. It sped away across the fiord and Winston turned and saluted.

I found Taff, a Rhondda valley pitman, next to me at the rail. 'There goes the bastard,' he said in a voice full of venom, 'back to his bloody brandy.' Startled, I turned and looked at him. Taff whipped round, glared defiantly and turned to the hatchway. 'And the best of bloody luck to him,' he added as he disappeared.[1]

From Iceland, the *Prince of Wales* proceeded to Scapa Flow. There, in his farewell speech to the officers and men of the battleship, Churchill declared: 'Many years ago there was a statesman who came back from a European Conference and said he had brought with him 'Peace with Honour'. We have not sought Peace on this occasion; and as for Honour, we have never lost it. But we have brought back a means of waging more effective war and surer hope of final and speedy victory'.[2]

From Scapa Flow Churchill crossed to Thurso, and then travelled south to London. During the train journey southward, Colville, who had come to Scotland with Clementine Churchill to welcome Churchill back, discussed recent Parliamentary criticisms and their effect on the Prime Minister with two other members of the welcoming party, Desmond Morton and Churchill's brother Jack. As Colville wrote in his diary:

Jack Churchill, Desmond and I discussed the rising annoyance in the House of Commons at the PM's personal resentment of criticism—which is meant to be helpful—and the offence which has been given to many people, including Ministers, by his treatment of them. Desmond goes so far as to say that the PM is losing many people's friendship. The PM himself does not expect to retain his popularity if he wins the war for us: he has before him the examples of Wellington and Disraeli amongst others. But that he should lose his personal friends owing to the impatience of his manner is unfortunate—and unfair to one so innately loveable and generous.[3]

The situation was a depressing one, its tensions heightened by con-

[1] 'Icelandic Encounter' by Squadron-Leader E. Ladbrooke: typescript sent to the author on 27 December 1968.

[2] 'The Prime Minister's Farewell Speech to HMS *Prince of Wales* at Scapa Flow', 18 August 1941: Premier papers, 4/71/1, folios 296–7.

[3] Colville diary, 18 August 1941: Colville papers.

tinuing and severe British bomber losses over Germany.[1] On the morning of August 19 Churchill warned the War Cabinet that the attacks 'should not be pressed too hard if the weather was unfavourable', and he suggested, with the approval of the War Cabinet, that consideration 'should also be given to attacking the less heavily defended centres'.[2]

More depressing still for Churchill was the prospect that Germany would destroy Russia before the United States entered the war. That night, as more news reached London of Russian reverses, Colville, who was on late duty at 10 Downing Street, found Churchill 'nodding his head gloomily', saying that the situation was 'very grim'.[3] The situation was so grim in fact that on the following day the War Cabinet approved a request by Lord Hankey to obtain assurances from the Soviet Government that 'the orders to destroy the Caucasian oil industry' would not be 'dangerously delayed' in the event of a German advance towards Baku. At the same time, Britian would compensate the Soviet Union for the destruction. If the war lasted two years after demolition, the War Cabinet were told, the sum involved would amount to about £100 million. 'It was impossible to foresee,' Kingsley Wood told his colleagues, 'what our position would be after the war, but it was not reasonable to suggest that we should be able to carry out such an undertaking without American help.'

Churchill did not feel, however, that Britain could press Russia to demolish its oil wells, telling the War Cabinet:

. . . he thought it was difficult for us, at a time when we were offering so little assistance to the Russians in the operational field, to press them to undertake this work of demolition. Russian agriculture was greatly dependent upon petrol. These oil fields produced 27 million tons a year, and their destruction would condemn large sections of the Russian people to starvation.'

Continuing, Churchill said:

. . . that the amount of help which we could give to the Russians by way of oil imports was so very small that he could not see that we had an effective inducement which we could offer them to destroy their oilfields, if they were not prepared to reach a decision themselves to do it. It was impossible for us to say what M. Stalin would do in regard to this issue.'

[1] In night raids over Germany in May 1941, 43 bombers had been shot down or crashed (out of 2,416 sorties). In June 1941 the losses were 91 (out of 3,288 sorties) and in August 166 (out of 3,344 sorties). After August, the number of sorties was reduced. For the whole of 1941, 1,054 bombers were lost in just over 30,000 sorties. (Sir Charles Webster and Noble Frankland, *The Strategic Air Offensive Against Germany 1939–1945*, Volume 4, London 1961, Appendix 40, page 431.)

[2] War Cabinet No. 84 of 1941, 19 August 1941, 11.30 a.m.: Cabinet papers, 65/19.

[3] Colville diary, 20 August 1941: Colville papers.

Churchill's personal feeling was that the British 'must be ready to bomb the oilfields ourselves if the Russians did not destroy them'.[1]

The Soviet distress was a spur to British action in North Africa. This was given an added sense of urgency on August 22, as Enigma decrypts made it clear that considerable German reinforcements were reaching Cyrenaica. Yet, as Churchill reminded Pound, Auchinleck 'is disinclined to move before November'. Churchill went on to ask: 'Are we then to wait and allow this ever-growing reinforcement, mainly of Italians and supplies to pile up in Libya.' If so, Auchinleck 'will be no better off, relatively to the enemy, when at last he considers himself perfectly ready, than he is now'. Churchill proposed a naval striking force to intercept supply ships on their way to Tripoli. His proposal was accepted, and 'Force K', consisting of two cruisers, *Aurora* and *Penelope*, and two destroyers, *Lance* and *Lively*, was formed at Malta in October.[2]

In an attempt to accelerate supplies to Auchinleck, Churchill had already proposed sending the lorries needed for two further infantry divisions direct from the United States to the Middle East. He was prepared, he now minuted to Dill and Leathers, to ask Roosevelt 'for the loan of this shipping for this particular purpose—and I daresay I can get it'.[3]

Yet Churchill continued to fret over Auchinleck's decision, telegraphing to Smuts on August 24: 'What do you say about Auchinleck's proposal not to strike until November? Are you convinced so long a delay is inevitable? Ought not wearing-down attacks to be made? If we accumulate for a set-piece battle, will not they do the same, in spite of their worse communications?'[4]

On August 25, to forestall a repetition further east of the pro-Nazi rebellion in Iraq, now crushed, British and Soviet forces moved into Persia. Landing that day from Basra, a British infantry brigade occupied the oil refinery at Abadan. Three days later, as British troops moved northwards, Churchill learnt that Wavell, now Commander-in-Chief in India, and commander of the forces fighting in Persia, proposed a visit to Britain on leave. Churchill telegraphed at once, urging him to wait until the Persian campaign was over. 'Although we have taken action to expel the Germans,' Churchill explained, 'our

---

[1] War Cabinet No. 85 of 1941, 11.30 a.m., 21 August 1941, Minute 7, Confidential Annex: Cabinet papers, 65/23.

[2] Prime Minister's Personal Minute, M.817/1, 22 August 1941: Churchill papers, 20/36.

[3] Prime Minister's Personal Minute, M.816/1, 22 August 1941: Churchill papers, 20/36.

[4] Prime Minister's Personal Telegram, T.507, 24 August 1941: Churchill papers, 20/49.

main object is to join hands with the Russians and establish a warm-water through route by which American supplies can reach the Caspian region. Nothing less than this will suffice.'[1] Two days later, the Persian forces surrendered.

Despite the swift occupation of Persia, Churchill still felt that the danger of a Russian defeat before America entered the war was considerable. On August 25 he had warned the War Cabinet of the dangers involved because the American public was being called upon 'to put up with all the inconvenience of war without the stimulus of being at war'. Churchill added:

He sometimes wondered whether the President realised the risk which the United States were running by keeping out of the war. If Germany beat Russia to a standstill and the United States had made no further advance towards entry into the war, there was a great danger that the war might take a turn against us. While no doubt we could hope to keep going, this was a very different matter from imposing our will on Nazi Germany.

Churchill then told the War Cabinet that he had on several occasions said to Roosevelt 'that he had rather the United States came into the war now, and that we got no more supplies from the United States for six months, than that supplies from the United States should be doubled but the USA kept out of the war'.[2]

In a live broadcast from Chequers on August 24, Churchill had spoken of Hitler's attempt to defeat Russia, a 'frightful business' which was now 'unfolding day by day before our eyes', with six or seven million soldiers 'locked in mortal struggle' from the Arctic Ocean to the Black Sea. Hitler had hoped for a swift victory, but, said Churchill, 'this time it was not so easy', and he went on to tell his listeners:

This time it was not all one way. The Russian armies and all the peoples of the Russian Republic have rallied to the defence of their hearths and homes. For the first time Nazi blood has flowed in a fearful torrent. Certainly

[1] Prime Minister's Personal Telegram, T.510, 26 August 1941: Churchill papers, 20/49. When Wavell replied that he wished to come back 'on duty' for consultation as Commander-in-Chief for India as well as for 'certain personal business' (Telegram No. 11947/C), Churchill replied that he agreed 'entirely' and considered 'visit will be invaluable', but added: 'Pray, however, do not go beyond Cairo till situation in Persia can be measured by us as well as by you.' (Prime Minister's Personal Telegram, T.518, 27 August 1941: Churchill papers, 20/49.)

[2] War Cabinet No. 86 of 1941, 25 August 1941, 5 p.m.: Cabinet papers, 65/19.

1,500,000, perhaps 2,000,000 of Nazi cannon-fodder have bit the dust on the endless plains of Russia.

The tremendous battle rages along nearly 2,000 miles of front. The Russians fight with magnificent devotion; not only that, our generals who have visited the Russian front line report with admiration the efficiency of their military organization and the excellence of their equipment.

The aggressor is surprised, startled, staggered. For the first time in his experience mass murder has become unprofitable. He retaliates by the most frightful cruelties. As his armies advance, whole districts are being exterminated. Scores of thousands—literally scores of thousands—of executions in cold blood are being perpetrated by the German police-troops upon the Russian patriots who defend their native soil. Since the Mongol invasions of Europe in the sixteenth century, there has never been methodical, merciless butchery on such a scale, or approaching such a scale.[1]

And this is but the beginning. Famine and pestilence have yet to follow in the bloody ruts of Hitler's tanks.

'We are in the presence,' Churchill ended, 'of a crime without a name.'[2]

The spectre of a German victory in Russia seemed to come even closer in the last week of August, when Russian forces were forced to evacuate Novgorod, only a hundred miles south of Leningrad, while in the south German forces on the Black Sea shore came within striking distance of the Caucasus. On August 28 Russian troops were forced to evacuate the Ukrainian industrial centre of Dnepropetrovsk, a major road and rail junction between the Ukraine and the Caucasus. That same day the great dam on the Dnieper at Zaporozhe was blown up on the eve of the arrival of German forces. 'I have been searching,' Churchill telegraphed that day to Stalin, 'for any way to give you help in your splendid resistance, pending the long term arrangements which we are discussing with the United States. . . .', and he went on to say that 40 Hurricanes should reach Murmansk on about September 6,

[1] Since July 18 German Police messages, decrypted at Bletchley, had revealed details of mass shootings of victims described variously as 'Jews', 'Jewish plunderers', 'Jewish bolshevists' or 'Russian soldiers' in numbers varying from under a hundred to several thousand at a time. On August 7 the SS Cavalry Brigade reported, as one decrypt revealed, that it had carried out 7,819 'executions' to date in the Minsk area, while on the same day a police decrypt revealed 30,000 executions in the central sector since the police had arrived in Russia. In the week following Churchill's speech the shooting of Jews in groups numbering from 61 to 4,200 was reported on 17 occasions in the southern sector. (F. H. Hinsley and others, *British Intelligence in the Second World War, Its Influence on Strategy and Operations*, volume 2, London 1981, Appendix 5, page 671.)

[2] Broadcast, 24 August 1941: Churchill papers, 9/152.

with a further 200, 'making 440 fighters in all', if the Soviet pilots 'could use them effectively'. Churchill's telegram continued:

We are instructing our advance guards to push on and join hands with your forces at a point to be fixed by the Military Commanders somewhere between Hamadan and Kasvin. It would be a good thing to let the world know that British and Russian forces had actually joined hands. In our view it would be better at this moment for neither of us to enter Teheran in force as all we want is the through route. We are making a large-scale base at Basra, and we hope to make this a well-equipped warm water reception port for American supplies, which can thus surely reach the Caspian and the Volga region.

Churchill's final words were of 'admiration' for the 'wonderful fight which the Russian armies and Russian people are making against the Nazi criminals', and he added: 'A very hard time lies before us, but Hitler will not have a pleasant winter under our ever-increasing Air bombardment'.[1]

The German air raids over British cities had lost their earlier intensity. In August 1941 British civilian deaths totalled no more than 169 killed for the whole month, the equivalent of a low toll for a single night of the Blitz when at its most intense. It was in the east that the civilian deaths were being reported in their thousands, and tens of thousands, the military deaths in millions. 'According to the best figures we have been able to obtain,' Churchill wrote to General Edmonds, 'the German losses in the ten weeks of their invasion of Russia approached two millions, killed, wounded and missing.[2]

With Persia being occupied by an Anglo-Soviet force, and Egypt held secure, it was Britain's hope, Churchill telegraphed to Lord Linlithgow, the Viceroy of India, on August 28, 'to be able to hold the half-circle from the Volga to the Nile'.[3] Inside Nazi-dominated Europe itself, in the Balkans, Churchill minuted to Dalton, there was 'widespread guerilla activity', and he urged that it be given 'cohesion, support and direction from outside'.[4] At Chequers that weekend there was, as Colville noted, 'considerable optimism' on Churchill's part. Churchill, he noted, compared the situation in the Middle East a year

[1] Prime Minister's Personal Telegram, T.523, 28 August 1941; Foreign Office Telegram to Moscow, No. 1136 of 29 August 1941: Premier papers, 3/170/1, No. 9.
[2] Prime Minister's Personal Minute, M.858/1, 31 August 1941: Churchill papers, 20/36.
[3] Prime Minister's Personal Telegram, T.528, 28 August 1941: Churchill papers, 20/42.
[4] Prime Minister's Personal Minute, M.837/1, 28 August 1941: Cabinet papers, 120/723.

earlier, 'when we had but 80,000 ill-equipped troops', with the situation of August 1941, when, apart from a 'tremendous army' of nearly a quarter of a million men, 'we were in possession of Syria, Iraq, Abyssinia, Eritrea, both Somalilands and Persia, and were confident in the Western Desert'.[1]

But Churchill was still disappointed about America, especially after Roosevelt's speech on his return from Argentia in which he had announced that America had made no commitments and was no nearer to war than before the ship board meeting. Churchill telegraphed his feelings to Hopkins, his telegram marked 'Personal, Secret and Private':

I ought to tell you that there has been a wave of depression through Cabinet and other informed circles here about President's many assurances about no commitments and no closer to war, &c. I fear this will be reflected in Parliament. If 1942 opens with Russia knocked out and Britain left again alone, all kinds of dangers may arise. I do not think Hitler will help in any way. To-night he has 30 U-boats in line from the eastern part of Iceland to northern tip of Ireland. We have lost 25,000 tons yesterday (27th) and to-day (28th), but he keeps clear of 26th meridian. You will know best whether anything more can be done. Should be grateful if you could give me any sort of hope.

Persia, Churchill ended, 'was okay'.[2]

Roosevelt, and even Hopkins, did not understand that the Cabinet's 'wave of depression' arose through fear of an unnecessarily prolonged war, which would destroy Europe while the United States remained neutral. After talking to Roosevelt about Churchill's telegram, Hopkins told the President, 'that not only Churchill but all the members of the Cabinet and all the British people I talked to believed that ultimately we will get into the war on some basis or other and if they ever reached the conclusion that this was not to be the case, that would be a very critical moment in the war and the British appeasers might have some influence on Churchill'.[3]

On August 29, while at Chequers, Churchill sent his son Randolph an account of recent developments:

... I had a very interesting and by no means unfruitful meeting with the President in Newfoundland, and in the three days when we were continually together I feel we made a deep and intimate contact of friendship. At the same time one is deeply perplexed to know how the deadlock is to be broken

---

[1] Colville diary, 29 August 1941: Colville papers.

[2] Prime Minister's Personal Telegram, T.526, 28 August 1941: Churchill papers, 20/49.

[3] Quoted in Robert E. Sherwood, *The White House Papers of Harry L. Hopkins*, volume 1, London 1948, page 374.

and the United States brought boldly and honourably into the war. There is a very dangerous feeling in America that they need not worry now as all will be well.[1]

Hitler will give no help in bringing things to a head by attacking American ships until at least he sees his way through the Russian miscalculation and morass. Meanwhile the larger pay envelopes spreading through the United States and the boom caused by our war necessities is leading to all kinds of consumptions which positively detract from the war effort. Besides this, the American people must now put up with taxation and many other of the inconveniences of war without its commanding stimuli.

The President, for all his warm heart and good intentions, is thought by many of his admirers to move with public opinion rather than to lead and form it. I thank God however that he is where he is. You will no doubt in time see the film of our meeting and of my inspection of Iceland, which I am sure you will find very interesting.

Turning to your part of the world, we have certainly been very successful in tidying up the Eastern Flank. Persia, though questionable as taking a leaf out of the German book, has given great pleasure here and enormously improved our situation. We have joined hands with the Russian armies and naval forces on the Caspian and in the Volga Basin, and I hope to make a good through route by which United States supplies can reach these vast regions and massive Russian forces. Compare this with the situation when Iraq was ablaze, Palestine quaking and Syria in the hands of the frogs. I lunched with Maisky today, all the representatives of the Allied defeated powers being present. He sent you friendly messages and enquired much after you.

Mackenzie King is with us now, and stayed here last week. He also sent you messages. He has made himself most friendly and helpful over here, and I am backing him up in every way.

Churchill continued his letter to Randolph with personal news:

Your mother is much better now. She was very tired, but retired for treatment to a home hard by, which has done her no end of good. She is, I know, sending you a letter by the same hand that bears this. Mary is now a gunner in the Anti-Aircraft Batteries, and is going to learn to work Predictors, etc. I thought it was better for her to do this than go into munitions or hospitals. She begins by being a private, but she has all the qualities to win her way, and is the greatest darling that can be imagined.

'Into Battle' has yielded much larger profits from the United States than I

---

[1] On 2 September 1941 Churchill minuted to the principal Ministers in receipt of United States supplies: 'It is imperative that the campaign now under weigh in the United States to discredit us and the administration by alleging that we make insufficient or improper use of American supplies should be promptly and fully countered. All Departments concerned should confer with the Ministry of Information in this matter and should provide the information which the Ministry requires to rebut attacks or promote an effective line of counter-propaganda.' (Prime Minister's Personal Minute, M.867/1, 2 September 1941: Premier papers, 4/17/3, folio 491.)

expected, and I shall be ready to give you £500 more on account of it, provided that you pay the income tax upon it on your appropriate scale when it falls due and also devote £400 of it to the payment of your bills and debts, to the bottom of which we never seem to be able to get. I have not told Pamela about this but I will do so during next week.

I do hope that you will make a success of your important work, which may easily broaden as time goes on. I have asked that the Commandos should be reconstituted and that Laycock should go out as DCO, and this I understand is being done. I do not wish you to rejoin him, because you are more useful where you are. General[1] Shearer tells me that for the purposes of your present work you are entitled to visit any part of the Front, and therefore you need not feel tied to an office stool when fighting is going on.[2]

On August 30 the process of aid to Russia took a forward step with the appointment of Beaverbrook and Harriman to represent Britain and America respectively in talks to take place in Moscow at the end of September aimed at establishing Russia's needs, and the Anglo-American ability to meet them.[3] The long term requirements of the Russian armies could only be achieved, Churchill wrote to Beaverbrook, 'almost entirely from American resources, though we have rubber boots etc'. A 'new, large installation' would have to be made in the United States; no large flow of material could begin until mid-1942 and 'the main planning will relate to 1943'. Churchill's letter continued: 'Your function will be not only to aid in the forming of the plans to help Russia, but to make sure that we are not bled white in the process, and even if you find yourself affected by the Russian atmosphere'. As for himself, Churchill added, 'I shall be quite stiff about it here.'[4]

Churchill was also reluctant to take undue risk in another area, that of the bomber offensive. In a daylight raid on merchant shipping in the docks at Rotterdam at the end of August, seven out of seventeen Blenheims had been lost. 'While I greatly admire the bravery of the pilots', he wrote to Portal, 'I do not want them to be pressed too hard.

[1] In fact, Brigadier. The First World War rank of Brigadier-General, of which Churchill was no doubt thinking, had been abolished in the 1920s.

[2] Letter of 29 August 1941: Churchill papers, 1/362. Randolph Churchill had been transferred from the Commandos to the General Staff 'I' (Information and Propaganda), GHQ, MEF, Cairo. Robert Laycock was Deputy (and from 1943 Chief) of Combined Operations.

[3] In the draft of a speech which he prepared in September for the Duke of Windsor, Churchill wrote: 'It had been decided that a British and United States Mission should be sent to confer in Russia with the leaders of the Russian Government. This was not because the Russians were Communists, but because they were brave and were fighting a righteous war to defend their native soil against brutal, unprovoked attack.' (Prime Minister's Personal Telegram' T.605, 22 September 1941: Churchill papers, 20/49.)

[4] Prime Minister's Personal Minute, M.847/1, 30 August 1941: Churchill papers, 20/36.

Easier targets giving a high damage return compared to casualties may be more often selected'.[1] To the mauled Squadrons themselves Churchill wrote: 'The devotion and gallantry of the attacks on Rotterdam and other objectives are beyond all praise. The Charge of the Light Brigade at Balaclava is eclipsed in brightness by these almost daily deeds of fame.'[2]

That weekend, at Chequers, Lord Halifax was among the guests.

Colville, who was on duty, recorded in his diary the conversation of the guests, and of their host:

Lord Halifax, whose reputation in this country and the US makes him out a reactionary and an obscurantist, seemed very Liberal in his conversation with the PM over the tea-table in the Long Gallery. He was emphatic that we must 'cough up supplies for Russia', and he said, in discussing the future of the Conservative party, that secondary schoolboys were on the whole better educated than Public Schoolboys. To this Winston said: 'They have saved this country; they have the right to rule it'. He was referring to the RAF pilots, the majority of whom have come from the Secondary Schools.

The PM considered that the only hope for the Tory party at the next election was to choose young candidates who had won their spurs in the war. To succeed in politics a man should enter the H of C if possible in the twenties.

They discussed the 4th point of the Atlantic Charter, which declares for freedom of trade and access to raw materials. The PM thought that this would in fact be achieved and foresaw a great increase in wealth as a result. Halifax said the Tories would not object, except perhaps Amery.

When he went to bed, after tea, the PM who is always talking about my joining up—with approval!—said, as he unlocked one of his 'buff boxes': 'You will have to forget a great many things. Be wise rather than well-informed. Give your opinion but not the reasons for it. Then you will have a valuable contribution to make.'

Colville went on to describe dinner that night at Chequers, at which Eden, Winant and Halifax were present:

Over the brandy, the PM, periodically supported by Halifax and Eden, made an impassioned appeal to Winant to realise the importance of the issues hanging on America entering the war. (Winant, of course, like Roosevelt, is no sufferer from illusions about this). The PM said that after the joint declaration, America could not honourably stay out. She could not fight with mercenaries.

Churchill continued, as Colville recorded, to say once more of the

---

[1] 'Action this Day', Prime Minister's Personal Minute, M.843/1, 29 August 1941: Churchill papers, 20/36.
[2] Prime Minister's Personal Minute, M.852/1, 30 August 1941: Churchill papers, 20/36.

United States: 'Better she should come in now and give us no supplies for six months than stay out and double her supplies. If she came in, the conviction of an allied victory would be founded in a dozen countries.' Churchill continued: 'we must have an American declaration of war, or else, though we cannot now be defeated, the war might drag on for another 4 or 5 years, and civilisation and culture would be wiped out. If America came in, she could stop this. She alone could bring the war to an end—her belligerency might mean victory in 1943.'

During the discussion, Winant told those assembled that, on the day Arthur Purvis had been killed, he had told Winant that he thought the US might be in the war next March.' This prospect, Colville noted, 'seemed to give Winston little satisfaction. He thought the delay too long.'

Colville now recorded the 'less serious epilogue' as the dinner came to an end, and Churchill 'discoursed on Egalitarianism and the White Ant', recommended Halifax to read Maeterlinck,[1] and told his guests: 'Socialism would make our society comparable to that of the White Ant'.[2]

On September 4 Maisky brought Churchill a letter from Stalin, in which the Soviet leader, after thanking Churchill for the promise of a total of 400 British fighters, warned that these war planes would no longer be able to effect 'serious changes' on the Russian front, as the situation of the Soviet forces had 'considerably deteriorated' in both the Ukraine and Leningrad. Stalin noted that 34 'fresh' German infantry Divisions had recently been transferred to the Russian front, as had 20 Finnish Divisions and 26 Rumanian Divisions, and he added: 'Germans consider danger in the West a bluff.'

If the 'mortal menace' of German pressure on Leningrad and the Ukraine were to be relieved, Stalin wrote, it was essential for 'a second front' to be set up before the end of the year 'somewhere in the Balkans or France', capable, as Stalin phrased it, 'of drawing away from the Eastern Front 30 to 40 Divisions'. At the same time, the Soviet Union wished to be assured of 30,000 tons of aluminium within the next twelve months, and a 'monthly minimum' of 400 aircraft and 500 small or medium tanks.

Without the second front and the aid, Stalin told Churchill, 'the Soviet Union will either suffer defeat or be weakened to such an extent

---

[1] Maurice Maeterlinck, the Belgian-French dramatist and poet, whose *Life of the Bee*, based on observations made in his own apiaries, was published in 1901.

[2] Colville diary, 30 August 1941: Colville papers.

that it will lose for a long period any capacity to render assistance to its Allies by its actual operations. . . .'[1]

In delivering this message to Churchill, Maisky stressed that this moment might be, as Churchill recalled his words, 'a turning-point in history'. If Russia were defeated, Maisky asked, how could Britain win the war, and he went on, as Churchill recalled, to emphasize the extreme gravity of the crisis on the western front 'in poignant terms which commanded my sympathy'. But, Churchill's account continued, 'when presently I sensed an underlying air of menace in his appeal I was angered', telling Maisky—whom he had known for nearly a decade:

Remember that only four months ago we in this Island did not know whether you were not coming in against us on the German side. Indeed, we thought it quite likely that you would, even when we felt sure we should win in the end. We never thought our survival was dependent on your action either way. Whatever happens, and whatever you do, you of all people have no right to make reproaches to us.

'As I warmed to my topic,' Churchill added, 'the Ambassador exclaimed, "More calm, please, my dear Mr Churchill",' but thereafter, Churchill noted, 'his tone perceptibly changed'.[2]

That same night Eden reported to Cripps that Churchill had told Maisky that from 'the day of the German invasion of Russia' he had asked the Chiefs of Staff 'to examine the possibility of an invasion of the French coast or the coast of Norway'. But, Churchill had explained to the Ambassador, British military opinion had been 'unanimously against such a course'.

If any action by Britain could relieve the pressure on the Russian front, Churchill assured Maisky, he would 'be ready to face the risks and the losses which would be involved'. If it were possible to 'draw the weight of attack off Russia', Churchill declared, 'he would not hesitate to take such action, even at the risk of losing 50,000 men'.

As regards 'winning the war', Churchill told Maisky, 'if the worst came to the worst, we would continue the fight in this island and wherever we could until victory was won'. Churchill continued:

. . . he had spent five hours that day examining with his advisers the means for greatly increasing the capacity of the Trans-Persian Railway. If this route could be assured and its capacity greatly increased, Russia would then have an assured warm-water channel for the receipt of American supplies. He saw

[1] 'Personal Message' sent from the Kremlin, 3 September 1941; delivered in London, 4 September 1941, 10 p.m.: Churchill papers, 20/42.

[2] Winston S. Churchill, *The Second World War*, volume 3, London 1950, page 406.

no alternative but that Russia should hold on through the winter and then maybe in the spring, with the help of our reinforced armies in the Middle East which would be in contact with the Russian armies, some offensive action might be possible, perhaps in conjunction with Turkey, who would be encouraged to join with us as she saw our strength grow.

Churchill went on to tell Maisky that he was 'convinced that there was no action which it was in our power to take which could affect events in Russia in the next two months'.[1]

Churchill now replied direct to Stalin. No Balkan front, he said, could be opened without the help of Turkey. No military landing in the West 'could draw the German forces from the east' before winter. Air action alone was possible. But the information 'at my disposal', Churchill added, 'gives one the impression that the culminating violence of the German invasion is already over and that winter will give your heroic armies a breathing space'. That, Churchill hastened to add, 'was a personal opinion'.

For the present, Churchill assured the Soviet Union, Britain would send, from its own production, one half of the monthly total of aircraft and tanks for which Stalin had asked, and would urge the United States to supply the other half. 'We shall use every endeavour,' Churchill wrote, 'to start the flow of equipment to you immediately.' After being converted to oil-burners, the first 48 railway engines and 400 wagons would start for the Persian railway, on the long journey round the Cape. The water supply along the railway would likewise have to be developed. From the existing capacity of only two trains a day each way, Britain intended to ensure that twelve trains a day each way could ferry the essential supplies from the Persian Gulf to the Caspian.

Surveying the strategic situation for 1942, as it would effect Russia, Churchill told Stalin:

Whether British armies will be strong enough to invade the mainland of Europe during 1942 must depend on unforeseeable events. It may be possible however to assist you in the extreme North when there is more darkness. We are hoping to raise our armies in the Middle East to a strength of three-quarters of a million before the end of the present year, and thereafter to a million by the summer of 1942. Once the German-Italian forces in Libya have been destroyed all these forces will be available to come into line on your southern flank, and it is hoped to encourage Turkey to maintain at the least a faithful neutrality.

'Meanwhile,' Churchill told Stalin, 'we shall continue to batter Ger-

[1] Foreign Office Telegram, No. 227 to Moscow, N.5096/78/G, 'Secret', SU/41/75, 4 September 1941: Foreign Office papers, 954/24, folio 388.

many from the air with increasing severity and to keep the seas open and ourselves alive.'[1]

In sending a copy of this telegram to Roosevelt, Churchill wrote: 'Hope you will not object to our references to possible American aid. I feel that the moment may be decisive. We can but do our best.'[2]

Answering in greater detail Stalin's appeal for a 'second front' in the west, Churchill wrote in a separate telegram to Sir Stafford Cripps, the British Ambassador in Moscow, for his use in speaking to Stalin or to Molotov:

If it were possible to make any successful diversion upon the French or Low Countries shore which would bring back German troops from Russia, we should order it even at the heaviest cost. All our generals are convinced that a bloody repulse is all that would be sustained, or, if small lodgments were effected, that they would have to be withdrawn after a few days.

The French coast is fortified to the limit,[3] and the Germans still have more divisions in the West than we have in Great Britain, and formidable air support. The shipping available to transport a large army to the Continent does not exist, unless the process were spread over many months. The diversion of our flotillas to such an operation would entail paralysis of the support of the Middle Eastern armies and a breakdown of the whole Atlantic traffic. It might mean the loss of the Battle of the Atlantic and the starvation and ruin of the British Isles.

Nothing that we could do or could have done would affect the struggle on the Eastern front.

From the 'very first day' of the German attack on Russia, Churchill told Cripps, 'I have not ceased to press the Chiefs of Staff to examine every form of action. They are united in the views expressed here.'

Of the Soviet demand for action in the Balkans, Churchill told Cripps:

. . . you should remember that even with the shipping then available in the Mediterranean it took us seven weeks to place two divisions and one armoured brigade in Greece, and that since we were driven out, the whole of the Greek and many of the island airfields have been occupied by the German and Italian Air Force and lie wholly outside the range of our fighter protection. I wonder that the losses sustained by our shipping and the Fleet in the evacuations of Greece and Crete have been forgotten.

[1] 'Personal and Most Secret', Foreign Office Telegram No. 1202 to Moscow, despatched 12.15 a.m., 6 September 1941: Foreign Office papers, 954/24, folio 394.

[2] 'Personal and Most Secret', Prime Minister's Personal Telegram, T.544, 5 September 1941: Premier papers, 4/469, folio 144.

[3] Even larger scale German construction of fortifications on the French coast began in the spring of 1942.

The conditions in the eastern Mediterranean were, Churchill wrote, 'far more adverse now than then, and our naval strength is reduced'.

As for a western front, Churchill told Cripps:

The situation in the West would be entirely different if the French front were in being, for then I have no doubt the invasion of Russia would have been impossible because of the enormous counter-attacks that could be immediately launched. No one wants to recriminate, but it is not our fault that Hitler was enabled to destroy Poland before turning his forces against France, or to destroy France before turning them against Russia.

Churchill also gave Cripps an account of the problems involved even in the sending of 400 fighter aircraft to Russia, telling the Ambassador:

The 400 fighter aircraft which we have taken from our seriously diminished reserve are no doubt petty compared with the losses sustained by the Russian Air Force. They constitute however a painful and dangerous sacrifice on our part. The attacks by the Royal Air Force both by day and by night are maintained with our utmost strength, and the even character of the fighting above the French coast shows the high degree of air-power still possessed by the Germans in the West.

Cripps had urged that Britain should make 'a superhuman effort to help Russia'.[1] By this phrase, Churchill wrote, 'you mean, I presume, an effort rising superior to space, time and geography. Unfortunately these attributes are denied us.'

'Neither sympathy nor emotion,' Churchill told Cripps, 'will overcome the kind of facts we have to face'.[2] To the War Cabinet, Churchill commented that he 'had the feeling that the possibility of a separate peace could not be altogether excluded'. Even so, Britain should make no promises to Russia 'which we could not possibly fulfil'.[3]

Because of the need to examine every possible source of supply for Russia, Churchill had already cancelled his departure for Ditchley that evening, and worked, as John Martin noted in his diary, 'till nearly 3

---

[1] Telegram No. 1090 from Moscow, 4 September 1941: Premier papers, 3/401/1, No. 18.

[2] Prime Minister's Personal Telegram, T.548, Churchill papers, 20/42. Foreign Office Telegram to Moscow, No. 1201, 5 September 1941: Premier papers, 3/401/1, No. 20.

[3] War Cabinet No. 90 of 1941, 5 September 1941, 12.30 p.m., Minute 1, Confidential Annex: Cabinet papers, 65/23. On the question of a possible Soviet negotiated peace. Colville noted in his diary six days later: 'Desmond Morton tells me that we know from secret sources that the Third International has given orders to its followers in this country to keep alive discontent with the alleged inadequacy of support for Russia in order to use this to overthrow the Churchill government when the time is ripe. Further he says that Stalin is lukewarm in his determination to go on fighting and Molotov definitely opposed to so doing; but there are others, representing Russian youth organisations, who are resolute.' (Colville diary, 11 September 1941: Colville papers.)

a.m.' at Downing Street, remarking as he worked: 'I feel the world vibrant again.'[1]

Churchill's assurance to Stalin on September 6 that the 'culminating violence' of the German attack was over and that winter would give the Soviet forces a 'breathing space' was not a mere 'personal opinion', as he had written, but was based upon the German Air Force Enigma decrypts. Between the middle of July and the middle of August these decrypts had shown that the German Air Force was suffering supply and maintenance difficulties. On August 26, after the German capture of Dnepropetrovsk in the southern Ukraine, Enigma decrypts, including the recently broken 'Vulture',[2] had also made it possible to forecast that the next major German thrust would be against Kiev. Further and regular decrypts throughout September not only provided a considerable amount of Intelligence about the fighting on the southern front, but also confirmation of diplomatic and Agents' reports that Germany was anxious about the degree of Russian resistance, and was now preparing for a winter campaign.[3]

On Saturday September 6 Churchill drove to Ditchley, visiting on the way 'the establishment at Bletchley'.[4] There, unknown to John Martin who accompanied him, the Enigma messages were decrypted, together with other high grade cypher messages, before being sent on to Broadway to be selected for Churchill's mysterious buff boxes.

On October 21 the four leading Enigma cryptanalysts[5] at Bletchley Park sent a jointly written memorandum to Churchill. It began: 'Dear Prime Minister, some weeks ago you paid us the honour of a visit, and we believe you regard our work as important. . . .' They went on to declare their conviction that this belief was not held in all quarters of the public service. This they regarded as responsible for their inability to obtain, despite repeated urgent requests through normal channels, some twenty additional typists and a similar number of women clerks, for want of which, they informed Churchill, some of their work was being seriously delayed and otherwise handicapped. They also asked Churchill if certain other bottlenecks could be removed.

---

[1] John Martin diary, 5 September 1941: Martin papers.

[2] The German Army Enigma key used for secret communication between front line headquarters and the German Army High Command, see page 1209.

[3] F. H. Hinsley and others, *British Intelligence in the Second World War, Its Influence on Strategy and Operations*, volume 1, London 1979, page 72.

[4] Martin diary, 6 September 1941: Martin papers.

[5] A. M. Turing, W. G. Welchman, C. H. O'D. Alexander and P. S. Milner-Barry.

The cryptanalysts apologized for communicating direct with the Prime Minister, twice stating that they meant no criticism of their superior in Bletchley Park. On receiving their letter, Churchill minuted to Ismay: 'Make sure they have all they want as extreme priority and report to me that this has been done.'[1]

After reaching Ditchley on September 6, Churchill received a personal telegram from Cripps in Moscow. 'I fully appreciate' Cripps said, 'that you are determined to do all that you consider possible to help the Russians and I hope very much it will enable them to hold on till next Spring'.[2]

Churchill also received that weekend welcome news from Roosevelt, who promised United States Navy transports, manned by US Navy crews, to transport up to 20,000 British troops to the Middle East. Roosevelt would also lend Britain ten or twelve cargo ships for the North Atlantic run to release British cargo ships for the Middle East supply routes. The American ships would, Roosevelt assured Churchill, be 'our best'.[3]

Replying from Ditchley on September 7, Churchill told Roosevelt that the supply of tanks to Russia, as Stalin had requested, was 'hitting ourselves very hard', but that the argument which had decided him was: 'If they keep fighting it is worth it; if they don't we don't have to send it.'[4]

With the spectre of a Russian defeat having been raised again by Stalin and Maisky, Churchill made plans to meet a German attack on British positions in Syria or Iraq. All depended upon the willingness of Turkey to remain neutral, and to be prepared to resist a German demand for the passage of troops. To this end, Britain had made plans, Churchill informed Menzies, to send a force of 17 squadrons of aircraft to Turkey, together with 'an immediate and special consignment' of a hundred 3.7 inch anti-aircraft guns. If the German threat to Turkey appeared to increase, Britain would also send, by December 1, 'at

---

[1] 'Action this day', 22 October 1941. Within a month 'C' reported that Bletchley's needs were well on the way to being met. F. H. Hinsley and others, *British Intelligence in the Second World War, Its Influence on Strategy and Operations*, volume 2, London 1981, Appendix 3, pages 655–7.

[2] Moscow Telegram No. 1105, 6 September 1941: Premier papers, 3/401/1, No. 21.

[3] 'Most Secret', 6 September 1941: Churchill papers, 20/42.

[4] Prime Minister's Personal Telegram, T.553, 7 September 1941: Premier papers, 3/469, folio 136.

latest', four Divisions and 'at least' one armoured brigade'. Meanwhile, in the western desert, Tobruk would be held, and an attack on German positions would be begun after November 1, although this would not 'preclude' Auchinleck from attacking sooner 'if a favourable opportunity were presented to him'.[1]

On September 9, British naval forces attacked German supply ships near Murmansk. 'From the moment,' Churchill told the House of Commons that day, 'now nearly 80 days ago, when Russia was attacked, we have cast about for every means of giving the most speedy and effective aid to our new Ally.' Of the supplies concerned, he added, 'the need is urgent, and the scale heavy'. A considerable part of the iron and steel production of Russia, and of its munitions industry, had fallen 'into the hands of the enemy'.[2] Also on September 9, Churchill informed Stalin, through Sir Stafford Cripps, that 5,000 tons of aluminium were to be sent to Russia from Canada 'as soon as arrangements for shipment are completed', to be followed by 2,000 tons a month, either through the Russian Far Eastern port of Vladivostok, or by the Persian route, if 'preferable to the Russian Government'.[3] As a result of Lord Beaverbrook's activities in London on Churchill's behalf, this aluminium supply, asked for by Stalin on September 4, had taken only five days to arrange.

On September 10 Eden sought Churchill's guidance on the question of peace overtures reaching London from Europe.[4] Churchill replied:

I am sure we should not depart from our policy of absolute silence. Nothing would be more disturbing to our friends in the United States or more dangerous with our new ally, Russia, than the suggestion that we were entertaining such ideas. I am absolutely opposed to the slightest contact.[5]

Not peacemaking, but a widening of the war, seemed most in prospect that week, for on September 11, in a further increase in United States involvement, Roosevelt broadcast to the world, following an unsuccessful torpedo attack on the American destroyer *Greer*, that henceforth any German or Italian vessels of war which entered the Atlantic zone under American protection did so 'at their own peril'. Roosevelt also declared: 'when you see a rattlesnake poised to strike, you do not

---

[1] Prime Minister's Personal Telegram, T.555, 7 September 1941: Churchill papers, 20/49.

[2] *Hansard*, 9 September 1941, columns 77–8.

[3] Prime Minister's Personal Telegram, T.558, 9 September 1941: Churchill papers, 20/42.

[4] Minute from Foreign Secretary, P.M./41/108.

[5] 'Most Secret', Prime Minister's Personal Minute, M.888/1, 10 September 1941: Churchill papers, 20/36.

wait until he has struck before you crush him'.[1] Churchill, who listened to Roosevelt's broadcast at Downing Street, wrote that day to the Governor General of Canada, the Earl of Athlone: 'Roosevelt this morning excellent. As we used to sing at Sandhurst "Now we *shan't* be long!"'[2]

That night, the first snow fell on the Russian front.

---

[1] Broadcast, Washington, 11 September 1941: B. D. Zevin (editor), *Nothing to Fear, The Selected Addresses of Franklin Delano Roosevelt, 1932–1945*, London 1947, pages 287–95. As well as the *Greer*, on 4 September 1941, a United States merchant ship, the *Steel Seafarer*, had been sunk in the Red Sea on 5 September 1941 by German aircraft, 220 miles south of Suez.

[2] Letter of 12 September 1941: Churchill papers, 20/22. Two days later Churchill telegraphed to Smuts, who had described Roosevelt's speech as 'a definite postponement of America's entry into the war', and 'very disappointing': 'Hitler will have to choose between losing the Battle of the Atlantic or coming into frequent collision with United States ships and warships. We know that he attaches more importance to starving us out than to invasion. American public have accepted the "shoot at sight" declaration without knowing the vast area to which it is to be applied, and in my opinion they will support President in fuller and further application of this principle, out of which at any moment war may come.' (Prime Minister's Personal Telegram, T.579, 14 September 1941: Premier papers, 3/474/1, folios 6–7.)

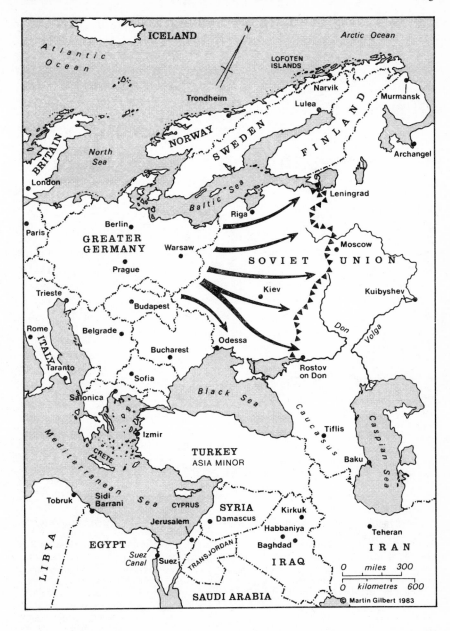

62

Support for the Soviet Union

O N September 15 Churchill received a further telegram from
Stalin, stating that the absence of a 'second front simply favours
the designs of our common enemy'. Stalin went on to ask, as German
forces drove ever further eastwards across the Ukraine, that twenty-five
to thirty British Divisions should be sent to Archangel, or transported
through Persia, in order to fight in the 'southern regions' of the Soviet
Union. This, Stalin added, would constitute 'a serious blow' against
German aggression.[1]

Reading this, Churchill later recalled his feelings. It was 'almost
incredible', he wrote, that the head of the Russian Government, with
all his military experts, 'could have committed himself to such absurd-
ities. It seemed hopeless to argue with a man thinking in terms of utter
unreality'.[2]

During the third week of September, Churchill briefed Beaverbrook
on his coming Mission to Moscow. Aid to Russia was not to be dimin-
ished, and among the first offerings of the Mission was to be the despatch to Russia of the whole of Britain's tank production for the week
ending September 27.[3]

On September 16 Royal Air Force bombers attacked German military and industrial targets in Hamburg, while on the following day a
newly established Royal Air Force wing in Russia was in action alongside Soviet air forces, near Murmansk.

That same day, to Churchill's consternation, the Australian Govern-

---

[1] Personal Message, dated Kremlin, 13 September 1941, received in London, 15 September
1941: Foreign Office papers, 954/24, folio 403.

[2] Winston S. Churchill, *The Second World War*, volume 3, London 1950, page 411.

[3] Tank production for that week was 20% above all previous records. All the tanks were sent to
Russia.

ment ordered the 9th Australian Division to be withdrawn from Tobruk.[1]

As soon as Auchinleck learnt of the Australian Government's decision, he drafted a telegram asking to be relieved of his command. It was only Oliver Lyttelton's personal intervention that persuaded him 'not to send it'.[2]

Twelve days later Churchill telegraphed to the Australian Prime Minister, Arthur William Fadden: 'Believe me, everyone here realizes your political embarrassments with a majority of only one. Nevertheless Australia might think this is a time to do and dare.' Churchill added: 'We have been greatly pained here by the suggestion, not made by you, but implied, that we have thrown an undue burden on the Australian troops. The debt to them is immense but the Imperial forces have suffered more casualties actually and relatively. Moreover, the British Submarine Service has lost nearly a third killed outright, and I could give you other instances.' Churchill's telegram ended with the assertion that as a result of Britain's losses 'we feel we are entitled to count upon Australia to make every sacrifice necessary for the comradeship of the Empire. But please understand that at whatever cost your orders about your own troops will be obeyed'.[3]

The Australian action opened up a new area of concern. Churchill very much 'grieved' at the Australian attitude, as he told Auchinleck in a telegram on September 17:

I have long feared the dangerous reactions on Australian and world opinion of our seeming to fight all our battles in the Middle East only with Dominion troops. For this reason, apart from desire to reinforce you, I have constantly pressed sending out some British infantry divisions. Your decision to put 50th

[1] On the following evening Harold Balfour, the Junior Minister selected for the Anglo-American Mission to Moscow, was present at a discussion between Churchill, Beaverbrook and others during which, as Balfour reported to Henry Channon, Churchill 'began to abuse everybody and everything, and said that we were at war with almost every country "including Australia". Then he attacked the Army, said it always refused to fight. . . .' Balfour also reported that Churchill had gone on to say: 'The Army always wants more divisions, more equipment,' that he had 'sacked Wavell', and now he would 'Sack Dill and go himself'. Dill 'was no use, little better than Wavell, etc. etc.' (Channon diary, 17 September 1941: Robert Rhodes James, editor, *Chips, The Diaries of Sir Henry Channon*, London 1967, page 311.)

[2] 'Most Secret and Personal', Nocop No. 2907 (Lyttelton to Churchill), 17 September 1941: Churchill papers, 20/42. Churchill replied to Lyttelton: 'I was astounded by Australian Government's decision, being sure it would be repudiated by Australia if the facts could be made known,' but, he added, all 'personal feelings' must be 'subordinated to appearance of unity' (Prime Minister's Personal Telegram, T.592, 'Personal and Secret', 18 September 1941: Churchill papers, 20/42).

[3] 'Personal and Secret', Prime Minister's Personal Telegram, T.620, 29 September 1941: Churchill papers, 20/43.

British Division in Cyprus was, as you know, painful to us. I know that when you put it there you thought Cyprus was a place of special danger, but the situation has been changed by Russian war, and I am sure you will continue to review employment of this British division in what looks like a safe defensive role. . . .

Churchill went on to express the hope that the Australian withdrawal would not 'further delay' Auchinleck's own proposed November offensive. But, he added:

The situation has already worsened. The enemy are far better supplied with petrol, Afrika Panzer Korps is now called Afrika Panzer Gruppe.[1] By waiting until you have an extra brigade you may well find you have to face an extra division. Your movements of transport and formation of dumps must be noted by the enemy.

The 'whole future' of the Middle East campaign of 1942, as well as Britain's relations with Turkey and Russia, were 'involved' in this, Churchill warned Auchinleck.[2] And on the following day he telegraphed to Auchinleck again:

Great allowances must be made for a Government with a majority of one playing politics with a bitter Opposition, part of whom at least are isolationist in sentiment. Whatever your and our personal feelings may be, it is our duty at all costs to prevent an open dispute with the Australian Government. Any public controversy would injure foundations of Empire and be disastrous to our general position in the war. Everything must be borne with patience, and in the end all will come right.

'You have all our sympathy,' Churchill added, 'and confidence.'[3]

There was a further and in many ways overriding factor of urgency in ensuring that 'Crusader' was begun as soon as possible. By September 12 German Enigma decrypts had made it almost certain that some special activity against Tobruk was being planned. On September 12 Panzergruppe Afrika had asked for maps and overlays of the Tobruk defences as a matter of urgency. Nine days later a further German Air Force Enigma decrypt referred to a 'special operation' against Tobruk.[4]

[1] Not entirely correct: the Deutsches Afrika Korps, which Churchill incorrectly calls the Afrika Panzer Korps, known to the British as the Africa Corps, had not changed its name. The Panzer Gruppe Afrika was a new, higher headquarters, almost equivalent to an Army Headquarters and about to become one. Rommel had been appointed to command this new HQ; it consisted of two corps, the Africa Corps and the XXI (Italian) Corps.

[2] Prime Minister's Personal Telegram, T.590, 17 September 1941: Churchill papers, 20/49.

[3] Prime Minister's Personal Telegram, T.593, 18 September 1941: Churchill papers, 20/42.

[4] OL 1108 of 12 September 1941 and OL 1241 of 21 September 1941: F. H. Hinsley and others, *British Intelligence in the Second World War: Its Influence on Strategy and Operations*, volume 2, London 1981, page 301.

The date of the operation was unknown. But successive decrypts made it clear that Rommel was planning, not merely to strengthen his own positions around the besieged port's defensive perimeter, but to seek to overrun it.

On September 18, as German forces prepared to enter the Ukrainian capital, Kiev, after forty-four days of intense fighting, Churchill informed Stalin that a survey was at that very moment being made before the departure of the Harriman–Beaverbrook Mission, to enable 'a definite programme of monthly delivery by every available route' of British and American munitions for Russia. According to Roosevelt's plan, Churchill explained, these deliveries would continue until the end of June 1942. But, Churchill assured Stalin, 'naturally we shall go on with you till victory'. The Staffs, Churchill told Stalin, had examined all possible theatres 'in which we might effect military co-operation with you', and he added:

The two flanks, North and South, certainly present the most favourable opportunities. If we could act successfully in Norway the attitude of Sweden would be powerfully affected but at the moment we have neither the forces nor the shipping available for this project.

Again in the south the great prize is Turkey; if Turkey can be gained another powerful army will be available. Turkey would like to come with us but is afraid, not without reason. It may be that the promise of considerable British forces and supplies of technical material in which the Turks are deficient will exercise a decisive influence upon them.

'We will study with you any other form of useful aid,' Churchill told Stalin, 'the sole object being to bring the maximum force against the common enemy.'[1]

When the Defence Committee met on September 19, it was to decide precisely what degree of aid the Mission to Moscow would be able to offer. The Under Secretary of State for Air, Harold Balfour, himself a First World War pilot of distinction, later recalled how, at the meeting:

At once it was clear that Churchill, Eden and Beaverbrook were the only ones on the positive side for aid. The Service Ministers and their Chiefs of

[1] Prime Minister's Personal Telegram, T.591, Foreign Office Telegram No. 1291 to Moscow, 'Personal and Secret', despatched 1.10 p.m., 18 September 1941: Foreign Office papers, 954/24, folio 404.

Staff were on the negative side. The Air Ministry case was, though invasion danger was past, the air defences of Britain had to be kept up to strength and further expanded to meet the threat of heavier enemy raids. Bomber Command had to be built up. The Middle East was crying out for Hurricanes and Spitfires for the Western Desert. As for the RAF, so for the Army and Navy. Not a rowing boat, a rifle or a Tiger Moth could be spared without weakening and without grave risk.

It was soon clear that the division between the positives and the negatives was acute. Discussion and argument went to and fro. After an hour and more Churchill made clear that in his view, an offer—a fair offer—of supplies from all three Services must be forthcoming; that the political and strategic importance of supporting Russia demanded this even at some risk to ourselves. Churchill did not neglect to remind the Service members that there were those in the room who had gone on record as saying that if Russia was attacked, she could not last three weeks against the German forces.

From the time of Churchill's declaration of the policy to be followed, the battle became one of what, and how much. Though the front had been narrowed, stubborn resistance was just as strong, even stronger.

At 7.30 p.m., the atmosphere of reason and debate seemed to deteriorate. I detected an acid note creeping into assertion, denial, exhortation. Churchill's shoulders became more hunched. A scowl on his brow deepened. His interjections were more frequent and impatient. On and on we went. Out-of-date aircraft were offered—and rejected. Old guns or tanks were likewise taken and thrown out of the Cabinet window. Unwanted naval craft were sunk without trace.

At around 8 p.m. the Prime Minister entered into the sad, pathetic role. His head sank lower. In a voice more of sorrow than anger, he made his little speech. 'Gentlemen, the role of a Prime Minister must always be difficult. In war it is more so. When his colleagues fail to agree, his role indeed becomes a harsh one. But these matters must be settled. We must stay at our task until we can agree. We will continue, and we will stay here all night if necessary.'

As Churchill spoke, a Marine messenger entered unnoticed, came up behind the Prime Minister's chair, and when he had finished speaking, bent down and whispered something in the Prime Minister's ear. Churchill turned round like a bulldog ready to growl and snap at an unexpected pat on the shoulder. The poor Marine jumped back about a yard and retreated from the room. It was clear to me what the domestic message had been. It was 8.15 and 'Mrs Churchill wants to know when you are coming to dinner'. Churchill paused; then again he spoke to us. 'Gentlemen, as I said, we have to decide these grave matters. But let us adjourn for a short while to obtain some sustenance. It is now 8.15. Let us meet again at 9 o'clock. Well, perhaps not 9—let us say 9.30. No, let us make it 10.30.'

As a young officer I had always been taught to be on parade five minutes before time, so at 10.25 I was back on the doorstep of No. 10. As I got there, two other Ministers joined me. The door was opened. Before I could walk down the passage to the Cabinet room I saw, coming towards me, a beaming figure in a blue siren-suit. The Prime Minister. He took me by the arm and said, 'Wait, my boy, wait.' I had never been called 'my boy' before by Churchill. 'I have something to show you.' He led me—and the others who had meanwhile arrived—to the little anteroom on the left of the passage. 'See,' he said, 'This has come for me today,' and he pointed to a large imitation Queen Anne-style cabinet, on the top of which was printed this inscription:

'To the Rt. Hon. Winston Churchill, PC, MP, Prime Minister of Great Britain. A tribute of admiration from the President and People of Cuba.'

'I have had some difficulty today in getting this through the Customs,' he said, as he opened one of the drawers to show lovely bundles of long Havana cigars. Turning to the waiting Ministers, he addressed us thus: 'Gentlemen, I am now going to try an experiment. Maybe it will result in joy. Maybe it will end in grief. I am about to give you each one of these magnificent cigars.' He paused. He continued with Churchillian rolling of sound and digestive enjoyment of the spoken word. 'It may well be that these each contain some deadly poison.' Then came the word picture which he alone could paint. 'It may well be that within days I shall follow sadly the long line of coffins up the aisle of Westminster Abbey.' Another pause before finale. 'Reviled by the populace; as the man who has out-Borgia-ed Borgia.'

Each of us was presented with a lovely—and in those days, extremely rare—Havana cigar. We lit up. We sailed into the Cabinet room. In half an hour we had settled all we had argued about for hours. Russian aid was safe and firm.[1]

At one moment during the Defence Committee's discussions, Churchill had entered a serious caveat, reminding his colleagues that the Russians had 'an immense army' and warning that:

Anything we could offer would appear like a drop in the ocean, though it might mean a great sacrifice on our part. He could never agree to any proposal which would mean cutting down the size of our Army below its present level. We could not build up new factories here and the Russians would have to look to the United States of America for large long term contracts.

---

[1] Lord Balfour of Inchrye, 'From Havana with Love': *The Times*, 28 September 1965. Eight days after the incident described here, Colville minuted to Churchill: 'I am sending one cigar from each box of the cabinet which you received from Cuba, to Lord Rothschild that they may be tested for poison or any other noxious content. Lord Cherwell hopes that you will not smoke any of the cigars until the result of the analysis is known. He points out that there has just been a round-up of undesirable elements in Cuba, which has shown that a surprisingly large number of Nazi agents and sympathisers exist in that country.' (Minute of 23 September 1941: Churchill papers, 2/434.)

'America, not ourselves,' Churchill warned, 'would have to be the arsenal for the Russian Army.'[1] But in a minute for the Chiefs of Staff later that night Churchill stressed that 'Assurances must be given to Russia of increased quotas for 1 July, 1942, to 30 June, 1943.'[2]

Churchill sought to help the Russians not only with equipment, but also by pursuing an offensive in the Middle East. On September 19 he pressed the Chiefs of Staff to send two complete additional British divisions as reinforcements to the Middle East. To their objection that there was a danger of these new troops being caught by a German advance through Turkey, Syria and Palestine, and possibly even from the Caucasus, Churchill replied that he doubted that the Germans would be able either to commit a large army to Turkey, or to break through the Caucasus within the next six months, 'unless we assume the surrender or collapse of Russia'.

Without a Russian collapse, the Black Sea and the Caspian Sea, both under Russian naval mastery, would form 'a great shield to the northward', protecting Britain from a German advance through Turkey or Syria.

Churchill then set out his reasons for sending these extra British troops to the Middle East. They concerned, he said, the need 'to give proper weight to the major political-strategic issues involved'. These were:

First, the moral need of our having a substantial recognisable British stake and contribution in the Middle East, and freeing ourselves from the imputation, however unjust, of always using other people's troops and blood.

Secondly, the effect produced upon Turkey by our being able to add two divisions to the forces already mentioned in the Staff conversations, thus appreciably increasing the chances of influencing Turkish action.

Thirdly, the basis of my appeal to the President, which I do not wish upset.

Fourthly, the possibility that these two divisions may move in by Basra in order to give an effective right-hand to the Russian reserve forces to the North of the Caspian.[3]

The tanks, aircraft and munitions already being sent to Russia, Churchill telegraphed to Smuts on September 20, involved Britain in

---

[1] Defence Committee (Operations), 19 September 1941, 6 p.m.: Cabinet papers, 69/2.
[2] Prime Minister's Personal Minute D.259/1, 2.30 a.m., 19 September 1941: Cabinet papers, 1/20/36.
[3] Minute to Colonel Hollis for Chiefs of Staff Committee, 1.30 a.m., 19 September 1941: Churchill papers, 4/240.

'terrible sacrifices' of war materials 'so sorely needed' by Britain itself. But he went on to say that it was not by supplies, but by an actual military campaign, that British help to Russia could be most effective. 'If we can clean up Cyrenaica,' he told Smuts, 'we shall have substantial forces to give right hand to Russia in Caspian region and/or influence action Turkey.' It was the procuring of Turkish resistance to any German demands of passage through Anatolia that Churchill regarded as the 'most immediate prize'.[1]

On September 21 Churchill gave his authority to operation 'Velvet', the despatch of air and military aid to the southern flank of the Russian front. All was to be prepared for a possible Soviet appeal, and Wavell, now Commander-in-Chief in India, Persia and Iraq, was designated commander of the force sent to Russia. As Churchill telegraphed to Beaverbrook, who was then on his way to Russia:

General Wavell proposes to go to Tiflis via Baghdad on his return to India. He speaks Russian, and I contemplate his directing or possibly, if the forces grow large enough, commanding, the right hand we shall give to the Russians in and about the Caspian Basin in the forthcoming campaign. It is therefore important that he should confer with high Russian military authorities on the whole position of their southern flank and in Persia.

You may bring this into your discussions, and see that the most is made of it. Actual dates can be settled later.[2]

By coincidence, on the day before this decision was taken in London, Wavell, in India, read an article in the *National Review* stating that it was Churchill's jealousy that had led to his removal from the Western Desert. 'I am writing to the sender of the magazine,' Wavell wrote, 'to say how much I resent this sort of thing and how harmful it is to our Cause; if there is anything else I can do to stop it I would of course do it.' Wavell added: 'You are carrying the heaviest burden of responsibility any man has ever shouldered, and I am very sorry if the Press add to your burdens in this way.'[3] Churchill replied by hand to Wavell:

I shall ever be grateful to you for all you have done to win the war, and I look forward with hope to your acting in a still wider field than the Nile Valley in the coming year.

It is a profound satisfaction to me to feel—as I have always felt—that you do not misjudge the spirit and motives with which I try to carry my burden.

[1] Prime Minister's Personal Telegram, T.600, 20 September 1941: Churchill papers, 20/49.
[2] Prime Minister's Personal Minute, T.604, 21 September 1941, 'The following for Lord Beaverbrook, to be put over the Scrambler to him via Flagship': Cabinet papers, 120/689.
[3] Letter of 20 September 1941, Churchill papers, 20/30.

My admiration for your character, conduct and military capacity is constant.[1]

German forces now entered Kiev, breaking the one point in the southern front where their advance had been checked. To Stalin, Churchill wrote again on September 21, in a letter to be delivered personally by Beaverbrook, that considerable weaponry and supplies would be sent to Russia. His letter continued:

You will understand however that our Army and its supply which has been planned is perhaps only one-fifth or one-sixth as large as yours or Germany's. Our first duty and need is to keep open the seas, and our second duty is to obtain decisive superiority in the air. These have the first claims upon the man-power of our 44,000,000 in the British Islands. We can never hope to have an army or army munition industries comparable to those of the great Continental military Powers. None the less we will do our utmost to aid you.

As an earnest of the seriousness of his intentions, Churchill told Stalin that General Ismay, who would accompany the Harriman–Beaverbrook Mission, was 'authorised to study with your commanders any plans for practical co-operation which may suggest themselves'. His letter continued: 'There is no doubt that a long period of struggle and suffering lies before our peoples, but I have great hopes that the United States will enter the war as a belligerent, and if so I cannot doubt that we have but to endure to conquer.'[2]

As Beaverbrook, Harriman, Balfour and Ismay prepared to leave for Moscow, Churchill issued a directive on what their task was to be. 'We must consider ourselves,' he began, 'pledged to fulfil our share of the tanks and aircraft which have been promised to Russia.' As to the offering of other equipment and material, Beaverbrook would have 'a considerable measure of discretion'. Assurance 'must be given' to Russia of increased British quotas from 1 July 1942 to 30 June 1943, and Beaverbrook should be 'free to encourage the prolonged resistance of Russia by taking a justifiably hopeful view of these more distant prospects'.

After setting out Britain's commitments at home and overseas, Churchill noted that it was intended to keep 25 Infantry Divisions and 4 or 5 armoured Divisions in Britain 'to repel invasion'[3] and to build up to 25 Divisions in the Middle East, leaving 6 or 7 Divisions, includ-

---

[1] 'Original in manuscript sent to General Wavell', (note by Leslie Rowan): Churchill papers, 20/30.

[2] Letter dated 21 September 1941: Premier papers, 3/401/7.

[3] It was with invasion in mind that Churchill now asked, of Britain's stocks of gas-filled weapons, whether the Chiefs of Staff were 'satisfied with the present position and our means of retaliating on the Germans if necessary'. (Prime Minister's Personal Minute, D.264/1, 21 September 1941: Premier papers, 3/88/1, folio 42.) He also learned, two days later, that the oil fuel and flame

ing two armoured Divisions, as the 'maximum that can be conceived' for any additional Expeditionary Force. All ideas of 20 or 30 Divisions 'being launched by Great Britain against the western shores of the continent', he warned, 'or sent round by sea for service in Russia have no foundation of reality on which to rest'. This, he said, 'should be made clear'. Churchill's directive ended:

The Russians will no doubt ask how you propose to win the war, to which our answer should be: 'By going on fighting till the Nazi system breaks up as the Kaiser's system broke up last time.' For this purpose we shall fight the enemy wherever we can meet them on favourable terms. We shall undermine them by propaganda; depress them with the blockade; and, above all, bomb their homelands ceaselessly, ruthlessly, and with ever-increasing weight of bombs.

We could not tell last time how and when we should win the war, but by not giving in and not wearying we came through all right. We did not hesitate to face Germany and Italy alone all last year, and the determination of the British masses to destroy the Nazi power is inflexible.

The phrases 'Nazi tyranny' and 'Prussian militarism' are used by us as targets rather than any implacable general condemnation of the German peoples. We agree with the Russian Government in hoping to split the Germans, and to isolate the criminal Nazi régime.[1]

Of course, we cannot predict what action the United States will take. The measures already sanctioned by President Roosevelt and his Government may at any time in the near future involve the United States in full war, whether declared or undeclared. In that case we might look forward to a general offensive upon Germany in 1943.

If German morale and unity were seriously weakened, and their hold upon the conquered European countries relaxed, it might be possible to land large numbers of armoured forces simultaneously on the shores of several of the conquered countries, and raise wide-spread revolts.

'Plans for this,' Churchill added, 'are now being studied by the British Staffs.'[2]

---

projectors for beaches, the 'F' schemes, had now been successfully tested, and were to be installed in eighteen different British ports, including Poole, Teignmouth, Looe, Yarmouth, Lowestoft, Penzance, Fowey, Padstow, Llanelly, Fishguard and Dartmouth. ('Secret', 23 September 1941: Admiralty papers, 1/17808.)

[1] In the second week of September, Churchill had learned of the shooting of the civilian hostages in Norway. 'Surely more stir ought to be made,' he wrote to Bracken, 'about Hitler shooting the Norwegian trade unionists, and sending others for long periods of penal servitude. Ought not the Trade Union Congress to pass resolutions of sympathy? Why don't you get into touch with Citrine and work up a steady outcry?' The names of the two victims, Churchill added, 'should be publicized as martyrs'. (Prime Minister's Personal Minute, M.894/1, 13 September 1941: Churchill papers, 20/36.)

[2] 'Anglo-American-Russian Conference', General Directive, Defence Committee Paper No. 12 of 1941, 22 September 1941: Cabinet papers, 69/3.

To Roosevelt, who had just offered to send Britain a substantial increase in United States tank production, Churchill replied: 'Your cheering cable about tanks arrived when we were feeling very blue about all we have to give up to Russia. The prospect of nearly doubling the previous figures encouraged everyone.'[1] And to Beaverbrook and Harriman Churchill telegraphed, as they left Britain's shores: 'All good wishes to you both and your colleagues for your memorable journey on which you carry with you the hope of the world.'[2]

The despatch of so large a supply of munitions to Russia was 'at great expense to ourselves', Colville wrote in his diary. But he added, 'as the PM says, it is worthwhile in order to keep Russia in the war'.[3]

The Anglo-American Mission to Russia left London at midday on September 21 going by train to Thurso, thence by boat to Scapa, and on from Scapa by cruiser to Archangel.[4] On September 25, while the mission was north of Bear Island, Churchill remembered that Beaverbrook, as well as Ismay, knew of the Enigma decrypts. To ensure that secrecy was maintained, he telegraphed to Beaverbrook: 'I am sure you realize that no one in Russia, including Cripps and all your party, must know about our special sources of information.'[5] Churchill's concern was not without cause: two months earlier, as Colville had noted in his disary, Desmond Morton had made 'the horrifying discovery that the Press, or at any rate Lord Camrose and his staff, have found out about the most closely guarded secret of the war: namely, the contents of those buff boxes which "C" sends to the P.M.' Leakages, Morton had told Colville, 'increase in number and seri-

---

[1] Prime Minister's Personal Telegram, T.603, 22 September 1941: Churchill papers, 20/43. The tanks available to Britain were 3,994 medium tanks and 1,953 light tanks between October 1941 and June 1942. These were 'minimum figures', Roosevelt explained a week later, 'because I have directed that production during the next nine months be increased by ten or fifteen percent' (Telegram of 26 September 1941: Churchill papers, 20/43.)

[2] Prime Minister's Personal Telegram, T.605, 22 September 1941: Churchill papers, 20/43.

[3] Colville diary, 22 September 1941: Colville papers.

[4] Harold Balfour wrote in his diary during the voyage to Archangel: 'we set forth with a real and genuine intention of helping Russia and have views as to what we shall offer which will make necessary a very real sacrifice to our air defence at home and in the Middle East and the ability of the RAF to expand as we had planned. However, if we succeed in encouraging Russia with the knowledge that she has our backing to an increasing degree and so stiffening her resistance, then her fight and ours against the Nazis is a mutual and joint effort. Commonly put, what we lose on the swings we will gain on the roundabouts'. (Balfour diary, 26 September 1941: Balfour of Inchrye papers.) The British Secretary to the Moscow Mission was William Gorell Barnes.

[5] 'Absolutely Personal and Secret', Prime Minister's Personal Telegram, T.610, 25 September 1941: Churchill papers, 20/43. Beaverbrook replied from Moscow: 'You may be sure that no word of mine, or look, or deed, will expose to anyone the secrets with which I am entrusted by you' (Linen No. 17, 29 September 1941: Churchill papers, 20/43.)

ousness'.[1] But, in fact, neither from Fleet Street nor from the Moscow Mission, did the secret break: it remained intact not only throughout the war, but for many years beyond, and even Colville, who saw those buff boxes daily, and knew their source, remained ignorant of their content.

On Thursday September 25 Churchill took a few hours off, to visit Walmer Castle, having been appointed Lord Warden of the Cinque Ports. From Walmer, Churchill and those accompanying him were taken on by car to Manston aerodrome, where Churchill inspected No. 615 Fighter Squadron of which he was the Honorary Commodore, looked at their Hurricanes, and saw a short film of the Squadron's most recent attack on German convoys in the Channel. The Squadron Leader was Denys Gillam, a Battle of Britain pilot who had already been awarded the Distinguished Flying Cross. For some time the Squadron had been stationed at Anglesey, until one of the pilots, without Gillam's knowledge, had written to Churchill asking for the Squadron to be sent south, to a more active station. Hence the transfer to Manston for 'Channel Stop duties' against German shipping. This was known to be a 'very hot' posting, Gillam later recalled, as the previous two Squadrons had only lasted about two weeks each 'before their casualties forced them to withdraw'.

Having reached Manston on September 12 the Squadron had begun a four week tour of Channel duty. More than a dozen pilots and some twenty-five aircraft had been lost, but a substantial number of German trawlers, flak ships and E-boats were sunk, effectively stopping German traffic in the Channel.[2]

At the end of Churchill's visit to Manston, tea was prepared for Churchill and those with him, the Squadron being 'very proud' as Gillam recalled, 'to get some cakes, a table cloth and several large teapots'. When Churchill and his wife entered the dispersal hut 'we proudly showed him our spread', Gillam added, 'and asked if he would like some tea, he replied "Good God no, my wife drinks that, I'll have a brandy".'[3]

That night Churchill and those with him spent the night, as Colville recorded, 'in a quiet siding, half a mile from a stone marking the

[1] Colville diary, 31 July 1941: Colville papers.

[2] Two weeks after Churchill's visit, 615 Squadron made a successful low level attack on shipping inside Ostend harbour. On November 23 Gillam was shot down by flak off Dunkirk and was rescued by a Royal Navy rescue launch. For his exploits during these Channel attacks Gillam was awarded the DSO and a bar to his DFC; he was subsequently awarded a bar to his DSO for attacks on V weapon sites.

[3] Group Captain Gillam, letter to the author, 20 January 1983.

centre of England and a few miles short of Coventry'. Colville added: 'The PM dictated half of his speech for the House of Commons next Tuesday. It promises to be one of his best.'[1]

The weekend, beginning on Friday September 26, was to be Colville's last weekend at Chequers for more than two years, for he had finally secured Churchill's agreement to join the Royal Air Force. After spending the night of September 25 on board the train in a railway siding, Colville wrote in his diary:

We arrived at Coventry platform and the PM was not dressed. He always assumes he can get up, shave and have a bath in $\frac{1}{4}$ hour whereas in reality it takes him 20 minutes. Consequently he is late for everything. Mrs C seethed with anger.

Lord Dudley (the Regional Commissioner) and the Mayor met us. We went to the centre of the town, where the PM inspected a parade of the Civil Defence Services, and then to the Cathedral. The German bombers assuredly did their worst at Coventry.

The PM *will* give the V sign with two fingers in spite of the representations repeatedly made to him that this gesture has quite another significance!

We toured very thoroughly the Armstrong Siddeley factory, where aircraft parts and torpedoes are made, and the PM had a rousing reception. As we entered each workshop all the men clanged their hammers in a deafening welcome.

I drove with Jack Churchill whom some of the crowd took for Maisky!

The Whitley bomber factory is a hotbed of communism and there was some doubt of the reception the PM would get. But his appearance with cigar and semi-top-hat quite captivated the workers who gave him vociferous applause. We saw the lines of finished bombers and amongst them a rickety biplane built in the same factory during the last war. A new Whitley took off and flew past, a Hurricane pilot did stunts, and No. 605 squadron of Hurricanes flew over in astonishingly tight formation. When we drove away the men and women of the factory quite forgot their communism and rushed forward in serried ranks to say good-bye. But I was disgusted to hear that their production-tempo had not really grown until Russia came into the war.

We lunched on the train, after visiting the cemetery where Coventry's air-raid dead are buried in one common grave. Lord Dudley lunched with us.

At 2.30 we reached Birmingham and there visited a tank factory, where the enthusiasm was even greater than at Coventry, and the Spitfire works at Castle Bromwich. Last of all we saw a display of aerobatics by two test pilots, one in a Hurricane and the other in a Spitfire. Their performance was so daring as to be positively frightening and we all shuddered as Henshaw, the Spitfire pilot, flew over us upside down, some 40 feet from the ground.

The drive back to the station was a triumphant procession. The crowds stood on the pavements, as thick as for the Opening of Parliament in London,

---

[1] Colville diary, 25 September 1941: Colville papers.

for miles and miles along the route. They waved, they cheered, they shouted: every face seemed happy and excited. I have seen the PM have many enthusiastic receptions, but never one to equal this. It is clear that his name and fame are as great to-day as they have ever been. He was deeply moved.

We spent the night in a siding. There was a storm cloud owing to the non-arrival of a pouch but after much lightning and many claps of thunder (some of which were telephoned to John Peck at No. 10!), the sky cleared with the advent of dinner and lots of champagne.[1]

That night Churchill worked on his speech for the following Tuesday. Then, on Saturday September 27, he visited Liverpool. Once more Colville recorded the day's events:

We reached Liverpool. The PM in his curious semi-naval garb, toured the new Aircraft-Carrier 'Indomitable'. After we had climbed up and down endless companions and seen the aircraft on deck, he made a speech to the assembled ship's company. I am always impressed by his skill in suiting his words to his audience. On this occasion he spoke of the man-of-war and his wife, or sweetheart, the aircraft carrier who goes out to find his dinner for him and sometimes cooks it or has it done to a turn so that the man-of-war may eat it. It was thus with the Bismarck, it might well be the same with the Tirpitz.

The docks at Liverpool are a scene of great devastation. Many acres have been entirely cleared of buildings by the bombs.

The PM visited C.-in-C. Western Approaches at his headquarters, where Lord Derby also awaited him, and then the party returned to the train for lunch.

In the afternoon we slept. . . .[2]

It was six o'clock in the evening before Churchill reached Chequers, where the film *Cottage to Let* provided the evening's entertainment.

The guests at Chequers on Sunday September 28 included the American Ambassador, Winant, the American representative at the Vatican, and the Leader of the Opposition of the Canadian Parliament.[3] That evening, Colville noted in his diary:

The PM talked to me while he was dressing for dinner. He said that so far the Government had only made one error of judgment: Greece. He had instinctively had doubts. We could and should have defended Crete and advised the Greek Government to make the best terms it could. But the campaign, and the Yugoslav volte-face which it entailed, had delayed Germany and might after all prove to have been an advantage.

I was surprised at the PM's assertion that he had doubted the wisdom of going to Greece. I seem to remember his influencing the decision in favour of

[1] Colville diary, 26 September 1941: Colville papers.
[2] Colville diary, 27 September 1941: Colville papers.
[3] Messrs. Winant, Taylor and Hanson respectively.

an expedition and Dill being against it.[1] Incidentally he has now got his knife right into Dill and frequently disparages him. He says he has an alternative CIGS in mind: Sir Alan Brooke, C-in-C Home Forces.

He went on to say that we cannot afford military failures. As regards all this talk of a diversion on the Western Front, a landing on the Continent could only have one outcome. The War Office would not do the job properly; indeed it was unfair to ask them to pit themselves against German organisation, experience and resources. They had neither the means nor the intelligence. But critics would ask how we were going to win the war and that was difficult to answer.

On one or two occasions lately I have heard him say he thinks it will last for several years more in all probability.

During dinner, Colville wrote in his diary:

> The PM launched an attack on Shinwell who had refused office in May 1940, because he thought the post offered him was inadequate to his deserts, and now took refuge in talking of the Government as a lot of 'pinchbeck Napoleons'. Then he reminisced about Harrow, where he said he had spent the unhappiest days of his life, and told how he and F. E. Smith had been booed when they went there in 1912. However he was going down again to hear the songs (he repeated several word-perfect by heart) and would recall me from wherever I then might be so that I could accompany him.
>
> After dinner we saw an American film called 'John Doe', which I enjoyed, and the PM then closeted himself with Oliver Lyttelton in the Hawtrey Room and talked so long, as well as dictating telegrams, that I did not get into bed till 25 to 4. The PM said he supposed I was looking forward to the RAF and lights out at 10.0 p.m.![2]

Neither the travel nor the entertainments of the weekend could block out the ever pressing demands of policy and planning. To Beaverbrook, who was about to reach Moscow with the Allied Mission on September 28, Churchill had held out the hope of a 'formidable Anglo-Russian force' which could, if German troops reached the Caucasus, already be in position. General Wavell was on his way to Tiflis, where, Churchill told Beaverbrook, 'he will hold out our right hand to the Russians'. One or even both of the two additional Infantry Divisions going to the Middle East before the end of the year would be sent to Persia 'if situation demands'. Lyttelton had taken an 'optimistic view' of Britain's

---

[1] On 12 February 1941 Churchill had indeed supported British military help for Greece, with Dill opposing it for fear of 'another Dunkirk'. But two weeks later it was Dill and Eden who, from Athens, had strongly urged the sending of a British expedition to Greece, and Churchill who had been hesitant (see pages 1010–13).

[2] Colville diary, 28 September 1941: Colville papers.

general strategic position in the Middle East. 'There is no doubt,' Churchill noted, 'that Germans are feeling the pinch.'[1]

In one area, as Churchill realized, on studying the reports put before him, the Germans were not as vulnerable as had been anticipated: this was the bombing campaign over Germany. As he had minuted to Portal:

> It is very disputable whether bombing by itself will be a decisive factor in the present war. On the contrary, all that we have learnt since the war began shows that its effects, both physical and moral, are greatly exaggerated. There is no doubt that the British people have been stimulated and strengthened by the attack made upon them so far. Secondly, it seems very likely that the ground defences and night fighters will overtake the Air attack. Thirdly, in calculating the number of bombers necessary to achieve hypothetical and indefinite tasks, it should be noted that only a quarter of our bombs hit the targets.

The 'most we can say', of the bomber offensive, Churchill ended, 'is that it will be a heavy and, I trust, a seriously increasing annoyance'.[2]

Ten days later, Churchill wrote to Portal again. His minute expressed in outspoken terms his doubts about the bombing offensive against Germany, which the Air Staff continued to champion. 'I deprecate,' Churchill wrote, 'placing unbounded confidence in this method of attack.' Even if 'all the towns of Germany were rendered largely uninhabitable, it does not follow that the military control would be weakened or even that war industry could not be carried on'.

Aware that Portal and his advisers wished to expand the scale and extend the scope of the bombing offensive, Churchill set out his criticisms in detail:

> The Air Staff would make a mistake to put their claim too high. Before the war we were greatly misled by the pictures they painted of the destruction that would be wrought by air raids. This is illustrated by the fact that 250,000 beds were actually provided for air-raid casualties, never more than 6,000 being required.
>
> This picture of air destruction was so exaggerated that it depressed the statesmen responsible for the pre-war policy, and played a definite part in the desertion of Czechoslovakia in August 1938.
>
> Again, the Air Staff, after the war had begun, taught us sedulously to believe that if the enemy acquired the Low Countries, to say nothing of France, our position would be impossible owing to the air attacks. However, by not paying too much attention to such ideas we have found quite a good means of keeping going.

[1] 'Most Secret and Personal', Prime Minister's Personal Telegram, T.611, 29 September 1941: Churchill papers, 20/43.

[2] 'Secret', Prime Minister's Personal Minute, M.940/1, 27 September 1941: Cabinet papers, 120/300.

It may well be that German morale will crack, and that our bombing will play a very important part in bringing the result about. But all things are always on the move simultaneously, and it is quite possible that the Nazi war-making power in 1943 will be so widely spread throughout Europe as to be to a large extent independent of the actual buildings in the homeland.

A 'different picture', Churchill believed, would be presented if the German Air Force were 'so far reduced' as a fighting force as to make possible heavy accurate British daylight bombing of German factories. But this, he had been told, would not be done 'outside the radius of fighter protection'. Churchill added: 'One has to do the best one can, but he is an unwise man who thinks there is any *certain* method of winning this war, or indeed any other war between equals in strength. The only plan is to persevere.'[1]

Monday September 29 was Colville's final day in the Private Secretariat. On the following day he said good-bye to Churchill in the Cabinet Room at 10 Downing Street, noting in his diary: 'He said it must only be "au revoir" as he hoped I should often come back and see him. He ought not to be letting me go, and Eden had been "very sour" about it and about recalling a trained officer from the army to take my place; but I had so much wanted to go and he thought I was doing a very gallant thing.' Churchill added: 'I have the greatest affection for you; we all have, Clemmie and I especially. Good-bye and God bless you.' Colville noted in his diary: 'I went out of the room with a lump in my throat such as I have not had for many years.'[2]

That evening a telegram reached Downing Street from Moscow. It was clear that Stalin was going to drive a hard bargain. As Beaverbrook explained: 'Moscow is asking for aircraft with cannon and I represent to you urgently that a good measure of Hispano production is desirable. Spitfires must be supplied before long in any circumstances.' Stalin, added Beaverbrook, 'is dissatisfied with Tomahawks and critical of the performance, declaring that the aircraft is unsuited to the Germans on this front. He says that ammunition supply is not adequate, particularly

---

[1] 'Secret', Prime Minister's Personal Minute, M.973/1, 7 October 1941: Cabinet papers, 120/300.

[2] Colville diary, 30 September 1941. Colville was succeeded by Francis Brown, whom a fellow member of the Private Office, Anthony Bevir, described as 'very much Wellington & Cambridge & FO & C of E—good presence & good manner—intelligent & a good draughtsman of civilities—very hardworking and amiable'. (Letter of 23 November 1941 to Eric Seal: Seal papers.)

no tracer. I recommend that this situation should be cleared up at the earliest possible moment.'[1]

On reaching the Moscow 'outer ring', Beaverbrook added, the Mission's aeroplane had been fired on by Soviet anti-aircraft at 600 feet, and was forced to dive 'to tree-tops, fleeing at full speed, brushing the autumn leaves away'. Beaverbrook added: 'We do not recommend any more anti-aircraft guns for Russia!'[2]

In his speech on the war situation on September 30, Churchill told the House of Commons of Britain's aid to Russia: not only the whole production of the Tank Week just ended, but 'precious aircraft and aluminium, rubber, copper, oil and many other materials vital to modern war, large quantities of which have already gone'.[3] That same day, having been apprised of the 'great delay' in the despatch of promised aircraft to Russia, Churchill minuted to the Paymaster-General, Lord Hankey: 'I hope that our programme of consignments to Russia is being carried out satisfactorily and that all the departments concerned realise the importance of getting the goods shipped before Archangel freezes up. Pray inform me if there is anything I could usefully do to expedite the process.'[4]

Another worry, of which Churchill told Roosevelt on September 30, was that British merchant shipping losses had become heavier as the months progressed, and some convoys had 'suffered severely'. Churchill added: 'I fear a hard time in October when the balance of light and darkness favours the U-boats.'[5]

Although serious, this setback in the Atlantic was, however, only temporary. In September the U-boats had attacked five convoys, sinking thirty-four merchant ships, despite Bletchley Park's successful decrypting of the German naval Enigma. This sudden increase in sinkings had been partly due to the greatly increased number of U-boats at sea—nearly double the number in the first six months of 1941—and partly because, on September 11, the U-boat command had introduced

[1] On the following day the Soviet leader changed his mind. 'Stalin has withdrawn his request for Spitfires,' Beaverbrook telegraphed to Churchill. 'He now says he wants only two types of fighters, Tomahawks and Hurricanes.' (Linen No. 21, 30 September 1941: Churchill papers, 20/43.)

[2] Linen No. 18, 29 September 1941: Churchill papers, 20/43.

[3] *Hansard*, 30 September 1941, columns 514–15. Among those who listened to Churchill's speech was Geoffrey Dawson, who described it in his diary as 'a very satisfactory performance, with good figures of the Atlantic battles and the Air'. It was Dawson's last day as Editor of *The Times*. (Dawson diary, 30 September 1941: John Evelyn Wrench, *Geoffrey Dawson and Our Times*, London 1955, page 446.)

[4] 'Action this Day', Prime Minister's Personal Minute, M.946/1, 30 September 1941: Churchill papers, 20/36.

[5] Prime Minister's Personal Telegram, T.623, 30 September 1941: Churchill papers, 20/49.

a more complex grid reference setting for the precise positions contained in the Enigma traffic. It took some weeks for this new setting to be mastered at Bletchley Park, whereupon the situation improved rapidly. During October only two convoys were attacked, and allied shipping losses fell to a quarter of their September level.[1]

As Churchill followed these naval developments, he also wished to give public recognition to those who were the victims of the war at sea. On October 22, at the Battle of the Atlantic Committee, he expressed the view 'that the number of awards made to the Merchant Navy and Fishing Fleet was inadequate', and asked that steps should be taken 'to ensure that Decorations should be distributed on a far larger scale'.[2]

To help Britain still further in the Atlantic, Roosevelt now authorized Defence Plan No. 5, whereby the United States Navy would undertake escort duties for Canadian Troop Convoys,[3] as well as for merchant shipping convoys, for the voyage from Canada to mid-Atlantic. United States forces were also authorized to escort the Empire Training Scheme convoys.[4] British naval forces, Pound explained to Churchill, were thus released in mid-Atlantic instead of making the passage the whole way across. In this way the five to six destroyers required for convoy escort duty would only be absent from the Western Approaches, where they were most needed, for about ten days, instead of three to four weeks for the full trans-Atlantic crossings.[5]

Churchill's naval concerns were also turned to future British offensives, and in a minute to Colonel Hollis for the Chief of Staff Committee, he gave instructions for the tank landing craft then under construction: 'These vessels must be hurried forward with the highest priority and special exertions.'[6]

On September 20 British Hurricanes of No. 151 Wing had been in action again against German Messerschmitts near Murmansk, in northern Russia. Three Messerschmitts were shot down, with no British casualties. Portal had sent an account of this engagement to Churchill on September 22.[7] But while Britain could not provide the far more

[1] F. H. Hinsley and others, *British Intelligence in the Second World War, Its Influence on Strategy and Operations*, volume 2, London 1981, page 173. In November the U-boats had even fewer successes, sinking only 62,000 tons of shipping, less than in any month since May 1940.

[2] Battle of the Atlantic Committee No. 16 of 1941, 5 p.m., 22 October 1941: Cabinet papers, 86/1.

[3] TC convoys.

[4] CT convoys.

[5] Notes on Plan 5, 1 October 1941, and Escort Forces—Benefits from Plans IV and V, 29 October 1941: Premier papers, 3/460/4.

[6] Prime Minister's Personal Minute, D.271/1, 3 October 1941: Premier papers, 3/260/1.

[7] Daily Operational Summary, No. 151 Wing, Murmansk to Air Ministry, London, received 4.55 p.m. 20 September 1941: Premier papers, 3/395/4, folio 85.

substantial forces for which Stalin had pressed earlier that month, she was able to provide something of far greater value: Intelligence, based upon the Enigma decrypts, relating to German military dispositions and plans on the eastern front. As early as June 24 Churchill had instructed 'C' to divulge certain Enigma Intelligence to the Russians 'provided no risks are run'.[1] Subsequently in scrutinizing the contents of his buff box, Churchill was often to ask 'C' whether a particular decrypt had been sent, or why it had been withheld.[2]

The Germans now planned to launch an all-out assault on Moscow. On September 20, when this became clear to Bletchley through the Enigma decrypts, a warning was at once sent through Bletchley and Broadway to the British Military Mission in Russia. Eight further warnings were sent to Moscow in the following four days, giving the Russian High Command more than a week's notice of German intentions and dispositions.

In addition to the German Air Force Enigma decrypts, British Intelligence had just begun to break the German Army Enigma key, code name 'Vulture'. This key was used for communications between armies and army groups on the eastern front, and the Army High Command. Vulture was broken a few times between June and September, and with some regularity from October until mid-December. It too, contributed, via Bletchley and Broadway, to the Intelligence help Britain was able to send to the Russians at this critical time. It was the Vulture decrypts that gave the numbers of German armoured and motorized divisions committed to the drive on Moscow, to be launched on October 2.

It was on October 2, the first day of the German offensive on the central front, that Churchill minuted to 'C': 'Are you warning the Russians of the developing concentration? Show me the last five messages you have sent out to our missions on the subject?'[3]

'C' was able to assure Churchill that the essential details had indeed been sent to Moscow, including information about German air and ground concentrations in the Smolensk area which had indicated impending major operations there.

Churchill continued to study the Enigma decrypts, and other Signals Intelligence sources, not only for what they told him, but for what they

---

[1] Dir/C Archive, 6863 of 24 June 1941: quoted in Hinsley and others *British Intelligence in the Second World War, Its Influence on Strategy and Operations*, volume 2, London 1981, page 59.

[2] Hinsley gives as an example Dir/C Archive, 7098, of 17 July 1941.

[3] Dir/C Archieve, 7706 of 2 October 1941: quoted in F. H. Hinsley and others, *British Intelligence in the Second World War, Its Influence on Strategy and Operations*, volume 2, London 1981, page 73.

might be able to tell the Russians, even in a disguised form. Thus a year later, on reading his daily box of decrypts, he minuted to 'C': 'Has any of this been passed to Joe?'[1]

Britain's provision of military aid to Russia affected the flow of supplies so essential for Britain herself; supplies secured after so much effort by Arthur Purvis and the British Purchasing Commission in 1940 and the first six months of 1941. 'The offers which we are both making to Russia,' Churchill telegraphed to Hopkins on October 2, 'are necessary and worthwhile.' But he added that there was 'no disguising the fact' that these offers made 'grievous inroads into what is required by you for expanding your forces and by us for intensifying our war effort. You know where the shoe will pinch most in the next nine months. We must both bend our efforts to making good the gaps unavoidably created.'

'We here,' Churchill added, 'are unlikely to be able to expand our programmes much above what is already planned. I earnestly hope that you will be able to raise the general level of yours by an immediate short-term effort.'[2]

During the first nine days of October, Soviet forces fell back to within 140 miles of Moscow. In response to Russia's agony, Clementine Churchill launched an Aid to Russia Appeal which, especially in the factories, as John Martin later noted, 'touched the feeling of popular sympathy for the Russians and their gallant resistance'.[3]

The extent of Britain's material pledge to Russia was formidable, covering every facet of the naval, air and land war. The Russians were to receive, in nine monthly deliveries, a total of 1,800 British Hurricanes and Spitfires, 900 American fighters and 900 American bombers.[4] For the Soviet Navy, 150 sets of 'Asdic' submarine detection sets were to be

[1] Dir/C Archive, 1645 of 6 December 1942: quoted in F. H. Hinsley and others, *British Intelligence in the Second World War, Its Influence on Strategy and Operations*, volume 2, London 1981, page 59, note 2.

[2] Foreign Office Telegram No. 5358 to Washington, 6.10 p.m., 2 October 1941: Foreign Office papers, 954/24, folio 427.

[3] John Martin recollections: Martin papers. By the end of October the Aid to Russia Appeal had raised (in twelve days), £370,000, and had already sent to Russia 53 emergency operating outfits, 30 blood-transfusion sets, 70,000 surgical needles, half a ton (one million doses) of the painkiller phenacetin (now known to be potentially damaging to the liver and the kidney, and largely discontinued) and seven tons of absorbent cotton-wool.

[4] 'Secret', 'Moscow Conference, 1941', 'Air Supply Committee, Report', 30 September 1941: Cabinet papers, 99/7.

supplied, as well as 1,500 naval guns, 3,000 anti-aircraft machine guns, and eight destroyers 'before the end of 1941'.[1] For the Red Army, the list of immediate requirements to be provided was staggering, eating into both Britain and America's essential war needs, and including 1,000 tanks a month together with 'a proper complement of accessories and spare parts', 300 anti-aircraft guns a month, 300 anti-tank guns a month, and 2,000 armoured cars a month, together with their anti-tank guns.[2]

Other Soviet needs which the British and American Governments promised to supply included 4,000 tons of aluminium a month, substantial quantities of copper, tin, lead, brass, nickel and cobalt, 13,000 tons monthly of steel bars for shells, industrial diamonds, machine tools, rubber, wool, jute and lead. For the soldiers of the Red Army, Britain was to provide 3 million pairs of army boots, immediately, followed by 400,000 pairs a month, the Americans sending in addition, also monthly, 200,000 pairs of army shoes. More than a million metres of army cloth were to be supplied each month.[3]

Other Anglo-American Committees in Moscow had agreed to supply 20,000 tons a month of petroleum products, including lubricating oil for aviation engines,[4] shipping to enable the transport of cargoes of up to half a million tons a month for food, oil and war material imports,[5] and medical supplies on a vast and comprehensive scale, including more than ten million surgical needles and half a million pairs of surgical gloves.[6]

Despite the renewed German offensive against Moscow on October 2, and a series of immediate Russian reverses, Churchill, with his close

[1] 'Secret', 'Moscow Conference, 1941', 'Naval Supply Committee, Report', 2 October 1941: Cabinet papers, 99/7.
[2] Also required were 2,000 anti-tank rifles a month, 12,000 Field Telephone sets, 100,000 kilometres of telephone cable, and 3,000 tons of Nitro-Glycerine powder a month. ('Russian Immediate Requirements', 'Moscow Conference 1941', 'Military Supply Committee', 1 October 1941: Cabinet papers, 99/7.)
[3] 'Secret', 'Moscow Conference, 1941', 'Raw Materials Committee, Report', 2 October 1941: Cabinet papers, 99/7.
[4] 'Petroleum Sub-Committee', report signed by E. A. Berthoud, 6 October 1941: Cabinet papers, 99/7.
[5] 'Transportation Committee, Report', 1 October 1941: Cabinet papers, 99/7.
[6] 'Medical Supply Committee, Report': Cabinet papers, 99/7. The British signatory of this report was Churchill's doctor, Sir Charles Wilson (later Lord Moran). Other medical supplies sent to Russia included 20,000 amputation knives, 15,000 amputation saws, 100 portable X-ray sets, 4,000 kilogrammes of local anaesthetics, more than a million doses of the recently discovered antibiotics (including M & B 693), sedatives, heart and brain stimulants, 800,000 forceps (including forceps for bone operations), instruments for brain and eye operations, and a million metres of oilcloth for covering wounds.

study of the Enigma decrypts, including the newly broken German Army 'Vulture' messages, remained in confident tone and mood.[1] On October 4 he telegraphed to Roosevelt:

Max and Averell seem to have had a great success at Moscow, and now the vital thing is to act up to our bargain in early deliveries. Hitler evidently feels the draught. We made almost exactly two thousand aircraft in September, and I think our first line strength tonight is slightly ahead of the Germans. Besides this the Russian Air Force is still very formidable.

'How I wish,' Churchill added, 'we could have another talk.'[2]

At the end of September Churchill had read a public statement by Smuts of his confidence in imminent American belligerency.[3] Churchill had replied at once: 'Would earnestly advise against public assumptions that United States will be in war. They say to me "Do let us declare war for ourselves." ' Churchill added: 'With patience "Alles sal reg kom." '[4]

Churchill was also kept informed of the attitude of others. Even the Duke of Windsor, Roosevelt told Halifax, was now 'very robust on war and victory' and showed in his attitude, 'a great improvement on the impression the President had found when he met him a year ago in the Bahamas'. Halifax at once sent Roosevelt's comments to Churchill.[5]

Churchill was worried about the speed with which supplies to Russia could be delivered. Of aircraft intended for despatch by sea to Archangel that month, he minuted for the Chiefs of Staff Committee: 'It is vital that delivery should begin at once. Pray let proposals and preparations be made for this forthwith . . .', including if necessary a

---

[1] The official historians of British Intelligence write of the messages encyphered in the 'Vulture' key, a form of Enigma used by the German Army: 'by disclosing the day-by-day movements and problems of enemy formations they also established that the advance was slowing down as it encountered increasingly bad weather, mounting fuel shortages, Soviet counter-attacks and evidence that the Soviet Air Force was gaining superiority'. 'Vulture' was the first German Army Enigma key to be broken with any regularity. (F. H. Hinsley and others, *British Intelligence in the Second World War: Its Influence on Strategy and Operations*, volume 2, London 1981, page 74.)

[2] 'Personal and Most Secret', Prime Minister's Personal Telegram, T.653, 4 October 1941: Churchill papers, 20/43.

[3] High Commissioner's Telegram No. 38 of 30 September 1941.

[4] 'All will come right', the motto of the former Boer President of the Orange Free State, Martinus Steyn (1857–1916), which Churchill frequently quoted. Prime Minister's Personal Telegram, T.640, 3 October 1941: Churchill papers, 20/43. Two weeks later, in a further move of American involvement, the House of Representatives passed a joint resolution to repeal the ban on the arming of United States merchant ships.

[5] 'Secret and Personal', Washington Telegram N.4551, (Halifax to Churchill), 4 October 1941: Churchill papers, 20/31.

'special convoy'. Churchill added: 'I cannot too strongly emphasise the vital importance and extreme urgency of this transaction.'[1]

Two days later Churchill telegraphed direct to Stalin: 'We intend to run a continuous cycle of convoys, leaving every ten days.' On the basis of the Chiefs of Staff proposals, he was able to tell Stalin that 20 heavy tanks and 193 fighters would arrive at Archangel on October 12. These would be followed on October 29 by 140 heavy tanks, 100 Hurricanes, 200 Bren carriers, 200 anti-tank rifles and ammunition, and 50 two-pounder guns and ammunition. The journey time for these supplies would be seventeen days, port to port. Churchill also told Stalin that on October 22 a third convoy would set off from Britain with 200 fighters and 100 heavy tanks. Churchill commented: 'Bis dat qui cito dat.'[2]

Sending a copy of this telegram to Beaverbrook, who was on his way back from Moscow, Churchill commented: 'We have not lost an hour in making good your undertakings.'[3]

The problem of how to take offensive action in an effort to relieve the pressures on Russian continued to worry Churchill. One plan which he favoured was Operation 'Ajax', a military landing at the Norwegian port of Trondheim, with a view to helping Russia by dislodging the Germans in northern Norway, and possibly even inducing Sweden to join the Allies. But after considerable discussion, in which Sir Alan Brooke and General Paget were the principal opponents of the plan, Churchill agreed to abandon it.[4]

Churchill had already offered Stalin a British force for the protection of the north Persian supply route, to liberate five or six Russian divisions 'for use on the battle front'.[5] Believing that the Middle East offensive could also be crucial for Russia, he had pressed, but in vain, for a

[1] Prime Minister's Personal Minute, D.274/1, 'Action this Day', 4 October 1941: Churchill papers, 20/36.

[2] Prime Minister's Personal Telegram, T.660, Foreign Office Telegram No. 1423 to Moscow, 6 October 1941: Premier papers, 3/170/1, No. 16. Churchill's Latin quotation states confidently: 'He gives twice who gives quickly.' The phrase is attributed to a first century Roman author, Publilius Syrus.

[3] Prime Minister's Personal Telegram, T.659, 6 October 1941: Churchill papers, 20/43.

[4] 'Ajax' was outlined by the Joint Planning Committee on September 29, but opposed by the Chiefs of Staff in their Paper No. 229 (O) of 1941 on October 12, their principal reason for opposition being the unlikelihood of overrunning the German aerodromes in the region of the proposed assault. (Premier papers, 3/40.) Churchill accepted its abandonment on October 15 (Defence Committee No. 64 of 1941, 14 October 1941, 10 p.m.: Cabinet papers, 92/2).

[5] Prime Minister's Personal Telegram, T.695, Foreign Office Telegram No. 1464 to Moscow, sent 12.20 a.m., 13 October 1941, 'Personal and Secret': Premier papers, 3/170/1, No. 17. Churchill added: 'I pledge the faith of Britain that we will not seek any advantage for ourselves at the expense of any rightful Russian interest during the war or at the end.'

reversal by the new Australian Prime Minister, John Curtin, of his predecessor's withdrawal of the remaining Australian troops then in Tobruk. Such a decision, he said, would be 'taken very kindly as an act of comradeship in the present struggle'.[1] He would be glad, Churchill told Auchinleck, 'for the sake of Australia and history', if the Australian Government would 'allow the troops to remain'. But the Australian Government adhered to its earlier decision, which was, Curtin telegraphed, 'apparently reached after fullest review of all considerations involved'.[2]

In planning the November offensive, Churchill told Auchinleck, all must go forward whatever the Australian response. 'The Russian news,' he told him, 'is increasingly grave. All now hinges on you.'[3]

In the third week of October, in order to ensure that aid to Russia was organized effectively, Churchill established an Allied Supplies Executive.[4] The Chairman was to be Lord Beaverbrook, and all relevant Ministries were represented.[5]

The pressures on Churchill were formidable. Those who took his dictation saw at close quarters his response at times of tension. On October 12 Elizabeth Layton wrote to her parents after a morning's dictation:

Not in a very good temper this morning. He suddenly said 'Gimme t—gr—spts—pk.' Interpreting this as 'Give me a toothpick' I leapt up, looked round and then started rummaging in the bag in which such necessities should be kept. After less than 30 seconds he said, very bored and superior 'now Miss Layton, just stop playing the bloody ass and ask Sawyers'.[6]

I couldn't help feeling amused. Presently, after having dictated something, he found I'd put 'Somehow I think it right' (which was what I thought he'd

---

[1] Prime Minister's Personal Telegram, T.697, 14 October 1941: Churchill papers, 20/43.

[2] Telegram No. 682, received on 16 October 1941: Churchill papers, 20/44.

[3] Prime Minister's Personal Telegram, T.700. 14 October 1941: Churchill papers, 20/43.

[4] 'Supplies to Russia and the Persian Gulf Area, Note by the Prime Minister', War Cabinet paper No. 111 of 1941, 15 October 1941: Cabinet papers, 111/27. The need for this Allied Supplies Executive, and the details of its composition, had been put to Churchill by Sir Edward Bridges on 1 October 1941, and approved by Churchill four days later. (Minute of 1 October 1941 and Churchill note of 5 October 1941: Premier papers, 4/32/11, folios 405–9.)

[5] The other members of the Allied Supplies Executive were David Margesson (Secretary of State for War), Colonel Llewellin (Parliamentary Secretary, Ministry of War Transport) and, specially co-opted, Eden and Sinclair. Lieutenant-Colonel Jacob served as representative of the Office of the Minister of Defence.

[6] Churchill's valet.

said). So, fairly patient, he said 'no, no, I said *now the time* is right' (with accents like that).

So I did it again. Gave it back. There was a roar of rage. 'God's teeth, girl, can't you even do it right the second time.' I said *ripe ripe ripe*—P *P P.*'

I should, perhaps, have realized, but he hadn't mentioned that 'right' was 'wrong'. However he forgave me and was very amiable for the rest of the day.[1]

Peter Kinna was also present at several moments of tension: 'If you had the temerity to ask him to repeat a word' Kinna later recalled 'he nearly killed you *with* words. It upset his train of thought. He never paused.' But with Churchill's 'slight impediment', Kinna noted, it was not always easy to hear what he said.[2]

There was yet another problem for those who took Churchill's dictation—the fascination of his remarks. 'Sometimes I just wanted to listen and not take it down,' Kinna remembered. 'I found myself listening instead of taking it down.'[3]

John Martin, who had succeeded Seal as Churchill's Principal Private Secretary, later recalled how it was sometimes 'difficult to interpret' Churchill's oral instructions. 'One didn't always understand what he said,' Martin explained. 'He just grunted or said "get me my minute"—and you had to know which one he had in mind.'[4]

All those who worked for Churchill at closest quarters saw his sternest moods, born of fearsome problems. They also saw the character that lay beneath those moods. 'I can't help feeling rather fond of him,' Elizabeth Layton wrote home, '—he is a loveable person, in spite of his impatience.'[5]

---

[1] Elizabeth Layton, letter of 12 October 1941: Nel papers.

[2] Since childhood, Churchill had had difficulty pronouncing the letter 's', which he frequently pronounced 'sh'.

[3] Peter Kinna, conversation with the author, 24 August 1982.

[4] Sir John Martin conversation with the author, 15 October 1982.

[5] Elizabeth Layton, letter of 12 October 1941: Nel papers.

63

The delay of 'Crusader':
'How bloody'

ON October 16 the Red Army evacuated Odessa, the principal
Black Sea port of the Soviet Union. Much now seemed to depend
on Auchinleck for a diversion in the Middle East. But in spite of
Churchill's repeated exhortations there were increasing hesitations in
Cairo as to when the offensive could begin, particularly as it emerged
that there were defects in the axles of the tanks which had been sent
out, and delays in their unloading.

There was a second reason for postponement: the fears of Air Chief
Marshal Tedder, the Air Officer Commanding-in-Chief, Middle East,
that 'Crusader' would not be able to go ahead at all in November on
account of German air strength in the Middle East, and the possible
arrival of German air reinforcements from the Russian front. Tedder's
assessment of German air strength differed from that of Churchill and
the Air Staff.

As Commanders-in-Chief, Middle East, both Auchinleck and Tedder
received Enigma decrypts direct from Bletchley, as did Admiral A. B.
Cunningham. As a result of this, Tedder and his staff knew the exact
order of battle and establishment of the German and Italian Air Forces
in the theatre. They differed from the Air Staff and Churchill, however,
on the probable percentage of serviceability, and the likelihood of reinforcement, including the possibility of reinforcement from the Russian
front.

To resolve the disagreement, Churchill decided to send Air Chief
Marshal Freeman to Cairo, to see Auchinleck, and to hand him a
letter setting out the air situation as it was believed to be, and the
wider hopes resting upon a prompt and successful offensive. Churchill's
letter read:

My dear General Auchinleck,

Tedder's estimate of strength, actual and relative, is so misleading and militarily untrue that I found it necessary at once to send Air Chief Marshal Freeman to Cairo. Only in this way can the facts be established, we here be properly informed and you yourself reassured as to the Air strength at your disposal. The Air Staff here know just as much and in some ways more than the Air Intelligence in Egypt. Their conviction is that you will have a substantial numerical superiority in the battle zone, even if all Italian planes are counted as if they were equal to German or British.

Moreover, Tedder's telegram assumed, on the basis of an estimate of September 7, that the Russian front would be stabilized by October 15, thus permitting reinforcement to begin. It will certainly not be stabilized for some weeks, if then, and thereafter several more weeks must elapse before any effective transference can be made of German Air Units already battered and worn.

I thought it very wrong that such mis-statements should be made by the Air authorities in Cairo on the eve of a decisive battle and I shall not conceal from you that such conduct has affected my confidence in their quality and judgement.

You will find Freeman an officer of altogether larger calibre and if you feel he would be a greater help to you and that you would have more confidence in the Air Command if he assumed it, you should not hesitate to tell me so.

The time has now come when for the purposes of the major operation impending, the Air is subordinated to you. Do not let any thought of Tedder's personal feelings influence you. This is no time for such considerations. On the other hand I am very glad to see that you and Tedder are in accord upon the tactical employment of the Air Force and that there is no danger of its being parcelled out among the various divisions, thus losing its power to make the characteristic contribution of its arm.

Churchill went on to tell Auchinleck how glad he was that he was sending an officer to Britain to tell Churchill and Dill 'something more of your plans'. Upon the outcome of 'Crusader' and the 'use made of it', Churchill wrote, depended issues affecting 'the whole immediate future of the war', and he went on to explain:

Turkey, French North Africa and Spain will pick their steps accordingly. The struggling Russian armies will feel that our long period of inaction has been at last broken and that they are not the only people engaging the enemy. Feeling here has risen very high against what is thought to be our supine incapacity for action. I am however fully in control of public opinion, and of the House of Commons. Nevertheless it seems to me, on military grounds alone, that everything should be thrown into this battle that can be made to play its part. This is also the view of the Defence Committee, both political and expert Members. God has granted us this long breathing space and I feel sure that if all is risked all may be won.

We have been considering how to help you exploit success, should it be granted to us. Any long delay after a victory in Cyrenaica in pushing on to Tripoli would seem fatal to that extension of your plan. It is rather a rapid dash forward, while the shock of the battle still reigns and before the enemy can bring new forces into Africa or into Italy, that seems alone possible.

Churchill's letter continued:

Directions have been given here to prepare an expedition to Norway and shipping for about four divisions, including one armoured division, is being gathered. Winter clothing is being issued to the troops assigned. This forms a real cover. However, from about the middle of November or perhaps even a little earlier I shall be holding a substantial force which can as easily steer south as north.

Should your operation change the attitude of Weygand we could enter by Casablanca at his invitation; or alternatively action against Sicily in conjunction with your army may be taken. This last plan is now being studied by the Chiefs of Staff and the Defence Committee. The situation in Italy, and particularly in Sicily, gives grounds for hope and audacity on our part.

'This letter,' Churchill added, 'is evidently most private and secret,' and should be shown to Lyttelton alone.[1]

Before Churchill's letter could reach Cairo, Auchinleck telegraphed, seeking a 'retardation' of the offensive from November 1 to November 18. Having been informed by Brigadier Shearer that an even earlier date than November 1 might have been possible, Churchill was, as he told Auchinleck, 'disquieted'. He also reported that, as far as the Australian troops in beseiged Tobruk were concerned, the Australian Government had sent 'an obdurate reply', and that these troops must now be relieved.[2]

On October 18 Churchill made one last effort to persuade Auchinleck to adhere to the November 1 date, which, he pointed out, had itself been fixed at Auchinleck's own insistence, postponing for two months an offensive which had originally been hoped for in September. Although 'we felt the delay most dangerous' then, Churchill noted,

---

[1] 'Private and Secret', 16 October 1941: Churchill papers, 20/20. Five days later Churchill telegraphed to Lyttelton: 'Tedder's alarmist figures about our air inferiority have now been corrected by Freeman, and it is agreed by Tedder that we have a large superiority at present even counting Italians as equals.' (Prime Minister's Personal Telegram, T.725, 'Personal and Secret', 21 October 1941: Premier papers, 3/282, folio 148.) In fact, after consultation, Freeman *increased* his figures substantially, *and* Tedder lowered his.

[2] Prime Minister's Personal Telegram, T.707, 17 October 1941: Churchill papers, 20/44.

'we accepted it and have worked towards it in our general plans'. Churchill's telegram continued:

It is impossible to explain to Parliament and the nation how it is our Middle East armies had to stand for 4½ months without engaging the enemy while all the time Russia is being battered to pieces. I have hitherto managed to prevent public discussion, but at any time it may break out. Moreover, the few precious weeks that remain to us for the exploitation of any success are passing. No warning has been given to me of your further delay, and no reasons. I must be able to inform War Cabinet on Monday number of days further delay you now demand.

Moreover, the Lord Privy Seal[1] leaves Monday for United States, carrying with him a personal letter to the President. In this letter, which would be handed to Mr Roosevelt for his eye alone and to be burnt or returned thereafter, I was proposing to state that in the moonlight of early November you intended to attack.

It is necessary for me to take the President into our confidence, and thus stimulate his friendly action. In view of the plans we are preparing for 'Whipcord',[2] I am in this letter asking him to send three or four United States divisions to relieve our troops in Northern Ireland, as a greater safeguard against invasion in the spring.

I fixed the date of the Lord Privy Seal's mission in relation to the date you had given us. Of course, if it is only a matter of two or three days the fact could be endured. It is not however possible for me to concert the general movement of the war if important changes are made in plans agreed upon without warning or reason.[3]

Eden shared Churchill's disappointment at Auchinleck's decision. 'AE much cast down this morning,' Oliver Harvey noted in his diary, 'by learning at Defence Committee that Western Desert Operation must be postponed three weeks owing to delay in unloading tanks and to necessity for altering axles.' Harvey added: 'Really, really, it is almost incredible that it should be so slow and that news of delay should not come till now. Whose fault is the muddle? Whilst on military grounds delay is bad, on the home front where the clamour for action to help Russia is increasing it is the very devil.'[4]

On October 21 Churchill telegraphed to Auchinleck: 'We have no

---

[1] Clement Attlee.

[2] The planned invasion of Sicily.

[3] 'Most Secret', 'Most Immediate', Prime Minister's Personal Telegram, T.711, 18 October 1941: Churchill papers, 20/44.

[4] Harvey diary, 20 October 1941: John Harvey, editor, *The War Diaries of Oliver Harvey*, London 1978, page 54.

choice but to accept your new proposal. I will not therefore waste further words upon it.'[1] But to Lyttelton he telegraphed angrily:

All here were astonished that we were not informed in good time of proposed further delay from which the very greatest dangers may arise. According to War Office and Ministry of Supply the axle story is without substance. The fact that a fortnight was taken to unload the 150 tanks of the 22nd Brigade is a scandal.[2]

'Most serious consequences have flowed from the breakdown in contacts between here and the Middle East,' Churchill minuted to Sir Andrew Duncan on October 26, 'and the responsibilities must be assigned, if only to prevent further misfortunes.'[3]

One reason for Churchill's sense of urgency in the date of Auchinleck's attack was his conviction, which he explained to Roosevelt on October 20, that Hitler intended, once the Russian front was stabilized, to 'gather perhaps fifty or sixty Divisions in the West for the invasion of the British Isles'. There had been reports 'which may be exaggerated' of the building up of perhaps 800 craft capable of carrying 'eight or ten tanks each' across the North Sea, and of 'landing anywhere upon the beaches'.[4] There would also be parachute and airborne descents 'on a yet unmeasured scale'.

In his telegram to Roosevelt, Churchill noted that a programme seemed to have emerged in Hitler's attacks: 1939, Poland; 1940, France; 1941, Russia; 1942, England; 1943——?'. At any rate, Churchill added,

[1] Prime Minister's Personal Telegram, T.723, 21 October 1941: Premier papers, 3/282. On October 20 Randolph Churchill had written to his father from Cairo, about Auchinleck: 'I have had a long talk with the Auk a few nights ago. I like him enormously and everyone out here is coming to have a tremendous admiration for him. One never can tell with Generals but he strikes me as being a really first class and intelligent human being. I trust that results will vindicate your choice.' (Churchill papers, 1/362.)

[2] Prime Minister's Personal Telegram, T.725, 'Personal and Secret', 21 October 1941: Premier papers, 3/282, folio 148.

[3] Premier papers, 3/282, folio 126. The enquiry was eventually carried out by Mr Justice Singleton, who reported in January 1942, listing a series of local errors and incompetence as the cause for the breakdowns.

[4] Having read at the end of January 1942 a Combined Intelligence Centre report (No. 506 of 26 January 1942) that the total of German landing craft both completed and being built in January 1942 did not exceed a hundred, and that there was 'no evidence so far of the intensified industrial effort which would be required to reach by the Spring the figure of 800', Churchill minuted to the Chief of the Imperial General Staff and the Commander in Chief Home Forces: 'If we are to believe the latest estimates of the Combined Intelligence Centre, all the stories about 800 specially constructed vessels and the deductions founded upon them as to the scale of invasion are obsolete. I was always sceptical about these 800 vessels, and have repeatedly questioned the trustworthiness of the rumours.' ('Most Secret', Prime Minister's Personal Minute M.116/2, 30 March 1942: Cabinet papers, 120/744.)

Britain must be prepared 'to meet a supreme onslaught from March onwards'.[1]

On October 20, German troops reached a point only sixty-five miles from Moscow. From his command post in the Kremlin, Stalin had already declared the capital to be in a state of siege, and now despatched the Soviet Government and administrative machinery eastwards to the city of Kuibyshev. That evening, in its search for every means to augment British help, the Defence Committee, in London, with Churchill in the Chair, agreed that every tank shipped to Russia under Britain's emergency aid programme should be furnished with three months' spares, 'whatever sacrifice this might entail'.[2]

As Churchill scrutinized, from hour to hour, the scale and nature of the aid sent to Russia, he was struck by one area where, as he saw it, too little had been attempted. This was in the despatch of two Royal Air Force squadrons to Murmansk. Writing to Portal, he commented:

I am not content with the arrangements made for the two Squadrons in Murmansk. I thought they were to take their aircraft and move to the south of the front where they might have come into action with the Russian Air force. Instead of this, the personnel only is being sent. When is it expected that these two Squadrons will again come into action, and where? The most serious mistake we have made about the Russians was in not sending eight Air Force Fighter Squadrons, which would have gained great fame, destroyed many German aircraft, and given immense encouragement all along the front.

But this criticism, Churchill added, was the only one among many that had been made 'which I feel strikes home'.[3]

On October 24, German forces captured Kharkov, the second largest city of the Ukraine. That same day, German troops in the south renewed their offensive against the Crimea. 'What in your opinion,' Churchill asked the Director of Military Operations that day, 'are the

---

[1] 'For yourself alone', 20 October 1941 (delivered by hand of Clement Attlee): Churchill papers, 20/20. On the following day Churchill told the Defence Committee of 'the importance of continuing photographic reconnaisance of the invasion ports'. The Germans, he said, 'would attempt to camouflage their concentrations of light craft and we might fail to penetrate their disguises unless photographs of all stages of their preparations were available'. (Defence Committee, Operations, No. 68 of 1941, 21 October 1941, 10 p.m.: Cabinet papers, 69/2.)

[2] Defence Committee (Operations) No. 67 of 1941, 20 October 1941, 10 p.m.: Cabinet papers, 69/2.

[3] Prime Minister's Personal Minute, M.1013/1, 24 October 1941: Premier papers, 3/395/4, folio 80. Portal replied, stressing the isolation of the men and machines in North Russia, and the danger of all five hundred men becoming 'stranded in Arctic Russia for the winter'. 'The story is most painful,' Churchill minuted in reply, and he added: 'The Russians would have welcomed the two squadrons intact in their fighting line.' (Premier papers, 3/395/4, folio 75.)

chances of Moscow being taken before the winter? I should be inclined to put it evens.'[1]

Such fears made 'Crusader' seem even more urgent. On October 24 Churchill had sent Auchinleck the final acceptance of November 18 as the date of the offensive, adding: 'Enemy is now ripe for sickle.' If successful, Churchill wrote, 'you should not hesitate to press on to Tripoli', but any 'lengthy delay' in doing so would 'almost certainly close this prospect'.

In his telegram to Auchinleck, Churchill declared: 'You will be justified in running extraordinary risks with your available fast forces while the going is good.' The invasion of Sicily, Operation 'Whipcord', a plan originally put forward by the Chiefs of Staff, would likewise be 'fitted in so as to act if all goes well'. Up to December 2, the forces assembled for 'Whipcord' could be turned back, 'but we cannot keep them hanging about indefinitely'.

The Russian situation, Churchill told Auchinleck, was at that moment favourable to 'Crusader'. The Russians were 'resisting very strongly in front of Moscow and winter is near'. 'This,' Churchill added, 'is the moment to strike hard. I have every confidence you will do so. Throw in all and count on me.'[2]

That night, when this telegram reached Auchinleck, Lyttelton telegraphed to Churchill: 'Its effect has been electric and I am more than grateful.' Everything, Lyttelton assured Churchill, 'will be put into the battle'.[3]

In sending details of the coming offensive to the Prime Minister of New Zealand, Churchill stressed that the Commanders were confident, unless the situation 'alters markedly', that 'we shall have good air superiority'.[4] There was also a substantial superiority in tanks. 'The armoured battle is what matters,' Churchill wrote, 'and we hope to force the enemy to it.'[5] The destruction of Rommel's armoured force

[1] Prime Minister's Personal Minute, M.1014/1, 24 October 1941: Churchill papers, 20/36.

[2] Prime Minister's Personal Telegram, T.732, War Office Telegram No. 111, 'Personal and Secret', 24 October 1941: Churchill papers, 20/44.

[3] Nocop No. 3344, 24 October 1941, 10.18 p.m.: Churchill papers, 20/44.

[4] In this telegram Churchill gave the New Zealand Prime Minister the 'agreed figures' of the British and Middle East Staffs on the opposing air strengths: 'British Air Forces, 660, Axis Forces 642. Probable serviceability of these forces Day 1, British Forces 528, Axis Forces 385. Of these latter little more than 100 are German. Moreover, all Axis forces are in shop window. We expect to have about 50 per cent reserves behind the counter. Germany has also in Aegean and Crete 156 all types, excluding all short-range fighters. In Malta we have 64 bombers. Serviceability 72 and 48 respectively.'

[5] Churchill noted: 'We shall have 658 infantry tanks, cruiser tanks and American cruisers of 12 tons or upwards against 168 comparable Axis vehicles. Axis has in addition 234 9-ton light tanks which play a serious part.'

'would bring ruin to the rest'. Unless the situation altered before the day of the attack, 'we are justified in sober confidence'.[1]

In a telegram to Lyttelton on October 25, Churchill expressed his belief that, for Operation 'Whipcord' to follow 'Crusader', it was 'probably a case of "Now or Never" ', and that by the end of December the prospects of following up a victory in Libya by the conquest of Sicily 'will be indefinitely closed'.

Success in Libya would, Churchill believed, open up the possibility of establishing Allied airfields not only in Tripoli and Sicily, but also in safety in Malta, and in prospect in Sardinia. This done, he told Lyttelton, 'a heavy and possibly decisive attack can be made upon Italy, the weaker partner in the Axis', by bombers from Britain based upon Libyan, Sicilian, Maltese and Sardinian airfields. The reaction upon French North Africa of such successes, including the arrival of British troops on the Tunisian border, 'might bring Weygand into action, with all the benefits that would come from that'. Hitler, confronted by Britain's Mediterranean successes, would be forced to try to occupy Spain. The Spaniards would 'resent and resist' any invasion of their country by the Germans, who were hated 'by the morose and hungry Spanish people', and it would be 'a very dangerous step' for Hitler to have to add Spain, and also Italy, 'to the already vast subjugated and rebellious areas over which his troops are spread'. Nothing would more effectively destroy Hitler's hopes of a German New Order in Europe than 'the continuance of the murders and reprisals, slaughters of hostages etc which is now going on in so many countries'.[2]

For these substantial prospects, Churchill told Lyttelton, the Libyan and Sicilian plans deserved 'close synchronization'. If this were not done, he warned, British military action would have to be transferred elsewhere, for, as he explained:

I am confronted with Russian demands for a British force to take its place in the line on the Russian left flank at the earliest moment. It will not be possible in the rising temper of the British people against what they consider our inactivity to resist such demands indefinitely. If therefore it were decided to abandon 'Whipcord' or alternative action in French North Africa at French

---

[1] Prime Minister's Personal Telegram, T.734, 'Most Secret', 24 October 1941: Churchill papers, 20/44. 'All the above', Churchill noted in this telegram, 'is of fateful secrecy'.

[2] On 20 October 1941 the German Military Commander of the Nantes region, Lieutenant-Colonel Hotz, had been assassinated by members of the French resistance. Two days later fifty hostages had been shot in Nantes as a reprisal. On 25 October 1941 both Roosevelt and Churchill condemned these reprisals, and pledged retribution.

invitation, as mentioned in Chiefs of Staff paper, it would be necessary to make preparations soon for moving a substantial force into Russia.[1]

That same day, October 25, Churchill read a report by his Parliamentary Private Secretary, George Harvie-Watt, that Aneurin Bevan had made 'a most bitter attack on the Government, which he considered was not prepared to take risks on behalf of Russia'.[2]

At Chequers on October 26, Churchill discussed his hopes for 'Crusader' and 'Whipcord' with General Brooke, whom he had asked to stay the night. It was their first time alone together since Brooke had resisted so strongly, successfully, and to Churchill's chagrin, the 'Ajax' operation against Trondheim. In his diary, Brooke recorded the evening's progress:

. . . I arrived about 7.45 p.m. I found that the only other guest was Lindemann. Dinner lasted on until about 11 p.m. by the time we had finished having snuff, etc. After dinner the PM sent for his dressing-gown to put over his 'siren-suit'. The dressing-gown is a marvellous garment, rather like Joseph's many-coloured robe. We then proceeded upstairs where he had a small cinema. There we watched Russian and German films till about midnight. We then came down and spent from midnight to 1 a.m. with an explanation of 'Bumper' Exercise which I had to give.

The PM then dismissed Lindemann and told him he wanted to speak to me. He proceeded to discuss impending operations in North Africa and Mediterranean and all the hopes he attached to them. From that he went on to discuss defence of this country against invasion and the strength of the forces left for this purpose. I told him of the forces I had, of being very short of tanks if we went on sending them to Russia as proposed. He assured me that I should have some 4,000 tanks in this country by the spring.

Finally at 2.15 a.m. he suggested we should proceed to the hall to have some sandwiches, and I hoped this might at last mean bed. But, no! We went on till ten to three before he made a move for bed. He had the gramophone turned on, and in the many-coloured dressing-gown, with a sandwich in one hand and watercress in the other, he trotted round and round the hall, giving occasional little skips to the tune of the gramophone.

On each lap near the fireplace he stopped to release some priceless quotation or thought. For instance he quoted a saying that a man's life is similar to a walk down a long passage with closed windows on either side. As you reach each window, an unknown hand opens it and the light it lets in only increases by contrast the darkness of the end of the passage.

---

[1] Prime Minister's Personal Telegram, T.743, 25 October 1941: Churchill papers, 20/44.
[2] 'Report by the Parliamentary Private Secretary', 24 October 1941: Harvie-Watt papers.

'Considering the burden of responsibility he was bearing,' Brooke added, 'his lightheartedness was unbelievable.'[1]

The decision to halt 'Ajax' had been a blow to Churchill, but worse was to come. On the night of October 27 the Chief of Staffs, and Pound in particular, successfully challenged 'Whipcord', and, as Cadogan noted in his diary, 'we buried it and put up a little headstone. Poor Winston very depressed'.[2] All the benefits which he had set out in his telegram to Lyttelton less than forty-eight hours before were now as if they had never been.

The three Commanders in Cairo had already telegraphed that 'Whipcord' could not be 'regarded as essential', and would indeed, if maintained, prove a 'drain' on resources needed in Libya itself.[3] In view of this telegram, Churchill minuted for the Chiefs of Staff on October 28, 'and of your own decisive abandonment of the project "Whipcord", which you advocated and which I espoused, I now consider that plan at an end.'

But the loss of one plan merely served to focus Churchill's mind on others, and from the ruin of 'Whipcord' he proposed the creation of 'Gymnast', to take advantage of a British victory in Libya being followed either by a change in French morale, or by a German demand on Vichy for the use of French North Africa in consequence of the loss of Tripoli. At such a moment, Churchill wrote, Weygand might ask for a British occupation of Bizerta or Casablanca. Britain 'must be ready to profit by so great a turn of fortune'. Churchill added:

I have received advices from America that our friends there are much attracted by the idea of American intervention in Morocco, and Colonel Knox[4] talked to Lord Halifax about 150,000 United States troops being landed there. We must be ready, if possible, with a simultaneous offer, or anyhow a British offer, to General Weygand at any moment which seems timely after a success in 'Crusader'. This might turn the scale in our favour. The offer should therefore be couched in most effective terms.[5]

All now depended upon the imminent battle in Libya. 'It may be,' Churchill wrote to Auchinleck on October 31, 'that the luck will hold and certainly the destruction of the enemy armour will open the door

---

[1] Brooke diary, 26 October 1941: Arthur Bryant, *The Turn of the Tide*, London 1956, page 263. 'Bumper' was an anti-invasion exercise.

[2] Cadogan diary, 27 October 1941: David Dilks (editor), *The Diaries of Sir Alexander Cadogan OM, 1938–1945*, London 1971, page 410.

[3] Tender No. 23, 'Most Immediate', 'Hush', Middle East No. 0/19301, 27 October 1941, received at 11 p.m.: Churchill papers, 20/44.

[4] United States Secretary of the Navy.

[5] Prime Minister's Personal Minute, D.288/1, 'Most Secret', 28 October 1941: Premier papers, 3/503/1, 2, folios 2–4.

to many possibilities.' At present Britain had 'scarcely any military credit', so that it was 'little use talking to the United States, to Russia, to Spain, to Turkey or to Weygand'. With success in Libya, he would try, Churchill explained, to 'win' Weygand by the offer 'of a substantial force', and to this end was not without hope 'of obtaining American support'. As to the abandonment of 'Whipcord', Churchill told Auchinleck: 'The Chiefs of Staff were so keen upon it and so were the appointed Commanders. It was, however, perhaps "a task beyond the compass of our stride",' nor, he added, did he think the opportunity would 'remain open'. Churchill's letter continued with a reference to one of Auchinleck's earlier reasons for the delay in his offensive:

I am going to have an enquiry for my personal information into the tragical lack of contact between the War Office and the Ministry of Supply on the one hand and Middle East reception on the other about the front axles of the 22nd Armoured Brigade. This is not so much for the purpose of fixing responsibility as for avoiding a recurrence of such break-downs. Considering the many months over which tanks have been passing from us to you, it is astonishing that no one at your end thought of saying "We distrust all your axles and are fitting on stubs to strengthen them thus taking (so many) days"; or that no one from our end arrived with the tanks able to answer all your questions and to give a good warrant. . . .

'On such mishaps,' Churchill commented, 'the fates of battles and of empires turn.' His letter ended:

I am greatly cheered by what the Brigadier has told me of the way in which you are concentrating all your power upon the destruction of the enemy's armour and of his armed force generally. Here is the true principle. '. . . seek ye first the kingdom of God; and all these things shall be added unto you'[1], or, as Napoleon put it, 'Frappez la masse et tout le reste vient par surcroît.'[2]

Brigadier Whiteley took this letter with him when he flew back to Auchinleck's headquarters in Cairo on October 31. He also took with him a personal letter from Churchill to his son, in which Churchill again surveyed both family and national panoramas, telling Randolph, on the personal front:

Your sisters have chosen the roughest roads they could find. Mary is Acting Temporary Unpaid Lance Bombadier and will in five or six weeks probably be promoted Sergeant. I hope she will presently be posted to a mixed battery

[1] St Matthew, chapter 6, verse 33.

[2] 'Most Secret', 30 October 1941: Churchill papers, 20/22. The Brigadier was Brigadier Whiteley, whom Auchinleck had sent to London to explain to Churchill the reasons for the final delay, and the detailed plan of attack.

in one of the parks near London so that we shall be able to see something of her on her leave. These two months of Amazonian Sparta have made a man of Judy[1] and also contrariwise improved her looks. Sarah, casting aside about £4,000 of contracts, is undergoing austerities with the WAAF. We think they are very heroic. They are certainly braver than the lady in 'The Black Mousquetaire' who 'did not mind death, but couldn't stand pinching'.

As for the wider war, Churchill told his son:

Things are pretty hard here now that the asthma season has come on and Max fights everybody and resigns every day. The Communists are posing as the only patriots in the country. The Admirals, Generals and Air Marshals chant their stately hymn of 'Safety First'. The Shinwells, Wintertons and Hore-Belishas do their best to keep us up to the mark. In the midst of this I have to restrain my natural pugnacity by sitting on my own head. How bloody![2]

October 1941 had ended with a fierce complaint from Cripps that Britain was not providing Russia with adequate aid or support, and that if Britain could not open a second front, then British troops, not less than a Corps, with an adequate proportion of Royal Air Force support, must be rushed to either the northern or southern extremities of the Russian battle front. 'Surely it is possible,' Cripps asked, 'to send either to Murmansk or through Iran at least 1 or 2 fully armed divisions to fight on the Russian front.'

Cripps proposed that he and General Mason-Macfarlane, head of the British Military Mission to Russia, should return to Britain to press and elaborate on this request. The Russians, he stressed, were deeply suspicious of Britain's lack of help, and motives.[3]

Churchill was deeply distressed by this complaint. He at once drafted a reply, which, after it had been amended in only two phrases, was telegraphed to Cripps at Kuibyshev. The telegram, sent on the afternoon of October 28, read, in full:

I fully sympathize with you in your difficult position, and also with Russia in her agony. They certainly have no right to reproach us. They brought their own fate upon themselves when by their Pact with Ribbentrop they let Hitler loose on Poland and so started the war. They cut themselves off from an effective second front when they let the French Army be destroyed. If prior to June 22 they had consulted with us beforehand, many arrangements could have been made to bring the great help we are now sending them in munitions earlier.

[1] Judy Montagu, daughter of Clementine Churchill's cousin, Venetia Montagu. Her father, Edwin Montagu, had died in 1921.

[2] Letter of 30 October 1941: Churchill papers, 1/362.

[3] Telegram No. 14 from Kuibyshev, 23 October 1941: Foreign Office papers, 954/24, folio 454.

We did not however know till Hitler attacked them whether they would fight or what side they would be on. We were left alone for a whole year while every Communist in England, under orders from Moscow, did his best to hamper our war effort. If we had been invaded and destroyed in July or August 1941, or starved out this year in the Battle of the Atlantic, they would [only have laughed[1] and] have remained utterly indifferent. If they had moved when the Balkans were attacked, much might have been done, but they left it all to Hitler to choose his moment and his foes.

That a Government with this record should accuse us of trying to make conquests in Africa or gain advantages in Persia at their expense, or being willing to fight to the last Russian soldier, leaves me quite cool.

If they harbour suspicions of us it is only because of the guilt and self-reproach in their own hearts.

We have acted with absolute honesty. We have done our very best to help them at the cost of deranging all our plans for rearmament and exposing ourselves to heavy risks when the Spring invasion comes. We will do anything more in our power that is sensible, but it would be silly to send two or three British or British-Indian divisions into the heart of Russia to be surrounded and cut to pieces as a symbolic sacrifice. Russia has never been short of man power, and has now millions of trained soldiers for whom modern equipment is required. That modern equipment we are sending and shall send to the utmost limit of the ports and communications.

Meanwhile we shall presently be fighting ourselves as the result of long-prepared plans, which it would be madness to upset. We have offered to relieve the five Russian divisions in Northern Persia, which can be done with Indian troops fitted to maintain internal order but not equipped to face Germans. I am sorry that Molotov rejects the idea of our sending modest forces to the Caucasus. We are doing all we can to keep Turkey a friendly neutral and prevent her being tempted by German promises of territorial gain at Russia's expense. Naturally we do not expect gratitude from men undergoing such frightful bludgeonings and fighting so bravely, but neither need we be disturbed by their reproaches. There is of course no need for you to rub all these salt truths into the Russian wounds, but you must have a robust conviction[2] of the loyalty, integrity and courage of the British nation.

I do not think it would be any use for you and Macfarlane to fly home now. I could only repeat what I have said here, and I hope I shall never be called upon to argue the case in public. I am sure your duty is to remain with these people in their ordeal, from which it is by no means certain that they will not emerge victorious. Any day now Hitler may call a halt in the East & turn his forces against us.[3]

[1] This phrase was deleted at Eden's suggestion.

[2] At Eden's suggestion this was changed to: 'you must do your utmost to convince the Russians'.

[3] Prime Minister's Personal Telegram, T.759, 28 October 1941: Churchill papers, 20/44. A copy of this telegram was sent to the King.

On November 1 German troops, having broken into the Crimea, captured Simferopol, the Crimean capital, and on November 3 entered the city of Kursk, in the eastern Ukraine. Despite these Soviet reverses, Churchill minuted to the Chiefs of Staff on November 3, 'There can be no question of our going back on our promises to Russia.' If Archangel froze up, 'we must do our best by other routes'. But it was too soon to 'raise any such issues now, when the ink is hardly dry on our promises, and we have been unable to do anything else to help the Russians'.[1]

'I do hope our supplies are being cleared from Archangel as fast as they come in,' Churchill telegraphed to Stalin on November 4. 'A trickle is now beginning through Persia. We shall pump both ways to our utmost.' Tanks and aircraft, Churchill wrote, 'are sent at our peril and we are anxious that they should have the best chance'. Direct orders from Stalin were therefore needed to ensure that the materials were not misused. 'I cannot tell you about our immediate military plans,' Churchill ended, 'any more than you can tell me about yours, but rest assured we are not going to be idle.'[2]

In order to 'plan for the future', Churchill telegraphed to Stalin on the following day, he was ready to send Wavell 'to meet you in Moscow, Kuibyshev, Tiflis or wherever you wish'. Wavell was Commander-in-Chief, not only in India, but in Persia and Iraq. He could come with General Paget, 'Commander-in-Chief secretly designate for the Far East', who had been 'in the centre of things here'. These two officers, Churchill added, 'can reach you in about a fortnight. Do you want them?'[3]

Churchill then turned to the appeal from Stalin for a British declaration of War on Finland, Hungary and Rumania. Such a declaration, he said, would only be 'a formality, because our extreme blockade is already against them'. His telegram continued.

My judgement is against it because, first, Finland has many friends in the United States and it is more prudent to follow Mr Cordell Hull's guidance about that. Secondly, Rumania and Hungary: these countries are full of our friends; they have been overpowered by Hitler and used as a catspaw. But if fortune turns against that ruffian they might easily come back to our side. A British declaration of war would only freeze them all and make it look as if Hitler were the head of a grand European alliance solid against us.

[1] Prime Minister's Personal Minute, M.1027/1, 3 November 1941: Churchill papers, 20/36.
[2] 'Personal and Secret', Prime Minister's Personal Telegram, T.776, Foreign Office Telegram No. 78 to Kuibyshev, 4 November 1941: Foreign Office papers, 954/24, folio 488.
[3] Stalin replied that he would only receive Wavell and Paget if they could include an understanding 'on war aims and on plans of the post-war organization of peace' and an agreement 'on mutual military assistance in Europe'. ('Personal Message', 8 November 1941: Premier papers, 3/170/1, folios 73–5.)

'Do not pray suppose,' Churchill continued, 'it is any want of zeal or comradeship that makes us doubt the advantage of this step.'[1]

In the first week of November, Churchill received a discouraging telegram from General Smuts. 'I am struck,' wrote Smuts, 'by the growth of the impression here and elsewhere that the war is going to end in stalemate and thus fatally for us.'

Smuts believed that the principal need and urgency was the entry of the United States into the war, which, he believed, 'may decisively warn off Japan and do more than anything else in keeping Russia in the war'. It was essential, Smuts argued, for Churchill to intervene personally with Roosevelt. 'I trust you are on the lookout,' Smuts added, 'for the right moment and manner of appeal to him for action.'[2]

Churchill replied that he did not think 'it would be any use' for him to make a personal appeal to Roosevelt, and he went on to explain to Smuts:

At the Atlantic Meeting I told his circle that I would rather have an American declaration of war now and no supplies for six months than double the supplies and no declaration. When this was repeated to him he thought it a hard saying. We must not underrate his Constitutional difficulties. He may take action as Chief Executive but only Congress can declare war. He went so far as to say to me: 'I shall never declare war; I shall make war. If I were to ask Congress to declare war they might argue about it for three months.

Churchill went on to point out to Smuts that in the American Congress 'it is all a matter of counting heads'. His telegram ended: 'Naturally if I saw any way of helping to lift this situation on to a higher plane I would do so. In the meanwhile we must have patience and trust to the tide which is flowing our way and to events.'[3]

While awaiting the Libyan offensive, planned for November 18, Churchill could respond no further to Russian requests for military aid. No British bombers or fighters could be sent to help Russia defend the Caucasus until 'Crusader' and its consequences had become clear. 'A plan should however be made,' Churchill minuted for the Chiefs of

---

[1] In the final version of this telegram as sent, Churchill added the sentence: 'Our Dominions, except Australia, are reluctant'. (Premier papers, 3/170/1, folio 78.)

[2] Telegram No. 1339, 'Secret', 4 November 1941: Premier papers, 3/476/3, folio 35.

[3] Prime Minister's Personal Telegram, T.794, 'Personal and Secret', 8 November 1941: Premier papers, 3/476/3, folios 31–2.

Staff on November 5, 'based on a large transference of Air from Libya to Persia,' so as to deny the Baku oilfields to Germany 'as long as possible.' One could not tell, Churchill added, how long Russian forces would retain command of the Black Sea, 'although with their forces it is inexcusable that they should lose it'.[1]

Stalin, angered that Britain had not yet declared war on Finland as he had asked, described this British delay as having created 'an intolerable situation'.[2] As for British military aid, he noted, 'although this is a minor matter', tanks, aeroplanes and artillery were arriving 'inefficiently packed', sometimes with parts of the same vehicles 'loaded in different ships', and with aeroplanes, on account of 'imperfect packing', reaching the Soviet Union broken. But it was the lack of any definite understanding between Britain and Russia 'on war aims and on plans of the post war organization of peace', as well as the lack of agreement on 'material military assistance against Hitler in Europe' that meant there would be difficulty 'to secure mutual confidence'.[3]

This telegram was delivered to Churchill and Eden by Maisky. Churchill, Eden noted in his diary, 'was, excusably, very angry and pretty rough with Maisky'.[4]

An abundance of problems were reaching Churchill's box. On November 8 he learnt that, in the heaviest British bombing raid of the war over Berlin, Cologne and Mannheim, of 300 bombers taking part, 37 had been lost owing to severe freak weather. He had already expressed in blunt terms his opposition to the continuing priority and scale of the bombing offensive. Now, angered by what he regarded as a false emphasis in air policy, he minuted to both Sinclair and Portal on November 11:

I have several times in Cabinet deprecated forcing the night bombing of Germany without due regard to weather conditions. There is no particular point at this time in bombing Berlin. The losses sustained last week were more grievous. We cannot afford losses on that scale in view of the short-fall of the

---

[1] Prime Minister's Personal Minute, D.293/1, 5 November 1941: Cabinet papers, 120/689.

[2] Churchill later replied to this charge: 'About Finland. I was quite ready to advise the Cabinet to declare war upon Finland when I sent you my telegram of September 4. Later information has made me think that it will be more helpful to Russia and the common cause if the Finns can be got to stop fighting and stand still or go home, than if we put them in the dock with the guilty Axis powers by a formal declaration of war and make them fight it out to the end. However, if they do not stop in the next fortnight and you still wish us to declare war on them, we will certainly do so.' (Prime Minister's Personal Telegram, T.844, Foreign Office No. 188 to Kuibyshev, 21 November 1941: Premier papers, 3/170/1, folios 61–4.)

[3] 'Personal Message', delivered on 11 November 1941: Premier papers, 3/170/1, folios 73–5.

[4] Eden diary, 11 November 1941: The Earl of Avon, *The Eden Memoirs, The Reckoning*, London 1965, page 280.

American bomber programme. Losses which are acceptable in a battle or for some decisive military objective ought not be incurred merely as a matter of routine. There is no need to fight the weather and the enemy at the same time.

It was now the 'duty' of both Fighter and Bomber command, Churchill added, 'to re-gather their strength for the spring'.[1]

The problems of confronting a German invasion attempt in the spring of 1942 were enormous, highlighted that same day when Roosevelt offered to send Churchill a confidential United States Army report critical of the condition of the defences in the British Isles.[2]

---

[1] Prime Minister's Personal Minute, M.1038/1, 11 November 1941: Churchill papers, 20/36. A week later, Portal wrote to Churchill: 'It is clearly understood that the November bombing programme will not be carried out unless the weather conditions are reasonable' (Premier papers, 3/11/3, folio 86). But the bomber programme itself was not to be curtailed.

[2] Message of 11 November 1941: Churchill papers, 20/45. Churchill minuted to Ismay: 'We should like to see this criticism, and will profit by any that we think are sound.'

64

'Crusader': 'a prolonged, wearing-down battle'

ON the night of November 8 Churchill learned of a British naval success. Two Italian convoys, bringing military supplies to Tripoli, were intercepted by the Malta-based naval 'Force K', and destroyed: a triumph for the use of Signals Intelligence. Nine out of ten of the supply ships were sunk, as were three of the four destroyers of the escort. It was also 'noteworthy', Churchill reported to Roosevelt, 'that the two Italian heavy cruisers would not face our two 6-inch light cruisers. . . .'[1]

But victory over the Italian convoy, like so many successful operations, provided only momentary satisfaction. On November 12 the aircraft carrier *Ark Royal*, returning to Gibraltar after having flown further aircraft into Malta, was struck by a torpedo from a German U-boat only twenty-five miles from Gibraltar itself. It sank on the following day. Fortunately, of its ships complement of 1,600, there was only a single casualty.

In preparation for 'Crusader', Tedder's pilots had bombed German positions throughout Cyrenaica. Churchill learned of their success from the Enigma decrypts. 'I am very glad to see,' he telegraphed to Tedder on the morning of November 13, 'from most secret sources, good effects

[1] Prime Minister's Personal Telegram, T.797, 'Personal and Secret', 9 November 1941: Churchill papers, 20/44. The destruction of the convoy had only been possible because of intercepted messages which, when decyphered, had given in advance the precise route and timing of the convoys and their escorts. Churchill was worried lest the secrecy of Britain's signals intelligence had been endangered. 'C' was asked about a signal from Malta giving details of the convoy, and replied reassuringly: 'The Malta signal was sent out as the result of an aircraft sighting, which quite naturally corresponded with our own Most Secret information. The signal, however, was based on the aircraft sighting and not on our material. No security, therefore, was disregarded'. ('Most Secret', C/8035, 12 November 1941: Cabinet papers, 120/766.)

of your attacks,' and he added: 'I hope it will be crescendo.'[1] To this, Tedder replied on the same morning: 'Thank you for your message. Real crescendo begins tomorrow.'[2]

In the third week of November, Churchill finally made a move he had long contemplated, the replacement of Sir John Dill as Chief of The Imperial General Staff. Early in October he had asked Oliver Lyttelton if he thought Lord Gort should return to the post which he had held from 1937 to 1939, before commanding the British Expeditionary Force in France, and Lyttelton had replied strongly in Gort's favour: 'Above all he is always thinking of soldiering and of getting at the enemy.'[3] But Churchill's choice was the Commander-in-Chief, Home Forces, General Sir Alan Brooke, whom he invited to Chequers on November 16 in order to ask if he was prepared to take over from Dill. Contemplating the magnitude of the task, and the extra work which it would entail, Brooke was silent for a while. In his diary he recorded the sequel:

The PM misunderstood my silence and said: 'Do you not think you will be able to work with me? We have so far got on well together.' I had to assure him that these were not my thoughts, though I am fully aware that my path will not be strewn with rose petals. But I have the greatest respect and real affection for him, so that I hope I may be able to stand the storms of abuse which I may well have to bear frequently.

He then went on to explain the importance he attached to the appointment, and the fact that the Chiefs of Staff Committee must be the body to direct military events over the whole world. He also stated that his relations with me must from now on approximate to those of a Prime Minister to one of his Ministers. Nobody could be nicer than he was, and finally, when we went to bed at 2 a.m., he came with me to my bedroom to get away from the others, took my hand and and looking into my eyes with an exceptionally kind look, said: 'I wish you the very best of luck'.[4]

In a minute to David Margesson, reporting Brooke's acceptance,

[1] Prime Minister's Personal Telegram, T.805, 'Most Secret', 'Most Immediate', Air Ministry No. X 319, 13 November 1941, sent 7.05 a.m.: Churchill papers, 20/45.

[2] 'Immediate', 'Most Secret', 13 November 1941, 11.41 a.m. (received 3.35 p.m.): Churchill papers, 20/45.

[3] Letter of 4 October 1941: Churchill papers, 20/27.

[4] Brooke diary, 16 November 1941: Arthur Bryant, *The Turn of the Tide 1939–1943*, London 1965, page 266.

Churchill commented, about Brooke himself: 'He is a combination of wisdom and vigour which I have found refreshing.'[1]

On receiving Brooke's formal acceptance of the new post, Churchill wrote to him:

My Dear Brooke,

Thank you for your kind letter. I did not expect that you would be grateful or overjoyed at the hard anxious task to which I summoned you. But I feel that my old friendship for Ronnie and Victor, the companions of gay subaltern days and early wars, is a personal bond between us, to which will soon be added the comradeship of action in fateful events.[2]

Perhaps the closest 'comradeship of action' between Churchill and any other single person during the Second World War was his friendship with Lord Cherwell. Churchill was therefore angered when, on November 11, a Conservative MP, Waldron Smithers, asked a number of critical questions in the House of Commons about Cherwell's salary and appointment, even hinting that the Professor was an alien. Churchill's Parliamentary Private Secretary, George Harvie-Watt, later recalled: 'The PM was livid, rightly so, and said in an aside to me, "Love me, love my dog, and if you don't love my dog you damn well can't love me."'[3]

*   *   *

[1] 'Most Secret', Prime Minister's Personal Minute, M.1052/1, 17 November 1941. Brooke was succeeded as Commander-in-Chief, Home Forces, by General Paget. Major-General Nye was appointed Vice-Chief of the Imperial General Staff. Sir John Dill was appointed Governor of Bombay, but in December 1941 he accompanied Churchill to Washington, remaining in the United States as Head of the British Joint Staff Mission until his death in November 1944.

[2] Letter dated 18 November 1941: Churchill papers, 20/22. Of Brooke's brother Victor, Churchill later wrote: 'Victor was a subaltern in the 9th Lancers when I joined the 4th Hussars, and I formed a warm friendship with him in 1895 and 1896. His horse reared up and he fell over backwards, breaking his pelvis, and he was sorely stricken for the rest of his life. However, he continued to be able to serve and ride, and perished gloriously from sheer exhaustion whilst acting as liaison officer with the French Cavalry Corps in the retreat from Mons in 1914'. Of Ronald Brooke, Churchill wrote: 'In the Boer War he was Adjutant of the South African Light Horse, and I for some months during the relief of Ladysmith was Assistant Adjutant, the regiment having six squadrons. Together we went through the fighting at Spion Kop, Vaal Krantz, and the Tugela. I learned much about tactics from him. Together we galloped into Ladysmith on the night of its liberation. Later on, in 1903, although I was only a youthful Member of Parliament, I was able to help him to the Somaliland campaign, in which he added to his high reputation. He was stricken down by arthritis at an early age, and could only command a reserve brigade at home during the First World War. Our friendship continued till his premature death in 1925'. (Winston S. Churchill, *The Second World War*, volume 2, London 1949, page 233, note 2.)

[3] G. S. Harvie-Watt, *Most of My Life*, London 1980, page 63. Harvie-Watt's account continued: 'Afterwards Winston left the Chamber of the House with me and went to the Smoke Room. I've never seen him in such a temper before. Later Waldron Smithers came up with his tail between

In the third week of November, Churchill was angered by a series of telegrams from Kuibyshev, in which Sir Stafford Cripps not only protested that Britain was not doing enough to help Russia, but informed Churchill that he wished to give up his post as Ambassador and return to Britain, to become the public champion of the Soviet cause. On November 16 Churchill telegraphed:

... I am sure it would be a mistake from your point of view to leave your post and abandon the Russians and the Soviet cause with which you are so closely associated while all hangs in the balance at Leningrad, Moscow and in the south. Your own friends here would not understand it.

I hope you will believe that I give you this advice not from any fear of political opposition which you might raise over here by making out we had not done enough, etc. I could face such opposition without any political embarrassment, though with much personal regret.

The Soviet Government, as you must see upon reflection, could never support you in an agitation against us because that would mean that we should be forced to vindicate our action in public which would necessarily be detrimental to Soviet interests and to the common cause. Force of circumstances would compel them to make the best of us.

'After all,' Churchill told Cripps, 'we have wrecked our Air and Tank expansion programmes for their sake, and in our effort to hold German Air power in the west we have lost more than double the pilots and machines lost in the Battle of Britain last year.' Churchill's telegram continued:

You must not underrate the strength of the case I could deploy in the House of Commons and on the broadcast, though I should be very sorry to do so. The Government itself was never so strong or unchallenged as it is now. Every movement of the United States towards the war adds to that strength.

'You should weigh all this,' Churchill ended, 'before engaging in a most unequal struggle which could only injure the interests to which you are attached'.[1]

On November 21 Churchill explained to Stalin the 'very solid understanding' he had established between himself and Roosevelt by personal correspondence, which 'has often helped in getting things done quickly'. Churchill added: 'My only desire is to work on equal terms of comradeship and confidence with you.' To make a 'broad survey' of

---

his legs and started grovelling to Winston who told him to get the hell out of here and not to speak to him again. Poor Smithers got the shock of his life.'

[1] 'Personal and Secret', 15 November 1941: Premier papers, 3/170/1, folios 67-8.

the war, he proposed sending Eden to Moscow 'in the near future' with high military and other experts.

On the question of Britain's aid to Russia, Churchill told Stalin that because of shipping and communication problems, 'you will have to choose between troops and supplies across Persia'. As for Stalin's wish to discuss the post-war organization of peace, Churchill told the Soviet Leader:

Our intention is to fight the war in alliance with you and in constant consultation with you, to the utmost of our strength and however long it lasts, and when the war is won, as I am sure it will be, we expect that Soviet Russia, Great Britain and the United States will meet at the Council table of the victors as the three principal partners and agencies by which Nazism will have been destroyed.

Naturally, the first object will be to prevent Germany and particularly Prussia breaking out upon us for a third time.

The fact that Russia is a Communist State and Britain and the United States are not and do not intend to be, is not any obstacle to our making a good plan for our mutual safety and rightful interests.

Churchill's telegram ended:

It may well be that your defence of Moscow and Leningrad, as well as the splendid resistance to the invader along the whole Russian front, will inflict mortal injuries upon the internal structure of the Nazi régime. But we must not count upon such good fortune, but simply keep on striking at them to the utmost with might and main.[1]

Churchill's confidence in the winter's war had increased in mid-November, not only by news of strong Russian resistance in front of Moscow, but by the amendment in Washington of the Neutrality Act, to allow United States merchant ships to be armed. 'The American decision,' wrote Beaverbrook, 'is worth more than many millions of tons of shipping. It is victory for you in the Battle of the Atlantic where you fought so long & such a lonely struggle.'[2] On the night that the Neutrality Act was amended, Churchill was dining at the Other Club. Among the Other Club members present was Lord Camrose, who wrote to his son Seymour:

I sat next to our friend last night. He seemed to be quite optimistic and thought things were going along rather well for us. On his advices,[3] Moscow is not likely to fall and, in any case, the Russians have made, and are making,

[1] Prime Minister's Personal Telegram, T.844; Foreign Office Telegram No. 188 to Kuibyshev, 21 November 1941: Premier papers, 3/170/1, No. 21.
[2] Letter dated 14 November 1941: Churchill papers, 20/24.
[3] In fact, a close reading of the Enigma decrypts, including 'Vulture'.

large preparations for munition works well to the East. He had nothing much to say about the South but did not seem to view it as too critical.

He feels that the country has settled down and is no longer resentful about the absence of the second front. . . .

I had a talk with him about his own position at the end of the war. His present decision is to retire immediately we have what he called 'turned the corner'. By this, of course, he means achieved victory. If he were 50 or 55 he would still be looking forward to a political career and would be planning his future; but as he was now nearing 70 he viewed his own future in quite a different way. He was fully determined not to make the ghastly error that LG had made, but he felt, in any case, that his age precluded him from planning to be a big figure in the long and complicated negotiations which the peace would involve.

While he did not say so, I am sure he also has in mind the idea that he should make provision for his family. To do this he would have to be able to write. I ventured to say to him that in all probability the country would demand that he continued in power in the absence of anybody arising of the same quality to take his place. He agreed that this might be the case, but maintained that he himself could not view such a thing with satisfaction having regard to his age.

I had arranged for the Telegraph to send me a message immediately they received the result of the Neutrality Act vote at Washington. I passed it across the table to Fred Lawson (who was in the Chair) to announce. Needless to say, it was received with great enthusiasm and Winston was highly delighted. He said he did not care a damn about the smallness of the Majority.[1] The thing was that the President now had power to act and the size of the majority would soon be forgotten. He anticipated great things from this new decision and I could see he feels that it cannot now be many days before America is finally in the war.[2]

Good news from the United States, hopeful news from Russia, the aid of a new Chief of the Imperial General Staff with whom he was very sure that he would be able to work 'in harmony'[3]: these combined to lessen Churchill's agitation.[4] And now at last his longed-for offensive was about to begin in the western desert. There, on the night of November 17, a British Commando force landed from the sea, two

[1] On the question of arming United States merchant ships, after a Senate vote of 50 to 37, the vote in the House of Representatives was 212 to 194. This gave Roosevelt less support from his own Democrats than he had obtained on Lend-Lease.

[2] Letter dated 14 November 1941: Camrose papers.

[3] Churchill to Margesson, 17 November 1941, Prime Minister's Personal Minute, M.1054/1, 'Secret': Churchill papers, 20/36.

[4] Churchill continued to make time to receive visitors from the United States. On November 21 Bebe Daniels and Ben Lyon brought him five special thumbs up badges which were being sold in New York by Mayor La Guardia on behalf of the British War Relief Society in the United States. Four days later he received John B. Snyder, Chairman of the Military Appropriations Sub-Committee of the House of Representatives.

hundred miles behind German lines, to attack Rommel's headquarters at Apollonia. Rommel, however, their target, was absent in Rome, and Lieutenant-Colonel Keyes, son of Admiral of the Fleet Sir Roger Keyes, was killed in the fighting inside one of the headquarter's houses, wrongly believed to be Rommel's.[1]

This setback, and the losses sustained, were but a prelude to the larger battle. 'I hope,' Randolph Churchill had written to his father from Cairo five days before the main attack on Rommel's forces, 'you will soon have some news which will make it easier for you to make a speech than it is at the moment.'[2] 'Now is the time', Churchill had telegraphed to Auchinleck for release on the eve of the battle, 'to strike the hardest blow yet struck for final victory, home, and freedom. The Desert Army may add a page to history which will rank with Blenheim and Waterloo.'[3]

In the early hours of November 18, in heavy rain, soldiers of the Eighth Army broke across the Libyan frontier, westwards into Cyrenaica. Operation 'Crusader' had begun. 'PM very impatient,' John Martin noted in his diary, 'at absence of news of its progress'.[4] But as Auchinleck explained that same day, wireless silence was being maintained for security, and weather was 'hampering air observation', so that there was 'no definite news of progress', but, Auchinleck added, 'we assume it to be satisfactory'.[5]

By nightfall on November 18, advances had been made of up to fifty miles towards Tobruk. 'I have forbidden all mention in Press of big offensive,' Churchill telegraphed to Auchinleck on November 19, 'but this cannot surely be necessary or possible for long,' and he added: 'We are puzzled at hearing nothing from you.'[6] When, however, that same day, Auchinleck issued from Cairo a communiqué on the battle, Churchill telegraphed again: 'I would rather you had not released a communiqué from Cairo in these circumstances, as we have to deal with

[1] An Enigma decrypt, disclosing that Rommel, having flown to Rome on November 1, would not return to North Africa until the evening of November 18, was sent to the Middle East in an emergency signal (OL 2008 of 17 November 1941), but must have arrived too late to stop the Commando attack (F. H. Hinsley and others, *British Intelligence in the Second World War: Its Influence on Strategy and Operations*, volume 2, London 1981, page 303). Colonel Keyes was awarded a posthumous Victoria Cross for his part in the raid.

[2] 'HQ, 8 Army, In the field', 13 November 1941: Churchill papers, 1/362. Randolph added: 'Is it true that the Abyssinians cabled you "We've finished the job; shall we send you the tools?" We all hope so'.

[3] Prime Minister's Personal Telegram, T.815, 15 November 1941: Churchill papers, 20/45.

[4] Martin diary, 18 November 1941: Martin papers.

[5] Susan No. 1593, sent 10.30 p.m., 18 November 1941: Churchill papers, 20/45.

[6] Prime Minister's Personal Telegram, T.827, 11.30 a.m., 19 November 1941: Churchill papers, 20/45.

press and public here.'[1] As for the text of the communiqué, Churchill added, it was 'perhaps precipitate in praising at so early a stage the skill and deception employed. It is much better to let events tell their own tale'.[2]

On November 19, advanced British units captured Sidi Rezegh, only ten miles south of Tobruk. It was, Churchill cautioned the House of Commons on November 20, 'far too soon to indulge in any exultation'. Positions had, however, been obtained of 'marked advantage'. All now depended on the battle which would follow.[3]

Even as Churchill spoke, Rommel's Panzergruppe Afrika, encircled by British forces, was giving battle with tanks over an area of more than forty square miles. 'Only now,' Churchill telegraphed to Roosevelt, did the enemy 'realise the large scale of our operations against him'. Orders had been given 'to press what is now begun to a decision at all costs'.

Churchill also sent Roosevelt his thoughts and hopes for the effect of the battle on French north Africa, and of the part which the United States itself would play in influencing the Vichy authorities there. As he explained to the President:

It would be disastrous if Weygand were to be replaced by some pro-Hun officer just at the moment when we are likely to be in a position to influence events in North Africa both from the East and from home. I hope you will try your utmost to persuade Vichy to preserve Weygand in his command.

If this cannot be achieved some friendly figure from retirement, like General Georges, might be agreed upon. I have not seen Georges since the collapse, but I have reasons to believe his heart is sound. I knew him very well.

Anyhow, Mr President, Tunis and all French North Africa might open out

[1] On the following day Churchill minuted to Bracken: 'G.H.Q., M.E., will issue its own communiqués to the world through London, and only through London. These communiqués can be either joint or from the Services individually. Only in very exceptional circumstances will any amendment be made. Special arrangements will be made to ensure no delay. There is no need to encypher communiqués. A special staff to be organised at W.O. No newspaper material is to emanate directly from Cairo. Whether Dominion or foreign, it is to come through here. There is no intention to censor or delay any Press matter passed by the Middle East censor. It will merely pass through our nozzle so as to ensure uniform delivery to the world. Only in very exceptional cases will any alteration be made here. Special arrangements are being made to ensure almost instantaneous release. Everything put out by Cairo should be sent *en clair* to us.' (Prime Minister's Personal Minute, M.1056/1A, 20 November 1941: Churchill papers, 20/36.)

[2] Prime Minister's Personal Telegram, T.831, 19 November 1941: Churchill papers, 20/45. 'I will ensure', Auchinleck replied, 'that communiqués issued from here are confined to bald statements and not embroidered in any way', and he went on strongly to urge that future communiqués, if issued in London, should be 'published as drafted here and not altered'. (Telegram No. I/28754, 20 November 1941, sent 5.54 p.m.: Churchill papers, 20/45.)

[3] *Hansard*, 20 November 1941, columns 467–8.

to us if we gain a good victory in Libya, and we must be ready to exploit success. I am afraid, on the other hand, lest Hitler may demand to occupy Bizerta in view of possible danger to Tripoli.

'It is now or never with the Vichy French,' Churchill ended, 'and their last chance of redemption.'[1]

On the evening of November 21 Auchinleck sent Churchill hopeful news. The Tobruk garrison had made a 'sally' that morning, and was said 'to be progressing slowly but steadily towards Sidi Rezegh'. A marked feature of all the operations to date, Auchinleck added, had been 'our complete air supremacy and excellent co-operation between ground and air'. As for the German tank losses, no firm estimate was possible 'as battle has moved and is moving with such speed, but there is no doubt that he has been hard hit'.[2]

Churchill was delighted with 'the very full information now flowing', for which he thanked Auchinleck on November 22, while asking Auchinleck for any material he might be able to use in a forthcoming broadcast. He was anxious, he said, while speaking only 'on most general lines', nevertheless:

. . . to make any success tell fully all over the world, and especially with the French. The moment we can really claim a victory I propose to address the President about an offer to Vichy. I fear very much the Germans may get hold of Bizerta unless we can rouse the French to a last effort. This can only be done through Roosevelt. It is not impossible he might offer troops.

Let me know for my most secret information how your mind is moving towards extensive exploitation westwards. It may be things will go with a run, in which case I presume you will run considerable risks with your light forces.

Everything seems to have gone splendidly so far.[3]

That same evening, Churchill learned from Auchinleck of the 'remarkable success in the fighting of the American Light tanks'.[4] That same night, Churchill repeated this information to Roosevelt.[5]

---

[1] Prime Minister's Personal Telegram, T.832, 20 November 1941: Churchill papers, 20/45.

[2] Susan No. 1600, despatched 9.55 p.m., received 10.50 p.m., 21 November 1941: Churchill papers, 20/45.

[3] Prime Minister's Personal Telegram, T.843, 3 p.m., 22 November 1941: Churchill papers, 20/45.

[4] Telegram No. CS/214, despatched 4.43 p.m., received 7.30 p.m., 22 November 1941: Churchill papers, 20/45.

[5] Prime Minister's Personal Telegram, T.852, 22 November 1941: Churchill papers, 20/45. But two days later he telegraphed to Sir Walter Monckton in Cairo: 'Broadcast tonight by an Australian speaking from battle headquarters referred four times to prowess of American tanks. It is quite right to pay these compliments, but proportion should be observed, remembering that four out of five tanks in the battle are of British manufacture. By overdoing a good thing you may

Ill-news, however, swiftly followed, for while these messages were being exchanged during November 22, Rommel had succeeded in re-capturing Sidi Rezegh, ending the prospect of an early link-up between Auchinleck's forces and the troops besieged in Tobruk. But all did not seem lost. 'Personally,' Churchill telegraphed to Auchinleck, late that night, 'I like the look of things and share your confidence. Prolongation of battle must wear down enemy with his limited resources.'[1]

Churchill's confidence was not mere bravado. As he read the daily batch of Enigma and other decrypts, it became clear that Rommel, for all his thrust and initiative, was running short of armour and fuel. The same decrypts were being sent to Auchinleck direct from Bletchley. Concerned to preserve intact this most secret source, Churchill tele-graphed to Auchinleck on November 23:

C is sending you daily our special stuff. Feel sure you will not let any of this go into battle zone except as statements on your own authority with no trace of origin and not too close a coincidence. There seem great dangers of docu-ments being captured in view of battle confusion.

Churchill's caution ended: 'Excuse my anxiety.'[2] In the event, no hint of Britain's possession of Enigma fell into German hands.

On November 23, as the 5th South African Infantry Brigade was overwhelmed, it became apparent that although German tank losses had been severe, Britain's losses had been even greater. On November 24 Auchinleck flew with Tedder to the Desert Headquarters, of the 8th Army. To their distress, as Auchinleck telegraphed to Churchill three days later, it was evident that General Cunningham 'has now begun to think defensively, mainly because of our large tank losses'.[3] This had already been reported by Lyttelton from Cairo, when he telegraphed to London: 'Cunningham, it appears, is shaken and now thinking in terms of withdrawal and defence.'[4]

Churchill replied at once to Lyttelton: 'General Auchinleck's auth-

---

create reaction and cause ill-feeling in our tank factories, which are working night and day.' (Prime Minister's Personal Telegram, T.860, 24 November 1941: Churchill papers, 20/36.)

[1] Prime Minister's Personal Telegram, T.850, despatched 2.20 a.m., 23 November 1941: Chur-chill papers, 20/45.

[2] Prime Minister's Personal Telegram, T.851, 23 November 1941: Churchill papers, 20/45. Two days later Churchill reiterated: 'Please burn all special stuff and flimsies, while up at the Front.' (Prime Minister's Personal Telegram, T.865, 25 November 1941: Churchill papers, 20/45.)

[3] Susan No. 1609, C.S. 233, 26 November 1941: Churchill papers, 20/45.

[4] Nocop No. 3724, 25 November 1941: Churchill papers, 20/45. On 1 December 1941 Auch-inleck telegraphed to Churchill that General Cunningham 'at my urgent request and much against his will agreed to go on sick list and enter hospital at Alexandria incognito where he still

ority over all Commanders is supreme and all his decisions during the battle will be confirmed by us.'[1] Auchinleck had already decided to appoint Major-General Ritchie in Cunningham's place, and at the same time to issue his own order of the day, to the 8th Army, to continue to press the offensive. The decision to give this order was neither foolhardy nor quixotic, but based upon Enigma decrypts which revealed without ambiguity the extent of Rommel's weakness in armour and reserves. A second intercepted signal was of equal importance: details of an air fuel cargo sailing on board the two oil transports *Maritza* and *Procida*. Churchill was most anxious, on reading this Intelligence, that Admiral Cunningham should see the decrypts themselves, in which the arrival of the fuel on board these two ships was described as of 'decisive importance'.[2] On November 23 he telegraphed to Auchinleck that he had asked Colonel Menzies 'to emphasise to you the importance' of the decrypt, and he added:

When one sees the invaluable cargoes of fuel now being directed upon Benghazi and the enemy air concentration at Benina, it would seem that quite exceptional risk should be run to sterilise these places, even for three or four days. The enemy's fear of this operation is obvious and well founded. The only time for such a venture is while he is in the throes of the battle. Chance of success will diminish as soon as he has been able to reinforce with troops withdrawing or escaping from the battle zone. There is a lot to be picked up cheap now, both at Benghazi and west of Agheila, which will rise in price enormously once the main battle is over. I am sure you will be considering this.

'Remember,' Churchill added, 'how much they got by brass and bluff at the time of the French collapse.'[3]

Churchill had already asked Sir Dudley Pound to signal to Admiral Cunningham about the 'vital importance' of intercepting the ships bringing reinforcements, supplies 'and above all, fuel to Benghazi'. That same day he signalled direct to Cunningham:

Our information here shows a number of vessels now approaching or starting. Request has been made by enemy for air protection, but this cannot be

---

is. Specialist report says that when admitted to hospital he was suffering from exhaustion and strain and that he will need a month to recuperate' (Susan No. 1629, 1 December 1941: Churchill papers, 20/46).

[1] Prime Minister's Personal Telegram, T.869, 26 November 1941: Churchill papers, 20/45.

[2] M.K. 96 of 23 November 1941 (Bletchley Park to GHQ Cairo, 8th Army, and Naval and Air Commanders).

[3] 'Personal and Most Strictly Secret', Prime Minister's Personal Telegram, T.856, 5.45 p.m., 23 November 1941: Churchill papers, 20/45.

given owing to absorption in battle of his African air force. All this information has been repeated to you. I shall be glad to hear through Admiralty what action you propose to take. The stopping of these ships may save thousands of lives, apart from aiding a victory of cardinal importance.

The primacy of the Enigma decrypts was clear, to those aware of their existence, in the phrase 'Request has been made by enemy for air protection. . . .'[1]

Within twenty-four hours of Churchill's telegrams, the *Maritza* and the *Procida* had been sunk. As a result, the fuel supplies of the air forces supporting Rommel were drastically curtailed.

A further Enigma decrypt of November 25 revealed that, in the opinion of the German air force, the sinking of the two ships had placed the German air operations in Libya in 'real danger'.[2] That same day Auchinleck issued his Order of the Day: 'Attack and pursue. All out everywhere.' A 'close grip upon the enemy by all units', Churchill telegraphed, 'will choke the life out of him'.[3]

Churchill now set out for the Chiefs of Staff Committee his 'forward view on the assumption of success': the immediate initiation of Operation 'Acrobat' for the capture of Tripoli and an advance to the frontiers of Tunisia; asking Roosevelt to offer then to land 150,000 American troops and Marines in Morocco 'if invited by the French', thus enabling the Vichy authorities in French North Africa to defy the Germans.[4] If, however, Vichy were to join with Germany in any active operations, it should be made clear that the British 'will hunt the Vichy Government with perpetual bombing wherever it moves', sinking every French ship 'at sight' and establish immediately 'the most complete blockade of France in our power'.

Alternatively, Churchill wrote, it might, after the conquest of Libya, be 'easier and cheaper in men and materials' to carry the war into Sicily, activating Operation 'Whipcord'.

These were all speculative ideas if Auchinleck and 'Crusader' were successful. But Churchill did not ignore the other possibility, adding:

[1] Prime Minister's Personal Telegram, T.858, 23 November 1941: Churchill papers, 20/36.
[2] MK 191 of 25 November 1941: F. H. Hinsley and others, *British Intelligence in the Second World War: Its Influence on Strategy and Operations*, volume 2, London 1981, page 321–2.
[3] Prime Minister's Personal Telegram, T.865, 25 November 1941: Churchill papers, 20/45.
[4] On November 30 Churchill minuted to Eden: 'I think it most important that the United States should continue their relations with Vichy and their supplies to North Africa and any other contacts unostentatiously for the present. It would be a great mistake to lose any contacts before we know the result of the battle in Libya and its reactions. There is always time to break but it is more difficult to renew contacts.' (Prime Minister's Personal Minute, M.1074/1, 30 November 1941: Premier papers, 3/187, folio 71.)

On the other hand, we may not win 'Crusader'; we may not decide to embark on 'Acrobat': we may fail in 'Acrobat': Pétain may go even more rotten than he is now; French North Africa may pass under German control; an Anglo-American effort may be made to take Dakar; Gibraltar harbour may be rendered untenable and we may have to carry out the island projects. These must be considered the bad developments in the West. Should they occur, the emphasis of our efforts in 1942 will be upon the Eastern Front.[1]

'Am immensely heartened,' Churchill telegraphed to Auchinleck on November 25, 'by your magnificent spirit and will-power. Say "Bravo" to Tedder and RAF on air mastery.'[2]

Hoping to divert the mounting pressure towards Tobruk, Rommel now sent a column of tanks in a deep penetration dash towards the Egyptian frontier. Alerted after the first push by the mass of radio signals in clear, Auchinleck allowed the column to charge ahead, like Rupert at Naseby, until even Rommel began to realise that he had been outwitted. One third of the attacking tanks were destroyed, and by nightfall on November 26 Rommel ordered his surviving tanks back towards Tobruk.

These orders for withdrawal were at once reflected in the decrypted German Enigma messages. 'From usual source,' Churchill telegraphed to Auchinleck on the afternoon of November 27, 'information just received that units 21st German Armoured Div. which have been raiding round Sidi-Omar were to be withdrawn urgently this morning to deal with position around Tobruk which was described as severely threatened.'[3]

Churchill now discussed with Brooke the possibility of a dramatic move. 'CIGS and I,' Churchill telegraphed to Auchinleck later on November 27, 'both wonder whether, as you saved the battle once, you should not go up again and win it now. Your presence on the spot will be an inspiration to all. However, this of course is entirely for you to judge.'[4]

Auchinleck replied that he had in fact, in relieving General Cunningham of command of the 8th Army, 'considered very carefully

[1] 'Most Secret', Prime Minister's Personal Minute, D.302/1, 24 November 1941: Churchill papers, 20/36.
[2] Prime Minister's Personal Telegram, T.865, Susan No. 132, sent 4.15 a.m., 25 November 1941: Churchill papers, 20/45.
[3] Prime Minister's Personal Telegram, T.884, 4 p.m., 27 November 1941: Churchill papers, 20/45.
[4] Prime Minister's Personal Telegram, T.882, 6.27 p.m., War Office No. 134, 27 November 1941: Churchill papers, 20/45.

whether I myself should take his place and command 8th', but had decided 'after much thought' to appoint General Ritchie in Cunningham's place. 'Ritchie is completely in my mind,' Auchinleck added, 'and his plans for future are exactly what I would do in his place.' To supersede Ritchie so soon after his appointment 'might have bad not good effect', Auchinleck added. He had appointed Ritchie after much thought, after concluding 'that I was more useful at GHQ where I could see the whole battle and retain a sense of proportion'.[1]

Churchill had no intention of overruling Auchinleck's judgement. But he did make one further effort to persuade him to change his mind, if only in his personal presence on the battlefield. His final telegram in the exchange read:

CIGS and I do not intend to suggest that you should in any way supersede Ritchie. What we still think would be wise is for you to visit the battlefield should a new impulse be clearly needed. Coming fresh to the scene with your drive and full knowledge of the situation you will put new vigour into the troops and inspire everyone to a supreme effort.

'Nevertheless,' Churchill ended, 'as I said before, this must be a matter for your judgement.'[2]

As to the Enigma and other decrypts, Auchinleck told Churchill he had 'made certain personally that every possible precaution is being taken in regard to your special stuff', the importance of which, he added, 'is fully realized by all concerned'.[3]

On the night of November 27, Randolph Churchill left Cairo to visit the forward zone. 'You will know that I am far from fanciful,' he wrote to his father six days later, and he added: 'I was lying awake in my bed at Battle HQ 7 Armoured Div: & the moon & the clouds combined to give the effect of your face on an enormous scale brooding over the battlefield. It was the most remarkable phenomenon I have ever seen.'[4]

On November 29 the 8th Army announced the capture of General von Ravenstein, the General Officer Commanding the 21st Panzer Division and 600 other ranks. That same morning Auchinleck's supply columns reached Tobruk and Lieutenant-General Godwin-Austen,

[1] Susan No. 1618, despatched 6.50 p.m., received 9.10 p.m., 28 November 1941: Churchill papers, 20/45.

[2] Prime Minister's Personal Telegram, T.895, 29 November 1941: Churchill papers, 20/43. Auchinleck replied (Susan No. 1623 of 29 November 1941): 'Thank you very much I quite understand and will certainly put every ounce of energy I can into maintaining momentum and in this will be ably seconded by Ritchie who has great drive' (Churchill papers, 20/43).

[3] Susan No. 1609, C.S.233, 26 November 1941: Churchill papers, 20/45.

[4] Letter of 3 December 1941: Churchill papers, 1/362.

Commanding 13 Corps, which had effected the relief of the besieged port, telegraphed to Churchill: 'Corridor to Tobruk clear and secure.' Tobruk, he added, 'is as relieved as I am.'[1]

'I am highly complimented by your message,' Churchill replied. '13 Corps have fought a great fight in this astounding battle.'[2]

November 30 was Churchill's 67th birthday.[3] That morning Auchinleck reported to him information from 'usual source', the German's own messages, that the position of the 21st Armoured Division had become 'untenable' owing to the 8th Army's artillery fire on their rear elements. Also 'in difficulties and shouting for help' was the Italian Ariete armoured division 'This looks favourable to me and all here hope it may develop into a real Birthday present for you'.[4] Two days earlier, at the start of their winter counter-offensive, the Russians had re-captured Rostov-on-Don, forcing the Germans under von Kleist to retreat towards Taganrog.

Many friends and colleagues wrote to congratulate Churchill that day. Sir Samuel Hoare wrote from Madrid:

What a year you have had! In some respects it has been like 1758, but far more dangerous to the British people. Today, with Rostov and the Libyan battle it looks as if your next year may follow its predecessor as 1759—a year of victories—followed 1758—a year of peril. May this be so. In any case you can look back with patriotic pride to many great achievements.[5]

'For those who have served with you,' wrote Lord Beaverbrook, 'it will be sufficient glory to be known as Churchill's man.'[6]

Desmond Morton, who had been Churchill's link with the world of Intelligence before the war, and was now his liaison with much Secret Service work, as well as with the Free French movement and other Governments-in-exile, wrote:

On your last birthday the great battle of the Air was won, though we hardly knew it.

[1] Susan No. 1627, paragraph 5, 30 November 1941: Churchill papers 20/46.

[2] Prime Minister's Personal Telegram, T.904, 1 December 1941: Churchill papers, 20/46.

[3] Among 120 birthday telegrams and letters which Churchill received and acknowledged were those from the King and Queen Mary, Bevin, Attlee, Averell Harriman and his daughter Kathleen, the headmaster of Harrow School, the boys of Harrow School, the destroyer HMS *Churchill*, Captain Hillgarth, Harry Hopkins, Lord Moyne, Sinclair, Winant, Wavell, Auchinleck, Smuts, Menzies, Maisky, de Gaulle, Dr Beneš, Dr Weizmann, Halifax, Sikorski, Mihailovic and Stalin. ('Birthday Telegrams and Letters of the Prime Minister': Churchill papers, 2/429.)

[4] Susan No. 1627, paragraph 6, 30 November 1941: Churchill papers, 20/46.

[5] 'Private and Personal', 30 November 1941: Churchill papers, 2/419.

[6] Churchill papers, 2/416.

On this birthday the great battle of the Atlantic is won, though we hardly dare own it.[1]

By next birthday may the great battle of the tank be won under your Leadership, is the prayer of yours most sincerely. . . .[2]

From Harry Hopkins came the telegram: 'Dear Winston. Happy birthday. How old are you anyway? I hope to celebrate the new one with you,'[3] and in a birthday broadcast that day, Leo Amery, who had known Churchill since schooldays at Harrow, told his radio listeners, of Churchill:

He is today the spirit of old England incarnate, with its unshakeable self confidence, its grim gaiety, its unfailing sense of humour, its underlying moral earnestness, its unflinching tenacity. Against that inner unity of spirit between leader and nation the ill-cemented moral fabric of Hitler's perversion of the German soul must be shattered in the end.[4]

On December 1 the newly appointed editor of *The Times*, Robin Barrington-Ward, was invited to lunch at 10 Downing Street. In his diary he recorded his impression of Churchill:

. . . looking (at 67) very fresh and young and spry. He is a different man altogether from the rather bloated individual whom I last saw (close to) before the war. His cheerful, challenging—not to say truculent—look is good to see just now; but it covers up a great deal of caution, even vacillation at times. Perhaps instinctively acquired.

Anyway it is good to see, and the public thinks so too, and it is the right 'face' to put on the vast responsibilities which he is discharging. A lack of the finer perceptions, no doubt! But no doubt either about vigour and purpose. He might and does contradict his appearance by hesitation over risks to be taken, but he would not be found wanting in the last ditch.[5]

While the offensive continued in the western desert, Churchill also followed the progress of two secret British initiatives. Early in December he learned of the success in Spain of the Naval Attaché, Captain Hillgarth, in continuing to seek out and encourage Spaniards who were opposed to any direct Spanish commitment to Germany. Three plans

[1] Morton's optimism was misplaced. Although the British use of the German Naval Enigma decrypts had substantially reduced U-boat attacks on trans-Atlantic merchant ships in the autumn and winter of 1941, a new Enigma machine for U-boats was instituted in February 1942 and not broken for ten months, during which time there were numerous sinkings in the Atlantic, and especially in United States coastal waters.

[2] 'Personal', Churchill papers, 2/420.

[3] Churchill papers, 2/416.

[4] Churchill papers, 2/416.

[5] Barrington-Ward diary, 1 December 1941: text by courtesy of the late Donald MacLachlan.

were evolved, as the Defence Committee were told at the beginning of December 'for stimulating Spanish resistance in the event of a German invasion of Spain'.[1]

The second area of clandestine activity concerned the various underground resistance groups in Yugoslavia. 'Everything in human power should be done,' Churchill had informed both Ismay and Portal on November 28 to help 'the guerilla fighters in Yugoslavia', both those led by General Mihajlovic, and the communist-led Partisans, who had recently come to an agreement to work together against the common foe. 'Please report what is possible,' Churchill asked.[2]

'The morale of the insurgents as a whole is now reported to be high,' Hugh Dalton informed Churchill on December 7. This was 'in spite of the occupation by the Germans of the upper Morava valley' in which many of the partisans had been operating. There was little doubt, Dalton added, that the partisans 'are immobilising not less than 7 German and 12 Italian Divisions. It seems, therefore, absolutely essential to keep the revolt going if we possibly can, and to regard it as an extension of the Libyan front.'[3]

The battles in Africa continued. In Ethiopia the last Italian forces were defeated at Gondar. These operations, Churchill telegraphed to General Fowkes, who had commanded them, 'appear to have been brilliantly conceived, and brilliantly executed'.[4] In Libya, the battle against Rommel continued to go in the 8th Army's favour, but with considerable difficulties in a fierce conflict, and with its objective, the Tunisian frontier, less and less likely of attainment.[5] 'It is too soon,' Churchill minuted for the Chiefs of Staff Committee on December 3, 'to decide how "Crusader" will go.' It was therefore 'no use' thinking about either 'Acrobat' against Tripoli nor 'Gymnast' against Morocco. 'If we are beaten in "Crusader"', he added, 'the enemy will also be severely mauled and we can revert to our defensive positions around Mersa Matruh and in Tobruk without danger of immediate disaster.' This being so, three divisions could be sent to the Russian southern

---

[1] 'SOE Plans for Spain', December 1941: Cabinet papers, 69/3. The first plan was to supply and store automatic weapons and ammunition for anti-Franco groups in Navarre, the second was to bring a number of Spaniards to London 'for training in wireless telegraph communications'. The third was to train in Britain seventy former Spanish Republicans 'to enable them to be landed in Spain and used for demolitions etc. in the event of a German invasion'.

[2] Prime Minister's Personal Minute D.303/1, 28 November 1941 Churchill papers 20/36.

[3] 'Yugoslav Revolt', letter dated 11 December 1941: Cabinet papers 69/3.

[4] Prime Minister's Personal Telegram, T.913, 2 December 1941: Churchill papers, 20/46.

[5] On 1 December 1941 Auchinleck had acceded to Churchill's request and gone to the Advanced Headquarters, where, for ten days, he remained with and supervised General Ritchie's operations.

flank, 'wherever it may rest', provided always that Stalin 'prefers troops to supplies'.[1]

Most pressing of all, for Stalin, was a British declaration of war on Finland. Churchill, hoping to avert this, had telegraphed direct to General Mannerheim, urging him to halt his troops at the 1939 Soviet border. 'I wish,' Churchill had telegraphed to Mannerheim on November 28, 'I could convince your Excellency that we are going to beat the Nazis. I feel far more confident than in 1917 or 1918,' and he added: 'It would be most painful to the many friends of your country in England if Finland found herself in the dock with the guilty and defeated Nazis. My recollections of our pleasant talks and correspondence about the last war lead me to send this purely personal and private message for your consideration before it is too late.'[2]

In reply, Mannerheim rejected Churchill's appeal, and the War Cabinet decided that the declaration of war must go ahead, despite Churchill's own continuing doubts. Indeed, at the midday War Cabinet on December 3 Churchill 'wished it to be on record', as the minutes noted, 'that in his view this declaration on Finland (and also on Hungary and Roumania) would not assist either our cause or that of the Russians. The sole justification for it was that it was necessary in order to satisfy the Russian Government.'

In support of his opposition to declaring war on Hungary, Churchill referred to a statement made by the Hungarian Under-Secretary of State for Foreign Affairs to the United States Minister at Budapest, when informed of Britain's intended declaration of war: 'Now we no longer have two roads, but only one we do not want to follow.'[3]

As to Russian pressure on Britain to open a 'second front', this, Dudley Pound told the Defence Committee that same day, 'we had now done in Libya, and very considerable air forces were being drawn away from the Russian front'. For this reason, and in view of the advantages to be gained 'by pressing on with the offensive in North Africa', the Defence Committee felt it would be 'unwise' to send British forces to the German-Soviet battleground on the Don. It would mean

---

[1] 'Most Secret,' Prime Minister's Personal Minute, D.307/1, 3 December 1941: Churchill papers, 20/36. The Divisions concerned were the 50th, the 18th and an unspecified Indian Division.

[2] Prime Minister's Personal Telegram, T.892, 'Personal, Secret and Private', 28 November 1941: Premier papers, 3/170/1, No. 25.

[3] War Cabinet No. 123 of 1941, 3 December 1941, 12.30 p.m., Minute 1, Confidential Annex: Cabinet papers, 65/24. Britain declared war on Finland, Hungary and Rumania at midnight on 5 December 1941.

'diverting them from the Libyan battle', and could at the same time 'choke the Persian supply line to Russia'.[1]

No British troops, therefore, would be sent to fight alongside the Red Army; and this decision was approved by the War Cabinet that same evening. Also at this War Cabinet, Churchill told his colleagues that whereas Britain had 'fulfilled' its promised deliveries to Russia, 'the American deliveries had lagged behind their undertakings', so much so that they now proposed to divert to Russia shipping which had previously been allocated 'to sustain the Import Programme' to Britain. He only wished, Churchill added, that at an earlier stage in the Russian campaign 'we had found it possible to send 10 squadrons of fighters to the Moscow front'.[2]

From Auchinleck came news of further successes, but without much chance now of a breakthrough towards Tripoli. Churchill took the news calmly. 'Although sudden swift success was desirable,' he replied, 'a prolonged wearing-down battle in Libya is useful and advantageous to us and unduly costly to enemy upon sea communications.' Churchill pointed out that the most recent news from the Russian front, the German retreat from Rostov and Taganrog, would give Auchinleck 'important easement upon your eastern flank', as the danger of a German drive through the Caucasus to Iraq and Syria receded, and, he wrote, 'as long as you are closely locked with the enemy, the Russians cannot complain about no second front'.

'The only thing that matters, Churchill ended, 'is to beat the life out of Rommel and Co.'[3] And to Eden he sent a 'directive' on December 6, that the 'prolongation' of the battle in Libya, 'which is drawing in so many Axis resources', would probably require the use both of the 50th and 18th British Divisions 'which we had hoped might be available for the defence of the Caucasus or for action on the Russian front'.

Churchill went on to note the increased importance of the 'attitude of Turkey' both to Russia and Britain. The Turkish army of fifty Divisions would require air support, and had already been promised a minimum of four and a maximum of twelve British Fighter squadrons should Germany attack Turkey. 'In this event,' Churchill told Eden, 'we might require to withdraw some of the squadrons proposed to be sent into action on the Russian southern front.' It was for the British

---

[1] Defence Committee (Operations) No. 71 of 1941, 3 December 1941, 5.30 p.m.: Cabinet papers, 69/2.

[2] War Cabinet No. 124 of 1941, 3 December 1941, 6 p.m., Minute 3, Confidential Annex: Cabinet papers, 65/24.

[3] Prime Minister's Personal Telegram, T.919, 4 December 1941: Churchill papers, 20/46.

and Soviet Governments and Staffs to consult together as to the 'best use of our aircraft on both shores of the Black Sea and the types to be employed. . . .'

Churchill's message to Eden continued:

The best form which our aid can take (apart from supplies) is the placing of a strong component of the Air Force, say ten squadrons, on the southern flank of the Russian armies, where, among other things, they can help protect the Russian naval bases on the Black Sea. These squadrons will be withdrawn from the Libyan battle at the earliest moment when success has been gained.[1]

But success in Libya was to prove elusive, and at sea the balance of naval triumphs tilted suddenly against the Royal Navy with the sinking of the *Barham* and the loss of more than 500 men, and against 'Force K' in particular with the sinking of the *Neptune*, of whose complement of more than 700, only 1 survived.[2] The *Neptune* had been struck by a mine at the very moment when she was about to intercept a supremely important supply convoy on its way to Tripoli. With these supplies, indeed, Rommel was able to avoid the prospect of retreat from Tripolitania.

On December 5, Hitler ordered the transfer of an Air Corps from Russia to the Sicily-Tripolitania area. 'Crusader' had finally drawn off essential German strength from the eastern battle. A 'second front' was indeed in being.

---

[1] Prime Minister's Personal Minute, D.308/1, 'Most Secret', 5 December 1941 (War Cabinet Paper No. 298 of 1941, 6 December 1941): Cabinet papers, 120/10.

[2] He survived as a prisoner-of-war, having been picked up by the Germans from a raft on which, during four days of drifting, the ship's Captain, R.C. O'Connor, and thirteen others, perished.

65

Japan, the road to war

<hr>

A T the end of July 1941 Japanese forces had occupied French Indo-China.

Roosevelt at once demanded the withdrawal of Japanese troops, and on July 26, after this had been refused, the United States imposed economic sanctions on Japan, freezing all Japanese assets in the United States. The British Government did likewise, as did the Dutch, thus depriving Japan of her essential oil supplies from the Dutch East Indies.

Roosevelt had confidence that this firm policy might deter Japan from further aggression. 'The President has asked me to tell you,' Hopkins wrote to Churchill on July 27, 'that he believes our concurrent action in Japan is bearing fruit. He hears their Government is much upset, and that they (the Japs) have formed no conclusive future policy. He wanted me to let you know, in great confidence, that he has suggested to Nomura, the Japanese Ambassador in Washington, that Indo-China be neutralized by Britain, Dutch, Chinese, Japan and ourselves, placing Indo-China somewhat in the status of Switzerland, the Japs to get rice, fertilisers, etc., but all on the condition that Japan withdraws all her armed forces from Indo-China.'[1]

During their meeting at Argentia, Churchill and Roosevelt agreed that a stern message to Japan, drafted by Churchill himself, was to be sent by Roosevelt to the Japanese Ambassador in Washington. Churchill's draft, accepted by Roosevelt as a statement of American policy, constituted an important step, albeit not a public one, on the way to an American commitment. The draft read: 'Any further encroachment by Japan in the South-West Pacific would produce a situation in which the United States Government would be compelled to take counter-

[1] 'Note to the Prime Minister from Mr Hopkins', 27 July 1941: Premier papers, 3/156/1, folios 36–7.

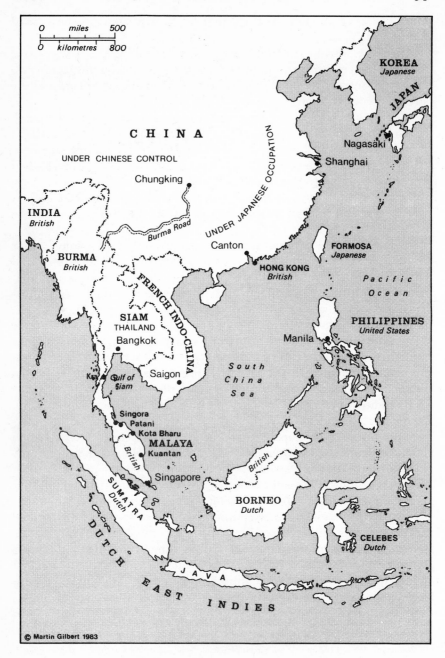

miles   500
kilometres   800

C H I N A

UNDER CHINESE CONTROL

Chungking

UNDER JAPANESE OCCUPATION

KOREA
Japanese

JAPAN

Nagasaki

Shanghai

INDIA
British

Burma Road

BURMA
British

Canton

FORMOSA
Japanese

HONG KONG
British

FRENCH INDO-CHINA

SIAM
THAILAND
Bangkok

Pacific
Ocean

PHILIPPINES
United States

Manila

 Kra   Gulf of
Siam

Saigon

South
China
Sea

Singora
Patani
Kota Bharu

MALAYA

Kuantan

British

Singapore

British

BORNEO
Dutch

SUMATRA
Dutch

CELEBES
Dutch

D U T C H   E A S T   J A V A   I N D I E S

© Martin Gilbert 1983

measures, even though these might lead to war between the United States and Japan.'[1]

America's warning to Japan was, Churchill told Eden, 'a very great advance towards the gripping of Japanese aggression by united forces'.[2] It was 'essential', he told Menzies 'to use the firmest language and the strongest combination'.[3]

Menzies understood the need for such a combination, and himself stressed the need for some naval activity if Japan were to be deterred from attacking Singapore and Malaya, with the resultant threat to Australia itself. Even while Churchill was with Roosevelt, Menzies had sent him an urgent appeal for the early despatch of five capital ships, to be sent East of Suez, and to act as 'the most powerful deterrent', as well as the 'first step' in the building up of naval reinforcements in the event of war.

Menzies wanted Britain to declare war on Japan if Japanese forces were to attack Thailand. If Thailand were abandoned, he wrote, 'and we delay our action, we will be one country nearer to war, and in that war, and in particular in the defence of Singapore, Japan will be relatively stronger and we relatively weaker than at present'.[4]

Battleships as a deterrent: the idea was pressed by Menzies at the same moment that Roosevelt made his commitment to a warning of possible American participation in a Far Eastern war. This commitment, the head of the Foreign Office, Sir Alexander Cadogan, noted in his diary, 'will give the Japanese a jar'.[5]

It seemed to Churchill that one way to encourage greater American involvement in the Far East was to put into operation the naval deterrent plan which Menzies had proposed, in the hope that, in conjunction with Roosevelt's warning to the Japanese, this plan would prevent any Japanese aggression for at least three months. By that time, November 1941, it was intended to have put a strong British naval force in Far Eastern waters, either to deter the Japanese permanently, or to act as the nucleus of a defensive war force in conjunction with the United States and Australian navies.

On August 25, Churchill sent A. V. Alexander and Pound his ideas of what was required for this new Far Eastern naval force: 'the smallest number', as he expressed it, 'of our best ships'. These ships, set at a

---

[1] See page 1160, note 5.
[2] Tudor No. 19, 11 August 1941: Churchill papers, 20/49.
[3] Tudor No. 33, 15 August 1941: Churchill papers, 20/49.
[4] 'Most Secret', No. 523, 11 August 1941: Churchill papers, 20/41.
[5] Cadogan diary, 11 August 1941: David Dilks (editor), *The Diaries of Sir Alexander Cadogan OM, 1938–1945*, London 1971, page 399.

minimum of two battleships and an aircraft carrier, would, Churchill wrote, 'exert a paralysing effect upon Japanese naval action' throughout the Indian Ocean, from Aden to Singapore. What was needed was 'a formidable, fast, high-class squadron', to be in place by the end of October. The American negotiations with Japan, he added, would probably 'linger on' for some time, and the Japanese 'may find it convenient to wait and see how things go in Russia'.[1]

Also on August 25, Churchill asked Pound to let him have on one sheet of paper a list of the 'effective Japanese fleet and flotillas', with rates of construction, and the ships 'which are ready now'.[2]

Replying three days later to Churchill's outline of a Far Eastern force, Pound revealed that the Admiralty had already been reviewing such a scheme 'before receipt of your minute'. It had emerged that the principal feature of the force, the King George V class battleships, could not in Pound's view be sent out at that time because sixty percent of the crews consisted of men under twenty-one 'who have never been to sea before', and that as a result it was inevitable 'that mishandling of material should occur at first'. At the same time, the Admiralty review had made clear that no aircraft carrier was then available, as *Illustrious* and *Formidable* had been damaged in action, and *Furious* and *Ark Royal* were receiving 'essential refits'.[3]

In the Admiralty's view, Churchill's proposed naval force could not be put together. After considering the proposal 'most carefully', Pound wrote, 'I cannot recommend it';[4] and Churchill bowed to the Admiral's judgement.

As Hitler's troops pressed back the Russians to the outskirts of Moscow, no one could tell whether Japan would keep the peace, attack Russia to the north, America to the East, or Britain and Holland to the south. 'The Jap situation is definitely worse,' Roosevelt warned Churchill on October 15, '& I *think* they are headed North.' Roosevelt added: 'you & I have two months of respite in the Far East'.[5]

The news on October 16, seemed, however, to bring the crisis suddenly much nearer, for it was learned that same evening that the moderate Konoye Cabinet had resigned, and this news, Eden's Private Secretary, Oliver Harvey, noted in his diary, 'seems to portend a for-

[1] Prime Minister's Personal Minute, M.819/1, 25 August 1941, 'Action this Day', 'Most Secret': Admiralty papers, 199/1934.
[2] 'Most Secret', Prime Minister's Personal Minute, M.820/1, 25 August 1941: Churchill papers, 20/36.
[3] The *Ark Royal* was later sunk, on 12 November 1941, see page 1233.
[4] 'Most Secret', 28 August 1941: Admiralty papers, 199/1934.
[5] Letter of 15 October 1941: Churchill papers, 20/20.

ward movement by Japanese extremists'.[1] Eden himself now revived, in a paper to the Defence Committee, Churchill's earlier idea of sending two British battleships to the Far East as an immediate deterrent force. At the same time, the Australian Government, which had originally pressed for such a force more than two months earlier, now asked for an assurance that it would include 'modern units'. At the Defence Committee meeting on October 17, where Eden's proposal was discussed, it was Churchill who raised the question of sending the *Prince of Wales* to the Far East, to join the *Repulse*, which was already in Singapore. According to Admiral Phillips, Japan's oldest battleships were 'inferior' to the R Class ships which Britain proposed to send out to the Far East. Phillips went on to tell the Defence Committee that these four R class ships, together with the *Rodney, Renown* and *Nelson* when repaired, 'should, in their own waters, and operating under cover of shore based aircraft, be a match for any forces the Japanese were likely to bring against them'.[2]

It was Clement Attlee who then said that it 'seemed sounder to send a modern ship' to the Far East, since Britain would find it very hard to 'remain on the defensive', as Phillips seemed to assume, even if Japan attacked Russia. 'We should find such action hard to justify in the circumstances,' Attlee added, whereupon Churchill invited A. V. Alexander 'to consider the proposal to send as quickly as possible one modern capital ship, together with an aircraft carrier, to join up with *Repulse* at Singapore'.[3]

On October 20, at a further meeting of the Defence Committe, it was decided 'that the importance of the early arrival of one of our latest battleships in Far Eastern waters outweighed the reasons put forward by the First Sea Lord for retaining all these King George V Class in Atlantic waters'. It was hoped, the minutes recorded, that the presence of the *Prince of Wales* and the *Repulse* at Singapore 'would act as a deterrent to Japan and avert war'. If, however, the Japanese were in fact 'on the point of taking the plunge', the presence of the two battleships would, the Committee hoped, prevent them 'from sending their expeditionary force to the southward'. Although the Japanese would be able to bring down 'a superior force', it was also felt by the Defence Committee 'that the containing power of the strong American

---

[1] Harvey diary, 16 October 1941: John Harvey (editor), *The War Diaries of Oliver Harvey*, London 1978, page 53.

[2] The four R class battleships to be sent to the Far East were the *Royal Sovereign, Revenge, Resolution* and *Ramilles*.

[3] Defence Committee (Operations) No. 21 of 1941, 17 October 1941: Cabinet papers, 69/2.

fleet at Hawaii would restrain them from any major venture into the Gulf of Siam'.[1]

The *Prince of Wales* prepared to steam eastward. Of Admiral Phillips, who was given command of the new force, Churchill telegraphed to Smuts: 'He is a great friend of mine and one of our ablest officers.'[2]

On October 20 Churchill gave Roosevelt a formal assurance that should the United States find itself at war with Japan, 'you may be sure that a British declaration of war upon Japan will follow within the hour'. He also told Roosevelt of Britain's hope to provide 'a considerable battle squadron' for the Indian and Pacific Oceans 'before Christmas'.[3]

Churchill persevered in believing that war could be averted in the Far East, telegraphing the new Australian Prime Minister, John Curtin, on October 25:

... in order further to deter Japan, we are sending forthwith our newest battleship, *Prince of Wales*, to join *Repulse* in Indian Ocean. This is done in spite of protests of Commander-in-Chief, Home Fleet, and is a serious risk for us to run. *Prince of Wales* will be noticed at Cape Town quite soon. In addition, the four R Battleships are being moved as they become ready to Eastern waters. Later on *Repulse* will be relieved by *Renown*, which has greater radius.

I agree with you that *Prince of Wales* will be the best possible deterrent, and every effort will be made to spare her permanently. . . .[4]

On October 31 an American destroyer on convoy duty for Britain, the *Reuben James*, was torpedoed in the North Atlantic, and 115 of her crew, including all the officers, were drowned. As with the sinking of the *Lusitania* in the First World War, however, this act of German aggression did not lead to any United States declaration of war on Germany. Churchill telegraphed to Roosevelt, on learning of the sinking: 'I am grieved at loss of life you have suffered with *Reuben James*. I salute the land of unending challenge'. As to the despatch of the *Prince of Wales* to the Indian Ocean 'as part of the Squadron we are forming there', Churchill told the President:

[1] Defence Committee (Operations) No. 66 of 1941, 12.30 p.m., 20 October 1941, Confidential Annex: Cabinet papers, 69/2.

[2] 'Personal and Secret', Prime Minister's Personal Telegram, T.774, 2 November 1941: Admiralty papers, 199/1934.

[3] 'Personal and Secret', 20 October 1941: Premier papers, 3/486/2.

[4] 'Most Secret', Prime Minister's Personal Telegram, T.742, Winch No. 4, 25 October 1941: Churchill papers, 20/44.

This ought to serve as a deterrent on Japan. There is nothing like having something that can catch and kill anything. I am very glad we can spare her at this juncture. It is more than we thought we could do some time ago.

'The firmer your attitude and ours,' Churchill added, 'the less chance of their taking the plunge.'[1]

To the War Cabinet on November 12, Churchill set out the United States' position, as he saw it, telling his colleagues of:

. . . the difficulties which faced President Roosevelt as a result of the slow development of American opinion and the peculiarities of the American Constitution. Nobody but Congress could *declare* war. It was, however, in the President's power to make war without declaring it.

President Roosevelt was a great leader. In the last twelve months American opinion had moved under his leadership to an extent which nobody could have anticipated. They had made immense credits available to us; they had made immense resources available to us under the Lease-Lend Act; their Navy was escorting the Atlantic convoys; and finally they were taking a firm line with the Japanese.

It would, however, Churchill warned, 'be a great error on his part to press President Roosevelt to act in advance of American opinion'.[2]

On November 25 Roosevelt informed Churchill of Japanese proposals for a 'modus vivendi', put forward by the Japanese Ambassador in Washington to Cordell Hull. Even America's demand for a withdrawal of Japanese troops from Indo-China had been held out to Hull as a possibility. Nor did Roosevelt dismiss the Japanese approach out of hand; instead, he suggested to Churchill a possible modification of the Anglo-American economic embargo on Japan, permitting the renewal of certain exports from the United States to Japan, and suggesting to Churchill that Britain, Australia and the Dutch East Indies do the same for a trial period of three months.

Roosevelt ended his telegram however: 'I am not very hopeful and we must all be prepared for real trouble, possibly soon.'[3]

[1] 'Personal and Secret', Prime Minister's Personal Telegram, T.773, 1 November 1941: Churchill papers, 20/44.

[2] War Cabinet No. 112 of 1941, 12 November 1941, 5.30 p.m., Minute 1, Confidential Annex: Cabinet papers, 65/24. John Peck later recalled a remark by Churchill at this time: 'The American Constitution was designed by the Founding Fathers to keep the United States clear of European entanglements—and by God it has stood the test of time' (Conversation with the author, 18 August 1982).

[3] Telegram received 25 November 1941: Premier papers, 3/156/5, folios 64–5.

In a minute to Eden on November 23, Churchill had already given his support to follow up the suggestions which Cordell Hull had put forward. As Churchill wrote:

My own feeling is that we might give Hull the latitude he asks. Our major interest is: no further encroachments and no war, as we have already enough of this latter. The United States will not throw over the Chinese cause, and we may safely follow them in this part of the subject. We could not of course agree to an arrangement whereby Japan was free to attack Russia in Siberia. I doubt myself whether this is likely at the present time. I remember that President Roosevelt himself wrote in, 'There must be no further encroachment in the North,' at the Atlantic Conference. I should think this could be agreed.

The formal denunciation of the Axis Pact by Japan is not in my opinion necessary. Their stopping out of the war is in itself a great disappointment and injury to the Germans. We ought not to agree to any veto on American or British help to China. But we shall not be asked to by the United States.

Subject to the above, it would be worth while to ease up upon Japan economically sufficiently for them to live from hand to mouth—even if we only got another three months. These, however, are only first impressions.

I must say I should feel pleased if I read that an American–Japanese agreement had been made by which we were to be no worse off three months hence in the Far East than we are now.[1]

Even while the negotiations continued in Washington, Roosevelt became aware, through intercepted Japanese messages, that preparations were being made by the Japanese for an early aggressive movement of some character.[2] But of where that movement would come, or what its strength would be, he did not know. An advance against Siam seemed most probable. But the Burma Road, the Malay Peninsula, the Dutch East Indies or the Philippines were all possibilities. That same day, pondering Roosevelt's report of the chances of agreement with Japan, Churchill telegraphed to the President:

Of course, it is for you to handle this business and we certainly do not want an additional war. There is only one point that disquiets us. What about Chiang Kai-shek? Is he not having a very thin diet? Our anxiety is about China. If they collapse, our joint dangers would enormously increase. We are sure that the regard of the United States for the Chinese cause will govern your action.

---

[1] 'Secret', Prime Minister's Personal Minute, M.1061, 23 November 1941: Premier papers, 3/156/6, folios 28–9.

[2] Roosevelt also received Intelligence material direct from Churchill, who used regularly to minute to 'C', on Enigma decrypts and interpretations, especially those referring to the Far East: 'Make sure the President knows this,' or 'Make sure the President sees this.' (Private Communication.)

'We feel,' Churchill added, 'that the Japanese are most unsure of themselves.'[1]

Unknown to Washington or to London, on November 26 a Japanese naval force set sail from the Kurile Islands, north of Japan, through fogs and gales, towards the Pearl Harbour naval base at Hawaii. Three days later, on November 29, while this force was still steaming secretly across the Pacific, the Chiefs of Staff Committee met in London. The first item of its discussion was Japanese intentions. Intelligence reports confirmed a higher state of military, naval and air alert. But it was now thought, by those who studied these indications, that Russia would be the principal, and perhaps the sole object, of Japan's attack. Hitler's forces were already in the Caucasus, halted, but within striking distance of Russia's main oil fields. Russia was thus a tempting target for Japan. But the Intelligence analysts also saw, to the South, a second possible target, Siam, which seemed to lie even more exposed to a Japanese descent, and which, if conquered, would then pose a direct threat to Malaya and Singapore.

The Chiefs of Staff Committee, Pound, Portal and the Vice Chief of the Imperial General Staff, Major-General Nye, were clear however, as their secret minutes expressed it, that 'unless our vital interests were directly affected we should avoid taking any action which would involve us in war with Japan unless'—and this was the often reiterated proviso, 'we were certain that America would join us'. The Chiefs of Staff Committee recommended, however, that in the event of a Japanese invasion of Thailand, Britain should 'carry out an operation designed to forestall them', by occupying the Isthmus of Kra. Such an operation should only be undertaken, however, if Britain could be sure that the United States 'would immediately join us should this move lead to war with Japan'.[2] Two days later, as indications of some Japanese forward movement intensified, but still in no clear direction, the Chiefs of Staff decided to approach the Canadian Government for the provision of the balance of an Infantry Brigade Group for Hong Kong.[3]

British policy still sought as its principal aim the avoidance of war in

[1] Prime Minister's Personal Telegram, T.871, No. 6462 to Washington, 26 November 1941, despatched 3.20 a.m.: Churchill papers, 20/45.
[2] Chiefs of Staff Committee No. 402 of 1941, 29 November 1941: Cabinet papers, 79/16.
[3] Chiefs of Staff Committee No. 403 of 1941, 1 December 1941: Cabinet papers, 79/16.

the Far East. 'The effect of war with Japan on our main war effort,' a secret War Office memorandum stated on November 30, 'might be so severe as to prejudice our chances of beating Germany. Our policy must therefore be—and is—avoidance of war with Japan.'[1]

Churchill still believed that a firm warning to Japan might avert war. He had often reflected upon the effect of such warnings in relation to the Rhineland crisis of 1936, when Hitler's move, unchallenged by Britain and France, had seemed to set a pattern for unchallenged aggression. He now set out for Roosevelt his final thoughts on what might still be done:

It seems to me that one important method remains unused in averting war between Japan and our two countries, namely, a plain declaration, secret or public, as may be thought best, that any further act of aggression by Japan will lead immediately to the gravest consequences. I realise your constitutional difficulties, but it would be tragic if Japan drifted into war by encroachment without having before her fairly and squarely the dire character of a further aggressive step. I beg you to consider whether, at the moment which you judge right, which may be very near, you should not say that 'any further Japanese aggression would compel you to place the gravest issues before Congress', or words to that effect. We would of course make a similar declaration or share in a joint declaration, and in any case arrangements are being made to synchronise our action with yours.

'Forgive me, my dear friend,' Churchill ended, 'for presuming to press such a course upon you, but I am convinced that it might make all the difference and prevent a melancholy extension of the war.'[2]

Even as Admiral Phillips approached Singapore in the *Prince of Wales*, the danger signals had intensified. On December 1 the Admiralty signalled Phillips that on his arrival he might send either the *Prince of Wales* or the *Repulse* 'away from Singapore to disconcert the Japanese'. Two days later, on December 3, the presence of Japanese submarines was reported in the Singapore area. The Admiralty at once signalled Phillips that he should request United States destroyers in the region to be sent to Singapore, and that he should get both the *Prince of Wales* and the *Repulse* 'away from Singapore to the eastwards'.[3]

Unfortunately, Phillips was unable to carry out this plan, since, as he explained in reply, the *Prince of Wales* had been taken in hand for repairs for seven days. During this seven-day period the warship would

---

[1] 'Far East—General Principles of Policy and Strategy', 'Secret', 30 November 1941: War Office papers, 208/3043.

[2] 'Personal and Secret', 'Action this Day', Prime Minister's Personal Telegram, T.902, 30 November 1941, 3 p.m.: Premier papers, 3/156/6, folios 25–6.

[3] Report of 27 January 1942: Premier papers, 3/163/2.

need 72 hours notice before being ready to leave. In the event, neither ship left Singapore until December 8.

On December 1 Halifax reported to Eden that, at a meeting with Roosevelt at which Hopkins was present, Roosevelt, 'threw in an aside that in the case of any direct attack on ourselves or the Dutch, we should obviously all be together, but he wished to clear up the matters that were less plain'. Halifax went on to report that Roosevelt had wished him to convey the suggestion that Britain should give Siam an undertaking 'that if they resisted Japanese attack or infiltration we would respect and guarantee for the future their full sovereignty and independence'. For constitutional reasons, Roosevelt explained, the United States could not give any such guarantee, but such an undertaking on Britain's part 'would be wholeheartedly supported by the United States'.[1]

When the War Cabinet met later in the afternoon of December 1, it was a possibly imminent Japanese threat to Siam that dominated its concern. 'PM against taking any forestalling action on Siam,' noted Cadogan. 'Think he is right. Japs evidently in a fix, and announce that they want to continue conversations in Washington.'[2] British policy, Churchill minuted to Eden on December 2, 'is not to take forward action in advance of the United States'. As far as a Japanese attack on the Kra Isthmus was concerned, Churchill wrote, if America moved, 'we will move immediately in support'. If America did not move, 'we must consider our position afresh'. But such an attack was, he thought, 'unlikely'. As for a Japanese attack on the Dutch East Indies:

If the United States declares war on Japan, we follow within the hour. If, after a reasonable interval, the United States is found to be incapable of taking any decisive action, even with our immediate support, we will nevertheless, although alone, make common cause with the Dutch. Having regard to the supreme importance of the United States being foremost, we must be the sole judge of timing the actual moment.

Any attack by Japan on a British possession, Churchill added, 'carries with it war with Great Britain as a matter of course'.[3]

Churchill reiterated these thoughts at the Defence Committee on December 3. He added that if Japan attacked the Dutch East Indies,

[1] 'Most Immediate', 'Most Secret', Washington Telegram No. 5519, sent 11.29 p.m., 1 December 1941, received 7.20 a.m., 2 December 1941: Premier papers, 3/156/5, folios 8–11.

[2] Cadogan diary, 1 December 1941: David Dilks (editor), *The Diaries of Sir Alexander Cadogan OM, 1938–1945*, London 1971, page 415.

[3] Prime Minister's Personal Minute, M.1078/1, 2 December 1941: Premier papers, 3/395/3, folio 41.

and Britain then declared war on Japan without giving the United States time to 'make up their minds what to do', there was a danger of giving the anti-British and Isolationist groups in America cause for saying that the United States was being 'dragged' into war.[1] A message from Roosevelt on December 4, however, was sufficiently strong in stating that, in the event of any direct attack on Britain or on the Dutch, the United States would consider herself directly involved, to 'induce Winston', Eden noted in his diary, 'to agree to full assurance to Dutch on the strength of it'.[2] He now had 'every confidence', Churchill told the War Cabinet that evening, that the United States would come to the aid of the Dutch should they be attacked by Japan.

Churchill also decided to authorize 'Matador', a British landing on the Kra Isthmus of Siam, either as a 'forestalling measure' if a Japanese attack on the Isthmus was imminent, or as an act of war if Japan invaded Siam.[3] 'We have authorized forestalling action at Kra Isthmus if necessary,' Churchill telegraphed to the Australian Prime Minister, John Curtin, 'and are about to assure Dutch that we will help them at once if they are attacked.' This, Churchill noted, 'meets your wishes in most respects'. But, he warned, 'Please treat President's attitude with utmost secrecy.'[4]

Despite rumours and counter rumours, no Japanese forces had yet attacked British, Dutch or Siamese territory. But Japanese naval troop movements, as shown by air reconnaisance and by Intelligence, were such that it suddenly became clear that a Japanese expedition was on its way southwards in the general direction of the Gulf of Siam. Its size was known: 35 troop transports, 8 cruisers and 20 destroyers. From the position of the transports however, it was not possible, General Brooke noted in his diary on December 6, 'to tell whether they were going to Bangkok, to the Kra Isthmus, or whether they were just cruising round as a bluff'. A second message from Singapore that evening 'did

[1] Defence Committee (Operations) No. 71 of 1941, 3 December 1941, 5.30 p.m.: Cabinet papers, 69/2.

[2] Eden diary, 4 December 1941: Earl of Avon, *The Eden Memoirs, The Reckoning*, London 1965, page 314.

[3] War Cabinet No. 124 of 1941, 4 December 1941, 6 p.m., Minute 4, Confidential Annex: Cabinet papers, 65/24.

[4] Winch No. 8, 'Most Secret and Personal', Telegram T.923, 5 December 1941: Churchill papers, 20/49.

not clear up the situation in the least and it only said that convoy had been lost and could not be picked up again'.[1]

That night Averell Harriman telegraphed to Harry Hopkins:

The President should be informed of Churchill's belief that in the event of aggression by the Japanese it would be the policy of the British to postpone taking any action—even though this delay might involve some military sacrifice—until the President has taken such action as, under the circumstances, he considers best. Then Churchill will act 'not within the hour but within the minute'. I am seeing him again tomorrow.[2]

On Sunday December 7 the three Chiefs of Staff, Pound, Portal and Brooke, meeting in London, minuted for Churchill that Britain was prepared to 'fire the first shot' on any Japanese expedition against Siam, 'before it reached its objective', provided—the eternal proviso—that Britain could be assured of 'US armed support', and also—and this was a new proviso—that if Britain fired the first shot this would not be represented by Isolationists in the United States 'as a deliberate attempt on our part to drag them into a British war'.[3]

As these discussions proceeded, and the Japanese threat seemed increasingly to point to Siam, Churchill was at Chequers with Averell Harriman.

A message was dictated over the telephone to London for the Chiefs of Staff, informing them that the Prime Minister and President were in agreement that, if a Japanese invasion force was seen moving south towards Siam, Britain 'should obviously attack Japanese transports'.

Churchill added, however, that no British troops would actually land in Siam unless a Japanese landing had either taken place, or was 'imminent'.[4] Nor would any British attack on Japanese transports take place, so the British Ambassador in Washington was informed, unless Roosevelt could give Britain 'some assurance of armed support', as he had already said he would provide in the event of a Japanese attack on Malaya.[5]

[1] Brooke diary, 6 December 1941: Arthur Bryant, *The Turn of the Tide, 1939–1943*, London 1957, page 281.

[2] Telegram of 6 December 1941: W. Averell Harriman and Elie Abel, *Special Envoy to Churchill and Stalin, 1941–1946*, London 1976, page 111.

[3] Minute of 7 December 1941: Premier papers, 3/163/2, report of 27 January 1942, Annex II.

[4] Report of 27 January 1942, Annex I: Premier papers, 3/163/2.

[5] Report of 27 January 1942, Annex III: Premier papers, 3/163/2.

Meanwhile, in London, the latest Intelligence reports made it clear that Japanese forces were preparing an immediate attack, not northwards against Russia, but southwards against Siam. At the same time, on the morning of December 7 in London, it was learned that Roosevelt was prepared to announce publicly that the United States would definitely regard it as a hostile act to the United States if Japan were to invade Malaya, Burma, the Dutch East Indies, or even Siam.

This new American commitment, so long sought by Churchill, was to be announced publicly by Roosevelt on Wednesday, December 10. 'This is an immense relief,' Churchill telegraphed to Auchinleck on December 7, 'as I had long dreaded being at war with Japan without or before the United States.' Churchill added: 'Now I think it is all right.'[1]

All but one of Churchill's luncheon guests had arrived by 1 o'clock on December 7. The missing guest was the American Ambassador, John Winant. 'When I reached Chequers,' he later recalled:

... the Prime Minister was walking up and down outside the entrance door—the others had gone in to lunch twenty minutes before. He asked me if I thought there was going to be war with Japan. I answered 'Yes.' With unusual vehemence he turned to me and said:

'If they declare war on you, we shall declare war on them within the hour.'

'I understand, Prime Minister. You have stated that publicly.'

'If they declare war on us, will you declare war on them?'

'I can't answer that, Prime Minister. Only the Congress has the right to declare war under the United States Constitution.'

He did not say anything for a minute, but I knew what was in his mind. He must have realised that if Japan attacked Siam or British territory it would force Great Britain into an Asiatic war, and leave us out of the war. He knew in that moment that his country might be 'hanging on one turn of pitch and toss'.

Nevertheless he turned to me with the charm of manner that I saw so often in difficult moments, and said, 'We're late, you know. You get washed and we will go in to lunch together.'[2]

To the Siamese Prime Minister, Churchill telegraphed just after midday on December 7: 'There is a possibility of imminent Japanese invasion of your country. If you are attacked, defend yourself. The preservation of the full independence and sovereignty of Siam is a Brit-

---

[1] Prime Minister's Personal Telegram, T.933, despatched 6.25 p.m., 7 December 1941, War Office No. 142: Churchill papers, 20/46.

[2] John G. Winant, *A Letter from Grosvenor Square: An Account of A Stewardship*, London 1947, pages 196–7.

ish interest and we shall regard an attack on you as an attack upon ourselves.'[1]

Even while this telegram was being despatched from London, the Japanese ships and aircraft had been continuing their crossing of the Pacific on the final stage of their attack on the American fleet at Pearl Harbour: that same 'strong American fleet at Hawaii' which the British had so recently believed would restrain the Japanese from any attack on British or Dutch possessions, or on Siam.

Early on the morning of December 7, Pacific time—early evening that same day in Britain—360 Japanese aircraft attacked the American fleet at Pearl Harbour. For an hour and a half they struck again and again at the ships at anchor, leaving in their wake four battleships destroyed, and two thousand American dead.

At nine o'clock on the evening of December 7, Churchill was still at Chequers, dining with Harriman and Winant. 'The Prime Minister seemed tired and depressed,' Harriman later recalled. 'He didn't have much to say throughout dinner and was immersed in his thoughts, with his head in his hands part of the time.'[2] Churchill himself later recalled: 'I turned on my small wireless set shortly after the nine o'clock news had started. There were a number of items about the fighting on the Russian front and on the British front in Libya, at the end of which some few sentences were spoken regarding an attack by the Japanese on American shipping at Hawaii, and also Japanese attacks on British vessels in the Dutch East Indies.'

Churchill recalled that there then followed a statement 'that after the news Mr Somebody would make a commentary, and that the Brains Trust programme would then begin, or something like this. I did not personally sustain any direct impression, but Averell said there was something about the Japanese attacking the Americans, and, in spite of being tired and resting, we all sat up.'

At that moment, Churchill's butler, Sawyers, who had likewise been listening to the news, came into the room. 'It's quite true,' he said, 'we heard it ourselves outside. The Japanese have attacked the Americans.'

Six years later, Winant recalled the ensuing scene:

We looked at one another incredulously. Then Churchill jumped to his feet and started for the door with the announcement, 'We shall declare war

[1] 'Most Immediate', 'Most Secret', Prime Minister's Personal Telegram, T.930A, Foreign Office to Bangkok No. 595, 7 December 1941, despatched 1.40 p.m.: Churchill papers, 20/46.

[2] W. Averell Harriman and Elie Abel, *Special Envoy to Churchill and Stalin, 1914–1946*, London 1976, page 111.

on Japan.' There is nothing half-hearted or unpositive about Churchill—certainly not when he is on the move. Without ceremony I too left the table and followed him out of the room.

'Good God,' I said, 'you can't declare war on a radio announcement.'

He stopped and looked at me half-seriously, half-quizzically, and then said quietly, 'What shall I do?' The question was asked not because he needed me to tell him what to do, but as a courtesy to the representative of the country attacked.

I said, 'I will call up the President by telephone and ask him what the facts are.'

And he added, 'And I shall talk with him too.'

We got through to the White House in a few minutes and the President told me very simply the story of the attack—so tragic in itself and yet the final mistake that was to end the power of the Axis. He could not, however, over the open transatlantic telephone, tell the extent of the crushing losses sustained by the fleet, or the heavy casualties.[1] I said I had a friend with me who wanted to speak to him. I said, 'You will know who it is, as soon as you hear his voice.'[2]

According to Churchill's account he then asked: 'Mr President, what's this about Japan,' to which Roosevelt replied: 'It's quite true. They have attacked us at Pearl Harbour. We are all in the same boat now.'[3]

In a note of this same conversation, John Martin wrote: 'The President confirmed that they had been attacked and said that he was going to ask Congress tomorrow, Monday, to declare a state of open hostility.' Churchill then asked Roosevelt 'what the President wanted him to do about his declaration'. This declaration, Churchill said, 'would follow the President's within the hour'.

Roosevelt also told Churchill that Japanese warships 'had been sighted between Hawaii and San Francisco'.[4]

His conversation with Roosevelt over, 'we then went back into the hall', Churchill later recalled, 'and tried to adjust our thoughts to the supreme world event which had occurred, which was of so startling a nature as to make even those who were near the centre gasp'. Harriman and Winant—'My two American friends'—'took the shock with ad-

---

[1] John Martin recalls 'Winant's excited "That's fine, Mr President, that's fine", not at that moment realising the extent of the blow to the US Navy (of which the President could not have spoken in detail on the telephone) but thinking only of the implication that now at last the US were in the war'. (Sir John Martin, letter to the author, 12 March 1983.)

[2] John G. Winant, *A Letter from Grosvenor Square: An Account of a Stewardship*, London 1947, pages 198–9.

[3] Winston S. Churchill, *The Second World War*, volume 3, London 1950, page 538.

[4] Note by John Martin, 7 December 1941: Premier papers, 3/158/1, folio 12.

mirable fortitude. We had no idea that any serious losses had been inflicted on the United States Navy. They did not wail or lament that their country was at war. They wasted no words in reproach or sorrow. In fact, one might almost have thought they had been delivered from a long pain.'[1]

It was not America alone whose territory had been attacked by Japan. 'Soon after the first excitement,' John Martin later recalled, 'I was able to obtain on the telephone from the Admiralty news of the Japanese attack on Malaya.'[2]

The message which Martin took down was a signal from the Commander-in-Chief of the China Station, Admiral Layton, to the Admiralty which read: 'Report from Kota Bharu. An attempt is being made to land from 3 or 5' (? transports). 'One landing craft already approaching mouth of river.'[3]

Both Britain and the United States had now been attacked by the same enemy. Churchill could go to bed that night knowing that it could only be a matter of a few more hours before America was at war with Japan. This was indeed so. 'The Senate passed the all-out declaration of war 82 to nothing,' Roosevelt telegraphed to Churchill on December 8, 'and the House has passed it 382 to 1.' Roosevelt added: 'Today all of us are in the same boat with you and the people of the Empire, and it is a ship which will not and cannot be sunk.'[4]

As the facts from Pearl Harbour accumulated, however, it became clear the immediate situation was grave. Of nine American battleships operational in the Pacific that morning, only two remained capable of any further immediate action, compared with ten Japanese battleships fully operational. Even counting the *Prince of Wales* and *Repulse*, the earlier Anglo-American marginal superiority of 11 to 10 had become a marked inferiority of 4 to 10. But in the area of the Malay peninsula, the two British warships still constituted the predominant naval force.

A month later, when Churchill was given details of the full extent of the American losses at Pearl Harbour, it was explained to him that these were 'considerably more than that given to the Press'. Churchill noted in red crayon: 'No one should be told who does not know already. What a holocaust!'[5]

[1] Winston S. Churchill, *The Second World War*, volume 3, London 1950, page 538.
[2] Sir John Martin, letter to the author, 3 September 1982.
[3] Martin papers.
[4] Telegram, 8 December 1941: Premier papers, 3/469, folio 13.
[5] Churchill's comment, dated 10 January 1942, on a note from Sir Dudley Pound of 8 January 1942: Admiralty papers, 205/13.

66

'KBO'

EVEN as the Japanese were striking at Pearl Harbour, information reached the British naval authorities in Singapore that a substantial Japanese expeditionary force had set off westwards from Indo-China, and was making for the coast of Siam. Although the *Prince of Wales* was still at Singapore, Admiral Phillips was at that moment in the Philippines conferring with his American opposite number. He immediately flew back to Singapore, where, at midday on December 8, he discussed the situation with his Flag-Captain, Captain J. C. Leach, and Captain Tennant of the *Repulse*. At their conference, Phillips described his plan to make a raid on the Japanese convoys in the Gulf of Siam, attacking those Japanese troop transports which were reinforcing the troops who had already landed, on December 7, at the Siamese ports of Singora and Patani, and at the northern Malayan port of Kota Bharu, where, after fierce fighting, a British force had been defeated. 'All were unanimous,' the secret Admiralty enquiry later revealed, 'that it was impossible for the Navy to do nothing while the Army and Air Forces were being driven back,' and that the plan for a sudden raid on Japanese lines of communication, 'though hazardous, was acceptable.'

The main hazard was a Japanese air attack on the *Prince of Wales* and the *Repulse* from Japanese air bases in and around Saigon. But at the conference on December 8, the 'cloudy and rainy weather' seemed to lessen that danger. There was also the Intelligence aspect. 'Owing to the policy of intensive secrecy implemented by Japan for some years past,' the Admiralty report noted, 'intelligence as to the capabilities of Japanese Naval and Air Forces left much to be desired.'

There was yet another factor. 'It may be,' the Admiralty report concluded, 'that the consistently adverse reports over a number of years of the capabilities of Japanese air personnel may have caused the Commander-in-Chief of the Eastern Fleet to underestimate the air threat, and discount the possibility of their delivering a heavy scale of attack at long range.'

A technical reason also led Phillips to conclude that a policy of attack, though hazardous, was acceptable. As the senior surviving staff officer on the *Prince of Wales*, acting Captain L. M. Bell, reported six weeks later, the Commander-in-Chief 'relied on the speed and surprise of the battleship attack to avoid damage to those ships, believing that the Japanese aircraft would not be carrying anti-ship bombs and torpedoes, and that the force on retirement would only have to deal with hastily organised long range bombers from bases in Indo-China'.[1]

Such were the arguments in favour of action rather than withdrawal. In London, however, Churchill and his advisers came to more cautious conclusions. At ten o'clock on the night of December 9, an emergency meeting was summoned in the Cabinet room to consider the future movements of the *Prince of Wales* and *Repulse*, and their four destroyers. Churchill put forward two suggestions. One, as Ismay later recalled, was that the ships 'should vanish into the ocean wastes and exercise a vague menace', acting as 'rogue elephants'. The other was that they should go across the Pacific 'and join the remnants of the American fleet'. No suggestion was made that the ships should remain in the war zone, or go on the offensive. Nor was any final decision reached, except to 'reconsider the problem in the morning light'.[2]

By morning light, however, two fateful decisions, the first for caution and the second for action, had been taken by Phillips himself. As the *Prince of Wales* and the *Repulse*, and four destroyers, steamed northwards towards the Siamese ports, the weather cleared. At that moment a Japanese reconnaissance aircraft located the force, and was itself seen by it. Phillips at once decided that the risk was unacceptable, and abandoned the operation. Thereupon, with Captain Leach's agreement, the warships shaped course at high speed southwards for Singapore.

At midnight on December 9, as Phillips steamed southward, he received a signal from Singapore that Japanese forces had landed half way down the Malayan coast, at Kuantan. He at once decided to change course, and to attack them. His reasoning was recalled six weeks later by acting Captain Bell. First, Kuantan lay four hundred miles from the Japanese aerodromes in Indo-China. Second, Kuantan was 'a

[1] Report of 27 January 1942: Premier papers, 3/163/2.

[2] Ismay to Churchill, 1948. Ismay wrote to Churchill, who was then writing his war memoirs: 'Hollis and I clearly remember the meeting to which you refer, but I think you might have summoned it unexpectedly and, for some reason or another, there is no record of what was said.' Ismay then set down the account quoted above. (Churchill papers, 4/233.)

key military position which every effort must be made to defend'. Third, the Japanese had last located his ships in the latitude of Singora, steaming *northwards*. They would not expect his force to be so far south. He therefore decided 'that a surprise at Kuantan was probable, and the risk justified'.

By one in the morning of December 10 Phillips had turned his ships towards Kuantan. Soon after daylight one of Phillips' destroyers, the *Express*, which had gone ahead, reached the harbour, found no sign of the Japanese, and rejoined the Admiral. Kuantan being uncaptured, Phillips prepared to continue his southward course to Singapore. But before doing so, at seven o'clock that morning, some time was spent searching for some tugs, barges and junks in convoy which had been sighted earlier. Thinking that these might be motor landing craft intended for a landing at Kuantan, Phillips steamed eastwards to examine them. Simultaneously, an aircraft was sighted, 'but not identified as enemy or friendly'. At ten to eleven the *Prince of Wales* radar picked up aircraft on its screen, and ten minutes later these same aircraft came into sight.

These Japanese aircraft had already flown as far south as Singapore in search of the British warships, and having sighted nothing were returning to Indo-China on a northerly course. It was by chance that their flight path had led them straight to their quarry. The first torpedos were dropped shortly after eleven in the morning, and for nearly an hour and a half the attack continued. At 12.33 p.m. the *Repulse* turned over and sank. The *Prince of Wales* capsized and sank at 1.20 p.m. Six hundred officers and men were drowned, including Phillips and Leach. More than two thousand were rescued by the four destroyers.

Fighter aircraft, sent from Singapore when the *Repulse* had signalled that an attack had begun, reached the scene only in time to witness the sinking of the *Prince of Wales*.

Three months later, reflecting on the loss of the *Prince of Wales* and *Repulse*, Dudley Pound wrote to Churchill:

Let us suppose for a moment that Kota Bharu aerodrome had been held by the Army and therefore not captured by the Japanese, and that the fighter protection asked for by Admiral Phillips had been available. Under these conditions there was a very fair chance of these battleships shooting up the invasion forces at Kota Bharu and Singora. If this had occurred the Army were in a position to drive those forces which had landed into the sea and we should then have been given the time required to put reinforcements into Malaya before the Japanese could have remounted their expeditions.

'If this had occurred,' Pound wrote, 'it is a fair assumption that Malaya, Sumatra and Java would still be in our hands to-day and that we should be in a far better position to deal with Japan than we are at the present moment.'[1]

On the morning of Wednesday, December 10, Churchill was in bed working on official papers when the telephone rang at his bedside. It was Dudley Pound. Churchill later recalled: 'His voice sounded odd. He gave a sort of cough and gulp, and at first I could not hear quite clearly. "Prime Minister, I have to report to you that the *Prince of Wales* and the *Repulse* have both been sunk by the Japanese—we think by aircraft. Tom Phillips is drowned." "Are you sure it's true?" "There is no doubt at all." So I put the telephone down. I was thankful to be alone. In all the war I never received a more direct shock.'[2]

Churchill was not alone. Mrs Hill was in the room when Pound's telephone call came. 'I sat in the corner of the room silently and unobtrusively,' she later recalled. 'When he was upset I used to try to be invisible. When the two ships went down, I was there. That was a terrible moment. "Poor Tom Phillips" he said.'[3]

That same day, the Russians launched a military offensive along the whole of the Eastern Front. For the first time since their onslaught in June, the Germans were being thrown back at dozens of different points, their winter plans in disarray. In Libya, the corridor to Tobruk, forced through two days earlier, was finally secured.

On Thursday December 11 Germany and Italy declared war on the United States. The United States Congress, in its turn, declared war on Germany and Italy, and voted to despatch United States forces to any part of the world. 'The stars in their courses are fighting for us,' John Martin quoted with relief in his diary that night,[4] while another of Churchill's Private Secretaries, John Peck, wrote to Eric Seal in Washington that despite the loss of the *Prince of Wales* and the *Repulse* 'the PM was soon full of bounce again, because the news from Russia and Libya more than balances our misfortunes'. Peck added that the Prime Minister's dictum was: 'We must just KBO,' which, he explained, meant 'Keep Buggering On'.[5]

On December 8, before the German declaration of war on the United

[1] 'Most Secret', 8 March 1942: Premier papers, 20/57.
[2] Winston S. Churchill, *The Second World War*, volume 3, London 1950, page 55.
[3] Kathleen Hill, conversation with the author, 15 October 1982.
[4] John Martin diary, 11 December 1941: Martin papers.
[5] Letter of 11 December 1941: Seal papers.

States, and the swift Congress response, had ensured that America would be Britain's ally in Europe as well as in Asia, Churchill told the House of Commons:

It is of the highest importance that there should be no underrating of the gravity of the new dangers we have to meet, either here or in the United States. The enemy has attacked with an audacity which may spring from recklessness, but which may also spring from a conviction of strength.

The ordeal to which the English-speaking world and our heroic Russian Allies are being exposed will certainly be hard, especially at the outset, and will probably be long, yet when we look around us over the sombre panorama of the world we have no reason to doubt the justice of our cause or that our strength and will-power will be sufficient to sustain it.

We have at least four-fifths of the population of the globe upon our side. We are responsible for their safety and for their future. In the past we have had a light which flickered, in the present we have a light which flames, and in the future there will be a light which shines over all the land and sea.[1]

After so many months of trying to bring America into the war, and almost despairing of being able to do so in time, Churchill's dilemma was resolved by the Japanese attack on Pearl Harbour and by Germany's declaration of war on the United States. On December 12 he telegraphed to Roosevelt: 'I am enormously relieved at turn world events have taken,'[2] and to Eden, who was on his way to Russia, Churchill signalled that same day: 'The accession of the United States makes amends for all, and with time and patience will give certain victory.'[3]

[1] *Hansard*, 8 December 1941, columns 1357-61.
[2] Prime Minister's Personal Telegram, T.969, 12 December 1941: Churchill papers, 20/46.
[3] Prime Minister's Personal Telegram, T.976, 12 December 1941: Churchill papers, 20/49.

Index

Compiled by the Author